Handbook of
Developmental
Psychopathology
Second Edition

Handbook of
Developmental Psychopathology
Second Edition

Edited by

Arnold J. Sameroff
University of Michigan
Ann Arbor, Michigan

Michael Lewis
Robert Wood Johnson Medical School
New Brunswick, New Jersey

and

Suzanne M. Miller
Fox Chase Cancer Center
Philadelphia, Pennsylvania

Kluwer Academic/Plenum Publishers
New York   Boston   Dordrecht   London   Moscow

Library of Congress Cataloging-in-Publication Data

Handbook of developmental psychopathology/edited by Arnold J. Sameroff, Michael
Lewis, and Suzanne M. Miller.—2nd ed.
    p. cm.
   Includes bibliographical references and index.
   ISBN 0-306-46275-3
    I. Child psychopathology—Handbooks, manuals, etc. 2. Child
development—Handbooks, manuals, etc. I. Sameroff, Arnold J. II. Lewis, Michael, 1937
Jan. 10– III. Miller, Suzanne M. (Suzanne Melanie), 1951–
    [DNLM: 1. Mental Disorders—Child. 2. Developmental Disabilities—Child. WS 350
H2359 2000]
   RJ499.3 .H332 2000
   618.92′89—dc21

                        00-028722

ISBN 0-306-46275-3

©2000 Kluwer Academic/Plenum Publishers, New York
233 Spring Street, New York, N.Y. 10013

http://www.wkap.nl/

10 9 8 7 6 5 4 3 2

A C.I.P. record for this book is available from the Library of Congress

Printed in the United States of America

Contributors

Thomas M. Achenbach, Department of Psychiatry, University of Vermont, Burlington, Vermont 05401-3456

Lauren B. Adamson, Department of Psychology, Georgia State University, Atlanta, Georgia 30303

Thomas F. Anders, Family and Infant Development Laboratory, Department of Psychiatry, University of California, Davis, Sacramento, California 95817

Judy A. Andrews, Oregon Research Institute, Eugene, Oregon 97403

Adrian C. Angold, Department of Psychiatry, Duke University Medical Center, Durham, North Carolina 27710

Steven R. Asher, Department of Psychology: Social and Health Sciences, Duke University, Durham, North Carolina 27708

Catherine Bagwell, Department of Psychology, Duke University, Durham, North Carolina 27710

Ronald G. Barr, McGill University–Montreal Children's Hospital Research Institute and Child Development Programme, Montreal Children's Hospital, Montreal Quebec, Canada H3H 1P3

Rowland P. Barrett, Department of Psychiatry and Human Behavior, Brown University School of Medicine, Emma Pendleton Bradley Hospital, East Providence, Rhode Island 02915

Andrew Baum, Behavioral Medicine and Oncology, University of Pittsburgh Cancer Institute, Pittsburgh, Pennsylvania 15219

Nicole L. Bickham, Department of Psychology, Syracuse University, Syracuse, New York 13244-2344

Neil W. Boris, Tulane University School of Medicine, New Orleans, Louisiana 70112-2715

Jeanne Brooks-Gunn, Center for Study of Children and Families, Teachers' College, Columbia University, New York, New York 10027

Melissa M. Burnham, Family and Infant Development Laboratory, Department of Psychiatry, University of California, Davis, Sacramento, California 95817

Beverley Cairns, Department of Psychology, University of North Carolina, Chapel Hill, North Carolina, 27514

Robert Cairns, Late of the Department of Psychology, University of North Carolina, Chapel Hill, North Carolina, 27514

Susan B. Campbell, Clinical Psychology Center, University of Pittsburgh, Pittsburgh, Pennsylvania 15260

Elizabeth Carlson, Institute of Child Development, University of Minnesota, Minneapolis, Minnesota 55455

Alice S. Carter, Department of Psychology, Yale University, New Haven, Connecticut 06520-8205

Steven T. Chermack, Detroit–VA Medical Center, Wayne State University School of Medicine, Detroit, Michigan 48201-1932

Dante Cicchetti, Mt. Hope Family Center, University of Rochester, Rochester, New York 14608

John D. Coie, Department of Psychology, Duke University, Durham, North Carolina 27710

Marietta H. Collins, Department of Psychiatry and Behavioral Sciences, Emory University School of Medicine, Atlanta, Georgia 30335

Bruce E. Compas, Department of Psychology, University of Vermont, Burlington, Vermont 05405

Elizabeth Jane Costello, Department of Psychiatry, Duke University Medical Center, Durham, North Carolina 27710

Geoffrey M. Curran, Central Arkansas Veterans Healthcare System, University of Arkansas for Medical Sciences, Little Rock, Arkansas 72205

Laura M. Davidson, Behavioral Medicine and Oncology, University of Pittsburgh Cancer Institute, Pittsburgh, Pennsylvania 15219

Kennth A. Dodge, Center for Child and Family Policy, Duke University, Durham, North Carolina 27708

Dennis D. Drotar, Department of Pediatrics, Rainbow Babies and Children's Hospital, Cleveland, Ohio 44106

Sunita Duggal, Institute of Child Development, University of Minnesota, Minneapolis, Minnesota 55455

Susan C. Duncan, Oregon Research Institute, Eugene, Oregon 97403

Terry E. Duncan, Oregon Research Institute, Eugene, Oregon 97403

Jacqueline S. Eccles, Achievement Research, Institute for Social Research, University of Michigan, Ann Arbor, Michigan 48106-1248

Barbara H. Fiese, Department of Psychology, Syracuse University, Syracuse, New York 13244-2344

Janet E. Fischel, Department of Pediatrics, State University of New York at Stony Brook, Stony Brook, New York 11794-8111

Gregory K. Fritz, Child and Family Psychiatry, Brown University School of Medicine, Rhode Island Hospital, Providence, Rhode Island 02903

Judy Garber, Department of Psychology and Human Development, Vanderbilt University, Nashville, Tennessee 37203

Cynthia García Coll, Department of Education, Brown University, Providence, Rhode Island 02912

Maria Garrido, Department of Psychology, University of Rhode Island, Providence, Rhode Island 02904

Beth L. Goodlin-Jones, Department of Psychiatry, Family and Infant Development Laboratory, University of California, Davis, Sacramento, California 95817

Julia A. Graber, Center for Study of Children and Families, Teachers' College, Columbia University, New York, New York 10027

Sara Harkness, School of Family Studies, University of Connecticut, Storrs, Connecticut 06269

Hyman Hops, Oregon Research Institute, Eugene, Oregon 97403

Sabra S. Inslicht, Department of Psychology, University of Pittsburgh, Pittsburgh, Pennsylvania 15219

Nadine Kaslow, Department of Psychiatry and Behavioral Sciences, Emory University School of Medicine, Atlanta, Georgia 30335

Benjamin Lahey, Department of Psychiatry, University of Chicago, Chicago, Illinois 60637-1470

Michael Lewis, Institute for the Study of Child Development, UMDNJ–Robert Wood Johnson Medical School, New Brunswick, New Jersey 08903

Alicia F. Lieberman, Department of Psychiatry, University of California, San Francisco, San Francisco, California 94110

Robert M. Liebert, Department of Psychology, State University of New York at Stony Brook, Stony Brook, New York 11794-2500

Rolf Loeber, Department of Psychiatry, University of Pittsburgh, Pittsburgh, Pennsylvania 15219

Angeline Maughan, Mt. Hope Family Center, University of Rochester, Rochester, New York 14608

Keith McBurnett, Department of Psychiatry, University of Chicago, Chicago, Illinois 60637-1470

Elizabeth L. McQuaid, Child and Family Psychiatry, Brown University School of Medicine, Rhode Island Hospital, Providence, Rhode Island 02903

Shari Miller-Johnson, Department of Psychology, Duke University, Durham, North Carolina 27710

Thomas G. O'Connor, Institute of Psychiatry, University of London, London SE5 8AF United Kingdom

Thomas H. Ollendick, Child Study Center, Virginia Polytechnic Institute and State University, Blacksburg, Virginia 24061-0355

Gerri Oppedisano, Department of Psychology, University of Vermont, Burlington, Vermont 05405

Robert Plomin, Institute of Psychiatry, University of London, London SE5 8AF United Kingdom

Rachel A. Pollock, Department of Psychology, Yale University, New Haven, Connecticut 06520-8205

Frank W. Putnam, Mayerson Center for Safe and Healthy Children, Children's Hospital Medical Center, Cincinnati, Ohio 45219-3039

Sharon Landesman Ramey, Departments of Psychiatry, Psychology, and Neurobiology, Civitan International Research Center, University of Alabama at Birmingham, Birmingham, Alabama 35233-0021

Jane Robinson, Department of Pediatrics, Rainbow Babies and Children's Hospital, Cleveland, Ohio 44106

Robert W. Roeser, School of Education, Stanford University, Stanford, California 94305

Karen D. Rudolph, Department of Psychology, University of Illinois, Champaign, Illinois 61820

Gene Sackett, Department of Psychology and Primate Center, University of Washington, Seattle, Washington 98195

Henry T. Sachs, Department of Psychiatry and Human Behavior, Brown University School of Medicine, Emma Pendleton Bradley Hospital, East Providence, Rhode Island 02915

Arnold J. Sameroff, Center for Human Growth and Development, University of Michigan, Ann Arbor, Michigan 48109

Ronald Seifer, Department of Psychiatry and Human Behavior, Brown University School of Medicine, Bradley Hospital, East Providence, Rhode Island 02915

Marian D. Sigman, Child and Adolescent Psychiatry, Neuropsychiatric Institute, University of California at Los Angeles, Los Angeles, California 90024-1759

L. Alan Sroufe, Institute of Child Development, University of Minnesota, Minneapolis, Minnesota 55455

Stephen J. Suomi, Laboratory of Comparative Ethology, National Institute of Child Health & Human Development, Bethesda, Maryland 20892

Charles M. Super, School of Family Studies, University of Connecticut, Storrs, Connecticut 06269

Elizabeth Tildesley, Oregon Research Institute, Eugene, Oregon 97403

Sheree L. Toth, Mt. Hope Family Center, University of Rochester, Rochester, New York 14608

Lisa L. Travis, Child and Adolescent Psychiatry, Neuropsychiatric Institute, University of California at Los Angeles, Los Angeles, California 90024-1759

Audrey R. Tyrka, Department of Psychiatry and Human Behavior, Brown University School of Medicine, Butler Hospital, Providence, Rhode Island 02906

Michael W. Vasey, Department of Psychology, Ohio State University, Columbus, Ohio 43210

Nancy Weinfeld, Institute of Child Development, University of Minnesota, Minneapolis, Minnesota 55455

Jay Wilder, Department of Psychology, Syracuse University, Syracuse, New York 13244-2344

Charles H. Zeanah, Tulane University School of Medicine, New Orleans, Louisiana 70112-2715

Kenneth J. Zucker, Child and Adolescent Gender Identity Clinic, Child and Family Studies Centre, Clarke Institute of Psychiatry, Toronto, Ontario M5T 1R8 Canada

Robert A. Zucker, Alcohol Research Center, University of Michigan, Ann Arbor, Michigan 48108-3318

Preface to the First Edition

The study of developmental psychopathology must combine questions about development on the one hand, and maladaptive behaviors on the other. Therefore, we offer, as have others, the definition of developmental psychopathology as *the study of the prediction of development of maladaptive behaviors and processes.*

The thrust of the definition of developmental psychopathology forces something more than a simple combination of two sets of interests. First and foremost, it is the study of change and development in maladaptive behaviors and processes. This goal stands as the basic definition of this domain. Second, however, is a much more important and interactive level of mutual informing. Combining the study of development with the study of psychopathology broadens the scope of each domain in unique and exciting ways. From a developmental perspective, it introduces the problems of change and transformation, and from a psychopathological perspective, it introduces the concept of individual difference, and with it the variety of possible processes and outcomes.

The study of developmental psychopathology begins with the realization that maladaptive behaviors often have an historical cause. Although most broad theories of maladaptive behaviors adhere to such a view, it is the psychoanalytic position which most clearly expresses the developmental perspective that disorders in adulthood have their roots in historical events, some of which occur in infancy and some in early childhood. Erikson's model of stages of development offers a viable framework for the factors which might be related to subsequently different forms of psychopathology.

The view that maladaptive developmental factors are the cause of subsequent psychopathology is so widely held that to argue its necessity seems redundant. Nevertheless, there is relatively little study, either in development or in clinical psychology, which touches upon this point. Thus, for example, in the study of development, most researchers tend to emphasize developmental processes and the normal course of growth. While there are studies on the development of pathological conditions, these remain few relative to the number of normative studies. The literature in clinical psychology, on the other hand, is full of studies of pathological conditions, yet has concerned itself relatively less with explorations of their initial causes or the stability and consistency of these conditions over time.

In part, the study of developmental psychopathology is hampered by at least two major factors. The first is that it is inherently difficult to conduct longitudinal investigations which could serve as a source for the understanding, not only of normal development, but of the development of psychopathology. There are few longitudinal studies currently available. Not surprisingly, therefore, this lack contributes to the dearth of information on the early causes of maladaptive behavior. This is due to the cost of such studies, both in terms of monetary expenditure and in terms of time an investigator must spend before there is sufficient payoff to facilitate a career.

The second major difficulty confronting the study of developmental psychopathology has to do with the problem of meaning. While we understand, at least in part, what we mean when we talk about a specific pathological condition in adults, we are often at a loss to understand what the same condition might mean for a young child. That is, it is not clear that the meaning of maladaptive behavior is consistent over age.

This problem of consistency of meaning over age is one that has plagued developmental science and psychopathology for some time. The basic tenet of developmental psychology is that the behaviors that underlie a given construct can change as a function of age. This is but one example of the way in which developmental principles can help elucidate critical issues in psychopathology.

At the same time, psychopathology, the study of individual differences, or deviant behavior, can inform developmental theory. Consider, for example, the problems that occur in the study of development when a normative approach is taken. A normative approach tends to force us into thinking that the developmental process has a single path leading to a specific outcome. A clinical perspective allows for a reconsideration of such a view. It draws us into understanding that multiple models of development are possible, where process as well as outcome can be variable.

It should be clear that the importance of the problem of developmental psychopathology necessitates continued investigation and we see this handbook serving as an important reference for those trying to study this domain. This volume should help to educate and inform those scholars interested in development and in problems related to psychopathology. Therefore, the scope of the handbook is extensive, especially since it captures the intellectual excitement and growth of two areas of study and application. The handbook not only addresses the academic community, but those who, during the course of their day, devote their time and energy to the treatment of maladaptive behavior. As articulated in individual chapters as well as in the volume as a whole, the multiple issues of theory and practice are considered. The book is also intended to provide a framework around which undergraduate and graduate courses can be structured.

Only a handbook broad in scope, bringing together experts across a wide area of problems and domains could hope to capture the challenge of the study of developmental psychopathology. We have undertaken this volume, in part, to meet this challenge. We have done so because there exists at the moment no comprehensive and single volume source in which these issues have been addressed. This is surprising, given the large and rapidly growing literature in developmental psychology and psychopathology. We therefore have attempted to fill this gap by including experts in developmental psychology who focus on maladaptive behaviors and processes. Likewise, we have found those scholars and practitioners of the study of psychopathology who are interested in the developmental perspective and have joined them together in this volume. It is, therefore, a unique effort aimed at addressing an important problem in the study and understanding of maladaptive development.

The integration of developmental and clinical psychology is an important step toward greater understanding, prediction, and management of normal and abnormal behavior. Accordingly, the present volume aims to provide a broad and comprehensive perspective on psychopathology in childhood, within a developmental context. It targets conceptual, diagnostic, and treatment issues as they relate to the field at large, and with respect to specific disorders and conditions. While we follow the broad outlines of current taxonomy, as reflected in the

Diagnostic and Statistical Manual of Mental Disorders (DSM), we also go beyond the limitations of this classification system.

In the current version (DSM-III-R), and in the ongoing revision, only certain problems are specifically identified as being relevant to childhood and early development. These include various disruptive behaviors (e.g., attention deficit disorder, conduct disorder), various forms of anxiety disorder (e.g., separation anxiety, avoidant disorder), eating disorders (e.g., anorexia nervosa, bulimia nervosa), gender identity disorders, tic and elimination disorders, mental retardation and autism. All of these problems play a central role in the growing field of developmental psychopathology and receive broad attention here. While these disorders can occur in adulthood, they usually have their origins in infancy, childhood, or adolescence.

The remainder of the diagnostic system includes disorders that have typically been associated with the psychopathology of adulthood. However, many of these problems—such as depression and schizophrenia—are relevant to the nature and course of early development. The current volume provides a focus on these phenomena, and explores the extent to which separate childhood diagnostic categories may be warranted. In future work, it will be exciting to examine if, and how, distinct adult classification diagnoses should be applied to the evolution or late appearance of disorders that usually have their first onset in the beginnings of life.

The book is divided into six major sections. The first section deals with key conceptual and theoretical issues in the story of developmental psychopathology, and provides an overview of the constructs, models, challenges, and cultural factors that are central to the field. Developmental psychopathology is conceptualized as a "macroparadigm," which can coordinate diverse theoretical models (e.g., biological, behavioral, psychoanalytic) and thereby serve to integrate the study of psychopathology from birth to maturity. A model is proposed that argues for the adoption of a "transformational" perspective, which not only emphasizes the way in which the child and environment interact, but also how each is transformed and changed by the other. Methodological strategies for predicting the cause and nature of pathology over time are highlighted. The application of cultural approaches to the nature of pathology is also considered, which helps alert us to how the culture defines notions of sickness and deviance and, in part, shapes the course and outcome of outlying behaviors. Important diagnostic and classification considerations are also highlighted. In particular, attention is given to the validity and usefulness of the diagnostic categories and to the need to specify the source from which diagnostic information is obtained.

Sections II through V explore the major specific clinical disorders that are relevant to childhood and development. The first section focuses on "undercontrolled" or disruptive disorders, specifically attention deficit disorder and conduct disorder. It begins with a focus on attention deficit disorder, which is one of the most common reasons children are referred for treatment. Conceptually, a model is proposed in which the deficits in sustained attention, impulse control, and poor regulation of activity level are seen as a result of more basic deficits in rule-governed behavior or in the way in which consequences regulate sustained responding. The importance of socialization influences to the etiology of the disorder, as well as of genetic and biomedical contributions, is also reviewed. Several chapters are devoted to conduct disorder and related problems of aggression. A range of issues is considered, including evidence for two main types of aggressive disorder: group (socialized) and solitary (unsocialized). While the role of genetics in the development of aggression is not well established, there is considerable evidence for the role of social cognitive deficits and for the influence of the family, the peer group, and the mass media. Furthermore, there is an impressive stability of aggressive behavior across time and generations. Finally, conduct-disturbed children appear to reason at lower levels of moral maturity than do nondisturbed children, which seems to be an important barrier to the development of prosocial behavior.

Section III deals with "overcontrolled" or anxiety-related conditions. Little research is currently available on the major clinical anxiety disorders that are specifically applied to children, such as separation anxiety, avoidant disorder, and overanxious disorder. The agenda for future research includes the development of multimethod assessment batteries and the broadening of psychological theories. In addition, temperamental characteristics appear to be important in some cases of anxiety disorder. For example, children who have a low threshold for fear and threat tend to react by displaying protective inhibitory behaviors. Peer relations are also central to and predictive of adaptive function in children. Among various anxiety conditions that are not specifically identified with but are relevant to childhood (e.g., test anxiety, posttraumatic stress, child maltreatment, and fears and phobias) important advances in conceptualization, treatment, and prevention are reviewed.

In Section IV, we present a perspective on depression as it related to early development, and review its etiology, psychobiology, and cognitive components. It is suggested that the manifestation of depression in childhood must be evaluated in terms of age-appropriate signs and symptoms. Future research is needed to establish criteria and assessment instruments for the diagnosis and subtyping of depressive episodes. Evidence which suggests that exposure to early loss and other adverse familial and personal experiences are risk factors for the development of depression in young children. The biological parameters of childhood depression appear to be more complex, with age and puberty exerting an important influence. Finally, as with adults, a variety of cognitive deficits have been identified in youngsters. However, these need to be considered and explored with respect to the child's stage of cognitive development.

Specific and pervasive disorders are presented in Section V. These range from more generalized conditions (e.g., borderline disorders, schizophrenia, autism, and mental retardation) to more delimited conditions (e.g., eating disorders, elimination disorders, physical disorders, and sexual disorders). Early childhood autism is the most common of the severe and pervasive childhood disorders and appears to be related to underlying biological and physiological disturbances. With respect to borderline disorders, the current literature needs to be supplemented by prospective longitudinal research, studies of high risk subjects, and more sophisticated etiological models. The study and management of mental retardation is particularly challenging, given the serious nature of the disorder and the fact that it is so frequently linked with other severe behavioral and psychological problems.

Among the more specific disorders, eating problems are prevalent and appear to be most likely to emerge in adolescence. This seems to be due, in part, to the convergence of particular physical changes and psychosocial stresses during this period, particularly in the lives of females. With regard to elimination problems, enuresis (bedwetting) is the most common form. Since these problems can be persistent, it is important to develop useful theoretical models and applied treatment modes. A number of other physical disorders are also considered in this section, including tics (which appear to have a genetic component) as well as sleep disorders and stuttering. Lastly, the development of a range of normal and pathological sexual patterns is explored, including masturbation, effeminate behavior, sexual identity, homosexuality, and paraphilias.

Finally, Section VI concludes with a focus on the management of psychopathology, and provides an evaluation of the effects of institutionalization as well as of the efficacy of a variety of psychotherapeutic intervention approaches. The effects of institutionalization on young children are considered first and it is concluded that the negative consequences can be at least partly offset by providing some stability in at least one close human contact. While treatment considerations are tackled throughout the volume with respect to specific disorders, the final chapters provide an overarching appraisal of critical aspects of the therapies themselves, as they are applied to children. Treatment approaches explored include dynamic, family, community and cognitive-behavioral modalities. These techniques need to consider the child in a developmental context in which social, emotional, and environmental influences are highlighted.

In conclusion, the volume provides a broad and in-depth coverage of the impact of developmental influences on clinical disorders in childhood and explores their linkages with subclinical and normal behaviors. For each disorder, its nature, origins, and evolution over the life cycle are explored, paying close attention to the confluence of behavioral, psychological, genetic, and social factors that are involved. As such, the volume presents a state-of-the field compendium of our current level of understanding of who is most vulnerable to disorder, the factors that predispose toward disorder, and the conditions that activate, exacerbate, or reverse disorder during the beginnings of life.

MICHAEL LEWIS
SUZANNE M. MILLER

Preface to the Second Edition

It has been ten years since the publication of the first edition of the *Handbook*. During these ten years, there has been a burgeoning of work in developmental psychopathology, so much so that what now exists bears little resemblance to what came before. A new edition of the *Handbook*, therefore, is badly needed—first, to capture the new developments that have occurred; second, to codify that which was already known. In Norman Garmezy's foreword to the first edition, he declared that developmental psychopathology was the "new kid on the block." What any reader of the new edition will discover is that the "kid on the block" is now an adolescent.

In the first edition, we sought to combine the fields of developmental science with that of psychopathology, arguing that the origins of psychopathology in adulthood could be found in childhood. We took as a model the psychiatric diagnostic scheme with its categories in order to explore this relationship. The maturation of the field has presented a new challenge, since we have increasingly come to see that the adult psychiatric diagnostic schemes are inadequate and new schemes for children have become necessary; thus, for example, a whole section on infancy, childhood, and adolescence has been added to the DSM system. Such advances in the field have moved us from a diagnostic framework toward more of a developmental one, for, indeed, given unique childhood classification, our task becomes more clearly developmental— that is, how do we understand childhood behavioral disturbances in their own right and how do these early childhood deviances become (or not) adult psychopathology? Thus, the challenge to merge developmental processes into the scheme of psychopathology becomes even more obvious.

Much of this challenge has been met in this new edition. While the focus of the *Handbook* remains on psychopathology, we have asked our authors to address the developmental considerations; thus, we have tried to embed maladaptive functioning into a general framework of development. In this regard, we have added and enlarged the first two sections to show that maladaptive behaviors in children have to be viewed from a cultural, historical, biological, and interpersonal framework, and that models and theories of normal development will serve us well in understanding the development of psychopathology.

As described in the first edition, we saw two major constraints on the study of developmental psychopathology. The first was an empirical one—the lack of longitudinal data on the trajectories leading to psychopathology. The second was a theoretical one—the lack of knowledge about how adult disorders might be expressed in children. In the last ten years, much has changed in dealing with these two problems. In regard to the first, there are an increasing number of longitudinal studies of the emotional, behavioral, and cognitive disorders that will help illuminate the etiology of many forms of psychopathology. In regard to the second, the meaning of disorder is becoming clearer as developmental linkages are found between early efforts at adaptive functioning and later disturbances.

Perhaps the most significant feature reflecting the maturation of the field has been our changing view of the nature of the developmental perspective. Whereas the earlier view took a trait perspective, one that stressed early individual characteristics or psychopathologies as somehow related in a nearly one-to-one fashion with later pathologies, a more mature view—one called a contextual or ecological perspective—has come to dominate our thinking. In this view, the context of children's lives and changes in their context are seen as the determining factors in subsequent pathology. Interestingly, there is growing support for the view that the concurrent context (rather than past events) may be better predictors of concurrent psychopathology. Such a view stresses the contextual features of each individual's life and represents truly a more interactive developmental perspective. Such a perspective, having much in common with dynamic systems theories, recognizes that children with the same initial deviances in behavior do not all end up with psychopathology. The differences between those who do and those who do not is increasingly explained by contextual factors and the experiences of the individual in the home, school, peer group, and community. As a result of the increasing appreciation within the field of developmental psychology of the need to understand general developmental processes within an ecological model, we have enhanced these aspects in the new edition of the *Handbook*. Thus, our new view on the nature of normal development informs us of the complexity of understanding the development of psychopathology.

Descriptions of childhood disorders were thin in DSM-III-R at the time of the first edition, and the ensuing revised DSM-IV did little to redress that problem, especially for the preschool age periods. We acknowledged their limitations in the first edition and do so again now. Imposing adult diagnostic categories on children is an intransigent problem. Nevertheless, the categories provide us with a starting point and a structure that will be helpful to the clinician as well as the researcher interested in childhood psychopathology. They will also contribute to its development not only to meet the needs of the clinician but also to meet the needs for a greater understanding of the developmental process.

The second edition of the *Handbook* contains 39 chapters by leading figures in the study of developmental psychopathology. There are nine major sections. Section I is about issues and theories and provides a basis for the underlying assumptions of a science of developmental psychopathology. Section II reflects our emphasis on experience and context. It is a new section for this edition because without an understanding of the lives of children and the contexts in which they exist, no strong theory about developmental psychopathology or even normal development is possible. Section III reflects our commitment to bring to bear the newest advances in biological research and how they may interact with context to provide a more realistic approach to understanding development. Section IV on disorders of early childhood highlights our understanding that childhood may have unique issues of mental health and that childhood psychopathology needs to be differentiated from those used for adults. Section V on disruptive behavior disorders, Section VI on emotional disorders, and Section VII on control disorders touch upon the psychopathologies associated with children and which also exist in adults. Sections VIII and IX deal with pervasive developmental and trauma disorders, and allow us to extend our understanding to more serious mental disorders.

In this new edition, we have continued to strive to provide a comprehensive description of the influences on child mental disorders. Our aim has been twofold: first, to provide a narrow enough description so that the reader can get a detailed understanding of the particulars of each mental health problem; second, to provide a broad enough framework to appreciate the developmental course of psychopathology in a contextual framework. Both the clinician and the academician will be able to gain from this approach.

MICHAEL LEWIS
ARNOLD J. SAMEROFF
SUZANNE M. MILLER

Contents

PART II. CONTEXT AND MENTAL HEALTH

PART IV. DISORDERS OF EARLY CHILDHOOD

20. The Early Caregiving Environment: Expanding Views on Nonparental Care and Cumulative Life Experiences

Sharon Landesman Ramey and Gene P. Sackettt

PART V. DISRUPTIVE BEHAVIORAL DISORDERS

Susan B. Campbell

Robert B. Cairns and Beverley D. Cairns

35. Psychopathology in Individuals with Mental Retardation 657

Henry T. Sachs and Rowland P. Barrett

36. Gender Identity Disorder 671

Kennth J. Zucker

PART IX. TRAUMA DISORDERS

37. An Ecological–Transactional Model of Child Maltreatment 689

Dante Cicchetti, Sheree L. Toth, and Angeline Maughan

I
ISSUES AND THEORIES

1

Toward a Development of Psychopathology
Models, Definitions, and Prediction

Michael Lewis

Developmental psychopathology can be defined in a variety of ways, all having to do with development on the one hand and the resulting set of maladaptive behaviors on the other. We, too, define developmental psychopathology as focusing on and integrating these two traditional areas; however, a third feature needs to be added, namely, maladaptive processes as well as behaviors. Thus, developmental psychopathology is the study of both the development of maladaptive behaviors (Sroufe & Rutter, 1984) and the maladaptive processes themselves. Underlying much of the study of developmental psychopathology is the principle of predictability (Kohlberg, LaCrosse, & Ricks, 1972). The prediction of maladaptive behavior has been viewed not only as possible, but also as an important feature in the study of developmental psychopathology. With this added feature, we now have a more complete definition: *Developmental psychopathology is the study and prediction of maladaptive behaviors and processes across time.*

If development, maladaptive behavior and processes, and prediction make up the important features of our inquiry, it is necessary that we consider each of them. In this chapter, the focus is first to look at developmental models and their application to psychopathology, then study the issue of the meaning of maladaptive behavior, and finally, the issue of prediction.

MODELS OF DEVELOPMENTAL PSYCHOPATHOLOGY

Models of development represent worldviews about human nature and environments that create a human life course (Lewis, 1997; Reese & Overton, 1970; Riegel, 1976). Models of

Michael Lewis • Institute for the Study of Child Development, UMDNJ–Robert Wood Johnson Medical School, New Brunswick, New Jersey 08903.

Handbook of Developmental Psychopathology, Second Edition, edited by Arnold J. Sameroff, Michael Lewis, and Suzanne M. Miller. Kluwer Academic/Plenum Publishers, New York, 2000.

abnormal development also reflect these views, and the data from normal and abnormal lives inform our theories of development. So, for example, the trait notion of personality (Block & Block, 1980) and the invulnerable child (Anthony, 1970; Garmezy, 1974; Rutter, 1981) both share the view that some fixed pattern of behavior may be unaffected by environmental factors. Likewise, information about the regression to old behavior patterns requires that we reconsider the notion that all developmental processes are transformations; that all old behavior patterns are changed into new ones. Clearly, models of development must be applicable for normal and for abnormal development.

Models of development have been considered by many writers, and the interested reader is referred to Reese and Overton (1970) and, more recently, Lewis (1997). We particularly like Riegel's (1978) scheme for considering models that involve the child and the environment. In this scheme, each of these elements can be active or passive agents. The passive child–passive environment model is of relatively less interest because it arose from John Locke and David Hume, and now receives little attention. In such a model, the environment does not try to affect behavior, and the child is a passive "blank tablet" upon which is received information from the world around it. Such models originally had some use, for example, in our understanding of short-term memory. These memories were likened to a small box that was sequentially filled. When a new memory was entered and there was no more room, the first (or oldest) memory dropped out. Although such a view of memory is no longer held, other views, especially in perception, share many of the features of this model. Gibson's (1969) notion of affordance, for example, suggests such a model because innate features of the child extract the given features of the environment. Such models are by their nature mechanistic.

The passive child–active environment model, is an environmental control view, because here the environment actively controls, by reward and punishment, the child's behavior. The characteristics of this environment may differ, as may the nature of the different reinforcers, but the child's behavior is determined by its environment. We are most familiar with this model in operant conditioning (Skinner, 1953). It is a model much favored by many therapists and is used in diverse areas, such as behavior modification treatment to alter maladaptive behavior, as well as in theories that explain normal sex-role learning by parental or peer reinforcement (Bem, 1987; Fagot & Patterson, 1969).

The third model is that of an active person and a passive environment. These models have in common an active child extracting and constructing its world from the material of the environment. Piaget's theory fits well within this framework (Piaget, 1952), although some have argued that Piaget may be a preformationalist (passive child–passive environment) in that all the structures children create are identical (Bellin, 1971). Given the active organismic view of Piaget, it is easy to see that although the child needs the environment to construct knowledge, the environment itself plays little role (Lewis, 1983). Linguistic theorists, such as Chomsky (1957, 1965) and Lennenberg (1967), believe that biological linguistic structures are available for children to use in their construction of language in particular environments. Whether such views are better placed in the passive child–passive environment model can be questioned, although the critical feature of this model should not be lost. In psychopathology and therapy, we often employ such a model when we attempt to help patients alter their behavior (active person) but discount the role of the environment.

The last model is most familiar to developmentalists because of its interactive nature. An active person and an active environment are postulated as creating, modifying, and changing behavior. These interactive models take many forms, varying from the interactional approach of Lewis (Lewis, 1972; Lewis & Feiring, 1991) to the transactional models of Sameroff and

Chandler (1975). They also include Chess and Thomas's (1984) and Lerner's (1984) goodness-of-fit model and, from a developmental psychopathology point of view, the notion of vulnerability and risk status (Garmezy, Masten, & Tellegen, 1984; Rutter, 1979). In his attempt to understand cognitive development, Luria (1976) argued that cognitive structures themselves are the consequence of an interaction between the nature of the environment and an active child. Such a view of interaction is often found in research on cultural differences (Cole, 1996).

Even though Riegel's (1978) approach is useful, other systems of classification are available. For example, both passive child and passive and active environment models are mechanistic in that either biological givens within the organism or environmental structures outside the organism act on the child. On the other hand, both active child models must be interactive because organisms almost always interact in some way with their environment, which, given its structure (whether active or passive), affects the ongoing interaction. In the models of development as they are related to maladaptive and abnormal behavior, we use a combination of approaches.

Developmental models of psychopathology have been considered recently, and three models of development have been suggested: these include a *trait model*, a *contextual or environmental model*, and an *interactional model*. Although each of these models has variations, the interactional model is the most variable. Because attachment theory remains central to normal and maladaptive development, it is used often as an exemplar in our discussion. These three models, which are prototypes of the various views of development, make clear how such models diverge and how they can be used to understand the etiology of psychopathology. Unfortunately, by describing sharp distinctions, we may draw too tight an image and, as such, may make them caricatures. Nevertheless, it is important to consider them in this fashion in order to observe their strengths and weaknesses.

Trait or Status Model

The trait or status model is characterized by its simplicity and holds to the view that a trait, or the status of the child at one point in time, is likely to predict a trait or status at a later point in time. A trait model is not interactive and does not provide for the effects of the environment. In fact, in the most extreme form, the environment is thought to play no role either in effecting its display or in transforming its characteristics. A particular trait may interact with the environment, but the trait is not changed by that interaction.

Traits are not easily open to transformation and can be processes, coping skills, attributes, or tendencies to respond in certain ways. Traits can be innate features, such as temperament or particular genetic codes, and can also be acquired through learning or through more interactive processes. However, once a trait is acquired, it remains relatively unaffected by subsequent interactions. The trait model is most useful in many instances, for example, when considering potential genetic or biological causes of subsequent psychopathology. A child who is born with a certain gene or a set of genes is likely to display psychopathology at some later time. This model characterizes some of the research in the genetics of mental illness. Here, the environment, or its interaction with the genes, plays little role in the potential outcome. The work of Kallman (1946), for example, on heritability of schizophrenia supports the use of such a model, as does the lack or presence of certain chemicals on depression (e.g., Puig-Antich, 1982). In each of these cases, the presence of particular features is hypothesized as likely to affect a particular type of pathology. Although a trait model is appealing in its simplicity, there are any number of problems with it; for example, not all people who possess a trait or have a particular status at one point in time are *all* likely to show subsequent psychopathology or the same type of psychopathology (Saudino, 1997).

That all children of schizophrenic parents do not themselves become schizophrenic, or that not all monozygotic twins show concordance vis-à-vis schizophrenia suggests that other variables need to be considered (Gottesman & Shields, 1982; Kringlon, 1968). We return to this point again; however, it is important to note that the failure to find a high incidence of schizophrenic children of schizophrenic parents leads to the postulation of such notions as resistance to stress, coping styles, and invulnerability. Each of these terms has a trait-like feature to them.

This model is also useful when considering traits that are not genetically or biologically based. For example, the attachment model as proposed by Bowlby (1969) and Ainsworth (1973) holds that the child's early relationship with its mother, in the first year of life, will determine the child's adjustment throughout life. The security of attachment that the child shows at the end of the first year of life is the result of the early interaction between the mother and the child. Once the attachment is established, it acts as a trait affecting the child's subsequent behavior. The following is an example of a trait that is established through the interaction of the child with its environment, but, once established, acts like any other trait; that is, it may interact with the environment but is not altered by it (see Ainsworth, 1989).

Figure 1.1 presents the trait model using the traditional attachment construct. Notice that the interaction of the mother and child at T_1 produces the intraorganism trait, C_{t_1}, in this case, a secure or an insecure attachment. Although attachment is the consequence of an interaction, once established, it is the trait (C_{t_1}) residing in the child that leads to C_{t_2}. There is no need to posit a role of the environment except as it initially produces the attachment. The problems with a trait view of the attachment model have been addressed by many (Lamb, Thompson, Gardner, & Charnov, 1985; Lewis, Feiring, & Rosenthal, 2000); nevertheless, it is a widely held view that the mother–child relationship in the first year of life can affect the child's subsequent social–emotional life as well as impact on its mental health.

FIGURE 1.1. Trait model using the attachment construct.

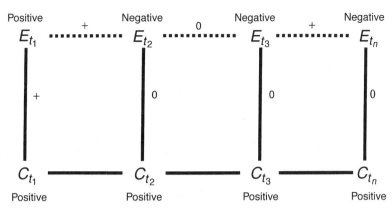

FIGURE 1.2. Invulnerability model from point of view of an acquired trait.

Moreover, there is the belief that a trait can act as a protective factor in the face of environmental stress. Secure attachment is seen as an invulnerability factor. The concept of invulnerability is similar to a trait model; that is, there are attributes of children that appear to protect them from subsequent environmental stress. These attributes (or traits) serve to make the child stress-resistant. Such a mechanism is used to explain why not all at-risk children develop psychopathology (Garmezy et al., 1984; Rutter, 1979). Garmezy (1989) and Rutter (1979) have focused on the factors that can protect the child against stress and, therefore, psychopathology.

Figure 1.2 presents the invulnerability model from the point of view of an acquired trait. Notice that at t_1, the environment is positive, so the child acquires a protective attribute. At t_2, the environment becomes negative (stress appears); however, the attribute acquired at t_1 protects the child (the child remains positive). At each additional point in time ($t_3, t_4, \ldots t_n$), the environment may change; however, it has little effect on the child because the intraorganism trait is maintained.

Of some question is the prolonged impact of a stress given the protective factor. It is possible to consider such a factor in several ways. In the first place, a protective factor can act to increase the threshold before a stress can affect the child. Stress will have an effect, but it will do so only after a certain level is past. A threshold concept applies not only for intensity but also for duration; that is, invulnerability may represent the ability to sustain one or two stress events, but not prolonged stress, or, alternatively, it may protect the child against long-term stress. Specific to secure attachment, it is increasingly clear that it is not a protective factor in terms of the child's reaction to subsequent stress (Lewis et al., 2000).

Trait models in personality theory are not new (Allport & Allport, 1921), and the problems identified in personality research apply here as well. The major problem related to trait models is the recognition that individual traits are likely to be situation-specific (Mischel, 1965). As such, they can only partially characterize the organism. For example, a child may be securely attached to its mother but insecurely attached to its father or its older sibling. It would therefore be hard to characterize the child as insecurely attached simply because it was insecurely attached to one family member but not to the others (Fox, Kimmerly, & Schafer, 1991). Prediction from an insecure attachment trait to subsequent psychopathology would be difficult without knowing the child's total attachment pattern. This would dilute attachment from a trait located within the individual to a set of specific relationships. Thus, to characterize the child in a simple way, such as secure or insecure, may miss the complex nature of traits, especially those likely to be related to subsequent psychopathology.

Equally problematic with the trait notion is the fact that such models leave little room for the impact of environment on subsequent developmental growth or dysfunction. Environments play a role in children's development in the opening year of life and continue to do so throughout the life span (Lewis, 1997).

The Environmental Model

The prototypic environmental model holds that exogenous factors influence development. Two of the many problems in using this model are (1) our difficulty in defining what environments are, and (2) the failure to consider the impact of environments throughout the life span. In fact, the strongest form of the environmental or contextual model argues for the proposition that adaptation to current environment, throughout the life course, is a major influence in our socioemotional life. As environments change, so too does the individual (Lewis, 1997). This dynamic and changing view of environments and adaptation is in strong contrast to the earlier models of environments as forces acting on the individual, and acting on the individual *only* in the early years of life. Let us consider them in detail, recognizing that the nature or the classification of types of environments lags behind our measurement of individual characteristics.

In the simplest model, behavior, normal or maladaptive, is primarily a function of the environmental forces acting on the organism at any point in time. In such a model, for example, a child does behavior *x* but not behavior *y*, because this behavior is positively rewarded by his parents and *y* is punished. Notice that, in this model, the environmental forces act continuously on the organism, and the behavior emitted is a direct function of this action. Although this model may apply for some behavior, it is more likely the case that environmental forces act on the child directly at that point in time and indirectly at later points in time. Our hypothetical child may do behavior *x*, not because of the immediate reward value, but because the child remembers that *x* is a rewarded behavior. Clearly, much of our behavior is controlled by this indirect form of environmental pressure. Many other forms of indirect reward and punishment have been observed. For example, consider the situation in which a child is present when the mother scolds the older sibling for writing on the walls of the house. The younger child, although not directly punished, does learn that writing on walls is not an action to be performed (Lewis & Feiring, 1981). Unfortunately, these indirect forms of reward and punishment receive little attention.

There are many different types of environmental pressures. For example, we see an advertisement for a product "that will make other people love us." We purchase such a product in the hopes that others will indeed love us. We can be rewarded or punished in many direct and indirect ways; however, it is important to note that the more the organism has to construct the nature or purpose of the environmental forces, the more we move from the passive child–active environment to the active child–active environment model. The social-cognitive theories of personality (Bandura, 1986; Mischel, 1965) are examples of this. In this case, the environment supplies the information that the child uses. Thus, the environment is passive, while the child is active in constructing meaning.

Because other people make up one important aspect of our environment, the work on the structures of the *social* environment is particularly relevant, and an attempt has been made to expand the numbers of potentially important people in the child's environment (Lewis, 1984) as well as to create an analysis of the structure of the social environment itself (Lewis, 1987b). Although considerable effort has been focused on the importance of the mother on the child, other persons, including fathers, siblings, grandparents, and peers, clearly have importance in shaping the child's life (Bronfenbrenner & Crouter, 1983; Dunn, 1993; Fox et al., 1991; Lewis, 1984).

Given these diverse features of environments and the important roles attributed to them, it is surprising that so little systematic work has gone into their study. For the most part, mothers and, to some extent, families (Belsky, Pensky, & Youngblade, 1990; Davies & Cummings, 1994; Howes & Markman, 1989; Waters, Posada, Crowell, & Lay, 1993) have received the most attention, and we therefore use them in our examples.

The role of environments in the developmental process has been underplayed because most investigators seek to find the structure and change within the organism itself. Likewise, in the study of psychopathology, even though we recognize that environments can cause disturbance and abnormal behavior, we prefer to treat the person—to increase coping skills or to alter specific behaviors—rather than change the environment (Lewis, 1997). Yet we can imagine the difficulties that are raised when we attempt to alter specific maladaptive behaviors in environments in which such behaviors are adaptive—a point well taken by Szasz (1961).

Our belief that the thrust of development resides in the organism rather than in the environment, in large part, raises many problems. At cultural levels, we assume that violence (and its cure) must be met in the individual—a trait model—rather than in the structure of the environment. The murder rate using handguns in the United States is many times higher than in any other Western society. We seek responsibility in the nature of the individual (e.g., XYY males, or the genetics of antisocial behavior), when the alternative of environmental structure is available. In this case, murders may be due more to the culture's nonpunishment of persons or nonrestriction of handguns. The solution to the high murder rate in the United States might be the elimination, through punishment, of the possession of weapons. Thus, we either conclude that Americans are by nature more violent than Europeans or that other Western societies do not allow handguns and therefore have lower murder rates (see Cairns & Cairns, Chapter 22, this volume).

A general environmental model suggests that children's behavior is a function of the environment in which the behavior occurs, because the task of the individual is to adapt to its current environment. As long as the environment appears consistent, the child's behavior will be consistent; if the environment *changes*, so, too, will the child's behavior. If a more active organism model is used, it is still the case that maladaptive environments produce abnormal behavior; however, the abnormal behavior is produced by the child's perception and construction of its reality. From a developmental psychopathology point of view, maladaptive behavior is caused by maladaptive environments; if we change those environments, we alter the behavior.

Figure 1.3 presents this model. The environment (*E*) at t_1, t_2, and t_3 all impact on the child's behavior at each point in time. The child's behavior at C_{t_1}, C_{t_2}, and C_{t_3} appears consistent, and it is, as long as *E* remains consistent. In other words, the continuity in *C* is an epiphenomenon of the continuity of *E* across time. Likewise, the lack of consistency in *C* reflects the lack of consistency in the environment. The child's behavior changes over t_1 to t_3 as the environment produces change. Even though it appears that *C* is consistent, it is so because *E* is consistent. Consistency and change in *C* are supported by exogenous rather than by endogenous factors.

Such a model of change as a function of the environment can be readily tested but rarely is it done. This failure reflects the bias of the trait model. Again, consider the case of the

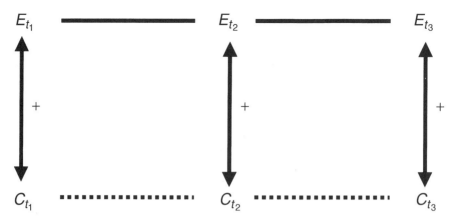

FIGURE 1.3. Model of change as a function of the environment.

attachment model. Although it is recognized that the environment affects the attachment at t_1, the child's status or trait at t_1 (C_{t_1}) is hypothesized to determine the child's other outcomes, C_{t_2}, C_{t_3}, and so forth. Rarely is the environment, and the consistency of the environment, factored into the model as a possible cause of subsequent child behavior. Consider that poor parenting produces an insecure child at C_{t_1} and this parenting remains poor at t_2, t_3. Without considering the continuing effects of poor parenting, it is not possible to make such a conclusion. That most research in this area fails in this regard constitutes evidence for the lack of interest in the environmental model.

Other forms of maladaptive behavior development have a similar problem. Depressed women are assumed to cause concurrent as well as subsequent depression in children (Zahn-Waxler, Cummings, McKnew, & Radke-Yarrow, 1984). What is not considered is the fact that depressed mothers at t_1 are also likely to be depressed at t_2 or t_3. What role does the mother's depression at these points play in the child's subsequent condition? We can only infer the answer given the limited data available. The question that needs to be asked is: What would happen to the child if the mother was depressed at t_1 but was not depressed at t_2 or t_3? This type of question suggests that one way to observe the effect of the environment on the child's subsequent behavior is to observe those situations in which the environment changes.

The environmental change can occur in two ways: a positive environment can become negative or a negative environment can become positive. In each case, the change in the child's behavior should inform us as to the role of the environment in affecting behavior. In the former case, we would expect an increase in the child's maladaptive behavior, whereas in the latter, we would expect to see a decrease. There are several studies that can be of help in answering this question. Thompson, Lamb, and Estes (1982), for example, examined children's attachment between 1 year and 18 months. They found that the change in the child was related to the mother's going back to work. When the child's environment changed by going from less to more stress, there was an increase in the negative behavior of the child. When there was no change in the stress environment, there was little change in the child's behavior. Unfortunately, there were no cases of the change from high to low stress, but a study by Lewis and Schaeffer (1981) bears on this issue. Abused children are found not to be securely attached (Schneider-Rosen & Cicchetti, 1984) and also have poor peer relationships. The trait model states that the insecure attachment produces subsequent poor peer relationships. Alternatively, an environmental model would state that abusive parents also are likely not to encourage or promote good peer relationships; thus, both insecure attachment and poor peer relationships are due to poor parenting at both points in time. Moreover, if peer relationships could be encouraged by placing these children in supervised day care, then peer relationships should improve even though the attachment characteristic did not change. Such findings would support an environmental model. Lewis and Schaeffer (1981) reported that although initial peer behavior in these abused children was different than that in a nonabused group, after 1 month, the behavior of the two groups could not be distinguished. Even so, the child–mother relationship remained poor. Findings such as these require that concurrent environmental influences be given more attention.

Although the environmental model can be made more complex, this model suggests, in all cases, that the child's concurrent health status is determined by the environment (Lewis, 1997). Should the environment change, then the child's status will change. The degree to which the environment remains consistent, and in our case psychopathogenic, is the degree to which psychopathology will be consistently found within the subject. Therefore, the environmental model is characterized by the view holding that the constraints, changes, and consistencies in children's psychopathology rest not so much with intrinsic structures located in the child as in the nature, structure, and environment of the child.

Degree of Prior Experience

The environmental model also raises the issue of the nature and degree of prior experience; that is, the notion of a critical period. Certain environmental influences may have a greater effect at some points in time, but not others. For example, a responsive environment in the first year and a less-responsive environment in the second year should lead to better consequences than a nonresponsive environment in the first year and a responsive environment in the second year. Although critical periods suggest some organismic characteristics, the effects of the environment as a function of past experience remain relevant here. In its simplest form, when a series of positive events is followed by a negative event, it is important to know whether the impact of the negative event depends on the number or the timing of the preceding positive ones. In similar fashion, the same question applies for a series of negative events.

For example, in Case A, if there are four positive environmental events prior to the negative one, whereas in Case B there are only two, is the negative event more negative for Case B than for Case A? The simplest environmental model would suggest no difference because such models argue for a passive child and, given such, past experiences have little effect. On the other hand, memory systems are likely to be ones in which past experiences are registered and processed. Given this fact, the four positive past experiences for Case A might dilute the effects of the negative event. A more complex model provides for a more active child, and here the child's memory of all the past positive events allows for a reconstruction of the negative one. The effect of the past events might serve to buffer the effect of the next event.

Besides the effects of past experiences on the behavior of the child, particular time periods may be critical for some environmental events (Bornstein, 1987). For example, a limited number of negative events in early life may have a greater impact than the same number of events later in life. Attachment theory suggests that the failure of the child to securely attach in the first year may predispose it to serious maladaptive behavior, even though the environment thereafter is altered in the positive direction. The data for this position are mixed (Lewis, 1997; Lewis et al., 2000) and suggest that, at least for socioemotional development, ongoing poor environments may be more critical than just the early ones. Nevertheless, the models of the effect of past experience, critical periods, and current environments are in need of serious testing if we are to understand the importance of an environmental model of developmental psychopathology.

Whatever model we choose, it is clear that the study and treatment of maladaptive behavior require that the environment across the life span be considered. Although some maladaptive behavior of the child may be altered within the therapeutic situation, the child usually returns to the same environment in which these maladaptive behaviors were formed. If such behavior is to be modified, we have to modify the environment. A strong environmental model suggests that, in many cases, this may be sufficient.

The Interactional Model

Interactional models vary; some researchers prefer to call them "interactional" and others "transactional" (Lewis, 1972; Sameroff & Chandler, 1975). As we shall see, all these models have in common the role of both child and environment in determining the course of development. In these models, the nature of the environment and the characteristics or traits of the child are needed to explain concurrent as well as subsequent behavior and adjustment. Such models usually require an active child and an active environment; however, they need not be so. What they do require is the notion that behavior is shaped by its adaptive ability and that this ability is related to environments. Maladaptive behavior may be misnamed because the behavior may be adaptive to a maladaptive environment. The stability and change in the child need to be viewed as a function of both factors, and, as such, the task of any interactive model is to draw us to the study of both features. In our attachment example, the infant who is securely attached, as a function of the responsive environment in the first year, will show competence at a later age as a function of the earlier events as well as the nature of the environment at that later age (see Lewis, 1999).

One of the central issues of the developmental theories that are interactive in nature is the question of transformation. Two models of concurrent behavior as a function of traits and environment can be drawn. In the first, both trait and environment interact and produce a new set of behaviors. However, neither the traits nor the environment are altered by the interaction. From a developmental perspective, this is an additive model because new behaviors are derived from old behaviors and their interaction with the environment, but these new behaviors are added to the repertoire of the set of old behaviors (Lewis, 1997). For example, an insecurely attached child ($-$ATT) can interact with a positive environment ($+$E) so that a positive outcome ($+$O) occurs:

$$(-\text{ATT}) \times (+\text{E}) \rightarrow +\text{O}$$

In this case, the trait of ($-$ATT) remains unaffected by the interaction and ($+$O) is added to the set of behaviors including ($-$ATT). Likewise ($+$E) is not altered by the interaction. This model is very useful for explaining such diverse phenomena as regression, vulnerability, and goodness of fit.

In the second model, both trait and environment interact, producing a new set of behaviors that transform themselves. From a developmental perspective, this is a transformational model because the old behaviors give rise to new behaviors and the environment itself is altered by the exchange. In our example, the insecurely attached child ($-$ATT) interacts with the positive environment ($+$E), which results in a positive attribute ($+$ATT) that leads to positive outcome ($+$O):

$$(-\text{ATT}) \times (+\text{E}) \rightarrow (+\text{ATT}) \rightarrow (+\text{O})$$

In this case, the trait of $(-ATT)$ is altered, and in like fashion, $(+E)$ might be altered as in the case $(-ATT) \times (+E) \rightarrow (-E) \rightarrow (-O)$. In fact, both might be possible:

$$(-ATT) \times (+E) \rightarrow [+ATT, -E] \rightarrow \text{outcome}$$

The result would be unclear, depending on the strength of change in each feature. Nevertheless, a transformation of structure has taken place.

The variety of interactional models is considerable. We focus on two of them in order to demonstrate their importance for our theories of developmental psychopathology.

Goodness-of-Fit Model

According to the goodness-of-fit model, discord arises when the child's characteristics do not match the environmental demand, or, stated another way, the environmental demand does not match the child's characteristic (Lerner, 1984; Thomas & Chess, 1977). Notice that maladjustment is the consequence of the *mismatch*. It is not located in either the nature of the child's characteristic or in the environmental demand. Because of this, such a model can be accused of "relativism." Some researchers would argue that certain environmental demands, by their nature, will cause pathology in the same way that certain child characteristics, by their nature, will cause them. Although this may be the case in extremes, the goodness-of-fit model suggests that psychopathology is the consequence of the mismatch between trait and environment, and, as such, it is an interactive model.

Consider the case of the temperamentally active child. If such a child is raised in a household where activity and noise are valued, where there is a match between the active child and the environment, no maladaptive behavior results. However, if this same child is raised in a household where quiet behavior and inhibition are valued, we would expect to see more adjustment problems. Similarly, for the quiet, lethargic child, again, dependent on the match between the behavior and the environment, different degrees of maladjustment would occur.

In terms of transformation, such a model is relatively silent. Even so, it would seem reasonable to imagine that new behaviors arise due either to the match or mismatch, but these new behaviors do not require the old behaviors to be transformed. The active child may learn to move more slowly, but the trait of activity is not lost or transformed. The environment, too, may change, because less is required of the child, but the values or goals underlying the requirement remain and are not changed.

In exploring early sex-role behavior in children and maternal attributes about sex role on subsequent adjustment, a goodness-of-fit model appeared to best explain the data. Lewis (1987a) observed the sex-role behavior of 2-year-olds in terms of how much the children played with male and female toys. There were large individual differences; some boys played more with boy toys than girl toys, and some boys played more with girl toys than boy toys. The same was true for the girls. Mothers were given the Bem Scales (1987), and we were able to determine their sex-role orientation. Some mothers were traditional, whereas others were more androgynous in their sex-role beliefs. We found that school adjustment, as rated by the teacher, was neither dependent on the mother's belief or the child's sex-role play. Rather, adjustment was dependent upon the goodness of fit between the child's play and the mother's belief. For example, boys showed subsequently better adjustment if their mothers were androgynous in belief, and they played equally with boy and girl toys, as well as if mothers were traditional and the boys played more with boy than girl toys. Adjustment at 6 years was worse if there was no fit; for example, if the mothers were traditional and the boys were androgynous, or if the mothers were androgynous and the boys were more male-toy oriented. The same was true for girls. The goodness of fit between the individual and its environment rather than the nature of the child's behavior itself may be more important for the development of maladaptive behavior. One therapeutic solution, then, is to alter the maladaptive behavior of the individual; the other is to alter the nature of the fit. Matching children by their characteristics to teachers' traits reduces educational mismatch and increases academic achievement.

The nontransformational feature of the goodness-of-fit model is particularly relevant for the development of psychopathology in two areas: the phenomenon of regression and the vulnerable child. Regression is a problem for any interactional model in which old behaviors are transformed and become new behaviors (Piaget, 1952). If old behaviors are transformed, they should disappear from the child's repertoire and should be unavailable for use once the new behaviors appear. This should be the case for the growth of intellectual or social behaviors. Nevertheless, it is clear that regression is a common occurrence in all domains and, as such, challenges the transformational model. It is not possible to use old behaviors if they were transformed. The appearance of regression requires that old behaviors do not disappear but are retained when new behaviors develop. New behaviors may have a greater likelihood of being elicited; however, old behaviors will occur, especially under stress.

The vulnerable child is another example of the usefulness of a nontransformational interactive model. A vulnerable child possesses some characteristics that places it at risk. If the environment is positive, the at-risk features are not expressed and the child appears to be adjusted. Over repeated exposures to the positive environment, the child appears adjusted; however, if given an instant or two of a negative environment, the child will appear maladjusted, showing abnormal behavior. It is obvious from this example that the positive environmental experiences were unable to transform the at-risk features that remained independent of their interaction with the environment. If the at-risk features remain independent of the environment and are displayed as positive or negative adjustment only as the environment changes, then a goodness-of-fit model, rather than a transformational model, best explains the data. It is possible that at-risk features are influenced by the environment such that repeated positive exposures make the response to a negative event less severe—a type of threshold view. Under such conditions, we approach a transformational model.

Transformational Model

The last model to be described often is captured in the contrast with earlier models, so a discussion of its unique features can be redundant. We try to avoid this here by our brevity. These types of models, which require that all features that make up an interaction are themselves comprised of all features and are transformed by their interaction, are called *transactional models* (Sameroff, 1975). For example, if we believe in Figure 1.3 that the child's characteristics at C_{t_1} interact with the environment E_{t_1} to produce a transformed C_{t_2} and E_{t_2}, then it is likely that C_{t_1} and E_{t_1} also were transformed from some earlier time $t_{(n-1)}$ and that, therefore, each feature is never independent of the other. The general expression of this, then is

$$(C_{t_1} \times E_{t_1}) \rightarrow C_{t_2}, E_{t_2}, \text{ where}$$
$$C_{t_1} = \int(C_{t_{n-1}} \times E_{t_{n-1}}) \text{ and}$$
$$E_{t_1} = \int(E_{t_{n-1}} \times C_{t_{n-1}}).$$

Such models reject the idea that child or environmental characteristics are ever independent or exist as "pure" forms; there is here an ultimate regression of effects. Moreover, these features interact and transform themselves at each point in development. The linear functions that characterize the other models are inadequate for the transformational view. The parent's behavior affects the child's behavior; however, the parent's behavior was affected by the child's earlier behavior.

Lewis and Feiring (1989), for example, have found that intrusive mothers of 3-month-olds are likely to have insecurely attached children at 1 year. However, their overstimulation appears to be related to their children's behavior. Children who do not appear socially oriented at 3 months prefer to play with and look at toys rather than people, and they are insecurely attached. These children have mothers who are overstimulating.

Insecure attachment at 1 year can be transformed given the proper environment, and an insecure attachment can transform a positive environment into a negative one. Consider the irritable child who interacts with a positive environment and produces a negative environment that subsequently produces a negative, irritable child. The causal chain does not simply pass in a continuous fashion either through the environment or through the irritable child as a trait or environmental model would have it. In fact, it is a circular pattern of child causes affecting the environment and the environmental causes affecting the child. Such models have intrinsic appeal, but are by their nature difficult to test. Nonlinearity requires a mathematics that still eludes us. However, recent theories of dynamic systems are now available that may allow us to explore this in more detail (Thelen & Ulrich, 1991; Thom, 1975; Zeeman, 1976). Even so, it is difficult not to treat a child or an environmental characteristic as a "pure" quantity, though we might know better. As such, we tend to test the interactive models that require less transformation.

As we have indicated earlier, other less extreme transformational models are possible. Transformational models rest on principles related to critical periods, threshold levels, and past experiences. Nevertheless, these models are transformational in nature and belong in any discussion of these types of effects.

WHAT IS MALADAPTIVE?

We have little trouble in defining psychopathology when we observe psychoses, since behaviors such as hallucinations or deeply disturbed thinking patterns indicate a clear pattern. On the other hand, there are behaviors we label as disturbed. In deciding whether we wish to call the behaviors psychotic or disturbed, our classification system becomes more of a problem (see Achenbach, Chapter 3, this volume). The issue here is whether all classes of psychopathology should be thought of as a yes–no, has or has not the disorder, or considered as a continuum. Psychotic disorders are usually thought of as yes–no; one cannot be a little psychotic. How about depression? It can be considered a yes–no disturbance, especially if we use a DSM-like classification system. On the other hand, it can be considered as a continuum, with the pathology classification representing one end of the continuum. Such problems continue to cause difficulties in the study of developmental psychopathology because of sampling and classification issues. The classification issues have to do with many problems, including what should be considered an outcome measure.

Sampling issues arise when we use a yes–no classification system given the relatively low base rate of most clinical disorders. In order to study the development of these disorders, very large samples need to be collected. Select subjects, who are at high risk for a disorder, can be used, but the likelihood of obtaining a high rate of disorder, through increased sample size, does not give us a very large number of subjects. Moreover, the selection of unique samples of high-risk children has its own problem. For example, the selection of a large schizophrenia sample for a study of development requires the examination of schizophrenic mothers (Garmezy & Rutter, 1983; Sameroff & Seifer, 1981). We know that the number of children showing early disorders, but not schizophrenia, is relatively lower than would be expected (Garmezy et al., 1984). Parenthetically, this fact results in our interest in stress resistance and the issue of invulnerability (Garmezy, 1981, 1989). Even when enough children are located, there are serious problems in logic when sampling procedures of this kind are employed.

Still another problem related to the outcome measures is the issue of not only what the classification of children should be, but also who classifies them. Typically, children themselves do not determine that they are disordered. Rather, a parent or teacher usually identifies signs of disorders and refers a child to a clinician (Lewis, 1990). An examination of childhood disorder must include parents' and teachers' perceptions of the child as well as the child's own perceptions. However, studies of child disorder, for example, depression, show that different people's assessments of the same child do not agree (Herjanic & Reich, 1982; Jensen, Salzberg, Richters, & Watanabe, 1993; Kazdin, French, Unis, & Esveldt-Dawson, 1983; Stavrakaki, Vargo, Roberts, & Boodoosingh, 1987). Patterns of agreement are no more consistent when outside raters such as clinicians, teachers, or peers are employed. Kazdin et al. (1983) found that parents and clinicians were in stronger agreement than children and clinicians, but Moretti, Fine, Haley, and Marriage (1985), Poznanski, Mokros, Grossman, and Freeman (1985), and Stavrakaki et al. (1987) reported the opposite. Research examining agreement between teachers and children also shows low levels of agreement (Achenbach, 1991; Jacobsen, Lahey, & Strauss, 1983; McConaughy, Stanger, & Achenbach, 1992; Saylor, Finch, Baskin, Furey, & Kelly, 1984). Peer ratings sometimes correlate with children's self-reported depression (Jacobsen et al., 1983; Lefkowitz & Testiny, 1980; Saylor et al., 1984), but only in normal samples. This raises the general issue of whether the assessment of the child's characteristics are consistent across raters or different measures. If this is not so, then factors that impact on individual differences may vary depending on the outcome measured (see Lewis, in press).

Raters may disagree about the same child for a number of reasons. First, different instruments are usually used to obtain ratings from different people, and the instruments might not be compatible (Achenbach, 1991; McConaughy et al., 1992; Stanger, McConaughy, & Achenbach, 1992). Second, low rates of agreement about child disorder also may be due to the fact that some raters might not know the child well enough to draw clinical conclusions. This is particularly important for syndromes such as depression, which may reflect a child's "inner state." Without knowing the inner state of the child, an observer might not be able to determine that a child is displaying symptoms of depression. A third reason for low rates of agreement may be due to the rater's own problems. For example, mothers who are more depressed perceive their children as more depressed (Richters, 1992).

Finally, it is likely that people's perceptions are based on the child's behavior in different situations. Teachers and parents experience the child in different circumstances that require different coping skills. That children are seen in different situations that elicit different behaviors is likely to be an important factor. Situationally determined behavior has been well documented (Snyder & Ickes, 1985). There is evidence that different observers base their judgments on different characteristics of the child (Routh, 1990). For example, Kazdin, Moser, Colbus, and Bell (1985) showed that parents and children emphasize different facets of the child's functioning. Children focused on internal feelings and expectancies for the future, while parents focused on the child's overt social behavior and outward manifestations of affect. Mischel (1990) has suggested that while behavior differs across situations, it may be consistent within situations. While parents, teachers, and children may disagree about the child, they may provide accurate assessments *within particular contexts*.

These problems support two ideas that need attention in any study of psychopathology. The first idea is that of an individual having characteristics that are enduring across situations and time. In general, while there may be some consistency across raters or scales and situations, the variance accounted for remains rather low considering the power of the idea of personality transcending situation, context, and other people. The second idea is that from a developmental point of view, the idea of predicting individual differences in psychopathology over time may be difficult if there is low agreement in terms of the classification of children and adults in terms of their psychopathology.

PREDICTION AND THE NOTION OF SUDDEN CHANGE

Predictability in the study of developmental psychopathology constitutes an important aspect of our definition (Santostefano, 1978; Sroufe & Rutter, 1984). Such a focus on prediction as a central feature is understandable because the origins of maladaptive behavior require an understanding of continuity and change. Even so, it is surprising that such a focus is required. Freud (1920/1955) doubted the ability of prediction. In truth, he appeared to be cognizant of the fact that retrospective prediction was much easier than prospective prediction (see also Freeman, 1984). His belief about the complexity involved in the development of maladaptive as well as normal behavior made him skeptical about the ability to predict outcome.

Even more important for our discussion is the recognition that elaborate debate exists within the domain of normal development to question the issue of continuity and therefore of prediction. It would be a mistake to assume that prediction is always possible or even a desired goal. The relationship between continuity and prediction allows us to view this problem from a developmental perspective. Much has been written on this topic (Brim & Kagan, 1980; Lewis, 1997; Reese & Overton, 1970).

The idea of continuity also involves the idea of gradualism. As espoused by Darwin (1871), gradualism assumes that a series of small changes can account for the development of complex outcomes. Gradualism in evolution has been attacked. Eldredge and Gould (1972), for example, proposed a theory of gradual change punctuated by sudden change. Alvarez (1982) and Raup (1986) demonstrated sudden change in evolutionary history. When applied to individual development, notions of continuity and gradualism take several forms, the most common form assuming that a person's development is an intraindividual process. Such theories assume that what the person is like now will determine what the person will be like in the future. It is a "trait" notion of development because the features residing within the individual lead to or become, in some one-to-one fashion, some other traits. Lewis (1987b, 1997) has shown that this model of development predominates, especially in theories of social development.

The alternative to a trait model, shared by most developmental theorists who consider themselves interactionalists, assumes that an individual's development is the result of a continuing interactive process in which people adapt to their changing environments, which, in turn, affect the environments themselves (Featherman, 1983). Such a model makes prediction difficult, if not impossible.

Prediction over time is limited in science in general (Heisenberg, 1962), and this may be true for development of psychopathology. The study of individual lives may have a greater degree of uncertainty than the study of physics, for example, but the principle is the same. For example, Faulconer and Williams (1985), after an analysis of positivism and historicism in human action, concluded that historicism is an illusion; that is, "true" history does not exist, only our reconstruction of it is real (see also Lewis, 1997; Spence, 1982). Given this condition, "such a goal (the search for certainty or prediction), in principle, is impossible for any science, especially a human science" (Faulconer & Williams, 1985, p. 1186). If historical prediction is not possible, it may be possible to understand individual differences from concurrent events or from current beliefs about historical events. Such a view does not endanger developmental study if we do not make prediction a criterion for development or developmental psychopathology (Lewis, 1997; Piaget, 1952; Wohlwill, 1973).

As for continuity in development, the answer remains in some doubt, even if we move from more specific traits to more general ones such as the coping strategies suggested by Sroufe and Rutter (1984). Consider the effect of wars and military service on men's lives. Wars are exogenous (and presumably random) and yet profoundly affect men's lives, altering them in ways not readily predicted even if we were to have an accurate historical record of men's lives before the war (Elder, 1986). We could consider less dramatic events, such as death, illness, floods, and fires, all of which are random to women's and men's lives and may profoundly alter them. For example, in therapy, an adolescent I knew had a terrible bicycle accident that resulted in permanent facial disfiguration. The change in her personality as a consequence of this accident could not have been predicted from her previous behavior or from knowledge of her coping style. Such data confirm a model of discontinuity due to environmental change not of the person's choosing and suggest that prediction may be impossible or difficult at best.

Any model that depicts development of psychopathology as a trajectory undisturbed by surrounding events, although created from the events earlier in time, needs reconsideration. Lewis (1997) suggests that the idea of contextualism, or environmental influences, does not require historicism. Individuals develop in the presence of random events and are more characterized by zigs and zags than by some predetermined connected and linear pattern. It is only when we understand how organism are influenced by their environments now and how people's ideas for their future can affect their desires and behaviors that we can understand the nature of pathology.

Even if some lives are not influenced by such strong exogenous events, prediction may be difficult. Implicit in Piaget's analysis of development and the nature of stages and change is the concept of discontinuity. We would agree with Piaget that there can be little prediction across the stages that make up early and normal life events. Within the first 2 years of life, we know that at 3, 8, and 15–18 months there occur significant central nervous system events that are likely to lead to discontinuities (Lewis, Jaskir, & Enright, 1986; McCall, Eichorn, & Hogarty, 1977). Such happenings, both within and without the organism, mean that the prediction of developmental psychopathology must be difficult, if not impossible.

In the chapters to follow, many of these ideas as well as specific content in the study of developmental psychopathology are explored. While some find agreement with the notions of models, processes, and prediction argued here, others do not. Nevertheless, it remains important to exercise our interests in developmental psychopathology by staying deeply grounded in the study of development in general. Indeed, it is impossible to conceptualize the study of developmental psychopathology without studying development and the models that underlie growth and change.

REFERENCES

Achenbach, T. M. (1991). *Manual for the Child Behavior Checklist and 1991 Child Behavior Profile.* Burlington: University of Vermont, Department of Psychiatry.

Ainsworth, M. D. S. (1973). The development of infant–mother attachment. In B. M. Caldwell & H. N. Ricciuti (Eds.), *Review of child development research* (Vol. 3, pp. 1–95). Chicago: University of Chicago Press.

Ainsworth, M. D. S. (1989). Attachment beyond infancy. *American Psychologist, 44,* 709–716.

Ainsworth, M. D. S., & Marvin, R. S. (1995). On the shaping of attachment theory and research: An interview with Mary D. S. Ainsworth. *Monographs of the Society for Research in Child Development, 62* (2–3, Serial No. 244).

Allport, F. H., & Allport, G. W. (1921). Personality traits: Their classification and measurement. *Journal of Abnormal and Social Psychology, 16,* 1–40.

Alvarez, L. W. (1982). Experimental evidence that an asteroid impact led to the extinction of many species 65 million years ago. *Proceedings of the National Academy of Science, 80,* 627.

Anthony, E. J. (1970). The behavior disorders of children. In P. H. Mussen (Ed.), *Carmichael's manual of child psychology* (pp. 667–764). New York: Wiley.

Bandura, A. (1986). *Social foundations of thought and action: A social cognitive theory.* Englewood Cliffs, NJ: Prentice-Hall.

Bellin, H. (1971). The development of physical concepts. In T. Michel (Ed.), *Cognitive development and epistemology* (pp. 85–119). New York: Academic Press.

Belsky, J., Pensky, E., & Youngblade, L. (1990). Childrearing history, marital quality and maternal affect: Intergenerational transmission in a low risk sample. *Development and Psychopathology, 1,* 291–304.

Bem, S. L. (1987). Masculinity and femininity exist only in the mind of the perceiver. In J. M. Reinish, L. A. Rosenblum, & S. A. Sanders (Eds.), *Masculinity/femininity: Basic perspectives* (pp. 304–314). New York: Oxford University Press.

Block, J., & Block, T. H. (1980). The role of ego control and ego resiliency in the organization of behavior. In W. Collins (Ed.), *Minnesota Symposium on Child Psychology* (Vol. 13, pp. 325–377). Hillsdale, NJ: Erlbaum.

Bornstein, M. (Ed.). (1987). *Sensitive periods in development: Interdisciplinary perspectives.* Hillsdale, NJ: Erlbaum.

Bowlby, J. (1969). *Attachment and loss: Vol. 1. Attachment.* New York: Basic Books.

Brim, O. G., Jr., & Kagan, J. (1980). Constancy and change: A view of the issues. In O. G. Brim, Jr. & J. Kagan (Eds.), *Constancy and change in human development* (pp. 1–25). Cambridge, MA: Harvard University Press.

Bronfenbrenner, U., & Crouter, A. C. (1983). The evolution of environmental models in developmental research. In W. Kessen & P. H. Mussen (Eds.), *History, theory, and methods: Handbook of child psychology* (Vol. 1, pp. 357–414). New York: Wiley.

Chess, S., & Thomas, A. (1984). *Origins and evolution of behavior disorders.* New York: Brunner/Mazel.

Chomsky, N. (Ed.). (1957). *Syntactic structures.* The Hague, Netherlands: Mouton.

Chomsky, N. (Ed.). (1965). *Aspects of the theory of syntax.* Cambridge, MA: MIT Press.

Cole, M. (1996). *Cultural psychology: A once and future discipline.* Cambridge, MA: Belknap Press of Harvard University Press.

Darwin, C. (1871). *On the origin of species.* London: John Murray.

Davies, P. T., & Cummings, E. M. (1994). Marital conflict and child adjustment: An emotional security hypothesis. *Psychological Bulletin, 116,* 387–411.

Dunn, J. (1993). *Young children's close relationships: Beyond attachment.* Newbury Park, CA: Sage.

Elder, G. J., Jr. (1986). Military times and turning points in men's lives. *Developmental Psychology, 22,* 233–245.

Eldredge, N., & Gould, S. J. (1972). Punctuated equilibria: An alternative to phyletic gradualism. In T. J. Schopf (Ed.), *Models in paleobiology* (pp. 83–115). San Francisco: Truman, Cooper.

Fagot, B. I., & Patterson, G. R. (1969). An *in vivo* analysis of reinforcing contingencies for sex role behaviors in the preschool child. *Developmental Psychology, 1,* 566–568.

Faulconer, J. E., & Williams, R. N. (1985). Temporality in human action: An alternative to positivism and historicism. *American Psychology, 40,* 1179–1188.

Featherman, D. L. (1983). *Biography, society and history: Individual development as a population process.* CDE Working Paper, University of Wisconsin.

Fox, N. A., Kimmerly, N. L., & Schafer, W. D. (1991). Attachment to mother/attachment to father: A meta-analysis. *Child Development, 62*(1), 210–225.

Freeman, M. (1984). History, narrative, and life-span development knowledge. *Human Development, 27,* 1–19.

Freud, S. (1955). The psychogenesis of a case of homosexuality in a woman. In J. Strachey (Ed. and Trans.), *The standard edition of the complete psychological works of Sigmund Freud* (Vol. 18, pp. 118–139). London: Hogarth. (Original work published 1920)

Garmezy, N. (1974). The study of competence in children at risk for severe psychopathology. In E. Anthony & C. Koupernik (Eds.), *The child in his family* (Vol. 3, pp. 77–98). New York: Wiley.

Garmezy, N. (1981). Children under stress: Perspectives on antecedents and correlates of vulnerability and resistance to psychopathology. In A. I. Rabin, J. Arnoff, A. M. Barclay, & R. A. Zucker (Eds.), *Further explorations in personality* (pp. 126–145). New York: Wiley.

Garmezy, N. (1989). Stress-resistant children: The search for protective factors. In J. E. Stevenson (Ed.), Aspects of current child psychiatry research (*Journal of Child Psychology and Psychiatry Book Supplement* No. 4, pp. 213–233). Oxford, UK: Pergamon Press.

Garmezy, N., Masten, A. S., & Tellegen, A. (1984). The study of stress and competence in children: A building block for developmental psychopathology. *Child Development, 55*, 987–1111.

Garmezy, N., & Rutter, M. (1983). *Stress, coping, and development in children*. New York: McGraw-Hill.

Gibson, J. J. (1969). *Principles of perceptual learning and development*. New York: Appleton–Century–Crofts.

Gottesman, I., & Shields, J. (Eds.). (1982). *Schizophrenia: The epigenetic puzzle*. New York: Cambridge University Press.

Heisenberg, W. (1962). *Physics and philosophy: The revolution in modern science*. New York: Helvetica Physica Acta (Supplementum IV, Basel, 1956).

Herjanic, B., & Reich, W. (1982). Development of a structured interview for children: Agreement between children and parents on individual symptoms. *Journal of Abnormal Child Psychology, 10*, 307–324.

Howes, P., & Markman, H. J. (1989). Marital quality and child functioning: A longitudinal investigation. *Child Development, 60*, 1044–1051.

Jacobsen, R. H., Lahey, B. B., & Strauss, C. C. (1983). Correlates of depressed mood in children. *Journal of Abnormal Child Psychology, 11*, 29–40.

Jensen, P. S., Salzberg, A. D., Richters, J. E., & Watanabe, H. K. (1993). Scales, diagnoses, and child psychopathology: I. CBCL and DISC relationships. *Journal of the American Academy of Child and Adolescent Psychiatry, 32*, 397–406.

Kallman, F. J. (1946). The genetic theory of schizophrenia: An analysis of 691 schizophrenic twin index families. *American Journal of Psychiatry, 103*, 309–322.

Kazdin, A. E., French, N. H., Unis, A. S., & Esveldt-Dawson, K. (1983). Assessment of childhood depression: Correspondence of child and parent ratings. *Journal of the American Academy of Child Psychiatry, 22*, 157–164.

Kazdin, A. E., Moser, J., Colbus, D., & Bell, R. (1985). Depressive symptoms among physically abused and psychiatrically disturbed children. *Journal of Abnormal Psychology, 94*, 298–307.

Kohlberg, L., LaCrosse, J., & Ricks, D. (1972). The predictability of adult mental health from childhood behavior. In B. Wolman (Ed.), *Manual of child psychopathology* (pp. 165–179). New York: McGraw-Hill.

Kringlon, E. (1968). An epidemiological twin study of schizophrenia. In D. Rosenthal & S. Kety (Eds.), *The transmission of schizophrenia* (pp. 49–63). New York: Pergamon Press.

Lamb, M. E., Thompson, R., Gardner, W., & Charnov, E. (1985). *Infant–mother attachment: The origins and developmental significance of individual differences in strange situation behavior*. Hillsdale, NJ: Erlbaum.

Lefkowitz, M. M., & Testiny, E. P. (1980). Assessment of childhood depression. *Journal of Consulting and Clinical Psychology, 48*, 43–50.

Lennenberg, E. H. (1967). *Biological foundations of language*. New York: Wiley.

Lerner, R. H. (1984). *On the nature of human plasticity*. New York: Cambridge University Press.

Lewis, M. (1972). State as an infant–environment interaction: An analysis of mother–infant interaction as a function of sex. *Merrill–Palmer Quarterly, 18*, 95–121.

Lewis, M. (1983). Newton, Einstein, Piaget, and the concept of self. In L. S. Liben (Ed.), *Piaget and the foundations of knowledge* (pp. 141–177). Hillsdale, NJ: Erlbaum.

Lewis, M. (1984). Social influences on development: An overview. In M. Lewis (Ed.), *Beyond the dyad* (pp. 1–12). New York: Plenum Press.

Lewis, M. (1987a). Early sex role behavior and school age adjustment. In J. M. Reinish, L. A. Rosenblum, & S. A. Sanders (Eds.), *Masculinity/femininity: Basic perspectives* (pp. 202–226). New York: Oxford University Press.

Lewis, M. (1987b). The social development of infants and young children. In J. Osofsky (Ed.), *Handbook of infant development* (2nd ed., pp. 419–493). New York: Wiley.

Lewis, M. (1990). Models of developmental psychopathology. In M. Lewis & S. Miller (Eds.), *Handbook of developmental psychopathology* (pp. 15–28). New York: Plenum Press.

Lewis, M. (1997). *Altering fate: Why the past does not predict the future*. New York: Guilford Press.

Lewis, M. (1999). On the development of personality. In L. Pervin & O. John (Eds.), *Handbook of personality* (2nd ed., pp. 327–346). New York: Guilford Press.

Lewis, M. (in press). Issues in the study of personality development. *Psychological Inquiry*.

Lewis, M., & Feiring, C. (1981). Direct and indirect interactions in social relationships. In L. Lipsitt (Ed.), *Advances in infancy research* (Vol. 1, pp. 131–163). New York: Ablex.

Lewis, M., & Feiring, C. (1989). Infant, mother, and mother–infant interaction behavior and subsequent attachment. *Child Development, 60,* 831–837.

Lewis, M., & Feiring, C. (1991). Attachment as personal characteristic or a measure of the environment. In J. L. Gewirtz & W. M. Kurtines (Eds.), *Intersections with attachment* (pp. 1–21). Hillsdale, NJ: Erlbaum.

Lewis, M., Feiring, C., & Rosenthal, S. (2000). Attachment over time. *Child Development, 7*(3).

Lewis, M., Jaskir, J., & Enright, M. (1986). Development of mental abilities in infancy. *Intelligence, 10,* 331–354.

Lewis, M., & Schaeffer, S. (1981). Peer behavior and mother–infant interaction in maltreated children. In M. Lewis & L. A. Rosenblum (Eds.), *The uncommon child* (Vol. 3, pp. 193–224). New York: Plenum Press.

Luria, A. R. (1976). *Cognitive development: Its cultural and social foundations.* Cambridge, MA: Harvard University Press.

McCall, R. B., Eichorn, D. H., & Hogarty, P. S. (1977). Transitions in early mental development. *Monographs of the Society for Research in Child Development, 42* (35, Serial No. 2).

McConaughy, S. H., Stanger, C., & Achenbach, T. M. (1992). Three-year course of behavioral/emotional problems in a national sample of 4- to 16-year-olds: I. Agreement among informants. *Journal of the American Academy of Child and Adolescent Psychiatry, 31,* 932–940.

Mischel, W. (1965). *Personality assessment.* New York: Wiley.

Mischel, W. (1990). Personality dispositions revisited and revised: A view after three decades. In L. Pervin (Ed.), *Handbook of personality: Theory and research* (pp. 111–134). New York: Guilford Press.

Moretti, M. M., Fine, S., Haley, G., & Marriage, K. (1985). Childhood and adolescent depression: Child-report vs. parent-report information. *Journal of the American Academy of Child Psychiatry, 24,* 298–302.

Piaget, J. (1952). *The origins of intelligence in children.* New York: International Universities Press.

Poznanski, E., Mokros, H. B., Grossman, J., & Freeman, L. N. (1985). Diagnostic criteria in childhood depression. *American Journal of Psychiatry, 142,* 1168–1173.

Puig-Antich, J. (1982). Psychobiological correlates of major depressive disorder in children and adolescents. In L. Greenspan (Ed.), *Psychiatry 1982: Annual Review* (pp. 41–64). Washington, DC: American Psychological Association.

Raup, D. M. (1986). Biological extinction in early history. *Science, 231,* 1528–1533.

Reese, H. W., & Overton, W. F. (1970). Models of development and theories of development. In L. R. Goulet & P. B. Baltes (Eds.), *Life-span developmental psychology: Research and theory* (pp. 115–145). New York: Academic Press.

Richters, J. E. (1992). Depressed mothers as informants about their children: A critical review of the evidence for distortion. *Psychological Bulletin, 112,* 485–499.

Riegel, K. F. (1976). *Psychology of development and history.* New York: Plenum Press.

Riegel, K. F. (1978). *Psychology, mon amour: A countertext.* Boston: Houghton Mifflin.

Routh, D. K. (1990). Taxonomy in developmental psychopathology: Consider the source. In M. Lewis & S. M. Miller (Eds.), *Handbook of developmental psychopathology* (pp. 53–62). New York: Plenum Press.

Rutter, M. (1979). Protective factors in children's responses to stress and disadvantage. In M. W. Kent & J. G. Rolf (Eds.), *Primary prevention of psychopathology: Vol. 3. Social competence in children* (pp. 150–162). Hanover, NH: University Press of New England.

Rutter, M. (1981). Stress, coping and development. Some issues and some questions. *Journal of Child Psychology and Psychiatry, 22,* 323–356.

Sameroff, A. (1975). Transactional models in early social relations. *Human Development, 18,* 65–79.

Sameroff, A., & Chandler, M. J. (1975). Reproductive risk and the continuum of caretaking causality. In F. D. Horowitz (Ed.), *Review of child development research* (Vol. 4, pp. 187–244). Chicago: University of Chicago Press.

Sameroff, A. J., & Seifer, B. (1981). The transmission of incompetence: The offspring of mentally ill women. In M. Lewis & L. Rosenblum (Eds.), *The uncommon child* (pp. 63–90). New York: Plenum Press.

Santostefano, S. (1978). *A biodevelopmental approach to clinical child psychology.* New York: Wiley.

Saudino, K. J. (1997). Moving beyond the heritability question: New directions in behavioral genetic studies of personality. *Current Directions in Psychological Science, 6*(4), 86–90.

Saylor, C. F., Finch, A. J., Baskin, C. H., Furey, W., & Kelly, M. (1984). Construct validity for measures of childhood depression: Application of a multitrait–multimethod methodology. *Journal of Consulting and Clinical Psychology, 52,* 977–985.

Schneider-Rosen, K., & Cicchetti, D. (1984). The relationship between affect and cognition in maltreated infants: Quality of attachment and the development of visual self-recognition. *Child Development, 55,* 648–658.

Skinner, B. F. (1953). *Science and human behavior.* New York: Macmillan.

Snyder, M., & Ickes, W. (1985). Personality and social behavior. In G. Lindzey & E. Aronson (Eds.), *Handbook of social psychology: Volume II. Special fields and applications* (pp. 883–947). New York: Random House.

Spence, D. P. (1982). *Narrative truth and historical truth meaning and interpretation in psychoanalysis*. New York: Norton.

Sroufe, L. A., & Rutter, M. (1984). The domain of developmental psychopathology. *Child Development, 55*, 17–29.

Stanger, C., McConaughy, S. H., & Achenbach, T. M. (1992). Three-year course of behavioral/emotional problems in a national sample of 4–16 year olds: II. Predictors of syndromes. *Journal of the American Academy of Child and Adolescent Psychiatry, 31*, 941–950.

Stavrakaki, C., Vargo, B., Roberts, N., & Boodoosingh, L. (1987). Concordance among sources of information for ratings of anxiety and depression in children. *Journal of the American Academy of Child and Adolescent Psychiatry, 26*, 733–737.

Szasz, T. S. (1961). *The myth of mental illness*. New York: Harper & Row.

Thelen, E., & Ulrich, B. D. (1991). Hidden skills: A dynamic systems analysis of treadmill stepping during the first year. *Monographs of the Society for Research in Child Development, 56* (1, Serial No. 223).

Thom, R. (1975). *Structural stability and morphogenesis*. Reading, MA: Benjamin.

Thomas, A., & Chess, S. (1977). *Temperament and development*. New York: Brunner/Mazel.

Thompson, R. A., Lamb, M. E., & Estes, D. (1982). Stability of infant–mother attachment and its relationship to changing life circumstances in an unselected middle class sample. *Child Development, 53*, 144–148.

Waters, E., Posada, G., Crowell, J., & Lay, K. (1993). Is attachment theory ready to contribute to our understanding of disruptive behavior problems? *Development and Psychopathology, 54*, 215–224.

Wohlwill, J. F. (1973). *The study of behavioral development*. New York: Academic Press.

Zahn-Waxler, C., Cummings, E. M., McKnew, D. H., & Radke-Yarrow, N. (1984). Altruism, aggression, and social interactions in young children with a manic–depressive parent. *Child Development, 55*, 112–122.

Zeeman, E. C. (1976). Catastrophe theory. *Scientific American, 234*, 65–83.

2

Dialectical Processes in Developmental Psychopathology

Arnold J. Sameroff

There is a set of dialectical contradictions inherent in any discipline that is not resolvable, and it is within these contradictions that the sources of progress can be found. Some of these contradictions are inherent in the study of psychology, others in the study of development, and still others are unique to the study of developmental psychopathology. One of the basic contradictions in each of these domains is between the labels we use to divide and categorize the phenomena with which we are concerned and the dynamic reality that comprises the phenomena themselves. Unique to the study of pathology is the contradiction between the abstracted diagnostic schemes we use for categorizing individuals and the complex dynamic processes of the individuals themselves.

Another dichotomy we must confront is the contrast between the study of serious mental disorders and mental health. Whereas clinicians have needed to center their attention on children who are in the greatest therapeutic need, most developmentalists who have entered the field have viewed the study of pathology in the few as a means for understanding the roots of mental health in the many. The study of mental disorder may be inseparable from the study of mental health, and it may be that the study of each is required for the understanding of the other (Sroufe, 1990).

The field is labeled with a concern for pathology, that is, disease. Here, we find another important dialectical contradiction in the name developmental psychopathology. By using a developmental approach in the study of pathology, we may find that the disease disappears when understood as one of many adaptational processes between the individual and life experiences.

The final contradiction lies in the nature–nurture dichotomy, where we find that by studying the environment, we obtain a better understanding of the individual, and by studying the individual, we obtain a better understanding of the environment. The better we understand

Arnold J. Sameroff • Center for Human Growth and Development, University of Michigan, Ann Arbor, Michigan 48109.

Handbook of Developmental Psychopathology, Second Edition, edited by Arnold J. Sameroff, Michael Lewis, and Suzanne M. Miller. Kluwer Academic/Plenum Publishers, New York, 2000.

the sources of these contradictions, the better will we be at understanding and changing the mental health of children.

THREE MAJOR ISSUES

The theoretical issues in developmental psychopathology can be captured in three major questions regarding conceptualizations of pathology, the individual development, and the role of the environment.

First, how do we define pathology? Is it a qualitative or quantitative judgment? Can individuals be placed on universal dimensions or are there qualitative distinctions to be made that place people in one category or another? Here, we find the important developmental issues of continuity and discontinuity, not only between one kind of individual and another, but also between the individual at one point in time and another.

Second, how do we understand individuals and their development? Is it through a search for stable characteristics of the individual independent of context, or is it the search for patterns of functioning in context? Moreover, do these characteristics change over time as the unfolding of some maturational pattern, or in reaction to new demands as each individual interacts with an expanding social domain?

Third, how do we conceptualize the environment? Is it a passive set of experiences that maximizes or minimizes innate individual potential, as in the concept of genetic ranges of reaction, or is experience transforming as it interacts and transacts with dynamic individual developmental processes?

Theories of Psychopathology

Developmental psychopathology arose as a new orientation to the etiology of psychopathology necessitated by the failure of more customary models to explain how disorders arise and are maintained. The traditional medical model of disorder is based on the presumption that there are identifiable somatic entities that underlie definable disease syndromes. Although within psychiatry the current dominant view of disease is still strongly biomedical, there is an increasing place allowed for social and psychological factors in the etiology of mental illness that may have an important role in the initiation, maintenance, and treatment of mental disorder. Traditionally, individuals were not seen as integrated systems of biological, psychological, and social functioning, but rather as divided into biological and behavioral selves. If the biology changes, either through infection or cure, the behavior changes. Three principles that emerge from this model are frequently applied to the study of psychopathology (Sameroff, 1995):

1. The same entity will cause the same disorder in all affected individuals, whether they be children or adults.
2. The same symptoms at different ages should be caused by the same entity.
3. Specific disorders of children should lead to similar adult disorders.

Unfortunately, none of these three principles can be generalized, especially with respect to the study of psychopathology. Regarding the first principle, the same biological problem can be related to quite different behaviors in children and adults, for example, the genetic deficit thought to underlie schizophrenia. Second, the same symptoms may be caused by quite different processes at different ages. The sadness that is a primary characteristic of adult affective disorders is a common reactive condition in childhood. Finally, for many emotional and behavioral problems in childhood, there is little evidence of continuity into adulthood. Most childhood emotional problems do not persist and there is little empirical evidence that connects adult disorders with childhood conditions. Even when continuities of symptoms are found, the connection to underlying entities is complex. Despite the fact that modern biology has moved beyond such a model in its own domain, there is a strong residue of such thinking when applied to the unknowns of behavioral functioning.

Developmental Psychopathology

The discipline of developmental psychopathology has been promoted as the foundation for major advances in our ability to understand, treat, and prevent mental disorders (Cicchetti, 1989). One assumption underlying this expectation is that the perspectives of developmentalists and psychopathologists offer different conceptualizations of the same phenomena and that their unification would produce a clarification of the appearance and etiology of psychological disturbances. In this vein, Rutter and Garmezy (1983) characterize this difference as the developmentalist's concern with *continuity* in functioning such that severe symptoms are placed on the same dimension as more normal behaviors in contrast to the pathologist's concern with *discontinuity*, where the abnormal is differentiated from the normal. The division of the field into those who approach the problem from a developmental perspective and those who approach from a clinical perspective has served to mask the fact that there are many different kinds of developmentalists and many different kinds of psychopathologists. These differences arise in contrasting interpretations of behavioral development and ultimately in contrasting views of the sources of behavioral deviation.

Recent progress in the technology of molecular genetics has led to a hope that the etiology of mental disorders will soon be revealed and that their treatment and prevention will follow. For example, Koshland (1993), the former editor of the journal *Science*, presents an optimistic picture in which the future will be better than the past because of expected "insights into the effect on complex processes such as IQ, bad behavior, and alcoholism by single genes or chemical reactions" (p. 1861). Although we may view this as a technological statement of fact, it can alternatively be interpreted as the expression of a particular belief system about the nature of the child and especially the nature of pathology. The basis for such linear hopes as Koshland's is a view of humans as determined by their biology and a view of development as an unfolding of predetermined lines of growth. Among these lines of development are those that produce the emotionally disturbed, such as schizophrenics and depressives, the cognitively disturbed, such as the learning disabled and the retarded, and the undisturbed, that is, normal individuals.

But would this model fit those individuals who do not stay on their predicted trajectories? There have been many full-term healthy infants who were predicted to have a happy course but instead ended up with a variety of mental disorders later in life. In these cases, one could argue that we have not yet developed the sophisticated diagnostic tools to identify their inherent deviancy at birth. However, how would one explain those infants who had already shown major disabilities and yet somehow did not progress to adult forms of disturbance (Sameroff & Chandler, 1975)?

The case of Helen Keller is probably the best-known counterpoint to the maturational view of development (Keller, 1904). The story of this deaf–blind woman required a model of development that went beyond the maturational blueprint to incorporate the powerful effect of environments on human potential. The biographies of many individuals that were certain candidates for a life of institutionalization but whose fate was altered to a happier end have been well documented (cf. Clarke & Clarke, 1976; Garmezy, 1985).

Because the fulfillment of most of the promises of molecular biology are still in the future, there is time to examine the gap between our current scientific knowledge and the elimination of mental disease. On the one hand, we can view this gap as a technical one that will be closed by the accomplishments of empirical initiatives such as the "Decade of the Brain." On the other hand, one can view this gap as a conceptual one that will continue to exist despite major advances in the biological understanding of developmental processes.

Notwithstanding vast scientific and technological advances over the last century, the solution to problems at both the individual and social level seems no closer. At the same time that there are major advances in our understanding of the biological underpinnings of such disorders as cancer, the rate of cancer increases. At the same time that major advances are made in the understanding of ecological systems, the rate of environmental devastation increases. And at the same time that major advances are made in our understanding of economic processes, the rate of poverty increases.

How can one explain such contradictions? At one level, the explanation may be that achievements in the laboratory are not readily translated into achievements in society at large, and that, eventually, scientific reason will prevail. At another level, the explanation may be that scientific reason itself may be at fault. A belief that scientific knowledge directly changes social behavior may be akin to a reductionistic belief that the action of atoms, molecules, and genes directly change human behavior. If such scientific reasoning is at fault, a different model of human and social action that respects the complexity of both may be necessary as an alternative view.

In recent years, a number of respected developmental psychologists have argued about the basic nature of the child and the correctness of our scientific models. For example, Kessen (1979, 1993), supporting the expansion of the contextualist view, proposes that the technological shifts in society are altering our scientific view of the child as an isolate that develops independent of experience to an image of the child as a continuous creation of social and biological contexts. In contrast, Scarr (1985) is able to reinterpret environmental influences from a reductionist perspective, arguing that theories that give context a major role in human development are based on underestimations of the power of genetic influences. She sees genes as directly influencing not only the characteristics of the child but also the child's environment.

My own view is that the appropriate model for understanding developmental psychopathology is one that matches the complexity of human behavior. Such a view is in accord with the beliefs of most of the founding voices of developmental psychopathology (Cicchetti, 1989; Cicchetti, Toth, & Maughan, Chapter 37, this volume; Sroufe & Rutter, 1984). Lewis, as well (see Chapter 1), describes the need for more complex explanatory models as he lists the inadequacies of linear models that focus on individual traits or simple environmental action. Many complexity approaches are based on general systems theory and similar attempts to integrate individual and contextual processes in a dynamic ecological model for understanding the sources of health and disorder that are the central concern of developmental psychopathology. In these views, if we find simplicity, it is an artifact. Although our goal should always be to find the signal in the noise, we need to make sure that it is noise and not music we have not yet learned to appreciate.

High-Risk Studies of Psychopathology

Developmental psychopathology has become a mainstream enterprise over the last decade. It began as an attempt to add some developmental content to the study and treatment of child psychopathology (Achenbach, 1974), which had, and still has in many camps, its main foundation in downward extensions of adult psychopathology. These simple beginnings represented an emerging revolution. Although a life-span perspective was implicit in the writings of Freud and Adolph Meyer, it was not explicit in general psychiatry. It took the high-risk movement to put the first cracks in the clay feet of traditional psychopathology. Although risk now is a field in its own right, in the late 1960s its meaning was restricted to risk for psychiatric disorder and grew out of an effort to understand the etiology of the then most diagnosed serious mental disease, schizophrenia.

Sarnoff Mednick and his colleagues (Mednick & McNeil, 1968) had argued that studying people with schizophrenia had not and would not illuminate the etiology of the disease because there were many things that happened to people after they got the diagnostic label that had little to do with how they got it. For example, they now had a label that led themselves and other people to think about and treat them differently, and the course of treatment from drugs to institutionalization had its own iatrogenic effects. Mednick argued that in order to really understand the factors directly associated with the disease, one had to study people before they got the label.

Whom to look at was the strategic question. It was not efficient to study everyone because only 1% of the population would become schizophrenic. The need was to find a subsample that was more likely to get the disorder than the general public, a subsample that was at "high risk." Mednick's answer was to study the offspring of schizophrenics because their risk for the disorder was 10 to 15 times higher than the general population. This was the answer adopted by the majority of the 14 or so projects that united in the Risk Research Consortium for the study of schizophrenia (Watt, Anthony, Wynne, & Rolf, 1984), under the intellectual leadership of Norman Garmezy (1974). Garmezy's career characterized the movement and evolution of the field from research wholly concerned with the roots of incompetence in a small segment of the population with serious mental disorders, to the study of the roots of competence in everyone.

Several stages in the growth of the field were consequences of the Risk Research Consortium. Each became a consequence of the dialectical contradiction between the question one was asking and the means one was using to answer it. In this case, it was a question of the etiological sequence leading to a disorder, schizophrenia, that did not appear until late adolescence. The means to an answer required studying younger children. Previously, there was little interest in children because they were presumed either to be too immature to have serious mental health problems or, in whatever problems they did have, to be identical to adults with psychopathology. The surprising results of actually studying children, in contradiction to old views, was that some children did have mental health problems and these problems did not readily map onto adult categories of mental illness.

The presumption in the case of later appearing schizophrenia was that there was an underlying biological continuity of disease, the schizotype, which manifested itself differently at different ages. Children with a schizotype would have different symptoms than adults with the same schizotype who had the disorder. The psychopathologist's research strategy was to identify markers of the schizotype during earlier periods that would be correlated with later schizophrenia. A number of hypotheses had arisen as to the nature of these markers, including birth complications (Mednick & Schulsinger, 1968), particular patterns of motor tonus (Fish, 1984), attentional patterns (Nuechterlein, 1984), and eye movement patterns (Holzman, Levy,

& Proctor, 1976). What is interesting about this strategy is that these markers need not be developmental links in the etiological chain; they are only markers of some underlying pathogenic process that has not yet been identified.

The Rochester Longitudinal Study (RLS) that my colleagues, Melvin Zax, Ronald Seifer, Ralph Barocas, and Alfred and Clara Baldwin have been involved in for almost 30 years (Sameroff, Seifer, Baldwin, & Baldwin, 1993; Sameroff, Seifer, & Zax, 1982) is an example of an old research model that centered on a linear analysis of the effects of parental psychopathology on child behavior. During the course of the study, however, adaptive changes were forced upon the investigators because of the lack of congruence between hypotheses and data. This dialectical process produced changes in the analytic strategy as well as the investigators' understanding of development—from a study of genetic influences on behavior to an investigation of the interaction of complex dynamic processes between individual and context. Bridging the gap between the unlimited complexity of dynamic developmental conceptualizations and the limited complexity of possible empirical investigations characterizes the scientific problematic for a discipline of developmental psychopathology.

In 1968, we (Sameroff & Zax, 1973) initiated a study using the high-risk approach developed by Mednick and Schulsinger (1968) in Denmark. We examined the early development of children of parents who had a variety of psychiatric diagnoses, with special attention to schizophrenia.

At the outset, we considered three major hypotheses: (1) that deviant behavior in the child would be attributed to variables associated with a specific maternal diagnosis (e.g., schizophrenia); (2) that deviant behavior would be attributable to variables associated with characteristics of mental illness in general, such as the severity and chronicity of the disorder, but no diagnostic group in particular; and (3) that deviant behavior would be associated with social status, exclusive of parental psychopathology.

In general, the first hypothesis found little support. Most of the significant differences found for the schizophrenic group occurred during the prenatal period, and these differences were in the mothers, not in the children. The schizophrenic mothers were the most anxious and least socially competent. They also had the worst prenatal obstetric status.

The second hypothesis, that mental illness in general would produce substantial effects, was supported more strongly. In almost every instance where there was a difference between diagnostic groups, it could be explained by a corresponding difference in the severity and/or chronicity of the illness. In addition, a large number of developmental effects produced by severity and/or chronicity differences did not have corresponding diagnostic differences.

When the number of significant outcomes was compared for differences in the diagnostic, mental illness, and social status dimensions, the highest density was found in the social class contrasts, the third hypothesis. One of the more interesting results was that the differences found between offspring of women with psychiatric diagnoses and those without were almost the same as those between offspring of lower and higher social status women.

From these analyses, a relatively clear picture could be seen. Among the mental illness measures, severity and chronicity of maternal disturbances were better predictors of risk than were specific diagnoses, but even stronger effects on development were found from social status variables.

High-Risk Conclusions

The excitement in the decade of the 1970s came from high-risk research targeting the offspring of schizophrenic women. As with most fads, the achievements rarely match the expectations and the study of those with high-risk schizophrenia was no exception. The last two major conference reports of the Risk Research Consortium (Goldstein & Tuma, 1987; Watt et al., 1984) contain sobering appraisals of the difficulties inherent in such research. Watt (1984) notes in his summary of this work that the various projects of the Risk Research Consortium had found hundreds of significant differences between children at high and low risk for schizophrenia. Unfortunately, this sensitivity does not extend to specificity because the same differences were found for children at risk for a variety of other psychiatric disorders. The inability of the RLS to find the roots of schizophrenia was not an exception in this research area. I return later to this issue of the universality of risk conditions for a variety of pathologies.

For most of the Risk Research Consortium, the concern with the etiology of schizophrenia was neither developmental nor social, nor was it concerned with understanding psychopathology in the light of normal behavior. But by engaging in the search for symptoms in children, the dialectical contradictions between hypotheses and reality led to new attention to the role of environmental experience and the importance of studying developmental processes in normal as well as abnormal children. The nonsymptomatic behavior of most children thought to be at risk led Garmezy (1985), for one, to transfer his concerns to the roots of competence in conditions of adversity. At Rochester, we were struck by how our attempts to study the child out of context were defeated by the profound effects of social variables on the lives of the children in our investigation. The contradiction here was that research devoted to understanding the nature of the child at risk for schizophrenia brought to the fore information that suggested it might be the nature of the environment that was as important as any biological heritage for their future mental health.

Pathology

There are two basic questions that need to be addressed for understanding childhood psychopathology: What does it mean to be disordered? Are disordered children different in kind or in degree? Here, the question has been best described by Zigler and Hodapp (1986) in their interpretation of mental retardation. In their view, there are two kinds of children with low intelligence scores. One group is dimensional and identified by the diagnostic test. They are part of the normal distribution of any attribute and, in the case of mental retardation, represent the less than 3% of individuals who are two standard deviations below the mean. Labeling them as retarded is an artifact of the normal distribution and not of the individuals themselves. It also produced the artifact of the 6-hour retarded child, who only manifests the difficulty when assessed through the lens of scholastic standards yet shows adequate social competence in the worlds of work and social relationships. This categorical view of retardation is further undermined by the major reduction in the percentage of mentally retarded individuals after 18 years of age, when they leave the academic environment and are no longer subject to normed tests of development (Berkson, 1978).

A second group of individuals that score in the retarded range is indeed different in kind from the first. They are organically impaired and the correlates of their low scores on the IQ test will be different than those of persons who are only at the low end of the normal distribution. Because their biology is different, the processes by which they develop may be different, and the therapeutic treatments required to improve their status may be different from the first group of children at the low end of the normal distribution. Behavioral genetic research has provided some confirmation for this dichotomy in that siblings of severely retarded children with IQs less than 50 tend to have normal average IQs of around 100, whereas siblings of mildly retarded children with IQs in the 60s had a lower average IQ of 85, and 20% were themselves retarded (Nichols, 1984).

When we move from mental retardation to mental illness, we are struck with the same question. Do the children with whom we are concerned represent the lowest part of a normal distribution or are they different in kind from the rest of the population? The answer to this question will have powerful implications for our understanding and treatment of their mental health problems. Community surveys of mental health routinely diagnose many more individuals as having psychopathology than make their way to clinical facilities. Are these results because of the lack of adequate services or because individuals' aberrant behavior is compensated by their life circumstances? Are there mental health criteria that distinguish those who are "really" deviant from those who are not? Moreover, will these criteria apply to individuals regardless of their context or only reflect deviance between individuals and their specific contexts?

Illness is generally associated with suffering. Although adult mental disorder is usually associated with suffering, in the case of children, it is usually the pain of others that brings them to clinical attention. It is the parents, teachers, and other caregivers who are the referral agents, especially for young children (Achenbach, 1974). The pain for them is that the child does not fit in. This is not to say that the children are not in distress, but when they are, it is usually the result of abuse and neglect. In these cases, we place the responsibility and the diagnosis on the parents and not on the child. In either case, we are confronted with the fact that mental illness in children is not an individual problem; it is a relationship problem in the conflict between the child and the context.

INDIVIDUAL DEVELOPMENT

Although absolutely necessary for scientific progress, one of the biggest problems for the field of psychology in general, and for developmental psychopathology in particular, is the use of operational definitions. These definitions require dividing the world into categories that can be easily grasped and catering to reductionist tendencies to view behavior as trait-like characteristics of the behaver. A number of developmental psychopathologists have been trying to counter this tendency.

One of the more articulate redefinitions of psychopathology in developmental terms has been provided by Sroufe and Rutter (1984), who saw the discipline as "the study of the origins and course of individual patterns of behavioral adaptation" (p. 18). Dante Cicchetti (1986) enlarged this concept by rooting it in Heinz Werner's (1948) classic organismic–developmental approach. He argues that

> it is necessary to engage in a comprehensive evaluation of those factors that may influence the nature of patterns, and the different pathways by which the same developmental outcomes may be achieved. It is important to map out the processes whereby the normal course of development in the social, emotional, and or cognitive domains, in dynamic transaction with the "inner" constitutional and "outer" environmental characteristics, may lead to outcomes that either inhibit or exacerbate early deviations or maintain or disrupt early adaptation. (p. vii)

However, such a degree of articulation is not easy to understand. Traits and their psychopathological analogs, diagnoses, are much easier. An individual is examined and a descriptor is applied—sad, manic, hyperactive, oppositional. Much like physical characteristics such as skin color, height, and body shape, they are thought of as inhering within the individual. If the individual moves from situation A to situation B, these attributes remain the same. A *pattern of adaptation* is far more complicated to assess. The implication of adaptation is that when situations change, the individual changes. Here, categories are not inherent in the individual but in relationships between the individual and situations.

Consider the practical difficulty in using such a system for understanding child development. One would have to know the general adaptive problems of children as they go through various life phases. Then, one would have to know the specific cultural variations and expectations for emotional and behavioral expression. And one would have to know the unique family parameters related to parent figures, caregiving figures, and finally, with our new understanding of the importance of nonshared environments within the family, one would need to have an additional understanding of the sibship patterns. In short, to have a scientific understanding of children's adaptive behavior, one would have to have the breadth of a good clinician.

Traits

A simpler alternative would be to use an assessment of traits of the child that are more easily classified through responses to a diagnostic interview or a behavioral questionnaire. The initial foray of psychiatry into child mental health involved a downward extension of adult categories, with the expectation that children would fit these classifications—to the extent that they would fit any categories. Costello and Angold (1996), in a review of the history of childhood psychopathology, point out that the first, most basic distinction for adults and children was between "imbeciles" and "lunatics," between the mentally retarded and the mentally ill. For children, the next distinction was between instinctive insanity, which was an aberration of instincts and passions, and moral insanity, which was a defect in moral qualities. What we have now is a much more elaborate schema with clear categories and descriptions and criteria for placing children in these categories described in the following sections of this handbook. Depression and conduct disorder are two of the most active research areas in developmental psychopathology so I would like to use these disorders as illustrations of problems in diagnosis.

Depression

The criteria that have been used to identify children with depression vary from high scores on a parent checklist to careful diagnostic interviews. Compas and Hammen (1994) have done an extensive analysis of the meaning of such scores. They raise three questions that overlap with our present concerns. The questions are whether a depressive disorder in childhood takes the same form as a depressive disorder in adulthood, whether high depression scores are different in quality or merely quantity from low depression scores, and a new issue involving the meaning of the correlation between symptoms of depression and symptoms of other disorders, the comorbidity question.

Their answers increase the complexity of the diagnostic problem because there appear to be three levels of depressive phenomena with similar degrees of sadness—depressed mood, depressive syndromes, and depressive disorders. It is only the latter, with criteria for an extended duration and accompanying functional impairment, that qualifies for the categorical diagnosis. But the bigger difficulty is that it is rare for children who have depression problems to have only depression problems. There is a tendency for emotional and behavioral problems to cluster or co-occur in the same individual. This co-occurrence can be variously thought of as covariation, interrelatedness, or comorbidity.

Comorbidity is a fascinating issue. It should be rare for an individual to have one serious disorder, much less two. Because one has diabetes should not make it more likely that he or she has cancer. But for psychiatric disorders, this seems to be the case. For depression, comorbidity is the rule not the exception. A review of community epidemiological studies found a range of comorbidity between 33% and 100% (Flemming & Offord, 1990). Anxiety conditions are most frequently comorbid with depression, so one might think that this could be easily explained because they are both internalizing disorders. But the co-occurrence with externalizing disorders is equally as high, ranging from 17% to 79%, including conduct disorders, oppositional defiant disorders, attention deficit disorder, and alcohol and drug abuse. Moreover, the worse the course of the child's depression, the more likely that she or he would have a concurrent, nonaffective comorbid condition (Keller et al., 1988).

For a while, when depression was first being discovered in children, it was believed that everything was a symptom of depression. The concept of masked depression was posited as an explanation for all these other symptoms (Cytryn & McKnew, 1979). Now, we understand that these other conditions are not simple expressions of underlying depression. They are symptoms and disorders in their own right.

Compas and Hammen end their review with a provocative idea that high rates of covariation and comorbidity of depressive phenomena are the result of the exposure of high-risk children to multiple sources of risk that contribute independently to negative outcomes. We return to this idea when we consider the whole issue of risk and resilience.

Conduct Disorder

Externalizing problems are much more intrusive into the lives of those around affected children than internalizing problems. Conduct disorders did not require a psychiatric revolution for their discovery and have long been a social as well as clinical concern. Crime is mostly committed by teenagers and young adults but it does not easily fit in with mental illness categories because, for most individuals, it is self-limiting. For one reason or another, children start and then stop, most within a 1-year period of time (Elliott, Huizinga, & Ageton, 1985).

Although adult antisocial behavior is generally preceded by childhood antisocial behavior, most antisocial children do not become antisocial adults, because most adults are not antisocial (Robins, 1978). There does appear to be a group of early offenders who are persistent through early adulthood. Stattin and Magnusson (1991) found that this group accounted for only 5% of their sample but 62% of the crimes. If there was going to be a valid diagnosis of conduct disorder, this would appear to be the group that would have it. Yet this group also has the highest levels of comorbidity. Boys who were only aggressive were less likely to become persistent offenders than boys who were aggressive and hyperactive, for example. They were also more likely to have a variety of nondiagnostic problems, including academic deficiencies, poor interpersonal relationships, and deficiencies in social problem-solving skills.

Developmental pathways associated with conduct disorder have had their best empirical demonstration in a developmental analysis of boys from childhood to adolescence by Rolf Loeber and his colleagues (Loeber et al., 1993). They were able to distinguish three pathways: (1) an early authority conflict pathway characterized by stubborn behavior, defiance, and authority avoidance; (2) a covert pathway characterized by minor covert behaviors, property damage, and moderate to serious forms of delinquency; and (3) an overt pathway characterized by aggression, fighting, and violence. This information is very important for appreciating the developmental trajectories that children follow through these behavior patterns, but does it throw light on any trait for conduct disorder in these youth? Not as much as we would hope. The worse the disorder, in this case, delinquency, the more likely the boys were to appear in more than one pathway, with the highest rates for youth in all three pathways.

As in the other studies, comorbidity is rampant in this sample with attention deficit/ hyperactivity disorder and substance abuse especially associated with the overt pathway. The result is that the more serious the disturbance, not only is comorbidity between disorders more likely, but also multiple deviant pathways within a disorder are more likely.

Patterns of Adaptation

What we have learned from this discussion of individual behavior is that children are integrated wholes rather than collections of traits. When they show evidence of serious dysfunction, it is not restricted to single domains unless we only measure single domains of dysfunction. The worse the problems, the more likely it is that more than one behavioral area is involved. The concept of patterns of adaptation does not provide an easy catalog of behavior but may be a better fit for understanding how children are negotiating their lives and the resulting positive or negative consequences. The pattern concept would require us to examine continually each element of the child's behavior in relation to the whole, a more complex but ultimately more useful way of viewing the child (Achenbach, 1995).

THE ENVIRONMENT

The early childhood data from the RLS had a transactional effect on the course of the rest of the study through adolescence. What had begun as a study of children was transformed into a study of environments. We had discovered, on the one hand, if the only developmental risk for a child was a mother with a mental illness, that child was doing fine. On the other hand, if the child had a mother who was mentally ill, who was also poor, uneducated, without social supports, and with many stressful life events, that child was doing poorly. But, we also found that children whose mothers were poor, uneducated, without social supports, and with many stressful life events had worse outcomes, even if the mother did not have a psychiatric diagnosis. In the RLS, social circumstance was a more powerful risk factor than any of the parental mental illness measures. What we learned was the overriding importance of attending to the context of the children in the study, in order to understand their development, but it was not yet clear what would be the best approach to understanding environmental influences.

The analysis of social ecologies proposed by Bronfenbrenner (1977) described a range of social influences, from the parent practices that have direct influence on the child to community and economic factors that can only impinge on the child through the action of others. Depending on disciplinary background, different sets of these social variables have been proposed to explain the sources of mental health problems. Economists have focused on poverty and deprivation, sociologists have implicated problems in the community and family structure, educators blame the school system, and psychologists have focused on processes within the family and its members as the environmental influences that most profoundly affect successful development. Rather than viewing these as competing hypotheses, each can be interpreted as a contributor to a positive or negative mental health trajectory. The ecological model emphasizes the contributions of multiple environmental variables at multiple levels of social organization to multiple domains of child development. To review even a fraction of the literature on parents, parenting, families, neighborhoods, cultures, and socioeconomic influences would be beyond the scope of this chapter, but such information can be found in the chapters to follow.

For the purposes of this discussion of issues in developmental psychopathology, I restrict the review to two environmental issues: the multiple risk model and the contrast among risk, protective, and promotive factors. Although a central role of epidemiology is the identification of the causes of poor health, Costello and Angold (Chapter 4, this volume) point out that in the study of complex physical disorders, the preponderance of studies has identified risk factors rather than causes. Moreover, such comprehensive efforts as the Framingham Study of heart disease have discovered that no single influence is either sufficient or necessary to produce the disorder. In the domain of mental illness, a variety of studies, beginning with Rutter (1979), have noted that it may be the quantity rather than the quality of risk factors that is most predictive when data from multiple environmental influences are combined.

In the RLS, we combined 10 environmental risk variables to calculate a multiple risk score for each child at the age of 4. These included (1) a history of maternal mental illness; (2) high maternal anxiety; (3) parental perspectives that reflected rigidity in the attitudes, beliefs, and values that mothers had in regard to their child's development; (4) few positive maternal interactions with the child observed during infancy; (5) head of household in unskilled occupations; (6) minimal maternal education; (7) disadvantaged minority status; (8) single parenthood; (9) stressful life events; and (10) large family size. The resulting score was highly correlated with child mental health. The more risk factors, the greater the prevalence of clinical symptoms in the preschoolers (Sameroff, Seifer, Zax, & Barocas, 1987). These effects were also found when multiple environmental risk scores were correlated to child mental health at 13 and 18 years of age (Sameroff, Bartko, Baldwin, Baldwin, & Seifer, 1998).

Another opportunity to examine the effects of multiple environmental risks on child development was provided by data emerging from a study of adolescents in a large sample of Philadelphia families (Furstenberg, Cook, Eccles, Elder, & Sameroff, 1999). We took a more conceptual approach in designing the project so that there were environmental measures at a series of ecological levels: parent–child interaction, parent personality, family process, peer influences, school quality, and neighborhood resources. As in the RLS, there were linear relations between a multiple risk score and adolescent mental health, problem behavior, and academic performance (Sameroff et al., 1998).

The concern with preventing developmental failures has often clouded the fact that the majority of children in every social class and ethnic group are not failures. They get jobs, have successful social relationships, and raise a new generation of children. The concern with the source of such success has fostered an increasing concern with the development of competence and the identification of protective factors, as in the work of Masten and Garmezy (1985). However, the differentiation between risk and protective factors is far from clear and there continue to be many theoretical and methodological limitations in their identification (Luthar & Zigler, 1991).

Although some have argued that protective factors can only have meaning in the face of adversity (Rutter, 1987), in most cases, protective factors appear to be simply the positive pole of risk factors (Stouthamer-Loeber et al., 1993). In this sense, a better term for the positive end of the risk dimension would be *promotive* rather than protective factors. To test this simplification, we created a set of promotive factors by identifying families at the positive pole of each of our risk factors (Sameroff, Seifer, & Bartko, 1997). For example, where a negative family climate had been a risk factor, a positive family climate now became a promotive factor, or where a parent's poor mental health was a risk factor, her good mental health became promotive. We then summed these promotive factors and examined their relation to adolescent outcomes. The results mirrored the effects of multiple risks. Families with many promotive factors did substantially better than families from contexts with few promotive factors. For the youth in this study, there did not seem to be much difference between the influence of risk and promotive variables. The more risk factors, the worse the outcomes; the more promotive factors, the better the outcomes. In short, when taken as part of a constellation of environmental influences on child development, most contextual variables in the parents, the family, the neighborhood, and the culture at large seem to be dimensional, aiding in general child development at one end and inhibiting it at the other.

Interpreting Environmental Action

Reviews of the environmental risk factors that lead to particular mental health problems have been converging on what at first appeared to be a startling conclusion. The lists of risks associated with depression, conduct disorder, substance abuse, and even schizophrenia look the same. Bad environmental elements that affect one outcome also affect others (Coie et al., 1993). This is certainly unsatisfying when one is searching for causal chains leading from antecedents to consequences. Developmental psychology has and should thrive on the study of processes. We need to know the details of how all pieces fit together. But when we are seeking pathology, those individuals who are at the end of the normal distributions, we may not be able to find it in single processes.

Development is composed of many-part processes, each requiring its own set of experiences. But these processes are integrated into a whole by the developing self. If one or another part of this progression goes awry, there are sufficient compensating processes in the average social environment. However, when the compensating processes as well as the nurturing processes are missing, regulation becomes more and more difficult. It is the accumulation of environmental adversity that combines with unusual needs of the child that produces initial patterns of maladjustment that then spin their way to diagnosable pathology. Multipathology, perhaps a better term than comorbidity, is usually associated with a plenitude of risk factors and a paucity of promotive ones.

We still have no answer to whether such psychopathology is found in children who differ in degree or in kind. What we do know is that the dimensions on which such judgments are based will not be simple ones.

REGULATORY SYSTEMS IN DEVELOPMENT

The developmental approach expands upon traditional models of mental disease by incorporating biological and behavioral functioning into a general systems model of developmental organization. Within this approach, underlying entities do not exist independent of developmental organization. The expression of biological vulnerabilities can occur only in relation to the balance between coping skills and stresses in each individual's life history

(Zubin & Spring, 1977). Continuities in competence or incompetence from childhood into adulthood cannot be simply related to continuities in underlying pathology or health.

The relations between earlier and later behavior have to be understood in terms of the continuity of ordered or disordered experience across time interacting with an individual's unique biobehavioral characteristics. To the extent that experience becomes more organized, problems in adaptation will diminish. To the extent that experience becomes more chaotic, problems in adaptation will increase. What the developmental approach contributes is the identification of factors that influence the child's ability to organize experience and, consequently, the child's level of adaptive functioning.

A theory that integrates our understanding of pathology and development must explain how the individual and the context work together to produce patterns of adaptive or maladaptive functioning and relate how such past or present functioning influences the future. The most basic principle to emerge in such a general theory of development is that individuals can never be removed from their contexts. Whether the goal is understanding causal connections, predicting outcomes, or intervention, it will not be achieved by removing the individual from the conditions that regulate development.

Growing attention is being given to the biological regulators of development. New advances in biological research are forcing researchers to pay more attention to analyzing environmental influences. At the molecular level, we have learned that despite the fact that every cell in an organism has the same genotype, each will have different characteristics and a different history. This differentiation is a function of the differing experiences of each cell; these are environmental effects.

Similarly, at the level of behavioral genetics, we have learned that each family member has a unique environment of his or her own (Plomin, 1994). The concept of nonshared environments forces us to move beyond socioeconomic status (SES) or family warmth as our primary indicators of the environment to measures of how each individual is experiencing his or her own niche. As the child develops, the number of proximal environments expands from the parents and siblings in the immediate family to the peer group, to the school and community, and each has its own set of influences on the course of development.

Environtypes

To alleviate our scientific distress at the multiplying number of documented influences on development, I have proposed a conceptual simplification that disguises a large measure of complexity (see Figure 2.1). In this model, there is an organization of the environment over time that captures the processes that are relevant to individual development. Just as there is a biological organization, the genotype, that regulates the physical outcome of each individual, there is a social organization that regulates the way human beings fit into their society. This organization operates through family and cultural socialization patterns and has been postulated to compose an "environtype" analogous to the biological genotype (Sameroff, 1995; Sameroff & Fiese, 1990).

The child's behavior at any point in time is a product of the transactions between the phenotype (i.e., the child), the environtype (i.e., the source of external experience), and the genotype (i.e., the source of biological organization). Traditional developmental research has emphasized the child's utilization of biological capacities to gain experience and the role of experience in shaping child competencies, but there has been far less attention to how that experience is organized. Indeed, the organization of experience is explicit in the great amount

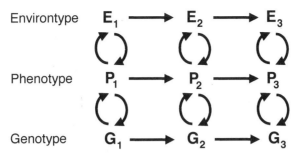

FIGURE 2.1. Regulation model of transactional development in which genotype and environtype change the phenotype as each is reciprocally changed by the phenotype over time.

of attention given to curriculum development and behavior modification plans, but far less attention is given to the implicit organization of experience found in the environtype.

From conception to birth, interactions with the biological system are most prominent. These processes continue less dramatically after birth, with some exceptions, for example, the initiation of adolescence and possibly senility. The period from birth to adulthood is dominated by interactions with the social system. The result of these regulatory exchanges is the expansion of each individual's ability for biological self-regulation and the development of behavioral self-regulation. Advances in motor development permit children to maintain thermal regulation and nutrition that initially needed to be provided by caregivers. Children soon are able to dress themselves and reach into the refrigerator.

There are clearly individual differences in developmental success, but it is the role of the environtype through the actions of parents, child care providers, educators, therapists, and other social agents to facilitate adaptation. If a parent or teacher is unresponsive or unadaptive to the needs of the child, this could result in a diagnosis of deviancy aimed at the parent or teacher as well as at the child. Successful assessments need to be directed at the environment to the same degree as to the child if we are to have successful interventions and treatments.

What is clear is that there is no emergent simplification on either the environmental or constitutional side that can explain how successful development occurs or how development can be changed. Single factors can be potent in destroying systems. An earthquake can destroy a city, or a gunshot can destroy a child. But single factors cannot create a child or any other living system. At the biological level 100,000 genes are required to transform an egg cell into an adult human body, each gene expressing itself in precise degrees at precise times in precise locations. It may take far more than 100,000 events to produce the complex psychological functioning of the adult human, integrating a wide variety of environmental experiences with a wide variety of developing capacities.

Contexts and Adaptation

The field of developmental psychopathology has introduced an important reorientation to the study of mental health and disorder. The principles of development that apply to the achievement of healthy growth are now seen as the same ones that apply to the achievement of illness (Sroufe & Rutter, 1984). In this view, most illnesses are indeed achievements that result from the active strivings of each individual to reach an adaptive relation to his or her environment. The nutrients or poisons that experience provides will flavor that adaptation. No complex human accomplishment has been demonstrated to arise without being influenced by experience. From this dynamic perspective, the discussion of developmental psychopathology can be summarized in three aspects: an adaptational process, a linkage between constitution and experience, and a linkage across time.

The study of the adaptational process emphasizes the constructive aspect of development in which each individual comes to terms with the opportunities and limitations of experience to produce a uniquely integrated outcome. The study of the linkage between constitution and experience contains the recognition that no individual can be understood apart from the context in which he or she lives, captured in the concept of an environtype that provides a locus for the many levels of influence at both family and societal levels that potentially regulate the adaptational process. The study of linkages across time perhaps most defines developmental psychopathology in that it contains the basis for continuities and discontinuities.

The perspective taken by developmental psychopathology offers a powerful alternative to nondevelopmental approaches, because principles of process are integrated into an understanding of behavioral deviancy. Where traditional views have seen deviancy as inherent in the individual, developmental views place deviancy in the dynamic relation between the individual and the internal and external context.

REFERENCES

Achenbach, T. M. (1974). *Developmental psychopathology*. New York: Ronald Press.

Achenbach, T. M. (1995). Developmental issues in assessment, taxonomy, and diagnosis of child and adolescent psychopathology. In D. Cicchetti & D. J. Cohen (Eds.), *Developmental psychopathology: Volume 1. Theory and minds* (pp. 57– 80). New York: Wiley.

Berkson, G. (1978). Social ecology and ethology of mental retardation. In G. P. Sackett (Ed.), *Observing behavior: Vol. I. Theory and applications in mental retardation* (pp. 403–409). Baltimore: University Park Press.

Bronfenbrenner, U. (1977). Toward an experimental ecology of human development. *American Psychologist, 32*, 513–531.

Cicchetti, D. (1986). Foreword in E. Zigler & M. Glick (Eds.), *A developmental approach to adult psychopathology*. New York: Wiley.

Cicchetti, D. (1989). Developmental psychopathology: Some thought on its evolution. *Development and Psychopathology* (pp. i–viii), *1*, 1–4.

Clarke, A. M., & Clarke, A. D. B. (1976). *Early experience: Myth and evidence*. London: Open Books and New York: Free Press.

Coie, J. D., Watt, N. F., West, S. G., Hawkins, J. D., Asarnow, J. R., Markman, H. J., Ramey, S. L., Shure, M. B., & Long, B. (1993). The science of prevention: A conceptual framework and some directions for a national research program. *American Psychologist, 48*, 1013–1022.

Compas, B. E., & Hammen, C. L. (1994). Child and adolescent depression: Covariation and comorbidity in development. In R. J. Haggerty, L. R. Sherrod, N. Garmezy, & M. Rutter (Eds.), *Stress, risk, and resilience in children and adolescents: Processes, mechanisms, and interventions* (pp. 225–267). New York: Cambridge University Press.

Costello, E. J., & Angold, A. (1996). Developmental psychopathology. In R. B. Cairns, G. H. Elder, Jr., & E. J. Costello (Eds.), *Developmental science* (pp. 168–189). New York: Cambridge University Press.

Cytryn, L., & McKnew, D. H. (1974). Factors influencing the changing clinical expression of the depressive process in children. *American Journal of Psychiatry, 131*, 879–881.

Elliott, D. S., Huizinga, D., & Ageton, S. S. (1985). *Explaining delinquency and drug use*. Beverly Hills, CA: Sage.

Fish, B. (1984). Characteristics and sequelae of the neurointegrative disorder in infants at risk for schizophrenia: 1952–1982. In N. F. Watt, E. J. Anthony, L. C. Wynne, & J. E. Rolf (Eds.), *Children at risk for schizophrenia: A longitudinal perspective* (pp. 423–439). New York: Cambridge University Press.

Flemming, J. E., & Offord, D. R. (1990). Epidemiology of childhood depressive disorders: A critical review. *Journal of American Academy of Child and Adolescent Psychiatry, 29*, 571–580.

Furstenberg, F. F., Jr., Cook, T. D., Eccles, J., Elder, G. H., Jr., & Sameroff, A. (1999). *Managing to make it: Urban families and adolescent success.* Chicago: University of Chicago Press.

Garmezy, N. (1974). Children at risk: The search for the antecedents of schizophrenia: Part 2. Ongoing research programs, issues and intervention. *Schizophrenia Bulletin, 9,* 55–125.

Garmezy, N. (1985). Stress-resistant children: The search for protective factors. In J. E. Stevenson (Ed.), *Recent research in developmental psychopathology* (pp. 213–233). Oxford, UK: Pergamon Press.

Goldstein, M., & Tuma, S. (1987). High risk research: Editors' introduction. *Schizophrenia Bulletin, 13,* 369–372.

Holzman, P. S., Levy, D. L., & Proctor, L. R. (1976). Smooth pursuit eye movements, attention, and schizophrenia. *Archives of General Psychiatry, 33,* 1415–1420.

Keller, H. (1904). *The story of my life.* New York: Doubleday, Page.

Keller, M. B., Beardslee, W., Lavori, P. W., Wunder, J., Dils, D. L., & Samuelson, H. (1988). Course of major depression in non-referred adolescents: A retrospective study. *Journal of Affective Disorders, 15,* 235–243.

Kessen, W. (1979). The American child and other cultural inventions. *American Psychologist, 34,* 815–820.

Kessen, W. (1993). The child and other cultural inventions. In F. S. Kessel & A. W. Siegel (Eds.), *The child and other cultural inventions* (pp. 26–47). New York: Praeger.

Koshland, D. E., Jr. (1993). The molecule of the year. *Science, 258,* 1861.

Loeber, R., Wung, P., Keenan, K., Giroux, B., Stouthamer-Loeber, M., Van Kammen, W. B., & Maughan, B. (1993). Developmental pathways in disruptive child behavior. *Development and Psychopathology, 5,* 103–133.

Luthar, S. S., & Zigler, E. (1991). Vulnerability and competence: A review of research on resilience in childhood. *American Journal of Orthopsychiatry, 61,* 6–22.

Masten, A. S., & Garmezy, N. (1985). Risk, vulnerability, and protective factors in psychopathology. In B. B. Lahey & A. E. Kazdin (Eds.), *Advances in clinical child psychology* (Vol. 8, pp. 1–52). New York: Plenum Press.

Mednick, S. A., & McNeil, T. F. (1968). Current methodology in research on the etiology of schizophrenia: Serious difficulties which suggest the use of the high-risk group method. *Psychological Bulletin, 70,* 681–693.

Mednick, S. A., & Schulsinger, F. (1968). Some premorbid characteristics related to breakdown in children and schizophrenic mothers. In D. Rosenthal & S. S. Kety (Eds.), *The transmission of schizophrenia* (pp. 267–292). Oxford, UK: Pergamon Press.

Nichols, P. (1984). Familial mental retardation. *Behavior Genetics, 14,* 161–170.

Nuechterlein, K. H. (1984). Sustained attention among children vulnerable to adult schizophrenia among hyperactive children. In N. F. Watt, E. J. Anthony, L. C. Wynne, & J. E. Rolf (Eds.), *Children at risk for schizophrenia: A longitudinal perspective* (pp. 327–332). New York: Cambridge University Press.

Plomin, R. (1994). *Genetics and experience: The interplay between nature and nurture.* Thousand Oaks, CA: Sage.

Robins, L. (1978). Sturdy childhood predictors of adult antisocial behaviour: Replications from longitudinal studies. *Psychological Medicine, 8,* 611–622.

Rutter, M. (1979). Protective factors in children's responses to stress and disadvantage. In M. W. Kent & J. G. Rolf (Eds.), *Primary prevention of psychopathology: Vol. 3. Social competence in children* (pp. 49–74). Hanover, NH: University Press of New England.

Rutter, M. (1987). Continuities and discontinuities from infancy. In J. Osofsky (Ed.), *Handbook of infant development* (2nd ed., pp. 1256–1296). New York: Wiley.

Rutter, M., & Garmezy, N. (1983). Development psychopathology. In E. M. Hetherington (Ed.), *Carmichael's manual of child psychology: Vol. 4. Social and personality development* (pp. 775–911). New York: Wiley.

Sameroff, A. (1995). General systems theories and developmental psychopathology. In D. Cicchetti & D. Cohen (Eds.), *Manual of developmental psychopathology* (Vol. 1, pp. 659–695). New York: Wiley.

Sameroff, A. J., Bartko, W. T., Baldwin, A., Baldwin, C., & Seifer, R. (1998). Family and social influences on the development of child competence. In M. Lewis & C. Feiring (Eds.), *Families, risk, and competence* (pp. 161–183). Mahwah, NJ: Erlbaum.

Sameroff, A., & Chandler, M. J. (1975). Reproductive risk and the continuum of caretaking casualty. In F. D. Horowitz, M. Hetherington, S. Scarr-Salapatek, & G. Siegel (Eds.), *Review of child development research* (Vol. 4, pp. 187–244). Chicago: University of Chicago Press.

Sameroff, A. J., & Fiese, B. H. (1990). Transactional regulation and early intervention. In S. J. Meisels & J. P. Shonkoff (Eds.), *Handbook of early childhood intervention* (pp. 119–149). New York: Cambridge University Press.

Sameroff, A. J., Seifer, R., Baldwin, A. L., & Baldwin, C. A. (1993). Stability of intelligence from preschool or adolescence: The influence of social and family risk factors. *Child Development, 64,* 80–97.

Sameroff, A. J., Seifer, R., Barocas, R., Zax, M., & Greenspan, S. (1987). IQ scores of 4-year-old children: Social–environmental risk factors. *Pediatrics, 79,* 343–350.

Sameroff, A. J., Seifer, R., & Bartko, W. T. (1997). Environmental perspectives on adaptation during childhood and adolescence. In S. S. Luthar, J. A. Barack, D. Cicchetti, & J. Weisz (Eds.), *Developmental psychopathology: Perspectives on risk and disorder.* Cambridge, UK: Cambridge University Press.

Sameroff, A. J., Seifer, R., & Zax, M. (1982). Early development of children at risk for emotional disorder. *Monographs of the Society for Research in Child Development, 47* (7, Serial No. 199).

Sameroff, A. J., Seifer, R., Zax, M., & Barocas, R. (1987). Early indicators of developmental risk: The Rochester Longitudinal Study. *Schizophrenia Bulletin, 13,* 383–393.

Sameroff, A. J., & Zax, M. (1973). Neonatal characteristics of offspring of schizophrenic and neurotically depressed mothers. *Journal of Nervous and Mental Diseases, 157,* 191–199.

Scarr, S. (1985). Constructing psychology: Making facts and fables for our times. *American Psychologist, 40,* 499–512.

Sroufe, L. A. (1990). Considering the normal and abnormal together: The essence of developmental psychopathology. *Development and Psychopathology, 2,* 335–347.

Sroufe, L. A., & Rutter, M. (1984). The domain of developmental psychopathology. *Child Development, 55,* 17–29.

Stattin, H., & Magnusson, D. (1991). Stability and change in criminal behaviour up to age 30. *British Journal of Criminology, 31*(4), 327–346.

Stouthamer-Loeber, M., Loeber, R., Farrington, D. P., Zhang, Q., van Kamman, W., & Maguin, E. (1993). The double edge of protective and risk factors for delinquency: Interrelations and developmental patterns. *Development and Psychopathology, 5,* 683–701.

Watt, N. F. (1984). In a nutshell: The first two decades of high-risk research in schizophrenia. In N. F. Watt, E. J. Anthony, L. C. Wynne, & J. E. Rolf (Eds.), *Children at risk for schizophrenia: A longitudinal perspective* (pp. 572–595). New York: Cambridge University Press.

Watt, N. F., Anthony, E. J., Wynne, L. C., & Rolf, J. E. (Eds.). (1984). *Children at risk for schizophrenia: A longitudinal perspective.* New York: Cambridge University Press.

Werner, H. (1948). *Comparative psychology of mental development.* New York: International Universities Press.

Zigler, E., & Hodapp, R. M. (1986). *Understanding mental retardation.* New York: Cambridge University Press.

Zubin, J., & Spring, B. (1977). Vulnerability: A new view of schizophrenia. *Journal of Abnormal Psychology, 56,* 103–126.

3

Assessment of Psychopathology

Thomas M. Achenbach

A developmental approach to psychopathology aims to advance our understanding of behavioral and emotional problems in relation to developmental tasks, sequences, and processes. Assessment must therefore take account of both the continuities and the discontinuities that occur across the life span. Assessment must also detect individual differences that occur within developmental periods and those that persist from one period to another.

The value of assessment procedures depends on their ability to identify characteristics of individuals that are important for making decisions about those individuals. The important characteristics may include both those that are manifest and those that underlie the manifest characteristics. Underlying patterns may be revealed by syndromes of manifest characteristics that are found to co-occur. Such syndromes can be tested for consistency across developmental periods in order to distinguish between patterns that persist versus those that change with development. Because different assessment procedures and sources of data may yield different results, we need ways of integrating variations in assessment data within and between developmental periods.

This chapter first presents a conceptual framework for assessing psychopathology. Two leading paradigms are then used to compare and contrast the implications of different forms of assessment for developmental understanding of behavioral and emotional problems.

CONCEPTUAL FRAMEWORK

Thousands of procedures are available for assessing characteristics that are assumed to be relevant to psychopathology. Some procedures, such as projective tests, generate ideographic personality portraits from clinical inferences. Other procedures, such as tabulations of overt behaviors in specific situations, eschew inferences about underlying variables. Still other procedures, such as personality inventories, measure hypothetical constructs in terms of responses to standardized stimuli.

Thomas M. Achenbach • Department of Psychiatry, University of Vermont, Burlington, Vermont 05401-3456.
Handbook of Developmental Psychopathology, Second Edition, edited by Arnold J. Sameroff, Michael Lewis, and Suzanne M. Miller. Kluwer Academic/Plenum Publishers, New York, 2000.

Interviews are the most common means for assessing psychopathology. Highly structured diagnostic interviews have been developed for research purposes, but most clinical interviews are relatively unstructured. Furthermore, clinicians differ greatly in their interview styles and in the information they seek from interviews. Clinicians also vary their interviews to take account of children's developmental levels and the nature of parental involvement.

Considering the many assessment possibilities, how can we advance our developmental understanding of individual cases, while also advancing developmental research on psychopathology? This chapter presents assessment procedures as ways of identifying both those characteristics that are important for current functioning and those that are important for further development. We focus mainly on assessment of behavioral and emotional problems during the period of rapid development from birth to maturity, but we also consider applications to adult psychopathology. For brevity, "children" refers to both infants and adolescents.

Taxonomic Targets for Assessment

To determine which characteristics to assess, we need to know (1) which ones can be reliably assessed, and (2) which of the reliably assessable characteristics are valid indices of variables that play key roles in disorders, in adaptive development, in responsiveness to interventions, and so on. In other words, we need to accumulate evidence regarding the utility of particular kinds of information for advancing our ways of helping troubled individuals. We also need to organize this information for effective applications. To organize the relevant information, we need to form taxonomic groupings of characteristics that will serve as targets for assessment. Such targets can be viewed as hypothetical constructs or latent variables that embody important patterns of functioning but that may not be exhaustively measured by any single assessment procedure.

Error of Measurement

By viewing assessment procedures as imperfect indices of taxonomic constructs, we can deal with the inevitability of measurement error. Variability in a measure's results over brief intervals (*test–retest unreliability*) is a well-known source of error. However, variability can arise from other sources as well. Meta-analyses of many studies have shown, for example, that the correlations between reports by different informants about children's problems are modest, even when the assessment procedures are quite reliable (Achenbach, McConaughy, & Howell, 1987). The modest correlations among different informants may reflect variations in children's behavior from one context and interaction partner to another, as well as differences among the informants' standards of judgment, perceptions of the children, memories of particular events, and candor.

Another source of variation is the type of assessment procedure that is used. Partly because assessment procedures may target different variables and partly because they differ with respect to method variance (e.g., interviews vs. questionnaires vs. observations), assessment procedures often differ in their results.

Still another source of variation is the time interval that is targeted for assessment. Observational procedures tap only the intervals (and locations) where the observations are carried out. Interviews may obtain observational data on behavior during the interview, plus self-reports spanning longer periods. Questionnaires usually specify particular baseline intervals that respondents are to consider, such as 6 months. Some taxonomically important characteristics may not be observable during observational or interview sessions. Other taxonomically important characteristics may not be accurately remembered over long periods.

From Assessment to Taxonomy (and Back Again)

Variations between different assessment procedures and between repetitions of the same procedure highlight the need to take account of measurement error in all assessment. Because we have no perfectly accurate gold standard, measurement error cannot be detected as deviation from perfect accuracy. Instead, we need to evaluate assessment procedures for psychopathology in terms of their contributions to taxonomic constructs whose value can then be tested. To improve assessment, we need to pursue an iterative, bootstrapping strategy whereby taxonomic constructs are derived from assessment procedures that may then be altered and refined to improve their ability to tap the taxonomic constructs.

The inevitability of measurement error (i.e., variation) argues for multiple procedures that provide different estimates of taxonomic constructs. Estimates of constructs may be improved by aggregating data from procedures having different error parameters. In this way, we can improve measurement of constructs that we can then analyze in relation to other variables. For rigorous aggregation, some form of quantification is needed, but this can be as simple as scoring characteristics as absent = 0 and present = 1. Quantitative procedures for aggregating assessment data are addressed later in the chapter. First, however, we consider the two most widely used paradigms for assessment and taxonomy of child psychopathology.

THE DSM PARADIGM

One influential paradigm is embodied in the American Psychiatric Association's (1994) *Diagnostic and Statistical Manual of Mental Disorders*, the DSM. The DSM classifies people's problems according to diagnostic categories. Each diagnostic category implies a taxonomic construct. Since 1980, the DSM has provided explicit criteria for each category (American Psychiatric Association, 1980, 1987, 1994). However, the DSM has not provided assessment procedures for determining which criteria are met. To determine whether criteria for the DSM categories are met, diagnostic interviews have been developed to operationalize the categories by questioning people about the absence versus presence of the criterial characteristics. Although neither the DSM nor the interviews have been explicitly formulated in terms of taxonomic constructs, Waldman, Lilienfeld, and Lahey (1995) have proposed a latent variable modeling approach to the constructs implied by the DSM categories of Attention-Deficit/Hyperactivity Disorder (ADHD), Conduct Disorder (CD), and Oppositional Defiant Disorder (ODD). Waldman et al. point out that the internal validity of the DSM categories has been taken too much for granted and that research is needed to determine whether the criterial characteristics specified for DSM diagnostic categories really represent coherent taxonomic constructs.

As indicated by Waldman et al., the DSM's categories and criteria were not derived by aggregating data from specific assessment procedures applied to relevant samples of children. Instead, they were negotiated among the committees responsible for the DSM. Although the DSM-IV field trials may have affected some diagnostic criteria and cutpoints (e.g., McBurnett, Lahey, & Pfiffner, 1993), the field trials did not derive the taxonomic constructs represented by DSM diagnostic categories, nor did they test the internal validity of these constructs. Rather than proceeding from data to constructs, the construction of the DSM can be described as working from "the top down." This top-down process started with concepts of disorders proposed by committees that then chose the criterial characteristics for defining each disorder. Once the diagnostic categories and their criteria were chosen, they provided the taxonomic targets for assessment procedures such as structured diagnostic interviews.

DSM Diagnostic Interviews

When explicit diagnostic criteria were tried out for major adult disorders in the 1970s, structured interviews were developed to question adult patients about the absence versus presence of each criterial symptom.

Diagnostic Interview Schedule for Children

Modeled on the adult interviews, the Diagnostic Interview Schedule for Children—Child Version (DISC-C; Costello, Edelbrock, Dulcan, Kalas, & Klaric, 1984) was developed to make DSM-III diagnoses of children. When it became clear that many children could not accurately report their own symptoms, a version of the DISC was developed to obtain parents' reports of their children's symptoms (DISC-P). As the DSM-III-R and DSM-IV changed the diagnostic criteria, new versions of the DISC-C and DISC-P were developed (Shaffer et al., 1996).

Test–Retest Reliability. A great deal of work has been invested in the DISC, especially in efforts to improve its test–retest reliability. Despite these efforts, the test–retest reliability of children's self-reports of symptoms has remained mediocre (Schwab-Stone et al., 1996). Especially troubling are large *test–retest attenuation* effects, which involve major declines in self-reported symptoms from initial interviews to repeat interviews (Edelbrock, Costello, Dulcan, Kalas, & Conover, 1985).

Parents' responses to the DISC-P show smaller but still significant test–retest attenuation effects (Jensen et al., 1995). Not restricted to the DISC, these effects also occur in other interviews, questionnaires, and rating forms. Nevertheless, test–retest attenuation effects create a major problem for assessing DSM constructs according to categorical criteria.

The problem is this: A change from an initial "yes" response regarding a criterial characteristis to a "no" response regarding the same characteristic can cause a change from first meeting a diagnostic threshold to later falling short of the threshold and therefore being considered free of the disorder. As an example, a DSM-IV diagnosis of ADHD requires that at least six out of nine descriptive criteria from either of two lists (Inattention or Hyperactivity–Impulsivity) be met, plus the following criteria:

> B. Some hyperactive–impulsive or inattentive symptoms that caused impairment were present before age 7 years.
> C. Some impairment from the symptoms is present in two or more settings.
> D. There must be clear evidence of clinically significant impairment in social, academic, or occupational functioning. (American Psychiatric Association, 1994, p. 84)

A change from "yes" to "no" regarding any one of the 18 descriptive criteria or criteria B, C, or D can thus change the diagnostic decision from "Yes, the child has ADHD," to "No, the child does not have ADHD." Furthermore, a child for whom the DISC affirms criteria B, C, and D, plus five descriptive criteria from each of the Inattentive and Hyperactive–Impulsive lists, is judged to be free of ADHD. By contrast, a child for whom the DISC affirms six descriptive criteria from one list but none from the other list is judged to have ADHD, despite meeting four fewer criteria than the 10 met by a child who meets five criteria from each of the two lists. Other DSM diagnoses of childhood disorders can also be changed from present to absent by denial of a single criterial characteristic. Test–retest attenuation effects can thus distort absent-versus-present assessment of diagnostic constructs.

Difficulty in Understanding DISC Questions.   Another potential source of error is children's difficulty in understanding DISC questions. For example, Breton et al. (1995) found that 9-year-olds understood only 16% of DISC questions for depressive diagnoses, increasing to only 31% at age 11. The children seldom understood DISC questions about the time when symptoms occurred. This can greatly affect many diagnoses, such as ADHD, which requires retrospective reports that impairment began before age 7. Other diagnostic categories require the co-occurrence of multiple symptoms during brief time intervals. For example, the criteria for Major Depressive Episode include: "A. Five (or more) of the following symptoms have been present during the same 2-week period and represent a change from previous functioning" (American Psychiatric Association, 1994, p. 327). Nine symptoms are then specified, such as "fatigue or loss of energy nearly every day."

It is not surprising that the 9- to 11-year-olds queried by Breton et al. (1995) could not accurately answer such questions. It would also not be surprising if older children and even parents could not accurately report multiple symptoms that (1) co-occur within a 2-week period and (2) represent a change from previous functioning.

The many factors that affect the yes-or-no conclusions about diagnoses made from the DISC-C and DISC-P may contribute to the low agreement between diagnoses obtained from child and parent interviews (Shaffer et al., 1996). These diagnoses also show low agreement with diagnoses made from clinical evaluations (Costello et al., 1984). Other diagnostic interviews that follow a format like the DISC, such as the Diagnostic Interview for Children and Adolescents (DICA), have generally yielded similar results, including large test–retest attenuation effects (Hodges, 1993; Welner, Reich, Herjanic, Jung, & Amado, 1987).

Child and Adolescent Psychiatric Assessment

A different type of structured diagnostic interview was developed in England (Angold, Cox, Prendergast, Rutter, & Simonoff, 1987). Called the Child and Adolescent Psychiatric Assessment (CAPA), it resembles the DISC in using a highly structured DSM-based protocol, including precisely specified questions and probes. However, the CAPA has more characteristics of an "interviewer based" protocol than the DISC, which is regarded as an entirely "respondent based" protocol. Being "interviewer based" means that the CAPA requires the interviewer to ensure that subjects (1) understand the questions, (2) provide clear information on behavior and feelings relevant to each symptom, and (3) have each symptom at a level of severity specified by an extensive glossary. By contrast, "respondent based" interviews, such as the DISC, tend to take the respondents' answers at face value, with minimal variations in interviewers' input and in their judgments of the answers.

Being interviewer-based, the CAPA requires much more interviewer training and sophistication than the DISC, plus extensive coding by the interviewer and thorough checking by a supervisor (Angold & Costello, 1995). The CAPA is 400 pages long, plus a 300-page glossary. Because the CAPA is so challenging and has not been available in a computerized version, it has been used mainly by its authors.

Test–Retest Reliability.   In a study of the CAPA's reliability, the only diagnosis that was common enough to permit analysis of test–retest attenuation effects was CD (Angold & Costello, 1995). Of the 16 subjects who were ever diagnosed with CD, six were diagnosed as having CD at Interview 1 but not at Interview 2, while three subjects showed the opposite pattern. Across the whole sample, CD symptoms showed a significant decline from Interview 1 to Interview 2.

In seeking reasons for the test–retest attenuation effect, Angold and Costello compared declines in symptoms for subjects who at Interview 1 reported that they had told at least two lies versus subjects who said that they did not tell lies. Significantly more of the admitted liars showed declines in self-reported CD symptoms from Interview 1 to Interview 2 (74% vs. 42% of those who denied lying). It thus appears that a tendency to lie may contribute to the attenuation effect on self-reports of CD symptoms in structured interviews such as the CAPA. However, lying cannot explain all of the attenuation effects that are found for many kinds of problems reported by different kinds of informants.

Whatever their causes, test–retest attenuation effects undermine interviews that operationalize DSM diagnoses in terms of absent-versus-present reports of criterial characteristics. This is true even when special efforts are made to ensure that subjects understand the questions, provide clear information, and have symptoms that meet precisely specified levels of severity, as in the CAPA. However, a semistructured clinical interview that does not impose the DSM's absent-versus-present dichotomies has been found to avoid test–retest attenuation effects (McConaughy & Achenbach, 1994). Furthermore, a quantitative approach to assessment and taxonomy is less affected by attenuation effects and by other variations in assessment data, as described in the following sections.

THE EMPIRICALLY BASED PARADIGM

A contrasting paradigm for assessment and taxonomy emerged to redress the neglect of childhood problems in early nosologies. In contrast to the "top down" approach of the DSM, this paradigm is designated as *empirically based*, because it works from the "bottom up" by starting with data obtained on specific problems in large samples of individuals. It then derives taxonomic constructs from statistical analyses of the problems actually found among the individuals who were assessed.

In early efforts to derive taxonomic constructs empirically, a combination of bivariate statistics and clinical judgments were applied to problems scored in the case histories of children referred to guidance clinics (Hewitt & Jenkins, 1946; Jenkins & Glockman, 1946). In the 1960s, these efforts were greatly advanced by the advent of electronic computers, which spawned multiple applications of factor analysis and principal components analysis to the derivation of syndromes of co-occurring problems (Achenbach, 1966; Dreger et al., 1964; Miller, 1967; Peterson, 1961). Despite differences in the instruments, samples of subjects, sources of data, and analytic procedures, reviews of many studies revealed considerable convergence on certain syndromes of problems that were repeatedly found to co-occur (Achenbach & Edelbrock, 1978; Quay, 1986).

The word *syndrome* is used here to designate sets of co-occurring problems in the sense of the original Greek root of syndrome, which means the "act of running together." Designation of a set of co-occurring problems as a syndrome does not imply any assumptions about whether the problems represent a disease nor about the reasons for their co-occurrence.

Statistically robust syndromes can serve as building blocks for a taxonomy of problem patterns. The procedures that were used to assess the samples from which the syndromes were derived can later be applied to new individuals for clinical and research purposes. The problems found for the new individuals can then be used to determine which syndromes best characterize these individuals. By testing correlates of the syndromes, we can determine which syndromes yield useful taxonomic constructs around which knowledge and hypotheses concerning psychopathology can be organized. We can also do longitudinal studies to identify developmental continuities and discontinuities in specific problems and syndromal constructs.

Quantitative Aspects of the Empirically Based Paradigm

A cornerstone of the empirically based paradigm is the statistical derivation of syndromes from associations among problem items scored for large samples of individuals. If problem items are judged as absent versus present, as is done in the DSM, they can be scored as 0 versus 1 for statistical analysis. However, because most problems vary in frequency and/or intensity, they are more effectively scored in gradations. Even a simple 3-step scale can make scoring easier, more reliable, and more sensitive than forced choices between absent versus present. For example, most problems can be scored as *Not true = 0, Somewhat or sometimes true = 1*, and *Very true or often true = 2*.

By quantifying problems, we can take account of measurement error more effectively than if we categorize each problem as either absent or present. Furthermore, multivariate methods such as factor analysis enable us to quantify *patterns* of problems and to assign items to syndromes on the basis of their quantitative associations.

After deciding which items to retain for each syndrome, we can construct scales for scoring the syndromes, such as by summing the scores that individuals obtain on the items of a syndrome. To evaluate a child's scores, we need norms to which the child's scores can be compared. Cutpoints on normative distributions can be established at scores that are found to discriminate between particular criterion groups, such as children who are judged to be clinically deviant according to external criteria versus children who are considered to be normal.

The quantitative assessment of specific problems, quantitative identification of syndromes, and quantitative scoring of individuals on syndrome scales can avoid difficulties posed by the DSM's categorical criteria. When specific problems and taxonomic constructs are viewed in quantitative terms, absent-versus-present judgments are replaced by quantitative indices of the *degree to which* individuals manifest certain problems and how high they score on measures of particular constructs, as compared to normative samples of peers. Measurement errors (variations) arising from test–retest attenuation effects, incomplete information about specific problems, differences in sources of data, and so on, do not affect quantitative indices as much as they affect absent-versus-present judgments. For example, small variations in scoring particular problems have minimal effects on the conclusions drawn from syndrome scores, whereas changing our judgment of one symptom from present to absent can change a DSM diagnosis into a clean bill of health. Furthermore, quantification offers abundant possibilities for deriving taxonomic constructs and for aggregating data from multiple sources, as illustrated in the following sections.

Cross-Informant Aspects of the Empirically Based Paradigm

All approaches must contend with variations in data from different sources. We must therefore take account of discrepancies between different informants and between different assessment procedures both when we formulate taxonomic constructs and when we assess individuals in terms of those constructs. For example, constructs formulated only on the basis of clinical interviews are apt to differ from constructs formulated on the basis of parent reports, teacher reports, or test scores. Similarly, interviews, parent reports, teacher reports, and tests may yield different conclusions about a child's standing on a particular construct.

Cross-Informant Syndrome Constructs

Many empirically based efforts have used data from only one source. However, data from parallel parent, teacher, and self-report instruments have been used to derive taxonomic constructs that incorporate multisource data. To derive constructs that embody problem patterns common to both genders, different ages, and different informants, separate principal components/varimax analyses were performed on problem scores for clinically referred boys and girls within different age ranges, as rated by parents on the Child Behavior Checklist (CBCL), teachers on the Teacher's Report Form (TRF), and the subjects themselves on the Youth Self-Report (YSR; Achenbach, 1991). Eight patterns of co-occurring problems found to have counterparts across genders, ages, and informants were used to define *cross-informant syndrome constructs*. These constructs comprise problem items that co-occurred in the analyses of both genders and multiple age groups, as rated by multiple informants. The eight constructs are designated as *Aggressive Behavior*, *Anxious/Depressed*, *Attention Problems*, *Delinquent Behavior*, *Social Problems*, *Somatic Complaints*, *Thought Problems*, and *Withdrawn*.

Most items of the eight syndromes are rated by parents, teachers, and the subjects themselves. However, because different informants are familiar with different aspects of the subjects' functioning, some items are rated by only certain types of informants. For example, problems that are on the CBCL but not on the TRF include *Disobedient at Home* and *Trouble Sleeping*. The rating forms for assessing children in terms of the constructs thus take advantage of the ability of different raters to assess different kinds of problems, as well as their ability to rate a core set of similar problems. Test–retest attenuation effects have been found on some scales but have accounted for very small percentages of variance, according to Cohen's (1988) criteria for effect sizes.

Using Cross-Informant Data for Assessing Individuals

Quantitative ratings of a child by multiple informants can be compared and combined in several ways. A computer program is available for entering data from the CBCL, TRF, and YSR (Arnold & Britting, 1999). For each informant, the program prints a profile that shows scores on each item of the eight cross-informant syndromes, raw scores and standard scores for each syndrome scale, and a graphic display that compares the child's syndrome scores with the scores of a national normative sample. Users can visually compare the profiles obtained from each informant to identify similarities and differences between patterns of syndrome scores.

Side-by-Side Displays of Scores.   To aid users in directly comparing the problem scores obtained from different informants, the program prints side-by-side displays of the scores on the items of each syndrome scale obtained from different informants, plus the standard scores computed for each scale from the ratings by each informant. This enables users to quickly identify specific problems and syndromes on which multiple informants agree or disagree. If users see important disagreements, they can explore them clinically to determine whether they reflect important differences in the child's functioning in different contexts or differences between informants' perceptions, which may then be targeted for interventions.

Using Cross-Informant Data for Research

Because no one source of data provides a true gold standard, multisource data are essential for research. A major advantage of the cross-informant syndromes is that they provide parallel multi-informant data for operationalizing a common set of taxonomic constructs.

Researchers can employ syndrome scores from multiple informants in several ways. If a researcher obtains ratings from mothers, fathers, teachers, and/or the subjects themselves, the mean of these ratings is likely to be more reliable and valid than ratings obtained from single informants. Because the distributions of scores differ between different types of informants, the mean of the ratings should be computed by first converting the raw syndrome scores to standard scores that provide a common numerical scale across the different types of informants. The computer program for the CBCL, TRF, and YSR automatically converts raw syndrome scores to T scores that indicate where each score stands in relation to national norms. To aggregate data from multiple informants, researchers can use the computer scoring program to obtain T scores for the CBCL, TRF, and/or YSR versions of a syndrome. These T scores can then be averaged for each subject to obtain composite standard scores for the syndrome. Structural equation modeling can also be used to create weighted combinations of data from multiple sources for measuring latent taxonomic constructs and for testing relations between the latent constructs over significant developmental periods.

Developmental Aspects of the Empirically Based Paradigm

The DSM lists certain disorders under the heading *Disorders Usually First Diagnosed in Infancy, Childhood, or Adolescence* (American Psychiatric Association, 1994). Among those that are defined primarily in terms of behavioral and emotional problems, the most prevalent include ADHD, CD, ODD, and Separation Anxiety Disorder. For certain other disorders, a few criteria that are intended primarily for adults can be modified for children. As an example, for children, "irritable mood" can be substituted for "depressed mood" in the criteria for Major Depressive Disorder (American Psychiatric Association, 1994, p. 327). Other than slight modifications like this, the DSM does not explicitly provide for developmental variations in its taxonomic constructs, the criteria for defining the constructs, nor the procedures for assessing the criterial attributes.

In contrast to the DSM paradigm, the empirically based paradigm derives syndromes from problem scores characterizing particular developmental periods. Even when the same assessment instruments and syndromes are applicable across long developmental spans, separate norms are constructed for each gender within each developmental period.

Developmental Analysis of Syndromes

Syndromes derived from data characterizing successive developmental periods, plus gender-specific quantitative scoring of the syndromes, offer abundant opportunities for developmental analyses of psychopathology, as illustrated in the following sections.

Path Analyses.   Path analyses can test the degree to which syndrome scores and other variables assessed at one developmental period predict syndrome scores at later developmental periods. As an example, it was found that the cross-informant Aggressive Behavior syndrome assessed in adolescence was a strong predictor of a similar syndrome found in young adults (Achenbach, Howell, McConaughy, & Stanger, 1995b). Furthermore, the Aggressive Behavior syndrome assessed in adolescence was also a strong predictor of a second young adult syndrome that had no clear counterpart among the adolescent syndromes. This syndrome, now designated as *Intrusive* (Achenbach, 1997), comprises socially obnoxious behaviors, such as showing off, bragging, demanding attention, talking too much, teasing, and loudness. Yet the absence of physically aggressive behaviors from the Intrusive syndrome indicates that some adolescents who score high on the Aggressive Behavior syndrome later reduce their physically aggressive behavior, despite continuing their socially obnoxious behavior into adulthood. Other adolescents who score high on the Aggressive Behavior syndrome remain physically aggressive in adulthood. This suggests that either certain characteristics of some aggressive youth or certain experiences that they undergo can reduce aggression during the transition to adulthood. By identifying these characteristics or experiences, we can design better interventions to reduce the persistence of aggression.

Accelerated Longitudinal Designs.   Another way to use empirically based syndromes in developmental analyses is via *accelerated longitudinal designs*. In these designs, several birth cohorts are assessed at multiple ages using the same standardized procedures. Individual subjects from each birth cohort are then matched to subjects from an adjoining birth cohort for demographic characteristics and for scores obtained at the Time 1 assessment. Longitudinal correlations are computed between scores obtained by subjects in each cohort at Time 1 and their own scores at each subsequent assessment through the last assessment at Time *N*. These *within-cohort* correlations indicate the degree to which subjects maintain consistent rank orderings of scores within their cohort.

To extend longitudinal analyses over longer developmental spans than the real time taken to do the study, we compute correlations between the Time 1 scores of subjects in the younger cohorts and the scores obtained by their matched partners in the adjoining older cohorts at each subsequent assessment. We then compare these *between-cohort* correlations to the within-cohort correlations for subjects' Time 1 scores and their own subsequent scores. If the between-cohort correlations are not significantly lower than the within-cohort correlations, we can use the between-cohort correlations to estimate what the within-cohort correlations would be. This enables us to estimate longitudinal correlations from the youngest age at which the young cohorts were assessed to the oldest ages at which their matched partners in older cohorts were assessed. The results thus provide correlations over developmental periods that are longer than the real time taken to do the study. If accelerated longitudinal analyses are successful, they can greatly expand the opportunities for developmental research on psychopathology, because they reduce the attrition of subjects, funding, and investigators that typically threaten long-term longitudinal research.

Accelerated longitudinal analyses were successfully applied to comparing the developmental course of the Aggressive Behavior versus Delinquent Behavior syndromes in seven cohorts of Dutch children (Stanger, Achenbach, & Verhulst, 1997). Aggressive behavior (e.g., fighting) and nonaggressive delinquent behavior (e.g., stealing) are interchangeable criteria for DSM diagnoses of CD. However, the accelerated longitudinal analyses yielded much higher within-cohort and between-cohort correlations for the Aggressive Behavior syndrome than for the Delinquent Behavior syndrome over periods of 2, 4, 6, and 8 years. The developmental trajectories of the two syndromes also differed: Aggressive Behavior scores declined steadily from age 4 to 18, whereas Delinquent Behavior scores increased in adolescence.

Other research has shown higher heritabilities for the Aggressive than the Delinquent syndrome (Edelbrock, Rende, Plomin, & Thompson, 1995; Van den Oord, Boomsma, & Verhulst, 1994). Higher correlations have also been found between the Aggressive syndrome and biochemical parameters in both boys (Gabel, Sadler, Bjorn, Shindledecker, & Bowden, 1993) and girls (Paikoff, Brooks-Gunn, & Warren, 1991). The finding of separate Aggressive Behavior and Delinquent Behavior syndromes via the empirically based "bottom-up" approach and their different developmental courses and correlates reveal important differences that are obscured when both kinds of problem behaviors are lumped together as interchangeable criteria for CD.

IMPLICATIONS FOR THE DEVELOPMENTAL UNDERSTANDING OF BEHAVIORAL AND EMOTIONAL PROBLEMS

This chapter presented a conceptual framework for assessing psychopathology in terms of characteristics that are indices of taxonomic constructs. The DSM and empirically based paradigms were presented as contrasting approaches to assessment and taxonomy. Table 3.1 summarizes similarities and differences between these two paradigms as they are applied to assessment and taxonomy of common behavioral and emotional problems.

As indicated in Table 3.1, the DSM paradigm (starting with DSM-III) and the empirically based paradigm both provide explicit statements of the problems to be assessed. There are also similarities between DSM categories such as ADHD, CD, and Somatization Disorder on the one hand, and the empirically based Attention Problems, Aggressive Behavior, Delinquent Behavior, and Somatic Complaints syndromes on the other. Furthermore, numerous studies have shown statistically significant associations between DSM diagnoses and scores on the corresponding empirically based syndromes (e.g., Chen, Faraone, Biederman, & Tsuang, 1994; Weinstein, Noam, Grimes, Stone, & Schwab-Stone, 1990). These important similarities

Table 1. Comparison of DSM and Empirically Based Paradigms for Common Behavioral and Emotional Problems

Similarities between Paradigms

1. Explicit statements of problems to be assessed.
2. Some DSM categories and empirically based syndromes comprise similar problems.
3. Statistically significant agreement between some diagnoses and syndrome scores.

Differences between Paradigms

DSM	Empirically based
1. Nosological model.	1. Psychometric model.
2. Problems are judged absent or present.	2. Problems are scored quantitatively.
3. "Top-down" approach: categories and criteria are chosen by committees.	3. "Bottom-up" approach: syndromes are derived from problem scores.
4. Clinical cutpoints are identical for both genders, all ages, and different informants.	4. Clinical cutpoints and norms vary by gender, age, and informant.
5. Diagnostician chooses sources of data, data to obtain, and assessment procedures.	5. Standardized procedures for obtaining multisource data.
6. No procedures are specified for comparing data from different sources	6. Explicit comparison of cross-informant scores and correlations.
7. End products are diagnoses judged to be absent or present.	7. End products are item and syndrome scores displayed on norm-referenced profiles.
8. Separate diagnostic categories for many types of problems ranging from Enuresis to Autistic Disorder.	8. Many specific problems are assessed, but are aggregated into a few statistically robust syndromes.

reflect convergence between the two paradigms with respect to certain patterns of problems. Nevertheless, the differences numbered 2 through 7 in Table 3.1 are apt to be important for our developmental understanding of behavioral and emotional problems, as follows:

2. Absent-or-Present versus Quantitative Scoring of Problems

It is difficult to accurately categorize each behavioral and emotional problem as absent or present. Because behavioral and emotional problems are not perfectly objective phenomena that can be mechanically recorded without error, they must be judged by people who are directly involved with the subjects and by subjects who can make such judgments about themselves. Many problems vary across occasions, situations, and interaction partners. In addition, the intensity and frequency of particular problems determine whether they are noticed, remembered, reported, and deemed severe enough to be pathological.

Quantification enables us to capture the inevitable variations in the nature, intensity, and frequency of behavioral and emotional problems, as well as variations in the information processing involved in reporting problems. By scoring problems on scales that are as simple as 0 = *Not true*, 1 = *Somewhat or sometimes true,* and 2 = *Very true or often true*, we can distinguish between those problems for which the evidence is the weakest (scores of 0), those for which the evidence is the strongest (scores of 2), and those that are between these extremes (scores of 1). Quantification also helps us aggregate data into scales that capture gradations in the construct on which the items converge.

3. "Top-Down" Approach versus "Bottom-Up" Approach

If the top-down process of formulating DSM diagnostic categories generated hypothetical constructs from an explicit theory, it could be called a *hypothetico-deductive* procedure. This is a widely used procedure for generating constructs and measures in many sciences. However, most of the DSM categories, rather than being derived from an explicit theory, were negotiated by the DSM committees. Once the categories were chosen, the diagnostic criteria were formulated via further negotiations, although data from field trials may also have played a role (e.g., McBurnett et al., 1993). Neither the choice of diagnostic categories nor the choice of defining criteria was based on evidence for the internal validity of the categories (Waldman et al., 1995).

The "bottom-up" approach of the empirically based paradigm can be described as *inductive empiricism*, because it proceeds from empirical findings on the co-occurrence of problems in relevant samples of subjects to the inductive derivation of taxonomic constructs. These constructs are then tested for validity and utility as markers for other important characteristics, for robustness across samples, for heritability, for developmental course, and so on. Over 3,000 publications report use of the empirically based procedures in over 48 cultures (Bérubé & Achenbach, 2000).

4. Clinical Cutpoints that are Identical across Genders, Ages, and Informants versus Gender, Age, and Informant-Specific Cutpoints

For each DSM category, the diagnostic criteria are the same for people of both genders and all ages, regardless of the sources of data. When the DSM's fixed cutpoints are applied, large gender and age differences in prevalence rates are found for some disorders. For example, the DSM states that ADHD "is much more frequent in males than in females, with male-to-female ratios ranging from 4:1 to 9:1" (American Psychiatric Association, 1994, p. 82). Owing perhaps to this gender difference in diagnostic prevalence, the literature on ADHD is based largely on males.

Because even nondeviant boys manifest more ADHD behaviors than do girls, the gender differences in ADHD diagnoses might be artifactual consequences of boys' higher base rates for salient ADHD behaviors. Declines in ADHD diagnoses with age may also reflect developmental declines in the base rates for salient ADHD behaviors.

In contrast to the use of the same diagnostic criteria for both genders, all ages, and different sources of data, gender, age, and informant-specific scores enable us to test correlates of the taxonomic constructs that may be obscured by uniform cutpoints. For example, adolescent girls who have significant attention problems are more likely to be identified by cutpoints for deviance from norms for their own gender and age than by the DSM's ADHD cutpoints that are based largely on young boys. Furthermore, gender- and age-specific analyses may reveal correlates that are obscured when scores for both genders and different ages are combined. For example, it has been found that high gender-specific scores on the Attention Problems syndromes predicted more problems over a 6-year period for girls than for boys (Achenbach et al., 1995a). In addition, principal components/varimax analyses of young adult problems have yielded a version of the Attention Problems syndrome that is strongly predicted by earlier gender-specific scores on the child/adolescent Attention Problems syndrome but that does not include problems of overactivity (Achenbach, 1997). For purposes of developmental research, quantitative scores with adjustable cutpoints are apt to be more sensitive to gender, age, and informant variations in the level and patterning of problems than are categorical diagnoses with fixed cutpoints.

5. Diagnostician Chooses Sources of Data, Data to Obtain, and Assessment Procedures versus Standardized Procedures for Obtaining Multisource Data

Because each case is in some respects unique, clinical assessment should be custom tailored to each case. On the other hand, standardization and norms enable us to compare each case to relevant reference groups. Standardization is also necessary to apply previously accumulated knowledge to new cases that share characteristics with previous cases. When standardized procedures are applied to every case, they can provide a framework within which customized assessment can contrast idiosyncratic features of individual cases with features that are like those of other cases.

The DSM paradigm has produced standardized interviews for uniformly making DSM diagnoses. Semistructured interviews, such as the Child Assessment Schedule (CAS; Hodges, 1993), are designed to obtain more diverse clinical data as well as DSM diagnoses. Both the highly structured and semistructured interviews require well-trained interviewers, plus considerable time with parent and child interviewees. Their use may therefore be limited to assessment situations that provide both extensive time and resources for obtaining basic diagnostic data, plus the time and resources needed for more customized assessment procedures.

By contrast, the parent, teacher, and self-report forms of the empirically based approach can be obtained without trained interviewers. They can therefore be used routinely without sacrificing the time and resources needed for customized assessment. They are also applicable across a wider age range than are DSM-based interviews, which are often too hard for children with mental ages below 12.

6. No Procedures for Comparing Data across Sources versus Explicit Cross-Informant Procedures

Some DSM diagnoses require judgments about multiple settings, such as "impairment from the symptoms is present in two or more settings (e.g., at school [or work] and at home)" (American Psychiatric Association, 1994, p. 84). However, the DSM does not specify procedures for assessing people in multiple settings. Instead, the diagnostician must decide how to assess people in multiple settings, and how to judge whether there is enough consistency to support a particular diagnosis. As outlined earlier, the empirically based paradigm provides explicit cross-informant comparisons.

7. End Products Are Diagnoses versus Item and Syndrome Scores Displayed on Norm-Referenced Profiles

In the DSM paradigm, assessment yields yes-or-no decisions about diagnoses. An individual may meet criteria for any number of diagnoses. Some disorders, such as CD, can be described as mild, moderate, or severe, depending on whether the diagnostic threshold is exceeded. However, the main end product of assessment is a conclusion about whether one or more disorders exists.

In the empirically based paradigm, on the other hand, the end products include a large number of problem scores and a smaller number of syndrome scores that are profiled in relation to norms. The almost infinite variations in profile patterns derivable from multi-informant data provide customized pictures of the problems reported for each subject. These profile patterns can be used to guide the choice of interventions. By readministering the empirically based procedures, we can track changes in specific problems and patterns of problems in response to interventions and over the course of development.

In summary, the DSM and empirically based paradigms converge in certain ways but diverge in others. For DSM categories such as ADHD, CD, Somatization Disorder, Depression, and Dysthymia, empirically based syndromes can provide evidence on the kinds of problems that are included in the DSM criteria. However, the empirically based paradigm assesses additional syndromes that do not have clear counterparts in DSM-IV, such as the Withdrawn and Social Problems syndromes. The empirically based paradigm also provides a customized picture of each case in terms of norm-referenced profiles from multiple sources of data. On the other hand, the DSM serves a variety of administrative purposes, such as record keeping and billing, that are not currently served by the empirically based paradigm. In addition, the DSM provides diagnostic categories for single-symptom problems, such as enuresis, and for other conditions that may not be readily identified by the statistical derivation of syndromes.

At our current stage of knowledge, an official nosology such as the DSM must serve many masters in ways that may not be consistent with scientific standards for knowledge. For purposes of advancing knowledge, it is therefore important to avoid reifying the DSM's categories as if they embody scientifically validated entities. Instead, to improve both the official nosology and our developmental understanding of psychopathology, we must recognize the tentativeness of existing taxonomic constructs and the need for continually testing and revising both our constructs and our procedures for assessing them.

REFERENCES

Achenbach, T. M. (1966). The classification of children's psychiatric symptoms. A factor-analytic study. *Psychological Monographs, 80*(No. 615).

Achenbach, T. M. (1991). *Integrative guide for the 1991 CBCL/4–18, YSR, and TRF profiles*. Burlington: University of Vermont, Department of Psychiatry.

Achenbach, T. M. (1997). *Manual for the Young Adult Self-Report and Young Adult Behavior Checklist*. Burlington: University of Vermont, Department of Psychiatry.

Achenbach, T. M., & Edelbrock, C. (1978). The classification of child psychopathology: A review and analysis of empirical efforts. *Psychological Bulletin, 85*, 1275–1301.

Achenbach, T. M., Howell, C. T., McConaughy, S. H., & Stanger, C. (1995a). Six-year predictors of problems in a national sample of children and youth: I. Cross-informant syndromes. *Journal of the American Academy of Child and Adolescent Psychiatry, 34*, 336–347.

Achenbach, T. M., Howell, C. T., McConaughy, S. H., & Stanger, C. (1995b). Six-year predictors of problems in a national sample of children and youth: III. Transition to young adult syndromes. *Journal of the American Academy of Child and Adolescent Psychiatry, 34*, 658–669.

Achenbach, T. M., McConaughy, S. H., & Howell, C. T. (1987). Child/adolescent behavioral and emotional problems: Implications of cross-informant correlations for situational specificity. *Psychological Bulletin, 101*, 213–232.

American Psychiatric Association (1980, 1987, 1994). *Diagnostic and statistical manual of mental disorders* (3rd ed., 3rd rev. ed., 4th ed.). Washington, DC: Author.

Angold, A., & Costello, E. J. (1995). A test–retest study of child-reported psychiatric symptoms and diagnoses using the Child and Adolescent Psychiatric Assessment (CAPA-C). *Psychological Medicine, 25*, 755–762.

Angold, A., Cox, A., Prendergast, M., Rutter, M., & Simonoff, E. (1987). *The child and adolescent psychiatric assessment (CAPA)*. London: MRC Child Psychiatry Unit, Institute of Psychiatry.

Arnold, J., & Britting, D. (1999). *The Cross-Informant Program for the CBCL/4–18, YSR, and TRF: Assessment Data Manager*. Burlington: University of Vermont, Department of Psychiatry.

Bérubé, R., & Achenbach, T. M. (2000). *ASEBA instruments: 2000 edition*. Burlington: University of Vermont, Department of Psychiatry.

Breton, J. J., Bergeron, L., Valla, J. P., Lepine, S., Houde, L., & Gaudet, N. (1995). Do children aged 9 through 11 years understand the DISC Version 2.5 questions? *Journal of the American Academy of Child and Adolescent Psychiatry, 34*, 954–956.

Chen, W. J., Faraone, S. V., Biederman, J., & Tsuang, M. T. (1994). Diagnostic accuracy of the Child Behavior Checklist scales for Attention-Deficit Hyperactivity Disorder: A receiver-operating characteristic analysis. *Journal of Consulting and Clinical Psychology, 62*, 1017–1025.

Cohen, J. (1988). *Statistical power analysis for the behavioral sciences* (2nd ed.). New York: Academic Press.

Costello, A. J., Edelbrock, C., Dulcan, M. K., Kalas, R., & Klaric, S. H. (1984). *Report on the Diagnostic Interview Schedule for Children (DISC)*. Pittsburgh, PA: University of Pittsburgh, Department of Psychiatry.

Dreger, R. M., Lewis, P. M., Rich, T. A., Miller, K. S., Reid, M. P., Overlade, D. C., Taffel, C., & Flemming, E. L. (1964). Behavioral classification project. *Journal of Consulting Psychology, 28*, 1–13.

Edelbrock, C., Costello, A. J., Dulcan, M. K., Kalas, R., & Conover, N. C. (1985). Age differences in the reliability of the psychiatric interview of the child. *Child Development, 56*, 265–275.

Edelbrock, C., Rende, R., Plomin, R., & Thompson, L. A. (1995). A twin study of competence and problem behavior in childhood and early adolescence. *Journal of Child Psychology and Psychiatry, 36*, 775–785.

Gabel, S., Stadler, J., Bjorn, J., Shindledecker, R., & Bowden, C. (1993). Dopamine-beta-hydroxylase in behaviorally disturbed youth: Relationship between teacher and parent ratings. *Biological Psychiatry, 34*, 434–442.

Hewitt, L. E., & Jenkins, R. L. (1946). *Fundamental patterns of maladjustment: The dynamics of their origin*. Springfield: State of Illinois.

Hodges, K. (1993). Structured interviews for assessing children. *Journal of Child Psychology and Psychiatry, 34*, 49–68.

Jenkins, R. L., & Glickman, S. (1946). Common syndromes in child psychiatry: I. Deviant behavior traits. II. The schizoid child. *American Journal of Orthopsychiatry, 16*, 244–261.

Jensen, P., Roper, M., Fisher, P., Piacentini, J., Canino, G., Richters, J., Rubio-Stipec, M., Dulcan, M., Goodman, S.,

Davies, M., Rae, D., Shaffer, D., Bird, H., Lahey, B., & Schwab-Stone, M. (1995). Test–retest reliability of the Diagnostic Interview Schedule for Children (ver. 2.1): Parent, child, and combined algorithms. *Archives of General Psychiatry, 52,* 61–71.

McBurnett, K., Lahey, B. B., & Pfiffner, L. J. (1993). Diagnosis of attention deficit disorders in DSM-IV: Scientific basis and implications for education. *Exceptional Children, 60*(2), 108–117.

McConaughy, S. H., & Achenbach, T. M. (1994). *Manual for the Semistructured Clinical Interview for Children and Adolescents.* Burlington: University of Vermont, Department of Psychiatry.

Miller, L. C. (1967). Louisville Behavior Checklist for males, 6–12 years of age. *Psychological Reports, 21,* 885–896.

Paikoff, R. L., Brooks-Gunn, J., & Warren, M. P. (1991). Effects of girls' hormonal status on depressive and aggressive symptoms over the course of one year. *Journal of Youth and Adolescence, 2,* 191–215.

Peterson, D. R. (1961). Behavior problems of middle childhood. *Journal of Consulting Psychology, 25,* 205–209.

Quay, H. C. (1986). Classification. In H. C. Quay & J. S. Werry (Eds.), *Psychopathological disorders of childhood* (3rd ed., pp. 1–41). New York: Wiley.

Schwab-Stone, M. E., Shaffer, D., Dulcan, M. K., Jensen, P. S., Fisher, P., Bird, H. R., Goodman, S. H., Lahey, B. B., Lichtman, J. H., Canino, G., Rubio-Stipec, M., & Rae, D. S. (1996). Criterion validity of the NIMH Diagnostic Interview Schedule for Children version 2.3 (DISC-2.3). *Journal of the American Academy of Child and Adolescent Psychiatry, 35,* 878–888.

Shaffer, D., Fisher, P., Dulcan, M. K., Davies, M., Piacentini, J., Schwab-Stone, M. E., Lahey, B. B., Bourdon, K., Jensen, P. S., Bird, H. R., Canino, G., & Regier, D. A. (1996). The NIMH Diagnostic Interview Schedule for Children version 2.3 (DISC-2.3): Description, acceptability, prevalence rates, and performance in the MECA study. *Journal of the American Academy of Child and Adolescent Psychiatry, 35,* 865–877.

Stanger, C., Achenbach, T. M., & Verhulst, F. C. (1997). Accelerated longitudinal comparison of aggressive versus delinquent syndromes. *Development and Psychopathology, 9,* 43–58.

van den Oord, E. J. C. G., Boomsma, D. I., & Verhulst, F. C. (1994). A study of problem behaviors in 10- to 15-year-old biologically related and unrelated international adoptees. *Behavior Genetics, 24,* 193–205.

Waldman, I. D., Lilienfeld, S. O., & Lahey, B. B. (1995). Toward construct validity in the childhood disruptive behavior disorders. Classification and diagnosis in DSM-IV and beyond. In T. H. Ollendick & R. J. Prinz (Eds.), *Advances in Clinical Child Psychology* (Vol. 17, pp. 323–344). New York: Plenum Press.

Weinstein, S. R., Noam, G. G., Grimes, K., Stone, K., & Schwab-Stone, M. (1990). Convergence of DSM-III diagnoses and self-reported symptoms in child and adolescent inpatients. *Journal of the American Academy of Child and Adolescent Psychiatry, 29,* 627–634.

Welner, Z., Reich, W., Herjanic, B., Jung, K. G., & Amado, H. (1987). Reliability, validity, and parent–child agreement studies of the Diagnostic Interview for Children and Adolescents (DICA). *Journal of the American Academy of Child and Adolescent Psychiatry, 26,* 649–653.

4

Developmental Epidemiology
A Framework for Developmental Psychopathology

Elizabeth Jane Costello and Adrian C. Angold

In this chapter, we show how epidemiology can help us to think about the causes of psychiatric disorders and to develop a coherent philosophy of intervention to prevent and ameliorate them. By the end of the chapter, we hope to have made the case that (1) the goal of epidemiological research is disease prevention, (2) understanding the development of a disease and intervening to prevent it are equally important aspects of epidemiological research, (3) understanding the development of a disease may point to different kinds of intervention at different stages in the developmental process, and (4) understanding individual development is a critical part of understanding and intervening in the disease process, because both risk for, and expression of, disorder change over the life course. Finally, taking as a model the Framingham study (Dawber, 1980), with its 50-year history of exploring risk for coronary heart disease, we argue the case for a "developmental Framingham": a longitudinal, community-based commitment to understanding and minimizing risk for emotional and behavioral disorders. At the same time, we point out that an epidemiological approach to the control of disease has often raised tremendous social and political controversies (think about the battle to put fluoride in the water supply), and that an epidemiological approach to developmental psychopathology is liable to raise even more violent debates.

Throughout this chapter, we unrepentantly use medical language to talk about developmental psychopathology. We do so in part because epidemiology developed its theory and methods as a branch of medicine, and we want to draw parallels with epidemiological thinking about, for example, smallpox or heart disease. We also use the language of disease because, however crude and inaccurate our current taxonomy of psychiatric disorders, it is a useful attempt to partition the inchoate mass of symptoms into categories that permit programs of research into the specificity of causes and correlates. However, as we hope that this chapter will make clear, an epidemiological approach necessarily involves understanding how the

Elizabeth Jane Costello and Adrian C. Angold • Department of Psychiatry, Duke University Medical Center, Durham, North Carolina 27710.
Handbook of Developmental Psychopathology, Second Edition, edited by Arnold J. Sameroff, Michael Lewis, and Suzanne M. Miller. Kluwer Academic / Plenum Publishers, New York, 2000.

development of the individual interacts with the development of the "disease," and how the manifestation of psychopathology at any time is the result of that interaction.

DEVELOPMENTAL EPIDEMIOLOGY

What Is Epidemiology?

Epidemiology is the study of patterns of distribution of disease in time and space. If we can figure out which groups of people are more vulnerable than others, and why, then we can begin developing ways to protect these vulnerable groups and possibly to understand more about the causes of the disease itself.

"Patterns in time," particularly important for developmental epidemiology, are the main focus of this chapter. For example, the prevalence of depression in young children is quite low, and probably higher in boys than in girls (Angold, Costello, & Worthman, 1998). By the late teens, the prevalence of depression is higher in girls, while remaining stable or even falling in boys (Angold et al., 1996). Observing these patterns in time, we are led to take a close look at puberty, a major developmental milestone with very different hormonal and social characteristics for boys and girls (Angold et al., 1998; Angold & Worthman, 1993; Brooks-Gunn, Graber, & Paikoff, 1994; Simmons & Blyth, 1992; Susman et al., 1985).

Epidemiology and Clinical Science

Of course, all of medical science, whether clinical or epidemiological, is concerned with understanding disease so as to eliminate it. However, epidemiology pursues somewhat different strategies from those of clinical medicine. Whereas the primary focus of clinical medicine is the *individual* patient, epidemiology concentrates on understanding and controlling disease processes in the context of the *population at risk*. This does not mean that epidemiology is not concerned with the individual; on the contrary, it is very much concerned with understanding the individual's illness and the causes of that illness. The difference lies in the context, or frame of reference. Put crudely, clinical medicine asks, "What is wrong with this person *and how should I treat him or her*?" Epidemiology asks, "What is wrong with this person and *what is it about him or her that has resulted in this illness*?" Such questions immediately set the individual child within a frame of reference of other children, or other family members, or other people of the same sex or race or social class, and have important effects on the way information is collected, the kind of information collected, the methods used to analyze it, and the conclusions about risk and prevention that may be drawn from it.

In the past half-century, epidemiology has turned its attention more and more to chronic and recurring diseases, such as cardiovascular disease and psychiatric illness. In the process, it has had to learn how rarely these diseases can be attributed to a single cause. When the Framingham Study of atherosclerotic disease was begun in 1946, the goal was to find the "cause" of coronary heart disease (Dawber, 1980). But it soon became clear that many conditions and behaviors increased the likelihood that an individual would later die of heart disease. No one factor was necessary, nor was any one factor sufficient. The Framingham Study researchers coined the phrase "risk factors" to describe the contributory role played by cigarette smoking, obesity, hypertension, lack of exercise, and so on. In the area of developmental psychopathology, parental alcohol abuse is strongly associated with substance abuse by children (Chassin, Curran, Husson, & Colder, 1996; Wills, DuHamel, & Vaccaro, 1995;

Wills, Schriebman, Benson, & Vaccaro, 1994), but there is no evidence that it is either necessary or sufficient as a cause; the relationship is best described in terms of risk factors.

What Is Developmental Epidemiology?

Figure 4.1 presents a developmental framework for talking about epidemiological research and intervention. It illustrates the developmental nature of epidemiological thinking, which arises naturally from the fact that the disease process itself has a developmental form, each stage arising out of the previous one in interaction with a range of contextual processes (Hay & Angold, 1993). The process of disease progression is "programmed" by the nature of the transformation of the organism that begins the process, and, in general, it follows a reasonably regular course, although with wide variations in its rate. Furthermore, there is hierarchical integration as diseases develop. Each stage in the progress of a given disease builds on the previous stages, and many of the manifestations of earlier stages are "integrated" into later symptomatology (Hay & Angold, 1993). Developmentalists will note that we have just described a key developmental concept: epigenesis (Gottlieb, 1991).

Not only do diseases have a developmental course, but they also develop in the context of a developing individual. While individual development may not be terribly important for the course of a brief illness such as a cold, it clearly becomes important when the diseases of interest are long-lasting, chronic, or recurrent, as are many psychiatric disorders. Developmental epidemiology is thus concerned with why vulnerability to, and expression of, different disorders change over the course of individual development. For example, there is a good deal of evidence that attachment disorders can be identified in the first few years of life (Zeanah & Emde, 1994). If they have not occurred then, they are highly unlikely to develop later in life, whereas the sequelae of early attachment problems can often be seen later in childhood and even into adulthood, with different overt manifestations (Main, Kaplan, & Cassidy, 1985). It

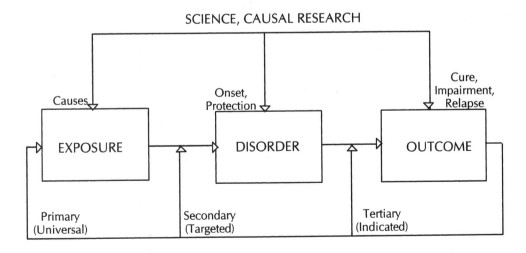

FIGURE 4.1. Relationship between scientific and public health epidemiology in understanding and preventing disease.

appears that at the developmental stage at which forming a strong relationship with key figures is a major developmental task, children are at that time vulnerable to failure of their environment to provide such stable figures in a way that they are not at later developmental stages (Carlson & Sroufe, 1995).

Thus, Figure 4.1 presents a framework for thinking about the development of disease in the developing individual. It also illustrates the interactive nature of scientific and applied epidemiology at every stage of the development of a disease. At each stage in the course of a disease, scientific epidemiology works to identify causes, while public health epidemiology works to prevent or ameliorate disease, using hypotheses from scientific research. These interventions in turn provide tests of the causal hypotheses. The scientific endeavors labeled "etiologic research" and "public health interventions" are thus two aspects of a single scientific process. In Figure 4.1 this process is divided into three sections, indexed by the three boxes. The boxes represent three stages of causation and have led to different strategies for prevention. The arrows between the boxes represent the transition probabilities, or the likelihood that an individual will move on to the next stage in the disease process, and are the points at which preventive interventions can be introduced. In this section, we provide a brief introduction to each part of the model separately, working through some of the issues associated with research into this stage of the disease process and the implications for developmental psychopathology.

Risk Exposure and Primary Prevention

The first stage of development of a disease is thought of in terms of *exposure to the causes of the disease*. At the first level in the model, this means exposure to a risk factor rather than to the disease itself. People who do not begin smoking cigarettes are never exposed to a major risk factor for lung cancer.

The most powerful preventive method at this stage of the model is to remove the risk factor from the environment altogether, as has been attempted, for example, with lead in paint and gas. This type of "primary" or "universal" prevention (Gordon, 1983; Mrazek & Haggerty, 1994) can be tremendously effective, as we have seen in the effects of eradicating the causes of most waterborne infectious diseases from industrialized nations. The key characteristic of primary or universal prevention is that it involves the whole population at risk, not just the people most likely to get the disease. It is most effective when the intervention is fairly inexpensive per capita (like fluoridation), or when there is no easy way of knowing who is likely to be or become exposed to the agent (as in the case of water pollution), or when there is a necessary causal agent against which it is possible to develop an inexpensive vaccine (like diphtheria). Primary prevention has been medicine's most powerful tool for reducing disease in the community. The dramatic increase in life expectancy in the industrialized world this century has been due very largely to the success of primary prevention methods to reduce or eradicate exposure to risk of infectious diseases. Community-based behavioral health interventions to encourage everyone to eat a healthy diet, get regular sleep and exercise, give up smoking, cut down alcohol, and so on, have resulted in a 25% reduction in mortality from coronary heart disease in the United States in the past 40 years (Califano, 1986; D'Agostino, Kannel, Belanger, & Sytkowski, 1989).

Costs and Benefits of Primary Prevention

Universal interventions are of benefit in that they do not stigmatize their targets and can often be designed to require little or no action by the individual, apart from paying taxes.

Sometimes it is possible to fine-tune the intervention by focusing on a particular demographic group known to be at increased risk; for example, women are at much greater risk of breast cancer than are men, so screening programs "target" women, to use Gordon's distinction (Gordon, 1983). But what about the costs? Apart from the tax burden, primary prevention can be fraught with social and political difficulties because it often requires individuals who do not perceive themselves as at risk to submit to additional costs or restrictions on their personal freedom. In the case of developmental psychopathology, these issues go to the foundations of people's views of the role of personal freedom and responsibility versus public responsibility for child rearing. Recent evidence from epidemiological research points to onset in adolescence or earlier for many of the severe psychiatric disorders of adulthood (Christie et al., 1988), indicating that primary prevention even of adult disorders needs to be directed to the early years of life, while those at risk are still dependents. But many of the risk factors so far identified are global ones affecting the whole family and seem to call for major social interventions for their eradication. For example, poverty appears to contribute to the causal cluster for several disorders, particularly conduct disorder and substance abuse and dependence. But how do we remove poverty as a risk factor? A family history of mental illness is another powerful risk factor, but there are terrible social costs associated with any attempt to interfere with the transgenerational transmission of genetic risk and very strong resistance to interference with families' rights to bring their children up as they see fit. We also have to bear in mind the very real risk that we may be wrong in our causal attributions.

The Risk of Disease and Secondary Prevention

The second box in Figure 4.1 represents what happens once a person has been exposed to a risk factor or cluster of factors (Kleinbaum, Kupper, & Morgenstern, 1982; Rothman, 1976). Some people exposed to risk will develop the disease, but others will not. For example, many young people used heroin and other addictive drugs in Vietnam, but only a few developed substance abuse disorders when they returned home (Robins, Davis, & Nurco, 1974). Scientific epidemiology is concerned here with why some are more vulnerable in the presence of risk, and public health epidemiology with how to prevent or delay the onset of disease in exposed or "high-risk" individuals. Secondary prevention efforts focus on those subgroups of the population believed to have been exposed to risk factors for the disease. For example, Beardslee et al. (1992) designed a targeted prevention for (currently healthy) children whose parents suffered from depression, and Dodge, Coie, and others are intervening to teach social skills to youth identified by teachers as being aggressive and at risk of developing conduct disorders (Coie, 1996).

Costs and Benefits of Secondary Prevention or High-Risk Interventions

Secondary prevention may be easier than primary prevention to sell politically, but it can also create tensions between individual rights and the public good. An individual, family, or group, may resent or resist being labeled as "high risk" or singled out for treatment, even if the intervention is benign in intention, just as families have resisted having their children identified as in need of remedial educational services, even when those services are provided with the best of intentions. Secondary prevention looks as though it should be cheaper than primary prevention, since it is provided only to a subgroup of the population rather than to everyone. However, the cost of identifying the high-risk group can be considerable, offsetting the reduction in the number for whom intervention is planned.

Minimizing Disease Impact and Tertiary Prevention

The third box in Figure 4.1 refers to the stage when an individual has succumbed to a disease, or when the disease becomes clinically identifiable. (Some epidemiologists define this third stage as occurring when the disease has actually been *identified*, for example, by a laboratory test. In child psychiatry, however, the amount of untreated psychopathology is so high [Burns et al., 1995; Costello et al., 1988] that we prefer to think about *identifiable* disorder in this context.) The goals of scientific epidemiology at this stage are to search for treatments and cures, and to understand why some people succumb to the disease, others survive, and others relapse. The boundary between prevention and treatment at this level is of course murky, and the distinction is rarely worth making. Public health epidemiology (often at this point synonymous with "clinical epidemiology") takes these ideas and turns them into clinical trials and effectiveness studies, or tests of promising treatments in real-world settings outside the research laboratory. At the level of tertiary prevention, epidemiological research and clinical trials become closely intertwined in both goals and methods, in the area where treatment of a disease and prevention of relapse or residual disability cannot usefully be disentangled.

Examples of tertiary prevention are programs to provide community support to schizo-phrenic patients to prevent relapse (Dincin, Wasmer, Witheridge, Sobeck, & Razzano, 1993; McFarlane, Stastny, & Deakins, 1992; Rosenheck, Neale, Leaf, Milstein, & Frisman, 1995). Multisystem treatment or wraparound programs (Clarke, Schaefer, Burchard, & Welkowitz, 1992; Eber, Osuch, & Redditt, 1996; VanDenBerg & Grealish, 1996) to keep severely emo-tionally disturbed children in their families and out of residential settings can be seen either as treatment of the child's (usually chronic) disorder or as prevention of a relapse that could lead to hospitalization.

Costs and Benefits of Tertiary Prevention

Interventions at the tertiary level are generally less controversial than those at primary or secondary levels, because the objects of the intervention are already clearly sick and interven-tion is socially acceptable. An area of controversy is the use of mandatory interventions for those seen to pose a risk to others or themselves, or compulsory removal from what are seen as damaging environments. The practical and ethical issues around outpatient commitment (Mulvey, Geller, & Roth, 1987) are examples of the costs and benefits of tertiary prevention in psychiatry; individuals involuntarily committed to inpatient treatment may be released into the community on the condition that they follow a court-approved treatment regimen; failure to comply is grounds for rehospitalization. Society benefits from reduced hospital costs, and patients from greater freedom, but there are questions about the morality of forcing people to undergo treatment or maintenance regimens under threat of legal action.

THE CURRENT STATE OF DEVELOPMENTAL EPIDEMIOLOGY

In this chapter so far, we have presented the skeleton of a research program. When it comes to describing work done to flesh out that program, we have to confess that in most places the bones still show through all too clearly. There is a shortage of empirical work that meets the model's requirements of being (1) informed by developmental principles, (2) formu-lated so as to test a causal hypothesis, and (3) capable of generating a prevention strategy.

There are very good reasons for this. First, diagnosing psychiatric disorders "in the field" is a complex business. Most of the past two decades have been devoted to developing reasonably accurate methods for doing epidemiological field research. Second is the high cost of field studies in which the object of interest may be a rare disorder and most hypotheses require longitudinal research with repeated assessments to test them. Third, psychologists and psychiatrists (even child psychiatrists) get little exposure to the principles of modern developmental science. Fourth is the historical split between child and adult research; different diagnostic instruments have been developed with different risk factors explored.

Prevalence and Continuity

Since the 1950s, there have been studies around the world attempting to establish the prevalence of "maladaptation" (Gould, Wunsch-Hitzig, & Dohrenwend, 1980), behavioral problems (Lapouse & Monk, 1964; Shepherd, Oppenheim, & Mitchell, 1971), or psychiatric disorders as defined by one or another taxonomy (Brandenburg, Friedman, & Silver, 1990; Costello, 1989). Most recent studies point to the presence of one or more DSM psychiatric disorders in one child in five in the community (Brandenburg et al., 1990; Costello, 1989). For the developmentalist, the more important question is the amount of continuity in these disorders. A review of nine studies (Costello & Angold, 1995), with a total of over 8,000 participants, showed that between 40% and 60% of children with a psychiatric disorder at one measurement point also had one when assessed a second time, 2 to 5 years later. A review of the literature published since that time shows remarkable consistency with the earlier studies (e.g., Achenbach, Howell, McConaughy, & Stanger, 1995; Feehan, McGee, Williams, & Nada-Raja, 1995; Ferdinand, Verhulst, & Wiznitzer, 1995; Fergusson & Horwood, 1995; Fergusson & Lynskey, 1995; Reinherz et al., 1995). Stability appears to be higher for behavioral disorders or symptom scale scores than for emotional problems (Ferdinand et al., 1995), although the Dunedin longitudinal study data suggest that this may be more true of boys than of girls (McGee, Feehan, Williams, & Anderson, 1992).

Prevalence of Different Disorders Across Childhood and Adolescence

Children appear to be differentially vulnerable to different disorders at different ages. For example, Figure 4.2 shows the 3-month prevalence of DSM-IV depression and anxiety disorders in a community sample studied between the ages of 9 and 16. Anxiety disorders have a downward trajectory, while the prevalence of depression is low until age 13, when it begins to move upward. A similar analysis of behavioral rather than emotional problems (Figure 4.3) shows attention-deficit hyperactivity disorder almost disappearing by midadolescence, while oppositional and conduct disorders remain fairly stable across the age range. Substance abuse shows a dramatic increase after age 13. These patterns are fairly similar in boys and girls, except for depression, where the adolescent increase is mainly caused by girls (Angold et al., 1998; Costello et al., 1996). The data presented are based on a single study, but the figures are consistent with other available data (e.g., Anderson, Williams, McGee, & Silva, 1987; Bird et al., 1988; Brown, Lewinsohn, Seeley, & Wagner, 1996; Cohen, Provet, & Jones, 1996; Costello & Angold, 1997; Esser, Schmidt, & Woerner, 1990; Feehan, McGee, & Williams, 1993; Feehan, McGee, Williams, & Nada-Raja, 1996; Fergusson, Horwood, & Lynskey, 1993; Fergusson, Lynskey, & Horwood, 1996; Kashani et al., 1987; Lewinsohn, Zinbarg, Lewinsohn,

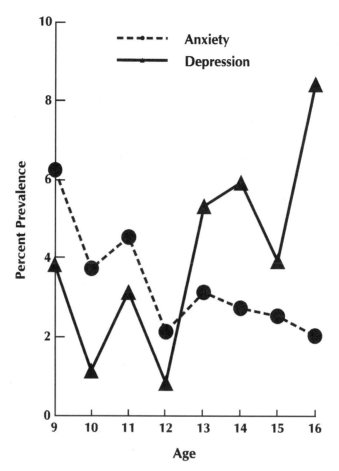

FIGURE 4.2. Prevalence of emotional disorders.

& Sack, 1997; Lewinsohn, Hops, Roberts, Seeley, & Andrews, 1993; McGee et al., 1992; Velez, Johnson, & Cohen, 1989; Wittchen, Nelson, & Lachner, 1998).

Risk Factors

Prevalence and continuity are, however, only the first step; we need studies that develop and test developmental hypotheses about risk exposure, onset and course of illness, and predictors of recovery and relapse, along the lines of Figure 4.1. A handful of risk factors have a robust relationship to the development of child and adolescent psychiatric disorders; however, there seems to be little specificity (Costello, 1989). For example, poverty has persistently been cited as a risk factor for both emotional and behavioral disorders (Duncan & Rodgers, 1988; McLeod & Shanahan, 1996). We know very little about the mechanisms by which poverty has its effect. Thus, in a comparison of rural white children ages 9–13 and American-Indian children living in the same area of southern Appalachia, where one-fourth of white

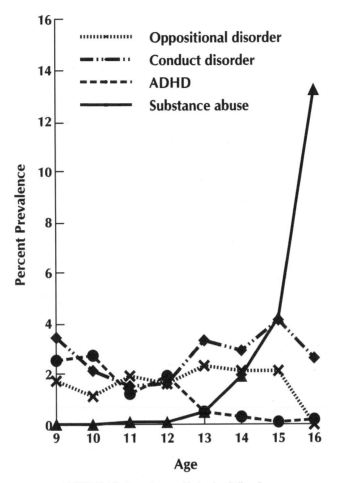

FIGURE 4.3. Prevalence of behavioral disorders.

children and two-thirds of American Indian children lived in poverty as defined by the federal guidelines, poverty was strongly associated with psychiatric disorder in the white children but not in the American Indian children (Costello, Farmer, Angold, Burns, & Erkanli, 1997). Is poverty only a risk factor if it is not the norm for the society in which one lives (a "relative deprivation" explanation of the findings)? Or are we seeing what Dohrenwend calls "social selection" at work in the white population (Dohrenwend et al., 1992); that over time, as the strong and healthy move up the social hierarchy, those left at the bottom are both poor and unhealthy in one way or another? In this case, the social isolation of the Indians would have prevented this kind of selection. Clearly, a great deal more work is needed to clarify the meaning of poverty as a risk factor.

It is perhaps worth nothing that clinical studies, while very useful for pointing to potential risk relationships, cannot be used to examine the importance of a risk factor or its temporal relationship with a specific disorder, because the factors that lead some children and not others into treatment settings may well be confounded with the role of those same factors in causing the disorder. Thus, our population-based studies showed that among children with a psychiatric disorder, those from families receiving Medicaid were twice as likely as those from families with private insurance to receive professional mental health services (Burns et al., 1995). This means that in a clinical study of treated children, poverty would appear to be an even stronger risk factor for psychopathology than it is in the general population.

A review of the epidemiological literature on disease onset shows that we do not even have a very clear sense of the causal significance of the timing of onsets for several disorders. This is because most studies have been cross-sectional rather than longitudinal, while problems with the reliability of interviews for children below the age of around 8 or 9 have limited the value of data on younger children. While cross-sectional studies can tell us something about the prevalence of different disorders at different ages, we do not know whether the early-onset cases are different in kind from later-onset cases or simply the first of the series. For example, most studies find that depression is rare before the early teens (Angold et al., 1998), but without good longitudinal data, we cannot say whether the rare prepubertal cases are precipitated by different risk factors from those with later onset, although a behavioral genetic study points in this direction (Silberg et al., 1999). Loeber and colleagues' work on the onset of conduct disorder in boys is a model of what is needed for the rest of psychopathology. In this longitudinal study of an urban community, Loeber (1991) identifies what he calls "pathways" into adolescent conduct disorder: an overt pathway, along which boys move from minor aggression via fighting to acts of physical violence; a covert pathway, along which they move from shoplifting and stealing, via vandalism and firesetting, to such acts as fraud, burglary, and serious theft; and an authority conflict pathway that begins earlier (before age 12) and moves from stubbornness, defiance, and disobedience, via truancy and running away, to end in serious overt and covert delinquency by the midteens.

Recovery and Relapse

The third focus of the developmental epidemiological model outlined in Figure 4.1 is recovery and relapse. Here, the clinical literature can be more helpful, at least for treated cases. A fine example is Kovacs's study of the course of childhood depressive disorder. She has followed the course of 55 children with dysthymia and 60 children with major depressive disorder over a period ranging from 3 to 12 years (mean 6 years) (Kovacs, Akiskal, Gatsonis, & Parrone, 1994). Major depressive disorder developed in 42 of the dysthymic children, usually on top of an ongoing dysthymic disorder. First episodes of dysthymia occurred at an earlier age, on average, than first episodes of major depression, while the average age of onset of the first episode of major depression was the same in the two groups, whether or not it was preceded by dysthymia. This study indicates that the prognosis for young people with diagnosed depression is not good; 80% of those with dysthymia and 48% of those with major depressive disorder had another depressive episode within the period of observation, and one in four attempted suicide (Kovacs, Goldston, & Gatsonis, 1993).

A community-based example of a study of tertiary intervention is McCord's follow-up of what would nowadays be called a multisystemic treatment program for high-risk inner-city boys, begun in the 1930s (McCord, 1992). This study is of great significance because it shows that the adult consequences of this extensive intervention program—unusual in incorporating random assignment and careful record keeping—was universally *worse* for the treated group. Illness, early mortality, suicide, criminal convictions, unemployment, divorce—all were significantly more common in the "experimental" than "control" group in the 30 years following the intervention. This is a somber warning that preventive efforts are not necessarily good or benign; they can actually cause harm.

This brief review of the early history of developmental epidemiology shows that although some of the groundwork has been done, we have very little information about what triggers the onset of disorder in vulnerable children. However, once a child reaches the treatment system (which may be for reasons quite outside the child's own symptomatology), the clinical literature on course, outcome, and relapse rate is far from encouraging. It would not be unreasonable to say that the developmental epidemiology of child and adolescent psychiatric disorders is very much in the position of cardiovascular epidemiology 50 years ago (Dawber, 1980).

THE FUTURE OF DEVELOPMENTAL EPIDEMIOLOGY

So far in this chapter, we have suggested that developmental epidemiology provides a set of principles and methods that (1) link etiological research with public health applications; (2) are concerned with preventing risk exposure and the onset of disease in exposed individuals, as well as with minimizing the disability caused by psychiatric illness; (3) set the development of psychiatric disorder in the context of "normal" development. In this section, we consider some areas to which developmental epidemiologists can contribute to the next phase in our understanding of developmental psychopathology. We concentrate on three areas: defining the phenotype; improving risk–disorder specificity; and integrating causal and preventive research.

Defining the Phenotype

Individuals presenting themselves to a clinician can be assumed to be suffering from some degree of symptomatology or distress. But epidemiologists have to be able to convince their clinical colleagues that a "case" as identified in their community sample would also be diagnosed as a case in the clinic. Since the psychiatric interview is still the main tool of child psychiatry and clinical psychology, epidemiologists working in the area of child psychiatric disorder have put immense effort over the past two decades into developing interview methods that have the desired characteristics of reliability (the interview produces the same responses in the hands of any trained interviewer) and clinical validity. Interviews include the Schedule for Affective Disorders and Schizophrenia: Child Version (K-SADS-E; Puig-Antich & Chambers, 1978), the Diagnostic Interview Schedule (DISC; Costello, Edelbrock, Kalas, Kessler, & Klaric, 1982; Shaffer et al., 1996), the Diagnostic Interview for Children and Adolescents (DICA; Welner, Reich, Herjanic, Jung, & Amado, 1987), and the Child and Adolescent Psychiatric Assessment (CAPA; Angold et al., 1995). There is still a great deal to be done, particularly in the area of developing shorter screening measures to identify potential cases for more detailed diagnosis and tools to select individuals on the basis of their exposure status for prospective studies, rather than on their outcome (diagnostic) status, for case-control studies. Problems with overdiagnosis using some psychiatric interviews (Breslau, 1987) have focused attention on other aspects of "casesness" besides the presence or absence of symptoms. For example, the DSM-IV taxonomy (American Psychiatric Association, 1994) requires symptoms to entail dysfunction, which is defined in terms of two key areas: *distress* and *disability*.

Distress is defined in the DSM-IV in terms of the pain that the symptom causes, while disability refers to impairment in one or more important areas of functioning. More work is needed to operationalize both of these aspects of dysfunction and improve the validity of epidemiological measures of psychopathology.

Equally important from the point of view of developmental psychopathology is the work needed to make assessments developmentally appropriate. We know extraordinarily little about how syndromes vary as children mature. At present, our measures assume an invariance that is methodologically convenient and conforms to the underlying ethos of the DSM but has almost no empirical underpinnings.

Improving Risk–Disorder Specificity

The mighty engine of epidemiological prevention described earlier in this chapter was designed to break the causal links between risk factors and disorders. One of the serious problems facing developmental epidemiology is the lack of specificity of the links so far identified. For example, maternal depression may increase the likelihood of childhood depression, but it also predicts a whole range of other psychiatric disorders, behavioral as well as emotional (Goodman, Adamson, Riniti, & Cole, 1994; Webster-Stratton & Hammond, 1988). One of the problems has been the dearth of longitudinal, prospective data sets with good risk and diagnostic data at several time points. Reviews of what is known to date can be found elsewhere (Costello, 1989; Costello & Angold, 1995). What is needed for the future is an organized program of research with large enough samples and a long enough time span to permit hypothesis testing with due respect for the complexities of correlated risk factors and comorbid diagnoses.

Integrating Etiologic Research and Prevention

This chapter has made the point that preventive interventions are tests of causal hypotheses, since they require the researcher to have a theory about the link between risk and outcome. Psychiatry has differed until now from other branches of medicine in the distance that has grown between the two disciplines of epidemiology and prevention science (Grob, 1985). In order to bring psychiatric epidemiology into line with other branches of medicine, we need to set up research programs that bring together researchers with expertise in both areas.

CONCLUSIONS

In this chapter, we have laid out the basic tenets of epidemiology as a set of methods for preventing and controlling the spread of disease in the community. The specific methods used—the research designs and statistical programs—are well known to most psychologists. What may be less familiar is the integration into a single model that links normal development, developmental psychopathology, etiological research, and prevention science. We have emphasized the role of epidemiology as a way of thinking about causes and prevention, rather than as a body of substantive knowledge about prevalence or incidence, the nose-counting aspect of epidemiology that is a useful step toward grasping the size and public health significance of a problem but only the first step toward preventing it. So what is the next step? To conclude this chapter, we describe a project that has been tremendously influential in the drive to reduce heart disease in the population, and dream about the effects that a similar project could have in shaping public policy toward child and adolescent psychopathology.

A "Developmental Framingham"

For the past 50 years, the National Institutes of Health (with support from industry at some points) have been studying a large sample of the population of Framingham, Massachusetts, with primary prevention of cardiovascular disease as the goal. Over 5,000 adult citizens of Framingham have been regularly evaluated for cardiovascular fitness and for a range of risk factors. Findings from the study have been translated into prevention trials, and thence into behavioral medicine programs (e.g., the American Heart Association's recommendations on diet, exercise, and smoking), and even into legislation (to limit smoking in public places and potentially to declare nicotine a dangerous drug). While the surgical treatment of coronary artery disease has increased the expectation of life of many people, its impact on the life expectancy of the population of the United States as a whole is trivial compared with the effects of the primary prevention strategies that emerged in large part from the Framingham Study. Yet looking back at the early study papers, it is fascinating to see how unfocused the preliminary hypotheses were. As Kannel pointed out in 1990, there was an initial belief that the Framingham Study would identify "a single etiology for atherosclerotic disease" (p. 206); the researchers had to invent the term "risk factors" to define the multiple contributory factors, none of them either necessary nor sufficient, that contributed to cardiovascular morbidity and mortality. Among the possible causal factors investigated early in the study were alcohol, exercise (thought at the time to be potentially harmful!), and high thyroid levels (thyroidectomy was sometimes used as a treatment for angina at the time). In his history of the Framingham Study, Dawber (1980) says that it was 10 years before a link between cigarette smoking and coronary heart disease was suspected.

An important message that Framingham taught us is that the aggregation of risk factors can be more important than any one separately. Investigators were able to use the representative, longitudinal sample to explore key developmental issues: the relative significance of *number* of risk factors compared with *severity* of risk factors, *length of exposure, age at onset,* or *effects of offset*. Because of the several age cohorts in the study, researchers were able to show, for example, that cigarette smoking exerted its strongest risk effect at the age when the absolute incidence of coronary heart disease was lowest; by the age of 65, smoking no longer exerted a separate risk effect, controlling for other factors (Dawber, 1980).

Summing up his impression of the impact of the first 24 years of the Framingham Study, Dawber points to its importance in *changing the attitudes of the medical profession,* moving doctors to concentrate on prevention rather than treatment. It is this *change in attitude* that we believe is needed in the area of mental illness and that a "developmental Framingham" could help to foster. There are important similarities between psychiatric and cardiovascular diseases. In both cases, we are talking about a group of disorders and a set of risk factors that appear to affect the course of several disorders. There is a clear genetic component to many disorders, but the expression of a genetic liability is very variable, under environmental control in ways not fully understood. With a few exceptions, the long-term success of most treatments currently available suggests strongly that prevention could be more cost-efficient than cure for several disorders, particularly disorders of childhood. Behavioral change, which has been so effective in preventing cardiovascular disease, is the obvious first line of attack in the prevention of some mental illnesses.

In our "Developmental Framingham," we envision that one or more study areas, preferably with a mixture of ethnic groups and social classes, would be selected to be representative of one or more communities, and great efforts would be made to involve the whole community in "their" study. This might involve regular, low-intensity screening of successive cohorts of families, with more detailed assessments of subgroups selected for case-control studies of various topics; for example, one might want to study all children who lost their mothers during the early years of life, or all the poorest children, or all the children with IQ or attainment below a certain level, and look over time at the predictive power of maternal loss, poverty, and developmental delay, separately and together, as risk factors. The latest developments in behavioral genetic research could be included in the study through the selection of genetically informative groups for more intensive study: twins, affected sib pairs, multigenerational clusters. One could also imagine regular, low-intensity community surveillance being supplemented by a more detailed assessment for everyone at specific ages, perhaps before and after puberty, or once in elementary school and once in high school. Ideas emerging from the study over time would be tested in other laboratories around the world, using different samples, different ethnic groups, and different investigators. Epidemiology, the study of patterns of distribution of disease in time and place, would for the first time become a truly developmental science.

REFERENCES

Achenbach, T. M., Howell, C. T., McConaughy, S. H., & Stanger, C. (1995). Six-year predictors of problems in a national sample: III. Transitions to young adult syndromes. *Journal of the American Academy of Child and Adolescent Psychiatry, 34*(5), 658–669.

American Psychiatric Association. (1994). *Diagnostic and statistical manual of mental disorders* (4th ed.). Washington, DC: Author.

Anderson, J. C., Williams, S., McGee, R., & Silva, P. A. (1987). DSM-III disorders in preadolescent children: Prevalence in a large sample from the general population. *Archives of General Psychiatry, 44*, 69–76.

Angold, A., Costello, E. J., & Worthman, C. M. (1998). Puberty and depression: The role of age, pubertal status, and pubertal timing. *Psychological Medicine, 28*, 51–61.

Angold, A., Erkanli, A., Loeber, R., Costello, E. J., Van Kammen, W., & Stouthamer-Loeber, M. (1996). Disappearing depression in a population sample of boys. *Journal of Emotional and Behavioral Disorders, 4*(2), 95–104.

Angold, A., Prendergast, M., Cox, A., Harrington, R., Simonoff, E., & Rutter, M. (1995). The Child and Adolescent Psychiatric Assessment (CAPA). *Psychological Medicine, 25*, 739–753.

Angold, A., & Worthman, C. W. (1993). Puberty onset of gender differences in rates of depression: A developmental, epidemiologic and neuroendocrine perspective. *Journal of Affective Disorders, 29*, 145–158.

Beardslee, W. R., Hoke, L., Wheelock, I., Rothberg, P. C., van de Velde, P., & Swatling, S. (1992). Initial findings on preventive intervention for families with parental affective disorders. *American Journal of Psychiatry, 149*(10), 1335–1340.

Bird, H. R., Canino, G., Rubio-Stipec, M., Gould, M. S., Ribera, J., Sesman, M., Woodbury, M., Huertas-Goldman, S., Pagan, A., Sanchez-Lacay, A., & Moscoso, M. (1988). Estimates of the prevalence of childhood maladjustment in a community survey in Puerto Rico: The use of combined measures. *Archives of General Psychiatry, 45*, 1120–1126.

Brandenburg, N. A, Friedman, R. M., & Silver, S. E. (1990). The epidemiology of childhood psychiatric disorders. *Journal of the American Academy of Child and Adolescent Psychiatry, 29*, 76–83.

Breslau, N. (1987). Inquiring about the bizarre: False positives in diagnostic interview schedule for children (DISC) ascertainment of obsessions, compulsions, and psychotic symptoms. *Journal of the American Academy of Child and Adolescent Psychiatry, 26*, 639–644.

Brooks-Gunn, J., Graber, J. A., & Paikoff, R. L. (1994). Studying links between hormones and negative affect: Models and measures. *Journal of Research on Adolescence, 4*(4), 469–486.

Brown, R., Lewinsohn, P. M., Seeley, J. R., & Wagner, E. F. (1996). Cigarette smoking, major depression, and other psychiatric disorders among adolescents. *Journal of the American Academy of Child and Adolescent Psychiatry, 35*(12), 1602–1610.

Burns, B. J., Costello, E. J., Angold, A., Tweed, D., Stangl, D., Farmer, E. M. Z., & Erkanli, A. (1995). Children's mental health service use across service sectors. *Health Affairs, 14*(3), 147–159.

Califano, J. A. (1986). *America's health care revolution: Who lives? Who dies? Who pays?* New York: Random House.

Carlson, E. A., & Sroufe, L. A. (1995). Contribution of attachment theory to developmental psychopathology. In D. Cicchetti & D. J. Cohen (Eds.), *Developmental psychopathology: Theory and methods* (Vol. 1; pp. 581–617). New York: Wiley.

Chassin, L., Curran, P. J., Husson, A. M., & Colder, C. R. (1996). The relation of parent alcoholism to adolescent substance use: A longitudinal follow-up study. *Journal of Abnormal Psychology, 105,* 70–80.

Christie, K. A., Burke, J. D., Regier, D. A., Rae, D. S., Boyd, J. H., & Locke, B. Z. (1988). Epidemiologic evidence for early onset of mental disorders and higher risk of drug abuse in young adults. *American Journal of Psychiatry, 145*(8), 971–975.

Clarke, R. T., Schaefer, M., Burchard, J. D., & Welkowitz, J. W. (1992). Wrapping community-based mental health services around children with a severe behavioral disorder: An evaluation of project wraparound. *Journal of Child and Family Studies, 1*(3), 241–261.

Cohen, P., Provet, A. G., & Jones, M. (1996). Prevalence of emotional behavior disorders during childhood and adolescence. In B. L. Lubotsky & J. Petrila (Eds.), *Mental health services: A public health perspective* (pp. 193–209). New York: Oxford University Press.

Coie, J. D. (1996). The prevention of violence and antisocial behavior. In R. DeV. Peters & R. J. McMahon (Eds.), *Prevention of psychological disorders* (pp. 1–18). London: Sage.

Costello, A. J., Edelbrock, C., Kalas, R., Kessler, M. D., & Klaric, S. H. (1982). *The National Institute of Mental Health Diagnostic Interview Schedule for Children (DISC).* Rockville, MD: National Institute of Mental Health.

Costello, E., Farmer, E., Angold, A., Burns, B., & Erkanli, A. (1997). Psychiatric disorders among American Indian and white youth in Appalachia: The Great Smoky Mountains Study. *American Journal of Public Health, 87*(5), 827–832.

Costello, E. J. (1989). Developments in child psychiatric epidemiology. *Journal of the American Academy of Child and Adolescent Psychiatry, 28,* 836–841.

Costello, E. J., & Angold, A. (1995). Developmental epidemiology. In D. Cicchetti & D. Cohen (Eds.), *Developmental psychopathology: Volume 1. Theory and methods* (pp. 23–56). New York: Wiley.

Costello, E. J., Angold, A., & Keeler, G. P. (1999). Adolescent outcomes of childhood disorders: The consequences of severity and impairment. *Journal of the American Academy of Child and Adolescent Psychiatry, 38,* 121–128.

Costello, E. J., Angold, A., Burns, B. J., Stangl, D. K., Tweed, D. L., Erkanli, A., & Worthman, C. M. (1996). The Great Smoky Mountains Study of youth: Goals, designs, methods, and the prevalence of DSM-III-R disorders. *Archives of General Psychiatry, 53*(12), 1129–1136.

Costello, E. J., Edelbrock, C. S., Costello, A. J., Dulcan, M. K., Burns, B. J., & Brent, D. (1988). Psychopathology in pediatric primary care: The new hidden morbidity. *Pediatrics, 82*(3), 415–424.

D'Agostino, R. B., Kannel, W. B., Belanger, A. J., & Sytkowski, P. A. (1989). Trends in CHD and risk factors at age 55–64 in the Framingham study. *International Journal of Epidemiology, 18*(3, Suppl. 1), S67–S72.

Dawber, T. R. (1980). *The Framingham Study: The epidemiology of coronary heart disease.* Cambridge, MA: Harvard University Press.

Dincin, J., Wasmer, D., Witheridge, T. F., Sobeck, L., Cook, J., & Razzano, L. (1993). Impact of assertive community treatment on the use of the state hospital inpatient bed-days. *Hospital and Community Psychiatry, 44*(9), 833–838.

Dohrenwend, B. P., Levav, I., Shrout, P. E., Schwartz, S., Naveh, G., Link, B. G., Skodol, A. E., & Stueve, A. (1992, February 21). Socioeconomic status and psychiatric disorders: The causation–selection issue. *Science, 255,* 946–952.

Duncan, G. J., & Rodgers, W. L. (1988, November). Longitudinal aspects of childhood poverty. *Journal of Marriage and the Family, 50,* 1007–1021.

Eber, L., Osuch, R., & Redditt, C. A. (1996). School-based applications of the wraparound process: Early results on service provision and student outcomes. *Journal of Child and Family Studies, 5*(1), 83–99.

Esser, G., Schmidt, M. H., & Woerner, W. (1990). Epidemiology and course of psychiatric disorders in school-age children: Results of a longitudinal study. *Journal of Child Psychology and Psychiatry, 31*(2), 243–263.

Feehan, M., McGee, R., & Williams, S. M. (1993). Mental health disorders from age 15 to age 18 years. *Journal of the American Academy of Child and Adolescent Psychiatry, 32*(6), 1118–1126.

Feehan, M., McGee, R., Williams, S. M., & Nada-Raja, S. (1995). Models of adolescent psychopathology: Childhood risk and the transition to adulthood. *Journal of the American Academy of Child and Adolescent Psychiatry, 34*(5), 670–679.

Ferdinand, R. F., Verhulst, F. C., & Wiznitzer, M. (1995). Continuity and change of self-reported problem behaviors from adolescence into young adulthood. *Journal of the American Academy of Child and Adolescent Psychiatry, 34*(5), 680–690.

Fergusson, D. M., & Horwood, L. J. (1995). Predictive validity of categorically and dimensionally scored measures of disruptive childhood behaviors. *Journal of the American Academy of Child and Adolescent Psychiatry, 34*(4), 477–485.

Fergusson, D. M., Horwood, L. J., & Lynskey, M. T. (1993, November). Prevalence and comorbidity of DSM-III-R diagnoses in a birth cohort of 15 year olds. *Journal of the American Academy of Child and Adolescent Psychiatry, 32*(6), 1127–1134.

Fergusson, D. M., & Lynskey, M. T. (1995). Childhood circumstances, adolescent adjustment, and suicide attempts in a New Zealand birth cohort. *Journal of the American Academy of Child and Adolescent Psychiatry, 34*(5), 612–622.

Fergusson, D. M., Lynskey, M. T., & Horwood, L. J. (1996). Origins of comorbidity between conduct and affective disorders. *Journal of the American Academy of Child and Adolescent Psychiatry, 35*(4), 451–460.

Goodman, S. H., Adamson, L. B., Riniti, J., & Cole, S. (1994). Mothers' expressed attitudes: Associations with maternal depression and children's self-esteem and psychopathology. *Journal of the American Academy of Child and Adolescent Psychiatry, 33*(9), 1265–1274.

Gordon, R. S., Jr. (1983). An operational classification of disease prevention. *Public Health Reports, 98*, 107–109.

Gottlieb, G. (1991). Epigenetic systems view of human development. *Developmental Psychopathology, 27*(1), 33–34.

Gould, M. S., Wunsch-Hitzig, R., & Dohrenwend, B. P. (1980). Formulation of hypotheses about the prevalence, treatment and prognostic significance of psychiatric disorders in children in the United States. In B. P. Dohrenwend (Eds.), *Mental illness in the United States: Epidemiological estimates* (pp. 9–44). New York: Praeger.

Grob, G. N. (1985). The origins of American psychiatric epidemiology. *American Journal of Public Health, 75*(3), 229–236.

Hay, D. F., & Angold, A. (1993). Introduction: Precursors and causes in development and pathogenesis. In D. F. Hay & A. Angold (Eds.), *Precursors and causes in development and psychopathology* (pp. 1–21). Chichester, UK: Wiley.

Kannel, W. B. (1990). Contribution of the Framingham Study to preventive cardiology. *Journal of the American College of Cardiology, 15*, 206–211.

Kashani, J. H., Beck, N. C., Hoeper, E. W., Fallahi, C., Corcoran, C. M., Mcallister, J. A., Rosenberg, T. K., & Reid, J. C. (1987). Psychiatric disorders in a community sample of adolescents. *American Journal of Psychiatry, 144*, 584–589.

Kleinbaum, D. G., Kupper, L. L., & Morgenstern, H. (1982). *Epidemiologic research: Principles and quantitative methods.* New York: Van Nostrand Reinhold.

Kovacs, M., Akiskal, H. S., Gatsonis, C., & Parrone, P. L. (1994). Childhood-onset dysthymic disorder: Clinical features and prospective naturalistic outcome. *Archives of General Psychiatry, 51*(5), 365–374.

Kovacs, M., Goldston, D., & Gatsonis, C. (1993). Suicidal behaviors and childhood-onset depressive disorders: A longitudinal investigation. *Journal of the American Academy of Child and Adolescent Psychiatry, 32*, 8–20.

Lapouse, R. L., & Monk, M. A. (1964). Behavior deviations in a representative sample of children. *American Journal of Orthopsychiatry, 34*, 436–447.

Lewinsohn, P., Zinbarg, J., Seeley, J. R., Lewinsohn, M., & Sack, W. (1997). Lifetime comorbidity among anxiety disorders and between anxiety disorders and other mental disorders in adolescents. *Journal of Anxiety Disorders, 11*(4), 377–394.

Lewinsohn, P. M., Hops, H., Roberts, R. E., Seeley, J. R., & Andrews, J. A. (1993). Adolescent psychopathology: I. Prevalence and incidence of depression and other DSM-III-R disorders in high school students. *Journal of Abnormal Psychology, 102*(1), 133–144.

Loeber, R. (1991). Questions and advances in the study of developmental pathways. In D. Cicchetti & S. Toth (Eds.), *Rochester Symposium on Developmental Psychopathology: Vol. 3. Models and integrations* (pp. 97–116). Rochester, NY: University of Rochester Press.

Main, M., Kaplan, N., & Cassidy, J. (1985). Security in infancy, childhood and adulthood: A move to the level of representation. In I. Bertherton & E. Waters (Eds.), Growing points of attachment theory and research (pp. 66–106). *Monographs of the Society for Research in Child Development, 50* (Serial No. 209).

McCord, J. (1992). The Cambridge–Somerville Study: A pioneering longitudinal experimental study of delinquency prevention. In J. McCord & R. E. Tremblay (Eds.), *Preventing antisocial behavior: Interventions from birth through adolescence* (pp. 196–206). New York: Guilford Press.

McFarlane, W. R., Stastny, P., & Deakins, S. (1992). Family-aided assertive community treatment: A comprehensive rehabilitation and intensive case management approach for persons with schizophrenic disorders. In *New Directions for Mental Health Services* (pp. 43–54). San Francisco: Jossey-Bass.

McGee, R., Feehan, M., Williams, S., & Anderson, J. (1992). DSM-III disorders from age 11 to age 15 years. *Journal of the American Academy of Child and Adolescent Psychiatry, 31*(1), 50–59.

McLeod, J. D., & Shanahan, M. J. (1996, September). Trajectories of poverty and children's mental health. *Journal of Health and Social Behavior, 37*, 207–220.

Mrazek, P. J., & Haggerty, R. J. (Eds.). (1994). *Reducing risks for mental disorders: Frontiers for preventive intervention research*. Washington, DC: National Academy Press.

Mulvey, E. P., Geller, J. L., & Roth, L. H. (1987). The promise and peril of involuntary outpatient commitment. *American Psychologist, 42*(6), 571–584.

Puig-Antich, J., & Chambers, W. (1978). *The Schedule for Affective Disorders and Schizophrenia for School-Aged Children (K-SADS)* (Unpublished Interview Schedule). New York: New York State Psychiatric Institute.

Reinherz, H. Z., Giaconia, R. M., Silverman, A. B., Friedman, A., Pakiz, B., Frost, A. K., & Cohen, E. (1995). Early psychosocial risks for adolescent suicidal ideation and attempts. *Journal of the American Academy of Child and Adolescent Psychiatry, 34*(5), 599–611.

Robins, L. N., Davis, D. H., & Nurco, D. N. (1974). How permanent was Vietnam drug addiction? *American Journal of Public Health, 64*, 38–43.

Rosenheck, R., Neale, M., Leaf, P., Milstein, R., & Frisman, L. (1995). A multi-site experimental cost study of intensive psychiatric community care. *Schizophrenia Bulletin, 21*(1), 129–140.

Rothman, K. J. (1976). Review and commentary: Causes. *American Journal of Epidemiology, 104*(6), 587–592.

Shaffer, D., Fisher, P. W., Dulcan, M., Davies, M. Piacentini, J., Schwab-Stone, M., Lahey, B. B., Bourdon, K., Jensen, P., Bird, H., Canino, G., & Regier, D. (1996). The NIMH Diagnostic Interview Schedule for Children (DISC 2.3): Description, acceptability, prevalences, and performance in the MECA study. *Journal of the American Academy of Child and Adolescent Psychiatry, 35*(7), 865–877.

Shepherd, M., Oppenheim, B., & Mitchell, S. (1971). *Childhood behaviour and mental health*. London: University of London Press.

Silberg, J., Pickles, A., Rutter, M., Kessler, R. J. H., Simonoff, E., & Eaves, L. (1999). The influence of genetic factors and life stress on depression among adolescent girls. *Archives of General Psychiatry, 56*, 225–232.

Simmons, R. G., & Blyth, D. A. (1992). Moving into adolescence: The impact of pubertal change and school context. In P. H. Rossi, M. Useem, & J. D. Wright (Eds.), *Social institutions and social change* (pp. 366–403). New York: Aldine De Gruyter.

Susman, E. J., Nottelmann, E. D., Inoff-Germain, G. E., Dorn, L. D., Cutler, G. B., Lorius, D. L., & Chrousos, G. P. (1985). The relation of relative hormonal levels and physical development and social–emotional behavior in young adolescents. *Journal of Youth and Adolescence, 14*(3), 245–264.

VanDenBerg, J. E., & Grealish, E. M. (1996). Individualized services and supports through the wraparound process: Philosophy and procedures. *Journal of Child and Family Studies, 5*(1), 7–21.

Velez, C. N., Johnson, J., & Cohen, P. (1989). A longitudinal analysis of selected risk factors of childhood psychopathology. *Journal of the American Academy of Child and Adolescent Psychiatry, 28*(6), 861–864.

Webster-Stratton, C., & Hammond, M. (1988). Maternal depression and its relationship to life stress, perceptions of child behavior problems, parenting behaviors, and child conduct problems. *Journal of Abnormal Child Psychology, 16*(3), 299–315.

Welner, Z., Reich, W., Herjanic, B., Jung, K. G., & Amado, H. (1987). Reliability, validity, and parent–child agreement studies of the Diagnostic Interview for Children and Adolescents (DICA). *Journal of the American Academy of Child and Adolescent Psychiatry, 26*, 649–653.

Wills, T. A., DuHamel, K., & Vaccaro, D. (1995). Activity and mood temperament as predictors of adolescent substance use: Test of a self-regulation mediational model. *Journal of Personality and Social Psychology, 68*(5), 901–916.

Wills, T. A., Schreibman, D., Benson, G., & Vaccaro, D. (1994). Impact of parental substance use on adolescents: A test of mediational model. *Journal of Pediatric Psychology, 19*(5), 537–556.

Wittchen, H.-U., Nelson, C. B., & Lachner, G. (1998). Prevalence of mental disorders and psychosocial impairments in adolescents and young adults. *Psychological Medicine, 28*, 109–126.

Zeanah, C. H., & Emde, R. N. (1994). Attachment disorders in infancy and childhood. In M. Rutter, E. Taylor, & L. Hersov (Eds.), *Child and adolescent psychiatry: Modern approaches* (pp. 490–504). Oxford: Blackwell Scientific.

5

Relationships, Development, and Psychopathology

L. Alan Sroufe, Sunita Duggal, Nancy Weinfield, and Elizabeth Carlson

Interpersonal relationships are pivotal for studying psychopathology in general and developmental psychopathology in particular. This is so at multiple levels of analysis, from defining psychopathology, to describing preconditions and contexts, and to understanding its origins and nature.

For example, relationship problems often are markers of disturbance, and the diagnosis of disorder often centers on relationship considerations. From social phobias to conduct problems to psychotic disorders, across the whole range of problems in childhood and adulthood, disturbances in interpersonal relationships are prominent criteria for classification in psychopathology. Thus, when there is psychological disturbance, interpersonal relationships also are likely to be disturbed. Given the critical importance of relationships in human adaptation, this is not surprising. This role of relationship problems as markers of pathology would, in and of itself, be sufficient grounds for emphasizing the developmental study of relationships for the field of psychopathology. But this is only the beginning.

Social relationships also are viewed by many theorists as important contexts within which psychopathology emerges and persists or desists. Psychogenic positions on pathology all focus on relationships, whether this be social learning experiences, the isolation and anomie emphasized by sociological models, or the emphasis on vital close relationships in psychodynamic and evolutionary positions (Lazare, 1973). Research on risk and protective factors in psychopathology, as well as process-oriented research involving moderator and mediator variables, commonly grants a prominent role for relationship variables. For some problems, such as conduct disorders (Dodge, Chapter 24, this volume), relationship experiences clearly play a dominant role. But all disorders develop in context (e.g., Lewis, 1984; Sameroff, 1997;

L. Alan Sroufe, Sunita Duggal, Nancy Weinfield, and Elizabeth Carlson • Institute of Child Development, University of Minnesota, Minneapolis, Minnesota 55455.
Handbook of Developmental Psychopathology, Second Edition, edited by Arnold J. Sameroff, Michael Lewis, and Suzanne M. Miller. Kluwer Academic/Plenum Publishers, New York, 2000.

Sroufe, 1997), and relationships with caregivers, peers, and others are a critical part of the child's developmental context.

Finally, a more thoroughgoing point of view has been proposed by some theorists (see, e.g., Bowlby, 1973; Sameroff & Emde, 1989). In this perspective, vital early relationships are seen as the progenitors of disorders; psychopathology is the outgrowth of relationship disturbances. Relationship disturbances themselves may constitute the roots of pathological processes that only later are manifest in individual behavior in broader contexts. A pathway to pathology is initiated and maintained by critical relationships in which the child participates. This viewpoint has some kinship with family systems perspectives, in which disorder is seen in the relationship system and not the individuals (e.g., Jackson, 1977). But in this relationship perspective, the reality of individual disorder is granted. However, the prototype for this disorder may lie in the patterns of relationships previously experienced.

In summary, relationship issues are not only important for defining pathology but also for understanding the origins and course of disorder. From a wide array of theoretical vantage points, social relationships have a key role in the etiology, maintenance, and remediation of disturbed behavior. In the following sections, we discuss relationships in terms of markers of disorder and as risk factors, protective factors, and contexts with regard to pathology. We end with a discussion of relationship disturbances as initiating pathways to psychopathology.

RELATIONSHIP PROBLEMS AS CRITERIA FOR DISORDER

Interpersonal relationships may be defined as patterns of interaction with specific partners, such as parents or peers, that are carried out over time and entail some degree of investment by participants (Hinde, 1979). Our definition of relationship problems is more inclusive, including failures to form relationships, incompetent social behavior, social withdrawal, social anxiety, and behavior that is noxious to others.

Even causal perusal of the current psychiatric classification system for disorders (American Psychiatric Association, 1994) reveals the centrality of interpersonal relationship problems in major disorders. While social relationship criteria commonly are more extensive and more clearly delineated for disorders first diagnosed in childhood, they are also quite prevalent in major adult disorders. Moreover, for all major child disorders and many adult disorders (including, for example, Major Depressive Disorder and Bipolar Disorder), one criterion for diagnosis is "significant impairment" in social functioning.

Many major childhood and adult disorders have relationship disturbance criteria (see Table 5.1). The very first criterion for Autistic Disorder, for example, is "qualitative impairment in social interaction." Failure to develop peer relationships, lack of emotional sharing with others, lack of social or emotional reciprocity, and communication deficits are specifically cited.

The Attention Deficit, Disruptive Behavior Disorders all have social features. While perhaps not obvious criteria of Attention Deficit/Hyperactivity Disorder, relationship features are nonetheless germane. As with many childhood problems, it is the impact of the child's behavior on others that leads to referral and diagnosis. Specific symptoms include "interrupting," "intruding," or "not listening" to others. In the case of Conduct Disorders, the child's bullying, threatening, cruel, or aggressive behavior toward others is often central. The severity specifications for this disorder explicitly refer to effects (especially amount of harm) caused to others. Oppositional Defiant Disorder, of course, is defined by arguing with, annoying, defying, and refusing to comply with parents, teachers, or other adults.

TABLE 5.1. DSM-IV Diagnostic Criteria with Implications for Relationships

DSM-IV disorder	Examples of relevant DSM-IV diagnostic criteria
Autistic Disorder	Qualitative impairment in social interaction. Delays or abnormal functioning in (1) social interaction, (2) language as used in social communication, or (3) symbolic or imaginative play.
Attention-Deficit/Hyperactivity Disorder	Often does not seem to listen when spoken to directly. Often interrupts or intrudes on others (e.g., butts into conversations or games)
Conduct Disorder	Often bullies, threatens, or intimidates others; often initiates physical fights; has been physically cruel to people.
Oppositional Defiant Disorder	A pattern of negativistic, hostile, and defiant behavior lasting at least 6 months.
Separation Anxiety Disorder	Developmentally inappropriate and excessive anxiety concerning separation from home or from those who whom the individual is attached.
Reactive Attachment Disorder of Infancy Early Childhood	Markedly disturbed and developmentally inappropriate social relatedness in most contexts.
Substance Abuse	Continued substance use despite having persistent or recurrent social or interpersonal problems caused or exacerbated by the effects of the substance.
Schizophrenia	Social/occupational dysfunction.
Social Phobia	A marked and persistent fear of one or more social or performance situations in which the person is exposed to unfamiliar poeple or to possible scrutiny by others. The avoidance, anxious anticipation, or distress in the feared social or performance situation(s) interferes significantly with the person's normal routine.
Posttraumatic Stress Disorder	Feelings of detachment or estrangement from others.

Separation Anxiety Disorder and Reactive Attachment Disorder were included in the DSM system specifically to capture explicit forms of relationship problems. The former entails excessive distress in the face of separation from an attachment figure or excessive worry with regard to possible or upcoming separations that may be manifest in a variety of ways. Reactive Attachment Disorder is defined by inappropriate social relatedness manifest either in (1) failure to appropriately initiate or respond to social encounters or (2) indiscriminate sociability or diffuse attachment. It is noteworthy that presumed pathogenic care also is a defining criterion for this disorder.

An array of adult disorders likewise have relationship problems as central features. From Social Phobias and Generalized Anxiety Disorders to psychosis, impairments in social relationships are prevalent. For example, one increasingly prominent anxiety disorder, Posttraumatic Stress Disorder (PTSD), is characterized by feelings of detachment or estrangement from others. The social withdrawal and inappropriate social behavior associated with many forms of schizophrenia are well known. Relationship problems are especially prominent in the personality disorders. All personality disorders, from Schizoid to Multiple Personality Disorder, are characterized by markedly deviating functioning in interpersonal relationships and/ or affectivity (dependency, antisocial behavior, etc.). Borderline Personality Disorder is characterized by profound abandonment worries and extreme lability in relationships, in which partners are alternately idealized and devalued. Those with Narcissistic Personality Disorder have superficial relationships and demand to be idealized.

Even disorders that on the surface are defined outside of the interpersonal domain often entail relationship criteria. Substance abuse, for example, requires for diagnosis continued use of the substance despite persistent or recurrent "social or interpersonal problems" caused or exacerbated by the effects of the substance (e.g., physical fights or arguments with spouse about the consequences of substance use).

In summary, throughout the DSM system, relationship problems play a key role in both determining that there is a problem warranting diagnosis and in determining the specific classification. This is testimony both to the centrality of social relationships in human functioning and to the merit of research in developmental psychopathology focusing on relationship issues. (A more complete tabular summary of relationship criteria for disorders is available from the authors.)

RELATIONSHIPS AS CONTEXTS FOR PSYCHOPATHOLOGY

When child problems and relationship problems co-occur, it is often difficult to establish causality. Clearly, child disturbance would have an impact on relationships with parents and peers, as implied by the preceding discussion of relationship criteria. Moreover, there is documentation of such child effects in the literature; for example, changes in parental behavior following reduction in child symptomatology (Hinshaw & McHale, 1991; Sroufe, 1997). Many models of child problems entail concepts of ongoing, mutual influence of parents and child (e.g., the work of Patterson, discussed later; see also Dodge, Chapter 24, this volume). Still, a persuasive case may be made for the role of relationships in the onset and course of psychopathology. Relationship disturbances often precede the manifestation of individual pathology, and relationship strengths predict differential resistance to adversity (e.g., Masten, 1994). Moreover, relationship change has been shown to precede change in individual disturbance and to influence the effect of other variables on psychopathology (e.g., Erickson, Sroufe, & Egeland, 1985). All of this is reflected in the literature on risk factors, protective factors, moderators, and mediators. Cause is complex in psychopathology. Rarely can one say that a certain pattern of parenting (or a certain relationship experience) directly led to a pathological outcome in a linear manner; yet it is certain that relationship experiences often are a crucial context for the emergence, waxing, and waning of pathology.

Relationships as Risk Factors for Disorder

Risk is a population concept. To say that an individual is "at risk" for pathology is to indicate that he or she is a member of a group that has an increased likelihood of later manifesting the disorder in question. A causal role is not necessarily implied, but risk factors are often seen as part of a causal network. Within this framework, both aspects of children's relationships with others and the broader relationship context in which they are developing have been identified as risk factors for psychopathology. From examining certain relationship variables it is possible to increment predictions of later pathology, sometimes dramatically.

Parent–Child Relationships as Risk Factors

Dimensions of Parenting.   More than three decades of research have established two basic dimensions of parenting as risk factors for psychopathology: (1) harsh treatment (hostility, criticality, rejection); and (2) lack of clear, firm discipline or supervision (e.g., Farrington et al., 1990; Maccoby & Martin, 1983; Patterson, Debaryshe, & Ramsey, 1989). These factors together, and in interaction with other variables, are often especially predictive and at times capable of differentiating various pathological outcomes.

Countless studies have underscored the predictive power of harsh treatment or rejection, with findings especially consistent for externalizing problems in boys (e.g., Campbell, 1997; Earls, 1994; Eron & Huesmann, 1990; Farrington et al., 1990; Harrington, 1994; Jenkins & Smith, 1990; see also Dodge, Chapter 24, this volume; Fiese, Wilder, & Bickham, Chapter 7, this volume). Rejection, lack of support, and hostility also have been consistently related to depression (e.g., Asarnow, Tompson, Hamilton, Goldstein, & Guthrie, 1994). Many of these studies are prospective, for example, predicting conduct problems throughout childhood and even into adulthood. Feldman and Weinberger (1994) found that parental rejection and power-assertive discipline predicted delinquent behavior of sixth-grade boys 4 years later. Ge, Best, Conger, and Simons (1996) found that parental hostility predicted 10th graders' behavior problems, even after controlling for 7th-grade symptom levels, and distinguished between those with conduct disorders and those with depression. Using a behavior genetic design, Reiss et al. (1995) found that the specific level of parental negativity directed to one member of a sibling pair predicted that child's level of conduct problems, thus showing this effect above and beyond any genetic contribution. Likewise, Patterson and Dishion (1988) reported that aggressive treatment of children was more predictive of conduct problems than parent trait measures of aggressiveness (a genetic surrogate). In our own research, we have found that low parental warmth predicted childhood depression, even after controlling for maternal depression (Duggal et al., in press).

Many of the studies cited here also demonstrated the impact of inconsistent discipline. One of the most powerful variables to be delineated in the last 15 years is the degree of parental "monitoring" (supervision and oversight; e.g., Dishion, Patterson, Stoolmiller, & Skinner, 1991). While some report only concurrent correlations, numerous prospective, longitudinal studies confirm the relation of lax discipline to later pathology, especially conduct disorders (e.g., Feldman & Weinberger, 1994; Ge et al., 1996; see also Fiese et al., Chapter 7, this volume) and association with deviant peers (e.g., Dishion et al., 1991). We discuss the role of monitoring as a moderator/mediator variable in the next major section.

A variable somewhat related to caregiver inconsistency has emerged from our own research: parent–child "boundary violation." This refers to an abdication by the adult of the parental role, especially when firm guidance is needed, and treating the child in a peer-like or spousal-like way (role reversal). Assessment of this variable at age 42 months was found to be a consistent predictor of attention deficit/hyperactivity symptoms in elementary school, and to predict above and beyond measures of temperament, perinatal difficulties, or other early child measures (Carlson, Jacobvitz, & Sroufe, 1995). Likewise, a comparable measure at age 13 years predicted subsequent conduct problems in boys (Nelson, 1994) and dating and sexuality problems in girls (Hennighausen, Collins, Anderson, & Hyson, 1998). Early pregnancy was predicted by the 42-month measure, and early impregnation (the comparable measure for boys) was predicted by the 13-year variable (Levy, 1998). A more general measure of parental boundary difficulties ("intrusiveness") obtained in infancy has been found to predict behavior problems throughout childhood and adolescence, being strikingly more powerful than infant temperament variables (Carlson et al., 1995; Egeland, Pianta, & Ogawa, 1996).

Child Maltreatment.   The substantial literature on child maltreatment (e.g., Cicchetti, Toth, & Maughan, Chapter 37, this volume) confirms the role for parental hostility and harshness outlined earlier. As Toth, Manly, and Cicchetti (1992) have suggested, maltreatment reflects "an extreme on the continuum of caretaking casualty" (p. 98). Prospective studies show that maltreatment (including physical abuse and emotional unavailability) is associated with conduct problems, disruptive behavior disorders, attention problems, anxiety disorders (including PTSD) and mood disorders (Cicchetti et al., Chapter 37, this volume; Cicchetti & Lynch, 1995). Egeland (1997) found that 90% of children with an observed history of child-hood maltreatment showed at least one diagnosable disorder at age 17½ years, compared to 30% of the poverty control subjects who were not maltreated.

Sexual abuse, the extreme of boundary violation, appears to be especially pathogenic, being related to a variety of problems (Kendall-Tackett, Williams, & Finkelhor, 1993; Toth & Cicchetti, 1996). Even in comparison to other maltreatment groups, those who are sexually abused manifest more forms of pathology and more extreme pathology (Egeland, 1997; Toth & Cicchetti, 1996). Sexual abuse is strongly and specifically associated with PTSD (Putnam, Chapter 39, this volume) and with depression. In our research, it accounted for depression in both childhood and adolescence, even after taking into account maternal depression and other potentially confounding factors (Duggal et al., in press).

Interpersonal Conflict.   Divorce, parental disharmony, and family violence all have been consistently associated with child behavioral and emotional problems (e.g., Amato & Keith, 1991; Emery & Kitzmann, 1995; Fiese et al., Chapter 7, this volume). Such conditions are overlapping and also co-occur with mistreatment or neglect of children, making causal conclusions difficult. Numerous studies have shown children of divorce to have more prob-lems than those in intact families (see Amato & Keith, 1991, for a meta-analysis). Researchers believe this is largely due to the conflict preceding and surrounding the marital breakup (e.g., Wallerstein & Kelly, 1982). It is the case that behavior problems often precede the divorce (Cherlin et al., 1991), and that parental conflict is consistently found to be a stronger predictor of child maladjustment than marital status (Emery & Kitzmann, 1995). Across eight studies reviewed, Amato and Keith (1991) found that children from high-conflict, intact families showed more problems (including depression and anxiety) than children from divorced families in general. They also reported more problems for children of divorce (where there was often conflict) than for those who lost a parent through death. Still, even if research to date shows little impact of divorce above and beyond the role of conflict, it remains an important marker variable and is a risk factor in the descriptive, population sense defined earlier.

Family violence has also been found to be associated with child pathology (e.g., Stern-berg et al., 1993). Here, a major problem is distinguishing the impact upon the child of witnessing violence from the consequences of direct maltreatment, which often co-occurs, or from the general life stress and chaos in which family violence is nested. However, in a recent analysis of prospective, longitudinal data, Dodds (1995) was able to control for these potential confounds. Presence of spousal abuse in early childhood predicted externalizing behavior problems in boys (but not girls, a common result), even with child maltreatment, socio-economic status (SES), and life stress statistically controlled.

Peer Relationships as Risk Factors

One reason for the power of family factors in predicting later pathology may be their impact upon peer relationships. Maltreatment, for example, is consistently associated with lack of competence with, and rejection by, peers (e.g., Cicchetti et al., Chapter 37, this volume; Cicchetti & Lynch, 1995), as have patterns of anxious attachment, especially the avoidant subtype (e.g., Sroufe, Egeland, & Carlson, 1999). Ample research shows that poor peer relationships and association with deviant peers themselves are risk factors for psychopathology (Rudolph & Asher, Chapter 9, this volume). Given the strong concurrent association between behavior problems and peer problems, our own review refers only to prospective studies in which peer measures precede later measures of psychopathology.

Numerous studies have found that general problems with peers, lack of social competence, or unpopularity (based on observation, teacher ratings, or peer sociometrics) are related to later behavioral and emotional problems (e.g., Masten & Coatsworth, 1995). For example, in one early study, a single item rated by teachers ("Fails to get along with other children") predicted psychiatric problems, including hospitalizations, 12 years later in adulthood (Janes, Hesselbrock, Myers, & Penniman, 1979). In our own research, we have found that teacher rankings of peer competence, beginning in early elementary school, predict behavior problems and psychopathology throughout childhood and adolescence (Sroufe et al., 1999).

Established patterns of sociometric status (e.g., rejected vs. neglected children) have proven to be very useful (see Rudolph & Asher, Chapter 9, this volume), predicting somewhat different problems later. Peer rejection is especially powerful, even in comparison to peer neglect (e.g., Ollendick, Weist, Borden, & Greene, 1992). Numerous studies have documented a relation between a history of peer rejection and later maladjustment, both externalizing and internalizing problems, sometimes even with earlier behavior problems controlled (e.g., Rudolph & Asher, Chapter 9, this volume; Burks, Dodge, & Price, 1995; Coie, Terry, Lenox, Lochman, & Hyman, 1995; Dodge, Chapter 24, this volume; Ollendick et al., 1992).

Finally, a great deal of recent research has emphasized the negative impact of deviant peer group membership (e.g., Cairns, Cairns, & Neckerman, 1989; Keenan, Loeber, Zhang, Stouthamer-Loeber, & Van Kammen, 1995; Patterson et al., 1989). Such a relationship experience is especially implicated in delinquency and school dropout.

Relationships as Protective Factors, Moderators, and Mediators

Technically, a protective factor, when present, moderates the impact of a risk variable; that is, protection is always particular to specific risks (Rutter, 1990). Thus, when factors are generally associated with positive outcomes (often simply being the other end of a risk dimension), they are best described as assets or, to use a term coined by Sameroff (1997), "promotive" factors. Of course, this distinction is not always easy to make, and the same variable may be viewed as an asset or protective factor depending on the context. This is certainly the case for certain relationship variables.

Relationship experiences may also moderate the impact of other risks or alter their impact (e.g., combine to lead to a distinctive outcome). In other circumstances, relationships may be the mechanism through which a certain risk factor has its impact. This is referred to as a mediator variable. While there is less information on relationships as moderators and mediators, compared to risks and assets, such research is of clear importance within a developmental perspective.

Family Relationships as Assets, Moderators, and Mediators

The most widely studied assets and protective factors in the parent–child relationship are parental warmth and emotional support, and the security of the attachment between infant and caregiver. Numerous studies have documented the link between parental warmth and psychological well-being and emotional health of the child (e.g., Campbell, 1997; Fiese et al., Chapter

7, this volume; Hetherington & Clingempeel, 1992; Sroufe, 1997). Infant attachment security has been linked with later self-esteem, social competence, prosocial behavior, ego resiliency, and overall adjustment (Sroufe, 1997; see also below).

Attachment security also is associated with recovery from behavioral problems (Sroufe, Egeland, & Kreutzer, 1990) and is a protective factor with regard to family life stress; that is, children with histories of secure attachment show fewer problems in the face of family stress than do children with histories of anxious attachment (Pianta, Egeland, & Sroufe, 1990).

Much of the research on family risk factors also contains evidence of other family relationship factors as moderators and mediators of such risk. Davies and Cummings (1994) propose that secure relationships with parents moderate the impact of marital conflict. Indeed, Miller, Cowan, Cowan, Hetherington, and Clingempeel (1993) found just that to be true for preschoolers and early adolescents. Other research suggests that the course or trajectory of problem behavior may be altered by parent–child relationship qualities. Campbell (1997), for example, reports that "authoritative parenting" accounts for desistance of behavior problems between preschool and elementary school. Finally, the research of Patterson and colleagues contains exemplary process analyses. They find, for example, that the impact of parental conflict and aggressiveness is mediated by (leads to) lax parental monitoring, which is then the more powerful influence on adolescent conduct problems (Capaldi & Patterson, 1991). They also describe the transactive nature of the developmental process between parents and peers (see below).

Peer Relationships as Assets, Moderators, and Mediators

As with family relationships, peer relationships may represent assets as well as risks. Peer competence is associated with low behavior problem scores or absence of pathology just as much as peer problems are associated with disorder. Moreover, peer competence measures have been associated with academic achievement and school completion, which themselves may be viewed as assets (Teo, Carlson, Mathieu, Egeland, & Sroufe, 1996), although reversed statements would be equally true and we could speak of risk.

Patterson and associates' work specifically points to a mediating role for peer experiences in the perpetuation of conduct problems. In their model (e.g., Dishion et al., 1991; Patterson et al., 1989), poor parental discipline and monitoring lead to conduct problems, which in turn are associated with peer rejection and academic failure. These factors converge to promote commitment to a deviant peer group, leading to consolidation of antisocial behavior. Problem behaviors (and peer competence) are best viewed as drawing upon the convergence of previous family and peer experiences.

Other Relationships and General Social Support

While not so widely studied, relationships with grandparents, other adults, and siblings have been suggested to serve protective or moderating roles in the face of stress or other risk factors (Lewis, 1984). For example, Jenkins and Smith (1990) reported that a close relationship with an adult outside of the family (usually a grandmother) moderated the effect of disharmonious marriages on child psychopathology. In our work, we found that an "alternative" close relationship with an adult (again, often a grandmother, and sometimes a therapist) predicted breaking the cycle of abuse; those parents who themselves were abused but did not mistreat their own children much more often had such a factor present (Egeland, Jacobvitz, & Sroufe, 1988).

Sibling relationships have been the subject of considerable interest to those studying peer relationships, parental conflict, and psychopathology. It is clear that there is an association between quality of sibling relationships and adjustment or behavior problems (e.g., Dunn, Slomkowski, Beardsall, & Rende, 1994; Stormshak, Bellanti, & Bierman, 1996). However, these findings may be interpreted in terms of troubled sibling relationships simply marking child disturbance. Patterson (1986) has argued that sibling conflict may play a role in "training for fighting" within coercive families. And there are some hints that siblings may play a protective role. East and Rook (1992), for example, reported that peer-isolated children were less anxious if they had a supportive sibling relationship, though they were still more anxious than average children. Jenkins (1992) found that in disharmonious homes, children with a close sibling relationship had less symptomatology than children without such a relationship. But this is not a widely reported finding; more often, the sibling relationship reflects the degree of parental conflict (Hetherington, 1988).

Finally, there is substantial literature concerning the importance of social support for individuals at risk for or already experiencing problems, and for caregivers during the child's development (e.g., Cohen & Wills, 1985; Nuechterlein et al., 1992; Robinson & Garber, 1995). For example, Windle (1992) found that (lower) perceived social support from the family predicted both internalizing and externalizing behaviors for adolescent girls. Using an indirect model of support, Goodyer, Herbert, Tamplin, Secher, and Pearson (1997) reported that mothers' lack of confiding relationships with partners was related to the maintenance of disorder in a clinical sample of 8- to 16-year-olds over a 36-week period.

RELATIONSHIP DISTURBANCES
AND PATHWAYS TO DISORDER

In the preceding discussion, relationship experiences have been viewed as contributors to psychopathology because of their role as risk factors, protective factors, mediators, or moderators. However, a more thoroughgoing and revolutionary view of the role of relationships in disturbance may be proposed. More than simply being risk factors, relationship disturbances may be the precursors of individual psychopathology, through their role in establishing fundamental patterns of emotional regulation. They may represent the initiation of developmental pathways probabilistically leading to disorder (Sroufe, 1997). Individual disturbance, in this view, begins as relationship disturbance. This view is in contrast to the DSM framework, in which the reality of relationship disturbances is allowed but sequestered into a few isolated categories (Attachment Disorders). Here, relationship disturbances are hypothesized to be the forerunners or *prototypes* of many major childhood disorders and adult personality disorders as well.

The Relationship Perspective on Psychopathology: Rationale

Problems in emotional regulation, like relationship disturbances, are pervasive markers of psychopathology. Such problems underlie most disorders of children and adults (Cole, Michel, & O'Donnell-Teti, 1994). Indeed, "emotional disturbance" often is used as a synonym for psychopathology. Moreover, difficulties in emotional regulation and relationship difficulties are intertwined. This is the starting point for our developmental–relationship perspective on psychopathology. Emotional regulation is the defining feature of all close relationships and the central goal of early primary relationships (Sroufe, 1996). Particular relationship experiences may be argued to be the progenitors of psychopathology precisely because of their role in early regulation.

Human infants are not very able to regulate their own arousal or emotional states. To be well regulated, they require ample assistance from caregivers. To be sure, they can express distress and contentment in the first weeks, and within a few months a greater range of feelings and needs. By the end of the first year, infants can signal many wishes with intention (raising their arms to be picked up, calling for caregivers when frightened, offering a toy for inspection). But throughout this time, they rely on caregivers to read these "signals," whether intended or not. Infants are equipped to play only a primitive role in their own regulation. They are not capable of self-regulation, but only "co-regulation" (Fogel, 1993). To be well regulated—to be competent as infants, they require sensitive, responsive caregivers (Ainsworth & Bell, 1974). In Sander's (1975) terms, there is an affective–behavioral organization early in life, but this organization lies in the infant–caregiver system, not the infant alone.

Thus, what will become functional self-regulation, or various forms of dysregulation, begins as caregiver–infant regulation (Lyons-Ruth & Zeanah, 1993). Researchers have now described this initial dyadic regulation process in great detail, including its changing form over time, as well as variations between particular infant–caregiver pairs (e.g., Brazelton, Koslowski, & Main, 1974; Fogel, 1993; Stern, 1985). Caregivers maintain smooth regulation by attending to the infant's changes in alertness or discomfort and signs of need, imbuing primitive infant behaviors with meaning. They quickly learn to "read" infant signals and to provide care that keeps distress and arousal within reasonable limits. By effectively engaging the infant and encouraging ever longer bouts of emotionally charged but organized behavior, they provide the infant with critical training in regulation. Within the secure "holding" framework of the relationship, infants learn something vital about "holding" themselves, containing behavior, and focusing attention (Brazelton et al., 1974).

In time, routine patterns of interchange are established. As the infant's capacities for engagement and repertoire of behaviors increase, a semblance of reciprocity—of back-and-forth communication—emerges. Caregiver and infant may, for example, engage in a series of mutual exchanges characterized by increasingly positive emotion expressed by both partners and a waxing and waning of engagement that helps the infant stay organized. In the early months, it is the caregiver that is adjusting behavior purposefully, always accommodating to the infant and creating space for the infant to fit in as well (Hayes, 1984). Such patterns of caregiver-orchestrated regulation set the stage for more truly dyadic regulation as new infant capacities emerge.

By the second half-year, the infant exhibits purposeful, goal-directed behavior (Sroufe, 1996). Infants at this age behave *in order to* elicit a particular response from the caregiver, for example, calling to the parent and raising their arms to indicate a desire to be picked up. They now actively participate in the regulation process. If the caregiver misreads a signal, the older infant will adjust the behavior, often until the desired response is received (e.g., crawling to parents if they do not come to the infant). Thus, dyadic regulation follows inevitably upon the heels of caregiver-orchestrated regulation. It requires only growth of intentional capacity, which occurs in all normal infants during this period. The form and structure of dyadic regulation is in place from the preceding period. What changes is the role of the infant, from reflexive or automatic signaling, to active, intentional signaling; the patterning is based on what was established earlier. In time, this patterning is carried forward, becoming the core of self-regulation.

Early relationship experiences are vital because they are the first models or *prototypes* for patterns of self-regulation. Infants have no choice but to generalize from what they experience. If they have experienced within their caregiving relationships that distress is routinely followed by recovery, that behavior can stay organized in the face of strong emotion, that positive experiences are shared, and that caregivers are central to all of these experiences, they will come to expect such contingencies (Lewis & Goldberg, 1969). One can turn to others when in need, and they will respond. At the same time, in a complementary manner, infants will come to believe in their own effectiveness in maintaining regulation and, because their needs are routinely met, in their own self-worth. Bowlby (1973) argues that this is inevitable. A sense of personal effectiveness follows automatically from routinely having one's actions achieve their purpose. So positive expectations toward others and a sense of connectedness, as well as self-confidence, all are logical outcomes of experiencing routinely responsive care. This provides an important motivational and attitudinal base for later self-regulation.

A history of responsive care does more than promote positive attitudes with regard to coping. In a well-regulated dyadic system, stimulation is appropriate to the capacities of the infant, disorganizing arousal is infrequent, and episodes of distress are short-lived. Within such a system, the infant is entrained into a pattern of modulated, flexible emotional responding at both the behavioral and the physiological levels (Sroufe, 1996). Recent research suggests that such experiences are vital for tuning and balancing excitatory and inhibitory systems in the brain (e.g., Cicchetti & Tucker, 1994; Schore, 1994). Thus, neither the nervous systems nor the behavioral capacities of children experiencing responsive care are easily overstimulated but, rather, remain flexibly responsive to challenge.

The movement toward self-regulation continues throughout the childhood years, as does a vital, though changing, role for caregivers. During the toddler period, the child acquires beginning capacities for self-control, tolerance for moderate frustration, and a widening range of emotional reactions, including shame and, later, pride and guilt (Lewis, Alessandri, & Sullivan, 1992; Sroufe, 1996). Practicing self-regulation in a supportive context is crucial. Emerging capacities are easily overwhelmed. Caregivers must allow children to master those circumstances within their capacities and yet anticipate circumstances beyond their abilities and help restore equilibrium when children are overtaxed. Such "guided self-regulation" is the foundation for the genuine self-regulation that will follow. As the child's capacities for self-regulation gradually emerge, parental tasks move toward providing optimal contexts for mastery, establishing guidelines for expected behavior, and monitoring the child's regulation efforts. Each of these tasks is important. The child's capacity for self-regulation can be compromised or enhanced at any point in development. But the entire developmental process builds upon the foundation laid out in infancy.

Bowlby's (1973) attachment theory is a useful framework for organizing this information. Indeed, attachment may be defined as the dyadic regulation of emotion (Sroufe, 1996). Variations in infant attachment are most centrally variations in dyadic regulation. In the usual case, Bowlby's starting point, infants develop what is called "secure attachment." Because their caregivers have been routinely available to them, sensitive to their signals, and reliably responsive (though by no means is perfect care required), these infants develop confidence that supportive care is available. They expect help when a need arises. If threatened or distressed, they are effective in utilizing caregivers to regain equilibrium. Such confident expectations are precisely what is meant by attachment security. They are secure in their attachment. This security supports confident exploration of the environment and ease of settling when distressed.

In other cases, when care is chaotic, notably inconsistent, neglectful or rejecting, or when the caregiver behaves in frightening or incoherent ways toward the infant, an anxious attachment relationship evolves. Infants facing inadequate care have few options (Main & Hesse,

1990). In the face of inconsistency, they may maximize the expression of attachment behaviors, hovering near the caregiver, emitting high-intensity signals, "punishing" the caregiver for nonresponsiveness. Such a pattern is known as *anxious/resistant* attachment, because these infants often mix strong seeking of contact with pushing away from the caregiver, squirming, or angrily pouting when they are distressed. Alternatively, in the face of chronic rebuff, infants may learn to cut off expression of attachment behaviors. This "strategy" characterizes *anxious/avoidant* attachment, so called because these infants turn away from, rather than go to, caregivers in the face of moderate stress (such as following a separation of a few minutes in an unfamiliar setting). Such avoidance may help the infant not alienate further an already rejecting caregiver, but, of course, it may initiate a pattern of rigid overcontrol in which real needs cannot be met. Finally, when caregivers are themselves the source of threat or fear, infants are placed in an irresolvable approach–avoidance conflict. Infants are strongly disposed to approach attachment figures when threatened, but if the attachment figure is the source of threat, they are simultaneously disposed to stay away from them. If routine, such conflict leads to what has been called *disorganized/disoriented* attachment. Each of these patterns of anxious attachment has been well described, with consequences for later dysregulation and emotional disturbance confirmed by long-term longitudinal research. Anxious attachment also repeatedly has been shown to be related to earlier insensitive care (e.g., National Institute of Child Health and Human Development, 1997; De Wolff & van IJzendoorn, 1997).

Attachment Outcome Research

Research has confirmed that infants with histories of secure attachment with their primary caregivers (that is, those who have experienced effective dyadic regulation of arousal and emotion) later are characterized by more effective self-regulation. For example, as preschoolers, they are judged by teachers and independent observers to have higher self-esteem, to be more self-reliant, and to be more flexible in the management of their impulses and feelings (e.g., Sroufe, 1983). They can be exuberant when circumstances permit and controlled when circumstances require it. They recover quickly following upset. They flexibly express the full range of emotions in context-appropriate ways. They positively engage and respond to other children, are able to sustain interactions even in the face of conflict and challenge, and are notably empathic. Though not unduly dependent, they are effective in using adults as resources, relating to them in an age-appropriate manner. These findings are supported by detailed behavioral data. Those with secure attachment histories are observed to seek less frequent physical contact or reassurance from teachers and to more often respond with positive emotion to peer initiations than do children with histories of anxious attachment. Moreover, those with different kinds of anxious attachment histories behave in distinctive ways. For example, those with histories of anxious/resistant attachment, who have become chronically aroused in the face of inconsistent, chaotic care, persistently hover near teachers, are easily frustrated, fall to pieces in the face of stress, and are unable to sustain interactions with peers, at times becoming a foil to those who are aggressive. Those with histories of avoidant attachment are disconnected from other children and/or show antipathy for them. They also are emotionally overcontrolled and/or aggressive, and they fail to seek out teachers precisely when disappointed or distressed.

In middle childhood and adolescence, those with histories of secure attachment carry forward patterns of effective emotional regulation. Such patterns enable them to meet the challenges of autonomous functioning and successful participation in ever more complex peer groups. In middle childhood, they form close relationships with friends as well as coordinate friendships with effective group functioning (Elicker, Englund, & Sroufe, 1992; Shulman, Elicker, & Sroufe, 1994). In adolescence, this evolves to the capacity for intimacy, self-disclosure, and successful functioning in the mixed-gender peer group (Sroufe et al., 1999). They are peer leaders, noted for interpersonal sensitivity (Weinfield, Ogawa, & Sroufe, 1997).

Throughout childhood and adolescence, research has now established a firm relation between established patterns of early regulation and later behavior problems and emotional disturbance. At each age assessed, those with secure attachment histories have been found to have fewer emotional problems. Those with anxious attachment histories have problems of one kind or another with greater frequency. Anxiety disorders are associated with histories of anxious/resistant attachment (Warren, Huston, Egeland, & Sroufe, 1997). Aggression, and conduct disturbances more generally, have been found to be related to anxious/avoidant attachment (Lewis, Feiring, McGuffog, & Jaskir, 1984; Sroufe, 1997). Both resistant and avoidant attachment appear to be related to depression, probably for different reasons (passivity and helplessness on the one hand, alienation on the other). Finally, disorganized/disoriented attachment shows the strongest overall relationship to disturbance in adolescence (Carlson, 1998). Given that this pattern reflects a major breakdown in early dyadic regulation, this finding was to be expected. The disorganized pattern also is related specifically to dissociative symptoms, that is, disruptions in orientation to the environment and failures to integrate various aspects of emotional and cognitive experience (Carlson, 1998).

EARLY RELATIONSHIPS IN DEVELOPMENTAL PERSPECTIVE

Despite the linkages described here, the relationship position derived from Bowlby is not deterministic but, rather, probabilistic. Anxious attachments do not directly cause later disorder. Rather, they initiate pathways, the pursuit of which is influenced by ongoing challenges and supports, as well as by the total prior history. Thus, assessments of child care in the years following infancy, life stress experienced by the family, and changes in caregiver support all increment predictions of outcome beyond early attachment assessment (Carlson, 1998; Sroufe, 1997). Psychopathology always is the result of the combination of risk and protective factors impacting on the individual's life over time.

Moreover, early care itself is multifaceted, with many aspects lying outside of the attachment domain (e.g., the socialization of impulse control; Sroufe, 1997). Some kinds of problems are not closely related to attachment history. For example, attention deficit disorder is at best only weakly related to attachment; however, it is predictably related to early patterns of overstimulation and parent–child boundary violation (Carlson et al., 1995).

Individual differences in early primary attachments are not viewed in themselves as manifestations of psychopathology, as direct causes, or as the only risk factors deriving from parenting history. At the same time, they are unique among risk factors in important ways. They embody core features of interpersonal connectedness and affective regulation that are central in psychopathology, and they entail patterns of motivational, behavioral, and emotional organization that often are prototypes for individual personality. In contrast to broad-based risk factors, such as poverty, attachment patterns may serve as templates for particular forms of disturbance when the confluence of risks outweighs the supports for the developing child.

REFERENCES

Ainsworth, M. D. S., & Bell, S. M. (1974). Mother–infant interaction and the development of competence. In K. Connolly & J. Bruner (Eds.), *The growth of competence* (pp. 97–118). New York: Academic Press.

Amato, P. R., & Keith, B. (1991). Parental divorce and the well-being of children: A meta-analysis. *Psychological Bulletin, 110,* 26–46.

American Psychiatric Association (1994). *Diagnostic and statistical manual of mental disorders* (4th ed.). Washington, DC: Author.

Asarnow, J. R., Tompson, M., Hamilton, E. B., Goldstein, M. J., & Guthrie, D. (1994). Family-expressed emotion, childhood-onset depression, and childhood-onset schizophrenia spectrum disorders: Is expressed emotion a nonspecific correlate of child psychopathology or a specific risk factor for depression? *Journal of Abnormal Child Psychology, 22,* 129–146.

Bowlby, J. (1973). *Attachment and loss: Vol. 2. Separation.* New York: Basic Books.

Brazelton, T. B., Koslowski, B., & Main, M. (1974). The origins of reciprocity: The early mother–infant interaction. In M. Lewis & L. Rosenblum (Eds.), *The effect of the infant on its caretaker* (pp. 49–76). New York: Wiley.

Burks, V. S., Dodge, K., & Price, J. (1995). Models of internalizing outcomes of early rejection. *Development and Psychopathology, 7,* 683–695.

Cairns, R. B., Cairns, B. D., & Neckerman, H. J. (1989). Early school dropout: Configurations and determinants. *Child Development, 60,* 1244–1257.

Campbell, S. B. (1997). Behavior problems in preschool children: Developmental and family issues. *Advances in Clinical Child Psychology, 19,* 1–26.

Capaldi, D. M., & Patterson, G. R. (1991). Relation of parental transitions to boys' adjustment problems: I. A linear hypothesis. II. Mothers at risk for transitions and unskilled parenting. *Developmental Psychology, 3,* 489–504.

Carlson, E. A. (1998). A prospective longitudinal study of attachment disorganization/disorientation. *Child Development, 69,* 1107–1128.

Carlson, E. A., Jacobvitz, D., & Sroufe, L. A. (1995). A developmental investigation of inattentiveness and hyperactivity. *Child Development, 66,* 37–54.

Cherlin, A. J., Furstenberg, F. F., Chase-Lansdale, P. L., Kiernan, K. E., Robins, P. K., Morrison, D. R., & Teitler, J. O. (1991). Longitudinal studies of effects on divorce on children in Great Britain and the United States. *Science, 252,* 1386–1389.

Cicchetti, D., & Lynch, M. (1995). Failures in the expectable environment and their impact on individual development: The case of child maltreatment. In D. Cicchetti & D. J. Cohen (Eds.), *Developmental psychopathology: Vol. 2. Risk, disorder, and adaptation* (pp. 3–31). New York: Wiley.

Cicchetti, D., & Toth, S. L. (1995). A developmental psychopathology perspective on child abuse and neglect. *Journal of the American Academy of Child and Adolescent Psychiatry, 34,* 541–565.

Cicchetti, D., & Tucker, D. (1994). Development and self-regulatory structures of the mind. *Development and Psychopathology, 6*(4), 533–549.

Cohen, S., & Wills, T. A. (1985). Stress, social support, and the buffering hypothesis. *Psychological Bulletin, 98,* 310–357.

Coie, J., Terry, R., Lenox, K., Kochman, J., & Hyman, C. (1995). Childhood peer rejection and aggression as predictors of stable patterns of adolescent disorder. *Development and Psychopathology, 7,* 697–713.

Cole, P., Michel, M., & O'Donnell-Teti, L. (1994). The development of emotion and regulation and dysregulation: A clinical perspective. *Monographs of the Society for Research in Child Development, 59* (2–3, Serial No. 240).

Davies, P. T., & Cummings, E. M. (1994). Marital conflict and child adjustment: An emotional security hypothesis. *Psychological Bulletin, 116,* 387–411.

De Wolff, M. S., & van IJzendoorn, M. (1997). Sensitivity and attachment: A meta-analysis on parental antecedents of infant attachment. *Child Development, 68*(4), 571–591.

Dishion, T. J., Patterson, G. R., Stoolmiller, M., & Skinner, M. L. (1991). Family, school, and behavioral antecedents to early adolescent involvement with antisocial peers. *Developmental Psychology, 27,* 172–180.

Dodds, M. F. (1995). *The impact of exposure to interparental violence on child behavior problems.* Unpublished doctoral dissertation, University of Minnesota, Minneapolis.

Duggal, S. R., Carlson, E., Sroufe, L. A., & Egeland, B. (in press). Depressive symptomatology in childhood and adolescence. *Development and Psychopathology.*

Dunn, J., Slomkowski, C., Beardsall, L., & Rende, R. (1994). Adjustment in middle childhood and early adolescence: Links with earlier and contemporary sibling relationships. *Journal of Child Psychology and Psychiatry, 35,* 491–504.

Earls, F. (1994). Oppositional-defiant and conduct disorders. In M. Rutter, E. Taylor, & L. Hersov (Eds.), *Child and adolescent psychiatry* (pp. 308–329). London: Blackwell.

East, P., & Rook, K. (1992). Compensatory patterns of support among children's peer relationships: A test using school friends, nonschool friends, and siblings. *Developmental Psychology, 28,* 163–172.

Egeland, B. (1997). Mediators of the effects of child maltreatment on developmental adaptation in adolescence. In D. Cicchetti & S. Toth (Eds.), *Rochester Symposium on Developmental Psychopathology: Vol. 7. The effects of trauma on the developmental process* (pp. 403–434). Rochester, NY: University of Rochester Press.

Egeland, B., Jacobvitz, D., & Sroufe, L. A. (1988). Breaking the cycle of abuse: Relationship predictors. *Child Development, 59*(4), 1080–1088.

Egeland, B., Pianta, R., & Ogawa, J. (1996). Early behavior problems: Pathways to mental disorders in adolescence. *Developmental Psychology, 8,* 735–749.

Elicker, J., Englund, M., & Sroufe, L. A. (1992). Predicting peer competence and peer relationships in childhood from early parent–child relationships. In R. Parke & G. Ladd (Eds.), *Family–peer relationships: Modes of linkage* (pp. 77–106). Hillsdale, NJ: Erlbaum.

Emery, R. E., & Kitzmann, K. M. (1995). The child in the family: Disruptions in family functions. In D. Cicchetti & D. J. Cohen (Eds.), *Developmental psychopathology: Vol. 2. Risk, disorder, and adaptation* (pp. 3–31). New York: Wiley.

Erickson, M. F., Sroufe, L. A., & Egeland, B. (1985). The relationship of quality of attachment and behavior problems in preschool in a high risk sample. In I. Bretherton & E. Waters (Eds.), Growing points in attachment theory and research. *Monographs of the Society for Research in Child Development, 50* (1–2, Serial No. 209).

Eron, L. D., & Huesmann, L. R. (1990). The stability of aggressive behavior—even unto the third generation. In M. Lewis & S. M. Miller (Eds.), *Handbook of developmental psychopathology* (pp. 147–156). New York: Plenum Press.

Farrington, D., Loeber, R., Elliot, D., Hawkins, D., Kandel, D., Klein, M., McCord, J., Rowe, D., & Tremblay, R. (1990). Advancing knowledge about the onset of delinquency and crime. In B. Lahey & A. Kazdin (Eds.), *Advances in clinical child psychology* (Vol. 13, pp. 283–342). New York: Plenum Press.

Feldman, S. S., & Weinberger, D. A. (1994). Self-restraint as a mediator of family influences on boys' delinquent behavior: A longitudinal study. *Child Development, 65,* 195–211.

Fogel, A. (1993). *Developing through relationships: Origins of communication, self, and culture.* Chicago: University of Chicago Press.

Ge, X., Best, K. M., Conger, R. D., & Simons, R. L. (1996). Parenting behaviors and the occurrence and co-occurrence of adolescent depressive symptoms and conduct problems. *Developmental Psychology, 32,* 717–731.

Goodyer, I. M., Herbert, J., Tamplin, A., Secher, S. M., & Pearson, J. (1997). Short-term outcome of major depression: II. Life events, family dysfunction, and friendship difficulties as predictors of persistent disorder. *Journal of the American Academy of Child and Adolescent Psychiatry, 36,* 474–480.

Harrington, R. (1994). Affective disorders. In M. Rutter, E. Taylor, & L. Hersov (Eds.), *Child and adolescent psychiatry: Modern approaches* (pp. 330–350). Cambridge, UK: Blackwell.

Hayes, A. (1984). Interaction, engagement, and the origins of communication: Some constructive concerns. In L. Feagans, C. Garney, & R. Golinkoff (Eds.), *The origins and growth of communications* (pp. 136–161). Norwood, NJ: Ablex.

Hennighausen, K., Collins, W. A., Anderson, F., & Hyson, D. (1998, February). *Longitudinal correlates of competence in romantic relationships and sexual behavior in later adolescence.* Paper presented at the biennial meeting of the Society for Research in Adolescence, San Diego, CA.

Hetherington, E. M. (1988). Parents, children and siblings: Six years after divorce. In R. Hinde & J. Stevenson-Hinde (Eds.), *Relationships within families* (pp. 311–331). Oxford, UK: Clarendon.

Hetherington, E. M., & Clingempeel, W. S. (1992). Coping with marital transitions: A family systems perspective. *Monographs of the Society for Research in Child Development, 57* (2–3, Serial No. 227).

Hinde, R. (1979). *Towards understanding relationships.* New York: Academic Press.

Hinshaw, S. P., & McHale, J. P. (1991). Stimulant medication and the social interactions of hyperactive children. In D. G. Gilbert & J. J. Connolly (Eds.), *Personality, social skills, and psychopathology: An individual differences approach* (pp. 229–253). New York: Plenum Press.

Jackson, D. (1977). The study of the family. In P. Watzlawick & J. H. Weakland (Eds.), *The interactional view* (pp. 2–20). New York: Norton.

Janes, C., Hesselbrock, B., Myers, D. G., & Penniman, J. (1979). Problem boys in young adulthood: Teachers' ratings and twelve-year follow-up. *Journal of Youth and Adolescence, 8,* 453–472.

Jenkins, J. (1992). Sibling relationships in disharmonious homes: Potential difficulties and protective factors. In F. Boer & J. Dunn (Eds.), *Children's sibling relationships: Developmental and clinical issues* (pp. 125–138). Hillsdale, NJ: Erlbaum.

Jenkins, J. M., & Smith, M. A. (1990). Factors protecting children living in disharmonious homes. *Journal of the American Academy of Child and Adolescent Psychiatry, 29,* 60–69.

Keenan, K., Loeber, R., Zhang, Q., Stouthamer-Loeber, M., & Van Kammen, W. (1995). The influence of deviant peers on the development of boys' disruptive and delinquent behavior: A temporal analysis. *Developmental Psychology, 7*, 715–726.

Kendall-Tackett, K. A., Williams, L. M., & Finkelhor, D. (1993). Impact of sexual abuse on children: A review and synthesis of recent empirical studies. *Psychological Bulletin, 113*, 164–180.

Lazare, A. (1973). Hidden conceptual models in clinical psychiatry. *New England Journal of Medicine, 288*, 345–350.

Lewis, M. (1984). *Beyond the dyad.* New York: Plenum Press.

Lewis, M., Alessandri, S., & Sullivan, M. (1992). Differences in shame and pride as a function of children's gender and task difficulty. *Child Development, 63*, 630–638.

Lewis, M., Feiring, C., McGuffog, C., & Jaskir, J. (1984). Predicting psychopathology in six-year-olds from early social relations. *Child Development, 55*, 123–136.

Lewis, M., & Goldberg, S. (1969). Perceptual–cognitive development in infancy: A generalized expectancy model as a function of mother–infant interaction. *Merrill–Palmer Quarterly, 15*, 81–100.

Levy, A. K. (1998, February). *Longitudinal predictors of adolescent pregnancy and impregnation.* Poster presented at the biennial meeting of the Society for Research in Adolescence, San Diego, CA.

Lyons-Ruth, K., & Zeanah, C. H. (1993). The family context of infant mental health: I. Affective development in the primary caregiver relationship. In C. H. Zeanah (Ed.), *The handbook of infant mental health* (pp. 14–37). New York: Guilford Press.

Maccoby, E. E., & Martin, J. A. (1983). Socialization in the context of the family. In E. M. Hetherington (Ed.), *Handbook of child psychology* (pp. 1–101). New York: Wiley.

Main, M., & Hesse, E. (1990). Parents' unresolved traumatic experiences are related to infant disorganized attachment status: Is frightened and/or frightening parental behavior the linking mechanism? In M. T. Greenberg, D. Cicchetti, & E. M. Cummings (Eds.), *Attachment in the preschool years* (pp. 161–182). Chicago: University of Chicago Press.

Masten, A. S. (1994). Resilience in individual development: Successful adaptation despite risk and adversity. In M. C. Wang & E. W. Gordon (Eds.), *Educational resilience in inner-city America: Challenges and prospects* (pp. 3–25). Hillsdale, NJ: Erlbaum.

Masten, A. S., & Coatsworth, J. D. (1995). Competence, resilience, and psychopathology. In D. Cicchetti & D. Cohen (Eds.), *Developmental psychopathology: Vol. 2. Risk, disorder, and adaptation* (pp. 715–752). New York: Wiley.

Miller, N. B., Cowan, P. A., Cowan, C. P., Hetherington, E. M., & Clingempeel, W. G. (1993). Externalizing in preschoolers and early adolescents: A cross-study replication of a family model. *Developmental Psychology, 29*, 3–18.

National Institute of Child Health and Human Development Early Child Care Research Network (1997). The effects of infant child care on mother–infant attachment security: Results of the NICHD early child care research network. *Child Development, 68*, 860–879.

Nelson, N. N. (1994). *Predicting adolescent behavior problems in late adolescence from parent–child interactions in early adolescence.* Unpublished doctoral dissertation, University of Minnesota, Minneapolis.

Nuechterlein, K. H., Dawson, M. E., Gitlin, M., Ventura, J., Goldstein, M. J., Snyder, K. S., Yee, C. M., & Mintz, J. (1992). Developmental processes in schizophrenic disorders: Longitudinal studies of vulnerability and stress. *Schizophrenia Bulletin, 18*, 387–424.

Ollendick, T., Weist, M., Borden, M. C., & Greene, R. (1992). Sociometric status and academic, behavioral, and psychological adjustment: A five year longitudinal study. *Journal of Consulting and Clinical Psychology, 60*, 80–87.

Patterson, G. R. (1986). The contribution of siblings to training for fighting: A microsocial analysis. In D. Olweus, J. Block, & M. Radke-Yarrow (Eds.), *Development of antisocial and prosocial behavior* (pp. 235–262). Orlando, FL: Academic Press.

Patterson, G. R., DeBaryshe, B. D., & Ramsey, E. (1989). A developmental perspective on antisocial behavior. *American Psychologist, 44*, 329–335.

Patterson, G. R., & Dishion, T. J. (1988). Multilevel family process models: Traits, interactions, and relationships. In R. A. Hinde & J. Stevenson-Hinde (Eds.), *Relationships within families: Mutual influences* (pp. 283–310). Oxford, UK: Clarendon Press.

Pianta, R., Egeland, B., & Sroufe, L. A. (1990). Maternal stress in children's development: Predictions of school outcomes and identification of protective factors. In J. E. Rolf, A. Masten, D. Cicchetti, K. Nuechterlein, & S. Weintraub (Eds.), *Risk and protective factors in the development of psychopathology* (pp. 215–235). New York: Cambridge University Press.

Reiss, D., Hetherington, M., Plomin, R., Howe, G. W., Simmens, S. J., Henderson, S. H., O'Connor, T. J., Bussell, D. A., Anderson, E. R., & Law, T. (1995). Genetic questions for environmental studies. *Archives of General Psychiatry, 52*, 925–936.

Robins, L. (1978). Sturdy childhood predictors of adult antisocial behavior: Replications from longitudinal studies. *Psychological Medicine, 8,* 611–622.

Robinson, N., & Garber, J. (1995). Social support and psychopathology across the life span. In D. Cicchetti & D. Cohen (Eds.), *Developmental psychopathology: Vol. 2. Risk, disorder, and adaptation* (pp. 162–209). New York: Wiley.

Rutter, M. (1990). Psychosocial resilience and protective mechanisms. In J. Rolf, A. S. Masten, D. Cicchetti, K. H. Nuechterlein, & S. Weintraub (Eds.), *Risk and protective factors in the development of psychopathology* (pp. 181–214). New York: Cambridge University Press.

Sameroff, A. (1997, April). *Developmental contributions to the study of psychopathology.* Master lecture presented at the biennial meetings of the Society for Research in Child Development, Washington, DC.

Sameroff, A. J., & Emde, R. N. (Eds.) (1989). *Relationship disturbances in early childhood: A developmental approach.* New York: Basic Books.

Sander, L. (1975). Infant and caretaking environment. In E. J. Anthony (Ed.), *Explorations in child psychiatry* (pp. 129–165). New York: Plenum Press.

Schore, A. N. (1994). *Affect regulation and the origin of the self: The neurobiology of emotional development.* Hillsdale, NJ: Erlbaum.

Shulman, S., Elicker, J., & Sroufe, L. A. (1994). Stages of friendship growth in preadolescence as related to attachment history. *Journal of Social and Personal Relationships, 11,* 341–361.

Sroufe, L. A. (1983). Infant–caregiver attachment and patterns of adaptation in preschool: The roots of maladaptation and competence. In M. Perlmutter (Ed.), *Minnesota Symposia in Child Psychology: Vol. 16. Development and policy concerning children with special needs* (pp. 41–83). Hillsdale, NJ: Erlbaum.

Sroufe, L. A. (1996). *Emotional development: The organization of emotional life in the early years.* New York: Cambridge University Press.

Sroufe, L. A. (1997). Psychopathology as an outcome of development. *Development and Psychopathology, 9,* 251–268.

Sroufe, L. A., Egeland, B., & Carlson, E. A. (1999). One social world. In W. A. Collins & B. Laursen (Eds.), *Minnesota Symposia on Child Psychology: Vol. 30. Relationships in developmental context* (pp. 241–262). Hillsdale, NJ: Erlbaum.

Sroufe, L. A., Egeland, B., & Kreutzer, T. (1990). The fate of early experience following developmental change: Longitudinal approaches to individual adaptation in childhood. *Child Development, 61,* 1363–1373.

Stern, D. (1985). *The interpersonal world of the infant: A view from psychoanalysis and developmental psychology.* New York: Basic Books.

Sternberg, K. J., Lamb, M. E., Greenbaum, C., Cicchetti, D., Dawud, S., Cortes, R. M., Krispin, O., & Lorey, F. (1993). Effects of domestic violence on children's behavior problems and depression. *Developmental Psychology, 29,* 44–52.

Stormshak, E., Bellanti, C., & Bierman, K. (1996). The quality of sibling relationships and the development of social competence and behavioral control in aggressive children. *Developmental Psychology, 32,* 79–89.

Teo, A., Carlson, E., Mathieu, P., Egeland, B., & Sroufe, L. A. (1996). A prospective longitudinal study of psychosocial predictors of achievement. *Journal of School Psychology, 34,* 285–306.

Toth, S. L., & Cicchetti, D. (1996). Patterns of relatedness, depressive symptomatology, and perceived competence in maltreated children. *Journal of Consulting and Clinical Psychology, 64,* 32–41.

Toth, S. L., Manly, J., & Cicchetti, D. (1992). Child maltreatment and vulnerability to depression. *Development and Psychopathology, 4,* 87–112.

Wallerstein, J. S., & Kelly, J. B. (1982). *Surviving the breakup: How children and parents cope with divorce.* New York: Basic Books.

Warren, S. L., Huston, L., Egeland, B., & Sroufe, L. A. (1997). Childhood anxiety disorders and attachment. *American Academy of Child and Adolescent Psychiatry, 36,* 637–644.

Weinfield, N. S., Ogawa, J. R., & Sroufe, L. A. (1997). Early attachment as a pathway to adolescent peer competence. *Journal of Research on Adolescence, 7,* 241–265.

Windle, M. (1992). A longitudinal study of stress and buffering for adolescent problem behaviors. *Developmental Psychology, 28,* 522–530.

6

Prevention Science

John D. Coie, Shari Miller-Johnson, and Catherine Bagwell

This chapter provides an overview of basic principles of prevention science and its relevance to the field of developmental psychopathology. The intellectual overlap between these two interdisciplinary sciences has become increasingly apparent over the past two decades. Prevention scientists now clearly recognize the central importance of developmental psychopathology research in the conceptualization, implementation, and evaluation of intervention strategies (Coie et al., 1993; Mrazek & Haggerty, 1994). From this perspective, the field of developmental psychopathology might be considered to be an essential domain of research within prevention science.

Arguments for a preventive approach to mental disorders invariably begin with a recitation of the astonishing prevalence and cost of these disorders in our society. The most recent epidemiological study places the prevalence of adult disorder in the United States at 20%, with a lifetime prevalence rate of 32% (Robins & Regier, 1991). Some estimates of disorder among children and adolescents range as high as 20% (Mrazek & Haggerty, 1994; Office of Technology Assessment, 1991). The economic costs relating to mental disorders are staggering, with estimated costs in 1990 of $147 billion, not including the $164 billion attributable to alcohol and drug abuse (Mrazek & Haggerty, 1994). This total includes 45% due to direct treatment costs, 43% to reduced productivity, 8% to mortality, and 4% to criminal justice costs.

Those who advocate the importance of prevention strategies in the face of the prevalence and costs of mental disorder offer three arguments. First, there will never be sufficient numbers of mental health professionals available to provide adequate treatment for the large number of individuals experiencing disorder at any given time; therefore, it is incumbent on our society to prevent disorder from occurring at such high prevalence rates. Second is the anticipation that when effective prevention strategies are found, they will prove to be relatively cost-effective compared to treatment strategies. The third argument is a moral one, namely, that preventing the human suffering and loss of personal productivity caused by mental disorder is itself a social value that outweighs some other cost–benefit considerations.

John D. Coie, Shari Miller-Johnson, and Catherine Bagwell • Department of Psychology, Duke University, Durham, North Carolina 27710.

Handbook of Developmental Psychopathology, Second Edition, edited by Arnold J. Sameroff, Michael Lewis, and Suzanne M. Miller. Kluwer Academic / Plenum Publishers, New York, 2000.

In this chapter, we provide a brief overview of the history and rationale for prevention science. Next, we discuss the major components of prevention science following the five-component model schematized in the Institute of Medicine report (Mrazek & Haggerty, 1994). Throughout the chapter, we illustrate most points with examples from the study of conduct problems, one of the most pervasive child and adolescent disorders, and a serious challenge to prevention science.

HISTORY AND RATIONALE FOR PREVENTION SCIENCE

Historically, the idea of prevention as it applies to mental disorders has been intrinsically intertwined with a community focus. This was true at the inception of the National Mental Health Association at the turn of the twentieth century and was especially true of the child guidance movement in the 1920s. The Joint Commission on Mental Illness and Health established by Congress in 1955 had as part of its mandate the development of prevention programs, along with more traditional treatment strategies (Felner, Jason, Moritsugu, & Farber, 1983). Numerous studies sponsored under the auspices of the Commission showed that mental health services were grossly inadequate, particularly in terms of service delivery to ethnic minorities. Less than one-fourth of the counties in the United States were found to have mental health centers (Cowen & Zax, 1967). In 1963, President Kennedy's Message on Mental Health and Mental Retardation to the U.S. Congress reflected recommendations from the Joint Commission's report in calling for prevention and treatment of mental illness as a community responsibility (Caplan, 1964). He called for establishment of comprehensive community mental health centers, with the focus of treatment being located in the community rather than in inpatient hospital settings. This led to passage of the Mental Retardation Facilities and Community Mental Health Centers Construction Act of 1963, which called for establishment of community mental health centers across the country. In this mandate, consultation and education, which included primary prevention, were among the five services to be provided by community mental health centers.

These events led to a need for professionals to be trained in community mental health, consultation, and prevention programs. In this spirit, the 1965 Swampscott Conference on the Education of Psychologists for Community Mental Health coined the term *community psychology*, with strong emphasis on prevention and the need to address social and contextual influences on mental health. The term *prevention* was adopted from public health principles, and three levels of intervention were delineated. *Tertiary* prevention most closely resembled traditional treatment approaches and focuses on the prevention of further disability. *Secondary* prevention emphasized early identification and intervention with individuals who display early signs of disorder but have not experienced full disorder or disability. *Primary* prevention emphasized the reduction of the incidence of onset of disorder.

Among psychologists, the cause of primary prevention was championed by those who saw themselves as community psychologists. The same was true for other mental health disciplines, because the expectation was that prevention would take place through changes in the way communities functioned and that prevention was as much a community responsibility as was treatment (Sarason, Levine, Goldenberg, Cherline, & Bennett, 1966). Less was known about the development of disorder in the 1960s than may have been necessary to realize this vision of prevention, but it is also true that in most community mental health centers, most of the available funding went to the treatment of existing disorders rather than to prevention activities. In addition, community mental health centers were never funded to the full extent intended by the original act. The deinstitutionalization of state psychiatric hospitals led to further pressure on community mental health centers to provide services to the chronically mentally ill.

These factors converged to hamper service delivery focused on the prevention of disturbance. This circumstance, in turn, led to renewed advocacy for primary prevention, as exemplified by the initiation of the Vermont Conference on Primary Prevention of Psychopathology in 1975 and the National Institute of Health Conference on Primary Prevention in 1976. There are still strong voices that would argue that primary prevention defines true prevention (Bower, 1987; Cowen, 1977; Peters, 1990) and only describes interventions to prevent onset among those without any sign of disorder. There are others (e.g., Coie, 1996) who argue that the distinction between primary and secondary prevention may apply better to physical disorders than to complex behavioral dysfunctions such as conduct disorder. This is because early signs of risk for conduct disorder almost always include some developmental approximation of the problem itself. Evidence for this view is provided by epidemiological studies suggesting that serious antisocial behavior in later life rarely occurs among children who do not exhibit earlier conduct problems (Robins, 1966).

Gordon's (1983) redefinition of prevention according to the population groups for whom intervention is thought to be most optimal redirects the issue from etiological to epidemiological considerations. *Universal* prevention, according to Gordon, includes all programs that are advisable for the general public, whereas *selective* prevention activities are for those whose risk of disorder is greater than average. *Indicated* preventions are for individuals not yet clinically disordered but at high risk and sometimes exhibiting early precursor signs. The Institute of Medicine report (Mrazek & Haggerty, 1994) recommended a classification system using Gordon's terminology but clarified that selective and indicated interventions, the latter in particular, are preventive only when the targets of these interventions do not meet diagnostic criteria, despite the presence of "symptoms foreshadowing mental disorder, or biological markers indicating predisposition to mental disorder" (p. 25). The adoption of this system does not resolve all disagreements about which intervention activities should be considered as prevention, but it does allow planners to consider prevention for a community in a comprehensive fashion, with components tailored to level of risk. It also permits definitional issues to become more subordinate to the more pressing need of getting national priorities attuned to prevention.

Throughout the 1980s, efforts at the federal level continued to give increased attention to prevention of mental disturbance, although the focus expanded beyond primary prevention. In 1982, the National Institutes of Mental Health (NIMH) established the Center for Prevention Research (CPR), and preventive efforts began to be coordinated through this center. The NIMH also began to sponsor yearly conferences on prevention. Initially, the focus was on community-level interventions. However, the 1980s and 1990s also saw an expansion of the prevention field beyond community psychology to include those scientists doing basic developmental psychopathology research who were interested in prevention. In 1989, the NIMH began a comprehensive review of research activities in the prevention of mental disorder. The outcome of this review was the NIMH report "The Prevention of Mental Disorders: A National Research Agenda" (NIMH Prevention Research Steering Committee, 1993). In 1990, the U.S. Congress initiated a separate but complementary review of research on the prevention of mental disorder. Congress mandated that the NIMH collaborate with the Institute of Medicine (IOM) to develop an integrated summary of current activities and recommendations for a prevention science agenda, the result being the report "Reducing Risk for Mental Disorders: Frontiers for Preventive Intervention Research" (Mrazek & Haggerty, 1994).

These two reports serve as a scientific framework for future development in this area and set a national agenda for the prevention of mental disorders. The major focus of both reports was on the critical need for a theoretical framework to organize prevention efforts, to delineate basic concepts guiding prevention science as a discipline, and to provide recommendations for future work.

THE COMPONENTS OF PREVENTION SCIENCE

The term *prevention science* reflects the fact that prevention is a research-based activity and recognizes the significance of multiple scientific disciplines for these efforts (Coie et al., 1993). Preventive intervention research deals with the identification and prevalence of disorder, the study of etiology and human development, the design of carefully controlled intervention trials addressing causal and mediating factors, the design and planning of field trials that attempt to address fully the essential process underlying disorder, and the implementation and evaluation of tested prevention programs in the community. These major components have been schematized as a cycle that is outlined in Figure 6.1 (Mrazek & Haggerty, 1994). While the figure suggests that components to the right build on the achievements of those to their left, it also pictures prevention science as a recursive process in which new learning emerges from clinical trials, field trials, and community implementations, and this new learning in turn influences the direction of the more "basic" science steps in the model. As we demonstrate, the success of prevention science depends on a careful integration of research from multiple disciplines, and movement toward closer collaboration among multi-disciplinary teams is essential for greater progress in prevention science.

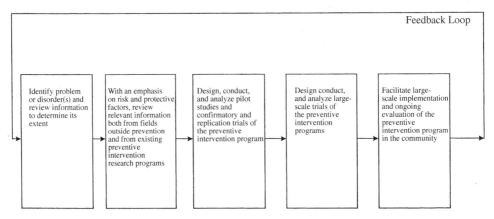

FIGURE 6.1. The preventive intervention research cycle. Preventive intervention research is represented in boxes three and four. Note that although information from many different fields in health research, represented in the first and second boxes, is necessary to the cycle depicted here, it is the review of this information, rather than the original studies, that is considered to be part of the preventive intervention research cycle. Likewise, for the fifth box, it is the facilitation by the investigator of the shift from research project to community service program with ongoing evaluation, rather than the service program itself, that is part of the prevention intervention research cycle. Although only one feedback loop is represented here, the exchange of knowledge among researchers and between researchers and community practitioners occurs throughout the cycle.

Epidemiology

Prevention of psychological disorder is a concept adapted from public health that received its most significant initial treatment in Gerald Caplan's 1964 volume *The Principles of Preventive Psychiatry*. At the core of this public health concept is the discipline of epidemiology, which is the study of the distribution of diseases by time and place (Costello & Angold, 1995). As patterns emerge among these distributions, it becomes possible to develop testable hypotheses about causal sequences in the development of disorder. For public health, this began with the solution to the 1853 epidemic of cholera in London by tracing prevalence rates of cholera to the Broad Street water pump as a source of infection (Snow, 1855). More contemporary efforts are reflected in an attempt to locate patterns of conduct problems by community and family characteristics (Offord, 1989) or by school and classroom (Kellam et al., 1991). The epidemiological search typically begins by assessing prevalence rates, the number of cases observed in a specific time period, or incidence rates, the number of new cases observed in a time period. Defining a case depends on the criteria adopted in a particular taxonomy, which, in this case, is the purview of psychiatry. Thus, changes in DSM-based standards can alter the epidemiological picture for psychiatric disorders. The problems of assessing prevalence become more complex where child psychiatric epidemiology is concerned (Costello & Angold, 1995), because the conception of a disorder must be reconciled with the physical, cognitive, social, and emotional changes that naturally occur across development.

Both theoretical advances and the conceptual dilemmas arising from epidemiological research related to prevention can be seen in important recent work on conduct disorder. Rates of child conduct disorder have been found to range from 4% to 10%, depending on the child's age and gender, with rates being higher for males and with rates for both genders increasing with age (Offord, 1989). Conduct disorder is a child psychiatric syndrome that is defined by the manifestation of three conduct problems within a 6-month period. The nature of these acts may change across time, such that by adolescence, they are not distinguishable from what by legal definition is delinquency (Tolan & Loeber, 1993). Thus, an important source of epidemiological data on this problem is also found in records of youthful criminal offenders.

According to 1995 official arrest data, the approximately 2.7 million juvenile arrests made in that year accounted for 18% of all arrests (Office of Juvenile Justice and Delinquency Prevention, 1996). Although juvenile arrests for violent crimes declined from 1994 to 1995, the numbers have increased 67% above the 1986 level. Arrests of juveniles accounted for 32% of robberies, 23% of weapons, and 15% of murder and aggravated assault charges in 1995. Females accounted for roughly one-fourth of juvenile arrests in 1995, and the relative proportion of arrests for girls has increased in recent years. In addition, rates of police contacts are estimated to represent only 3–10% of self-reported offenses (Elliot & Voss, 1974; Gold, 1966). Thus, antisocial behavior represents a growing and substantial problem among juveniles.

From a prevention standpoint, one of the most important findings about conduct problems is their high degree of stability within individuals. This stability is a two-sided coin. On the one hand, it is rare to find an antisocial adult who did not exhibit conduct problems as a child (Robins, 1966). On the other hand, no more than half of the children who engage in these behaviors go on to become involved in serious antisocial activities as adolescents or adults. This fact suggested to theorists such as Moffitt (1993) and Patterson (Patterson, Capaldi, & Bank, 1991) that there may be a group of early starting conduct problem youth who merit the strongest attention of preventionists. Further support for this idea comes from longitudinal studies that show a pool of 5–6% of the child population who display early conduct problems and go on to account for approximately half of all adolescent or adult crimes (Stattin & Magnusson, 1991c; Wolfgang, Figlio, & Sellin, 1972).

One of the dilemmas involving these youth is that although they certainly represent a high-risk group worthy of prevention efforts, the high stability and frequency of their delinquency make their behavior difficult to change. This, in fact, has been the consistent outcome of most treatment efforts, with successful short-term results generally fading over time (Kazdin, 1993). The second dilemma is whether intervention programs for this group can properly be construed as prevention activities. On the one hand, many of these children might be diagnosable as being conduct disordered at the time of recruitment into a prevention program, so that intervention might be more properly construed as treatment, rather than as prevention. On the other hand, many of the childhood behaviors qualifying the child for a conduct disorder diagnosis would not lead to arrest if exhibited in adolescence and constitute classes of behavior that are not all that atypical among younger children. Seen in this light, intervention could be viewed as preventing the more serious antisocial acts that are ultimately society's main concern. All too often, this debate has taken place, not over any disagreement about the importance of intervening with youth at high risk for chronic conduct problems, but over whether these efforts should be funded from what is an all-too-limited a pot of prevention monies.

There are other youth who would not have qualified as conduct disordered children but who engage in delinquent acts as adolescents. Moffitt (1990) found that 32% of a sample of previously nondelinquent boys became delinquent in early adolescence. There is little question about intervention being considered as prevention with this group, but the dilemma here is now to identify them prior to onset. One of the central mechanisms cited by both Patterson and Moffitt in explanation of the delinquency of this latter group is the role of deviant peers (Cairns, Cairns, Neckerman, Ferguson, & Gariepy, 1989; Elliot, Huizinga, & Ageton, 1985; Patterson et al., 1991). Since it is the early starters who may play the most influential role in the delinquency of the late starter group, the irony is that the best preventive strategy for the late starter group is effective intervention with the early starting group.

Risk and Protective Factors: Developmental Psychopathology

The second component of the prevention research cycle involves an analysis of the potential risk factors emerging from epidemiological studies for their causal significance to the development of disorder. There are two important aspects to this analysis. One involves the determination of a factor's actual causal or mediating role, as opposed to a determination that it is associated with a disorder. The second is a careful articulation of the process by which a factor influences either the emergence of a disorder, the frequency or seriousness of its manifestation, or its longevity. Some risk factors may serve an initiating role in causing disorder in that they place an individual in a life circumstance that in turn increases the probability of disorder. Other risk factors may mediate a predisposition to disorder or serve as triggers to the onset of disorder. These, of course, are exactly the issues addressed by developmental psychopathology. Rather than elaborating on the discipline that is the topic of this volume, we will address the implications of developmental psychopathology for prevention science.

Concepts of risk and protection are at the core of prevention science. At the 1991 NIMH-sponsored National Prevention Conference, the term *prevention science* was coined to describe a field "focused primarily on the systematic study of potential precursors for dysfunction and health, called risk factors and protective factors, respectively, [with the] aim to counteract risk factors and reinforce protective factors in order to disrupt processes that contribute to human dysfunction" (Coie et al., 1993, p. 1013). Research on modifiable risk and protective factors serves as the foundation of prevention science and informs the development of controlled prevention trials. Well-conducted risk research informs us as to who should be the primary focus of prevention trials. It also provides a clear statement of the developmental trajectory of the disease process, so that questions of timing and content of intervention can be answered.

Briefly, risk factors are those characteristics of the individual or of the social or physical environment that increase the likelihood of either the onset, severity, or duration of a disorder. In contrast, protective factors are those characteristics that promote resistance to disturbance and provide a buffer against the development of disorder (Mrazek & Haggerty, 1994). The delineation of risk factors informs the design of intervention strategies, in that prevention programs have as their goal the reduction of risk factors and the promotion of protective factors. Therefore, basic research on risk and protective factors elucidates causal chains and processes that would be expected to change as a result of the preventive intervention (Cicchetti & Cohen, 1995). Results from controlled prevention trials in turn inform us about the validity of developmental models that specify the causal role of variables designated as risk factors. In this way, research on risk factors and preventive interventions are reciprocally interdependent and cyclical in nature.

While the concept of risk factor is apparently quite simple and suggests a direct causal relation between risk and disorder, these connections are rarely straightforward in the case of mental disorders. First of all, it is rare to find isomorphic relations between risk factors and disorders. Equifinality and multifinality are two principles from the developmental psychopathology perspective that are particularly relevant to this issue (Cicchetti & Cohen, 1995). First, equifinality reflects the fact that multiple early risk factors may lead to the same outcome. Thus, multiple risk factors are usually related to any single disorder (Coie et al., 1993; Reiss & Price, 1996). For example, risk factors for substance abuse include individual, peer, school, family, and genetic influences (Hawkins, Catalano, & Miller, 1992). As such, if the goal of a prevention program is to prevent the emergence of a specific outcome, interventions must address multiple risk factors and the diverse set of causal chains that have been shown to lead to a disorder.

Multifinality, on the other hand, refers to the process by which any particular risk factor or early maladaptive developmental phenomenon may lead to quite diverse outcomes. Risk factors are often not specific to a particular disorder, and different disorders may share risk factors in common. For example, many of the same factors that create risk for substance abuse are also implicated in the development of conduct problems, and some of these same factors also create risk for depression (Kazdin, 1993). Thus, some risk factors can be thought of as generic, in that they serve as antecedents to multiple disorders. One question, then, for prevention planning is whether all risk factors must be addressed by interventions and, if so, whether timing should be considered in relation to multiple risk factors. A second question is whether generic risk factors are the most potent influences and, hence, should be at the heart of intervention activities, or whether they are less mutable (e.g., SES) and serve as proxies for factors that can be altered (McLoyd, 1990). It is only through prospective longitudinal research from a developmental psychopathology framework that prevention scientists can understand the emergence and course of a disorder, as well as the processes through which risk and protective factors operate. In turn, this knowledge is essential for designing effective interventions to prevent the disorder.

Knowledge about early precursors is especially important when considering the popula-tion of children to whom the interventions will be directed, and thus evaluating the issue of false positives and false negatives. Ideally, cost-effective prevention efforts are designed to intervene with children who display a particular set of risk factors and would eventually develop the particular disorder of interest. Unfortunately, prevention programs, especially those that begin with very early risk factors (e.g., prenatal care and nutrition), must also address the risks of false positives, or intervening with children who are identified as at risk but who would not eventually develop the disorder, as well as false negatives, or failing to intervene with those who develop the disorder without evidencing the early risk factors.

Developmental considerations are also important to consider in understanding risk and protective factors. Some risk factors indicate risk across the life span, while other factors sig-nal risk at only certain developmental periods (Coie et al., 1993). As a general rule, compo-nents of comprehensive prevention programs must be designed in synchrony with normative developmental processes. An intervention at one developmental stage may not be equally effective at all ages, since the importance of particular risk factors varies at different periods in development. The effectiveness of a particular preventive intervention will thus depend, in part, on its adherence to temporal issues in development (Cicchetti & Cohen, 1995). Preven-tive interventions should take place as a risk factor becomes manifest, generally, rather than after it has had a prolonged impact on development (Reiss & Price, 1996). In addition, once a risk factor has been determined to be a salient precursor of disorder, prevention should occur when that risk factor is most amenable to alteration. Therefore, the issue of timing is one of balancing the problems of identification with those of change.

One example of this timing issue appears in the way that deviant peer influences may influence early adolescent delinquency. Dishion, Patterson, Stoolmiller, and Skinner (1991) found that having deviant friends at age 12 reliably predicted increased antisocial activity, but at age 10, boys in their longitudinal study did not show this effect. Instead, it was aggression, poor parental monitoring, and peer rejection at age 10 that predicted both subsequent antisocial activity and deviant peer relations. These findings suggest that interventions prior to age 12 that were designed to reduce aggression, bolster parental monitoring skills, and improve peer relations to the point where the target children had prosocial friendship possibilities, would be a strategic way to preclude negative peer influences when these high-risk youth enter middle school.

It is relatively rare that a single risk factor is responsible for a psychological disorder. Rather, combinations of risk factors working at the level of child, family, peer network, or community characteristics have been found to be related to most such disorders. Rutter (1979) concluded that for many childhood psychological disorders, the risk of dysfunction increases exponentially with the number of risk factors, at least to some limit. In one important test of this hypothesis, Sameroff, Seifer, Baldwin, and Baldwin (1993) created a multiple risk score for children of the Rochester Longitudinal Study and found that scores were related to the child's IQ score and clinical symptoms at preschool. Similar evidence for multiple risk factor influence comes from the Philadelphia longitudinal study of urban youth (Sameroff, 1997).

As the developmental study of psychopathology has progressed, it is becoming clear that multiple risk factors do not simply add up like weights hung around the child's neck, but they interact with each other across time. Complex associations may exist among biological and psychosocial risk factors; therefore, integrated developmental models are necessary to de-scribe these interactions. Sometimes the interactions can be quite simple and directly sugges-tive of intervention strategies. For example, Caspi, Lynam, and Moffitt (1993) found that early maturing girls in mixed-sex school settings were at greater risk for delinquency than early maturing girls from same-sex school settings. The social context, in combination with biological maturation, may provide increased opportunities for involvement in risk-taking behaviors through contact with older males. In other cases, the interaction of person and environment characteristics may not be so straightforward. Scarr and McCartney (1983) have observed that individuals are not randomly distributed across contexts, and certain individual risk factors may be more likely to co-occur with other environmental risk factors. We describe an extended example of the way this point may operate in the case of many children who are at high risk for persistent, life-course conduct disorder. The developmental model we summarize serves as a guide to major prevention trials for conduct problems (Conduct Problems Prevention Research Group, 1992).

In the preschool years, the high-risk child exhibits high levels of irritable, inattentive, and impulsive behaviors (Bates, Bayles, Bennett, Ridge, & Brown, 1991; Campbell, Breaux, Ewing, & Szumowski, 1986). In some cases, these characteristics may be due to genetic influence or gene–environment interactions (Raine, 1993). In other cases, neurological deficits due to trauma or toxins in the environment (Needleman & Bellinger, 1991) may be factors. Parents may be marginally employed and have a history of psychopathology or criminality (Farrington, 1995; Rutter & Giller, 1983). Such families tend to reside in high-poverty communities that lack adequate services to address their needs (Offord, Alder, & Boyle, 1986; Shaw & Emery, 1988). This combination of parent and child factors leads to early coercive patterns, during which the child is negatively reinforced for aversive behaviors (Patterson, 1982). Inadequate parenting may also be reflected in poor support for the child's cognitive and emotional development (Cook, Greenberg, & Kusche, 1994). In addition, families are often socially isolated, with low levels of neighborhood cohesion and support (Dumas & Wahler, 1983).

High-risk children thus enter school with a host of learned negative behaviors (Campbell, 1990). They are highly aggressive, inattentive, and disruptive in the classroom. These behaviors often lead to rejection by peers (Coie, Dodge, & Kupersmidt, 1990), which, if it remains stable, can lead to social stigma and expectational biases by other peers that, in turn, lead to increased aggressiveness (Dodge, Bates, & Pettit, 1990). High-risk children are often unprepared in terms of academic readiness, and they tend to be enrolled in schools with a high density of behavior-problem children, resource-poor facilities, and inexperienced teachers. Over the course of elementary school, these high-risk children become increasingly defeated academically and are likely to be chronically rejected by teachers, peers, and parents (Dodge, Coie, & Brakke, 1982; Patterson & Bank, 1989). As a result, they may become alienated from mainstream values (Hawkins & Weiss, 1985) and are prone to become involved with deviant peer cliques that support and promote involvement in delinquent activities.

Up to this point, little has been said about protective factors. One reason for this is that the research on risk and protective factors has tended to focus more on risk factors than on protective factors. A second reason is that, all too often, ostensible protective factors appear, on closer scrutiny, to be the opposite pole of a risk factor continuum. Stouthamer-Loeber, Loeber, Farrington, and Zhang (1993) demonstrated this point in their analyses of contextual and child risk factors related to antisocial outcomes. For the most part, there was a great deal of symmetry to the prediction of delinquency and the promotion of nondelinquency from risk variable scores that were treated categorically to reflect either the negative or the positive quartiles of the distribution. They found that these variables "were more likely to show *both* protective and risk effects than either one alone" (p. 68, emphasis in original). They found some variables had only risk effects, but no variables had only protective effects; however, the data did come from a study designed to assess risk processes.

On the other hand, there is often great value in articulating what the positive pole of a risk factor might represent in terms of identifying competencies of the child or family, or in specifying the kinds of positive activities that are protective, rather than focusing exclusively on the avoidance of negative experiences. For example, while it may have some utility to establish that a major risk factor for inner-city adolescents is the participation in deviant peer groups, it may be more useful to determine whether certain alternatives (e.g., regular participation in an organized team sport or other group activity) are more protective than others (e.g., a low supervision, after-school program). Likewise, while having a substance-abusing parent may be a risk factor for a whole constellation of problem behaviors, this is not to say that teetotalling parents are a better protective factor than having parents who drink in moderation. Sameroff (1997) has suggested that the term *promotive* be substituted for *protective*, to reflect the importance of understanding the active ingredient(s) that operate at the positive pole.

Most questions relating to protective factors remain unanswered. It is an area of research that has not been developed very well, and this fact may be related to another deficiency in prevention science that we discuss later on, namely, the development of innovative intervention components to address issues of risk. The fact that we know more about factors that undermine effective personal functioning than we do about the enhancement and promotion of competence is a serious problem for preventionists. Nonetheless, there are some useful illustrations of the importance of thinking in terms of both risk and protective factors. Thornberry, Huizinga, and Loeber (1995) reported the effects of protective factors on adolescent offending among Rochester youth. Adolescents with five or more risk factors in childhood had rates of serious delinquency that were three times as high as those children with no risk factors. Single protective factors assessed in eighth or ninth grade had only a small impact on reducing delinquency among the high-risk portion of the sample. However, among the children not at high risk, those adolescents who had 75% or more of the protective factors had only an 18% chance of delinquency, while youth with less than half of the protective factors had a 78% chance of delinquency. Conceptualizing risk and protective factors developmentally rather than concurrently, as Thornberry et al. have done, provides a solid basis for prevention planning.

THE STAGES OF PREVENTION TRIAL IMPLEMENTATION

Initial Pilot Research

The cycle of prevention research schematized in Figure 6.1 describes the third stage of prevention research as the design, conduct, and analysis of pilot studies and confirmatory or replication trials. At this stage, prevention planning requires the selection of a theoretical model that specifies the target group (those at highest risk), the timing of intervention, and the factors to be altered by the intervention (risk determinants or mediators and protective or promotive factors). The purpose of a pilot study is twofold. It is to determine whether the intervention procedure can alter risk factors in the appropriate directions and, having achieved that, whether it reduces the frequency or severity of the disordered outcome.

For many social scientists, a pilot study connotes an effort that is limited in time—a quick test of the efficacy of an experimental procedure. For the prevention researcher, a pilot study can represent a substantial time commitment. This is because it is necessary to follow-up on samples across time to determine whether changes in risk or protective factors at the end of the intervention period yield a positive impact on the incidence of disorder in a subsequent period.

The important distinction here is between testing the effectiveness of the intervention on reducing the risk factor and testing its effects on the outcome variable (Lorion, 1991). Outcomes that occur with some frequency or density in a population can be evaluated within a shorter time than those that occur less frequently. Sometimes investigators settle for an approximation of the disorder to deal with this problem, as, for example, in measuring the number of depression symptoms rather than diagnosable cases of depression. For disorders that represent continuous dimensions of dysfunction other than truly categorical entities, this approach may be valid.

The growing sophistication of prevention research today can be traced in large part to the increased reliance on developmental theory as a guide for action. The concept of prevention is inherently developmental in nature, with the purpose of prevention trials being the alteration of either initial causal factors or the reduction or elimination of factors that mediate the transition from initial risk factors to disordered outcomes. One can, therefore, plan the interruption of this dysfunctional process only if one is informed about the way this aberrant development takes place, or, in other words, by having a developmental theory (Lorion, Myers, Cartels, & Dennis, 1994). Reciprocally, a carefully designed and comprehensively evaluated prevention trial with a sufficient sample size can inform developmental theory, providing that the intervention procedure has been effective in reducing the hypothesized risk factors. If, for example, the intervention does forestall or reduce disorder rates relative to the control group, and corresponding reductions in risk factors can be attributed to the intervention, then tests for the effects of risk factors as mediators (Baron & Kenny, 1986) can confirm or disconfirm the theory in a way that is more convincing than longitudinal evidence alone. This is true for both selective and universal interventions. In the latter case, interventions specified by theory as having possible benefits and no anticipated iatrogenic effects can be evaluated with subsamples of the population that have been chosen to represent varying levels of risk. In turn, findings from these evaluations are critical for refining the theory and informing future prevention efforts. Specifically, by examining differences in these subsamples, preventionists can identify boundary conditions on the intervention's effectiveness and conduct follow-up studies to "test these boundary conditions, evaluate the validity of earlier findings, and inform the theory further" (Coie et al., 1993, p. 1017). Even when a prevention trial fails to reduce disorder, if there has been a significant reduction in the putative risk factors, the trial has value for theory building in that it tends to disconfirm the hypothesized relation between risk factors and disordered outcome (Cicchetti & Cohen, 1995; Heller, 1996; Lorion, 1991).

Having selected an empirically based developmental theory, the next step is to identify interventions that have demonstrated positive impact on one or more of the critical risk factors. In the case of conduct disorder, an established risk factor in the period of middle childhood to preadolescence is parental discipline and monitoring of activities and peer associations (Patterson & Bank, 1989). Dishion, Patterson, and Kavanagh (1991) successfully tested the use of parent training in contingency management to improve parental discipline with preadolescents. It is this careful fitting of intervention methods to risk factor constructs that creates the building blocks for the foundation of a prevention trial.

There are a number of reasons why carefully conducted prevention trials may fail using procedures that have been tested previously. Methods that have been successful with one population may be less appropriate with others. The significance of person × environment interactions in developmental research (Scarr & McCartney, 1983) is equally applicable to prevention research designs. Cultural, gender, and developmental differences are among the major reasons why prevention methods need to fit the population. Parent training methods for preventing conduct disorder may need to differ in some ways for African-American and European-American parents, given some evidence (Deater-Deckard, Dodge, Bates, & Pettit, 1996) that spanking is less predictive of later aggressive behavior in African-American children, for example. Norms for adaptive and maladaptive behavior may differ from one sociocultural context to another, as well as the socialization patterns that produce them, and the types of preventive interventions that are effective in some contexts may not be effective in others (Wilson, Rodrigue, & Taylor, 1997). Similar problems may arise in adapting prevention strategies that are effective at an earlier age for use with older youth, such as certain social skills training methods or the "Turtle" technique for teaching anger control (Robin, Schneider, & Dolnick, 1976). The same issue may hold true for interventions with girls and boys. This possibility presents still further challenges to prevention researchers, who find themselves with too few well-tested prevention methods as it is.

Prevention activities with high-risk children and youth are sometimes conducted in a group format because group process is a desired aspect of the program, but often for purposes of economy of staff time and funds. This can inadvertently lead to negative results for reasons that are somewhat unexpected and may undermine the purposes of the intervention. Dishion and his colleagues (Dishion & Andrews, 1995) have found iatrogenic effects for group-based preventive intervention to reduce problem behaviors among high-risk young teens, including increased levels of tobacco use, more favorable attitudes toward substance use, and higher teacher ratings of behavior problems. They suggest that during adolescence, preventive interventions that aggregate high-risk youth in groups may actually increase contact among high-risk teens and promote problem behaviors, and that parent interventions may be more effective at this developmental stage. Alternatively, high-risk-youth-based interventions may need to be embedded with a peer context in which the influence process can work against deviant attitudes, that is, by having well-functioning youth outnumber the high-risk youth in order to set positive norms for group behavior. This is a serious issue for many prevention programs with children and adolescents because the most commonly used strategies involve group training modalities for social skills training (Schneider, 1992) or anger control and social cognitive approaches (Lochman, 1992; Lochman, Lampron, Gemmer, & Harris, 1987). In general, these programs have had at least moderate short-term success, so that the question of iatrogenic influences is one that needs to be explored in some detail. It is entirely possible that two kinds of opposing influences are at work within the same paradigms, thus accounting for some unevenness in results. It is also possible that ages of the children may be a factor in determining how feasible it is to combine disruptive youth in group training paradigms.

If there is a particularly undeveloped area of prevention science, it is here, at the point where prevention researchers have articulated the conditions they want to change, based on empirically validated theory, and are searching for methods to bring about this change. All too often, prevention researchers are forced to rely on intuition about what is called for, or to borrow methods from clinical trials or from educational paradigms. These are all good sources of ideas, but further validation is called for before they are thrust into use in a full-scale prevention trial. In addition, a careful analysis of the risk or protective factor dynamics may suggest that there is more to be dealt with than would be met by a simple adaptation of an existing procedure. For example, parent training might be a useful intervention for parental neglect by young adolescent mothers, but if part of the dynamic behind this neglect is that these mothers have unmet needs for a more active social life, but no one to provide alternative child care for them, parent training may not be the full answer to the problems of neglect.

There are a number of steps that might be considered in adapting existing methods or devising new ones. First, consider whether the developmental model, or the research on which it is based, reflects more of an emphasis on reducing risk, on the promotion of competency, or on the enhancement of protective circumstances. The latter two types of approaches are less likely than the former to be intrusive or to expose the targets of prevention to additional risk. As noted earlier in discussing the Stouthamer–Loeber findings, it is often possible to reframe risk issues in terms of promotion, and the latter are usually more palatable to consumers of prevention activities. Thus, given the choice between focusing on promotion or enhancement versus eliminating risk, the former might be preferable, but the latter should not be ignored if research findings suggest this is what is at issue. A second step would be to examine patterns of change in the presence of later disordered outcomes. It is rare for more than half of a designated risk group to become disordered, and this fact suggests that much can be learned from a developmental study of children who start out with a risk factor but do not continue to show the risk factor across time and do not become disordered. For example, in a recent study of children who were socially rejected by peers at two time points in fourth grade, retrospective interviews with mothers and children revealed that those who improved their peer relations by fifth grade were more likely to have been involved in out-of-school activities of a group nature (Sandstrom & Coie, 1999).

Third, it is important to distinguish between skills deficits and motivational deficits. The research on aggressive boys who are socially rejected by their peers, a group at high risk for adolescent conduct problems and depression (Coie, Terry, Zakriski, & Lochman, 1995), suggests that they are deficient in important social skills that may account for their rejected status (Coie et al., 1990). However, a second literature (Boivin & Begin, 1989; Zakriski & Coie, 1996) suggests these same boys do not recognize that they are having problems with peers and may be unmotivated to use social skills training if it is offered (Parkhurst & Asher, 1992). This means that a social skills intervention designed to provide alternative strategies for dealing with peer conflict or influence will have to be framed as having additional advantages beyond those of getting along well with peers. Fourth, prevention researchers should consider analyzing the component processes related to risk-based deficits in order to develop new skills building procedures that can be tested rather than using methods that have only a marginal fit with risk factors. New procedures are often required.

The discussion thus far has focused on the selection or development of single intervention components. It is relatively rare to find behavioral or psychological disorders that are traceable to single risk factors. This means that preventionists usually need to think in terms of multiple intervention components. This has led to some confusion over the place of factorial designs in prevention trials or designs that allow the investigator to compare the effects of different intervention components. If one's developmental theory postulates a causal role to multiple risk factors, operating either sequentially or in combination, then factorial designs may be ill-advised unless the goal is to test the developmental theory by determining whether the control of a single risk factor has as much impact as controlling multiple risk factors. The latter conclusion would then suggest that only one risk factor is truly causal, and the other putative risk factors either serve as marker variables or have effects correlated with those of the true risk factor. If one is operating from a theory for which there is solid longitudinal evidence for the independent or multiplicative effects of more than one risk factor, then an adequate prevention design should include components to address each of these risk processes, and a factorial test of their relative importance may be inappropriate.

The Montreal longitudinal–experimental study (Tremblay, Kurtz, Masse, Vitaro, & Pihl, 1995) demonstrates the value of a multiple component intervention for preventing serious antisocial behavior. Boys in their study were identified as high risk based on teacher ratings at the end of kindergarten, and intervention took place over a 2-year period. The prevention program consisted of two intervention components. First, parents received individualized home-based training sessions based on the Oregon Social Learning Center's work (Patterson, 1982). Second, boys participated in social skills training that took place at school in a small-group setting of prosocial peers. Initial follow-up results showed positive intervention effects in terms of decreased levels of teacher-reported aggression, greater likelihood of placement in age-appropriate classroom, lower levels of school adjustment problems, and fewer delinquent behaviors among boys in the treatment condition (Tremblay et al., 1992). However, later follow-up through age 15 (Tremblay et al., 1995) showed that although a higher percentage of treatment boys continued to be placed in age-appropriate classrooms, effects disappeared from age 13 onward. Boys' self-reported delinquency did significantly decrease 1- to 6-years postintervention. The authors suggest that more intensive and earlier intervention may be warranted for some families and recommended booster sessions for all boys in order to maintain treatment effects over time, particularly to deal with age-related developmental issues, such as deviant peer influences in early adolescence.

Large-Scale Field Trials

Once carefully controlled, smaller sample, prevention trials have yielded results that suggest that the theoretical model and its translation into an intervention design have validity for reducing disorder, the next logical step in the prevention research cycle is to extend the implementation of this design into community settings. There are several purposes to this step. The most obvious is to see whether results from carefully controlled studies, often conducted with graduate assistants or individuals experienced in the demands of research projects, can be replicated in conditions that are less optimal. The scale of a field trial itself introduces more variation in application. Variation among participants provides an important test of gener-alizability, and large sample sizes may permit a systematic examination of the effects of cultural or geographic factors, as well as gender or other factors that may influence the degree of risk. Most field trials involve collaborations or interactions with community organizations, such as schools, clinics, or service agencies, and provide a test of the community's response to the program. The training of personnel from the community adds variation to the design, as well as a test of the potential for eventually locating the program within the community rather than in the research center. As a result of all these factors, the prevention researcher gives up a substantial amount of control of the total operation, which is also a reflection of real-world circumstances.

The large-scale field trial often provides the opportunity for testing the effects of multiple component designs on problems whose causes seem to implicate several levels of risk factors. The developmental research on chronic, early starting conduct disorder, as noted earlier, implicates community (e.g., neighborhood, school), family, and individual factors. In addition, these factors change as the child grows older, with new factors entering the equation at later points in development (e.g., peer influences, parental monitoring). An adequate test of a complex model such as this requires resources and sample sizes that are beyond the scope of the third stage of the prevention research cycle (i.e., pilot and confirmatory trials).

The Fast Track project for preventing serious and chronic antisocial behavior represents just such a design. Based on a conceptual developmental model (Conduct Problem Prevention Research Group, 1992) that called for interventions at the level of school, family, and child, the design combines both universal and selective interventions in order to address the significant developmental risk factors. While the primary goal of the project is to reduce the incidence of serious antisocial behavior in a high-risk sample, the design recognizes the negative influences of high-risk youth on their school classmates as well as the reciprocal negative effects on the high-risk youth of a typical school serving a high poverty and crime neighborhood. Thus, a secondary goal was to reduce conduct problems in the classrooms attended by the high-risk children who were the primary targets of the project.

A second feature of the Fast Track design was to take seriously the cumulative risk process outlined in the developmental model by extending the intervention beyond the transition into first grade (where the parent and child components were most intensive) and continuing it through the second major transition into adolescence and middle school. The assumption was that risk processes begun well before school entry would not be dramatically altered by a relatively brief intervention of a year and that the interactions of children and families in their high-risk environment would continue to pull the children into antisocial patterns without continued, age-appropriate interventions, a conclusion prompted by the Montreal study (Tremblay et al., 1995). The early results for the Fast Track project seem to support this reasoning. The initial effects of the intervention on important child- and parent-mediating factors were consistently positive but moderate (Conduct Problems Prevention Research Group, 1997a). Classroom effects were also consistently positive, suggesting that both universal and selective interventions were working. It is important to note, parenthetically, that the design does not make it possible to separate out the impact of the universal component or the selective components on either the high-risk targets or their nonrisk classmates, since the selection of high-risk intervention children was nested within classrooms receiving the PATHS curriculum (Greenberg, Kusche, Cook, & Quamma, 1995). Support for the longitudinal aspect of the design comes from growth curve analyses of child conduct problems at home and school, each of which reflects a significant and increasingly greater reduction in conduct problems by the intervention group relative to the control group from baseline (end of kindergarten) through the end of third grade (Conduct Problems Prevention Research Group, 1997b). The ultimate test of the effectiveness of this design, of course, will come in the adolescent years, when data on arrests, substance use, and related dysfunctions are assessed.

A full discussion of the issues relating to the conduct of prevention research trials is beyond the scope of this chapter. The Institute of Medicine report (Mrazek & Haggerty, 1994) is an important resource for a fuller discussion of these issues, including the structure and duration of prevention trials, staffing and sample considerations, measurement decisions, statistical analyses, documentation of implementation, cultural factors, ethical considerations, and cost–benefit issues. The latter issues are of particular importance in making the transition from large-scale field trials to the last stage of the prevention cycle, the dissemination of tested field trial programs into the community. Community leaders will look for evidence of benefits outweighing costs, although it must be recognized that benefits will be weighted differently in different communities and by different segments of the community. Differences in values and ideas about how community agencies should function will also effect the dissemination process, as Rappaport, Seidman, and Davidson (1979) have documented in the case of a juvenile diversion program.

Community Implementation

A graphic illustration of the problems of disseminating a successful prevention trial is provided by the Prenatal/Infancy Project (Olds, Henderson, Tatelbaum, & Chamberlin, 1986). The nurse home-visiting program was designed to address problems of abuse and infant health by providing education about fetal and infant development, promoting a support network for the mother, and linking the family to community services. The initial randomized trial in Elmira resulted in less child abuse and better cognitive functioning. It also had impact on mothers' smoking and delay of subsequent child births. When the health prevention department took over the program, it lost all of the original staff and most of its effectiveness as the philosophy of the program changed in ways that diluted services to the high-risk mothers (Government Accounting Office, 1990). A replication of the original program in Memphis, with primarily African-American families fitting the original high-risk criteria, has yielded similar positive findings in caregiving behavior (Olds, Henderson, Kitzman, & Tatelbaum, 1998). A third replication is currently under way in Denver. This series of studies provides both a caution about the transition of field trials to the demonstration phase and an exemplary model of replication across cultural and geographical settings.

One ingenious strategy for moving to the demonstration stage in a broad sample of communities is being used in the Communities That Care project (Hawkins et al., 1992). The purpose of this project is to introduce to communities packages of tested prevention components for prevention of substance abuse and related antisocial activities. Panels of community leaders are asked to take the lead in evaluating the risk factors operating in their community and then are given the opportunity to select components from among those designated to be best suited to remediating the risk profile they have endorsed. In this way, community leaders participate fully in the design of the prevention trial without sacrificing the value of science-based linkages between prevention components and risk factors. While it is possible for a number of unique combinations of prevention components to emerge from this process, so that some total packages that have never been field tested will be implemented at the demonstration level, this strategy represents a substantial advance in the merger of community decision making with research-based prevention planning.

Perhaps the most important feature of the prevention cycle outlined in Figure 6.1 is the feedback loop. As outlined, the feedback loop goes from the demonstration stage back to the epidemiology/taxonomic stage. While this particular linkage may reflect the significance of demonstration trials for new understandings about the identity and prevalence of disorders in the community, the feedback loop actually operates at all levels of the cycle, as we sometimes have indicated in this chapter. Data from prevention trials, at all levels, provide the occasion for testing theories of the development of psychopathology, if the measurement design has been adequate and appropriate. At an informal level, the experiences of investigators in the conduct of a prevention trial can suggest new hypotheses regarding both the theory of disorder and the conceptualization of the intervention design. This latter point is one reason it is important for the prevention researcher to be in close touch with all facets of the prevention trial, especially those involving the intervention itself. A second point that should be obvious to the reader by now is that prevention research calls for a wide diversity of knowledge and skill. The multidisciplinary nature of good prevention research calls for research teams that reflect not only that diversity but also a breadth of training and experience on the part of individual researchers. This is the challenge of being part of the prevention science enterprise.

REFERENCES

Baron, R. M., & Kenny, D. A. (1986). The moderator–mediator variable distinction in social psychological research: Conceptual, strategic, and statistical considerations. *Journal of Personality and Social Psychology, 51,* 1173–1182.

Bates, J. E., Bayles, K., Bennett, D. S., Ridge, B., & Brown, M. (1991). Origins of externalizing behavior problems at eight years of age. In D. J. Pepler & K. H. Rubin (Eds.), *The development and treatment of childhood aggression* (pp. 93–120). Hillsdale, NJ: Erlbaum.

Boivin, M., & Begin, G. (1989). Peer status and self-perception among early elementary school children: The case of rejected children. *Child Development, 60*, 591–596.

Bower, E. M. (1987). Prevention: A word whose time has come. *American Journal of Orthopsychiatry, 57*, 4–5.

Cairns, R. B., Cairns, B. D., Neckerman, H. J., Ferguson, L. L., & Gariepy, J. L. (1989). Growth and aggression: Childhood to early adolescence. *Developmental Psychology, 25*, 320–330.

Campbell, S. B. (1990). *Behavior problems in preschool children: Clinical and developmental issues.* New York: Guilford Press.

Campbell, S. B., Breaux, A. M., Ewing, L. D., & Szumowski, E. K. (1986). Correlates and prediction of hyperactivity and aggression: A longitudinal study of parent-referred problem preschoolers. *Journal of Abnormal Child Psychology, 14*, 217–234.

Caplan, G. (1964). *Principles of preventive psychiatry.* New York: Basic Books.

Caspi, A., Lynam, D., & Moffitt, T. E. (1993). Unraveling girls' delinquency: Biological, dispositional, and contextual contributions to adolescent misbehavior. *Developmental Psychology, 29*, 19–30.

Cicchetti, D., & Cohen, D. J. (1995). Perspectives in developmental psychopathology. In D. Cicchetti & D. J. Cohen (Eds.), *Developmental psychopathology* (pp. 2–20). New York: Wiley.

Coie, J. D. (1996). Prevention of violence and antisocial behavior. In R. DeV. Peters & R. J. McMahon (Eds.), *Prevention of psychological disorders* (pp. 1–18). Thousand Oaks, CA: Sage.

Coie, J. D., Dodge, K. A., & Kupersmidt, J. B. (1990). Peer group behavior and social status. In S. R. Asher & J. D. Coie (Eds.), *Peer rejection in childhood* (pp. 17–59). New York: Cambridge University Press.

Coie, J. D., Terry, R., Zakriski, A., & Lochman, J. E. (1995). Early adolescent social influences on delinquent behavior. In J. McCord (Ed.), *Coercion and punishment in long-term perspectives* (pp. 229–244). New York: Cambridge University Press.

Coie, J. D., Watt, N. F., West, S. G., Hawkins, J. D., Asarnow, J. R., Markman, J. H., Ramey, S. L., Shure, M. B., & Long, B. (1993). The science of prevention: A conceptual framework and some directions for a national research program. *American Psychologist, 48*, 1013–1022.

Conduct Problems Prevention Research Group (1992). A developmental and clinical model for the prevention of conduct disorder: The FAST Track Program. *Development and Psychopathology, 4*, 509–527.

Conduct Problems Prevention Research Group (1997a, April). *Prevention of antisocial behavior: Initial findings from the Fast Track Project.* Symposium presented at biennial meetings of Society of Research in Child Development, Washington, DC.

Conduct Problems Prevention Research Group (1997b, August). *Testing developmental theory of antisocial behavior with outcomes from the Fast Track Prevention project.* Paper presented in symposium (G. Patterson, Chair), Using Randomized Prevention Trials to Test Developmental Theory, at the annual meeting of American Psychological Association, Chicago, IL.

Cook, E. T., Greenberg, M. T., & Kusche, C. A. (1994). The relations between emotional understanding, intellectual functioning, and disruptive behavior problems in elementary school-aged children. *Journal of Abnormal Child Psychology, 22*, 205–219.

Costello, E. J., & Angold, A. (1995). Developmental epidemiology. In D. Cicchetti & D. J. Cohen (Eds.), *Developmental psychopathology: Vol. 1. Theory and methods* (pp. 23–56). New York: Wiley.

Cowen, E. L. (1977). Baby-steps toward primary prevention. *American Journal of Community Psychology, 5*, 1–22.

Cowen, E. L., & Zax, M. (1967). The mental health fields today: Issues and problems. In E. L. Cowen, E. A. Gardner, & M. Zax (Eds.), *Emergent approaches to mental health problems* (pp. 1–14). New York: Appleton–Century–Crofts.

Deater-Deckard, K., Dodge, K. A., Bates, J. E., & Pettit, G. S. (1996). Physical discipline among African-American and European-American mothers: Links to children's externalizing behaviors. *Developmental Psychology, 32*, 1065–1072.

Dishion, T. J., & Andrews, D. W. (1995). Preventing escalation in problem behaviors with high-risk young adolescents: Immediate and 1-year outcomes. *Journal of Consulting and Clinical Psychology, 63*, 538–548.

Dishion, T. J., Patterson, G. R., & Kavanagh, K. (1991). An experimental test of the coercion model: Linking theory, measurement, and intervention. In J. McCord & R. Tremblay (Eds.), *Preventing antisocial behavior: Interventions from birth through adolescence* (pp. 253–282). New York: Guilford Press.

Dishion, T. J., Patterson, G. R., Stoolmiller, M., & Skinner, M. L. (1991). Family, school, and behavioral antecedents to early adolescent involvement with antisocial peers. *Developmental Psychology, 27*, 172–180.

Dodge, K. A., Bates, J. E., & Pettit, G. S. (1990). Mechanisms in the cycle of violence. *Science, 250*, 1678–1683.

Dodge, K. A., Coie, J. D., & Brakke, N. P. (1982). Behavior patterns of socially rejected and neglected preadolescents: The roles of social approach and aggression. *Journal of Abnormal Child Psychology, 18*, 389–409.

Dumas, J. E., & Wahler, R. G. (1983). Predictors of treatment outcome in parent training: Mother insularity and socioeconomic disadvantage. *Behavioral Assessment, 5,* 301–313.

Elliott, D. S., Huizinga, D., & Ageton, S. S. (1985). *Explaining delinquency and drug use.* Beverly Hills, CA: Sage.

Elliot, D. S., & Voss, H. L. (1974). *Delinquency and dropout.* Lexington, MA: Lexington Books.

Farrington, D. P. (1995). The development of offending and antisocial behavior from childhood: Key findings from the Cambridge study in delinquent development. *Journal of Child Psychology and Psychiatry, 36,* 1–36.

Felner, R. D., Jason, L. A., Moritsugu, J., & Farber, S. S. (1983). Preventive psychology: Evolution and current status. In R. D. Felner, L. A. Jason, J. N. Moritsugu, & S. S. Farber (Eds.), *Preventive psychology: Theory, research, and practice* (pp. 3–10). New York: Pergamon Press.

Gold, J. (1966). Undetected delinquency behavior. *Journal of Research in Crime and Delinquency, 3,* 27–46.

Gordon, R. S. (1983). An operational classification of disease prevention. *Public Health Reports, 98,* 107–109.

Government Accounting Office (1990). *Home visiting: A promising early intervention strategy for at-risk families.* Report of the Chairman, Subcommittee on Labor, Health and Human Services, Education, and Related Agencies, Committee on Appropriations, U.S. Senate GAO/HRD-90-93.

Greenberg, M. T., Kusche, C. A., Cook, E. T., & Quamma, P. (1995). Promoting emotional competence in school-aged children: The effects of the PATHS Curriculum. *Development and Psychopathology, 7,* 117–136.

Hawkins, J. D., Catalano, R. F., & Miller, J. Y. (1992). Risk and protective factors for alcohol and other drug problems in adolescence and early adulthood: Implications for substance abuse prevention. *Psychological Bulletin, 12,* 64–105.

Hawkins, J. D., & Weiss, J. G. (1985). The social development model: An integrated approach to delinquency prevention. *Journal of Primary Prevention, 6,* 73–95.

Heller, K. (1996). Coming of age of prevention science: Comments on the 1994 National Institute of Mental Health–Institute of Medicine Prevention Reports. *American Psychologist, 51,* 1123–1127.

Kazdin, A. E. (1993). Adolescent mental health: Prevention and treatment programs. *American Psychologist, 48,* 127–141.

Kellam, S. G., Werthamer-Larsson, L., Dolan, L. J., Brown, C. H., Mayer, L. S., Rebok, G. W., Anthony, J. C., Laudolff, J., Edelsohn, G., & Wheeler, L. (1991). Developmental epidemiologically-based preventive trials: Baseline modeling of early target behaviors and depressive symptoms. *American Journal of Community Psychology, 19,* 563–584.

Lochman, J. E. (1992). Cognitive-behavioral intervention with aggressive boys: Three-year follow-up and preventive effects. *Journal of Consulting and Clinical Psychology, 60,* 426–432.

Lochman, J. E., Lampron, L. B., Gemmer, T. C., & Harris, R. (1987). Anger coping intervention with aggressive children: A guide to implementation in school settings. In P. A. Keller & S. R. Heyman (Eds.), *Innovations in clinical practice: A source book* (pp. 339–356). Sarasota, FL: Professional Resource Exchange.

Lorion, R. P. (1991). Targeting preventive interventions: Enhancing risk estimates through theory. *American Journal of Community Psychology, 19,* 859–866.

Lorion, R. P., Myers, T. G., Cartels, C., & Dennis, A. (1994). Preventive intervention research: Pathways for extending knowledge of child/adolescent health and pathology. In T. H. Ollendick & R. J. Prinz (Eds.), *Advances in clinical child psychology* (Vol. 16, pp. 109–139). New York: Plenum Press.

McLoyd, V. C. (1990). The impact of economic hardship on black families and children: Psychological distress, parenting, and socioemotional development. *Child Development, 61,* 311–346.

Moffitt, T. E. (1990). Juvenile delinquency and attention deficit disorder: Boys' developmental trajectories from age 3 to age 15. *Child Development, 61,* 893–910.

Moffitt, T. E. (1993). Adolescence-limited and life-course-persistent and social behavior: A developmental taxonomy. *Psychological Review, 100,* 674–701.

Mrazek, P. G., & Haggerty, R. J. (Eds.). (1994). *Reducing risks for mental disorders: Frontiers for preventive intervention research.* Washington, DC: National Academy Press.

National Institute of Mental Health Prevention Research Steering Committee. (1993). *The prevention of mental disorders: A national research agenda.* Bethesda, MD: NIMH.

Needleman, H. L., & Bellinger, D. (1991). The health effects of low level exposure to lead. *Annual Review of Public Health, 12,* 111–140.

Office of Juvenile Justice and Delinquency Prevention. (1996). *Female offenders in the juvenile justice system.* National Center for Juvenile Justice, Washington, DC.

Office of Technology Assessment, U.S. Congress. (1991). Adolescent health: Vol. II. Background and the effectiveness of selected prevention and treatment services. Washington, DC: U.S. Government Printing Office.

Offord, D. R. (1989). Conduct disorder: Risk factors and prevention. In D. Shaffer, I. Philip, and N. B. Enzer (Eds.), *Prevention of mental disorders, alcohol and other drug use in children and adolescents.* Rockville, MD: Office for Substance Abuse Prevention.

Offord, D. R., Alder, R. J., & Boyle, M. H. (1986). Prevalence and socio-demographic correlates of conduct disorder. *American Journal of Social Psychiatry, 6,* 272–278.

Olds, D., Henderson, C., Kitzman, H., & Tatelbaum. R. (1998). The promise of home visitation: Results of two randomized trials. *Journal of Community Psychology, 26,* 5–27.

Olds, D. L., Henderson, C. R., Tatelbaum, R., & Chamberlin, R. (1986). Preventing child abuse and neglect: A randomized trial of nurse home visitation. *Pediatrics, 78,* 65–78.

Parkhurst, J. T., & Asher, S. R. (1992). Peer rejection in middle school: Subgroup differences in behavior, loneliness, and interpersonal concerns. *Developmental Psychology, 28,* 231–241.

Patterson, G. R. (1982). *Coercive family process.* Eugene, OR: Castalia.

Patterson, G. R., & Bank, C. L. (1989). Some amplifying mechanisms for pathologic processes in families. In M. Gunnar & E. Thelen (Eds.), *Systems and development: The Minnesota Symposia on Child Psychology* (pp. 167–210). Hillsdale, NJ: Erlbaum.

Patterson, G. R., Capaldi, D. M., & Bank, L. (1991). An early-starter model for predicting delinquency. In D. J. Pepler & K. H. Rubin (Eds.), *The development and treatment of childhood aggression* (pp. 139–168). Hillsdale, NJ: Erlbaum.

Peters, R. DeV. (1990). Adolescent mental health promotion: Policy and practice. In R. J. McMahon & R. DeV. Peters (Eds.), *Behavior disorders of adolescence: Research, intervention, and policy in clinical and school settings* (pp. 207–223). New York: Plenum Press.

Raine, A. (1993). *The psychopathology of crime: Criminal behavior as a clinical disorder.* San Diego: Academic Press.

Rappaport, J., Seidman, E., & Davidson, W. S. (1979). Demonstration research and manifest versus true adoption: The natural history of a research project to divert adolescents from the legal system. In R. F. Muñoz, L. R. Snowden, & J. G. Kelly (Eds.), *Social and psychological research in community settings* (pp. 101–144). San Francisco: Jossey-Bass.

Reiss, D., & Price, R. H. (1996). National research agenda for prevention research: The National Institute of Mental Health Report. *American Psychologist, 51,* 1109–1115.

Robin, A. L., Schneider, M., & Dolnick, M. (1976). The turtle technique: An extended case study of self-control in the classroom. *Psychology in the Schools, 73,* 449–453.

Robins, L. N. (1966). *Deviant children grown up.* Baltimore: Williams & Wilkins.

Robins, L. N., & Regier, D. A. (Eds.). (1991). *Psychiatric disorders in America: The epidemiologic catchment area study.* New York: Free Press.

Rutter, M. (1979). Protective factors in children's responses to stress and disadvantage. In M. W. Kent & J. E. Rolf (Eds.), *Primary prevention of psychopathology: Vol. 3. Social competence in children* (pp. 49–74). Hanover, NH: University Press of New England.

Rutter, M., & Giller, H. (1983). *Juvenile delinquency: Trends and perspectives.* New York: Penguin Books.

Sameroff, A. (1997, April). *Developmental contributions to the study of psychopathology.* Master lecture presented at the biennial meetings of the Society for Research in Child Development, Washington, DC.

Sameroff, A. J., Seifer, R., Baldwin, A., & Baldwin, C. (1993). Stability of intelligence from preschool to adolescence: The influence of social and family risk factors. *Child Development, 64,* 80–97.

Sandstrom, M. J., & Coie, J. D. (1999). A developmental perspective on peer rejection: Mechanisms of stability and change. *Child Development, 70,* 955–966.

Sarason, S. B., Levine, M., Goldenberg, I., Cherline, D. I., & Bennett, E. M. (1966). *Psychology in community settings.* New York: Wiley.

Scarr, S., & McCartney, K. (1983). How people make their own environments: A theory of genotype greater than environment effects. *Child Development, 54,* 424–435.

Schneider, B. H. (1992). Didactic methods for enhancing children's peer relations: A quantitative review. *Clinical Psychology Review, 12,* 363–382.

Shaw, D. S., & Emery, R. E. (1988). Chronic family adversity and school-age children's adjustment. *Journal of the American Academy of Child and Adolescent Psychiatry, 27,* 200–226.

Snow, J. (1855). *On the mode of communication of cholera, second edition.* London: Churchill.

Stattin, H., & Magnusson, D. (1991). Stability and change in criminal behavior up to age 30. *British Journal of Criminology, 31,* 327–346.

Stouthamer-Loeber, M., Loeber, R., Farrington, D. P., & Zhang, W. (1993). The double edge of protective and risk factors for delinquency: Interrelations and developmental patterns [Special Issue: Milestones in the development of resilience]. *Development and Psychopathology, 5,* 683–701.

Thornberry, T. P., Huizinga, D., & Loeber, R. (1995). The prevention of serious delinquency and violence: Implications from the program of research on the causes and correlates of delinquency. In J. C. Howell, B. Krisberg, J. D. Hawkins, & J. J. Wilson (Eds.), *Sourcebook on serious violent and chronic juvenile offenders* (pp. 147–166). Thousand Oaks, CA: Sage.

Tolan, P. H., & Loeber, R. (1993). Antisocial behavior. In P. H. Tolan & B. J. Cohler (Eds.), *Handbook of clinical research and practice with adolescents* (pp. 307–331). New York: Wiley.

Tremblay, R. E., Kurtz, L., Masse, L. C., Vitaro, F., & Pihl, R. O. (1995). A bimodal preventive intervention for disruptive kindergarten boys: Its impact through mid-adolescence. *Journal of Consulting and Clinical Psychology, 63*, 560–568.

Tremblay, R. E., Vitaro, F., Bertrand, L., LeBlanc, M., Beauchesne, H., Boileau, H., & David, L. (1992). Parent and child training to prevent early onset of delinquency: The Montreal Longitudinal–Experimental Study. In J. McCord & R. Tremblay (Eds.), *Preventing antisocial behavior: Interventions from birth through adolescence* (pp. 117–138). New York: Guilford Press.

Wilson, D. K., Rodrigue, J. R., & Taylor, W. C. (Eds.). (1997). *Health-promoting and health-compromising behaviors among minority adolescents*. Washington, DC: American Psychological Association.

Wolfgang, M. E., Figlio, R. M., & Sellin, T. (1972). *Delinquency in a birth cohort*. Chicago: University of Chicago Press.

Zakriski, A. L., & Coie, J. D. (1996). A comparison of aggressive-rejected and nonaggressive-rejected boys' interpretations of self-directed and other-directed rejection. *Child Development, 67*, 1048–1070.

II
CONTEXT AND MENTAL HEALTH

7

Family Context in Developmental Psychopathology

Barbara H. Fiese, Jay Wilder, and Nicole L. Bickham

Few would disagree that families affect children's development. The theoretical basis for this assumption, however, has evolved over time, with increasing recognition that children live in complex and multidetermined environments (Bronfenbrenner, 1977; Sameroff, 1997). Despite these concerns, historical factors, theoretical limitations, and restricted diagnostic systems have limited the understanding of family-context effects in developmental psychopathology. To address these limitations, we have organized the chapter to examine the historical, theoretical, and diagnostic challenges encountered in studying families and their effects on children's adaptation and maladaptation. Our overview is necessarily brief and the interested reader is directed to more extensive discussions found in other sources (e.g., Cowan, 1991; Crockenberg, Lyons-Ruth, & Dickstein, 1993; Lewis, 1987; Lewis & Feiring, 1992; Wagner & Reiss, 1995).

HISTORICAL DEPICTIONS OF THE FAMILY IN DEVELOPMENTAL PSYCHOPATHOLOGY

Prior to the 1950s and 1960s, when prominent child psychiatrists began to include family members in psychotherapy, there was little concern with family functioning when a child was the identified patient, although John Bowlby (1949) published an early article describing family interviews in treating problematic teenagers. Based on observations (and sometimes speculations) of family interactions involving disturbed children, theories were developed identifying the family's contribution to child dysfunction (Broderick & Schrader, 1981). Usually, the family was equated with the mother–child relationship, and child problems were proposed to result from deficiencies in the mother, giving rise to such terms as schizophrenogenic mothers. These models were consistent with psychoanalytic theories that empha-

Barbara H. Fiese, Jay Wilder, and Nicole L. Bickham • Department of Psychology, Syracuse University, Syracuse, New York 13244-2344.

Handbook of Developmental Psychopathology, Second Edition, edited by Arnold J. Sameroff, Michael Lewis, and Suzanne M. Miller. Kluwer Academic/Plenum Publishers, New York, 2000.

sized the pivotal role of the mother–child relationship in the development of the child's psyche. Thus, overcontrolling and domineering mothers were seen as destructive to their child's mental health (Lidz, Cornelison, Fleck, & Terry, 1957). The child's symptoms were recast as predictable outcomes to tensions in the family, giving rise to concepts such as the emotionally disturbed child as a family scapegoat (Vogel & Bell, 1960).

These early theories were particularly influential for clinicians, who began to see the family as important informants in the diagnosis and treatment of children. However, developmental processes were rarely included as a central component to these theories, and linear models of the direct effects of mothers on children prevailed. Indeed, in many instances, case formulations were based on speculation rather than direct observation of parent–child interactions (Hoffman, 1981).

Whereas the early family therapy movement, in general, did not conduct extensive observations of asymptomatic families, developmental psychologists were immersed in prospective studies of children in families and relied upon observational research techniques restricted to dyads, usually the mother and child. These studies emphasized dyadic exchanges and did not include observations of the whole family. Two major themes were prevalent during the early studies of family effects on child adaptation: family structure and parent–child interaction patterns.

Family Structure

Studies of disruptions in family structure were based on the premise that healthy children come from two-parent households and that they remain with the same parents throughout their childhood. Despite frequently divergent findings, the weight of the current evidence suggests that children from divorced families do exhibit, overall, *modest* decrements in academic, social, psychological, and behavioral adjustment relative to their peers from intact families (Amato & Keith, 1991). A number of moderating variables have been explored, including child sex and age. For example, boys have generally been shown to exhibit more serious behavior problems in the aftermath of divorce (Hetherington, Cox, & Cox, 1982), whereas a "sleeper effect" has been observed in the adjustment of girls, with problems fading in the short-term only to reemerge in adolescence (Hetherington, 1982; Wallerstein & Blakeslee, 1989). Sex and age differences, however, have not been demonstrated consistently. The adjustment of boys and girls of different ages is likely influenced by a variety of other factors such as parenting variables, available resources, economic conditions, and the type of developmental outcome assessed (Amato, 1993; Hetherington, Stanley-Hagan, & Anderson, 1989). Studies that focus on divorce as a distinct event, discontinuous from earlier development, may have overestimated the effects of changes in family structure on child adaptation. It is more likely that predivorce family functioning and family process variables are more closely linked to child adjustment than the event of divorce (e.g., Block, Block, & Gjerde, 1986). Mediating and moderating effects are often called upon to explain how disruptions in structural aspects of the family influence child adaptation. Many of these effects are linked to distinct parent–child interaction patterns.

Parent–Child Interaction

Beginning in infancy, there are clear indications that the ways in which family members interact with each other affect child adjustment. At least two aspects of family interaction are pertinent to the concerns of developmental psychopathology: warmth and demandingness (Maccoby & Martin, 1983). Warmth is a parental characteristic that is often studied in the context of either mother–child or father–child interaction. Again, the focus has been on the dyad. Mothers who engage in mutual turn taking with their infants in a warm and responsive manner have children who are described as socially competent (Field, 1987), securely attached (Sroufe, 1983), and successful in school (Grolinck & Ryan, 1989). Similar patterns of adjustment have been identified in relation to father–child interactions (Parke, 1981). The positive relation between parental warmth and child adjustment extends from the toddler period (Belsky, Woodworth, & Crnic, 1996), to the preschool years (Campbell, 1994), and into adolescence (Allen, Hauser, O'Connor, Bell, & Eickholt, 1996). The reverse pattern also holds true, where hostile or rejecting patterns of interaction between parent and child are associated with insecure attachment (Sroufe, 1983), externalizing problems in preschool (Campbell, Pierce, Moore, Marakovitz, & Newby, 1996), and antisocial behavior in adolescence (Patterson, DeBaryshe, & Ramsey, 1989).

The second aspect of parent–child interaction related to child adjustment is the degree of control or demandingness that parents exert in getting children to comply to their requests. Parents who use excessive control to manage child behavior are often faced with an escalating pattern of noncompliance, which is related to externalizing behavior in toddlers (Belsky et al., 1996) and preschool-age children (Campbell, 1994), and conduct disorder in adolescents (Patterson et al., 1989).

Patterns of parent–child interaction have been consistently linked to child adjustment in a variety of domains. However, a focus on how parents and children behave with each other may be insufficient in describing the family interactional context of developmental psychopathology. The most obvious limitation concerns equating family factors with interactions between dyads. The exclusion of other family members in direct observation severely limits conclusions that can be drawn about family effects on child adjustment. In most cases, the dyad under investigation has been the mother and child. Fathers are represented in a very small proportion of studies, and these studies focus on fathers as risk factors, rarely including direct observation of fathers in an interactional context (Phares & Compas, 1992). The second limitation concerns the singular focus on adults as parents. Although parenting is an important aspect of family life, it is not the only relationship that affects child adjustment. Parenting in itself is a multidimensional role that is influenced by a variety of factors (e.g., work stress, marital distress, and life-span issues) that may directly or indirectly affect parent–child interaction (Cowan, Cowan, Heming, & Miller, 1991; Hooker, Fiese, Jenkins, Morfei, & Schwagler, 1996). The third limitation is the isolation of the parent–child dyad from the family context. Multiple combinations of dyads (e.g., mother–child, father–child, mother–father) are a part of the family context that extends into triads and whole-family functioning (Emde, 1994). Furthermore, the effects of one dyad on another (i.e., mother–father effects on mother–child) are rarely considered from a strictly parent–child interactional stance and neglect indirect effects on child adjustment (Lewis & Feiring, 1992).

Focusing on interaction patterns alone may not give a complete picture of family factors associated with child adjustment. Families also make use of symbols and create representations that are enduring across generations (Csikszentmihalyi & Rochberg-Halton, 1981). Families create and maintain representations of family relationships that are typically expressed in verbal accounts of family experiences. Working models of relationships highlight yet another aspect of family symbolic life. Mothers who describe their relationship with their parents in a coherent fashion tend to have children who are more secure (e.g., Crowell & Feldman, 1988). Indirect effects on child behavior problems have been identified, where coherence in the narrative account of caregiving experiences was related to parenting behaviors, which in turn were predictive of child externalizing and internalizing behaviors (Cowan, Cohn, Cowan, & Pearson, 1996). The ways in which family members think about, or symbolically represent, relationships are important for child adjustment. However, just as studies that focus on parent–child interactions are limited by focusing on the dyad, representations of dyadic relationships may be only one aspect of the family context associated with developmental psychopathology.

The family context in developmental psychopathology can be understood from a historical perspective that calls for an integration of family therapy and developmental principles. In order to provide a more coherent synthesis of these two fields, it is important to have a theoretical framework. Family systems theory offers one such perspective.

FAMILY SYSTEMS PRINCIPLES

General systems theory has been an important perspective for the field of developmental psychopathology (Sameroff, 1995), but it has been pivotal to the understanding of families in general (e.g., Bateson, Jackson, Haley, & Weakland, 1956; Hoffman, 1981). As an open living system, the family is faced with challenges of maintaining order during times of change and finding a balance between environmental and individual needs. Little wonder that family life is often described as a juggling act, requiring that each piece is balanced with another while still in motion. Three major principles of systems theory are important for understanding family context in developmental psychopathology: organization, morphostasis, and morphogenesis (Steinglass, 1987).

Families Are Organized Systems

Organized systems share three characteristics: wholeness, boundaries, and hierarchical structure. Wholeness is summarized by the axiom, the whole is greater than the sum of its parts, which takes on additional meaning when relationships between parts are added (Sameroff, 1987). For developmental psychopathologists, this principle suggests that the functioning of a child at any point in time cannot be adequately explained by characteristics of the child or parents alone, but the transactional processes that arise when parents and children assemble as a family. Wholeness may be accessed through such concepts as family cohesion, flexibility, dominance, and control (Markman & Notarius, 1987). Wholeness and order are also related to symbolic aspects of the family to include their shared paradigms, beliefs, and sense of coherence (Reiss, 1981).

The second aspect of family organization is the concept of boundaries. Family therapists and systems theorists discuss how families are bounded in space and time (Minuchin, 1974; Steinglass, 1987). In families, marital, parental, and sibling relationships constitute subsystems that are distinct from, but also influence, each other. Families can be described in terms of the degree of permeability evident in their subsystem boundaries. Healthy families are characterized by semipermeable boundaries. Information exchange is neither so rigid as to prevent dialogue among the subsystems nor so fluid as to lose definitional boundaries. When boundaries become either too rigid or too permeable, the wholeness of the system is threatened and there may be a cost to individual functioning.

Boundaries are also created between the family and larger systems. The degree to which families are open to the outside social world and engage in neighborhood, school, and community activities reflect the relative permeability of family boundaries. The interactional aspects of boundaries include how information is exchanged among family members. The symbolic aspect of boundaries includes how representations of past generations influence current practices (Bowen, 1976).

Although the concept of boundaries is considered metaphorical, recent research suggests that clear parent–child boundaries are important to child adjustment. Sroufe, Jacobvitz, Mangelsdorf, DeAngelo, and Ward (1985) have demonstrated that when the boundaries between child and parent are diffuse there are effects on the child directly involved in the interaction, as well as other children in the family. When mothers behave in a seductive manner toward their sons, thus violating parent–child boundaries, they also tend to be more hostile with their daughters.

The third aspect of organization is hierarchical structure. families are composed of subsystems that are organized in a hierarchical fashion and influence each other. Hierarchies are characterized by a distribution of power such that healthy family systems include a strong parental subsystem that influences the child and sibling subsystems. The relative health of each subsystem may influence subsystems lower in the hierarchy. For example, high levels of hostility in the marital relationship may be related to harsh discipline in the parent–child relationship, suggesting a system that is organized around the regulation of negative affect. From an interactional perspective, hierarchical organization is evident when similar patterns of interaction are examined in different subsystems. From a symbolic perspective, hierarchies are implicit in examining the beliefs that individuals hold about family roles and relationships.

Morphostasis

Given that families are hierarchically arranged systems with distinct elements that form a whole, it is important to consider how the parts of the system are regulated. Families are considered patterned wholes that are regulated to establish stability and maintain balance in the face of disruptions. In order to maintain order, families create repetitive patterns of interaction and symbolic representations that allow for predictability and ease of communication. One of the ways in which families maintain wholeness is through homeostatic regulation. Families typically have a "set-point" of comfort; when an internal or external stressor threatens balance within the family, family members are mobilized to act in such a way that the system's balance is restored. Clinical examples of this process abound. For example, an anorexic's restricted eating behavior can be seen as a way to distract family members from ongoing marital conflict and refocus attention on the identified patient (Minuchin, Rosman, & Baker, 1978).

Morphogenesis

Although families are regulated to maintain balance, they are also developmental systems that undergo change. On a daily, or even moment-to-moment basis, families make minor adjustments in their response to change using preexisting patterns of behavior (Watzlawick, Weakland, & Fisch, 1974) but must also redefine roles throughout the family life cycle (McGoldrick, Heiman, & Carter, 1993). The developmentalist will recognize that these types of change are similar to Piaget's notions of assimilation and accommodation (Lyddon, 1990). Just as the child's development may be characterized by the interplay between assimilation and accommodation, families maintain patterns of organization until faced with a challenge that calls for reorganization. These challenges may be met through alterations in both behavior and beliefs.

FAMILY PRACTICES AND REPRESENTATIONS

A common thread running throughout many family theories is that behavior and beliefs are two equally important domains in understanding family effects on child adaptation. Whether referred to as family style and worldview (Minuchin, 1988), parenting practices and style (Darling & Steinberg, 1993), or the representing and practicing family (Reiss, 1989), these descriptions share the perspective that family life is organized around interactions and beliefs that extend across generations and are altered with time. Reiss's (1989) distinction between the practicing and representing family is especially pertinent to developmental psychopathology. Family practices stabilize and regulate family members through directly observed interaction patterns. The interaction patterns are repetitive and serve to provide a sense of family coherence and identity. Family interaction patterns may remain relatively stable until there is a perturbation, for example, an adolescent's striving for autonomy or a change in family composition such as death or divorce. Adolescents, for example, are undergoing rapid physical and cognitive changes that may alter their position in the family. As adolescents mature, family adaptation requires interaction patterns that once revolved around close monitoring of children's behavior to be altered to include adolescents as more independent members of the family (Grotevant & Cooper, 1985). Should the previous family patterns persist, adolescents may not develop the autonomy necessary to successfully transition into young adulthood (Allen & Hauser, 1996; Barber, 1996). Families reorganize their interaction patterns until stability is once again reached, thus reflecting the joint roles of morphostasis and morphogenesis.

Family beliefs, representations that guide behavior, are created by family practices. Representations are relatively stable but may be altered through developmental changes in the family and individual changes experienced in reconstructing past experiences, as in some forms of psychotherapy.

Family Practices

Family practices have direct and indirect effects on dyadic interaction, triadic interaction, and whole-family practices that influence child adaptation (Lewis & Feiring, 1992). Considered together, a complex weave of interactions between husbands and wives, mothers and fathers, and parents and children is found to be important to developmental psychopathology.

Marital Interaction and Child Adaptation

Resolving conflict is part of family life. Husbands and wives disagree with each other, parents and children do not always see eye to eye, and sibling relationships frequently involve rivalry. The characteristic ways in which families resolve conflict are an important part of the practicing family and influence child development (Downey & Coyne, 1990). Children are sensitive to anger and conflict even when adults other than their parents express it. In a programmatic series of studies, Cummings and colleagues have demonstrated that when exposed to adult anger, children are physiologically aroused (El-Sheikh, Cummings, & Goetsch, 1989), engage in verbal and physical aggression toward their peers (Cummings, 1987), and show signs of emotional distress (Ballard & Cummings, 1990). When adults engage in unresolved, angry interchanges, children are particularly vulnerable to feelings of anger, sadness, and fear (Cummings, Simpson, & Wilson, 1993). Unresolved marital conflict is more predictive of child functioning than marital satisfaction alone, suggesting that the specific ways that husbands and wives resolve conflict may be related to child social and emotional functioning (Cummings & Davies, 1994).

Easterbrooks, Cummings, and Emde (1994) have demonstrated that even during infancy, children are responsive to patterns of marital conflict resolution. Children visually track the back-and-forth exchanges between parents when they are engaged in a disagreement and may respond differentially to maritally satisfied versus dissatisfied fathers (Dickstein & Parke, 1988). Not all marital conflict is detrimental to children, however. Exposure to low levels of marital conflict may provide one avenue for children to learn how to solve interpersonal problems effectively. While Easterbrooks et al. (1994) demonstrated that constructive parental conflict can aid healthy development, an overwhelming number of studies show that destructive forms of parental conflict are related to adverse outcomes such as antisocial behavior (Patterson et al., 1989), maladaptive social skills (Grych & Fincham, 1990), and academic difficulties (Long, Forehand, Fauber, & Brody, 1987).

Particular patterns of marital interaction have been found to be related to couple distress, the likelihood of divorce, and child behavior problems. Couples whose conflict is typified by mutually hostile exchanges, or one partner making demands while the other withdraws from further discussion, are less satisfied in their marriages and are at greater risk for divorce (Christensen, 1988; Gottman, 1994). Katz and Gottman (1993) have proposed that children raised in families with high levels of marital conflict may become fearful that their parents are on the road to divorce and dissolution of important family relationships. Consequently, the child is motivated to reduce marital conflict by distracting the parents with acting-out behavior. The child's acting-out behavior serves to reunite the parents into the parental subsystem and decrease the conflict expressed in the marital subsystem. In this regard, the battling husband and wife are enlisted as cooperative mother and father, and the result is a temporary reduction in marital negative affect. Although there may be increased negative affect between parent and child, the system has retained its order and the subsystem of parent–child regulation temporarily overrides the marital subsystem and preserves the family as a whole (Fincham & Osborne, 1993).

Parent–Child Interaction as Mediator of Marital Conflict Effects

Interactions in one portion of the family will more than likely influence other interactions in the family. The cost to children can be quite high when there is disruption in the marital relationship, as it effects the parents' ability to engage in mutually pleasing interactions with their children. Marital difficulties are proposed to lead to inconsistent parenting and discipline, which in turn create situations conducive to child behavior problems (Fauber & Long, 1991; Kendziora & O'Leary, 1993). Externalizing problems in elementary-school-age boys have been found to be best predicted by a model of family stress (including marital satisfaction and divorce) mediated by negative maternal control and disciplinary interactions (Campbell et al., 1996). In some cases, there is a cascading effect, where specific aspects of marital conflict "spill over" into parent–child interactions. For example, Katz and Gottman (1995) reported that when husbands withdrew in angry conflicts with their wives, the wives (mothers) tended to be critical and intrusive with their children, which in turn was related to internalizing problems reported by teachers 3 years later.

Sibling Interactions

There has been increasing recognition that the sibling subsystem plays an important role in child outcome. Indeed, the birth of a sibling may set into motion a series of changes in family interaction patterns (Feiring, Lewis, & Jaskir, 1983; Lewis & Feiring, 1992). Much of this interest has been fueled by studies in behavioral genetics (Hetherington, Reiss, & Plomin, 1994). In terms of the practicing family, it has been documented that parents interact differentially with siblings (Plomin & Daniels, 1987) and that these patterns may have differential effects on child mental health (Dunn, Stocker, & Plomin, 1990). A recent report suggests that when mothers in maritally distressed households exert control over older siblings, there is increased negativity between siblings (Erel, Margolin, & John, 1998). The inclusion of siblings in the study of the family context can highlight how different subsystems influence each other and affect child mental health.

Triadic Interactions

Family systems theorists have long been interested in triadic interaction and its significance for psychopathology. Bowen (1976) proposed that a three-member system is inherently more stable than a two-member system, for should stability in the system be threatened by a disruptive interchange between two members, a third party can intervene to return the system to homeostasis. When a child is the third member in an exchange, maladaptive consequences are possible. Parents may attempt to draw the child into an argument by having the child side with one parent over the other, thus creating a parent–child coalition (Minuchin et al., 1978). Parents may also try to outdo each other in an attempt to win their child's affection, a process often reported in divorce cases. Or parents may avoid addressing the conflict altogether, directing their negative affect to an identified child, who serves as a scapegoat for family conflict. Families may use one or more forms of triadic interaction at different points: The youngest child serves as a scapegoat when an older child and parent have a disagreement; children enlist the support of one parent over another when attempting to gain approval for a desired activity; parents may dole out special favors to a child when trying to influence a spouse's decision. However, when the triadic boundaries become too rigid and scapegoating is a repetitive form of interaction, there is often a psychological cost to the child (Minuchin et al., 1978).

Although family triangles are rich in clinical reports, there is little direct empirical support documenting the form or effects of triadic interaction and child adjustment. An exception is the work conducted by Vuchinich and colleagues (Vuchinich, Emery, & Cassidy, 1988), in which family interactions were videotaped during dinner. Vuchinich and colleagues found that there was a tendency for a third party to intervene in approximately one-third of the recorded conflicts. Furthermore, alliances were identified in which it was more likely for mothers and fathers to side with each other than with a child. In a study of distressed and nondistressed families, Gilbert, Christensen, and Margolin (1984) found that marital alliances were weaker in distressed families, partially supporting Bowen's theory. These studies point to the importance of considering multiple family members as a part of the practicing family.

Family Rituals

Family rituals are one way to access whole-family practices that affect child mental health. Family rituals range from highly stylized religious observances, such as first communion, to less articulated daily interaction patterns such as dinnertime. Two dimensions have been identified as important in understanding family rituals: the degree to which roles and routines are an integral part of the ritual, and the degree to which the rituals include symbolic meaning and are an important part of family life (Fiese, 1995; Fiese & Kline, 1993). During the child-rearing years, creating and maintaining family rituals on a daily basis can be a central part of family life (Bennett, Wolin, & McAvity, 1988) and change over time (Fiese, Hooker, Kotary, & Schwagler, 1993). For example, families with preschool-age children established more dinnertime, weekend, and annual celebration rituals than families whose oldest child was an infant. Furthermore, families of preschool-age children reported more meaning associated with their rituals, including more frequent occurrence, a stronger attachment of affect and symbolic significance to family rituals, more deliberate planning around ritual events, and a stated commitment to continue the family rituals into the future, than families of infants.

Family rituals may also serve a protective function for families undergoing transitions or involved in high-risk child-raising environments such as parental alcoholism. When family gatherings are deliberately planned and made distinct from parental alcoholism, children tend to develop a stronger sense of self and are less likely to report problematic drinking patterns (Bennett, Wolin, Reiss, & Teitelbaum, 1987; Fiese, 1993). Family rituals may also preserve relationships during times of transition and protect couples from marital dissatisfaction during the early stages of parenthood. Couples who are able to practice meaningful rituals in the context of raising children are more satisfied in their marriages than couples who find their rituals hollow and lacking in meaning (Fiese et al., 1993).

Developmental Pathways and the Practicing Family

The practicing family is composed of several components that influence child adaptation. Healthy adjustment is associated with warm and consistent limit setting in parent–child interactions, resolved conflicts between husband and wife, clear boundaries and hierarchically organized relationships involving more than two members, and deliberate planning and meaningful interchanges when the family is gathered as a group. A disruption in any aspect of the practicing family may potentially affect the child. Disruptions in marital relationships have received the greatest attention in this regard. From a developmental psychopathology perspective, it is beneficial to consider that disruption in any one aspect of the practicing family may lead to maladaptive or adaptive consequences depending on the relative health and functioning of other aspects of the system. Several protective factors already have been identified when one aspect of the system is malfunctioning. Effective and sensitive mother–child interactions have been found to protect children from the harmful effects of marital conflict (Campbell et al., 1996), and meaningful family rituals have been found to protect offspring from the harmful effects of parental alcoholism (Bennett et al., 1987).

Family Representations

Family representations include working memories of relationships and family experiences that serve to regulate behavior. Just as the domain of family practices may be examined according to the relative influence of different subsystems, it is possible to consider the domain of family representations across different relationships and their relation to child adaptation. Here, we consider recollected interpretations of caregiving experiences, marital and sibling relationships, and whole family functioning as examples of the represented family.

Caregiving Representations

Recent work of attachment researchers has pointed to the relation between parents' working memories of caregiving experiences and current attachment relationships. In a meta-analytic review of the attachment representation literature, Van IJzendoorn and Bakermans-Kranenburg (1996) conclude that parents of disturbed children represent their own attachment experiences as more insecure than parents of nondisturbed children. A central component of the working models of attachment paradigm is the degree to which past events are reconstructed in a coherent fashion. It is not the details of the past that are as crucial to the formation of new attachment relationships (i.e., between parent and child) but the degree to which individuals are able to create a coherent, well-organized, and interpretable account of close relationships in the present. Regulation implicit in the narrative is aligned with regulation in dyadic family relationships. The interpretive component of working memories may also be important in the child's understanding of family relationships. Children who provide narrative representations of their mothers as positive and responsive are less likely to exhibit behavior problems (Oppenheim, Emde, & Warren, 1997). The effects of the child's representations on adaptation extend beyond the caregiving relationship and include the child's perception of his or her parent's marital relationship.

Just as the study of parent–child interaction patterns has focused primarily on mother–child exchanges, the study of caregiving representations has centered on maternal working memories. There are exceptions, however, (e.g., Steele, Steele, & Fonagy, 1996) that point to the importance of including the father's working models of relationships in predicting child attachment status. There may be differential effects of mothers' and fathers' attachment representations on child adaptation, with fathers' attachment relationships more closely aligned with success in peer relationships and mothers' attachment relationships linked to ego development (Van IJzendoorn, Bakermans-Kranenburg, Swart-Woudstra, Van Busschebach, & Lambermom, 1991). A more extensive study of representations throughout the family system is needed to more clearly assess the effects on child mental health.

Children's Perceptions of Marital Conflict

Children who create images of warm and responsive caregiving tend to consider themselves as worthy of love and affection, and develop a sense of confidence in relating to others. When children are exposed to marital conflict, feelings of anger, shame, and fear often evolve. Children may then create images of themselves as either potential mediators or provocateurs of the marital conflict. In this regard, children place blame on themselves that may then be integrated into a view of the self as unworthy of rewarding relationships, and feelings of shame and guilt predominate their self-perceptions (Grych & Fincham, 1993). Recent evidence suggests that adolescents exposed to marital hostility interpret parent–child relationships in a more negative and hostile manner than do children who have not been exposed to such conflict (Harold, Fincham, Osborne, & Conger, 1997). Thus, children exposed to marital conflict may perceive their relationship with their parents as threatened and insecure, expecting hostile exchanges with their parents (Cummings & Davies, 1994). Representational models created in the context of marital hostility and parent–child negative affect have been found to be related to both internalizing and externalizing behavior problems in both boys and girls (Grych & Fincham, 1990; Harold et al., 1997).

Perceptions of Sibling Relationships

Although raised in the same family, siblings perceive their relationships with their parents differently. The differential perception of family relationships by siblings has been found to be linked to patterns of fearfulness and may affect the choice of peer groups (Daniels, 1986). Thus, how the individual children perceive their relationship with siblings as well as their role in the family may influence choice of peer group, which in turn may affect mental health.

Perceptions of Triadic Relationships

In Minuchin's (1974) model of structural family relationships, children are proposed to be caught in the middle of triangulated exchanges among mother, father, and child. In addition to children "acting out" or altering interaction patterns in response to triangulation, there is recent evidence to suggest that children create representations of triadic interactions that may be related to child adjustment. Kerig (1995) reports that the majority of families in a normative sample described their own families as cohesive, representing triadic relationships as relatively well balanced and in harmony with each other. Families that perceived themselves as triangulated (i.e., with coalitions between mother and child, father and child, or child in the middle) reported lower levels of marital satisfaction, and children in triangulated families perceived their parents' quarrels as more intense, frequent, and unresolved than did children in cohesive families. Although not directly addressing the types of representations that are formed within different triadic settings, the findings suggest that children maintain representations of triadic relationships that can be reliably identified and are related to aspects of family functioning.

Family Stories and Representations of Family Relationships

Family stories deal with how the family makes sense of its world, expresses rules of interaction, and creates beliefs about relationships that have implications for mental health. When family members are called upon to recount an experience, they set an interpretive frame reflecting how individuals grapple with understanding events, how the family works together, and how the ascription of meaning is linked to beliefs about relationships in the family and social world. It is possible to consider family stories from a variety of perspectives, including their thematic content, the coherence of the narrative, and the ways in which relationships are depicted to reflect expectations in social settings.

Thematic Content of Family Stories. The formation of close personal relationships and striving for success are two central themes in adult and child development (Erikson, 1963; Gilligan, 1982; McAdams & de St. Aubin, 1992). How the family goes about imparting values of relationships and achievement is tempered by the family's developmental stage and personal values. Mothers and fathers tell stories with different themes to children at different developmental levels (Fiese, Hooker, Kotary, Schwagler, & Rimmer, 1995). Fathers tend to talk about their childhood experiences, with an emphasis on achievement themes; mothers tend to talk about childhood experiences that emphasize affiliation themes. Furthermore, parents of infants have been found to tell family stories with strong affiliation themes, whereas parents of preschool-age children tell family stories with achievement themes. Representations of family events may alter with the developmental demands of the family. Families with infants, focused on intense caregiving and nurturing demands, may impart images that revolve around close relationships with others. Families with preschool-age children, on the other hand, may be preparing their children for the role of achiever and student, and relay messages that emphasize the importance of persistence in the face of obstacles.

Narrative Coherence and Family Relationships. The degree to which parents present coherent images of family life may be another component to our understanding of representations of relationships. Just as coherence has been found to be a central feature in attachment relationships, it has also been found to be important in understanding the context of whole-family relationships. Coherence is defined as the degree to which narratives are internally consistent and well organized, and provide an understanding of multiple perspectives, with the expressed affect matching the content of the story (Fiese & Sameroff, 1999). The coherence of family narratives is related to the likelihood that couples will remain married (Wamboldt, 1999), maternal marital satisfaction (Fiese & Marjinsky, 1999), and it is distinguished among groups of parents who have undergone open or closed adoption (Grotevant, Fravel, Gorall, & Piper, 1999). The coherence of family narratives imparts to children that not only is the world an understandable place but also that there are ways to make sense of a variety of experiences. In the case of mothers with a psychiatric illness and current reports of depression, the child may be at risk because of the transmission of family messages that are inconsistent, poorly organized, and demonstrate a mismatch between affect and content (Dickstein, St. Andre, Sameroff, Seifer, & Schiller, 1999). A child presented with incoherent images may then create representations that are difficult to understand and provide poor models for behavior.

Relationship Depictions in Family Narratives. Another aspect of family stories with mental health significance is the degree to which relationships are described as trustworthy and reliable or whether the social world is considered a dangerous place. Narrative depictions of rewarding family relationships are related to marital satisfaction (Wamboldt, 1999), signs of mental health (Dickstein et al., 1999), and family interaction patterns (Fiese & Marjinsky, 1999). Just as the effects of marital conflict on child adaptation appear to be mediated by parent–child interaction patterns, the relation between family narratives and child adaptation appears to be mediated by family interaction and practices.

Integrating Family Practices and Representations

Externalizing Behavior Problems as an Example. Family practices and representations influence each other and can be considered part of the transactional process in developmental psychopathology (Fiese, 1997; Sameroff & Fiese, 2000). Transition points in family life have been identified as vulnerable periods for relationships and child adjustment (Cowan, 1991). Marital relationships, in particular, are vulnerable to feelings of decreased satisfaction following the birth of a child (Cowan et al., 1991), which in turn may affect other children in the family. Dissatisfied marital relationships are marked by representations of others as unreliable and unworthy of attention (Wamboldt, 1999). During family meals, couples in dissatisfied marriages may engage in less meaningful rituals, and family practices may be disrupted (Fiese et al., 1993). Within this context of disrupted family practices and marital conflict, the children

FAMILY REPRESENTATIONS

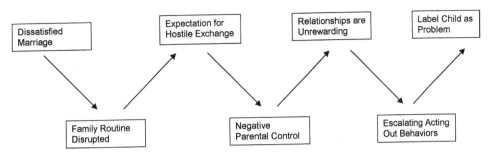

FAMILY PRACTICES

FIGURE 7.1. Transactions between family representations and practices predicting child outcome.

develop cognitive expectations for hostile exchanges (Cummings & Davies, 1994). When the family is gathered together as a group, negative affect marks the interactions and the child attempts to decrease marital conflict through acting-out behaviors (Katz & Gottman, 1993). These behaviors are integrated into the parents' representations of relationships as unrewarding and unfulfilling (Fiese & Marjinsky, 1999). The parents attempt to decrease the child's acting-out behaviors through increased control, which increases the likelihood the child will act out (Campbell et al., 1996). The child's escalating negative behavior invokes an image of the child as disruptive and eventually the label "problem behavior child" is assigned. The transactional process resulting in labeling the child as having externalizing problems is presented in Figure 7.1.

There is, however, an optimistic side to this somewhat daunting picture. At any point within the process, intervention could alter the child's developmental trajectory. For example, interventions aimed at creating new family rituals during times of transition may aid in stabilizing family practices (Imber-Black, Roberts, & Whiting, 1988); effective means of resolving marital conflict may alter how parents view each other and family relationships (Markman, Renick, Floyd, Stanley, & Clements, 1993); and training in effective limit setting may alter family practices and decrease negative affect (Patterson et al., 1989). Just as problems may develop in transactions between family practices and representations, effective forms of prevention and intervention may be implemented to decrease the likelihood that problems will arise.

DIAGNOSTIC CONCERNS

Our description of the family context in developmental psychopathology has focused on the effects of multiple relationships on child adaptation. Disruptions in marital, parent–child, and whole-family relationships are associated with markers of child mental health. The most widely used diagnostic system, DSM-IV (American Psychiatric Association, 1994), restricts identification of relationship problems to V. codes entitled "Other Conditions That May Be A Focus Of Clinical Attention." Within this category are codes identifying parent–child and sibling relational problems. These codes are primarily descriptive and are not considered reimbursable diagnoses. It is unclear whether extension of the DSM-IV would result in a useful diagnostic system for family psychologists as "the theoretical foundations for diagnosing individual psychopathology and relational disorders are markedly different and may not be compatible" (Kaslow, 1996, p. 13). There have been recent efforts, however, to place relationship functioning as central to understanding child adaptation. We highlight three of these systems to illustrate how the family context is reflected in diagnostic decisions.

Diagnostic Classification of Mental Health and Developmental Disorders in Infancy and Early Childhood (National Center for Clinical Infant Programs, 1994)

This diagnostic system places relationship functioning on the second axis of diagnoses. The authors of this system state, "When a disorder exists, it is *specific to a relationship*" (p. 46). A unique aspect of this system is the equal weight given to parent and child behaviors. Accurate diagnosis results from a careful examination of how parent and child behave within the context of the relationship; thus, the relationship (e.g., overinvolved, underinvolved, abusive), rather than the individual, is characterized. There are considerable strengths in this approach. However, relational diagnoses based on parent–child interaction do not take into account the effects of other relationships on the child (e.g., the marital relationship).

Relational Diagnosis and Dysfunctional Family Patterns (Kaslow, 1996)

In anticipation of a revision of the DSM and concern over the relative neglect of family issues in previous editions of the diagnostic manual, a multidisciplinary coalition on family diagnoses was formed (Kaslow, 1996). The efforts of this group have been collected in an edited volume, of which a portion is dedicated to child- and adolescent-focused diagnoses. The proposed diagnostic criteria include attention to whole-family variables such as family cohesion, conflict, and control (Kaslow, Deering, & Ash, 1996). Developmental trajectories are also described, and the manifestation of disruptive behaviors is recognized to alter with age (Alexander & Pugh, 1996). These promising efforts have yet to be employed on a large basis or be the subject of validity studies.

Global Assessment of Relationship Functioning (GARF, 1996)

The Committee on the Family of the Group for the Advancement of Psychiatry developed the GARF. Drawing on conceptual models of the family, three domains were identified as important in family functioning: joint problem solving, organization, and emotional climate. Preliminary reports suggest that the GARF may be used reliably and distinguishes among families according to measures of expressed emotion (Dausch, Miklowitz, & Richards, 1996). To date, reports on the GARF have not included the child as the index family member.

Although these relational approaches to diagnosis are an improvement over existing systems, there are still several limitations that may ultimately limit their influence on developmental psychopathology. The first limitation concerns developmental history. Diagnostic classification systems necessarily emphasize current functioning, but rarely view it as part of a transactional process involving the individual and his or her environment. Extensions to include family factors must also incorporate transitions and change as important aspects of the child's environment (Jensen & Hoagwood, 1997). A second limitation is the emphasis on family practices and exclusion of family representations as important to child adaptation. Family representations may serve as important markers of the family's meaning-making system that will influence not only child adaptation but also how the family interacts with other members of the social world, such as schools and the health care system. Integrative approaches to diagnosis must also consider the significance of meaning-making systems and how they guide behavior in close relationships (Jensen & Hoagwood, 1997; Lyons-Ruth, 1995).

CONCLUSIONS

Focusing attention on whole families, either as a clinician or researcher, can be an overwhelming experience. Educational and clinical traditions have been wedded to the notion that it is individuals who experience distress and effective remediation should be aimed at changing individuals. Although there have been repeated calls to expand the scope of developmental studies beyond the dyad (e.g., Feinman & Lewis, 1984), the family context remains an understudied area for developmental psychopathology. This may be due in part to a methodological heritage that has developed sophisticated technologies for the direct observation of dyads but falls short when attempting to observe the whole family. The problem extends beyond method, however, and may revolve around the expectation that a single theory can be applied to explain family effects on child mental health. It is likely that a more productive approach is to identify the multiple domains that constitute family effects and generate predictions within each domain. We have discussed family practices and representations as two such domains that may contribute to the relative health of different subsystems within the family. These domains extend across different subsystems of the family, are sensitive to developmental changes, and may influence one another in a transactional manner. We have not addressed how characteristics of the individual such as gender, personality, and temperament may also transact within these domains and should be included in future developmental psychopathology studies.

Although family effects may extend across multiple domains, they are accessible and crucial to understanding child mental health. By including the family context in the study of developmental psychopathology, it is possible to identify multiple pathways of adaptation and dysfunction. Therefore, the family context can offer an optimistic perspective suggesting several avenues for prevention and intervention. Families provide one context for healthy development and, in their complexity, may further our understanding of child adaptation.

ACKNOWLEDGMENT.   Preparation of this chapter was supported, in part, by a grant from the National Institute of Mental Health to the first author.

REFERENCES

Allen, J. P., & Hauser, S. T. (1996). Autonomy and relatedness in adolescent–family interactions as predictors of young adults' states of mind regarding attachment. *Development and Psychopathology, 8,* 793–809.

Allen, J. P., Hauser, S. T., O'Connor, T. G., Bell, K. L., & Eickholt, C. (1996). The connection of observed hostile family conflict to adolescents' developing autonomy and relatedness with parents. *Development and Psychopathology, 8,* 425–442.

Alexander, J. F., & Pugh, C. A. (1996). Oppositional behavior and conduct disorders in children and youth. In F. W. Kaslow (Ed.), *Handbook of relational diagnosis and dysfunctional family patterns* (pp. 210–224). New York: Wiley.

Amato, P. R. (1993). Children's adjustment to divorce: Theories, hypotheses, and empirical support. *Journal of Marriage and the Family, 55,* 23–38.

Amato, P. R., & Keith, B. (1991). Parental divorce and the well-being of children: A meta-analysis. *Psychological Bulletin, 110,* 26–46.

American Psychiatric Association. (1994). *Diagnostic and statistical manual of mental disorders* (4th ed.). Washington, DC: Author.

Ballard, M., & Cummings, E. M. (1990). Response to adults' angry behavior in children of alcoholic and non-alcoholic parents. *Journal of Genetic Psychology, 151,* 195–210.

Barber, B. K. (1996). Parental psychological control: Revisiting a neglected construct. *Child Development, 67,* 3296–3319.

Bateson, G., Jackson, D. D., Haley, J., & Weakland, J. H. (1956). Toward a theory of schizophrenia. *Behavioral Science, 1,* 251–264.

Belsky, J., Woodworth, S., & Crnic, K. (1996). Trouble in the second year: Three questions about family interaction. *Child Development, 67,* 556–578.

Bennett, L. A., Wolin, S. J., & McAvity, K. J. (1988). Family identity, ritual and myth: A cultural perspective on lifecycle transitions. In C. J. Falicov (Ed.), *Family transitions* (pp. 211–234). New York: Guilford Press.

Bennett, L. A., Wolin, S. J., Reiss, D., & Teitelbaum, M. A. (1987). Couples at risk for transmission of alcoholism: Protective influences. *Family Process, 26,* 111–129.

Block, J. H., Block, J., & Gjerde, P. F. (1986). The personality of children prior to divorce: A prospective study. *Child Development, 57,* 827–840.

Bowen, M. (1976). Theory in the practice of psychotherapy. In P. Guerin (Ed.), *Family therapy: Theory and practice* (pp. 42–90). New York: Gardner.

Bowlby, J. (1949). The study and reduction of group tension in the family. *Human Relations, 2,* 123–128.

Broderick, C. B., & Schrader, S. S. (1981). The history of professional marriage and family therapy. In A. S. Gurman & D. P. Kniskern (Eds.), *Handbook of family therapy* (pp. 5–35). New York: Brunner/Mazel.

Bronfenbrenner, U. (1977). Toward an experimental ecology of human development. *American Psychologist, 32,* 513–531.

Campbell, S. B. (1994). Hard-to-manage preschool boys: Externalizing behavior, social competence, and family context at two year follow-up. *Journal of Abnormal Child Psychology, 22,* 147–166.

Campbell, S. B., Pierce, E. W., Moore, G., Marakovitz, S., & Newby, K. (1996). Boys' externalizing problems at elementary school age: Pathways from early behavior problems, maternal control, and family stress. *Development and Psychopathology, 8,* 701–719.

Christensen, A. (1988). Dysfunctional interaction patterns in couples. In P. Noller & M. A. Fitzpatrick (Eds.), *Perspectives on marital interaction* (pp. 31–52). Avon, UK: Multilingual Matters.

Cowan, P. A. (1991). Individual and family life transitions: A proposal for a new definition. In P. A. Cowan & M. Hetherington (Eds.), *Family transitions* (pp. 3–30). Hillsdale, NJ: Erlbaum.

Cowan, P. A., Cohn, D., Cowan, C. P., & Pearson, J. (1996). Parents' attachment histories and children's externalizing and internalizing behaviors: Exploring family systems models of linkage. *Journal of Consulting and Clinical Psychology, 64,* 53–63.

Cowan, P. A., Cowan, C. P., Heming, G., & Miller, N. B. (1991). Becoming a family: Marriage, parenting, and child development. In P. A. Cowan & M. Hetherington (Eds.), *Family transitions* (pp. 79–109). Hillsdale, NJ: Erlbaum.

Crockenberg, S., Lyons-Ruth, K., & Dickstein, S. (1993). The family context of infant mental health: II. Infant development in multiple relationships. In C. H. Zeanah (Ed.), *Handbook of infant mental health* (pp. 38–55). New York: Guilford Press.

Crowell, J. A., & Feldman, S. S. (1988). Mothers' internal models of relationships and children's behavioral and developmental status: A study of mother–child interaction. *Child Development, 59,* 1273–1285.

Csikszentmihalyi, M., & Rochberg-Halton, E. (1981). *The meaning of things: Domestic symbols and the self.* Cambridge, UK: Cambridge University Press.

Cummings, E. M. (1987). Coping with background anger in early childhood. *Child Development, 58,* 976–984.

Cummings, E. M., & Davies, P. (1994). *Children and marital conflict.* New York: Guilford Press.

Cummings, E. M., Simpson, K. S., & Wilson, A. (1993). Children's response to interadult anger as a function of information about resolution. *Developmental Psychology, 29,* 978–985.

Daniels, D. (1986). Differential experiences of siblings in the same family as predictors of adolescent sibling personality differences. *Journal of Personality and Social Psychology, 51,* 239–246.

Darling, N., & Steinberg, L. (1993). Parenting style as context: An integrative model. *Psychological Bulletin, 113*, 487–496.

Dausch, B. M., Miklowitz, D. J., & Richards, J. A. (1996). Reliability and validity in a sample of families of bipolar patients. *Family Process, 35*, 175–190.

Dickstein, S., & Parke, R. (1988). Social referencing: A glance at fathers and marriage. *Child Development, 59*, 506–511.

Dickstein, S., St. Andre, M., Sameroff, A. J., Seifer, R., & Schiller, M. M. (1999). Maternal depression, family functioning, and child outcomes: A narrative assessment. In B. H. Fiese, A. J. Sameroff, H. D. Grotevant, F. Wamboldt, S. Dickstein, & D. L. Fravel (Eds.), The stories that families tell: Narrative coherence, narrative interaction, and relationship beliefs. *Monographs of the Society for Research in Child Development, 64*(2), 84–104.

Downey, G., & Coyne, J. C. (1990). Children of depressed parents: An integrative review. *Psychological Bulletin, 108*, 50–76.

Dunn, J., Stocker, C., & Plomin, R. (1990). Nonshared experiences within the family: Correlates of behavioral problems in middle childhood. *Development and Psychopathology, 2*, 113–126.

Easterbrooks, M. A., Cummings, E. M., & Emde, R. N. (1994). Young children's responses to constructive marital disputes. *Journal of Family Psychology, 8*, 160–169.

El-Sheikh, M., Cummings, E. M., & Goetsch, V. L. (1989). Coping with adults' angry behavior: Behavioral, physiological, and verbal response in preschoolers. *Developmental Psychology, 25*, 490–498.

Emde, R. N. (1994). Individuality, context, and the search for meaning. *Child Development, 65*, 719–737.

Erel, O., Margolin, G., & John, R. S. (1998). Observed sibling interaction: Links with the marital and the mother–child relationship. *Developmental Psychology, 34*, 288–298.

Erikson, E. H. (1963). *Childhood and society.* New York: Norton.

Fauber, R. L., & Long, N. (1991). Children in context: The role of the family in child psychotherapy. *Journal of Consulting and Clinical Psychology, 59*, 813–820.

Feinman, S., & Lewis, M. (1984). Is there social life beyond the dyad? In M. Lewis (Ed.), *Beyond the dyad: The genesis of behavior series* (pp. 13–41). New York: Plenum Press.

Feiring, C., Lewis, M., & Jaskir, J. (1983). Birth of a sibling: Effect on mother–first born child interaction. *Developmental and Behavioral Pediatrics, 4*, 190–195.

Field, T. M. (1987). Affective and interactive disturbances in infants. In J. Osofosky (Ed.), *Handbook of infant development* (2nd ed., pp. 972–1005). New York: Wiley.

Fiese, B. H. (1993). Family rituals in alcoholic and nonalcoholic households: Relations to adolescent health symptomatology and problem drinking. *Family Relations, 42*, 187–192.

Fiese, B. H. (1995). Family rituals. In D. Levinson (Ed.), *Encyclopedia of marriage and the family* (pp. 275–278). New York: Macmillan.

Fiese, B. H. (1997). Family context in pediatric psychology from a transactional perspective: Family rituals and stores as examples. *Journal of Pediatric Psychology, 22*, 183–196.

Fiese, B. H., Hooker, K. A, Kotary, L., & Schwagler, J. (1993). Family rituals in the early stages of parenthood. *Journal of Marriage and the Family, 55*, 633–642.

Fiese, B. H., Hooker, K. A., Kotary, L., Schwagler, J., & Rimmer, M. (1995). Family stories in the early stages of parenthood. *Journal of Marriage and the Family, 57*, 763–770.

Fiese, B. H., & Kline, C. A. (1993). Development of the Family Ritual Questionnaire: Initial reliability and validity studies. *Journal of Family Psychology, 6*, 290–299.

Fiese, B. H., & Marjinsky, K. A. T. (1999). Dinnertime stories: Connecting family practices with relationship beliefs and child adjustment. In B. H. Fiese, A. J. Sameroff, H. D. Grotevant, F. Wamboldt, S. Dickstein, & D. L. Fravel (Eds.), The stories that families tell: Narrative coherence, narrative interaction, and relationship beliefs. *Monographs of the Society for Research in Child Development, 64*(2), 52–68.

Fiese, B. H., & Sameroff, A. J. (1999). The family narrative consortium: A multidimensional approach to narratives. In B. H. Fiese, A. J. Sameroff, H. D. Grotevant, F. Wamboldt, S. Dickstein, & D. L. Fravel (Eds.), The stories that families tell: Narrative coherence, narrative interaction, and relationship beliefs. *Monographs of the Society for Research in Child Development, 64*(2), 1–36.

Fincham, F., & Osborne, L. (1993). Marital conflict and children: Retrospect and prospect. *Clinical Psychology Review, 13*, 75–88.

Gilbert, R., Christensen, A., & Margolin, G. (1984). Patterns of alliances in nondistressed and multiproblem families. *Family Process, 23*, 75–87.

Gilligan, C. (1982). *In a different voice: Psychological theory and women's development.* Cambridge, MA: Harvard University Press.

Gottman, J. M. (1994). *What predicts divorce?* Hillsdale, NJ: Erlbaum.

Grolinck, W. S., & Ryan, R. M. (1989). Parent styles associated with children's self-regulation and competence in school. *Journal of Educational Psychology, 81,* 143–154.

Grotevant, H. D., & Cooper, C. R. (1985). Patterns of interaction in family relationships and the development of identity exploration in adolescence. *Child Development, 56,* 415–428.

Grotevant, H. D., Fravel, D. L., Gorall, D., & Piper, J. (1999). Narratives of adoptive parents: Perspectives from individual and couple interviews. In B. H. Fiese, A. J. Sameroff, H. D. Grotevant, F. Wamboldt, S. Dickstein, & D. L. Fravel (Eds.), The stories that families tell: Narrative coherence, narrative interaction, and relationship beliefs. *Monographs of the Society for Research in Child Development, 64*(2), 69–83.

Grych, J. H., & Fincham, F. D. (1990). Marital conflict and children's adjustment: A cognitive-contextual framework. *Psychological Bulletin, 108,* 267–290.

Grych, J. H., & Fincham, F. D. (1993). Children's appraisals of marital conflict: Initial investigations of the cognitive-contextual framework. *Child Development, 64,* 215–230.

Harold, G. T., Fincham, F. D., Osborne, L. N., & Conger, R. D. (1997). Mom and Dad are at it again: Adolescent perceptions of marital conflict and adolescent psychological distress. *Developmental Psychology, 33,* 333–350.

Hetherington, E. M. (1982). Effects of fathers' absence on personality development in adolescent daughters. *Developmental Psychology, 7,* 313–326.

Hetherington, E. M., Cox, M., & Cox, R. (1982). Effects of divorce on parents and children. In M. Lamb (Ed.), *Nontraditional families* (pp. 233–288). Hillsdale, NJ: Erlbaum.

Hetherington, E. M., Reiss, D., & Plomin, R. (1994). *Separate social worlds of siblings: Impact of the nonshared environment on development.* Hillsdale, NJ: Erlbaum.

Hetherington, E. M., Stanley-Hagan, M., & Anderson, E. R. (1989). Marital transitions: A child's perspective. *American Psychologist, 44,* 303–312.

Hoffman, L. (1981). *Foundations of family therapy.* New York: Basic Books.

Hooker, K., Fiese, B. H., Jenkins, L., Morfei, M. Z., & Schwagler, J. (1996). Possible selves among parents of infants and preschoolers. *Developmental Psychology, 32,* 542–550.

Imber-Black, E., Roberts, J., & Whiting, R. (1988). *Rituals in families and family therapy.* New York: Norton.

Jensen, P. S., & Hoagwood, K. (1997). The book of names: DSM-IV in context. *Development and Psychopathology, 9,* 231–249.

Kaslow, F. W. (1996). History, rationale, and philosophic overview of issues and assumptions. In F. W. Kaslow (Ed.), *Handbook of relational diagnosis and dysfunctional family patterns* (pp. 3–18). New York: Wiley.

Kaslow, F. W., Deering, C. G., & Ash, P. (1996). Relational diagnosis of child and adolescent depression. In F. W. Kaslow (Ed.), *Handbook of relational diagnosis and dysfunctional family patterns* (pp. 171–185). New York: Wiley.

Katz, L. F., & Gottman, J. M. (1993). Patterns of marital conflict predict children's internalizing and externalizing behaviors. *Developmental Psychology, 29,* 940–950.

Katz, L. F., & Gottman, J. M. (1995). Marital interaction and child outcomes: A longitudinal study of mediating and moderating processes. In D. Cicchetti & S. L. Toth (Eds.), *Emotion, cognition, and representation: Rochester Symposium on Developmental Psychopathology* (pp. 301–342). Rochester, NY: University of Rochester Press.

Kendziora, K. T., & O'Leary, S. G. (1993). Dysfunctional parenting as a focus for prevention and treatment of child behavioral problems. *Advances in Child Clinical Psychology, 15,* 175–206.

Kerig, P. K. (1995). Triangles in the family circle: Effects of family structure on marriage, parenting, and child adjustment. *Journal of Family Psychology, 9,* 28–43.

Lewis, M. (1987). Social development in infancy and early childhood. In J. Osofsky (Ed.), *Handbook of infant development* (pp. 419–493). New York: Wiley.

Lewis, M., & Feiring, C. (1992). Direct and indirect effects and family interaction. In S. Feinman (Ed.), *Social referencing and the social construction of reality in infancy* (pp. 297–321). New York: Plenum Press.

Lidz, T., Cornelison, A., Fleck, S., & Terry, D. (1957). The intrafamilial environment of schizophrenic patients: II. Marital schism and marital skew. *American Journal of Psychiatry, 114,* 241–248.

Long, N., Forehand, R., Fauber, R., & Brody, G. H. (1987). Self-perceived and independently observed competence of young adolescents as a function of parental marital conflict and recent divorce. *Journal of Abnormal Child Psychology, 15,* 15–27.

Lyddon, W. J. (1990). First- and second-order change: Implications for rationalist and constructivist cognitive therapies. *Journal of Counseling and Development, 69,* 122–127.

Lyons-Ruth, K. (1995). Broadening our conceptual frameworks: Can we reintroduce relational strategies and implicit representational systems to the study of psychopathology? *Developmental Psychology, 31,* 432–436.

Maccoby, E. E., & Martin, J. A. (1983). Socialization in the context of the family: Parent–child interaction. In P. M. Mussen (Series Ed.) & E. M. Hetherington (Vol. Ed.), *Handbook of child psychology: Vol. 4. Socialization, personality, and social development* (4th ed., pp. 1–101). New York: Wiley.

Markman, H. J., & Notarious, C. I. (1987). Coding marital and family interaction: Current status. In T. Jacob (Ed.), *Family interaction and psychopathology* (pp. 329–390). New York: Plenum Press.

Markman, H. J., Renick, M. J., Floyd, F. J., Stanley, S. M., & Clements, M. (1993). Preventing marital distress through communication and conflict management training: A 4- and 5-year follow-up. *Journal of Consulting and Clinical Psychology, 61,* 70–77.

McAdams, D. P., & de St. Aubin, E. (1992). A theory of generativity and its assessment through self-report, behavioral acts, and narrative themes in autobiography. *Journal of Personality and Social Psychology, 62,* 1003–1015.

McGoldrick, M., Heiman, M., & Carter, B. (1993). The changing family life cycle: A perspective on normalcy. In F. Walsh (Ed.), *Normal family processes* (2nd ed., pp. 405–443). New York: Guilford Press.

Minuchin, P. (1988). Relationships within the family: A systems perspective on development. In R. A. Hinde & J. Stevenson-Hinde (Eds.), *Relationships within families* (pp. 7–26). Oxford, UK: Clarendon Press.

Minuchin, S. (1974). *Families and family therapy.* Cambridge, MA: Harvard University Press.

Minuchin, S., Rosman, B., & Baker, L. (1978). *Psychosomatic families.* Cambridge, MA: Harvard University Press.

National Center for Clinical Infant Programs. (1994). *Diagnostic classification of mental health and developmental disorders of infancy and early childhood.* Arlington, VA: Zero to Three.

Oppenheim, D., Emde, R. N., & Warren, S. (1997). Children's narrative representations of mothers: Their development and associations with child and mother adaptation. *Child Development, 68,* 127–138.

Parke, R. D. (1981). *Fathers.* Cambridge, MA: Cambridge University Press.

Patterson, G. R., DeBaryshe, B. D., & Ramsey, E. (1989). A developmental perspective on antisocial behavior. *American Psychologist, 44,* 329–335.

Phares, V., & Compas, B. E. (1992). The role of fathers in child and adolescent psychopathology: Make room for daddy. *Psychological Bulletin, 111,* 387–412.

Plomin, R., & Daniels, D. (1987). Why are children in the same family so different from one another? *Behavioral and Brain Sciences, 10,* 1–16.

Reiss, D. (1981). *The family's construction of reality.* Cambridge, MA: Harvard University Press.

Reiss, D. (1989). The practicing and representing family. In A. J. Sameroff & R. Emde (Eds.), *Relationship disturbances in early childhood* (pp. 191–220). New York: Basic Books.

Sameroff, A. J. (1987). The social context of development. In N. Eisenberg (Ed.), *Contemporary topics in developmental psychology* (pp. 273–291). New York: Wiley.

Sameroff, A. J. (1995). General systems theories and developmental psychopathology. In D. Cicchetti & D. Cohen (Eds.), *Developmental psychopathology* (Vol. 1, pp. 659–695). New York: Wiley.

Sameroff, A. (1997, April). *Developmental contributions to the study of psychopathology.* Master lecture presented at the biennial meeting of the Society for Research in Child Development, Washington, DC.

Sameroff, A. J., & Fiese, B. H. (2000). Transactional regulation and early intervention. In S. J. Meisels & J. P. Shonkoff (Eds.), *Handbook of early childhood intervention* (2nd ed., pp. 119–149). New York: Cambridge University Press.

Sroufe, L. A. (1983). Infant–caregiver attachment and patterns of adaptation in preschool: The roots of maladaptation and competence. In M. Perlmutter (Ed.), *Minnesota Symposia in Child Psychology, 16,* 41–81. Hillsdale, NJ: Erlbaum.

Sroufe, L. A., Jacobvitz, D., Mangelsdorf, S., DeAngelo, E., & Ward, M. J. (1985). Generational boundary dissolution between mothers and their preschool children: A relationship systems approach. *Child Development, 56,* 317–325.

Steele, H., Steele, M., & Fonagy, P. (1996). Associations among attachment classifications of mothers, fathers, and their infants. *Child Development, 67,* 541–555.

Steinglass, P. (1987). A systems view of family interaction and psychopathology. In T. Jacob (Ed.), *Family interaction and psychopathology* (pp. 25–66). New York: Plenum Press.

Van IJzendoorn, M. H., & Bakermans-Kranenburg, M. J. (1996). Attachment representations in mothers, fathers, adolescents, and clinical groups: A meta-analytic search for normative data. *Journal of Consulting and Clinical Psychology, 64,* 8–21.

Van IJzendoorn, M. H., Bakermans-Kranenburg, M. J., Swart-Woudstra, M. J., Van Busschebach, A. M., & Lambermom, W. E. (1991). Parental attachment and children's socioemotional development: Some findings on the validity of the Adult Attachment Interview in the Netherlands. *International Journal of Behavioral Development, 14,* 375–394.

Vogel, E. F., & Bell, N. W. (1960). The emotionally disturbed child as the family scapegoat. In N. W. Bell & E. F. Vogel (Eds.), *The family* (pp. 382–397). Glencoe, IL: Free Press.

Vuchinich, S., Emery, R. E., & Cassidy, J. (1988). Family members as third parties in dyadic family conflict: Strategies, alliances, and outcomes. *Child Development, 59,* 1293–1302.

Wagner, B. M., & Reiss, D. (1995). Family systems and developmental psychopathology: Courtship, marriage or divorce? In D. Cicchetti & D. J. Cohen (Eds.), *Developmental psychopathology: Vol. 1. Theory and methods* (pp. 696–730). New York: Wiley.

Wallerstein, J. S., & Blakeslee, S. (1989). *Second chances: Men, women, and children a decade after divorce.* New York: Ticknor & Fields.

Wamboldt, F. S. (1999). Co-constructing a marriage: Analyses of young couples' relationship narratives. In B. H. Fiese, A. J. Sameroff, H. D. Grotevant, F. Wamboldt, S. Dickstein, & D. L. Fravel (Eds.), The stories that families tell: Narrative coherence, narrative interaction, and relationship beliefs. *Monographs of the Society for Research in Child Development, 64*(2), 37–51.

Watzlawick, P., Weakland, J., & Fisch, R. (1974). *Change: Principles of problem formation and problem resolution.* New York: Norton.

8

Schooling and Mental Health

Robert W. Roeser and Jacquelynne S. Eccles

Schools hold a central place in the "developmental agenda" set forth for children and adolescents throughout the world (Rogoff, 1990; Sameroff, 1987).[1] Children's experiences in school have the capacity to promote developmental competencies associated with learning and achievement motivation, emotional functioning, and social relationships, and in some instances can potentiate difficulties in these aspects of functioning. In this chapter, we focus on the relation between children's academic and emotional functioning, and on how school, as a central context of development, can shape both academic and mental health outcomes in children. The chapter is comprised of three main sections. First, we discuss the relevance of schooling to those interested in development, mental health, and psychopathology. Second, we briefly discuss linkages between children's academic and emotional functioning. Third, we provide a description of the interpersonal, instructional, and organizational processes through which schools can influence the developmental course of children's achievement-related behaviors, academic motivation, and their mental health.

STUDYING SCHOOLING, DEVELOPMENT, AND MENTAL HEALTH

The development of an interdisciplinary approach to the study of atypical and normative child development in the context of school could make an important contribution to educational, developmental, and clinical theory and practice. The lines of inquiry we envision at the center of such an interdisciplinary approach include research on (a) the interdependent, individual-level processes that underlie academic success, difficulty, or disability at different times in development; and (b) the impact of different educational settings on the academic–

---

[1]Children and adolescents are henceforth referred to as children for reasons of simplicity.

Robert W. Roeser • Department of Education, Stanford University, Stanford, California 94305-3096.   **Jacquelynne S. Eccles** • Achievement Research, Institute for Social Research, University of Michigan, Ann Arbor, Michigan 48106-1248.
Handbook of Developmental Psychopathology, Second Edition, edited by Arnold J. Sameroff, Michael Lewis, and Suzanne M. Miller. Kluwer Academic / Plenum Publishers, New York, 2000.

intellectual and social–emotional development of diverse populations of children. Several practical concerns highlight the need to develop these lines of inquiry, including the prevalence of adjustment problems among school-age children, the impact of student problems on teachers, and the need for more effective, sustainable school-based programs that address student and teacher needs related to mental health issues.

Prevalence of Problems among School-Age Children

Many children attending schools in the United States today have significant academic difficulties, emotional/behavioral difficulties, or most likely both (Dryfoos, 1994; Knitzer, Steinberg, & Fleisch, 1991; Weist, 1997). According to current epidemiological estimates, between 12% and 30% of school-age children experience moderate to serious social–emotional difficulties that can interfere with daily functioning in and outside of school (Institute of Medicine, 1994; Verhulst & Koot, 1992; Weist, 1997). Additionally, many of the children who require services for mental health difficulties will never receive them either within schools or in service provision centers outside the schools (Knitzer et al., 1991; Tuma, 1989; Weist, 1997). The near-term educational costs of social–emotional difficulties in children are great: Kessler, Foster, Saunders, and Stang (1995) estimate that early-onset psychiatric disorders (especially conduct disorders in males and anxiety disorders in females) are related to truncated educational attainments in about 7.2 million Americans.

Equally important, poor motivation and academic failure are problems that continue to plague large numbers of children in U.S. primary and secondary schools. It is estimated that approximately 25% of all 10- to 17-year-olds in the United States are behind their "modal grade" in school (Dryfoos, 1990), and up to 20% of all students are retained a grade at least once in their academic careers (see Durlak, 1995). Research has also documented declines in children's achievement motivation as they progress from elementary into middle and high school (Eccles, Midgley, & Adler, 1984; Eccles, Wigfield, & Schiefele, 1998). The near-term emotional and behavioral costs of these educational problems include an increased likelihood of drug use and abuse, engagement in delinquent activities, teenage pregnancy, and dropping out of school during late adolescence (Cairns, Cairns, & Neckerman, 1989; Dryfoos, 1990; Fine, 1991).

Research that focuses on the developmental course of co-occurring mental health and academic problems, and the processes that underlie them, may inform the next generation of school-based reforms that aim to enhance students' readiness to learn and remove social–emotional barriers to learning through systems-level reforms (Adelman & Taylor, 1998). Designing a new generation of programs that address co-occurring problems in school-age children is essential given that the long-term costs of such problems include personal suffering, unemployment, and poverty, and social costs such as lost productivity and increased burdens on the criminal justice, social welfare, and health care systems (Cowen, 1991; Carnegie Council on Adolescent Development, 1995).

Impact of Student Problems on Teachers

Untreated academic and social–emotional problems in children undermine not only student learning but also teachers' capacity to teach (Adelman & Taylor, 1998). Roeser and Midgley (1997) found that approximately two-thirds of a sample of elementary- and middle-school teachers in Michigan reported feeling "somewhat to very overwhelmed" by the kinds of emotional and behavioral difficulties some of their students presented in class. Analysis of a subsample of teachers and children revealed that the teachers who felt the most overwhelmed did in fact teach in classrooms where children reported the poorest academic motivation and the highest levels of emotional distress. In addition, teachers in these classrooms nominated approximately 13% of their students as showing problems significant enough to warrant mental health services (a figure close to national estimates; Institute of Medicine, 1994). Given the lack of mental health services in most schools, students with untreated problems present a daily challenge to many teachers. Providing clinical insights and supports to teachers and educational insights and supports to clinicians in schools that are derived from interdisciplinary scholarship may ultimately ease the burdens felt by the many teachers and administrators who serve vulnerable children (Close-Conoley & Conoley, 1991).

Enhancing Effectiveness of School-Based Mental Health Programs

Finally, although schools have long been recognized as efficient and cost-effective sites for efforts to promote developmental competence and for identifying and redressing developmental difficulties, school-based programs often prove difficult to implement and sustain (Cowen, 1980, 1991; Cowen, Gardner, & Zax, 1967; Dryfoos, 1994; Durlak, 1995; U.S. Department of Education, 1995). Interdisciplinary scholarship may lead to new insights into how mental health programs can be integrated into the fabric of everyday life in classrooms and school, and thereby, enhance the school ownership and effectiveness of such programs (Meyers, 1989).

The needs of vulnerable children, the need to assist teachers and other school personnel serve such children, and the larger need to create long-lasting programs in the schools that address children's and teachers' needs all underscore the importance of a more integrated study of educational and mental health issues. For the remainder of this chapter, we describe two issues that relate to both education and mental health concerns. First, we describe person-level research on the connection between achievement behavior and emotional distress, the cognitive processes that underlie co-occurring academic and emotional problems in normative children, and how some children who experience elevated levels of emotional distress can nonetheless maintain good grades and demonstrate positive conduct in school (Roeser, Eccles, & Strobel, 1998). Second, we describe context-level research on general school influences on child development. In this section, we focus on how particular school-contextual processes can affect students' mental health. We conclude with our thoughts on future directions for research on schooling and mental health issues.

THE RELATION OF ACADEMIC FUNCTIONING AND MENTAL HEALTH: INDIVIDUAL-LEVEL PROCESSES

In order to understand connections between academic and mental health outcomes, it is important to differentiate between two different conceptualizations of academic functioning: one quantitative and the other qualitative (Ames, 1987; see also Kellam, Rebok, Mayer, Ialongo, & Kalodner, 1994). Quantitative conceptualizations of school functioning are centered around notions of *what* students *do* in academic settings. A focus on quantitative behaviors, ones that can be judged by observers of the child such as teachers, parents, or peers, is central to this conceptualization. Behaviors such as performance on classroom and standardized assessments, effort investment and time on task, choice of challenging work, and positive conduct in school settings are viewed as quantitative indicators of functioning. The more children manifest such behaviors, the more academically competent they are thought to be (e.g., Masten et al., 1995).

Researchers who study children's achievement motivation emphasize the importance of considering not only the quantitative indicators of what children *do* in school, but also *qualitative* indicators that assess *why* they do what they do. Such a distinction affords, for instance, an opportunity to differentiate between the high achiever motivated by anxiety and perfectionistic tendencies, and the high achiever motivated by a love of learning. Process measures such as children's beliefs about the causes of academic success or failure, their goals, their beliefs about their academic competence and the value of school, and their use of particular learning and metacognitive strategies are viewed as qualitative indicators of functioning (see Ames, 1987; Eccles et al., 1998). A qualitative perspective focuses attention on underlying processes as well as manifest behavior, and is in keeping with the focus of developmental psychopathologists on the overall organization of behavior.

Manifest Academic Problems and Internalized Distress

Children who report frequent feelings of internalized distress show diminished academic functioning in terms of (quantitative) achievement-related behaviors. Symptoms of depression are associated with lower teacher-rated grades and standardized test scores, challenge avoidance and lack of persistence in the face of academic difficulties, and a lack of classroom participation among both children and adolescents (Blechman, McEnroe, Carella, & Audette, 1986; Dweck & Wortman, 1982; Kellam et al., 1994; Kovacs, 1992; Nolen-Hoeksema, Girgus, & Seligman, 1986). Symptoms of test anxiety are also associated with lower teacher-rated grades and standardized test scores, with these negative associations growing stronger with age (for reviews, see Dweck & Wortman, 1982; Hill & Wigfield, 1984; Wigfield & Eccles, 1989). Finally, although discrepancies exist in the literature (see Parker & Asher, 1987), there is some indication that children who manifest high levels of internalized distress and concomitant poor peer relations during the elementary school years also show academic difficulties such as lower academic grades, lower standardized test scores, and a greater likelihood of dropping out during high school (Ollendick, Greene, Weist, & Oswald, 1990).

Manifest Academic Problems and Externalized Distress

Children with externalized distress in the form of conduct problems, attention problems, or both, also show poorer behavioral functioning in school. Externalizing difficulties in children are associated with poorer teacher-rated grades and standardized test scores, more time off-task in the classroom, and more behavioral problems within and outside class at school (Astor, 1998; Barkley, 1998; Dishion, French, & Patterson, 1995; Hinshaw, 1992; Ollendick, Weist, Borden, & Greene, 1992; Parker & Asher, 1987; Roeser, Eccles, & Strobel, 1998). Aggressive children are also more likely to experience social difficulties at school, such as rejection by peers and disfavor on the part of teachers (Parker & Asher, 1987; Wentzel & Asher, 1995), and there is strong evidence of long-term academic difficulties such as poor achievement, poor attendance, and school dropout among children who manifest high levels of externalized distress earlier in development (Cairns et al., 1989; for review, see Parker & Asher, 1987).

In summary, there is evidence that emotional distress and academic problems often co-occur among what is likely a small (e.g., 12% of school-aged children) but socially significant minority of school-age children. Although it is not yet clear when and how co-occurring problems in the intellectual and social–emotional domains of functioning emerge prior to school entry, and though issues of causal direction in the link between intellectual and social–emotional difficulties continue to be debated (e.g., Hinshaw, 1992), co-occurring problems do become more evident as vulnerable children move through school. Thus, the next section focuses attention on some of the cognitive processes that serve to maintain co-occurring academic and emotional–behavioral difficulties, whatever their origins, during the elementary and secondary school years.

Qualitative Processes Linking Academic Problems and Emotional Distress

Research on achievement motivation and child mental health have illuminated several psychological processes that explain, in part, why academic and emotional–behavioral problems co-occur in some children, and why such problems are mutually reinforcing over time (Eccles, Wigfield, & Schiefele, 1998; Kendall & Dobson, 1993; Weiner, 1986). Some of these psychological processes are depicted in Figure 8.1.

Academic Problems Lead to Distress

In one pathway, certain cognitive processes translate academic problems into subsequent emotional distress. One such process involves the manner in which children cognitively

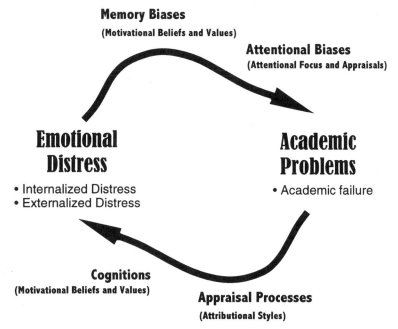

FIGURE 8.1. Psychological processes linking academic problems and emotional distress.

appraise their academic difficulties, with specific kinds of attributions for difficulty leading directly to feelings of internalized or externalized distress (Ames & Archer, 1988; Weiner, 1994). Children who do poorly in school, and who attribute such difficulties to a fixed sense of personal incompetence, generate feelings of shame, self-doubt, low esteem, and alienation from learning (e.g., internalized distress, see Dweck & Wortman, 1982). Alternatively, children who attribute academic problems to the influence of hostile or unsupportive people generate feelings of anger, academic alienation, and hostility toward others (see Connell & Wellborn, 1991; Roeser, Eccles, & Strobel, 1998; Weiner, 1994).

Children's appraisals of academic difficulty can also contribute indirectly to their mental health through the impact of such appraisals on their developing self-perceptions of academic competence, academic value, and beliefs about the relative supportiveness of others in learning situations. Competence beliefs, values, and feelings of support are associated with feelings of esteem, interest, and belonging, whereas feelings of incompetence, low value, and low support are associated with feelings of shame and doubt, disinterest and boredom, and isolation or victimization (Ames, 1992; Eccles et al., 1998; Roeser, Eccles, & Strobel, 1998).

Distress Leads to Academic Problems

In a second pathway, emotional distress influences cognitive processes, which in turn lead to subsequent academic problems. As Lazarus (1991) reminded us, emotion is not only an outcome of cognitive processes, but it also shapes them. Thus, children who experience predominant negatively emotions sometimes show mood-congruent biases of memory and attention (e.g., Gotlib & MacLeod, 1997) that can affect academic functioning. For instance, feelings of distress can activate negative academic motivational beliefs in memory during learning activities. For sad or anxious students, this biasing may be reflected in pervasive worries about incompetence in learning situations, whereas angry students may perseverate on presumed hostile intentions of others (Cole, 1991; Crick & Dodge, 1994; Dweck & Wortman, 1982; Gotlib & MacLeod, 1997). Negative, mood-induced biases of this sort can divert the investment of psychological resources into self-protective goals and coping efforts rather than into academic mastery goals and learning strategies (Boekaerts, 1993). Reduced attentional, cognitive, and emotional investments in learning can precipitate subsequent academic problems.

A second, related process by which negative mood can influence academic functioning involves the biasing effect of mood on attention. Distress-induced attentional biases operate to filter out information that is at odds with any particular, prevailing negative emotional state (Segal & Cloitre, 1993). Thus, children experiencing high levels of either internalized or externalized distress in academic settings may discount positive experiences (e.g., moments of academic success or support by others), and focus instead on mood-consistent experiences (e.g., difficulties with learning and garnering social support), thereby maintaining the original negative emotional state.

The reciprocal nature of the processes in Figure 8.1 helps to explain why many children with academic difficulties also show emotional difficulties, and vice versa. In the next section, we describe two maladaptive patterns of in-school functioning, one involving internalized and one involving externalized forms of distress. In addition, because the cognitive processes presented in Figure 8.1 not only link academic problems with particular forms of distress, but also positive academic outcomes with positive mental health, we describe an optimal pattern of in-school functioning that co-occurs with feelings of wellness and enthusiasm.

Academic Internalizing Pattern

One pattern of co-occurring academic and emotional problems that can arise in educational settings involve children who show academic difficulty joined with internalized symptoms of emotional distress. Studies have shown that academic difficulty can cause subsequent internalized distress (Dweck & Leggett, 1988; Weiner, 1986); and internalized distress can cause subsequent academic difficulties (Nolen-Hoeksema et al., 1986). In Table 8.1, we have summarized some of the academic behaviors, beliefs, emotions, and self-regulatory processes that characterize such children.

Achievement-related behavioral characteristics of such children include avoidance of academic challenges, failure to persist on difficult tasks, withdrawal from classroom activities, and poor achievement. These are all signs of learned helplessness, here manifest in educational settings; thus, such children have been labeled as "helpless" by those who initially described such a subgroup (see Dweck & Elliott, 1983; Nolen-Hoeksema et al., 1986; Seligman et al., 1984). Qualitative cognitive, emotional, and self-regulatory processes associated with this pattern include (1) the adoption of goals in which the concealment of one's perceived sense of inability relative to others is the main focus (called "ego avoidance goals"); (2) low self-perceptions of academic competence; (3) frequent worries about incompetence and concomitant feelings of sadness or low esteem; (4) a tendency to use ineffective learning strategies; (5) a tendency to attribute academic difficulties to a personal, stable inability to achieve; and (6) a tendency to cope with academic difficulties by blaming oneself (Connell & Wellborn, 1991; Covington, 1992; Dweck & Leggett, 1988; Dweck & Wortman, 1982; Nolen-Hoeksema et al., 1986; Urdan, 1997; Weiner, 1986). In general, an organizational pattern of behavior that could be characterized as somewhat avoidant, ruminative, rigid, and overcontrolled would describe the functioning of such children in educational settings (Block & Block, 1980; Deci & Ryan, 1985; Dweck & Leggett, 1988). Such a pattern may describe not only a small percentage of normative children who show primarily academic difficulties but also some unknown percentage of children who manifest clinical levels of depression and anxiety.

Academic Externalizing Pattern

A second pattern of academic and emotional problems that is seen among some children in educational settings involves achievement difficulties that co-occur with externalized forms of distress such as disruptive behavior and aggression (e.g., Hinshaw, 1992). Such children do poorly in school, show academic skills deficits and a great deal of time off-task in learning settings, have poor peer relations, and are disruptive in the classroom (Dishion et al., 1995; Hinshaw, 1992). Less research has been devoted to understanding this particular pattern in school settings, so our description of it remains somewhat speculative and preliminary.

Empirical research has shown that, among some children, academic difficulty can cause subsequent feelings of frustration, inferiority, anger, and aggression that can result in behavior problems in and out of school (Connell & Wellborn, 1991; Graham, 1997; Hinshaw, 1992; Weiner, 1997). There is some indication that symptoms of externalized distress such as anger and aggression can also cause subsequent academic problems. Angry children often show heightened fears, concerns, and attention to issues of victimization, provocation, and control by others. These heightened sensitivities distract such children from focusing on academic work and learning academic skills. If such sensitivities are accompanied by aggression toward others, such children actually create conditions in which peers and teachers are less willing to

TABLE 8.1. Selective Properties of Maladaptive and Optimal Patterns of Academic Functioning

	Maladaptive academic functioning		Optimal academic functioning
	Academic internalizing pattern	Academic externalizing pattern	Intrinsic-mastery pattern
Quantitative properties			
Academic behaviors			
Preferred level of academic challenge	Easy tasks		Moderately challenging tasks
Response to academic difficulty	Lack of persistence		Redoubled effort
Classroom behaviors	Withdrawal	Disruption/acting out	Participation
Level of achievement	Low	Low	Moderate to high
Qualitative properties			
Academic-related cognitions and emotions			
Achievement-related goals	Ego avoidance goals		Task mastery goals
Achievement-related self perceptions	Low academic confidence	High academic confidence	High academic confidence
Achievement-related task beliefs			High value for school
Predominant classroom emotion	Academic worry	Boredom/anger	Interest
Academic regulatory processes			
Learning strategies	Poor learning strategies		Deep learning strategies
Self-regulatory process	Rumination	Reaction	Reflection-action
Academic coping processes			
Coping with academic difficulties	Self blame	Projection	Problem-focused
Attributions for academic difficulties	Lack of ability	Influence of others	Lack of effort

offer assistance. Inattention and lack of support due to the child's misconduct can in turn precipitate subsequent academic problems (Coie & Jacobs, 1993; Dishion et al., 1995; Graham, 1997).

Table 8.1 summarizes some of the qualitative cognitive, emotional, and regulatory features of what we call the "academic externalizing pattern." Note that there is some indication that, despite their academic difficulties, such children may report high levels of perceived academic competence. This seems to be a function of the fact that such children attribute blame to others when they receive poor grades, and thus use such occasions not as an opportunity for self-relevant feedback, but rather as an opportunity to confirm their beliefs about the controlling, unsupportive qualities of others (see Coie & Jacobs, 1993). In general, children who manifest the "academic externalizing" organizational pattern of behavior could be characterized as somewhat reactionary, rigid, and undercontrolled in classroom situations (Block & Block, 1980; Crick & Dodge, 1994; Graham, 1997). The "academic externalizing pattern" may characterize not only a small percentage of normative children who show primarily academic difficulties but also an unknown percentage of children with externalizing disorders.

Intrinsic-Mastery Pattern

A third pattern noted among some school children involves co-occurring academic success and emotional well-being. The same set of processes depicted in Figure 8.1 that link academic problems with emotional distress also link academic successes with emotional well-being. In this case, positive attributions for success (e.g., effort and hard work) contribute to these children's sense that they are competent and school is valuable. These beliefs in turn lead to feelings of pride, high self-esteem, and enjoyment of learning (Covington, 1992; Deci & Ryan, 1985; Weiner, 1986). Feelings of psychological well-being in turn activate positive motivational beliefs (e.g., competence beliefs, values) and serve to focus such children's attention on mood-congruent, positive aspects of the classroom environment such as moments of success, the intrinsically motivating qualities of tasks, and supports for learning. These motivational beliefs, in concert with attention to supportive contextual factors and experiences, predict subsequent academic successes (Eccles, 1983; Pintrich & De Groot, 1990).

Table 8.1 summarizes some of the characteristics of such children. They tend to show a preference for moderately challenging tasks, a redoubling of effort following difficulty, participation in classroom activities, free-time choice of academic activities, and high achievement. In terms of qualitative processes, such children pursue goals associated with the academic mastery and self-improvement, attribute successes to hard work, and cope with the inevitable setbacks that occur during learning by redoubling their efforts and seeking help. In general, children who manifest the intrinsic-mastery organizational pattern of behavior can be characterized as somewhat optimistic, reflective, flexible, and intrinsically self-regulating (Ames, 1992; Block & Block, 1980; Deci & Ryan, 1985; Dweck & Leggett, 1988; Nicholls, 1984). We believe this pattern of academic functioning should form an integral part of any definition of mental health in children insofar as it reflects a form of "optimal functioning" (Kazdin, 1993) and "wellness" (Cowen, 1991).

Academic Resilience

Table 8.1 lists holistic patterns of academic functioning that are likely to describe the classroom adjustment of children who manifest internalizing problems, externalizing problems, or positive mental health. Just how tightly linked such motivational patterns of academic functioning are to broader patterns of social–emotional functioning that extend beyond the classroom context remains an open question. Possibilities exist for youth to show mixed patterns of functioning in relation to school and more general mental health. For instance, in a recent series of studies, we found that some adolescents who reported high levels of emotional distress compared to their peers nonetheless continued to show the intrinsic-mastery pattern of academic functioning described in Table 8.1 (Roeser, Eccles, & Sameroff, 1998; Strobel & Roeser, 1998). Somehow these youth, despite other life adversities, retained their capacity to learn and to behave appropriately in school: Their academic functioning was not "tightly coupled" with their broader feelings of emotional distress. Such resilience may have been due to factors such as intelligence (Masten & Braswell, 1991), self-affirmation through school achievement (Eccles, 1983; Steele, 1988), an interest-induced cognitive space of functioning that is protected from the disruptive effects of sadness and anger (Roeser, Eccles, & Strobel, 1998), a positive school climate (Roeser, Eccles, & Sameroff, 1998; Rutter, 1980), or a combination of these factors and others. Just how some children with emotional difficulties manage to stay motivated to learn, get high grades, and act appropriately in school is an important topic for future research on what can be considered "academic resilience." In the next section, we consider how school environments probabilistically cultivate or potentiate these three coherent patterns of academic–emotional functioning in the classroom.

SCHOOL ECOLOGY AND MENTAL HEALTH

Our understanding of how the ecology of the classroom and the school as a whole influence children's cognitive, emotional, and social development remains underdeveloped at the present time. For the most part, researchers interested in children's education have focused on the impact of schools on intellectual rather than social–emotional outcomes in children (Eccles, Lord, & Roeser, 1996), and researchers interested in children's social–emotional development have focused mainly on the socializing influence of the family, peer group, and neighborhood rather than the school (Maughan, 1988). Thus, it has proven difficult to build an integrated body of knowledge about school effects on child development, especially non-academic aspects of development. Below we summarize findings from research on school effects and then use this summary to build a descriptive model of schooling that can be applied to the study of children's education and mental health. A discussion of how *changes* in school factors affect *changes* in different aspects of children's development can be found in Eccles and Roeser (1998).

Modeling School Influence

The presence or absence of adequate physical and curricular resources in schools is an important aspect of how they influence children, but this seems more a political than a scientific issue at this time (Speece & Keogh, 1996). Therefore, we focus here on research that documents how particular curricular, instructional, interpersonal, and organizational processes that occur in classrooms and schools on a daily basis influence aspects of children's mental health (see Good & Weinstein, 1986; Rutter, 1983). Several broad generalizations can be made regarding research on school effects. First, proximal contextual processes are as important as distal school resources in assessing school influences on children (Rutter, 1980). Second, school effects operate at different levels: at the interpersonal, classroom, school, and district levels (Zalatimo & Sleeman, 1975). Third, school contexts change or "develop" as children move through different types of schools (Eccles & Midgley, 1989; Simmons & Blyth, 1987). Fourth, children's perceptions of the classroom or the school environment are stronger predictors of their adjustment than are more "objective" indicators of the environment such as observers' ratings (see Eccles, 1983; Maehr, 1991; Ryan & Grolnick, 1986; Weinstein, 1989). Fifth, school effects on achievement and other achievement-related behaviors are mediated through children's perceptions of the environment, as well as their motivational beliefs (e.g., confidence), goals (e.g., to master material), and emotions (e.g., interest; for a review, see Eccles et al., 1998).

With these generalizations in mind, we now turn to a description of some of the processes by which schools influence children's mental health. Based upon conceptions of systems theory (Sameroff, 1987), Figure 8.2 depicts the school environment as a set of hierarchical and interdependent levels of organization, and emphasizes our assumptions that schools are systems comprised of structural levels, each characterized by organized processes (inter-personal, instructional, and organizational in nature); that these levels of organization are interrelated vertically; and that the processes corresponding to these levels are more or less dynamic in nature, sometimes being worked out each moment between social actors (e.g., teachers and students). The time dimension along the bottom of Figure 8.2 denotes the fact that these processes "develop" or change as children move through different types of schools (elementary, middle, and high school). Finally, we assume that it is through children's explicit

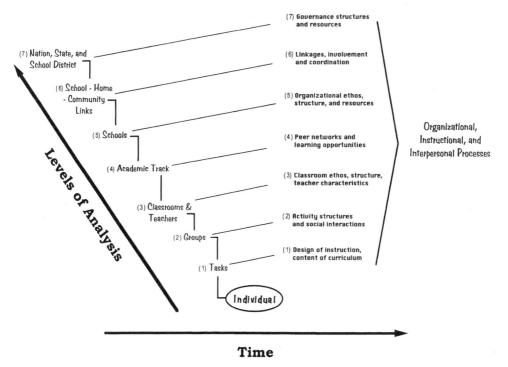

Time

FIGURE 8.2. Multilevel description of school ecology.

or implicit experience of such processes that schools probabilistically exert an impact on their cognitive, social–emotional, and behavioral development. Together, these systems-theory concepts define a process-oriented, multilevel, developmental, and phenomenological view of schooling and its potential influence on children's mental health.

Level 1: Academic Tasks

The nature of academic work is at the heart of schooling and includes both the design of instruction and the content of the curriculum. Poorly designed instruction can reinforce cycles of failure in children who need well-structured academic tasks and explicit instruction in the strategies required for successful learning. Such children include those with poor achievement histories and those with learning disabilities in the areas of short-term memory, language, attention, or spatial perception (Adelman, 1989; Brophy, 1988; Schumm & Vaughan, 1995; Silver, 1996). Given that interest seems to be an important factor in how some children maintain their engagement in school despite other life difficulties, the meaningfulness of the curriculum in relation to children's developmental needs and contemporary experiences seems to be another important factor at this level of analysis, one that can keep some troubled students engaged in school and prevent others from dropping out (Fine, 1991; Glasgow, 1980; Roeser, Eccles, & Sameroff, 1998a).

Level 2: Groups

Classroom instruction is delivered through different activity structures, including whole-group instruction, individualized instruction, and grouped instruction. Cooperative grouping in classrooms can enhance learning, self-esteem, and interethnic relations, and can diversify the number of friendships that form in the classroom (Cohen & Lotan, 1997; Slavin, 1983). In contrast, the use of whole-class instruction and within-class ability groups can make ability differences more salient, increase social comparison among students, make differential teacher treatment of high and low achievers in the classroom more noticeable, and lead to more social isolation among students who are not high achievers (Eccles et al., 1984; Karweit & Hansell, 1983; Marshall & Weinstein, 1984).

Level 3: Classroom Practices and Teacher Characteristics

Classroom instructional practices, teachers' pedagogical beliefs, and teachers' ability to relate to students all can influence children's cognitive and social–emotional development (for extensive reviews, see Ames, 1992; Berliner, 1985; Brophy, 1988). Here we highlight a few relevant findings from research on these processes.

Teacher Role Beliefs. Teachers' beliefs about their role can influence the nature of the interactions they have with students. In a study of 98 elementary school teachers, Brophy (1985) found that teachers who saw themselves primarily as "instructors" (e.g., oriented toward teaching academic content and fostering the "good student") responded the most unfavorably to scenarios involving students who were underachievers, academically unmotivated, or disruptive during learning activities. In contrast, "socializers" (e.g., those oriented toward addressing children's social–emotional needs and fostering the "good citizen") responded the most unfavorably to scenarios involving aggressive students or those who thwarted teachers' efforts to form close personal relationships. These findings require further research in actual classroom settings with children who manifest different types of academic maladjustment (e.g., academic internalizing vs. externalizing patterns) but suggest the possibility that teacher–student transactions that potentiate such maladaptive patterns may occur partially as a function of teachers' beliefs concerning their role (see Greene, 1996; Roeser & Midgley, 1997).

Teacher Efficacy. Teachers who believe they are able to reach even the most difficult students and feel they can influence developmental outcomes in students above and beyond other social influences tend to communicate such positive expectations and beliefs to their students. In turn, these messages enhance children's own beliefs about their ability to master academic material, thereby promoting effort investment, achievement, and feelings of self-worth (Ashton, 1985; Covington, 1992; Midgley, Feldlaufer, & Eccles, 1989a; Rutter, 1980). The building of student confidence by highly efficacious teachers is likely to be particularly important for children who are having academic difficulties due to personal feelings of incompetence (e.g., academic internalizing pattern) or victimization and neglect (e.g., academic externalizing pattern).

Teacher Academic Goal Orientation. Teachers' beliefs about the goals of learning and the instructional practices that follow from such goals also can affect students' mental health. Some teachers emphasize the demonstration of ability relative to others in the classroom through instructional practices such as grouping by ability, differential rewards for high achievers, public evaluative feedback, academic competitions, and other practices that promote social comparison. Children who display the academic internalizing style described earlier (see Table 8.1) are likely to be more vulnerable in such environments because, by the very nature of these classrooms, the threat of public displays of incompetence are more likely (Ames, 1992; Covington, 1992; Dweck & Elliott, 1983; Midgley, 1993; Nicholls, 1984). Additionally, if these kinds of ability-focused, competitive classroom practices are perceived as controlling, they may also exacerbate feelings of victimization and anger among children manifesting the academic-externalizing pattern described earlier.

Other teachers emphasize what are called "task-mastery goals" in their classrooms through practices such as the recognition of individual effort and improvement regardless of a child's current ability level, provisions for choice and collaborative work, opportunities for revision, and an emphasis on learning from mistakes, mastering content, and investing effort in learning (Ames, 1992; Midgley, 1993). Such practices reduce children's concerns about their ability relative to peers and the feelings of self-consciousness, anxiety, or disenfranchisement that can accompany such concerns. In mastery-focused environments, children are more likely to show the kinds of behaviors and psychological characteristics associated with the intrinsic-mastery pattern described earlier (Ames, 1992) and may explain why some distressed students maintain a positive orientation toward schooling (Roeser, Eccles, & Strobel, 1998). Some students who appear "academically resilient" may actually be in resilience-enhancing school settings (Roeser et al., 1998a).

Teacher Autonomy Support and Control. A related classroom practice concerns the structure of authority in the classroom (Ames, 1992; Deci & Ryan, 1985). In classrooms where teachers assert a great deal of control by offering students few provisions for self-determined behavior and by using frequent rewards, punishments, competitions, and praise, children are more likely to feel that their behavior is being controlled by factors outside themselves. Controlling practices can potentiate both the academic internalizing and externalizing patterns described earlier. Some children may feel unable to live up to expectations and external demands, and thus feel inadequate in such settings (academic internalizing pattern; Boggiano et al., 1992; Deci, Vallerand, Pelletier, & Ryan, 1991; Flink, Boggiano, & Barrett, 1990). Other children (e.g., those manifesting the academic externalizing pattern) may respond to frequent punishments and competitions with defiance, especially if they are often the target of negative feedback and punishments (Coie & Jacobs, 1993; Deci et al., 1991; Rutter, 1980).

Other teachers design their classes so as to support student autonomy. They do this by giving students opportunities to make choices, pursue their interests, and contribute to classroom discussions and decisions. Such practices promote a sense of autonomous, self-determined behavior on the part of children in relation to their schoolwork and are related to children's intrinsic valuing of school, quality of cognitive engagement during learning, performance, and feelings of self-esteem and personal control (Deci & Ryan, 1985). Such environments, in essence, foster the intrinsic-mastery pattern of academic functioning and, again, seem protective for some children who experience high levels of emotional distress (Roeser et al., 1998a,b).

The authority structure in the classroom also has important effects on children's social relationships with each other. In secondary classrooms, opportunities for students to participate in academic decisions are associated with less social isolation, a broader range of acquaintances, and less status-based friendship networks (e.g., Epstein, 1983). Thus, it could be that autonomy support in the classroom reduces peer neglect, though little research on this has been done to date.

Orderliness and Predictability.   In rooms where teachers have established smoothly running and efficient procedures for monitoring student progress, providing feedback, enforcing accountability for work completion, and organizing group activities, student achievement and conduct are enhanced (Moos, 1979; Rutter, 1980). On the other hand, ineffective classroom organization reflected in a lack of clear and consistent behavioral rules, routines, and procedures for transitioning between activities is related to behavior problems at school (Rutter, 1980) and has a particular disorganizing influence on the behavior and learning of children with attention-deficit/hyperactivity disorder and conduct disorder (Dishion et al., 1995; Hechtman, 1996; Kasen, Johnson, & Cohen, 1990).

Teacher–Student Relationships.   Quality teacher–student relationships positively affect students' motivation to learn and their "bonding" with the institution of school (Goodenow, 1993; Midgley, Feldlaufer, & Eccles, 1989b; Moos, 1979; Roeser, Midgley, & Urdan, 1996). Conversely, a lack of supportive teacher relationships can fuel students' alienation from school and is an oft-cited reason among dropouts for why they decided to withdraw from school (Fine, 1991). Evidence shows that school environments designed to provide a smaller community to students within the larger context of secondary schools, and thereby enhance teacher–student relationships, can reduce emotional distress, behavioral problems, and school dropout (Carnegie Council on Adolescent Development, 1995; Felner et al., 1993).

Level 4: Academic Tracks

Academic tracks or "curriculum differentiation policies" refer to a widespread, if not controversial, set of practices in American schools in which different students are given different sets of learning experiences based upon some estimation of their abilities (Oakes, Gamoran, & Page, 1992). Tracking takes different forms, though here we concentrate on between-class ability grouping, in which students of different abilities are assigned to different classrooms. Such differentiated curricular experiences affect children in two main ways: first, they determine the quality and kind of opportunities to learn available to the child; and second, they determine exposure to different peer groups (Karweit & Epstein, 1983; Oakes et al., 1992).

At the elementary-school level, one effect of between-classroom ability grouping is to concentrate children with similar academic or behavioral vulnerabilities in the same room (Kellam, Rebok, Wilson, & Mayer, 1994). This organizational practice may reinforce negative behavior by promoting friendships and peer influence among similarly troubled children, and by creating social environments in which aggression or poor academic performance seems normative and is rewarded by peers.

At the secondary level, between-class ability grouping that involves several classes (e.g., academic programs or tracks) may have similar effects. Adolescents in noncollege preparatory tracks achieve at lower levels, have poorer motivation, are more likely to associate with deviant peers, and engage in more problem behaviors than those in the general or college preparatory sequence of courses (Oakes et al., 1992). Whether curriculum tracking promotes such outcomes or reflects preexisting differences is hotly debated, though it does appear that the curriculum in lower track classes is characterized by less demanding and imaginative tasks and more teacher control, and that lower track classes enhance opportunities for students to befriend peers with similarly poor academic histories (Oakes et al., 1992).

Level 5: Schools as Organizations

Schools function as overall organizations and have "climates" or "cultures" that can affect students in ways over and above their unique classroom experiences (Fine, 1991; Maehr, 1991; Rutter, 1980). For example, competition in middle and high schools has been associated with higher rates of delinquency, emotional distress, and diminished motivation among adolescents (Fiqueira-McDonough, 1986; Roeser et al., 1998a). In contrast, when students perceive their secondary schools as places where teachers hold high expectations for all students regardless of their ability level, and where effort, improvement, and task mastery are emphasized as the hallmarks of success, adolescents act out less, experience less emotional distress, and are motivated to learn more (Roeser et al., 1996, 1998a; Rutter, 1980; Urdan & Roeser, 1993). These findings suggest that the organizational culture of a school may exacerbate maladaptive patterns of academic functioning or enhance the intrinsic-mastery pattern of academic functioning (Maehr & Midgley, 1996; Rutter, 1980).

Level 6: School–Home–Community Linkages

Home–School Linkages. Parental involvement in their child's schooling has consistently emerged as an important factor in promoting both academic and emotional well-being (Comer, 1988; Eccles & Harold, 1993; Epstein, 1992). Such involvement communicates positive educational expectations, interest, and support to the child. Parental involvement can also help to establish a "safety net" of concerned adults (parents and teachers) that can support children's academic and social–emotional development, and assist children if adjustment problems should arise. Unfortunately, home–school connections are relatively infrequent during the elementary years and become almost nonexistent during the middle and high school years (e.g., Carnegie Council on Adolescent Development, 1995; Eccles & Harold, 1993).

School-Community Lineages. Closer ties between schools and communities may be especially important in high-risk neighborhoods for preventing behavioral problems among youth. Both researchers and policymakers have become concerned with the lack of structured opportunities for youth after school, and the use of school sites as activity centers and as homes to after-school programs could do much to address some adolescents' involvement in deviant behavior during the after-school hours (Bryce-Heath & McLaughlin, 1996; Carnegie Corporation of New York, 1992; Dryfoos, 1994).

CONCLUSIONS

School functioning is a central aspect of children's developmental competence or mal-adjustment, and the ecology of schooling is a central context of children's development that both cultivates and directs attentional, cognitive, and emotional energies. The need for a more integrated understanding of schooling, development, mental health, and psychopathology is underscored by current cultural needs, our fragmentary understanding of children's developmental competence and maladjustment across various psychological domains and ecological contexts, and the fragmentary nature of our public policies concerning youth development and education (Millstein, Petersen, & Nightingale, 1994). In concluding this chapter, we provide some thoughts on how an integrated study of schooling, development, mental health, and psychopathology might proceed.

Architecture of an Integrated Study

Child-Level Studies

One line of inquiry associated with such an integrated approach is research on the psychological processes that predictably forecast academic success, difficulty, or disability among atypical and normative populations of children. "Atypical trajectories" refer to the life paths of children characterized by clinically significant cognitive, emotional, social, or behavioral difficulties that are likely to (but do not necessarily) meet educational disability or psychiatric diagnostic criteria (e.g., learning disabilities, conduct disorders, etc.). "Normative trajectories" refer to life paths of children with adequate or optimal functioning in the cognitive, emotional, social, and behavioral areas of functioning. Such integrated research would provide a more holistic conception of the intrapsychic factors that contribute to children's school functioning by (1) focusing research attention on the interdependence among attentional, cognitive, emotional–motivational, and regulatory processes in the prediction of school learning, peer relationships, and behavioral conduct; and (2) integrating our understanding of these interconnected, intrapsychic processes across atypical and normative populations of children (e.g., Case, 1988; Hinshaw, 1992; Rourke & Fuerst, 1995).

Child-in-Context Studies

A second important line of inquiry in such an integrated approach would be research on atypical and normative trajectories of child development in the context of atypical or normative educational settings. "Atypical educational settings" refer to alternative schools, special education classrooms, day-treatment centers, schools in mental health clinics and juvenile justice centers, and so on, whereas "normative educational settings" refer to regular classrooms and schools. The goal of this work would be to provide a thorough description of how interpersonal, instructional, and organizational features of different educational settings influence the course of academic–intellectual *and* social–emotional development among different populations of children.

Public Policy Studies

Finally, we view research on the links between child mental health (Knitzer et al., 1991; Tuma, 1989), special education (Alpert, 1985; Speece & Keogh, 1996), and public school reform (Adelman & Taylor, 1998; Dryfoos, 1994; Weist, 1997) policies as a central component of such an integrated study. These areas of policy share many important interconnections. Those who are concerned with the lack of mental health services for children in general are also involved in thinking about schools as viable centers for mental health service provision and coordination (Adelman & Taylor, 1998; Dryfoos, 1994; Weist, 1997); those who work on school reforms are also interested in the mental health of children (Deci et al., 1991; Eccles et al., 1996; Maehr & Midgley, 1991), and so on.

In conclusion, as we look to the future and toward a new generation of reforms and policies aimed at enhancing children's mental health and learning simultaneously (e.g., Cowen, 1991), we believe research that adopts an integrated and interdisciplinary approach to schooling, development, mental health, and psychopathology could do much to inform educators, social workers, clinicians, and policymakers on how to make schools even more effective and efficient in their efforts to improve the lives of children.

REFERENCES

Adelman, H. S. (1989). Prediction and prevention of learning disabilities: Current state of the art and future directions. In L. A. Bond & B. E. Compas (Eds.), *Primary prevention and promotion in schools* (pp. 106–145). Newbury Park, CA: Sage.

Adelman, H. S., & Taylor, L. (1998). Reframing mental health in schools and expanding school reform. *Educational Psychologist, 33*, 135–152.

Alpert, J. (1985). Change within a profession: Change, future, prevention, and school psychology. *American Psychologist, 40*, 1112–1121.

Ames, C. (1987). The enhancement of student motivation. In *Advances in motivation and achievement: Enhancing motivation* (Vol. 5, pp. 123–148). Greenwich, CT: JAI Press.

Ames, C. (1992). Achievement goals and the classroom motivational climate. In D. H. Schunk & J. L. Meece (Eds.), *Student perceptions in the classroom* (pp. 327–348). Hillsdale, NJ: Erlbaum.

Ames, C., & Archer, J. (1988). Achievement goals in the classroom: Student's learning strategies and motivation processes. *Journal of Educational Psychology, 80*, 260–267.

Ashton, P. (1985). Motivation and the teacher's sense of efficacy. In C. Ames & R. Ames (Eds.), *Research on motivation in education: Vol. 2. The classroom milieu* (pp. 141–171). Orlando, FL: Academic Press.

Astor, R. A. (1998). Moral reasoning about school violence: Informational assumptions about harm within school subcontexts. *Educational Psychologist, 33*, 207–221.

Berliner, D. C. (1985). Effective classroom teaching: The necessary but not sufficient condition for developing exemplary schools. In G. R. Austin & M. Garber (Eds.), *Research on exemplary schools* (pp. 127–154). Orlando, FL: Academic Press.

Barkley, R. A. (1998). Attention-deficit hyperactivity disorder. *Scientific American, 279*, 66–71.

Blechman, E. A., McEnroe, M. J., Carella, E. T., & Audette, D. P. (1986). Childhood competence and depression. *Journal of Abnormal Psychology, 95*, 223–227.

Block, J. H., & Block, J. (1980). The role of ego-control and ego-resiliency in the organization of behavior. In W. A. Collins (Ed.), *Minnesota symposia on child psychology* (Vol. 13, pp. 39–101). Hillsdale, NJ: Erlbaum.

Boekaerts, M. (1993). Being concerned with well-being and with learning. *Educational Psychologist, 28*, 149–167.

Boggiano, A. K., Shields, A., Barrett, M., Kellam, T., Thompson, E., Simons, J., & Katz, P. (1992). Helplessness deficits in students: The role of motivational orientation. *Motivation and Emotion, 16*, 271–296.

Brophy, J. (1985). Teachers' expectations, motives, and goals for working with problem students. In C. Ames & R. Ames (Eds.), *Research on motivation in education: Vol. 2: The classroom milieu* (pp. 175–213). New York: Academic Press.

Brophy, J. (1988). Research linking teacher behavior to student achievement: Potential implications for instruction of Chapter 1 students. *Educational Psychologist, 23*, 235–286.

Bryce-Heath, S., & McLaughlin, M. W. (1996). The best of both worlds: Connecting schools and community youth organizations for all-day, all-year learning. In J. G. Cibulka & W. J. Kritek (Eds.), *Coordination among schools, families, and communities: Prospects for educational reform* (pp. 69–93). Albany: State University of New York Press.

Cairns, R. B., Cairns, B. D., & Neckerman, H. J. (1989). Early school dropout: Configurations and determinants. *Child Development, 60*, 1437–1452.

Carnegie Corporation of New York. (1992). *A matter of time: Risk and opportunity in the non-school hours.* New York: Author.

Carnegie Council on Adolescent Development. (1995). *Great transitions: Preparing adolescents for a new century.* New York: Carnegie Corporation of New York.

Case, R. (1988). The whole child: Toward an integrated view of young children's cognitive, social, and emotional development. *Psychological Bases for Early Education*, 155–184.

Close-Conoley, J., & Conoley, C. W. (1991). Collaboration for child adjustment: Issues for school- and clinic-based child psychologists. *Journal of Consulting and Clinical Psychology, 59*, 821–829.

Cohen, E. G., & Lotan, R. A. (1997). *Working for equity in heterogeneous classrooms: Sociological theory in practice.* New York: Teachers College Press.

Coie, J. D., & Jacobs, M. R. (1993). The role of social context in the prevention of conduct disorder. *Development and Psychopathology, 5*, 263–275.

Cole, D. A. (1991). Preliminary support for a competency-based model of depression in children. *Journal of Abnormal Psychology, 100*, 181–190.

Comer, J. (1988). Educating poor minority children. *Scientific American, 259*, 42–48.

Connell, J. P., & Wellborn, J. G. (1991). Competence, autonomy and relatedness: A motivational analysis of self-system processes. In M. R. Gunnar & L. A. Sroufe (Eds.), *Self-processes in development: Minnesota Symposium on Child Psychology, 23*, 43–77. Hillsdale, NJ: Erlbaum.

Covington, M. V. (1992). *Making the grade: A self-worth perspective on motivation and school reform.* New York: Cambridge University Press.

Cowen, E. L. (1980). The Primary Mental Health Project: Yesterday, today, and tomorrow. *Journal of Special Education, 14*, 133–154.

Cowen, E. L. (1991). In pursuit of wellness. *American Psychologist, 46*, 404–408.

Cowen, E. L., Gardner, E. A., & Zax, M. (1967). *Emergent approaches to mental health problems.* New York: Appleton–Century–Crofts.

Crick, N., & Dodge, K. (1994). A review and reformulation of social-information processing mechanisms in children's social adjustment. *Psychological Bulletin, 115*, 74–101.

Deci, E., & Ryan, R. (1985). *Intrinsic motivation and self-determination in human behavior.* New York: Academic Press.

Deci, E. L., Vallerand, R. J., Pelletier, L. G., & Ryan, R. M. (1991). Motivation and education: The self-determination perspective. *Educational Psychologist, 26*, 325–346.

Dishion, T. J., French, D. C., & Patterson, G. R. (1995). The development and ecology of antisocial behavior. In D. Cicchetti & D. J. Cohen (Eds.), *Developmental psychopathology: Volume 2. Risk, disorder, and adaptation* (pp. 421–471). New York: Wiley.

Dobson, K. S., & Kendall, P. C. (1993). *Psychopathology and cognition.* San Diego: Academic Press.

Dryfoos, J. G. (1990). *Adolescents at risk: Prevalence and prevention.* New York: Oxford University Press.

Dryfoos, J. G. (1994). *Full service schools: A revolution in health and social services for children, youth, and families.* San Francisco: Jossey-Bass.

Durlak, J. A. (1995). *School-based prevention programs for children and adolescents.* Thousand Oaks, CA: Sage.

Dweck, C. S., & Elliott, E. S. (1983). Achievement motivation. In P. H. Mussen (Ed.), *Handbook of child psychology* (Vol. 4, pp. 643–691). New York: Wiley.

Dweck, C. S., & Leggett, E. (1988). A social-cognitive approach to motivation and personality. *Psychological Review, 95*, 256–273.

Dweck, C. S., & Wortman, C. B. (1982). Learned helplessness, anxiety, and achievement motivation: Neglected parallels in cognitive, affective, and coping responses. In H. Krohne & L. Laux (Eds.), *Achievement, stress, and anxiety* (pp. 93–125). Washington, DC: Hemisphere.

Eccles, J. S. (1983). Expectancies, values and academic behaviors. In J. T. Spence (Ed.), *The development of achievement motivation* (pp. 283–331). Greenwich, CT: JAI Press.

Eccles, J. S., & Harold, R. D. (1993). Parent–school involvement during the early adolescent years. *Teachers' College Record, 94,* 568–587.

Eccles, J. S., Lord, S., & Roeser, R. W. (1996). Round holes, square pegs, rocky roads, and sore feet: A discussion of stage–environment fit theory applied to families and school. In D. Cicchetti & S. L. Toth (Eds.), *Rochester Symposium on Developmental Psychopathology: Volume VII. Adolescence: Opportunities and challenges* (pp. 47–92). Rochester, NY: University of Rochester Press.

Eccles, J. S., & Midgley, C. (1989). Stage–environment fit: Developmentally appropriate classrooms for young adolescents. In C. Ames & R. Ames (Eds.), *Research on motivation in education: Volume 3. Goals and cognitions* (pp. 13–44). New York: Academic Press.

Eccles, J. S., Midgley, C, & Adler, T. (1984). Grade-related changes in the school environment: Effects on achievement motivation. In J. Nicholls (Ed.), *Advances in motivation and achievement* (Vol. 3, pp. 283–331). Greenwich, CT: JAI Press.

Eccles, J. S., & Roeser, R. W. (1998). School and community influences on human development. In M. H. Boorstein & M. E. Lamb (Eds.), *Developmental psychology: An advanced textbook* (2nd ed., pp. 503–554). Hillsdale, NJ: Erlbaum.

Eccles, J. S., Wigfield, A., & Schiefele, U. (1998). Motivation to succeed. In W. Damon (Ed.), N. Eisenberg (Series Ed.), *Handbook of child psychology: Vol. 3. Social, emotional, and personality development* (5th ed., pp. 1017–1095). New York: Wiley.

Epstein, J. L. (1983). Selection of friends in differently organized schools and classrooms. In J. L. Epstein & N. Karweit (Eds.), *Friends in school: Patterns of selection and influence in secondary schools* (pp. 73–92). New York: Academic Press.

Epstein, J. L. (1992). School and family partnerships. In M. Atkins (Ed.), *Encyclopedia of educational research* (pp. 1139–1151). New York: Macmillan.

Felner, R. D., Brand, S., Adan, A. M., Mulhall, P. F., Flowers, N., Sartain, B., & Dubois, D. L. (1993). Restructuring the ecology of the school as an approach to prevention during school transitions: Longitudinal follow-ups and extensions of the School Transitional Environment Project (STEP). In L. A. Jason, K. E. Danner, & K. S. Kurasaki (Eds.), *Prevention and school transitions* (pp. 103–136). New York: Haworth Press.

Fine, M. (1991). *Framing dropouts: Notes on the politics of an urban public high school.* Albany: State University of New York Press.

Fiqueira-McDonough, J. (1986). School context, gender, and delinquency. *Journal of Youth and Adolescence, 15,* 79–98.

Flink, C., Boggiano, A. K., & Barrett, M. (1990). Controlling teaching strategies: Undermining children's self-determination and performance. *Journal of Personality and Social Psychology, 59,* 916–924.

Glasgow, D. G. (1980). *The Black underclass: Poverty, unemployment, and entrapment of ghetto youth* (1st ed.). San Francisco: Jossey-Bass.

Good, T. L., & Weinstein, R. S. (1986). Schools make a difference: Evidence, criticisms, and new directions. *American Psychologist, 41,* 1090–1097.

Goodenow, C. (1993). Classroom belonging among early adolescent students: Relationships to motivation and achievement. *Journal of Early Adolescence, 13,* 21–43.

Gotlib, I. H., & MacLeod, C. (1997). Information processing in anxiety and depression: A cognitive–developmental perspective. In J. A. Burack & J. T. Enns (Eds.), *Attention, development, and psychopathology* (pp. 350–378). New York: Guilford Press.

Graham, S. (1997). Using attribution theory to understand social and academic motivation in African American youth. *Educational Psychologist, 32,* 21–34.

Greene, R. W. (1996). Students with attention-deficit hyperactivity disorder and their teachers: Implications of a goodness-of-fit perspective. In T. H. Ollendick & R. J. Prinz (Eds.), *Advances in clinical child psychology* (Vol. 18, pp. 205–230). New York: Plenum Press.

Hechtman, L. (1996). Developmental, neurobiological, and psychosocial aspects of hyperactivity, impulsivity, and attention. In M. Lewis (Ed.), *Child and adolescent psychiatry: A comprehensive textbook* (2nd ed., pp. 323–334). Baltimore: Williams & Wilkins.

Hill, K. T., & Wigfield, A. (1984). Text anxiety: A major educational problem and what can be done about it. *Elementary School Journal, 85,* 105–126.

Hinshaw, S. P. (1992). Externalizing behavior problems and academic underachievement in childhood and adolescence: Causal relationships and underlying mechanisms. *Psychological Bulletin, 111,* 127–155.

Institute of Medicine. (1994). *Reducing risks for mental disorders: Frontiers for preventive intervention research.* Washington, DC: National Academy Press.

Karweit, N., & Hansell, S. (1983). School organization and friendship selection. In J. L. Epstein & N. Karweit (Eds.),

Friends in school: Patterns of selection and influence in secondary schools (pp. 29–38). New York: Academic Press.

Kasen, S., Johnson, J., & Cohen, P. (1990). The impact of school emotional climate on student psychopathology. *Journal of Abnormal Child Psychology, 18,* 165–177.

Kazdin, A. E. (1993). Adolescent mental health: Prevention and treatment programs. *American Psychologist, 48,* 127–141.

Kellam, S. G., Rebok, G. W., Mayer, L. S., Ialongo, N., & Kalodner, C. R. (1994). Depressive symptoms over first grade and their response to a developmental epidemiologically based preventive trial aimed at improving achievement. *Development and Psychopathology, 6,* 463–481.

Kellam, S. G., Rebok, G. W., Wilson, R., & Mayer, L. S. (1994). The social field of the classroom: Context for the developmental epidemiological study of aggressive behavior. In R. K. Silbereisen & E. Todt (Eds.), *Adolescence in context: The interplay of family, school, peers, and work in adjustment* (pp. 390–408). New York: Springer-Verlag.

Kendall, P. C., & Dobson, K. S. (1993). On the nature of cognition and its role in psychopathology. In K. S. Dobson & P. C. Kendall (Eds.), *Psychopathology and cognition* (pp. 1–18). San Diego, CA: Academic Press.

Kessler, R. C., Foster, C. L., Saunders, W. B., & Stang, P. E. (1995). Social consequences of psychiatric disorders: I. Educational attainment. *American Journal of Psychiatry, 152,* 1026–1032.

Knitzer, J., Steinberg, Z., & Fleisch, B. (1991). Schools, children's mental health, and the advocacy challenge. *Journal of Clinical Child Psychology, 20,* 102–111.

Kovacs, M. (1992). *Children's depression inventory manual.* North Tonawanda, NY: Multi-Health Systems.

Lazarus, R. S. (1991). *Emotion and adaptation.* New York: Oxford University Press.

Maehr, M. L. (1991). The "psychological environment" of the school: A focus for school leadership. In P. Thurstone & P. Zodhiates (Eds.), *Advances in educational administration* (Vol. 2, pp. 51–81). Greenwich, CT: JAI Press.

Maehr, M. L., & Midgley, C. (1991). Enhancing student motivation: A school-wide approach. *Educational Psychologist, 26,* 399–427.

Marshall, H. H., & Weinstein, R. S. (1984). Classroom factors affecting students' self-evaluations: An interactional model. *Review of Educational Research, 54,* 301–325.

Masten, A. S., & Braswell, L. (1991). Developmental psychopathology: An integrative framework. In P. R. Martin (Ed.), *Handbook of behavior therapy and psychological science: An integrative approach* (pp. 35–56). New York: Pergamon Press.

Masten, A. S., Coatsworth, J. D., Neemann, J., Gest, S. D., Tellegen, A., & Garmezy, N. (1995). The structure and coherence of competence from childhood to adolescence. *Child Development, 66,* 1635–1659.

Maughan, B. (1988). School experiences as risk/protective factors. In M. Rutter (Ed.), *Studies of psychosocial risk: The power of longitudinal data* (pp. 200–220). New York: Cambridge University Press.

Meyers, J. (1989). The practice of school psychology in the schools for the primary prevention of learning and adjustment problems in children: A perspective from the field of education. In L. A. Bond & B. E. Compas (Eds.), *Primary prevention and promotion in the schools* (pp. 391–422). Newbury Park, CA: Sage.

Midgley, C. (1993). Motivation and middle level schools. In P. Pintrich & M. L. Maehr (Eds.), *Advances in motivation and achievement: Vol. 8. Motivation in the adolescent years* (pp. 217–294). Greenwich, CT: JAI Press.

Midgley, C., Feldlaufer, H., & Eccles, J. S. (1989a). Change in teacher efficacy and student self- and task-related beliefs during the transition to junior high school. *Journal of Educational Psychology, 81,* 247–258.

Midgley, C., Feldlaufer, H., & Eccles, J. S. (1989b). Student/teacher relations and attitudes towards mathematics before and after the transition to junior high school. *Child Development, 90,* 981–992.

Millstein, S. G., Petersen, A. C., & Nightingale, E. O. (1994). *Promoting the health of adolescents: New directions for the twenty-first century.* New York: Oxford University Press.

Moos, R. H. (1979). *Evaluating educational environments.* San Francisco: Jossey-Bass.

Nicholls, J. G. (1984). Achievement motivation: Conceptions of ability, subjective experience, task choice, and performance. *Psychological Review, 91,* 328–346.

Nolen-Hoeksema, S., Girgus, J. S., & Seligman, M. E. P. (1986). Learned helplessness in children: A longitudinal study of depression, achievement, and explanatory style. *Journal of Personality and Social Psychology, 51,* 435–442.

Oakes, J., Gamoran, A., & Page, R. N. (1992). Curriculum differentiation: Opportunities, outcomes, and meanings. In P. Jackson (Ed.), *Handbook of research on curriculum* (pp. 570–608). New York: Macmillan.

Ollendick, T. H., Greene, R. W., Weist, M. D., & Oswald, D. P. (1990). The predictive validity of teacher nominations: A five year follow-up of at-risk youth. *Journal of Abnormal Child Psychology, 18,* 699–713.

Ollendick, T. H., Weist, M. D., Borden, M. C., & Greene, R. W. (1992). Sociometric status and academic, behavioral, and psychological adjustment: A five-year longitudinal study. *Journal of Consulting and Clinical Psychology, 60,* 80–87.

Parker, J. G., & Asher, S. R. (1987). Peer relations and later personal adjustment: Are low-accepted children at risk? *Psychological Bulletin, 102*, 357–389.

Pintrich, P., & De Groot, E. V. (1990). Motivational and self-regulated learning components of classroom academic performance. *Journal of Educational Psychology, 82*, 33–40.

Roeser, R. W., Eccles, J. S., & Sameroff, A. J. (1998a). Academic and emotional functioning in early adolescence: Longitudinal relations, patterns, and prediction by experience in middle school. *Development and Psychopathology, 10*, 321–352.

Roeser, R. W., Eccles, J. S., & Strobel, K. (1998b). Linking the study of schooling and mental health: Selected issues and empirical illustrations at the level of the individual. *Educational Psychologist, 33*, 153–176.

Roeser, R. W., & Midgley, C. M. (1997). Teacher's views of aspects of student mental health. *Elementary School Journal, 98*(2), 115–133.

Roeser, R. W., Midgley, C. M., & Urdan, T. C. (1996). Perceptions of the school psychological environment and early adolescents' psychological and behavioral functioning in school: The mediating role of goals and belonging. *Journal of Educational Psychology, 88*, 408–422.

Rogoff, B. (1990). *Apprenticeship in thinking: Cognitive environment in social context*. New York: Oxford University Press.

Rourke, B. P., & Fuerst, D. R. (1995). Cognitive processing, academic achievement, and psychosocial functioning: A neurodevelopmental perspective. In D. Cicchetti & D. J. Cohen (Eds.), *Developmental psychopathology: Volume 1. Theory and methods* (pp. 391–423). New York: Wiley.

Rutter, M. (1980). School influences on children's behavior and development: The 1979 Kenneth Blackfan Lecture, Children's Hospital Medical Center, Boston. *Pediatrics, 65*, 208–220.

Rutter, M. (1983). School effects on pupil progress: Research findings and policy implications. *Child Development, 54*, 1–29.

Ryan, R. M., & Grolnick, W. (1986). Origins and pawns in the classroom: Self-report and projective assessments of individual differences in children's perceptions. *Journal of Personality and Social Psychology, 50*, 550–558.

Sameroff, A. J. (1987). The social context of development. In N. Eisenberg (Ed.), *Contemporary topics in developmental psychology* (pp. 273–291). New York: Wiley.

Schumm, J. S., & Vaughn, S. (1995). Getting ready for inclusions: Is the stage set? *Learning Disabilities Research and Practice, 10*, 169–179.

Segal, Z. V., & Cloitre, M. (1993). Methodologies for studying cognitive features of emotional disorder. In K. S. Dobson & P. C. Kendall (Eds.), *Psychopathology and cognition* (pp. 19–50). San Diego: Academic Press.

Seligman, M. E. P., Peterson, C., Kaslow, N. J., Tanenbaum, R. L., Alloy, L. B., & Abramson, L. Y. (1984). Attributional style and depressive symptoms among children. *Journal of Abnormal Psychology, 93*, 235–238.

Silver, L. B. (1996). Developmental learning disorders. In M. Lewis (Ed.), *Child and adolescent psychiatry: A comprehensive textbook* (2nd ed., pp. 520–526). Baltimore: Williams & Wilkins.

Simmons, R. G., & Blyth, D. A. (1987). *Moving into adolescence: The impact of pubertal change and school context*. Hawthorne, NY: Aldine de Gruyter.

Slavin, R. E. (1983). *Cooperative learning*. New York: Longman.

Speece, D. L., & Keogh, B. K. (1996). *Research on classroom ecologies: Implications for inclusion of children with learning disabilities*. Mahwah, NJ: Erlbaum.

Steele, C. M. (1988). The psychology of self-affirmation: Sustaining the integrity of the self. In L. Berkowitz (Ed.), *Advances in experimental social psychology* (pp. 261–302). San Diego: Academic Press.

Strobel, K., & Roeser, R. W. (1998, April). *Patterns of motivation and mental health in middle school: Relation to academic and emotional regulation strategies*. Paper presented at the Annual Meeting of the American Educational Research Association, San Diego.

Tuma, J. M. (1989). Mental health services for children: The state of the art. *American Psychologist, 44*, 188–199.

United States Department of Education. (1995). *School-linked comprehensive services for children and families*. Washington, DC: National Center for Education Statistics, Office of Educational Research and Improvement.

Urdan, T. C. (1997). Achievement goal theory: Past results, future directions. In M. L. Maehr and P. R. Pintrich (Eds.), *Advances in Motivation and Achievement* (Vol. 10, pp. 99–141). Greenwich, CT: JAI Press.

Urdan, T. C., & Roeser, R. W. (1993, April). *The relations among adolescents' social cognitions, affect, and academic self-schemas*. Paper presented at the annual meeting of the American Educational Research Association, Atlanta, GA.

Verhulst, F. C., & Koot, H. M. (1992). *Child psychiatric epidemiology: Concepts, methods and findings*. Newbury Park, CA: Sage.

Weiner, B. (1986). *An attributional theory of motivation and emotion*. New York: Springer-Verlag.

Weiner, B. (1990). History of motivational research in education. *Journal of Educational Psychology, 82*, 616–622.

Weiner, B. (1994). Integrating social and personal theories of achievement striving. *Review of Educational Research*, *64*, 557–573.

Weinstein, R. (1989). Perceptions of classroom processes and student motivation: Children's views of self-fulfilling prophecies. In C. Ames & R. Ames (Eds.), *Research on motivation in education: Vol. 3. Goals and cognitions* (pp. 13–44). New York: Academic Press.

Weist, M. D. (1997). Expanded school mental health services: A national movement in progress. In T. H. Ollendick & R. J. Prinz (Eds.), *Advances in clinical child psychology* (Vol. 19, pp. 319–352). New York: Plenum Press.

Wentzel, K. R., & Asher, S. R. (1995). The academic lives of neglected, rejected, popular, and controversial children. *Child Development, 66*, 754–763.

Wigfield, A., & Eccles, J. S. (1989). Test anxiety in elementary and secondary school students. *Educational Psychologist, 24*, 159–183.

Zalatimo, S. D., & Sleeman, P. J. (1975). *A systems approach to learning environments*. Pleasantville, NY: Redgrave.

9

Adaptation and Maladaptation in the Peer System
Developmental Processes and Outcomes

Karen D. Rudolph and Steven R. Asher

INTRODUCTION

Decades of scientific inquiry have yielded a wealth of information about normative patterns of growth in peer relationships as well as the antecedents and consequences of peer difficulties (for reviews, see Asher & Coie, 1990; Bukowski, Newcomb, & Hartup, 1996). This research has been fueled in part by evidence of a link between social disturbance in childhood and later maladjustment in adolescence and adulthood. Reviews of this research on long-term risk (e.g., Coie, Dodge, & Kupersmidt, 1990; Parker & Asher, 1987; Parker, Rubin, Price, & DeRosier, 1995) converge in their conclusion that problematic peer relations forecast maladaptive developmental outcomes. These long-term difficulties are foreshadowed by problems during early and middle childhood, including negative school attitudes (Ladd, 1990), low self-esteem (Patterson, Kupersmidt, & Griesler, 1990), social anxiety (Hymel & Franke, 1985), depression (Boivin, Poulin, & Vitaro, 1994), and loneliness (Asher, Hymel, & Renshaw, 1984; Cassidy & Asher, 1992; Crick & Ladd, 1993; Parkhurst & Asher, 1992).

Early research on peer relationships primarily consisted of descriptive analyses of developmental trends and perturbations. More recently, however, theory-driven approaches have emerged. Consistent with this trend has been the evolution of the field of developmental psychopathology, which has provided a comprehensive theoretical and interpretive framework for conceptualizing and studying adjustment, risk, and disorder (Cicchetti, 1993; Lewis, 1990; Sameroff, 1987). The explicit application of developmental psychopathology principles to the peer relationships literature is reflected in several contemporary models (e.g., Dodge, 1993; Parker et al., 1995; Rubin, Bukowski, & Parker, 1997) and in recent empirical work

Karen D. Rudolph • Department of Psychology, University of Illinois, Champaign, Illinois 61820.   **Steven R. Asher** • Department of Psychology: Social and Health Sciences, Duke University, Durham, North Carolina 27708.

Handbook of Developmental Psychopathology, Second Edition, edited by Arnold J. Sameroff, Michael Lewis, and Suzanne M. Miller. Kluwer Academic/Plenum Publishers, New York, 2000.

(Cicchetti & Bukowski, 1995b). Despite these promising leads, the integration of theory and research on peer relationships and childhood disorder remains a relatively uncultivated area.

As we discuss, the complementary strengths of these two research domains make this a particularly appealing union. Our primary goal in this chapter is to describe a developmental process-oriented approach designed to nurture an alliance between the study of peer relationships and developmental psychopathology. We demonstrate how the principles of developmental psychopathology can be invoked as an organizational framework for (1) understanding and studying peer relationships, (2) generating and testing theories of etiology of childhood disorder, and (3) examining the processes that link peer maladjustment and psychopathology. First, we describe overarching models of peer relationship difficulties that emanate from a developmental psychopathology perspective. Next, we identify specific developmental processes hypothesized to underlie both peer difficulties and associated psychopathology, and we summarize the evidence for the proposed processes. Finally, we provide an integrative developmental perspective on peer relationship problems and childhood disorder.

OVERARCHING MODELS OF PEER RELATIONSHIP DIFFICULTIES AND PSYCHOPATHOLOGY

Understanding the disparate roles played by peer relationships in normative patterns of growth is essential for constructing theories of peer–psychopathology linkages. Peer relationships may serve as socialization contexts that guide critical aspects of intra- and interpersonal development, learning, and skills acquisition. For example, experiences within the peer group help to shape the emergence of self-concept and social perception (Dunn & Slomkowski, 1992), emotion regulation (Katz, Kramer, & Gottman, 1992), language and social communication (Garvey, 1984), cognitive development (Hartup, 1985), moral reasoning (Berndt, 1987), interpersonal orientation (Sullivan, 1953), and many other competencies necessary for successful adaptation (Lewis, Young, Brooks, & Michalson, 1975; reviewed in Asher & Parker, 1989; Hartup & Sancilio, 1986; Rubin et al., 1997). Peers, especially friends, also serve as social support networks that have been hypothesized to compensate for poor family relationships (Sullivan, 1953) and have been found to buffer children during times of stress (Dubow & Tisak, 1989). These and other normative functions of the peer system can act as a backdrop against which to understand the links between peer disturbance and psychopathology. Below, we summarize implicit and explicit models that have guided research on the association between social impairment and mental health problems; these models alternately view peer difficulties as indicators, antecedents, or consequences of maladjustment and psychopathology.

Peer Functioning as a "Detection System" for Psychopathology

Much of the early theory and research on peer relations emerged from an "incidental" model (Parker & Asher, 1987), wherein peer relationship problems are viewed as a by-product of an underlying pathogenic process arising from genetic or early environmental factors. This perspective presupposes that precursors of disorder—reflected in problematic child behavior or characteristics—impair relationships with peers, yielding an incidental association between earlier peer relationship dysfunction and later maladjustment. One basic assumption of this model is that most, if not all, forms of developmental deviation or delay would be detected in some way by the peer system; hence, the nature of children's peer relationships would serve as a litmus test of overall behavioral and emotional adjustment. For example, impulsivity resulting from constitutional factors or ineffective parenting would likely create interpersonal difficulties during early childhood. Any association between early peer problems and later psychopathology would be an epiphenomenon resulting from continuity in children's behavioral style across development. According to an incidental model, therefore, peer difficulties have concurrent and predictive validity—that is, they can serve as a useful marker of risk for contemporaneous and future mental health problems—but they make no actual contribution to disorder.

Psychopathology as a Consequence of Disturbances in the Peer System

An alternative "causal" model assumes that early peer difficulties can cause later maladjustment (see Parker & Asher, 1987; Parker et al., 1995). This perspective is based on the presumed role of peer interactions and friendships in normative socialization processes. According to a causal model, restricted or negative experiences within the peer group would interfere with the development of critical age-appropriate competencies or relationship-enhancing cognitive representations and would thereby contribute directly to subsequent maladaptive outcomes. For example, a history of being excluded or victimized by peers may impede the growth of prosocial interaction skills or may lead to views of peers as hostile, resulting in later aggressive or withdrawn behavior. Peer relationship problems also may lead to loneliness, anxiety, and depression (e.g., Boivin, Hymel, & Bukowski, 1995; Panak & Garber, 1992; Renshaw & Brown, 1993). Moreover, interpersonal rejection or isolation may undermine the stress-buffering effect of peer relationships and may act as an independent source of stress (e.g., Burks, Dodge, & Price, 1995; Panak & Garber, 1992). Thus, a causal view highlights the more direct impact of peer experiences on mental health.

Interactional Models

"Incidental" and "causal" explanations offer relatively simple main-effects models (Parker & Asher, 1987; Parker et al., 1995), with the former focused primarily on stable features of children and the latter focused primarily on the nature of children's peer experiences as determinants of disorder. However, a developmental psychopathology perspective involves a more complex conceptualization of vulnerability and risk. For instance, "diathesis–stress" models (e.g., Sameroff, 1987) acknowledge the disparate pathways to disorder that emerge from the joint influence of children and their environments. Such models hold that peer disturbances would produce the most serious negative outcomes in youngsters with predisposing vulnerabilities. Although diathesis-stress models have not been well-studied in the peer relationship literature, some potential sources of individual vulnerability to peer rejection and interpersonal stress have been identified, such as depressive attributional styles (Panak & Garber, 1992), negative attachment cognitions (Hammen et al., 1995), rejection sensitivity (Downey & Feldman, 1996), and behavioral style (Bierman, Smoot, & Aumiller, 1993).

Preliminary efforts to articulate diathesis–stress models represent a significant theoretical advance in that they (1) consider child characteristics that may moderate the impact of peer experiences on future outcomes, and (2) provide a framework for understanding differential stability and expression of adjustment problems across children and over time. Thus, these models have the potential to explain the heterogeneity of outcomes observed within groups of youngsters who experience similar peer difficulties in early childhood.

Transactional Models

Due to their view of child and environmental contributions as orthogonal, albeit interacting, sources of influence, diathesis–stress conceptualizations still do not fulfill the potential of a developmental psychopathology approach to peer relationships. Peer researchers have therefore begun to advocate the construction and empirical validation of transactional models of early interpersonal disruption and later psychopathology (e.g., Cicchetti & Bukowski, 1995a; Parker et al., 1995; Rubin et al., 1997). Transactional models are predicated on the assumption that children and their environments participate in reciprocal interchanges over time, resulting in feedback loops that stimulate continuous structural reorganization and change at both the individual and environmental levels (Cicchetti, 1993; Lewis, 1990; Parker et al., 1995; Sameroff, 1975). Thus, such models may contribute insight into the processes through which children and their environments jointly guide the course of development.

Several emerging models of peer relationships conform to a transactional framework. For example, Parker and colleagues (1995) and Dodge and colleagues (e.g., Crick & Dodge, 1994; Dodge, 1993) have proposed models that depict the mutual influences among impaired social behavior, social-cognitive impairment, and peer relationship problems. According to these models, disruption within each domain and interactions among domains gain momentum over time, setting youngsters upon a developmental trajectory to disorder. Rubin and colleagues (Rubin, LeMare, & Lollis, 1990; Rubin et al., 1997) also have advanced a model in which ongoing transactions among characteristics of children (e.g., temperamental styles), their families (e.g., family stress and mental health, parent–child interactions and attachment), and their environments (e.g., stressful experiences within and outside of the peer group) precipitate and perpetuate peer difficulties and consequent maladjustment. Thus, transactional models emphasize not only how children and their environments work together to determine outcomes (as reflected in interactional models), but also how children and their environments actually influence each other.

DEVELOPMENTAL PROCESSES UNDERLYING PEER ADAPTATION AND MALADAPTATION

Efforts to understand the developmental context of peer adjustment have generated theory and research on the processes that drive social behavior and peer interaction. We present a selective synopsis of the most prominent conceptual models and empirical studies. Our central aim is to illustrate how a process-oriented approach can facilitate a synthesis of the peer relationships and psychopathology literatures. In light of this goal, we do not attempt an inclusive review of each research area. Rather, we provide representative examples and refer the reader to more detailed reviews where available. First, we discuss proximal influences on social adjustment that may exert direct effects on peer interactions, peer group acceptance, and friendships. These proximal influences include social-cognitive, motivational, affective, and social-behavioral processes. Next, we discuss a more distal influence, namely, the contribution of family processes to the development of interpersonal competence. We touch briefly on several recurring themes within each section but reserve a more complete integrative commentary for our concluding comments.

Social-Cognitive Processes

Several social-cognitive models of peer interaction have been proposed (e.g., Dodge, Pettit, McClaskey, & Brown, 1986; Rubin & Krasnor, 1986). Early versions of these models elucidated a series of sequential information-processing steps hypothesized to underlie interpersonal response patterns: (1) encoding of situational and internal cues, (2) mental representation and interpretation of cues, (3) response access or construction, (4) response selection, (5) behavioral enactment, and (6) outcome evaluation. In accord with a developmental psychopathology perspective, more recent reformulations of these models (e.g., Crick & Dodge, 1994; Parker et al., 1995) have emphasized the bidirectional, nonlinear, and recursive nature of these steps.

Most contemporary social-cognitive models of relationships distinguish between (1) online processing of ongoing social interactions, and (2) latent knowledge structures or belief systems that have been conceptualized using constructs such as interpersonal schemas (e.g., Safran, 1990), mental, internal, or cognitive representations (e.g., Main, Kaplan, & Cassidy, 1985; Rudolph, Hammen, & Burge, 1995), and social scripts (e.g., Nelson, 1981). Both active social information processing and organized knowledge structures are presumed to influence patterns of interpersonal relatedness. For example, the accurate processing of social information and an optimistic view of the self and relationships may promote competent behavior and may increase children's likelihood of forming positive social bonds, whereas processing biases and deprecating social perceptions may trigger interpersonal impairment and consequent alienation from peers (Crick & Dodge, 1994; Rubin et al., 1997; Rudolph et al., 1995). Unsuccessful experiences within the peer group may then reinforce maladaptive social-cognitive tendencies, thereby creating a self-perpetuating cycle of dysfunction (Safran, 1990).

Substantial research has implicated impaired social-cognitive processes in peer adjustment problems (for a review, see Crick & Dodge, 1994). With regard to social information processing, peer relationship difficulties have been found to be related to deficits at each stage of social interaction. For instance, peer rejection and aggressive behavior have been linked to intention–cue detection deficits (Dodge, Murphy, & Buchsbaum, 1984), hostile attributional biases (Dodge, 1980; Milich & Dodge, 1984), social problem-solving deficits (Asher, Renshaw, & Geraci, 1980; Quiggle, Garber, Panak, & Dodge, 1992), maladaptive self-efficacy expectations (Erdley & Asher, 1996), and internal attributions for social failure (Goetz & Dweck, 1980; Hymel & Franke, 1985). With regard to belief systems, research has linked self- and interpersonal representations with social behavior and sociometric status. Overall, rejected and neglected children report negative and biased views of relationships (Patterson et al., 1990), whereas popular children possess more positive perceptions and social expectations of self and peers (Ladd & Price, 1986; Rudolph et al., 1995).

Despite the large amount of evidence supporting a link between problematic social-cognitive processes and peer relationship difficulties, two important questions remain. First, there is some controversy concerning the pervasiveness of social-cognitive dysfunction. Whereas some research has suggested that the negative perceptions held by unpopular children were limited to familiar peers or specific friendships (Rabiner, Keane, & MacKinnon-Lewis, 1993), other research has suggested that less popular children possessed more negative generalized assumptions about peers and relationships that predicted the quality of interactions with unfamiliar peers (Rudolph et al., 1995). Moreover, experimental manipulation of interpersonal expectations has been found to affect the success of peer-rejected children during interactions with unfamiliar peers (Rabiner & Coie, 1989). Additional research is therefore necessary to determine the extent to which negative belief systems generalize beyond the familiar peer group and affect peer interactions in novel social settings.

Second, relatively little is known about the direction of association between maladaptive social-cognitive processes and peer relationship problems. On the one hand, social-cognitive tendencies may emerge from prior interpersonal experiences. On the other hand, negative perceptions and inaccurate information processing may exert an adverse influence on children's social competence and peer status. As reflected in transactional models, the most inclusive explanation is likely to involve bidirectional effects, but research that directly addresses this issue is scarce.

Motivational Processes

Diverse conceptual and empirical approaches have been employed to study the influence of motivational tendencies on children's social behavior and sociometric status (e.g., Crick & Dodge, 1994; Dodge, Asher, & Parkhurst, 1989; Erdley & Asher, 1996; Goetz & Dweck, 1980; Renshaw & Asher, 1983). For example, Dweck (e.g., Dweck & Leggett, 1988) has distinguished between performance goals—that is, the pursuit of outcomes that allow individuals to provide evidence for their ability or to avoid evidence of inadequacy—and learning goals— that is, the pursuit of outcomes that facilitate learning, growth, and the actual development of competencies. Studies support a link between children's goal orientations and their behavior in social situations. Specifically, naturally occurring and experimentally induced performance goals have been found to predict helpless responses to social failure, whereas learning goals have been found to predict mastery-oriented responses (Erdley, Cain, Loomis, Dumas-Hines, & Dweck, 1997). In a slightly different vein, several investigators (Chung & Asher, 1996; Erdley & Asher, 1996; Hinshaw & Melnick, 1995) have linked specific types of social goals to interpersonal behavior. These investigators have discovered that positive social adjustment is correlated with relationship-enhancing and cooperative goals, whereas social maladjustment is correlated with hostile or social avoidance goals. For example, Rose and Asher (1999) found that the endorsement of revenge goals in conflict-of-interest situations with a friend was associated with having fewer friends and having more conflictual friendships.

Elaborating on the antecedents and consequences of social goals, reformulated social-cognitive models now include goal clarification as one component of the social information-processing cycle (see Crick & Dodge, 1994; Dodge et al., 1989). For instance, children's goal orientations may both influence and be influenced by causal attributions, interpretations of social events, and generation and selection of response alternatives (e.g., Chung & Asher, 1996; Crick & Dodge, 1994; Erdley et al., 1997). Further research is necessary to determine the causal nature of the pathways among goals, information processing, and social adjustment. In addition, more sophisticated conceptualizations of the adaptiveness of social goals are needed. For example, adjustment may be linked not only to the particular content of children's goals, but also to flexibility in the formulation of goals across various social contexts and to the effective coordination of multiple goals (see Crick & Dodge, 1994; Dodge et al., 1989).

Affective Processes

In their lives with peers, children are confronted with social tasks that have the potential to elicit powerful emotions. Even routine tasks such as joining a group or maintaining a conversation can be emotionally challenging for some children. Still other tasks, such as managing disagreement, dealing with being teased or rejected, or having a good friend move away, can be very challenging for most children. Sadness, embarrassment, hurt, anger, and shame are just some of the emotions that children experience in their day-to-day lives (e.g., Lewis, 1993; Parker & Gottman, 1989).

Affective processes are receiving increasing attention in the peer relations literature. Several aspects of emotional competence have been studied in relation to children's social interaction style or sociometric status, including the ability to identify emotions in self and others, to empathize, to appropriately display emotion, and to regulate emotion (for reviews, see Denham, 1998; Hubbard & Coie, 1994; Saarni, 1999; Underwood, 1997). For example, deficiencies in children's encoding and decoding of emotions (Parke et al., 1989), and ineffective coping with negative emotional arousal (Eisenberg et al., 1997) have been found to be associated with decreased social competence and increased peer rejection.

In a related line of inquiry, researchers have studied the link between temperament, which often is construed in part as dispositional differences in emotional arousal and regulation (e.g., Thomas & Chess, 1977), and functioning in peer relationships. These studies indicate that a difficult or active temperament in infancy and toddlerhood is a prelude to future aggressive and impulsive social behavior, whereas behavioral inhibition (i.e., a tendency toward vigilant and fearful reactions to social novelty) predicts future social withdrawal (reviewed in Rubin et al., 1997). Thus, whether due to socialization processes or to genetic differences in emotional reactivity, regulation of affect may play an important role in the development of peer competence.

Social-Behavioral Processes

Behavioral style is one of the most frequently studied predictors of social adjustment. Ample evidence derived from multiple methods of assessment (e.g., peer evaluations, teacher ratings, direct observations by trained observers) across a range of interpersonal contexts (e.g., cooperative and competitive play, peer group entry, interpersonal conflict) has enabled researchers to identify the behavioral characteristics associated with peer acceptance versus rejection (reviewed in Coie et al., 1990; Newcomb, Bukowski, & Pattee, 1993). Overall, popularity has been found to be associated with assimilating one's behavior into the peer group's frame of reference, active engagement in group activity, prosocial behavior, constructive leadership, and having a good sense of humor. In contrast, rejection has been linked to high rates of disruptive and attention-seeking actions; verbal, physical, and relational aggression; behavioral withdrawal and submissiveness; immature forms of solitary play; and low levels of prosocial behavior (e.g., Coie & Kupersmidt, 1983; Crick, 1996; Dodge, 1983; Parkhurst & Asher, 1992; Putallaz & Gottman, 1981).

Once again, the direction of causality can be called into question. To be sure, behavioral differences may arise in part from experiences in the peer group. For instance, rejected children have been found to display increases in inappropriate activity and decreases in prosocial behavior over time (Coie & Kupersmidt, 1983; Dodge, 1983). Through the innovative use of previously unacquainted peers as play partners, however, convincing evidence attests to the fact that social status is acquired in a surprisingly short period of time as a consequence of specific interactional styles (Coie & Kupersmidt, 1983; Dodge, 1983). Further support comes from longitudinal studies that implicate social-behavioral differences as antecedent to emerging social status (Little & Garber, 1995; Panak & Garber, 1992) and from intervention studies that show increases in peer acceptance in response to social-behavioral changes (e.g., Bierman, 1986; for a recent review of intervention research, see Asher, Parker, & Walker, 1996).

Another challenging issue concerns the extent to which the social-behavioral inadequacies of unpopular children reflect deficits in social knowledge versus social performance. Interestingly, observations of peer entry attempts have revealed that children in all status groups do at some point display a variety of social bids (Putallaz & Gottman, 1981). A question that arises, then, is why unpopular children engage in higher levels of troublesome behavior if they do in fact possess prosocial skills in their behavioral repertoires. A variety of processes, such as emotional arousal, causal attributions, self-efficacy cognitions, social goals, or outcome expectations may mediate between the availability and the production of appropriate behavioral responses (Crick & Dodge, 1994). For example, experimental manipulation of social goals by prompting preschoolers (Rudolph & Heller, 1997) and adolescents (Freedman, Rosenthal, Donahoe, Schlundt, & McFall, 1978) for prosocial responses to hypothetical interpersonal dilemmas uncovered social knowledge that was not apparent in spontaneous response generation. Thus, intervening variables may impede children's ability or motivation to translate their social knowledge into action, thereby yielding social-behavioral differences above and beyond those due to knowledge deficits.

Family Processes

In addition to identifying processes that exert a more immediate influence on peer adjustment, researchers have begun to explore the family origins of interpersonal competence (for reviews, see Parke & Ladd, 1992). Several theoretically and empirically disparate approaches implicate the parent–child relationship as a critical factor in shaping peer competence. The attachment paradigm has stimulated considerable research on family–peer linkages. In particular, theorists have speculated that interpersonal attitudes, expectancies, and behaviors that develop within the context of the attachment relationship may underlie continuity in relationships across development (Main et al., 1985). Indeed, past and concurrent insecure attachment has been found to predict decreased sociability and likability with peers, increased aggression, and disturbances in problem solving, affect regulation, and conflict resolution; in contrast, secure attachment predicts peer competence and higher quality friendships (see Cohn, Patterson, & Christopoulos, 1991; Erickson, Sroufe, & Egeland, 1985; for a recent review, see Kerns, 1996). In a separate line of research, investigators have attempted to pinpoint particular features of parent–child relationships—such as parenting attitudes, discipline practices, and socialization-related behaviors—that may influence the emergence of competent or dysfunctional social behavior. Evidence has suggested that parental warmth, responsivity, engagement, and affection are associated with social self-confidence and prosocial behavior; parental hostility, overcontrol, intrusiveness, coercion, unpredictability, and uninvolvement are associated with aggression and peer difficulties (Cohn et al., 1991; Dishion, 1990; MacDonald & Parke, 1984; Putallaz, 1987). In addition, researchers have proposed that parental behaviors may directly affect peer relationships (e.g., Lewis, 1990). For example, success with peers has been linked to more effective parental management and supervision of peer interactions (Ladd & Golter, 1988).

Thus, a solid theoretical and empirical basis has been established for continuity between early experiences within the family and later peer relationships. The next step is to understand *how* the family may contribute to social adjustment. For example, family factors may influence adaptation in the peer group through specific instruction or modeling (e.g., teaching a child the importance of sharing and cooperation) or through the transmission of internalized modes of functioning (e.g., exposure to consistent and predictable parenting promoting a sense of self-efficacy and control over the environment). In particular, family relationships and experiences are presumed to give rise to adaptive or maladaptive social-behavioral styles, social-cognitive orientations, affective tendencies, and motivational orientations, which then shape children's interpersonal competence and adjustment.

With regard to social-behavioral mediators, inconsistent, punitive, and coercive discipline and insecure attachment history have been linked to increased antisocial and aggressive behavior in children and adolescents. These behaviors then lead to peer rejection and association with deviant peer groups (Dishion, 1990; French, Conrad, & Turner, 1995; Patterson, Reid, & Dishion, 1992).

With regard to social-cognitive mediators, attachment history and other experiences within the family may lead to characteristic social-cognitive orientations or internal working models of relationships (Cassidy, Kirsh, Scolton, & Parke, 1996); that is, secure attachment and rewarding parent–child relationships are presumed to cultivate positive social expectations and a sense of self-efficacy and personal self-worth that facilitate success with peers. In support of this pathway, researchers have discovered that some aspects of social information processing (e.g., social problem-solving ability) may mediate between family experiences and peer competence (Pettit, Dodge, & Brown, 1988; Putallaz, 1987). Furthermore, pessimistic expectations and perceptions of peers have been found to mediate between negative representations of the family and peer rejection (Rudolph et al., 1995).

With regard to affective mediators, secure attachment has been found to predict emotional openness in young children, as reflected in the spontaneous expression of appropriate emotions in response to stories about parent–child separations (Main et al., 1985). Furthermore, Parke and colleagues (1989) have reported that emotion encoding and decoding skills may be acquired in the context of family interactions. As mentioned earlier, adaptive emotional expression and regulation in turn predict positive peer adjustment; however, direct mediational analyses are needed to confirm this pathway.

Perhaps the most compelling evidence for the impact of family experiences on the processes hypothesized to underlie peer competence comes from the child maltreatment literature. Child maltreatment represents an extreme case of family dysfunction and may therefore provide a useful paradigm for studying the peer consequences of adverse parent–child relationships (Parker et al., 1995; Rogosch, Cicchetti, & Aber, 1995). Indeed, maltreatment has been linked to profound difficulties in peer relationships (for a review, see Cicchetti, Lynch, Shonk, & Manly, 1992). Moreover, maltreated children manifest disturbances in multiple domains of socioemotional adjustment associated with peer competence, including aberrant social-cognitive processes (e.g., intention–cue detection deficits, hostile attributional biases, negative self and interpersonal perceptions), maladaptive behavioral styles (e.g., aggression, social withdrawal), and deviations in emotional organization, regulation, understanding, communication, and expression; these disturbances mediate between a history of maltreatment and peer difficulties (e.g., Rogosch et al., 1995; Weiss, Dodge, Bates, & Pettit, 1992).

Theory and research therefore support a connection between early family experiences and peer competence, and indicate that a focus on developmental processes can shed additional light on this link. Once again, however, only minimal evidence has been brought to bear on the direction of effects (e.g., Rogosch et al., 1995). It is possible that incipient psychopathology in children may interfere with parent–child attachment, contribute to parents' selection of maladaptive discipline practices, and evoke aversive responses during parent–child interactions. Thus, additional longitudinal research is needed to examine possible transactional relations.

PEER RELATIONSHIPS AND PSYCHOPATHOLOGY

Much of the existing research on peer relationships has been based on sociometrically or behaviorally defined groups of children, with less focus on the interpersonal characteristics and experiences of children with psychiatric symptoms or disorders; this gap in our knowledge is especially large for the internalizing disorders, such as depression and anxiety. However, peer relationship problems do appear to be a central feature of many forms of childhood disorder. For example, children with disruptive behavior disorders, such as attention-deficit/ hyperactivity disorder (ADHD), experience higher rates of peer rejection than non-ADHD children (Hinshaw & Melnick, 1995; reviewed in Parker et al., 1995). Conduct disorder (CD), antisocial behavior, and substance use also are associated with affiliation with deviant peer groups and rejection by mainstream peers (Dishion, Capaldi, Spracklen, & Li, 1995; French et al., 1995). Likewise, interpersonal theories of depression (Coyne, 1976) emphasize the role played by social impairment in depressive disorders. In support of such theories, depressed youngsters experience higher rates of unpopularity, isolation, and rejection (reviewed in Hammen & Rudolph, 1996), poor quality friendships (Goodyer, Wright, & Altham, 1990), and interpersonal—including peer—stressors (Rudolph et al., in press). Anxious children have been found to experience analogous social problems, including low peer acceptance and loneliness (Strauss, Frame, & Forehand, 1987; Strauss, Lease, Kazdin, Dulcan, & Last, 1989). Evidence from longitudinal studies also has revealed that peer difficulties predict future internalizing outcomes, including loneliness, anxiety, and depression (Boivin et al., 1995; Panak & Garber, 1992; Renshaw & Asher, 1983).

Developmental Processes and Psychopathology

Not surprisingly, examination of the correlates of psychiatric disorders has yielded social-cognitive, motivational, affective, social-behavioral, and family profiles similar to those obtained in studies of children with peer relationship difficulties. With regard to social-cognitive and motivational processes, children with ADHD have been noted to demonstrate information-processing deficits and distortions (Milich & Dodge, 1984) and deviant social agendas, characterized by sensation-seeking and trouble-making goals (Melnick & Hinshaw, 1996), that parallel those exhibited by aggressive and rejected youngsters. Moreover, preschoolers with elevated levels of externalizing behavior problems on Achenbach's Child Behavior Checklist (e.g., oppositional behavior, attention problems, conduct problems) (Rudolph & Heller, 1997) and delinquent adolescents (Freedman et al., 1978) have been found to show interpersonal problem-solving deficits that are similar to those observed in children with peer relationship problems. Internalizing disorders, such as depression and anxiety, have been associated with diminished perceptions of interpersonal competence and perceived control (e.g., Messer & Beidel, 1994; reviewed in Hammen & Rudolph, 1996), negative cognitive representations of peers (Rudolph, Hammen, & Burge, 1997), problematic social problem-solving styles (Rudolph, Hammen, & Burge, 1994), attributional biases (Quiggle et al., 1992), and distortions in social information processing (Rudolph et al., 1997; Shirk, Van Horn, & Leber, 1997).

As to affective processes, children with psychiatric symptoms and disorders demonstrate less effective emotion-regulation and coping styles. For example, contemporary models of ADHD incorporate difficulties in self-regulation of affect as a critical factor underlying maladaptive emotional and behavioral response styles (Barkley, 1996). However, preliminary empirical work in this area has yielded some qualifications. For example, findings have suggested that higher emotional reactivity and poorer emotion modulation in youth with ADHD may be limited to an aggressive subgroup (Hinshaw & Melnick, 1995). Additional research is therefore needed to determine whether emotion dysregulation in ADHD youth can be attributed to comorbid aggression. In contrast to these deficits in affect regulation, depressed children may exhibit deviant coping styles, such as lower levels of active or problem-focused coping and higher levels of passive, avoidant, ruminative, and emotion-focused coping (Ebata & Moos, 1991; Garber, Braafladt, & Zeman, 1991). Observations of dysphoric children in the context of dyadic interactions also have indicated less adaptive affect regulation, as reflected in higher levels of anger and sadness (Rudolph et al., 1994). Finally, proneness to anxiety disorders has been found to be associated with the temperamental style of behavioral inhibition early in life, characterized by difficulties in the regulation of emotional responses to social novelty (see Albano, Chorpita, & Barlow, 1996).

Social-behavioral deficits also are common across different types of psychiatric disorder. Children with disruptive behavior disorders manifest a variety of aversive behaviors in the peer context. Parallel to patterns observed in rejected youngsters, these problems include intrusive, impulsive, annoying, aggressive, and antisocial behavior (e.g., Hinshaw & Melnick, 1995; Whalen & Henker, 1992). Studies also have yielded consistent support for correlations between depression and social-behavioral impairment, but contradictions have emerged as to the nature of these deficits. Whereas some studies have revealed impulsivity and peer aggression, others have indicated decreased social activity and withdrawal (for a review, see Hammen & Rudolph, 1996). Anxious children also demonstrate higher levels of social withdrawal than nonanxious youngsters (reviewed in Rubin & Stewart, 1996).

Finally, many of the dimensions of family relationships linked to peer difficulties are associated in similar ways with psychopathology. For instance, concurrent and prospective relations have been reported between insecure attachment and a host of psychiatric symptoms (e.g., Erickson et al., 1985; Lewis, Feiring, McGuffog, & Jaskir, 1984). Specific parenting styles related to peer problems, such as inconsistency, intrusiveness, punitiveness, hostility, and low positive affect, also have been observed in families of children with externalizing disorders (e.g., Hinshaw & Melnick, 1995; reviewed in Rothbaum & Weisz, 1994) and internalizing disorders (for a review, see Hammen & Rudolph, 1996).

Limitations of Existing Research on Peer Relations and Psychopathology

Specificity of Outcomes

Although peer relations problems are associated with various types of psychopathology, previous research provides minimal information about the unique peer predictors and interpersonal profiles characteristic of particular disorders. In fact, many of the processes reviewed here appear to be associated with a wide array of interpersonal difficulties and adjustment problems. Constructing more refined models of the developmental paths to dysfunction will require the identification of specific sets of predictors and outcomes.

Preliminary advances toward this goal are reflected in Rubin and colleagues' (1990, 1997) speculations about the pathways to externalizing versus internalizing problems. One hypothesized pathway is characterized by a progression from a difficult temperament and nonresponsive or rejecting parenting to insecure-avoidant attachment and hostility within the family setting, to aggressive and inappropriate behavior with peers, culminating in externalizing difficulties, such as antisocial behavior. The second hypothesized pathway is characterized by a progression from an inhibited temperament and insensitive parenting, to insecure-resistant or insecure-avoidant attachment and a lack of self-confidence, to fearful and avoidant social behavior and negative self-perceptions, culminating in internalizing difficulties, such as anxiety and depression. This approach represents an exemplary starting point for future theory and empirical work. However, in order to better understand the association between peer difficulties and psychopathology, peer relationship researchers will need to consider the evidence (for reviews, see Caron & Rutter, 1991; Hammen & Compas, 1994) for the prevalence of diagnostic comorbidity—that is, the co-occurrence of multiple disorders. In light of this evidence, it will be important to learn how some children develop both internalizing and externalizing conditions.

Transactional Models

Interpersonal models typically have sought to explain the mechanisms by which early peer relationship difficulties and their psychosocial consequences may set children on a developmental trajectory to disorder. Most of these models assume that peer adjustment problems serve as a precursor and perhaps contributor to psychopathological outcomes. Following from this conceptual standpoint, the majority of prospective empirical studies have examined the prediction of disorder from earlier sociometric status or interpersonal behavior (e.g., Coie, Terry, Lenox, Lochman, & Hyman, 1995; Kupersmidt, Burchinal, & Patterson, 1995; Rubin, Chen, McDougall, Bowker, & McKinnon, 1995). An obvious, but often conceptually overlooked and empirically understudied, facet of transactional models is the disruptive influence of psychopathology itself on children's social competence, experiences in the peer group, and interpersonal development. Undoubtedly, the experience of chronic or even episodic disorder, regardless of its origin, is likely to undermine children's functioning in many life domains; thus, psychopathology that emerges as a result of causes other than peer relationship problems (e.g., genetic predisposition, stressful life experiences) may precipitate interpersonal impairment in children with prior adequate social adjustment.

The case of childhood depression provides a useful example of the potential susceptibility of interpersonal relationships to disorder-induced disruption. Although some theories contend that impaired interpersonal functioning and low rates of social reinforcement may constitute a risk factor for depression (e.g., Lewinsohn, 1974), others argue for a reciprocal influence of depression on social relationships (e.g., Coyne, 1976). It seems plausible that aspects of depression, such as anhedonia, lack of interest in social activities, negative self-regard, and irritability, would interfere with the development and maintenance of successful peer relationships. Indeed, depressive symptoms and behaviors displayed in videotapes (Peterson, Mullins, & Ridley-Johnson, 1985) and in face-to-face interactions (Rudolph et al., 1994) have been found to evoke negative reactions from age-mates. Furthermore, research has suggested that depressed youngsters may generate stress and conflict within their interpersonal relationships (Rudolph et al., in press), and depressive symptoms may predict subsequent peer rejection (Little & Garber, 1995). Similarly, children with ADHD have been described as " 'negative social catalysts' who fuel discordant interactions in social partners" (Hinshaw & Melnick, 1995, p. 629). Thus, research is needed to clarify the direction of the association between peer difficulties and psychopathology. In addition, future work should investigate whether the impact of psychopathology on peer adjustment differs across developmental stages. For instance, disorders may have more severe and longer-term effects on children's social relationships when they occur during critical periods of interpersonal growth.

INTEGRATIVE SUMMARY

The application of a developmental psychopathology perspective presents unique possibilities for advancing theory and research on children's peer relationships and social functioning. The strong resemblance between the configuration of personal characteristics and social environments of children with peer relationship difficulties and children with various forms of disorder clearly points to the utility of integrated efforts that unite these two strands of research. In fact, contemporary ideas about the developmental pathways to social risk and associated impairment borrow extensively from, and contribute to, the field of developmental psychopathology (e.g., Dodge, 1993; Parker et al., 1995; Rubin et al., 1990, 1997). Collectively, research to date emphasizes the intimate connections among temperamental characteristics; parental beliefs, attitudes, and behaviors; early experiences within the family; emerging social-behavioral, social-cognitive, and affective styles; social interactions and relationships in the peer group; and general behavioral and emotional adjustment. In the process, the following portrait has emerged of the likely developmental sequence of events.

Early attachment and socialization experiences are presumed to serve as a basis for the development of future interpersonal competence. Specifically, aversive parent–child interactions, insecure attachment, and inadequate modeling and coaching of prosocial values and skills would contribute to a negative interpersonal orientation, characterized by pessimistic beliefs about the self and others, negatively biased processing of interpersonal situations, dysfunctional emotion regulation strategies, and a problematic behavioral style. This triad of social-cognitive, affective, and behavioral deficiencies would conspire to undermine children's acceptance by their peers and their participation in close friendships. This experience of problematic peer relationships would then confirm and, perhaps, intensify prior critical attitudes about the self and relationships. Repeated failure in the peer group also may cause children to modify their goals for social interaction. For example, children may choose to pursue goals that ensure a higher likelihood of success (e.g., antagonistic acts that attract attention or place them in a position of dominance) or that remove the threat of direct censure or social stress (e.g., avoidant behaviors that promote social isolation). Pursuit of deviant goals may cause prosocial behavior to be relegated to a lower position in children's response hierarchies. As peer interactions begin to demand more advanced social skills with age, troublesome behaviors presumably become more conspicuous and stigmatized. Furthermore, dysfunctional social-cognitive, affective, and behavioral styles, and resulting peer reputation, may become increasingly entrenched and resistant to change over time. Throughout this process, unsuccessful social experiences would act as a source of stress and would deprive youngsters of socialization opportunities that are instrumental to healthy development. Lack of participation in normative socialization and rejection by the mainstream peer group may then lead to affiliation with deviant peers. This constellation of maladaptive processes and outcomes would culminate in increased risk for a range of adjustment problems and psychopathology in later years. Finally, psychopathology and associated impairment would further disrupt social interactions and relationships.

Reflecting the preponderance of peer relationships research, this model emphasizes continuity in disturbance across the life span. In line with a continuity approach, evidence has accrued for the relative cross-temporal stability in particular patterns of interpersonal disturbance, such as rejection and aggression (Bierman & Wargo, 1995; Coie & Dodge, 1983). Considerably less theory and research on peer relationships have addressed determinants of, or explanations for, developmental discontinuity, or instability in patterns of competence or disturbance over time. Yet a developmental psychopathology perspective strives not only to understand processes underlying vulnerability and risk, but also to account for resilience in the face of adversity and for positive transformations that could not be predicted from earlier challenging circumstances. For example, why do some children who experience peer relationship problems in early childhood escape relatively unscathed in adulthood, showing little sign of ongoing interpersonal disturbance or ensuing psychopathology? As noted earlier, a few investigators have begun to explore personal and environmental characteristics that might increase or decrease children's sensitivity to the long-term detrimental effects of peer relationship difficulties (e.g., Downey & Feldman, 1996; Hammen et al., 1995; Panak & Garber, 1992). Further research on the processes underlying risk and resilience at different points in development, and on the potential contributions of corrective experiences even after serious problems have developed, is likely to reap fruitful results.

Finally, future research would benefit from considering between-group variability in the nature and consequence of peer acceptance and friendships. First, the form and function of peer relationships shift across gender (Berndt, 1982) and across development (for reviews, see Parker et al., 1995; Rubin et al., 1997). Specifically, peer relationships in early adolescence, particularly in girls, are marked by a heightened importance of close friendships based on intimacy and disclosure, rather than larger peer groups based on companionship and affiliation; thus, adolescent girls may place a higher value on intimate dyadic friendships than do boys (Laursen, 1996; Parker et al., 1995). Perhaps as a result, the deleterious effects of peer friendship quality versus general rejection by the peer group may vary across age and gender (e.g., see Burks et al., 1995; Oldenberg & Kerns, 1997). Second, developmental norms or gender socialization influences or may lead certain forms of behavior to be viewed as more or less acceptable within older versus younger or female versus male peer groups (see Parker et al., 1995; Rubin et al., 1997); thus, the consequences of particular patterns of social behavior also may differ across age and gender. For example, attention-seeking behavior (Putallaz & Wasserman, 1989) and withdrawal or solitary activity (Younger, Schwartzman, & Ledingham, 1985) may not be perceived as deviant by younger children. In terms of gender, engagement in gender nonnormative forms of aggression (i.e., overt aggression in girls and relational aggression in boys) has been linked to higher levels of maladjustment (Crick, 1997). Third, research on both normative and atypical development in the peer context would benefit from a deeper understanding of the influence of developmental transitions on interpersonal adjustment. Many transitions, such as the move to middle school or high school, are characterized by significant interpersonal disruption and change; analysis of transformations in peer relationships during this time may prove useful for understanding risk onset and individual differences in reactivity to social stress. Much could be contributed to research on peer relationships by more systematic efforts to incorporate the moderating impact of gender, age, and other developmental factors into conceptual models of peer adjustment.

CONCLUSIONS

This chapter highlights how a conceptual and empirical emphasis on the developmental underpinnings of adjustment and maladjustment can help to clarify the links between peer dysfunction and psychopathology. In particular, the application of a developmental psychopathology approach to the study of peer adjustment and the identification of processes underlying risk have yielded a rich and growing body of literature concerning the developmental context and implications of early peer relationship problems. Still, there are many formidable challenges that lie ahead for investigators interested in exploring the new frontier of research that represents the intersection between literature on peer relationships and developmental psychopathology. We hope that this analysis stimulates further conceptual and empirical exploration of the interface between these two thriving areas of research.

REFERENCES

Albano, A. M., Chorpita, B. F., & Barlow, D. H. (1996). Childhood anxiety disorders. In E. J. Mash & R. A. Barkley (Eds.), *Child psychopathology* (pp. 196–241). New York: Guilford Press.

Asher, S. R., & Coie, J. D. (1990). *Peer rejection in childhood.* New York: Cambridge University Press.

Asher, S. R., Hymel, S., & Renshaw, P. D. (1984). Loneliness in children. *Child Development, 55,* 1456–1464.

Asher, S. R., & Parker, J. G. (1989). The significance of peer relationship problems in childhood. In B. H. Schneider, G. Attili, J. Nadel, & R. P. Weissberg (Eds.), *Social competence in developmental perspective* (pp. 5–23). Amsterdam: Kluwer Academic.

Asher, S. R., Parker, J. G., & Walker, D. L. (1996). Distinguishing friendship from acceptance: Implications for intervention and assessment. In W. M. Bukowski, A. F. Newcomb, & W. W. Hartup (Eds.), *The company they keep: Friendship during childhood and adolescence* (pp. 366–405). New York: Cambridge University Press.

Asher, S. R., Renshaw, P. D., & Geraci, R. L. (1980). Children's friendships and social competence. *International Journal of Linguistics, 7,* 27–39.

Barkley, R. A. (1996). Attention-deficit/hyperactivity disorder. In E. J. Mash & R. A. Barkley (Eds.), *Child psychopathology* (pp. 63–112). New York: Guilford Press.

Berndt, T. J. (1982). The features and effects of friendships in early adolescence. *Child Development, 53,* 1447–1460.

Berndt, T. J. (1987). The distinctive features of conversations between friends: Theories, research, and implications for socio-moral development. In W. M. Kurtines & J. L. Gewitz (Eds.), *Moral development through social interaction* (pp. 281–300). New York: Wiley.

Bierman, K. L. (1986). Process of change during social skills training with preadolescents and its relation to treatment outcome. *Child Development, 57,* 230–240.

Bierman, K. L., Smoot, D. L., & Aumiller, K. (1993). Characteristics of aggressive-rejected, aggressive (nonrejected), and rejected (nonaggressive) boys. *Child Development, 64,* 139–151.

Bierman, K. L., & Wargo, J. B. (1995). Predicting the longitudinal course associated with aggressive-rejected, aggressive (nonrejected), and rejected (nonaggressive) status. *Development and Psychopathology, 7,* 669–682.

Boivin, M., Hymel, S., & Bukowski, W. M. (1995). The roles of social withdrawal, peer rejection, and victimization by peers in predicting loneliness and depressed mood in childhood. *Development and Psychopathology, 7,* 765–785.

Boivin, M., Poulin, F., & Vitaro, F. (1994). Depressed mood and peer rejection in childhood. *Development and Psychopathology, 6,* 483–498.

Bukowski, W. M., Newcomb, A. F., & Hartup, W. W. (1996). *The company they keep: Friendship in childhood and adolescence.* New York: Cambridge University Press.

Burks, V. S., Dodge, K. A., & Price, J. M. (1995). Models of internalizing outcomes of early rejection. *Development and Psychopathology, 7,* 683–696.

Caron, C., & Rutter, M. (1991). Comorbidity and child psychopathology: Concepts, issues, and research strategies. *Journal of Child Psychology and Psychiatry, 32,* 1063–1080.

Cassidy, J., & Asher, S. R. (1992). Loneliness and peer relations in young children. *Child Development, 63,* 350–365.

Cassidy, J., Kirsh, S. J., Scolton, K. L., & Parke, R. D. (1996). Attachment and representations of peer relationships. *Developmental Psychology, 32,* 892–904.

Chung, T., & Asher, S. R. (1996). Children's goals and strategies in peer conflict situations. *Merrill–Palmer Quarterly, 42,* 125–147.

Cicchetti, D. (1993). Developmental psychopathology: Reactions, reflections, projections. *Developmental Review, 13,* 471–502.

Cicchetti, D., & Bukowski, W. M. (1995a). Developmental processes in peer relations and psychopathology. *Development and Psychopathology, 7,* 587–589.

Cicchetti, D., & Bukowski, W. M. (Eds.). (1995b). Developmental processes in peer relations and psychopathology [Special issue]. *Development and Psychopathology, 7.*

Cicchetti, D., Lynch, M., Shonk, S., & Manly, J. T. (1992). An organizational perspective on peer relations in maltreated children. In R. D. Parke & G. W. Ladd (Eds.), *Family-peer relationships: Modes of linkage* (pp. 345–383). Hillsdale, NJ: Erlbaum.

Cohn, D. A., Patterson, C., & Christopoulos, C. (1991). The family and children's peer relations. *Journal of Social and Personal Relationships, 8,* 345–346.

Coie, J. D., & Dodge, K. A. (1983). Continuities and changes in children's social status: A five-year longitudinal study. *Merrill–Palmer Quarterly, 29*, 261–281.

Coie, J. D., Dodge, K. A., & Kupersmidt, J. B. (1990). Peer group behavior and social status. In S. R. Asher & J. D. Coie (Eds.), *Peer rejection in childhood* (pp. 17–59). New York: Cambridge University Press.

Coie, J. D., & Kupersmidt, J. (1983). A behavioral analysis of emerging social status in boys' groups. *Child Development, 54*, 1400–1416.

Coie, J. D., Terry, R., Lenox, K., Lochman, J., & Hyman, C. (1995). Childhood peer rejection and aggression as predictors of stable patterns of adolescent disorder. *Development and Psychopathology, 7*, 697–713.

Coyne, J. C. (1976). Depression and the response of others. *Journal of Abnormal Psychology, 85*, 186–193.

Crick, N. R. (1996). The role of overt aggression, relational aggression, and prosocial behavior in the prediction of children's future social adjustment. *Child Development, 67*, 2317–2327.

Crick, N. R. (1997). Engagement in gender normative versus nonnormative forms of aggression: Links to social-psychological adjustment. *Developmental Psychology, 33*, 610–617.

Crick, N. R., & Dodge, K. A. (1994). A review and reformulation of social-information processing mechanisms in children's social adjustment. *Psychological Bulletin, 115*, 74–101.

Crick, N. R., & Ladd, G. W. (1993). Children's perceptions of their peer experiences: Attributions, loneliness, social anxiety, and social avoidance. *Developmental Psychology, 29*, 244–254.

Denham, S. A. (1998). *Emotional development in young children.* New York: Guilford Press.

Dishion, T. J. (1990). The family ecology of boys' relations in middle childhood. *Child Development, 61*, 874–892.

Dishion, T. J., Capaldi, D., Spracklen, K. M., & Li, F. (1995). Peer ecology of male adolescent drug use. *Development and Psychopathology, 7*, 803–824.

Dodge, K. A. (1980). Social cognition and children's aggressive behavior. *Child Development, 51*, 162–170.

Dodge, K. A. (1983). Behavioral antecedents of peer social status. *Child Development, 54*, 1386–1399.

Dodge, K. A. (1993). Social-cognitive mechanisms in the development of conduct disorder and depression. *Annual Review of Psychology, 44*, 559–584.

Dodge, K. A., Asher, S. R., & Parkhurst, J. T. (1989). Social life as a goal-coordination task. In C. Ames & R. Ames (Eds.), *Research on motivation in education: Goals and cognitions* (pp. 107–135). New York: Academic Press.

Dodge, K. A., Murphy, R. R., & Buchsbaum, K. (1984). The assessment of intention–cue detection skills in children: Implications for developmental psychopathology. *Child Development, 55*, 163–173.

Dodge, K. A., Pettit, G. S., McClaskey, C. L., & Brown, M. M. (1986). Social competence in children. *Monographs of the Society for Research in Child Development, 51*, 1–85.

Downey, G., & Feldman, S. I. (1996). Implications of rejection sensitivity for intimate relationships. *Journal of Personality and Social Psychology, 70*, 1327–1343.

Dubow, E. F., & Tisak, J. (1989). The relation between stressful life events and adjustment in elementary school children: The role of social support and social problem solving skills. *Child Development, 62*, 583–599.

Dunn, J., & Slomkowski, C. (1992). Conflict and the development of social understanding. In C. U. Shantz & W. W. Hartup (Eds.), *Conflict in child and adolescent development* (pp. 70–92). New York: Cambridge University Press.

Dweck, C. S., & Leggett, E. L. (1988). A social-cognitive approach to motivation and personality. *Psychology Review, 95*, 256–273.

Ebata, A. T., & Moos, R. H. (1991). Coping and adjustment in distressed and healthy adolescents. *Journal of Applied Developmental Psychology, 12*, 33–54.

Eisenberg, N., Fabes, R. A., Shepard, S. A., Murphy, B. C., Guthrie, I. K., Jones, S., Friedman, J., Poulin, R., & Maszk, P. (1997). Contemporaneous and longitudinal prediction of children's social functioning from regulation and emotionality. *Child Development, 68*, 642–664.

Erdley, C. A., & Asher, S. R. (1996). Children's social goals and self-efficacy perceptions as influences on their responses to ambiguous provocation. *Child Development, 67*, 1329–1344.

Erdley, C. A., Cain, K. M., Loomis, C. C, Dumas-Hines, F., & Dweck, C. S. (1997). Relations among children's social goals, implicit personality theories, and responses to social failure. *Developmental Psychology, 33*, 263–272.

Erickson, M. F., Sroufe, L. A., & Egeland, B. (1985). The relationship of quality of attachment and behavior problems in preschool in a high-risk sample. In I. Bretherton & E. Waters (Eds.), Growing points in attachment theory and research. *Monographs of the Society for Research in Child Development, 50*, 147–166.

Freedman, B. J., Rosenthal, L., Donahoe, C. P., Schlundt, D. G., & McFall, R. M. (1978). A social-behavioral analysis of skill deficits in delinquent and nondelinquent adolescent boys. *Journal of Consulting and Clinical Psychology, 46*, 1448–1462.

French, C. D., Conrad, J., & Turner, T. M. (1995). Adjustment of antisocial and nonantisocial rejected adolescents. *Development and Psychopathology, 7*, 857–874.

Garber, J., Braafladt, N., & Zeman, J. (1991). The regulation of sad affect: An information-processing perspective. In

J. Garber & K. Dodge (Eds.), *The development of emotion regulation and dysregulation* (pp. 208–240). New York: Cambridge University Press.

Garvey, C. (1984). *Children's talk*. Cambridge, MA: Harvard University Press.

Goetz, T. E., & Dweck, C. S. (1980). Learned helplessness in social situations. *Child Development, 39*, 246–255.

Goodyer, I., Wright, C., & Altham, P. (1990). The friendships and recent life events of anxious and depressed school-age children. *British Journal of Psychiatry, 156*, 689–698.

Hammen, C. L., Burge, D., Daley, S. E., Davila, J., Paley, B., & Rudolph, K. D. (1995). Interpersonal attachment cognitions and prediction of symptomatic responses to interpersonal stress. *Journal of Abnormal Psychology, 104*, 436–443.

Hammen, C., & Compas, B. (1994). Unmasking unmasked depression: The problem of comorbidity in childhood depression. *Clinical Psychology Review, 14*, 585–603.

Hammen, C., & Rudolph, K. D. (1996). Childhood depression. In E. J. Mash & R. A. Barkley (Eds.), *Child psychopathology* (pp. 153–195). New York: Guilford Press.

Hartup, W. W. (1985). Relationships and their significance in cognitive development. In R. A. Hinde, A. Perret-Clermont, & J. Stevenson-Hinde (Eds.), *Social relationships and cognitive development* (pp. 66–82). Oxford, UK: Clarendon Press.

Hartup, W. W., & Sancilio, M. F. (1986). Children's friendships. In E. Schopler & G. B. Mesibov (Eds.), *Social behavior in autism* (pp. 61–80). New York: Plenum Press.

Hinshaw, S. P., & Melnick, S. M. (1995). Peer relationships in boys with attention-deficit hyperactivity disorder with and without comorbid aggression. *Development and Psychopathology, 7*, 627–647.

Hubbard, J. A., & Coie, J. D. (1994). Emotional correlates of social competence in children's peer relationships. *Merrill–Palmer Quarterly, 40*, 1–20.

Hymel, S., & Franke, S. (1985). Children's peer relations: Assessment self-perceptions. In B. H. Schneider, K. H. Rubin, & J. E. Ledingham (Eds.), *Children's peer relationships: Issues in assessment and intervention* (pp. 75–92). New York: Springer-Verlag.

Kagan, J. (1989). Temperamental contributions to social behavior. *American Psychology, 44*, 668–674.

Katz, L. F., Kramer, L., & Gottman, J. M. (1992). Conflict and emotions in marital, sibling, and peer relationships. In C. U. Shantz & W. W. Hartup (Eds.), *Conflict in child and adolescent development* (pp. 122–149). New York: Cambridge University Press.

Kerns, K. A. (1996). Individual differences in friendship quality: Links to child–mother attachment. In W. M. Bukowski, A. F. Newcomb, & W. W. Hartup (Eds.), *The company they keep: Friendship during childhood and adolescence* (pp. 137–157). New York: Cambridge University Press.

Kupersmidt, J. B., Burchinal, M., & Patterson, C. J. (1995). Developmental patterns of childhood peer relations as predictors of externalizing behavior problems. *Development and Psychopathology, 7*, 825–843.

Ladd, G. W. (1990). Having friends, keeping friends, making friends, and being liked by peers in the classroom: Predictors of children's early school adjustment? *Child Development, 61*, 1081–1100.

Ladd, G. W., & Golter, B. S. (1988). Parents' initiation and monitoring of children's peer contacts: Predictive of children's peer relations in school and nonschool settings? *Developmental Psychology, 24*, 109–117.

Ladd, G. W., & Price, J. W. (1986). Promoting children's cognitive and social competence: The relation between parents' perceptions of task difficulty and children's perceived and actual competence. *Child Development, 57*, 446–460.

Laursen, B. (1996). Closeness and conflict in adolescent peer relationships: Interdependence with friends and romantic partners. In W. M. Bukowski, A. F. Newcomb, & W. W. Hartup (Eds.), *The company they keep: Friendship in childhood and adolescence* (pp. 186–210). New York: Cambridge University Press.

Lewinsohn, P. M. (1974). A behavioral approach to depression. In R. Friedman & M. Katz (Eds.), *The psychology of depression: Contemporary theory and research* (pp. 157–185). Washington, DC: Winston–Wiley.

Lewis, M. (1990). Models of developmental psychopathology. In M. Lewis & S. M. Miller (Eds.), *Handbook of developmental psychopathology* (pp. 15–27). New York: Plenum Press.

Lewis, M. (1993). Self-conscious emotions: Embarrassment, pride, shame, and guilt. In M. Lewis & J. M. Haviland (Eds.), *Handbook of emotions* (pp. 563–573). New York: Guilford Press.

Lewis, M., Feiring, C., McGuffog, C., & Jaskir, J. (1984). Predicting psychopathology in six-year-olds from early social relations. *Child Development, 55*, 123–136.

Lewis, M., Young, G., Brooks, J., & Michalson, L. (1975). The beginning of friendship. In M. Lewis & L. A. Rosenblum (Eds.), *Friendship and peer relations* (pp. 27–66). New York: Wiley.

Little, S. A., & Garber, J. (1995). Aggression, depression, and stressful life events predicting per rejection in children. *Development and Psychopathology, 7*, 845–856.

MacDonald, K., & Parke, R. (1984). Bridging the gap: Parent–child play interaction and peer interactive competence. *Child Development, 55*, 1265–1277.

Main, M., Kaplan, N., & Cassidy, J. (1985). Security in infancy, childhood, and adulthood: A move to the level of representation. In I. Bretherton & E. Waters (Eds.), Growing points in attachment theory and research. *Monographs of the Society for Research in Child Development, 50* (1–2, Serial No. 209), 66–104.

Melnick, S. M., & Hinshaw, S. P. (1996). What they want and what they get: The social goals of boys with ADHD and comparison boys. *Journal of Abnormal Child Psychology, 24,* 169–185.

Messer, S. C., & Beidel, D. C. (1994). Psychosocial correlates of childhood anxiety disorders. *Journal of the American Academy of Child and Adolescent Psychiatry, 33,* 975–983.

Milich, R., & Dodge, K. (1984). Social information processing in child psychiatric populations. *Journal of Abnormal Child Psychology, 12,* 471–490.

Nelson, K. (1981). Social cognition in a script framework. In J. H. Flavell & L. Ross (Eds.), *Social cognitive development* (pp. 97–118). New York: Cambridge University Press.

Newcomb, A. F., Bukowski, W. M., & Pattee, L. (1993). Children's peer relations: A meta-analytic review of popular, rejected, neglected, controversial, and average sociometric status. *Psychological Bulletin, 113,* 99–128.

Oldenberg, C. M., & Kerns, K. A. (1997). Associations between peer relationships and depressive symptoms: Testing moderator effects of gender and age. *Journal of Early Adolescence, 17,* 319–337.

Panak, W. F., & Garber, J. (1992). Role of aggression, rejection, and attribution in the prediction of depression in children. *Development and Psychopathology, 4,* 145–165.

Parke, R. D., & Ladd, G. W. (1992). *Family–peer relationships: Modes of linkage.* Hillsdale, NJ: Erlbaum.

Parke, R. D., MacDonald, K. B., Burks, V. M., Carson, J., Bhavnagri, N., Barth, J. M., & Beitel, A. (1989). Family and peer system: In search of linkages. In K. Kreppner & R. M. Lerner (Eds.), *Family systems and life span development* (pp. 65–92). Hillsdale, NJ: Erlbaum.

Parker, J. G., & Asher, S. R. (1987). Peer relations and later personal adjustment: Are low accepted children at risk? *Psychological Bulletin, 102,* 357–389.

Parker, J. G., & Gottman, J. M. (1989). Social and emotional development in a relational context. In T. J. Berndt & G. W. Ladd (Eds.), *Peer relationships in child development* (pp. 95–131). New York: Wiley.

Parker, J. G., Rubin, K. H., Price, J. M., & De Rosier, M. E. (1995). Peer relationships, child development, and adjustment: A developmental psychopathology perspective. In D. Cicchetti & D. Cohen (Eds.), *Developmental psychopathology: Vol. 2. Risk, disorder, and adaptation* (pp. 96–161). New York: Wiley.

Parkhurst, J. T., & Asher, S. R. (1992). Peer rejection in middle school: Subgroup differences in behavior, loneliness, and interpersonal concerns. *Developmental Psychology, 28,* 231–241.

Patterson, C. J., Kupersmidt, J. B., & Griesler, P. C. (1990). Children's perceptions of self and of relations with others as a function of sociometric status. *Child Development, 61,* 1335–1349.

Patterson, G. R., Reid, J. B., & Dishion, T. J. (1992). *Antisocial boys.* Eugene, OR: Castalia Press.

Peterson, L., Mullins, L. L., & Ridley-Johnson, R. (1985). Childhood depression: Peer reactions to depression and life stress. *Journal of Abnormal Child Psychology, 13,* 597–609.

Pettit, G. S., Dodge, K. A., & Brown, M. M. (1988). Early family experience, social problem solving patterns, and children's social competence. *Child Development, 59,* 107–120.

Putallaz, M. (1987). Maternal behavior and children's sociometric status. *Child Development, 58,* 324–340.

Putallaz, M., & Gottman, J. M. (1981). An interactional model of children's entry into peer groups. *Child Development, 52,* 986–994.

Putallaz, M., & Wasserman, A. (1989). Children's naturalistic entry behavior and sociometric status: A developmental perspective. *Developmental Psychology, 25,* 297–305.

Quiggle, N., Garber, J., Panak, W., & Dodge, K. A. (1992). Social-information processing in aggressive and depressed children. *Child Development, 63,* 1305–1320.

Rabiner, D., & Coie, J. D. (1989). Effect of expectancy inductions on rejected children's acceptance by unfamiliar peers. *Developmental Psychology, 25,* 450–457.

Rabiner, D. L., Keane, S. P., & MacKinnon-Lewis, C. (1993). Children's beliefs about familiar and unfamiliar peers in relation to their sociometric status. *Developmental Psychology, 29,* 236–243.

Renshaw, P. D., & Asher, S. R. (1983). Children's goals and strategies for social interaction. *Merrill–Palmer Quarterly, 29,* 353–374.

Renshaw, P. D., & Brown, P. J. (1993). Loneliness in middle childhood: Concurrent and longitudinal predictors. *Child Development, 64,* 1271–1284.

Rogosch, F., Cicchetti, D., & Aber, J. L. (1995). The role of child maltreatment in early deviations in cognitive and affective processing abilities and later peer relationship problems. *Development and Psychopathology, 7,* 591–609.

Rose, A. J., & Asher, S. R. (1999). Children's goals and strategies in response to conflicts within a friendship. *Developmental Psychology, 35,* 69–79.

Rothbaum, F., & Weisz, J. R. (1994). Parental caregiving and child externalizing behavior in nonclinical samples: A meta-analysis. *Psychological Bulletin, 116,* 55–74.

Rubin, K. H., Bukowski, W. M., & Parker, J. G. (1998). Peer interactions, relationships, and groups. In W. Damon (Series Ed.), & N. Eisenberg (Vol. Ed.), *Handbook of child psychology. Social, emotional, and personality development* (5th ed., pp. 619–700). New York: Wiley.

Rubin, K. H., Chen, X., McDougall, P., Bowker, A., & McKinnon, J. (1995). The Waterloo longitudinal project: Predicting internalizing and externalizing problems in adolescence. *Developmental Psychology, 7,* 751–764.

Rubin, K. H., & Krasnor, L. R. (1986). Social cognitive and social behavioral perspectives on problem-solving. In M. Perlmutter (Ed.), *Minnesota's Symposium on Child Psychology* (Vol. 18, pp. 1–68). Hillsdale, NJ: Erlbaum.

Rubin, K. H., LeMare, L. J., & Lollis, S. (1990). Social withdrawal in childhood: Developmental pathways to peer rejection. In S. R. Asher & J. D. Coie (Eds.), *Peer rejection in childhood* (pp. 217–249). New York: Cambridge University Press.

Rubin, K. H., & Stewart, S. L. (1996). Social withdrawal. In E. J. Mash & R. A. Barkley (Eds.), *Child psychopathology* (pp. 277–307). New York: Guilford Press.

Rudolph, K. D., Hammen, C., & Burge, D. (1994). Interpersonal functioning and depressive symptoms in childhood: Addressing the issues of specificity and comorbidity. *Journal of Abnormal Child Psychology, 22,* 355–371.

Rudolph, K. D., Hammen, C., & Burge, D. (1995). Cognitive representations of self, family, and peers in school-age children: Links with social competence and sociometric status. *Child Development, 66,* 1385–1402.

Rudolph, K. D., Hammen, C., & Burge, D. (1997). A cognitive–interpersonal approach to depressive symptoms in preadolescent children. *Journal of Abnormal Child Psychology, 25,* 33–45.

Rudolph, K. D., Hammen, C., Burge, D., Lindberg, N., Herzberg, D., & Daley, S. E. (in press). Toward an interpersonal life-stress model of depression: The developmental context of stress generation. *Development and Psychopathology.*

Rudolph, K. D., & Heller, T. L. (1997). Interpersonal problem solving, externalizing behavior, and social competence in preschoolers: A knowledge–performance discrepancy? *Journal of Applied Developmental Psychology, 18,* 107–118.

Saarni, C. (1999). *The development of emotional competence.* New York: Guilford Press.

Safran, J. D. (1990). Towards a refinement of cognitive therapy in light of interpersonal theory: I. Theory. *Clinical Psychology Review, 10,* 87–105.

Sameroff, A. J. (1975). Transactional models in early social relations. *Human Development, 18,* 65–79.

Sameroff, A. J. (1987). The social context of development. In N. Eisenberg (Ed.), *Contemporary topics in developmental psychology* (pp. 273–291). New York: Wiley.

Shirk, S. R., Van Horn, M., & Leber, D. (1997). Dysphoria and children's processing of supportive interactions. *Journal of Abnormal Child Psychology, 25,* 239–249.

Strauss, C. C., Frame, C. L., & Forehand, R. (1987). Psychosocial impairment associated with anxiety in children. *Journal of Clinical Child Psychology, 16,* 235–239.

Strauss, C. C., Lease, C. A., Kazdin, A. E., Dulcan, M. L., & Last, C. G. (1989). Multimethod assessment of the social competence of children with anxiety disorders. *Journal of Clinical Child Psychology, 18,* 184–189.

Sullivan, H. S. (1953). *The interpersonal theory of psychiatry.* New York: Norton.

Thomas, A., & Chess, S. (1977). *Temperament and development.* New York: Brunner/Mazel.

Underwood, M. K. (1997). Top ten pressing questions about the development of emotion regulation. *Motivation and Emotion, 21,* 127–146.

Weiss, B., Dodge, K. A, Bates, J. E., & Pettit, G. S. (1992). Some consequences of early harsh discipline: Child aggression and a maladaptive social information processing style. *Child Development, 63,* 1321–1335.

Whalen, C. K., & Henker, B. (1992). The social profile of attention-deficit hyperactivity disorder: Five fundamental facets. *Child and Adolescent Psychiatric Clinics of North America, 1,* 395–410.

Younger, A., Schwartzman, A., & Ledingham, J. (1985). Age-related changes in children's perceptions of aggression and withdrawal in their peers. *Developmental Psychology, 21,* 70–75.

10

Minorities in the United States

Sociocultural Context for Mental Health and Developmental Psychopathology

Cynthia García Coll and Maria Garrido

The history and definition of minority status in this country is a central consideration in our analysis of the conditions that affect the etiology, identification, assessment, incidence, and treatment of developmental psychopathology in these populations. As history clearly illustrates, the status of a minority in a country is not a function of numerical representation. In South Africa, the "minority" population created by the system of apartheid was actually the numerical majority of its habitants. Minority status is not a matter of numbers: It is a matter of access to resources and the power to determine their allocation and distribution.

In the United States, as a result of the civil rights movement in the 1960s, there was recognition of the history of this country's systematic exclusion of various groups from access to resources and power. As a consequence, the Federal Government placed in the category of minorities the following groups: African Americans, Hispanics, American Indians, Alaskan Natives, Asian or Pacific Islander (U.S. Code, Title 42, Section 714 [f]). Programs such as Affirmative Action, Bilingual Education, mandatory desegregation, and busing in schools were some of the consequences of this recognition. Although some advances have been achieved in the socioeconomic, educational, and health status of these populations in the last 30 years, their relative status still lags behind that of the majority population in many indices of well-being and, in fact, they are overrepresented in many high-risk categories.

It is our position that the systematic exclusion from critical resources and power experienced by many minority populations places these children and their families on less favorable developmental pathways from the very beginning (García Coll, 1990; García Coll et al., 1996; García Coll & Magnuson, 1997b; García Coll and Vázquez García, 1995). By not having access to good prenatal care, by being exposed to environmental toxins *in utero* and thereafter,

Cynthia García Coll • Department of Education, Brown University, Providence, Rhode Island 02912.   **Maria Garrido** • Department of Psychology, University of Rhode Island, Providence, Rhode Island 02904.

Handbook of Developmental Psychopathology, Second Edition, edited by Arnold J. Sameroff, Michael Lewis, and Suzanne M. Miller. Kluwer Academic / Plenum Publishers, New York, 2000.

and by experiencing on a day-to-day basis the cumulative effects of other poverty-related factors (such as limited nutrition, exposure to violence in local communities, parental un- or underemployment, inadequate housing, etc.), these children are placed at a higher risk for developmental psychopathology. In addition, the present deficit models that are used to interpret cultural, ethnic, and racial differences in parenting, family functioning, developmental outcome, and so forth, and the ensuing racism, exacerbates their risk status. Thus, their interactions with institutions such as mental health clinics, hospitals, early intervention programs, and schools might not be as effective as needed and, in fact, may contribute to their tracking into less than optimal life trajectories. These developmental pathways and the expectations for their presence and occurrence (from both the members of the majority and the minority groups) are further influenced by their relatively high frequency among these populations and by the failure of many systems to adequately address them in spite of many preventive and remediative interventions.

In this chapter we examine how the unique sociocultural context of minorities in this country contributes to their relatively high-risk status and the failure of many systematic interventions at both the population and individual level. However, several caveats have to be proposed before we examine how the sociocultural context of minority status influences developmental psychopathology.

First, the federal government coined the word *minority*, yet the uniformity that this term implies is far from the truth. Minorities in this country are comprised of very heterogeneous groups of people from different ethnic, racial, cultural, and migration histories, who have in common a broad historically based systematic exclusion from resources and power in this country. As such, language usage, generational status, socioeconomic background in the country of origin, racial features, and so on, vary considerably within these populations. These groups comprise families who have been in this country for four generations or more (i.e., Mexican Americans, African Americans, and Native Americans), relatively recent refugees (i.e., Southeast Asians, Cubans), undocumented immigrants (i.e., some Mejicanos), and U.S. citizens at birth, born outside the mainland and a product of conquest (i.e., Puerto Ricans). Different immigration statuses (i.e., undocumented, U.S. citizen by birth, etc.), reasons for being in this country (U.S. expansionism vs. voluntary migration, etc.) and conceptualizations of their relationship to this country ("I will go back to my country as soon as I can") have major implications for developmental outcomes (García Coll & Magnuson, 1997b; Ogbu, 1978). As such, generalizations are hard to come by as well as to document, and individual assessments of families and children within these processes are critical for effective diagnosis and intervention.

Second, even if legislation and government intervention have made it illegal to discriminate against these groups and to impede their access to educational, health, mental health, and economic resources, the power of racism in this country maintains many barriers. More subtle messages and methods of exclusion have replaced the more explicit, institutionally based ones (Duckitt, 1992; Ogbu, 1991). Terms such as *symbolic racism* (McConahay & Hough, 1976; Sears, 1988), *microaggressions* (Pierce, 1995), and social and *psychological segregation* (García Coll et al., 1996) have been used to refer to the more subtle, seemingly harmless expressions of racism currently prevalent. These theoretical positions argue that (1) the cumulative burden of these transgressions can theoretically contribute to morbidity or at least to undermining mental health by inducing negative expectations, self-doubt, anger, hatred, conflict, and so on, and that (2) they preclude meaningful and sustained access to resources that would otherwise promote mental health or prevent or ameliorate developmental psychopathology (García Coll et al., 1996; Jones, 1992; Willie, Rieker, Kramer, & Brown, 1995).

Unfortunately, there is still a lack of systematic research that documents the link between these more subtle processes and developmental psychopathology. Moreover, some authors have warned that inattention to diversity may result in the obsolesce of behavioral sciences to address the needs of these populations (Hall, 1997). Most research is descriptive and inferential, or it does not document how racism operates as one of the mechanisms in explaining developmental psychopathology in these populations. Moreover, in an era of "political correctness," racist attitudes and exclusionary practices are even more difficult to document. In contrast to this lack of empirical documentation, it has been clearly delineated how sources of bias exist in assessment, diagnostic, and treatment processes (Cervantes & Arroyo, 1994; Gopaul-McNicol, Clark-Castro, & Black, 1997; Lopez, Lamar, & Scully-DeMartini, 1997). Thus, although empirical evidence is lacking at the etiological level, negative biases have been clearly documented at the assessment, diagnostic, and treatment levels.

The third caveat is that the extant literature on developmental processes in these populations is skewed toward psychopathology, so we know much more about problems than strengths and resources in these populations. There are a variety of reasons for this. Although most minority families are thriving and healthy, as defined by traditional standards, minority children and families tend to be overrepresented in some categories of developmental psychopathology. For example, there is a long history of minority students being overrepresented among special education classes, the maladjusted, underachievers, and high school dropouts (Dunn, 1968; Mercer, 1972, 1978; Oakland, 1977; Oakland & Phillips, 1973; Samuda, 1975, 1976; Tucker, 1980). Other categories include teenage pregnancies and involvement with the criminal justice system.

In part because of this overrepresentation, we know very little about what contributes to positive outcomes in these populations. In other words, most of the extant literature documents the risk factors and not the protective factors within these populations. However, there is an increasing recognition that most of these groups maintain an adaptive culture that distinguishes them from mainstream North American culture and that this adaptive culture might perform a protective role. This culture is expressed through language, beliefs, values, and daily practices that respond to traditions, legacies, and immediate circumstances. Both researchers and clinicians need to learn about the relevant coping mechanisms and sociocultural values of the groups they work with and identify aspect of those values. This knowledge should then be employed in the assessment and treatment efforts.

For instance, among Latino families, values such as *respeto* (or respect, the positive interpersonal regard of others and especially the respectful treatment of elders and persons of authority) and *familismo* (or familism, the sense of loyalty toward the family as a group and concern for its honor and common good) represent key cultural imperatives that are understood, supported, and often invoked by clinicians who work effectively with these children and families (Rosado, 1986). In so doing, the therapeutic work beginning at the assessment phase fosters appropriate parent–child boundaries, promotes the development of appropriate authority in the parents, and helps the child view the family as a source of strength and protection.

Fourth, the lack of a systematic, non-deficit-oriented *body of literature* that addresses both risk and protective factors creates the need to be open to other ways of documenting these processes in minority populations. Emic approaches are necessary when the use of more standard methods might bring biases into the inquiry. This follows the call of authors such as Vargas and Koss-Chioino (1992), Ramirez (1998), and Dana (1993), who indicate that more culturally congruent modes of inquiry need to be employed in order to achieve a more socioculturally competent understanding of these populations. Thus, they encourage researchers and clinicians alike to be open to methodologies such as observations, interviews, case studies, and the integration of an understanding of indigenous values into research and practice.

The last caveat is that the course of identification and treatment of developmental psychopathology in these populations might be different than in others, where parents are the main sources of referrals. In many instances, the school setting is the first place minority children get identified for diagnosable conditions, ranging from behavioral adjustment and attentional issues such as attention-deficit/hyperactivity disorder (ADHD) to other behavioral problems and developmental disorders or delays. Unless the health care settings where primary pediatric care is delivered are equipped to identify in these diverse populations the range of early manifestations of developmental psychopathology, it is in the school settings that this recognition first takes place. It is during these referrals also that the issues of assessment and diagnosis become critical, along with the need to differentiate them from more educationally related issues (Cervantes & Arroyo, 1994; Rosado, 1986).

In this chapter, we first present a theoretical framework that provides a way to understand developmental processes and outcomes in these populations. A theoretical framework is needed to allow for the heterogeneity within these populations to emerge and to specify the unique influences on developmental psychopathology derived from the sociocultural context of minority status in this country. Additionally, we describe in more detail the specific sources of risk and protection for minority children derived from this theoretical framework. Subsequently, more clinically relevant issues such as assessment, diagnosis, and treatment for developmental psychopathology in minority populations are discussed. Because of the lack of a unified body of literature on these topics that does not espouse a deficit model about the populations under study, individual cases[1] are presented as illustrations of the issues and strategies to address them.

A THEORETICAL FRAMEWORK

Figure 10.1 shows a schematic of the proposed theoretical model (for a more detailed explanation of the model, see García Coll et al., 1996). Although this model was conceived to increase our understanding of developmental competencies, it can also be applied to the understanding of developmental psychopathology. In other words, our society's social stratification system and its derivatives should be conceptualized as major sources of influence in the development of normative as well as deviant behavior, especially in populations that are considered minorities in this country. These influences will also be important as they support or undermine corrective efforts. The failure of many preventive efforts as well as intervention or therapeutic efforts can be a function of the lack of attention given to these macrosystemic factors in the etiology and maintenance of such behaviors.

The main theoretical premise of this hypothetical model is that the social stratification of any society (the rules used to place individuals in the social hierarchy) is a powerful influence on developmental outcome. In our society, these factors include, but are not limited to, race, social class, ethnicity, and gender. For example, included within consideration of race are factors such as skin color and racial features that carry a social construction that leads to differential treatment and opportunities. These position factors represent social addresses that

---

[1]Most of the illustrative cases are drawn from the clinical experience of the second author, primarily with Latino clients. Although both authors' research and clinical experience has been mostly with Latino populations, it is our position that minority populations of diverse racial, ethnic, and cultural backgrounds share similar developmental processes in this country while maintaining community-specific expressions.

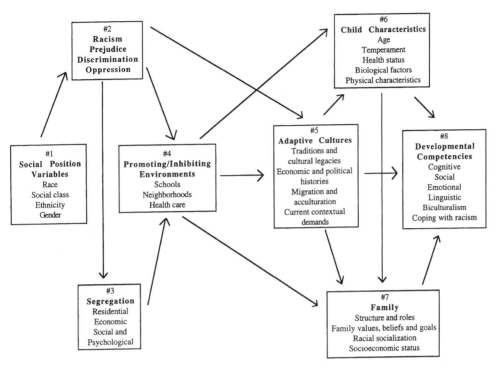

Figure 10.1. An integrative model for the study of developmental competencies in children of color (adapted from Garcia Coll et al., 1996).

influence the ecocultural niche of the family (Weisner, 1984) and/or create alternative developmental pathways to competence in children.

Furthermore, we propose that these social-position factors might not simply be additive (Rutter, 1979; Sameroff, 1994), but have the potential to interact and magnify or diminish the influence of others. So, for example, the fact that you are an African American in a school context where coming from a single head of household, large family is also viewed uniquely as a detrimental source of influence, would place you at risk for developmental psychopathology.

Although considered a primary construct, social position does not directly affect developmental outcomes and the immediate environments in which children grow. Rather, the effect of social position is mediated through the pervasive social mechanisms of racism, prejudice, discrimination, and oppression. There is evidence that these factors continue to be part of the daily life of many minority individuals and that they might undermine mental health status (Basic Behavioral Science Research for Mental Health, 1996; Jones, 1992; Willie et al., 1995). By creating chronic levels of stress that have both physical and mental health consequences, by placing an individual's sense of identity under constant attack, by having to develop psychological adaptations to maintain positive identities and self-esteem, by creating self-fulfilling prophecies and undermining mental health treatment and other interventions, experiencing/expecting racism in a chronic or episodic manner can lead to negative mental states and social behaviors. Most of the work, however, has been conducted with adults and has not included a developmental perspective. Very little systematic research has addressed how these chronic and episodic sources of stress translate into developmental psychopathology, or how cultural influences serve as buffers and contribute to mental health status in these populations.

These factors in turn create the segregated environments to which children and their families have access. Segregation must be considered as multifaceted, combining residential, economic, and social and psychological dimensions. For example, a child can experience social and psychological segregation in a seemingly racially or ethnically integrated school (García Coll & Magnuson, 1997a). On the other hand, socioeconomic integration or variability at the neighborhood level has been shown to support the development of competencies in families of low socioeconomic background (Brooks-Gunn & Duncan, 1997). The interplay of these three major derivatives of social stratification (social position, racism, and segregation) creates the unique conditions faced by all children and affects the nature of the developmental processes that operate and the eventual competencies that result.

Moreover, we propose that segregation (residential, economic, social, and psychological) directly influences the various inhibiting and promoting environments (e.g., the school, the neighborhood, and other institutions such as health care), and mediates the effects of macrosystem factors on children and families. Although, previously, we have posited that racism and its concomitant processes provide a macrosystem context that *indirectly* influences the nature of the opportunities available to children and families of diverse cultural backgrounds, processes such as racism, discrimination, and prejudice *directly* affect children's experience through social interactions in specific inhibiting and promoting environments. Through these social interactions, the influence of the macrosystem factors (derived from the social stratification system in place) directly affects developmental processes in all children. It is in these proximal environments that children will directly experience chronic and episodic expressions of racism (Waters, 1996), as well as exposure to a lack of appropriate resources, that will undermine their developmental potential and contribute to maladaptations and psychopathology.

Inhibiting and promoting environments—or those immediate settings such as school, neighborhood, church, and so on, that can have both positive and/or negative influences on development—in turn directly influence the adaptive cultures that are created in response to children's and families' experiences within these environments. An adaptive culture involves a social system defined by sets of goals, values, attitudes, and daily practices that might differ from or reflect the dominant culture. The adaptive culture evolves from a combination of both historical forces and current demands. It is our position that these cultural influences are major sources of both strengths and weaknesses in these populations, and that they need to be incorporated into our analyses of the etiology, maintenance, and modification of developmental psychopathology.

Both inhibiting and promoting environments and the adaptive culture directly influence the nature of specific individual family processes (the day-to-day interactions and experiences) and interact with children's biological, constitutional, and psychological characteristics. Children are not simply passive recipients of their experience; rather, they influence their family processes and contribute to their own socialization and developmental outcomes. Likewise, families are not static either: They reflect their own developmental and cultural histories, as well as their adaptations to current demands.

Finally, children's developmental competencies emerge as a direct function of individual contributions of adaptive culture, family processes, and children's own characteristics operating through the interactions among these systems of influence. As such, models that do not capture the influence of social stratification variables in the day-to-day lives of minority families, but instead concentrate on individual characteristics, miss an important set of influences that permeate people's daily lives and can affect the onset and course of developmental psychopathology.

RISK AND PROTECTIVE FACTORS

As it is argued in this theoretical framework, the unique sociocultural position of minority groups and the pervasiveness of the social stratification derivatives in the United States create particular conditions for mental health and developmental psychopathology for these populations. Some of these conditions affect the children directly (i.e., reproductive risk, lead poisoning, poor educational opportunities, cultural insensitivity, discrimination); others affect their family members (i.e., job and housing discrimination) and consequently the resources (social, emotional, educational, and material) available to them to prevent, remediate, or correct psychopathological conditions.

We hypothesize that the main risk factors for developmental psychopathology in these populations are the compounding effects of poverty expressed through problems such as malnutrition, exposure to environmental toxins, and diminished resources to promote development, and racism, as expressed through the systematic segregation to poor educational and health care systems, and the consequent preclusion of social mobility. These are sources of both chronic and acute stress.

In addition, some populations (more recent immigrants and migrants) are also subjected to acculturative stress, compounding even further these other sources of stress. It has been proposed that acculturative stress can occur as a result of the adoption of cultural beliefs, customs, behaviors, and identity of an alternate culture (Berry, 1990; Padilla, 1980) and include issues such as language problems, perceived discrimination, perceived cultural incompatibilities, cultural distrust, and commitment or lack thereof to culturally prescribed protective values, such as familism and cultural pride (Gil, Vega, & Dimas, 1994).

There is a body of literature that explores the psychological consequences of acculturation for individuals and families. This literature has documented the complexity of the interaction between the acculturative process and the psychological functioning of children and families (Rogler, Cortes, & Malgady, 1991). For instance, in a study of Mexican American families representing different levels of acculturation, Rueschenberg and Buriel (1995) found that level of acculturation was positively related to external family system variables such as independence and achievement, intellectual–cultural, and active recreational orientation. At the same time, they found that level of acculturation was not related to internal family system variables such as family cohesion, expressiveness, conflict management, and control. Therefore, the basic pattern of interactions within the family is not necessarily altered by acculturative experiences, lending support to the notion that acculturation is not an all-or-nothing process. Additionally, these findings suggest that families facing the process of acculturation might still preserve functional patterns that are guided primarily by their native culture's values. This, in turn, could have a protective effect for its members that might face external acculturation-related stressors such as discrimination and prejudice (Zinn, 1975).

The complexity in the relationship between acculturative stress and mental health for children and adolescents has also been increasingly recognized. Gil et al. (1994) have studied the impact of acculturation on Hispanic adolescents born in and outside the United States, and found that different sources of acculturative strain affect U.S. and foreign-born adolescents differently. For instance, foreign-born Hispanic adolescents with higher levels of acculturation experienced reduced family pride, while for adolescents born in the United States, family pride was low regardless of their level of acculturation. The authors also found that among U.S.-born adolescents, low levels of acculturation were linked to internalized negative self-images, whereas bicultural U.S.-born adolescents presented the best adaptive and self-esteem profiles. In general, these findings illustrate the complexity of influences to which those who experience the process of acculturation are exposed. These findings also highlight the need to think about the effects of acculturation as a multifaceted process rather than in simple linear terms and to consider the effects of racism as a moderator of the effects of acculturative stress on mental health.

Finally, intercultural, ethnic, and racial differences and conflict may also take a toll on these populations. Transactional costs, or the internal costs of transactions with an environment that devalues individuals and their contributions, can also be high for these populations. This is particularly the case for children and adolescents that are forging a sense of self and identity, and receiving, for the most part, mixed messages—subtle and not so subtle—from their family, schools, communities, peers, and media regarding what is valued and what is not. Although recent research points to the fact that minority children can maintain a positive sense of self even if they have the cultural knowledge that devalues their group (see Cross, 1991), there can still be negative consequences of such successful adaptations. The work by Steele (1995) has documented how black students in predominantly white environments maintain a positive identity when faced with persistent and expected devaluation in the academic arena by disidentifying with academic domains. Thus, even if the sense of self is maintained by substituting either more global self-referents or equally important alternative domains, the use of these cognitive strategies may often result in underperformance in important areas in which such biases may take place (Jones, 1992).

Moreover, even if these environments are benign and promote developmental competencies, navigating multiple worlds is a given demand for minority children and youth (Cooper, Jackson, Azmitia, & Lopez, 1998). The myriad of inhibiting and promoting environments that these children need to negotiate, including racially integrated or segregated schools, churches, gangs, and neighborhoods, require particular skills, including bilingualism, code switching, and biculturalism. We know very little about the strengths and vulnerabilities that accompany mastering code switching, negotiating cultural differences and conflicts, and developing bicultural orientations in these populations, and the possible internal cost associated with these transactions.

However, even if many conditions contribute to their overrepresentation in risk categories, the majority of minority children and families thrive, and some go on to excel in spite of all odds. What do we know about the factors that counteract or prevent the development of psychopathology in these populations?

As we have stated before, much less is known about the protective factors operative within these populations than about the risk conditions. Are the same protective factors operative for minority and majority populations? What about righting and promoting processes? For now, we will assume that the same protective factors will operate but that some will be more necessary than others, or that their impact will be different or community-specific. For example, positive family relationships, which are universally thought of as a protective factor, might be more crucial in the prevention of developmental psychopathology in minority populations. Given the lack of access to compensatory or remediative resources in other contexts, or the presence of even inhibiting or hostile factors in others, strong parental investment and advocacy, and exposure to positive role models in the home might be more critical for these children and adolescents than for those in the mainstream.

In addition, parental monitoring, an aspect of family functioning that has been found to be related to developmental outcome in various populations, might be more important for minority children and adolescents given the conditions of many of the neighborhoods in which these children live (Jarrett, 1997). The systematic housing segregation observed in this country (Massey & Denton, 1988) relegates a large percentage of these populations to neighborhoods where crime and violence are frequent occurrences. Monitoring the peer group, school attendance and performance, as well as connecting children and youth with critical resources outside their immediate surroundings, might be critical in prevention and early remediation.

In contrast, there are other protective factors that might operate only within minority groups or be more salient for these populations. Strong connection with an extended family system, due in part to a more collective sense of self and a definition of well-being in relational terms, seems to play a major role in family functioning. Lacking a strong family system, or in addition to it, community resources typically identified as sources of support, such as ministers and religious groups, have also been identified as promoting well-being in these populations. Finally, the ethnic enclave and the sharing of an adaptive culture and sense of belonging and connection to a community seems also to buffer stress and its many negative consequences. These more collective mechanisms that go beyond the nuclear family and the parents as sole caretakers can be supported and/or provided by the adaptive cultures. While segregation into these communities may deprive minority families of many critical resources, it may also contribute to well-being by providing minority children and their families with other sources of support that are more congruent with their ancestral roots.

ISSUES AROUND ASSESSMENT AND DIAGNOSIS

Because of the complexity of the sociocultural matrix in which many of these children and families are imbedded, practitioners need to implement assessment paradigms that go beyond the universalistic–relativistic dichotomy of cultural understanding (emic vs. etic) in order to be able to identify and delineate both risk and protective factors. Vargas and Koss-Chioino (1992) have proposed a multidimensional model that includes *culture* (as both content and context) and *structure* (as the form and process of interventions). The content dimension, for instance, includes values that differ from one cultural group to another, role expectations, spiritual beliefs, and developmental expectations. The context dimension consists of socio-economic factors, immigration factors, racism, discrimination, and expectations of the therapeutic work determined by both the client's and clinician's culturally patterned expectations that may have an impact on the content. Although the model was initially proposed to understand culturally responsive therapies, we argue that it could be implemented at the assessment phase to help clinicians identify risk and protective factors, especially in the cultural dimension. Therefore, a clinician might identify content of the client's or family's cultural values (e.g., beliefs about developmental milestones, parenting, family relations, spirituality) and their protective or inhibiting qualities while simultaneously understanding the impact of the family's (cultural) context (defined by a broader set of influences, such as poverty, experiences of discrimination, violence) that might in turn interfere with the normal enactment and implementation of the family's cultural values. Consideration of these dimensions in relation to elements of assessment, diagnosis, and intervention can facilitate the choice of appropriate approaches and may reduce the risk of implementing approaches that focus on risk or deficiency at the expense of mobilizing protective factors that are culturally congruent.

In response to these issues, a number of professional associations in the behavioral sciences have adopted guidelines to ensure the ethical conduct of assessment, treatment, research, and educational activities that involve ethnic minority populations. For instance, the American Psychological Association (APA) and the National Association of Social Workers (NASW) have established ethical standards that call for practitioners to obtain education relevant to working with diverse populations, to understand the cultural backgrounds of their clients, and to use this knowledge appropriately (American Psychological Association, 1993;

NASW, 1996, p. 9). Additionally, the APA "Guidelines for Providers of Psychological Services to Ethnic, Linguistic, and Culturally Diverse Populations" was drafted in 1993, with the purpose of helping practitioners eliminate unethical and inappropriate practices when working with culturally diverse clients.

These guidelines establish the need for practitioners to obtain knowledge and skills for multicultural assessment and intervention, and specify the tasks in which practitioners who work with these populations should be proficient. While these guidelines clearly recognize the diversity and sociocultural complexity of consumers of psychological services, including the socioculturally diverse children and families we are concerned with in this chapter, they also represent a challenge for both the scientists and practitioners who work with these populations. The challenge consists of formulating theoretical models that guide the socioculturally competent assessment, diagnosis, and treatment of these children and of developing assessment instruments whose application to these children and families will not result in inappropriate diagnoses or further stigmatization.

However, clinicians who work with minority children and families have few specific guidelines for culturally appropriate evaluation, assessment, diagnostic, and intervention strategies. As Cervantes and Arroyo (1994) indicate, inattention to cultural factors that may affect diagnosis and the relative paucity of practical knowledge about culturally competent assessment, diagnosis, and intervention strategies has led to inappropriate referrals for services, academic placements (e.g., special education), and perhaps more alarmingly, to clinical diagnostic errors that have resulted in the overpathologizing of minority children and adolescents (Canino & Spurlock, 1994; Cervantes & Arroyo, 1994).

In addition, the use of standard definitions of developmental psychopathology sometimes introduces biases that contribute to the overrepresentation of these populations within some diagnostic categories. Cervantes and Arroyo (1994) reviewed the DSM-IV diagnostic categories relevant to children and adolescents, and have identified several sources of potential diagnostic bias that they alert clinicians to consider. For instance, they indicate that many limited English proficiency (LEP) children who are referred for cognitive/educational evaluations may be inaccurately found to be cognitively delayed on the basis of having limited second-language proficiency and also on the basis of cognitive testing that is not adequately normed on populations similar to the child's population of origin.

Additionally, many second-language children are referred for testing due to "reading/ writing developmental disorders" and often tested in English before adequate native and second-language proficiency testing is performed in order to determine the most appropriate language in which to test them. The failure to determine the appropriate language in which to perform diagnostic testing of a second-language child and the application of English instruments normed on English-speaking populations may yield results that significantly underestimate the child's actual level of functioning. Lopez et al. (1997) have also identified some of these problems and recommend that the assessment of LEP children include informal prereferral assessment of their language capabilities and usage in different contexts (i.e., school, family, community); assessment of their language dominance and proficiency; the integration of multiple assessment tools; and the adaptation of existing instruments and appropriate norming.

The following case illustrates the extreme difficulties that practitioners may encounter when asked to perform comprehensive psychological evaluations of children from sociocultural backgrounds that are radically different from that of the practitioner even when he or she is of the same ethnic background: Luisa, a 12-year-old undocumented child, is originally from a remote village in Central America. Spanish is Luisa's second language; a native indigenous language is her first. At the time of the referral, made by a state child protective agency, Luisa had given birth to a child, the product of an alleged rape in her village. The evaluation was requested to help determine if Luisa would be an appropriate parent for this infant.

The background referral information stated that, much like her mother, Luisa had at most a year of formal schooling in her country of origin and at a very early age was working on her aunt and uncle's ranch. Upon interview, her mother explained that in her society of origin, there is a sharp distinction between those families who own land and those who do not. Among the families who own land, the priority is that everyone works the land or otherwise contributes to the family's livelihood. Those families without land cannot afford to send their children to school. She added that, in her village, it is normative for very young girls to marry, have children, and learn how to take care of their children. However, she felt that Luisa was rather immature and not ready to assume these responsibilities. Luisa's mother was also appropriately distressed about her daughter being raped but felt powerless to prosecute the offender, who allegedly remains in his country of origin.

The individual assessment of Luisa presented several challenges, mostly due to the absence of Spanish-language instruments with norms that could be applied to her. In particular, the cognitive testing was performed utilizing the Spanish version of a known instrument that had recently been normed for use in Puerto Rico. Luisa obtained scores in the mentally deficient range in both the verbal and nonverbal parts of this instrument. On a test of basic literacy in Spanish, Luisa also performed significantly below her age expectations. Finally, projective drawings and a projective test involving a storytelling task indicated that Luisa holds a rather chaotic perception of herself and social environment around her, and also appears to have severe organic deficits.

On the basis of these results, Luisa could be determined to be in need of special education services and most likely not ready to assume parenting responsibilities independently. Nevertheless, her sociocultural background makes it necessary to consider that these results may also be explained by her lack of exposure to academic tasks and environments normative in her host society, the impact of the instability Luisa experienced as a result of the poverty in her family and the specific experiences of trauma in her life. It is also important to point out that the measures employed to evaluate cognitive functioning may have been inappropriate in that they represented "etic" means. Thus, her mother's assessment of Luisa's capabilities based on the expectations of their culture of origin is important here.

Given the complexity of these factors, it is imperative for clinicians to point out the severe limitations inherent in the existing testing instruments and in the validity of the resulting reports. Additionally, this was an assessment situation that required that the clinician learn about the values, assumptions, and, especially, the ways in which families like Luisa's have had to cope with poverty, social and political oppression in their countries of origin, and with the implications of having an undocumented status in this country.

Bilingual/bicultural clinicians can often be asked to perform cognitive–educational evaluations to determine school placement of children who are bilingual or speak a language other than English at home. Oftentimes, the child is lagging behind in reading and writing skills. However, referrals of children who have no significant delay (relative to their white peers) are also received because those responsible for the academic placement of these children feel that their use of a language other than English outside of school might interfere with the development of their English language competencies. Oftentimes the referral question is, "Which is this child's dominant language?" In the clinical experience of one author, suburban school districts in particular refer minority children to determine language competency, even though many of these children have been born in the United States, have attended an English-speaking school but come from either Spanish only or bilingual homes. In many of these cases, bilingual testing of cognitive–academic language proficiency (CALP) often reveals that English is the language in which these children are proficient for school-related tasks, and just as often, they have inadequate Spanish language competencies for academic tasks. The reverse has been seen almost exclusively in the cases of children who have spent most of their schooling in a Spanish-speaking country and have recently arrived in the United States. Thus, the issue of testing referrals reflects, on one hand, well-defined (or well-intentioned) efforts at clarifying or confirming a child's language dominance for school in the interest of serving the educational needs of this population. On the other hand, some of these referrals may reflect a prejudice: that exposure to and family use of a native language other than English can be detrimental to the academic progress of minority children.

Contrary to the prejudices underlying some of these referrals, research in the area of the effects of bilingualism on the academic and cognitive development of children has provided evidence that bilingualism does not necessarily interfere with children's academic or cognitive functioning. In fact, bilingual children may be at an advantage over monolingual children in certain aspects of cognitive functioning (Diaz & Klinger, 1991; Padilla & Lindholm, 1984). As an example, research by Umbel, Pearson, Fernandez, and Oller (1992) found that among bilingual first graders in Miami who spoke both English and Spanish at home, scores on a measure of receptive vocabulary in English was nearly average, suggesting that the simultaneous learning of two languages is not harmful in the development of language competencies in English. These children also scored within the average range in a parallel measure of receptive vocabulary in Spanish.

It is also important to note that research on the relationship between bilingualism and cognition in the United States has suffered from several methodological problems that have likely contributed to contradictory results. Bilingual and monolingual children might differ on a number of relevant contextual variables, which may have confounded some of the findings that exist in the literature. These variables, such as the family's socioeconomic status and its ability to effectively participate in their children's education, should be controlled for in future studies.

In summary, the context of minority children and their families has profound implications for the identification and assessment of developmental psychopathology, inclusive of etiological factors. Both theoreticians and practitioners are faced with the challenge presented by the relatively limited research and knowledge base of the complex interplay of the unique sociocultural context of minority children and families, and developmental problems. Nevertheless, recent contributions to the area of assessment, such as the model proposed by Vargas and Koss-Chioino (1992), represent emerging alternatives responses to this challenge. Other alternative and perhaps complementary approaches that we feel facilitate the balanced identification of risk and protective factors in assessment and treatment are discussed in the next section.

TREATMENT AND THERAPEUTIC ISSUES

There are several ways in which the sociocultural context of minority children and families impacts treatment considerations. One of them is the family's agreement and cooperation in regard to the diagnosis and treatment of developmental psychopathology. Even if parents agree with the fact that there is a "problem" and with the etiology of the problem, there is still potential for disagreement in how to treat and resolve this problem (García Coll, Meyer, & Brillon, 1995).

For example, the involvement of parents in educational supportive or remedial interventions might be deemed inappropriate in minority groups, where the teachers are seen as being in charge of promoting learning and the parents as being either nurturers (mothers) or disciplinarians (fathers). Rosado (1986), in particular, discusses the need to bring to bear knowledge of the complex interplay of Hispanic families' cultural values around child rearing and the ecological variables they encounter to the process of treating and placing children in the appropriate school services. These variables may include migration experiences, socio-economic stressors, and access to indigenous supports and resources. Unfortunately, as with the assessment and diagnostic issues discussed earlier, there is also a relative lack of knowledge on how ethnocultural variables and values relevant to parenting practices impact the developmental and learning experiences of Hispanic children (Rosado, 1986).

On the other hand, particular therapeutic orientations might be well fitted to these family systems. For example, family systems therapy might be very welcome and accepted in some families, where the collective sense of self defines an individual member's problem as everybody's problem, but it might need to be adapted in a hierarchical family system with rigid age and gender roles. For instance, the structural model of family therapy (Minuchin, 1974), which is based on the understanding of subsystems of function and authority within the family, may provide a culturally congruent model for Hispanic families. Specifically, this family therapy orientation formulates family dysfunction on the basis of breakdowns in the family structure and the violation of boundaries between parent and child subsystems. The therapeutic intervention consequently consists of restoring and finding support for the function of the parental roles and the allocation of appropriate roles for the children.

As an example, Szapocznik, Scopetta, Aranalde, and Kurtines (1978) have applied principles based on the structural model of family therapy to the assessment and treatment of Hispanic (particularly Cuban) families facing behavioral and emotional difficulties with their children. Their experience with these families indicates that these problems are often associated with children's rejection of parental authority (which in turn might be associated with the process of acculturation and the developmental demands of adolescence), particularly when the parents adopt ineffective (i.e., extremely restrictive) roles. Szapocznik et al. recommend that clinicians provide the families with skills to address the problems while simultaneously supporting the traditional hierarchical structure of Hispanic families. They also recommend that clinicians who work with these families facilitate a dialogue between parents and children about the different acculturation-related challenges they are each facing.

The following case illustrates the application of family therapy using an approach that recognizes the hierarchy of the family and also mobilizes traditional protective aspects, as illustrated by the family's accessing the help of an aunt, thus strengthening the adult subsystem by tapping the extended family. Ana is a Puerto Rican, bilingual adolescent who lives with both parents in a Northeastern city. Ana recently ran away from home, causing her mother a great deal of distress. Her mother affirmed that she would never have expected this behavior from Ana: "She has always been obedient and a good student." Ana had been diagnosed as "conduct disordered" by a non-Hispanic clinician following the incident, when she was referred for evaluation by her school. Ana and her family were subsequently referred for outpatient treatment.

When Ana was interviewed, she was reluctant to disclose her reasons for running away, where she went, or what took place during the time she was AWOL. Her mother, in her great distress, frequently asked, "What did I do wrong? Where did I fail?" By the time the family came into therapy, Ana's aunt, who was living in a distant state, had come to help the family and made plans to move in until the situation was normalized.

As the circumstances around this event were assessed, it became clear that a thorough understanding of this family's value assumptions surrounding parent–child relations, and especially the expected role of women in their society of origin, was essential. Ana's parents, being somewhat older than most parents in Ana's age group, described their own upbringing as very traditional in that young women would only go out if chaperoned, and that children of both genders would, first and foremost, be obedient and respectful of parental authority.

In subsequent meetings, Ana complained rather emphatically that she was being raised in the same way her parents had been, and she felt that she was the only one in her peer group that "couldn't do anything!" Ana explained that she finally ran away with a girlfriend because of this, as she felt that there was no other way for her to join in on the activities that most of her peers enjoyed without the same restrictions.

Further assessment of Ana's parents revealed that they had in fact hoped to raise Ana and her older sister (now a college student) under the same guidelines and assumptions under which they were raised. Ana's mother found the ideas of adolescent dating, sleepovers, and after-school activities to be quite foreign to her experience, "unnecessary, and even dangerous." Additionally, Ana's mother often expressed that she did not know most of Ana's friends or their parents.

The more helpful therapeutic interventions in this case combined an assessment and understanding of Ana's parents' traditional value-based assumptions about parenting practices, their perspectives on the process of acculturation (which they had basically rejected altogether for themselves), and the pressures Ana was trying to negotiate, namely, adolescent development, acculturation, and her family's values. Validation of how these issues impacted both Ana and her parents facilitated dialogue and significantly reduced the anger and distress the family was experiencing at the time they presented for treatment.

Additionally, Ana's aunt, who had raised her now-adult children both in Puerto Rico and in the mainland United States, added important and empathic insights that Ana's parents could utilize and also served as a source of support for Ana. Eventually, the family was able to discuss making a contract together with Ana, in which expectations and privileges were established. This allowed the parents to implement their authority in a values-congruent fashion while becoming responsive to the developmental and acculturative imperatives with which Ana was contending. At this point in the therapy, it was clear that the initial diagnosis of conduct disorder did not accurately reflect Ana's need to negotiate the developmental and acculturation pressures that precipitated her running away.

Ana was also able to see that her parents were willing to work with her and to function more effectively in light of the challenges they were all facing. The therapy ended after a 2-month period, during which Ana and her parents were seen in a combination of individual and conjoint sessions with the purpose of providing support as they implemented the contract, were assisted with problem-solving tasks, and were reaffirmed regarding the parents' capacity to function with authority but also with empathic understanding of Ana's developmental stage challenges. By the end of the therapy, Ana's parents reported that they had begun to meet and socialize with some of her friends' parents and were thoroughly enjoying this experience. Within it, they also found support and validation for their efforts to raise their daughter in a culturally congruent but also developmentally appropriate fashion.

Aside from family considerations, the sociocultural context of minority children and youth can have implications for the actual therapeutic interventions utilized with the individual child and youth. For example, the approach of "cuento therapy," developed for Hispanic children with behavioral disorders by Costantino, Malgady, and Rogler (1985), illustrates how the content of Puerto Rican culture is integrated into the broader social context in which these children live.

These authors' premise is that traditional therapeutic approaches that do not incorporate culture as a potentially therapeutic tool may not be effective for Hispanic children and adolescents diagnosed as having behavioral disorders and also facing the pressures of acculturation. Additionally, the authors designed a therapeutic approach that could respond to the problem of access to therapeutic services, often encountered by cultural and linguistic minorities, that could be applied in school settings to facilitate the participation of the parent from a linguistic and sociocultural standpoint. Specifically, this therapeutic approach uses culture as content by employing Puerto Rican short stories, which in turn contain expressed cultural values and roles definitions that typify the stories' themes. The short stories are read by the clinician and, in some cases, by the parent. This is then followed by a role-play exercise where the child takes on the role of the folk hero/heroine and implements prosocial, adaptive problem-solving strategies. This form of intervention affirms cultural identity for these children and families who are in the midst of powerful acculturative pressures. Storytelling is also a culturally congruent way of transmitting values and traditions, and of modeling functional family and child behaviors.

The authors evaluated the effect of this approach on the behavior of 200 children, from grades K to 3, found to be "high-risk" in a public school system in New York City. The children had been found to exhibit maladaptive behaviors in school, including aggression and other forms of anxiety. Utilizing Puerto Rican folktales, therapists and the children's mothers participated in small, weekly group sessions of 90 minutes' duration for 20 weeks. The folktales were chosen for content in which the main character(s) modeled prosocial, adaptive behaviors. The stories were read to the children, who subsequently engaged in a role-play exercise based on the content of the stories. Outcome measures of trait anxiety revealed that at the end of the treatment period, the scores of children who participated in the therapy experienced a significant reduction in trait anxiety, increased on the comprehension subtest of the Wechsler Intelligence Scale for Children, and showed less aggression in their role plays compared to the scores obtained before the intervention (Costantino, Malgady, & Rogler, 1985).

These same authors have developed techniques to address behavioral disorders in Hispanic adolescents that can also be used as preventive mental health interventions (Costantino, Malgady, & Rogler, 1988). In these cases, adult Puerto Rican role models are utilized in order to promote ethnic identity, improved self-concept, and to reduce anxiety. Finally, Costantino and his colleagues have developed a projective personality assessment technique, the Tell Me a Story (TEMAS), consisting of cards containing brightly illustrated, unambiguous situations that they have shown to be highly relevant to Hispanic and other minority and nonminority children who live in inner-city environments. The authors have developed age and culture-specific norms for this test to assist in diagnosis and to help clinicians arrive at a formulation of personality and behavioral issues. Their main construct is the child's perception of the surrounding social and familial environment, and of commonly experienced situations.

CONCLUSIONS

The social, economic, and cultural contexts of minority children and their families in the United States create special conditions for mental health and developmental psychopathology. These unique conditions, derived from subjects' relatively low position in the social stratification system in this country, need to be placed centrally in our understanding of these populations' relative overrepresentation in high-risk categories and the failure of many preventive and remediative efforts on their behalf.

The pervasiveness of these factors, from conception on, requires interventions at all levels of society for the prevention and amelioration of developmental psychopathology in minority children. Working with individual children solely in an educational or psychotherapeutic setting will be sufficient only for certain resilient, high-functioning families and their children, or for those with relatively minor conditions. More systemic efforts, inclusive of multigenerational strategies, will be needed for some families in which the parental contribution to the child's developmental conditions might be more readily identifiable. For interventions to be effective for some children, parental employment, underemployment, isolation from the extended family, mental health problems, or even many conflicting demands placed on the parents by the lack of emotional, social, and material resources to support their own family, need to be addressed.

Strengthening community resources is another level of intervention that might be necessary in order to prevent or remedy some conditions. Although it has been relatively hard to identify neighborhood effects on developmental outcome, several lines of research suggest aspects of community resources that support positive developmental outcome (Sampson, Raudenbush, & Earls, 1997).

Another level of intervention refers to fostering the opportunities for social mobility and integration of these populations. More uniformity of educational and health care opportunities should exist in this country. It is appalling that in one of the wealthiest countries of the world, many families do not have access to basic critical resources that would serve as protective factors and lead to the prevention of developmental psychopathology and the promotion of positive developmental outcome. The roles of racism and other derivatives of our social stratification system need to be addressed at every societal level.

Practitioners who work with culturally diverse subjects must implement assessment, diagnostic, and treatment approaches that reflect a thorough integration of the complex cultural and sociopolitical imperatives and conditions experienced by these children and families. Theoretical models, such as the ones proposed by Vargas and Koss-Chioino (1992), provide clinicians with a practical framework that can assist them in this task.

In particular, practitioners need to identify the specific effects of the acculturation process on the adult and child subsystems of the families with which they work and should also assess the strengths, or protective factors, that most families have in spite of the adversities they might face. Moreover, they need to gain a full understanding of these families' experiences of discrimination and racism in order to establish the level of trust that they will have in mainstream institutions and interventions. Knowledge and understanding of these factors is closely linked to an understanding of the family's sociocultural values and how these values are supported or challenged in the new environment.

Practitioners should also remember that the existing knowledge base on how to provide assessment and therapy services in a socioculturally competent manner is still relatively limited. This might be due to the complexity of the issues and the methodological challenges that their systematic assessment presents (García Coll & Magnuson, 1999). For example, measuring the effects of discriminatory/racist practices in a school setting requires both direct and indirect assessments from multiple viewpoints, such as direct observation by an unbiased observer, children's reports of actual acts of discrimination, children's projective responses to hypothetical situations, and so on (Akiba, García Coll, & Magnuson, submitted). In addition, most extant theoretical models and research efforts have applied deficiency driven models that continue to document primarily the negative aspects of functioning in these populations, disregarding the well-functioning areas and the protective factors found in their adaptive culture. Therefore, practitioners should also derive from their collective experiences the fundamentals of socioculturally competent work with diverse populations and disseminate this knowledge among the academic and practitioner communities.

REFERENCES

Akiba, D., García Coll, C. T., & Magnuson, K. (submitted). Children of color and children from immigrant families: The development of social identities, school engagement and interethnic social attribution during middle childhood.

American Psychological Association. (1993). Guidelines for providers of psychological services to ethnic, linguistic, and culturally diverse populations. *American Psychologist, 48*(1), 45–48.

Basic Behavioral Science Research for Mental Health. (1996). Sociocultural and environmental processes. *American Psychologist, 51*(7), 722–731.

Berry, J. (1990). Acculturation and adaptation: A general framework. In W. H. Holtzman & T. H. Borneman (Eds.), *The mental health of immigrants and refugees* (pp. 90–102). Austin: Hogg Foundation for Mental Health, University of Texas.

Brooks-Gunn, J., & Duncan, G. J. (1997). The effects of poverty on children. *Children and Poverty, 7*(2), 55–71.

Canino, I. A., & Spurlock, J. (1994). *Culturally diverse children and adolescents.* New York: Guilford Press.

Cervantes, R. C., & Arroyo, W. (1994). DSM-IV: Implications for Hispanic children and adolescents. *Hispanic Journal of Behavioral Sciences, 16*(1), 8–27.

Constantino, G., Malgady, R., & Rogler, L. (1985). *Cuento therapy: Folktales as a culturally sensitive psychotherapy for Puerto Rican children.* (Hispanic Research Center Monograph No. 12). Maplewood, NJ: Waterfront Press.

Constantino, G., Malgady, R., & Rogler, L. (1988). Folk hero modeling therapy for Puerto Rican adolescents. *Journal of Adolescence, 11,* 155–165.

Cooper, C., Jackson, J. F., Azmita, M., & Lopez, E. M. (1998). Multiple selves, multiple worlds: Three useful strategies for research with ethnic minority youth. In V. McLoyd & L. Steinberg (Eds.), *Studying minority adolescents: Conceptual, methodological, and theoretical issues.* Mahwah, NJ: Erlbaum.

Cross, W. (1991). *Shades of black: Diversity in African American identity.* Philadelphia: Temple University Press.

Dana, R. H. (1993). *Multicultural assessment perspectives for professional psychology.* Needham Heights, MA: Allyn & Bacon.

Diaz, R. M., & Klinger, C. (1991). Towards an explanatory model of interaction between bilingualism and cognitive development. In E. Bialystok (Ed.), *Language processing in bilingual children* (pp. 167–192). New York: Cambridge University Press.

Duckitt, J. (1992). Psychology and prejudice. *American Psychologist, 47*(10), 1182–1193.

Dunn, L. M. (1968). Special education for the mildly retarded: Is much of it justifiable? *Exceptional Children, 56*(2), 154–158.

García Coll, C. T. (1990). Developmental outcome of minority infants: A process-oriented look into our beginnings. *Child Development, 61,* 271–289.

García Coll, C. T., Lamberty, G., Jenkins, R., McAdoo, H. P., Crnic, K., Wasik, B. H., & Vázquez García, H. (1996). An integrative model for the study of developmental competencies in minority children. *Child Development, 67*(5), 1891–1914.

García Coll, C. T., & Magnuson, K. (1997a, April 4). *To be or not to be: Racial and ethnic identity during middle childhood.* Paper presented to the Society for Research on Child Development, Washington, DC.

García Coll, C. T., & Magnuson, K. (1997b). The psychological experience of immigration: A developmental perspective. In A. Booth (Ed.), *Immigration and the family: Research and policy on U.S. immigrants.* Hillsdale, NJ: Erlbaum.

García Coll, C. T., & Magnuson, K. (1999). Cultural influences on child development: Are we ready for a paradigm shift? In C. Nelson and A. Masten (Eds.), *Minnesota Symposium on Child Psychology, 29.*

García Coll, C. T., & Vázquez García, H. A. (1995). Hispanic children and their families: On a different track from the very beginning. In H. E. Fitzgerald, B. M. Lester, & B. Zuckerman (Eds.), *Children of poverty: Research, health care and policy issues* (pp. 57–83). New York: Garland.

García Coll, C. T., Meyer, E. C., & Brillon, L. (1995). Ethnic and minority parents. In M. H. Bornstein (Ed.), *Handbook of parenting* (Vol. 2, pp. 189–209). New York: Erlbaum.

Gil, A. G., Vega, W. A., & Dimas, J. M. (1994). Acculturative stress and personal adjustment among Hispanic adolescent boys. *Journal of Community Psychology, 22,* 43–53.

Gopaul-McNicol, S. A., Clark-Castro, S., & Black, K. (1997). Cognitive testing with culturally diverse children. *Cultural Diversity and Mental Health, 3*(2), 113–116.

Hall, S. (Ed.). (1997). *Representation: Cultural representations and signifying practices.* London: Sage.

Jarrett, R. (1997). African American family and parenting strategies in impoverished neighborhoods. *Qualitative Sociology, 20,* 275–288.

Jones, J. M. (1992). Understanding the mental health consequences of race: Contributions of basic social psychological processes. In D. N. Ruble, P. R. Costanzo, & M. E. Oliveri (Eds.), *The social psychology of mental health* (pp. 199–240). New York: Guilford Press.

Lopez, E. C., Lamar, D., & Scully-Demartini, D. (1997). The cognitive assessment of limited-English-proficient children: Current problems and practical recommendations. *Cultural Diversity and Mental Health, 3*(2), 117–130.

Massey, D. S., & Denton, N. A. (1988). Suburbanization and segregation in U.S. metropolitan areas. *American Journal of Sociology, 94,* 592–626.

McConahay, J. B., & Hough, J. C. (1976). Symbolic racism. *Journal of Social Issues, 32*(2), 23–45.

Mercer, J. R. (1972). *Sociocultural factors in the educational evaluation of black and Chicano children.* Paper presented at the 10th Annual Conference on Civil and Human Rights of Educators and Students, Washington, DC.

Mercer, J. R. (1978). Test validity, bias, and fairness: An analysis from the perspective of the sociology of knowledge. *Interchange, 9*(1), 1–16.

Minuchin, S. (1974). *Families and family therapy.* Cambridge, MA: Harvard University Press.

National Association of Social Workers. (1996). *Code of ethics.* Washington, DC: Author. @http//:www.naswdc.org/code/ethics.htm

Oakland, T. (1997). *Psychological and educational assessment of minority children.* New York: Brunner/Mazel.

Oakland, T., & Phillips, B. N. (1973). *Assessing minority group children.* New York: Behavioral Publications.

Ogbu, J. U. (1978). *Minority education and caste: The American system in a cross-cultural perspective.* New York: Academic Press.

Ogbu, J. U. (1991). Low school performance as an adaptation: The case of blacks in Stockton, California. In M. A. Gibson & J. U. Ogbu (Eds.), *Minority schooling and status* (pp. 249–285). New York: Garland.

Padilla, A. M. (Ed.). (1980). *Acculturation: Theory, models, and some new findings.* Boulder, CO: Westview.

Padilla, A. M., & Lindholm, K. J. (1984). Child bilingualism: The same old issues revisited. In J. L. Martinez & R. H. Mendoza (Eds.), *Chicano psychology* (pp. 369–408). New York: Academic Press.

Pierce, K. A. (1995). Aggressors and their victims: Toward a contextual framework for understanding children's aggressor–victim relationships. *Developmental Review, 15*(3), 292–310.

Ramirez, M. (1998). *Multicultural/multiracial psychology: Mestizo perspectives in personality and mental health.* Northook, NJ: Aronson.

Rogler, L. H., Cortes, D. E., & Malgady, R. G. (1991). Acculturation and mental health status among Hispanics. *American Psychologist, 46*(6), 585–597.

Rosado, J. W., Jr. (1986). Toward an interfacing of Hispanic cultural variables with school psychology service delivery systems. *Professional Psychology: Research and Practice, 17*(3), 191–199.

Rueschenberg, E. J., & Buriel, R. (1995). Mexican American family functioning and acculturation. In A. M. Padilla (Ed.), *Hispanic psychology: Critical issues in theory and research* (pp. 15–25). Thousand Oaks, CA: Sage.

Rutter, M. (1979). Protective factors in children's responses to stress and disadvantage. In M. W. Kent & J. E. Rolf (Eds.), *Primary prevention of psychopathology: Vol. 3. Social competence in children.* Hanover, NH: University Press of New England.

Sameroff, A. (1994). Ecological perspectives on longitudinal follow-up studies. In S. L. Friedman & H. C. Haywood (Eds.), *Developmental followup: Concepts, domains, and methods.* New York: Academic Press.

Sampson, R. J., Raudenbush, S. W., & Earls, F. (1997). Neighborhoods and violent crime: A multilevel study of collective efficacy. *Science, 277,* 918–924.

Samuda, R. (1975). From ethnocentrism to a multicultural perspective in educational testing. *Journal of Afro-American Issues, 3,* 4–17.

Samuda, R. (1976). Problems and issues in assessment of minority group children. In R. L. Jones (Ed.), *Mainstreaming and the minority child* (pp. 65–76). Reston, VA: Council for Exceptional Children.

Sears, D. O. (1988). Symbolic racism. In P. A. Katz & K. A. Taylor (Eds.), *Eliminating racism: Profiles in controversy. Perspectives in social psychology* (pp. 53–84). New York: Plenum Press.

Steele, C. (1995). A threat in the air: How stereotypes shape intellectual identity and performance. *American Psychologist, 52,* 613–629.

Szapocznik, J., Scopetta, M. A., Aranalde, M., & Kurtines, W. (1978). Cuban value structure: Treatment implications. *Journal of Consulting and Clinical Psychology, 46,* 961–970.

Tucker, J. A. (1980). *Nineteen steps for assuring non-biased placement of students in special education.* Reston, VA: ERIC Clearinghouse on Handicapped and Gifted Children.

Umbel, V. M., Pearson, B. Z., Fernandez, M. C., & Oller, D. K. (1992). Measuring bilingual children's receptive vocabularies. *Child Development, 63,* 1012–1020.

Vargas, L. A, & Koss-Chioino, J. D. (Eds.). (1992). *Working with culture: Psychotherapeutic interventions with ethnic minority children and adolescents.* San Francisco: Jossey-Bass.

Waters, M. C. (1996). The intersection of gender, race, and ethnicity in identity development of Caribbean American teens. In B. J. R. Leadbetter & N. Way (Eds.), *Urban girls: Resisting stereotypes, creating identities* (pp. 65–81). New York: New York University Press.

Weisner, T. S. (1984). Ecocultural niches of middle childhood: A cross-cultural perspective. In W. Andrew Collins (Ed.), *Development during middle childhood: The years from six to twelve* (pp. 335–369). Washington, DC: National Academy Press.

Willie, C. V., Rieker, P. P., Kramer, B. M., & Brown, B. S. (Eds.). (1995). *Mental health, racism, and sexism.* Pittsburgh: University of Pittsburgh Press.

Zinn, M. B. (1975). Political familism: Toward sex role equality in Chicano families. *Aztlan, 6*(1), 13–26.

11

Culture and Psychopathology

Sara Harkness and Charles M. Super

Anthropological research and, more recently, cross-cultural studies in general have played a delicate combination of roles as they converse with psychological theory. On the one hand, they provide a method of answering questions about human behavior and development, which are central to contemporary thought; on the other, they often return only partial answers and, in addition, a new set of questions. The interplay of psychological theory contributing to the agenda for anthropological research, and cross-cultural findings challenging accepted theories of the person, has shifted from time to time, responding in part to the needs and opportunities of the larger disciplines. Throughout the interdisciplinary dialogue are woven the complementary themes of human universals and cultural particulars, or, in modern developmental terms, how and to what degree general universals become the particular specifics. This is no less true for research on psychopathology than for studies of normal development.

The challenge from one perspective is to collect and integrate comparative data about human behavior into a theory that accounts for both the universal and the particular; from another, it is to understand the role of culture in both the normal and the deviant. In both cases, a focus on *development* recasts the dichotomy into a question of process. In the case of psychopathology, as other chapters in this volume illustrate, a developmental approach substantially alters the terms of understanding from the earlier, adult-oriented model of diagnosis and therapy. With regard to the oft-posed dichotomy in culture and development, we concluded in an earlier review that "it no longer seems appropriate to ask which behaviors are universal and which are culturally variable; all behaviors probably are both, at different levels" (Harkness & Super, 1987, p. 238). An understanding of culture and psychopathology is in many ways only a more specific case of understanding culture and development.

In this chapter, we review the intellectual history of anthropological contributions to the study of psychopathology across cultures and relate these contributions to current work in developmental psychology and psychiatry that address issues of individual functioning in social context. At this point, three generalizations are evident. First, culture as the meaningful,

Sara Harkness and Charles M. Super • School of Family Studies, University of Connecticut, Storrs, Connecticut 06269.

Handbook of Developmental Psychopathology, Second Edition, edited by Arnold J. Sameroff, Michael Lewis, and Suzanne M. Miller. Kluwer Academic/Plenum Publishers, New York, 2000.

shared, and immediate structuring of daily life, contributes to the development and manifestation of psychological distress and mental dysfunction. Second, distress and dysfunction are organized into categories through cultural processes, thus further influencing their development and expression. Third, culture structures the responses to distress and dysfunction by other persons and institutions through shared implicit or explicit theories of causality and intervention. As theories of culture, development, individuality, and psychopathology have themselves evolved in this century, our understanding of the phenomena and processes that lie behind these generalizations has increased substantially.

EARLY FORMULATIONS OF CULTURE AND PSYCHOPATHOLOGY: BENEDICT AND MEAD

A point of departure for much thinking about culture and psychopathology in twentieth-century anthropology was established by Ruth Benedict. In an article first published in the *Journal of General Psychology* in 1934, Benedict (1934/1973) argued that mental illness exists only in relation to cultural definitions of normal and abnormal. Each culture, she proposed, chooses a portion of the spectrum of possible human behavior as socially appropriate, labeling as "abnormal" those other behaviors that would conflict with the dominant ethos. Benedict suggested further, building on her theory of "patterns of cultures" (Benedict, 1934), that the degree of cultural integration in any particular society should coincide with a greater tendency to sanction behavior that from the perspectives of other cultures would appear aberrant.

Benedict made her case on the basis of ethnographic accounts such as the following description of reaction to the death of loved ones among the Kwakiutl, an American Indian group of the Pacific Coast, whose mores had been recorded by ethnographers starting in the late nineteenth century:

> A chief's sister and her daughter had gone up to Victoria, and either because they drank bad whiskey or because their boat capsized they never came back. The chief called together his warriors. "Now I ask you, tribes, who shall wail? Shall I or shall another?" The spokesman answered, of course, "Not you, Chief. Let some other of the tribes." Immediately they set up the warpole to announce their intention of wiping out the injury, and gathered a war party. They set out, and found seven men and two children asleep and killed them. Then they felt good when they arrived at Sebaa in the evening. (Benedict, 1934/1973, p. 90)

Benedict (1934/1973, p. 90) commented, "The point which is of interest to us is that in our society those who on that occasion would feel good when they arrived at Sebaa that evening would be the definitely abnormal." Benedict's larger point here was that individual variation in personality and behavior exists across all cultures, and that it is thus somewhat arbitrary just which kinds of orientations are regarded locally as "good," "normal," or deviant.

Ruth Benedict's younger colleague and friend Margaret Mead shared with her, and with their mentor Franz Boas, an interest in individual psychological functioning in cultural context, and her first field research, which became an American classic, was directed to exploring the role of culture not only in labeling psychopathology but in actually creating it (Mead, 1928). Among adolescent girls of Samoa, as Mead described them, there was no evidence of the social and psychological upheavals that had come to be expected in American society. Mead contrasted the permissive cultural environment of adolescence in Samoa to the strictures of the late Victorian Era in the United States. Far from being the normal expression of biological forces, she argued, the troubles of American adolescence could be seen as cultural artifacts (Mead, 1928).

Mead shared with Benedict a view of culture as a larger version of personality. In Benedict's words, "Cultures from this point of view are individual psychology thrown large upon the screen, given gigantic proportions and a long time span" (Benedict, 1932, p. 24). The lessons to be derived from this observation, in their views, were twofold: on the one hand, that "human nature is not rigid and unyielding" (Mead, 1939, p. 2)—thus, cultural forces could be used to improve as well as to diminish emotional well-being; on the other hand, those who were deviant by the standards of their own societies should be regarded with greater sympathy by people aware that in other times or other places, these same individuals might not be considered abnormal. Mead further developed this perspective on culture and psychopathology to address the issues of goodness of fit between individuals of varying temperaments and their culturally constructed environments. As Mead (1972) later described this thinking, she and Ruth Benedict had come to the conclusion that

> there are a limited number of temperamental types, each of which is characterized by an identifiable cluster of inborn traits, and ... these several types are systematically related to one another. If this was so, it seemed clear that an individual whose temperament was incompatible with the type (or types) emphasized in the culture in which he was born and reared would be at a disadvantage—a disadvantage that was systematic and predictable for that culture. (p. 219)

We return later in this chapter to the issue of temperament, culture, and goodness of fit as it has been addressed in more recent research.

FREUDIAN THEORY IN THE "CULTURE AND PERSONALITY" SCHOOL

The consideration of culture as a magnified version of individual dispositions set the stage for the application of theories drawn from psychopathology to the study of human social groups. This, coupled with the dominance of Freud in both lay and professional circles during the years between the two World Wars, led to a period of close collaboration between anthropologists and their colleagues in clinical psychology and psychiatry. A central event in this period was Abram Kardiner's seminar, organized in 1936 at the New York Psychoanalytic Institute, which brought together practicing analysts with major anthropological figures of the day (see Harris, 1968, pp. 435–448). Drawing from Freudian theory, Kardiner (1939) suggested that different societies were characterized by particular "basic personality structures" derived from culturally shared early childhood experience. To pursue this approach required the collection of field data that could be subjected to clinical analysis. This was provided by Cora DuBois, an anthropologist participant in Kardiner's seminar, who returned in 1939 from 2 years of field research among the people of Alor in the Dutch East Indies. Dubois's data included Rorschach test protocols, children's drawings, and eight extensive life histories, including a great deal of detailed interview material on the recalled experiences of early childhood. These materials were given to Kardiner and his colleagues in psychiatry for independent analysis; strikingly, all came up with rather similar portrayals of Alorese personality. A description by psychiatrist Emil Oberholzer, based on the Rorschach drawings, is representative:

From this we assume that the Alorese are suspicious and distrustful; they are so not only toward everything that is new and unknown to them, such as foreigners, for instance, but also among themselves. No one will trust another. Moreover, they are fearful and timid in their heart of hearts, feeling uneasy and insecure.... The Alorese must be lacking in individual personal contact, living beside one another but not with one another .... Either there are no friendships and relationships or there are none that are deeply rooted. (DuBois, 1944, pp. 598–600)

From the idea of a shared personality structure, as this quotation indicates, anthropologists and their colleagues in psychiatry had moved to the next logical inference: shared psychopathologies. Interestingly, the validity of this notion was not questioned by contemporary and even some later anthropologists, who focused their questions instead on trying to explain the *cause* of the proposed adult personalities—whether they were due to "oral deprivation" of infants when their mothers went off to the fields to work or, alternatively, whether frequent illness during childhood was to blame (e.g., Barnouw, 1973, p. 159). The fact that societies where there were truly "no friendships and relationships" could not long survive did not seem to occur to these observers.

The primacy of early experience in the etiology of adult personality was to remain an organizing principle for research in psychological anthropology for the next three decades, and along with it, a continuing identification among the constructs of culture, personality, and psychopathology. Building from Kardiner's hypothesized "primary" and "secondary" institutions, John Whiting proposed a model for psychocultural research that placed child-rearing practices as the crucial connecting link between the culturally constructed environments of early childhood and the development of adult personality, expressed at the cultural level in turn by "projective systems" such as religion and belief systems (for a recent statement of this position, see Whiting, 1977). Whiting and his colleagues put these hypothesized relationships to the test through a series of cross-cultural analyses on the co-occurrence of different kinds of cultural practices such as mother–child sleeping arrangements and adolescent circumcision ceremonies (Whiting, Kluckhohn, & Anthony, 1958), and early childhood socialization practices and adult customary behavior (Whiting, 1961). Although the studies were correlational, the researchers proposed causal relationships following the proposed cultural sequences, usually with Freudian theories providing specific proposed mechanisms. In Whiting and Child's (1953) landmark study, *Child Training and Personality*, for example, the authors found that strict socialization practices were associated with cultural attributions of guilt in the event of illness; on the other hand, extremely permissive rearing was not related to a particular pattern of illness beliefs. Whiting and Child concluded that while the cross-cultural data supported Freud's idea of negative fixation, the idea of positive fixation was not upheld.

Some projective systems such as adolescent circumcision ceremonies were hypothesized as antidotes to the otherwise pathogenic effects of early childhood experience (in this case, extended mother–child sleeping practices), thus freeing adults of psychopathology. In other cases, however, it seems that the projective systems were themselves regarded as manifestations of culturally shared psychopathology. Thus, for example, Herbert Barry, a prominent cross-cultural researcher, entitled a review paper on much of this literature "Cultural Variations in the Development of Mental Illness" (Barry, 1969). It is important to note, however, that the identification of certain cultural beliefs or practices as pathological (due to unhealthy experiences in childhood) did not seem to imply that one should expect to find whole societies of nonfunctional adults or even large numbers of adults needing psychological treatment. This apparent contradiction is perhaps best understood as a metaphorical use of the concepts of clinical theory for the purpose of understanding cultural dynamics. Reliance on poorly differentiated concepts of culture, personality, and psychopathology, however, led to so many problems of data collection and analysis that their use contributed significantly to the eventual decline of this approach (see LeVine, 1973).

CULTURAL MODELS OF THE SELF

In recent years, the interface between individual and culture has been rediscovered through thinking and research on the cultural construction of the self (see, e.g., Shweder & LeVine, 1984). Although psychopathology has not been a focus in most of this work, cultural differences in ideas about the normative self are a key component to understanding what can be construed as deviant or unhealthy—an issue of increasing practical importance in the current context of growing cultural diversity within communities. At the core of cultural perspectives on the self is the question of how the individual person is conceptualized in relation to the social context, particularly other people. Shweder and Bourne's research on Asian Indian and American concepts of the person, for example, led them to the conclusion that Indians conceptualize persons as embedded in their own social context, defined by relationships and rules, to a greater extent than do Americans (Shweder & Bourne, 1991). Similar contrasts have been drawn in comparative studies of Japanese and American cultural models of the self (Azuma, 1984; Caudill & Schooler, 1973).

In its most widely used version, cross-cultural variability in concepts of the self has been framed in terms of individualism (or independence) and collectivism (or interdependence) (Greenfield & Cocking, 1994; Markus & Kitayama, 1991; Triandis, 1989). In a nutshell, parents in collectivist cultures are said to train their children to value the welfare of the group over that of the individual, whereas parents in individualistic cultures train their children to be independent and unique (Gardiner, Mutter, & Kosmitzki, 1998). Not surprisingly, the collectivist orientation is attributed to non-Western or Third World cultures, whereas the individualistic orientation is attributed to postindustrial Western cultures, especially mainstream American culture.

This formulation has already been recognized as too simple: Research in both "individualistic" and "collectivistic" cultures has shown that both kinds of values are present in all cultures, although they may be configured differently (Harkness, Raeff, & Super, 2000). For example, Harkness, Super, and van Tijen (2000) have contrasted parents' descriptions of their children in communities in The Netherlands and the United States; they find that the Dutch parents' descriptions combine features of individualism, such as being strong-minded, with concern for social qualities, in contrast to the U.S. parents, who characterize their children in more exclusively individualistic terms, especially regarding intelligence. The contrast between individualism and collectivism, when viewed from a Western perspective, can also lead to erroneous conclusions about the psychological functioning of people in "collectivistic" cultures: For example, as Kagitçibasi (1996a) points out, achievement motivation in societies such as India and Japan goes beyond individual achievement to achievement for the benefit of the group. This "socially oriented achievement motivation" (p. 68) is not tapped by measures based on individualistic conceptualizations.

Kagitçibasi (1996a, p. 64) has proposed that a dimension of "separateness–relatedness" captures the cross-cultural contrast in conceptualizations of the self more adequately than individualism versus collectivism, because "separateness–relatedness of the self is a basically psychological dimension, whereas individualism–collectivism is not." She further critiques the adequacy of the Western insistence on separateness—evident in psychological theories as well as popular thinking—for defining what is truly most adaptive for healthy human development. In this critique, Kagitçibasi calls on her own cross-cultural observations from a Turkish point of view on the oddities of American family lifestyles and ideas; for example, she notes that "in parent education classes in the United States, young mothers are often taught to 'let go' of their toddlers. This early separation must go against some (natural?) tendencies of mothers to 'merge' with their young children (considered to be harmful), because they are asked to make a calculated effort to control these tendencies" (p. 69).

Kagitçibasi argues that although separation is construed as necessary for the achievement of independence, a primary goal of American child-rearing practices, it is neither necessary in the American context nor a prescription for health in other cultural groups who value relatedness more highly. In such groups, "enmeshment" can be a normal state of relationships rather than a sign of pathology (Coll, 1990). Therapists working with families from these cultural backgrounds, it has been pointed out, need to take other perspectives on individuation in recommending action: For example, as Falicov (1982, p. 159) notes,

> A therapist perceiving a need for greater individuation in a 9-year-old Mexican American boy may encourage him—in the Anglo pattern—to seek friendships outside the home by joining a neighborhood club or take more responsibility by getting a newspaper route. On the other hand, his parents may feel that giving him a few household chores or allowing him to run an occasional errand—duties that do not warrant payment or an allowance—are sufficient acknowledgement of more maturity.

The contrast between cultural belief systems that emphasize separateness versus relatedness can also be found within the broad parameters of Western middle-class societies, as was demonstrated in an analysis of Dutch and American parents' ideas about their children (Harkness & Super, 2000; Harkness et al., 2000). Although parents in both cultural samples described their children equally in terms of dependence and independence, the American parents tended to see both kinds of behavior as involving difficult relationship issues, whereas the Dutch parents did not. It appears that the Dutch parents conceptualized independence more in terms of autonomy—knowing one's own mind and making one's own choices—rather than separation. The Dutch parents' ideas about personal independence within the context of a close family and community are consistent with Kagitçibasi's formulation of the "autonomous relational self" (Kagitçibasi, 1996b) as a resolution to the universal human needs for both freedom and social relatedness.

CROSS-CULTURAL EPIDEMIOLOGY

In contrast to the long-standing relationship between anthropology and clinical approaches to psychopathology, the epidemiological study of psychopathology cross-culturally is still young. Until fairly recently, indeed, the question in this literature was whether mental illness existed at all in preindustrial societies, or whether it was, as Freud had proposed, a by-product of "civilization and its discontents" (Freud, 1930). Strong counterevidence has been provided by epidemiological research in diverse cultures, such as J. M. Murphy's (1976) study showing that rates of mental illness among Canadian villagers in Nova Scotia, Eskimos, and members of the Yoruba tribe in Nigeria were very similar despite the many differences among these cultures. More recently, the drive to establish standardized diagnostic techniques has provided the basis for large-scale, cross-cultural psychiatric epidemiology surveys, most notably those carried out by the World Health Organization (WHO) (e.g., Sartorius, Jablensky, Gulbinat, & Ernberg, 1980; World Health Organization, 1973, 1983).

Epidemiological studies of psychopathology start with a template of symptoms recognized as representing a distinct disease category and attempt to match individual patients to it. The difficulties inherent in this process are greatly magnified when the category system is applied across cultures, but researchers differ on their interpretation of this fact. For example, Berne (1959) suggested that the differences among patients with the same major disorder in different countries could be thought of as variants of the same phenomenon. Similarly, Draguns (1997) concluded, based on a review of epidemiological and cross-cultural studies of psychopathology, that cultural factors have a quantitative but not qualitative impact on psychiatric symptoms. Other researchers, such as Kleinman and Good (1985), however, argue that cultural differences in the experience of mental illnesses such as depression are much more profound. Specifically, as summarized by Marsella, Sartorius, Jablensky, and Fenton (1985, p. 306): "Results indicate ... the experience and expression of depression varies across ethnocultural boundaries. Reviewers concur that feelings of guilt, self-deprecation, suicidal ideas, and feelings of despair are often rare or absent among non-European populations, whereas somatic and quasi-somatic symptoms, including disturbances of sleep, appetite, energy, body sensation, and motor functioning, are more common." Given these basic differences, these researchers question whether it is useful to apply categories of psychopathology across cultures. Kleinman (1987, p. 450) has concluded that "the anthropological model of an idiom of distress offers a more accurate mapping of the experience of culture-bound disorder, and its sources and consequences, than does the medical model." Consequently, he argues, the application of psychiatric disease categories across cultures can lead to a "category fallacy," or "the reification of a nosological category developed for a particular cultural group that is then applied to members of another culture for whom it lacks coherence and its validity has not been established." Furthermore, despite considerable efforts by cross-cultural researchers, the challenge of how to incorporate cultural perspectives into standard psychiatric nosology such as the *Diagnostic and Statistical Manual of Mental Disorders* (DSM; American Psychiatric Association, 1994) remains largely unmet (Good, 1996).

In spite of these difficulties, there is a growing literature on cross-cultural differences in the prevalence of disorders that are similar enough to be compared. For example, Weisz and his colleagues have compared the prevalence of child and adolescent behavior disorders in Thailand and the United States (Weisz, Chaiyasit, Weiss, Eastman, & Jackson, 1995). In a formulation reminiscent of earlier anthropological approaches, they proposed that the Buddhist ethos of Thai culture leads adults to be "unusually intolerant of aggression, disobedience, and disrespectful acts in children" (Weisz, McCarty, Eastman, Chaiyasit, & Suwanlert, 1997, pp. 570–571). On this basis, the researchers expected to find a higher rate of "overcontrolled" problems such as shyness, somaticizing and depression in Thai children, and, conversely, a higher rate of "undercontrolled" problems such as disobedience, fighting and impulsivity in U.S. children. The researchers used several different approaches for their comparative analyses, including parent and teacher reports based on standardized measures (the Child Behavior Checklist for parents and the Teacher's Report Form, developed by Achenbach, 1991a, 1991b), clinic reports of referrals, and direct observation of children in classrooms. The results are interesting but complex (for a summary, see Weisz et al., 1997). Parent reports showed broad cross-cultural similarities in child problems, although there were significant differences in the expected direction with respect to overcontrolled and undercontrolled problems. Clinic referrals showed a high proportion of undercontrolled problems for U.S. children, whereas overcontrolled problems accounted for more than half the top 12 problems for which Thai children were referred. Teacher reports on children's problem behaviors showed a prevalence rate twice as high for Thai children as for American children, but observers found exactly the opposite.

The inconsistencies among different findings from this research led Weisz and his colleagues to draw several "lessons" about methodology in cross-cultural epidemiological research (Weisz et al., 1997). In particular, these researchers suggest that parent reports of child problems are culturally influenced in that parents may have different cultural ideas about what behavior is appropriate or usual for children at a certain age. In addition, they draw attention to the long-recognized problem of translation of items in instruments used cross-culturally. To these concerns can be added two more caveats. First, the cross-cultural use of measures such as the Child Behavior Checklist is problematic in that reporters who are members of the culture inevitably judge the behavior of a particular child in relation to their own cultural world rather than in relation to a worldwide population. This is important because responses such as "disobedient at school" or "impulsive" may signal rather different levels of problem behavior in different cultural contexts. It would be logical to imagine that in all cultures, variability in behavior is organized around what is locally normative; but what is normative, on the other hand, may differ considerably. If this is the case, then one would expect parent or teacher reports to produce "similar" results based on possibly rather different population baselines.

A second caveat relates to the issue of parental (or teacher) perceptions raised by Weisz and colleagues. The study of parental perceptions of children's behavior problems is certainly colored by cultural models of the normative child; it is reasonable to expect, therefore, that these perceptions might follow the same principles as parent descriptions of their own children (see Harkness & Super, 1996). In cross-cultural research on parents' ideas about their own children, Harkness, Super, and their colleagues have repeatedly found that there are meaningful differences in the characteristics that parents focus on, and these differences are reflected in the frequency with which certain kinds of descriptors are used by parents in different cultural settings. For example, American parents have been found to characterized their children more frequently as intelligent in contrast with a sample of Dutch parents, who more often describe their children in terms of social and temperament qualities (Harkness et al., 2000). Asian Indian immigrant parents use a group of descriptors including obedient, respectful, and (conversely) argumentative in describing their daughters by contrast with a matched group of American parents living in the same community (Raghavan, Harkness, & Super, 2000). These findings have not been interpreted as reflecting real population differences in child qualities; rather, the group differences in descriptor profiles are thought to indicate different aspects of the child that are culturally more salient, whether they are perceived as negative or positive in the individual case. Applying this perspective to parent reports of children's behavior problems, it would be reasonable to conclude that a higher prevalence of "overcontrolled" problems as reported by Thai parents reflects, among other things, the high salience of these behaviors as they relate to traditional values of modesty and self-control. If this is true, it would provide yet another way to understand the apparently inconsistent results of these cross-cultural studies.

In summary, although epidemiological approaches to the study of culture and psychopathology would seem at first blush to be relatively straightforward, the results of research indicate a far different scenario in which culture plays a pervasive role. Nevertheless, the study of child and adolescent psychopathology using a standardized frame of reference can be very informative, both for what it indicates about real cultural differences and for what it reveals about ideas and perceptions held by members of the culture.

CULTURE-BOUND SYNDROMES

The problems encountered in cross-cultural epidemiological studies of psychopathology intersect with issues identified through research on mental illness from an "emic" perspective, that is, as defined by members of the cultures where they occur. Anthropologists and other observers have long recognized the existence of culturally distinctive forms of psychopathology (Marsella, 1993). The list of these illnesses, which have come to be known as "culture-bound syndromes," includes such oft-cited examples as *windigo* psychosis among Canadian Indian groups (Fogelson, 1965; Parker, 1960), *latah* among Malay groups (H. B. M. Murphy, 1976; Simons, 1980, 1983), *susto* (O'Neill, 1975) and *ataques de nervios* (Guarnaccia, Rivera, Franco, & Neighbors, 1996) among Hispanic populations, and *taijin-kyofu-sho* ("fear of other people," or TKS syndrome) in Japan (Prince & Tcheng-Laroche, 1987). Although these syndromes have exotic qualities, some can be compared to standard Western illness categories. For example, TKS syndrome is similar to social phobia as defined by the DSM-III-R (Prince, 1991), with the important difference that Asian patients with this disorder tend to be mainly concerned about causing discomfort to others, whereas North American patients tend to focus their concern on being embarrassed and rejected by others. Miyake and Yamazaki (1995) have suggested that this disorder, and others common in Japanese society, may be related to the socialization of self-conscious emotions such as shame, guilt, embarrassment, and shyness in Japanese child rearing.

Although psychopathology has universal dimensions, the particular forms and meanings of culture-bound syndromes are best understood in relation to culturally shaped experience of the patients. Minturn (1993), for example, describes "transition trauma" of young women in Rajput families as they enter arranged marriages and are separated from their homes and communities. In this cultural setting, young women are traditionally expected to leave their families of origin to marry a man they might never have seen or spoken to, to be subject to the absolute authority of their mothers-in-law, and to live their lives confined to the women's courtyards of their marital home. In the community studied by Minturn, this was expected to be a difficult transition, and it was common to find young women weeping in a corner of the house while the older women discussed marriage arrangements. For some young women, however, distress was severe and was manifested in psychiatric symptoms including possession and coma, as well as severe depression. Minturn notes, as have other observers, that suffering from a culturally recognized illness has the useful effect of mobilizing family resources to help the young bride and give her some relief from the stress of her abrupt life transition.

As researchers and clinicians have become more familiar with patterns of mental health and disorder in other cultures, they have increasingly recognized the cultural aspects of disorders common in Western societies. It has recently been suggested, for example, that both premenstrual syndrome and postpartum depression are disorders of Western society rarely found in traditional non-Western settings, although this picture is changing with rapid social transformations in Third World countries (Harkness, 1987; Johnson, 1987). In both these cases, several aspects of the culturally shaped environment play a role in the development or prevention of disorder. For example, Harkness's research on the psychology of childbirth in a rural Kipsigis community of Kenya found that there are many ways that the community provided social and instrumental support to "new mothers," thus mitigating the stress of the postpartum period.

The status of eating disorders (anorexia and bulimia) as culture-bound syndromes is especially intriguing, as there appears to be rapid culture change associated with these disorders worldwide. Whereas earlier observers had found eating disorders almost exclusively in Western societies, there has been a rapid increase in the incidence of anorexia nervosa worldwide during the past two decades, which may be attributable to the influence of Western cultural values or an emerging transnational culture of modernity (Iancu, Spivak, Ratzoni, Apter, & Weizman, 1994; Lee, 1995). Cross-cultural studies have found that young people in the United States perceive a slender figure as more desirable than do their peers in Ghana and Malayasia (Cogan, Bhalla, Sefa-Dedeh, & Rothblum, 1996; Indran, 1995); in the Ghanian–U.S. study, these cultural differences in attitudes and perceptions were associated with different rates of self-reported eating disorders.

Given the increasing level of international communication and the "contagiousness" of some disorders such as anorexia and bulimia through the media, it seems likely that the truly exotic, culture-bound syndromes found in cultures isolated from the modern world will become increasingly rare. On the other hand, recognizing the roles of culture as a meaning system and provider of response to distress is important in relation to all disorders. From this perspective, as Hughes (1998) argues, it may not be useful to maintain a separate diagnostic category of culture-bound syndromes in classification systems such as the DSM-IV (American Psychiatric Association, 1994).

THE "NEW MORBIDITY" AS CULTURAL EPIDEMIOLOGY

The cultural construction of developmental and epidemiological patterns of psychopathology is more broadly seen in "the new morbidity," a term proposed by Haggerty, Roghmann, and Pless (1975) to describe the growing clinical workload presented by psychosocial, behavioral, and related problems in U.S. society. For pediatricians, whose profession has been dramatically altered in a single generation by antibiotics and public health measures (Pawluch, 1983; Russo & Varni, 1982), the shift toward syndromes that involve processes outside the traditionally medical domain is profound. In some settings, as much as 10% of pediatricians' time with patients in primary health care is devoted to psychosocial issues (Korsch, Negrete, Mercer, & Freemon, 1971), even though they may overlook the majority of such problems (Starfield & Borkowf, 1969). For specialists in mental and behavioral problems, that is, for psychiatrists, clinical psychologists, and social workers, the great majority of professional effort is spent with similar issues, including hyperactivity, conduct disorder, functional enuresis, depression, and school failure. The cultural construction, labeling, and responsiveness to each of these syndromes are inherent in their briefest description. Although culture also plays a critical role in the more severe psychopathologies, it is the new morbidity, a specifically cultural construction, that dominates the front lines of professional clinical practice. Epidemiological evidence suggests approximately one-fifth of all children in Western settings suffer psychosocial morbidity (Earls, 1981; Starfield et al., 1984), and only a portion of them receive professional treatment.

Attention deficit disorder (ADD, or ADHD with hyperactivity) is a prime example of the new morbidity as a cultural construction. Although ADD was earlier thought to be due to minimal brain damage, the recent Consensus Conference did not establish any basis for this disorder in brain functioning (National Institutes of Health, 1998). Instead, current definitions of ADHD are behavioral, covering a wide range of readily recognizable behaviors, such as not appearing to listen when spoken to; not finishing, or forgetting, school assignments; fidgeting; and having trouble staying seated when it is appropriate (Miller & Castellanos, 1998). Since many children, especially boys, could be described in these terms, the crucial diagnostic criterion becomes how "often" or "excessively" these incidences occur, and operationally, how much they interfere with the lives of the children and others in their environments, especially school. In spite of the broad definition of symptoms and their lack of either an established connection with brain functioning or even stable behavioral traits (evident in all situations), however, the treatment of choice for ADD/ADHD has become medication. From 1990 to 1995, the annual U.S. production of methylphenidate (marketed as Ritalin) increased 500%, and the sharp upward trend in production—and, presumably, use—of this drug has continued unabated, indicating an epidemic of ADHD (Diller, 1996). Informal reports from teachers are that in some classrooms, as many as 30% of all children are on Ritalin for control of ADHD.

A variety of explanations has been proposed for the rapid increase in diagnosis of ADHD, including broadening of the diagnostic criteria, increased expectations for children's early academic performance, changes in parents' schedules that leave parents less tolerant of children's disruptive behavior, and increases in the amount of time that young children spend in group care settings where controlled behavior is necessary and where, additionally, deviance can be recognized and referred earlier (Diller, 1996). In addition, the efficacy of medications such as Ritalin in subduing the behavior of *all* children, not just those with ADHD, makes it an easy solution for issues of control, especially in school settings with large and diverse groups of students in each classroom. Finally, parents may embrace a diagnosis of ADHD as a means of obtaining needed extra services for their children (Diller, 1996).

The medicalization of a broad range of children's behavior as captured in use of the ADHD diagnosis has been critiqued by Rubenstein and Perloff (1986), who argue that the disease-oriented approach represented by inclusion in the DSM-III is erroneous. Instead, they point to the possibility that "hyperactivity is not a disease of the child, but rather the reification of social processes which result in the labeling as sick of children who act badly" (p. 319). Given the structure of the helping professions in America, this becomes the "medicalization" of psychosocial problems, for the mechanism of response in the primary health care system, and in most psychosocial referral networks, is to treat deviant behavior as sick.

An alternative approach to ADHD, which takes culture as well as individual child differences into account, is proposed by pediatrician William Carey (see Carey & McDevitt, 1995), who argues that most of what gets diagnosed as ADD is actually behavior at the far ends of the normal distribution of child temperament characteristics such as activity level and distractibility. If this is the case, then the most adequate response to a child's difficult behavior is to improve the "goodness of fit" between the child's own temperament and the demands of the environment, as Carey and McDevitt recommend. In this approach, cultural, individual, and clinical perspectives are combined insofar as caretakers and health care providers are able to analyze the cultural dimensions of the child's "developmental niche," along with particular elements of family history and circumstance, parental characteristics, and child temperament in devising a strategy for improved functioning (see Harkness, Keefer, & Super, 1999).

Individual Differences and the Goodness of Fit

The discussion of ADD highlights two important and related observations that should be kept in mind when considering the epidemiology of dysfunction and the nature of culture-bound syndromes. First, it is obviously not the case that all members of a given community suffer from whatever syndromes might be specific to their home culture. Not all Hispanics have symptoms of *susto*, and not all Japanese suffer from TKS syndrome. Exposure to a pattern of risk, in this sense, does not affect all persons equally. As is often the case in studies of the distribution of disease, therefore, one must consider individual differences in vulnerability to the predisposing or contextual factors.

The second observation follows directly: Any individual case of psychopathology will necessarily reflect both features of the individual (temperament or personal history) and features of the cultural surround (availability of particular types of dysfunctional relationships, trauma-inducing experiences, or shared meaning systems). As we comment at several points in this chapter, it is an old but still frequent error to imagine that some pathologies emerge in the absence of culturally structured forces, while others are solely cultural (as opposed to individual) products. Like all normal psychological development, all developmental psychopathology is both individual and cultural. A cultural perspective on developmental psychopathology, therefore, must include an understanding of individual differences that elucidates the interaction of individuality and cultural environment as they create or modify the risk of psychopathology.

The study of individual differences in temperamental disposition is now an established and energetic enterprise, having started, in the modern era, with the pioneering work of psychiatrists Thomas and Chess and their colleagues in the New York Longitudinal Study (NYLS; Chess & Thomas, 1984; Thomas & Chess, 1977; Thomas, Chess, Birch, Hertzig, & Korn, 1963). The initial context of the project was a clinical one, with the goal of understanding the importance of inborn, constitutionally based behavioral dispositions (such as activity level, approach to new situations, and overall mood) in the emergence of psychosocial symptoms. This perspective was in part a reaction to the prevailing emphasis on early experience, particularly maternal care. One of the first major contributions of the NYLS was the identification of the "difficult infant syndrome," a constellation of irregular biorhythms, avoidance of change, slow adaptability to new situations, negative mood, and intensity of expression that was particularly demanding and upsetting for parents. This disposition, coupled with common parental responses of frustration, anger, and despair, seemed to put a child at heightened risk for a variety of psychosocial disorders.

As the NYLS progressed, the emphasis shifted from establishing the existence and importance of temperamental differences to understanding the secondary but more critical issue of "goodness of fit" (Chess & Thomas, 1984). This shift was accelerated by parallel research with working-class Puerto Rican families in New York City that provided a striking contrast with the original middle-class, largely Jewish sample. Because bedtimes were not scheduled and enforced with the same regularity in the Puerto Rican families as was the case in the initial sample, differences in the children's disposition toward a regular schedule were of less significance. Hence this dimension of temperament did not contribute to parental difficulties and concern (Thomas, Chess, Sillen, & Mendez, 1974). But when the children reached school age and the demands for regularity increased, more families encountered temper tantrums at bedtime and related problems. In contrast, in the middle-class sample, bedtime problems had been faced and largely resolved, by some means or another, much earlier. In a related analysis that focused more explicitly on the relationship of temperament to behavioral symptomatology, Korn and Gannon (1983) found that clinical problems at age 5 years were significantly related to the original cluster of "difficult" temperament scores in the middle-class group for whom this definition of difficulty was initially derived, but that symptomatology and "difficult temperament" were not related for the Puerto Rican children. For these families, clinical referrals were more likely to involve excessive motor activity—a disposition possibly related to nutritional and medical factors, but certainly more difficult to handle in small, crowded apartments than in the more spacious middle-class environment. In the original sample, there were virtually no clinical referrals for this cluster that was so problematic for the Puerto Rican families. More detailed study of individual cases within the original sample further supported the idea that how families handled their children's behavioral style was critical in determining whether potentially poor fit of temperament to environment did ultimately result in the development of behavioral pathology.

Although this early work presented a cogent example of cultural differences in what might constitute a good fit, subsequent research has moved very unevenly toward understanding the matrix of individual and contextual contributions. On the one hand, there is now a substantial literature on what might be the most reliable dimensions of temperamental variation (Buss & Plomin, 1984; Rothbart, 1989) and their physiological underpinnings (Fox, 1994; Kagan, Resnick, & Snidman, 1987). On the other hand, the ethnographic literature that explicitly outlines the culturally constructed niches into which individuals must fit remains very small indeed.

We have presented an extended example of rural Kenya in the 1970s, where the pattern of family life in the Kipsigis community of Kokwet made a quite different set of temperamental dispositions "difficult" (Harkness & Super, 1983; Super & Harkness, 1981, 1982, 1994b). The customs of caring for infants and toddlers in this setting drew heavily on older sisters for constant attention and involved frequent use of back-carrying for quieting as well as transportation. Thus, infants who were not comforted by back-carrying, or who demanded more attention from the mother, presented a difficult situation for the family in Kokwet, as this disposition was one that upset the smooth functioning of family routines. On the other hand, the irregularities of sleeping that are so difficult for American families (and which constitute a major element in Thomas and Chess's "difficult infant syndrome") were of little consequence in Kokwet. This is the cultural construction of poor fit based on the infant's developmental niche.

In summary, the role of temperamental disposition in the developmental pathways to psychological health or dysfunction must be appreciated in the context of the culturally organized responses to those differences. Parents' interpretations of what is problematic or deviant, their attributions of causality, the availability of particular persons to help, the techniques used to address the problem, and how other aspects of the human environment are consequently altered are all possibilities that are culturally prepared in broad outline long before they become activated for any particular child. In this regard, it can be said that what culture does is embed individual temperamental variation in a matrix of potential responses, personal and institutional, which may lessen, or in some cases heighten, the risks of developmental psychopathology.

It follows that in the clinical diagnosis of any particular case of dysfunction, the clinician is better able to identify causal conditions to the degree that he or she is able to understand how the child's and family's pattern of behavior is (or is not) consonant with an elaborated, culturally supported set of beliefs. Cases that appear to be "purely individual" when looked at by an insider from the same background become instances of culturally shaped patterns when a more objective lens is used. For this reason, we and others have argued that an ethnographic posture is helpful in the diagnosis and intervention for all developmental problems (Harkness et al., 1999; Super & Harkness, 1994a).

CULTURE AND DEVELOPMENTAL PSYCHOPATHOLOGY

Anthropological and cross-cultural research on psychological development and psychopathology, as reviewed here, suggest three main functions of culture in relation to developmental psychopathology. First, cultural settings contribute to the development and manifestation of mental illness and distress. This view of individual variation in relation to cultural context was modern anthropology's first and best-known contribution to the study of psychopathology, and it was further elaborated by the cross-cultural study of child-rearing practices and cultural "projective systems" or aspects of adult behavior. More recently, research in temperament and "goodness of fit" has provided a new framework for analyzing the mutual adaptations—or lack thereof—in a developmental framework (Super & Harkness, 1986b).

The relativistic view of psychopathology that lies behind this work is supported by a second function of culture in relation to psychological illness: Culture labels psychological distress or dysfunction, organizing it into categories, thus further influencing its manifestations. This principle, derived from anthropological and epidemiological research on psychopathology across cultures, does not deny the reality of the biological dimension of psychological illness. In contrast to disease-based epidemiological research, however, recognition of the cultural organization of psychopathology leads to the conclusion that there is no universal "ultimate reality" of mental disorders that can be captured by purely medical models. As the examples of TKS syndrome and depression illustrate, disease categories in different cultures may bear resemblances to each other, but the imposition of strict universal categories would involve considerable loss of specificity for identifying illnesses where they occur and where they are problematic, that is, within particular cultural contexts.

Finally, culture structures responses to mental distress and problematic behavior through the provision of shared formal and informal theories for understanding by individuals, and through institutions and professional roles accorded the responsibility and power to intervene. At the microscopic level, as indicated in the previous discussion, culturally organized responsiveness to individual differences plays a role in the evolution of illness conditions. More broadly, however, social responses to a fully developed problem are overtly structured by the social context. The kinds of interventions that are permitted are socially defined, and the networks for seeking help are socially constructed.

These three functions operate concurrently; the more they reinforce each other, the greater the likelihood of an altered surface of prevalence rates, and an emicly unique interior of distress. Thus, Harkness's (1987) study of postpartum depression, for example, illustrates the intertwining of socially defined settings for pregnancy and birth that promote the illness, of local theories of distress that label the relevant emotion states, and of social values and folk theories of disease that determine the societal response.

Culture—the socially organized human environment—is the major determinant of the developmental niche of young humans (Super & Harkness, 1986a, 1999), and this is as true for the emergence and elaboration of problematic behavior as it is of the harmless and normative behavior. The physical and social settings, the customs of child care and rearing, and the psychology of caretaking together define what kinds of behavior will be experienced as stressful to the child's family, and what behaviors will be problematic for the child's development. They structure the adaptations that a family and community can make to improve a poor fit of individual and environment. The sequence of adjustments are the ingredients for learning, for the development of self, and for the acquisition of coping skills. At the same time, the growing child is following his or her own parameters of change. The process of adaptation is a mutual one, and at each step of the way, cultural meaning and local logistics shape the progression. Some kinds of problems are more likely to occur in a particular context, and some kinds of responses are more likely to be given. Specific institutions for intervention may be activated. The resulting coevolution of individual and environmental systems, in other words, is pointed in one direction or another by cultural forces. Waddington's (1971) epigenetic landscape, in this regard, is an elastic one, responsive to the shape and texture of the rolling ball; however, the particular channeling and the pattern of elasticity vary from one human group to another. The outcome, summed over many individuals, yields culture-bound syndromes and the epidemiological landscape, that is, the cultural patterning of developmental psychopathology.

REFERENCES

Achenbach, T. M. (1991a). *Manual for the Child Behavior Checklist and 1991 Profile*. Burlington: University of Vermont, Department of Psychiatry.

Achenbach, T. M. (1991b). *Manual for the Teacher's Report Form and 1991 Profile*. Burlington: University of Vermont, Department of Psychiatry.

American Psychiatric Association. (1994). *Diagnostic and statistical manual of mental disorders* (4th ed., rev.). Washington, DC: Author.

Azuma, H. (1984). Secondary control as a heterogeneous category. *American Psychologist, 39*, 970–971.

Barnouw, V. (1973). *Culture and personality* (rev. ed.). Homewood, IL: Dorsey.

Barry, H., III. (1969). Cultural variations in the development of mental illness. In S. C. Plog & R. B. Edgerton (Eds.), *Changing perspectives in mental illness* (pp. 155–178). New York: Holt, Rhinehart & Winston.

Benedict, R. F. (1932). Configurations of culture in North America. *American Anthropologist, 34*, 1–27.

Benedict, R. F. (1934). *Patterns of culture*. New York: Houghton Mifflin.

Benedict, R. F. (1973). Anthropology and the abnormal. *Journal of General Psychology, 10*, 59–80. Reprinted in A. K. Romney & P. L. DeVore (Eds.), *You and others: Readings in introductory anthropology* (pp. 82–95). Cambridge, MA: Winthrop. (Original published in 1934)

Berne, E. (1959). Difficulties of comparative psychiatry. *American Journal of Psychiatry, 116*, 104–109.

Buss, A. H., & Plomin, R. (1984). *Temperament: Early developing personality traits*. Hillsdale, NJ: Erlbaum.

Carey, W. B., & McDevitt, S. C. (1995). *Coping with children's temperament*. New York: Basic Books.

Caudill, W. A., & Schooler, C. (1973). Child behavior and child rearing in Japan and the United States: An interim report. *Journal of Nervous and Mental Disease, 157*, 323–338.

Chess, S., & Thomas, A. (1984). *Origins and evolution of behavior disorders*. New York: Brunner/Mazel.

Cogan, J. C., Bhalla, S. K., Sefa-Dedeh, A., & Rothblum, E. D. (1996). A comparison study of United States and African students on perceptions of obesity and thinness. *Journal of Cross-Cultural Psychology, 27*(1), 98–113.

Coll, C. T. G. (1990). Developmental outcome of minority infants: A process-oriented look into our beginnings. *Child Development, 61*, 270–289.

Diller, L. H. (1996). The run on Ritalin: Attention deficit disorder and stimulant treatment in the 1990s. *Hastings Center Report, 26*(2), 12–18.

Draguns, J. G. (1997). Abnormal behavior patterns across cultures: Implications for counseling and psychotherapy. *International Journal of Intercultural Relations, 21*(2), 213–248.

DuBois, C. (1944). *The people of Alor: A social-psychological study of an East-Indian Island*. Minneapolis: University of Minnesota Press.

Earls, F. (1981). Cultural and national differences in the epidemiology of behavior problems of preschool children. *Culture, Medicine, and Psychiatry, 6*, 9–20.

Falicov, C. J. (1982). Mexican families. In M. McGoldrick, J. K. Pearce, & J. Giordano (Eds.), *Ethnicity and family therapy* (pp. 134–163). New York: Guilford Press.

Fogelson, R. D. (1965). Psychological theories of *windigo* "psychosis" and a preliminary application of a models approach. In M. E. Spiro (Ed.), *Context and meaning in cultural anthropology* (pp. 74–99). New York: Free Press.

Fox, N. A. (Ed.). (1994). The development of emotion regulations: Biological and behavioral considerations. *Monographs of the Society for Research in Child Development*, Serial No. 240, Vol. 59.

Freud, S. (1930). *Civilization and its discontents*. New York: Jonathan Cape & Harrison Smith.

Gardiner, H. W., Mutter, J. D., & Kosmitzki, C. (1998). *Lives across cultures: Cross-cultural human development*. Boston: Allyn & Bacon.

Good, B. J. (1996). Culture and the DSM-IV: Diagnosis, knowledge, and power. *Culture, Medicine, and Psychiatry, 20*(2), 127–132.

Greenfield, P. M., & Cocking, R. R. (1994). *Cross-cultural roots of minority child development*. Hillsdale, NJ: Erlbaum.

Guarnaccia, P. J., Rivera, M., Franco, F., & Neighbors, C. (1996). The experiences of *ataques de nervios*: Towards an anthropology of emotions in Puerto Rico. *Culture, Medicine, and Psychiatry, 20*, 343–367.

Haggerty, R. J., Roghmann, K., & Pless, I. (1975). *Child health and the community*. New York: Wiley.

Harkness, S. (1987). The cultural mediation of postpartum depression. *Medical Anthropology Quarterly, 1*, 194–209.

Harkness, S., Keefer, C. H., & Super, C. M. (1999). Culture and ethnicity. In M. D. Levine, W. B. Carey, & A. C. Crocker (Eds.), *Developmental–behavioral pediatrics* (3rd ed., pp. 107–117). New York: Saunders.

Harkness, S., Raeff, C., & Super, C. M. (Eds.). (2000). *Variability in the social construction of the child*. New Directions for Child Development. San Francisco: Jossey-Bass.

Harkness, S., & Super, C. M. (1983). The cultural construction of child development: A framework for the socialization of affect. *Ethos, 11*, 221–231.

Harkness, S., & Super, C. M. (1987). The uses of cross-cultural research in child development. In G. J. Whitehurst & R. Vasta (Eds.), *Annals of child development* (Vol. 4, pp. 209–244). Greenwich, CT: JAI Press.

Harkness, S., & Super, C. M. (1996). Introduction. In S. Harkness & C. M. Super (Eds.), *Parents' cultural belief systems: Their origins, expressions, and consequences* (pp. 1–24). New York: Guilford Press.

Harkness, S., & Super, C. M. (1999). From parents' cultural belief systems to behavior: Implications for the development of early intervention programs. In L. Eldering & P. Leseman (Eds.), *Effective early education: Cross-cultural perspectives* (pp. 67–90). New York: Falmer Press.

Harkness, S., Super, C. M., & van Tijen, N. (2000). Individualism and the "Western mind" reconsidered: American and Dutch parents' ethnotheories of the child. In S. Harkness, C. Raeff, & C. M. Super (Eds.), *Variability in the social construction of the child*. New Directions for Child Development (pp. 23–39). San Francisco: Jossey-Bass.

Harris, M. (1968). *The rise of anthropological theory*. New York: Thomas Y. Crowell.

Hughes, C. C. (1998). The glossary of "culture-bound syndromes" in DSM-IV: A critique. *Transcultural Psychiatry, 35*(3), 413–421.

Iancu, I., Spivak, B., Ratzoni, G., Apter, A., & Weizman, A. (1994). The sociocultural theory in the development of anorexia nervosa. *Psychopathology, 27*(1–2), 29–36.

Indran, S. K. (1995). Brief report: Eating attitudes among adolescent girls in Malaysian secondary school using the EAT questionnaire. *International Journal of Social Psychiatry, 41*(4), 299–303.

Johnson, T. M. (1987). Premenstrual syndrome as a Western culture-specific disorder. *Culture, Medicine, and Psychiatry, 11*(3), 337–356.

Kagan, J., Reznick, S., & Snidman, N. (1987). The physiology and psychology of behavioral inhibition in young children. *Child Development, 58*, 1459–1473.

Kagitçibasi, C. (1996a). *Family and human development across cultures: A view from the other side*. Mahwah, NJ: Erlbaum.

Kagitçibasi, C. (1996b). The autonomous–relational self: A new synthesis. *European Psychologist, 1*(3), 180–186.

Kardiner, A. (Ed.). (1939). *The individual and his society*. New York: Columbia University Press.

Kleinman, A. (1987). Anthropology and psychiatry: The role of culture in cross-cultural research on illness. *British Journal of Psychiatry, 151*, 447–454.

Kleinman, A., & Good, B. (Eds.). (1985). *Culture and depression: Studies in the anthropology and cross-cultural psychiatry of affect and disorder*. Berkeley: University of California Press.

Korn, S., & Gannon, S. (1983). Temperament, culture variation, and behavior disorders in preschool children. *Child Psychiatry and Human Development, 13*, 203–212.

Korsch, B. M., Negrete, V. F., Mercer, A. S., & Freemon, B. (1971). How comprehensive are well child visits? *American Journal of Diseases of Children, 122*, 483–488.

Lee, S. (1995). Reconsidering the status of anorexia nervosa as a Western culture-bound syndrome. *Social Science and Medicine, 42*(1), 21–34.

LeVine, R. A. (1973). *Culture, behavior, and personality*. Chicago: Aldine.

Markus, H., & Kitayama, S. (1991). Culture and the self: Implications for cognition, emotion, and motivation. *Psychological Bulletin, 98*, 199–337.

Marsella, A. J. (1993). Sociocultural foundations of psychopathology: An historical overview of concepts, events and pioneers prior to 1970. *Transcultural Psychiatric Review, 30*(2), 97–142.

Marsella, A. J., Sartorius, N., Jablensky, A., & Fenton, R. F. (1985). Cross-cultural studies of depressive disorders: An overview. In A. Kleinman & B. Good (Eds.), *Culture and depression: Studies in the anthropology and cross-cultural psychiatry of affect and disorder* (pp. 299–324). Berkeley: University of California Press.

Mead, M. (1928). *Coming of age in Samoa*. New York: Morrow.

Mead, M. (1939). *From the South Seas*. New York: Morrow.

Mead, M. (1972). *Blackberry winter: My earlier years*. New York: Simon & Schuster.

Miller, K. J., & Castellanos, F. X. (1998). Attention deficit/hyperactivity disorders. *Pediatrics in Review, 19*(11), 373–384.

Minturn, L. (1993). *Sita's daughters*. Cambridge, MA: Harvard University Press.

Miyake, K., & Yamazaki, K. (1995). Self-conscious emotions, child rearing, and child psychopathology in Japanese culture. In J. P. Tangney & K. W. Fischer (Eds.), *Self-conscious emotions: The psychology of shame, guilt, embarrassment, and pride* (pp. 488–504). New York: Guilford Press.

Murphy, J. M. (1976). Psychiatric labeling in cross-cultural perspectives (Yoruba and Eskimo). *Science, 191*, 1019–1028.

National Institutes of Health. (1998, November 16–18). Diagnosis and treatment of attention deficit hyperactivity disorder. *NIH Consensus Statement, 16*(2).

O'Nell, C. W. (1975). An investigation of reported "fright" as a factor in the etiology of *susto*, "magical fright." *Ethos, 3*, 268–283.

Parker, S. (1960). The Wiitiko psychosis in the context of Ojibwa personality and culture. *American Anthropologist, 62*, 620.

Pawluch, D. (1983). Transitions in pediatrics: A segmental analysis. *Social Problems, 30*, 449–465.

Prince, R., & Tcheng-Laroche, F. (1987). Culture-bound syndromes and international disease classifications. *Culture, Medicine, and Psychiatry, 11*(1), 3–20.

Prince, R. H. (1991). Transcultural psychiatry's contribution to International Classification Systems: The example of social phobias. *Transcultural Psychiatry Research Review, 28*, 124–131.

Raghavan, C., Harkness, S., & Super, C. M. (2000). *The role of parental ethnotheories in the child's developmental niche: A study of Asian immigrant and American mothers and daughters*. Manuscript in preparation.

Rothbart, M. K. (1989). Temperament and development. In G. A. Kohnstamm, J. E. Bates, & J. K. Rothbart (Eds.), *Temperament in childhood* (pp. 187–247). London: Wiley.

Rubenstein, R. A., & Perloff, J. D. (1986). Identifying psychosocial disorders in children: On integrating epidemiological and anthropological understandings. In C. R. Janes, R. Stall, & S. M. Gifford (Eds.), *Anthropology and epidemiology* (pp. 303–332). Dordrecht, Holland: Reidel.

Russo, D. C., & Varni, J. W. (1982). *Behavioral pediatrics: Research and practice*. New York: Plenum Press.

Sartorius, N., Jablensky, A., Gulbinat, W., & Ernberg. (1980). WHO Collaborative Study: Assessment of depressive disorders. *Psychosomatic Medicine, 10*, 743–749.

Shweder, R. A., & Bourne, E. J. (1991). Does the concept of the person vary cross-culturally? In R. A. Shweder (Ed.), *Thinking through cultures: Expeditions in cultural psychology* (pp. 113–155). New York: Cambridge University Press.

Shweder, R. A., & LeVine, R. A. (Eds.). (1984). *Culture theory: Essays on mind, self, and emotion*. New York: Cambridge University Press.

Simons, R. C. (1980). The resolution of the lata paradox. *Journal of Nervous and Mental Disease, 168*, 195–206.

Simons, R. C. (1983). Latah II: Problems with a purely symbolic interpretation. *Journal of Nervous and Mental Disease, 171*, 168–175.

Starfield, B., & Borkowf, S. (1969). Physician's recognition of complaints made by parents about their children's health. *Pediatrics, 43*(2), 168–172.

Starfield, B., Katz, H., Gabriel, A., Livingston, G., Benson, P., Hankin, J., Horn, S., & Steinwachs, D. (1984). Morbidity in childhood: A longitudinal view. *New England Journal of Medicine, 310*, 824–829.

Super, C. M., & Harkness, S. (1981). Figure, ground, and gestalt: The cultural context of the active individual. In R. M. Lerner & N. A. Busch-Rossnagel (Eds.), *Individuals as producers of their development: A life-span perspective* (pp. 69–86). New York: Academic Press.

Super, C. M., & Harkness, S. (1982). The infant's niche in rural Kenya and metropolitan America. In L. L. Adler (Ed.), *Cross-cultural research at issue* (pp. 47–55). New York: Academic Press.

Super, C. M., & Harkness, S. (1986a). The developmental niche: A conceptualization at the interface of child and culture. *International Journal of Behavioral Development, 9*, 545–569.

Super, C. M., & Harkness, S. (1986b). Temperament, development, and culture. In R. Plomin & J. Dunn (Eds.), *The study of temperament: Changes, continuities, and challenges* (pp. 131–150). Hillsdale, NJ: Erlbaum.

Super, C. M., & Harkness, S. (1994a). Temperament and the developmental niche. In W. B. Carey & S. A. McDevitt (Eds.), *Prevention and early intervention: Individual differences as risk factors for the mental health of children—a Festschrift for Stella Chess and Alexander Thomas* (pp. 115–125). New York: Brunner/Mazel.

Super, C. M., & Harkness, S. (1994b). The cultural regulation of temperament–environment interactions. *Researching Early Childhood, 2*(1), 19–58.

Super, C. M., & Harkness, S. (1999). Culture as environment. In T. Wachs & S. Friedman (Eds.), *Measurement of the environment in developmental research* (pp. 279–323). Washington, DC: American Psychological Association.

Thomas, A., & Chess, S. (1977). *Temperament and development*. New York: Brunner/Mazel.

Thomas, A., Chess, S., Birch, H. G., Hertzig, M., & Korn, S. (1963). *Behavioral individuality in early childhood*. New York: New York University Press.

Thomas, A., Chess, S., Sillen, J., & Mendez, O. (1974). Cross cultural study of behavior in children with special vulnerabilities to stress. In D. Ricks, A. Thomas, & M. Roff (Eds.), *Life history research in psychopathology* (Vol. 3, pp. 53–67). Minneapolis: University of Minnesota Press.

Triandis, H. C. (1989). The self and social behavior in differing cultural contexts. *Psychological Bulletin, 96*, 506–520.

Waddington, C. H. (1971). Concepts of development. In E. Tobach, L. R. Aronson, & E. Shaw (Eds.), *The biopsychology of development*. New York: Academic Press.

Weisz, J. R., Chaiyasit, W., Weiss, B., Eastman, K. L., & Jackson, E. W. (1995). A multimethod study of problem behavior among Thai and American children in school: Teacher reports versus direct observations. *Child Development, 66*, 402–415.

Weisz, J. R., McCarty, C. A., Eastman, K. L., Chaiyasit, W., & Suwanlert, S. (1997). Developmental psychology and culture: Ten lessons from Thailand. In S. S. Luthar, J. A. Burack, D. Cicchetti, & J. R. Weisz (Eds.), *Developmental psychopathology: Perspectives on adjustment, risk, and disorder* (pp. 568–592). Cambridge, UK: Cambridge University Press.

Whiting, J. W. M. (1977). A model for psychocultural research. In P. H. Leiderman, S. R. Tulkin, & A. Rosenfeld (Eds.), *Culture and infancy: Variations in the human experience* (pp. 29–48). New York: Academic Press.

Whiting, J. W. M. (1961). Socialization process and personality. In F. L. K. Hsu (Ed.), *Psychological anthropology: Approaches to culture and personality* (pp. 355–380). Homewood, IL: Dorsey Press.

Whiting, J. W. M., & Child, I. (1953). *Child training and personality: A cross-cultural study*. New Haven, CT: Yale University Press.

Whiting, J. W. M., Kluckhohn, R., & Anthony, A. (1958). The function of male initiation ceremonies at puberty. In E. E. Maccoby, T. M. Newcomb, & E. L. Hartley (Eds.), *Readings in social psychology* (3rd ed., pp. 359–370). New York: Holt, Rhinehart and Winston.

World Health Organization. (1973). *International pilot study of schizophrenia* (Vol. 1). Geneva: World Health Organization.

World Health Organization. (1983). *Depressive disorders in different cultures*. Geneva: World Health Organization.

III
BIOLOGY AND MENTAL ILLNESS

12

Developmental Behavioral Genetics

Thomas G. O'Connor and Robert Plomin

Since the previous edition of this volume (Plomin, Nitz, & Rowe, 1990), there have been significant advances in our understanding of genetic influences on psychopathology. Gains are notable not only in our understanding of which dimensions of behavioral and emotional disturbance are under genetic influence, but also in our understanding of *how* genetic influences operate in the development of psychopathology. In tandem with those advances is progress in conceptualizing environmental risk and protective factors.

In this chapter, we highlight advances in behavioral genetics research on psychopathology and offer a selective rather than exhaustive review of available data. The aim is to provide the reader with an update on recent findings and an overview of their conceptual and methodological implications for further research and theory for developmental psychopathology. Texts and reviews are available that provide more extensive coverage of findings and background to behavioral genetics methodology (Gottesman, 1991; McGuffin, Owen, O'Donovan, Thapar, & Gottesman, 1994; Plomin, DeFries, McClearn, & Rutter, 1997; Plomin & McClearn, 1993; Rutter, Silberg, O'Connor, & Simonoff, 1999).

The goals of this chapter are to (1) highlight the methodological and conceptual lessons from the past decade of research; (2) provide a brief overview of the genetics of developmental psychopathology since the last edition (Plomin et al., 1990); (3) explicate the developmental themes in behavioral genetics research; (4) review the current models for detecting how genetic influences are associated with psychopathology; and (5) trace the import of molecular genetics research into developmental psychopathology, especially concerning children and adolescents, and discuss why this is a critical area of research for all those interested in developmental psychopathology.

Thomas G. O'Connor and Robert Plomin • Institute of Psychiatry, University of London, London SE5 8AF United Kingdom.

Handbook of Developmental Psychopathology, Second Edition, edited by Arnold J. Sameroff, Michael Lewis, and Suzanne M. Miller. Kluwer Academic/Plenum Publishers, New York, 2000.

INTRODUCTION TO BEHAVIORAL GENETICS RESEARCH

Background to Behavioral Genetics Methods

Behavioral genetics research decomposes individual differences in the variation of behavior into genetic, shared environmental, and nonshared environmental sources of influence. This is possible based on phenotypic or observed patterns of similarity in genetically informative designs that vary genetic or environmental relatedness, most notably twin and adoption designs. The estimate of genetic influence indicates the extent to which variation in individual differences is accounted for by genetic differences. Of the two remaining sources of environmental influence, shared environment estimates the extent to which variation in individual differences is accounted for by shared experiences *independent of genetic factors*; nonshared environment is what is left over, or those experiences that make siblings different from one another. Further discussion of these estimates and the models underlying them may be found in Plomin et al. (1997).

Concerns have been raised about the models and samples used in behavioral genetics research (for a review, see O'Connor, Deater-Deckard, & Plomin, 1998). In the case of twins, for example, there have been criticisms regarding twin and nontwin differences in the rate of language difficulties and experience of perinatal complications (Rutter & Redshaw, 1991), rates of psychopathology (Simonoff, 1992; Van den Oord, Koot, Boomsma, & Verhulst, 1995), and prevalence of maternal depression (Thorpe, Golding MacGillivray, & Greenwood, 1991), which may adversely affect family processes. A different set of concerns has been raised regarding adoption studies. However, despite these criticisms, there is considerable evidence that the methodological approaches in behavioral genetics analyses are robust (Plomin et al., 1997). Nonetheless, it is important to consider that the estimate of genetic influence is a population parameter derived from a particular sample at a particular time. Like any other statistic, it can vary depending on sample characteristics, methodology, and historical context.

Replication of Findings in Multiple Designs

There is no single best design to estimate genetic or environmental influences, or the effects of genotype–environment interactions or correlations (discussed later). Twin, adoption, family history, parent–offspring and, more recently, the stepfamily design (Van den Oord & Rowe, 1997) each provides strengths and weaknesses with respect to such matters as availability and feasibility, estimation of nonadditive genetic influence, and the degree to which genetic, shared environmental, and nonshared environmental influences can be directly assessed (i.e., are unconfounded). Inevitably then, it follows that there is a need to replicate findings in multiple designs (for antisocial behavior, see Gottesman & Goldsmith, 1994). The reason is that because different designs have different strengths and weakness, it is possible that methodological differences will give rise to different results. For example, extant findings on personality and social development generally suggest stronger genetic influence in twin compared with adoption studies (e.g., Plomin, Corley, Caspi, Fulker, & DeFries, 1998). However, despite the need to compare findings across methods and designs, attempts to include data from adoption and twin studies within the same analysis are relatively rare (Bouchard & McGue, 1981; Miles & Carey, 1997).

The Need for Multimethod, Multirater Designs

Methodological problems such as rater bias and other forms of measurement error are as vexing in behavioral genetics research as they are on psychosocial research. We know now, for example, that the magnitude of association between parenting behavior and child adjustment varies considerably depending on who provides the information; this has led to the use of multimethod latent models (e.g., Reiss et al., 1995). The same is true for estimating genetic, shared, and nonshared environmental influences. Compared to child self-report data, there is a general tendency for parent ratings to indicate more shared and less nonshared environmental effects. This was recently highlighted in a meta-analysis of behavioral genetics studies of aggression that found substantial method effects (Miles & Carey, 1997). A notable example of rater effects in behavioral genetics research is given by Thapar and McGuffin (1995), who reported that the heritability of anxious symptoms in children based on parental report was 59% but 0% according to children's self-reports!

There is a striking degree of nonoverlap among parent, teacher, and child self-reports; consequently, multiple-reporter designs rarely yield simple findings. What is significant about more recent research is the interest in examining the extent to which findings vary according to source (e.g., Eaves et al., 1997). One important finding to emerge is that variance shared by different reporters is largely explained by genetics, thus providing cross-method validity for genetic influence (see, e.g., Schmitz, Saudino, Plomin, Fulker, & DeFries, 1996).

RECENT FINDINGS IN BEHAVIORAL GENETICS STUDIES OF PSYCHOPATHOLOGY

The major question for genetic research in psychopathology is no longer whether or how much genetic factors play a role in the development of a disorder or disturbance. This is perhaps the most obvious difference between behavioral genetics research conducted just a few years ago and contemporary reports. There are now well-documented genetic influences on a wide range of major mental disorders using a variety of twin, adoption, family history, and, more recently, molecular genetic approaches (Plomin et al., 1997).

Behavioral genetics findings that have attracted the most attention in recent years address fundamental questions about the etiology and nature of psychopathology. Our review of recent findings relevant to developmental psychopathology is shaped by four key questions: How do environmental risks operate? Are genetic influences more prominent at the extreme than within the normal range of disturbance? Do genetic influences explain co-occurring disorders? Are gender differences in the rates and associated features of psychopathology mediated by different patterns of genetic–environmental influence? Questions concerning development and change are examined in the subsequent section.

Environmental Risks Operate on an Individual and Not on a Familywide Basis

A main lesson from behavioral genetics findings is that environmental risks are individual-specific. The reason is that a wealth of research demonstrates that environmental risks that are shared by siblings, operationalized as "shared environment" in the analytic models, play little role in the development of psychopathology. Perhaps the only exceptions noted to date are conduct disorder, aggression (Gottesman & Goldsmith, 1994), and certain anxiety disorders, including separation anxiety and overanxious disorder (Eaves et al., 1997). The finding that estimates of shared environment in behavioral genetic studies is often zero or minimal does not, of course, suggest that there are no effects of the family environment. That is, "shared environment" is neither conceptually nor methodologically equivalent to "family environment" in the analytic models. Instead, the often minimal effect of shared environment simply indicates that growing up in the same home per se appears to matter remarkably little in shaping children's *similarity* in behavioral traits.

It is important to note here that estimates of shared environment are based on *effects* rather than *measures*. The consequence is that shared environmental influences are detected only insofar as experiences have a *functionally equivalent effect* on siblings. Which specific environmental experiences function to make siblings similar to one another is rarely examined in research, and identifying such processes can be very difficult. For example, the same experience (e.g., parental divorce) may not result in similar outcomes for siblings, and it is even possible that different experiences could function to make siblings similar to one another for a particular outcome.

Environmental influences that exert a substantial role in development and psychopathology are those that make siblings different from one another. Over a decade of research supports the view that *non*shared or individual-specific environmental factors exert considerable influence on behavioral adjustment (Plomin & Daniels, 1987; Rodgers, Rowe, & Li, 1994). This finding, which resulted from behavioral genetics research, is now increasingly incorporated into investigations that seek to synthesize lessons from behavioral genetic and environmental research. For example, the Nonshared Environment and Adolescent Development (NEAD; Reiss et al., 1994) project documented the varied ways in which nonshared factors contribute to development and psychopathology. Reports from that project have indicated, for instance, that nonshared effects are implicated in a wide range of developmental outcomes (e.g., McGuire, Neiderhiser, Reiss, Hetherington, & Plomin, 1995) and partly mediate the association between parenting and adjustment (Pike, McGuire, Reiss, Hetherington, & Plomin, 1996), and the overlap in behavioral and emotional difficulties (O'Connor, McGuire, Reiss, Hetherington, & Plomin, 1998).

The core implication is that risk needs to be conceptualized as individual-specific. Consequently, greater attention needs to be focused on how siblings are exposed to different levels of, for example, parental hostility and peer rejection, and more research is required that examines how siblings make sense of the same experiences differently. Little is known whether "shared" risks (e.g., maternal depression, divorce) have different (i.e., nonshared) consequences, and what cognitive mechanisms mediate this effect. In other words, it is no longer satisfactory to define family risks such as conflict and parental psychopathology in global terms; it is important to define family risk as experienced by individual family members.

Genetic Factors Operate along the Continuum of Psychopathology

The discipline of developmental psychopathology has continually emphasized the need to study the normal alongside the abnormal (Cicchetti, 1984). Behavioral genetics researchers have also been interested in this issue because it is a fundamental question of etiology: Are the same genetic influences operating within the normal and clinical (extreme) range of functioning? The concepts and methods underlying the behavioral genetics approach to this topic are reviewed by Plomin (1991).

Findings from a number of studies using different analytical approaches converge on the same conclusion: Genetic influences are equally salient in the normal and clinical levels of psychopathology. Using an approach called the DF analyses (DeFries & Fulker, 1985), several investigators failed to find greater genetic (or environmental) influence in the elevated compared to the normal range in nonselected samples (Deater-Deckard, Reiss, Hetherington, & Plomin, 1997; Eley, 1997). Similarly, different diagnostic thresholds to define caseness result in broadly similar estimates of genetic influence (Kendler, Neale, Kessler, Heath, & Eaves, 1992b; Slutske et al., 1997; see also Gjone, Stevenson, Sundit, & Eilertsen, 1996). Attempts to bring together research on personality and that on personality disorder and psychopathology has also emphasized that there is very little evidence suggesting discontinuity in genetic influence on the continuum of normal–abnormal (Nigg & Goldsmith, 1994).

A separate line of research makes a similar point using different strategies. Rutter (1994), among others, has noted that genetic influences are not limited to the disorder but also extend beyond traditional diagnostic boundaries. For example, first-degree relatives of schizophrenic probands are more likely to exhibit not only schizophrenia but also schizophrenic-related symptoms such as neurological impairments and schizoid symptoms (e.g., Kendler, Gruenberg, & Kinney, 1994). A parallel pattern is found among first-degree relatives of autistic individuals, who exhibit elevated levels of pervasive developmental disorder (Bolton et al., 1994) and neuropsychiatric and cognitive symptoms (e.g., Piven & Palmer, 1997).

Although the available evidence underscores strong continuity in genetic influences on the continuum of psychopathologies, a number of issues remain for this line of research. For example, many of the studies to date suffer from small samples and have little power to detect discontinuities in genetic influences across the range of functioning. Accordingly, there is a need to assess larger and more extreme groups. In addition, further research is needed that selects individuals as a function of environmental adversity (rather than symptom severity), in order to test whether extreme psychosocial stress modifies the impact of genetics (Scarr, 1992).

Finally, it is also important that researchers not assume that a condition that manifests dimensionally cannot also have etiologically distinct states. A well-accepted example of this is found in research on cognitive delay, in which the genetic etiology of mild mental retardation (sometimes referred to as "cultural–familial") is qualitatively different from the many distinct genetic sources of severe mental retardation (Plomin, 1991; Rutter, 1994). Some family history research suggests the same with respect to mild, compared with severe, psychotic depression (Coryell, 1997), although further investigation of this issue is needed.

Genetic Influences Explain Co-occurring Dimensions and Disorders

Dimensions of psychopathology and disorders covary at rates far higher than would be expected by chance, and this appears to be the case across the life span (Kessler et al., 1994). Elevated rates of co-occurring disorders or dimensions may be explained by diagnostic overlap of specific symptoms, one disorder acting as a risk factor for a second disorder, or multiple disorders sharing common psychosocial risks; other explanations are also possible (Caron & Rutter, 1991).

One recently has research examined whether two (or more) disorders or dimensions correlate because of a shared genetic liability. The assumption underlying this approach is that genetic influences are not necessarily diagnosis- or dimension-specific; that is, genes do not code for complex behaviors directly. Instead, it may be the case that there is a genetic correlation between disorders or dimensions because disorders share a common biological substrate that is genetically influenced, such as neurotransmitter systems (Collier & Sham, 1997).

Quantitatively, a common genetic diathesis underlying two (or more) syndromes is possible if each syndrome is genetically influenced and the syndromes are correlated; it is most directly assessed in twin studies by examining the cross-twin cross-correlation (see Neale & Cardon, 1992). For example, if the correlation between twin A's depression and twin B's anxiety is greater in monozygotic (MZ) than in dizygotic (DZ) twin pairs, a genetic correlation between the two is suggested.

Recent research documents the pervasiveness of genetic correlations for psychopathology. Kendler and his colleagues have examined this issue in detail in their study of adult female twins in the Virginia twin registry. Findings from that group indicate that there is a genetic correlation between depression and generalized anxiety disorder (Kendler, Neale, Kessler, Heath, & Eaves, 1992a), alcoholism (Kendler, Heath, Neale, Kessler, & Eaves, 1993), and smoking (Kendler, Neale, MacLean, et al., 1993). Although in most cases the magnitude of the genetic correlation is modest, for depression and generalized anxiety, the genetic correlation is very high, suggesting that the same genes affect both dimensions.

Research on psychopathology in childhood and adolescence leads to similar conclusions regarding the importance of genetic correlations underlying overlapping symptom clusters. For example, the robust phenotypic correlation between depressive symptoms and antisocial behavior in children and adolescents is well known, and there is evidence from a national study using a multimethod measurement design that approximately 50% of the phenotypic correlation between these dimensions is explained by genetic influences (O'Connor, McGuire, et al., 1998; O'Connor, Neiderhauser, et al., 1998). In addition, analyses of data of juvenile twins revealed a genetic correlation between hyperactivity and oppositional/conduct problems (Silberg et al., 1996).

Evidence for genetic correlations between disorders is also derived from family history studies that report, for example, that first-degree relatives of depressed probands are at elevated risk not only for depression but also for a second disorder compared to first-degree relatives of nondepressed probands. There are a number of examples of this sort, and links have been drawn between depression and alcoholism or antisocial behavior (Kovacs, Devlin, Pollock, Richards, & Mukerji, 1997) and attention deficit disorder (Biederman, Faraone, Keenan, & Tsuang, 1991), as well as between anxiety and attention deficit disorder (Perrin & Last, 1996). It is important to note, however, that the family history design is unable to differentiate shared genetic from shared family environmental risks.

Research suggesting genetic correlations between disorders also provides the clearest evidence of specificity of genetic influences; that is, in addition to examining the extent to which overlap between disorders is accounted for by genetic factors, the models also estimate the complement—the extent to which one disorder is explained by genetic influences that are independent of a second dimension. With few exceptions (notably, Kendler et al., 1992a), the genetic correlation between disorders is modest, suggesting that there is a limit to the generality of genetic influences. Support for the relative specificity of genetic risks is also supported by family history studies, which indicate that, for example, first-degree relatives of schizophrenic individuals are at greater risk for schizophrenia and schizophrenia-related conditions but *not* for bipolar disorder; similarly, genetic influences underlying liability to bipolar disorder are not linked to those associated with unipolar depression (see Tsuang & Faraone, 1990).

In a similar way, genetic data have been able to distinguish syndromes that are highly correlated phenotypically. For example, although aggression and delinquency are highly intercorrelated, behavioral genetic evidence indicates that whereas the former is under substantial genetic influence, the latter appears not to be (Edelbrock, Rende, Plomin, & Thompson, 1995). Thus, behavioral genetics research may help to specify the phenotype and demarcate the boundaries between dimensions.

Are There Sex Differences in the Patterns of Genetic and Environmental Influence?

Sex differences are marked in most forms of psychopathology, but it is not clear whether these differences can be attributable to genetic and or environmental factors, or how sex or gender may modify genetic etiology.

Available data on sex differences are mixed. For example, in their study of 3-year-old twins, Van den Oord, Verhulst, and Boomsma (1996) found significant sex differences only for one (Overactive) of seven subscales of the Child Behavior Checklist, with genetic effects slightly greater for girls. Greater genetic risk for externalizing behavior in girls has been found by some investigators, but others report the reverse pattern (e.g., Silberg et al., 1994). For depression, Murray and Sines (1996) reported that the genetic influences were greater for boys than for girls (see also Silberg et al., 1994). Still other studies have found no sex differences in the genetic–environmental patterns of influence for either depression or antisocial behavior, or their co-occurrence, despite marked differences in prevalence of each disorder between boys and girls (O'Connor, McGuire, et al., 1998).

Findings from family history and adoption studies suggest that sex may moderate genetic risk. For example, Cadoret et al. (1996) found that genetic risk manifested differently for adult males and females, as the latter but not the former with an alcoholic biological parent were more likely to exhibit depression in the presence of environmental adversity. This is consistent with the authors' argument that depression and alcoholism are part of the same genetic spectrum for females but not for males. A second example of how sex (or gender) may moderate genetic risk is also suggested by Kovacs et al. (1997), who report first-degree female but not male relatives of depressed probands to be more likely to exhibit depression themselves.

Whether the difference between boys and girls can be attributed to biologically or socially based processes is unclear, nor is it certain if the sex or gender effects operate directly, as some authors have suggested, or in terms of the intersection of genes and the environment. Furthermore, sex or gender differences may be modified by age if, for example, pubertal timing and development are etiologically involved in psychological disturbance. Thus, there remain a number of central and unresolved questions for behavioral genetic investigations of the rate and developmental course of psychopathology in males and females.

WHAT IS DEVELOPMENTAL ABOUT DEVELOPMENTAL BEHAVIORAL GENETICS?

Interest in integrating behavioral genetics with developmental and clinical psychology is not new (e.g., Gottesman, 1974), but the concepts and methods necessary for this synthesis have been developed and applied in empirical research only relatively recently (Plomin, 1986,

1994). Fortunately, developmental questions that lie at the heart of developmental psycho-pathology (Cicchetti, 1990) are now beginning to be addressed. This section examines the evidence for developmental change in the genetic–environmental profile of influences on certain forms of psychopathology and surveys findings on genetic influences mediating stability (and change) in psychopathology.

Developmental Change in the Genetic Influence on Psychopathology

An increase in genetic influence for cognitive abilities across the life span is now reasonably well-accepted, but the evidence for developmental change in social development, personality, and psychopathology has been less clear (Plomin et al., 1997; see also McCartney, Harris, & Bernieri, 1990). This is partly due to the relative absence of longitudinal behavioral genetic studies of psychosocial outcomes and the greater difficulties in defining and measuring behavioral phenotypes across the first decades of life. Nonetheless, despite the methodological problems in conducting longitudinal behavioral genetics investigations, there is growing support for increasing genetic influence on psychopathology with age.

Perhaps the strongest evidence for developmental change in genetic influence is found for antisocial behavior and aggression. Miles and Carey's (1997) meta-analysis suggested that genetic influences increase over time and play a greater role in adult versus juvenile crimi-nality; the opposite effect was found for shared environment. That conclusion is exemplified in the detailed report of Lyons and colleagues (1995), based on a retrospective twin study of Vietnam Era adults. The Lyons et al. report is noteworthy for its analysis of not only disorder but also individual symptoms characteristic of juvenile and adult antisocial individuals.

However, there is some evidence that the developmental change in genetic influence on antisocial behavior and aggression may be anything but linear. DiLalla and Gottesman (1989) hypothesized that whereas adolescence-limited and late-onset delinquency may derive from largely psychosocial factors, antisocial behavior exhibited by individuals who exhibit an early emerging and stable trajectory may be genetically mediated. Their genetic argument antici-pated Moffitt's (1993) developmental taxonomy of antisocial individuals that incorporated a large body of research on antisocial behavior and provided a compelling example of how behavioral genetics findings may be brought to bear on rudimentary questions about hetero-geneity of the phenotype. If DiLalla and Gottesman's hypothesis is correct, then genetic estimates of antisocial behavior in studies that do not differentiate according to developmental course—that is, all studies to date—would be difficult to interpret.

Age-based differences in genetic influence have also been reported for depression, with at least two studies suggesting greater genetic influence in adolescence than in childhood (Murray & Sines, 1996; Thapar & McGuffin, 1994). However, the marked change in estimates of genetic influences in both of these studies is striking (e.g., .18 compared to .78 in the Thapar & McGuffin, 1994 study), and neither the rationale for the age groupings nor what may account for this large age difference is clear. The family study of Harrington et al. (1997) contributed an important element to this line of investigation by suggesting that puberty may mediate age-based differences in genetic influence. Their findings are important but require replication in twin or adoption designs that are able to distinguish genetic and environmental influences.

Thus, age-based change in the genetic influence on depressive symptoms may be less complicated than that suggested for antisocial symptoms, but a clear developmental picture has yet to emerge. More importantly, for both antisocial and depressive symptoms, it is not yet apparent what mechanisms in development account for reported changes, as age per se has little explanatory value (Rutter, 1989). Furthermore, the proposal that genetic influences increase with age must be considered in light of recent studies suggesting substantial genetic influence on behavioral problems in very young children. A recent twin study reported that significant genetic influence is found at age 5 (Zahn-Waxler, Schmitz, Robinson, Fulker, & Emde, 1996), and a separate twin study reported that genetic factors accounted for between .38 to .77 of the variance in problem behavior in 3-year-olds (Van den Oord et al., 1996). What is striking is that the magnitude of genetic influence in these two studies is comparable to published reports on adolescents and even adults. It is possible that children exhibiting behavioral problems at a very young age may be at particular genetic risk (a theme developed later), or that methodological problems such as rater bias inflated genetic estimates, or that the level and types of problems in the two studies of nonclinic samples are more akin to and indistinguishable from temperament characteristics rather than psychopathology. Exploring these possibilities in future research may help elucidate the nature of developmental change in the genetic–environmental etiology of psychopathology.

A complementary line of research on developmental change examines the hypothesis that early age of onset is an index of increased genetic risk. In the early studies of this kind, the label "early onset" was defined as young adult onset (Weissman et al., 1984; see also Kendler, Neale, Kessler, Heath, & Eaves, 1992c), but the term has been increasingly applied to distinguish childhood from adolescent onset (e.g., Harrington et al., 1997). Harrington et al. reported that individuals with early (defined as adolescent but not prepubertal) onset may be at greater genetic risk than those with later-onset depression, and that prepubertal depressed probands are less likely than postpubertal depressed probands to have depressed first-degree relatives, suggesting a different pattern of genetic–environmental influence as a function of pubertal status. It is not yet clear whether the evidence that depressed individuals vary in the degree of genetic etiology can be translated into treatment, but studies of this sort are on the horizon.

Genetic Influence on Stability and Change

Longitudinal research findings convincingly demonstrate that there is considerable continuity in psychopathology. Numerous explanations for the continuity are possible, such as the stability of psychosocial risks and the tendency to carry forward maladaptive behavioral patterns to new developmental challenges. Recently, investigators have examined the genetic influences underlying stability of psychopathology.

Two studies found that both genetic and environmental factors contribute to stability in psychopathology in adolescence. Van den Oord and Rowe (1997) reported that genetic and shared environmental influences contribute to the stability of antisocial, anxious/depressed, and hyperactivity symptoms. O'Connor, Neiderhiser, et al. (1998) found that genetic influences explained approximately half of the stability in antisocial and depressive symptoms; stability of antisocial behavior was also explained by shared environmental factors, and nonshared influences also contributed to stability for both syndromes. Genetic influences on continuity have also been reported in research on depression in adulthood (e.g., Kendler, Neale, Kessler, Heath, & Eaves, 1993). Moreover, the retrospective study of adult male twins reported by Lyons et al. (1995) indicated that genetic influences common to both juvenile and adult forms of antisocial behavior accounted for approximately one-fourth of the phenotype correlation, with the remainder explained equally by shared and nonshared environmental influences.

Finally, the finding from family history studies that diagnosed child probands have an elevated proportion of similarly disordered first-degree relatives compared to a control group suggests that the genes associated with the disorder in childhood are the same as those that underlie its manifestation in adulthood. Examples of this sort for depression are given by Harrington et al. (1997) and Kovacs et al. (1997).

A number of questions remain for longitudinal behavior genetics research. For example, recent reports suggest that there is continuity between temperament assessed at age 3 and psychiatric diagnoses assessed in young adulthood, and that there is considerable support for specificity in these patterns (Caspi, Moffitt, Newman, & Silva, 1996). A longitudinal behavioral genetics approach is needed to determine to what extent these long-term patterns may be genetically mediated.

It is also important to note that there is also growing evidence for genetic influences on change. This is most clearly seen in those disorders under substantial genetic control that appear primarily postpubertally (e.g., schizophrenia and bipolar disorder) or later in adulthood (such as Alzheimer's disease, Huntington's disease). Empirical findings on genetic mediation of behavioral change in childhood and adolescence, and their implications, have only recently received attention, and this remains a fruitful area of further research.

UPDATING MODELS OF GENETIC AND ENVIRONMENTAL INFLUENCES ON PSYCHOPATHOLOGY

Genetic research has provided two of the most challenging and important insights into the role of the environment. First, as noted earlier, both behavioral genetics and nonbehavioral genetics studies highlight the role of nonshared environmental influences in behavioral development, including differential parenting and involvement in different peer groups (Plomin, 1995; Plomin & Daniels, 1987). Second, there are genetic influences on so-called environmental measures (Plomin & Bergeman, 1991; Rowe, 1981). This is so because individuals are provided with environments from parents with whom they also share genes, and because individuals actively seek out and respond to their environments in a way that is consistent or correlated with genetic predispositions (Plomin, 1994; Scarr & McCartney, 1983). These advances have not only significantly altered the way in which research on risk and protective factors is conducted but also have brought investigators closer to answering the critical "how" question (Bronfenbrenner & Ceci, 1993; Rutter, 1997) in behavior genetics.

Developing a cohesive model for testing how genetic influences shape behavioral development is increasingly important, as the list of so-called environmental measures showing genetic influence has grown considerably in recent years to include divorce (McGue & Lykken, 1992), life events (Plomin, Lichtenstein, Pedersen, McClearn, & Nesselroade, 1990), social support (Kessler, Kendler, Heath, Neale, & Eaves, 1992), and even television viewing (Plomin, Corley, DeFries, & Fulker, 1990). Moreover, genetic influences are not limited to questionnaire methods, as even dynamic parent–adolescent problem-solving interactions are influenced to a significant degree by genetic factors (O'Connor, Hetherington, Reiss, & Plomin, 1995). Whether or how much genes influence development is therefore no longer the central issue for psychopathologists.

Models for determining how genes influence behavioral development are no longer based on main effects models in which genes directly shape behavior. Such a model is neither empirically correct nor biologically plausible. Moreover, the models of genetic action and gene–environment interplay based on such diseases as phenylketonuria (PKU) and Huntington's disease are equally implausible and misleading for psychopathology. For complex and common medical disorders as well as psychological disorders, no evidence has emerged suggesting that single-gene effects are necessary and sufficient for the development of the disorder. Instead, it is generally accepted that such disorders involve multiple genes as well as multiple environmental factors of varying but small effect size. Research data that tell us most about the action of genes, environment, and their interplay are those directly examining genotype–environment correlations and interactions.

Genotype–Environment Correlations

Genotype–environment correlations arise in different forms (Plomin, DeFries, & Loehlin, 1977; Scarr & McCartney, 1983). Passive genotype–environment correlations exist because related parents provide both their genes and the environment for their children. Consequently, the higher rates of psychopathology in children of parents with a mental disorder are difficult to interpret from an etiological standpoint because these children are likely not only to inherit genetic risks but also to be exposed to pathogenic environments (Rutter & Quinton, 1984).

Genotype–environment correlation also occurs because individuals are active participants in, and create and select, their own environments. As a result, individual differences in behavior styles are sustained, in part, through the dynamic interactions between persons and their environments (Caspi, Moffitt, et al., 1996b); that is, so-called active and evocative genotype–environment correlations arise because behaviors that shape the way in which individuals elicit, select, and respond to their environments are themselves partly genetically influenced (Plomin, 1994; Rutter et al., 1997).

One implication of the pervasiveness of genotype–environment correlations in development is that genetic influences mediate predictor–outcome relationships that were hitherto believed to be entirely environmentally mediated. Adoption study results reported by Plomin (for a review, see Plomin, 1994), McGue (McGue, Sharma, & Benson, 1996) and others indicate with remarkable consistency that the phenotypic associations between parenting and child adjustment outcomes in biological parent–child dyads are much reduced in adoptive parent–child dyads; that is, in the absence of genetic influences, there is quite modest evidence of an association between parenting behavior and children's well-being. A similar conclusion was derived in a twin–sibling design (Pike et al., 1996).

Studies of evocative genotype–environment correlations similarly suggest that environmental risks may be genetically mediated. In a high-risk adoption study, Ge and colleagues (Ge et al., 1996) reported that adolescents at genetic risk for antisocial behavior (by virtue of having a biological parent with diagnosed disorder) were more likely to evoke hostile parenting and were less likely to receive warm, supportive parenting from their adoptive parents compared with adoptees not at genetic risk. The critical finding was that this effect was entirely mediated by genetic influences on the adoptees' aggressive, antisocial behavior. In other words, genetic influences give rise to behavioral problems that increase the likelihood of, and may sustain, environmental risks. However, it was not possible to unambiguously decipher the direction of effects in the Ge et al. study because of its cross-sectional design.

A study based on the Colorado Adoption Project (CAP) used a similar design and reached a broadly similar conclusion: Children with a biological parent having a history of antisocial behavior were more likely to evoke negative, coercive parenting from their adoptive parent compared to adoptees not at genetic risk (O'Connor, Deater-Deckard, Fulker, Rutter, &

Plomin, 1998). Although the tendency for parents to display more aversive parental behavior toward the at-risk adoptees was mediated by the children's aggressive behavior, the mediating effect was modest. In addition, despite the longitudinal design that covered five occasions of measurement, it was still not possible to unambiguously determine the direction of effects. The authors concluded that effects were likely to be bidirectional (i.e., child effects on the parents and parent effects on the child).

Scarr and McCartney (1983) advanced the hypothesis that passive genotype–environment correlations would predominate in infancy and early childhood and that there would be a gradual developmental shift toward evocative and active genotype–environment correlations as individuals increasingly gain greater autonomy in selecting their own environments. This developmental hypothesis complements that proposed by Plomin (1986) and others that genetic influences increase with age (McCartney et al., 1990). However, to date, few data support age-based changes in the magnitude or type of genotype–environment correlations (O'Connor, Deater-Deckard et al., 1998), and passive as well as evocative and active genotype–environment correlations may be salient throughout the first two decades of life and may be so throughout the life span (Lytte, 1977; McGue et al., 1996). The developmental hypothesis regarding genotype–environment correlations therefore awaits supporting findings.

Genotype–Environment Interactions

A second type of finding that has provided important insights into gene–environment interplay is studies documenting genotype–environment interactions. These studies generally suggest that there are genetic influences on the sensitivity to the environment. Stated differently, individuals at genetic risk are more likely than individuals not at genetic risk to react maladaptively to psychosocial stresses. Although evidence of genotype–environment interactions for psychopathology was minimal a decade ago, there are now several reports on a range of disorders.

Cadoret, Yates, Troughton, Woodhouse, and Stewart (1995) reported that adversity in the adoptive home environment was associated with adoptee antisocial outcome only in the presence of genetic risk for antisocial behavior. In a separate paper, Cadoret et al. (1996) reported that those women most likely to develop depression were those at genetic risk (defined by alcoholism) and who experienced environmental adversity; however, no such effects were found for men. Similarly, Kendler et al. (1995) found that the likelihood of experiencing depressive symptoms was especially pronounced in those at genetic risk who recently experienced stressful, severe life events; however, only women were assessed in that study. Wahlberg et al. (1997) reported a genotype–environment interaction for schizophrenia-related symptoms: Only those at genetic risk and who experienced environmental risk (defined in this case as communicative deviance in the adoptive family) exhibited elevated levels of thought disorder symptoms. An additional empirical example is provided in the Swedish study by Bohman (1996), who reported that the rate of antisocial behavior among adoptees was considerably greater (40%) in those with both genetic and environmental risks (i.e., in the adoptive home) than in those with only environmental (approximately 6%) or only genetic (12%) sources of risk. Finally, Slutske et al. (1997) reported a genotype–environment interaction, but the effect was different from that reported above. They found substantial genetic influence on conduct disorder in males based on retrospective reports in adulthood, but only if the twins had the same friends as children.

Thus, in contrast to a decade ago, there is now substantial evidence for genotype–environment interactions. These findings, like those suggesting substantial genotype–environment correlations, have significantly altered the questions posed by behavioral genetic approaches to psychopathology and have spurred interest in identifying the mechanisms underlying the genetic findings.

MOLECULAR GENETICS RESEARCH ON PSYCHOPATHOLOGY

Undoubtedly, the biggest change in behavioral genetics research on psychopathology since the previous edition of this volume is the increasing role of molecular genetics. The journals *Psychiatric Genetics* and *Molecular Psychiatry*, among others, regularly include new findings regarding the molecular genetic basis of psychopathology.

Space limits do not allow a detailed methodological overview of the methods and assumptions in this line of research, but four general points are worth noting. First, molecular genetics studies of psychopathology should not be equated with reductionistic approaches. The most obvious reason for this is that specific genes, like specific environments, will account for only a small percentage of the total variance in psychopathology. Second, identifying the genes provides no answers to the processes through which genetic influences lead to psychopathology: results from molecular genetics studies will heighten the need and lead to an increased focus for research on environmental as well as biological processes.

Third, there is an important distinction to be made between research that examines genes previously identified in research (e.g., in the case of replication studies or research examining whether a gene associated with one disorder is also implicated in a related disorder) and research that seeks to identify a new candidate gene for a disorder (e.g., through genomewide scans; Plomin & Rutter, 1998). Whereas it is relatively easy and inexpensive to use previously identified genes in research, it is difficult and expensive to identify a new finding linking genes and behavior. Fourth, molecular genetic research on complex dimensions and disorders has required new analytic paradigms from the single-gene approaches (Plomin, Owen, & McGuffin, 1994). The essence of these new methods is to identify genes in multiple-gene systems that are of modest effect size, which have been called quantitative trait loci (QTL), or susceptibility genes. These advances include QTL linkage approaches that attempt to locate general regions of a chromosome where a QTL resides (Fulker & Cherny, 1996) as well as association analyses that correlate candidate genes with complex traits (e.g., Risch & Merikangas, 1996).

To date, most of the robust molecular genetic evidence concerns personality. Novelty seeking or sensation seeking, a well-established personality characteristic included in many models of personality, was reported in two studies in 1996 to be associated with the gene for dopamine receptor (DRD4; Benjamin et al., 1996; Ebstein et al., 1996). Subsequent studies of DRD4 have continued to show some replications (Ebstein, Nomanov, Klotz, Gritsenko, & Belmaker, 1997) as well as some failures to replicate (Jonsson et al., 1997), although the direction of results and effect sizes of the failures to replicate are within the range to be expected for a QTL of small effect size given the studies' sample sizes (Plomin & Caspi, in press). Moreover, an association between DRD4 and heroin addiction has been consistently found in three studies, because there is an extensive literature relating sensation seeking to drug use, including opiate abuse (Zuckerman, 1986). Alcoholism shows mixed results (Ebstein & Belmaker, 1997) and one study of smoking shows an association with DRD4 (Lerman et al., 1999).

For the personality trait of neuroticism, an association has also been reported with a functional polymorphism in a serotonin transporter promoter, although other studies have failed to replicate the finding (see Ball et al., 1997; Ebstein et al., 1997). Finally, although there has been progress in molecular genetic studies of more severe psychopathology such as schizophrenia and bipolar disorder (Manki et al., 1996), there has been less consistent replication.

Relatively few molecular genetic studies have targeted disorders in childhood, but there are some encouraging results. For example, DRD4 has been linked to attention-deficit/ hyperactivity disorder (ADHD; LaHoste et al., 1996; Sunohara et al., 1997), although failures to replicate have also been reported (Asherson et al., 1997; Castellanos et al., 1998). Another dopamine gene that codes for a molecule that transports dopamine from the synapse has also been reported to be associated with ADHD (Gill, Daly, Heron, Hawi, & Fitzgerald, 1997; Palmer et al., 1997). The connection between ADHD and dopamine is especially interesting because pharmacological evidence also implicates the dopaminergic system in ADHD, suggesting that this system is what links genetic influence and the disorder.

Replicated molecular genetic findings were reported for reading disability; two studies suggested a QTL on chromosome 6 (Cardon et al., 1994; Grigorenko et al., 1996). Progress is also being made on the molecular genetics front with autism, a disorder also known to have a significant genetic etiology (Folstein & Rutter, 1977). For example, Cook et al. (1997) reported a linkage between the serotonin transporter gene and autism, a finding that is also consistent with what is known about the biological basis of the disorder. A final example, and one that requires replication, is a link between a 10 repeat allele of the dopamine transporter gene (DAT1) and internalizing disorders, including generalized anxiety and social phobia, obsessive–compulsive disorder and Tourette syndrome (Rowe et al., 1998). As in the earlier autism example, the genetic finding reported by Rowe et al. is interesting because it is consistent with previously reported neurotransmitter evidence.

More recently, molecular genetic investigations have focused not only on what genes are implicated in which forms of psychopathology but also on genetic mechanisms that might be implicated in developmental changes such as age of onset. A recent example of such a genetic mechanism was found in the case of Alzheimer's disease. Meyer and colleagues (1998) extended the previously reported connection between Alzheimer's disease and the apolipro-tein (APOE) genotype. They found that the number of e4 alleles (there are three alleles of APOE, e2, e3, and e4; only e4 has been implicated in the disease) was associated with the age of onset of Alzheimer's disease in vulnerable individuals rather than with the diagnosis of the disease. Further research of this kind may help explain other strong age-based trends in the rates of certain forms of psychopathology.

CONCLUSIONS

Much has changed in behavioral genetic research on developmental psychopathology in the past decade. Major changes include the increasing appreciation of genotype–environment correlation and interactions in development and the emergence of molecular genetic strategies as a viable and important step forward in research. Basic scientific issues have not changed, however, as there is continuing great need for further longitudinal research, careful measurement of psychosocial risk and protective factors, and the testing of alternative models to clarify the nature of gene–environment interplay. Moreover, it is now even clearer that neither a significant heritability nor a significant association between a specific gene and disorder necessarily provides direct clues as to how genetics shape development. Only when investigators have specified the biological and social pathways through which genetic vulnerabilities respond to psychological stresses that then lead to maladjustment can it be said that we know "how" genes influence the development of psychopathology.

REFERENCES

Ball, D., Hill, L., Freeman, B., Eley, T., Strelau, J. Riemann, R., Spinath, F. M., Angleitner, A., & Plomin, R. (1997). The serotonin transporter gene and peer-rated neuroticism. *Neuroreport, 8*, 1301–1304.

Benjamin, J., Li, L., Patterson, C., Greenberg, B., Murphy, D. L., & Hamer, D. H. (1996). Population and familial association between the D4 dopamine receptor gene and measures of novelty seeking. *Nature Genetics, 12*, 81–84.

Biederman, J., Faraone, S. V., Keenan, K., & Tsuang, M. T. (1991). Evidence of familial association between attention deficit disorder and major affective disorders. *Archives of General Psychiatry, 48*, 633–642.

Bohman, M. (1996). Predisposition to criminality: Swedish adoption studies in retrospect. In G. R. Bock & J. A. Goode (Eds.), *Genetics of criminal and antisocial behavior* (pp. 99–114). Chichester, UK: Wiley.

Bolton, P., MacDonald, H., Pickles, A., Rios, P., Goode, S., Crowson, M., Bailey, A., & Rutter, M. (1994). A case-control family history study of autism. *Journal of Child Psychology and Psychiatry, 35*, 877–900.

Bouchard, T., & McGue, M. (1981). Familial studies of intelligence: A review. *Science, 212*, 1055–1059.

Bronfenbrenner, U., & Ceci, S. J. (1993). Heredity, environment, and the question "how?"—a first approximation. In R. Plomin & G. E. McClearn (Eds.), *Nature, nurture, and psychology* (pp. 313–324). Washington, DC: APA Books.

Cadoret, R. J., Winokur, G., Langbehn, D., Troughton, E., Yates, W., & Stewart, M. A. (1996). Depression spectrum disease I: The role of gene–environment interaction. *American Journal of Psychiatry, 153*, 892–899.

Cadoret, R. J., Yates, W. R., Troughton, E., Woodworth, G., & Stewart, M. A. (1995). Genetic–environmental interactions in the genesis of aggressivity and conduct disorders. *Archives of General Psychiatry, 52*, 916–924.

Cardon, L. R., Smith, S. D., Fulker, D. W., Kimberling, W. J., Pennington, B. F., & DeFries, J. C. (1994). Quantitative trait loci for reading disability on chromosome 6. *Science, 266*, 276–279.

Caron, C., & Rutter, M. (1991). Comorbidity in child psychopathology: Concepts, issues and research strategies. *Journal of Child Psychology and Psychiatry, 32*, 1063–1080.

Caspi, A., & Moffitt, T. E. (1995a). The continuity of maladaptive behaviour: From description to understanding in the study of antisocial behaviour. In D. Cicchetti & D. Cohen (Eds.), *Developmental psychopathology* (Vol. 2, pp. 472–511). New York: Wiley.

Caspi, A., Moffitt, T. E., Newman, D. L., & Silva, P. A. (1996). Behavioral observations at age 3 years predict adult psychiatric disorders. *Archives of General Psychiatry, 53*, 1033–1039.

Castellanos, F. X., Lau, E., Tayebi, N., Lee, R., Long, R. E., Giedd, J. N., Sharp, W., Marsh, W. L., Walter, J. M., Hamburger, S. D., Ginns, E. I., Rappaport, J. L., & Sidrinsky, E. (1998). Lack of an association between a dopamine-receptor polymorphism and attention-deficit hyperactivity disorder. *Molecular Psychology, 3*, 431–434.

Cicchetti, D. (1984). The emergence of developmental psychopathology. *Child Development, 55*, 1–7.

Cicchetti, D. (1990). A historical perspective on the discipline of developmental psychopathology. In J. Rolf, A. S. Masten, D. Cicchetti, K. H. Nuechterlein, & S. Weintraub (Eds.), *Risk and protective factors in the development of psychopathology* (pp. 2–28). New York: Cambridge University Press.

Collier, D. A., & Sham, P. C. (1997). Catch me if you can: Are catechol- and indoamine genes pleiotropic QTLs for common mental disorders? *Molecular Psychiatry, 2*, 181–183.

Cook, H., Courchesne, R., Lord, C., Cox, N. J., Tan, S., Lincoln, A., Haas, R., Courchesne, E., & Leventhal, B. L. (1997). Evidence of linkage between the serotonin transporter and autistic disorder. *Molecular Psychiatry, 2*, 247–250.

Coryell, W. (1997). Do psychotic, minor and intermittent depressive disorders exist on a continuum? *Journal of Affective Disorders, 45*, 75–83.

Deater-Deckard, K., Reiss, D., Hetherington, E. M., & Plomin, R. (1997). Dimensions and disorders of adolescent adjustment: A quantitative genetic analysis of unselected samples and selected extremes. *Journal of Child Psychology and Psychiatry, 38*, 515–525.

DeFries, J. C., & Fulker, D. W. (1985). Multiple regression analysis of twin data. *Behavior Genetics, 15*, 467–473.

DiLalla, L. F., & Gottesman, I. I. (1989). Heterogeneity of causes for delinquency and criminality: Lifespan perspectives. *Development and Psychopathology, 1*, 339–350.

Eaves, L. J., Silberg, J. L., Meyer, J. M., Maes, H. H., Somonoff, E., Pickles, A., Rutter, M., Neale, M. C., Reynolds, C. A., Erikson, M. T., Heath, A. C., Loeber, R., Truett, T. R., & Hewitt, J. K. (1997). Genetics and developmental psychopathology: 2. The main effects of genes and environment on behavioral problems in the Virginia Twin Study of Adolescent Behavioral Development. *Journal of Child Psychology and Psychiatry, 38,* 965–980.

Ebstein, R. P., & Belmaker, R. H. (1997) Saga of an adventure. Novelty seeking, substance abuse and the dopamine D4 receptor (DRD4) exon III repeat polymorphism. *Molecular Psychiatry, 2,* 381–384.

Ebstein, R. P., Nemanov, L., Klotz, I., Gritsenko, I., & Belmaker, R. H. (1997). Additional evidence for an association between the dopamine D4 receptor (DRD4) exon III repeat polymorphism and the human personality trait of novelty seeking. *Molecular Psychiatry, 2,* 472–477.

Ebstein, R. P., Novick, O., Umansky, R., Priel, B., Osher, Y., Blaine, D., Bennett, E., Nemanov, L., Katz, I., & Belmaker, R. H. (1996). Dopamine D4 receptor (DRD4) exon III polymorphism associated with the human personality trait of novelty seeking. *Nature Genetics, 12,* 78–80.

Edelbrock, C., Rende, R., Plomin, R., & Thompson, L. A. (1995). A twin study of competence and problems behaviours in childhood and early adolescence. *Journal of Child Psychology and Psychiatry, 36,* 775–786.

Eley, T. C. (1997). Depressive symptoms in children and adults: Etiological links between normality and abnormality: A research note. *Journal of Child Psychology and Psychiatry, 38,* 861–865.

Folstein, S., & Rutter, M. (1977). Genetic influences and infantile autism. *Nature, 265,* 726–728.

Fulker, D. W., & Cherny, S. S. (1996). An improved multipoint sib-pair analysis of quantitative traits. *Behavior Genetics, 26,* 527–532.

Ge, X., Conger, R. D., Cadoret, R. J., Neiderhiser, J. M., Yates, W., Troughton, E., & Stewart, M. A. (1996). The developmental interface between nature and nurture: A mutual influence model of child antisocial behavior and parent behaviors. *Developmental Psychology, 32,* 574–589.

Gill, M., Daly, G., Heron, S., Hawi, Z., & Fitzgerald, M. (1997). Confirmation of association between attention deficit hyperactivity disorder and a dopamine transporter polymorphism. *Molecular Psychiatry, 2,* 311–313.

Gjone, H., Stevenson, J., Sundet, J. M., & Eilertsen, D. E. (1996). Changes in heritability across increasing levels of behavior problems in young twins. *Behavior Genetics, 26,* 419–426.

Gottesman, I. I. (1974). Developmental genetics and ontogenic psychology: Overdue detente and propositions from a matchmaker. In A. D. Pick (Ed.), *Minnesota Symposium on Child Psychology* (pp. 55–80). Minneapolis: University of Minnesota Press.

Gottesman, I. I. (1991). *Schizophrenia genesis: The origins of madness.* New York: Freeman.

Gottesman, I. I., & Goldsmith, H. H. (1994). Developmental psychopathology of antisocial behavior: Inserting genes into its ontogenesis and epigenesis. In C. A. Nelson (Ed.), Threats to optimal development. *Minnesota Symposium on Child Psychology, 27,* 20–44. Hillsdale, NJ: Erlbaum.

Grigorenko, E. L., Wood, F. B., Meyer, M. S., Hart, L. A., Speed, W. C., Schuster, A., & Pauls, D. (1996). Susceptibility loci for distinct components of dyslexia on chromosomes 6 and 15. *American Journal of Human Genetics, 59* (A219 abstract).

Harrington, R., Rutter, M., Weissman, M., Fudge, H., Groothues, C., Bredenkamp, D., Pickles, A., Rende, R., & Wickramaratne, P. (1997). Psychiatric disorder in the relatives of depressed probands: I. Comparison of prepubertal, adolescent and early adult onset cases. *Journal of Affective Disorders, 42,* 9–22.

Jonsson, E. G., Nothen, M. M., Gustavsson, J. P., Neidt, H., Brene, S., Tylec, A., Propping, P., & Sedvall, G. C. (1997). Lack of evidence for allelic association between personality traits and the dopamine D4 receptor gene polymorphisms. *American Journal of Psychiatry, 154,* 697–699.

Kendler, K. S., Gruenberg, A. M., & Kinney, D. K. (1994). Independent diagnoses of adoptees and relatives as defined by DSM-III in the provincial and national samples of the Danish Adoption Study of schizophrenia. *Archives of General Psychiatry, 51,* 456–468.

Kendler, K. S., Heath, A. C., Neale, M. C., Kessler, R. C., & Eaves, L. J. (1993). Alcoholism and major depression in women: A twin study of the causes of comorbidity. *Archives of General Psychiatry, 50,* 690–698.

Kendler, S. K., Kessler, R. C., Walters, E. E., MacLean, C., Neale, M. C., Heath, A. C., & Eaves, L. J. (1995). Stressful life events, genetic liability, and onset of an episode of major depression in women. *American Journal of Psychiatry, 152,* 833–842.

Kendler, K. S., Neale, M. C., Kessler, R. C., Heath, A. C., & Eaves, L. J. (1992a). Major depression and generalized anxiety disorder: Same genes, (partly) different environments? *Archives of General Psychiatry, 49,* 716–722.

Kendler, K., Neale, M., Kessler, R., Heath, A., & Eaves, L. (1992b). A population-based twin study of major depression in women: The impact of varying degrees of illness. *Archives of General Psychiatry, 49,* 257–266.

Kendler, K., Neale, M. C., Kessler, R. C., Heath, A. C., & Eaves, L. J. (1992c). Familial influences on the clinical characteristics of major depression: A twin study. *Acta Psychiatrica Scandinavica, 86,* 371–378.

Kendler, K., Neale, M. C., Kessler, R. C., Heath, A. C., & Eaves, L. J. (1993). A longitudinal study of 1-year prevalence of major depression in women. *Archives of General Psychiatry, 50,* 843–852.

Kendler, K. S., Neale, M. C., MacLean, C. J., Heath, A. C., Eaves, L. J., & Kessler, R. C. (1993). Smoking and major depression: A causal analysis. *Archives of General Psychiatry, 50,* 36–43.

Kessler, R. C., Kendler, K. S., Heath, A. C., Neale, M. C., & Eaves, L. J. (1992). Social support, depressed mood, and adjustment to stress: A genetic epidemiological investigation. *Journal of Personality and Social Psychology, 62,* 257–272.

Kessler, R. C., McGonagle, K. A., Zhao, S., Nelson, C. B., Hughes, M., Eshleman, S., Wittchen, H.-U., & Kendler, K. S. (1994). Lifetime and 12-month prevalence of DSM-III-R psychiatric disorders in the United States. *Archives of General Psychiatry, 51,* 8–19.

Kovacs, M., Devlin, B., Pollock, M., Richards, C., & Mukerji, P. (1997). A controlled family history study of childhood-onset depressive disorder. *Archives of General Psychiatry, 54,* 613–623.

LaHoste, G. J., Swanson, J. M., Wigal, S. S., Glabe, C., Wigal, T., King, N., & Kennedy, J. L. (1996). Dopamine D4 receptor gene polymorphism is associated with attention deficit hyperactivity disorder. *Molecular Psychiatry, 1,* 128–131.

Lerman, C., Caporaso, N., Main, D., Audrain, J., Boyd, N. R., Bowman, E. D., & Shields, P. G. (1999). Depression and self-medication with nicotine: The modifying influence of the dopamine D4 receptor gene. *Health Psychology, 18,* 14–20.

Lyons, M. J., True, W. R., Eisen, S. A., Goldberg, J., Meyer, J. M., Faraone, S. V., Eaves, L. J., & Tsuang, M. T. (1995). Differential heritability of adult and juvenile antisocial traits. *Archives of General Psychiatry, 52,* 906–915.

Lytten, H. (1977). Do parents create, or respond to, differences in twins? *Developmental Psychology, 13,* 456–459.

Manki, H., Kanba, S., Muramatsu, T., Higuschi, S., Suzuki, E., Matsushita, S., Ono, Y., Chiba, H., Shintani, F., Nakamura, M., Tagi, G., & Asai, M. (1996). Dopamine D2, D3 and D4 receptor gene polymorphisms and mood disorders. *Journal of Affective Disorders, 40,* 7–13.

McCartney, K., Harris, M. J., & Bernieri, F. (1990). Growing up and growing apart: A developmental meta-analysis of twin studies. *Psychological Bulletin, 107,* 226–237.

McGue, M., & Lykken, D. T. (1992). Genetic influence on risk for divorce. *Psychological Science, 3,* 368–373.

McGue, M., Sharma, A., & Benson, P. (1996). The effect of common rearing on adolescent adjustment: Evidence from a U.S. adoption cohort. *Developmental Psychology, 32,* 604–613.

McGuffin, P., Owen, M. J., O'Donovan, M. C, Thapar, A., & Gottesman, I. I. (1994). *Seminars in psychiatric genetics.* London: Gaskell Press.

McGuire, S., Neiderhiser, J., Reiss, D., Hetherington, E. M., & Plomin, R. (1994). Genetic and environmental influences on perceptions of self-worth and competence in adolescence: A study of twins, full siblings, and step siblings. *Child Development, 65,* 785–799.

Meyer, M. R., Tschanz, J. T., Norton, M. C., Welsh-Bohmer, K., Steffens, D. C., Wyse, B. W., & Breitner, J. C. S. (1998). APOE genotype predicts when—not whether—one is predisposed to develop Alzheimer disease. *Nature Genetics, 19,* 321–322.

Miles, D. R., & Carey, G. (1997). Genetic and environmental architecture to human aggression. *Journal of Personality and Social Psychology, 72,* 207–217.

Moffitt, T. E. (1993). Adolescence-limited and life-course-persistent antisocial behavior: A developmental taxonomy. *Psychological Review, 100,* 674–701.

Murray, K. T., & Sines, J. O. (1996). Parsing the genetic and nongenetic variance in children's depressive behavior. *Journal of Affective Disorders, 38,* 23–34.

Neale, M. C., & Cardon, L. R. (1992). *Methodology for genetic studies of twins and families.* Boston, MA: Kluwer Academic.

Nigg, J. T., & Goldsmith, H. H. (1994). Genetics of personality disorders: Perspectives from personality and psychopathology research. *Psychological Bulletin, 115,* 346–380.

O'Connor, T. G., Deater-Deckard, K., Fulker, D., Rutter, M., & Plomin, R. (1998). Genotype–environment correlations in late childhood and early adolescence: Antisocial behavioral problems and coercive parenting. *Developmental Psychology, 34,* 970–981.

O'Connor, T. G., Deater-Deckard, K., & Plomin, R. (1998). Contributions of behavioral genetics research to clinical psychology. In E. Walker (Ed.), *Handbook of clinical psychology: Vol. 1. Foundations* (pp. 87–114). New York: Pergamon.

O'Connor, T. G., Hetherington, E. M., Reiss, D., & Plomin, R. (1995). A twin-sibling study of observed parent–adolescent interactions. *Child Development, 66,* 812–829.

O'Connor, T. G., McGuire, S., Reiss, D., Hetherington, E. M., & Plomin, R. (1998). Co-occurrence of depressive symptoms and antisocial behaviour in adolescence: A common genetic liability. *Journal of Abnormal Psychology, 107,* 27–37.

O'Connor, T. G., Neiderhiser, J. M., Reiss, D., Hetherington, E. M., & Plomin, R. (1998). Genetic contributions to continuity, change and co-occurrence of antisocial and depressive symptoms in adolescence. *Journal of Child Psychology and Psychiatry, 39,* 323–326.

Palmer, C. G., Bailey, J. N., Ramey, C., Cantwell, D., DeHomme, M., McGough, J., Woodward, J., Saranow, R.,

Asarnow, J., Smalley, S., Nelson, S. (1997). Possible evidence of DAT1 gene by sex interaction in susceptibility to dopamine transporter. *American Journal of Medical Genetics (Neuropsychiatric Genetics)*, *74*, 620. (Abstract)

Perrin, S., & Last, C. (1996). Relationships between ADHD and anxiety in boys: Results from a family study. *Journal of the American Academy of Child and Adolescent Psychiatry*, *35*, 988–996.

Pike, A., McGuire, S., Reiss, D., Hetherington, E. M., & Plomin, R. (1996). Family environment and adolescent depressive symptoms and antisocial behaviour: A multivariate genetic analysis. *Developmental Psychology*, *32*, 590–603.

Piven, J., & Palmer, P. (1997). Cognitive deficits in parents from multiple-incidence autism families. *Journal of Child Psychology and Psychiatry*, *38*, 177–183.

Plomin, R. (1986). *Development, genetics, and psychology*. Hillsdale, NJ: Erlbaum.

Plomin, R. (1991). Genetic risk and psychosocial disorders: Links between the normal and abnormal. In M. Rutter & P. Casear (Eds.), *Biological risk factors for psychosocial disorders* (pp. 101–138). Cambridge, UK: Cambridge University Press.

Plomin, R. (1994). *Genetics and experience*. Newbury Park, CA: Sage.

Plomin, R. (1995). Genetics and children's experiences in the family. *Journal of Child Psychology and Psychiatry*, *36*, 68.

Plomin, R., & Bergeman, C. S. (1991). The nature of nurture: Genetic influences on "environmental" measures. *Behavioral and Brain Sciences*, *14*, 373–427.

Plomin, R., & Caspi, A. (in press). DNA and personality. *European Journal of Personality*.

Plomin, R., Corley, R., Caspi, A., Fulker, D. W., & DeFries, J. (1998). Adoption results for self-reported personality: Evidence for nonadditive genetic effects? *Journal of Personality and Social Psychology*, *75*, 211–218.

Plomin, R., Corley, R., DeFries, J. C., & Fulker, D. W. (1990). Individual differences in television viewing in early childhood: Nature as well as nurture. *Psychological Science*, *1*, 371–377.

Plomin, R., & Daniels, D. (1987). Why are children in the same family so different from one another? *Behavioral and Brain Sciences*, *10*, 1–16.

Plomin, R., DeFries, J. C., & Loehlin, J. C. (1977). Genotype–environment interaction and correlation in the analysis of human behavior. *Psychological Bulletin*, *84*, 309–322.

Plomin, R., DeFries, J. C., McClearn, G. E., & Rutter, M. (1997). *Behavioral genetics* (3rd ed.). New York: Freeman.

Plomin, R., Lichtenstein, P., Pedersen, N. L., McClearn, G. E., & Nesselroade, J. R. (1990). Genetic influences on life events during the last half of the life span. *Psychology and Aging*, *5*, 25–30.

Plomin, R., & McClearn, G. E. (1993). *Nature, nurture, and psychology*. Washington, DC: American Psychological Association.

Plomin, R., Nitz, K., & Rowe, D. C. (1990). Behavioral genetics and aggressive behavior in childhood. In M. Lewis & S. M. Miller (Eds.), *Handbook of developmental psychopathology* (pp. 119–133). New York: Plenum Press.

Plomin, R., Owen, M. J., & McGuffin, P. (1994). The genetic basis of complex human behaviors. *Science*, *264*, 1733–1739.

Plomin, R., Reiss, D., Hetherington, E. M., & Howe, G. (1994). Nature and nurture: Genetic contributions to measures of the family environment. *Developmental Psychology*, *30*, 32–43.

Plomin, R., & Rutter, M. (1998). Child development and molecular genetics: What do we do with the gene once they are found? *Child Development*, *69*, 1223.

Reiss, D., Hetherington, E. M., Plomin, R., Howe, G. W., Simmens, S. J., Henderson, S. H., O'Connor, T. G., Bussell, D. A., Anderson, E. R., & Law, T. C. (1995). Genetic questions for environmental studies: Differential parenting of siblings and its association with depression and antisocial behavior in adolescence. *Archives of General Psychiatry*, *52*, 925–936.

Reiss, D., Plomin, R., Hetherington, E. M., Howe, G., Rovine, M., Tryon, A., & Stanley, M. (1994). The separate worlds of teenage siblings: An introduction to the study of the nonshared environment and adolescent development. In E. M. Hetherington, D. Reiss, & R. Plomin (Eds.), *Separate social worlds of siblings: Importance of nonshared environment on development* (pp. 63–109). Hillsdale, NJ: Erlbaum.

Risch, N., & Merikangas, K. (1996). The future of genetic studies of complex human disease. *Science*, *273*, 1516–1517.

Rodgers, J. L., Rowe, D. C., & Li, C. (1994). Beyond nature versus nurture: DF analysis of nonshared influences on problem behaviors. *Developmental Psychology*, *30*, 374–384.

Rowe, D. (1981). Environmental and genetic influences on perceived parenting: A twin study. *Developmental Psychology*, *17*, 203–208.

Rowe, D. C., Stevens, C., Gard, J., Cleveland, H. H., Sanders, M., Abramovitz, A., Kozol, S. T., Mohr, J. M., Sherman, S. L., & Waldman, I. D. (1998). The relation of the dopamine transporter gene (DAT1) to symptoms of internalizing disorders in children. *Behavior Genetics*, *28*, 215–225.

Rutter, M. (1989). Age as an ambiguous variable in developmental research: Some epidemiological considerations from developmental psychopathology. *International Journal of Behavioural Development*, *12*, 1–34.

Rutter, M. (1994). Psychiatric genetics: Research challenges and pathways forward. *American Journal of Psychiatric Genetics (Neuropsychiatric Genetics)*, *54*, 185–198.

Rutter, M. (1997). Nature–nurture integration: The example of antisocial behavior. *American Psychologist, 52*, 390–398.

Rutter, M., Dunn, J., Plomin, R., Simonoff, E., Pickles, A., Maughan, B., Ormel, H., Meyer, J., & Eaves, L. (1997). Integrating nature and nurture: Implications of person–environment correlations and interactions for developmental psychopathology. *Development and Psychopathology, 9*, 335–364.

Rutter, M., & Plomin, R. (1997). Opportunities for psychiatry from genetic findings. *British Journal of Psychiatry, 171*, 209–219.

Rutter, M., & Quinton, D. (1984). Parental psychiatric disorder: Effects on children. *Psychological Medicine, 14*, 853–880.

Rutter, M., & Redshaw, J. (1991). Annotation: Growing up as a twin: Twin-singleton differences in psychological development. *Journal of Child Psychology and Psychiatry, 32*, 885–895.

Rutter, M., Silberg, J., O'Connor, T., & Somonoff, E. (1999). Genetics and child psychiatry: II. Empirical research findings. *Journal of Child Psychology and Psychiatry, 40*, 19–55.

Scarr, S. (1992). Developmental theories for the 1990s: Development and individual differences. *Child Development, 63*, 1–19.

Scarr, S., & McCartney, K. (1983). How people make their own environments: A theory of gene→environment effects. *Child Development, 54*, 424–435.

Schmitz, S., Suadino, K., Plomin, R., Fulker, D. W., & DeFries, J. C. (1996). Genetic and environmental influences on temperament in middle childhood: Analyses of teacher and tester ratings. *Child Development, 67*, 409–422.

Silberg, J. L., Erickson, M. T., Meyer, J. M., Eaves, L. J., Rutter, M. L., & Hewitt, J. K. (1994). The application of structural equation modelling to maternal ratings of twins' behavioural and emotional problems. *Journal of Consulting and Clinical Psychology, 62*, 510–521.

Silberg, J. L., Rutter, M., Meyer, J., Maes, H., Hewitt, J., Simonoff, E., Pickles, A., Loeber, R., & Eaves, L. (1996). Genetic and environmental influences on the covariation between hyperactivity and conduct disturbance in juvenile twins. *Journal of Child Psychology and Psychiatry, 37*, 803–816.

Simonoff, E. (1992). A comparison of twins and singletons with child psychiatric disorders: An item sheet study. *Journal of Child Psychology and Psychiatry, 33*, 1319–1332.

Slutske, W., Heath, A. C., Dinwiddie, S., Madden, P., Bucholz, K., Dunne, M., Statham, D., & Martin, N. G. (1997). Modeling genetic and environmental influences in the etiology of conduct disorder: A study of 2,682 adult twin pairs. *Journal of Abnormal Psychology, 106*, 266–279.

Sunohara, G., Bar, C. L., Jin, U., Scahcher, R., Roberts, W., Tannock, R., Malone, M., & Kennedy, J. L. (1997). Is the dopamine D4 receptor gene associated with children and adults with attention-deficit-hyperactivity disorder? *American Journal of Medical Genetics (Neuropsychiatric Genetics), 74*, 629. (Abstract)

Thapar, A., & McGuffin, P. (1994). A twin study of depressive symptoms in childhood. *British Journal of Psychiatry, 165*, 259–265.

Thapar, A., & McGuffin, P. (1995). Are anxiety symptoms in childhood heritable? *Journal of Child Psychology and Psychiatry, 36*, 439–447.

Thorpe, K., Golding, J., MacGillroy, I., & Greenwood, R. (1991). Comparison of prevalence of depression in mothers of twins and mothers of singletons. *British Medical Journal, 302*, 875–878.

Tsuang, M., & Faraone, S. D. (1990). *The genetics of mood disorders*. Baltimore: Johns Hopkins University Press.

Van den Oord, E. J., Koot, H. M., Boomsma, D., & Verhulst, F. C. (1995). A twin-singleton comparison of problem behavior in 2–3-year-olds. *Journal of Child Psychology and Psychiatry, 36*, 449–458.

Van den Oord, E. J., & Rowe, D. C. (1997). Continuity and change in children's social maladjustment: A developmental behavior genetic study. *Developmental Psychology, 33*, 319–332.

Van den Oord, E. J., Verhulst, F. C., & Boomsma, D. (1996). A genetic study of maternal and paternal ratings of problem behaviors in 3-year-old twins. *Journal of Abnormal Psychology, 105*, 349–357.

Wahlberg, K. E., Wynne, L. C., Oja, H., Keskitalo, P., Pykalainen, L., Lahti, I., Moring, J., Naarala, M., Sorri, A., Seitmaa, M., Laksy, K., Kolassa, J., & Tienari, P. (1997). Gene–environment interaction in vulnerability to schizophrenia: Findings from the Finnish adoptive family study of schizophrenia. *American Journal of Psychiatry, 154*, 355–362.

Weissman, M. M., Wickramaratne, P., Merikangas, K. R., Leckman, J. F., Prusoff, B. A., Caruso, K. A., Kidd, K. K., & Gammon, G. D. (1984). Onset of major depression in early adulthood: Increased familial loading and specificity. *Archives of General Psychiatry, 41*, 1136–1143.

Zahn-Waxler, C., Schmitz, S., Robinson, J., Fulker, D. W., & Emde, R. (1996). Behavior problems in 5-year-old monozygotic and dizygotic twins: Genetic and environmental influences, patterns of regulation, and internalization of control. *Development and Psychopathology, 8*, 103–122.

Zuckerman, M. (1986). Sensation seeking and the endogenous deficit theory of drug use. *NIDA Research Monographs, 74*, 59–70.

13

A Biobehavioral Perspective on Developmental Psychopathology

Excessive Aggression and Serotonergic Dysfunction in Monkeys

Stephen J. Suomi

It can be persuasively argued that few topics of scientific inquiry pose more formidable challenges—theoretical, empirical, or applied—than the development of behavioral abnormalities, especially in organisms whose nervous systems remain relatively plastic throughout ontogeny. Researchers and clinical workers in this area are frequently faced with decisions as to whether the phenomenon under investigation or treatment truly represents a pathology or is merely unusual or extreme in the statistical sense—or perhaps simply reflects a phase of development that eventually will be outgrown. In addition, those who study psychopathological disorders in children and adolescents must routinely deal with behavioral and biological systems that often express themselves in diverse (and sometimes seemingly independent) fashions not only at different ages but also at different levels of analysis. For this population, obvious changes in behavior are not always reflected by systematic changes in physiology—or vice versa. Moreover, profound complications accompany rigorous study of any developing systems or individuals, relative to those that are already stable or mature, be they normal or anomalous. As stated by Sackett, Sameroff, Cairns, and Suomi (1981):

> The study of development poses a major paradox for students of behavior. The problem arises from the fact that change is an essential property of development. Virtually all features of the organism undergo modification during its life span. On the other hand, continuity over time seems essential for individual uniqueness, organization, and the maintenance of integrated patterns of behavior. The paradox is simply this: How can

Stephen J. Suomi • Laboratory of Comparative Ethology, National Institute of Child Health & Human Development, Bethesda, Maryland 20892.

Handbook of Developmental Psychopathology, Second Edition, edited by Arnold J. Sameroff, Michael Lewis, and Suzanne M. Miller. Kluwer Academic/Plenum Publishers, New York, 2000.

continuity and persistence be achieved in an organismic system that necessarily undergoes maturational, interactional, and social–cultural change? (p. 23)

In this chapter, I describe an important mental health problem that has attracted widespread attention in recent years—the development of excessive physical aggression and violence in children and adolescents, with an emphasis on recent findings linking such behavior to an apparent deficit in central serotonin metabolism. I show that although this problem presents major ethical and practical obstacles to basic and applied research with human subjects and patients, it is nevertheless possible to model essential features of the phenomenon in nonhuman primates with considerably greater research latitude. Next, I summarize evidence that demonstrates a striking association between excessive physical aggression and similar deficits in central serotonin metabolism for rhesus monkeys and other primate species. I then describe some new findings demonstrating that variations in a specific gene implicated in serotonin metabolism can have dramatically different developmental consequences for monkeys as a function of their early social-rearing history. I conclude by arguing that biobehavioral research with animals can help investigators disentangle the complex issues of nature–nurture and continuity–discontinuity in order to advance our understanding of developmental psychopathology in humans.

DEVELOPMENT OF EXCESSIVE PHYSICAL AGGRESSION IN CHILDREN

To illustrate some of the problems for researchers and clinicians trying to investigate and understand any developmental psychopathology, consider the case of children and adolescents who exhibit excessive physical aggression toward their peers. A large body of prospective and retrospective evidence accumulated over the past two decades indicates that children, especially boys, who display high levels of physical aggression upon entry into the school system are disproportionately likely to continue to be highly aggressive for the rest of their childhood and may even become violent as adolescents or adults (e.g., Olweus, 1979; Tremblay, 1992). Other studies (e.g., Rutter, Giller, & Hagell, 1998) have shown that such individuals are also at greatly increased risk for developing a wide range of other behavioral problems or even more serious psychopathologies, including attentional difficulties and both externalizing and internalizing behavior disorders during childhood, and delinquency, substance abuse, violent criminality, and suicide in adolescence and adulthood.

Recently, Tremblay et al. (1998) reported what generations of parents have long suspected—that 2-year-olds exhibit higher rates of physical aggression, much of it seemingly unprovoked, than do children during any other phase of development. Fortunately, most 2-year-olds lack the physical strength to inflict serious injury in any of their frequent aggressive outbursts, and, even more fortunately, most somehow outgrow their terrible-2 phase, such that their aggressive behaviors decline in frequency, are less likely to involve overt physical attack, and become increasingly limited to specific situations as they grow older. A few children, however, continue to exhibit high levels of physical aggression well beyond toddlerhood. These are the individuals who appear most likely to show excessive and socially inappropriate aggression upon entry into the school system and thereafter, as well as being at high risk for developing the other comorbid problems listed earlier.

However, only a relatively small proportion of children who display high levels of physical aggression when they start school actually maintain such high levels throughout the rest of childhood and adolescence. Instead, the vast majority of highly aggressive kinder-gartners also show the normative developmental decline in physical aggression (described earlier) in subsequent years. For example, in a recent prospective longitudinal study that followed a large cohort of boys from low socioeconomic scale (SES) areas in Montreal from 6 to 18 years of age, Negin and Tremblay (1999) found that whereas approximately 33% of their sample were reported by their kindergarten teachers to exhibit excessive physical aggression, only 4% continued to show high levels throughout the rest of grade school. Moreover, those same boys not only had the highest teacher-reported incidence of physical aggression during high school as well but also self-reported much higher rates of violence (e.g., gang fighting, assault with a deadly weapon) and serious delinquency (e.g., breaking and entering, arson, other property destruction, nonpetty theft) than the rest of their cohort. What other characteristics differentiate such chronically aggressive individuals from their peers, and what factors might contribute to such characteristics?

One line of research has focused on the patterns of social interaction these children and adolescents develop with their parents and peers, and the perceptions and attitudes that presumably emerge from those interactions. For example, Patterson and his colleagues (e.g., Patterson, Reid, & Dishion, 1992) have identified escalating interaction sequences in which a misbehaving child elicits coercive disciplinary parental responses, which in turn elicit aggressive child responses that lead to further parental coercion. Other investigators (e.g., Rubin & Rose-Krasnor, 1992) have described patterns of peer interaction in which aggressive children who engage in bullying are increasingly avoided by peers and as a consequence become progressively isolated socially, with few opportunities to acquire the interactive skills normally involved in the socialization of aggressive tendencies. Dodge (1980; Chapter 24, this volume) has shown that highly aggressive children are disproportionately likely to perceive ambiguous social stimulation from peers as aggressive in intent and to respond in kind; MacKinnon, in turn, has described similar social–perceptual biases for aggressive children in interactions with their mothers (MacKinnon, Lamb, Arbuckle, Baradan, & Volling, 1992).

Detailed descriptions of characteristic interaction patterns and biased perceptions of highly aggressive children have provided the foundation for a number of seemingly effective interventions for these children—and their parents and peers (cf. Reiss & Roth, 1993). Yet relatively little is known about the actual origins of such patterns and perceptions (e.g., Do they predate, emerge concurrently, or begin only after the child's excessive aggression first becomes apparent?), in large part because few longitudinal studies can sample often enough to catch the phenomenon as it emerges. Similarly, little is known about the developmental trajectories of such patterns and perceptions, even though relevant information might prove invaluable for designing intervention strategies that could take advantage of potential develop-mental windows to identify optimal periods for targeted interventions.

Other researchers have searched for potential causes of excessive childhood aggression. Some investigators have looked to community, demographic, and economic factors to account for differences in incidence rates among children from different populations (e.g., Offord, Alder, & Boyle, 1987). Others have focused on within-family factors. Excessive physical aggression *does* seem to run in families, but there is scant consensus as to precisely *which* factors within the family might be responsible. For example, numerous developmental and clinical studies have reported strong links between excessive childhood aggression and problems in parenting. A disproportionately high number of aggressive children grow up in basically dysfunctional families, in which the attachment relationship with their primary caregiver is likely to be insecure or disorganized. Thus, incompetent, neglectful, or abusive parenting is thought to contribute to the excessive physical aggression exhibited by children.

On the other hand, any parent's role can be rendered more daunting by a temperamentally difficult child. A consistent finding from prospective longitudinal studies is that infants with certain temperamental characteristics (e.g., high irritability and/or poor state control) are disproportionately likely to develop subsequent problems controlling their aggression. Of course, only a small proportion of the infants who exhibit such temperamental characteristics actually grow up to be violent adolescents and adults. Nevertheless, these data regarding temperament have encouraged some investigators to search for heritable factors that might promote or even cause excessive physical aggression to remain in some children's repertoires throughout development. Recent findings from well-designed behavioral genetics studies have, in fact, demonstrated significant heritability for many of the behavioral features and common concomitants of high physical aggressivity (cf. Rutter, Silberg, O'Connor, & Simonoff, 1999). Thus, it appears that both nature and nurture are implicated in the etiology of this phenomenon, but we currently know precious little about how heritable and experiential factors actually act and/or interact to influence its development.

BIOLOGICAL CORRELATES
OF PHYSICAL AGGRESSION IN CHILDREN

In recent years, a number of investigators have turned to biology in their search for potential causes of excessive physical aggression and violence. To date, evidence in support of a biological basis for such behaviors has been mixed at best. Most of the prime suspects that have been studied by these researchers (e.g., excessive testosterone titers or elevated cortisol concentrations) have not been found to be particularly useful in differentiating highly aggressive individuals from others. On the other hand, considerable research interest has been generated by the finding of an apparent link between extreme cases of aggression and abnormalities in central nervous system (CNS) metabolism of the inhibitory neurotransmitter *serotonin*. For example, unusually low concentrations of the primary CNS serotonin metabolite 5-hydroxyindoleacetic acid (5-HIAA) in cerebrospinal fluid (CSF) have been found in children who are unusually aggressive toward peers and hostile toward their mothers (Kruesi et al., 1990), children who torture animals (Kruesi, 1989), and children and adolescents with severely disruptive behavioral disorders (Kruesi et al., 1990). This pattern characterizes older individuals as well, including young adult males convicted of violent acts and/or property destruction (Linnoila et al., 1983), men with personality disorders who have extreme scores for aggression, irritability, hostility, and psychopathic deviance on standardized interviews (Brown, Linnoila, & Goodwin, 1990; Linnoila, 1988), men expelled from the Marines for excessive violence and psychopathic deviance (Brown, Goodwin, Ballenger, Goyer, & Major, 1979), suicide victims (e.g., Mann, Arango, & Underwood, 1990), men with impulse-mediated Type II alcoholism (Cloninger, 1987), and, interestingly, sons of men arrested for violence and arson (Linnoila, DeJong, & Virkkunen, 1989).

In order to understand the precise nature of this apparent linkage between low CSF 5-HIAA concentrations and excessive physical aggression and violence (e.g., what causes what), it becomes necessary to ask some basic developmental questions concerning the initial appearance of abnormalities in serotonin metabolism and the developmental trajectories and long-term stabilities of such abnormalities. The answers to such questions have obvious theoretical, clinical, and perhaps even societal interest, yet, to date, definitive answers have largely remained elusive. One major obstacle to research in this area has been the difficulty of obtaining repeated CSF samples from human subjects, especially nonclinical populations of infants, children, and adolescents. Without such samples, it is not possible to determine normative ranges for or to describe developmental changes in CSF 5-HIAA concentrations, precluding meaningful interpretation of findings from clinical populations. Indeed, long-term longitudinal measures of CSF 5-HIAA concentrations are not presently available even for clinical populations. The absence of such data makes it difficult, if not impossible, to characterize any relationship between abnormalities in serotonergic functioning and the development of excessive physical aggression, let alone come to conclusions regarding potential causality, long-term developmental course, or possible modes of transmission across successive generations.

Many of the problems confronting researchers investigating biological aspects of excessive childhood aggression and its long-term concomitants and consequences are emblematic of basic issues common to the rigorous scientific study or empirically based treatment of any developmental disorder. The ethical and practical difficulties typically encountered in characterizing symptoms, identifying etiologies, and fashioning effective treatments for developing young humans are trying enough even without considering long-term outcomes or possible intergenerational transmission. Developmental psychopathology ideally should be examined in prospective longitudinal fashion over multiple generations (e.g., Sackett et al., 1981), but virtually all of our current knowledge about these issues has been limited to retrospective reports.

ANIMAL MODELS OF PSYCHOPATHOLOGY

Faced with the difficulties of carrying out perspective, long-term longitudinal research with humans, some investigators have turned to *animal models* for answers to basic questions about the development of psychopathology. Animal models, broadly defined, are experimental efforts to reproduce in nonhuman subjects the essential features of various human disorders or conditions (Kornetsky, 1977; Suomi, 1982). Historically, animal models have been widely utilized throughout the biomedical sciences; indeed, few major medical advances during the past century have been achieved without employing some form of animal model in at least some phase of the relevant research. Nevertheless, one might reasonably ask why any researcher interested in learning more about a particular human psychopathological disorder would choose to study its apparent existence or attempted reproduction in a different species, when presumably plenty of affected human cases exist for possible study.

Perhaps the most powerful motivation for developing animal models stems from the many ethical and practical problems inherent in almost all developmental studies involving humans. Research with animals is not subject to the same limitations and restrictions that characterize most human clinical research. Although there presently exist numerous legal regulations and formal ethical standards governing animal research, and they are now far more rigorous than they were a decade ago, such regulations and standards nevertheless allow for manipulations and measurements with animals that are simply not ethically permissible or, in many cases, practically possible with human subjects or patients.

For example, animals can be selectively bred or genetically manipulated (e.g., via knock-out gene procedures) to possess genetic features that put them at risk for developing biological and/or behavioral abnormalities. Animal subjects can be placed in prospective studies specifically designed to induce psychopathology via experimental manipulations such as brain lesions or intraventricular drug injections. They can be reared, maintained, and observed in well-controlled laboratory environments every day of their lives, and in these settings a variety of measures of biological and behavioral functioning too extensive or obtrusive to be easily gathered from human subjects can be routinely collected on a daily or even more frequent basis. Various pharmacological treatments or therapeutic interventions can be systematically administered to animal subjects and their effects objectively determined via careful comparisons with scientifically appropriate controls. Finally, and perhaps most significantly from a developmental perspective, because most animals used in laboratory studies develop far more rapidly and have much shorter natural life spans than humans, the long-term and even intergenerational consequences of a particular pathology or the effectiveness of a specific treatment can be assessed in a fraction of the time it would take to obtain comparable longitudinal human developmental data.

Animal models, of course, are meaningful theoretically and useful clinically only to the extent that they *generalize* to the human phenomenon or condition being modeled. Several authors (e.g., Abramson & Seligman, 1977; Harlow & Suomi, 1974; Kornetsky, 1977; McKinney & Bunney, 1969; Suomi & Immelmann, 1983) have posited specific criteria by which the validity of any animal model can be objectively judged. In general, animal models are considered more valid to the extent to which they are able to reproduce (or at least simulate) the presumed etiology, behavioral symptoms, physiological concomitants, and effective therapies for the human disorder under study. Of course, in most cases, not all of these factors are well known or fully understood at the human level. In addition, for cases of pathology per se, assertions of generality between humans and animals seem more compelling when there exist naturally occurring animal analogs (or, better yet, homologs) of the human disorder, independent of any symptoms or syndromes produced in a laboratory setting.

For many phenomena, pathological or otherwise, the most compelling generalizations between animals and humans are usually found when the animal data come from our closest evolutionary relatives—nonhuman simian primates. Monkeys and apes share most of our genes (e.g., the genetic overlap between humans and Old World monkeys ranges between 90% and 95%, depending on the monkey species, while the genetic overlap between humans and chimpanzees approaches 99%; Lovejoy, 1981; Sibley, Comstock, & Alquist, 1990). As a result, many aspects of their morphology and physiology are essentially homologous with ours. The basic patterns and sequences of brain development are also highly conserved across the primate order, especially among Old World monkeys, apes, and humans. Moreover, the rich behavioral repertoires, emotional expressions, cognitive capabilities, and complex social relationships characteristic of most monkey and ape species provide opportunities for modeling aspects of human socioemotional development that simply do not exist for rodents or other nonprimate animals (Suomi, 1986).

Some of the most compelling primate models of human psychopathology developed to date have centered on anxiety and depressive disorders (e.g., McKinney & Bunney, 1969; Suomi, 1986). For the phenomenon of excessive physical aggressiveness—and its apparent link with deficits in serotonin metabolism, a growing body of evidence also presents a powerful case for substantial cross-species generality between humans and advanced nonhuman primates. Much of the relevant research has been carried out with rhesus monkeys (*Macaca mulatta*).

SPECIES-NORMATIVE DEVELOPMENT AND SOCIALIZATION OF AGGRESSION IN RHESUS MONKEYS

By way of background, rhesus monkeys are a highly successful Old World monkey species indigenous to the Indian subcontinent. In their natural habitats, these monkeys typically reside in large, distinctive social groups (termed troops) that range in size from several dozen to several hundred individuals. Every troop is composed of several female-headed families (matrilines) that each span several generations of kin, plus numerous immigrant adult males. This form of social organization derives from the fact that all rhesus monkey females spend their entire lives in the troop in which they were born, whereas virtually all males emigrate from their natal troop around the time of puberty and never return. Rhesus monkey troops, in addition to their obvious organization around maternal kinship relationships, are also characterized by multiple dominance hierarchies, including distinctive hierarchies both between and within matrilines, as well as among the immigrant adult males.

Numerous systematic longitudinal behavioral studies of rhesus monkeys have been carried out in both captive and naturalistic settings over the past 35 years, and as a result, a great deal is known about species-normative behavioral development, which transpires approximately four times more rapidly than in humans. Rhesus monkey infants spend virtually all of their initial days and weeks of life in physical contact with or within arm's reach of their biological mother, during which time they form a strong, specific attachment bond with her. In their second month of life, rhesus monkey infants begin to explore their immediate physical and social environment, typically using their mother as a secure base to support such exploration (cf. Harlow, Harlow, & Hansen, 1963; Suomi, 1995). Over the next few months, these infants spend increasing amounts of time engaging in extensive social interactions with other group members, especially peers. Weaning to solid food typically begins during the fourth month and is usually completed by the age of 6 months. Shortly thereafter, play with peers becomes their predominant social activity and remains so until puberty. During this time, play interactions become increasingly complex and involve patterns of behavior that appear to simulate virtually all adult social activities, including courtship and reproductive behaviors as well as dominance/aggressive interactions.

The onset of puberty, usually during the fourth year for rhesus monkeys living in the wild, is associated with major life transitions for both genders. Although females remain in their natal troop throughout adolescence and thereafter, their postpubertal interactions with peer decline dramatically as they redirect most of their social activities toward matrilineal kin, including the infants they subsequently bear and rear. Pubertal males, by contrast, leave both their family and their natal troop permanently, typically joining all-male gangs for varying periods before attempting to enter a different troop. This period of transition represents a time of major stress for adolescent and young males, with a mortality rate that approaches 50% in some monkey populations (e.g., Dittus, 1979). Some surviving males remain in their new troop for the rest of their lives, whereas other males may transfer from one troop to another several times during their adult years. This overall pattern of social group organization and general sequence of behavioral development is relatively common among Old World monkey species, especially within the genus *Macaca* (Lindburg, 1991).

Aggression is a normal and necessary part of every rhesus monkey's overall behavioral repertoire—indeed, rhesus monkeys are usually ranked by primatologists as among the most aggressive of all primate species. Rhesus monkey aggression can range in intensity from mere facial threats and vocalizations to vigorous chases and actual physical aggression, including slapping, hitting, hair-pulling, and biting with sufficient intensity to produce lasting tissue damage or even death. The capability for aggression is crucial for survival in the wild, not only from the standpoint of defending oneself and offspring from predators and conspecific competitors but also in maintaining social order and enforcing the complex dominance hierarchies characteristic of all rhesus monkey troops. However, uncontrolled, unpredictable, and violent aggression within any troop could drive members apart and destroy it as a social unit. Therefore, as with humans, aggression must be *socialized*—it must be minimized or at least largely ritualized in intragroup interactions, but it also must remain a viable response in order to counter external threats or other dangers. Socialization of aggression for young rhesus monkeys involves not only learning in which circumstances and toward what targets aggressive behavior might be appropriate, but also gauging the relative intensity of the attack or response called for and the appropriate time and means for terminating an aggressive bout or avoiding it altogether. Indeed, learning whom *not* to attack, as well as how to moderate aggressive impulses, is as important in the socialization process as is honing one's fighting skills.

Numerous studies carried out in both captive and field settings suggest that the socialization of aggression is largely accomplished during the childhood years through instrumental learning in agonistic interactions with adults, as well as in the context of peer play. Aggression typically emerges in a rhesus monkey infant's behavioral repertoire around the time of weaning. Virtually all infants at this age may try to bite their mother when their efforts to obtain nipple contact with her are rebuffed; such biting typically results in immediate physical punishment by the mother, usually in the form of a cuff, swat, or even a reciprocal nip. An infant's attempts to hit or bite other adults in the troop may lead to even harsher retaliation, especially if those adults are socially dominant over the infant's mother. Consequently, most young monkeys soon learn to inhibit their biting activity and even to avoid many other direct interactions with adults outside of their matriline.

In contrast, biting, hair-pulling, wrestling, and other forms of physical contact are basic components of rough-and-tumble play directed toward peers, which occurs with increasing frequency among males in the second half of their first year of life and becomes the predominate type of play for the rest of their juvenile years. Although some form of virtually all behavioral components of adult aggressive exchanges can be seen in the rough-and-tumble play bouts of young males, the intensity of such interactions is usually quite controlled and seldom escalates to the point of potential physical injury; if it does, the play bout is almost always terminated immediately, either via adult intervention or by one or more of the participants backing away themselves. The importance of these play bouts with peers for the socialization of aggression becomes apparent when one considers that rhesus monkey infants reared in laboratory environments that deny them regular access to peers during their initial months inevitably exhibit excessive and socially inappropriate aggression later in life (e.g., Alexander & Harlow, 1965; Harlow & Harlow, 1969).

In naturalistic settings, both prepubertal males and females readily join their mothers and other relatives in actual aggressive exchanges involving other matrilines or monkeys from other troops. Such exchanges are typically precipitated by challenges to existing dominance hierarchies and usually are brief in duration and more likely to involve threats, bluffs, and chases than actual tissue-damaging physical contact. These dominance-related agonistic exchanges are a normal part of the rhesus monkey's everyday troop life, and it is through participation in such exchanges that most juveniles learn about the complexities of rhesus monkey dominance hierarchies and associated interactions, including the development and maintenance of social coalitions, the use of submissive responses in the face of likely defeat, and the ability to back away from or terminate rapidly escalating agonistic exchanges prior to the point of potential tissue damage. Most juveniles also eventually learn that sudden, seemingly impulsive behaviors can readily provoke aggressive reactions from more dominant troop members with obvious negative consequences, and most become increasingly proficient in inhibiting such activities in potentially dangerous social circumstances, but others do not.

INDIVIDUAL DIFFERENCES
IN RHESUS MONKEY AGGRESSIVENESS

As in human children, there is considerable interindividual variability among rhesus monkey juveniles in their expression and control of aggressive behavior. Recent studies of free-ranging rhesus monkey troops have identified a subset of young monkeys, mostly males, who appear to be unusually impulsive and physically aggressive in their interactions with other troop members. These individuals, typically comprising no more than 5–10% of a troop's juvenile population, begin to distinguish themselves from same-sex peers in their early play interactions. They seem to lack the ability to moderate their responses to playful invitations from peers, and by late childhood, their rough-and-tumble play interactions frequently escalate into tissue-damaging aggressive exchanges, disproportionately at their own expense. Not surprisingly, most of these individuals come to be avoided by their peers, and as a result, they become increasingly isolated socially. In addition, many of these juvenile males often appear unwilling (or unable) to follow social rules inherent in rhesus monkey social dominance hierarchies. For example, they may directly challenge a dominant adult male, a foolhardy act that can result in serious injury, especially when the juvenile refuses to back away or exhibit submissive behavior once defeat becomes obvious. Many of these aggressive young males also display a propensity for making dangerous leaps from treetop to treetop, occasionally with painful or even crippling consequences (Mehlman et al., 1994).

Analyses of CSF samples obtained from preadolescent male rhesus monkeys living in free-ranging troops have revealed that the males' 5-HIAA concentrations, while statistically unrelated to their overall rates of aggression, are negatively correlated with the frequencies of both dangerous leaps and those aggressive bouts that escalate into assaults, wounds, and prolonged chase sequences. The 5-HIAA concentrations of preadolescent males are also negatively correlated with the ratio of their rate of impulsive aggression to their overall rate of aggression, as well as with the number and severity of scars resulting from bite wounds and fractures (Higley, Mehlman, et al., 1996; Higley et al., 1992; Mehlman et al., 1994). These findings clearly show that those young male rhesus monkeys who are most likely to exhibit excessive and inappropriate aggression, and who make the greatest number of dangerous leaps, also tend to have the lowest CSF 5-HIAA concentrations within their birth cohort. In contrast, CSF free testosterone concentrations tend to be positively correlated with the incidence of socially appropriate aggressive bouts and other behaviors indicative of high social dominance, but not with the incidence of bouts of escalating aggression or the other impulsive behavior patterns described earlier (Higley, Mehlman, et al., 1996). As such, these monkey data from the field strongly parallel the previously cited human clinical findings linking excessive physical aggression with low CSF 5-HIAA concentrations, but not with testosterone levels, in juvenile, adolescent, and young adult males.

Over the past decade, extensive laboratory studies with rhesus monkeys and several other Old World monkey species have both replicated and considerably extended this finding of a strong inverse relationship between the incidence of excessive aggression and CSF 5-HIAA concentrations. Several cross-sectional and longitudinal studies have tracked this relationship developmentally, and its consistency across different ages is striking. In rhesus monkeys, CSF 5-HIAA concentrations are at their highest immediately after birth, when aggression does not exist in the neonate's behavioral repertoire, and they drop by more than half over the first 5 months, a time when aggression emerges in the infant's repertoire and is typically in its least socialized form. CSF 5-HIAA concentrations continue to decline, albeit considerably more slowly, until around 18 months of age, at which point they become relatively stable until puberty. Some monkeys experience another pronounced drop in 5-HIAA concentrations around puberty, and for most individuals, there is a slight rise throughout the adult years. The developmental trajectory for physical aggression is exactly the reverse: Aggression directed toward peers typically increases in frequency from 6 to 18 months of age, basically stabilizes until puberty, increases (at least in intensity) for some individuals during and shortly after puberty, and then generally declines monotonically throughout the adult years. Thus, developmental changes in the nature and incidence of physical aggression are temporally linked to developmental changes in CSF 5-HIAA concentrations throughout the life span. More importantly, individual differences in aggressivity have been found to correlate negatively with individual differences in CSF 5-HIAA concentrations at every age studied. In summary, there is a strong and significant developmental *continuity* in this inverse relationship that remains robust in the face of major developmental changes in both measures throughout the life span.

The inverse relationship between excessive aggression and central serotonin metabolism appears to generalize beyond individuals of different ages to monkeys of different genders, strains, and even species. For example, rhesus monkey males generally begin to exhibit noticeably more physical aggression in play than females at about 6 months of age, the same point at which significant gender differences in CSF 5-HIAA concentrations (females higher) first emerge. Both sets of gender differences are maintained throughout the juvenile years and then increase in magnitude around puberty. Moreover, at every age, separate, within-gender analyses have consistently revealed similarly strong negative correlations between inappropriate aggression and 5-HIAA levels for males and females alike. This inverse relationship has also been found for rhesus monkeys of different geographical origin (Champoux, Higley, & Suomi, 1997), as well as in every other Old World monkey species in which the phenomenon has been investigated, including bonnet, crab-eating, pigtail macaques, and vervet monkeys (Raleigh & McGuire, 1994; Rosenblum et al., 1994; Shively, Fontenot, & Kaplan, 1995; Westergaard, Mehlman, Suomi, & Higley, in press). In summary, the basic finding that variation in CSF 5-HIAA concentrations is negatively associated with variation in aggressiveness is exceedingly consistent across a wide range of ages and species of primates.

Longitudinal studies of rhesus and other Old World monkeys have also shown that individual differences in CSF 5-HIAA concentrations are remarkably *stable* throughout ontogeny, despite the dramatic developmental changes in such concentrations from infancy to adulthood described earlier. Rhesus monkeys who have the lowest CSF 5-HIAA concentrations as infants also tend to have relatively low 5-HIAA concentrations as juveniles, adolescents, and even adults (Higley, King, et al., 1996; Higley, Suomi, & Linnoila, 1991; Mehlman et al., 1995). The remarkable stability of individual differences in 5-HIAA concentrations throughout development, along with the aforementioned robust inverse relationship with escalating aggression, makes it possible to predict individual differences in such aggression exhibited by juvenile, adolescent, and adult rhesus monkeys on the basis of individual differences in the CSF 5-HIAA concentrations assessed when they were infants.

Furthermore, unlike most other measures of biobehavioral function (e.g., heart rate patterns, adrenocortical output, catecholamine metabolite concentrations, or activity levels), all of which tend to be highly context-dependent, CSF 5-HIAA concentrations show relatively little change across dramatically different situations, even those involving such obvious stressors as involuntary social separation or repeated episodes of intense aggression (e.g., Higley et al., 1992; Mehlman et al., 1994). These findings therefore suggest that an individual's CSF 5-HIAA concentration may serve as a useful marker of the propensity to engage in excessive aggressive activity, even when the CSF sample is collected under relatively benign circumstances.

Finally, several studies with rhesus monkeys whose genetic backgrounds were well-characterized, and who were raised from birth in controlled laboratory environments, have demonstrated significant heritability for individual differences in CSF 5-HIAA concentrations. One investigation compared paternal half-siblings (same father, different mother) with unrelated individuals reared under identical conditions, with no physical exposure to their fathers at any time. Heritability analyses revealed significantly greater concordance of 5-HIAA concentrations among same-sex, paternal half-siblings than among unrelated, same-sex control subjects matched for age and rearing background. Another study utilized cross-fostering procedures, in which newborn rhesus monkey infants were separated from their biological mothers within the first 4 days of life and foster-reared thereafter by unrelated multiparous females. CSF 5-HIAA concentrations for the cross-fostered infants, assessed at both 6 and 18 months of age, more closely resembled the CSF 5-HIAA concentrations of their biological mothers, with whom they shared many genes but little experience, than those of their foster mothers, with whom they shared fewer genes but much more experience (Higley et al., 1993). These findings provide compelling (albeit indirect) evidence of heritable influences on central serotonin metabolism and, by extension, on the risk for the development of impulsive aggressivity in laboratory-reared rhesus monkeys.

CORRELATES, PREDICTORS, AND CONSEQUENCES OF EXCESSIVE AGGRESSIVITY

Many of the laboratory studies linking low concentrations of CSF 5-HIAA to high rates of physical aggressin also examined the possible relationships of these characteristics to other measures of rhesus monkey biobehavioral activity, and from these studies a more complete profile of high aggressive–low 5-HIAA individuals can be drawn. For example, juvenile, adolescent, and adult females displaying these characteristics tend to initiate and receive significantly fewer bouts of social grooming than other members of their social group, and they also spend less time in close physical proximity to other group members. Perhaps not surprisingly, these females usually remain at the bottom of their group's dominance hierarchy (Higley, King, et al., 1996). Moreover, when previously unfamiliar females are brought together to form new social groups, the resulting dominance hierarchies can be predicted with surprising precision on the basis of these females' CSF 5-HIAA concentrations assessed *prior* to group formation (Higley, Suomi, & Linnoila, 1996). Similar findings have been reported for adult males across several different monkey species (e.g., Raleigh, McGuire, Brammer, Pollack, & Yuwiler, 1991).

Other studies have investigated possible relationships between CSF 5-HIAA concentrations and various sleep, activity, and metabolic parameters in captive groups of rhesus monkeys. For example, Zajicek, Higley, Suomi, and Linnoila (1997) reported a significant negative correlation between sleep latencies and 5-HIAA levels, such that individuals with the lowest 5-HIAA levels tended to be the last members of their group to fall asleep each night and were, on average, more active during both daytime and evening hours than were other group members. Doudet et al. (1995) found that adult male monkeys with relatively low CSF 5-HIAA concentrations required higher doses of the anesthetic sodium pentobarbital than same-age and -sex peers to reach a comparable state of sedation. They also reported a significant negative correlation between rates of whole brain glucose utilization, as assessed via positron-emission tomography (PET) under mild isoflurane anesthesia, and CSF 5-HIAA concentrations, as well as a significant positive correlation between whole-brain glucose metabolism and ratings for aggressiveness in those adult male monkeys. Finally, several studies have demonstrated statistically significant relationships between rates of physical aggression and 5-HIAA concentrations, on the one hand, and patterns of alcohol consumption, on the other, such that adolescent and young adult monkeys who consume the most alcohol in a daily happy hour *ad libitum* situation also tend to have the highest rates of physical aggression and the lowest concentrations of CSF 5-HIAA within their age–sex cohort (Higley, Hasert et al., 1991; Higley, Suomi, & Linnoila, 1996).

How early in life can one identify individual monkeys who are at high risk for developing excessive physical aggression in their juvenile, adolescent, and adult years? Some of the prospective longitudinal studies cited here revealed that CSF 5-HIAA concentrations assessed during the first month of life were predictive of individual differences in 5-HIAA concentrations in subsequent years; those values, in turn, were significantly correlated with concomitant measures of physical aggression (e.g., Higley, King et al., 1996). Another prospective longitudinal study (Champoux et al., 1997) examined the predictive relationship between composite scores for individual clusters of a standardized Brazelton-like neonatal test battery administered repeatedly to rhesus monkey neonates at 7, 14, 21, and 28 days of age (cf. Schneider, Moore, Suomi, & Champoux, 1991) and measures of biobehavioral functioning throughout the first 2 years of life. Champoux et al. (1997) found that those monkeys who had the lowest CSF 5-HIAA concentrations from 3 to 4 months onward, as well as the highest frequencies of impulsive and aggressive behaviors in subsequent months, had exhibited significant deficits in their activity state control and their visual orienting capabilities during their first month relative to the norms established for like-reared infants born in the laboratory colony over the previous decade. These findings suggest that it may be possible to identify infants who are at risk for developing inappropriate aggression later in life not only by measuring their CSF 5-HIAA concentrations, an admittedly invasive procedure for individuals under a month of age, but also by assessing their specific response patterns on a relatively noninvasive standardized test that can be used as a screening device for a large number of subjects. In this respect, the monkey findings parallel the previously cited human studies reporting links between certain infant temperament characteristics and later externalizing behavioral problems, although the risk of misclassifying false positives appears substantially less for the monkey infants.

What are the long-term developmental consequences of low CSF 5-HIAA concentrations and excessive physical aggression displayed early in life? For rhesus monkey males with these characteristics, the prognosis is not particularly promising if they grow up in naturalistic settings. Ostracized by their peers and frequently attacked by adults of both sexes, most of these excessively aggressive young males are physically driven out of their natal troop prior to 3 years of age, long before the onset of puberty. At that point, these young males seemingly lack the social skills to join any all-male gang, let alone become a member of another full-fledged rhesus monkey troop. As a result, most remain solitary after expulsion from their natal troop, and virtually all of them perish within a year, well before becoming physically capable of reproduction.

Moreover, those few solitary males who do survive beyond puberty appear unlikely to make significant contributions to any troop's gene pool. Mehlman et al. (1997) found that those males tended to be actively avoided by most females, and in the few instances in which mating was actually observed, the males engaged in fewer mounts per copulatory sequence (rhesus monkey males must mount a female repeatedly in order to ejaculate), were less likely to ejaculate before the mounting sequence was terminated, and had a lower probability of inseminating the females when they did ejaculate, than other males in the population. Given the findings that individual differences in CSF 5-HIAA concentrations are highly heritable and that males with the lowest 5-HIAA concentrations do not appear to be making significant contributions to the next generation's gene pool, an obvious conclusion is that cross-generational transmission of this characteristic (which appears in as much as 10% of the population) must be occurring largely via females.

Like their male counterparts, rhesus monkey females who have unusually low CSF 5-HIAA concentrations typically develop a wide range of socially inappropriate behaviors, and they too become relatively isolated within their respective social groups, especially with respect to reciprocal grooming patterns and time spent within arm's reach of fellow group members. Unlike their male counterparts, low 5-HIAA females are not expelled from either their matriline or natal troop. Instead, they remain in the same social group in which they were reared, appear to reproduce in species-typical fashion, and subsequently raise their own offspring in that very group. Thus, their offspring not only share many of their genes but also typically grow up in a physical and social environment much like, if not essentially identical to, that which they have experienced themselves.

Relatively little is presently known about the overall maternal competence of females with chronically low CSF 5-HIAA concentrations who raise their infants in natural habitats. However, recent studies of rhesus monkey females residing in captive social groups have found that mothers with chronically low CSF 5-HIAA concentrations also tend to exhibit significant deficits in several aspects of their maternal behavior. For example, around and immediately following the time of weaning, these females appear to overly restrict their infants' efforts to break contact and explore the environment, often precipitating rapidly escalating conflicts between mother and offspring. Perhaps as a result, these mothers often develop insecure- and/or disorganized-like attachment relationships with their infants (Tsai, Lindell, Shannon, & Higley, 1998). It also appears that those infants who develop the least secure attachment relationships with their mothers are also the most likely to exhibit deficits in their central serotonin metabolism.

Thus, an alternative possible mechanism for cross-generational transmission of 5-HIAA deficits could be via the aberrant maternal care that offspring might experience during development. According to this view, the mother's maternal behavior may be at least as relevant for cross-generational transmission of this characteristic as her genes. Of course, these two potential etiological pathways are neither mutually exclusive nor necessarily independent. Unfortunately, prospective longitudinal studies of low 5-HIAA females in the wild, no matter how detailed or long-lasting, will never be able to provide the specific information necessary to disentangle those or any other possible genetic and environmental influences.

EFFECTS OF EARLY PEER REARING ON THE DEVELOPMENT OF EXCESSIVE AGGRESSION

In contrast to the limitations of observational field studies described earlier, it is possible to identify and characterize specific etiological pathways in laboratory settings in which both genetic and environmental factors can be explicitly manipulated and/or controlled. In recent years, several studies of this sort have been carried out with rhesus monkeys and other primate species. One set of studies has focused on rhesus monkey infants raised with peers instead of their biological mothers. These peer-reared infants are typically separated from their biological mothers at birth, raised in a neonatal nursery, and housed with same-age, like-reared peers for their first 6 months, and are then moved into larger social groups containing both peer-reared and mother-reared age-mates. During their initial months, they readily develop strong social attachment bonds to each other, much as mother-reared infants develop attachments to their own mothers (Harlow, 1969). However, because peers are not nearly as effective as typical monkey mothers in reducing fear in the face of novelty or in providing a "secure base" for exploration, the attachment relationships that these peer-reared infants develop are almost always "anxious" in nature (Suomi, 1995). As a result, while peer-reared monkeys exhibit normal physical and motor development, their early exploratory behavior is usually rather limited. They appear reluctant to approach novel objects, and they tend to be shy in initial encounters with unfamiliar peers (Suomi, 1999).

Even when peer-reared youngsters interact with their same-age cage-mates in familiar settings, their emerging social play repertoires are often retarded in both frequency and complexity. One explanation for their relatively poor play performance is that their cage-mates must serve both as attachment figures and playmates, a dual role that neither mothers nor mother-reared peers have to fulfill; another is that they develop their play repertoires with basically incompetent play partners. Perhaps as a result of either or both of these factors, peer-reared youngsters typically drop to the bottom of their group's dominance hierarchy when housed with mother-reared monkeys their own age (Higley, King, et al., 1996).

Several prospective longitudinal studies have found that peer-reared monkeys tend to become excessively aggressive, especially if they are males. Like the previously described monkeys with low CSF 5-HIAA concentrations growing up in the wild, peer-reared males initially exhibit excessive aggression in the context of juvenile play; as they approach puberty, the frequency and severity of their aggressive episodes typically exceed those of most mother-reared group members of similar age. Peer-reared females tend to groom (and be groomed by) others in their social group less frequently and for shorter durations than their mother-reared counterparts, and they usually remain at the bottom of their respective dominance hierarchies. These overall group differences between peer-reared and mother-reared monkeys in aggression, grooming, and dominance remain relatively robust throughout the preadolescent and adolescent years (Higley, Suomi, & Linnoila, 1996). Importantly, peer-reared monkeys also consistently have lower CSF 5-HIAA concentrations than most of their mother-reared counterparts. Significant rearing-group differences appear well before 6 months of age, and they remain stable throughout adolescence and into early adulthood (Hidley & Suomi, 1996). Thus, peer-reared monkeys in general resemble excessively aggressive mother-reared monkeys not only behaviorally but also in terms of decreased serotonergic functioning (Suomi, 1997).

Other laboratory studies utilizing peer-reared monkeys have disclosed additional differences with their mother-reared counterparts in domains that are not readily apparent in free-ranging populations. For example, peer-reared adolescent and adult males require larger doses of the anesthetic ketamine to reach a comparable state of sedation. They also exhibit significantly higher rates of whole-brain glucose metabolism under mild isoflurane anesthesia, as determined by PET imaging, than mother-reared controls (Doudet et al., 1995). Finally, peer-reared adolescent monkeys consistently consume larger amounts of alcohol under comparable *ad libidum* conditions than their mother-reared agemates (Higley, Hasert et al., 1991). Recent follow-up studies have demonstrated that the peer-reared subjects quickly develop a greater tolerance for alcohol, which can be predicted by their CNS serotonin turnover rates (Higley et al., in press), and which in turn appears to be associated with differential serotonin transporter availability (Heinz et al., 1998).

An additional risk that peer-reared females carry into adulthood concerns their maternal behavior. Peer-reared mothers are significantly more likely to exhibit neglectful and/or abusive treatment of their firstborn offspring than are most of their mother-reared counterparts, although their care of subsequent offspring tends to improve dramatically (Ruppenthal, Arling, Harlow, Sackett, & Suomi, 1976). Nevertheless, most multiparous mothers who experienced early peer-rearing continue to exhibit nonnormative patterns of maternal care throughout the whole of their reproductive years (Champoux, Byrne, Delizio, & Suomi, 1992), and such patterns appear to be highly similar to those characteristic of mother-reared females with chronically low CSF 5-HIAA concentrations.

To summarize, early peer-rearing has significant short- and long-term behavioral and physiological consequences for rhesus monkeys. Indeed, the developmental trajectories of peer-reared subjects strongly resemble those of excessively aggressive mother-reared monkeys, even after their period of exclusive exposure to peers has been completed and they are living in more species-typical social groups. Moreover, some effects of early peer rearing may well be passed on to the next generation via aberrant patterns of maternal care, as appears to be the case for mothers who experienced poor early attachment relationships in nature (Suomi & Levine, 1998). Thus, as noted by Bowlby (1988) for the human case, the effects of inadequate early attachments may be both lifelong and cross-generational in nature.

SPECIFIC GENE–ENVIRONMENT INTERACTIONS

The findings summarized here provide compelling evidence that both heritable and early experiential factors can influence the development of excessive physical aggression and abnormal serotonin metabolism in rhesus monkeys. Do these factors operate independently, or do they interact in some fashion in shaping individual developmental trajectories? Ongoing research capitalizing on recently discovered polymorphisms in one specific gene—the serotonin transporter gene—suggests that gene–environment interactions not only occur but also can be expressed in multiple forms.

The serotonin transporter gene (5-HTT) is a candidate gene for impaired serotonergic function in that it mediates serotonin neurotransmission and is a target for both antidepressant compounds such as fluoxetine (Prozac) and certain drugs of abuse (Lesch et al., 1996). Lesch and his colleagues have shown that length variation of the 5-HTT gene-linked polymorphic region (5-HTT-LPR) results in allelic variation in 5-HTT expression, such that the short allele of the gene confers low transcriptional efficiency to the 5-HTT gene promoter (relative to the long allele), raising the possibility that low 5-HTT expression may result in decreased serotonergic function (Heils et al., 1996), although evidence supporting this hypothesis in humans has been decidedly mixed to date (e.g., Furlong et al., 1998). These specific 5-HTT alleles were first characterized in humans, but they also appear in homologous form in rhesus monkeys; indeed, this particular genetic polymorphism is found only in simian primates (Lesch et al., 1997).

With the help of Lesch and his colleagues, most of the adult rhesus monkeys in my laboratory at the National Institutes of Health have recently been genotyped with respect to the 5-HTT polymorphism. Some of these genotyped monkeys had been peer-reared for their first 6 months, while others had been reared by their biological mothers. The genotypic analyses revealed that the relative frequency of subjects possessing the short (LS) versus the long (LL) 5-HTT allele did not differ significantly between these two rearing groups, an expected finding given that those monkeys had been randomly assigned to their respective rearing conditions at birth. Because extensive observational data and biological samples were previously collected from these monkeys throughout development, it has become possible to examine a wide range of behavioral and physiological measures for potential 5-HTT polymorphism main effects and interactions with early rearing history. Analyses completed to date suggest that such interactions are widespread and diverse.

For example, Bennett et al. (1998) found that CSF 5-HIAA concentrations did not differ as a function of 5-HTT status for mother-reared subjects, whereas among peer-reared monkeys, individuals with the LS allele had significantly lower CSF 5-HIAA concentrations than those with the LL allele. One interpretation of this interaction is that mother-rearing appeared to buffer any potentially deleterious effects of the LS allele on serotonin metabolism. A different form of gene–environment interaction was suggested by the analysis of alcohol consumption data: Whereas peer-reared monkeys with the LS allele consumed more alcohol than peer-reared monkeys with the LL allele, the reverse was true for mother-reared subjects, with individuals possessing the LS allele actually consuming *less* alcohol than their LL counterparts. In other words, the LS allele appeared to represent a risk factor for excessive alcohol consumption among peer-reared monkeys but a protective factor for mother-reared subjects. Analysis of dominance-related assertive behavior revealed a third form of gene–environment interaction that was basically additive in nature: Across all subjects, peer-reared monkeys with the LL allele were the least assertive, peer-reared LS and mother-reared LL monkeys were intermediate, and mother-reared LS monkeys were the most assertive (Bennett et al., 1998).

A specific gene–environment interaction was thus identified for each of the measures examined by Bennett et al. (1998), but the precise nature of the interaction was different for each measure. Moreover, the consequences of having the LS allele differed dramatically for peer-reared and mother-reared monkeys: Whereas peer-reared individuals with the LS allele exhibited deficits in serotonin metabolism and excessive alcohol consumption, mother-reared subjects with the very same allele showed normal serotonin metabolism, reduced risk for excessive alcohol consumption, and high social dominance. Indeed, it could be argued on the basis of these findings that having the short allele of the 5-HTT gene may well lead to psychopathology among monkeys with poor early rearing histories but might actually be adaptive for monkeys who develop secure early attachment relationship with their mothers.

Additional analyses involving other behavioral and physiological measures that have already been collected on those mother- and peer-reared monkeys whose 5-HTT polymorphic status has been determined suggest that gene–environment interactions are ubiquitous, diverse in nature, and detectable even within the first month of life, whereas genetic main effects represent the exception rather than the rule. Thus, the development of excessive physical aggression and deficits in serotonin metabolism in rhesus monkeys appears to be the exclusive product of neither nature nor nurture, but rather the result of both, interacting in complex and dynamic fashion throughout development.

IMPLICATIONS FOR A BIOBEHAVIORAL PERSPECTIVE ON HUMAN DEVELOPMENTAL PSYCHOPATHOLOGY

Earlier in this chapter, I argued that many of the obstacles to rigorous study of human developmental psychopathology could be overcome or even avoided by investigating parallel phenomena in nonhuman primates. To what extent can studies of inappropriate aggression and its biological correlates in rhesus monkeys enhance our understanding of children who display excessive physical aggression toward peers and parents and who are at risk for becoming violent later in life? To be sure, rhesus monkeys are clearly *not* furry little humans with tails but rather members of another (albeit closely related) species that lack not only language but also other basic human capacities such as self-reflection and even self-awareness (cf. Gallup, 1977). Indeed, one should be especially cautious when making comparisons between humans and other primate species regarding aggressive phenomena, particularly when there exist obvious age, gender, and cultural differences in what is considered excessive or abnormal for humans. Nevertheless, there appear to be some general principles emerging from research with rhesus monkeys that are likely to be relevant for the human case.

First, aggression per se is neither abnormal nor necessarily undesirable, but rather represents a behavioral capacity present in every individual, with both biological underpinnings and adaptive features that usually follow an orderly pattern of ontogenic change. However, to be adaptive, it must be socialized during the childhood years, and problems in the socialization process usually result in alterations in its developmental trajectory, with long-term behavioral and biological consequences that are likely to be adverse for both the individual and society. Indeed, aggression becomes excessive when it fails to change with increasing age.

Second, excessive physical aggression appears to be associated with deficits in central serotonin metabolism. This is *not* to say that deficits in serotonin metabolism actually cause excessive physical aggression (or vice versa), but rather that both are closely linked throughout development and across genders. The inverse relationship between CSF 5-HIAA concentrations and excessive physical aggression is exceedingly robust, such that factors that can alter the expression of physical aggression also typically alter CSF 5-HIAA concentrations (and vice versa). Moreover, individual differences in CSF 5-HIAA concentrations appear to be relatively stable throughout development, despite major normative ontogenic changes in the concentrations themselves, and they also tend to be stable across situations. These trait-like characteristics make it possible to predict individual differences in physical aggression throughout development on the basis of CSF 5-HIAA values obtained early in life.

A third basic principle is that deficits in serotonin metabolism (and associated behavioral tendencies) are the exclusive product of neither nature nor nurture, but rather reflect the interaction of both. It is possible to demonstrate significant heritability for individual differences in 5-HIAA concentrations, and it is also clear that certain rearing experiences often result in deficits in serotonin metabolism. However, the recent findings that specific polymorphisms in the serotonin transporter gene are associated with different behavioral and biological outcomes for rhesus monkeys as a function of their early social rearing histories suggest that more complex gene–environment interactions actually are responsible for the phenomenon. It is hard to imagine that the situation would be any less complex for humans.

REFERENCES

Abramson, L. Y., & Seligman, M. E. P. (1977). Modeling psychopathology in the laboratory: History and rationale. In J. D. Maser & M. E. P. Seligman (Eds.), *Psychopathology: Experimental models* (pp. 1–26). San Francisco: Freeman.

Alexander, B. K., & Harlow, H. F. (1965). Social behavior of juvenile rhesus monkeys subjected to different rearing conditions during the first 6 months of life. *Zoologia Jahr Physiologia, 60,* 167–174.

Bennett, A. J., Lesch, K. P., Heils, A., Long, J., Lorenz, J., Shoaf, S. E., Champoux, M., Suomi, S. J., Linnoila, M., & Higley, J. D. (1998). Serotonin transporter gene variation, strain, and early rearing environment affect CSF 5-HIAA concentrations in rhesus monkeys (*Macaca mulatta*). *American Journal of Primatology, 45,* 168–169.

Bowlby, J. (1986). *A secure base*. New York: Basic Books.

Brown, G. L., Goodwin, F. K., Ballenger, J. C., Goyer, P. F., & Major, L. F. (1979). Aggression in humans correlates with cerebrospinal fluid amine metabolites. *Psychiatry Research, 1*, 131–139.

Brown, G. L., Linnoila, M., & Goodwin, F. K. (1990). Clinical assessment of human aggression and impulsivity in relation to biochemical measures. In H. M. Van Praag, R. Plutchik, & A. Apter (Eds.), *Violence and suicidality: Perspectives in clinical and psychobiological research* (pp. 184–217). New York: Brunner/Mazel.

Champoux, M., Byrne, E., Delizio, R. D., & Suomi, S. J. (1992). Motherless mothers revisited: Rhesus maternal behavior and rearing history. *Primates, 33*, 251–255.

Champoux, M., Higley, J. D., & Suomi, S. J. (1997). Behavioral and physiological characteristics of Indian and Chinese-Indian hybrid rhesus macaque infants. *Developmental Psychobiology, 31*, 49–63.

Cloninger, C. R. (1987). Neurogenic adaptive mechanisms in alcoholism. *Science, 236*, 410–416.

Dittus, W. P. J. (1979). The evolution of behaviours regulating density and age-specific sex ratios in a primate population. *Behaviour, 69*, 265–302.

Dodge, K. (1980). Social cognition and children's aggressive behavior. *Child Development, 51*, 162–170.

Doudet, D., Hommer, D., Higley, J. D., Andreason, P. J., Moneman, R., Suomi, S. J., & Linnoila, M. (1995). Cerebral glucose metabolism, CSF 5-HIAA, and aggressive behavior in rhesus monkeys. *American Journal of Psychiatry, 152*, 1782–1787.

Furlong, R. A., Ho, L., Walsh, C., Rubinsztein, J. S., Jain, S., Pazkil, E. S., Easton, D. F., & Rubinsztein, D. C. (1998). Analysis and meta-analysis of two serotonin transporter gene polymorphisms in bipolar and unipolar affective disorders. *American Journal of Medical Genetics, 81*, 58–63.

Gallup, G. G. (1977). Self-recognition in primates: A comparative approach to the bidirectional properties of consciousness. *American Psychologist, 32*, 329–338.

Harlow, H. F. (1969). Age-mate or peer affectional system. In D. S. Lehrman, R. A. Hinde, & E. Shaw (Eds.), *Advances in the study of behavior* (Vol. 2, pp. 333–383). New York: Academic Press.

Harlow, H. F., & Harlow, M. K. (1969). Effects of various mother–infant relationships on rhesus monkey behaviors. In B. M. Foss (Ed.), *Determinants of infant behaviour* (Vol. 4, pp. 15–36). London: Metheun.

Harlow, H. F., Harlow, M. K., & Hansen, E. W. (1963). The maternal affectional system of rhesus monkeys. In H. L. Rheingold (Ed.), *Maternal behavior in mammals* (pp. 254–281). New York: Wiley.

Harlow, H. F., & Suomi, S. J. (1974). Induced depression in monkeys. *Behavioral Biology, 12*, 273–296.

Heils, A., Teufel, A., Petri, S., Stober, G., Riederer, P., Bengel, B., & Lesch, K. P. (1996). Allelic variation of human serotonin transporter gene expression. *Journal of Neurochemistry, 6*, 2621–2624.

Heinz, A., Higley, J. D., Gorey, J. G., Saunders, R. C., Jones, D. W., Hommer, D., Zajicek, K., Suomi, S. J., Weinberger, D. R., & Linnoila, M. (1998). *In vivo* association between alcohol intoxication, aggression, and serotonin transporter availability in nonhuman primates. *American Journal of Psychiatry, 155*, 1023–1028.

Higley, J. D., Hasert, M. L., Suomi, S. J., & Linnoila, M. (1991). A new nonhuman primate model of alcohol abuse: Effects of early experience, personality, and stress on alcohol consumption. *Proceedings of the National Academy of Sciences, 88*, 7261–7265.

Higley, J. D., Hommer, D., Lucas, K., Shaof, S., Suomi, S. J., & Linnoila, M. (in press). CNS serotonin metabolism rate predicts innate tolerance, high alcohol consumption, and aggression during intoxication in rhesus monkeys. *Archives of General Psychiatry*.

Higley, J. D., King, S. T., Hasert, M. F., Champoux, M., Suomi, S. J., & Linnoila, M. (1996). Stability of individual differences in serotonin function and its relationship to severe aggression and competent social behavior in rhesus macaque females. *Neuropsychopharmacology, 14*, 67–76.

Higley, J. D., Mehlman, P. T., Taub, D. M., Higley, S., Fernald, B., Vickers, J. H., Suomi, S. J., & Linnoila, M. (1996). Excessive mortality in young free-ranging male nonhuman primates with low CSF 5-HIAA concentrations. *Archives of General Psychiatry, 53*, 537–543.

Higley, J. D., Mehlman, P. T., Taub, D. M., Higley, S. B., Vickers, J. H., Suomi, S. J., & Linnoila, M. (1992). Cerebrospinal fluid monoamine and adrenal correlates of aggression in free-ranging rhesus monkeys. *Archives of General Psychiatry, 49*, 436–444.

Higley, J. D., & Suomi, S. J. (1996). Reactivity and social competence affect individual differences in reaction to severe stress in children: Investigations using nonhuman primates. In C. R. Pfeffer (Ed.), *Intense stress and mental disturbance in children* (pp. 3–58). Washington, DC: American Psychiatric Press.

Higley, J. D., Suomi, S. J., & Linnoila, M. (1991). CSF monoamine metabolite concentrations vary according to age, rearing, and sex, and are influenced by the stressor of social separation in rhesus monkeys. *Psychopharmacology, 103*, 551–556.

Higley, J. D, Suomi, S. J., & Linnoila, M. (1996). A nonhuman primate model of Type II alcoholism? (Part 2): Diminished social competence and excessive aggression correlates with low CSF 5-HIAA concentrations. *Alcoholism: Clinical and Experimental Research, 20*, 643–650.

Higley, J. D., Thompson, W. T., Champoux, M., Goldman, D., Hasert, M. F., Kraemer, G. W., Scanlan, J. M., Suomi, S. J., & Linnoila, M. (1993). Paternal and maternal genetic and environmental contributions to CSF monoamine metabolites in rhesus monkeys (*Macaca mulatta*). *Archives of General Psychiatry, 50*, 615–623.

Kornetsky, C. (1977). Animal models: Problems and promises. In I. Hanin & E. Usdin (Eds.), *Animal models in psychiatry and neurology* (pp. 1–23). New York: Pergamon Press.

Kruesi, M. J. (1989). Cruelty to animals and CSF 5-HIAA. *Psychiatry Research, 28*, 115–116.

Kruesi, M. J., Rapoport, J. L., Hamburder, S., Hibbs, E., Potter, W. Z., Lenane, M., & Brown, G. L. (1990). Cerebrospinal fluid monoamine metabolites, aggression, and impulsivity in disruptive behavior disorders of children and adolescents. *Archives of General Psychiatry, 47*, 419–426.

Lesch, K. P., Bengel, D., Heils, A., Sabol, S. Z., Greenberg, B. D., Petri, S., Benjamin, J., Muller, C. R., Hamer, D. H., & Murphy, D. L. (1996). Association of anxiety-related traits with a polymorphism in the serotonin transporter gene regulatory region. *Science, 274*, 1527–1531.

Lesch, L. P., Meyer, J., Glatz, K., Flugge, G., Hinney, A., Hebebrand, J., Klauck, S. M., Poustka, A., Poustka, F., Bengel, D., Mossner, R., Riederer, P., & Heils, A. (1997). The 5-HTT transporter gene-linked polymorphic region (5-HTTLPR) in evolutionary perspective: Alternative biallelic variation in rhesus monkeys. *Journal of Neural Transmission, 104*, 1259–1266.

Lindburg, D. G. (1991). Ecological requirements of macaques. *Laboratory Animal Science, 41*, 315–322.

Linnoila, M. (1988). Monoamines and impulse control. In J. A. Swinkels & W. Blijeven (Eds.), *Depression, anxiety, and aggression* (pp. 167–172). Houten, The Netherlands: Medidact.

Linnoila, M., DeJong, J., & Virkkunen, M. (1989). Monoamines, glucose metabolism, and impulse control. *Psychopharmacy Bulletin, 25*, 404–406.

Linnoila, M., Virkkunen, M., Scheinin, M., Nuutila, A., Rimon, R., & Goodwin, F. K. (1983). Low cerebrospinal fluid 5-hydroxyindoleacetic acid concentration differentiates impulsive from nonimpulsive violent behavior. *Life Sciences, 33*, 2609–2614.

Lovejoy, C. O. (1981). The origins of man. *Science, 211*, 341–350.

MacKinnon, C. E., Lamb, M. E., Arbuckle, B., Baradan, L. P., & Volling, B. (1992). The relationship between biased maternal and filial attributions and the aggressiveness of their interactions. *Development and Psychopathology, 4*, 403–415.

Mann, J. J., Arango, V., & Underwood, M. E. (1990). Serotonin and suicidal behavior. *Annals of the New York Academy of Science, 600*, 476–485.

McKinney, W. T., & Bunney, W. E. (1969). Animal model of depression: Review of evidence and implications for research. *Archives of General Psychiatry, 21*, 240–248.

Mehlman, P. T., Higley, J. D., Faucher, I., Lilly, A. A., Taub, D. M., Vickers, J. H., Suomi, S. J., & Linnoila, M. (1994). Low cerebrospinal fluid 5 hydroxyindoleacetic acid concentrations are correlated with severe aggression and reduced impulse control in free-ranging primates. *American Journal of Psychiatry, 151*, 1485–1491.

Mehlman, P. T., Higley, J. D., Faucher, I., Lilly, A. A., Taub, D. M., Vickers, J. H., Suomi, S. J., & Linnoila, M. (1995). CSF 5-HIAA concentrations are correlated with sociality and the timing of emigration in free-ranging primates. *American Journal of Psychiatry, 152*, 901–913.

Mehlman, P. T., Higley, J. D., Fernald, B. J., Sallee, F. R., Suomi, S. J., & Linnoila, M. (1997). CSF 5-HIAA, testosterone, and sociosexual behaviors in free-ranging male macaques during the breeding season. *Psychiatric Research, 72*, 89–102.

Negin, D., & Tremblay, R. E. (1999). Trajectories of boys' physical aggression, opposition, and hyperactivity on the path to physically violent and nonviolent juvenile delinquency. *Child Development*.

Offord, D. R., Alder, R. J., & Boyle, M. H. (1987). Prevalence and sociodemographic correlates of conduct disorder. *American Journal of Social Psychiatry, 6*, 272–278.

Olweus, D. (1979). Stability of aggressive reaction patterns in males: A review. *Psychological Bulletin, 86*, 852–875.

Patterson, G. R., Reid, J. B., & Dishion, T. J. (1992). *Antisocial boys*. Eugene, OR: Castalia.

Raleigh, M. J., & McGuire, M. T. (1994). Serotonin, aggression, and violence in vervet monkeys. In R. D. Masters & M. T. McGuire (Eds.), *The neurotransmitter revolution* (pp. 129–145). Carbondale: Southern Illinois University Press.

Raleigh, M. J., McGuire, M. T., Brammer, G. L., Pollack, D. B., & Yuwiler, A. (1991). Serotonergic mechanisms promote dominance acquisition in vervet monkeys. *Brain Research, 559*, 181–190.

Reiss, A. J., & Roth, J. A. (1993). *Understanding and preventing violence*. Washington, DC: National Academy Press.

Rosenblum, L. A., Coplan, J. D., Friedman, S., Bassoff, T., Gorman, J. M., & Andrews, M. W. (1994). Adverse early experiences affect noradrenergic and serotonergic functioning in adult primates. *Biological Psychiatry, 35*, 221–227.

Rubin, K., & Rose-Krasnor, L. (1992). Interpersonal problem-solving and social competence in children. In V. Van Hasselt & M. Hersen (Eds.), *Handbook of social development: A lifespan perspective* (pp. 117–144). New York: Plenum Press.

Ruppenthal, G. C, Arling, G. L., Harlow, H. F., Sackett, G. P., & Suomi, S. J. (1976). A 10-year perspective on motherless mother monkey mothering behavior. *Journal of Abnormal Psychology, 88*, 341–349.

Rutter, M., Giller, H., & Hagel, A. (1998). *Antisocial behaviour by young people*. Cambridge, UK: Cambridge University Press.

Rutter, M., Silberg, J., O'Conner, T., & Simonoff, E. (1999). Genetics and child psychiatry: II. Empirical research findings. *Journal of Child Psychology and Psychiatry, 40*, 19–56.

Sackett, G. P., Sameroff, A. S., Cairns, R. B., & Suomi, S. J. (1981). Continuity in behavioral development: Theoretical and empirical issues. In K. Immelmann, G. W. Barlow, L. Petrinovich, & M. Main (Eds.), *Behavioral development: The Bielefeld interdisciplinary project* (pp. 395–431). New York: Cambridge University Press.

Schneider, M. L., Moore, C. F., Suomi, S. J., & Champoux, M. (1991). Laboratory assessment of temperament and environmental enrichment in rhesus monkey infants (*Macaca mulatta*). *American Journal of Primatology, 25*, 137–155.

Shivley, C. A., Fontenot, M. B., & Kaplan, J. R. (1995). Social status, behavior, and central serotonergic responsibility in female cynomolgus monkeys. *American Journal of Primatology, 37*, 333–340.

Sibley, C. O., Comstock, J. A., & Alquist, J. E. (1990). DNA hybridization evidence of hominid phylogeny: A reanalysis of the data. *Journal of Molecular Evolution, 30*, 202–236.

Suomi, S. J. (1982). Animal models of human psychopathology: Relevance for clinical psychology. In P. Kendall & J. Butcher (Eds.), *Handbook of research methods in clinical psychology* (pp. 249–271). New York: Wiley.

Suomi, S. J. (1986). Anxiety-like disorders in young primates. In R. Gittelman (Ed.), *Anxiety disorders of childhood* (pp. 1–23). New York: Guilford Press.

Suomi, S. J. (1995). Influence of Bowlby's attachment theory on research on nonhuman primate biobehavioral development. In S. Goldberg, R. Muir, & J. Kerr (Eds.), *Attachment theory: Social, developmental, and clinical perspectives* (pp. 185–201). Hillsdale, NJ: Analytic Press.

Suomi, S. J. (1997). Early determinants of behaviour: Evidence from primate studies. *British Medical Bulletin, 53*, 170–184.

Suomi, S. J. (1999). Developmental trajectories, early experiences, and community consequences: Lessons from studies with rhesus monkeys. In D. Keating & C. Hertzman (Eds.), *Developmental health: The wealth of nations in the Information Age* (pp. 185–200). New York: Guilford Press.

Suomi, S. J., & Immelmann, K. (1983). On the product and process of cross-species generalization. In D. W. Rajecki (Ed.), *Studying man studying animals* (pp. 203–223). New York: Plenum Press.

Suomi, S. J., & Levine, S. (1998). Psychobiology of intergenerational effects of trauma: Evidence from animal studies. In Y. Daniele (Ed.), *International handbook of multigenerational legacies of trauma* (pp. 623–637). New York: Plenum Press.

Tremblay, R. E. (1992). The prediction of delinquent behavior from childhood behavior: Personality theory revisited. In J. McCord (Ed.), *Facts, frameworks, and forecasts: Advances in criminological theory* (Vol. 3, pp. 192–230). New Brunswick, NJ: Transactions.

Tremblay, R. E., Japel, C., Perusse, D., Boivin, M., Zoccolillo, M., Montplaisir, J., & McDuff, P. (in press). The search for the age of onset of physical aggression: Rousseau and Bandura revisited. *Criminal Behavior and Mental Health*.

Tsai, T., Lindell, S. G., Shannon, C., & Higley, J. D. (1998). Aggression to infants and maternal competence by female rhesus monkeys with low CNS serotonin functioning. *American Journal of Primatology, 45*, 211.

Westergaard, G. T., Mehlman, P. T., Suomi, S. J., & Higley, J. D. (in press). CSF 5-HIAA and aggression in female primates: Species and interindividual differences. *Biological Psychiatry*.

Zajicek, K., Higley, J. D., Suomi, S. J., & Linnoila, M. (1997). Rhesus macaques with high CSF 5-HIAA concentrations exhibit early sleep onset. *Psychiatric Research, 77*, 15–25.

14

Temperament and Goodness of Fit
Implications for Developmental Psychopathology

Ronald Seifer

The style of infant and child behavior is a nexus where many factors affecting normative and pathological development converge, providing a unique opportunity for understanding a variety of children's pathways through development. During the past 40 years, temperament in infants and children has been a focus of normative work in human development and has been advanced as a potential contributor to psychopathology in children and adolescents. As such, it is an ideal focus of those interested in pursuing the developmental psychopathology agenda. Of particular interest is the extension of temperament to the relationship processes between children and their caregivers, particularly during the first years of life. In this chapter, I provide a brief overview of issues addressed by temperament researchers, review knowledge about basic developmental phenomena related to temperament, identify empirical evidence that temperament is associated with incompetence and/or psychopathology, and discuss goodness-of-fit models as a coherent framework for understanding the interplay of infant characteristics and parental behavior in the context of explaining variations in developmental outcomes.

Temperament is often presented as an individual differences construct closely related to personality that is presumed to have strong biological roots. In contrast, the perspective I take in this review is less individualistic and less biologically deterministic than is typically found in today's human development literature. Moreover, I embed this review of temperament research in a functionalist perspective (Campos, Mumme, Karmoian, & Campos, 1994), concentrating on the importance of infant behavioral characteristics in the social and nonsocial tasks of daily life.

Ronald Seifer • Department of Psychiatry and Human Behavior, Brown University School of Medicine, Bradley Hospital, East Providence, Rhode Island 02915.

Handbook of Developmental Psychopathology, Second Edition, edited by Arnold J. Sameroff, Michael Lewis, and Suzanne M. Miller. Kluwer Academic/Plenum Publishers, New York, 2000.

DOMAIN OF TEMPERAMENT

The publication of the original Thomas and Chess reports (Thomas, Chess, Birch, Hertzig, & Korn, 1963) spurred an interest in temperament that has exploded to become a major focus of human development research. Since that time, a wide variety of methods has been applied to the domain. Implicit in these methods, and often explicit in associated theoretical explications, is the domain covered by temperament researchers; temperament researchers typically make the assumption that some infant behavioral dispositions transcend time and setting, and are relatively independent of contextual support (Goldsmith et al., 1987).

In addition to their role in driving basic research, temperament assessments inform clinical research and practice as well. Several research programs have noted a relation of difficult temperament during infancy to later social competence and behavior problems. Furthermore, some have used temperament conceptualizations to provide a frame of reference for understanding some aspects of psychopathology. The multiple agendas of temperament assessment constitute a good example of the developmental psychopathology approach in that assessments are simultaneously designed to illuminate normative developmental phenomena and to discern whether behavioral style characteristics of children are important in understanding the etiology and maintenance of specific disorders. Still, there remains substantial variation among different groups in how they have conceptualized the domain of temperament, ranging from strong emphasis on individual genetic factors to concentration on dyadic social processes.

Theoretical Approaches

The current dominant approach to the field of temperament research may be traced back to the work of Thomas and Chess that began in the late 1950s (Thomas et al., 1963). At that time, they attempted to define characteristics of individuals that were presumed to be important to infant and child development. This was in contrast to the prevailing environmentalism manifest in psychodynamic and learning theory approaches to development. What has set this temperament approach apart from other constitutional theories of development is that it has always emphasized the dynamic interactions between individual constitution and developmental context. More recently, alternatives have emerged to the behavioral style approach to temperament (Rothbart & Bates, 1998). The most notable of these alternatives are the bio-behavioral regulation approach of Rothbart and Goldsmith (Goldsmith & Campos, 1982; Rothbart & Derryberry, 1982) and the typology approach of Kagan (Kagan, Resnick, & Gibbons, 1989). Characteristics of these three approaches are described here.

Behavioral Style

Behavioral style refers to *how* an individual behaves, in contrast to the person's *motivation*, *success*, or the *specific content* of the behavior. Several basic assumptions underlie this approach: (1) aspects of style are important individual differences in behavior; (2) these behavioral styles are relatively stable over time; and (3) these stylistic aspects of behavior generalize across situations. The early work of Thomas and Chess yielded nine temperament dimensions that continue to be widely used: Activity, Rhythmicity, Approach, Adaptability, Intensity of Behavior, Mood, Persistence, Distractibility, and Threshold to Stimulation. Most of these dimensions are self-evident from their labels, but a few require a bit of comment. Approach and Adaptability are similar in their focus on response to novelty, the distinction being that the former refers to initial exposure to novelty, and the latter refers to repeated exposure to a new stimulus. Distractibility, when measured at older ages, conforms more closely to the common usage of the term to describe a sometimes-intrusive level of attention to background stimuli; in infancy, this dimension refers more to soothability or the ability to be distracted by comforting strategies when distressed.

These dimensions range from simple descriptions of behavior (such as Activity level) to complex descriptions of change over time in response to new situations (such as Adaptability). By "simple," it is meant that the behavior may be directly observed in discrete time frames and referenced against "norms" displayed by other children of similar age. Complex descriptions require integration of multiple elements, such as reference to specific contexts, attention to repeated encounters with a situation, or attention to sequences over time. Thus, there would be reason to believe that informants might have an easier task with the "simple" dimensions and a potentially more difficult task with the "complex" dimensions.

Biobehavioral Regulation

This approach to temperament is concerned with examining behavioral indicators of regulatory processes important in everyday interactions with one's environment. The processes include regulation of arousal and attention, response to fear-inducing stimuli, adjustment to environmental limitations, and modulation of affect. The specific behaviors observed are of interest primarily because they provide insight into otherwise nonobservable internal regulation processes.

From this perspective, temperament behaviors are always interpreted in a conditional framework; that is, what are the environmental constraints operative when the behaviors are observed? This distinction from the behavioral style perspective is important because it implies more situational specificity in the expression of temperament behaviors (Rothbart & Derryberry, 1982). Furthermore, relations to other processes, such as attention, are basic to understanding the more stylistic aspects of behavior: Understanding the style is dependent on appreciating the attentional substrates, and full understanding of processes such as attention is not complete without considering how factors such as mood or activity level might affect focusing or shifting of attention.

Typology

There are many potential typologies that could be applied to the domain of temperament. One approach has been to classify individual children as *difficult* versus *easy* based on five of the nine Thomas and Chess dimensions (Carey & McDevitt, 1978; Thomas et al., 1963). This approach, however, was intended more as a summary of a large set of behavioral style information than as a statement about the nature of individual children.

A stronger approach to temperament typology is found in Kagan's theory of behavioral inhibition (Kagan, 1998; Kagan et al., 1989). He asserts that a small group of children (10–20%) exhibit a well-defined syndrome of extremely shy, inhibited behaviors in response to novel situations and are highly physiologically reactive to such novelty. Furthermore, this behavioral pattern is strongly linked to underlying nervous system properties. Individual differences outside of this extreme range are not of interest, as the focus is on identifying individual children who fit this particular category. This research agenda has been pursued by others, expanding it to include factors such as EEG activation in specific brain regions, serotonin levels, and long-term behavioral outcomes (Calkins, Fox, & Marshall, 1996; Higley et al., 1996).

ASSESSMENT OF TEMPERAMENT

Before exploring how temperament and child adaptation are related, it is useful to address issues of measurement and assessment, because conclusions from this literature often hinge on the assessment strategies employed. Empirical support for the proposition that infants and children exhibit individual differences in behavioral style that endure across time and setting has been discovered in both direct observations and parental reports (Hubert, Wachs, Peters-Martin, & Gandour, 1982; Seifer, Sameroff, Barrett, & Krafchuk, 1994). The importance of the concept of temperament is that even in the earliest months of life, infants are seen to behave in part according to internal agendas, and not to be totally driven by external contextual events.

In general, temperament assessments are designed to be descriptions of child behaviors. Furthermore, the range of behaviors examined is presumed to have some structure, consistent with the dimensions described in previous sections. Thus, the assessments of child behavior follow a model much like that in personality theory. Behaviors characteristic of individuals, generally stable across time and setting, with some definable structure, are the focus of assessments (Epstein & O'Brien, 1985).

Instruments and Assessment Technology

There are three basic methods used to assess temperament in infants and children: (1) parent or teacher report questionnaire, (2) direct observation of the child, and (3) structured parent interview. Obviously, the questionnaire approach is the most economical and has been the method of choice in the vast majority of work on temperament. However, serious questions about the utility of this approach have been raised (discussion to follow). Several methods for direct observation are available for home and laboratory, but they are mostly used during the infancy and early childhood years. Parent interviews, while of historical significance as the method used in Thomas and Chess's New York Longitudinal Study (NYLS), are rarely used in current practice.

The instrument developed by Carey and associates for infants (Carey & McDevitt, 1978), toddlers (Fullard, McDevitt, & Carey, 1984), and 3- to 7-year-old children (McDevitt & Carey, 1975) were the first widely used questionnaires, which led a much wider audience to apply the Thomas and Chess perspective. On the heels of these NYLS-based questionnaires, several other groups developed instruments as well. Bates and colleagues developed a series of questionnaires for children 6 months to 2 years of age (Bates, Freeland, & Lounsbury, 1979), focusing primarily on infant Difficulty. Another set of instruments based on the NYLS is the Dimensions of Temperament Surveys (DOTS), which are designed for older children and adults, and have both parent-report and self-report versions (Lerner, Palermo, Spiro, & Nesselroade, 1982). Motivated by behavior genetics findings, Buss and Plomin (1984) developed a set of instruments to be used as a self-report (adults), teacher-report, or parent-report measure from infancy to adulthood, assessing three areas where strong evidence of heritability was available: Emotionality, Activity, and Sociability. From still another theoretical perspective, biobehavioral regulation, Rothbart (1981) developed a parent-report scale to assess temperament in children during the first year of life, with subsequent extensions for preschool-age children (Goldsmith, 1987) and 3- to 7-year-olds (Rothbart, Ahadi, & Hershey, 1994).

The common features of these questionnaires are as follows: (1) They are parent-report measures (although some have self-report versions); (2) all require generalizations about children's behavior over a time period, although that time frame is almost always unspecified (phrases such as "usually" or "during feeding" are characteristic of the instruments rather than an emphasis on "during the past 24 hours" or "in the previous month"); (3) they have in common some core constructs (e.g., activity, adaptability to people and events, and quality of affect show up in one form or another on most of the instruments).

Despite the large set of existing questionnaires relying on parental report (many of which were not explicitly mentioned here) there are substantial problems with their use. The validity of this parental-report approach has been seriously questioned because (1) parent and observer reports show modest correspondence at best and (2) parental characteristics have strong impact on the reports of their infant's temperament (Bates, 1980; Hubert et al., 1982; Sameroff, Seifer, & Elias, 1982; Seifer et al., 1994; Vaughn, Bradley, Joffe, Seifer, & Barglow, 1987; Vaughn, Taraldson, Crichton, & Egeland, 1981; Zeanah, Keener, Stewart, & Anders, 1985). The measurement difficulties in this research area are well demonstrated in a careful study by Goldsmith, Rieser-Danner, and Briggs (1991). Samples of infants, toddlers, and preschoolers were rated by parents and by teachers on each of three different instruments. Multitrait–multimethod analysis revealed moderate to good evidence of convergent and discriminant validity of three constructs (Activity, Mood, and Approach); however, there was still low correspondence between parents and teachers, even though the samples were from university settings and largely composed of undergraduate- and graduate-student parents. Thus, even when parent-report instruments appeared well-behaved *internally* and *across instruments*, the results were less encouraging when compared *across informants*.

Observation Methods

Current observational methods to assess temperament require highly structured protocols and detailed scoring procedures. García-Coll and colleagues report on a 20-minute laboratory sequence in which progressively intrusive stimuli (e.g., putting a hat on the baby, a large toy that has intense light and sound effects) are presented to 3- and 9-month-old children. Summary scores include Positive, Negative, Approach, and Inhibition (García-Coll, Halpern, Vohr, Seifer, & Oh, 1992). In a similar vein, Kagan has laboratory procedures that index behavioral inhibition when challenging stimuli are presented (Kagan et al., 1989), procedures that have been modified by Fox and colleagues (Calkins et al., 1996). Goldsmith and Rothbart's (1990) LABTAB battery assesses Fear, Anger–Frustration, Joy–Pleasure, Interest–Persistence, and Activity. Seifer and Sameroff have developed procedures designed for use in the home during the first year of life. Multiple observations are used to derive scores for Mood, Approach, Activity, Intensity and Total Difficulty (Seifer et al., 1994). All of these observation methods are expensive to administer in terms of assessment time, laboratory space, equipment, and scoring time. Thus, they are best suited to clinical or research protocols in which temperament is a central concern.

As noted earlier, a core feature of temperament theory is that behaviors evidence some stability across time and setting. All methods support the contention; the magnitude of the stability is, however, modest when single time points are considered. This should not be surprising, as personality assessments reveal a similar phenomenon. High levels of consistency are apparent when multiple assessments are considered simultaneously in aggregate form (Bornstein, Gaughran, & Homel, 1986; Seifer et al., 1994; for similar findings in personality assessment, see also Epstein & O'Brien, 1985).

In summary, several classes of behavior are assessed across most temperament instruments. These include activity level, some aspect of negative emotionality (with a lesser emphasis on positive emotionality), regulatory behavior (in the realms of emotion expression, response to novelty or change, and attention), some combination of shyness and inhibition in social and nonsocial settings, and the intensity of behavioral responses in general.

Developmental Considerations

All of the different approaches to temperament and its assessment share a bias that dimensions or types of temperaments apply across a broad span of development. This does not imply that these theories are insensitive to developmental change (Rothbart & Ahadi, 1994). Rather, they have attempted to identify common processes that are manifest across different developmental periods, even though they may be expressed in vastly different specific behaviors. With one notable exception (Buss & Plomin, 1984), assessment batteries typically include a series of instruments employing different sets of items that measure temperament at different points in development.

An important developmental consideration to keep in mind is that the bulk of work in temperament has occurred in the infancy and early childhood period, with only a few substantial bodies of work conducted with older, school-age children. Relatively little work has been done with adolescents (the DOTS instrument [Lerner et al., 1982] is a major exception). This places some limits on our understanding of temperament as a developmental phenomenon. Perhaps of more concern from the perspective of developmental explanation is that temperament theories have been largely nondevelopmental in nature. The primary agenda has been to define similarities across age rather than systematic transformations that may occur with development. To cite just one example, I noted earlier that the Thomas and Chess dimension of Distractibility shifted in emphasis from soothability early in life to more attentional processes later on. Still, there is little theoretical explication for this shift in emphasis, and just as little data to support a contention that soothability and level attention to environmental stimuli are empirically related or emanating from some common process.

One of the few areas in which developmental models have begun to emerge is in the analysis of temperament and social systems. When temperament is viewed from the perspective of biobehavioral regulation and coupled with the idea that interactive partners contribute to this regulatory process (discussed in more detail later), temperament and social developmental processes may be viewed as highly interconnected (Calkins, 1994; Hinde, 1982; Kochanska, 1995; Seifer & Schiller, 1995). This becomes increasingly important as consideration of developmental adaptation becomes central. For many theories of child development and pathology, placing social processes within families, peer groups, and school setting is essential to understanding developmental trajectories.

TEMPERAMENT AND PSYCHOPATHOLOGY

With the establishment of a base of measurement strategies and well-regarded models of the structure of the behavior, one can address questions about how the normative phenomenon might be related to variations in developmental outcome. Several research programs have noted a relation of difficult temperament during infancy to later social competence and behavior problems. However, the findings have been complicated, with consensus in only a few areas on the most important temperament predictors. There are also a number of major methodological drawbacks.

Externalizing and Internalizing Problems

Most work on temperament and psychopathology has focused on relations with externalizing symptoms. In the earliest longitudinal study of temperament–adaptation associations, Thomas and Chess described longitudinal relations of early temperament with behavior problem outcomes in middle childhood and adolescence (Thomas & Chess, 1977; Thomas, Chess, & Birch, 1968). However, their difficult temperament assessment was aggregated over the first several years of life, and their reports are vague as to whether any specific time during the infancy and preschool years was a better predictor of childhood behavioral outcomes (see Bates, 1989). Subsequent studies, which minimize these shortcomings, have found similar associations of difficult or negative temperamental characteristics and subsequent outcomes— usually the realm of externalizing problems—although substantial overlap with internalizing symptoms is evident as well. Caspi, Henry, McGee, Moffitt, and Silva (1995) identified three factors of temperament scales in their New Zealand sample. One of the Caspi et al. factors, *lack of control* (emotional lability, negativity, restlessness, short attention span) in preschool years, was associated with hyperactivity, attention problems, antisocial behavior, and conduct disorder at ages 9–15. Bates and colleagues found similar results, with early hostility and difficulty, along with low parental involvement, predicting externalizing problems several years later (Bates & Bayles, 1988; Bates, Bayles, Bennett, Ridge, & Brown, 1991). In still another large longitudinal study, Sanson, Smart, Prior, and Oberklaid (1993) found early difficult temperament related to later hyperactive and aggressive behavior in their Australian sample.

Relations between temperament (either measured early in life or contemporaneously with behavior problems) have also been reported by Maziade et al. (1989, 1990), Campbell, March, Pierce, Ewing, and Szumowski (1991), Graham, Rutter, and George (1973), Earls (1981), Lerner (1983), Lerner, Lerner, and Zabski (1985), Spangler (1990), Matheny (1989), and Martin, Olejnik, and Gaddis (1994). Difficult temperament has also been related to higher rates of physician visits, accidents, abdominal pain, sleep disturbance, and absences from school (Carey, 1985). In nonhuman primates, there is strong evidence that behavioral style characteristics, along with biological processes underlying the behavioral variation, are related to important outcomes, ranging from establishment of early social relationships to ultimate survival into adulthood, where early death is often associated with aggressive, impulsive behavior (Higley et al., 1996; Suomi, 1997).

Temperament is also an important factor in children's school performance. Activity Level, Persistence, Distractibility, and General Difficulty have been related to IQ, grades, classroom behavior, and interaction with teachers (Keough, 1989; Martin et al., 1994; McClowry et al., 1994).

Other investigators have identified more complicated associations of temperament with later behavior outcomes. Bates, Maslin, and Frankel (1985) found that infant temperament ratings at 6 months and 13 months were correlated with mothers' reports of behavior problems with 3-year-olds. Unadaptive infants were later seen as anxious at age 3, and high-active infants were viewed as hostile and hyperactive at 3 years. Frankel and Bates (1990) report that social competence (measured in the Matas, Arend, and Sroufe [1978] problem-solving paradigm) was related to infant unadaptability, and that infant difficulty was related to *competent* behavior by boys and *incompetent* behavior by girls. It should be noted there are studies in the literature that fail to find relations between temperament and behavior problems (e.g., Olson, Bates, & Bayles, 1990).

Fewer specific predictors of internalizing behavior problems are apparent, although some evidence exists that shyness and low sociability may be antecedents (Hagekull, 1994). Also, behavioral inhibition has ben related to risk for anxiety disorder (Rosenbaum et al., 1988; see also Biederman et al., 1990). In the Caspi et al. (1995) study described earlier, their *Approach* factor (ease with strangers, adjustment to new situations, friendliness, self-confidence) negatively predicted anxiety in boys and their *Sluggishness* factor (flat affect, passivity, malleability) predicted anxiety in girls.

Three drawbacks of many of these studies are (1) the reliance on parental reports for the temperament ratings, (2) single-time-point measurements of child temperament, and (3) informant bias in having the same person rate temperament and behavior problems. Rothbart and Bates (1998) discuss methods that could potentially reduce the confounds in such research (such as multiple informants and longitudinal designs) but conclude that no single ideal design will always be effective. Rather, a reliance on evidence from converging viewpoints and methods is required to arrive at valid, potentially replicable, and theoretically consistent findings.

The vast majority of the literature relating temperament to child adaptation reports on direct linear effects. There are, however, many other ways that temperament might influence child adaptation, which have been well articulated by Rothbart and Bates (1998). Briefly, other possibilities include indirect linear effects, interactions of temperament with other contextual factors, interactions among different temperament characteristics, and common etiological pathways resulting in both temperament and behavior problems.

Indirect Effects of Temperament on Behavior Problems

Considering that temperament influences might be more varied and indirect than has been implicit in most empirical work, it is useful to consider what is known in the realm of nondirect influences. For example, in the domain of temperament by context interactions, the contextual variable of most importance in the lives of young children is the family. The theoretical work of Thomas and Chess clearly indicates how temperament might interact with parental expectations and behavior to influence developmental trajectories. The scant empirical investigation of such transactions supports their ideas. For example, Maziade (1989) reports that the combination of difficult temperament and dysfunctional family behavior control is a better predictor of behavior disorder outcome than temperament alone. In studies of positive adaptation (internalized conscience in preschoolers), Kochanska (1995) has demonstrated replicable interactions of fearfulness with maternal control style and attachment security in predicting levels of internalized control. High fearfulness, coupled with gentle, noncontrolling parenting styles, predicted more internalized conscience (control style was not important for low-fearful children); low fearfulness coupled with secure attachment also predicted internalized conscience, with no effect detected among the fearful children. Many other studies report these types of interaction effects but, in general, they are less embedded in programmatic research efforts and have less theoretical basis and replicability (Rothbart & Bates, 1998).

Such findings lead to consideration of how children's behavior affects their developmental context. In the following section is a more detailed explication of the association of temperament and emerging social relationships in the first years of life, much of it from the perspective of attachment theory. Using this example, directions for future theoretical and empirical work integrating temperament in a developmental psychopathology framework can emerge.

Temperament Contributions to Social Systems

Mental health or illness may be broadly viewed as individual variation in general adaptation. From this perspective, temperament is conceived as one way that individual children contribute to their future adaptation. Such temperament contributions to child adaptation may (as described earlier) be examined by directly relating temperament characteristics and specific child outcomes. What may be equally important, however, is the influence temperament exerts on other systems throughout development. Thus, this alternative approach to understanding the role of temperament in psychopathology emphasizes indirect effects on psychopathology outcomes, affecting the development of social relationships within families.

One domain where infant contributions to parent–child relationship systems have been carefully considered may be broadly described in the context of attachment theory (Ainsworth, Blehar, Waters, & Wall, 1978). Beginning with the first relationships between infants and their caregivers, this approach provides a general model for understanding relationship processes across the life span. Attachment theory emphasizes the organization of thoughts and behaviors that underlie relationship processes, invoking the construct of working models as a heuristic for understanding these structures that describe how relationship partners think about and behave with one another. These working models become explicit in the expressed emotions, proximity maintenance, and intensity of behavior among relationship partners.

Within the framework of these organizational constructs (Sroufe & Waters, 1977), temperament is best viewed as a moderating influence on the development of relationship processes rather than a fundamental characteristic that linearly predicts status among relationship partners (Seifer & Schiller, 1995). It is important to emphasize again that viewing the child's contributions to the attachment relationship as unidirectional vastly oversimplifies the developmental process. Such child characteristics should instead be examined in terms of their impact on the dyadic system and the manner in which they contribute to a caregiver–child co-construction of the relationship (Hinde, 1982).

Behavioral Style and Social Interaction

Of particular interest in this context is to identify the differences in motivations or goals that different investigators have proposed as governing individual and social-interactive systems. Several investigators have microanalytically examined early social interactions, carefully describing the sequence of infant and parent behavior. In this context, Tronick (1989) proposes that achieving and maintaining an optimal state of arousal is a basic set-goal of young infants that motivates interactive behavior. Thus, expression of mood, intensity of responses, soothability when distressed, and activity level all likely contribute to the flow of early social interactions.

In a slightly different vein, Fogel and Thelen (1987) invoke the notion of a set of frequently changing control parameters, which may be endogenous or exogenous, that spur transitions during early development; that is, the characteristics of the infant self-regulatory and communicative systems change over time, and these changes in themselves may spur developmental shifts. This type of approach may be especially useful in beginning to understand temperament in a developmental context. What remains is to identify more explicitly the types of organized infant behaviors that might follow such patterns and begin to validate empirically that such transformations indeed occur.

One useful way of beginning to understand such developmental transformations and, more specifically, how temperament may be implicated in adaptive systems, is in terms of a functional analysis. Adaptation models of the type invoked here have as a basic agenda understanding behavior motivated to achieve systemic goals (Sameroff, 1983; Waters & Sroufe, 1983). As Campos and colleagues (1994) elaborated in the context of understanding emotion regulation, several key propositions are held. Central among these are the focus of goal-oriented explanations of behavior (cf. Waters & Sroufe, 1983) and evaluations of bidirectional individual–context influences. Thus, the specific behaviors of the child in combination with parenting practices and sensitivity (i.e., the ability to recognize and respond to the child behavior appropriately) become the key building blocks of relationship systems (Ainsworth et al., 1978; Seifer & Schiller, 1995).

From an explicit functional perspective, several key issues may be identified regarding the role of temperament in emerging adaptive processes, including the *social signals* to others that may be implicit in behavioral style, the ways that behavioral style *regulates the behavior of others*, how the *behavior of others affects an individual's behavioral style*, the *hedonic features* that characterize the behavioral style, the *past history* affecting present behavioral style, *physiological processes* implicated in behavioral style, and the *cultural forces* affecting behavioral style. These issues emanating from a functional analysis are used to guide discussion of the role of temperament in emerging child adaptation.

Development of Social Attachments

One early social relationship presumed to have significance for later adaptation is attachment with primary caregivers. This is an interesting example to pursue in the present context, since many researchers and theorists have attempted to understand the overlap of the disparate constructs of temperament and attachment. Temperament definitions typically include behaviors within the domains of affect; activity; approach to novel objects, events, or people; intensity of behavioral expressions; and general interactive difficulty. All of these are behaviors that overlap with those considered to be central in indexing individual differences in infants' social behavior (to be discussed). Thus, a specific domain in which temperament may be particularly important is the development of infant–caregiver attachment.

Attachment is often assessed using home-based observations (Waters, 1995) or, more often, the laboratory-based Strange Situation (Ainsworth et al., 1978). The latter procedure examines exploration and return to secure base in the context of stressful separation from parents and introduction of unfamiliar adults, along with reunions with the parents. Many temperament behaviors are central to the way we understand attachment; behaviors characterized as temperamental attributes of Fear (Rothbart, 1981) or Approach (Thomas et al., 1963) should relate to infants' reaction to the introduction of an unfamiliar adult in the laboratory assessment. Temperamental Soothability and Distractibility (Thomas et al., 1963) will be involved in the degree to which infants return to baseline arousal if they become distressed during separations (as is presumed in the laboratory protocol). Activity level (Bates et al., 1979; Rothbart, 1981; Thomas et al., 1963) may influence the degree of exploration and returns to the attachment figure that are observed both in the laboratory and in the home. Orientation,

Threshold to Stimulation, Distractibility, and Persistence (Thomas et al., 1963) should all be related to the quality of interactions with both objects and people during the exploration phases of secure base behavior. Thus, there is ample reason to believe that temperament will somehow be implicated in the behaviors observed in attachment assessments. Furthermore, Connell and Thompson (1986) and Bridges, Connell, and Belsky (1988) provide evidence that emotional reactivity has cross-episode and cross-age stability in Strange Situation assessments of attachment quality, consistent with temperament phenomena.

Probably of more importance than a mapping of temperament constructs onto organized attachment behaviors is the role of behavioral style in development of the *goal-corrected partnership*. Within attachment theory in particular, and dynamic developmental models in general, the principle of ongoing redefinition of systems properties is a key feature. Thus, the notion of a goal-corrected partnership reflects the presumed shared goals of relationship partners that motivate ongoing adaptation across development. Such adaptive partnership, when described within the functional perspective outlined earlier, leads to several key points. First, children's behavior will affect their caregivers: Social signaling associated with fear may result in caregiver behavior that amplifies the arousal generated by the stressful situation, which in turn may exacerbate fearful, agitated behavior of the child. One may consider these influences as they affect measurement at any one point in time, as well as how they affect parent–infant interaction across developmental time. Also, if indeed the separations and introduction of strangers in attachment assessment are stressful, infants may exhibit behavioral styles that maximize the hedonic qualities of the immediate experience. In a similar vein, the past experience of infants with caregivers in similar situations will differentially promote behavioral styles that have been more successful in those situations (e.g., nonactive, nonsocial behavior for some infants; highly active, fussy, difficult behaviors for others). Note how similar this view is to attachment theorists' views that the accumulated history of behavioral expression and caregiver response to those behaviors in large part determines quality of attachment behavior (Seifer & Schiller, 1995). Finally, the shaping of behavioral style by different cultural practices (Super & Harkness, 1986) may be related to variation of attachment behaviors in different cultures (Posada et al., 1995).

Viewed as regulatory systems, temperamental "types" also have a substantial surface relevance to the operation of social relatedness from a functional perspective. The behaviorally inhibited children described earlier (those who are physiologically reactive, fearful, wary, and behaviorally timid in response to novelty) may be analyzed in terms of functional characteristics (Kagan et al., 1989). In particular, where novelty and stress may play a role (as has been suggested when activation of the attachment system [arousal] occurs in procedures such as the Ainsworth Strange Situation), the interaction of individual behavioral response and the social partner become important. The heightened arousal of inhibited children in the novel Strange Situation experience may promote more amplified attachment behavior, perhaps even interfering with their presumed goal of modulating that arousal via secure base behavior. Interactions of this type, where there is discordance among various regulators of behavioral style and goal-corrected behavior, may be early indicators of maladaptation. Furthermore, caregivers who are sensitive to these properties of their infant, and who have the techniques for modulating arousal, may be more successful in correcting the relationship partnership in the service of achieving broad relationship goals. This is now considered in more detail.

Temperament Influences on Sensitivity–Attachment Associations

An analysis of temperament–attachment associations is not complete without considering the antecedents of infant–caregiver attachment. Within attachment theory, the most significant hypothesized predictor of early attachment is parenting sensitivity. Sensitivity is a constellation of parenting behaviors, including prompt response to infant signals, appropriate timing and pacing of behavior, flexible adaptation to specific infant cues, and contextual embedding of parenting behavior. To date, however, parenting sensitivity has been treated as though it occurred in an interactive vacuum: Little attention has been given to the contribution of infant behavior to the parenting process. Thus, it is useful to consider the relation between the two influences on attachment—child characteristics and parenting sensitivity (Seifer & Schiller, 1995).

Characteristics of both the child and the parent contribute to the dyadic interaction process, even when considering the limited domain of interactions relevant to sensitivity (Gable & Isabella, 1992; Isabella & Gable, 1991; Mangelsdorf, Gunnar, Kestenbaum, Lang, & Andreas, 1990). Infants with more positive mood, who adapt well to new situations, and whose behavior is predictable and well-regulated, will (in the short term) more often elicit behaviors from parents that are themselves positive in nature, well-tuned with the infant's ongoing behavior, and are not tinged with distress and frustration. In the longer term, such "easy" infants will more likely have parents who are themselves at ease, comfortable with their parenting skills, and approaching the tasks of parenting with a positive outlook and motivation to meet the emergent needs of their child. In contrast, when infants are difficult, fussy, hard to soothe, intense in their responses, and unpredictable, parents are more likely to find ineffective strategies and generally behave in the context of frustration, self-doubt, and perhaps even distaste for their child. Our own empirical work suggests that there is indeed a relation between positive infant mood and greater parenting sensitivity at 6 and 9 months of age (Seifer et al., 1994), similar to the relations described by Mangelsdorf et al. (1990). Unfortunately, few studies have focused on such questions and there is very little empirical data to address this issue with authority.

Finally, I have presented much of this material in terms of how temperament might influence parenting, attachment quality, and/or measurement. It is equally important to consider that parenting behavior and felt security will also likely influence the behavioral style of infants. For example, infants secure in their belief that caregivers will provide a safe haven may be more likely to approach novel social or physical contexts, exhibit generally more positive affective demeanor, or engage in persistent, focused explorations of the environment. As noted earlier, these very behaviors may also promote sensitive parenting and secure attachment behavior. It is these very types of transactions that could become the focus of the next wave of developmentally sensitive research on early social relationships.

GOODNESS-OF-FIT MODELS

When considering developmental psychopathology, the Thomas and Chess goodness-of-fit model is extremely useful in organizing the often disparate issues surrounding individual differences in behavioral style. What is most useful about this goodness-of-fit perspective on temperament is that it integrates the individually based behavioral style model with its functional consequences related to the most important context for infants and young children—their family. Within this model, individual differences in behavioral style are viewed less as linear predictors of outcome and more as systems properties that moderate the ongoing adaptation of the caregiver–child relationship systems. Thus, when attempting to understand psychopathology outcomes, such a model provides an integrated framework in which the major individual and contextual influences on maladaptive behavior can be examined.

Goodness of fit is a *relationship* construct whose formal properties can be described in terms of a functional perspective. The dyadic partners behave with each other according to set goals for a variety of infant temperament behaviors that are determined in part by infant self-regulation, prior expectations, cultural background, and immediate context. When the dyadic system operates close to these set goals, there is a high degree of fit; when their interactions consistently violate these goals, the fit is poor. Hinde (1982) has discussed how the match between characteristics of the dyad and the larger social context must be considered in attachment research, a point well taken in the domain of understanding goodness-of-fit models.

It is important to note that goodness of fit should not be construed as a static construct, akin to matching the pieces of a precut jigsaw puzzle. Rather, the partners in the relationship must be viewed as dynamic and changing on the basis of their accumulated interactive histories, and capable of influencing one another in fundamental ways. Furthermore, the degree of fit is not established at some point to remain fixed thereafter but may repeatedly change over time as perturbations and repairs of the interactions and goal-corrected partnership take place. The concept of goodness of fit typically is used to describe parents adapting to difficulties presented by their infants; however, it can be applied equally well to the resilient child who adapts to less than optimal caregiving circumstances and hence promotes healthier development of the relationship. In summary, goodness of fit characterizes the "personality" of caregiver–infant relationships in ways that may be enduring over time (i.e., trait-like dimensions) as well as ways that are sensitive to the interactive history at a particular point in time (i.e., state-like dimensions). The theoretical presumption is that the dyads that function best will be those that fit well together, naturally, in smoothly maintaining set goals and/or those that adapt well to perturbations during interactions.

Operationalizing Goodness of Fit

Thomas and Chess originally proposed their goodness-of-fit model in their earliest publications on infant temperament, presenting it as a heuristic for understanding the mechanism by which temperamental variability might be translated into later behavior problems (Thomas et al., 1963). Despite the importance of the model for their perspective on temperament, Thomas and Chess never fully defined or operationalized this construct. They did identify some important features: (1) The parent–child system is characterized by dynamic interactions, where neither partner has a stable developmental course independent of the other; and (2) a fundamental characteristic of the health of this parent–child interaction system is the degree of fit of the child's temperament with the parent's expectations or cultural boundaries. This model implies a high degree of complexity. Point 1 implies that there are child effects on parents (Bell & Harper, 1977) and that developmental progress is *not* linear. Point 2 implies that goodness of fit must be examined at the familial level of organization (Bronfenbrenner, 1986), and that parenting experience, beliefs, and values will be important determinants of the level of fit. Also apparent is the strong similarity to Sameroff's transactional and systems models (Sameroff, 1983; Sameroff & Seifer, 1983).

The study of goodness of fit presents formidable problems because of the complexity I just described. First, the phenomenon has many components that are affected by at least two individuals. Second, much of what is encompassed in the goodness-of-fit construct is inherently subjective; for example, parental perceptions of child behavior sometimes have little in common with the child's observed behavior (Seifer et al., 1994). Third, because of the multidimensional and multidetermined nature of the phenomenon, research design and analysis are inherently complex, which in turn requires that measurements must be especially precise and free from error if the analyses are to be meaningful. Thus, in addition to specific behavioral manifestations, goodness of fit has a cognitive component (i.e., how is the behavior interpreted) and an affective component (i.e., how do these observations and appraisals make one feel). We have thus identified three distinct ways that goodness of fit may be operationalized: (1) objective behavior matching, (2) objective matching of expectations and behavior, and (3) subjectively reported stress–appraisal–coping models.

Behavior Matching (Objective)

The most concrete approach to goodness of fit is at the level of *behavioral matching*, where temperaments of parents and children are compared for level of fit (e.g., Wallander, Hubert, & Varni, 1988). These matching paradigms have often been discussed in terms of statistical interactions of child temperament by some contextual factor used in the prediction of child outcome (Bates, 1989). Wallander et al. (1988) used the approach of matching child and parent temperament and found no evidence that goodness of fit so defined was predictive of behavior problems in a sample of handicapped children. Sprunger, Boyce, and Gaines (1985) also found generally nonsignificant effects when degree of match on infant and family rhythmicity was related to family adjustment and infant behavior problems. Another study operationalized goodness of fit as infant temperament in conjunction with certain parent personality characteristics (i.e., whether infant behavior matches with a *different* parent characteristic). Mangelsdorf et al. (1990) found that infants prone to distress, who had mothers low on the personality factor of Constraint, were more likely to have secure attachment classifications. This general approach, however, does not fully capture the theoretical spirit of the Thomas and Chess construct, being more concerned with exact comparability rather than the developmental implications of degree of match.

Matching Expectations and Behavior (Objective)

Lerner and Lerner's "matching of expectations and behavior" approach to the issue of goodness of fit has the virtue of straightforward operationalization and ease of interpretation. The research design typically involves measuring the degree of behavioral match with teacher or peer expectation and relates it to some measure of competence or adjustment. The processes that mediate how mismatches are experienced or how they impact on social systems are not considered. In general, the ability to predict outcomes from these goodness-of-fit measures has been modest, with little unique predictive variance that is independent of ordinary temperament ratings (Lerner, 1983; Lerner, Lerner, & Zabski, 1985). Several potential factors might work against strong prediction in these studies. The expectations provided by teachers are general: They relate to children in general and not to individual subjects in the studies. This lack of individual specificity may introduce error.

Stress–Appraisal–Coping Model (Subjective)

Another way of approaching the goodness-of-fit issue is examining the degree to which infants have lived up to the individual and cultural expectations of their families. In addition, the specific impact of infants on their family system may be examined in terms of such qualities as stress, affective quality, or quality of daily life. With minor exceptions, these latter approaches have not been examined in the goodness-of-fit approach to infant temperament, although research is currently in progress in our laboratory (Seifer, 1996). One model that might be applied to goodness of fit comes from the life stress literature, where three components are considered in the *stress–appraisal–coping* model: amount of objective stressors, the cognitive and affective appraisal of those stressors, and the social supports available to aid in adaptively coping with the stress (Cobb, 1976; Cutrona & Troutman, 1986; Hammen, 1992; Schaefer, Coyne, & Lazarus, 1981). If the impact of infant temperamental qualities is viewed as life stresses in the model, then a logical approach to study of goodness of fit is available: the objective qualities of the child behavior; the nature of the parent's appraisal (e.g., reports of child behavior matching with expectations); and adaptation strategies for dealing with mismatches (cf. Power, Gershenhorn, & Stafford, 1990). Such an analysis of goodness of fit aligns well with the functional perspective. The bidirectional social processes related to parenting, often emotion-laden and stressful, include appraisal and coping mechanisms in the regulation of parents' emotions that may influence the quality of adaptation in the transition to parenting a new child.

In their study of the appraisal aspect of temperament ratings, Power et al. (1990) examined how different attributions regarding a standard set of early negative behaviors led to differences in later reports of child temperament. Power et al. found that those mothers who, when asked about negative behaviors of their 6-week-old children, attributed physical discomfort to that behavior, later rated their children as difficult at 4 months. However, other mothers who attributed resistance or disinterest to the same negative behaviors at 6 weeks, later rated the children's temperament as unpredictable. The importance of these findings is that differences among parents' appraisal processes are related to differences in how they view their children's temperament, even when the behavior being appraised is identical. Prior, Sanson, Carroll, and Oberklaid (1989) found that parents' appraisal of difficult behavior differed as a function of social status. In their Australian sample, lower status parents rated their children as more difficult, but they expressed less displeasure regarding these behaviors. Prior et al. also noted that the temperament ratings were related to reported parenting practices, which indicates that difficulty must be interpreted in a family, rather than an individual, context. Thus, the little evidence available suggests some of the questions posed by the functional perspective will have relevance to understanding early temperament and relationship processes.

Parental Working Models and Goodness of Fit

Recent methodological developments have facilitated more direct assessment of adults' current working models of their past relationships, termed adult attachment (George, Kaplan, & Main, 1985; Main & Goldwyn, 1988). These cognitive models of relationships are viewed as a key component in influencing the many ways that parents provide developmental contexts for their children. Such cognitive working models of attachment relationships are analogous to the cognitive goodness-of-fit models in the domain of temperament, particularly when goodness of fit is understood via the stress–appraisal–coping model. Understanding the attitudes and beliefs that parents hold about their individual children may prove to be as important as understanding the actual behaviors that occur during parent–child interactions (Sameroff & Seifer, 1983).

This recognition leads to understanding temperament and relationship processes in ways that overlap. First, the confluence of actual experience with cognitive construction of the experience becomes a central theme when the notion of working models is invoked. This is consistent with assertions made earlier regarding how temperament may influence emerging dyadic systems. Furthermore, it provides a positive perspective for what has been termed *bias* in parental reports: Systematic variation from the objective observation of behavior to the actual reporting of the behavior to others may reflect the parent's working model of that infant. To the extent that working models have overarching effects and guide behavior in multiple contexts, such cognitive understanding could provide an important window to explain the individuality in relationship development.

As noted earlier, previous studies indicate that difficult infant temperament reported by parents predicts later childhood social competence and behavior problems (usually reported by parents as well). It is also true that these reports by parents (of both temperament and behavior problems) are not very accurate measures of the children's actual behavior; further-more, they are correlated with the parents' own characteristics. One explanation of this set of results is that the correlations of temperament and behavior problems are as much a function of the parents' appraisal and feelings about their children's behavior as of the behavior itself. Stated another way, the *degree of fit* between parent and child may be one of the operative factors in explaining the relation of reports of early behavior and reports of later problems.

GOODNESS OF FIT AND PSYCHOPATHOLOGY

Considering the full range of adaptation in functional models applied to goodness of fit allows for understanding how temperament may be implicated in pathological developmental processes. Borrowing from Sameroff and Emde's (1989) relationship model, early goodness-of-fit perturbations may be set up in many ways: violation of expectations (e.g., giving birth to a boy when a girl was preferred); difficult-to-manage behavior (e.g., waking in the night); or pathology in the parent that impedes inability to adapt easily to demands of parenting (e.g., postpartum depression), to cite a few examples. In family systems that can flexibly adapt to such perturbations, early difficulties will likely be of little long-term consequence. In contrast, in families where working models are inflexible (perhaps in parents' overattending to diffi-culties or, alternatively, defensively dismissing areas of mismatch), perturbations may persist, simultaneously exacerbating difficult child behaviors and negatively influencing parental goodness-of-fit appraisals/working models. If such cycles become ingrained (akin to the coercive cycles described by Patterson, 1982), long-term relationship and behavior problems may become more likely.

Such theoretical formulations may have internal logical consistency. Still, the field is far from providing substantial bodies of evidence that this approach will eventually prove useful in understanding (at least in part) the emergence of maladaptive behavior in young children. The significance of this approach, however, is that it is a first step in addressing the complexity of how infant behavioral style operates in family context to influence variation in levels of child adaptation.

To conclude, the continuing growth of interest in infant and child behavioral style likely reflects the multiple agendas associated with this research endeavor. The behavioral phenom-ena, underlying genetic factors, physiological correlates, interaction with parenting practices, and associations with outcomes all support interests in the area. The history of conceptualizing linear relations of child behavior with these associated factors has, to a small extent, begun to be supplanted by more dynamic and complex models that more accurately reflect the intricate developmental trajectories that are the focus of interest for many in the field. In particular, when psychopathology outcomes are of central concern, full integration of child behavioral style in the context of parenting, working models, physiological responsibility, as well as other, yet to be identified, factors, holds the promise of enlightening us about the roots of adaptive and maladaptive behavior.

ACKNOWLEDGMENT. This research was supported by grants from the National Institute of Mental Health.

REFERENCES

Ainsworth, M. D. S., Blehar, M. C., Waters, E., & Wall, S. (1978). *Patterns of attachment: A psychological study of the strange situation.* Hillsdale, NJ: Erlbaum.

Bates, J. E. (1980). The concept of difficult temperament. *Merrill–Palmer Quarterly, 26,* 299–319.

Bates, J. E. (1989). Applications of temperament concepts. In G. A. Kohnstamm, J. E. Bates, & M. K. Rothbart (Eds.), *Temperament in childhood* (pp. 321–355). New York: Wiley.

Bates, J. E., & Bayles, K. (1988). The role of attachment in the development of behavior problems. In J. Belsky & T. Nezworski (Eds.), *Clinical implications of attachment* (pp. 253–299). Hillsdale, NJ: Erlbaum.

Bates, J. E., Bayles, K., Bennett, D. S., Ridge, B., & Brown, M. M. (1991). Origins of externalizing behavior problems at eight years of age. In D. Pepler & K. Rubin (Eds.), *Development and treatment of childhood aggression* (pp. 93–120). Hillsdale, NJ: Erlbaum.

Bates, J. E., Freeland, C. A., & Lounsbury, M. L. (1979). Measure of infant difficultness. *Child Development, 50,* 794–803.

Bates, J. E., Maslin, C. A., & Frankel, K. A. (1985). Attachment security, mother–child interaction, and temperament as predictors of behavior problem ratings at three years. In I. Bretherton & E. Waters (Eds.), Growing points of attachment theory and research. *Monographs of the Society for Research in Child Development, 50* (Serial No. 209), 167–193.

Bell, R. Q., & Harper, L. V. (1977). *Child effects on adults.* Hillsdale, NJ: Erlbaum.

Biederman, J., Rosenbaum, J. F., Chaloff, J., & Kagan, J. (1995). Behavioral inhibition as a risk factor for anxiety disorders. In J. L. March (Ed.), *Anxiety disorders in children and adolescents* (pp. 16–81). New York: Guilford Press.

Biederman, J., Rosenbaum, J. F., Hirshfeld, D. R., Faraone, S. V., Bolduc, E. A., Gersten, M., Meminger, S. R., Kagan, J., Snideman, N., & Reznick, S. (1990). Psychiatric correlates of behavioral inhibition in young children of parents with and without psychiatric disorders. *Archives of General Psychiatry, 47,* 21–26.

Bornstein, M. H., Gaughran, J., & Homel, P. (1986). Infant temperament: Theory, tradition, critique, and new assessments. In C. E. Izard & P. B. Read (Eds.), *Measuring emotions in infants and children* (Vol. 2, pp. 172–199). New York: Cambridge University Press.

Bridges, L. J., Connell, J. P., & Belsky, J. (1988). Similarities and differences in infant–mother and infant–father interaction in the Strange Situation: A component process analysis. *Developmental Psychology, 24,* 92–100.

Bronfenbrenner, U. (1986). Ecology of the family as a context for human development: Research perspectives. *Developmental Psychology, 22,* 723–742.

Buss, A. H., & Plomin, R. (1984). *Temperament: Early developing personality traits.* Hillsdale: NJ: Erlbaum.

Calkins, S. D. (1994). Origins and outcomes of individual differences in emotion regulation. In N. Fox (Ed.), The development of emotion regulation: Biological and behavioral considerations. *Monographs of the Society for Research in Child Development, 59* (Serial No. 240), 53–72.

Calkins, S. D., Fox, N. A., & Marshall, T. R. (1996). Behavioral and physiological antecedents of inhibited and uninhibited behavior. *Child Development, 67,* 523–540.

Campbell, S. B., March, C. L., Pierce, E. W., Ewing, L. J., & Szumowski, E. K. (1991). Hard-to-manage preschool boys: Family context and the stability of externalizing behavior. *Journal of Abnormal Child Psychology, 19,* 301–318.

Campos, J. J., Mumme, D. L., Kermoian, R., & Campos, R. G. (1994). A functionalist perspective on the nature of emotion. In N. A. Fox (Ed.), The development of emotion regulation: Biological and behavioral considerations. With Commentary by Joseph J. Campos et al. *Monographs of the Society for Research in Child Development, 59* (2–3, Serial No. 240), 284–303.

Carey, W. B. (1985). Interactions of temperament and clinical conditions. *Advances in Development and Behavioral Pediatrics, 6,* 83–115.

Carey, W. B., & McDevitt, S. C. (1978). Revision of the Infant Temperament Questionnaire. *Pediatrics*, *61*, 735–739.

Caspi, A., Henry, B., McGee, R. O., Moffitt, T. E., & Silva, P. A. (1995). Temperamental origins of child and adolescent behavior problems: From age three to age fifteen. *Child Development*, *66*, 55–68.

Caspi, A., & Silva, P. A. (1995). Temperamental qualities at age three predict personality traits in young adulthood: Longitudinal evidence from a birth cohort. *Child Development*, *66*, 486–498.

Clark, L. A., Watson, D., & Mineka, S. (1994). Temperament, personality, and the mood and anxiety disorders. *Journal of Abnormal Psychology*, *103*, 103–116.

Connell, J. P., & Thompson, R. (1986). Emotion and social interaction in the Strange Situation: Consistencies and asymmetric influences in the second year. *Child Development*, *54*, 733–745.

Cutrona, C. E., & Troutman, C. R. (1986). Social support, infant temperament, and parenting self-efficacy: A mediational model of postpartum depression. *Child Development*, *57*, 1507–1518.

Earls, F. (1981). Temperament characteristics and behavior problems in three-year-old children. *Journal of Nervous and Mental Disease*, *169*, 367–373.

Epstein, S., & O'Brien, E. J. (1985). The person–situation debate in historical and current perspective. *Psychological Bulletin*, *98*(3), 513–537.

Fogel, A., & Thelen, E. (1987). Development of early expressive and communicative action: Reinterpreting the evidence from a dynamic systems perspective. *Developmental Psychology*, *23*, 747–761.

Frankel, K. A., & Bates, J. E. (1990). Mother–toddler problem solving: Antecedents in attachment, home behavior, and temperament. *Child Development*, *61*, 810–819.

Fullard, W., McDevitt, S. C., & Carey, W. B. (1984). Assessing temperament in one-to-three-year-old children. *Journal of Pediatric Psychology*, *9*, 205–216.

Gable, S., & Isabella, R. A. (1992). Maternal contributions to infant regulation of arousal. *Infant Behavior and Development*, *15*, 95–107.

García-Coll, C. T., Halpern, L. F., Vohr, B. R., Seifer, R., & Oh, W. (1992). Stability and correlates of change of early temperament in preterm and full-term infants. *Infant Behavior and Development*, *15*, 137–154.

George, C., Kaplan, N., & Main, M. (1985). *Adult attachment interview*. Berkeley, CA: University of California at Berkeley.

Goldsmith, H. H. (1987). *Toddler Behavior Assessment Questionnaire*. Eugene: University of Oregon.

Goldsmith, H. H., Buss, A. H., Plomin, R., Rothbart, M. K., Thomas, A., Chess, S., Hinde, R. A., & McCall, R. B. (1987). Roundtable: What is temperament? Four approaches. *Child Development*, *58*, 505–529.

Goldsmith, H. H., & Campos, J. (1982). Toward a theory of infant temperament. In R. N. Emde & R. J. Harmon (Eds.), *The development of attachment and affiliative systems* (pp. 161–193). New York: Plenum Press.

Goldsmith, H. H., Rieser-Danner, L. A., & Briggs, S. (1991). Evaluating convergent and discriminant validity of temperament questionnaires for preschoolers, toddlers, and infants. *Developmental Psychology*, *27*, 566–579.

Goldsmith, H. H., & Rothbart, M. (1990). *The laboratory temperament assessment battery (Version 1.3; Locomotor Version)*. Eugene: University of Oregon.

Graham, P., Rutter, M., & George, S. (1973). Temperamental characteristics as predictors of behavior disorders in children. *American Journal of Orthopsychiatry*, *43*, 328–339.

Hagekull, B. (1994). Infant temperament and early childhood functioning: Possible relations to the Five-Factor Model. In C. J. Halverson, Jr., G. A. Kohnstamm, & R. P. Martin (Eds.), *The developing structure of temperament and personality* (pp. 277–240). Hillsdale, NJ: Erlbaum.

Hammen, C. (1992). Cognitive, life stress, and interpersonal approaches to a developmental psychopathology model of depression. *Development and Psychopathology*, *4*, 189–206.

Higley, J. D., Mehlman, P. T., Higley, S. B., Fernald, B., Vickers, J., Lindell, S. G., Taub, D. M., Suomi, S. J., & Linnoila, M. (1996). Excessive mortality in young free ranging male nonhuman primates with low cerebrospinal fluid 5-hydroxyindoleacetic acid concentrations. *Archives of General Psychiatry*, *53*, 537–543.

Hinde, R. A. (1982). Attachment: Some conceptual and biological issues. In C. M. Parkes & J. Stevenson-Hinde (Eds.), *The place of attachment in human behavior* (pp. 60–76). New York: Basic Books.

Hubert, N. C., Wachs, T. D., Peters-Martin, P., & Gandour, M. J. (1982). The study of early temperament: Measurement and conceptual issues. *Child Development*, *53*, 571–600.

Isabella, R. A., & Gable, S. (1991, April). *Infant behavior and the origins of infant–mother attachment*. Paper presented at the meeting of the Society for Research in Child Development, Seattle, WA.

Kagan, J. (1998). Biology and the child. In N. Eisenberg (Ed.), *Handbook of child psychology: Social, emotional, and personality development* (5th ed., pp. 117–236). New York: Wiley.

Kagan, J., Resnick, J. S., & Gibbons, J. (1989). Inhibited and uninhibited types of children. *Child Development*, *60*, 838–845.

Keough, B K. (1989). Applying temperament research to school. In G. A. Kohnstamm, J. E. Bates, & M. K. Rothbart (Eds.), *Temperament in childhood* (pp. 451–462). New York: Wiley.

Kochanska, G. (1995). Children's temperament, mothers' discipline, and security of attachment: Multiple pathways to emerging internalization. *Child Development, 66,* 597–615.

Lerner, J. V. (1983). The role of temperament in psychosocial adaptation in early adolescents: A test of a "goodness of fit" model. *Journal of Genetic Psychology, 143,* 149–157.

Lerner, J. V., Lerner, R. M., & Zabski, S. (1985). Temperament and elementary school children's actual and rated academic performance: A test of a "goodness of fit" model. *Journal of Child Psychology and Psychiatry, 26,* 125–136.

Lerner, R. M., Lerner, J. V., Windle, M., Hooker, K., Lenerz, K., & East, P. L. (1986). Children and adolescents in their contexts: Tests of a goodness of fit model. In R. Plomin & J. Dunn (Eds.), *The study of temperament: Changes, continuities, challenges* (pp. 99–114). Hillsdale, NJ: Erlbaum.

Lerner, R. M., Palermo, M., Spiro, A., & Nesselroade, J. R. (1982). Assessing the dimensions of temperamental individuality across the life span: The Dimensions of Temperament Survey (DOTS). *Child Development, 53,* 149–159.

Main, M., & Goldwyn, R. (1988). *Adult attachment classification system (Version 3).* Unpublished manuscript, University of California at Berkeley.

Mangelsdorf, S., Gunnar, M., Kestenbaum, R., Lang, S., & Andreas, D. (1990). Infant proneness-to-distress temperament, maternal personality, and mother–infant attachment: Associations and goodness of fit. *Child Development, 61,* 820–831.

Martin, R. P., Olejnik, S., & Gaddis, L. (1994). Is temperament an important contributor to schooling outcomes in elementary school? Modeling effects of temperament and scholastic ability on academic achievement. In W. B. Carey & S. C. McDevitt (Eds.), *Prevention and early intervention: Individual differences as risk factors for the mental health of children* (pp. 59–68). New York: Brunner/Mazel.

Matas, L., Arend, R. A., & Sroufe, L. A. (1978). Continuity of adaptation in the second year: The relationship between quality of attachment and later competence. *Child Development, 49,* 547–556.

Matheny, A. P. (1989). Temperament and cognition: Relations between temperament and mental test scores. In G. A. Kohnstamm, J. E. Bates, & M. K. Rothbart (Eds.), *Temperament in childhood* (pp. 263–281). New York: Wiley.

Maziade, M. (1989). Should adverse temperament matter to the clinician? An empirically based answer. In G. A. Kohnstamm, J. E. Bates, & M. K. Rothbart (Eds.), *Temperament in childhood* (pp. 421–436). New York: Wiley.

Maziade, M., Caron, C., Cote, R., Boutin, P., & Thivierge, J. (1990). Extreme temperament and diagnosis: A study in a psychiatric sample of consecutive children. *Archives of General Psychiatry, 47,* 477–484.

Maziade, M., Cote, R., Bernier, H., Boutin, P., & Thivierge, J. (1989). Significance of extreme temperament in infancy for clinical status in pre-school years. I: Value of extreme temperament at 4–8 months for predicting diagnosis at 4.7 years. *British Journal of Psychiatry, 154,* 535–543.

McClowry, S. G., Giangrande, S. K., Tommasini, N. R., Clinton, W., Foreman, N. S., Lynch, K., & Ferketich, S. L. (1994). The effects of child temperament, maternal characteristics, and family circumstances on the maladjustment of school-age children. *Research in Nursing and Health, 17,* 25–35.

McDevitt, S. C., & Carey, W. B. (1975). The measurement of temperament in 3–7 year old children. *Journal of Child Psychology and Psychiatry, 19,* 245–253.

Olson, S. L., Bates, J. E., & Bayles, K. (1990). Early antecedents of childhood impulsivity: The role of parent–child interaction, cognitive competence, and temperament. *Journal of Abnormal Child Psychology, 18,* 317–334.

Patterson, G. R. (1982). *Coercive family process.* Eugene, OR: Castalia.

Posada, G., Gao, Y., Wu, F., Posada, R., Tascon, M., Schoelmerich, A., Sagi, A., Kondo-Ikemura, K., Haaland, W., & Synnevaag, B. (1995). The secure-base phenomenon across cultures: Children's behavior, mothers' preferences, and experts' concepts. In E. Waters, B. E. Vaughn, G. Posada, & K. Kondo-Ikemura (Eds.), *Caregiving, cultural, and cognitive perspectives on secure-base behavior and working models: New growing points of attachment theory and research. Monographs of the Society for Research in Child Development, 60* (Serial No. 244), 27–48.

Power, T. G., Gershenhorn, S., & Stafford, D. (1990). Maternal perceptions of infant difficultness: The influence of maternal attitudes and attributions. *Infant Behavior and Development, 13,* 421–437.

Prior, M., Sanson, A., Carroll, R., & Oberklaid, F. (1989). Social class differences in temperament ratings by mothers of preschool children. *Merrill–Palmer Quarterly, 35,* 239–248.

Rosenbaum, J. F., Biederman, J., Gerstern, M., Hirshfeld, D. R., Meminger, S. R., Herman, J. B., Kagan, J., Reznick, J. S., & Snidman, N. (1988). Behavioral inhibition in children of parents with panic disorder and agoraphobia. *Archives of General Psychiatry, 45,* 463–470.

Rothbart, M. K. (1981). Measurement of temperament in infancy. *Child Development, 52,* 569–587.

Rothbart, M. K. (1989). Temperament and development. In G. A. Kohnstamm, J. E. Bates, & M. K. Rothbart (Eds.), *Temperament in childhood* (pp. 187–248). New York: Wiley.

Rothbart, M. K., & Ahadi, S. A. (1994). Temperament and the development of personality. *Journal of Abnormal Psychology, 103,* 55–66.

Rothbart, M. K., Ahadi, S. A., & Hershey, K. L. (1994). Temperament and social behavior in childhood. *Merrill–Palmer Quarterly, 40,* 21–39.

Rothbart, M., & Bates, J. E. (1998). Temperament. In W. Damon (Ed.), *Handbook of child psychology* (5th ed., Vol., 3, pp. 105–176). New York: Wiley.

Rothbart, M. K., & Derryberry, D. (1982). Theoretical issues in temperament. In M. Lewis & L. T. Taft (Eds.), *Developmental disabilities: Theory, assessment, and intervention* (pp. 383–400). New York: Spectrum.

Sameroff, A. J. (1983). Developmental systems: Contexts and evolution. In W. Kessen (Ed.), *Handbook of child psychology: History, theories and method* (4th ed., pp. 237–294). New York: Wiley.

Sameroff, A. J., & Emde, R. N. (1989). *Relationship disturbances in early childhood: A developmental approach.* New York: Basic Books.

Sameroff, A. J., & Seifer, R. (1983). Familial risk and child competence. *Child Development, 54,* 1254–1268.

Sameroff, A. J., Seifer, R., & Elias, P. K. (1982). Sociocultural variability in infant temperament ratings. *Child Development, 53,* 164–171.

Sanson, A. V., Smart, D., Prior, M., & Oberklaid, F. (1993). Precursors of hyperactivity and aggression. *Journal of the American Academy of Child and Adolescent Psychiatry, 32,* 1207–1216.

Schaefer, C., Coyne, J. C., & Lazarus, R. S. (1981). The health-related functions of social support. *Journal of Behavioral Medicine, 4,* 381–406.

Seifer, R. (1996). *Temperament fit, attachment, and depressed mothers.* National Institute of Mental Health Grant R01-MH51301.

Seifer, R., Sameroff, A. J., Barrett, L. C., & Krafchuk, E. (1994). Infant temperament measured by multiple observations and mother report. *Child Development, 65,* 1478–1490.

Seifer, R., & Schiller, M. (1995). The role of parenting sensitivity, infant temperament, and dyadic interaction in attachment theory and assessment. In E. Waters, B. E. Vaughn, G. Posada, & K. Kondo-Ikemura (Eds.), Caregiving, cultural, and cognitive perspectives on secure-base behavior and working models: New growing points of attachment theory and research. *Monographs of the Society for Research in Child Development, 60* (Serial No. 244), 146–174.

Spangler, G. (1990). Mother, child, and situational correlates of toddlers' social competence. *Infant Behavior and Development, 13,* 405–419.

Sprunger, L. W., Boyce, W. T., & Gaines, J. A. (1985). Family–infant congruence: Routines and rhythmicity in family adaptation to a young infant. *Child Development, 56,* 564–572.

Sroufe, L. A., & Waters, E. (1977). Attachment as an organizational construct. *Child Development, 48,* 1184–1199.

Suomi, S. J. (1997). Early determinants of behavior: Evidence from primate studies. *British Medical Bulletin, 53,* 170–184.

Super, C. M., & Harkness, S. (1986). Temperament, development, and culture. In R. Pluming & J. Dunn (Eds.), *The study of temperament: Changes, continuities and challenges* (pp. 131–149). Hillsdale, NJ: Erlbaum.

Thomas, A., & Chess, S. (1977). *Temperament and development.* New York: Brunner/Mazel.

Thomas, A., Chess, S., & Birch, H. G. (1968). *Temperament and behavior disorders in children.* New York: New York University Press.

Thomas, A., Chess, S., Birch, H. G., Hertzig, M. E., & Korn, S. (1963). *Behavioral individuality in early childhood.* New York: New York University Press.

Tronick, E. Z. (1989). Emotions and emotional communication in infants. *American Psychologist, 44,* 112–119.

Vaughn, B. E., Bradley, C. F., Joffe, L. S., Seifer, R., & Barglow, P. (1987). Maternal characteristics measured prenatally predict ratings of temperamental "difficulty" on the Carey Infant Temperament Questionnaire. *Developmental Psychology, 23,* 152–161.

Vaughn, B. E., Taraldson, B. J., Crichton, L., & Egeland, B. (1981). The assessment of infant temperament: A critique of the Carey Infant Temperament Questionnaire. *Infant Behavior and Development, 4,* 1–17.

Wallander, J. L., Hubert, N. C., & Varni, J. W. (1988). Child and maternal temperament characteristics, goodness of fit, and adjustment in physically handicapped children. *Journal of Clinical Child Psychology, 17,* 336–344.

Waters, E. (1995). The Attachment Q-Set. In E. Waters, B. E. Vaughn, G. Posada, & K. Kondo-Ikemura (Eds.), Caregiving, cultural, and cognitive perspectives on secure-base behavior and working models: New growing points of attachment theory and research. *Monographs of the Society for Research in Child Development, 60* (Serial No. 244), 234–246.

Waters, E., & Sroufe, L. A. (1983). Social competence as a developmental construct. *Developmental Review, 3,* 79–97.

Zeanah, C. H., Keener, M. A., Stewart, L., & Anders, T. F. (1985). Prenatal perception of infant personality: A preliminary investigation. *Journal of the American Academy of Child and Adolescent Psychiatry, 24,* 204–210.

15

Chronic Medical Conditions

Impact on Development

Gregory K. Fritz and Elizabeth L. McQuaid

The past decade has seen a marked increase in recognition of both the degree to which chronic medical conditions affect the psychological functioning of children and adolescents, and the complexity of these interactions. The inclusion of the present chapter in the second edition of this book reflects the growing awareness of the impact of illness and psychopathology on psychological development. In the sections that follow, we review the definitions, methodological issues, and conceptual approaches to considering chronic pediatric problems, from which follow prevalence data that indicate the scope of the problem. We review available evidence on the association of psychopathology, psychological symptoms, and adjustment problems with chronic medical conditions. Theoretical, clinical, and empirical data form the basis for a discussion of the impact of chronic conditions on specific developmental stages. Finally, we discuss conceptual models that usefully integrate potentially confounding issues in the field and point the way for future research efforts.

A comprehensive consideration of all the topics relevant to psychosocial aspects of pediatric chronic illness is beyond the scope of this chapter. The impact of illness on parents and siblings; particular issues regarding the dying child; ethical, legal, and policy issues affecting chronically ill children; the full range of identified and potential psychopathology mechanisms; and problems and solutions regarding psychological assessment in the medically ill are highly relevant. The reader is referred to several comprehensive monographs that deal with these topics (Pless & Pinkerton, 1975; Stein, 1988).

Gregory K. Fritz and Elizabeth L. McQuaid • Child and Family Psychiatry, Brown University School of Medicine, Rhode Island Hospital, Providence, Rhode Island 02903.

Handbook of Developmental Psychopathology, Second Edition, edited by Arnold J. Sameroff, Michael Lewis, and Suzanne M. Miller. Kluwer Academic / Plenum Publishers, New York, 2000.

DEFINITIONS

"Illness," "disease," "disorder," "disability," and "medical condition" are often used interchangeably despite subtle differences in meaning. The Research Consortium on Chronic Illness in Childhood advocates the use of "condition" as the most neutral and encompassing term, avoiding the implication that active symptoms are necessary (as an "illness" or "disease") or (as in "handicap" or "disability") that a deficit or incapacity is inevitable (Perrin et al., 1993).

Chronic illnesses, having a duration of 3 months or more, are distinguished from acute illnesses in several important ways. With an acute illness, the *diagnostic process* is of primary importance and consumes considerable energy, in contrast to a chronic illness, where the diagnosis typically was made some time earlier. An acute illness is assumed to be *curable* in a time frame of days to weeks, whereas a chronic illness is expected to be *managed* over months to years. With an acute illness such as pneumonia or appendicitis, children and their parents expect to *delegate the caretaking responsibilities* to the medical system, whereas parents and children with chronic conditions often gain considerable expertise and assume significant management responsibility. While these differences are important and seem readily apparent, the medical system has long been based on the acute care model. This is reflected in medical training, where residents rotate on a monthly basis (to the dismay of chronically ill patients), in the preponderance of cross-sectional research when longitudinal studies are needed, and in the way medical funding fails to deal with "preexisting conditions." Although the medical system is gradually changing, the problems of fitting a chronic condition into a system with an acute care focus present additional challenges to affected children and their families.

In the past, children were identified as having a chronic health condition through the use of diagnostic lists: If their specific condition was on the list, they were included in public programs, educational efforts, and research protocols. Such an approach was criticized for being arbitrary, inevitably incomplete, inequitable, prone to bias, and promoting fragmentation. Stein and Jessop (1989) have proposed an alternative, "noncategorical" framework in which children with various conditions are considered together and grouped across, rather than within diagnostic categories with regard to psychological and social aspects of their chronic conditions. This approach recognizes the common experiences associated with having a chronic illness, no matter what the specific condition. It permits the inclusion of children with rare or difficult-to-define conditions, encourages the design of inclusive programs, and minimizes competition for resources. Recognizing the considerable variation in how individual children are affected even within a particular illness category, Perrin et al. (1993) have advocated applying a broad, noncategorical approach initially and then evaluating a number of dimensions with regard to their impact on a given child, as summarized in Table 15.1. This two-step evaluation maximizes the benefits of both the categorical and noncategorical approaches, while minimizing artificial distinctions.

Clearly, each of these variables cannot be examined and controlled for in every study. Acknowledging their relevance adds complexity to an already challenging area. If researchers collectively consider these variables in detail, however, progress will be made toward a comprehensive understanding of how chronic medical conditions affect the developing child.

EPIDEMIOLOGY

The prevalence of chronic illness within the pediatric population is a subject open to considerable debate. Depending on the definitions applied (severity threshold, whether psychi-

TABLE 15.1. Dimensions of Chronic Medical Conditions in Children

A. Duration	Brief	Lengthy
B. Age of onset	Congenial	Acquired
C. Limitation of activities	None	Unable to conduct
D. Visibility	Not visible	Highly visible
E. Expected survival	Usual longevity	Immediate threat to life
F. Mobility	Not impaired	Extremely impaired
G. Physiological functioning	Not impaired	Extremely impaired
H. Cognition	Normal	Extremely impaired
I. Emotional/social	Normal	Extremely impaired
J. Sensory functioning	Not impaired	Extremely impaired
K. Communication	Not impaired	Extremely impaired
L. Course	Stable	Progressive
M. Uncertainty	Episodic	Predictable
N. Stigma	None	Extremely stigmatized
O. Pain	Painless	Extremely painful

SOURCE: Modified from Perrin et al. (1993).

atric disorders are included, etc.), the assessment methods employed (parental reports, multiple informants, medical records) and whether the study is population based or clinic based, published prevalence rates vary from less than 5% to more than 30% (Cadman, Boyle, Szatmari, & Offord, 1987; Pless & Roghman, 1971; Stewart, 1967). Chronic health conditions in children are increasing, largely due to more careful diagnosis and improved treatment resulting in longer survival. For example, children with cystic fibrosis now live more than seven times longer than they did in 1950, and lymphocytic leukemia, nearly always fatal in 1970, now has the expectation of over 80% survival at 5 years (Gortmaker & Sappenfield, 1984). Newacheck and Taylor (1992) studied data from 17,110 children in the 1988 National Health Interview Survey. As summarized in Table 15.2, 31% of children under 18 years of age were affected by chronic health conditions. When severity is considered, 20% of the population have mild conditions that result in little or no bother or activity limitation, 9% have conditions of moderate severity, and 2% have severe conditions associated with frequent bother and limitation of activity.

The degree to which a chronic medical condition constitutes a risk factor for childhood psychopathology or adjustment problems is of considerable importance for mental health professionals and policymakers. Unfortunately, even after a number of years of interest in this issue and many studies and articles on the subject, findings remain contradictory and firm answers are elusive. The same methodological problems that make it complicated to define the prevalence of chronic illnesses in childhood, when combined with the difficulties in psychiatric diagnosis and the assessment of behavior problems, result in contradictory reports of psychosocial morbidity among chronically ill children. For example, several studies (Breslau, 1985; Drotar et al., 1981; Tavormina, Kastner, Slater, & Watt, 1976) have reported little or no increased risk in psychopathology. However, these studies have all been based in tertiary care centers, where access to comprehensive services may negate much of the risk associated with the condition. Other studies are hard to interpret because chronically ill children are compared to norms for a particular instrument rather than appropriate controls.

TABLE 15.2. Prevalence of Childhood Chronic Conditions
in Cases for 1,000 by Age and Gender

Condition	Overall $N = 5,332$	Age		Gender	
		Under 10 years	10 to 17 years	Boys	Girls
All children with chronic conditions	307.60	302.20	315.00	326.20	288.20
Impairments					
Musculoskeletal impairments	15.20	10.90	20.90	16.70	13.60
Deafness and hearing loss	15.30	14.10	17.00	18.30	12.30
Blindness and vision impairment	12.70	10.30	16.00	11.40	14.20
Speech defects	26.20	31.60	18.90	35.30	16.70
Cerebral palsy	1.80	2.20	1.2*	2.00	1.5*
Diseases					
Diabetes	1.00	0.6*	1.5*	1.50	0.5*
Sickle-cell disease	1.20	1.3*	0.9*	0.9*	1.40
Anemia	8.80	11.00	5.80	8.40	9.10
Asthma	42.50	39.30	46.80	50.70	33.90
Respiratory allergies	96.80	71.80	130.30	106.50	86.70
Eczema and skin allergies	32.90	31.10	35.20	30.10	35.80
Epilepsy and seizures	2.40	1.7*	3.30	1.7*	3.10
Arthritis	4.60	1.5*	8.70	4.20	4.90
Heart disease	15.20	13.60	17.40	16.40	13.90
Frequent or repeated ear infection	83.40	120.60	33.60	88.50	79.10
Frequent diarrhea/bowel trouble	17.10	22.60	9.60	18.10	15.90
Digestive allergies	22.30	23.20	21.10	25.60	18.90
Frequent or severe headaches	25.30	9.90	45.80	22.80	27.90
Other	19.80	12.10	30.00	19.30	20.30

SOURCE: Original tabulations of the 1988 National Health Interview Survey. Modified from Newacheck and Taylor (1992).
*Standard error exceeds 30% of estimate value.

Several population-based studies are available that show substantially increased risks for psychosocial morbidity in children with chronic medical conditions. The work by Cadman et al. (1987) from the Ontario Child Health Study is illustrative. A modified version of the Child Behavior Checklist was administered by interview to parents, teachers, and children (those over 12 years of age). Data on the sample of 3,294 children ages 4–16 are summarized in Table 15.3. Clearly, children with disability resulting from their chronic illness are, as a group, at heightened risk for diagnosable psychopathology and for social and school problems. Children without associated disability are at lower but still increased risk compared to healthy children. While this study is not methodologically perfect (assessment of over 3,000 children was, of necessity, relatively brief; some DSM-IV diagnoses were not considered, etc.) and is far from the "final answer" (relationships between type of illness, duration, and specific psychosocial problems were not addressed), it is consistent with earlier population-based studies in demonstrating a heightened association between chronic medical conditions and children's mental health or adjustment problems.

Lavigne and Faier-Routman (1992) conducted a meta-analytic review of 87 studies of children's adjustment to a variety of physical disorders. They concluded that children with chronic medical conditions are at increased risk for overall adjustment problems, including both internalizing and externalizing symptoms, with a mean change in effect sizes of approximately one standard deviation. Studies of children's self-concept were more variable, but

TABLE 15.3. Odds Ratios (Age- and Sex-Adjusted) for Specific Problems in Chronically Ill Compared to Health Children

Disorder or problem	Children with chronic illness and disability	Children with chronic illness alone
Neurosis	4.7	2.2
Conduct disorder	2.5	2.2
ADHD	5.1	2.2
Any psychiatric disorder	3.4	2.1
Isolated child	5.4	1.4
Peer difficulties	1.9	1.1
Low participation	1.8	0.9
Low competence	5.5	1.4
Repeated grade/remediation	2.9	1.4
Not doing well at school	4.7	1.3

SOURCE: Modified from Cadman et al. (1987).

across all studies, the children with chronic medical conditions had significantly lower self-concept than healthy children. For all outcome variables, the magnitude of the risk varied by informant (parent, teacher, mental health professional), and the authors cited a lack of studies using structured interviews with the children themselves as a glaring omission in the literature.

Granting that despite methodological shortcomings, the available empirical data confirm an overall increased risk of psychopathology and adjustment problems associated with chronic illness, questions arise as to what specific factors are associated with the increased risk. There is consistent evidence that conditions affecting the brain itself are more problematic in terms of adjustment than other conditions. This has been demonstrated in children with head injuries (Brown, Chadwick, Shaffer, Rutter, & Traub, 1981), epilepsy (Hoare, 1984), and leukemia treated with cranial irradiation (Sawyer, Toogood, Rice, Haskell, & Baghurst, 1986). However, various other physiological variables that may moderate behavioral outcomes have been largely ignored (Gortmaker, Walker, Weitzman, & Sobol, 1990). Results are contradictory in the few areas that have been examined. For example, early research in pediatric asthma suggested that the absence of allergies might be a marker for psychological vulnerability (Block, Jennings, Harvey, & Simpson, 1964). This distinction between "extrinsic" (environmentally triggered) and "intrinsic" (nonallergic asthma) persists to date despite greater understanding of the multifactorial etiology of asthma. However, recent genetic research has linked allergy to increased risk of behavior problems in children (Wamboldt & Schmitz, 1998). Clearly, the complicated interplay between physiological disease variables and behavioral outcomes requires further investigation and may lead to a greater understanding of the mechanisms underlying both.

Despite the commonsense appeal of the concept that more severe conditions are associated with greater psychosocial dysfunction, study results are also contradictory. In pediatric asthma, for example, more severe asthma has been (1) associated with poorer social competence and more behavior problems (MacLean, Perrin, Gortmaker, & Pierre, 1992); (2) found to have no relationship with psychopathology and self-concept (Kashani, Kovig, Shepperd, Wilfley, & Morris, 1988); and (3) part of a bimodal distribution (with mild asthma) associated with worse adaptation compared to moderate asthma (Perrin, MacLean, & Perrin, 1989).

The concept of marginality, in which mild or marginally affected individuals have more psychosocial impairment that moderately or even severely affected individuals, has been supported in studies of children with hemophilia, hearing loss, thalidomide deformities, and other physical defects (Midence, 1994). This phenomenon can be understood in several ways. Children who are marginally affected by an illness or disability may try to "pass" as un-affected, keeping their problem a secret and not making even small accommodations to their condition. The sense of isolation as well as self-criticism and frustration when the conditions prevent full function may lead to social or psychological difficulties. If adults in the child's life (teachers, coaches, neighbors, as well as parents) make no acknowledgments or necessary allowances for a mild condition, the child may experience insensitivity and inappropriate expectations. Other evidence suggests that it is the subjective experience of severity on the part of affected children and/or their parents rather than objectively determined severity that is most strongly related to psychosocial adaptation. Clearly, the relationship between illness severity and psychological functioning is complicated, depending to a great extent on whether functioning is assessed via direct observation, on child interview or parent report, and on how severity is defined.

PHYSICAL ILLNESS AND DEVELOPMENT STAGES

In the section that follows, we provide general guidelines regarding the developmental issues that may exert influence on the link between physical illness and behavioral functioning in childhood. A more comprehensive review of this topic can be found in Garrison and McQuiston (1989).

Infancy and Toddlerhood

Critical developmental tasks during infancy include the development of attachment rela-tionships to caretaking adults and the integration of various regulatory systems such as motoric activity, autonomic regulation, and arousal. Significant medical difficulties during this period pose risk for the disruption of these developmental tasks. For premature infants, motoric development and autonomic regulation may be compromised by physiological and neurologi-cal immaturity and associated dysfunction. The aversive and intrusive level of stimulation required for basic survival, especially in the intensive care nursery, adds additional challenges to the development of biobehavioral regulation. As the infant begins to recognize the consis-tency of the individuals in his or her world, an acute medical crisis requiring hospitalization can challenge the development of a stable attachment relationship.

For older infants and toddlers, the development of social relationships and trust can be challenged by the experience of the separation from parents and exposure to painful medical procedures associated with physical illness (Brown, Fritz, & Herzog, 1997). A review of young children's reactions to hospitalization and illness indicates that the reaction to hospital-ization is most marked for children between the ages of 1 and 4 years (Theut & Mrazek, 1997). At this age, separation from parents can result in continual crying, apprehensive behavior toward adults, and a variety of somatic symptoms. Previously attained milestones, such as toilet training, may fall victim to regression in the face of the stress of hospitalization.

Pediatric feeding disorders represent an example of a disruption of normative develop-mental sequence that can be caused by neuromuscular, metabolic, skeletal, and/or psycho-social dysfunction (Palmer & Horn, 1978). Dysfunctional parent–child interactions at meal-times can develop subsequent to physiological vulnerability such as esophageal lesions or hypotonia from chronic neurological conditions (Babbitt et al., 1994). In their attempts to coax children to eat, parents may inadvertently reinforce negative behavior, such as food refusal. These patterns may persist during or even after basic causes for the feeding problem have been addressed through medical intervention. Early behavioral intervention can often have a significant impact on behavioral patterns and subsequent weight gain. However, if untreated, more severe cases of feeding disorders place children at risk for multiple poor outcomes, including malnutrition, retarded growth, and impaired intellectual and social development (Budd, McGraw, & Farbisz, 1992).

Acute or severe chronic illness in young children can also pose challenges for new parents (Theut & Mrazek, 1997), who may face numerous stressors, including financial challenges, disruptions in regular routines, and fluctuating perceptions of their child's health. The need to monitor physical symptoms, arrange extra visits to the physician, and provide special care can engender feelings of loss and grief. Early perceptions of their child as "fragile" can lay the groundwork for later dysfunctional family patterns, inhibiting parents from allowing their child sufficient autonomy and independence.

As children grow through toddlerhood toward early school age, developmental tasks include increased socialization outside the family and the development of appropriate behavioral inhibition. At this stage, chronic illness and repeated hospitalizations may impair early socialization. Restriction of children's participation in play activities with siblings and peers can deprive them of the opportunity to learn the skills necessary to negotiate early social interactions. Misbehavior, which often emerges at this stage, can interfere with regular disease management, such as in the child who continually scratches due to atopic dermatitis despite parent protests, or the preschooler who refuses to cooperate with regular insulin injections. Parental misguided beliefs that "the poor child is too sick" to have behavioral limits imposed may inadvertently worsen the misbehavior.

School-Age Children

For school-age children, key developmental tasks include the achievement of age-appropriate academic goals and the establishment of peer relationships. There is some evidence to suggest that school and academic achievement are more likely to be affected in younger children with medical conditions compared to adolescents (Rovet, Ehrlich, & Hoppe, 1987). As was evident in the previous epidemiological review, despite increased risk, the majority of children with chronic illnesses do not have significant intellectual impairments. However, the risk of intellectual impairment and/or learning difficulties is increased for children with diseases involving the central nervous system (CNS), such as seizure disorder, spina bifida, neurofibromatosis, and pediatric AIDS (Eiser, 1990; Hobbs, Perrin, & Ireys, 1985). Even diseases not commonly thought of as having substantial neurological involvement, such as diabetes and sickle-cell disease, may have subtle neuropsychological sequelae (Brown, Armstrong, & Eckman, 1993; Rovet et al., 1987). For illnesses requiring certain types of treatment, such as CNS irradiation for cancer, the treatments themselves may have enduring side effects such as slowed cognitive processing and specific learning disabilities (MacLean et al., 1995).

The restriction of children's various activities due to illness, and frequent absences from school due to illness and hospitalization, have important implications for the development of social competence. In researching the associations between chronic illness, school absences, and behavioral adjustment, Stein and Jessop (1984) found moderate, but significant associations between psychological adjustment and number of days absent from school. Traditional measures of functional impairment (such as days hospitalized) were not found to be related to adjustment. These findings suggest that school absence due to illness may be a risk factor for increased difficulties in behavioral adjustment. However, survey research by Wallander, Varni, Babani, Banis, and Wilcox (1988) demonstrated that although children with chronic conditions may be able to participate in fewer activities, their mothers do not report that the children have fewer friends than healthy children. The relationships between disease severity, school adjustment, and social competence in children with acute and chronic illness clearly merit further investigation.

Adolescents

During adolescence, acute and chronic medical conditions can challenge the development of autonomy, development of peer and romantic relationships, and the consolidation of a positive self-image. During a time in which they are beginning to establish independence from parents, adolescents with medical conditions often find themselves dependent on adults for medical care, instrumental aid, and emotional support.

Clinical examples and research findings indicate that the assumption of responsibilities for medical treatment (such as taking medications, monitoring symptoms) is an area in which many adolescents experience particular difficulty. Research on diabetes demonstrates that although parents begin to withdraw responsibility for illness management as children reach adolescence, adolescents do not necessarily begin to assume more responsibility for their own self-care (Ingersoll, Orr, Herrold, & Golden, 1986). Adherence to medical regimens has been shown to decline in adolescence in a number of different conditions, including diabetes (Bond, Aiken, & Somerville, 1992; Hanson, Henggeler, & Burghen, 1990), cancer (Dolgin, Klatz, Doctors, & Siegel, 1986; Tebbi et al., 1986), and asthma (Christiaanse, Lavigne, & Lerner, 1989). Clinical interpretation of these data suggest that adolescents with medical conditions may exert their growing independence in ways that are potentially life threatening, such as the teenager with asthma who smokes despite repeated warnings not to do so.

Adolescence is a time of rapid physical and sexual maturation. Delays in physical development, disfigurement due to illness, or side effects of treatment, such as hair loss, may exacerbate feelings of self-consciousness in adolescents with medical conditions. The development of romantic and sexual relationships may be challenged by concerns regarding body integrity. Some research indicates that adolescent body image may be affected by the existence of certain chronic illnesses. Morgan and Jackson (1986) found that, in comparison to matched controls, adolescents with sickle-cell anemia (SCA) reported less satisfaction with their bodies. In a similar study, Zeltzer, Kellerman, Ellerberg, Dash, and Rigler (1980) found that adolescents with cancer and rheumatological diseases had more body-image concerns than did adolescents with diabetes.

Although specific difficulties in adherence and body-image disturbance have been demonstrated in adolescents with medical conditions, studies investigating global indices of social adjustment and self-esteem have yielded conflicting findings. Although some research on specific conditions has demonstrated lower self-esteem and impaired adjustment (e.g., in SCA; Morgan & Jackson, 1986), much of the well-controlled research indicates that adolescents with medical conditions do not have lowered self-esteem compared to healthy controls (McAnarney, 1985). Research in diabetes has indicated that adolescents may utilize different methods of coping with illness than younger children. In a study comparing coping strategies in latency-age children and adolescents with diabetes, Band (1990) found that adolescents were more likely to use secondary control coping (i.e., adjusting to circumstances as they are, as opposed to trying to directly change stressful conditions). Such findings indicate that the emergence of more sophisticated cognitive strategies during adolescence may serve to facilitate adaptation to disease.

THEORETICAL MODELS

As demonstrated by the studies outlined earlier in this review, much of the extant literature on illness and psychological adjustment in children has addressed global epidemiological questions, such as whether children with chronic medical conditions are at increased risk for psychiatric disorder (e.g., Cadman et al., 1987; Gortmaker et al., 1990). Although such studies have provided general information regarding the adjustment difficulties encountered by these children, from the data provided, one can only generate hypotheses regarding the mechanisms accounting for these associations. However, over the past several decades, theoreticians have utilized the rich information resulting from clinical work with these families to propose theoretical models to explain the complex relations among disease type, illness severity, and patterns of individual and family adaptation. A brief overview of these models and the empirical data available for their support are presented below.

Individual Psychosomatic Models

Early theorists working in the fields of psychology, psychiatry, and medicine viewed certain disease as arising from specific individual variables (e.g., Alexander, 1950) or particular personality types as concordant with certain illnesses (Dunbar, 1954). From this perspective, illness was seen as an expression of underlying psychological conflict, or as arising from predisposing personality type. For example, in one classic study, Grace and Graham (1952) utilized clinical interviews to assess the relation of specific attitudes to particular diseases. They linked particular attitudes (e.g., an individual's sense that "he must be constantly prepared to meet all threats") to specific physical conditions (e.g., arterial hypertension).

These models were groundbreaking attempts to address the integration of psychological and physiological factors in disease adaptation. Their ongoing influence can be seen in the current conceptualizations of certain disorders. For example, research in asthma has assessed the existence of a "panic–fear" dimension of personality that is thought to affect rates of health care utilization and health management behavior (Kinsman, Dirks, & Jones, 1982). Similarly, Dunbar's theories regarding "the ulcer personality" and "the arthritic personality" are seen as predecessors to the "Type A" personality that is at increased risk for high blood pressure and cardiac arrest (Brown et al., 1997). However, these theories were largely based on individual models of development and proposed a unidirectional model in which individual factors of personality influenced illness.

Family Systems Models

Conceptualizations of familial response to childhood illness have been largely influenced by systems models of family functioning (Minuchin et al., 1975). These models have their roots in clinical observations of families with chronically ill children and thus often emphasize more dysfunctional patterns of adaptation to illness. The most well-known of these theories is Minuchin's classic model of the "psychosomatic family," which arises from a physiological vulnerability (predisposition to illness) on the part of the child, a certain kind of family organization, and the involvement of the ill child in regulating patterns of parental conflict. Patterns of symptom expression interact with individual and family behavior to maintain family "homeostasis." These patterns in turn have influence on the expression of disease symptoms and illness behavior in the child.

Minuchin's model was revolutionary in that it posed a framework for understanding levels of reciprocal influence between biological and familial factors in illness adaptation. Despite its compelling clinical significance, it has been difficult to evaluate and validate empirically. Subsequent critiques by Coyne and Anderson (1988, 1989) and Wood (1993) note the model's emphasis on family dysfunction, the lack of testable hypotheses that arise from the model, and the inadequate empirical validation of the constructs. Coyne and Anderson (1989) further outline the pitfalls of misapplying the "psychosomatic family" model in discussing its implications for families in which a child has diabetes that is difficult to control even with a logical insulin regimen and dietary recommendations. By utilizing a model that emphasizes maladaptive family interactions, it is possible for clinicians to miss physiological differences in the ability to achieve metabolic control and to underestimate the role of overall family dysfunction in illness management.

Coyne and Anderson (1989) propose a model that integrates variations in medical functioning as well as family functioning independent of illness, which contribute to disease adaptation. This serves to contextualize the family's functioning within the acknowledged demands of chronic illness. For example, in diabetes, the family's premorbid functioning and attempts to adapt to the complex demands of the illness are considered key elements in predicting adjustment to illness. Coyne and Anderson also note that new research regarding certain physiological variables, such as insulin resistance during puberty, calls for some reinterpretation of the "psychosomatic family" model initially proposed by Minuchin and colleagues.

Similarly, Kazak's (1989) systems and social–ecological approach builds on many of the strengths of the original Minuchin et al. (1975) model in its conceptualization of family adaptation to disease. From the systems perspective, changes in one family member (such as a chronic illness) affect all members of the system. Adjustments are then made by various members that result in homeostasis, or stability. This model's additional emphasis on the child and family within various social–ecological contexts, such as the neighborhood, school, and community, distinguish it from prior family-based models. This conceptualization allows for the generation of testable hypotheses regarding family functioning, such as the potential for social and community supports to buffer family adaptation to illness.

Biopsychosocial Models

Family systems models represent significant advancements over individual psycho-somatic models in their representation of multiple levels of reciprocal influences on adaptation. However, perhaps due to their foundation in psychological principles, they often fail to describe fully physiological factors that may influence child functioning and family interactions.

More recently, a few theorists have proposed integrating genetic and biological factors into their conceptualizations of child and family adjustment to illness. For example, Wood

(1993) proposes a "biobehavioral family model" of pediatric illness, in which biological, psychological, and social processes are seen as reciprocal and interactive. Central to this model is the construct of "responsivity," which is seen as the strength with which an individual responds to physiological stimuli, and the intensity with which family members respond to one another. Similarly, Creer and colleagues' "transactional model of asthma" integrates biological, emotional, and neuroimmunological factors on both disease outcome and psychological adjustment (Creer, Stein, Rappaport, & Lewis, 1992).

Models such as these draw on research findings regarding individual responsivity to stress and the impact of individual physiological variables on health outcomes. The integration of individual physiological factors, such as patterns of reactivity to stress, adds a new dimension to prior models that accounts for individual variation in response to illness. Biobehavioral models allow for explicit hypotheses regarding the interrelationships among biology, temperament, and family in predicting adaptation to illness.

CONCLUSIONS

Substantial progress has been made in recent years regarding the epidemiology of chronic pediatric disorders in relation to psychological development. Theoretical models to explain the complex interactions among physiological, familial, and temperamental factors have been posed. Recent conceptualizations have evolved to integrate individual physiological factors, such as reactivity to stress in autonomic and immune systems, thereby adding an important dimension that may account for individual variations in response to illness. Challenges for the future include refining the mechanisms for interaction and bringing complex developmental perspectives more fully to bear on the study of children with physical conditions.

REFERENCES

Alexander, F. G. (1950). *Psychosomatic medicine, its principles and applications*. New York: Norton.

Babbitt, R. L., Hoch, T. A., Coe, D. A., Cataldo, M. F., Kelly, K. J., Stackhouse, C., & Perman, J. A. (1994). Behavioral assessment and treatment of pediatric feeding disorders. *Developmental and Behavioral Pediatrics, 15*, 278–291.

Band, E. B. (1990). Children's coping with diabetes: Understanding the role of cognitive development. *Journal of Pediatric Psychology, 15*, 27–41.

Block, J., Jennings, P. H., Harvey, E., & Simpson, E. (1964). Interaction between allergic potential and psychopathology in childhood asthma. *Psychosomatic Medicine, 26*, 307–320.

Bond, G. G., Aiken, L. S., & Somerville, S. C. (1992). The health belief model and adolescents with insulin-dependent diabetes mellitus. *Health Psychology, 11*, 190–198.

Breslau, N. (1985). Psychiatric disorder in children with physical disabilities. *Journal of the American Academy of Child and Adolescent Psychiatry, 24*, 87–94.

Brown, R. T., Armstrong, F. D., & Eckman, J. R. (1993). Neurocognitive aspects of pediatric sickle-cell disease. *Journal of Learning Disabilities, 26*, 33–45.

Brown, G. Chadwick, O., Shaffer, D., Rutter, M., & Traub, M. (1981). A retrospective study of children with head injuries: III. Psychiatric sequelae. *Psychological Medicine, 11*, 63–78.

Brown, L. K., Fritz, G. K., & Herzog, D. B. (1997). Psychosomatic disorders. In J. W. Wiener (Ed.), *Textbook of child and adolescent psychiatry* (pp. 621–633). Washington, DC: American Psychiatric Press.

Budd, K. S., McGraw, T. E., & Farbisz, R. (1992). Psychosocial concomitants of children's feeding disorders. *Journal of Pediatric Psychology, 17*, 81–94.

Cadman, D., Boyle, M., Szatmari, P., & Offord, D. R. (1987). Chronic illness, disability and mental and social well-being: Finding of the child health study. *Pediatrics, 79*, 805–813.

Christiaanse, M. E., Lavigne, J. V., & Lerner, C. V. (1989). Psychosocial aspects of compliance in children and adolescents with asthma. *Developmental and Behavioral Pediatrics, 10*, 75–80.

Coyne, J. C., & Anderson, B. J. (1988). The "psychosomatic family" reconsidered: Diabetes in context. *Journal of Marital and Family Therapy, 14,* 113–123.

Coyne, J. C., & Anderson, B. J. (1989). The "psychosomatic family" reconsidered: II. Recalling a defective model and looking ahead. *Journal of Marital and Family Therapy, 15,* 139–148.

Creer, T. L., Stein, R. E. K., Rappaport, L., & Lewis, C. (1992). Behavioral consequences of illness: Childhood asthma as a model. *Pediatrics, 90,* 808–815.

Dolgin, M. J., Katz, E. R., Doctors, S. R., & Siegel, S. E. (1986). Caregivers' perceptions of medical compliance in adolescents with cancer. *Journal of Adolescent Health Care, 7,* 22–27.

Drotar, D., Doershuk, C. F., Stern, R. C., Boat, T. F., Boyer, W., & Mattheus, L. (1981). Psychosocial function of children with cystic fibrosis. *Pediatrics, 67,* 338–342.

Dunbar, F. (1954). *Emotions and bodily changes.* New York: Columbia University Press.

Eiser, C. (1990). Psychological effects of chronic disease. *Journal of Child Psychology and Psychiatry, 31,* 85–98.

Garrison, W. T., & McQuiston, S. (1989). *Chronic illness during childhood and adolescence: Psychological aspects.* Beverly Hills, CA: Sage.

Gortmaker, S. L., & Sappenfield, W. (1984). Chronic childhood disorders: Prevalence and impact. *Pediatric Clinics of North America, 31,* 3–18.

Gortmaker, S. L., Walker, D. K., Weitzman, M., & Sobol, M. A. (1990). Chronic conditions, socioeconomic risks and behavioral problems in children and adolescents. *Pediatrics, 85,* 267–276.

Grace, W. J., & Graham, D. T. (1952). Relationship of specific attitudes and emotions to certain bodily diseases. *Psychosomatic Medicine, 14,* 243–251.

Hanson, C. L., Henggeler, S. W., & Burghen, G. A. (1990). Social competence and parental support as mediators of the link between stress and metabolic control in adolescents with insulin dependent diabetes mellitus. *Journal of Consulting and Clinical Psychology, 55,* 529–533.

Hoare, P. (1984). The development of psychiatric disorder among school children with epilepsy. *Developmental Medicine and Child Neurology, 26,* 3–13.

Hobbs, N., Perrin, J. M., & Ireys, H. T. (1985). *Chronically ill children and their families.* San Francisco: Jossey-Bass.

Ingersoll, G. M., Orr, D. P., Herrold, A. J., & Golden, M. P. (1986). Cognitive maturity and self-management among adolescents with insulin-dependent diabetes mellitus. *Behavioral Pediatrics, 108,* 620–623.

Kashani, J. H., Konig, P., Shepperd, J. A., Wilfley, D., & Morris, D. A. (1988). Psychopathology and self-concept in asthmatic children. *Journal of Pediatric Psychology, 13,* 509–520.

Kazak, A. E. (1989). Families of chronically ill children: A systems and social–ecological model of adaptation and challenge. *Journal of Consulting and Clinical Psychology, 57,* 25–30.

Kinsman, R. A., Dirks, J. F., & Jones, N. (1982). Psychomaintenance of chronic physical illness: Clinical assessment of personal styles affecting medical management. In T. Millon, C. Grew, & R. Meagler (Eds.), *Handbook of clinical health psychology* (pp. 435–466). New York: Plenum Press.

Lavigne, J. V., & Faier-Routman, J. (1992). Psychological adjustment to pediatric physical disorders: A meta-analytic review. *Journal of Pediatric Psychology, 17,* 133–157.

MacLean, W. E., Noll, R. B., Stehbens, J. A., Kaleita, T. A., Schwartz, E., Whitt, J. K., Cantor, N. L., Waskerwitz, M., Ruymann, R., & Novak, L. J. (1995). Neuropsychological effects of cranial irradiation in young children with acute lymphoblastic leukemia nine months after diagnosis. *Archives of Neurology, 52,* 156–160.

MacLean, W. E., Perrin, J. M., Gortmaker, S., & Pierre, C. B. (1992). Psychological adjustment of children with asthma: Effects of illness severity and recent life events. *Journal of Pediatric Psychology, 17,* 159–171.

McAnarney, E. R. (1985). Social maturation: A challenge for handicapped and chronically ill adolescents. *Journal of Adolescent Health Care, 6,* 90–101.

Midence, K. (1994). The effects of chronic illness on children and their families: An overview. *Genetic, Social and General Psychology Monographs, 120,* 311–326.

Minuchin, S., Baker, L., Rosman, B. L., Liebman, R., Milman, L., & Todd, T. C. (1975). The conceptual model of psychosomatic illness in children: Family organization and family therapy. *Archives of General Psychiatry, 32,* 1031–1038.

Morgan, S. A., & Jackson, J. (1986). Psychological and social concomitants of sickle-cell anemia. *Journal of Pediatric Psychology, 11,* 429–440.

Newacheck, P. W., & Taylor, N. R. (1992). Childhood chronic illness: Prevalence, severity and impact. *American Journal of Health, 82,* 364–371.

Palmer, S., & Horn, S. (1978). Feeding problems in children. In S. Palmer & S. Ekvall (Eds.), *Pediatric nutrition in developmental disorders* (pp. 107–129). Springfield, IL: Thomas.

Perrin, J. M., & MacLean, W. E. (1988). Children with chronic illness: The prevention of dysfunction. *Pediatric Clinics of North America, 35,* 1325–1337.

Perrin, J. M., MacLean, W. E., & Perrin, E. C. (1989). Parental perceptions of health status and psychological adjustment of children with asthma. *Pediatrics, 83,* 26–30.

Perrin, E. C., Newacheck, P., Pless, B., Drotar, C., Gortmaker, S. L., Leventhal, J., Perrin, J. M., Stein, R. E. K., Walker, D. K., & Weitzman, M. (1993). Issues involved in the definition and classification of chronic health conditions. *Pediatrics, 91,* 787–793.

Pless, I. B., & Pinkerton, P. (1975). *Chronic childhood disorder: Promoting patterns of adjustment.* London: Henry Kimpton.

Pless, I. B., & Roghmann, K. (1971). Chronic illness and its consequences: Observations based on three epidemiologic surveys. *Journal of Pediatrics, 79,* 351–359.

Rovet, J. F., Ehrlich, R. M., & Hoppe, M. (1987). Intellectual deficits associated with early onset of insulin-dependent diabetes mellitus in children. *Diabetes Care, 10,* 510–515.

Sawyer, M. G., Toogood, I., Rice, M., Haskell, C., & Baghurst, P. (1986). School performance and psychological adjustment of children treated for leukemia. *American Journal of Pediatric Hematology/Oncology, 8,* 200–207.

Stein, R. (Ed.). (1988). *New directions in care of children with chronic illness.* New York: Springer.

Stein, R. E. K., & Jessop, D. J. (1984). Relationship between health status and psychological adjustment among children with chronic conditions. *Pediatrics, 73,* 169–174.

Stein, R. E. K., & Jessop, D. J. (1989). What diagnosis does not tell: The case for a noncategorical approach to chronic illness in childhood. *Social Science and Medicine, 29,* 769–778.

Stewart, W. (1967). The unmet needs of children. *Pediatrics, 39,* 157–160.

Tavormina, J. B., Kastner, L. S., Slater, P. M., & Watt, S. L. (1976). Chronically ill children: A psychologically and emotionally deviant population? *Journal of Abnormal Child Psychology, 4,* 99–110.

Tebbi, C. K., Cummings, M., Zevon, M. A., Smith, L., Richards, M., & Mallon, J. (1986). Compliance of pediatric and adolescent cancer patients. *Cancer, 58,* 1179–1184.

Theut, S. K., & Mrazek, D. A. (1997). Infants and toddlers with medical conditions and their parents: Reactions to illness and hospitalization and models for intervention. In J. D. Noshpitz (Ed.), *Handbook of child and adolescent psychiatry* (pp. 428–438). New York: Wiley.

Wallander, J. L., Varni, J. W., Babani, L., Banis, H. T., & Wilcox, K. T. (1988). Children with chronic physical disorders: Maternal reports of their psychological adjustment. *Journal of Pediatric Psychology, 13,* 197–212.

Wamboldt, M. Z., & Schmitz, S. (1998). Genetic association between atopy and behavioral symptoms. *Journal of Child Psychology and Psychiatry, 39,* 1007–1016.

Wood, B. L. (1993). Beyond the "psychosomatic family": A biobehavioral family model of pediatric illness. *Family Process, 32,* 261–278.

Zeltzer, L. K., Kellerman, J., Ellerberg, L., Dash, J., & Rigler, D. (1980). Psychological effects of illness in adolescents: II. Impact of illness on adolescents—crucial issues and coping styles. *Journal of Pediatrics, 97,* 132–138.

IV
DISORDERS OF EARLY CHILDHOOD

16

Attachment Disorders of Infancy

Charles H. Zeanah, Neil W. Boris, and Alicia F. Lieberman

John Bowlby's influential theory of attachment (1969/1982, 1973, 1980) grew out of concern among clinicians and researchers in the early to mid-twentieth century about problems of young children raised in contexts of less-than-adequate caregiving, with difficulties in social relatedness (Bowlby, 1951; Call, 1980; Goldfarb, 1945; Kempe, Silverman, Steele, Droege-mueller, & Silver, 1962; Rutter, 1972; Skeels, 1966; Spitz, 1945, 1946; Tizard & Tizard, 1971). The formal classification of clinical disorders of attachment, however, is a relatively recent development. In fact, there has been almost no systematic research devoted to clinical disorders of attachment, and until recently, these disorders have been cited in the literature only rarely. In this chapter, we begin by reviewing research demonstrating some of the deviant and unusual attachment behaviors evident in young children raised in extraordinary caregiving contexts. Afterward, we review several different approaches to defining and classifying disorders of attachment. Then, we turn to what is known about the etiology, epidemiology, differential diagnosis, and course and prognosis. We conclude by describing issues salient to assessment and treatment of attachment in infants and toddlers. Throughout, we emphasize the importance of the integration of theory, research, and clinical application.

CLINICAL TRADITION OF DISORDERED ATTACHMENT

The relatively common practice of institutionalization of infants in orphanages in the first half of the century unwittingly provided more evidence of the detrimental effects of what has been called maternal deprivation. Although pediatricians had argued against the practice of institutionalization of young children for years (see Chapin, 1915), it was not until Spitz (1945, 1946), Robertson and Robertson (1989), and Skeels (1966) in midcentury used more rigorous studies (including control groups) that the wider community of health care providers took

Charles H. Zeanah and Neil W. Boris • Tulane University School of Medicine, New Orleans, Louisiana 70112.   **Alicia F. Lieberman** • Department of Psychiatry, University of California, San Francisco, California 94110.

Handbook of Developmental Psychopathology, Second Edition, edited by Arnold J. Sameroff, Michael Lewis, and Suzanne M. Miller. Kluwer Academic/Plenum Publishers, New York, 2000.

notice of the untoward effects on social and emotional development caused by institution-alization.

These studies also led Spitz (1945) to propose a diagnostic entity he called "anaclitic depression," one that foreshadowed subsequent criteria for clinical disorders of attachment in psychiatric nosologies and is consistent with some of the features of current approaches to attachment disorders. Anaclitic depression seemed to occur following the prolonged separa-tion of an infant from his or her primary caregiver and was most severe if the infant was old enough to have already developed a preference for that caregiver. The eventual recognition of the clinically meaningful consequences of institutionalization led to a marked decrease in state-run orphanages in many industrialized countries (Provence, 1989). Nevertheless, the recent influx of young children from Romania and some Russian states has renewed interest in studying this population of children (Chisholm, Carter, Ames & Morison, 1995; Fisher, Ames, & Chisholm, 1995; Fisher, Ames, Chisholm, & Savoie, in press; Morison, Ames, & Chisholm, 1995; Rosenberg, Pajer, & Rancurello, 1992; Rutter, 1996).

Another major source of concern about clinical disorders of attachment came from research on child maltreatment. Recognition of the scope of this problem, on the other hand, did not begin until the relatively recently, spurred initially by Kempe et al.'s (1962) classic article on the "battered child syndrome." Since the early 1960s, there has been a great deal of research on the developmental effects of maltreatment on young children (Carlson & Cic-chetti, 1989; Cicchetti & Toth, 1995; Mrazek, 1993). Though research on the effects of maltreatment is made difficult by the number of competing variables influencing observed outcome, disturbed attachment patterns have been consistently documented in a range of sam-ples of maltreated young children (Carlson, Cicchetti, Barnett, & Braunwald, 1989; Cicchetti & Barnett, 1991). On the other hand, it is not yet clear what percentage of these children might meet criteria for a clinical disorder of attachment at any given developmental stage. Neverthe-less, it is clear that many of the descriptions of the socially deviant behaviors observed in maltreated infants and toddlers became incorporated into the criteria used to define clinical disorders of attachment (Zeanah & Emde, 1994).

DEFINITION AND CLASSIFICATION
OF ATTACHMENT DISORDERS

Although some clinical efforts to describe disordered attachments have been proposed (see Call, 1980; Greenspan & Lieberman, 1988), the formal nosological criteria for clinical disorders of attachment have a rather brief history. The diagnosis of Reactive Attachment Disorder (RAD) was first introduced in modern nosologies in 1980, with the publication of DSM-III (American Psychiatric Association, 1980). This early version of the disorder in-cluded as central features growth failure and lack of social responsivity, and these had to be evident prior to 8 months of age.

The link between failure to thrive and RAD was eliminated in DSM-III-R (American Psychiatric Association, 1987), and the age of onset was changed to appearance in the first 5 years. Thus, the rather curious requirement that there be evidence of an attachment disorder before there was evidence of a focused attachment was dropped. Two subtypes of the disorder, "inhibited" and "disinhibited," also were introduced with DSM-III-R (American Psychiatric Association, 1987).

In DSM-IV (American Psychiatric Association, 1994), the two subtypes were main-tained. The etiological link between the disorder and evidence of "pathogenic care" at the hands of young children's primary caregivers and the exclusion of children whose symptoms might be accounted for by cognitive delay or one of the Pervasive Developmental Disorders (PDD) remained an emphasis of the criteria as well. All of these changes were made without the benefit of data, as there were no published studies evaluating or even using the criteria for attachment disorders between 1980 and 1994. In fact, the criteria received virtually no attention until Richters and Volkmar (1994) published a series of case studies illustrating RAD.

One of the difficulties in considering psychopathology in the first 3 years of life is determining caseness (Zeanah, 1996); that is, at what point do an infant's attachment disturbances constitute a clinical disorder rather than merely a risk for subsequent disorder? Given the importance and ubiquity of attachment under usual developmental circumstances, at what point do we designate a specific attachment to be disordered? Although the nosologies do not address this question specifically, they do usually require some degree of functional impairment as well as the presence of a constellation of symptoms and signs in order to constitute a disorder. Given the uniqueness of the first 3 years of life as they impact conceptualizations of psychopathology (Emde, Bingham, & Harmon, 1993; Zeanah, Boris, & Scheeringa, 1997), the initial question is how to define clinical disorders of attachment in the early years. Zeanah, Mammen, and Lieberman (1993) offered the following definition of attachment disorders: "Attachment problems become psychiatric disorders for infants when emotions and behaviors displayed in attachment relationships are so disturbed as to indicate, or substantially to increase the risk for, persistent distress or disability in the infant" (p. 338). Admittedly, this definition allows wide latitude for clinicians, although clinical flexibility is probably desirable given the paucity of our current knowledge base.

DSM-IV

Reactive Attachment Disorder of Infancy and Early Childhood, as described in DSM-IV (American Psychiatric Association, 1994), is characterized by "markedly disturbed and developmentally inappropriate social relatedness in most contexts" (p. 116). These findings are presumed to be due to "grossly pathogenic care." The disorder must begin before 5 years of age to meet criteria and cannot be solely due to developmental delay. Similarly, those who meet criteria for PDD are explicitly excluded from consideration for RAD in DSM-IV criteria and are implicitly excluded by ICD-10 criteria.

Zeanah and Emde (1994) suggested that criteria describing this pattern of emotionally withdrawn nonattachment were derived from documented social abnormalities in maltreated (especially neglected) young children (e.g., Gaensbauer & Sands, 1979; George & Main, 1979; Powell, Low, & Speers, 1987) and from a subgroup of institution-reared children who were noted to be markedly withdrawn and unattached (Provence & Lipton, 1962; Tizard & Rees, 1975). The pattern of emotional withdrawal and absence of an attachment figure also have been observed in children in foster care (Hinshaw-Fuselier, Boris, Guttierez, & Zeanah, in press; Zeanah et al., 1993).

Since RAD first appeared in DSM-III (American Psychiatric Association, 1980), the criteria have undergone substantial revision, but the current criteria describe two general patterns of disorder (Boris & Zeanah, in press). The first pattern is characterized by inhibition of the normal developmental tendency to seek comfort from a select group of caregivers. Responses to social interactions are "excessively inhibited, hypervigilant, or highly ambivalent" (p. 116) reflecting the overall inhibition of the attachment system in affected children at times when attachment behaviors ordinarily are activated. The second pattern is characterized by a relative hyperactivation of the attachment system, but with little discrimination, resulting in "diffuse" and unselective attachments. The disinhibited subtype is marked by a lack of selectivity in choosing social partners, resulting in diffuse attachments and a peculiar over-friendliness that has been labeled "indiscriminate sociability." Caregivers may remark on their own subjective sense that the child is not truly attached to them. This pattern has been observed both in some young children in foster care with multiple placements (Hinshaw-Fuselier et al., 1999; Zeanah et al., 1993) and in young children raised in institutions (Chisholm, Carter, Ames, & Morison, 1995; Hodges & Tizard, 1989b; Tizard & Rees, 1975).

ICD-10

Criteria for attachment disorders in ICD-10 (World Health Organization, 1992) are largely similar to criteria in DSM-IV. Instead of describing absence of a preferred attachment figure, manifest either by emotional withdrawal or by indiscriminate sociability, ICD-10 proposes two separate disorders: RAD and Disinhibited Attachment Disorder.

RAD, according to ICD-10 criteria, is characterized by contradictory or ambivalent social responsiveness across social situations associated with emotional distress and/or withdrawal, and abnormalities in reciprocal social responsiveness. It is essentially equivalent to the emotionally withdrawn subtype of RAD described in DSM-IV and shares the same database for indirect validation.

Disinhibited Attachment Disorder is similar to the indiscriminate pattern of RAD described by DSM-IV. Specifically, the diagnosis requires a normal tendency to seek comfort from others when distressed but an abnormal tendency to seek comfort nonpreferentially (indiscriminately). Following the findings of Tizard and Rees (1975) about some institution-reared young children, the ICD-10 criteria describe overly clingy behavior in infancy, followed by indiscriminately friendly behavior in later childhood as manifestations of the indiscriminate pattern. Again, the same indirect validity data regarding the indiscriminate pattern described in DSM-IV apply equally well to the ICD-10 Disinhibited Attachment Disorder.

Interestingly, ICD-10 does not explicitly link attachment disorders to pathogenic care in its criteria, though a warning against making the diagnosis without evidence of abuse or neglect is included in the clinical description attached to the criteria. Furthermore, the child is expected to display some "elements of normal social relatedness" with reasonably responsive adult caregivers. There is no explicit exclusion of children with mental retardation or PDD in the ICD-10 criteria. However, because the clinician is required to document that the child demonstrate the capacity for normal social relatedness, the latter diagnosis essentially is precluded.

Diagnostic Classification: Zero to Three

Zero to Three, a national advocacy, social policy, and professional development organization, formulated a task force several years ago charged with developing a nosology of infancy disorders. Curiously, although the description of this disorder in *DC: 0-3* (1994), is explicitly modeled after Reactive Attachment Disorder in DSM-IV, most of the descriptions are about environmental abnormalities rather than infant behaviors that define the syndrome. Thus, the disorder is present in the context of "parental deprivation or maltreatment" (p. 29), such as might occur in "long-term hospitalization, multiple or changing caregivers, or parents who are depressed or afflicted with substance abuse" (p. 29). These conditions are asserted to "prevent stable attachments" (p. 30) at least under some circumstances. The description does make clear that not all maltreated children develop the disorder and that improved environmental support is expected to ameliorate the condition. Given the absence of explicit infant behavioral criteria to define the disorder, this version of clinically disordered attachment is difficult to evaluate formally except by using DSM-IV criteria as a rough equivalent.

Alternative Criteria for Disorders of Attachment

Because these other approaches seemed oddly removed from the hundreds of studies conducted in developmental research on attachment, a group of investigators proposed an alternative set of criteria describing disorders of attachment drawn from developmental attachment research (Lieberman & Zeanah, 1995; Zeanah, 1996; Zeanah et al., 1993). Building upon Lieberman's (Lieberman & Pawl, 1988, 1990) descriptions of clinical disturbances of the secure base phenomena, these investigators proposed an alternative set of criteria to describe a broader range of attachment disorders than any of the previous approaches (Lieberman & Zeanah, 1995; Zeanah et al., 1993). These descriptions have been modified somewhat over time, and the description in this chapter represents an update of the previous description of alternative criteria for clinical disorders of attachment.

A number of findings from developmental attachment research have been used to construct principles to inform descriptions of clinical attachment disorders:

1. Infants construct different kinds of attachment relationships with different caregivers. Therefore, there is no reason to expect generalization of disturbed attachment behaviors across different attachment relationships. If an infant demonstrates a particular form of disturbed attachment to a caregiver, there is no reason to expect the disturbance to generalize to other attachment relationships.
2. Attachment encompasses specific behaviors designed to promote proximity to the caregiver for purposes of attaining comfort, support, and nurturance. There is no reason to assume that other problems with social relatedness necessarily reflect attachment disturbances.
3. The attachment relationship in early toddlerhood reflects the toddler's use of the caregiver as a secure base and as a safe haven. In later toddlerhood, the toddler's enhanced representational capacities ushers in the goal-corrected partnership whose hallmark is cooperation. This may be observed in either clinic or naturalistic settings.
4. Although attachment features prominently in many different kinds of interpersonal relationships, in parent–child relationships, attachment is an unequal partnership. The caregiver is responsible for the care, nurturance, and protection of the child, but not vice versa.

These principles, together with observations of clinically referred and high-risk children, were used to develop an alternative approach to classification of attachment disorders, described below. This approach involves three broad types of attachment disorders: Disorders of Nonattachment, which are similar to the DSM-IV and ICD-10 disorders, Secure Base Distortions, in which the child has a seriously unhealthy attachment relationship with a caregiver, and Disrupted Attachment Disorders, in which the child reacts to the loss of an attachment relationship.

Disorders of Nonattachment

In keeping with the DSM-IV and ICD-10 criteria, the alternative approach maintains two types of disorders in which there is no preferred attachment figure: Nonattachment with Emotional Withdrawal, a pattern in which the child is emotionally withdrawn, inhibited, and unattached, and Nonattachment with Indiscriminate Sociability, a pattern in which the child seeks comfort and social interaction with relative strangers, without the developmentally appropriate discrimination and reticence. The comfort seeking function of attachment is almost always seriously problematic in each of these patterns, although other components of attachment, including showing affection, reliance for help, cooperation, and disturbances of exploration are also evident in affected children. Not surprisingly, given these interpersonal and social relatedness problems, affected children also may demonstrate serious problems in self-regulation and self-protection.

There is no expectation relationship variability in these disorders of nonattachment; that is, their behavioral disturbances should be similar in different relationships, because children with either of these patterns have no attachment figure. The alternative criteria introduce a requirement that affected children have a mental age of at least 10 months, in order that the failure to demonstrate a preferred attachment figure is not due to cognitive limitations. Furthermore, the link to pathogenic care is not a part of the criteria because of the unreliability of histories of caregiving in many of the affected children (see Hinshaw-Fuselier et al., 1999; Zeanah et al., 1993).

Although these disorders are described and conceptualized categorically, some data, especially regarding indiscriminate sociability, raise questions about whether or not they may be more usefully conceptualized dimensionally. For example, in the Tizard study of children raised in institutions in London, persistence of indiscriminate sociability was noted in all three groups that spent 2–4 years in an institution. Some of the children were adopted out of the institution, others were returned to their biological families who had placed them in the institution originally, and still others remained in the institution. Although some of the children in all three of these groups retained features of indiscriminate friendliness, none of the inner-city London comparison children (who had not been raised in an institution) exhibited this pattern of behavior (Hodges & Tizard, 1989b; Tizard & Rees, 1975). Similarly, in a study of Romanian babies adopted from orphanages into Canada, "indiscriminate friendliness" was noted both at 11 months and 39 months postadoption (Chisholm & Ames, 1995; Chisholm et al., 1995). Interestingly, indiscriminate friendliness measured concurrently was inversely related to attachment security at 11 months postadoption but unrelated to concurrently measured attachment security at 39 months postadoption. Furthermore, although attachment security significantly increased from 11 to 39 months, there were no differences in the levels of indiscriminate friendliness from 11 to 39 months postadoption, adding further evidence of the persistence of this unusual behavior pattern even after attachment develops. One implication of these findings is that indiscriminate sociability may be more usefully considered dimensionally rather than categorically.

Secure Base Distortions

A second general type of disordered attachment, grouped under the heading of Secure Base Distortions, arose from observing patterns of clinically disturbed attachment relationships between young children and their caregivers. What distinguishes these disorders from the disorders of nonattachment is that the child with a Secure Base Distortion does have a preferred attachment figure, but the relationship with this caregiver is seriously disturbed. The disturbed attachment behaviors that characterize these disorders is relationship specific, in keeping with the important finding from developmental attachment research that infants may construct different types of relationships with different caregivers (Lyons-Ruth, Zeanah, & Benoit, 1996; Zeanah, 1996).

Four different types of Secure Base Distortions are evident: Attachment Disorder with Self-Endangerment, Attachment Disorder with Clinging/Inhibited Exploration, Attachment Disorder with Vigilance/Hypercompliance, and Attachment Disorder with Role Reversal. In each of these disorders, the observed disturbances in the child's behavior are anticipated to be relationship-specific rather than general characteristics of how the child interacts socially.

Attachment Disorder with Self-Endangerment. The primary function of the attachment behavioral system is to maintain proximity to the caregiver. This function is closely tied to safety and survival as the infant's capacities for mobility increase dramatically in the second year, and the infant must balance the motivation to explore with the motivation to maintain proximity to the attachment figure.

The self-endangering pattern of attachment disorder is characterized by expected ventures away from the attachment figure for purposes of exploration, but the exploration is unchecked by the opposing tendency to maintain proximity or to return to the putative safe haven of the attachment figure. In addition, the child may engage in a variety of exceedingly dangerous and provocative behaviors in the presence of the attachment figure, such as running out into traffic, deliberately running away in crowded public places, climbing up on ledges, and so on. Bold, active, or uninhibited children may exercise poor judgement at times, but provocative and self-endangering behaviors constitute signs of an attachment disorder only if they are relationship-specific.

Accompanying behaviors include aggression that may be self-directed or directed at the caregiver, especially if the aggressive behaviors are displayed in the place of comfort-seeking behaviors. Case reports have suggested that family violence, either physical abuse, partner violence, or both, may be strongly associated with Self-Endangering Attachment Disorder (Lieberman & Zeanah, 1995; Zeanah et al., 1993). It appears as if the young child is attempting to attract the attention and protection of an unavailable or undependable caregiver, although what combination of intrinsic and environmental features might predispose to self-endangering behaviors and the mechanisms responsible for their production remains unknown.

Attachment Disorder with Clinging/Inhibition. At the other end of the clinical spectrum, some young children do not venture away from the attachment figure to engage in age-expectable exploration. Here, the secure base function of the attachment figure appears to be deficient, and the child's willingness to venture away and explore the object world is impaired. Curiously, this inhibition is not pervasive but, rather, is situation-specific. The inhibited behaviors and high levels of accompanying anxiety are observed when the child is in the presence of the attachment figure in an unfamiliar setting, or especially in the presence of the attachment figure *and* an unfamiliar adult. In a case report illustrating this pattern, Zeanah et al. (1993) described a 28-month-old girl who was extremely clingy and inhibited when she was with her mother and an unfamiliar adult, although with her mother alone, or with other familiar adults (such as her day care providers), she showed neither distress nor inhibition.

Attachment Disorder with Vigilance/Hypercompliance. Another form of disordered attachment behavior associated with strong inhibition of exploration occurs in Attachment

Disorder with Vigilance/Hypercompliance. In this pattern, however, there is no clinging. Instead, the child is emotionally constricted, vigilant of the caregiver, and hypercompliant with caregiver requests and commands. Instead of fearing to leave the caregiver as in the clinging/inhibited pattern, the child instead gives the impression of fearing to displease the caregiver. Virtually all the child's spontaneity is gone in the service of vigilance, creating the impression of a little automaton, or that the child may be obviously terrified of the caregiver. Although the behavioral pattern is specific to interactions with the attachment figure, it is not necessarily always evident. It is likely that certain cues trigger the response in young children, such as displays of intense or prolonged anger and frustration by the caregiver.

In the child abuse literature, this pattern has been described as "frozen watchfulness" (Steele, 1983), and it is believed to be an effort by the child to minimize the chances of harsh, punitive, or frankly abusive responses by the caregiver. Crittenden and DiLalla (1988) demonstrated that a closely related pattern of "compulsive compliance" was indeed relationship-specific and was related to intrusive caregiving. The disorder is distinguished by both the intensity of the fearful reactions in the child and their relationship specificity.

Attachment Disorder with Role Reversal.   A final distortion of the secure base occurs when the attachment relationship is inverted (Bowlby, 1980). Instead of the caregiver providing emotional support, nurturance, and protection to the child, the emotional well-being of the caregiver is a preoccupation and even responsibility of the child. To a developmentally inappropriate degree, the child assumes the emotional burden of the relationship. This may be associated with the child's efforts to control the caregiver's behavior, either punitively, over-solicitously, or in some other role-inappropriate manner (Main & Cassidy, 1988; Solomon, George, & DeJong, 1995).

Case reports have implied that this pattern is easily recognized (Lieberman & Pawl, 1988; 1990; Lieberman & Zeanah, 1995; Zeanah & Scheeringa, 1997; Zeanah et al., 1993), although in a recent investigation, interrater reliability was lower for Attachment Disorder with Role Reversal than for any other type of attachment disorder (Boris et al., 1998). It seems clear that despite the putative developmental costs of such a relationship structure to the child, there are also positive features. The child in a role-reversed relationship is noticed and valued, albeit in a restricted and functionally specific manner. The problem clinically is determining under what circumstances the closeness in such relationships is developmentally compromising to the child.

Disrupted Attachment Disorder

A third general type of disorder is also proposed, one called Disrupted Attachment Disorder. Its criteria are applied in cases in which the child experiences the sudden loss of the attachment figure. Criteria for the disorder are consistent with the descriptions by Robertson and Robertson (1989) of young children, separated from their caregivers for days to weeks, who develop the well-known sequence of protest, despair, and detachment.

The rationale for this disorder is that loss of the attachment figure for an infant or toddler is so devastating that it is qualitatively different from loss at another point in the life cycle. This disorder has not been well studied, although it has been described in children who have lost their only attachment figure through death or through changes in foster placement (Gaensbauer, Chatoor, Drell, Siegel, & Zeanah, 1995; Lieberman & Zeanah, 1995). Clinical experience suggests that the presence of other caregivers may buffer the loss of the primary attachment figure but to what degree and under what circumstances remains unclear. An interesting question for the field is whether young children with healthier attachments may be more vulnerable to disruptions than children with more disturbed attachments (see Gaensbauer et al., 1995).

ETIOLOGY

Although disorders of nonattachment typically occur in the context of grossly neglectful or overtly abusive care, the critical elements of this care and their relationship to the onset of the disorder are unclear. DSM-IV includes pathogenic care as a criterion for RAD, despite the explicitly phenomenological nature of its approach. As Volkmar (1999) and others (Richters & Volkmar, 1994; Rutter, 1995; Zeanah, 1996) have noted, this serves to preclude the possibility of discovering other possible pathways.

In any case, the relationship between adverse caregiving and attachment disorders is certainly probabilistic rather than linear. Research highlighting the importance of nonshared environments reminds us that children institutionalized in the same facility, or siblings raised together in a markedly disturbed family, may have divergent experiences and outcomes. Individual differences in temperament or other characteristics may interact with corrective experiences to predict a nonpathological outcome in some children who experience extremes of care. For example, Emde and Spitz (1965) reported a case of an infant whose difficult temperament in the context of an orphanage may have enhanced his opportunities for attachment to caregivers who were compelled to respond to his irritability. The individual fit between the caregiving environment and an infant or young child is likely to be critical in determining which children develop symptoms consistent with an attachment disorder.

Secure Base Distortions, as relationship disorders, reflect complex disturbances in the infant–caregiver relationship, as manifest both at the level of interactive behavior and at the level of representational processes. Substantial indirect evidence implicates both of these levels of relationship disturbance as salient to any consideration of clinical disorders (van IJzendoorn, 1995; van IJzendoorn & Bakermans-Kranenburg, 1996, 1997).

EPIDEMIOLOGY

Because of the lack of agreement about the criteria used to define attachment disorders and the lack of available methodologies for assessing their presence or absence, there are virtually no data available on the prevalence of clinical disorders of attachment.

As many as 40% of children in unselected samples are insecurely attached (van IJzendoorn, 1995) and perhaps as many as 70–80% of clinic-referred children are insecurely attached (Goldberg, 1997; Greenberg, DeKlyen, Speltz, & Endriga, 1997; van IJzendoorn, Goldberg, Kroonenberg, & Frenkel, 1992). Nevertheless, it is likely that only a small proportion of insecurely attached children meet criteria for clinical disorders of attachment (Zeanah, 1996). In one recent study (Boris et al., 1998), as many as one-third of consecutively diagnosed patients in an infant psychiatry clinic met criteria for attachment disorders as defined by Lieberman and Zeanah (1995), but this clinic received a large number of referrals from child protective services of maltreated, symptomatic children and clearly is not representative.

Because pathogenic care is more likely to occur within broad risk factors such as poverty, family violence and disruption, and low social support in clinical samples, these nonspecific risks are likely to be associated with the diagnosis. By extrapolating from data in the Tizard investigation (Tizard & Rees, 1974, 1975), as many as two-thirds of young children raised in institutions in which there is limited opportunity to form selective attachments to caregivers may develop clinical pictures resembling attachment disorders.

The paucity of data about prevalence underscores the importance of developing well-validated methods for defining and assessing attachment disorders. This, of course, will require more of a consensus about the nature of such disorders than currently exists, although the clear operationalization of constructs and the rapid development of methods of assessing attachment suggest that this is a particularly ripe area for research.

DIFFERENTIAL DIAGNOSIS

Young children with marked disinterest in social interaction pose a diagnostic challenge for clinicians. Evidence of stereotypies, grossly restricted range of interests, and poor response to changes in routines suggest the spectrum of PDD; cognitive impairment is frequently moderate to severe in these children. The clinical challenge is how to make distinctions between the socially deviant behaviors in PDD and in attachment disorders. There are few data available to address this question directly, in part because of the vagueness about the abnormalities in social behavior that characterize descriptions of disorders.

ICD-10 suggests that the attachment disorders may be distinguished from PDD by (1) a normal capacity for social relatedness in reactive attachment disorder, (2) remission of social abnormalities in a normal rearing environment in reactive attachment disorder, (3) distinctive communicative and language abnormalities in PDD, (4) improved cognitive deficits with improvements in the caregiving environment only in reactive attachment disorder, and (5) persistently restricted, repetitive, and stereotyped patterns of behavior, interests, and activities as features of PDD but not attachment disorders (World Health Organization, 1992). An obvious problem with these assertions is that it is not possible to know whether abnormal behaviors will persist or ameliorate at the time of assessment (see Zeanah et al., 1993). Still, the limited data available suggest that these assertions may be used as clinical diagnostic guides, although a subgroup of children raised in Romanian orphanages who exhibit features of autistic spectrum disorders suggests that the distinction between attachment abnormalities and PDD is not always readily made (Rutter, 1996). A detailed examination of the characteristics of children with reactive attachment disorders as compared to those diagnosed with PDD, who live in stable, secure environments, will be a useful start for exploring this question further.

There is evidence that many children with PDD do form attachments with their primary caregivers, despite some deviance in the features of their attachment-related behaviors (Capps, Sigman, & Mundy, 1994). Distinguishing between deviant attachment behaviors associated with PDD and those associated with attachment disorders is an important clinical challenge. Children with severe receptive and expressive language delays also may present clinically with difficulties in social relatedness. Nevertheless, grossly inappropriate care is unusual in these cases, and as communication improves, relatedness also improves.

Some types of externalizing behavior disorders may appear similar to Self-Endangering Attachment Disorder. It is not uncommon for the young child's aggressive behavior to be more prominent as a complaint than self-endangering behavior, which may be revealed only with direct questioning. Relationship specificity in Self-Endangering Attachment Disorder distinguishes it from disruptive behavior disorders in which the externalizing symptomatology is manifest cross-contextually.

Relationship specificity is also the key to distinguishing inhibited attachment disorders from a more pervasive temperamental disposition to inhibition (Kagan, Reznick, & Snidman,

1988). Significant variability of the inhibition in different relationships is expected with an attachment disorder but not with a temperamental attribute.

COURSE AND PROGNOSIS OF DISORDERS OF ATTACHMENT

To date, there have been no investigations on the course of clinical disorders of attachment as defined by standard nomenclature. As a result, data from longitudinal investigations of the consequences of institutional rearing and investigations from developmental research are the most relevant data available to address questions of the course and prognosis of disordered attachments. These data have supported many (though not all) of Bowlby's (1951) original assertions about the effects of maternal deprivation on social relationships, on behavioral problems, and on intelligence.

Results from a considerable amount of research on the developmental sequelae of insecure attachment converge well with data on the sequelae of early institutional rearing or situations in which there have been limited opportunities for infants to develop selective attachments (reviewed in Zeanah & Emde, 1994). Several tentative conclusions about the course and prognosis of attachment disorders can be drawn from these data. First, the failure to form selective attachments to a relatively small number of caregiving individuals in the early years is a significant risk factor for subsequent functioning. Second, quality of attachment relationships once formed are important mediators between early experiences and subsequent functioning. There is even some evidence suggesting that the effects of poor quality attachment relationships are additive in that infants securely attached to both parents have the best preschool adjustment, infants insecurely attached to both parents have the worst outcomes, and infants securely attached to one parent and insecurely attached to the other have intermediate outcomes (Suess, Grossman, & Sroufe, 1992). Third, more profound effects are apparent in the area of social adaptation and less profound effects in the cognitive domain, with intermediate effects on symptoms of behavioral disturbances. This is in keeping with Sroufe's (1988) emphasis on attachment as a precursor of the child's sense of self-worth, capacity for emotional intimacy, and interpersonal competence rather than broadly predictive of developmental functioning in many domains. The link between early disturbances of attachment and antisocial tendencies, particularly lack of empathy, was first made by Bowlby (1944) himself and remains of interest (Fonagy, Steele, Steele, Higgit, & Target, 1994). Evidence that disorganized attachment classifications predict subsequent aggressive behavior (Lyons-Ruth, Alpern, & Repacholi, 1993) are an initial step toward longitudinal studies of this association needed to clarify the pathway.

Data suggesting that, in children with a history of adverse early experiences, the choice of marital partners selected in later life strongly influences eventual adult psychological functioning (Quinton, Rutter, & Liddle, 1985) beg the question of individual differences in how those choices are made. Despite great interest, the vital questions of when and under what circumstances seriously disturbed attachment experiences can be overcome by subsequent more optimal caregiving experiences remain unanswered.

CONCLUSIONS

Some young children who have experienced extremes of caregiving are not merely insecurely attached; they have clinical disorders of attachment. These are profound and pervasive disturbances in the child's sense of safety and security that require intervention not to prevent subsequent disorder but to ameliorate current symptomatology.

How best to conceptualize these disorders of attachment remains controversial. There is widespread agreement about the clinical picture of young children who lack attachments entirely and tend to appear either emotionally withdrawn and unresponsive or indiscriminately to seek attention and comfort. Whether children who have established attachments but serious relationship disturbances with their caregiver should also be included is less clear.

What is clear is the need for more research to clarify the most appropriate and most useful ways of defining and classifying these disorders and, especially, to develop and demonstrate effective interventions for affected children. No doubt the complexity of the problems will need to be matched by complexity in our approaches to them.

REFERENCES

American Psychiatric Association. (1980). *Diagnostic and statistical manual of mental disorders* (3rd ed.). Washington, DC: Author.

American Psychiatric Association. (1987). *Diagnostic and statistical manual of mental disorders* (3rd ed., rev.). Washington, DC: Author.

American Psychiatric Association. (1994). *Diagnostic and statistical manual of mental disorders* (4th ed.). Washington, DC: Author.

Boris, N., & Zeanah, C.H. (in press). Reactive attachment disorder. In A. Kaplan & B. Sadock (Eds.), *Comprehensive textbook of psychiatry*. Philadelphia: Williams & Wilkins.

Boris, N., Zeanah, C.H., Larrieu, J., Scheeringa, M., & Heller, S. (1998). Attachment disorders in infancy and early childhood: A preliminary study of diagnostic criteria. *American Journal of Psychiatry, 155,* 295–297.

Bowlby, J. (1944). Forty-four juvenile thieves. *International Journal of Psychoanalysis, 25,* 19–53.

Bowlby, J. (1951). *Maternal care and child health.* Geneva: World Health Organization.

Bowlby, J. (1982). *Attachment.* New York: Basic Books. (Original published in 1969)

Bowlby, J. (1973). *Separation.* New York: Basic Books.

Bowlby, J. (1980). *Loss.* New York: Basic Books.

Call, J. D. (1980). Attachment disorders of infancy. In H. I. Kaplan, A. M. Freedman, & B. J. Sadock (Eds.), *Comprehensive textbook of psychiatry* (pp. 2586–2597). Baltimore: Williams & Wilkins.

Capps, L., Sigman, M., & Mundy, P. (1994). Attachment security in children with autism. *Development and Psychopathology, 6,* 249–262.

Carlson, V., & Cicchetti, D. (Eds.). (1989). *Child maltreatment: Theory and research on the causes and consequences of child abuse and neglect.* Cambridge, UK: Cambridge University Press.

Carlson, V., Cicchetti, D., Barnett, D., & Braunwald, K. (1989). Finding order in disorganization: Lessons from maltreated infant's attachments to their caregivers. In D. Cicchetti & V. Carlson (Eds.), *Child maltreatment: Theory and research on the causes and consequences of child abuse and neglect* (pp. 494–528). Cambridge, UK: Cambridge University Press.

Chapin, H. D. (1915). Are institutions for infants necessary? *Journal of the American Medical Association, 64,* 1–3.

Chisholm, K., & Ames, E. W. (1995, March). *A follow-up study of attachment security and indiscriminately friendly behavior in Romanian adoptees.* Paper presented to the Biennial Meetings of the Society for Research in Child Development, Indianapolis, IN.

Chisolm, K., Carter, M. C., Ames, E. W., & Morison, S. J. (1995). Attachment security and indiscriminately friendly behavior in children adopted from Romanian orphanages. *Development and Psychopathology, 7,* 283–294.

Cicchetti, D., & Barnett, D. (1991). Attachment organization in maltreated preschoolers. *Development and Psychopathology, 3,* 397–411.

Cicchetti, D., & Toth, S.L. (1995). A developmental psychopathology perspective on child abuse and neglect. *Journal of the American Academy of Child and Adolescent Psychiatry, 34,* 541–565.

Crittendon, P., & Dilalla, D. L. (1988). Compulsive compliance: The development of an inhibitory coping strategy in infancy. *Journal of Abnormal Child Psychology, 16,* 585–599.

Crowell, J. A., & Fleischmann, M. A. (1993). Use of structured research procedures in clinical assessments of infants. In C. H. Zeanah (Ed.), *Handbook of infant mental health* (pp. 210–221). New York: Guilford Press.

Emde, R. N., Binghman, R., & Harmon, R. (1993). Classification and the diagnostic process. In C. H. Zeanah (Ed.), *Handbook of infant mental health* (pp. 225–235). New York: Guilford Press.

Emde, R. N., Polak, P. R., & Spitz, R. A. (1965), Anaclitic depression in an infant raised in an institution. *Journal of the American Academy of Child Psychiatry, 4*, 545–553.

Fisher, L., Ames, E. W., & Chisholm, K. (1995, June). *Child behavior problems and parent stress in Romanian adoptees.* Paper presented to the Annual Meeting of the Canadian Psychological Association.

Fisher, L., Ames, E. W., Chisholm, K., & Savoie, L. (in press). Problems reported by parents of Romanian orphans adopted to British Coloumbia. *International Journal of Behavioral Development.*

Fonagy, P., Steele, M., Steele, H., Higgit, A., & Target, M. (1994). The Emmanuel Miller Memorial Lecture 1992: The theory and practice of resilience. *Journal of Child Psychology, Psychiatry and Allied Disciplines, 35*, 231–257.

Gaensbauer, T., Chatoor, I., Drell, M., Siegel, D., & Zeanah, C.H. (1995). Traumatic loss in a one-year-old girl. *Journal of the American Academy of Child and Adolescent Psychiatry, 34*, 94–102.

Gaensbauer, T., & Sands, K. (1979). Distorted affective communications in abused/neglected infants and their potential impact on caregivers. *Journal of the American Academy of Child and Adolescent Psychiatry, 18*, 236–250.

George, C., & Main, M. (1979). Social interactions in young abused children: Approach, avoidance, and aggression. *Child Development, 50*, 306–318.

Goldberg, S. (1997). Attachment and child behavior problems in normal, at-risk and clinical samples. In L. Atkinson & K. J. Zucker (Eds.), *Attachment and psychopathology* (pp. 171–195). New York: Guilford Press.

Goldfarb, W. (1945). Effects of psychological deprivation in infancy and subsequent stimulation. *American Journal of Psychiatry, 102*, 18–33.

Greenberg, M. T., DeKlyen, M., Speltz, M. L., & Endriga, M. C. (1997). The role of attachment processes in externalizing psychopathology in young children. In L. Atkinson & K. J. Zucker (Eds.), *Attachment and psychopathology* (pp. 196–222). New York: Guilford Press.

Greenspan, S. I., & Lieberman, A. F. (1988). A clinical approach to attachment. In J. Belsky & T. Nezworski (Eds.), *Clinical implications of attachment* (pp. 327–424). Hillsdale, NJ: Erlbaum.

Hinshaw-Fuselier, S., Boris, N., Guttierez, A., & Zeanah, C. H. (1999). Trauma dissociation and attachment disorder in twins. *Infant Mental Health Journal, 20*, 42–59.

Hodges, J., & Tizard, B. (1989a). IQ and behavioural adjustment of ex-institutional adolescents. *Journal of Child Psychology, Psychiatry, and Allied Disciplines, 30*, 53–75.

Hodges, J., & Tizard, B. (1989b). Social and family relationships of ex-institutional adolescents. *Journal of Child Psychology, Psychiatry, and Allied Disciplines, 30*, 77–97.

Kagan, J., Reznick, J. S., & Snidman, N. (1988). Biological bases of childhood shyness. *Science, 240*, 167–173.

Kempe, C. H., Silverman, F. N., Steele, B. B., Droegemueller, W., & Silver, H. K. (1962). The battered child syndrome. *Journal of the American Medical Association, 181*, 17–24.

Lieberman, A., & Zeanah, C. H. (1995). Disorders of attachment in infancy. In K. Minde (Ed.), *Infant psychiatry: Child psychiatric clinics of North America* (pp. 571–588). Philadelphia: Saunders.

Lieberman, A. F., & Pawl, J. H. (1988). Clinical applications of attachment theory. In J. Belsky & T. Nezworski (Eds.), *Clinical implications of attachment* (pp. 327–351). Hillsdale, NJ: Erlbaum.

Lieberman, A. F., & Pawl, J. H. (1990). Disorders of attachment and secure base behavior in the second year of life: Conceptual issues and clinical intervention. In M. T. Greenburg, D. Cicchetti, & E. M. Cummings (Eds.), *Attachment in the preschool years* (pp. 375–398). Chicago: University of Chicago Press.

Lyons-Ruth, K., Alpern, L., & Repacholi, B. (1993). Disorganized infant attachment classification and maternal psychosocial problems as predictors of hostile–aggressive behavior in the preschool classroom. *Child Development, 64*, 572–585.

Lyons-Ruth, K., Zeanah, C. H., & Benoit, D. (1996). Disorder and risk for disorder during infancy and toddlerhood. In E. J. Mash & R. A. Barkley (Eds.), *Child psychopathology* (pp. 457–491). New York: Guilford Press.

Main, M., & Cassidy, J. (1988). Categories of response to reunion with the parent at age 6: Predictable from infant attachment classifications and stable over a 1-month period. *Developmental Psychology, 24*, 1–12.

Morison, S. J., Ames, E. W., & Chisholm, K. (1995). The development of children adopted from Romanian orphanages. *Merrill–Palmer Quarterly, 41*, 411–430.

Mrazek, P. (1993). Maltreatment and infant development. In C. H. Zeanah (Ed.), *Handbook of infant mental health* (pp. 159–170). New York: Guilford Press.

Powell, G. F., Low, J. F., & Speers, M. A. (1987). Behavior as a diagnostic aid in failure to thrive. *Journal of Developmental and Behavioral Pediatrics, 8*, 18–24.

Provence, S. (1989). Infants in institutions revisited. *Zero to Three, 9*, 1–4.

Provence, S., & Lipton, R. C. (1962). *Infants reared in institutions.* New York: International Universities Press.

Quinton, D., Rutter, M., & Liddle, C. (1985). Institutional rearing, parenting difficulties, and marital support. *Psychological Medicine, 14*, 107–124.

Richters, M. M., & Volkmar, F. (1994). Reactive attachment disorder of infancy or early childhood. *Journal of the American Academy of Child and Adolescent Psychiatry, 33*, 328–332.

Robertson, J., & Robertson, J. (1989). *Separations and the very young.* London: Free Association Books.

Rosenberg, D. R., Pajer, K., & Rancurello, M. (1992). Neuropsychiatric assessment of orphans in one Romanian orphanage for "unsalvageables." *Journal of the American Medical Association, 268*, 3489–3490.

Rutter, M. (1972). *Maternal deprivation reassessed.* London: Penguin.

Rutter, M. (1995). Clinical implications of attachment concepts: Retrospect and prospect. *Journal of Child Psychology, Psychiatry, and Allied Disciplines, 36*, 549–571.

Rutter, M. (1996, April). *Romanian orphans adopted early: Overcoming deprivation.* Paper presented to the International Conference on Infant Studies, Providence, RI.

Solomon, J., George, C., & DeJong, A. (1995). Children classified as controlling at age six: Evidence of disorganized representational strategies and aggression at home and at school. *Development and Psychopathology, 7*, 447–464.

Skeels, H. M. (1966). Adult status of children with contrasting early life experiences. *Monographs of the Society for Research in Child Development, 31* (Serial No. 105).

Spitz, R. (1945). Hospitalism: An inquiry into the genesis of psychiatric conditions in early childhood. *Psychoanalytic Study of the Child, 1*, 53–74.

Spitz, R. (1946). Anaclitic depression: An inquiry into the genesis of psychiatric conditions in early childhood II. *The Psychoanalytic Study of the Child, 2*, 313–342.

Sroufe, L.A. (1988). The role of infant–caregiver attachment in development. In J. Belsky & T. Nezworski (Eds.), *Clinical implications of attachment* (pp. 18–40). Hillsdale, NJ: Erlbaum.

Steele, B. (1983). Psychological effects of child abuse and neglect. In J. D. Coll, E. Galenson, & R. E. Tyson (Eds.), *Frontiers of infant psychiatry* (pp. 235–244). New York: Basic Books.

Suess, G. J., Grossman, K. E., & Sroufe, L. A. (1992). Effects of infant attachment to mother and father on quality of adaptation in preschool: From dyadic to individual organization of self. *International Journal of Behavioral Development, 15*, 43–65.

Tizard, B., & Hodges, J. (1978). The effect of early institutional rearing on the development of eight-year-old children. *Journal of Child Psychology and Psychiatry, 19*, 99–118.

Tizard, B., & Rees, J. (1974). A comparison of the effects of adoption, restoration of the natural mother, and continued institutionalization on the cognitive development of four-year-old children. *Child Development, 45*, 92–99.

Tizard, B., & Rees, J. (1975). The effect of early institutional rearing on the behavior problems and affectional relationships of four-year-old children. *Journal of Child Psychology and Psychiatry, 27*, 61–73.

Tizard, J., & Tizard, B. (1971). Social development of 2-year-old children in residential nurseries. In: H. R. Schaeffer (Ed.), *The origins of human social relations.* London: Academic Press.

van IJzendoorn, M. H. (1995). Adult attachment representations, parental responsiveness, and infant attachment: A meta-analysis on the predictive validity of the Adult Attachment Interview. *Psychological Bulletin, 117*, 411–415.

van IJzendoorn, M. H., & Bakersman-Kranenberg, M. J. (1996). Attachment representations in mothers, fathers, adolescents, and clinical groups: A meta-analytic search for normative data. *Journal of Consulting and Clinical Psychology, 64*, 8–21.

van IJzendoorn, M. H., & Bakersman-Kranenberg, M. J. (1997). Intergenerational transmission of attachment: A move to the contextual level. In L. Atkinson & K. J. Zucker (Eds.), *Attachment and psychopathology* (pp. 135–170). New York: Guilford Press.

van IJzendoorn, M. H., Goldberg, S., Kroonenberg, P. M., & Frenkel, O. J. (1992). The relative effects of maternal and child problems on the quality of attachment: A meta-analysis of attachment in clinical samples. *Child Development, 50*, 971–975.

Volkmar, F. (1999). Reactive attachment disorders: Issues for DSM-IV. *DSM-IV Source Book.* Washington, DC: American Psychiatric Association.

World Health Organization. (1992). *The ICD-10 classification of mental and behavioral disorders: Clinical descriptions and diagnostic guidelines.* Geneva: Author.

Zeanah, C. H. (1996). Beyond insecurity: A reconceptualization of clinical disorders of attachment. *Journal of Consulting and Clinical Psychology, 64*, 42–52.

Zeanah, C. H., Boris, N., & Scheeringa, M. (1997). Infant development: The first three years of life. In A. Tasman, J. Kay, & J. Lieberman, (Eds.), *Psychiatry* (pp. 75–100). New York: Saunders.

Zeanah, C. H., & Emde, R. N. (1994). Attachment disorders in infancy. In M. Rutter, L. Hersov, & E. Taylor (Eds.), *Child and adolescent psychiatry: Modern approaches* (pp. 490–504). Oxford: Blackwell.

Zeanah, C. H., Mammen, O., & Lieberman, A. (1993). Disorders of attachment. In: C. H. Zeanah (Ed.), *Handbook of infant mental health* (pp. 332–349). New York: Guilford Press.

Zeanah, C. H., & Scheeringa, M. (1997). The experience and effects of violence in infancy. In J. D. Osofsky (Ed.), *Children, youth and violence: Searching for solutions* (pp. 97–123). New York: Guilford Press.

Zero to Three. (1994). *Diagnostic classification of mental health and developmental disorders of infancy and early childhood.* Arlington, VA: Zero to Three Task Force on Diagnostic Classification.

17

Sleep and Sleep Disturbances

Regulatory Processes in Infancy

Beth L. Goodlin-Jones, Melissa M. Burnham, and Thomas F. Anders

The first 2 years of an infant's life involve significant changes in sleep and waking state organization. Traditionally, sleep has been viewed as a characteristic of an individual. However, the infant's biological sleep–wake system is regulated, in large part, by parent–infant interaction and is affected by the infant's cognitive, emotional, and social experiences. How do the developing infant's biological systems, such as the circadian, nutritional, and fatigue systems, interact with environmental experiences to produce nighttime "self-soothing" or "signaling" behavior in the first year of life? Does the process of infant sleep–wake state regulation in the first year predict infant sleep disturbance in the second year or sleep problems in later childhood? The study of sleep–wake state maturation in infancy provides an extraordinary opportunity to examine the complexity of influences that are associated with the processes of regulation and, in turn, the sleep–wake problems (outcomes) that may result.

In the following presentation, we discuss sleep–wake state maturation and sleep disturbances in infancy and early childhood. We adopt a transactional sleep–wake model (Sameroff & Chandler, 1975; Sameroff & Fiese, 1990) to categorize the array of factors that seem to be associated with sleep–wake state regulation and outcomes. Each domain in the model represents a conceptual grouping of explanatory factors hypothesized to precede and influence the process of sleep–wake state "*consolidation*," a construct that has been equated with the major milestone of "sleeping through the night." The model incorporates physiological, environmental, cultural, psychological, and relationship domains hypothesized to play a role in sleep–wake state consolidation.

Beth L. Goodlin-Jones, Melissa M. Burnham, and Thomas F. Anders • Family and Infant Development Laboratory, Department of Psychiatry, University of California, Davis, Sacramento, California 95817.

Handbook of Developmental Psychopathology, Second Edition, edited by Arnold J. Sameroff, Michael Lewis, and Suzanne M. Miller. Kluwer Academic/Plenum Publishers, New York, 2000.

DESCRIPTION AND DEFINITION
OF SLEEP–WAKE CONSOLIDATION

Before focusing on the model, it is important to describe the significant differences between the less mature sleep–wake state organization of infants and the more mature organization of adults. Two interrelated mechanisms, timing and sleep bout length, summarized in Table 17.1, comprise the process of consolidation.

Timing is regulated by two clocks. The *circadian* clock is involved in the regulation of the diurnal sleep–wake cycle, while the *ultradian* clock is involved in the regulation of the shorter cycles of rapid eye movement (REM) and nonrapid eye movement (NREM) states within the sleep cycle itself. In adults, the circadian clock is "set" so that sleep and waking episodes alternate one time in each 24-hour period. In our culture, the typical young adult sleeps uninterruptedly for 8–10 hours, most often at night, without any prolonged awakenings. The remainder of the time is spent awake. Typically, in adults, sleep onset is rapid, within 5 to 10 minutes of going to bed, and waking in the morning is spontaneous. It is important to note, however, that circadian periodicity is very sensitive to environmental influence. For example, the pattern differs in cultures that embrace an afternoon siesta and it also differs in adults who regularly work at night.

How does the circadian clock function in infancy? At birth, sleep–wake states are organized polyphasically. The circadian clock does not appear to function. The infant's sleep–wake cycle seems to be regulated more by a hunger–satiety cycle rather than a light–dark cycle. Awakenings occur from sleep every 3 to 4 hours, usually for a feeding. In prematurely born infants recorded in the intensive care nursery, sleep–wake cycles also seem related to cycles of feeding and intervention rather than to a circadian clock (Glotzbach, Edgar, & Ariagno, 1995). By 3 months of age, however, evidence of circadian periodicity is present. More sleep occurs at night and more wakefulness occurs during the day, even though the lengthening of sustained sleep and waking periods has not changed appreciably. Melatonin, thought to be associated with the regulation of the circadian clock, begins to demonstrate a diurnal secretion pattern at 3 months of age and diurnal rhythms in activity, crying, and core body temperature become evident (Sadeh, 1997; Walker & Menahem, 1994). Nevertheless, the process of consolidation does not become fully adult-like until the child stops napping, usually between the ages of 3 to 5 years (Weissbluth, 1995).

The second mechanism involved in the regulation of sleep is the ultradian clock. Within the sleep portion of the diurnal cycle, the ultradian clock regulates the periodicity of REM and NREM states. In adults, one REM–NREM sleep cycle lasts 90 minutes, on average, before the next begins (Kripke, 1982). In the neonate, the REM–NREM cycle lasts only 50 to 60 minutes. In contrast to the circadian clock, the ultradian clock seems to function *in utero*, regulating the fetal rest–activity cycle (Groome, Swiber, Atterbury, Bentz, & Holland, 1997). After birth, the ultradian clock regulates the infant's REM–NREM cycle.

TABLE 17.1. Consolidation of Sleep–Wake States

Timing	Neonate	Adult
Circadian clock	Polyphasic sleep–wake cycles/24 hours	1 sleep–wake cycle/24 hours
Ultradian clock	REM/NREM cycle is 50–60 minutes	REM/NREM cycle is 90 minutes
Sleep bout length	4 hours	6–10 hours

Sustained sleep and waking episodes increase in length during development. The length of wakeful periods becomes extended from 15-minute bouts in the newborn period to 16-hour bouts, on average, in adulthood. The sleep period demonstrates less dramatic lengthening, from 3-hour bouts in the newborn period to 6- to 10-hour bouts in adulthood, although there is controversy about even this length. As with infants, arousals and brief awakenings periodically interrupt adult sleep before the morning awakening, often at times of sleep cycle transitions. The "sleeping" adult is generally unaware of these awakenings and, thus, sustained sleep in adults, like in year-old infants, may not lengthen beyond 6 hours. Sleep–wake states organize over time and the process of organization is influenced by a number of external factors. Before reviewing these factors, we next examine what is known about infant sleep problems as possible outcomes of disturbances in sleep–wake state regulation.

SLEEP PROBLEMS

Definitions of what constitutes a sleep problem in infancy vary widely. Some professionals view sleep difficulties as nearly universal and benign, while others suggest that they are more serious, serving as indicators of possible psychological disturbance or relationship dysfunction (Anders, 1994; Benoit, Zeanah, Boucher, & Minde, 1992). In infants and young children, sleep disruption is one of the most common concerns discussed by parents with professionals (Ferber, 1987; Messer & Richards, 1993). The disruptions comprise problems of night waking, difficulty in falling asleep, or both, and are classified by sleep clinicians as dyssomnias (American Psychiatric Association, 1994; American Sleep Disorders Association, 1990). However, because the criteria for dyssomnias are not well defined at young ages, they may be better characterized as "protodyssomnias" (Anders & Eiben, 1997). The classification of infant protodyssomnias has been based on parental complaints that, in turn, are influenced by parental attitude, experience, expectations, and behaviors, and by cultural practices. Night awakenings constitute a problem only for those parents who expect their infants to "sleep though the night." Similarly, having lengthy delays in settling for the night is not viewed as a problem if parents enjoy their child's persistent requests for company (Jaffa, Scott, Hendriks, & Shapiro, 1993).

Parental report measures have been suggested as accurate for characterizing problematic awakenings but a poor method to develop scientific knowledge about the causal factors involved in sleep–wake state regulation (Messer & Richards, 1993; Sadeh, 1996a). In a study conducted in England, 10% of the parents who reported frequent nighttime awakenings by their toddlers did not report them as problems (Scott & Richards, 1990). An epidemiological survey in Bavaria indicated that while 23% of the 5-month-olds in the sample had night waking problems, only 10–15% of parents reported family distress with these patterns (Wolke, Meyer, Ohrt, & Riegel, 1995). In our laboratory, using time lapse video to record infant sleep in the home, we have attempted to define potential precursors of sleep problems. We have noted that "sleeping through the night" as reported by parents is a misnomer. Rarely do infants sleep continuously for more than 6 hours on average. On videotape, the 10- to 12-hour sleeping through the night periods reported by parents are actually punctuated by one or more brief arousals that may last from 30 seconds to 4 minutes or longer. Because some infants do not cry upon awakening, parents are often unaware that the awakening occurred. Seventy percent of 1-year-old infants return to sleep after such an arousal, while 30% begin to cry. We have termed the former group "self-soothers" and the latter group "signalers." We use the terms *signaling* and *self-soothing* to categorize learned patterns of behavior, not characteristics of individual infants. We speculate that signaling infants may continue their signaling pattern and develop a sleep problem in the second year of life (Anders, Halpern, & Hua, 1992).

Richman (1981) provided operational criteria for parent complaints. She indicated that a diagnosis of sleep disorder can be made if, for at least 3 consecutive months and for 5 or more nights per week, one of the following is present: The child (1) awakens three or more times per night; (2) awakens for more than 20 minutes during the night; (3) is taken into the parent's bed; or (4) refuses to go to sleep at bedtime or requires the presence of the parents to fall asleep. Moore and Ucko's (1957) criteria for an infant sleep problem included awakening and signaling between midnight and 5:00 A.M. on at least 4 of 7 nights for at least 4 consecutive weeks.

These operational definitions are based on the observation that the family is sufficiently concerned by the problem to bring the child for an evaluation. Some studies have found that only a minority of parents view night waking as problematic or distressing (Wolke et al., 1995). Conversely, Anders and colleagues (1992) reported that close to 78% of mothers with 8-month-olds who signaled in the middle of the night perceived the infants as problem sleepers. Thus, the perception of night waking as a problem may be more important than the night waking itself in influencing outcomes.

PREVALENCE AND PERSISTENCE OF SLEEP PROBLEMS

Given the varied definitions of sleep complaints derived from parent reports, the literature is remarkably consistent about their prevalence. A brief review of the prevalence and persistence of infant and toddler sleep problems is warranted. Discussion of sleep problems in later childhood and adolescence have been discussed elsewhere (Carskadon, Anders, & Hole, 1988). In a survey of three developed nations (United States, Great Britain, and New Zealand), the prevalence of night waking as a sleep problem during infancy and early childhood was approximately the same, averaging 28% over all ages (Scher et al., 1995). Another survey of parents of 2-year-old children found that 23% had settling problems at the beginning of the night (Hewitt, Powell, & Tait, 1989). In another large survey conducted in Australia, 28% of parents reported that they perceived a significant problem with their infant or toddler's pattern of night waking or inability to settle (Armstrong, Quinn, & Dadds, 1994). Furthermore, sleep that is fragmented by awakenings or arousals has been shown to cause problems in approximately 25% of 1-year-olds and 25–50% of 2- to 3-year-olds (Douglas, 1989; Kataria, Swanson, & Trevanthan, 1987; Sadeh, 1996a, 1996b; Scher, Steppe, & Banks, 1996). Over the first 4 years of life, Wolfson and colleagues (1992) estimated that one out of three children experienced settling and/or night waking problems. Similarly, in a survey of parents with infants age 1–3 years, 42% reported settling problems and 35% reported night waking problems (Johnson, 1991). Additionally, physicians practicing pediatrics report that 26% of their office visits involve sleep questions, and physicians practicing child psychiatry report that 61% of their patients experience sleep problems (Wolfson, Lacks, & Futterman, 1992).

The continuity of sleep problems during childhood is difficult to determine because many reports rely on parent recall a few years after the problem began. Retrospective histories often provide biased information and there is a paucity of prospective longitudinal data reporting on the persistence of sleep disturbances (Guedeney & Kreisler, 1987). In the few longitudinal studies that have been conducted, the results indicate that infant sleep problems often persist and may lead to chronic sleep problems later in life. In the Bavarian study mentioned earlier, data from parent reports indicated that 30% of full-term nightwakers at 5 months were also nightwakers at 20 months (Wolke et al., 1995). Of those infants waking at 20 months, 17% continued to be nightwakers at 56 months. For the preterm infant group, the persistence of night waking was similar, with 28% of nightwakers remaining so at the 20 month assessment, and 24% of them remaining so at 56 months of age (Wolke et al., 1995). Previous researchers with samples of full-term infants have noted that approximately 40% persist with night waking into the preschool and early elementary school years (Zuckerman, Stevenson, & Bailey, 1987). It is clear that sleep problems in infancy are fairly common, with a large portion persisting to childhood. The following discussion reviews what is known about the factors that may mediate the process of sleep maturation.

THE TRANSACTIONAL SLEEP–WAKE MODEL

We have employed a transactional model to understand the developmental processes involved in sleep maturation and how the factors involved interact over time (Fig. 17.1). The transactional model reflects the concepts of dynamic systems theory. It assumes that the regulation of sleep–wake states is mediated through parent–infant interactions that, in turn, are responsive to a larger system of dynamic contextual influences. The more proximal influences include (1) indicators of marital satisfaction, social support, and family economic circumstances; (2) the primary caregiver's current state of physical health, psychological well-being and childhood representations; and (3) the infant's temperament and state of physical health. More distal factors include the broader set of cultural values related to sleep as well as both direct and indirect environmental influences that are assumed to disrupt sleep. In other words, maturation of infant sleep–wake states involves an interplay of factors that dynamically interact. Outcomes in infant sleep–wake state organization continuously reflect and affect both infant and family well-being. According to this model, proximal stressors, such as maternal depression, marital dysfunction, or a chaotic lifestyle affect parent–infant interaction, the process of infant sleep–wake regulation and, reactively, the family context. In the sections that follow, we review what is known about the process of consolidation of sleep–wake states, and the relationship between consolidation and outcome from the perspective of our transactional model.

Culture

Cultures vary in child-rearing attitudes and techniques. Cultural attitudes dictate whether a specific set of behaviors is defined as a sleep problem. Cultural beliefs also influence family sleeping arrangements that affect sleep–wake regulation (McKenna et al., 1993). In fact, cosleeping and solitary sleeping decisions are much more a function of cultural values than physical space considerations (Harkness & Super, 1995). Parent–child cosleeping is considered a normal practice in most cultures of the world (Mosko, Richards, McKenna, & Drummond, 1996). In Japanese families, a cross-sectional study found that children slept with their parents until approximately age 13, at which point they began to sleep more independently (Harkness & Super, 1995). Cosleeping in Japan, however, is not the same as cosleeping in the United States. In Japan, mothers, fathers, and infants each sleep on their own futons, placed adjacent to each other (K. Nishihara, personal communication, June 17, 1997). In the United States, cosleeping most often refers to sharing a family bed. In a study comparing Korean, American, and Korean-American children, it was apparent that as families became accultur-

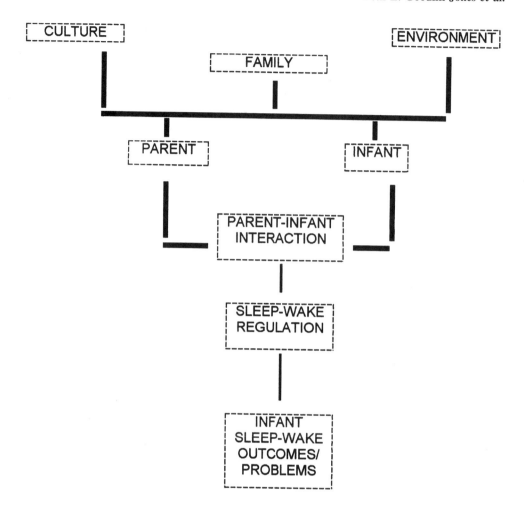

FIGURE 17.1. The transactional model of sleep–wake regulation. Both proximal and distal factors influence regulation and outcome in a bidirectional way.

ated to the Western belief in solitary sleeping, they changed from cosleeping to solitary sleeping arrangements. The American families in this sample used solitary sleeping arrangements for children by the age of 3 months (Hong & Townes, 1976). Clearly, cultural sanctions in regard to cosleeping are important. It has been observed, for example, that in the United States, white families more often cosleep as a reaction to a child's sleep problem, while nonwhite families cosleep at higher rates as part of their customary practices (Medoff & Schaefer, 1993).

When cosleeping, the organization of sleep–wake states and the nature of parent–infant nighttime interactions differ significantly (McKenna et al., 1993). Cosleeping infants are physiologically more aroused, with a greater proportion of sleep time spent in NREM stages 1 and 2, and less time in the less aroused, deeper sleep of NREM stages 3 and 4 (Mosko et al., 1996). Cosleeping infants and solitary sleeping infants under 1 year of age, however, are awake for similar total amounts of time (Mosko et al., 1996). Interestingly, parents who cosleep seldom report sleep disturbances or night waking problems (Kawasaki, Nugent, Miyashita, Miyahara, & Brazelton, 1994). Another recent study found that cosleeping infants experienced more sensory exchanges (movement, touch, sound, smell) with their mothers. Furthermore, these infants were never observed sleeping in the prone position (Richards, Mosko, McKenna, & Drummond, 1996). Thus, it has been suggested that cosleeping may reduce the possibility of sudden infant death syndrome (SIDS).

Professional beliefs also can influence cultural values. For example, in 1992, the American Academy of Pediatrics (AAP) recommended that all healthy infants be positioned on their backs (supine) or on their sides for the first year of life (American Academy of Pediatrics Task Force, 1992). Research reviews indicate that placing an infant on his or her back or side at the beginning of the night significantly reduces the risk of SIDS (Gilbert-Barness & Barness, 1995; Mitchell, 1993). The AAP has actively promoted a "Back to Sleep" campaign by providing education on positioning to both the professional community and the general public. Recent surveys of pediatricians have indicated that they have changed their sleeping position advice in accordance with the AAP recommendations (Kohler & Markestad, 1993; Rainey & Lawless, 1994). It seems relatively clear that Western cultural practices regarding the positioning of infants can be impacted by professional recommendations. Furthermore, it is also clear from the cross-cultural cosleeping literature that encompassing cultural beliefs can impact the sleep environment of young children. Thus, in accordance with the transactional model, culture both influences and is influenced by factors related to infant sleep.

Environment

Environmental factors can also influence infant sleep–wake outcomes. The environment is broadly defined by elements that may act as direct (light–dark periods, external schedules) or indirect (maternal employment, socioeconomic status) regulators of sleep in the young child. Few studies have examined environmental factors such as the family's schedule for bedtime interaction and their availability during the night (Anders & Taylor, 1994). The studies that have looked at environmental factors have primarily focused on such variables as socioeconomic status (SES) or maternal employment as they impact sleep. One study observed a socioeconomic class difference among parents' response to night waking (Scott & Richards, 1990). Middle-class parents were more likely than working-class parents to let a night-waking infant "cry it out." Working-class parents preferred to go to the infant immediately. Another study found that during the first year of life, mothers employed outside of the home had greater difficulty separating from their infants at night and had more concern about their child's sleep than mothers who were not employed (Van Tassel, 1985). This difference disappeared during the child's second year of life. An additional investigation found a higher rate of night waking among infants in families with employed mothers compared to families with mothers who did not work outside the home (Scher et al., 1995). Generally, in families in which both parents work all day, the evening may be an important time for family socialization (Sadeh & Anders, 1993b). For young children, going to bed early means missing out on opportunities for interacting with their parents.

Family

Family characteristics also represent a significant set of factors that contribute to sleep regulation. As with the impact of employment-related stress on infant sleep, there is a paucity of information regarding the influences of marital relationship quality or presence–absence of extended family on infant sleep consolidation. The evidence that is available suggests that marital conflict may alter sleep behavior in infants and young children. In those families where severe family conflict was identified as a major source of distress, 12 of 18 infants suffered from a sleep problem (Guedeney & Kreisler, 1987). Additionally, maternal reports of unsupportive marital relationships were commonly reported in mothers of 1- to 2-year-old infants with sleep problems (Richman, 1981). Also, in a case history presentation, the presence of marital conflict and dissatisfaction with the maternal role for a new mother who decided to remain at home with her infant were identified as contributors to her infant's settling problem (Shonkoff & Brazelton, 1993). Unfortunately, there are no systematic data available on the role of extended family members and their contribution to the regulation of sleep. More research is needed to better understand the impact of family characteristics on infant sleep patterns.

Maternal Characteristics

Maternal psychopathology, especially anxiety and depression, has been identified as a contributing factor to infants' sleep problems. Richman (1981) found that mothers of 1- to 2-year-old infants with sleep problems were more anxious than mothers of control infants. In addition to anxiety, maternal depression has been repeatedly identified as a significant correlate of infant sleep problems (Gjerdingen & Chaloner, 1994; Seifer, Dickstein, et al., 1994). Zuckerman and colleagues (1987) reported that depression was more common in mothers of 8-month to 3-year-old children with sleep problems. Guedeney and Kreisler (1987) also found a significant correlation between maternal depression and infant sleep disturbances during the first 18 months of life. Additionally, separating from the infant at bedtime was identified as difficult for the depressed mother in Shonkoff and Brazelton's case study (1993). Similarly, negative attitudes toward motherhood and feelings of stress and depression in mothers have also been associated with night waking problems in young children (Scott & Richards, 1990). Unfortunately, the paucity of longitudinal data makes causal inferences difficult. It is not clear whether maternal depression influences infant sleep, whether infant sleep problems lead to maternal depression, or whether both are influenced by a third factor.

Our recent longitudinal study identified a significant relationship between higher levels of maternal depressive feelings and fewer bouts of self-soothing during the middle of the night in infants under 1 year of age (Goodlin-Jones, Eiben, & Anders, 1997). Depressive feelings in mothers may be worsened by loss of sleep associated with infant waking. Loss of sleep, in turn, may hamper the nighttime interaction patterns with their infants. This pattern is an example of the hypothesized bidirectional process involved in the regulation of sleep.

Another study examining maternal characteristics found a significant association between insecure adult attachment classifications in mothers and maternal reports of sleep problems in their toddlers (Benoit et al., 1992). The significant association between how a mother represents her early relationship history in interaction with her toddler's sleep problem is assumed to reflect a difficulty in the mother's ability to separate and is posited to impact the toddler's night waking behavior (Benoit et al., 1992). Minde (1988) has also suggested that a mother who overresponds at night to the infant's waking may be responding from her own previous experience and memory of family trauma. These results on the effects of maternal past experiences on infant sleep disturbances await replication and must be interpreted cautiously.

Maternal age also may be a significant factor that contributes to infant sleep problems. Younger adult mothers are reported to experience more depressive feelings during the first postpartum year than older adult mothers (Gjerdingen & Chaloner, 1994). Additionally, younger adult mothers have also been found to have infants who wake up significantly earlier in the morning than infants of older mothers (Scher et al., 1995). Finally, in a study comparing adult and teenage primiparous mothers, it was found that infants of teenage mothers had shorter sleep bouts at night at 4 months of age, and that this correlated with higher levels of perceived stress by their mothers (Becker, Chang, Kameshima, & Bloch, 1991). The differences were nonsignificant by 12 months of age.

In summary, the quality of maternal well-being seems to be key in the regulation of infant sleep. In fact, the most consistent findings from several studies suggest that maternal depression, experienced by the infant through day and nighttime interactions, may be one pathway to the development of sleep problems. Marital conflict, financial stress, and employment outside of the home all appear to play somewhat less significant roles in infant and early childhood bedtime and night-waking problems, although more adequately controlled longitudinal studies need to be completed to understand how these factors interact.

Infant Characteristics

As with the other domains in the transactional model, most studies have not adequately accounted for the contributions of infant characteristics such as gender, temperament, and feeding style to sleep–wake patterns. There are no consistently reported gender differences in prevalence rates for sleep problems in the literature. While one study found that a greater proportion of "problem sleepers" at 8 months were males (Anders et al., 1992), Scher and colleagues (1995) found that more females than males in their sample were reported as night wakers. A consensus has not been reached on the role of gender in sleep disturbances.

Birth order has been associated with sleep problems. For example, firstborn infants experience a greater proportion of night-waking problems than later born infants (Walters, 1993) and have shorter sleep duration (St. James-Roberts & Plewis, 1996). Also, firstborn infants were found to have a later bedtime than later born infants, suggesting greater difficulty with settling (Scher et al., 1995). However, other studies have not observed a preponderance of sleep problems in firstborn infants (Van Tassel, 1985). The changes in parenting behavior and parenting expectations as parity increases may significantly influence how parents interact with their children at bedtime and in the middle of the night but the data remain inconclusive. It has been suggested that parental attitudes and behaviors are more likely to shift in relation to their third child, not their second (Anders & Keener, 1985).

Research studies comparing sleep–wake differences between breast- and bottle-fed infants have yielded conflicting results. Breast feeding has been associated with more night waking for additional feedings and longer waking bouts, which continue to older ages compared to bottle-fed infants (Daws, 1993; Scher et al., 1995). However, Pinilla and Birch (1993) reported that breast feeding bouts at night are modifiable and infants may be taught with simple techniques to lengthen their sleep periods to those comparable to bottle-fed infants. In his review, Messer (1993) found little support for a relationship between method of feeding and sleep problems. Additionally, there appears to be little impact on sleep when solid food is added to the diet or when a feeding is given just prior to bedtime, despite the folklore that suggests otherwise (Anders, 1994).

A number of studies have indicated that a child's temperament is an important factor in the cause and maintenance of sleep problems (Atkinson, Vetere, & Grayson, 1995; Sadeh, Lavie, & Scher, 1994; Schaefer, 1990). For example, Weissbluth (1984) reported that children with "difficult" temperaments slept less than children with "easy" temperaments. Furthermore, significant associations have also been reported between a high rate of night-waking problems and "difficult" temperaments (Atkinson et al., 1995; Schaefer, 1990). Minde (1988; Minde et al., 1993) suggests from his research that the failure of poor sleepers to use self-soothing techniques in the middle of the night may be related to temperamental differences and difficulties in state regulation. The mothers in another study also described their night-waking infants as less adaptive, having a lower sensory threshold, being more distractible, and as more demanding compared to controls (Sadeh et al., 1994).

In contrast, Keener, Zeanah, and Anders (1990) did not find temperamental differences by parental report in infants who cried upon awakening at night compared to infants who did not cry in their review of the literature. Other researchers have also reported no significant relationship between maternal reports of temperament and sleep problems (Messer, 1993; St. James-Roberts & Plewis, 1996). However, these studies relied on questionnaire ratings of temperament. The validity of temperament categorization by parental report has been discussed frequently (e.g., Zeanah, Keener, & Anders, 1986). One study compared both sources and found that observational ratings of temperament at 3 months, in contrast to questionnaire ratings, *were* correlated with sleep–wake measures (Halpern, Anders, García-Coll, & Hua, 1994). Specifically, infants who spent more time awake at night were less sociable, and infants with lower active sleep percentages were more irritable.

Despite the lack of a clear, direct relationship between temperament and sleep, differences in temperament *are* likely to be associated with different interaction patterns with parents (Sigman, Beckwith, Cohen, & Parmelee, 1989). Infants who have smoother state transitions may be easier to care for, with less disruptive social interactions and less need for assistance in maintaining an organized sleep period. Again, more research is needed to clarify this relationship.

Temperament has also been posited to interact with colic by increasing the likelihood of a mother's negative perception of her infant. Infants with colic are typically described as having periods of low soothability, high activity, and persistent crying (Lester, 1997). In Western cultures, infantile colic is reported in approximately one out of four infants. Colic begins at about 2–3 weeks of age and persists until 3–6 months of age (Lester, 1997). Brazelton (1990) has proposed that for 3- to 12-week-old infants, crying may be a normal discharge phenomenon when the central nervous system is overstimulated. It is interesting to note that a peak in crying, clustered at evening time, at approximately 4–6 weeks postnatally has also been observed in non-Western cultures and in premature infants (Barr, Chen, Hopkins, & Westra, 1996). Lehtonen, Korhonen, and Korvenranta (1994) found that mothers of colicky infants had a more negative impression of their infant's temperament at 3 months and again at 12 months, even though the infant's actual behaviors did not differ on sleep measures at 12 months. Thus, the mother's perception of temperament was apparently affected by the early parenting experience involving colic.

In addition to the data suggesting an interaction between temperament and colic, sleep may be impacted directly by colic. Specifically, a recent study found that colicky infants had significantly less quiet sleep, more active sleep, and more awake fussy time in the crib when compared to noncolicky infants during the first 4 months of life (Keefe, Kotzer, Froese-

Fretz, & Curtin, 1996). Parental report measures also indicate significantly less sleep time in 2-month-old colicky infants as compared to noncolicky infants (White, Gunnar, Larson, Donzella, & Barr, 1998). A recent longitudinal study that followed infants from age 2 weeks to 9 months suggested that "high fussers" at 6 weeks remain "high fussers" at 9 months, but there was little impact on sleep behavior (St. James-Roberts & Plewis, 1996). In another prospective longitudinal study, little support for this association in infancy was demonstrated (Lehtonen et al., 1994). Specifically, few sleep differences were observed between groups of colicky versus normal infants at 8 and 12 months of age as measured by maternal perception. However, when these same families were interviewed again, when the children were 3 years of age, the families reported more distress with daily parenting tasks and more sleeping problems as measured by a standardized questionnaire, the Child Behavior Checklist 2–3 (CBCL2–3). The problems with sleep reported by these families involved both settling at night and night-waking issues (Rautava, Lehtonen, Helenius, & Sillanpaa, 1995). Thus, the role that colic plays in impacting sleep is uncertain. What appears clear is colic's impact on maternal perception, which then may influence nighttime behavior.

Young children with neurodevelopmental disorders also display more sleep disturbances (Stevenson, 1993). In a recent study using direct observation, Piazza, Fisher, and Kahng (1996) reported that the children with mental retardation and severe behavioral disorders in their sample slept for significantly shorter periods of time compared to expected durations. Furthermore, 88% of the children with developmental disorders had problems with night waking or difficulty settling. Similarly, children with learning disorders and developmental delay have been reported to have high rates of night waking (50% to 85% of sample) and settling problems, requiring an average of 2 hours to settle (Quine, 1992; Saxby & Morgan, 1993). Sleep problems also have been observed in children diagnosed with attention-deficit/hyperactivity disorder (ADHD; Dahl, Pelham, & Wierson, 1991). Interestingly, it has recently been suggested that for a sub-group of children with ADHD, disturbed sleep may be the primary problem. The resulting sleepiness then causes the hyperalert behavior, inattention, and impulsiveness (Sadeh & Gruber, 1998).

The risk of developmental disorders is particularly salient for infants born prematurely. Several studies have examined the sleep characteristics of preterm infants during the neonatal period to determine whether their sleep parameters differ from those of full-term infants. The frequency of night-waking problems among preterm infants at 7 months of age has been compared to that of full-term infants. Ju, Lester, García-Coll, Oh, and Vohr (1991), for example, employed a 24-hour diary completed by mothers, to study infants' sleep. They found that the mean number of night awakenings was greater for preterm infants. In contrast, Anders and Keener (1985), using time-lapse video equipment to study the sleep–wake patterns of preterm and full-term infants in the first year of life, found that the two groups of infants were similar with regard to all sleep parameters when they were compared at corrected conceptional ages. It is unclear, then, whether sleep–wake measures differ between preterm and full-term infants. It may be that the different outcomes found in other studies comparing preterm and full-term infants are more related to maternal well-being than gestational age.

Sleep measures have also been found to differ in infants exposed to alcohol or illicit substances *in utero* compared to their nonexposed counterparts. While alcohol exposure alone has been reported to lessen the sleep duration and increase waking times in exposed infants, cocaine exposure *in utero* has a different effect (Regalado, Schechtman, Del Angel, & Bean, 1995; Scher, Richardson, Coble, Day, & Stoffer, 1988). Cocaine-exposed, 2-week-old infants have been found to have the same amount of total sleep and wake time as nonexposed infants, but they exhibit significantly less active sleep and more indeterminate sleep. Substance use by mother clearly affects newborn sleep patterns. In summary, infant characteristics, such as neurodevelopmental status, do exert significant influence on sleep–wake patterns.

Parent–Infant Interaction

The significance of parent–infant interaction as an important "regulator" in the transactional system of sleep–wake consolidation is clear. It is one of the more consistent findings regarding sleep problems in infancy and early childhood (Anders, 1994; Ware & Orr, 1992). At bedtime, the manner in which the parent interacts with the infant influences how or if settling occurs and the infant's behavior upon subsequent night waking. Specifically, difficulty in returning to sleep at night following an awakening often recapitulates the difficulty experienced in falling asleep at bedtime. A routine of rocking or rubbing may be associated with sleep onset at bedtime and then is expected again in the middle of the night. In one study, a parent's presence at bedtime was significantly related to requiring the parent's presence after a night waking in 9-month-olds (Adair, Bouchner, Philipp, Levenson, & Zuckerman, 1991). Furthermore, 8-month-old infants who did not "signal" in the middle of the night upon awakening were more likely to have been put into their crib awake at the beginning of the night, have gone to sleep on their own, and were more likely to have used a sleepaid while falling asleep (Anders et al., 1992). Parental presence at bedtime has also been found to lessen the infant's likelihood of using an object to self-soothe at night (Wolf & Lozoff, 1989). Finally, the absence of a regular bedtime routine has been noted as a significant correlate of night-waking problems (Anders 1994; Quine 1992).

Parent–child bedtime interaction may include encouraging the use of a sleepaid. Helping the infant to find a "lovey" to use when tired or going to sleep has been recommended as an effective strategy for infants with settling problems (Shonkoff & Brazelton, 1993). Anders and colleagues (1992) observed that infants at both 3 and 8 months of age who used a sleepaid were more likely to be placed in their bed awake at the beginning of the night and to use the object to self-soothe both when settling and in the middle of the night after an awakening. Paret (1983) observed that 9-month-old infants who did not have night-waking problems were more likely to use their fingers or an object in the middle of the night to soothe themselves. Thus, although somewhat controversial among some groups of parents (e.g., Sears, 1985), the use of a sleepaid has consistently been found to relate to "better" sleep outcomes in infancy.

SUMMARY AND CONCLUSIONS

Do the studies reviewed support a transactional model of sleep–wake state development? What is the relationship between signaling and self-soothing behavior in the first year of life to mother–infant nighttime interaction and to longer term outcomes of poorly regulated sleep and sleep problems later in development? Unfortunately, the designs of most studies to date preclude a definitive understanding of sleep–wake state regulation leading to consolidation and outcome. Moreover, the specific mechanisms and pathways underlying the processes remain unknown. Design issues, such as small sample sizes, studies of clinical populations of complaining parents instead of population-based samples, and reliance on one-dimensional data-collection methods, confound the results. Since the posited contextual variables, such as maternal depression, marital dysfunction, and poor social support, are often highly intercorrelated, studies with large sample sizes, in which the partial effects of these confounds can be controlled or aggregated, need to be undertaken.

The question of stability of individual differences also remains problematic. Seifer, Sameroff, Barrett, and Krafchuk (1994) have suggested that temperament measurements collected between 4 and 14 months need to be repeated at least seven times to ascertain stability. Similarly, Acebo and Carskadon (1997) reported that a minimum of four nights of home-recorded sleep, using the actigraph, is required to determine significant consistency in night-to-night sleep–wake measures. In support of these recommendations, our own studies with videosomnography suggest that infants' response to awakenings at young ages change from one night to another, as do their parents in interaction with them during the night. Moreover, even on the same night, infants may signal after some awakenings and self-soothe after others (Goodlin-Jones et al., 1997). Finally, we do not know whether poorly regulated sleep at an early age really predicts significant sleep disorder at a later age, and what potential risk and protective factors might contribute to the outcome. Parental reports, especially retrospective reports, are inadequate. Multimethod longitudinal studies, using population-based samples, including large enough samples to partial the effects of contextual variables, and sufficient recording opportunities to ensure stability are required. These are stringent and costly criteria but worth the investment if one believes that understanding optimal parent–infant relationships and their regulation are significant determinants of the future well-being of children.

The prevalence rates discussed earlier in the chapter suggest that problems in sleeping through the night or settling for the night are disruptive to approximately one out of three young families in Western, industrialized populations. The concurrent impact of these sleep disturbances usually involves exhausted or frustrated parents who are likely to exhibit less-than-optimal parenting behavior. This less-than-optimal parenting may increase the likelihood of early sleep problems developing into later sleep problems. It has been shown that young children with sleep problems early in life may exhibit emotional problems in later childhood (Stevenson, 1993). Thus, sleep problems may be viewed as potential indicators of an under-lying psychological problem in the individual or a problem in his or her relationships (Pollock, 1994). If the sleep problem is a symptom of a poor parent–child relationship early in life, later emotional and behavioral problems would be expected as the poor relationship continues to impact the child's development (Anders, 1994; Benoit et al., 1992).

A better understanding of the processes involved in early parent–infant regulation in general, and around sleep–wake state consolidation in particular, should provide significant new knowledge that will enhance optimal development for the child and family. Our view of the development of sleep-state regulation and the emergence of sleep problems in infants and young children remains relational, in that the social context (caregiving relationship) must be examined first and foremost in both evaluating the cause and designing the intervention of a sleep difficulty. What is clear from the literature examined is that sleep–wake outcomes are related to a number of complex and interacting factors, and, thus, fit more clearly with a systems, rather than a linear, perspective. The details of each element in the model are what need the most attention in future research.

ACKNOWLEDGMENTS.   Supported, in part, by the Hibbard E. Williams Fund, University of California, Davis (BGJ), and Grant No. MH50741 (TFA).

REFERENCES

Acebo, C., & Carskadon, M. A. (1997). Reliability of actigraph measures in children and adolescents. *Associated Professional Sleep Societies Abstracts, 11*, 347.

Adair, R., Bouchner, H., Philipp, B., Levenson, S., & Zuckerman, B. (1991). Night waking during infancy: Role of parental presence at bedtime. *Pediatrics, 87*(4), 500–504.

American Academy of Pediatrics Task Force. (1992). Positioning and SIDS. *Pediatrics, 89*(6), 1120–1126.

American Psychiatric Association. (1994). *Diagnostic and statistical manual of mental disorders* (4th ed.). Washington, DC: Author.

American Sleep Disorders Association. (1990). *The international classification of sleep disorders: Diagnostic and coding manual* (2nd ed.). Lawrence, KS: Allen Press.

Anders, T. F. (1994). Infant sleep, nighttime relationships, and attachment. *Psychiatry, 57*, 11–21.

Anders, T. F., & Eiben, L. A. (1997). Pediatric sleep disorders: A review of the past 10 years. *Journal of the American Academy of Child and Adolescent Psychiatry, 36*, 9–20.

Anders, T. F., Halpern, L. F., & Hua, J. (1992). Sleeping through the night: A developmental perspective. *Pediatrics, 90*, 554–560.

Anders, T. F., & Keener, M. A. (1985). Developmental course of nighttime sleep–wake patterns in full-term and premature infants during the first year of life. *Sleep, 8*(3), 173–192.

Anders, T. F., & Taylor, T. R. (1994). Babies and their sleep environment. *Children's Environments, 11*(2), 123–134.

Armstrong, K. L., Quinn, R. A., & Dadds, M. R. (1994). The sleep patterns of normal children. *Medical Journal of Australia, 161*, 202–206.

Atkinson, E., Vetere, A., & Grayson, K. (1995). Sleep disruption in young children: The influence of temperament on the sleep patterns of pre-school children. *Child: Care, Health and Development, 21*(4), 233–246.

Barr, R. G., Chen, S., Hopkins, B., & Westra, T. (1996). Crying patterns in preterm infants. *Developmental Medicine and Child Neurology, 38*, 345–355.

Becker, P. T., Chang, A., Kameshima, S., & Bloch, M. (1991). Correlates of diurnal sleep patterns in infants of adolescent and adult single mothers. *Research in Nursing and Health, 14*, 97–108.

Benoit, D., Zeanah, C. H., Boucher, C., & Minde, K. K. (1992). Sleep disorders in early childhood: Association with insecure maternal attachment. *Journal of the American Academy of Child and Adolescent Psychiatry, 31*(1), 86–93.

Brazelton, T. B. (1990). Crying and colic. *Infant Mental Health Journal, 11*(4), 349–356.

Carskadon, M. A., Anders, T. F., & Hole, W. (1988). Sleep disturbances in childhood and adolescence. In H. E. Fitzgerald, B. M. Lester, & M. W. Yogman (Eds.), *Theory and research in behavioral pediatrics* (Vol. 4, pp. 221–247). New York: Plenum Press.

Crawford, C. J. (1994). Parenting practices in the Basque country: Implications of infant and childhood sleeping location for personality development. *Ethos, 22*(1), 42–82.

Dahl, R. E., Pelham, W. E., & Wierson, M. (1991). The role of sleep disturbances in attention deficit disorder symptoms: A case study. *Journal of Pediatric Psychology, 16*, 229–239.

Daws, D. (1993). Feeding problems and relationship difficulties: Therapeutic work with parents and infants. *Journal of Child Psychotherapy, 19*(2), 69–83.

Douglas, J. (1989). Training parents to manage their child's sleep problem. In C. E. Schaefer & J. M. Briemeister (Eds.), *Handbook of parent training* (pp. 13–37). New York: Wiley.

Ferber, R. (1987). Sleepless child. In C. Guilleminault (Ed.), *Sleep and its disorders in children* (pp. 41–163). New York: Raven Press.

Gilbert-Barness, E., & Barness, L. (1995). Sudden infant death. *Contemporary Pediatrics, 12*(4), 88–107.

Gjerdingen, D. K., & Chaloner, K. M. (1994). The relationship of women's postpartum mental health to employment, childbirth, and social support. *Journal of Family Practice, 38*(5), 465–472.

Glotzbach, S. F., Edgar, D. M., & Ariagno, R. L. (1995). Biological rhythmicity in preterm infants prior to discharge from neonatal intensive care. *Pediatrics, 95*(2), 231–237.

Goodlin-Jones, B. L., Eiben, L. A., & Anders, T. F. (1997). Maternal well-being and sleep–wake behaviors in infants: An intervention using maternal odor. *Infant Mental Health Journal, 18*, 378–393.

Groome, L. J., Swiber, M. J., Atterbury, J. L., Bentz, L. S., & Holland, S. B. (1997). Similarities and differences in behavioral state organization during sleep periods in the perinatal infant before and after birth. *Child Development, 68*(1), 1–11.

Guedeney, A., & Kreisler, L. (1987). Sleep disorders in the first 18 months of life: Hypothesis on the role of mother–child emotional exchanges. *Infant Mental Health Journal, 8*(3), 307–318.

Halpern, L. F., Anders, T. F., García-Coll, C., & Hua, J. (1994). Infant temperament: Is there a relation to sleep–wake states and maternal nighttime behavior? *Infant Behavior and Development, 17*, 255–263.

Harkness, S., & Super, C. (1995). Culture and parenting. In M. H. Bornstein (Ed.), *Handbook of parenting* (Vol. 2, pp. 211–234). Mahwah, NJ: Erlbaum.

Hewitt, K., Powell, I., & Tait, V. (1989). The behavior of 9-month and 2-year-olds as assessed by health visitors and parents. *Health Visitor, 62*, 52–54.

Hong, K. M., & Townes, B. D. (1976). Infants' attachment to inanimate objects: A cross-cultural study. *Journal of the American Academy of Child Psychiatry, 15*(1), 49–61.

Jaffa, T., Scott, S., Hendriks, J. H., & Shapiro, C. M. (1993). Sleep disorders in children. *British Medical Journal, 306,* 640–643.

Johnson, C. M. (1991). Infant and toddler sleep: A telephone survey of parents in one community. *Developmental and Behavioral Pediatrics, 12*(2), 108–114.

Ju, S.-H., Lester, B., García-Coll, C., Oh, W., & Vohr, B. R. (1991). Maternal perceptions of the sleep patterns of premature infants at seven months corrected age compared to full-term infants. *Infant Mental Health Journal, 12*(4), 338–346.

Kataria, S., Swanson, M. S., & Trevanthan, G. E. (1987). Persistence of sleep disturbances in preschool children. *Journal of Pediatrics, 110,* 642–646.

Kawasaki, C., Nugent, J. K., Miyashita, H., Miyahara, H., & Brazelton, T. B. (1994). The cultural organization of infants' sleep. *Children's Environments, 11*(2), 135–141.

Keefe, M R., Kotzer, A. M., Froese-Fretz, A., & Curtin, M. (1996). A longitudinal comparison of irritable and nonirritable infants. *Nursing Research, 45*(1), 4–9.

Keener, M. A., Zeanah, C. H., & Anders, T. F. (1990). Infant temperament, sleep organization, and nighttime parental interventions. In S. Chess & M. E. Hertzig (Eds.), *Annual progress in child psychiatry and child development* (pp. 257–274). New York: Brunner/Mazel.

Kohler, L., & Markestad, T. (1993). Consensus statement on prevention program for SIDS. *Acta Pediatrica Supplement, 82*(389), 126–127.

Kripke, D. F. (1982). Ultradian rhythms in behavior and physiology. In F. M. Brown & R. C. Graeber (Eds.), *Rhythmic aspects of behavior* (pp. 313–343). Hillsdale, NJ: Erlbaum.

Lehtonen, L., Korhonen, T., & Korvenranta, H. (1994). Temperament and sleeping patterns in colicky infants during the first year of life. *Developmental and Behavioral Pediatrics, 15*(6), 416–420.

Lester, B. M. (1997). Definition and diagnosis of colic. In *Colic and excessive crying* (pp. 18–29). Report of the 105th Ross Conference on Pediatric Research. Columbus, OH: Ross Products Division, Abbott Laboratories.

McKenna, J. J., Thoman, E. B., Anders, T. F., Sadeh, A., Schechtman, V. L., & Glotzbach, S. F. (1993). Infant–parent co-sleeping in an evolutionary perspective: Implications for understanding infant sleep development and sudden infant death syndrome. *Sleep, 16,* 263–282.

Medoff, D., & Schaefer, C. E. (1993). Children sharing the parental bed: A review of the advantages and disadvantages of cosleeping. *Psychology: A Journal of Human Behavior, 30,* 1–9.

Messer, D. (1993). The treatment of sleeping difficulties. In I. St. James-Roberts, G. Harris, & D. Messer (Eds.), *Infant crying, feeding, and sleeping* (pp. 194–210). New York: Harvester Wheatsheaf.

Messer, D., & Richards, M. (1993). The development of sleeping difficulties. In I. St. James-Roberts, G. Harris, & D. Messer (Eds.), *Infant crying, feeding, and sleeping* (pp. 150–173). New York: Harvester Wheatsheaf.

Minde, K. (1988). Behavioral abnormalities commonly seen in infancy. *Canadian Journal of Psychiatry, 33,* 741–747.

Minde, K., Popiel, K., Leos, N., Falkner, S., Parker, K., & Handley-Derry, M. (1993). The evaluation and treatment of sleep disturbances in young children. *Journal of Child Psychology and Psychiatry, 34,* 521–533.

Mitchell, E. A. (1993). Sleeping position of infants and the sudden infant death syndrome. *Acta Paediatrica Supplement, 389,* 26–30.

Moore, T., & Ucko, L. E. (1957). Night waking in early infancy. *Archives of Disease in Childhood, 32,* 333–342.

Mosko, S., Richards, C., McKenna, J., & Drummond, S. (1996). Infant sleep architecture during bedsharing and possible implications for SIDS. *Sleep, 19*(9), 677–684.

Paret, I. (1983). Night waking and its relationship to mother–infant interaction in nine-month-old infants. In J. Call, E. Galenson, & R. Tyson (Eds.), *Frontiers of infant psychiatry* (pp. 171–177). New York: Basic Books.

Piazza, C. C., Fisher, W. W., & Kahng, S. W. (1996). Sleep patterns in children and young adults with mental retardation and severe behavior disorders. *Developmental Medicine and Child Neurology, 38,* 335–344.

Pinilla, T., & Birch, L. L. (1993). Help me make it through the night: Behavioral entrainment of breast-fed infants' sleep patterns. *Pediatrics, 91*(2), 436–444.

Pollock, J. I. (1994). Night-waking at five years of age: Predictors and prognosis. *Journal of Child Psychology and Psychiatry, 35*(4), 699–708.

Quine, L. (1992). Severity of sleep problems in children with severe learning difficulties: Description and correlates. *Journal of Community and Applied Social Psychology, 2,* 247–268.

Rainey, D. Y., & Lawless, M. R. (1994). Infant positioning and SIDS. *Clinical Pediatrics, 33*(6), 322–324.

Rautava, P., Lehtonen, L., Helenius, H., & Sillanpaa, M. (1995). Infantile colic: Child and family three years later. *Pediatrics, 96*(1), 43–47.

Regalado, M. G., Schechtman, V. L., Del Angel, A. P., & Bean, X. D. (1995). Sleep disorganization in cocaine-exposed neonates. *Infant Behavior and Development, 18,* 319–327.

Richards, C., Mosko, S., McKenna, J., & Drummond, S. (1996). Sleeping position, orientation, and proximity in bedsharing infants and mothers. *Sleep, 19*(9), 685–690.

Richman, N. (1981). A community survey of characteristics of one- to two-year-olds with sleep disruptions. *Journal of the American Academy of Child and Adolescent Psychiatry, 20,* 281–291.

Sadeh, A. (1996a). Evaluating night wakings in sleep-disturbed infants: A methodological study of parental reports and actigraphy. *Sleep, 19*(10), 757–762.

Sadeh, A. (1996b). Stress, trauma, and sleep in children. *Child and Adolescent Psychiatric Clinics of North America, 5*(3), 685–700.

Sadeh, A. (1997). Sleep and melatonin in infants: A preliminary study. *Sleep, 20,* 185–191.

Sadeh, A., & Anders, T. F. (1993a). Infant sleep problems: Origins, assessment, interventions. *Infant Mental Health Journal, 14*(1), 17–34.

Sadeh, A., & Anders, T. F. (1993b). Sleep disorders. In C. H. Zeanah (Ed.), *Handbook of infant mental health* (pp. 305–316). New York: Guilford Press.

Sadeh, A., & Gruber, R. (1998). Sleep disorders. In A. Bellack & M. Hersen (Eds.), *Comprehensive clinical psychology.* New York: Pergamon Press.

Sadeh, A., Lavie, P., & Scher, A. (1994). Sleep and temperament: Maternal perceptions of temperament of sleep-disturbed toddlers. *Early Education and Development, 5*(4), 311–322.

Sameroff, A. J., & Chandler, M. (1975). Reproductive risk and the continuum of caretaking casualty. In F. D. Horowitz, E. M. Hetherington, S. Scarr-Salapatek, & G. Siegel (Eds.), *Review of child development research* (Vol. 4, pp. 187–244). Chicago: University of Chicago Press.

Sameroff, A. J., & Fiese, B. H. (1990). Transactional regulation and early intervention. In S. J. Meisels and J. P. Shankoff (Eds.), *Handbook of early childhood intervention* (pp. 119–149). New York: Cambridge University Press.

Saxby, H., & Morgan, H. (1993). Behaviour problems in children with learning disabilities: To what extent do they exist and are they a problem? *Child: Care, Health and Development, 19,* 149–157.

Schaefer, C. E. (1990). Night waking and temperament in early childhood. *Psychological Reports, 67,* 192–194.

Scher, A., Tirosh, E., Jaffe, M., Rubin, L., Sadeh, A., & Lavie, P. (1995). Sleep patterns of infants and young children in Israel. *International Journal of Behavioral Development, 18*(4), 701–711.

Scher, M., Richardson, G., Coble, P., Day, N., & Stoffer, D. (1988). The effects of prenatal alcohol and marijuana exposure: Disturbances in neonatal sleep cycling and arousal. *Pediatric Research, 24,* 101–105.

Scher, M. S., Steppe, D. A., & Banks, D. L. (1996). Prediction of lower developmental performances of healthy neonates by neonatal EEG-sleep measures. *Pediatric Neurology, 14*(2), 137–144.

Scott, G., & Richards, M. P. M. (1990). Night waking in 1-year-old children in England. *Child: Care, Health and Development, 16,* 283–302.

Sears, W. (1985). *Nighttime parenting.* New York: Plume.

Seifer, R., Dickstein, S., Sameroff, A. J., Hayden, L., Magee, K., & Schiller, M. (1994). Sleep in toddlers whose parents have psychopathology. *Sleep Research, 23,* 145.

Seifer, R., Sameroff, A. J., Barrett, L. C., & Krafchuk, E. (1994). Infant temperament measured by multiple observations and mother report. *Child Development, 65*(5), 1478–1490.

Shonkoff, J. P., & Brazelton, T. B. (1993). Paradise lost: Delayed parenthood in the carefully planned life. In E. Fenichel & S. Provence (Eds.), *Development in jeopardy* (pp. 177–202). Madison, CT: International Universities Press.

Sigman, M., Beckwith, L., Cohen, S. E., & Parmelee, A. H. (1989). Stability in the biosocial development of the child born preterm. In M. H. Bornstein & N. A. Krasnegor (Eds.), *Stability and continuity in mental development: Behavioral and biological perspectives* (pp. 29–42). Hillsdale, NJ: Erlbaum.

St. James-Roberts, I., & Plewis, I. (1996). Individual differences, daily fluctuations, and developmental changes in amounts of infant waking, crying, fussing, and sleeping. *Child Development, 67*(5), 2527–2540.

Stevenson, J. (1993). Sleep disturbance in children and its relationship to non-sleep behaviour problems. In I. St. James-Roberts, G. Harris, & D. Messer (Eds.), *Infant crying, feeding, and sleeping* (pp. 174–193). New York: Harvester Wheatsheaf.

Van Tassel, E. B. (1985). The relative influence of child and environmental characteristics on sleep disturbances in the first and second years of life. *Developmental and Behavioral Pediatrics, 6*(2), 81–86.

Walker, A. M., & Menahem, S. (1994). Intervention of supplementary carrying on normal baby crying patterns: A randomized study. *Journal of Developmental and Behavioral Pediatrics, 15*(3), 174–178.

Walters, J. (1993). Sleep management: The hidden agenda. *Child: Care, Health and Development, 19,* 197–208.

Ware, J. C., & Orr, W. C. (1992). Evaluation and treatment of sleep disorders in children. In C. E. Walker & M. C. Roberts (Eds.), *Handbook of clinical child psychology* (2nd ed., pp. 261–282). New York: Wiley.

Weissbluth, M. (1984). Sleep duration, temperament, and Conner's ratings of three-year-old children. *Journal of Developmental and Behavioral Pediatrics, 5*(3), 120–123.

Weissbluth, M. (1995). Naps in children: 6 months–7 years. *Sleep, 18*(2), 82–87.

White, B., Gunnar, M., Larson, M., Donzella, B., & Barr, R. (in press). Behavioral and physiological responsivity and patterns of sleep and daily salivary cortisol in infants with and without colic. *Child Development.*

Wolf, A. W., & Lozoff, B. (1989). Object attachment, thumbsucking, and the passage to sleep. *Journal of the American Academy of Child and Adolescent Psychiatry, 28,* 287–292.

Wolfson, A., Lacks, P., & Futterman, A. (1992). Effects of parent training on infant sleeping patterns, parents' stress, and perceived parental competence. *Journal of Counseling and Clinical Psychology, 60*(1), 41–48.

Wolke, D., Meyer, R., Ohrt, B., & Riegel, K. (1995). The incidence of sleeping problems in preterm and fullterm infants discharged from neonatal special care units: An epidemiological investigation. *Journal of Child Psychology and Psychiatry, 36*(2), 203–223.

Zeanah, C. H., Keener, M. A., & Anders, T. F. (1986). Developing perceptions of temperament and their relation to mother and infant behavior. *Journal of Child Psychology and Psychiatry, 27*(4), 499–512.

Zuckerman, B., Stevenson, J., & Bailey, V. (1987). Sleep problems in early childhood: Continuities, predictive factors, and behavioral correlates. *Pediatrics, 80,* 664–671.

18

Excessive Crying

Ronald G. Barr

INTRODUCTION

All infants cry, and some cry much more than others. Indeed, the differences are so apparent that it has been tempting to consider "excessive" amounts of crying as an individual difference characteristic of early infancy. In fact, differences among infants in crying duration are reasonably stable across the first few months of life (Keller, Lohaus, Volker, Cappendberg, & Chasiotis, 1998; St. James-Roberts, Conroy, & Wilsher, 1997a). However, the value of these differences as markers of an "excessive cryer" are importantly qualified by the recognition that whether and when crying is considered excessive is subject to a variety of influences other than amount of crying.

First, crying duration is significantly dependent on caregiving practices, such as carrying, holding, interfeed interval, nutritional intake, and responsivity to infant crying signals (Barr & Elias, 1988; Bell & Ainsworth, 1972; Bensel, 1996; Hubbard & van IJzendoorn, 1989; Hunziker & Barr, 1986). Consequently, differences in amounts of crying may be more characteristic of the behavior of the infant–caregiver dyad than of the infant itself (Acebo & Thoman, 1992, 1994). Second, for any particular infant, the amount of crying will not be the same at different ages. Because of an early crying "peak," most infants will cry more in the first 3 months of life than ever again (Barr, 1990a; Brazelton, 1962; St. James-Roberts & Halil, 1991). Third, some crying is "explicable" and some is not. A lot of crying following a fall or in the presence of a fever is not usually considered "excessive," but the same amount of crying in the absence of an apparent explanation may well be. Fourth, crying in some contexts may be particularly appropriate for the infant. For example, temperamentally difficult, irritable infants were more likely to survive a famine than their less difficult, more placid peers (DeVries, 1984). This is a sobering reminder that what is excessive in one context may be life saving in another. For all of these (and other) reasons, determining whether crying is "excessive" remains elusive, conceptually problematic, and possibly clinically useless (Barr, 1993).

Ronald G. Barr • McGill University–Montreal Children's Hospital Research Institute and Child Development Programme, Montreal Children's Hospital, Montreal, Quebec, Canada H3H 1P3.

Handbook of Developmental Psychopathology, Second Edition, edited by Arnold J. Sameroff, Michael Lewis, and Suzanne M. Miller. Kluwer Academic/Plenum Publishers, New York, 2000.

Despite these considerations, the concept of an "excessively crying infant" as a clinical disorder remains robustly entrenched in our approaches to infant psychopathology. Its clinical presentation tends to be manifest in different guises, however, depending in part on the age of the infant. Interestingly, the first (or "birth") cry is rarely, if ever, considered excessive. It is morphologically and perceptually different than crying that comes later (Wasz-Hockert, Lind, Vuorenkoski, Partanen, & Valanne, 1968). A robust, loud cry is welcomed by parents and clinicians alike, and interpreted as a sign of a healthy infant. Probably the most common and notorious clinical manifestation of excessive crying is the syndrome of infant colic (or persistent crying) that occurs during the infant's first 4 months (Barr, 1996). For the majority of these infants, the excessive crying "resolves." For a minority, however, caregiver–infant interaction may be so disrupted that excessive crying persists and the distress becomes generalized to both infant and caregiver (Papousek & von Hofacker, 1995, 1998), which might be dubbed the "persistent infant–mother distress syndrome" (Barr, 1998). By the middle of the first year of life, infants who cry excessively may be thought of as irritable (van den Boom, 1994; van den Boom & Hacksma, 1994), fearful and shy (Kagan & Snidman, 1991a,b), temperamentally difficult (Bates, Freeland, & Lounsbury, 1979; Carey, 1972; Rothbart & Derryberry, 1981) or regulatory disordered (DeGangi, DiPietro, Greenspan, & Porges, 1991; Maldonado-Duran & Sauceda-Garcia, 1996). For each of these constructs, crying behavior is not defining in and of itself, but is considered a phenotypic behavioral manifestation of some underlying and relatively stable constitutional property of the infant. Toward the end of the first year, crying may increase (become excessive) in the context of infant–caregiver separation (separation anxiety [Kagan]) and as unexplained nighttime crying (Bernal, 1973; St. James-Roberts, 1994; St. James-Roberts & Halil, 1991). In the second year of life (and later), excessive crying is a salient manifestation of increasingly prominent temper tantrums (Potegal, Kosorok, & Davidson, 1996). Some of these may progress to breath holding and even loss of consciousness (Lombroso & Lerman, 1967). Excessive crying is also a salient manifestation of "resistant" attachment, a behavioral pattern considered to be characteristic of a behavioral strategy adopted by infants in the absence of a caregiving context that facilitates confidence in infants that their needs for comfort will be met (Ainsworth, Blehar, Waters, & Wall, 1978). Equally problematic, but less age-dependent, is excessive crying as a time-honored clinical clue to "real" or organic disease, especially in nonverbal infants. Although this clinical presentation has received little systematic analytical study, it has been the subject of an informative case series (Poole, 1991).

Common to all of these manifestations is the assumption that "excessive" crying directly maps onto something negative, wrong, or at least nonoptimal, either in the infant, the caregiver's response to crying, or infant–caregiver interactions. In this type of discourse, the historical report of excessive crying is taken as a *symptom*, or observation of this behavior is taken as a *sign*, of a pathological process. However, unless crying that is excessive is defined a priori and circularly as crying *due to* an abnormal process, its value as a symptom or sign is severely limited by what might be referred to as the crying paradox. This paradox may be stated as follows: that, namely, the same crying behavior (or amounts of crying) may function to bring about good or bad consequences for the infant (alternatively, more crying may be better than less crying) depending on the context. The increased survival of temperamentally difficult, irritable infants in the face of famine is only one good illustration of the paradox. Thoman and Acebo (1992) provide another. When held in their mother's arms, higher crying infants receive more patting, caressing, moving, or rocking stimulation. More interesting, however, is that there are "n-shaped" dose–response relationships between amounts of crying and indices of positive maternal attention. Up to a point, the mothers of infants who cry more increase their talking to, looking at, mutual gaze, and use of opportunities to coordinate mutual gaze with their infants. Such manifestations of maternal attention tend to lessen in the highest crying infants, but they still remain greater than with lower crying infants. These findings nicely illustrate that in contrast to the typical clinical stance, more crying is not necessarily bad. From this standpoint, crying acts not as a symptom or as a sign, but as a *signal* to which the caregiving environment may (or may not) respond. Whether caregivers do so, and in what ways, determines whether or not the signal will benefit the infant.

Because of the signaling function of crying, its role is highly context-dependent. As a result, there is no one-to-one "normative" relationship between amount or intensity of crying and psychopathology. Consequently, rather than any particular amount of crying per se, psychopathology related to crying is primarily a function of how the individual differences and developmental changes in the amounts of crying behavior *are experienced* within the context of the caregiving environment specific to the individual infant.

Attention will be drawn to three aspects of the clinical manifestations of crying. This chapter focuses first on the behavioral syndrome of colic. Colic is typically thought of as benign and self-limited, having resolved by the fourth month of age (Barr, 1996). However, it is the paradigmatic syndrome of "excessive crying," the only clinical presentation for which crying is the defining symptom, and nicely illustrates developmental issues concerning crying. For other clinical presentations, crying is one of a cluster of problematic behaviors (e.g., crying when waking at night; crying with temper tantrums), some of which are dealt with elsewhere. Next, other clinically relevant constructs (persistent mother–infant distress syndrome, difficult temperament, regulatory disordered infants) are considered with the aim of understanding how they might be continuous or discontinuous with colic, and how these concepts may be related in meaningful ways. Finally, we consider how various conceptual approaches (behavioral state, responsivity, evolution) might contribute to our understanding of the behavioral phenomenology of excessive crying.

A TAXONOMIC NOTE

Discussion of crying problems is hampered by the lack of a widely accepted taxonomy for describing crying phenomenology. One proposal that integrates various levels of description argues that crying phenomena can be arranged hierarchically and defined by different levels of aggregations of voiced expirations and the (usually) unvoiced inspirations (Figure 18.1; Barr, 1990b). The basic building blocks are voiced expirations interpreted as expressing negative emotion, in contrast to neutral sounds (such as grunting) and positive sounds (such as cooing). Thus, a single cry *cycle* consists in part of a negative vocalization and in part of a quiet inspiration, and lasts on the order of one or a few seconds (Zeskind, Parker-Price, & Barr, 1993). A cry *event* consists of a consecutive "series" of cry cycles, occurs on the order of seconds to a few minutes, and consists of negative vocalizations and interdigitated quiet expirations. A crying *bout* consists of a "cluster" of cry events, occurring on the order of one to many minutes, and includes cycles of negative vocalizations as well as intervening quiet periods. The term *cluster* (instead of series) is used at this level to indicate the important distinction that the sequence of cry cycles ("events") that contribute to the bout need *not* be consecutive, and that a sequence of nonnegative vocalization inspiratory–expiratory cycles may be included in the bout. Consequently, a crying bout is made up of a *cluster* of nonconsecutive cry events, while the events in turn are composed of a consecutive *series* of cry cycles.

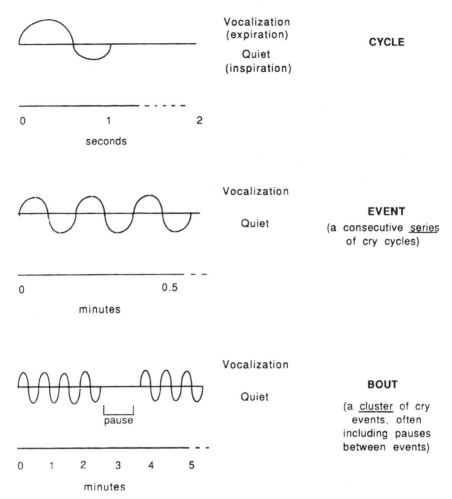

FIGURE 18.1. Three levels of description of cry phenomena. At all levels, crying consists of expiratory vocalizations alternating with (usually) quiet inspirations. Levels differ in regard to how many of these expiratory–inspiratory cycles are included, and whether they are consecutive. Note the differences in time scale at each level. (Reproduced with permission from R. G. Barr, 1990b.)

This hierarchic classification corresponds to three levels of measurement found in cry studies. Most spectrographic and listener perception studies describe cry cycles (usually one); direct observation studies describe cry events; and diary studies, recall history, and question-naire studies describe crying bouts. It also illustrates that what constitutes a measure of "excessive crying" in a psychologically real sense may have a number of meanings. There is no definitional correspondence between duration and frequency indices at one level with the same indices at another. To illustrate this, *bout* durations described in diary records do not "match" the *event* durations obtained by audiotaped recordings. Brazelton (1962) is often cited as having shown that the typical 6-week-old cries 2¾ hours/day on the basis of diary records. Direct comparisons of diary and audiotaped recordings indicate that about 120 minutes of diary-recorded crying and fussing correspond to approximately 30 minutes of "negative vocalizations" (Barr, Kramer, Leduc, et al., 1988; St. James-Roberts, Hurry, &

Bowyer, 1993). Clearly, the durations of the "same" amount of crying are quite different. Diary-recorded crying bouts include the duration of within-cycle and between-event non-vocalization quiet as well as "recorder error." However, it remains unclear which measure is more important for the caregiver, since it is not obvious that the parent would find much meaning (or comfort) in being told that she "only" heard 30 minutes of crying.

Another unresolved taxonomic issue concerns what is meant by fretting, fussing, and crying. These terms have been differentiated variously but not consistently on dimensions of intensity, persistence, rhythmicity, presumed message, and associated motor activity or behavioral states (Barr & Desilets, 1990; St. James-Roberts, Conroy, & Wilsher, 1996), but the exact behavioral constituents or qualities to which the terms refer (validity) remain elusive. This is a potentially important issue. Where distinctions have been made, however arbitrarily, crying and fussing have been differentially related to stability (Fish & Crockenberg, 1981; St. James-Roberts et al., 1997) and manipulability (Barr, Woolridge, & Hanley, 1991), and could be important in distinguishing clinical conditions. It is also unresolved as to whether these gradations in crying behavior are better understood as qualitative and discontinuous (categorical) or as quantitative and continuous (noncategorical) dimensions (Barr, 1995c). This has implications for the study of cry phenomenology, and for assessment of clinical crying. Parents will, if asked, make a distinction between "fussing," "crying," and "colic" on diary records (Forsyth, 1989; St. James-Roberts, Conroy, & Wilsher, 1995a; Stifter & Braungart, 1992). However, diary-recorded bouts of crying (compared to fussing) matched audiorecorded negative vocalization events that were somewhat more frequent but of the same duration, and the range was the same for both (Barr et al., 1988b). In a similar comparison of parent diary–designated "colic" compared to "cry/fuss" distress, there was no difference in audiorecorded negative vocalization events (St. James-Roberts et al., 1996). At least on these measures, evidence that there are discontinuous, qualitatively distinct types of distress is not compelling.

EARLY EXCESSIVE CRYING: COLIC (PERSISTENT CRYING)

The language used to describe the clinical manifestations of excessive crying continues to be confusing for a number of reasons. One of these is that the term *colic* has traditionally been used in medical discourse to refer to pain in the abdomen regardless of etiology, age, or the specific organ involved (such as "renal" colic or lead intoxication; McConaghey, 1967). In pediatrics and everyday speech, however, it usually refers to an age-specific condition in the first 3 months of life whose primary symptom is excessive crying. Even within this more restricted domain, the term *colic* may be used to refer to a presumably distinct *type* of crying (or, more accurately, crying bout—see earlier taxonomic note), to a presumably distinct *behavioral crying syndrome*, and to a clinical *complaint* about crying. To add to the confusion, "colic" is limited by some to crying that is due to organic (or, even more specifically, gastrointestinal) causes and by others to crying in infants in whom organic disease has been ruled out or who are "otherwise well." In this discussion, the phrase "colic syndrome" (to distinguish it from questions related to types of crying) refers to the presumably distinct behavioral crying syndrome regardless of whether an organic etiology, pathophysiological process, or disease underlies the syndrome. Whether organic pathologies account for some cases of colic syndrome is an empirical, rather than a definitional, question. Our discussion indicates further that this behavioral syndrome is not as distinct as usually assumed.

In the "classical" picture of colic syndrome, the clinical descriptions have focused on three dimensions. First, the syndrome has characteristic *age-dependent* and *diurnal* features.

Crying typically begins to increase about 2 weeks after birth, reaches a peak sometime in the second month, and declines to baseline by the fourth month. Within the day, crying tends to cluster during the late afternoon and evening hours. Second, the syndrome is typified by a number of *behavioral* characteristics, some of which are common and some more variable. The common behaviors are that the infant manifests prolonged bouts of crying (sometimes called "colic" bouts) (Barr, 1990c; St. James-Roberts et al., 1996) that are resistant to soothing, including feeding. More variable behaviors include the infant clenching its fists, flexing its legs over its abdomen, arching its back, having an active and grimacing face, and being flushed. This concatenation of behaviors tends to invoke the perception that the infant is in pain (has a "pain facies"). The abdomen may be hard and distended, and the crying bout may include regurgitation and the passing of gas per rectum. The third dimension refers to *unpredictability* of the crying. The bouts are typically described as "paroxysmal," meaning variably that their onset is sudden, they begin and end without warning, and they are unrelated to other events in the environment, or appear to be spontaneous.

This qualitative description is widely accepted, but capturing the complexity of the syndrome in a quantifiable way has been more difficult. The most widely used definition has come to be known as "Wessel's rule of threes." An infant is considered to "have colic" if it cries for more than 3 hours per day for more than 3 days per week for more than 3 weeks (Wessel, Cobb, Jackson, Harris, & Detwiler, 1954). This definition helpfully focuses on quantifiable measures of the *duration* of crying, obtainable with reasonable accuracy from diary recordings (Barr, Kramer, Leduc, et al., 1988; Hunziker & Barr, 1986; St. James-Roberts et al., 1993). However, even this simple definition has been modified frequently (Barr, 1995a; Canivet, Hagander, Jakobsson, & Lanke, 1996). It is subject to a number of recognized limitations: (1) Few parents or clinicians are willing to wait for 3 weeks to see whether the excessive crying persists; (2) the "cut-off" is arbitrary; (3) infants of mothers who have been "working overtime" soothing their infants may not meet criteria, whereas infants whose mothers leave them to "cry out" may; and (4) the definition takes no account of qualitative differences in cries. To date, evidence implicating a distinctly different "colic" cry, either by listener perception or by acoustical analysis, is mixed (Barr, Rotman, Yaremko, Leduc, & Francoeur, 1992; Lester, Boukydis, García Coll, Hole, & Peucker, 1992; St. James-Roberts, 1999; St. James-Roberts et al., 1996; Zeskind & Barr, 1997). However, it is likely that the quality of the cry contributes, perhaps independently or additively with quantity, to whether the infant is brought to a clinician with a crying complaint (Barr et al., 1992; Gormally & Barr, 1997).

Etiological Considerations

Detecting organic pathology is a crucial responsibility for clinicians, a challenge made more difficult by the fact that crying can be the presenting complaint for almost any disease condition in infants. As a result, long lists of organic causes accompany clinical descriptions of colic. The amount of crying, its unsoothability and the apparent pain understandably support the notion that something "must" be wrong and that an organic etiology should be present. Most reports of organic causes refer to highly selected or specialized samples, giving the impression that organic etiologies are frequent (Miller & Barr, 1991). However, colic syndrome is relevant only to afebrile infants who have crying complaints during the first 3 months and are chronic. In such infants, the number of causal organic diseases and the number of cases that can be attributed to them are considerably fewer than suspected (Gormally & Barr, 1997).

All organic diseases together probably account for no more than 5% of cases with colic syndrome, depending on the clinical setting (Gormally & Barr, 1997; Sauls & Redfern, 1997; Treem, 1994).

Of these, by far the most prevalent is sensitivity to cow's milk protein to which the infant may be exposed through infant formulae or maternal breast milk. The evidence supporting a causal role of cow's milk protein intolerance has been extensively reviewed (Barr, 1996; Geertsma & Hyams, 1989; Miller & Barr, 1991; Sauls & Redfern, 1997; Treem, 1994). On current evidence, it is probable that cow's milk protein is a real, but relatively rare (< 5%), cause of colic syndrome. By comparison, other organic causes are rarer still (Gormally & Barr, 1997). However, there are fairly well-documented cases due to isolated fructose intolerance (Wales, Primhak, Rattenbury, & Taylor, 1989), maternal antidepressant use (fluoxetine hydrochloride, Prozac; Lester, Cucca, Andreozzi, Flanagan, & Oh, 1993), and, rarely, reflux esophagitis (Heine, Jaquiery, Lubitz, Cameron, & Catto-Smith, 1995) or infant migraine (Katerji & Painter, 1994). Infant abuse (shaken baby syndrome), congenital glaucoma (Talbot, Pitts, Dudgeon, & Lee, 1992), and central nervous system abnormalities (Listernick & Tomita, 1991) are also rare, but important, causes. A few general principles may be useful as clinical clues (Gormally & Barr, 1997). First, behaviorally, infants whose cries are high pitched, who regularly arch their back, and whose crying does not manifest a diurnal pattern may be more at risk for having an organic etiology. Second, the principle may hold that colic syndrome is never due to organic disease in the absence of additional signs and symptoms. Third, onset of increased crying late in the third month may raise the likelihood of cow's milk protein intolerance as a cause. Finally, persistence of excessive crying beyond 3 months is typical with organic disease, though not diagnostic. Though rare, the relative severity of such entities heightens the importance of careful diagnosis and, especially, monitoring.

Developmental Considerations

Colic syndrome is variously described as occurring in 4–40% of infants (Canivet et al., 1996; Hide & Guyer, 1982; Lehtonen & Korvenranta, 1995; Stahlberg, 1984; Stifter & Braungart, 1992), depending on whether the broader definition of crying as a complaint or narrower more specific definitions are used, whether the behavior is assessed by parent report or diary, and whether the report is prospective or retrospective. As discussed, few of these cases will be accounted for by organic pathologies, and evidence is also increasing that most cases of colic syndrome will not be accounted for by preexisting maternal personality characteristics, postpartum depression, or inappropriate and nonoptimal caregiving. The role of the primary caregiver (usually the mother) in the etiology of colic has long been controversial, with some early reports supporting such a role (Carey, 1968) and some not (Paradise, 1966). However, the real question is whether colic syndrome can occur in the absence of maternal determinants. A number of observations support this. Maternal inexperience may result in the first infant being brought to a clinician as a concern, but there is no difference in crying amounts between firstborn and laterborn infants (St. James-Roberts & Halil, 1991). Furthermore, third trimester emotional lability in mothers is not different in infants that subsequently meet clinical criteria for colic syndrome (Miller, Barr, & Eaton, 1993). Most importantly, mothers with "persistently" crying infants do the same things that other mothers do and, if anything, hold and soothe them more, and receive equivalent optimality ratings for interactive sensitivity and affection during direct observations (St. James-Roberts, Conroy, & Wilsher, 1998). This does not imply that maternal personality or caregiving style never causes colic syndrome, nor that such factors may not exacerbate otherwise normal infant crying behavior. Indeed, excessive stimulation and parental emotional and life stresses are often evident in referred samples of infants with colic syndrome (Mckenzie, 1991; Papousek & von Hofacker, 1995, 1998). Consequently, colic syndrome can occur despite optimal caregiving and is most often not accounted for by pathological processes in the infant, the caregiver, or the caregiving environment, but can be associated with significant psychopathology in subgroups and clinically referred samples.

The inability to account for colic syndrome by traditional clinical means has been a significant impetus to reconsidering its developmental origins. This shift was presaged by Wessel et al.'s (1954) astute observation that "the time distribution and frequency of diurnal regularity are similar for the mild fussy periods of the 'contented babies,' and for the more prolonged periods of the 'fussy infants' " (p. 428). Subsequently, Brazelton's (1962) study of "normal" crying demonstrated that the total duration of crying per 24 hours tended to increase in the first month, peak in the second, and then decrease to a more stable level by the fourth month. These observations provided an essential normative description of early crying against which to judge the clinical presentation of colic syndrome from a developmental perspective. They suggested that two of the defining temporal characteristics of colic syndrome—the early "peak" and the diurnal distribution—could be a manifestation of normal developmental processes. This raised the important possibility that etiologically "unexplained" cases could be infants whose crying was at the upper end of a spectrum of crying of normal infants who came to clinical attention because they exceeded some level of tolerance in the caregiver.

A number of systematic studies have supported the presence of an n-shaped curve for crying, usually including evening clustering (Barr, 1990a). Almost 25 years later, Hunziker and Barr (1986) found the same pattern of daily crying and fussing duration, depicted in Figure 18.2, which also illustrates the considerable individual variability within and among infants. Thus, the "normal crying curve" is a modal curve for groups of infants; individual infants show much more variability. Understood in this sense, the curve has been remarkably robust, being found in the majority of studies of sufficient sample size, whether the measurement was by questionnaire (Emde, Gaensbauer, & Harmon, 1976; St. James-Roberts & Halil, 1991), diary (Alvarez & St. James-Roberts, 1996; Brazelton, 1962; Hunziker & Barr, 1986; St. James-Roberts & Halil, 1991), direct observation (Bloom & McDowell, 1972), or audio recordings (Rebelsky & Black, 1972). In a few samples, evidence for the ascending part of the crying curve has been less apparent (Bensel, 1997; St. James-Roberts, Hurry, Bowyer, Varghese, & Sawdon, 1995b). Whether this is due to methodological differences, changing caregiving practices, or other factors is unclear. In all studies, however, daily crying duration has been greater in the first 2 months than later.

Such robustness suggests that this early crying pattern is importantly constrained by developmental determinants common to the human species. Indeed, it is arguably the case that it is a behavior universal of infancy in the sense that human infants share a propensity for increased crying that is characteristic of all groups of infants in the human species, if not of all infants (Konner, 1989). Two lines of evidence support this contention. Similar temporal characteristics are present in cultures where caregiving practices differ substantially from that in Western contexts. In !Kung San hunter-gatherers of Botswana, caregiving practices include constant carrying, direct body contact, upright positioning, "continuous" feeding (3 to 4 times/hour for 1–2 minutes/feed), and contingent responsivity (responding to 92% of frets and cries within 10 seconds) (Barr, Bakeman, Konner, & Adamson, 1991). On the basis of experimental studies, all of these caregiving practices might be expected to reduce crying duration (Barr, 1990b). Interestingly, some characteristics of crying differ from Western

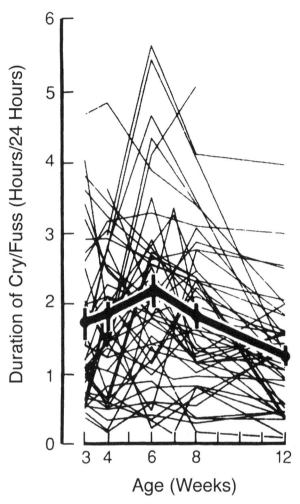

FIGURE 18.2. Cry/fuss duration by week of age of 50 infants, with superimposed mean and standard error of the mean (S.E.M.) values for the whole group. Data are from Hunziker and Barr control group. (Figure reproduced with permission from R. G. Barr, 1990a.)

patterns, but not all. First, relative to Dutch and American infants, the duration of crying was about half as long, and prolonged crying bouts were rare. Second, cry frequency remained the same. Third, !Kung San infants still manifested an early crying/fretting peak within the first 3 months. These findings suggest that caregiving style can affect crying, but that crying duration was specifically affected, while frequency and the early crying curve were not. In Manali, India, mothers are more responsive to infant cries, more likely to cosleep and to breast feed than mothers in London, England. Despite these differences, Manali and London infants have an evening peak, an increase in crying from 2 to 6 weeks, with a tendency to decline between 6 and 12 weeks (St. James-Roberts, Bowyer, Varghese, & Sawdon, 1994). In Korean infants, whose mothers are in direct contact with their infants more than 90% of the time, crying is greater during the second month than later (Lee, 1994).

A second line of evidence comes from preterm infants. If the crying pattern is determined by postnatal experience, then preterm infants should manifest their crying curve earlier. Alternatively, if the pattern is constrained by developmental processes, it should occur at "corrected" ages. A cohort of relatively well preterms born 8 weeks early manifested both their crying peak and evening clustering at 6-weeks corrected age (i.e., 14 weeks postnatally) (Barr, Chen, Hopkins, & Westra, 1996; see also Malone, 1997). The timing was unrelated to a variety of postnatal medical complications, suggesting that the developmental pattern was quite resilient.

This similarity in temporal patterning strongly suggests that the crying of infants with colic syndrome is not a distinctly different pattern of behavior, but rather is continuous with the crying of normal infants. The same is true for other behavioral manifestations of the syndrome. Behaviors thought to be distinctive of colic syndrome are otherwise normal behaviors, but there are more of them. In one study, infants who met Wessel's criteria differed in total duration from controls (by definition), but this was due to longer bout lengths of crying and fussing, while bout frequency was the same (Barr, Rotman, Yaremko, Ledne, & Francoeur, 1992). This dissociation suggests that what differentiates infants with colic is that they cry longer once started. Similarly, infants with colic syndrome exhibited more facial activity and "pain facies" than control infants, but these patterns were also present in infants without colic. Crying after feeds, a behavior thought to be diagnostically helpful, occurred more often in infants with colic but also occurred in 70% of control infants. Similarly, infants with colic are more likely to manifest unsoothable crying bouts, but such bouts also occur in infants without colic in proportion to the overall amount of crying and fussing that infants do (St. James-Roberts, Conroy, & Wilsher, 1995a). There have been fewer studies of cry quality in infants with colic. Parents are more likely to perceive cries differently, and some acoustical features (such as dysphonation) are more common, but none of these features are specific to infants with colic (Barr et al., 1992; Lester et al., 1992; St. James-Roberts, 1999; Zeskind & Barr, 1997). Rather than infants with colic syndrome being distinctly different, it is more likely that they do what otherwise normal infants do, but more so, because they cry for longer periods of time.

If both temporal and behavioral characteristics of colic syndrome are continuous with normal behavioral development, then the syndrome is better understood in terms of normative than pathological developmental processes. Given the individual differences in crying patterns (Figure 18.2), it is understandable that only some infants come to clinical attention or meet clinical criteria for "having" the syndrome. Furthermore, some crying features, especially bout duration, are amenable to influence by caregiving style and/or differentiate infants with colic syndrome. From this developmental perspective, it is arguably more appropriate to conceptualize colic as sets of behaviors that infants "do" rather than as a distinct clinical syndrome that infants "have."

LATER EXCESSIVE CRYING

There is an important "developmental shift" in crying following the third month. The level of crying is dramatically reduced, and its form and function change. Cry phonation becomes sensitive to the communicative context in which it occurs (Franco, 1984), crying is more coordinated with visual regard and gestures (Gustafson & Green, 1991), and a new form of "interrupted fussing" appears transiently, occurring only when the infant is alone (Hopkins & Palthe, 1987). These and other observations (Bell & Ainsworth, 1972; Gekoski, Rovee-

Collier, & Carulli-Rabinowitz, 1983) have contributed to the general concept that crying is at first relatively undifferentiated ("expressive") and later more intentional or communicative.

Clinically, excessive crying after 3 months has been variously captured in the notions of the so-called persistent mother–infant distress syndrome (Barr, 1998; Papousek & von Hofacker, 1995) the temperamentally difficult infant (Bates et al., 1979; Carey, 1982; Thomas, Chess, & Birch, 1968), and the regulatory disordered infant (DeGangi et al., 1991). These overlapping concepts complicate systematic description. However, crying features as a prominent, but not isolated, behavior in all of them. Whether and, if so, in what way, early colic syndrome might be either a manifestation (in the case of temperamental difficultness) or a precursor (in the case of persistent mother–infant distress syndrome and the regulatory disordered infant) of these later syndromes remains an intriguing but as yet unanswered question (Barr & Gunnar, in press).

Persistent Mother–Infant Distress Syndrome

Papousek and her colleagues describe in detail the clinical characteristics of families presenting to the Munich Interdisciplinary Research and Intervention Programme because of excessive crying (Papousek & Papousek, 1990, 1996; Papousek & von Hofacker, 1995, 1998). Most presented after the crying peak at 2 months, but showed no decrements in crying that remained at or greater than crying levels of infants with Wessel's colic. These infants often had disturbances in feeding and/or sleeping, mild developmental delay, and organic risk factors. Their parents often reported significant psychosocial risk factors, prenatal emotional distress in mothers of the "extreme" criers, a high rate of maternal psychopathology, and postnatal parental conflicts. In direct parent–infant observations, parents (especially those with psychopathology) were less likely to show sensitive and appropriate interactions, and the infants were less likely to be ready to interact. Papousek et al. propose that this syndrome has its genesis in the concatenation of significant parental, infant, and familial risk factors that serve to disrupt "intuitive parenting," the normal interactive and coregulatory capacities of the infant and its caregivers.

An interesting issue is whether these infants and families represent a "worst case" scenario for the outcome of colic syndrome, or a distinct syndrome that would have occurred anyway whether or not the infant had earlier colic. A number of pathways are possible. In one, colic syndrome simply might not resolve in some infants. The prolonged unresolved crying would lead to increased frustration, familial stress, and caregiving breakdown in an otherwise normal family. In a second "double hit" scenario, an infant with colic syndrome is a perturbation in an already fragile family that serves to disrupt normative caregiving in an escalating cycle of frustration. In a third, stressed families may elevate a normal crying curve to the status of a colic syndrome through overstimulation that worsens and generalizes to other behavioral domains. In other scenarios, this syndrome may have occurred anyway, independent of earlier colic. These families' retrospective reports might be colored by current frustrations, so that an earlier mild increase or atypical later onset in crying is reported as colic syndrome. In others, the syndrome may develop without a preceding colic syndrome. Interestingly, 20% of a sample that presented after 6 months did not report earlier colic syndrome (Papousek & von Hofacker, 1998). Finally, persistent infant–parent distress syndrome may simply have occurred anyway due to different developmental factors that contribute to infants becoming temperamentally "difficult" after 4 months (see below). In this case, the earlier experience with increased crying is coincidental. Regardless of the pathway, the task of reestablishing responsive "intuitive" parenting is a challenge for all of these families. With the possible exception of parents with frank psychopathology, this may be doable (Papousek & von Hofacker, 1998).

"Difficult" Temperament

A similar uncertainty attends the notion of the "temperamentally difficult" infant. The concept of temperament has gained wide acceptance as a way of capturing individual behavioral differences that are primarily constitutional and biological in origin, present early in life, and relatively stable across time and situations, albeit expressed differently at different developmental stages (Goldsmith et al., 1987; Thomas et al., 1968). Within the broader temperament construct, "difficultness" is conceptualized as a dimension that includes a predisposition to negative affect, poor adaptability, greater intensity of reactions, and unpredictability. Not surprisingly, crying contributes prominently to all assessments of this dimension. In the widely used Infant Characteristics Questionnaire, the "fussy–difficult" factor contributes almost 60% of the variance to this temperamental dimension (Bates et al., 1979).

As a result, it is reasonable to ask whether and to what extent the dimension of temperamental "difficultness" contributes to early colic syndrome, later persistent mother–infant distress syndrome, or dysregulatory syndrome in later infancy. Infants with colic syndrome and persistent mother–infant distress syndrome usually are rated as temperamentally difficult (Barr et al., 1992; Carey, 1972, 1984; Papousek & von Hofacker, 1998; Weissbluth, Christoffal, & Davis, 1984). However, the importance of difficult temperament in these clinical syndromes is subject to a methodological caveat. Since crying is a predominant behavior both in the clinical syndromes and the measures of temperament, the two are likely to be associated "by definition." Convincing evidence for the role of temperamental difficulty in these syndromes requires measures that are independent of amounts of crying (White, Gunnar, Larson, Donzella, & Barr, in press).

If colic syndrome is a manifestations of a temperamental dimension of "difficultness," the supporting evidence is surprisingly weak, or paradoxical at best, even in the face of this methodological bias. For one thing, the stability of crying and fussing is at best weakly associated between early and later infancy. Development (age) accounts for 40% of cry–fuss variance over the first year, and individual differences account for only 16%. For another, individual differences for crying are stable before 3 months, but not after, and are not stable for fussing until after 6 weeks (St. James-Roberts & Plewis, 1996). Also, temperament indices have not been associated with colic syndrome when assessed before or after the colic period. A temperament index at 2 weeks accounted for only 7% of the variance in crying and fussing at 6 weeks (Barr, Kramer, Pless, Boisjoly, & Leduc, 1989). There were no differences in 5- and 10-month temperament ratings, nor in newborn, 5-, and 10-month measures of reactivity to sensory and social stimuli in infants who did, or did not, develop colic syndrome (Stifter & Braungart, 1992). In fact, infants with prior colic cried only 70% as long as noncolic infants in response to stimuli at 5 and 10 months. In addition, infants with prior colic were rated by their mothers as "more difficult" on global impressions at 1 year but not by their own responses to standardized temperament scales focusing on specific behavioral reactions (Lehtonen, Korhonen, & Korvenranta, 1994). Another approach would be to measure physiological responses presumed to be substrates for temperamental differences (Boyce, Barr, & Zeltzer, 1992). One of these—salivary cortisol response to pain stimuli—shows dramatic developmental shifts around 3 months remarkably parallel to changes in crying level. There is a significant "dampening" of cortisol response between 2 and 4 months, and stable individual differences appear only after 4 months (Gunnar, Broderson, Krueger, & Rigatuso, 1994; Lewis & Ramsay, 1995, in press; Lewis & Thomas, 1990). In response to a mock physical exam, infants with colic do not differ in their cortisol response. However, their daily diurnal rhythms of cortisol production were suppressed relative to controls (White et al., in press). Whether these differences persist beyond the dampening that occurs by 4 months is unknown.

These findings suggest that there may be a significant discontinuity between early and later infancy for temperament measures of "difficultness" and for clinical presentations of excessive crying. Interestingly, the most widely used measures of temperamental difficultness were only established on infants 4 months and older (Bates et al., 1979; Rothbart, 1981). Although adjustments in scoring permit the Infant Behavior Questionnaire (Rothbart, 1981) to be used in younger infants (Worobey & Blajda, 1989), all dimensions but one (irritability) were only stable between 2 weeks and 2 months, but not between 2 weeks and 1 year (Worobey & Blajda, 1989). Consequently, the notion of the temperamentally "difficult" infant may account for excessive crying presenting later in the first year, but it may not be appropriate to assume that the same biologically stable characteristics are operative earlier.

Regulatory Disordered Child

A closely related concept is that of the regulatory disordered child. Clinically, these infants are characterized as exhibiting fussiness, irritability, poor self-calming, intolerance to change, and a hyperalert state of arousal, with difficulties manifest across domains of affect regulation, feeding, sleeping, motor activity, and attention (DeGangi et al., 1991). Physiologically, both hyper- and hyposensitivity to sensory stimuli in any channel are postulated to characterize the regulatory deficit. Initial investigations have raised the possibility of atypical vagal system responsiveness (DeGangi, Porges, Sickel, & Greenspan, 1993; DeGangi et al., 1991). Conceptually, the core concept is that regulatory control and, in particular, the ability to inhibit both behavioral and physiological reactivity is atypical or maladaptive. This concept has been incorporated as a descriptive diagnostic category in the Zero to Three Diagnostic Classification (National Center for Clinical Infant Programs, 1994) with four subcategories: (1) hypersensitive, (2) underreactive, (3) motorically disorganized–impulsive, and (4) processing–behavior undefined.

This category recognizes that earlier problems with crying and sleeping may be transient (as in colic syndrome) and stipulates that regulatory disorder must be persistent, with the result that the diagnosis is only considered appropriate after 6 months. Whether these infants will be shown to be those with prior colic and/or persistent mother–infant distress syndromes that does not resolve is simply unknown. This "clinical" concept overlaps the individual-differences concept of difficult temperament to such an extent that substantive differences between them remain obscure. Conceptually, the temperamentally difficult infant is a variation of normal development, while the regulatory disordered infant is a clinical classification implying abnormality or atypicality. Empirically, however, validation of the distinctness of regulatory disordered infants—especially when they present with excessive crying—from those who are temperamentally difficult has yet to be addressed. In the one comparison, almost all of those studied longitudinally to date also met criteria on the fussy–difficult subscale of the Infant Characteristics Questionnaire (ICQ) (Bates, 1984; DeGangi et al., 1991). To the extent that the clinical concept is a recognition of how difficult and stressful infants with excessive crying can be (Maldonado-Duran & Sauceda-Garcia, 1996), however, the clinical classification provides important avenues to assessment, treatment, and future study.

INTERPRETIVE CONTEXTS AND UNDERLYING PROCESSES

The developmental perspective contributes to understanding clinical features of the temporal course and some behavioral characteristics of colic syndrome, but reasonable accounts of other clinical features contributing to caregiver frustration remain unfulfilled. In this section, we consider some clinical and developmental phenotypic characteristics of crying from the point of view of three related sets of concepts: (1) infant behavioral states; (2) "responsivity"; and (3) crying as an adaptive behavior in evolutionary time. These concepts suggest approaches to understanding the determinants and processes contributing to excessive crying.

Infant Behavioral States and Nonlinear Dynamic Systems

One unexplained feature is the so-called "paroxysmal" nature of crying bouts. Although widely cited, the term is used loosely, referring variously to crying bouts that have a sudden onset, that begin and end without warning (are unpredictable), and that appear to be unrelated to other events in the environment. Being unrelated to environmental events includes (but is not limited to) another frustrating feature, namely, that the infants are unsoothable, even by feeding. These features contribute to the clinical mystery of early excessive crying, and to the question of whether there is a specific type of "colic" crying bout.

Although a given in developmental studies (Korner, 1972; Prechtl & O'Brien, 1982; Wolff, 1987), the concept of infant behavioral states may provide some understanding of this clinical feature. The concept captures the important insight that infant behavior, at least in the early postnatal period, is not organized as a continuum of arousal but rather as a finite set of discontinuous and distinctly organized modes. Three important characteristics of behavioral states are that (1) they are self-organizing in the sense that a behavioral state is maintained until that pattern of necessary and/or sufficient events occurs that results in a transition to another behavioral state; (2) they are relatively stable over time (on the order of minutes rather than seconds); and (3) a stimulus experienced in one state has a different effect than when it is experienced in another state (the responses are "state specific" and nonlinear). In Wolff's classification, the crying state is defined behaviorally in terms of persistent cry vocalizations (from whimpering to loud screaming), diffuse motor activity or rigid, extended trunk posture, resistance of the limbs to passive movement, and a facial cry grimace that is sometimes accompanied by flushing (Wolff, 1987). One of the waking states (waking activity) is characterized by bursts of generalized motor activity and open eyes. Occasional vocalizations (moaning, grunting or whimpering) can occur, but they are always unsustained. Fussing, characterized by intermittent vocalizations and less intense, nonrhythmical motor activity, is conceptualized as transitional between these two behavioral states. More recently, Wolff has proposed that behavioral state organization can be helpfully construed as the output of an organism that is a "well-behaved" nonlinear dynamic system (Wolff, 1987, 1993).

If correct, the phenomenology of paroxysmal, unsoothable crying bouts can be understood in terms of the dynamics of two stable states and transitions between them (see Figure 18.3). Assume that the abscissa represents (undefined) determinants of behavioral states,

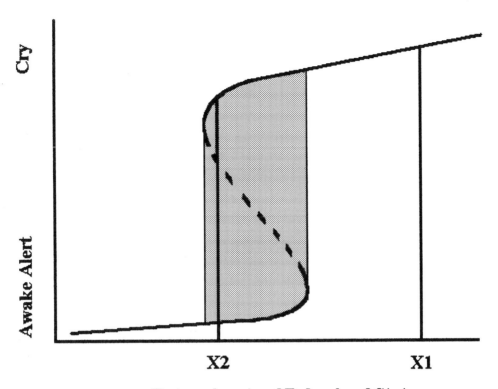

Determinants of Behavioral State

FIGURE 18.3. Illustration of possible nonlinear relationship between determinants of infant behavioral state (abscissa) and the Awake Alert and Crying states, two organized modes of behavior that are preferentially assumed by the organism (ordinate). As the infant "moves" from left to right, its behavioral state remains stably "Awake Alert" through many values of X, unstably oscillates between Awake Alert and Crying when values of X correspond to the shaded area ("fussing"), and becomes stably "Crying" through many values of X to the right of the shaded area. X_1 represents a region where the addition of a soothing maneuver would not affect a change in behavioral state, whereas the same maneuver would if applied at X_2.

whose possible modes of organization are represented on the ordinate. The curve illustrates that, in the region to the left of the shaded section, the infant will stably (predictably) remain in a state of waking activity; in the region to the right, the infant will stably remain in a crying state. In the shaded region, the infant can be in either state, waking activity or crying; however, which behavioral organization it assumes is unstable and unpredictable. Having more than one organizational mode under the same determinant conditions is a defining feature of a system whose behavior is nonlinear rather than linear. Note that if the infant "stays" in the shaded area for a while, it will transition back and forth between its two preferred states, being sometimes (intermittently) in a crying state and sometimes in an awake, active state. This intermittent switching might be seen as fussing.

The curve illustrates the dynamics of stable behavioral states and transitions among them, not the structural mechanisms. However, the dynamics may be critical to understanding the clinical phenomenology. Infants who tend to "live" to the left of the abscissa would have less intense or prolonged crying bouts; those to the right (with, say, colic syndrome), would have more intense and prolonged crying bouts. Paroxysmal bouts would occur when the infant transitions from the left to the right relatively quickly; fussing would occur when the infant remains in the shaded area. Unsoothable crying would occur to the right of the shaded area, when the crying state is well organized and stable over a range of determinant conditions. A soothing stimulus (say, picking up and holding the infant) would have little effect when applied at X_1 but enough to be an effective soothing maneuver when applied at X_2. Where the infant tends to "live" can change over (real and developmental) time as a function of the interaction among intrinsic physiological reorganizations and extrinsic caregiving contributions. What this kind of perspective might contribute is an account of some of the dynamic features of crying in terms of principles that are common to infants with and without excessive crying, and without the need to posit abnormal or aberrant processes.

Responsivity

Another potentially important notion is that of "responsivity," a concept widely applied in the fields of temperament and emotional regulation in infancy (for excellent reviews, see Rothbart & Derryberry, 1981; Thompson, 1994) but rarely to clinical syndromes of excessive crying. The concept has the advantages that it is applicable to different dimensions of temperament (such as activity and affect), different levels of description (behavior and physiology) and to both behavioral systems and neurological systems that may underlie them (Lewis, 1989; Rothbart & Derryberry, 1981). Responsivity is usually the superordinate category that refers to three conceptually and sometimes empirically distinguishable response properties on which individuals can differ. Behaviorally, individuals can differ in the *type* and/ or the *dynamics* of response. In infants, type of response refers primarily to whether the response has positive (e.g., smiling) or negative (e.g., crying) valence. Dynamics usually refer to the quality, intensity, and timing characteristics thought to reflect biological adaptiveness of graded, flexible (rather than stereotypical), situationally responsive and adaptable functioning (Hofer, 1994; Thompson, 1994). Dynamics includes *reactivity*, operationalized by measures of threshold, intensity, and time of onset; and *regulation* (or inhibition), operationalized as duration or rate of recovery of the response. Emotional responses consists of subjective–experiential, behavioral, and physiological components that are integrally related in complex ways but whose reactive and regulatory properties are not isomorphic (Fox, 1989; Stansbury & Gunnar, 1994). In human infants, subjective–experiential components are available only by inference, but the balance and dynamics of behavioral and some physiological systems are accessible in noninvasive ways (for a review, see Fox, 1994).

Such concepts (and their measures) should be able to be meaningfully applied to generate testable predictions concerning the clinical and developmental phenomenology of excessive crying syndromes. Thus, for example, Barr and Gunnar (in press) have proposed the transient responsivity hypothesis in regard to colic syndrome. According to this hypothesis, infants with colic will manifest increased responsivity (increased reactivity and/or decreased regulation) on measures of negative affectivity compared to infants without colic, but this responsivity will be *transient* (that is, present at 2 months, but no different from control infants at 5 months). This hypothesis differs from the traditional temperament hypothesis in which colic is regarded as an early manifestation of a *stable* temperamental predisposition, which would predict that infants with colic will show increased responsivity both at 2 and 5 months. These concepts permit even more specific predictions. What differentiates infants with colic syndrome may be not simply that they are more responsive but, more specifically, that they are normally reactive but have diminished regulatory responses. This would be consistent with clinical observations that infants with colic syndrome have longer duration, but not more frequent, crying bouts (Barr et al., 1992), that increased carrying shortens crying bout length in normal infants but not in those with colic syndrome (Barr, McMullan, et al., 1991; Hunziker & Barr, 1986), and that infants with colic are more difficult to soothe (Barr, Young, Wright, Gravel, & Alkawaf, 1999; St. James-Roberts, Conroy, & Wilsher, 1995; White et al., in press). Analogously, such concepts might accommodate findings in an important series of observations on so-called "irritable" infants by van den Boom (1994; van den Boom & Hoecksma, 1994). Infants were chosen as irritable at 2 weeks of age on the basis of the excitement peak, rapidity of buildup, and irritability items of the Brazelton Neonatal Behavioral Assessment Scale (NBAS; Brazelton, 1973) that could be seen as measures of reactivity. During an intervention between 6 and 9 months, low-income mothers were coached to increase sensitive responsiveness to their infant, including (but not limited to) effective soothing. Infants who received the intervention cried less and improved on measures of self-soothing, sociability, and exploration (van den Boom, 1994). In terms of responsivity, these results could be indicating that such "irritable" infants are highly reactive but, in contrast to infants with colic syndrome, have the capacity for normal regulation given a caregiving environment sensitive to their signals.

Although widespread, the application of responsivity notions is not without its difficulties, especially when it comes to operationalizing reactivity and regulation by appropriate measures (Barr & Gunnar, in press; Rothbart & Derryberry, 1981). Nevertheless, these notions applied at the behavioral level may well map onto neurological systems implicated in affect. A predisposition to respond with crying (rather than smiling) may be related to asymmetry in right–left hemispheric activation (Davidson & Fox, 1989; Fox & Davidson, 1988). Similarly, the crying response to the taste of sucrose may be useful as a biobehavioral probe of central, opioid-dependent soothing systems (Barr et al., 1994; Blass & Ciaramitaro, 1994; Blass & Smith, 1992). Interestingly, sucrose is differentially effective in calming infants with and without colic and may be specifically different in regard to regulation rather than reactivity to the taste stimulus (Barr & Young, 1997; Barr et al., 1999). Such observations provide the possibility of relating behavioral responsivity characteristics to neurological processes implicated in excessive crying syndromes.

Crying as an Adaptive Behavior in Evolutionary Time

Since crying acts as a signal that elicits caregiving responses, it may determine the infant's access to available resources and parental investment. This makes it likely that at least some aspects of crying are evolved characteristics that serve adaptive functions for survival and/or reproduction (Barr, 1990b, 1995b, 1999; Lummaa, Vuorisalo, Barr, & Lehtonen, 1998). If at least some aspects of phenotypic crying behavior are subject to evolutionary pressures (the so-called "phenotypic gambit" assumption), then a number of recognized evolutionary mechanisms may be contributing to behavior that in Western contexts is considered excessive.

The observation that irritable, difficult infants were more likely to survive a famine (DeVries, 1984) underlines the important point that the Western ideal of an infant who does not cry may not be the most adaptive strategy in all contexts. To the extent that different "crying strategies" may be more or less appropriate to different contexts, one might expect that there would be individual differences in propensity to cry. Other mechanisms may also be operative. Trivers (1974) argued that parents and offspring are likely to be in conflict as to how long and to what degree parents should invest in providing resources to their offspring. Crying could be seen as one of the infant's "psychological weapons" for competing for resources that could be employed, for example, during weaning conflicts. In this case, it is in the infant's interest to have parental investment via breastfeeding continue, whereas it is in the mother's interest to discontinue allocating this resource to the distressed infant, either because of her own health or because it may be more advantageously allocated to a younger sibling. Another relevant evolutionary principle is that of "honest signaling." In evolutionary terms, signals are "honest" if there is a correlation between the information in the signal and the individual's fitness, if the signals are costly to produce, and if they are more costly for less fit individuals (Grafen, 1991). Arguably, infant cries act as honest signals (Barr, 1998; Bryant Furlow, 1997; Lummaa et al., 1998). Crying increases energy expenditure by 13% (Rao, Blass, Brignol, Marino, & Glass, 1993), a level of investment that is marginal for healthy infants but may be important in compromised ones. Two features of crying may be useful in relation to signaling fitness. On the one hand, a number of acoustical features, including pitch (fundamental frequency) do seem to correlate to the infant's neurological condition (Bryant Furlow, 1997; Zeskind, Platzman, Coles, & Schuetze, 1996; Zeskind & Lester, 1981; Zeskind, Sale, Maio, Huntingdon, & Weiseman, 1985). These could be used by the caregiver to decide whether (or not) to increase parental investment. On the other hand, strong early crying might well have been selected for as an honest signal of robustness and good health, very much as it is currently interpreted at the birth of an infant.

Assuming these mechanisms contribute to some of the features of early crying, they may also help to account for characteristics of excessive crying. Arguably, many of the presumably positive and adaptive functions of early crying (such as assuring optimal nutrition, protection from predators, and encouraging positive attachment relationships; Bowlby, 1969) are most likely to occur when crying bouts are frequent and short (e.g., as in the !Kung San) rather than prolonged, as is more common with Western caregiving strategies (Barr, 1990b). Assuming the organism's predispositions to cry were matched (or "coadapted") to expectable environments in which it evolved, prolonged crying that is energetically expensive and more likely to attract predators would be rare. The recent and relatively rapid (in evolutionary terms) shift toward a Western "separation" caregiving style could increase bout length that would otherwise be "inappropriate" in evolutionarily expectable environments. The prolonged crying bouts that distinguish the crying of Western infants from the !Kung San is the same feature that distinguishes infants with and without colic syndrome (Barr, 1990b, 1995b), but the early curve and frequency are the same. If so, evolutionarily defined determinants in interaction with recently changed caregiving practices may help to account for some of the clinical aspects of excessive crying.

SUMMARY AND CONCLUSIONS

In preverbal infants, crying is a salient signal that commands attention and is often effective in recruiting caregiver responses. Because of signaling functions and developmental changes in amounts, forms, and functions of crying behavior, there is no one-to-one relationship between the amount of crying and pathology in the infant or the caregiver–infant relationship. Consequently, the extent to which crying is "excessive" is critically dependent on the context in which it occurs, how it is perceived, and how the context responds. Analogously, crying behavior becomes clinically relevant when the contextual responses no longer function in the best interests of the infant and reflects a breakdown in caregiving relationships and/or contributes to worse outcomes for the infant.

ACKNOWLEDGMENTS. The author would like to thank Megan Gunnar and Liisa Lehtonen for helpful discussions concerning these issues, and the Louis Sessenwein Foundation for the Academic Award supporting this work.

REFERENCES

Acebo, C., & Thoman, E. B. (1992). Crying as a social behavior. *Infant Mental Health Journal, 13*(1), 67–82.

Acebo, C., & Thoman, E. B. (1994). Role of infant crying in the early mother–infant dialogue. *Physiology and Behavior, 57*(3), 541–547.

Ainsworth, M. D. S., Blehar, M. C., Waters, E., & Wall, S. (1978). *Patterns of attachment: A psychological study of the Strange Situation.* Hillsdale, NJ: Erlbaum.

Alvarez, M., & St. James-Roberts, I. (1996). Infant fussing and crying patterns in the first year in an urban community in Denmark. *Acta Paediatrica, 85,* 463–466.

Barr, R. G. (1990a). The normal crying curve: What do we really know? *Developmental Medicine and Child Neurology, 32,* 356–362.

Barr, R. G. (1990b). The early crying paradox: A modest proposal. *Human Nature, 1,* 355–389.

Barr, R. G. (1990c). The "colic" enigma: Prolonged episodes of a normal predisposition to cry. *Infant Mental Health Journal, 11,* 340–348.

Barr, R. G. (1993). Normality: A clinically useless concept: The case of infant crying and colic. *Journal of Developmental and Behavioral Pediatrics, 14,* 264–270.

Barr, R. G. (1995a). Infant crying and colic: It's a family affair: Invited commentary. *Infant Mental Health Journal, 16*(3), 218–220.

Barr, R. G. (1995b). Infant cry behaviour and colic: An interpretation in evolutionary perspective. In W. Tevathan, J. J. McKenna, & E. O. Smith (Eds.), *Evolutionary medicine* (pp. 27–51). New York: Oxford University Press.

Barr, R. G. (1995c). The enigma of infant crying: The emergence of defining dimensions. *Early Development and Parenting, 4*(4), 225–232.

Barr, R. G. (1996). Colic. In W. A. Walker, P. R. Durie, J. R. Hamilton, J. A. Walker-Smith, & J. B. Watkins (Eds.), *Pediatric gastrointestinal disease: Pathophysiology, diagnosis, and management* (pp. 241–250). St. Louis: Mosby.

Barr, R. G. (1998). Reflections on measuring pain in infants: Dissociation in responsive systems and "honest signalling." *Archives of Disease in Childhood: Fetal and Neonatal Edition, 79,* F152–F156.

Barr, R. G. (1998). Crying in the first year of life: Good news in the midst of distress. *Child: Care, Health and Development, 24*(5), 425–439.

Barr, R. G., Bakeman, R., Konner, M., & Adamson, L. (1991). Crying in !Kung infants: A test of the cultural specificity hypothesis. *Developmental Medicine and Child Neurology, 33,* 601–610.

Barr, R. G., Chen, S., Hopkins, B., & Westra, T. (1996). Crying patterns in preterm infants. *Developmental Medicine and Child Neurology, 38,* 345–355.

Barr, R. G., & Desilets, J. (in press). The normal crying curve: Hoops and hurdles. In B. M. Lester (Ed.), *Biological and social aspects of infant crying.* New York: Plenum Press.

Barr, R. G., & Elias, M. F. (1988). Nursing interval and maternal responsivity: Effect on early infant crying. *Pediatrics, 81,* 529–536.

Barr, R. G., & Gunnar, M. R. (in press). Colic—the transient responsivity hypothesis. In R. G. Barr, B. Hopkins, & J. Green (Eds.), *Crying as a sign, a signal and a symptom: Clinical, emotional and developmental aspects of infant and toddler crying.* London: MacKeith Press.

Barr, R. G., Kramer, M. S., Leduc, D. G., Boisjoly, C., McVey-White, L., & Pless, I. B. (1988). Parental diary of infant cry and fuss behaviour. *Archives of Disease of Children, 63,* 380–387.

Barr, R. G., Kramer, M. S., Pless, I. B., Boisjoly, C., & Leduc, D. (1989). Feeding and temperament as determinants of early infant cry/fuss behaviour. *Pediatrics, 84,* 514–521.

Barr, R. G., McMullan, S. J., Spiess, H., Leduc, D. J., Yaremko, J., Barfield, R., Francoeur, T. E., & Hunziker, U. A. (1991). Carrying as colic "therapy": A randomized controlled trial. *Pediatrics, 87,* 623–630.

Barr, R. G., Quek, V., Cousineau, D., Oberlander, T. F., Brian, J. A., & Young, S. N. (1994). Effects of intraoral sucrose on crying, mouthing, and hand–mouth contact in newborn and six-week-old infants. *Developmental Medicine and Child Neurology, 36,* 608–618.

Barr, R. G., Rotman, A., Yaremko, J., Leduc, D., & Francoeur, T. E. (1992). The crying of infants with colic: A controlled empirical description. *Pediatrics, 90*(1), 14–21.

Barr, R. G., Wooldridge, J. A., & Hanley, J. (1991). Effects of formula change on intestinal hydrogen production and crying and fussing behavior. *Journal of Development and Behavioural Pediatrics, 12,* 248–253.

Barr, R. G., & Young, S. N. (1997). A two phase model of the soothing taste response: Implications for a taste probe of temperament and emotion regulation. In M. Lewis & D. Ramsay (Eds.), *Soothing and stress.* Hillsdale, NJ: Erlbaum.

Barr, R. G., Young, S. N., Wright, J. H., Gravel, R., & Alkawaf, R. (1999). Differential calming response to sucrose taste in crying infants with and without colic. *Pediatrics, 103*(5), 1–9. http://www.pediatrics.org/cgi/content/full/103/5/e68.

Bates, J. E. (1984). *Infant characteristics questionnaire, revised.* Bloomington: Indiana University Press.

Bates, J. E., Freeland, C. A., & Lounsbury, M. L. (1979). Measurement of infant difficultness. *Child Development, 50,* 794–803.

Bell, S. M., & Ainsworth, D. S. (1972). Infant crying and maternal responsiveness. *Child Development, 43,* 1171–1190.

Bensel, J. (1996). Early crying—developmental constant or civilizatory artifact? [Abstract]. *Program of the 13th International Conference for Human Ethology, Communication, Cognition and Evolution,* p. 29.

Bensel, J. (1997). Culture meets nature: How much early crying is "normal"? [Abstract]. *Program of the 6th International Cry Research Workshop,* p. 4.

Bernal, J. (1973). Night waking in infants during the first 14 months. *Developmental Medicine and Child Neurology, 15,* 760–769.

Blass, E. M., & Ciaramitaro, V. (1994). A new look at some old mechanisms in human newborns: Taste and tactile determinants of state, affect and action. *Monographs of the Society for Research in Child Development, 59*(1), 1–80.

Blass, E. M., & Smith, B. A. (1992). Differential effects of sucrose, fructose, glucose, and lactose on crying in 1- to 3-day-old human infants: Qualitative and quantitative considerations. *Developmental Psychology, 28*(5), 804–810.

Bloom, K., & McDowell, E. E. (1972). Time-sampling caretaker and infant behaviours in the first five weeks of life. *Journal of Psychology, 80,* 111–120.

Bowlby, J. (1969). *Attachment and loss* (1st ed.). New York: Basic Books.

Boyce, W. T., Barr, R. G., & Zeltzer, L. K. (1992). Temperament and the psychobiology of childhood stress. *Pediatrics, 90*(3), 483–486.

Brazelton, T. B. (1962). Crying in infancy. *Pediatrics, 29,* 579–588.

Brazelton, T. B. (1973). *Neonatal Behavioral Assessment Scale.* London: William Heinemann Medical Books.

Bryant Furlow, F. (1997). Human neonatal cry quality as an honest signal of fitness. *Evolution and Human Behavior, 18,* 175–193.

Canivet, C., Hagander, B., Jakobsson, I., & Lanke, J. (1996). Infantile colic—less common than previously estimated? *Acta Paediatrica, 85,* 454–458.

Carey, W. B. (1968). Maternal anxiety and infantile colic: Is there a relationship? *Clinical Pediatrics, 7*(10), 590–595.

Carey, W. B. (1972). Clinical applications of infant temperament measures. *Behavioral Pediatrics, 81*(4), 823–828.

Carey, W. B. (1984). "Colic": Primary excessive crying as an infant–environment interaction. *Pediatric Clinics of North America, 31,* 993–1005.

Davidson, R. J., & Fox, N. A. (1989). Frontal brain asymmetry predicts infants' response to maternal separation. *Journal of Abnormal Psychology, 98*(2), 127–131.

DeGangi, G. A., DiPietro, J. A., Greenspan, S. I., & Porges, S. W. (1991). Psychophysiological characteristics of the regulatory disordered infant. *Infant Behavior and Development, 14,* 37–50.

DeGangi, G. A., Porges, S. W., Sickel, R. A., & Greenspan, S. I. (1993). Four-year follow-up of a sample of regulatory disordered infants. *Infant Mental Health Journal, 14*(4), 330–343.

DeVries, M. W. (1984). Temperament and infant mortality among the Masai of East Africa. *American Journal of Psychiatry, 141,* 1189–1194.

Emde, R. N., Gaensbauer, T. J., & Harmon, R. J. (1976). *Emotional expression in infancy: A biobehavioral study.* New York: International Universities Press.

Fish, M., & Crockenberg, S. (1981). Correlates and antecedents of nine-month infant behavior and mother–infant interaction. *Infant Behavior and Development, 4,* 69–81.

Forsyth, B. W. C. (1989). Colic and the effect of changing formulas: A double-blind, multiple-crossover study. *Journal of Pediatrics, 115,* 521–526.

Fox, N. A. (1989). Psychophysiological correlates of emotional reactivity during the first year of life. *Developmental Psychology, 25*(3), 364–372.

Fox, N. A. (1994). *The development of emotion regulation: Biological and behavioral considerations* (1st ed.). Chicago: University of Chicago Press.

Fox, N. A., & Davidson, R. J. (1988). Patterns of brain electrical activity during facial signs of emotion in 10-month-old infants. *Developmental Psychology, 24*(2), 230–236.

Franco, F. (1984). Differences in manner of phonation of infant cries: Relationship to communicative context. *Language and Speech, 27*, 59–78.

Geertsma, M. A., & Hyams, J. S. (1989). Colic—a pain syndrome of infancy? *Pediatric Clinics of North America, 36*, 905–919.

Gekoski, M. J., Rovee-Collier, C. K., & Carulli-Rabinowitz, V. (1983). A longitudinal analysis of inhibition of vocal distress: The origins of social expectations? *Infant Behavior and Development, 6*, 339–351.

Goldsmith, H. H., Buss, A. H., Plomin, R., Rothbart, M. K., Thomas, A., Hinde, R. A., & McCall, R. B. (1987). Roundtable: What is temperament? Four approaches. *Child Development, 58*, 505–529.

Gormally, S. M., & Barr, R. G. (1997). Of clinical pies and clinical clues: Proposal for a clinical approach to complaints of early crying and colic. *Ambulatory Child Health, 3*(2), 137–153.

Grafen, A. (1991). Modelling in behavioural ecology. In J. R. Krebs & N. B. Davies (Eds.), *Behavioural ecology* (pp. 5–31). London: Blackwell Scientific.

Gunnar, M., Broderson, L., Krueger, K., & Rigatuso, J. (1994). Dampening of adrenocortical and behavioral reactivity during early infancy: Normative changes and individual differences. *Child Development, 67*, 877–889.

Gustafson, G. E., & Green, J. A. (1991). Developmental coordination of cry sounds with visual regard and gestures. *Infant Behaviour and Development, 14*, 51–57.

Heine, R. G., Jaquiery, A., Lubitz, L., Cameron, D. J. S., & Catto-Smith, A. G. (1995). Role of gastro-oesophageal reflux in infant irritability. *Archives of Disease in Childhood, 73*, 121–125.

Hide, D. W., & Guyer, B. M. (1982). Prevalence of infantile colic. *Archives of Disease of Children, 57*, 559–560.

Hofer, M. A. (1994). Hidden regulators in attachment, separation and loss. In N. A. Fox (Ed.), *The development of emotion regulation: Biological and behavioral considerations* (pp. 192–207). Chicago: University of Chicago Press.

Hopkins, B., & Palthe, T. V. (1987). The development of the crying state during early infancy. *Developmental Psychobiology, 20*, 165–175.

Hubbard, F. O. A., & van IJzendoorn, M. H. (1989). *Maternal unresponsiveness and infant crying: Frequency measures.* Paper presented at the Society for Research in Child Development, Kansas City, Missouri.

Hunziker, U. A., & Barr, R. G. (1986). Increased carrying reduces infant crying: A randomized controlled trial. *Pediatrics, 77*, 641–648.

Kagan, J., & Snidman, N. (1991a). Infant predictors of inhibited and uninhibited profiles. *Psychological Science, 2*, 40–44.

Kagan, J., & Snidman, N. (1991b). Temperamental factors in human development. *American Psychologist, 46*, 856–862.

Katerji, M., & Painter, M. (1994). Infantile migraine presenting as colic. *Journal of Child Neurology, 8*, 336–337.

Keller, H., Lohaus, A., Volker, S., Cappendberg, M., & Chasiotis, A. (1998). Relationships between infant crying, birth complications, and maternal variables. *Child: Care, Health and Development, 24*(5), 377–394.

Konner, M. (1989). Spheres and modes of inquiry: Integrative challenges in child development research. In P. H. Zelazo & R. G. Barr (Eds.), *Challenges to developmental paradigms: Implications for theory, assessment and treatment* (pp. 227–258). Hillsdale, NJ: Erlbaum.

Korner, A. F. (1972). State as variable, as obstacle, and as mediator of stimulation in infant research. *Merrill–Palmer Quarterly, 18*, 77–94.

Lee, K. (1994). The crying pattern of Korean infants and related factors. *Developmental Medicine and Child Neurology, 36*, 601–607.

Lehtonen, L., Korhonen, T., & Korvenranta, H. (1994). Temperament and sleeping pattern in infantile colic during the first year of life. *Journal of Development and Behavioral Pediatrics, 15*(6), 416–420.

Lehtonen, L., & Korvenranta, H. (1995). Infantile colic: Seasonal incidence and crying profiles. *Archives of Pediatrics and Adolescent Medicine, 149*, 533–536.

Lester, B. M., Boukydis, C. F. Z., García-Coll, C. T., Hole, W. T., & Peucker, M. (1992). Infantile colic: Acoustic cry characteristics, maternal perception of cry, and temperament. *Infant Behavior and Development, 15*, 15–26.

Lester, B. M., Cucca, J., Andreozzi, L., Flanagan, P., & Oh, W. (1993). Possible association between fluoxetine hydrochloride and colic in an infant. *Journal of the American Academy of Child and Adolescent Psychiatry, 32*(6), 1253–1255.

Lewis, M. (1989). Culture and biology: The role of temperament. In P. R. Zelazo & R. G. Barr (Eds.), *Challenges to developmental paradigms: Implications for theory, assessment and treatment* (pp. 203–226). Hillsdale, NJ: Erlbaum.

Lewis, M., & Thomas, D. (1990). Cortisol release in infants in response to inoculation. *Child Development, 61*, 50–59.

Lewis, M., & Ramsay, D. S. (1995). Developmental change in infants' responses to stress. *Child Development, 66*, 657–670.

Lewis, M., & Ramsay, D. S. (1995). Stability and change in cortisol and behavioral response to stress during the first 18 months of life. *Developmental Psychobiology, 28*(8), 419–428.

Listernick, R., & Tomita, T. (1991). Persistent crying in infancy as a presentation of Chiari type I malformation. *Journal of Pediatrics, 118*(4, Pt. 1), 567–569.

Lombroso, C. T., & Lerman, P. (1967). Breathholding spells (cyanotic and pallid infant syncope). *Pediatrics, 39*(4), 563–581.

Lummaa, V., Vuorisalo, T., Barr, R. G., & Lehtonen, L. (1998). Why cry? Adaptive significance of intensive crying in human infants. *Evolution and Human Behavior, 19*, 193–202.

Maldonado-Duran, M., & Sauceda-Garcia, J. M. (1996). Excessive crying and regulatory disorders in infants. *Bulletin of the Menninger Clinic, 60*(1), 62–78.

Malone, A. (1997). The crying pattern of preterm infants [Abstract]. *Program of the 6th International Cry Research Workshop*, p. 4.

McConaghey, R. M. S. (1967). Sir George Baker and the Devonshire colic. *Medical History, 11*, 345–360.

Mckenzie, S. (1991). Troublesome crying in infants: Effect of advice to reduce stimulation. *Archives of Disease in Childhood, 66*(12), 1416–1420.

Miller, A. R., & Barr, R. G. (1991). Infantile colic: Is it a gut issue? *Pediatric Clinics of North America, 38*(6), 1407–1423.

Miller, A. R., Barr, R. G., & Eaton, W. O. (1993). Crying and motor behavior of six-week-old infants and postpartum maternal mood. *Pediatrics, 92*, 551–558.

National Center for Clinical Infant Programs. (1994). *Diagnostic Classification: 0–3*. Arlington, VA: Zero to Three/ National Center for Clinical Infant Programs.

Papousek, M., & Papousek, H. (1990). Excessive infant crying and intuitive parental care: Buffering support and its failures in parent–infant interaction. *Early Child Development and Care, 65*, 117–125.

Papousek, M., & Papousek, H. (1996). Infantile persistent crying, state regulation, and interaction with parents: A systems view. In M. H. Bornstein & J. L. Genevro (Eds.), *Child development and behavioral pediatrics* (pp. 11–32). Mahwah, NJ: Erlbaum.

Papousek, M., & von Hofacker, N. (1995). Persistent crying and parenting: Search for a butterfly in a dynamic system. *Early Development and Parenting, 4*(4), 209–224.

Papousek, M., & von Hofacker, N. (1998). Persistent crying in early infancy: A non-trival condition of risk for the developing mother–infant relationship. *Child: Care, Health and Development, 24*(5), 395–424.

Paradise, J. L. (1966). Maternal and other factors in the etiology of infantile colic. *Journal of the American Medical Association, 197*, 123–131.

Poole, S. R. (1991). The infant with acute, unexplained, excessive crying. *Pediatrics, 88*(3), 450–455.

Potegal, M., Kosorok, M. R., & Davidson, R. J. (1996). The time course of angry behaviour in the temper tantrums of young children. *Annals of the New York Academy of Sciences, 794*, 31–45.

Prechtl, H. F. R., & O'Brien, M. J. (1982). Behavioural states of the full-term newborn. The emergence of a concept. In P. Stratton (Ed.), *Psychobiology of the human newborn* (pp. 53–73). New York: Wiley.

Rao, M., Blass, E. M., Brignol, M. J., Marino, L., & Glass, L. (1993). Effect of crying on energy metabolism in human neonates. *Pediatric Research, 33*, 309.

Rebelsky, F., & Black, R. (1972). Crying in infancy. *Journal of Genetic Psychology, 121*, 49–57.

Rothbart, M. K. (1981). Measurement of infant temperament. *Child Development, 52*, 569–578.

Rothbart, M. K., & Derryberry, D. (1981). Development of individual differences in temperament. In A. L. Brown & M. E. Lamb (Eds.), *Advances in developmental psychology* (pp. 37–86). Hillsdale, NJ: Erlbaum.

Sauls, H. S., & Redfern, D. E. (1997). *Colic and excessive crying*. Columbus, OH: Ross Products Division, Abbott Laboratories.

St. James-Roberts, I. (in press). Infant crying levels, and maternal patterns of care, in normal community and clinically referred samples. In B. Lester (Ed.), *Biological and social aspects of infant crying*. New York: Kluwer Academic/ Plenum.

St. James-Roberts, I. (1999). What's distinct about infants' "colic" cries? *Archives of Disease in Childhood, 80*, 56–62.

St. James-Roberts, I., Bowyer, J., Varghese, S., & Sawdon, J. (1994). Infant crying patterns in Manali and London. *Child: Care, Health and Development, 20*, 323–337.

St. James-Roberts, I., Conroy, S., & Wilsher, K. (1995). Clinical, developmental and social aspects of infant crying and colic. *Early Development and Parenting, 4*(4), 177–189.

St. James-Roberts, I., Conroy, S., & Wilsher, K. (1996). Bases for maternal perceptions of infant crying and colic behaviour. *Archives of Disease in Childhood, 75*, 375–384.

St. James-Roberts, I., Conroy, S., & Wilsher, C. (1998). Stability and outcome of persistent infant crying. *Infant Behavior and Development, 21*(3), 411–435.

St. James-Roberts, I., Conroy, S., & Wilsher, K. (1998). Links between maternal care and persistent infant crying in the early months. *Child: Care, Health and Development, 24*(5), 353–376.

St. James-Roberts, I., & Halil, T. (1991). Infant crying patterns in the first year: Normal community and clinical findings. *Journal of Child Psychology and Psychiatry, 32*(6), 951–968.

St. James-Roberts, I., Hurry, J., & Bowyer, J. (1993). Objective confirmation of crying durations in infants referred for excessive crying. *Archives of Disease in Childhood, 68*(1), 82–84.

St. James-Roberts, I., Hurry, J., Bowyer, J., & Barr, R. G. (1995). Supplementary carrying compared with advice to increase responsive parenting as interventions to prevent persistent crying. *Pediatrics, 95*(3), 381–388.

St. James-Roberts, I., & Plewis, I. (1996). Individual differences, daily fluctuations, and developmental changes in amounts of infant waking, fussing, crying, feeding and sleeping. *Child Development*, 1–36.

Stahlberg, M. (1984). Infantile colic: Occurrence and risk factors. *European Journal of Pediatrics, 143*, 108–111.

Stansbury, K., & Gunnar, M. (1994). Adrenocortical activity and emotion regulation. In N. A. Fox (Ed.), *The development of emotion regulation: Biological and behavioral considerations* (pp. 108–134). Chicago: University of Chicago Press.

Stifter, C. A., & Braungart, J. (1992). Infant colic: A transient condition with no apparent effects. *Journal of Applied Developmental Psychology, 13*, 447–462.

Talbot, E. M., Pitts, J. F., Dudgeon, J., & Lee, W. R. (1992). A case of developmental glaucoma presenting with abdominal colic and subnormal intraocular pressure. *Journal of Pediatric Ophthalmology and Strabismus, 29*(2), 116–119.

Thomas, A., Chess, S., & Birch, H. (1968). *Temperament and behavior disorders in children.* New York: New York University Press.

Thompson, R. A. (1994). Emotion regulation: A theme in search of definition. In N. A. Fox (Ed.), *The development of emotion regulation: Biological and behavioral considerations* (pp. 25–52). Chicago: University of Chicago Press.

Treem, W. R. (1994). Infant colic: A pediatric gastroenterologist's perspective. *Pediatric Clinics of North America, 41*(5), 1121–1138.

Trivers, R. L. (1974). Parent–offspring conflict. *American Zoologist, 14*, 249–264.

van den Boom, D. C. (1994). The influence of temperament and mothering on attachment and exploration: An experimental manipulation of sensitive responsiveness among lower-class mothers with irritable infants. *Child Development, 65*, 1457–1477.

van den Boom, D. C., & Hoecksma, J. B. (1994). The effect of infant irritability on mother–infant interaction: A growth-curve analysis. *Developmental Psychology, 30*, 581–590.

Wales, J. K. H., Primhak, R. A., Rattenbury, J., & Taylor, C. J. (1989). Isolated fructose malabsorption. *Archives of Disease in Childhood, 65*(2), 227–229.

Wasz-Hockert, O., Lind, J., Vuorenkoski, V., Partanen, T., & Valanne, E. (1968). The infant cry: A spectrographic and auditory analysis. In *Clinics in developmental medicine* (pp. 1–42). Lavenham, Suffolk, UK: Spastics International Medical Publications.

Weissbluth, M., Christoffel, K. K., & Davis, T. (1984). Treatment of infantile colic with dicyclomine hydrochloride. *Journal of Pediatrics, 104*(6), 951–955.

Wessel, M. A., Cobb, J. C., Jackson, E. B., Harris, G. S., & Detwiler, A. C. (1954). Paroxysmal fussing in infancy, sometimes called "colic." *Pediatrics, 14*, 421–434.

White, B. P., Gunnar, M. R., Larson, M. C., Donzella, B., & Barr, R. G. (in press). Physiological reactivity and daily rhythms in infants with and without colic. *Child Development.*

Wolff, P. H. (1987). *The development of behavioral states and the expression of emotions in early infancy: New proposals for investigation.* Chicago: University of Chicago Press.

Wolff, P. H. (1993). Behavioral and emotional states in infancy: A dynamic perspective. In L. B. Smith & E. Thelen (Eds.), *A dynamic systems approach to development: Applications* (pp. 189–208). Cambridge, MA: MIT Press.

Worobey, J., & Blajda, V. M. (1989). Temperament ratings at 2 weeks, 2 months, and 1 year: Differential stability of activity and emotionality. *Developmental Psychology, 25*(2), 257–263.

Zeskind, P. S., & Barr, R. G. (1997). Acoustic characteristics of naturally occurring cries of infants with "colic." *Child Development, 68*(3), 394–403.

Zeskind, P. S., & Lester, B. M. (1981). Analysis of cry features in newborns with differential fetal growth. *Child Development, 52*, 207–212.

Zeskind, P. S., Parker-Price, S., & Barr, R. G. (1993). Rhythmic organization of the sound of infant crying. *Developmental Psychobiology, 26*(6), 321–333.

Zeskind, P. S., Platzman, K., Coles, C. D., & Schuetze, P. A. (1996). Cry analysis detects subclinical effects of prenatal alcohol exposure in newborn infants. *Infant Behavior and Development, 19*, 497–500.

Zeskind, P. S., Sale, J., Maio, M. L., Huntingdon, L., & Weiseman, J. R. (1985). Adult perceptions of pain and hunger cries: A synchrony of arousal. *Child Development, 56*, 540–554.

19

Developmental Psychopathology of Failure to Thrive

Dennis Drotar and Jane Robinson

The term *failure to thrive* (FTT), also known as growth deficiency, describes an infant or toddler whose weight is more than two standard deviations below the mean for age, or less than the 5th percentile based on National Center for Heath Statistics norms (Hammill et al., 1979), corrected for gestational age, parental growth patterns (genetic growth potential), and gender (Casey, 1992). The term *nonorganic FTT* has been erroneously used to refer to children whose growth deficiency does not relate primarily to organic disease. However, informed pediatricians recognize that a simple dichotomy between organic and "nonorganic," or environmental influences, on growth is highly misleading (Bithoney & Dubowitz, 1985).

The condition of FTT has significance for the field of developmental psychopathology in several respects. For example, deceleration in rate of weight gain early in life in the absence of primary organic disease is a potential marker for problematic adaptation in parent–child relationships and risk to the child's psychological development (Drotar, 1995). In addition, as in other research with young children at psychological risk (Garmezy, Masten, & Tellegen, 1984), the study of FTT can illuminate the biological and environmental risk factors that threaten children's cognitive, affective, and social development at critical times in their development. In contrast to many other problems that disrupt young children's psychological development, FTT can be identified objectively by pediatric caregivers early in the child's life. This potential for early recognition provides an important opportunity for preventive intervention to reduce the consequences of FTT and associated risk factors on children's physical health and psychological development (Drotar, 1991b; Silverman & Levin, 1985).

Dennis Drotar and Jane Robinson • Department of Pediatrics, Rainbow Babies and Children's Hospital, Cleveland, Ohio 44106.

Handbook of Developmental Psychopathology, Second Edition, edited by Arnold J. Sameroff, Michael Lewis, and Suzanne M. Miller. Kluwer Academic/Plenum Publishers, New York, 2000.

DEVELOPMENTAL INFLUENCES ON FAILURE TO THRIVE

It is useful to distinguish between two types of influences that affect the development of FTT, as well as the psychological outcomes of children with this problem: (1) inadequate caloric intake, which is recognized as a final common pathway for FTT (Frank & Drotar, 1994); and (2) the specific factors that disrupt the provision of food and attention to the child, and eventually limit caloric intake (Drotar, 1988). These latter influences are complex and multifaceted. One of the lingering misconceptions concerning FTT is the equation of this problem with maternal deprivation (Patton & Gardner, 1962). While a subgroup of children with FTT are neglected and deprived (Frank & Drotar, 1994), the evidence for inadequate parenting as a single or universal etiological factor in FTT is lacking (Boddy & Skuse, 1988; Drotar, 1988, 1995). Modern pediatric thinking emphasizes a multidimensional etiological model involving both biological and environmental risk factors (Bithoney & Dubowitz, 1985; Frank & Drotar, 1994).

One comprehensive conceptual framework that we have found useful in considering the origins of FTT is Belsky's (1984) process-oriented, contextual model of parental competence. In this framework, parental competence is defined as sensitivity to the child's developing repertoire and communications, and involvement with the child. These core dimensions of parental competence are assumed to be influenced by three sets of factors: (1) parental resources, especially early developmental experiences and personality development; (2) child characteristics, including temperament, physical health, illness, and age; and (3) the social context of parent–child relations, which includes the parents' quality of the relationship, family social networks and resources, employment, and community resources. Belsky hypothesizes that parental competence is multiply determined, rarely undermined by problems in a single domain, but is most vulnerable when all three sets of influences (e.g., parental resources, child characteristics, and family resources) are compromised in some way (Belsky & Isabella, 1988). This model can be extrapolated to the problem of FTT, where evidence suggests that parental competence is undermined by risks and problems in each of the following domains:

Parental Personal Resources

Clinical observers have suggested that some mothers of infants who fail to thrive have experienced traumatic childhoods that would be expected to disrupt their identification with the maternal role and their learning of effective parenting skills, and also interfere with the quality of their attachment to and relationship with their children (Fraiberg, 1980; Gorman, Leifer, & Grossman, 1993; Lieberman & Birch, 1985). The strongest evidence for this hypothesis has been provided by Altemeier et al.'s (1979) prospective study of high risk mothers who were initially interviewed during their pregnancies and then followed through their child's first year. Mothers of children who eventually developed FTT reported more problematic childhoods, including more reports of feeling abused as a child than mothers of children who achieved age-appropriate physical growth.

Other evidence suggests that continuing maternal vulnerabilities for problematic early relationships with their children may culminate in FTT. Benoit, Zeanah, and Barton (1989) found that almost all of the mothers of infants with FTT in their sample were classified as insecure in their attachments, based on the Adult Attachment Interview, compared to a smaller number of mothers of thriving infants. Polan et al. (1991) found that mothers of infants with FTT reported more current or past psychiatric symptoms, especially major depression, than mothers of physically healthy infants. While almost no research has been conducted on the psychological characteristics of fathers of infants who fail to thrive, clinical observations have suggested that they may also demonstrate problems in parent to child attachment (Drotar & Sturm, 1988).

Child Characteristics

Various infant physical and psychological characteristics may interact with vulnerable parental resources and contribute to the development of FTT, perhaps by increasing the complexity of parents' child-rearing burdens. For example, several studies have demonstrated that children with FTT have lower birth weights than children with similar sociodemographic and family characteristics who have achieved normal growth patterns (Pollitt & Leibel, 1980). Prematurity and low birth weight may affect infant behavior or physical growth potential directly, intensify family stress, and/or engender early separation between mother and child, all of which may increase the risk for parenting problems and, potentially, FTT.

Infants' acute physical illnesses may also contribute to the development of growth deficiency by contributing to a vicious cycle of illness and malnutrition (Frank & Drotar, 1994). Newberger, Reed, Daniel, Hyde, and Kotelchuck (1977) and Kotelchuck (1979) reported that children with FTT made more visits to a doctor in their first year of life and were hospitalized longer than a comparison group of infants with normal growth patterns. In a prospective study, Sherrod, O'Connor, Vietze, and Altemeier (1985) also found that young children who experienced subsequent abused or developed FTT were ill more often than control children, particularly during their first few months of life.

Other physical problems also may contribute to growth deficiency in various ways. For example, problems such as cerebral palsy can interfere with the child's ability to feed and/or necessitate treatment procedures such as a gastrostomy or nasogastric feedings that impede the development of normal feeding patterns and eventually disrupt physical growth (Geertsma, Hyams, Pelletier, & Reiter, 1985). In a carefully done prospective, population-based study, Mathisen, Skuse, Wolke, and Reilly (1989) identified a higher frequency of physical problems (i.e., oral–motor deficits) in young children who were eventually identified as growth deficient compared with normally growing infants.

The evidence that infant behavioral characteristics operate as risk factors for the development of FTT is not as strong as it is for physical characteristics. However, lethargic, listless infant behavior and easy temperament may elicit less responsive behavior from parents and eventually contribute to FTT (Pollitt, 1973). Unresponsive, withdrawn behavior, which reflects the combined influence of undernutrition and limited stimulation, is often associated with FTT (Drotar, 1989). However, such behavior appears to be a consequence rather than antecedent of FTT. In what is, to our knowledge, the only prospective study to assess infant behavior prior to the development of FTT, Vietze et al. (1980) found no differences in newborn behavior (vocalization, visual attention, cry, and no response) on the Brazelton Neonatal Assessment Scale between infants who were subsequently diagnosed as failing to thrive and those who eventually achieved normal growth.

The Social and Family Context of Parent–Child Relations

Salient resources of the child's social and family context such as poverty, problematic food allocation strategies, and strained family relationships appear to interact with the threats to parental competence posed by limited parental resources and burdensome child characteristics to disrupt caloric intake and contribute to FTT (Drotar, 1991a; Drotar & Eckerle, 1989). Although a causal relationship between economic disadvantage and FTT has not been clearly established (Skuse, 1993), increasing numbers of U.S. families live in poverty that is severe enough to limit the quantity and quality of food that is available for children's consumption (Frank, Allen, & Brown, 1985; Frank & Drotar, 1994).

In families where sufficient food is consistently available to adequately support the child's growth, parents may not allocate it effectively, because they are not aware of the child's nutritional needs or the consequences of feeding and nutritional practices on children's growth and development. For example, parents from cultural and ethnic groups who believe that weaning children from the breast or bottle and/or introducing solid foods at an early age will enhance their children's development may not appreciate that their children may have problems taking in a sufficient number of calories solely through solid foods (Cassidy, 1980). In other families, a zealous parental commitment to "healthy" dietary practices may limit the child's caloric intake. For example, Pugiliese, Weyman-Daum, Moses, and Lifshitz (1987) reported a series of cases in which maternal concerns about obesity and atherosclerosis caused them to limit their children's caloric intake to 60–90% of that recommended for age and culminated in FTT.

Patterns of family relationships and caretaking patterns such as inconsistent feeding schedules, faulty or incomplete response to the child's feeding initiatives, or serious family conflict that pervades mealtimes, may also limit the child's caloric intake by interfering with a concentrated, organized approach to feeding and by affecting the quality of the child's response to food. Family conflict may limit family members' abilities to monitor their children's feeding behavior and caloric intake effectively, to recognize the early signs of limited caloric intake or feeding problems, or to make necessary adjustments to correct these problems (Drotar, 1991b; Hertzler & Vaughn, 1979). At least one controlled home observational study (Heptinstall et al., 1987) has documented a link between familial feeding and caretaking patterns and FTT. Families of growth-deficient infants were observed to have less consistent mealtimes and to limit their children's food intake more than families of normally growing children.

THE ROLE OF DEVELOPMENTAL PROCESSES IN FAILURE TO THRIVE

While multiple risk factors appear to contribute to the development of FTT, the specific processes that actually trigger and maintain reduced caloric intake among young children are not at all clear, partially because it is very difficult to observe carefully children who fail to thrive and their families prior to the development of this problem. Identification of the origins of FTT is further complicated by the fact that different subtypes of FTT may reflect different etiologies and very different patterns of disruption in early relationships (Drotar & Sturm, 1994a). For example, the child's diminished caloric intake may reflect parental underfeeding based on faulty nutritional knowledge and/or practices, problematic family food allocation, extreme poverty that occurs in the context of a reasonably intact mother–child relationship, or a highly dysfunctional parent–child relationship (Drotar, 1991a; Drotar & Sturm, 1994a).

Experienced practitioners have observed consistent patterns of individual differences in the clinical presentations of FTT that can be differentiated by the developmental stage at which the problems occur. For example, FTT that presents in the first several months of life often reflects problems of homeostasis, for example, regulation of sleep, feeding, and/or elimination

(Chatoor & Egan, 1983; Lieberman & Birch, 1985). Patterns of noncontingent or anticontingent maternal–child interactions (Greenspan & Lieberman, 1980) that do not provide a consistent and predictable response to infants' signals for hunger and social interaction have been observed in clinical populations of young (2- to 5-month-old) FTT infants and parents (Lieberman & Birch, 1985).

Other cases of FTT, especially those that occur during the latter part of the child's first year, may reflect a breakdown of age-appropriate parent–child interactional processes concerning separation and individuation. For example, Chatoor, Dickson, Schaefer, and Egan (1985) have observed feeding disorders that begin in the second half of the first year of life, with a peak incidence around 9 months of age among children with fail to thrive. Such disorders are characterized by well-reinforced patterns of maladaptive parent–infant interaction, as shown in the following interactional scenario: The infant grabs for the spoon to participate in feeding. In her zeal to get the food into the infant's mouth, the mother ignores this signal. However, the infant responds with anger and frustration and refuses to open his mouth. The mother then becomes increasingly anxious about the infant's behavior and tries harder and harder to get the food into the infant, only to be met by steadfast and escalating refusals.

Such contrasting developmental presentations of FTT may reflect the end point of very different patterns of early learning experiences and social reinforcement (Linscheid & Rasnake, 1985). For example, the type of FTT that reflects a disturbance in early regulation of sleep and feeding patterns is characterized by deficits in mutual contingency experiences, which are important building blocks of the infant's experience of efficacy (Lewis & Goldberg, 1969). On the other hand, eating disorders in older infants are more likely to reflect maladaptive learning habits that involve classical conditioning; for example, the presentation of food is repeatedly paired with maternal anxiety (or other negative emotions, e.g., frustration) or operant learning; for example, food presentation becomes an antecedent event for reinforcing consequences such as the withdrawal of the disliked food and prolonged attention from the caregiver to reinforce (Linscheid & Rasnake, 1985). At the point at which they present to practitioners, some FTT infants and parents may have engaged in literally thousands of maladaptive interactions that as a consequence are very difficult to interrupt (Drotar & Sturm, 1994a).

DEVELOPMENTAL PROBLEMS ASSOCIATED WITH AN EARLY HISTORY OF FAILURE TO THRIVE

One of the core tenets of developmental psychopathology is the coherence and stability of basic developmental processes across different ages, despite changes in manifest behavior (Sroufe, 1979). One hallmark of FTT is the wide range of developmental, cognitive, and social–emotional outcomes that are disrupted by this problem and associated risk factors during infancy and the preschool years (Drotar, 1988, 1995).

Cognitive Development

Research has consistently indicated that beginning in early infancy, children with early histories of FTT are at risk for global deficits in their cognitive development (Drotar & Sturm, 1988; Singer & Fagan, 1984). Moreover, the level of impairment in cognitive development in young children with early histories of FTT increases from early infancy to age 4, which may reflect the influence of economic disadvantage often associated with FTT (Drotar & Sturm, 1994b). For example, Dowdney, Skuse, Heptinstall, Puckering, and Zur-Szpiro (1987) surveyed an inner-city population in London to assess the association between physical growth and developmental delay in preschool children with growth delay and a closely matched comparison group. Children with nonorganic growth problems were significantly more delayed in their level of cognitive development than controls. Based on standardized tests, one-third were identified as intellectually retarded and in need of specialized education. While there have been no prospective studies of the cognitive development of school-age children with early histories of FTT to our knowledge, retrospective studies of children of this age reveal significant academic deficits (Oates, Peacock, & Forest, 1985).

Socioemotional Development

A wide range of problems in socioemotional development, including feeding disorders (Chatoor & Egan, 1983), insecure attachment (Crittenden, 1987), and deficits in social responsiveness (Drotar, 1989), have been described among infants and toddlers with histories of FTT. Consistent with the association of FTT with problematic mother–child interactions (Drotar, 1995) and even neglect in some cases (Frank & Drotar, 1994), high rates of insecure attachments (45–90%) have been identified in several studies. Differences in the prevalence of insecure attachment probably reflect variation in sampling characteristics, such as differences in risk factors in specific populations (Drotar, 1990).

In a well-controlled study, Ward, Kessler, and Altman (1993) compared the responses of 26 children ages 12–25 months with FTT (10 with nonorganic FTT, 16 with nonorganic FTT) and 28 normally growing same-age children to the Strange Situation procedure. Children with FTT were more likely to show anxious (especially disorganized) attachments (40%) than normally growing controls. Only 35% of children with FTT had secure attachments. In contrast, 64% of normal controls were securely attached and only 7% were disorganized. On the other hand, Crittenden's (1987) finding of a very high incidence (92%) of insecure attachments in infants with FTT may reflect the fact that children in this sample had also been referred to county welfare protective services for evaluation of neglect.

Feeding difficulties have been identified among infants who present with FTT during infancy (Benoit, 1993) especially during the second half of the first year of life. In what, to our knowledge, is the only study to assess age differences concerning feeding interactions in this population, Hutcheson, Black, and Starr (1993) observed that mothers of toddlers with nonorganic FTT (ages 13–26 months) experienced more difficulty in feeding interactions than mothers of younger (ages 8–13 months) infants.

Because the families of infants who fail to thrive are difficult to recruit and maintain in prospective follow-up, there is relatively little information concerning the socioemotional outcomes of preschool children with early histories of FTT and almost no information about school-age children. Our prospective research has indicated that 3-year-old children with early histories of FTT demonstrated lower ego resiliency and ego control (Block & Block, 1980), and a higher frequency of behavioral problems than normally growing children who were matched on sociodemographic factors (Drotar & Sturm, 1992). Oates et al. (1985) found that older school-age children with early histories of FTT had a higher frequency of behavioral problems as reported by parents and teachers than a comparison group of normally growing children.

RISK AND PROTECTIVE INFLUENCES CONCERNING PSYCHOLOGICAL OUTCOMES OF CHILDREN WITH EARLY HISTORIES OF FAILURE TO THRIVE

There is considerable variation in such potential risk factors as age at onset, duration, severity of malnutrition, associated psychological deficits at the time of diagnosis, and parent–child and family problems among children who fail to thrive and their families (Drotar, 1988; 1995). Consistent with a transactional model (Sameroff & Chandler, 1975), a range of biological and environmental factors predict individual variation in the psychological outcomes of children with early histories of FTT (Drotar & Sturm, 1994b).

Influences on Cognitive Development and Behavior

Severity and History of Growth and Nutritional Deficiency

Although many children with early histories of FTT gain weight following diagnosis and nutritional intervention, not all of these children recover completely from their weight and nutritional deficits. Our studies of children who were hospitalized and treated for FTT as infants (average age of 5 months at time of diagnosis) indicated that although the majority attained normal nutritional status at age 3 (as assessed by weight for height), a subgroup (nearly one-third) still demonstrated at least mild nutritional wasting (Sturm & Drotar, 1989). The presence of continuing nutritional deficits in children with early histories of FTT is potentially important in light of research conducted among children in developing countries indicating that early episodes of severe malnutrition have long-lasting negative effects on cognitive development and behavior, especially in suboptimal family environments (Black & Dubowitz, 1991). For example, school-age children with early histories of severe malnutrition have been shown to be less responsive to peers and to have attentional deficits as well as difficulties containing their impulses and organizing their behavior (Galler, Ramsey, Solimano, & Lowell, 1983).

Among other factors, better nutritional status, as measured by weight for height at point of hospitalization, predicted cognitive development at 18 months of age among children with early histories of FTT (Drotar, Nowak, Malone, & Negray, 1985). However, at least one study has shown that early nutritional deficits (as assessed by weight for height) at the time of the diagnosis of FTT did not predict cognitive development or behavioral symptoms in preschool children (Drotar & Sturm, 1988). These findings may reflect the milder nutritional deficits among children who are treated for FTT in the United States as compared with malnourished children who have been studied in developing countries.

Impact of the Chronicity of Growth Failure

There are often delays of several months or more between the time that the child's growth delay is severe enough to be categorized as FTT and the point of treatment, diagnosis, and institution of treatment (Drotar, Nowak, et al., 1985). In some cases, such as among children who present with the serious condition known as psychosocial or deprivational dwarfism, the child's growth failure and associated deprivation may have lasted for years (Money, 1992). We have found that the chronicity of FTT prior to diagnosis and treatment was positively associated with the subsequent development of insecure attachment, especially in association with early onset of FTT (Drotar, Nowak, et al., 1985).

Family–Environmental Factors

Studies have consistently revealed that the quality of their home environments predicts the cognitive development of children with FTT, just as it does for other children. For example, lower maternal educational levels and a higher frequency of placements outside the home were associated with lower levels of cognitive development at age 3 among children with histories of FTT (Singer & Fagan, 1984). In addition, children with histories of early FTT whose mothers were less nurturant and demonstrated a lower quality of stimulation had less optimal cognitive developmental outcomes (Black, Hutcheson, Dubowitz, & Berenson-Howard, 1994; Puckering et al., 1995).

Multifactorial Influences

Our research has generally found that biological and environmental risk factors predict cognitive developmental outcomes among children with early histories of FTT. For example, better nutritional status, higher family income, and a higher ratio of adults to children were associated with better cognitive development outcomes among 18-month-old infants (Drotar, Malone, et al., 1985). In a subsequent follow-up, higher income and later age of onset of FTT predicted better cognitive development at 24 months (Drotar, Novak, et al., 1985b). Children with higher Bayley scores had a later age of onset of FTT and were from families with higher incomes. Finally, family environmental characteristics (family income and maternal educational level) accounted for statistically significant, though relatively small, amounts of variance (22% and 10%, respectively) in cognitive development at age 3 (Drotar & Sturm, 1988).

Consistent with studies of physically healthy children, family environmental factors and early patterns of attachment have been shown to predict socioemotional development among children with early histories of FTT. For example, children who were rated as securely attached at 12 months of age demonstrated higher standards of performance, less rigidity under stress, and were rated more competent and more creative at 42 months than children with early histories of FTT who had been rated as insecurely attached (Brinich, Drotar, & Brinich, 1989). However, no differences were found between securely versus insecurely attached children on several other behaviors, including an overall index of ego resiliency. Drotar and Sturm (1994b) found that the quality of family relationships 6 months prior to the assessment (but not at a time of diagnosis) predicted frequency of behavioral problems on the Child Behavior Checklist in 4-year old children with early histories of nonorganic FTT. Positive family relationships (e.g., lower conflict, greater cohesion) were associated with fewer behavioral problems. Finally, Puckering et al. (1995) found that among preschool children with a history of growth delay, less adequate behavioral adjustment, as measured by the Behavioral Screening Questionnaire, was associated with high maternal negative affect based on home observation.

RISK AND PROTECTIVE FACTORS AND MODERATORS OF THE EFFECTS OF INTERVENTION

One of the most important but as yet unanswered questions in research on FTT concerns the role of risk and protective factors in moderating children's response to interventions that are designed to ameliorate the psychological deficits that are associated with this problem. Black and her colleagues found that the impact of intervention on cognitive development was greater among children who were younger (1–12 months) versus older (12–25 months) at recruitment (Black, Dubowitz, Hutcheson, Berenson-Howard, & Starr, 1995). This finding suggests that FTT and associated risk factors (e.g., understimulation) have a cumulative negative influence on children's psychological development that coincides with findings of the powerful effects of chronic as opposed to transient risk factors on the development of maltreated children (Rizley & Cicchetti, 1981).

In a recent study, Black et al. (1997) found that the level of maternal depressive symptoms moderated the effects of home-based intervention on the cognitive behavior during play and development of preschool children with histories of FTT. Children whose mothers reported low levels of negative affectivity showed beneficial effects of the home intervention, whereas mothers with high levels of negative affect did not. Finally, clinical observations have suggested that subtypes of FTT that differ in etiology (e.g., underfeeding vs. relationship problems) respond differentially to interventions that are tailored to address these problems (Drotar & Sturm, 1994), but as yet such evidence is anecdotal.

METHODOLOGICAL AND LOGISTICAL CONSTRAINTS ON UNDERSTANDING THE DEVELOPMENTAL PSYCHOPATHOLOGY OF FAILURE TO THRIVE

Our reviews of research concerning psychosocial influences and consequences of FTT have identified several important methodological and logistical problems that have limited progress in scientific knowledge related to the developmental psychopathology of this condition (Drotar & Robinson, 1999). For example, the fact that children who fail to thrive are often recruited from small clinical samples that vary considerably in age (sampling from infancy to 8 years), has imposed significant constraints on the study of developmental influences (Drotar, 1995; Drotar & Robinson, 1999). Owing to problems in recruiting and maintaining samples of children in research, prospective studies of this population, which afford the best window to study developmental psychopathology, have been few and far between. Moreover, the small sample sizes that have characterized research on FTT generally precluded assessment of age on the presentation of symptoms or outcomes.

A particularly troubling obstacle to knowledge is that it is difficult to study the processes that give rise to FTT. By the time children are diagnosed with the condition, they may have been exposed to undernutrition for significant periods of time, which makes it very difficult to disentangle the cause and effect. Finally, for the most part, research on FTT has been atheoretical, focusing on clinical description rather than on tests of hypotheses concerning specific developmental processes that give rise to FTT and associated outcomes.

FUTURE DIRECTIONS

Scientific knowledge concerning the developmental psychopathology of FTT would be enhanced by research that focuses on the following key issues: (1) describing developmental processes affected by FTT and associated risks; (2) identifying how parent–child and family relationships processes affect the psychological outcomes of children who fail to thrive; and (3) identifying moderators of response to interventions that are designed to ameliorate the psychological deficits associated with FTT.

Description of Developmental Processes Affected by Failure To Thrive

Descriptive refinement and empirical validation of developmentally relevant classifications of subtypes of FTT is a priority area for future research. In this regard, studies that document the relationship of clinically relevant descriptive characteristics of FTT (e.g., age of onset, duration, level of malnutrition) to important psychological attributes (e.g., behavioral responsiveness and security of attachment) will be especially instructive and applicable to practice (Drotar, 1995; Whitt & Runyan, 1993).

While FTT is associated with a range of problems, the impact of this condition and associated risk factors on key developmental outcomes such as self-regulation and self-concept, development of peer relationships, and moral development, has not been studied (Cicchetti & Toth, 1995). Moreover, the relationship of FTT to developmental psycho-pathological conditions such as Reactive Attachment Disorder or Feeding Disorder of Infancy or Early Childhood (Chatoor, 1997) in the *Diagnostic and Statistical Manual of Mental Disorders* (DSM-IV; American Psychiatric Association, 1994) and Disorders of Affect, Eating, and Relationship in the *National Center for Clinical Infants Program's Classification of Mental Health and Developmental Disorders of Infancy and Early Childhood* (Greenspan & Wieder, 1994), or feeding and nutritional problems in the newly published *Diagnostic and Statistical Manual for Primary Care* (DSM-PC; Wolraich, Felice, & Drotar, 1995) needs to be established with detailed descriptive research.

Moreover, very little information is available concerning comorbidities of mental health and cognitive developmental problems among children who present with FTT. Such studies are important because children with early histories of FTT are at risk for problems in multiple domains of development, all of which need to be addressed in assessment and intervention (Drotar, 1989, 1995). Finally, it is critical that researchers extend their studies of children with early histories of FTT beyond the infancy and preschool years to school-age children and adolescents to assess key developmental tasks (e.g., interpersonal relationships, self-regulation) that have not yet been assessed in this population, but would be expected to be influenced by problematic parenting and child maltreatment (Rogosch, Cicchetti, & Aber, 1995).

Identifying How Parent–Child and Family Relationship Processes Affect the Psychological Outcomes of Children Who Fail to Thrive

Insofar as the condition of FTT signals clinically salient problems in early parent–child relationships, the problem provides a context in which to describe and evaluate the consequences of early relationship disturbances (Sameroff & Emde, 1989). However, the link between critical components of early relationship experiences, for example, parental emotional unavailability and children's socioemotional status (Emde, 1989), is not well understood in FTT. Anders (1989) has proposed the following criteria to classify disordered parent–child relationships that could be applied to prospective studies of children who fail to thrive: (1) Symptoms are expressed in significant problems in relationship tasks; (2) symptoms are problematic and disruptive to the routines of daily living and/or developmental milestones for one or both partners; (3) pervasive disturbance are evident across a range of interactional contexts and functional domains; and (4) patterns are rigid and not easily altered. One would predict that the risk to children's development, and hence the necessity for intervention, would be much greater for children with FTT who demonstrate disordered parent–child relationships than for those who do not.

Research on FTT would benefit from greater understanding of the processes by which key dimensions of parental behavior (e.g., emotional responsiveness) affect the development of children with this condition. For example, Donovan and Leavitt's (1989) conceptual model, which describes how a mother's depression-prone attributional style and negative mood state can interact with the perceived difficulty of an infant to affect maternal self-efficacy and response to her infant's behavior and eventual security of attachment, would appear to have applicability to the problem of FTT. Similarly, the Wahler and Dumas (1989) framework, which suggests that deficits in parental attention are closely linked to problematic family relationships and lack of social support, should be studied in families whose children are failing to thrive.

Another important, highly relevant area of research in the problem of FTT, as well as other conditions that reflect various forms of child maltreatment, concerns the impact of inconsistent stimulation, neglect, and trauma on the developing brain. In particular, children who are exposed to vicious cycles of negative early experience (e.g., lack of critical early nurturing and pervasive physical threat) may be vulnerable to neuroendocrine and neuro-developmental disturbances that have pervasive effects (Perry, 1997).

Identifying Moderators of Child and Family Response to Intervention

One of the most important directions for research on developmental influences on FTT is to assess factors that influence response to intervention with this condition. Do children with greater severity and comorbidity of associated problems have poorer outcomes? What factors affect family responsiveness to intervention, including their understanding of the problem and acceptance of intervention? Progress in understanding the problem of FTT and preventing associated short- and long-term psychological deficits (Drotar, 1995) will require much closer integration of research and practice than has been typical of work in this field.

REFERENCES

Altemeier, W. A., III, Vietze, P. M., Sherrod, K. B., Sandler, H. M., Falsey, S., & O'Connor, S. (1979). Prediction of child maltreatment during pregnancy. *Journal of the American Academy of Child Psychiatry, 18*, 205–218.

American Psychiatric Association. (1994). *Diagnostic and statistical manual of mental disorders* (4th ed.). Washington, DC: Author.

Anders, T. F. (1989). Clinical syndromes: Relationship disturbances and their assessment. In A. J. Sameroff & R. N. Emde (Eds.), *Relationship disturbances in early childhood: A developmental approach* (pp. 125–144). New York: Basic Books.

Belsky, J. (1984). The determinants of parenting: A process model. *Child Development, 55*, 83–96.

Belsky, J., & Isabella, R. (1988). Maternal, infant, and social–contextual determinants of attachment security. In J. Belsky & T. Nezworski (Eds.), *Clinical implications of attachment* (pp. 40–94). Hillsdale, NJ: Erlbaum.

Benoit, D. (1993). Failure to thrive and feeding disorders. In C. H. Zeanah (Ed.), *Handbook of infant mental health* (pp. 317–331). New York: Guilford Press.

Benoit, D., Zeanah, C. H., & Barton, M. L. (1989). Maternal attachment disturbances in failure to thrive. *Infant Mental Health Journal, 10*, 185–202.

Bithoney, W. G., & Dubowitz, H. (1985). Organic concomitants of nonorganic failure to thrive: Implications for research. In D. Drotar (Ed.), *New directions in failure to thrive: Implications for research and practice* (pp. 47–69). New York: Plenum Press.

Black, M. M., & Dubowitz, H. (1991). Failure to thrive: Lessons from animal models and developing countries. *Journal of Developmental and Behavioral Pediatrics, 12*, 259–267.

Black, M. M., Dubowitz, H., Hutcheson, J., Berenson-Howard, J., & Starr, D. H. (1995). A randomized clinical trial of home intervention for children with failure to thrive. *Pediatrics, 95*, 807–814.

Black, M., Hutcheson, J., Dubowitz, H., & Berenson-Howard, J. (1994). Parenting style and developmental status among children with nonorganic failure to thrive. *Journal of Pediatric Psychology, 19*, 689–707.

Block, J. R., & Block, J. M. (1980). The role of ego resiliency in the organization of behavior. In W. A. Collins (Ed.), Development of cognition: Affect and social relations (pp. 39–100). *Minnesota Symposium of Child Psychology.* Hillsdale, NJ: Erlbaum.

Boddy, J. M., & Skuse, D. H. (1994). Annotation: the process of parenting in failure to thrive. *Journal of Child Psychology and Psychiatry, 19*, 689–707.

Brinich, E., Drotar, D., & Brinich, P, (1989). Relationship of security of attachment to the physical and psychological outcome of preschool children with early histories of nonorganic failure to thrive. *Journal of Clinical Child Psychology, 18*, 142–152.

Casey, P. H. (1992). Failure to thrive. In M. D. Levine, W. B. Carey, & A. C. Crocker (Eds.), *Developmental behavioral pediatrics* (2nd ed., pp. 375–383). Philadelphia: Saunders.

Cassidy, C. M. (1980). Benign neglect and toddler malnutrition. In C. Greene & F. E. Johnston (Eds.), *Social and biological predictors of nutritional status, physical growth and neurological development* (pp. 109–139). New York: Academic Press.

Chatoor, I. (1977). Feeding and eating disorders of infancy and early childhood. In J. M. Wiener (Ed.), *Textbook of child and adolescent psychiatry* (pp. 527–542). Washington, DC: American Psychiatric Press.

Chatoor, I., Dickson, L., Schaefer, S., & Egan, J. (1985). A developmental classification of feeding disorders associated with failure to thrive: Diagnosis and treatment. In D. Drotar (Ed.), *New directions in failure to thrive: Implications for research and practice* (pp. 235–258). New York: Plenum Press.

Chatoor, I., & Egan, J. (1983). Nonorganic failure to thrive and dwarfism due to food refusal: A separation disorder. *Journal of the American Academy of Child Psychiatry, 22*, 294–301.

Cicchetti, D., & Toth, S. L. (1995). A developmental psychopathology perspective on child abuse and neglect. *Journal of the American Academy of Child and Adolescent Psychiatry, 34*, 541–515.

Crittenden, P. M. (1987). Nonorganic failure to thrive: Deprivation or distortion? *Infant Mental Health Journal, 8*, 51–64.

Donovan, W. L., & Leavitt, L. A. (1989). Maternal self-efficacy and infant attachment: Integrating physiology, perceptions, and behavior. *Child Development, 60*, 460–472.

Dowdney, L., Skuse, D., Heptinstall, E., Puckering, C., & Zur-Szpiro, S. (1987). Growth retardation and developmental delay amongst inner-city children. *Journal of Child Psychiatry and Psychology, 28*, 529–541.

Drotar, D. (1988). Failure to thrive. In D. K. Routh (Ed.), *Handbook of pediatric psychology* (pp. 71–106). New York: Guilford Press.

Drotar, D. (1989). Behavioral diagnosis in nonorganic failure to thrive. A critique and suggested approach to psychological assessment. *Journal of Developmental and Behavioral Pediatrics, 10*, 48–55.

Drotar, D. (1990). Sampling considerations in nonorganic failure to thrive. *Journal of Pediatric Psychology, 15*, 255–272.

Drotar, D. (1991a). The family context of failure to thrive. *American Journal of Orthopsychiatry, 61*, 23–34.

Drotar, D. (1991b). Prevention of neglect and nonorganic failure to thrive. In D. J. Willis, E. W. Holden, & M. Rosenberg (Eds.), *Prevention of child maltreatment* (pp. 115–149). New York: Wiley.

Drotar D. (1995). Failure to thrive (growth deficiency). In M. C. Roberts (Ed.), *Handbook of pediatric psychology* (2nd ed., pp. 516–533). New York: Plenum Press.

Drotar, D., & Eckerle, D. (1989). Family environment in nonorganic failure to thrive: A controlled study. *Journal of Pediatric Psychology, 14*, 245–257.

Drotar, D., Malone, C. A., Devost, L., Brickell, C., Mantz-Clumpner, C., Negray, J., Wallace, M., Woychik, J., Wyatt B., Eckerele, D., Bush, M., Finlon, M. A., El-Amin, D., Nowak, M., Satola, J., & Pallotta, J. (1985). Early preventive intervention in failure to thrive: Methods and early outcome. In D. Drotar (Ed.), *New directions in failure to thrive: Implications for research and practice* (pp. 119–138). New York: Plenum Press.

Drotar, D., Nowak, M., Malone, C. A., Negray, J. (1985). Early psychological outcome in failure to thrive: Predictions from an interactional model. *Journal of Clinical Child Psychology, 9*, 236–240.

Drotar, D., & Robinson, J. (1999). Researching failure to thrive: Progress, problems, and recommendations. In B. Kessler & P. Dawson (Eds.), *Failure to thrive and pediatric undernutrition: A transdisciplinary approach to nutritional adequacy in childhood* (pp. 72–98). Baltimore: Paul H. Brookes.

Drotar, D., & Sturm, L. (1987). Paternal influences in non-organic failure to thrive: Implications for psychosocial management. *Infant Mental Health Journal, 8*, 37–50.

Drotar, D., & Sturm, L. (1988). Prediction of intellectual development in young children with early histories of nonorganic failure to thrive. *Journal of Pediatric Psychology, 13*, 281–295.

Drotar, D., & Sturm, L. (1992). Personality development, personality solving and behavioral problems among preschool children with early histories of nonorganic failure to thrive: A controlled study. *Journal of Developmental and Behavioral Pediatrics, 13*, 266–273.

Drotar, D., & Sturm, L. (1994a). Failure to thrive: Psychological issues. In R. A. Olson, L. L. Mullins, J. B. Gillman, & J. M. Chaney (Eds.), *The sourcebook of pediatric psychology* (pp. 26–41). Needham Heights, MA: Allyn & Bacon.

Drotar, D., & Sturm, L. (1994b). Psychological outcomes of children with early histories of failure to thrive. In B. Stabler & L. Underwood (Eds.), *Growth stature and adaptation: Behavioral, cognitive, and social aspects of growth delay* (pp. 211–233). Chapel Hill: University of North Carolina, Office of Continued Medical Education.

Emde, R. N. (1989). The infant's relationship experience: Developmental and affective aspects. In A. J. Sameroff & R. N. Emde (Eds.), *Relationship disturbances in early childhood: A developmental approach* (pp. 33–51). New York: Basic Books.

Fraiberg, S. (Ed.). (1980). *Clinical studies in infant mental health.* New York: Basic Books.

Frank, D. A., Allen, D., & Brown, J. L. (1985). Primary prevention of failure to thrive: Social policy implications. In D. Drotar (Ed.), *New directions in failure to thrive: Implications for research and practice* (pp. 337–358). New York: Plenum Press.

Frank, D. A., & Drotar, D. (1994). Failure to thrive. In R. M. Reece (Ed.), *Child abuse: Medical diagnosis and management* (pp. 298–325). Philadelphia: Lea & Febiger.

Galler, J. R., Ramsey, F., Solimano, G., & Lowell, W. C. (1983). Influence of early malnutrition on subsequent behavioral development: II. Classroom behavior. *Journal of the American Academy of Child Psychiatry, 22,* 58–64.

Garmezy, N., Masten, A. S., & Tellegen, A. (1984). The study of stress and competence in children: A building block for developmental psychopathology. *Child Development, 55,* 97–111.

Geertsma, M. A., Hyams, J. S., Pelletier, J. M., & Reiter, L. (1985). Feeding resistance after parental alimentation. *American Journal of Diseases of Children, 139,* 255–256.

Gorman, J., Leifer, M., & Grossman, G. (1993). Nonorganic failure to thrive: Maternal history and current maternal functioning. *Journal of Clinical Child Psychology, 23,* 322–336.

Greenspan, S. I., & Lieberman, A. F. (1980). Infants, mothers and their interaction: A quantitative approach to developmental assessment. In S. Greenspan & G. Pollock (Eds.), *The course of life: Vol. I. Infancy and early childhood* (pp. 271–312). Washington, DC: U.S. Department of Human Services.

Greenspan, S. I., & Wieder, S. (1994, June–July). Diagnostic classification of mental health and developmental disorders of infancy and early childhood. *Zero to Three,* pp. 34–41.

Hammill, P. V. V., Drizd, T. A., Johnson, C. L., Reed, R. B., Roche, A. F., & Moore, W. M. (1979). Physical growth: National Center for Health Statistics percentiles. *American Journal of Clinical Nutrition, 32,* 607–629.

Heptinstall, F., Puckering, C., Skuse, D., Start, K., Zur-Szpiro, S., & Dowdney, L. (1987). Nutrition and mealtime behavior in families of growth-retarded children. *Human Nutrition: Applied Nutrition, 41A,* 390–402.

Hertzler, A. A. & Vaughn, C. W. (1979). The relationship of family structure and interaction to nutrition. *Journal of the American Dietetic Association, 74,* 23–27.

Hutcheson, J. J., Black, M. M., & Starr, R. H. (1993). Developmental differences in interactional characteristics of mothers and their children with failure to thrive. *Journal of Pediatric Psychology, 18,* 453–466.

Hutcheson, J. J., Black, M. M., Talley, M., Dubowitz, H., Berenson-Howard, J., Starr, D. H., & Thompson, B. S. (1997). Risk status and home intervention among children with failure to thrive: Follow-up at age 4. *Journal of Pediatric Psychology, 22,* 651–668.

Kotelchuck, M. (1979). Child abuse and neglect: Prediction and misclassification. In R. H. Starr (Ed.), *Child abuse prediction: Policy implications* (pp. 67–104). Cambridge, MA: Ballinger.

Lewis, M., & Goldberg, S. (1969). Perceptual–cognitive development in infancy: A generalized expectancy model as a function of the mother–infant interaction. *Merrill–Palmer Quarterly, 15,* 81–100.

Lieberman, A. F., & Birch, M. (1985). The etiology of failure to thrive: An interactional developmental approach. In D. Drotar (Ed.), *New directions in failure to thrive: Implications for research and practice* (pp. 259–278). New York: Plenum Press.

Linscheid, T., & Rasnake, L. K. (1985). Behavioral approaches to the treatment of failure to thrive. In D. Drotar (Ed.), *New directions for failure to thrive: Implications for research and practice* (pp. 279–294). New York: Plenum Press.

Mathisen, B., Skuse, D., Wolke, D., & Reilly, S. (1989). Oral–motor dysfunction and failure to thrive among inner-city infants. *Developmental Medicine and Child Neurology, 31,* 193–302.

Money, J. M. (1992). *The Kasper Hauser syndrome of psychosocial dwarfism: Deficient structural, intellectual, and social growth induced by child abuse.* Buffalo, NY: Prometheus Books.

Newberger, E. H., Reed, R. P., Daniel, J. H., Hyde, J., & Kotelchuck, M. (1977). Pediatric social illness: Toward an etiologic classification. *Pediatrics, 60,* 175–185.

Oates, R. K., Peacock, A., & Forest, D. (1985). Long-term effects of non-organic failure to thrive. *Pediatrics, 75,* 36–40.

Patton, R. G., & Gardner, L. E. (1962). Influences of family environment of growth: The syndrome of "maternal deprivation." *Pediatrics, 30,* 957–962.

Perry, B. D. (1997). Incubated in terror: Neurodevelopmental factors in the cycle of violence. In J. Osopsky (Ed.), *Children youth and violence: The search for solutions* (pp. 124–144). New York: Guilford Press.

Polan, H. J., Kaplan, J., Kessler, D. B., Shindeldecker, R., Newmark, M., Stem, D., & Ward, M. J. (1991). Psychopathology in mothers of children with failure to thrive. *Infant Mental Health Journal, 12,* 55–64.

Pollitt, E. (1973). Behavior of the infant in causation of nutritional marasmus. *American Journal of Clinical Nutrition, 26,* 264–270.

Pollitt, E., & Leibel, R. (1980). Biological and social correlates of failure to thrive. In L. Greene & F. E. Johnston (Eds.), *Social biological predictors of nutritional status, physical growth and neurological development* (pp. 171–196). New York: Academic Press.

Puckering C., Pickles, A., Skuse, D., Heptinstall, E., Dowdney, L., & Zur-Szpiro, S. (1995). Mother–child interaction and the cognitive and behavioral development of four-year-old children with poor growth. *Journal of Child Psychology and Psychiatry, 56,* 575–595.

Pugiliese, M. T., Weyman-Daum, M., Moses, N., & Lifshitz, F. M. (1987). Parental health beliefs as a cause of non-organic failure to thrive. *Pediatrics, 80,* 175–181.

Rizley, R., & Cicchetti, D. (1981). *Developmental perspectives on child maltreatment.* San Francisco: Jossey-Bass.

Rogosch, F. A., Cicchetti, D., & Aber, L. A. (1995). The role of child maltreatment in early deviations in cognitive and affective processing abilities and later peer relationship problems. *Development and Psychopathology, 7,* 591–609.

Sameroff, A. (1975). Transactional models in early social relations. *Human Development, 18,* 65–79.

Sameroff, A., & Chandler, M. J. (1975). Reproductive risk and the continuum of caretaking casualty. In F. D. Horowitz (Ed.), *Review of child development research* (Vol. 4; pp. 187–244). Chicago: University of Chicago Press.

Sameroff, A. J., & Emde, R. N. (Eds.). (1989). *Relationship disturbances in early childhood: A developmental approach.* New York: Basic Books.

Sherrod, K. B., O'Connor, S., Vietze, P. M., & Altemeier, W. A. (1985). Child health and maltreatment. *Child Development, 55,* 1174–1183.

Silverman, M. M., & Levin, V. S. (1985). Research on the prevention of psychological disorders of infancy: A federal perspective. In D. Drotar (Ed.), *New directions in failure to thrive: Implications for research and practice* (pp. 3–16). New York: Plenum Press.

Singer, L., & Fagan, J. (1984). Cognitive development in the failure to thrive infant: A three-year longitudinal study. *Journal of Pediatric Psychology, 9,* 363–383.

Skuse, D. (1993). Epidemiologic and definitional issues in failure to thrive. *Child and Adolescent Psychiatric Clinics of America, 1,* 37–59.

Sroufe, L. A. (1979). The coherence of individual development. *American Psychologist, 34,* 834–841.

Sturm, L., & Drotar, D. (1989). Prediction of weight for height Following intervention in three year-old children with early histories of nonorganic failure to thrive. *Child Abuse and Neglect, 13,* 19–28.

Vietze, P. M., Falsey, S., O'Connor, S., Sandler, H., Sherrod, K., & Altemeier, W. A. (1980). Newborn behavioral and interactional characteristics of non-organic failure to thrive infants. In T. M. Field, S. Goldberg, D. Stern, & A. M. Sostek (Eds.), *High risk infants and children* (pp. 3–17). New York: Academic Press.

Wahler, R. G., & Dumas, J. E. (1989). Attentional problems in dysfunctional mother–child interactions. *Psychological Bulletin, 105,* 116–130.

Ward, M. J., Kessler, D. B., & Altman, S. C. (1993). Infant–mother attachment in children with failure to thrive. *Infant Mental Health Journal, 14,* 208–220.

Whitt, J. K., & Runyan, D. (1993, March). *Infant nonorganic failure to thrive: A developmental model for subgroup classification.* Paper presented at the biennial meeting of the Society of Research in Child Development, New Orleans, LA.

Wolraich, M., Felice, M. A., & Drotar, D. (1995). *The classification of child and adolescent mental diagnosis in primary care: Diagnostic and statistical manual for primary care: DSM-PC Child and adolescent version.* Elk Grove, IL: American Academy of Pediatrics.

20

The Early Caregiving Environment

Expanding Views on Nonparental Care and Cumulative Life Experiences

Sharon Landesman Ramey and Gene P. Sackett

The study of the effects of nonparental care—especially care in orphanages, institutions, and foster care—has been affected profoundly by residential care practices for infants and young children, and by changing conceptualizations of what comprises an optimal early caregiving environment. Dramatic descriptions of child maltreatment in orphanages, from Dickens's *David Copperfield* and *Oliver Twist* in mid-nineteenth century England to Gray's "Little Orphan Annie" in the 1920s, captured vividly the plight of many children who were once placed in the care of strangers. The reasons for seeking out-of-home care for very young children relate strongly to economic, political, and health conditions of the times. Those who bear the responsibility for direct care of children in group settings have been portrayed alternatively as highly opportunistic and nonnurturing *or* angelic, heroic, and totally devoted. The latter, however, were by far the rarer set of attributes ascribed to caregivers in institutional settings. Typically, nonparental caregivers have had opportunities for monetary gain and for deriving perverse pleasures from abusing children outside the purview of the conventional world.

In the late 1930s and early 1940s, disturbing clinical observations surfaced about the grave effects of institutionalization on children. These led to the seminal studies of Bowlby (1940, 1944, 1951, 1958, 1969), Spitz (1945, 1946, 1947), Bender (1947), Bender and Yarnell (1941), Crissey (1937), Skodak and Skeels (1949), and Skeels (1966). These pioneers opened the field of systematic inquiry about the effects of early care on the long-term outcomes for children. The primary concern was that absence of the mother would lead to lifelong pathology, especially in establishing positive and enduring social relationships.

Sharon Landesman Ramey • Departments of Psychiatry, Psychology, and Neurobiology, Civitan International Research Center, University of Alabama at Birmingham, Birmingham, Alabama 35294-0021. **Gene P. Sackett** • Department of Psychology and Primate Center, University of Washington, Seattle, Washington 98195.

Handbook of Developmental Psychopathology, Second Edition, edited by Arnold J. Sameroff, Michael Lewis, and Suzanne M. Miller. Kluwer Academic/Plenum Publishers, New York, 2000.

EARLY THEMES IN THE STUDY OF NONPARENTAL CARE

Two themes dominated the early scientific inquiry in this field. The first was concern about the child's tragic loss of mother, synonymous with a signaled disruption in the child's primary source of nurturance. The mother–child relationship was assumed to be essential, universal, and unique in setting the stage for the child's emerging trust in others, confidence in self, responsiveness to cognitive and linguistic stimulation, and willingness to explore the world beyond this first and compelling dyadic relationship. Accordingly, the most pressing question was: Will maternal loss prevent normal development of the child's sense of self and social–emotional understanding? The second theme revolved around what actually happened to children when they grew up in an atypical context rather than in a nuclear family. The atypical context of group care for young children was characterized by a complex array of worrisome environmental conditions. These included (1) the fluctuating presence of multiple careproviders (usually referred to as custodians and only rarely viewed as surrogate mothers); (2) the lack of appropriate and diverse cognitive stimulation and feedback; (3) the regimentation and restriction of daily activities; (4) the absence of privacy; (5) the depersonalization of most social interactions; (6) the large and often strongly influential peer groups; and (7) the ever-present possibility of neglect and abuse—a possibility all too frequently realized and concealed from public knowledge. The paramount aim of these landmark investigations was to measure the nature and extent of psychological damage inflicted upon children who experienced such deviant and depriving environments and, ultimately, to learn how to provide effective social and cognitive remediation for children exposed to nonoptimal early environments.

The early investigations sought to provide a clinically rich documentation of the effects of institutionalization, both immediate and long-term consequences. The psychopathology ranged from apathy, failure to thrive, and death from "tristeza" (infant depression) to social withdrawal, intellectual deficiency, and rebellion in adolescence and adulthood. At that time, orphanages existed in almost every American and European community as places of refuge for children who lost connection with one or both parents through death, insanity, illness, or poverty. Institutions for individuals with mental retardation also were starting their ascent to a peak occupancy in the mid-1960s, an increase largely attributable to two successive factors: (1) a vigorous eugenics movement in the early part of this century that led to massive institutionalization of "intellectual and moral degenerates" to prevent their reproduction; and (2) widespread professional endorsement of institutionalization for "defective" children, directed mostly toward white, middle-class parents who were urged to make this decision as early as possible to avoid inflicting harm and likely psychopathology on other family members. Many parents also saw institutionalization as the only source of education or habilitation for children with mental retardation, who were routinely excluded from public education and had few or no alternative treatment settings. Thus, institutions for children who were "mentally defective" became society's refuge for a very heterogeneous group of children who did not readily fit in. Many of these children were minimally retarded intellectually or showed early behavioral disturbances that parents alone could not treat.

These prevailing practices of placing large numbers of children in nonparental group care contributed to the considerable interest of child psychiatrists, developmental psychologists, and pediatricians in ascertaining developmental consequences of early caregiving environments. It is noteworthy that this interest in the effects of institutionalization was not merely academic. In 1949 and 1950, Bowlby was invited by the World Health Organization to summarize the mental health aspects of the world's homeless children. His conclusions (Bowlby, 1951) affirmed

1. The importance of early bonding in the first 6 months of life.
2. The vigorous protest and subsequent emotional retreat displayed by well-attached infants when they lost their mothers.
3. A range of severe disturbances in older orphaned children who were not permitted to mourn their loss openly or to maintain contact with siblings and other close relatives.

The child's presumed feeling of abandonment was hypothesized to be central, lifelong, and extremely difficult to resolve—a feeling later manifest in adult symptomatology. The most commonly reported adult psychopathology involved severe separation anxiety, recurrent bouts of depression, and lifelong difficulties in forming and maintaining positive intimate relationships. Other, less frequent reactions included open rebellion and antisocial acts, manifest especially during adolescent years; suicidal inclinations and attempts; and elevated rates of psychosomatic complaints. Bowlby's review set the stage for the development of an enhanced construct of "attachment," which hypothesized that variation in both the *continuity* and the *quality* of the relationship between an infant and primary caregiver could have far-reaching, long-lasting consequences on psychological development. This construct, with clear origins in the work of Freud and his students, has had a profound influence on the field of developmental psychology and has theoretical implications that extend far beyond questions about orphanages and institutions per se. Today, the conceptualization of early attachment guides research on the effects of child care, foster families, adoption, and disrupted families.

EXPERIMENTAL STUDIES OF THE EFFECTS OF EARLY EXPERIENCE

A rich naturalistic and experimental animal literature on the effects of early experience complements the (fortunately) more limited studies of human development in orphanages and institutions. A broad biobehavioral theoretical framework shaped much of the nonhuman primate research on the effects of early experience (e.g., Harlow & Harlow, 1965; Harlow & Zimmerman, 1959; Rosenblum & Kaufman, 1968; Suomi & Harlow, 1978) in contrast to the predominantly psychoanalytic perspective in the early human literature (for a sharply delineated psychodynamic view of the child's attachment to the mother, see Bowlby, 1958). The work of leading ethologists also fueled the interest in identifying critical time periods and critical experiences for normal development (e.g., Hinde, 1974; Lorenz, 1935; Tinbergen, 1963), as did seminal work by learning theorists working with rodent models and enriched environments (e.g., Hebb, 1949; Rosenweig, Krech, Bennett, & Diamond, 1961). The central questions asked were as follows:

1. What are the effects of specific types of social and sensory deprivation (alone and in combination) on the developing organism?
2. Do these effects occur only during critical or sensitive periods in development?
3. Can subsequent normative environments compensate for earlier deprivation?

Nobel prizes were awarded for the work of the European ethologists Lorenz and Tinbergen who observed that organisms were "primed" for certain types of social experiences at particular times in development, proven through environmental alterations that disrupted normal behavioral processes. Furthermore, the nature, magnitude, and irreversibility of these effects related systematically to timing (i.e., the organism's stage of development).

Other Nobel Prize winning research by Hubel and Weisel (Hubel, 1979; Weisel & Hubel, 1974) also provided compelling evidence for the long-term consequences of early experience. Lack of visual stimulation early in life was shown to produce functional or behavioral blindness in otherwise healthy animals. This environmentally induced behavioral disability was accompanied by abnormal distribution of responses in neurons and morphological abnormalities in the brain. Thus, a critical period for visual experience was delineated, with proof that damage attributable to environmental deprivation was irreversible. The possibility that similar consequences occurred in the social–emotional realm was further strengthened by these findings.

Behavioral Effects in Nonhuman Primates

Important research on monkeys provided an experimental model that more closely paralleled the life situation of infants who suffered maternal loss followed by institutional care. Early social deprivation was shown to produce extremely aberrant, species-atypical forms of behavior (e.g., Capitanio, 1986; Harlow & Harlow, 1965; Harlow & Zimmerman, 1959; Sackett, 1968, 1972). The magnitude and persistence of these effects depended on the nature as well as the timing of the deprivation. Maternal deprivation *and* total isolation produced the most extreme effects, while partial isolation produced less severe effects. Also, relatively brief and early periods of deprivation did *not* produce the severe consequences observed in animals that experienced longer periods (6 months or more) of social deprivation. For rhesus monkeys, the age of 6–9 months appeared to be an especially sensitive time period for the development of normative social–emotional behavior. Most impressively, these effects of early maternal and social deprivation appeared to be lifelong. Even after 25 years of social living, a substantial period during which social habilitation was expected to occur, the rhesus monkeys reared in isolation for the first 9 months of life did *not* recover. They continued to show high levels of stereotypy, lack of prosocial behavior, and avoidance of novel situations (Lewis, Gluck, Beauchamp, Keresztury, & Mailman, 1990; Martin, Spicer, Lewis, Gluck, & Cork, 1991). For males, sexual performance was deviant and nonproductive. For females, the effects extended to their own competency as mothers: 80% of the "motherless mothers" were unable to provide adequate care for their offspring, and many were extremely abusive (Ruppenthal, Arling, Harlow, Sackett, & Suomi, 1976). See Sackett, Novak, and Kroeker (1999) for a detailed, up-to-date review of this literature.

Biological Effects of Variation in Early Experience

Over the past four decades, the animal research has provided an extraordinary amount of detail about the range of permanent structural and functional consequences of variation in early rearing environments on the brain and at least one gene (zenk) that affects brain growth and development (e.g., Comery, Shah, & Greenough, 1995; Fuchs, Montemaor, & Greenough, 1990; Greenough, Volkmar, & Juraska, 1973; Jones & Greenough, 1996; Jones, Klintsova, Kilman, Sirevaag, & Greenough, 1997; Wallace et al., 1995). Collectively, a large and diverse body of experimental research provides impressive evidence that early experience is vital for normal brain development (cf. Sackett et al., 1999; Shore, 1997).

Lessons Learned from Controlled Studies on Early Experience

Some important caveats about what has been learned from the experimental research on early experience warrant mention. First, there is substantial variation in how different species respond to early social and sensory deprivation. Closely related species often show wide variation in the form and severity of effects, with some species apparently remarkably resilient to negative effects of even extreme isolation and deprivation. Second, individuals within the same species and strain can differ in their response to early deprivation. For reasons not adequately understood, some are far more vulnerable to negative and persistent effects than are others. Third, the important ethological construct of a critical period for social development or attachment—that is, a single time period when certain experiences *must* occur in order for normative behavior patterns to develop—was never confirmed as dramatically in primates as it was in ducks and other birds. Perhaps this is because of the much longer and more complex processes of attachment and socialization that occur in primates, as well as the near impossibility of manipulating all of the relevant dimensions of social experience across all time periods. Genetic and other biological factors undoubtedly are intertwined as well. Fourth, there is substantial experimental evidence that benefits associated with environmental enrichment are lifelong; that is, enrichment effects are not limited just to an early time period when many basic neurodevelopmental processes are particularly active. This underscores the importance of viewing development in its broad context and longitudinally, rather than focusing only on the effects of early experience. Fifth and finally, the controlled animal research, as informative as it is, can never adequately answer the key questions about what types, amounts, and timing of social and sensory experiences very young children need to develop normally. Rather, this research is invaluable in identifying broad principles about the central role of experience in shaping the course of development and in elucidating more about the interdependence of behavioral and biological development.

"INSTITUTIONALIZATION" AS A METAPHOR FOR INADEQUATE SOCIAL EXPERIENCE

At first glance, clinicians, developmental scientists, and policymakers might be inclined to discount the large historical literature on the effects of orphanages and institutions as outdated and not relevant to children's lives today. Such a perspective, however, ignores two major facts. One is that many children still are being placed in nonmaternal care for significant portions of their lives, often beginning quite early in life. The most prevalent form in the United States and worldwide is foster care. The quality and length of foster care varies tremendously across and within locales, and serious concerns about its effects surface regularly in the policy arena. Less well known is that hundreds of thousands of children still are being placed in orphanages and institutions—many of which are as deplorable as those studied earlier this century. These orphanages are most likely to exist in countries experiencing extremely oppressive political and economic conditions. Sometimes they operate because of negative cultural attitudes toward adoption (e.g., that parents should invest only in biological offspring) and because of prejudice about certain ethnic groups. In the United States, new types of orphanages, often referred to as baby centers or children's havens, have opened in response to crises associated with maternal substance abuse and AIDS. Other forms of nonparental care include family care or group homes and a form of "child care" that lasts 5 days and nights each week—used extensively in some former Soviet bloc countries (personal experience) as a means of child care for working mothers. In the United States as well, there are many infants and children who receive child care for 10 or more hours per day. Accordingly, a careful review of the earlier literature on the effects of institutionalization is informative.

Effects of Extended Institutionalization on Young Children

By the early 1950s, more than enough evidence existed from observations of children to confirm the conclusion that extreme forms of neglect, abuse, and deprivation could cause permanent damage in infants born without defects. Freudian concepts of the mother–child relationship evolved into a broader conceptual framework about early attachment. The quality of the mother–child attachment was hypothesized to have a central role in the emergence of children's social and emotional competence, as well as to be vital for scaffolding young children's early learning experiences and their social contacts beyond the family. The ethological notion of critical periods was modified to one of sensitive periods, which identified optimal or favorable (rather than exclusive) time periods for certain types of environmental input. Anecdotal and clinical evidence were consistent with this, such as the observation that infants born profoundly deaf have markedly different courses of development depending on when they begin to learn and use sign language—a formal system of symbolic communication. Children who had earlier and more extensive experience with sign language in infancy showed much higher levels of abstract reasoning and cognitive performance in adolescence and adulthood than did those who began later (Bates, O'Connell, & Shore, 1987). Indeed, such findings refuted the long-accepted clinical prognosis that children born deaf were also "dumb"—a prophecy that was fulfilled when the early environment was lacking in communicative experiences essential for normal intellectual development. Similarly, the provision of corrective lenses *in infancy* to children with certain forms of visual impairment prevents lifelong impairment that results from lack of early treatment.

A tremendous amount of information has been gathered about the average ages when particular sensory and perceptual competencies emerge, as well as when infants demonstrate a large array of social, emotional, linguistic, and cognitive skills (cf. Osofsky, 1987; C. Ramey & Ramey, 1999). The implicit inference from these discoveries about infant competencies is that children need to have experiences that use and challenge their emerging skills in order for development to proceed well. In fact, a vast literature has documented extensive delays and below-average performance of children from very low-resource environments (cf. Huston, 1992; S. Ramey & Ramey, 1999b). In essence, most institutions for children were low resource, as indexed by the amount and quality of interactions with caring adults, and by the opportunities to explore and learn. Besides being low in resources, institutions often included highly atypical experiences, such as exposure to peer groupings, and rules and regulations that were far from normative. Accordingly, institutionalization often represented a distinctive cultural experience, one that seldom was designed to prepare the children for successful living in the outside community.

The early studies of institutionalization effects on children with mental retardation sought to delineate which behavioral processes were disrupted as a result of the institutional experience. Careful inquiry that included more sophisticated designs and took into account variation across institutions, as well as in the types and ages of children and caregivers, confirmed wide variation in outcomes (e.g., Balla, Butterfield, & Zigler, 1974; Butterfield & Zigler, 1965; Klaber, 1969). Accordingly, subsequent efforts to make sweeping generalizations about the effects of institutions per se were considered far too simplistic. Even more germane was the finding, replicated in several diverse settings, that some children actually showed gains in intelligence *after* institutionalization (Clarke & Clarke, 1953, 1954; Clarke, Clarke, & Reiman, 1958; Klaber, 1969; Zigler, Butterfield, & Capobianco, 1970), whereas other children within the same institutions showed declines. The explanation for this differential effect of a given institution on children from different family backgrounds was both developmental and relativistic. Specifically, children's development progresses as a function of the amount and quality of stimulation received; yet whether environmental stimulation is "enriching" versus "depriving" is a function of what the child has previously experienced. Thus, children from very low-resource families experienced institutions as relatively more stimulating, and thus showed greater developmental advances, whereas those from high-resource families showed detrimental effects because of the comparative decrease in stimulation in the institutional environment.

Thorough and insightful critiques and commentaries provided suggestions for future research (cf. Baumeister, 1967; Butterfield, 1967, 1987; Crissey, 1975; Heal, Sigelman, & Switzky, 1978; Klaber, 1969; Windle, 1962; Zigler & Balla, 1977). To conduct well-conceptualized, well-designed studies about institutionalization was truly challenging, especially given the heterogeneity of children served by institutions, the biases in placement of children in different types of institutions, the difficulty in documenting the quality of children's preinstitutional experiences, and the lack of sound instrumentation to guide the measurement of the adaptation process and the environment itself.

Since the 1970s, when deinstitutionalization was widely practiced and an increasing number of alternative, community-based residences were established, a new wave of environmental effects research has begun. The questions remained essentially the same, although the focus was on distinctive populations and phrased more in positive than in negative terms. Leading questions included the following:

1. What comprises an optimal social environment to support normative experiences, developmental progress in adaptive behavior, and decreases in undesirable behavior?
2. What variables predict *who* will benefit from *particular types* of residential experiences?

Consistent with the earlier human and experimental animal literatures, however, most studies comparing community versus institutional placements suffered from serious flaws in design, measurement, and analysis; that is, the children who were placed in different living arrangements had different prior life experiences as well as presenting signs and symptoms, thus making the groups nonequivalent. Furthermore, the dynamic components of the community-based residences were rarely measured adequately to understand differential behavioral outcomes. Finally, much of the inquiry was motivated by a desire to prove that "community living" was good and demonstrably better than that in institutions (cf. Landesman & Butterfield, 1987), rather than to understand the developmental processes and person–environment transactions under diverse conditions. Some research, however, sought to test plausible mechanisms to account for individual differences observed in responses to similar environments (cf. Landesman & Vietze, 1987). These mechanisms were offered to explain how (1) traditional institutions fostered high rates of bizarre, atypical, and undesirable social behavior that could be linked clearly to environmental antecedents and consequences; (2) well-controlled environmental manipulations—especially increasing positive attention and opportunities for interesting activities—could significantly reduce such aberrant behavior, at least for the short term; and (3) the behavioral competence of individuals was, to a considerable extent, a function of environmental opportunities. Thus, individuals were observed to behave in more or less intelligent and adaptive ways as a function of the expectations or behavioral standards of the settings where they spent time. The most dramatic examples of this derived from observations of the same individuals across different settings at the same time in their lives. Many of these individuals appeared apathetic, nonverbal, and nonpurposive in their behavior when in their residential institutional environment, but became verbal, socially responsive, and actively engaged in learning or productive work when in high-quality school or vocational settings (Landesman-Dwyer, 1987).

INDIVIDUAL DIFFERENCES IN RESPONSE TO ENVIRONMENTS

Interestingly, the repeated finding of variation in response to institutional experiences or to community living was in many ways quite encouraging, though seldom discussed in the research literature in these terms; that is, some children appear to survive quite well, despite tremendous environmental oppression or lack of normative growth-promoting opportunities. More systematic inquiry into the processes by which these seemingly "invulnerable" children achieve positive outcomes has important theoretical and clinical value. Are these children truly *not* affected by extreme environments or do they have special coping strategies to offset the difficulties, obstacles, and inadequacies identified in their environments? Alternatively, would more refined assessment of these children's environments reveal the presence of supportive elements that previously were not recognized? To the extent that compensatory behavioral and/or environmental variables can be identified for certain children or certain situations, new treatment interventions can be designed to incorporate these protective elements and test whether they can minimize negative effects of nonoptimal environments for other children as well.

Although the effects of institutional environments were related in various studies to children's earlier experiences and to such variables as age, sex, and level of mental retardation, a consistent pattern did not emerge regarding long-term prognosis (Windle, 1962). Because of life circumstances, the preinstitutional or preorphanage lives of infants and young children were rarely documented with any credible details, thus preventing post hoc study of how temperamental and previous environmental experiences contribute to individual differences in developmental outcomes.

One fascinating source of information comes from biographies of accomplished people who survived the loss of one or both parents early in life and frequently endured a series of nonparental family homes and orphanages, sometimes entering into a life of independence even before reaching adolescence. Simpson (1987) wrote an interesting popular book on orphans that highlights many of these lives and provides thoughtful insights about individual differences and coping mechanisms, including the use of fantasy, denial, and fabrication. She also posited that all children may endure some "degrees of the parentless state" better because of having had crucial positive attachment with a mother early in life. In literature, this is captured by Dickens's *David Copperfield*, who starts life with a mother who herself is still a child and then traverses through many disruptions and disappointments, with mother's love being more or less available at different times (e.g., due to other lovers and being sent away to school). Somewhat ironically, his mother's true death is portrayed as allowing David Copper-field to see his mother idealistically, returning to the mother of his infancy. This interpretation is compatible with a scientific conceptualization of a continuum of care-providing environments, which is associated with differential effects depending on a combination of individual and historical variables, as well as differential responses to stressful life situations (e.g., Garmezy, 1989; Garmezy & Rutter, 1983; Sameroff & Chandler, 1975). Even outside the walls of institutions, institutional experiences and a sense of parental abandonment may occur. What contributes to variations in these feelings and how these feelings are transformed over time and influence the life course of individuals is still, to a large extent, not understood.

Modern Forms of "Institutionalization": Distinguishing Features

An explicit definition of what comprises an institutional environment or an institutional experience was seldom provided in the earlier scientific literature. This was because orphanages and children's institutions were so obviously distinguished from natural family homes and so inextricably associated with a relatively constant set of negative qualitative attributes ("blandness, drabness, uniformity, and lack of individual attention," Flexner, 1987) that further definition seemed superfluous. The oppressively inhumane institutions and impoverished orphanages of the mid-twentieth century have been closed or transformed markedly (e.g., Rothman & Rothman, 1984; Wolins & Wozner, 1982). Efforts to provide truly habilitative and individualized care within group settings for children with special needs have increased. At the same time, the success of these modifications in residential care settings has been uneven, and structural reforms have often not resulted in functional improvements or a higher quality of life (Landesman, 1987; Landesman & Butterfield, 1987).

The possibility that institution-like environments can exist outside traditionally recognized large institutions has been raised (Edgerton, 1988; Landesman, 1988); that is, the environmental elements hypothesized to contribute to negative behavior and poor developmental progress may be present in such places as foster homes, group homes, day care settings, or even nuclear family homes. From this perspective, the *functional characteristics* of children's primary care-providing environments (e.g., amount and quality of social interactions, availability of developmentally appropriate activities, opportunities for choice and variety) are hypothesized to be the critical mediating factors in producing institutional effects rather than the structural characteristics (e.g., administrative category, caregiver, child ratio, size of facility).

From this functional perspective, the most salient negative features associated with institutional environments (Landesman, 1988), including modern residential and child care facilities, are as follows:

1. A rigid and slow-to-change administrative organization with inflexible operating policies.
2. Lack of frequent positive, individualized, and response-contingent social interactions.
3. Instability and unpredictability in the presence and behavior of adult care providers.
4. Poor resource utilization, often associated with a closed system and relative isolation.

In essence, these features define institutional environments in a way that underscores the child's day-to-day experiences, the social and physical resources within the environment, and the opportunities for learning. This places the study of institutional effects in a broad developmental framework.

One of the most prevalent forms of institutional care in present times is poor-quality day care for infants and toddlers. The recent surge of systematic study of day care environments has resulted from the same concerns that guided the earlier research on the effects of institutionalization. Indeed, scientific inquiry on the topic of day care has benefitted from careful review of the serious flaws that plagued decades of research on institutionalization. Thus, to understand the role of young children's early and multiple care-providing environments, the scientific questions must be integrated within a biosocial and ecological framework that seeks to discover dynamic patterns of individual development that emerge within functionally cohesive environments (e.g., Bronfenbrenner, 1977; Landesman & Ramey, 1989; C. Ramey & Ramey, 1998). A child's nonparental care experiences need to be evaluated within the context of his or her other life experiences, including the quality of parental caregiving and the rate and nature of changes in the social and physical environment over time.

In theory, there are many caregiving environments—including children's own family homes—at risk for having at least some of the institutional qualities of regimentation, insensitivity in social interactions, instability, unpredictability, and inadequacy of resources. It is important to remember that environments always represent the joint product of people and physical resources, and that environments are not static. A caregiving environment may be highly effective at one time during a child's development, but not necessarily at other times. Similarly, a certain combination of environmental features may produce positive developmental outcomes for the majority of children, yet fail to do so for others. What is vitally important is a taxonomy of developmentally supportive environments that is based on explanatory mechanisms that can account for individual variation in response to environments.

The most recent information about the consequences of different types, amounts, and quality of early experience derives from an ongoing 10-site longitudinal study on early child care coordinated by the National Institute of Child Health and Human Development (NICHD). Since 1991, approximately 1,300 children from diverse ethnic and socioeconomic groups have been followed from birth through school age. The study (NICHD Study of Early Child Care, 1998) has documented in detail the complexity and unpredictability of child care for many families. Just as importantly, the quality of nonparental care varies tremendously, with many infants and young children receiving care that is of poor quality, based on direct observations and assessments of the caregiving environments. The quality of care shows a consistent, although modest, association with children's language and intellectual development. The higher the quality of child care, as indexed by language stimulation and interactions between adult caregivers and children, the more advanced the child's developmental competencies. It is important to note that such analyses take into account the differences in children's families and the quality of their home environments. One of the most practical implications of this study is that what matters for young children is their cumulative life experiences. A compartmentalized analysis of environmental effects that considers only parental care or nonparental care would yield conclusions that are incomplete and sometimes erroneous.

Recent study of orphanages in Romania also provides informative findings about present-day effects of early experience. In a special issue of the *International Journal of Behavioral Development* (1997), descriptions of the institutional conditions and case studies indicate that the degree of deprivation and neglect is extreme for most of these children. Research by Groze and Ileana (1996) indicates that the age when children are placed in foster or adoptive homes relates to the severity of social and cognitive impairments. Children who were institutionalized for shorter periods of time and received supportive care beginning at earlier ages showed significantly better outcomes. An important caveat, however, is that there were tremendous individual differences in the observed long-term outcomes. S. Ramey et al. (1995) reported that infants and toddlers in Romanian orphanages responded positively to systematic, daily enrichment. The results were based on two randomized, controlled trials. A treated group received enrichment for 6 hours per day, 5 days per week, for 11–13 months. A comparison group received additional training supports and materials for their caregivers to help promote more positive, response-contingent experiences. The investigators reported the following conclusions: (1) When previously deprived children receive frequent, high-quality stimulation, they show developmental advances that correspond to approximately the duration of treatment. For example, on average, children showed 11–13 months of growth in terms of *developmental age* in social, language, fine motor, and gross motor development when they received adequate stimulation, while the comparison children showed only 6–9 months of developmental advance during the same time period; and (2) there was no evidence of true "catch up," even after receiving enrichment; that is, although children responded positively to enrichment, they did not show superaccelerated development, such that the delays already experienced could be corrected. Rather, the enrichment appeared to prevent further accumulation of delays that were largely associated with environmental inadequacies. These findings are consistent with those reported earlier by Groze and Ileana.

Collectively, the results of more recent studies of new forms of nonparental caregiving affirm the same principles detected in the early studies of institutional effects and in the controlled experimental research. Despite the repeated observation that there are individual differences in the response to enrich mental deprivation or enrichment, there is a strong and consistent finding that the quality and type of stimulation received in early life makes a difference. How long-lasting and permanent these effects are does vary, in part because of hypothesized individual differences, and in part because of subsequent life experiences that serve to minimize, sustain, or exacerbate earlier effects. There is still much to be learned from careful, theory-guided inquiry about life courses, documenting the ways in which children's everyday transactions with the environment at one age affect their transactions at later ages.

TOWARD A DEVELOPMENTAL TAXONOMY OF CARE-PROVIDING ENVIRONMENTS

That the measurement of care-providing environments and environmental variables has lagged far behind the measurement of individuals has been well recognized and vigorously lamented. The number of standardized tools is few, and the range of environmental variables considered is limited. Yet the developmental literature continues to rely on relatively simplistic, and predominantly structural and demographic variables to describe children's environments. Furthermore, the cultural biases in selecting environmental variables to include in longitudinal research are not adequately recognized as restricting our theoretical advances about child–environment transactions. For example, the present-day values and parenting practices of upper-middle-class white families are those most frequently assessed because they are hypothesized to be the environmental variables that promote children's development. Although children in these environments typically display better-than-average developmental progress on the outcome measures obtained, notably, IQ scores, language skills, and school achievement, there is a serious flaw in conducting an essentially historical and ethnocentric study; that is, the evidence is compelling that the structural and demographic features of families have changed dramatically within this century. Many children today are living in environments considered pathological by the normative standards of earlier generations (e.g., only-child families, single-parent families, mothers who work full-time outside the home), yet many children are continuing to develop well; that is, they do not show major negative effects (at least as defined by the investigators and parents) and they do progress well cognitively, socially, and emotionally. What, then, have been the surviving functional features of successful children's early environments, despite the marked structural changes? Have there been new environmental variables that have been added that, in turn, have provided functional equivalents to elements no longer assured in children's everyday lives? Are there some classes of environmental variables that have developmental consequences only when certain other resources are present or absent, or only for certain types of children?

Increasingly, answers to questions about the effects of maternal absence and institutional environments indicate the potential value of a more formalized taxonomy of care-providing environments (Landesman, 1986). Arbitrary categorizations of home and other care-providing environments that are based primarily on current standards or labels are highly vulnerable to cohort effects and thus limit the potential accumulation of valuable scientific information about human adaptation. Similarly, classification schemes derived from statistical groupings of a large number of environmental variables have not demonstrated good utility or validity. To date, no single broad-based theory has been transformed into a method for measuring and describing (1) the objective external features of children's home and out-of-home environments; (2) the subjective or experiential environments of children, which may or may not be compartmentalized by geographical location; and (3) the relationship between objective and subjective environments. Increasingly, children spend large amounts of time in two or more primary residences during their early development, with significant changes in the adults who are their primary or shared care providers. Assessing the continuities and changes in children's environments across settings and sequentially is vital. We must incorporate the multidimensional and variable environment as a significant codeterminant, along with biological maturational influences, of a child's development, a codeterminant leading to the development of theoretically cohesive and psychometrically strong measurement tools and classification schemes.

CONCLUSIONS

Institutionalization as an exemplar of an extremely aberrant environment for rearing children provided an important historical opportunity to identify themes related to normative experiences and their correlates within specified environmental contexts. The deep, lasting psychological consequences that originally motivated investigators to study the effects of institutionalization remain worthy of continued scientific inquiry. What happens when children's individuality is ignored? If feelings of loss and anger, especially toward parents and other primary caregivers, cannot be expressed, in what ways will children's emotional sensitivity and subsequent interpersonal attachments be affected? When cognitive challenges and environmental stimulation are inadequate to support developmental advances, how effective can subsequent remedial efforts be to correct for the consequences of earlier environmental deficiencies? Do alterations in brain structure and function attributable to very low resource environments—or very high resource environments—leave a lasting legacy that further limits—or enhances—a child's opportunities?

Reflections on the combined human and animal literature on the effects of early deprivation, especially maternal deprivation, and subsequent studies on institutionalization confirm three broad conclusions. Interestingly, these conclusions have important implications for understanding person–environment transactions and the consequences of experiences within a contextual life-span framework. They are not unique to children who have lived in orphanages or those with disabilities but extend to children who spend significant amounts of time in settings that have institution-like features. These conclusions are that (1) environments are not inherently good or bad; (2) the consequences of a given environmental experience are as much determined by what follows and what precedes it as by the experience itself; and (3) the negative consequences associated with disruptions and environmental changes can be offset, at least in part, by providing some stability in at least one primary, close human contact. These findings now need to be integrated with a biosocial functional taxonomy of environments to further specify the means by which children develop competencies and emotional maturity and trust.

REFERENCES

Balla, D., Butterfield, E. C., & Zigler, E. (1974). Effects of institutionalization on retarded children: A longitudinal cross-institutional investigation. *American Journal of Metal Deficiency, 78,* 530–549.

Bates, E., O'Connell, B., & Shore, C. (1987). Language and communication in infancy. In J. Osofsky (Ed.), *Handbook of infant development* (2nd ed., pp. 149–204). New York: Wiley.

Baumeister, A. A. (Ed.). (1967). *Mental retardation: Appraisal, education, and rehabilitation.* Chicago: Aldine.

Bender, L. (1947). Psychopathic behavior disorders in children. In R. Linderner & R. Seliger (Eds.), *Handbook of correctional psychology* (pp. 360–377). New York: Philosophical Library.

Bender, L., & Yarnell, H. (1941). An observation nursery: A study of 250 children on the Psychiatric Division of Bellevue Hospital. *American Journal of Psychiatry, 97,* 1158–1174.

Bowlby, J. (1940). The influence of early environment in the development of neurosis and neurotic character. *International Journal of Psychoanalysis, 21,* 154–178.

Bowlby, J. (1944). Forty-four juvenile thieves: Their characters and home life. *International Journal of Psychoanalysis, 25,* 107–127.

Bowlby, J. (1951). *Maternal care and mental health.* New York: Columbia University Press.

Bowlby, J. (1958). The nature of the child's tie to his mother. *International Journal of Psychoanalysis, 39,* 250–373.

Bowlby, J. (1969). *Attachment and loss: Vol. 1. Attachment.* New York: Basic Books.

Bronfenbrenner, U. (1977). Toward an experimental ecology of human development. *American Psychologist, 32,* 513–531.

Burchinal, M. R., Campbell, F. A., Bryant, D. M., Wasik, B. H., & Ramey, C. T. (1997). Early intervention and mediating processes in cognitive performance of children of low-income African American families. *Child Development, 68,* 935–954.

Butterfield, E. C. (1967). The role of environmental factors in the treatment of institutionalized mental retardates. In A. A. Baumeister (Ed.), *Mental retardation: Appraisal, education, and rehabilitation* (pp. 120–137). Chicago: Aldine.

Butterfield, E. C. (1987). Why and how to study the influence of living arrangements. In S. Landesman & P. M. Vietze (Eds.), *Living environments and mental retardation* (pp. 43–59). Washington, DC: American Association on Mental Retardation.

Butterfield, E. C., & Zigler, E. (1965). The influence of differing institutional social climates on the effectiveness of social reinforcement in the mentally retarded. *American Journal of Mental Deficiency, 70,* 48–56.

Caldwell, B. M., & Bradley, R. H. (1984). *Home observation for measurement of the environment.* Little Rock: University of Arkansas.

Capitanio, J. P. (1986). Behavioral pathology. In G. Mitchell & J. Erwin (Eds.), *Comparative primate biology: Vol. 2. Part A. Behavior, conservation, and ecology* (pp. 411–454). New York: Alan R. Liss.

Carnegie Task Force on Meeting the Needs of Young Children. (1994). *Starting points: Meeting the needs of our youngest children.* New York: Carnegie Corporation.

Clarke, A. D. B., & Clarke, A. M. (1953). How constant is the IQ? *Lancet, 2,* 877–880.

Clarke, A. D. B., & Clarke, A. M. (1954). Cognitive changes in the feebleminded. *British Journal of Psychology, 45,* 173–179.

Clarke, A. D. B., Clarke, A. M., & Reiman, S. (1958). Cognitive and social changes in the feebleminded: Three further studies. *British Journal of Psychology, 49,* 144–157.

Comery, T. A., Shah, R., & Greenough, W. T. (1995). Differential rearing alters spine density on medium-sized spiney neurons in the rat striatum: Evidence for association of morphological plasticity with early response gene expression. *Neurobiology of Learning and Memory, 63,* 217–219.

Crissey, M. S. (1975). Mental retardation: Past, present, and future. *American Psychologist, 30,* 800–808.

Crissey, O. L. (1937). The mental development of children of the same IQ in different institutional environments. *Child Development, 8,* 217–220.

Edgerton, R. B. (1988). Community adaptation of persons with mental retardation. In J. F. Kavanagh (Ed.), *Understanding mental retardation: Research accomplishments and new frontiers* (pp. 331–318). Baltimore: Paul H. Brookes.

Flexner, S. B. (Ed. in Chief). (1987). *The Random House dictionary of the English language* (2nd ed., unabridged). New York: Random House.

Fuchs, J. L., Montemayor, M., & Greenough, W. T. (1990). Effect of environmental complexity on size of the superior colliculus. *Behavioral and Neural Biology* (pp. 198–203).

Galinsky, E. (1992). The impact of child care on parents. In A. Booth (Ed.), *Child care in the 1990s: Trends and consequences* (pp. 159–171). Hillsdale, NJ: Erlbaum.

Garmezy, N. (1989). Stress-resistant children: The search for protective factors. In J. E. Stevenson (Ed.), Aspects of current child psychiatry research. *Journal of Child Psychology and Psychiatry Book Supplement, 4,* 213–233. Oxford, UK: Pergamon Press.

Garmezy, N., & Rutter, M. (1983). *Stress, coping, and development in children.* New York: McGraw-Hill.

Greenough, W. T., Volkmar, F. R., & Juraska, J.M. (1973). Effects of rearing complexity on dendritic branching in frontal and temporal cortex of the rat. *Experimental Neurology, 41,* 371–378.

Groze, V., & Ileana, D. (1996). A follow-up study of adopted children from Romania. *Child Adolescent Social Work Journal, 13,* 541–565.

Guralnick, M. J. (Ed.). (1997). *The effectiveness of early intervention.* Baltimore: Paul H. Brookes.

Harlow, H., & Harlow, M. (1965). The affectional systems. In A. Schrier, H. Harlow, & F. Stollnitz (Eds.), *Behavior of nonhuman primates* (Vol. 2, pp. 287–334). New York: Academic Press.

Harlow. H., & Zimmerman, R. (1959). Affectional responses in the infant monkey. *Science, 130,* 421.

Heal, L. W., Sigelman, C. K., & Switzky, H. N. (1978). Research on community residential alternatives for the mentally retarded. In N. R. Ellis (Ed.), *International review of research in mental retardation* (Vol. 9, pp. 209–149). New York: Academic Press.

Hebb, D. O. (1949). *The organization of behavior: A neurophysiological theory.* New York: Wiley.

Hinde, R. (1974). *Biological bases of human social behavior.* New York: McGraw-Hill.

Hofferth, S. (1992). The demand for and supply of child care in the 1990s. In A. Booth (Ed.), *Child care in the 1990s: Trends and consequences* (pp. 3–25). Hillsdale, NJ: Erlbaum.

Hubel, D. H. (1979). The visual cortex of normal and deprived monkeys. *American Scientist, 67,* 532–543.

Hunt, J. McV. (1961). *Intelligence and experience.* New York: Ronald Press.

Infant Health and Development Program. (1990). Enhancing the outcomes of low-birth-weight, premature infants. *Journal of the American Medical Association, 263,* 3035–3042.

Jones, T. A., & Greenough, W. T. (1996). Ultrastructural evidence for increased contact between astrocytes and synapses in rats reared in complex environments. *Neurobiology of Learning and Memory, 65,* 48–56.

Jones, T. A., Klintsova, A. Y., Kilman, V. L., Sirevaag, A. M., & Greenough, W. T. (1997). Induction of multiple synapses by experience in the visual cortex of adult rats. *Neurobiology of Learning and Memory, 68,* 13–20.

Klaber, M. M. (1969). *Retardates in residence: A study of institutions.* West Hartford, CT: University of Hartford Press.

Kraemer, G. W., & Clarke, A. S. (1990). The behavioral neurobiology of self-injurious behavior in rhesus monkeys. *Progress in Neuro-Pharmacology and Biological Psychiatry, 14,* 141–168.

Landesman, S. (1986). Toward a taxonomy of home environments. *International Review of Research in Mental Retardation, 14,* 259–289.

Landesman, S. (1987). Introduction. In S. Landesman & P. Vietz (Eds.), *Living environments and mental retardation* (pp. ix–xv). Washington, DC: American Association on Mental Retardation.

Landesman, S. (1988). Preventing "institutionalization" in the community. In M. P. Janicki, M. W. Krauss, & M. M. Seltzer (Eds.), *Community residence for persons with developmental disabilities: Here to stay* (pp. 105–116). Baltimore: Paul H. Brookes.

Landesman, S., & Butterfield, E. C. (1987). Normalization and deinstitutionalization of mentally retarded individuals: Controversy and facts. *American Psychologist, 42,* 309–816.

Landesman, S., & Ramey, C. (1989). Developmental psychology and mental retardation: Integrating scientific principles with treatment practices. *American Psychologist, 44,* 409–415.

Landesman, S., & Vietze, P. (Eds.). (1987). *Living environments and mental retardation.* Washington, DC: American Association on Mental Retardation.

Landesman-Dwyer, S. (1987). Living in community. *American Journal of Mental Deficiency, 86*, 223–234.

Laudenslager, M. L., Reite, M., & Harbeck, R. J. (1982). Suppressed immune response in infant monkeys associated with maternal separation. *Behavioral and Neural Biology, 36*, 40–48.

Lewis, M. H., Gluck, J. P., Beauchamp, A. J., Keresztury, M. F., & Mailman, R. P. (1990). Long-term effects of early social isolation in *Macaca mulatta*: Changes in dopamine receptor function following apomorphine challenges. *Brain Research, 513*, 67–73.

Lorenz, K. (1935). DerKumpan in der Umvelt des Vogels. Reprinted in C. Schiller (Ed.), *Instinctive behavior (1957)*. New York: International Universities Press.

Martin, J. L., Spicer, D. M., Lewis, M. H., Gluck, J. P., & Cork L. C. (1991). Social deprivation of infant rhesus monkeys alters the chemoarchitecture of the brain. I. Subcortical Regions. *Journal of Neuroscience, 11*, 3344–3358.

NICHD Early Child Care Research Network. (1998). Results of the NICHD Study of Early Child Care. *Child Development, 108*, 860–879.

Osofsky, J. (Ed.). (1987). *Handbook of infant development* (2nd ed.). New York: Wiley.

Ramey, C. T., & Campbell, F. A. (1992). Poverty, early childhood education, and academic competence: The Abecedarian experiment. In A. Huston (Ed.), *Children in poverty* (pp. 190–221). New York: Cambridge University Press.

Ramey, C. T., & Ramey, S. L. (1997a). The development of universities and children. Commissioned paper for the Harvard Project on Schooling and Children. Cambridge, MA: Harvard University Press.

Ramey, C. T., & Ramey, S. L. (1997b). Early childhood experiences and developmental competence. Commissioned paper for the Ford Foundation. New York: Russell Sage.

Ramey, C. T., & Ramey, S. L. (1998). Early intervention and early experience. *American Psychologist, 53*, 109–120.

Ramey, C. T., & Ramey, S. L. (1999). *Right from birth: Building your child's foundation for life*. New York: Goddard Press.

Ramey, S. L., & Ramey, C. T. (1992). Early educational intervention with disadvantaged children: To what effect? *Applied and Preventive Psychology, 1*, 131–140.

Ramey, S. L., & Ramey, C. T. (1999a). *Going to school*. New York: Goddard Press.

Ramey, S. L., & Ramey, C. T. (1999b). Early experience and early intervention for children "at risk" for developmental delay and mental retardation. *Mental Retardation and Developmental Disabilities Research Reviews, 5*, 1–10.

Ramey, S. L., & Ramey, C. T. (2000). Effects of early childhood experiences in developmental competence. In J. Waldfogel & S. Danziger (Eds.), *Securing the future: Investing in children from birth to college* (pp. 122–150). New York: Russell Sage.

Ramey, S. L., Sparling, J., Dragomir, C., Ramey, C., Echols, K., & Soroceanu, L. (1995, March). *Recovery by children under 3 years old from depriving orphanage experiences*. Symposium presentation at the Society for Research in Child Development, Indianapolis, IN.

Rosenblum, L. A., & Kaufman, I. C. (1968). Variations in infant development and response to maternal loss in monkeys. *American Journal of Orthopsychiatry, 38*, 418–426.

Rosenzweig, M. R., & Bennett, E. L. (1996). Psychobiology of plasticity: Effects of training and experience on brain and behavior. *Behaviour Brain Research, 78*, 57–65.

Rosenzweig, M. R., Krech, D., Bennett, M. L., & Diamond, M. C. (1961). Effects of environmental complexity and training on brain chemistry and anatomy: A replication and extension. *Journal of Comparative Physiology and Psychology, 55*, 429–437.

Rothman, D. J., & Rothman, S. M. (1984). *The Willowbrook wars: A decade of struggle for social justice*. New York: Harper & Row.

Ruppenthal, G. C., Arling, G. L., Harlow, H. F., Sackett, G. P., & Suomi, S. J. (1976). A ten year perspective of motherless-mother monkey behavior. *Journal of Abnormal Psychology, 85*, 341–349.

Sackett, G. P. (1968). Abnormal behavior in laboratory-reared monkeys. In M. Fox (Ed.), *Abnormal behavior in animals* (pp. 293–331). Philadelphia: Saunders.

Sackett, G. P. (1970). Innate mechanisms, rearing conditions and a theory of early experience effects in primates. In M. R. Jones (Ed.), *Miami Symposium on Prediction of Behavior: Early experience* (pp. 11–60). Coral Gables, FL: University of Miami Press.

Sackett, G. P. (1972). Isolation rearing in monkeys: Diffuse and specific effects on later behavior. In R. Chauvin (Ed.), *Animal models of human behavior* (pp. 61–110). Paris: Colloques Internationaux du C.N.R.S.

Sackett, G. P., Novak, M. F., & Kroeker, R. (1999). Early experience effects on adaptive behavior: Theory revisited. *Mental Retardation and Developmental Disabilities Research Reviews, 5*, 30–40.

Sameroff, A., & Chandler, M. J. (1975). Reproductive risk and the continuum of caretaking casualty. In F. D. Horowitz (Ed.), *Review of child development research* (Vol. 4, pp. 187–244). Chicago: University of Chicago Press.

Shore, R. (1997). *Rethinking the brain: New insights into early development*. New York: Families and Work Institute.

Simpson, E. (1987). *Orphans: Real and imaginary*. New York: Weidenfeld & Nicolson.

Skeels, H. (1966). Adult status of children with contrasting early life experiences: A follow-up study. *Monographs of the Society for Research in Child Development, 31* (Serial No. 105), 1–65.

Skodak, M., & Skeels, H. M. (1949). A final follow-up study of one hundred adopted children. *Journal of Genetic Psychology, 75,* 85–125.

Smith, S. (Ed.). (1995). *Two generation programs for families in poverty: A new intervention strategy.* Norwood, NJ: Ablex.

Spitz, R. (1945). Hospitalism: An inquiry into the genesis of psychiatric conditions in early childhood. *Psychoanalytic Study of the Child, 1,* 53.

Spitz, R. (1946). Anaclitic depression: An inquiry into the genesis of psychotic conditions in early childhood. *Psychoanalytic Study of the Child, 2,* 313–341.

Spitz, R. (1947). *Grief: A peril in infancy* [Film]. New York: New York University Film Library.

Suomi, S. J., & Harlow, H. F. (1978). Early experience and social development in the rhesus monkeys. In M. E. Lamb (Ed.), *Social and personality development.* New York: Holt, Rinehart & Winston.

Wallace, C. S., Withers, G. S., Weiler, I. J., George, J. M., Clayton, D. F., & Greenough, W. T. (1995). Correspondence between sites of NGFI-A induction and sites of morphological plasticity following exposure to environmental complexity. *Brain Res Molec Brain Res, 32,* 211–220.

Wiesel, T. N., & Hubel, D. H. (1974). Ordered arrangement of orientation columns in monkeys lacking visual experience. *Journal Comp Neurol, 158,* 307–318.

Windle, C. (1962). Prognosis of mental subnormals. *American Journal of Mental Deficiency, 66* (Monograph Supplement to No. 5).

Wolins, M., & Wozner, Y. (1982). *Revitalizing residential settings.* San Francisco: Jossey-Bass.

Zigler, E., & Balla, D. (1977). Impact of institutional experience on the behavior and development of retarded persons. *American Journal of Mental Deficiency, 82,* 1–11.

Zigler, E., Butterfield, E. C., & Capobianco, R. (1970). Institutionalization and the effectiveness of social reinforcement: A five and eight year follow-up study. *Developmental Psychology, 3,* 255–263.

V
DISRUPTIVE BEHAVIORAL DISORDERS

21

Attention-Deficit/Hyperactivity Disorder

A Developmental View

Susan B. Campbell

Attention-deficit/hyperactivity disorder (ADHD), among the most common disorders of childhood, has been the subject of research for nearly a century (Barkley, 1990, 1996; Campbell & Werry, 1986; Schachar, 1986). Indeed more studies have been published on ADHD and its variations than on any other disorder of childhood, and despite the continuing gaps in our knowledge, it is probably safe to assert that more is known about ADHD than about any other childhood disorder as well.

Throughout the last 60 years, various terms have been used to define this disorder, including hyperkinetic impulse disorder, organic driveness, minimal brain dysfunction, hyperactivity, attention deficit disorder, and now attention-deficit/hyperactivity disorder (Barkley, 1990; 1996; Campbell & Werry, 1986; Schachar, 1986). Despite these differences in terminology, there is general agreement that the core features of inattention, impulsivity, and hyperactivity define ADHD. However, changing conceptions have led to somewhat different definitions and emphases. In the 1950s and 1960s, emphasis was placed on the activity component (Laufer, Denhoff, & Solomons, 1957); by the 1970s, the focus had shifted to attentional problems (Campbell & Werry, 1986; Douglas, 1972, 1983; Douglas & Peters, 1978); most recently, more weight has been placed on the poor impulse control (lack of inhibition) that characterizes ADHD (Barkley, 1996, 1997).

Although researchers and clinicians may debate the fine points of this disorder, to the parent or teacher dealing with an ADHD child, these are of only passing interest unless they lead to prescriptions for dealing with the difficult behavior of these youngsters. The high energy level, constant movement, poor organizational skills, lack of persistence, poor social skills, lack of social judgment, and frequent shifting of attention that ADHD children display lead to a myriad of social and academic problems. Difficulties are evident at home, where

Susan B. Campbell • Clinical Psychology Center, University of Pittsburgh, Pittsburgh, Pennsylvania 15260.

Handbook of Developmental Psychopathology, Second Edition, edited by Arnold J. Sameroff, Michael Lewis, and Suzanne M. Miller. Kluwer Academic/Plenum Publishers, New York, 2000.

ADHD children often have a hard time following rules, often create disturbances at mealtime, bedtime, or on family outings, are in frequent conflict with siblings, and rarely complete homework without a struggle or in the absence of parental supervision. In the classroom, ADHD children often stand out because of their lack of concentration, failure to follow class routines, fidgetiness, inappropriate verbalizations and disruptiveness, and difficulty working independently. In the peer group, ADHD children are often avoided by others, may provoke fights, may disrupt other children's activities by barging in or calling attention to themselves, or may act as the class clown, eliciting a mixture of amusement and disdain from other children.

A detailed review of the cognitive and social difficulties associated with ADHD is beyond the scope of this chapter. Suffice it to say that numerous studies document difficulties in focused and sustained attention (e.g., Seidel & Joschko, 1990), the organization and effortful processing of complex information (e.g., Tannock, Purvis, & Schachar, 1993), the inhibition of ongoing motor responding (e.g, Iaboni, Douglas, & Baker, 1995), and the control of impulsive responding on cognitive tasks (e.g., Barkley, Grodzinsky, & DuPaul, 1992). Debates have focused on the specific nature of the attentional deficit, for example, whether it is really a deficit in sustained attention or one of focusing attention and persisting on demanding tasks, or a reflection of lack of inhibitory control (for a discussion of this issue and for a review of the cognitive functioning of ADHD children, see Barkley, 1996, 1997). The many social deficits these children experience may well emerge from their documented cognitive deficits. These are reflected in the social information-processing difficulties of ADHD children as well as in their inappropriate social behavior with family members and peers (e.g., Barkley, 1996; Campbell, 1990; Milich & Dodge, 1984; Pelham & Bender, 1982; Whalen & Henker, 1985, 1992).

DIAGNOSTIC CRITERIA

In the DSM-IV (American Psychiatric Association, 1994), ADHD is defined by nine symptoms classified under the rubric of inattention: six symptoms considered indicative of hyperactivity, and three symptoms considered to reflect impulsivity (see Table 21.1). Subtypes, included in DSM-III (American Psychiatric Association, 1980) and dropped in DSM-III-R (American Psychiatric Association, 1987), have been redefined in DSM-IV. Thus, to meet criteria for ADHD, *predominantly inattentive type*, the child must show six symptoms of inattention. Children who display six symptoms from the hyperactivity–impulsivity cluster

TABLE 21.1. Symptoms of ADHA Included in the DSM-IV

Inattention	Hyperactivity	Impulsivity
Fails to attend to details	Fidgets	Blurts out answers
Difficulty sustaining attention	Leaves seat inappropriately	Difficulty awaiting turn
Does not listen	Runs about or climbs	Interrupts
Does not follow instructions	Difficulty playing quietly	
Difficulty organizing tasks	On the go	
Avoids tasks requiring sustained mental effort	Talks incessantly	
Often loses things		
Distracted by external stimuli		
Forgetful		

meet criteria for ADHD, *predominantly hyperactive–impulsive type*. Those who meet both sets of criteria are considered to be showing ADHD, *combined type*. In order to meet criteria for any subtype of ADHD, the symptoms must have been present before age 7, persist for at least 6 months, and be judged as both maladaptive and inappropriate for the child's developmental level. In addition, impairment in functioning should be evident in at least two settings (e.g., home and school). These criteria are meant to ensure that children with transient problems related to anxiety or acute reactions to stressful life events are not misdiagnosed and to facilitate differentiating between children with learning problems (who may show difficulties at school, but not home) and children living with parents with limited understanding of normal development (who may see problems that are age-related and minor or not evident in the classroom). Concerns have been expressed about the age-of-onset criterion, however, which may rule out children whose symptoms of inattention go unnoticed until the demands of school become more salient (Applegate et al., 1997). Before discussing other issues in diagnosis and developmental course, I turn to the question of how many children actually show this disorder.

PREVALENCE

A number of studies have examined the prevalence of ADHD in representative samples of children. Not surprisingly, rates have varied widely based on the age range of the children, the definition of ADHD used, how ADHD was measured, and who was reporting on the symptoms. In particular, the use of DSM-III, DSM-III-R, and DSM-IV criteria (American Psychiatric Association, 1980, 1987, 1994) have led to different estimates of prevalence (e.g., August & Garfinkel, 1993; Lahey et al., 1990; Wolraich, Hannah, Pinnock, Baumgaertel, & Brown, 1996). It appears that the move to DSM-IV criteria and the inclusion of three subtypes, two with somewhat lower symptom thresholds, has led to a slight increase in prevalence (e.g., Wolraich et al., 1996) over earlier prevalence rates based on DSM-III and III-R criteria. Rates also vary depending upon whether rating scales or structured interviews are used to assess symptoms (see Bird, 1996; Szatmari, Offord, & Boyle, 1989), whether one informant or two are used (e.g., Anderson, Williams, McGee, & Silva, 1987), how their data are combined (e.g., Anderson et al., 1987; Boyle et al., 1996; Shaffer et al., 1996), and whether symptom counts alone are used or impairment in functioning and/or pervasiveness of symptoms are included as additional criteria (e.g., August & Garfinkel, 1993; Boyle et al., 1996; Shaffer et al., 1996). Of course, the estimated rates of ADHD are lower when more stringent criteria are used to define disorder, for example, symptoms apparent across settings ("pervasiveness") or indices of functional impairment. Thus, even among the more recent and carefully conducted epidemiological studies, rates have varied fairly widely from about 1% to 9% (see review by Bird, 1996). The DSM-IV estimates prevalence at between 3% and 5% (American Psychiatric Association, 1994).

Studies also indicate that this disorder is more prevalent in boys than girls (Anderson et al., 1987; Cohen et al., 1993; Szatmari et al., 1989; Wolraich et al., 1996). Gender differences appear to be especially strong when teacher reports are used to define disorder. For example, Szatmari et al. (1989) reported that teachers rated many more children, especially boys under the age of 12, as meeting their criteria for ADHD than did parents; the gender ratio in this study, according to teacher reports, was greater than 3:1, with more than three times as many boys receiving elevated ratings. The DSM-IV estimates the gender ratio at from 4:1 to 9:1 in favor of boys. Because ADHD is more common in boys, most of the extant research is either focused entirely on boys with ADHD or fails to address gender differences because of small numbers of girls. However, there is suggestive evidence that ADHD in girls may be more closely associated with learning problems than with oppositional and conduct problems, and that in girls, only the more severe cases come to clinical attention (Arnold, 1996). Preliminary data from the DSM-IV field trials and other recent studies indicate that the diagnosis of ADHD–inattentive subtype identifies more girls (Lahey et al., 1994; Wolraich et al., 1996), so these revised criteria may lead to the inclusion of more girls in research on ADHD. Finally, a recent meta-analysis by Gaub and Carlson (1997a) of 18 studies in which gender differences could be examined confirmed that girls with ADHD are more likely to experience intellectual difficulties and less likely to show comorbid oppositional and conduct disorders as well as high levels of hyperactivity than ADHD boys. On the other hand, academic and social deficits and family dysfunction did not appear to differentiate ADHD boys and girls. However, referral biases and developmental issues (e.g., age of referral as it relates to subtypes) need to be addressed in future studies before firm conclusions can be drawn.

Finally, cross-sectional studies indicate that rates of ADHD decline with age (Cohen et al., 1993; Szatmari et al., 1989). Although this widely replicated finding has been interpreted to suggest that this disorder is age-related, longitudinal studies suggest that the manifestations of ADHD change somewhat with development and new cases are rarely diagnosed after age 10 or 11. However, this cannot be taken to mean that the problems disappear by adolescence (Barkley, Fischer, Edelbrock, & Smallish, 1990; Cohen, Cohen, & Brook, 1993). This issue is discussed in more detail later.

COMORBIDITY

Comorbidity, or the tendency of children diagnosed with one disorder to also manifest symptoms of other disorders, is a complex dilemma for researchers and clinicians alike. Which symptoms are primary? What should be the focus of treatment? What are the implications of this for defining a particular disorder, distinguishing it from other disorders, and identifying its unique correlates and pathology or etiology? These issues are beyond the scope of this chapter and they apply equally to most childhood disorders. Thoughtful discussions of this issue may be found in Caron and Rutter (1991) and Angold and Costello (1993).

The co-occurrence of ADHD with other disorders has become a major concern in the study of ADHD (e.g., Hinshaw, 1987; Hinshaw, Lahey, & Hart, 1993; Jensen, Martin, & Cantwell, 1997). The epidemiological studies discussed earlier indicate that over half the children identified as having ADHD also meet criteria for another disorder, especially conduct disorder and/or oppositional defiant disorder (CD/ODD), but also depression and anxiety (Anderson et al., 1987; August & Garfinkel, 1993; August, Realmuto, MacDonald, Nugent, & Crosby, 1996; Szatmari et al., 1989; Wolraich et al., 1996). In clinical samples, rates of comorbidity are even higher (e.g., Barkley et al., 1990; Biederman et al., 1992), and overlap also is apparent with most other childhood disorders, including oppositional disorder, conduct disorder, depression, and anxiety.

Recent research examining subgroups of children with ADHD alone and ADHD plus CD/ODD suggests that many of the factors thought to characterize ADHD may actually be accounted for either by the co-occurring CD/ODD or by the combination of ADHD and conduct problems (e.g., Barkley, Fischer, Edelbrock, & Smallish, 1991; Hinshaw & Melnick, 1995; Lahey et al., 1988). This raises important questions about the distinctness of ADHD in and of itself; it also raises the possibility that when ADHD occurs in tandem with another disorder, this complex of problems forms a distinct disorder, with its own pattern of correlates, developmental course, and set of etiologies. Jensen et al. (1997) have recently suggested that co-occurring ADHD and CD/ODD reflect a distinct disorder. In addition, ADHD often covaries with learning problems (Hinshaw, 1992), and it is well established that children with an ADHD diagnosis often experience severe academic problems (Barkley, 1996; Faraone et al., 1993). This pattern of difficulties may form yet another distinct subtype.

Interestingly, these patterns of comorbidity appear to map onto the subtypes proposed in the DSM-IV, which Barkley (1996) posits may have different causes and consequences: The inattentive subtype appears to co-occur very often with learning problems, and the hyperactive–impulsive subtype may co-occur with CD/ODD or with subthreshold disruptive, aggressive, and antisocial behavior. Those with combined inattentive and hyperactive–impulsive symptoms may show co-occurring deficits in both cognitive functioning and self-regulation and social behavior, reflecting oppositional, antisocial behavior as well as learning problems. Several recent studies of clinical samples provide some support for this formulation of subtypes and comorbidity (Gaub & Carlson, 1997b; Lahey et al., 1994; Morgan, Hynd, Riccio, & Hall, 1996). In particular, there is some consensus that children with the inattentive subtype often experience learning problems, whereas children with the combined inattentive and impulsive–hyperactive subtypes often show antisocial and aggressive behavior (Lahey et al., 1994; Morgan et al., 1996). Gaub and Carlson (1997b)also reported that children with combined inattention and impulsivity–hyperactivity showed a combination of academic and social problems. Additional large-scale studies of clinical samples using the DSM-IV subtypes and also examining patterns of comorbidity are sorely needed to determine whether children with "pure" ADHD subtypes can be identified, or whether comorbidity is the rule. This is clearly an important issue, one that must be addressed if meaningful subtypes are to be validated and if we are to determine whether conclusions from prior and current research apply to the comorbid condition, to ADHD specifically independent of the co-occurring problem, or to something about the combination of ADHD and the other disorder.

ETIOLOGICAL FORMULATIONS

Although a good deal is known about the correlates and course of ADHD and its co-occurrence with other childhood disorders, we have a relatively poor understanding of its cause or causes. Research has emphasized possible biological factors, although early attempts to identify specific brain damage were unsuccessful (Barkley, 1996; Campbell & Werry, 1986; Zametkin & Rapoport, 1986). Thus, assumptions about specific lesions in various brain areas were not supported; in the absence of localized damage, hypotheses about "minimal" or "diffuse" brain damage were put forth (e.g., Clements & Peters, 1962), but these notions have not stood up to empirical scrutiny either. Despite this, there is general agreement that some biological mechanism must be involved in at least some cases of ADHD, presumably related to central nervous system functioning, and there is also accumulating evidence for genetic transmission of ADHD. Recent research suggests that frontal lobe functioning ("executive function deficits") may be implicated in ADHD (Barkley, 1996; 1997; Moffitt, 1993a; Pennington & Ozonoff, 1996) given the predominance of inattention, poor planning, and poor regulation of behavior in the symptom picture. However, it is not entirely clear how specific the identified deficits in planning and organization are to ADHD, as opposed to co-occurring learning problems (Barkley et al., 1992) and aggressive, antisocial behavior (Moffitt, 1993a), and whether they reflect one or several underlying neural mechanisms. In general, it is likely that more than one cause of ADHD will ultimately be identified. What remains unclear at this time is whether there will be multiple causes for ADHD generally defined, or specific causes for specific subtypes, possibly defined partly in terms of their comorbid conditions (Barkley, 1996; Hinshaw, 1994). A number of possible etiological factors are discussed briefly.

Neurotransmitters

A growing body of research has postulated a role for various neurotransmitters in the development of psychopathology in general, and ADHD is no exception. It may be that the central processing deficits that are reflected in inattention and poor impulse control result from an underlying imbalance, deficit, or dysregulation in certain neurotransmitter systems. Although several reviews by Zametkin and Rapoport (1986, 1987) have been inconclusive, the complexity and importance of this area make it a fertile one for research and new models continue to appear. For example, Pliszka, McCracken, and Maas (1997) have recently proposed a comprehensive and complex two-stage model implicating the interactions among norepinephrine, epinephrine, and dopamine in attentional processes, and they caution against overly simplistic models hypothesizing too much or too little of one or another neurotransmitter. As neuroscience progresses and we understand more about the complex role of neurotransmitters in cognitive functioning and behavioral self-regulation, this area may prove fruitful. Still, it will be necessary to demonstrate that any dysfunction in neurotransmitters and their interactions are a cause rather than a correlate or effect of the ADHD symptoms.

Behavioral Inhibition

Barkley (1997) has developed an integrative model of ADHD that emphasizes behavioral inhibition as the core deficit underlying the constellation of ADHD symptoms (hyperactive–impulsive and combined subtypes). Although others have also focused on poor inhibition as the central feature of ADHD (e.g., Quay, 1988), Barkley has gone much further in examining how data on cognitive functioning are consistent with such a model. He posits that, as a result of this core deficit, a range of difficulties in memory, planning, temporal organization of behavior, affect regulation, self-reflection, and goal-directed behavior emerge. Presumably, this deficit is neurologically based and is most apparent behaviorally in executive function deficits, which in turn should reflect some neurophysiological dysfunction in the prefrontal cortex and its projections to other brain areas. Whereas this view is consistent with some biological evidence (Zametkin et al., 1993), much research remains to be conducted to determine its accuracy. However, Barkley has managed to put together a large and diverse literature on ADHD children and to make specific predictions that can be followed up with programmatic research.

An especially interesting aspect of Barkley's model is his proposal that the attention deficits characterizing the two specific subtypes of ADHD are different, with a different etiology and course. Whereas deficits in sustained attention characterize the *inattentive* subtype, poorly focused attention and lack of persistence (resulting from poor inhibitory control) characterize the attentional deficit of the *hyperactive–impulsive* subtype. It will be necessary to determine how well this model fits with new cognitive, biological, and behavior genetic data; to demonstrate unequivocally that ADHD children with hyperactive–impulsive symptoms fit the model's predictions, whereas those with ADHD, inattentive subtype, and with other disorders (such as "pure" oppositional disorder or "pure" learning disorders) do not; and that deficits in inhibitory control are causally related to the emergence of symptoms rather than a reflection of the symptoms themselves.

Familial Aggregation of ADHD/Behavior Genetics

There is growing evidence that ADHD runs in families (Biederman et al., 1992; Levy, Hay, McStephen, Wood, & Waldman, 1997). A series of studies by Biederman and colleagues on a sample of clinically referred children meeting diagnostic criteria for ADHD indicates higher rates of ADHD and a range of other disorders, including antisocial personality, depression, and anxiety in family members (Biederman et al., 1990, 1992). Siblings of ADHD probands had elevated rates of both ADHD and oppositional disorder (Faraone, Biederman, Mennin, Gershon, & Tsuang, 1996); parents were likely to have a history of ADHD and to have current antisocial personality, depression, and/or anxiety disorders. These data have been interpreted as evidence for the genetic transmission of ADHD (Biederman et al., 1992) and although they are consistent with a genetic model, familial aggregation studies cannot rule out environmental causes. This requires twin or adoption studies.

Several recent twin studies do provide quite dramatic support for the contention that the dimensions of inattention and hyperactivity–impulsivity that characterize ADHD show higher correlations in monozygotic than dizygotic twin pairs (Goodman & Stevenson, 1989; Levy et al., 1997; Sherman, Iacono, & McCue, 1997); these studies have been conducted primarily on children of school age. Zahn-Waxler, Schmitz, Fulker, Robinson, and Emde (1996) recently reported similar findings from a study of preschool-age twins. Moreover, in the Levy et al. (1997) work, ADHD was examined both as a dimension and a categorical diagnosis, with similar findings. Thus, whether ADHD is conceptualized as a continuum of symptoms reflecting poor regulation of activity, attention, and impulses, or as a categorical diagnosis that is present in some children and absent in others, the results from twin studies suggest high heritability. Several of these twin studies also show evidence, albeit less consistently so, for small nonshared environmental influences (Goodman & Stevenson, 1989; Levy et al., 1997; Zahn-Waxler et al., 1996).

Twin studies that include a larger sample of clinically diagnosed ADHD children and adoption studies examining the offspring of ADHD adults (diagnosed as children) will be needed to address fully issues of genetic transmission. More important, most research to date has relied on parent and teacher report measures of symptoms, which are subject to bias, rather than on more objective laboratory measures of cognitive functioning reflecting attentional, planning, organizational, and self-regulatory abilities. Finally, given the emphasis on subtypes in DSM-IV, it will be important to determine whether the inattentive and hyperactive–impulsive subtypes "breed true." These will be important next steps, if the diverse findings on the familiality of ADHD and the attendant underlying deficits in information processing and inhibitory control are to be integrated into a coherent picture.

Environmental Risk Factors

Numerous studies have documented an association between ADHD in children and family adversity (e.g., Barkley et al., 1991; Biederman, Milberger, & Faraone, 1995; Campbell, 1990). The environmental correlates examined include poor parenting, as reflected in more

negative, intrusive, overstimulating, and harsh behavior, greater use of commands and direc-
tives, and fewer positive, supportive responses to children's compliance (Anderson, Hinshaw,
& Simmel, 1994; Barkley, 1990; Campbell, 1990; 1997; Heller, Baker, Henker, & Hinshaw,
1996; Jacobvitz & Sroufe, 1987). Studies have also identified more marital dysfunction and
family breakup (Barkley et al., 1990; Campbell, Pierce, Moore, Marakovitz, & Newby, 1996);
more general family stress (Biederman et al., 1995; Campbell, 1997; Campbell et al., 1996);
more family stress related specifically to difficulties raising a noncompliant child (Fischer,
1990; Mash & Johnston, 1990) as well as parental disagreements over child rearing (Jouriles et
al., 1991); and more family psychopathology, especially mood disorders, anxiety disorders,
antisocial personality and substance abuse (Biederman et al., 1992). However, there is also
some evidence suggesting that family history of psychiatric disorder (Lahey et al., 1988) and
negative parenting (Barkley et al., 1990) may be more closely related to comorbid CD/ODD
than to the presence of ADHD alone. Most studies of family correlates of ADHD and related
problems have neglected to examine comorbidity or tease apart the ADHD symptoms from co-
occurring noncompliance and aggression. Thus, family adversity, especially at the extremes,
may be more clearly associated with extreme cases of ADHD (as in the DSM-IV combined
type) or with ADHD that occurs in combination with aggressive and antisocial behavior. This
issue is far from resolved at present.

Taken together, these data indicate that at least some children with a diagnosis of ADHD
grow up in riskier environments, and often in more dysfunctional families. However, cause–
effect relations among variables are difficult to determine. On the one hand, some data suggest
that inept parenting and lack of positive engagement play a role in fueling noncompliance,
aggression, and poor self-regulation in young children with behavior problems (e.g., Anderson
et al., 1994; Campbell et al., 1996; Dumas, 1996; Gardner, 1987; 1989). On the other hand,
some studies suggest the reverse; that is, child noncompliance and lack of behavioral control
lead to increasingly more angry and controlling parental behavior (Barkley, 1990; Fischer,
1990; Lytton, 1990). From a transactional perspective, it seems logical to suppose that both
processes are going on simultaneously (Barkley, 1996; Campbell, 1990; Sameroff, 1995; Shaw
& Bell, 1993): Angry and punitive parental behavior leads to escalating noncompliance on the
part of the child, and the child's out of control and provocative behavior leads to increased
attempts at limit setting and control. Similarly, marital problems, including lack of agreement
about child rearing and family breakup may be partly a response to dealing with a very difficult
child, as well as a contributor to the child's distress (Cummings & Davies, 1994; Jouriles et al.,
1991). Finally, although full-blown disorders in parents are not likely to result from children's
problems, there is some evidence suggesting that self-reported depression and alcohol use may
increase when children are difficult to handle (Cunningham, Benness, & Siegel, 1988; Pelham
& Lang, 1993). These findings underscore the complexity of disentangling cause–effect
relations. They also point to the fact that risk factors tend to co-occur (Sameroff, Seifer,
Baldwin, & Baldwin, 1993), with children's problems, marital distress, parental disorder, and
stressful life events often going together in the same families regardless of who is the identified
patient (parent or child) or what the diagnosis is (maternal depression, paternal antisocial
personality disorder, childhood ADHD). Furthermore, most risk factors that have been associated with ADHD, with the exception of family history of childhood ADHD in parents, tend to
be nonspecific; that is, they are associated with ADHD and other childhood disorders as well,
most notably conduct and oppositional disorders (Patterson, DeBaryshe, & Ramsey, 1989;
Reid, 1993) and depression (Hammen, 1992). This may suggest that all or many of these
problems co-occur in the context of multiple genetic and psychosocial risks.

MULTIPLE PATHWAYS AND DEVELOPMENTAL COURSE

Although several possible etiological mechanisms have been discussed, there is also general agreement that ADHD results from multiple causes (e.g., Barkley, 1996; Cantwell, 1996; Hinshaw, 1994; Ross & Ross, 1982). At a minimum, most would agree that a mixture of biological–genetic, family environment, and community factors interact to lead to variations in age-of-onset of problems, symptom expression and severity, comorbid conditions, developmental course, and response to treatment. A number of issues make it difficult to be explicit about exactly what combination of factors at what point in time will lead to which outcome (Cicchetti & Cohen, 1995). Moreover, because of the marked overlap between symptoms of ADHD and symptoms of oppositional and conduct disorders, it is not always obvious, especially when the focus is on younger children, which outcome is being predicted. Thus, many studies examine behavior problems that are a combination of oppositional, defiant, aggressive, inattentive, impulsive, and high-intensity behaviors. It is likely that youngsters with an early onset of problems reflecting both impulsive and noncompliant behavior (i.e., early co-occurring signs of both ADHD and oppositional/conduct problems) are at highest risk for continuing difficulties at school age and beyond (Campbell, 1990; Campbell et al., 1996; Loeber, Green, Lahey, Christ, & Frick, 1992; Moffitt, 1990, 1993b; Richman, Stevenson, & Graham, 1982).

Based on a developmental psychopathology perspective (Cicchetti & Cohen, 1995; Sroufe & Rutter, 1984) and accumulating evidence, it is possible to speculate about the developmental course of ADHD and about different pathways that may reflect differing subtypes (or patterns of comorbidity). There is some evidence that highly arousable, irritable, and difficult to console infants are more likely to be seen as problematic in toddlerhood and the preschool period (Rothbart, Posner, & Hershey, 1995; Sanson, Oberklaid, Pedlow, & Prior, 1991; Thomas, Chess, & Birch, 1968) than more tractable and less reactive babies. One possible outcome of this high level of reactivity and negative affect, and low consolability may be ADHD, which ultimately reflects difficulties regulating attention, motor activity, and impulsivity. Data consistent with this come from the Australian Temperament Project (Kyrios & Prior, 1990; Prior, Smart, Sanson, Pedlow, & Oberklaid, 1992; Sanson, Smart, Prior, & Oberklaid, 1994; Sanson et al., 1991) in which temperamental difficultness assessed in infancy was specifically examined as a precursor of later problems in a representative sample of newborns in Australia. Although temperament did predict later ratings of problem behavior generally and ADHD-related symptoms specifically at preschool age (Sanson et al., 1991) and age 8 (Sanson et al., 1994), temperament was an especially good predictor of ratings of inattention and overactivity in the context of other child risk factors (birth complications, prematurity, male gender). Although research on specific birth complications and prematurity as predictors of later childhood behavior problems has been equivocal at best (for a review, see Campbell, 1995), it does appear that difficult and inconsolable boys with birth complications or prematurity may be at higher risk to develop ADHD and related behavior and learning problems at school age. This may be one pathway to ADHD in at least a small subset of children who eventually receive a diagnosis. Moreover, this outcome is probably more likely in the context of adverse family circumstances (Biederman et al., 1995; Campbell, 1997; Hinshaw, 1994; Kyrios & Prior, 1990; Sanson et al., 1991) in which parental psychopathology, marital and other stresses, and inconsistent or harsh parental behavior combine to exacerbate early difficulties with self-regulation. There is reason to believe that this pattern of early temperament and family environment will be associated with both impulsivity and overactivity as well as early oppositional behavior (Campbell, 1990; Patterson et al., 1989; Reid, 1993). Moreover, there is some evidence to suggest that symptoms of impulsivity and hyperactivity are identified earlier than inattention, with the age of onset of these symptoms most often in infancy or toddlerhood (Applegate et al., 1997).

The difficult infant growing up in a supportive environment may totally outgrow early problems with organization and modulation of activity and attention, or may show only some mild problems later on. The same infant growing up in a family with high rates of family pathology, disorganization, and conflict will almost certainly have difficulty learning to control impulses, focus attention, regulate arousal, and delay gratification. Maturational factors, biological–genetic predispositions, and the rearing environment interact to determine outcomes. The behavior genetic and familial findings, as well as Barkley's model of response inhibition, are consistent with this formulation in pointing to genetic–familial factors associated with both biological predispositions in the child (poor behavioral and attentional control) and less optimal family factors (inconsistent parenting, inability of the parent to help the child learn to manage negative emotions and curb impulsive responding in infancy and toddlerhood, use of punishment, modeling of poor impulse control) that interact to fuel symptom expressions in young children that are exacerbated over time as the child copes with new challenges.

Although few studies have examined early precursors of ADHD, it is generally agreed that symptoms are often first evident in toddlerhood or the preschool period (Applegate et al., 1997; Barkley, 1990). Symptoms of ADHD and of noncompliance and defiance are especially likely to co-occur in young children (Campbell, 1990). In my own longitudinal study of hard-to-manage preschool boys identified by parents and/or preschool teachers as showing early signs of overactivity and poor impulse control, most were seen as both overactive–impulsive and noncompliant–aggressive (Campbell, March, Pierce, Ewing, & Szumowski, 1991). When problem boys were compared with age-matched controls on behavior observed in the laboratory, problem boys were rated as more active during both free play and structured tasks, less focused during play, more impulsive on tasks requiring self-regulation, and less compliant during a toy cleanup procedure. In the preschool classroom, independent and blind observers rated problem boys as more disruptive with peers and more noncompliant with teachers (Campbell, Pierce, March, Ewing, & Szumowski, 1994); families with problem boys also reported more recent negative (stressful) life events and were more likely to report a family history of psychiatric disorder and use of mental health services (Campbell et al., 1991). Thus, these preschool boys appeared to be showing early signs of ADHD and co-occurring behavior problems, and their families were having more problems as well.

Problems persisted in about 30% of the early-identified problem boys at age 9. In general, continuing problems were predicted by higher rates of self-reported maternal depression and marital distress, higher rates of separation, divorce, and remarriage, more negative maternal discipline, and higher initial levels of inattention–overactivity and co-occurring aggression–noncompliance in the children (Campbell, 1990, 1994; Campbell et al., 1996). Thus, these data suggest that early-emerging symptoms of ADHD may persist when they occur with other externalizing symptoms, such as aggression and noncompliance, and in the context of multiple indicators of family adversity.

At school age, ADHD children have particular problems managing the demands of school and the peer group. Teachers note their poor school achievement and disruptive classroom behavior (Barkley, 1996; Campbell, 1994). ADHD children may have special difficulties making the transition from preschool or kindergarten to first grade, where the expectations that they follow rules, cooperate with others, remain quiet, and focus attention for long periods of time make particular demands on their capacities for behavioral control and self-regulation. In addition, children with the inattentive subtype of ADHD, as defined in

DSM-IV, may only begin to have serious difficulties when they enter first grade and must master the demands of early reading and other academic skills (e.g., Applegate et al., 1997).

Studies of the peer relations of children with ADHD indicate that they are more likely to be rejected by peers than comparison youngsters, and that in group situations, their inappropriate, provocative, and demanding behavior often leads to peer rejection early in group formation (Pelham & Bender, 1982; Whalen & Henker, 1985, 1992). For example, when entering a new group, ADHD children are more likely to call attention to themselves, to try to change the focus of group activities, or to engage in norm-violating behavior (Pelham & Bender, 1982; Whalen & Henker, 1985, 1992). Whether because of their inattention or their poor modulation of arousal and impulses, ADHD children tend to be oblivious to cues from others and they have difficulty working cooperatively with other children to reach group goals. This appears to be the case regardless of whether they are also aggressive (Hinshaw & Melnick, 1995). Thus, these difficulties in peer relations may fuel additional problems in adolescence when the ADHD child may be more likely to join a less desirable and more antisocial peer group (Hinshaw & Melnick, 1995; Patterson et al., 1989) or to become socially isolated (Hinshaw & Melnick, 1995). Moreover, recent research linking inept and inappropriate behavior in the peer group to patterns of child rearing may suggest that some of the social problems that ADHD youngsters encounter in school partly emerge from aggressive and provocative social problem-solving strategies and ways of relating to peers that were initially learned in dysfunctional families (e.g., Dodge, Pettit, Bates, & Valente, 1995; Strassberg, Dodge, Pettit, & Bates, 1994). Thus, early problems first evident in the family may become more pronounced and pervasive with development, affecting the child's functioning in family, peer, school, and community contexts.

Follow-up studies of ADHD children indicate that problems are likely to persist, and this is especially the case for ADHD children with co-occurring oppositional and aggressive behavior, living in more conflict-ridden and dysfunctional families. Biederman et al. (1996) provided data on a large clinically diagnosed sample of children followed up 4 years after initial diagnosis. A full 85% of the sample continued to meet diagnostic criteria for ADHD, and of these, over 70% also met criteria for OD or CD. Predictors of continuing ADHD included comorbid oppositional behavior, a family history of ADHD, and family conflict. Barkley and colleagues have conducted the largest and most comprehensive longitudinal study of ADHD children first diagnosed in childhood and followed up 8 years later at a mean age of 15 (Barkley et al., 1990). Consistent with the shorter-term follow-up of Biederman et al. (1996), 72% of these ADHD youngsters still met DSM-III-R diagnostic criteria for ADHD at follow-up and of these, two out of three also met DSM-III-R criteria for oppositional disorder and/or conduct disorder. Slightly higher rates of alcohol and drug use were found in the ADHD group, but they were accounted for by adolescents with co-occurring conduct problems.

In addition, Barkley and associates assessed cognitive and academic functioning. ADHD boys, especially those with comorbid conduct problems, were more likely to have been expelled or suspended from school (Barkley et al., 1990). ADHD children also performed more poorly than controls on standard measures of reading, spelling, and mathematics achievement, even with child IQ and maternal education covaried (Fischer, Barkley, Edelbrock, & Smallish, 1990). Furthermore, ADHD children did more poorly than controls on measures of sustained attention and impulsivity; observations of behavior during these tasks indicated that they remained more fidgety and off-task than controls. Younger and older ADHD adolescents showed similar patterns of differences. Thus, older adolescents with ADHD were not more likely to have outgrown these particular cognitive difficulties than younger ADHD children.

Barkley et al. (1991) also assessed mother–adolescent interaction and family climate at follow-up using observational and self-report measures. Mothers of ADHD children reported more family conflict, marital distress, stressful life events, and psychological symptoms of depression and hostility, but these were primarily accounted for by differences between the control group and those families with an ADHD and oppositional adolescent. Observations of dyadic interaction revealed similar results, with mothers of comorbid adolescents showing higher levels of negativity than mothers of controls and both members of these problem dyads communicating less. ADHD children were also more likely to be living with only one biological parent and, therefore, to have experienced separation/divorce and changes in residence more often than controls (Barkley et al., 1990). Other follow-up studies have yielded results consistent with this work in that ADHD children did not outgrow their symptoms and their cognitive and academic functioning remained impaired (Gittelman, Mannuzza, Shenker, & Bonagura, 1985; Hoy, Weiss, Minde, & Cohen, 1978; McGee, Partridge, Williams, & Silva, 1991). In addition, in the Gittelman et al. cohort, although only 40% of boys met criteria for a diagnosis of ADHD in adolescence, these boys were also more likely to show symptoms of antisocial personality disorder and higher rates of substance use.

Although these studies all suggest that symptoms persist, they also indicate that comorbidity plays a major role in predicting outcome, as does family stress and adversity. Thus, most research supports the growing consensus that especially poor outcome may be specific to children with ADHD and co-occurring conduct/oppositional disorder (Barkley, 1996; Hinshaw, 1994; Moffitt, 1990, 1993b) and that children living in more dysfunctional families are more likely to have a poor outcome. The cause–effect relations among these have not been clearly disentangled, but one possibility is that ADHD children in more dysfunctional families are more likely to develop comorbid conduct problems (e.g., Lahey et al., 1988) and that together, the more severe and pervasive symptoms and the family problems fuel more severe and continuing disorder. Among the processes implicated in this sequence, modeling of negative and aggressive behavior by angry parents, and limited monitoring and supervision (e.g., Patterson et al., 1989) are important. In addition, these rejected and poorly achieving children seem to gravitate toward more deviant peers (e.g., Patterson et al., 1989). These complex determinants also appear to reflect biological vulnerability (e.g., Biederman et al., 1992), as indexed by parental psychopathology and cognitive deficits. Moreover, these configurations of co-occurring problems within families appear to illustrate patterns of gene–environment correlation and gene–environment interaction (Plomin, 1995).

The two major studies of adult outcome in children with ADHD are consistent with this formulation and suggest different outcomes for those with and without co-occurring ODD/CD. Mannuzza and colleagues (Mannuzza, Klein, Bessler, Malloy, & Hynes, 1997; Mannuzza, Klein, Bessler, Malloy, & LaPadula, 1993) followed two cohorts of ADHD boys and demographically matched controls into early adulthood. Weiss and Hechtman (1993) followed the Montreal sample of hyperactive children and controls. Results of these follow-up studies indicated that ADHD children fared more poorly than nonpsychiatric controls in terms of educational and occupational attainment in adulthood. For example, Mannuzza et al. (1997) reported that the ADHD boys had on average 2 fewer years of education than control boys and about 25% did not finish high school (vs. 1% of controls). Additional analyses indicated that the poor educational and occupational attainment in the ADHD group could not be accounted for by either antisocial personality or lower IQ. In the Weiss and Hechtman study, ADHD adults also showed poorer job stability and employment satisfaction, as well as poorer interpersonal functioning, and they had more difficulty forming stable intimate relationships.

These studies also documented higher rates of antisocial personality disorder and other symptoms. In the Mannuzza et al. (1993) sample, there were also higher rates of substance abuse among the ADHD probands, and overall, 33% met criteria for some psychiatric diagnosis at follow-up (vs. 16% of controls). In the Weiss and Hechtman sample, 66% of hyperactives reported continuing symptoms of restlessness, impulsivity, and/or inattention that interfered with their functioning, and 23% met criteria for antisocial personality disorder in adulthood (vs. 2.4% of controls). In general, early indicators of aggression and poor family relationships were associated with poorer adult outcomes in the Weiss and Hechtman study. Thus, across numerous studies, assessing ADHD children at different ages, patterns of comorbidity and family functioning are associated with different outcomes. Children whose ADHD symptoms are not associated with long-standing aggressive and oppositional behavior, and who are not growing up in disturbed families appear to function better in adulthood, even if they are not totally problem-free.

SUMMARY AND CONCLUSIONS

There is continuing speculation about the role of neurobiological, genetic, and other family (child-rearing, modeling) influences on ADHD and its developmental course. There is also interest in the onset and developmental course of comorbid oppositional and aggressive behavior and learning problems. Delineation of the multiple determinants of ADHD and related problems may provide insights into different developmental pathways from early symptoms to later functioning and also have relevance for understanding subtypes and comorbidity. For example, a different "mix" of child factors and family factors may characterize different patterns of symptoms and comorbidities and predict different developmental pathways.

In addition, the new formulation of ADHD delineated in the DSM-IV includes two distinct subtypes of ADHD, and several recent papers suggest that they may have different etiologies, correlates, and responses to treatment (Barkley, 1997; Jensen et al., 1997). However, the subtypes also appear to overlap considerably with early-emerging oppositional and conduct disorder (impulsive–hyperactive and combined subtypes) and with learning disorders (inattentive subtype). Thus, it may be that ADHD in its current guise is superfluous. Because research on these subtypes of ADHD is just beginning to appear, firm conclusions cannot be drawn at this stage of our knowledge. However, it will be important to demonstrate that the symptoms of these ADHD subtypes occur in "pure" form, independent of comorbid oppositional and learning disorders, and that they provide more information than the comorbid diagnoses alone, once severity and pervasiveness of impairment are considered. These different subtypes, when combined with information on degree of impairment, may also suggest different pathways from early symptoms to later outcomes.

For example, some children with early signs of aggression, noncompliance, overactivity, and poor impulse control in toddlerhood may outgrow their problems. When these symptomatic behaviors occur at only a moderate level of severity in children residing in fairly well-functioning families, problems may be less likely to persist. This may be particularly the case if parents are able to provide relatively supportive and nonconfrontational parenting, while still setting age-appropriate limits (Campbell, 1997). In such cases, the problems may become less salient with development and may be seen as a transient developmental phase.

In a second instance, children may not appear different early on, but their difficulties may emerge in the preschool period or even in first grade, when demands for performance on challenging cognitive tasks become salient. These may be the children who are ultimately seen as ADHD, inattentive subtype, possibly with co-occurring learning problems. They may or may not have a family history of language or reading problems. These may be the youngsters who perform adequately in follow-up studies or show poorer academic and occupational functioning, but not symptoms of antisocial disorder or poor impulse control (e.g., Weiss & Hechtman, 1993).

The third group may be those with the impulsive–hyperactive or combined subtype, with co-occurring CD/ODD. These may be the youngsters whose problems are evident early, as reflected in difficult temperament, or those who are especially defiant, aggressive, and impulsive by toddlerhood. When these behaviors occur in the context of family dysfunction, especially when it includes parental depression, antisocial personality, or deficits in impulse control, the stage is set for parent–child conflict. Whereas some parents with these characteristics might provide "good enough" parenting for an easy toddler, this is unlikely to be the case when the toddler is difficult and demanding. Parental depression may be associated with inconsistent parental behavior or lack of adequate limit setting (Kochanska, Kuczynski, Radke-Yarrow, & Welsh, 1987); antisocial personality or parental impulsivity is likely to be associated with more inconsistent, harsh, and punitive parental behavior (e.g., Patterson et al., 1989) that escalates in the face of other stressors (e.g., Campbell et al., 1996; Snyder, 1991). Thus, the combination of parental and child difficulties begins a process whereby early child problems with poor regulation of emotion and arousal become symptomatic, in the absence of patient and supportive parenting behavior. This is consistent with several models of ODD/CD (Greenberg, Speltz, & DeKlyen, 1993; Moffitt, 1993b; Patterson et al., 1989; Reid, 1993) in which early-onset symptoms of both hyperactivity and aggression in the context of other risk factors predict more chronic and ongoing difficulties in academic and interpersonal functioning into early adulthood.

Given the considerable comorbidity between ADHD impulsive–hyperactive subtype and ODD/CD, much of what we know about ADHD children's behavior problems across contexts (family, peer group, school), family history of psychopathology, developmental course of the disorder, and adult outcome appears to refer either to the comorbid condition (i.e., ODD/CD) or to the combination of ADHD and oppositional disorder (Jensen et al., 1997). Moreover, given the relative nonspecificity of most risk factors, these may be the same children described in many studies targeting either parental pathology or child symptoms (either early aggression–noncompliance or early hyperactivity–impulsivity) and then examining the developmental course of problems.

Taken together, then, the literature reviewed and the formulation presented here suggest that children with early signs of ADHD may have different outcomes depending on the particular constellation of symptoms, their age of onset and pervasiveness, and the severity and chronicity of co-occurring risk factors (or conversely, the presence of protective factors) in the family. A developmental psychopathology perspective on ADHD and related problems seems necessary if we are to make progress in understanding the different developmental pathways that children with these symptoms follow from childhood to adulthood.

REFERENCES

American Psychiatric Association. (1980). *Diagnostic and statistical manual of mental disorders* (3rd ed.) Washington, DC: Author.

American Psychiatric Association. (1987). *Diagnostic and statistical manual of mental disorders* (3rd ed., rev.). Washington, DC: Author.

American Psychiatric Association. (1994). *Diagnostic and statistical manual of mental disorders* (4th ed.). Washington, DC: Author.

Anderson, C., Hinshaw, S., & Simmel, C. (1994). Mother–child interactions in ADHD and comparison boys: Relationships with overt and covert externalizing behavior. *Journal of Abnormal Child Psychology, 22,* 247–265.

Anderson, J. C., Williams, S., McGee, R., & Silva, P. A. (1987). DSM-III disorders in preadolescent children. *Archives of General Psychiatry, 44,* 69–76.

Angold, A. & Costello, E. J. (1993). Depressive co-morbidity in children and adolescents: Empirical, theoretical, and methodological issues. *American Journal of Psychiatry, 150,* 1779–1791.

Applegate, B., Lahey, B. B., Hart, E. L., et al. (1997). Validity of the age-of-onset criterion for ADHD: A report from the DSM-IV field trials. *Journal of the American Academy of Child and Adolescent Psychiatry, 36,* 1211–1221.

Arnold, L. E. (1996). Sex differences in ADHD: Conference summary. *Journal of Abnormal Child Psychology, 24,* 555–570.

August, G., & Garfinkel, B. (1993). The nosology of attention-deficit hyperactivity disorder. *Journal of the American Academy of Child and Adolescent Psychiatry, 32,* 155–165.

August, G., Realmuto, G. M., MacDonald, A. W., Nugent, S. M., & Crosby, R. (1996). Prevalence of ADHD and comorbid disorders among elementary school children screened for disruptive behavior. *Journal of Abnormal Child Psychology, 24,* 571–596.

Barkley, R. A. (1990). *Attention-deficit hyperactivity disorder: A handbook for diagnosis and treatment.* New York: Guilford Press.

Barkley, R. A. (1996). Attention-deficit/hyperactivity disorder. In E. Mash & R. A. Barkley (Eds.), *Child psychopathology* (pp. 63–112). New York: Guilford Press.

Barkley, R. A. (1997). Behavioral inhibition, sustained attention, and executive functions: Constructing a unifying theory of ADHD. *Psychological Bulletin, 121,* 65–94.

Barkley, R. A., Fischer, M., Edelbrock, C. S., & Smallish, L. (1990). Adolescent outcome of hyperactive children diagnosed by research criteria: I. An 8 year prospective follow-up study. *Journal of the American Academy of Child and Adolescent Psychiatry, 29,* 546–557.

Barkley, R. A., Fischer, M., Edelbrock, C. S., & Smallish, L. (1991). Adolescent outcome of hyperactive children diagnosed by research criteria: III. Mother–child interaction, family conflict, and maternal psychopathology. *Journal of Child Psychology and Psychiatry, 32,* 233–256.

Barkley, R. A., Grodzinsky, G., & DuPaul, G. J. (1992). Frontal lobe functions in ADD with and without hyperactivity: A review and research report. *Journal of Abnormal Child Psychology, 20,* 163–188.

Biederman, J., Faraone, S., Keenan, K., et al. (1992). Further evidence for family–genetic risk factors in ADHD: Patterns of co-morbidity in probands and relatives in psychiatrically and pediatrically referred samples. *Archives of General Psychiatry, 49,* 728–738.

Biederman, J., Faraone, S., Milberger, S., et al. (1996). Predictors of persistence and remission of ADHD into adolescence: Results from a four-year prospective follow-up. *Journal of the American Academy of Child and Adolescent Psychiatry, 35,* 343–351.

Biederman, J., Milberger, S., & Faraone, S. (1995). Family–environment risk factors for attention-deficit hyperactivity disorder: A test of Rutter's indicators of adversity. *Archives of General Psychiatry, 52,* 464–470.

Bird, H. (1996). Epidemiology of childhood disorders in a cross-cultural context. *Journal of Child Psychology and Psychiatry, 37,* 35–50.

Boyle, M., Offord, D., Racine, Y., Szatmari, P., Fleming, J. E., & Sanford, M. (1996). Identifying thresholds for classifying childhood psychiatric disorder. *Journal of the American Academy of Child and Adolescent Psychiatry, 35,* 1440–1448.

Campbell, S. B. (1990). *Behavior problems in preschool children: Clinical and developmental issues.* New York: Guilford Press.

Campbell, S. B. (1994). Hard-to-manage preschool boys: Externalizing behavior, social competence, and family context at two-year follow-up. *Journal of Abnormal Child Psychology, 22,* 147–166.

Campbell, S. B. (1995). Behavior problems in preschool children: A review of recent research. *Journal of Child Psychology and Psychiatry, 36,* 113–149.

Campbell, S. B. (1997). Behavior problems in preschool children: Developmental and family issues. In T. H. Ollendick & R. Prinz (Eds.), *Advances in clinical child psychology, 19* (pp. 1–26). New York: Plenum Press.

Campbell, S. B., March, C. L., Pierce, E. W., Ewing, L. J., & Szumowski, E. K. (1991). Hard-to-manage preschool boys: Family context and the stability of externalizing behavior. *Journal of Abnormal Child Psychology, 19,* 301–318.

Campbell, S. B., Pierce, E. W., March, C. L., Ewing, L.J., & Szumowski, E. K. (1994). Hard-to-manage preschool boys: Symptomatic behavior across contexts and time. *Child Development, 65,* 836–851.

Campbell, S. B., Pierce, E. W., Moore, G., Marakovitz, S., & Newby, K. (1996). Boys' externalizing problems at elementary school age: Pathways from early behavior problems, maternal control, and family stress. *Development and Psychopathology, 8,* 701–720.

Campbell, S. B., & Werry, J. S. (1986). Attention deficit disorder (hyperactivity). In H. C. Quay & J. S. Werry (Eds.), *Psychopathological disorders of childhood* (3rd ed., pp. 111–155). New York: Wiley.

Cantwell, D. (1996). ADHD: A review of the past 10 years. *Journal of the American Academy of Child and Adolescent Psychiatry, 35,* 978–987.

Caron, C., & Rutter, M. (1991). Co-morbidity in child psychopathology: Concepts, issues, and research strategies. *Journal of Child Psychology and Psychiatry, 32,* 1063–1080.

Cicchetti, D., & Cohen, D. (1995). Perspectives in developmental psychopathology. In D. Cicchetti & D. Cohen (Eds.), *Developmental psychopathology: Vol. I. Theory and methods* (pp. 3–20). New York: Wiley.

Clements, S. D., & Peters, J. (1962). Minimal brain dysfunctions in the school age child. *Archives of General Psychiatry, 6,* 185–197.

Cohen, P., Cohen, J., & Brook, J. (1993). An epidemiological study of disorders in late childhood and adolescence: II. Persistence of disorders. *Journal of Child Psychology and Psychiatry, 34,* 869–878.

Cohen, P., Cohen, J., Kasen, S., et al. (1993). An epidemiological study of disorders in late childhood and adolescence: I. Age- and gender-specific prevalence. *Journal of Child Psychology and Psychiatry, 34,* 851–868.

Cunningham, C. E., Benness, B. B., & Siegel, L. S. (1988). Family functioning, time allocation, and parental depression in families of normal and ADHD children. *Journal of Clinical Child Psychology, 17,* 169–177.

Davies, P., & Cummings. E. M. (1994). Marital conflict and child adjustment: An emotional security hypothesis. *Psychological Bulletin, 116,* 387–411.

Dodge, K. A., Pettit, G. S., Bates, J. E., & Valente, E. (1995). Social information processing patterns partially mediate the effect of early physical abuse on later conduct problems. *Journal of Abnormal Psychology, 104,* 632–643.

Douglas, V. I. (1972). Stop, look, and listen: The problem of sustained attention and impulse control in hyperactive and normal children. *Canadian Journal of Behavioural Science, 4,* 259–282.

Douglas, V. I. (1983). Attention and cognitive problems. In M. Rutter (Ed.), *Developmental neuropsychiatry* (pp. 280–329). New York: Guilford Press.

Douglas, V. I., & Peters. K. G. (1978). Toward a clearer definition of the attentional deficit in hyperactive children. In G. A. Hale & M. Lewis (Eds.), *Attention and the development of cognitive skills* (pp. 173–248). New York: Plenum Press.

Dumas, J. E. (1996). Why was this child referred? Interactional correlates of referral status in families of children with disruptive behavior problems. *Journal of Clinical Child Psychology, 25,* 105–115.

Faraone, S. V., Biederman, J., Lehman, B. K., et al. (1993). Intellectual performance and school failure in children with attention deficit hyperactivity disorder and in their siblings. *Journal of Abnormal Psychology, 102,* 616–623.

Faraone, S. V., Biederman, J., Mennin, D., Gershon, J., & Tsuang, M. T. (1996). A prospective four-year follow-up study if children at risk for ADHD: Psychiatric, neuropsychological, and psychosocial outcome. *Journal of the American Academy of Child and Adolescent Psychiatry, 35,* 1449–1459.

Fischer, M. (1990). Parenting stress and the child with attention deficit hyperactivity disorder. *Journal of Clinical Child Psychology, 19,* 337–346.

Fischer, M. E., Barkley, R. A., Edelbrock, C. S., & Smallish, L. (1990). Adolescent outcome of hyperactive children diagnosed by research criteria: II. Academic, attentional, and neuropsychological status. *Journal of Consulting and Clinical Psychology, 58,* 580–588.

Frankel, K. A., & Bates, J. E. (1990). Mother-toddler problem solving: Antecedents in attachment, home behavior, and temperament. *Child Development, 60,* 810–819.

Gardner, F. E. (1987). Positive interaction between mothers and conduct-problem children: Is there training for harmony as well as fighting? *Journal of Abnormal Child Psychology, 15,* 283–293.

Gardner, F. E. (1989). Inconsistent parenting: Is there evidence for a link with children's conduct problems? *Journal of Abnormal Child Psychology, 17,* 223–233.

Gaub, M., & Carlson, C. L. (1997a). Gender differences in ADHD: A meta-analysis and critical review. *Journal of the American Academy of Child and Adolescent Psychiatry, 36,* 1036–1045.

Gaub, M., & Carlson, C. L. (1997b). Behavioral characteristics of DSM-IV ADHD subtypes in a school-based population. *Journal of Abnormal Psychology, 25,* 103–111.

Gittelman, R., Mannuzza, S., Shenker, R., & Bonagura, N. (1985). Hyperactive boys almost grown up: I. Psychiatric status. *Archives of General Psychiatry, 42,* 937–947.

Goodman, R., & Stevenson, J. (1989). A twin study of hyperactivity: II. The aetiological role of genes, family relationships and perinatal adversity. *Journal of Child Psychology and Psychiatry, 30,* 691–709.

Greenberg, M. T., Speltz, M. L., & DeKlyen, M. (1993). The role of attachment in the early development of disruptive behavior problems. *Development and Psychopathology, 5,* 191–213.

Hammen, C. (1992). Cognitive, life stress, and interpersonal approaches to a developmental psychopathology model of depression. *Development and Psychopathology, 4,* 189–206.

Heller, T. L., Baker, B. L., Henker, B., & Hinshaw, S. P. (1996). Externalizing behavior and cognitive functioning from preschool to first grade: Stability and predictors. *Journal of Clinical Child Psychology, 25*, 376–387.

Hinshaw, S. P. (1987). On the distinction between attentional deficits/hyperactivity and conduct problems/aggression in child psychopathology. *Psychological Bulletin, 101*, 443–463.

Hinshaw, S. P. (1992). Externalizing behavior problems and academic underachievement in children and adolescents: Causal relationships and underlying mechanisms. *Psychological Bulletin, 111*, 127–155.

Hinshaw, S. P. (1994). *Attention deficits and hyperactivity in children.* Thousand Oaks, CA: Sage.

Hinshaw, S., Lahey, B. B., & Hart, E. (1993). Issues of taxonomy and co-morbidity in the development of conduct disorder. *Development and Psychopathology, 5*, 31–50.

Hinshaw, S. P., & Melnick, S. (1995). Peer relationships in boys with attention-deficit hyperactivity disorder with and without co-morbid aggression. *Development and Psychopathology, 7*, 627–647.

Hoy, E., Weiss, G., Minde, K. K., & Cohen, N. J. (1978). The hyperactive child at adolescence: Cognitive, emotional, and social functioning. *Journal of Abnormal Child Psychology, 6*, 311–324.

Iaboni, F., Douglas, V. I., & Baker, A. G. (1995). Effects of reward and response costs on inhibition in ADHD children. *Journal of Abnormal Psychology, 104*, 232–240.

Jacobvitz, D., & Sroufe, L. A. (1987). The early caregiver–child relationship and attention deficit disorder with hyperactivity in kindergarten. *Child Development, 58*, 1488–1495.

Jensen, P. S., Martin, D., & Cantwell, D. P. (1997). Comorbidity in ADHD: Implications for research, practice, and DSM-V. *Journal of the American Academy of Child and Adolescent Psychiatry, 36*, 1065–1079.

Jouriles, E. N., Murphy, C. M., Farris, A. M., Smith, D. A., Richters, J. E., & Waters, E. (1991). Marital adjustment, parental disagreements about child rearing, and behavior problems in boys: Increasing the specificity of the marital assessment. *Child Development, 62*, 1424–1433.

Kochanska, G., Kuczynski, L., Radke-Yarrow, M., & Welsh, J. (1987). Resolution of control episodes between well and affectively ill mothers and their young child. *Journal of Abnormal Child Psychology, 15*, 441–456.

Kyrios, M., & Prior, M. (1990). Temperament, stress, and family factors in behavioural adjustment of 3–5-year-old children. *International Journal of Behavioral Development, 13*, 67–93.

Lahey, B. B., Applegate, B., McBurnett, K., et al. (1994). DSM-IV field trials for attention deficit hyperactivity disorder in children and adolescents. *American Journal of Psychiatry, 151*, 1673–1685.

Lahey, B. B., Loeber, R., Stouthamer-Loeber, M., et al. (1990). Comparison of DSM-III and DSM-III-R diagnoses for prepubertal children: Changes in prevalence and validity. *Journal of the American Academy of Child and Adolescent Psychiatry, 29*, 620–626.

Lahey, B. B., Piacentini, J. C., McBurnett, K., Stone, P., Hartdagen, S., & Hynd, G. (1988). Psychopathology in the parents of children with conduct disorder and hyperactivity. *Journal of the American Academy of Child and Adolescent Psychiatry, 27*, 163–170.

Laufer, M., Denhoff, E., & Solomons, G. (1957). Hyperkinetic impulse disorder in children's behavior problems. *Psychosomatic Medicine, 19*, 38–49.

Lee, C. L., & Bates, J. E. (1985). Mother–child interaction at age two years and perceived difficult temperament. *Child Development, 56*, 1314–1325.

Levy, F., Hay, D., McStephen, M., Wood, C., & Waldman, I. (1997). Attention-deficit hyperactivity disorder: A category or a continuum? Genetic analysis of a large-scale twin study. *Journal of the American Academy of Child and Adolescent Psychiatry, 36*, 737–744.

Loeber, R., Green, S. M., Lahey, B. B., Christ, M. A., & Frick, P. J. (1992). Developmental sequences in the age of onset of disruptive child behaviors. *Journal of Child and Family Studies, 1*, 21–41.

Lytton, H. (1990). Parent and child effects in boys' conduct disorder: A reinterpretation. *Developmental Psychology, 26*, 683–697.

Mannuzza, S., Klein, R. G., Bessler, A., Malloy, P., & Hynes, M. E. (1997). Educational and occupational outcome of hyperactive boys grown up. *Journal of the American Academy of Child and Adolescent Psychiatry, 36*, 1222–1227.

Mannuzza, S., Klein, R. G., Bessler, A., Malloy, P., & LaPadula, M. (1993). Adult outcome of hyperactive boys: Educational achievement, occupational rank, and psychiatric status. *Archives of General Psychiatry, 50*, 565–576.

Mash, E. J., & Johnston, C. (1990). Determinants of parenting stress: Illustrations from families of hyperactive and families of physically abused children. *Journal of Clinical Child Psychology, 19*, 313–328.

McGee, R., Partridge, F., Williams, S., & Silva, P. A. (1991). A twelve year follow-up of preschool hyperactive children. *Journal of the American Academy of Child and Adolescent Psychiatry, 30*, 224–232.

Milich, R., & Dodge, K. A. (1984). Social information processing in child psychiatric populations. *Journal of Abnormal Child Psychology, 12*, 471–489.

Moffitt, T. E. (1990). Juvenile delinquency and attention deficit disorder: Boys' developmental trajectories from age 3 to 15. *Child Development, 61,* 893–910.

Moffitt, T. E. (1993a). The neuropsychology of conduct disorder. *Development and Psychopathology, 5,* 135–152.

Moffitt, T. E. (1993b). "Adolescent-limited" and "life-course-persistent" antisocial behavior: A developmental taxonomy. *Psychological Review, 100,* 674–701.

Morgan, A. E., Hynd, G. W., Riccio, C., & Hall, J. (1996). Validity of DSM-IV ADHD predominantly inattentive and combined types: Relationship to previous DSM diagnoses/subtype differences. *Journal of the American Academy of Child and Adolescent Psychiatry, 35,* 325–333.

Offord, D., et al. (1996). Integrating assessment data from multiple informants. *Journal of the American Academy of Child and Adolescent Psychiatry, 35,* 1078–1085.

Patterson, G., DeBaryshe, B., & Ramsey, E. (1989). A developmental perspective on antisocial behavior. *American Psychologist, 44,* 329–335.

Pelham, W., & Bender, M. E. (1982). Peer relations in hyperactive children: Description and treatment. In K. Gadow & I. Bialer (Eds.), *Advances in learning and behavioral disabilities* (Vol. 1, pp. 365–436). Greenwich, CT: JAI Press.

Pelham, W. E., & Lang, A. R. (1993). Parental alcohol consumption and deviant child behavior: Laboratory studies of reciprocal effects. *Clinical Psychology Review, 13,* 763–784.

Pennington, B., & Ozonoff, S. (1996). Executive functions and developmental psychopathology. *Journal of Child Psychology and Psychiatry, 37,* 51–88.

Pliszka, S. R., McCracken, J. T., & Maas, J. W. (1997). Catecholamines in attention-deficit hyperactivity disorder: Current perspectives. *Journal of the American Academy of Child and Adolescent Psychiatry, 35,* 264–272.

Plomin, R. (1995). Genetics and children's experiences in the family. *Journal of Child Psychology and Psychiatry, 36,* 33–68.

Prior, M., Smart, D., Sanson, A., Pedlow, R., & Oberklaid, F. (1992). Transient versus stable behavior problems in a normative sample: Infancy to school age. *Journal of Pediatric Psychology, 17,* 423–443.

Quay, H. (1988). Attention deficit disorder and the behavioral inhibition system: The relevance of the neuropsychological theory of Jeffrey A. Gray. In L. Bloomingdale & J. Sergeant (Eds.), *Attention deficit disorder: Criteria, cognition, and intervention* (pp. 117–126). New York: Pergamon Press.

Reid, J. (1993). Prevention of conduct disorder before and after school entry: Relating interventions to developmental findings. *Development and Psychopathology, 5,* 243–262.

Richman, N., Stevenson, J., & Graham, P. (1982). *Preschool to school: A behavioural study.* London: Academic Press.

Ross, D. M., & Ross, S. A. (1982). *Hyperactivity: Research, theory, and action.* New York: Wiley.

Rothbart, M. K., Posner, M. I., & Hershey, K. L. (1995). Temperament, attention, and developmental psychopathology. In D. Cicchetti & D. Cohen (Eds.), *Developmental psychopathology: Vol. I. Theory and methods* (pp. 315–339). New York: Wiley.

Sameroff, A. (1995). General systems theories and developmental psychopathology. In D. Cicchetti & D. Cohen (Eds.), *Developmental psychopathology: Vol. I. Theory and methods* (pp. 659–695). New York: Wiley.

Sameroff, A. J., Seifer, R., Baldwin, A., & Baldwin, C. (1993). Stability of intelligence from preschool to adolescence: The influence of social and family risk factors. *Child Development, 64,* 80–97.

Sanson, A., Oberklaid, F., Pedlow, R., & Prior, M. (1991). Risk indicators: Assessment of infancy predictors of preschool behavioural maladjustment. *Journal of Child Psychology and Psychiatry, 32,* 609–626.

Sanson, A., Smart, D., Prior, M., & Oberklaid, F. (1993). Precursors of hyperactivity and aggression. *Journal of the American Academy of Child and Adolescent Psychiatry, 32,* 1207–1216.

Schachar, R. (1986). Hyperkinetic syndrome: Historical development of the concept. In E. Taylor (Ed.), *The overactive child* (pp. 19–40). Philadelphia: Lippincott.

Seidel, W., & Joschko, M. (1990). Evidence of difficulties in sustained attention in children with ADHD. *Journal of Abnormal Child Psychology, 18,* 217–229.

Shaffer, D., Fisher, P., Dulcan, M., et al. (1996). The NIMH Diagnostic Interview Schedule for Children Version 2.3 (DISC-2.3): Description, acceptability, prevalence rates, and performance in the MECA study. *Journal of the American Academy of Child and Adolescent Psychiatry, 35,* 865–877.

Shaw, D. S., & Bell, R. Q. (1993). Developmental theories of parental contributors to antisocial behavior. *Journal of Abnormal Child Psychology, 21,* 493–518.

Sherman, D. K., Iacono, W. G., & McCue, M. K. (1997). Attention-deficit hyperactivity disorder dimensions: A twin study of inattention and impulsivity–hyperactivity. *Journal of the American Academy of Child and Adolescent Psychiatry, 36,* 745–753.

Snyder, J. (1991). Discipline as a mediator of the impact of maternal stress and mood on child conduct problems. *Development and Psychopathology, 3,* 263–276.

Sroufe, L. A., & Rutter, M. (1984). The domain of developmental psychopathology. *Child Development, 55,* 17–29.

Strassberg, Z., Dodge, K., Pettit, G., & Bates, J. (1994). Spanking in the home and children's subsequent aggression toward kindergarten peers. *Development and Psychopathology, 6*, 445–462.

Szatmari, P., Offord, D. R., & Boyle, M. H. (1989). Ontario Child Health Study: Prevalence of attention deficit disorder with hyperactivity. *Journal of Child Psychology and Psychiatry, 30*, 219–230.

Tannock, R., Purvis, K. L., & Schachar, R. J. (1993). Narrative abilities in children with ADHD and normal peers. *Journal of Abnormal Child Psychology, 21*, 103–118.

Thomas, A., Chess, S., & Birch, H.G. (1968). *Temperament and behavior disorders in children.* New York: New York University Press.

Weiss, G., & Hechtman, L. (1993). *Hyperactive children grown up.* New York: Guilford Press.

Whalen, C. K., & Henker, B. (1985). The social worlds of hyperactive (ADHD) children. *Clinical Psychology Review, 5*, 447–478.

Whalen, C. K., & Henker, B. (1992). The social profile of attention-deficit hyperactivity disorder: Five fundamental facts. In G. Weiss (Ed.), *Child and adolescent psychiatric clinics of North America: Attention-deficit hyperactivity disorder* (pp. 395–410). Philadelphia: Lippincott.

Wolraich, M. L., Hannah, J. N., Pinnock, T. Y., Baumgaertel, A., & Brown, J. (1996). Comparison of diagnostic criteria for ADHD in a county-wide sample. *Journal of the American Academy of Child and Adolescent Psychiatry, 35*, 319–324.

Zahn-Waxler, C., Schmitz, S., Fulker, D., Robinson, J., & Emde, R. (1996). Behavior problems in 5-year-old monozygotic and dizygotic twins: Genetic and environmental influences, patterns of regulation, and internalization of control. *Development and Psychopathology, 8*, 103–122.

Zametkin, A. J., Liebenauer, L. L., Fitzgerald, G. A., et al. (1993). Brain metabolism in teenagers with attention-deficit hyperactivity disorder. *Archives of General Psychiatry, 50*, 333–340.

Zametkin, A. J., & Rapoport, J. L. (1986). The pathophysiology of attention deficit disorder with hyperactivity. In B. B. Lahey & A. E. Kazdin (Eds.), *Advances in clinical child psychology* (Vol. 9, pp. 177–216). New York: Plenum.

Zametkin, A. J., & Rapoport, J. L. (1987). Neurobiology of attention deficit disorder with hyperactivity: Where have we come in 50 years? *Journal of the American Academy of Child and Adolescent Psychiatry, 26*, 676–686.

22

The Natural History and Developmental Functions of Aggression

Robert B. Cairns and Beverly D. Cairns

Stories of antiquity indicate that aggression and violence have deep historical roots in human nature, or at least in the nature of human storytelling. The *Odyssey* and the *Iliad* are laced with heavy doses of bloody violence, hate, jealousy, and retribution. But popular fascination with themes of aggression and violence are not vestigial if the subject matter of motion pictures of the 1990s are any indication. And beyond fiction and fantasy, virtually all significant military and political leaders in modern history—from George Washington and Franklin D. Roosevelt to Napoleon Bonaparte and Adolf Hitler—have achieved greatness (or infamy) partly because of their willingness to direct others into war, death, and destruction.[1] Accordingly, there may be an element of doublespeak in viewing aggression and violence as "inhuman." The historical record indicates that aggression is thoroughly human and often romanticized. It has even been seen as banal (Arendt, 1963).

Yet aggression is rarely admired or encouraged in everyday interchanges. Depending upon context and circumstance, aggression may be cause for arrest, dismissal, separation, expulsion, or litigation. The low societal tolerance for interpersonal aggression is reflected in its modest frequency of occurrence in normal interactions and its sharp diminution with age. From naturalistic observations of children, it has been estimated that about 50% of peer-initiated contacts in 1-year-olds are "negative" (Holmberg, 1980), with the proportion of the negative peer interactions diminishing to 3–6% by the age of 10 years (Cairns, 1979; Cairns & Cairns, 1994; Patterson, 1982). Aggressive acts occur even less frequently among adults. To be

[1]There are at least two important exceptions in the twentieth century to the might-makes-fame generalization, namely, Mahatma Gandhi and Martin Luther King. Both were assassinated.

Robert B. Cairns • Late of the Department of Psychology, University of North Carolina at Chapel Hill, Chapel Hill, North Carolina 27514. **Beverly D. Cairns** • Department of Psychology, University of North Carolina at Chapel Hill, Chapel Hill, North Carolina 25714.

Handbook of Developmental Psychopathology, Second Edition, edited by Arnold J. Sameroff, Michael Lewis, and Suzanne M. Miller. Kluwer Academic / Plenum Publishers, New York, 2000.

sure, problems of definition and operational measurement exist when one aspires to compile and validate such statistics. To use a single variable—aggression—is parsimonious and appeals to common sense and understanding. But the term may be too economical for scientific precision, since it may encompass diverse and developmentally independent phenomena (Sears, Whiting, Nowliss, & Sears, 1953). One and the same construct is used to refer to acts that are reviled in interpersonal exchanges but seen as heroic in literature and history.

Efforts to establish a general definition of aggression have been likened to "taking a stroll through a semantic jungle" (Bandura, 1973). Consider, for example, the definition of aggression as "unprovoked actions that are intended to produce harm or injury." Embedded in that general definition—in scientific use in the twentieth century; in common English use since the seventeenth century and derived directly from the Latin *aggressio*—are a number of pitfalls for operational scientific measures. These pitfalls involve the following characteristics:

- *Nondevelopmental.* The construct of aggression categorizes into one bin the negative acts of toddlers in grabbing another 2-year-old's chair, fights on the schoolyard between 9-year olds, the brutal attacks of teenage gangs, and international atrocities of "ethnic cleansing" by armed troops. That is a lot of developmental ground for a single construct to cover.
- *Nonsocial.* Since aggression refers to acts of individuals toward other persons, it is an inherently social construct. Yet common language and scientific definitions uniformly point to individualistic acts, motives, and responsibility.
- *Attribution of intentionality.* The definition implies *motivation* and/or *intention* to create injury, yet the establishment of intentionality has been as elusive for the discipline as it has been for courts of law and international tribunals.
- *Overinclusion.* The definition *inclusive*, in that it encompasses qualitatively and quantitatively distinct behaviors over contexts, gender, and ages, implies monothetic generalization, where commonality in function and development is assumed because of similarity in outcome (i.e., harm and injury). This problem is closely linked to the nondevelopmental nature of the construct.
- *Evaluative.* The definition is evaluative (i.e., "unprovoked" actions). Ambiguity arises when it is unclear who is to make the evaluative judgment, since in the eyes of the actor, virtually all hurtful acts are provoked. Along with this judgmental ambiguity, there is a pervasive tendency for investigators and clinicians to view "aggression" as an index of individual or societal psychopathology.

Bandura and Walters (1963) propose that identification of "aggressive" acts reflect social judgments on the part of persons who make the identification. The social judgment involves a complex weighting of contextual, developmental, and interactional norms, along with evaluations of whether there is a just cause for the actions and their intensity. Despite the complexity of the judgmental process and the opportunities for error, empirical studies indicate that such judgments can usually be made rapidly and reliably across independent observers (Cairns & Lewis, 1962; Radke-Yarrow & Zahn-Waxler, 1979). The apparent ease of classification belies the complexity of the judgmental processes, including the ability of observers to take into account the current context and history of relationship, to assess the motivation of the actors, and to judge whether the nature and intensity of acts are justified by antecedents. While recognition of the role of social consensus facilitates measurement, it does not address the vexing conceptual issues surrounding the use of the construct.

That task is a central concern of this chapter. To adumbrate one of our conclusions, the data now available seriously challenge the assumption that aggression is a unitary and psychopathological disposition. The nondevelopmental, unitary definition has handicapped the scientific analysis of phenomena it purports to clarify, obscuring important distinctions and providing answers when questions are required. In contrast, a functional, developmental analysis of aggressive patterns serves to clarify the interactional principles that give rise to, maintain, and change aggressive behaviors across time and contexts. This framework presupposes a new perspective on establishment, prevention, and intergenerational transmission.

TAKING STOCK

The slim volume *Frustration and Aggression* (Dollard, Doob, Miller, Mowrer, & Sears, 1939) was a landmark publication that transformed the scientific study of aggression. This book by an interdisciplinary group of investigators at Yale University appeared on the eve of World War II. It appeared at the right time and in the right place, and it gained immediate attention and broad influence that extended over much of the rest of the century. Although the basic hypothesis of the volume that "aggression is always a consequence of frustration" (p. 27) was soon amended by the authors themselves (see Miller, 1941), the new social learning framework that helped justify the study of aggressive phenomena was itself enthusiastically endorsed. The original model of social learning theory involved the melding of psychoanalytic propositions and Hullian learning assumptions to account for meaningful social adaptations.

In the second half of the twentieth century, empirical studies of aggression and aggressive phenomena have expanded enormously in number, breadth, and complexity. The story of the transformation of the social learning model and its derivatives is best told in the writings of its primary contributors, including the work of Albert Bandura and Richard Walters (Bandura, 1973, 1977; Bandura & Walters, 1959, 1963), Gerald Patterson (1982), Seymour Feshbach (1970), and Dan Olweus (1979, 1994). Beyond the theoretical contributions, there have been a large number of empirical studies, with thorough literature reviews appearing periodically in successive editions of the *Handbook of Child Psychology* (e.g., Coie & Dodge, 1998; Feshbach, 1970; Parke & Slaby, 1983), the *Annual Review of Psychology*, and the *Handbook of Antisocial Behavior* (Stoff, Breiling, & Maser, 1997). Although the social learning model gained hegemony, competing statements have noted sources of control that were originally muted or ignored in the model. These include the role of genetics (Rutter, 1996), biosocial and neurobiological factors (Stoff & Cairns, 1996), evolution (Lorenz, 1966; Maynard Smith, 1974), empathy and emotion (Zahn-Waxler, Cummings, & Iannotti, 1986), and cognition and mass media (Eron, Huesmann, Lefkowitz, & Walder, 1972).

Taken together, these contributions have underscored the shortcomings of a perspective that was built primarily on learning assumptions, and the view that aggressive acts can be accounted for as primarily learned phenomena. The evidence also indicated that the substitution of other single factors for learning as a primary explanation was similarly unsatisfactory. This held regardless of the single factor or single system proposed, whether it was essentially genetic, neurobiological, endocrinological, cognitive, a social network process, or cultural. It became recognized that aggressive phenomena are multidetermined and that each of these factors plays a role in their establishment, maintenance, and change. As a consequence, it became possible to find statistical support for any sane hypothesis, even when apparently contradictory. To make a meaningful progress, one must know how these factors fit together to produce aggressive actions, not how they can be teased apart. This task presupposes an integrated or holistic analysis of the phenomena in the context where they occur, with attention given to the magnitude of the effects rather than merely whether the effects were statistically significant. This recognition brought with it the new problem of how to build a coherent model that permitted the integration of these influences. Such a model should not only yield a more adequate fit to extant data, but it should also generate fresh research designs and new insights about ways to prevent and modify aggressive phenomena and their sequelae.

IS AGGRESSION A UNITARY CONCEPT?

Issues of development and regulation are directly linked to the problem of how "aggression" may be conceptualized. Two different approaches have been followed in historical conceptualizations of aggressive behavior that have radically different consequences for how the phenomenon can be studied and understood. One approach, consistent with ordinary language and with common sense, views aggression as a unitary structure, depicting the individual's propensity to harm or injure others. It is seen as a stable and enduring feature of personality that is established early in life. A second approach views aggressive patterns in a pluralistic framework, with the assumption that the term *aggression* has been applied to diverse phenomena, some of which have only the faintest degree of centrality. Examination of the concrete phenomena is assumed to yield information about circumstances that lead to the establishment of specific patterns, their maintenance, and their prevention.

Aggression and Reification

In modern accounts of personality and social behavior, constructs of social behavior—such as aggression and attachment—tend to be viewed as latent structures or traits, with specifiable origins, functions, and goals. For example, the related construct of a general "antisocial behavior syndrome" (ABS) has been proposed to account for both individual differences in irritability and aggressive behavior among young children and violence and delinquency in adolescents (Moffitt, 1993; Stoff, et al., 1997). Across developmental stages and over contexts, it is assumed that the forms of antisocial behavior may shift, but the underlying syndrome and its functions and goals remain virtually unchanged. The view that there are latent stable personality structures with definable functions and goals that remain unmodified despite changing circumstances and developmental status has had an enormous influence on methods in the social and behavioral sciences. The impact extends from the use of research measures or data transformations that eliminate the effects of age and context at the first stage of assessment, to the widespread adoption of statistical analyses designed to reveal the latent structures. In this regard, advances in multivariate statistical models—such as LISREL—have helped fuel the theoretical view that there are hidden but stable underlying "latent variables" of personality and behavior. Accordingly, "latent variable analyses" refer to statistical procedures that may be employed to identify the structures underlying, say, "aggression," and "attachment."

There is only a small step from statistical labeling to the theoretical conceptualization of enduring, fixed structures of personality. What is modified over time and context are the various expressions promoted by changes in developmental stages or by gender status, not by changes in the latent variable or its functions. The reified view of aggression as a unitary disposition has been highly influential in accounts of criminal and antisocial behaviors. It has been presumed that aggression is an organized system or personality structure that is established by early experiences in the home and/or biological–genetic factors. As a unitary system/structure, it potentially provides an economical summary for a large number of observations, measures, and outcomes. That is no small gain given the complexity of social behavior and how it develops. In addition, the proposal that aggression becomes organized by events and circumstances early in life is consistent with the dominant model of personality development.

The unitary model of aggression has historical precedent. From the 1940s through the 1960s, a parallel account of aggression was offered. It was called a secondary drive that was both unitary and consolidated by early experiences (for reviews, see Sears et al., 1953; Cairns, 1983). Even further back, McDougall's (1908) concept of "pugnacity instinct" was, on formal and operational grounds, virtually parallel to the current proposal of aggression as a "latent variable." A main difference between McDougall's formulation and later ones was the assumption that the basic energy source was instinctual and genetic, as opposed to learning theory proposals on the early development of an acquired drive. Recent proposals have recycled history by focusing on the genetic determinants of criminal and aggressive behavior (Rutter, 1996).

Despite obvious gains in simplicity and parsimony of explanation, certain empirical problems have arisen for the unitary concept of aggression. First, the use of a single term invites the assumption that a single organizing source may account for the multiple manifestations of negative, antisocial, alienating, aggressive, and violent behaviors over time. While there are reasonable commonalties within subsets of these behaviors under certain conditions (e.g., when age is held constant), there is only modest predictability over the life course from measures of infancy and early childhood to adulthood. Second, the model biases research toward the early developmental study of factors that give rise to the construct and how the construct remains stable over time. However, a large body of information from animal and human investigations indicates that potent social and biological factors arise in adolescence that directly contribute to violence. Failure to attend to these factors can preclude attention to some of the more powerful immediate constraints and controls on violent behaviors. Third, the unitary conceptualization promotes the use of measures and statistical transformations that get rid of age-, gender-, or context-linked changes at the first stage of assessment, so as to better focus on underlying differences in aggression. It goes hand in hand with the assumption that, once established, aggression represents enduring, unmodifiable motives and "essences" of the individual (see also Lewis, 1997; Kagan, 1998).

Multiple Phenomena and Multiple Constructs

In a remarkable book entitled *The Dynamics of Behavior Development*, Zing-Yang Kuo argues that the unitary concept of aggression is a myth. Kuo (1967) has been one of the few researchers to demonstrate experimentally the situational supports and relativity of fighting. The dog that is a terror in its own yard becomes a docile visitor in another area. He also found that chows could be trained to attack cats outside the laboratory, and to treat them entirely civilly inside the laboratory. The reverse effect was also demonstrated: the same dogs that would eat and sleep with a feline companion inside the laboratory viciously attacked cats outside the laboratory. Kuo called the phenomenon the Dr. Jekyll–Mr. Hyde effect. More generally, Kuo argued that the very concept of "aggression" should be abandoned. It carries too much surplus meaning, obfuscates the immediate regulation of the behavior to be explained, draws attention away from its functions, diminishes focus on the developmental dynamics of change, and promotes the false idea that a general disposition to harm is fixed irreversibly early in life or by genes.

Beyond Kuo, a significant number of researchers have expressed reservations about the unitary concept of aggression, whether as an instinct, secondary drive, trait, or latent construct (e.g., Bandura, 1962; Cairns, 1979; Hinde, 1959). What sorts of research strategies are implied by this multifunctional and multidimensional view of aggressive phenomena? In brief, focus must be upon understanding the concrete phenomena to be explained, not upon the early development of the construct. Operationally, the investigator is challenged to identify with some precision the phenomenon of interest, whether it be toddlers grabbing each others' crayons, an 8-year-old boy yelling "Stop it" to an older brother, two elementary school boys fighting, a daughter talking back to her mother, adolescent girls spreading rumors, teenage boys shooting rival gang members, or a linebacker breaking the leg of a quarterback in a vicious tackle in high school football. In a developmental–functional framework, it cannot be assumed that these different behaviors are equivalent forms of aggression, each with similar functions and underlying determinants.

Investigators in the functional–developmental framework must address the general problem of what outcomes the behaviors produce for individuals or their groups, for good or for ill. The challenge is to identify the antecedents and consequences of the behaviors and what purposes these outcomes may serve for the individuals. This analysis, in turn, is part of a more general research strategy that presupposes a need to identify the developmental origins of the behaviors to be explained and to clarify the factors that maintain or reverse it over time. The framework recognizes that social actions are multidetermined and inevitably modified over time and context.

What gains accrue from a multidimensional approach to aggressive phenomena? At the least, the concrete phenomena and their primary determinants are brought into focus for precise and detailed analysis. Rather than explaining the origins and functions of a disposition that may itself have only modest centrality and stability over time, attention is drawn to real actions and outcomes. In addition, as Kuo (1967) proposed, the approach brings to the fore a concern with developmental dynamics of the establishment and modification of specific behaviors. It points to the need for understanding stability and modification over the life course, along with implications for prevention and intervention.

Failures to distinguish among the forms and functions of behaviors that have been variously labeled aggressive promote the commonsense bias that the entire class of actions is "inhuman" and/or psychopathological. It takes only a slight conceptual step to assume that the negative interpersonal patterns subsumed by the rubric aggression reflect deficiencies or anomalies in normal development, whether cognitive, emotional, social, or genetic. Accordingly, aggressive patterns (and the underlying forces that give rise to them) have been attributed to developmental anomalies such as early childhood abuse, attachment insecurity, genetic anomalies, social-cognitive deficits, peer rejection, emotional disturbance, or some combination of these. In brief, negative interpersonal actions of children tend to be attributed to the operation of dysfunctional or psychopathological processes, or normal processes and functions gone awry in much of the recent developmental literature (Coie & Dodge, 1998).

A Modern Example: Social Aggression

Beginning in late childhood/early adolescence (10–13 years of age), there is an accentuation of gender differences. The onset of puberty and romantic and sexual interests in adolescence is associated with a fresh social-role differentiation. This accentuation of gender differences has two profound consequences for aggressive expression. For females, there is the rapid development of adult-like, nonconfrontational aggressive strategies of anger expression that may coexist with the direct confrontational actions of childhood. For males, there is an inevitable increase in the intensity of confrontations due, in part, to gender-relative differences in masculine role, sexual dimorphism, and weapon availability.

At approximately 10–11 years of age, girls begin to employ nonconfrontational strategies in aggressive expression to supplement the confrontational acts of childhood (Cairns, Cairns, & Neckerman, 1989). In adolescence, this takes the form of social aggression—including rumor spreading, social ostracism, and group alienation. These "indirect" forms of aggression are themselves correlated and serve as nonconfrontational forms of attack. As we have observed elsewhere, indirect or social aggression has some remarkable advantages over confrontational attacks by reducing the likelihood of immediate escalation and overt physical violence. The victim may not be able to distinguish between friend or enemy given that the originators of the attacks are concealed by the fabric of the social framework. The findings indicate that these "hidden" techniques rapidly become a preferred strategy for aggressive expression in midadolescence and later, particularly among girls. From the 4th grade to the 10th grade, the percentage of female-to-female conflicts involving themes of alienation, ostracism, or character defamation rose from 14% to 56%.

While nonconfrontational strategies become increasingly dominant in female conflicts, it would be inaccurate to indicate that adolescent females lose the capability to produce serious harm and damage. Confrontational and nonconfrontational strategies seem to coexist for girls throughout adolescence. What about males during early and midadolescence? One remarkable feature of male–male aggressive expression in this age range is the failure to develop and employ nonconfrontational strategies. They persist in the strategy of childhood, but with new and more powerful physical resources for creating injury and maiming. With this quantitative shift in intensity, there is a qualitative shift in consequences. The "aggression" of childhood becomes the "violence" of adolescence and adulthood.

Relative to girls, boys in the late childhood and early adolescent period seem "socially retarded" in the use of indirect forms of aggressive expression. They rarely report the use of nonconfrontational strategies in their conflicts with other boys or girls. Factor-analytic methods indicate that the gender difference in strategies was not present at 10 years of age, but it was clearly present by 13 years of age and beyond. One consequence of the failure to shift to nonconfrontational strategies is that males in this age range become more vulnerable to assaults and escalation in the intensity of fights. For adolescent males, this means that a mere insult or being "dissed" can escalate to physical assaults or to life-threatening conflicts involving lethal weapons.

Over the past 5 years, discussions of the construct of "relational aggression" have helped bring into focus the nature of gender differences in human aggressive expression. As employed by Crick and her colleagues (e.g., Crick & Grotpeter, 1995), relational aggression refers to the employment of interpersonal relations in aggressive expression. In contrast to the construct of "social aggression," relational aggression may be direct and confrontational as well as indirect and hidden. The inclusive nature of the construct and its assessment is nontrivial, since it appears to be responsible for (1) high correlations between physical aggression and relational aggression, and (2) modest differences between developmental and gender differences in relational aggression. By contrast, social aggression refers to the use of the social network to ostracize, defame, or otherwise create distress in another person without direct confrontation. The "hidden" or nonconfrontational feature of social aggression is key. Longitudinal studies of social aggression indicate large gender differences in age of onset and frequency of use, low correlations with physical aggression, and virtually no prediction of adult psychopathology associated with childhood and adolescent use (Cairns & Cairns, 1994;

Xie, 1998). In brief, the constructs of physical and social aggression are only linked by slender common threads: They represent different short-term determinants and long-term consequences.

THE FUNCTIONS OF AGGRESSIVE PATTERNS

The view that aggressive acts are necessarily dysfunctional and maladaptive tends to close doors on research inquiries when further distinctions are required. This recognition presupposes an inquiry into the multiple functions of behaviors that have been classified as aggressive. While at first blush this may seem to be a curious pursuit, the answers may help one to understand why negative actions are so ubiquitous in individual development and evolution. Four sets of functions can be examined: namely, (1) interactional and psychological, (2) physical, (3) evolutionary, and (4) social. On examination, these functions may prove to be complementary rather than conflictual.

Interactional and Individual Psychological Functions

It has been proposed that a primary developmental function of negative or aggressive actions is to produce rapid and effective change in the ongoing behavior of other persons (Cairns, 1979). In most interchanges, there is a tug-of-war between maintaining the integrity of one's own behavior patterns and thoughts while simultaneously synchronizing them with the behavior patterns and thoughts of others. That interpersonal synchrony occurs virtually without effort and outside consciousness from infancy through adulthood is something of a miracle. In the absence of role hierarchies and other structures, inevitable tensions arise within interpersonal units—mother and infant, a schoolmate pair, collegial collaboration—in determining whose actions are to be modified and whose will prevail. When the tensions become great as compromises fail and/or overt conflicts arise, the interaction/collaboration may dissolve because of dyssynchrony. In the case of infants, children, and adolescents, where escape is not possible, the use of negative or coercive feedback is a common mechanism to modify the behavior of others. The negative coercion, though mild in the initial stages, can escalate to be labeled punishment or aggression.

A closely related function of negative actions is to remove threats to one's self or one's concept of oneself. Any perceived threat from another person, if it cannot otherwise be accommodated or the individual cannot escape, may become the target of negative acts that lead to removal. Homer justified the bloody rage of Odysseus because of the disrespect shown him by the suitors. More up to date, being "dissed" or disrespected appears to be a primary reason for violence among youth in inner-city neighborhoods.

Physical and Survival Functions

With development and maturation, the protective functions of aggressive acts extend beyond psychological considerations and include protection of one's physical self, and one's living space and possessions. How these protective functions operate are relative to such basic parameters as species, age, gender, and ecology. Beyond the specific and species-typical considerations, there are some general principles that provide a surprisingly close fit to human beings. For instance, the right to use just force to protect oneself, one's home, and one's possessions against intruders is one of the primary justifications for aggression accepted by law. The protection of one's physical self against harm—and by extension, one's family and their physical well-being and access to resources—complements the protection of one's behavioral and psychological integrity.

Survival by protecting one's resources and well-being are not simply inventions of human beings. It is, for example, well established in comparative and ethological studies of animal behavior that (1) physical attacks by conspecifics, under a wide range of conditions and species, tend to promote counterattacks, and (2) violations of living space by an intruder tend to provoke threats and attempts to remove the invader. These two conditions—physical attacks directed toward the self and the violation of territorial boundaries—tend to provoke attacks among nonhuman mammalian males.

Evolutionary Functions

Protection of one's offspring constitutes a special case that combines certain features of physical protection and possession protection, and addresses the basic problem of how species reproduce themselves and maintain continuity across generations. To protect one's offspring, and one's distinctive genetic material, may be an evolutionary extension of the protection of one's self (Wilson, 1975). However, sociobiologists have also raised key questions on the certainty of parentage. Among mammalian species, there is necessarily less ambiguity in the neonatal period and infancy with respect to infants' motherhood than to their fatherhood. Accordingly, the function of physical protection of young offspring typically is the responsibility of mothers in nonhuman mammals. This phenomenon is seen across species and has been labeled "brood defense" (e.g., Green, 1978).

What else can aggressive acts do for individuals in fulfilling their "ultimate" assignment of conveying their genes to later generations? One insight in recent formulations is that individuals can perpetuate their genes by enhancing both the survival of their own offspring *and* the offspring of their close relatives (many of whose genes are the same as the individual's own). Whatever behavior patterns do the job most effectively—whether aggression or passivity, altruism or selfishness—should be favored in the course of evolution.

But the specific problem remains: Why do most individuals stop short of killing competitors who are not closely related to them (or doing away with obnoxious second cousins)? One individual-selection answer to this question has been offered by the game theory analysis of geneticist John Maynard Smith (1974). To determine the genetic consequences of a behavior pattern that is almost universal in a population, Maynard Smith argues, it is necessary to take into account the nature of the counterresponses that will be provided and initiated by other individuals. For instance, a "hawk strategy" (fighting to the death) has been calculated by Maynard Smith to be a low-payoff interpersonal strategy if all of one's opponents are likely to reciprocate with the same strategy. Alternative patterns, such as "conventional competition" or a "dove strategy" (running away and making love, not war), would usually yield higher genetic payoffs. If such an "optimal" strategy persists across generations, it is called an "evolutionarily stable strategy" (ESS).

Social Functions

One of the primary lessons of social group organization is the unifying effect of identifying a common enemy or an outgroup. Sherif and Sherif (1970), in their brilliant study of how to organize children into subgroups with deep loyalties, found that the creation of outgroups or common enemies was an especially effective device. Conversely, the barriers between groups were broken down when cooperation was necessary to reach common goals. For example, the Nazi party discovered in the 1930s that children and adolescents could be effectively mobilized to help promote national chauvinism and the goals of national socialism. Having specific outgroups—or enemies of the nation—helped unify not only the youth but also served to consolidate broader public support, with eventually disastrous consequences. Parallel discoveries were made about the same time in the former Soviet Union and, later, in the Chinese cultural revolution. It may be the case that the same principle underlying the maintenance of personal integrity helps account for the use of negative acts and aggression to consolidate and maintain the integrity of social groups. On this count, the most egregious and extended acts of violence in modern history have occurred in societal and national conflicts and wars. Stripped of individual identify, the victims became representatives of a threatening outgroup, and the outgroup could be identified by religion, ethnicity, or nationality. Ordinary people thereby become both the instruments and the victims of mass destruction.

To sum up, an overview of the interpersonal, psychological, physical, evolutionary, and social properties of aggressive acts indicate that they serve multiple functions, depending on the nature of the action and the circumstances in which they occur. It cannot be gainsaid that some grievous instances of violence are the outcomes of hallucinatory or delusional processes and seemingly without adaptive functions. Unfortunately, these exceptional instances have paradoxically become the model for normal development. The error has been to classify all negative actions together into a unitary construct and to fail to recognize that they have multiple normative and functional properties in development and evolution.

In light of the multiple functions of aggression, perhaps the classic question of Nobelist Konrad Lorenz (1966) should have been "Why not aggression?" rather than "Why aggression?" Because of the attractive hazards of negative and aggressive acts, there exists a broad network of practices and controls that are built within the very fabric of society. The network includes not only the criminal codes of society but, more broadly, the conventions of etiquette and civility that guide everyday exchanges. In conventional settings, these controls are maintained by the social networks of peers through the internalization and enforcement of mutually protective standards of behaviors that diminish direct and harmful aggressive acts.

A DEVELOPMENTAL ACCOUNT
OF AGGRESSIVE PHENOMENA

The emergent developmental model of aggressive patterns builds upon the conceptual and functional distinctions that were anticipated, in large measure, by the work of Bandura and Walters (1959, 1963; Bandura, 1973). While developmental science provides a framework for proceeding, it offers an orientation to phenomena rather than a specific substantive theory. The specific developmental theory should be informed by systematic empirical investigations conducted over time, using multilevel procedures. Moreover, the assumptions should be explicit enough to guide research and to specify the grounds for empirical verification or disconfirmation of the model. Such a model has been outlined by Cairns (1979; Cairns & Cairns, 1994) and Magnusson (1988, 1995; Magnusson & Cairns, 1996).

Five propositions from the developmental model are of special interest in this chapter because they point to directions for fresh inquiry.

Interpersonal Alignment

The principle of interactional alignment is that individuals tend to synchronize their interpersonal actions with the salient and compelling acts of others directed toward the individual. This principle appears to hold even in the early postnatal stages of mammalian young and is supported by highly evolved biobehavioral predispositions and interactions that are critical for survival, reproduction, and defense. For instance, interactional alignment underlies the early harmony of mother nurturance–infant suckling, and it is seen in the attachment of the infant to the mother (Cairns, 1966). It is reflected as well in the mutual engagement and passion required for the synchronization of sexual arousal and performance in adults.

But more to the point of this chapter, interpersonal synchrony does not necessarily lead to harmony and happiness. Acts of anger, hate, and rage directed toward individuals can organize negative interpersonal reactions in an unhappy escalatory cycle. The recurrent finding that "aggression begets aggression" reflects the ubiquity of negative escalatory sequences in animals and humans (Cairns, 1973). In this regard, vigorous actions by others toward the individual—including those that produce intentional or unintentional harm—tend to elicit synchronous counterresponses, even in infancy. If unchecked, these interactions can escalate in vigor, intensity, and hurtfulness. This interactional principle is consistent with Holmberg's (1980) observation that approximately half of the interactions among infants at 1 year of age are negative. By contrast, the infant's negative reciprocity with parents (and other adults) is virtually zero. With adults, the child's synchronous negative responses are either checked or not permitted to occur in the first place.

This proposition has counterintuitive implications for the origins of aggressive behaviors. On this score, a distinction may be drawn between events necessary for the initial establishment of aggressive behaviors and the events necessary for their maintenance and generalization. The practical implications for prevention may be nontrivial. For instance, parental behaviors that have been broadly viewed as necessary and sufficient for aggressive development in children (e.g., use of corporal punishment) may be less responsible for the *origin* of childhood aggression than for its *consolidation* and *recurrence*; that is, coercive parental punishment appears to be part of a package of parental failures to regulate, control, or otherwise modify the inevitability of the child's hurtful and hostile actions toward siblings and peers. Hence, the main antecedents to childhood aggression may lie in parental failures to modulate aggression escalation in young children and/or failures to support alternative, nonaggressive strategies for regulating peer actions. On this view, parental passive acceptance of peer-directed or sib-directed aggression could be more fundamental to childhood peer aggression than active coercive parental punishment.

Multiple Trajectories

The phenomena labeled "aggression" refers to diverse patterns of interpersonal and social activity that emerge across development. Although some of these patterns may overlap in determinants and functions, there is sufficient dissimilarity across developmental stages and contexts to view them as separable constructs. Accordingly, attempts to plot a single trajectory for the growth of aggression are inherently flawed. On the other hand, it is entirely feasible and productive to track the emergence and course of specific strategies of social control and negative behaviors as a function of age and gender. Due to emergent sexual dimorphism and gender-identified roles, it is expected that there will be identifiable developmental differences in modal strategies of social control among females and males as a function of interactional partners.

Adolescent Risk

Some of the more serious patterns of aggressive behavior are organized primarily in adolescence and early adulthood. There are three developmental factors that combine to bring about this heightened level of brutality.

1. There is the relative freedom of individuals and social groups of peers from external constraints, whether parental or societal. Without constraints, male adolescents tend to synchronize their behaviors and actions around vigorous, salient, risky, and/or deviant themes (Cairns, 1979).

2. Another factor is the increased access to firearms and other destructive weapons in some countries. According to one investigation, over half of adolescent males in the southern United States claim gun ownership, with 12.5 years being the mean age of firearm acquisition (Livingston & Lee, 1992; Sadowski, Cairns, & Earp, 1989).

3. The final factor is the "brutality norm" for adolescent males, where confrontational, aggressive behavior is broadly held as the measure of adolescent manhood (Ferguson & Rule, 1980). This "norm" serves to support the propensities of groups to organize their behaviors and attitudes around "vigorous, salient, risky, and/or deviant themes."

When the interactional social dynamics of groups are combined with social isolation and access to weapons of injury and destruction in teenage males, they can have explosive consequences for the youths and persons around them.

Developmental Shifts in Group Relevance

The social agents and internal factors that support and maintain aggressive behaviors differ as a function of age and circumstances. For example, the parental and family factors that are pivotal for aggressive expression in infants and children inevitably diminish in significance as youth become adolescents and young adults, and peer social groups and peer interactional patterns gain hegemony. To the extent that designs for prevention and intervention become informed by such developmental changes in social organization and influence, fresh avenues can be identified and ineffective ones avoided.

Prevention and Change

Recognizing the functional significance and embedded nature of aggressive patterns is key to formulating programs of prevention and change, regardless of age. Since negative patterns are supported by biological and psychological factors within the individual and the social network, there are multiple potential avenues for modification. However, the correlated constraints in development also provide barriers to change, whereby biological dispositions, beliefs and attitudes, and social network relationships become intertwined in the support of direct aggressive strategies.

CREATING AGGRESSION

Is it possible to create aggressive individuals under experimental conditions? This may seem like a frivolous and leading question given what is known about the developmental determinants of aggression. Perhaps. On the other hand, an inability to provide firm evidence on the matter may expose gaps in our fundamental knowledge.

How to Create Aggressive Animals

Thirty years ago, my students and I believed the development of aggressive mice would be a straightforward and easy first step toward assessing a more complex issue. That proved to be a classic case of overconfidence. After nearly a year of research, we were ready to give up because of our repeated failures to produce aggressive animals. This occurred despite the fact that we followed then-standard guides for eliciting aggression, including a "boot camp" training sequence (Scott, 1967). Moreover, we used inbred mice (C57/BL), which had a reputation for being highly aggressive, and adopted the classical frustration and reinforcement techniques to produce the phenomenon. In fact, our efforts to create aggression by frustration, punishment, and training, paradoxically, produced the opposite of aggression; to the contrary, we were successful only in creating inhibited, frightened animals (e.g., Cairns, 1973, 1979).

The happy ending—if one can ever view the generation of aggression a positive outcome—occurred when we abandoned conventional psychological wisdom and adopted a rearing procedure employed by ethologists to prove that aggression is innate. In brief, we found that the key to producing highly aggressive mice was to rear them alone after they were weaned—in isolation from other conspecifics. Beyond isolation rearing, no special training seemed required; that is, there was no need to "train" the animal to fight through observation, reinforcement, frustration, or punishment. The isolation manipulation, taken by itself, yielded robust, consistent, and powerful effects on the generation of aggressive behaviors.

Once we discovered the isolation manipulation, the production of aggressive animals became as simple and efficient as we had originally anticipated. The problem was that we had been misled by adopting the dominant psychobiological and social learning theories on the necessary and sufficient conditions to produce aggressive behavior in humans. In our assessments of the implications of those models, none of the key manipulations of modeling, punishment, and reinforcement produced aggression and fighting. In contrast, the robust effects of isolation rearing upon creating aggressive behavior in males have been broadly replicated in diverse nonhuman mammalian species, from dogs and sheep to monkeys.

Why does isolation rearing work so well to enhance the likelihood of aggression? The effect was originally interpreted as evidence for the innateness of aggression (Eibl-Eibesfeldt, 1961; Lorenz, 1966). It was intended to prove that, in the absence of experience, the phenomenon must reflect the operation an of immanent, instinctual drive. But does it really? An alternative, developmental account focused upon what isolation rearing promotes in behavior and biology rather than what it omits (Cairns, 1973). Compared to group-reared peers, isolated animals are more reactive and more readily startled, more responsive to tactile and chemical social stimulation, and more alert to the presence of novel peers. These heightened behavioral reactivities are, in turn, associated with isolation-induced changes in neurotransmitters (e.g., dopamine, serotonin) and hormones (e.g., testosterone, corticosterone). Moreover, direct observations indicate that previously isolated males are more readily aroused by unfamiliar males than nonisolated sibs. Microanalysis of the interactional events that lead to the first attack indicates that fighting reflects an escalatory sequence in which both individuals become engaged. Typically, the isolated male has a lower threshold for arousal and a greater tendency to escalate the intensity of social stimulation. Hence, previously isolated males are the first to behave as if they were dominant and "king of the hill" in this first encounter. The isolation rearing conditions, in effect, mimic the naturalistic living circumstances of dominant animals of this species (i.e., males isolate themselves physically from male peers). The consequent alignment of biobehavioral conditions and behavioral reactivities promoted by isolation—whether self-created or imposed experimentally—create psychobiological conditions optimally suited for escalation and attacks. All this occurs, it should be noted, without prior frustration, punishment, or social learning experiences.

Once fighting patterns are established, social learning experiences are important for their consolidation and generalization. Learning processes can be key to short-cut escalatory sequences and determine when and where attacks occur, and toward whom they are directed (Cairns & Scholz, 1973).

Creating Aggressive Adolescents

While general interactional and developmental principles may be studied in animals, it is folly to leap from mice to monkeys to humans in accounts of aggressive behavior. The distinctively human characteristics of communication, thinking, deception, and social organization demand parallel studies of human ontogeny. Perhaps the most important lesson to be learned from comparative investigations is that a coherent account of aggressive behavior is within grasp in at least one mammalian species, and a scientific account of aggressive behavior in humans may be possible. While general principles of social and biological interaction that hold across species may be clarified, it is unlikely that specific generalizations will survive critical examination.

On this score, we noted earlier that aggressive attitudes and behavior patterns could be effectively organized in human adolescents. Evidence for this proposition may be found in changes produced in the attitudes and behaviors of children and adolescents during wartime and during periods of national reorganization. The effectiveness of government-organized organizations, such as Hitler's youth corps in the 1930s and 1940s, is a case in point. Children were transformed into extremist patriots, willing and able to fight and die for the Fatherland. But social transformations were not limited to totalitarian governments. The Allied propaganda during World War II was almost as effective for their youth, including this writer. Propaganda messages in posters and the media were effective in encouraging fear and hatred of entire classes of people, nations, and leaders. The same holds for the perpetuation of the "troubles" in Ireland, where religious discrimination takes firm hold in early adolescence (Cairns, 1986), or Serbian hostility toward the Kosovars. The science can learn from society as well as the reverse. The record of the twentieth century suggests that late childhood and adolescence is a prime time for creating prejudiced attitudes and aggressive patterns.

On a broader scale, societies may simply take advantage of naturally occurring phenomena that create the confrontational aggression of adolescence. The developmental principles underlying this propensity were noted earlier—the relative isolation in adolescence from parental and social controls, and the inherent interactional bias of social groups toward alignment with violent, vigorous, and risky behaviors. When this interactional propensity is coupled with ready access to weapons of destruction and a societal adoption of brutality norms for young males—norms reinforced by heroic fiction and famed leaders, small wonder that adolescent males constitute the most violent subgroups of modern society. As the experiments of Milgram (1964) suggest, there may be a banality in evil when there is strong authoritarian support for violence (Arendt, 1963). This brings up a reconsideration of the role of social networks in the promotion of aggression.

SOCIAL NETWORKS AND AGGRESSION

The roles that social groups play in the adoption, support, and activation of violence demand special attention. That most serious forms of violence tend to occur when two or more persons act together suggests the potential for violence in the social unit—whether in the dyad, group, or gang. In an extension of the Gestalt holistic idea of social behavior, it appears that the group may add a critical dimension to individual propensities. This phenomenon has been labeled "group contagion" and the concept has been employed to account for riots, lynchings, and other unhappy mob behaviors.

"Contagion," or catalytic group interactional effects on violence, may be derived from a consideration of basic interactional processes, including the "aggression begets aggression" phenomenon (Cairns & Cairns, 1994). The principle of interactional alignment holds that vigorous, salient acts directed toward individuals are more likely to elicit interpersonal synchrony between individuals than are weak, passive acts, all things equal (Cairns, 1966, 1979). Whether the synchronous engagement involves reciprocal or complementary acts depends, in part, upon the relative status of persons in the relationship and the nature of the acts. The principle seems to apply to group processes as well as individual exchanges. Accordingly, forcefully presented dogma, attitudes, or beliefs within a group, or vigorous, aggressive actions against a group from the outside can serve to catalyze group cohesion and collective counteractions. In late childhood and adolescence, such events can heighten the formation and consolidation of groups and, in the more extreme case, gangs. The bias toward aligning behind the more vigorous, risky alternatives can promote behaviors that are increasingly risky and/or deviant. When there are few or no curbs on group contagion—as when conventional society abdicates responsibility for overseeing neighborhoods or schools, or when parents and peers abdicate responsibility—there is a potential for escalation. In filling the void, adolescent groups may create their own control codes of conduct and sanctions. As in the fictional *Lord of the Flies*, such groups and their norms can become increasingly disaffiliated from the society, and in some cases, increasingly violent.

The current empirical literature has demonstrated that affiliation with delinquent peers is closely related to adolescents' aggressive behavior (e.g., Cairns, Cairns, Neckerman, Gest, & Gariépy, 1988), delinquency (e.g., Clarke-McClean, 1996; Elliot, Huizinga, & Menard, 1989; Giordano, Cernkovich, & Pugh, 1986), school dropout (Cairns et al., 1989), teenage parenthood (Cairns & Cairns, 1994), and substance abuse (e.g., Dishion, Reid, & Patterson, 1988). Not only in adolescence do peer social networks play a supportive role in the development of aggression, it is also true in childhood. Analyses of peer social networks of children and adolescents indicated that group members are similar in their levels of aggression (e.g., Cairns & Cairns, 1994); aggressive children tend to hang around with other aggressive children. This finding has been replicated in both cross-context and cross-cultural studies (e.g., Farmer et al., 1999; Leung, 1996; Sun, 1995). Beside aggression, members of the same peer group resemble each other on multiple behavioral dimensions, such as popularity, academic competence, and athletic ability (Cairns, Xie, & Leung, 1998; Edwards, 1990; Leung, 1996; Neckerman, 1996). The strong evidence of "homophily" may reflect both the opportunities afforded in the community and school and the continuing impact of common background and value structures.

Other evidence is consistent with the proposition that reciprocal relationships in dyads and in groups play a significant role in aggressive behaviors of both children and adolescents. In suburban and rural American schools, there is virtually no difference among highly aggressive children and adolescents in terms of whether they are nuclear members of social groups, or whether they have reciprocal friendships (Cairns et al., 1988), though in some inner-city schools, highly aggressive boys have even higher centrality in the peer social networks (Xie, Cairns, & Cairns, 1999). Large differences appear, however, in the kinds of friendships they form. Aggressive youth tend to form friends and groups with other aggressive youth (Cairns et al., 1988; Coie, Terry, Lenox, Lochman, & Hyman, 1995; Kupersmidt & Coie, 1990).

The current literature suggests that the supportive role that peer social networks play in the development of aggression may differ across gender. In comparisons of male groups relative to female groups, there is a modest yet consistent gender difference in group size. Boys tend to form slightly larger groups than girls (e.g., Eder & Hallinan, 1978; Lagerspetz, Björkqvist, & Peltonen, 1988). In terms of group homophily, girls within a group tend to share a broader web of similarities than boys (e.g., Neckerman, 1992; Xie, Cairns, & Cairns, 1999). These results support the proposal that girls form more cohesive, exclusive groups relative to those of boys. Gender difference also exists in the type of behavior that is associated with centrality in the social networks. In an inner-city sample, it was reported that high social network centrality in girls was associated with high levels of popularity; however, high social network centrality in boys was associated with high levels of aggressive behavior (Xie, Cairns, & Cairns, 1999). All this suggests that peer social networks may play a more supportive role in the development of aggressive patterns in males than in females.

PREDICTING AGGRESSIVE BEHAVIOR FROM CHILDHOOD TO MATURITY[2]

One of the success stories of behavioral study in the twentieth century has been the completion of carefully conducted prospective longitudinal studies of behavior across childhood and adolescence and much of the life span. This goal for the science was outlined by Mills (1899), and it has taken almost a full century to accomplish. Our knowledge about basic issues of developmental change and prediction now extend beyond common sense, speculation, or selective recall; it is based on a firm body of replicated findings across settings, populations, and generations. In brief, these longitudinal data indicate that aggressive behaviors tend to occur in specific configurations or packages, and so do their developmental sequelae. When aggressive behaviors co-occur with particular other phenomena in childhood, notably, academic failure in school, the boy or girl is at risk for a range of problem behaviors in late adolescence or early adulthood. These problem behaviors include early school dropout, arrests for both violent and property crime, and teenage parenthood. For girls, there is some indication that the predictions show a significant increase in magnitude with age, such that predictions from these configurations are more robust in early adolescence, say, than in middle childhood. For boys, there is a somewhat higher continuity in prediction from childhood through adolescence.

While the predictions are moderately high, the error rate in predicting subsequent pathology is about 50%, in that about half of the persons fail to show serious problem behaviors in adulthood. When the age of first assessment is extended downward, to early school age, or prior to school entry, the prediction relations are weak, though sometime statistically reliable. In general, the pattern of relations in aggressive prediction fits the overall

[2]This section is revised from a recent selection published by Cairns, Mahoney, Xie, and Cadwallader (1999).

first empirical "law" of developmental prediction, namely, "The shorter the interval between two assessments, the more likely it is that the individual's relative position in the distributions of score will be similar" (Cairns & Cairns, 1994, p. 61). Although this empirical generalization was first enunciated for intelligence test performance, it has held for other psychological characteristics. Contrary to the assumption of early fixation of personality, it assigns greater weight to more recent events in the prediction of future behavior. The logical implications of this robust empirical generalization have rarely been explored in systematic accounts of aggressive behavior development.

Twenty years ago, Olweus (1979) published an influential review of longitudinal studies that focused upon the developmental stability of aggressive behavior. In his overview, Olweus concluded that measures of aggressive behavior were about as stable in terms of development as measures of intelligence. The evidence was mostly from males, but the implication was that a similar pattern would hold for females. This review was particularly important at the time, because it was one of the first demonstrations that social development could be viewed as being as lawful as cognitive development or otherwise more "fundamental" behavior systems.

The longitudinal research completed over the past two decades permits a critical evaluation of Olweus's assertion. Different research teams throughout the world have now reported evidence relevant to the issue. The groups have been directed by Pulkkinen (1982) in Finland, Magnusson (1988) in Sweden, Farrington and West (1990) in England, Patterson (Patterson, Reid, & Dishion, 1992) in Oregon, Eron and Huesmann (1987) in New York, Huizinga and Elliot (Elliot et al., 1989) in the National Youth Study, Werner (Werner & Smith, 1986) in Kauai, Block (1971) in California, and Masten (Masten & Braswell, 1991) in Minnesota, among others.

The Carolina Longitudinal Study (CLS), a project begun in 1981, provides focus on findings that pertain to risk and resilience in childhood and adolescence. The goal was to track the pathways of risk and resilience from childhood to early maturity in a representative population of rural and suburban youth. The investigation involved 695 children in two school-grade cohorts (Cairns & Cairns, 1994). At the beginning of the study, the two samples of children were enrolled in the fourth and seventh grades of public schools in counties that had been designated as suburban or rural in the 1980 census. The mean age of the 220 subjects of Cohort I was 10.3 years of age, and that of the 475 subjects of Cohort II was 13.3 years of age.

Embedded within the total sample, a subgroup of 40 children was identified at the outset as being at extremely high risk for violent behavior. A comparison group of 40 children was individually matched to the high-risk subjects with respect to gender, race, classroom, physical size, and neighborhood residence. Children were seen individually on an annual basis through the end of high school, regardless of whether they had changed residence or dropped out of school. The longitudinal tracking in this study has been exhaustive over the several years of the investigation, with 100% of the original subjects located and 98% interviewed at the end of high school.

Recall the Olweus speculation that aggressive behavior is virtually as stable as intelligence. Do our findings support or refute that claim? Yes and no. Yes, in that correlations between the same measures are consistently significant over periods of 5 to 10 years, from childhood to adolescence and early maturity. This is a nontrivial accomplishment for the science. No, in that the magnitude of individual-difference predictions in aggressive behavior do not rival the stability of intelligence measures. Moreover, the modest levels of the correlations observed from childhood to maturity do not support the proposition that there exist robust individual-difference predictions. One of the problems is that variable-to-variable analyses leave out contextual information that, in a developmental framework, is the key to whether or not stability is observed. The characteristic is analyzed as if it were an independent component, divorced from the person and his or her environmental circumstances.

It has been broadly assumed that there are cycles of aggression across generations that inevitably link parents to offspring. As Widom (1989) observed, the empirical evidence for this proposition is less than compelling. Two longitudinal studies on this issue have used rigorous criteria to assess the extent to which there is inter-generational similarity. This required two successive longitudinal studies in which both parents and offspring were seen in childhood using identical assessment devices. The studies indicated that the aggressive patterns of children are not closely linked to the aggressive patterns of the mothers when they were children (e.g., Cairns, Cairns, Leung, Xie, & Hearne, 1998; Serbin, Cooperman, Peters, Lehoux, Stack, & Schwartzman, 1998). When the results of the two investigations are scrutinized, there is surprising agreement in the two data sets on the modest level of inter-generational similarities in aggressive behavior when the same measures were used for both generations. On the one hand, these studies confirm that there are reliable continuities in aggressive behavior *within* each generation (i.e., from a girl's aggressive behavior in child-hood to her behavior in adolescence and adulthood). But there are few continuities *across* generations (i.e., from the mother's aggressive behavior in childhood to her offspring's aggressive behavior in childhood). Instead, there appear to be significant windows of change that occur in the adolescence-to-parenthood transition, and this transition provides an opportunity for change in the adult and prevention for the offspring.

DOES AGGRESSION INCREASE OR DECREASE OVER TIME?

One of the conundrums of the aggression literature concerns the shape of the developmental trajectory of aggressive behaviors. Does aggression increase, decrease, or remain the same over development? The question arises because evidence has been reported for all three possibilities. Paradoxically, empirical support may be claimed for each of the three seemingly contradictory answers. On the possible increase, there is a sharp rise in arrests for assaults and violent crimes for persons ages 10 through 19 years, with a gradual drop-off through later maturity (Cairns & Cairns, 1994; Crime in the United States, 1998). Eron, Huesmann, Brice, Fischer, and Mermelstein (1983, see also Huesmann, Lagerspetz, & Eron, 1984) show a developmental increase in peer nominations for aggression. Furthermore, Ferguson and Rule (1980) have identified the rise of a brutality norm in adolescence (i.e., acceptability of physical aggression). With regard to a developmental decrease, Loeber (1982) has indicated that most longitudinal studies of children typically show decrements in ratings of aggressive behavior as they enter adolescence. Consistent with this report, longitudinal assessments by teacher ratings and self ratings show a consistent drop in the frequency of aggressive expression from early childhood through late adolescence (Cairns & Cairns, 1994).

Why the diversity of findings? The answer is that the confusion has arisen because researchers have used the same term—aggression—to refer to different concepts of aggression and different operational definitions. Once these concepts and operations are distinguished, the data are quite lawful and consistent.

Consider first the assertion that aggressive and violent behaviors increase from childhood to adolescence. The primary evidence for this generalization comes from reports of arrests for violence and the incidence of interpersonal acts that lead to serious injury and hospitalization.

According to successive years of reports of national arrest data in the Department of Justice publication, *Crime in the United States* (1998), the initial rise in arrests for assaultive and violent behaviors begins at ages 10–12 years. There is a dramatic increase in the incidence of arrests for crimes of violence in males from 11 to 18 years of age. The drop-off in arrests for violence and victimization begins in the twenties and decreases steadily until senescence. For females, there is a rise in arrests for violence at adolescence, but the increase is modest compared to males. These national statistics have yielded the same curves each year since the age by sex breakdown was first reported in the Uniform Crime Reports in the 1970s. These phenomena are wholly consistent with the proposition that key events in the organization of violent behavior occur during late childhood and early adolescence for many youth (Cairns & Cairns, 1994; Loeber & Hay, 1997). By "organization of violent behavior," we refer to the time in development when individuals ordinarily gain the capability and motivation to intentionally inflict by their own actions serious and permanent physical injuries to another person.

Other regional and national data—including murder and victimization information—yield parallel outcomes. In this regard, Wolfgang, Figlio, and Sellin (1972) show the age-related rise over adolescence in both index and nonindex crimes in their study of a 1945 birth cohort of Philadelphia boys. In this monograph, Wolfgang et al. conclude that "both whites and nonwhites commit a greater number of violent crimes as they age, although the rate of increase is greater for nonwhites" (p. 251). Tracy, Wolfgang, and Figlio (1990) reported a follow-up study by this research team using a Philadelphia birth cohort born 13 years later. Comparisons between the two cohorts show that there is increasing occurrence of serious crimes (i.e., weighted for seriousness) as a function of age, with the median asymptote occurring at 16 years. There is, in addition, a marked cohort difference in the occurrence of serious offenses at all age levels. Philadelphia boys born in 1958 were much more likely to be arrested for serious crimes than boys born in 1945. More broadly, Hirschi and Gottfriedson (1983) have employed national, cross-national, and historical data sets to demonstrate the ubiquity of the age–delinquency function. Although the asymptote of the curve has shifted over time and context, its basic configuration seems to have remained constant.

Is adolescence a bloody battleground that gains its distinction in the life span as a special period of violence, with increasingly severe levels of violence from late childhood through late adolescence? If the criminological, injury, and suicide statistics are taken as criteria, the answer is yes. But a different picture is obtained when psychological and interpersonal measures are employed. In general, the picture is one of decreasing rather than increasing rates of aggression. In self-evaluations of aggressive behavior (e.g., fighting, arguing) from large representative populations, individuals show a strong, replicable, and significant tendency to see themselves as becoming *less aggressive* in the years from childhood to adolescence and early adulthood. This trend holds for both males and females. The same effects are observed regardless of whether self or teacher ratings are employed.

Return to the primary question for this section: Does aggression increase or decrease with development? The "arrest for violence" measure presupposes that the aggressive actions have produced serious outcomes for the victim. Hence, the criminological measure has a built-in severity criterion; it calls for absolute (i.e., age-independent) judgments by courts of injury or harm to the victim rather than relative (i.e., age-dependent) judgments of severity by the self or others. With age and maturation, the consequences of aggressive acts can become increasingly severe.

Simply stated, the stakes of aggression get higher with age. Older youth gain access to lethal weapons, they form gangs, and there is an age-related increase in the capability to produce harm by brute force, particularly for males. Since the risks associated with any given conflict become higher, there could be increasing selectivity in whom one confronts, and when. Consider, for example, the possibility that access to lethal weapons is a factor in the aggressive intensity–age relationship. In this regard, the mortality rate for unintentional or "accidental" firearm deaths is highest among 15- to 19-year-old youth, and firearms are involved in the majority of teenage suicides and homicides (Fingerhut & Kleinman, 1989).

Since the mortality rates for males significantly exceed female rates in all accidents involving firearms, we were curious as to how this pattern emerged in a general population. In the CLS investigation, we were surprised at the number of participants who lived in households where firearms were accessible to them. Depending on whether the respondent was male or female, firearms were available in 84% or 65% of the households. Over half of these suburban and rural subjects claimed firearm ownership themselves. How did the boys get the guns in the first place? Of those boys who claimed gun ownership, the age of first gun ownership was 12.5 years of age. The primary giver was the father or some other male relative. Mothers rarely were identified as the agent who gave the child the firearm (Cairns & Cairns, 1994). In contrast, few girls claimed gun ownership of any kind (9%), and they tended to be vague about the nature of the weapons that were available in the home (Sadowski et al., 1989).

CONFIGURATIONS OF ANTECEDENTS, CONSEQUENCES, AND PATHWAYS

One of the key contemporary advances in studies of aggression has been the discovery that developmental variables derive their meaning in combination rather than in isolation. In a contemporary developmental framework, the researcher's goal shifts from the identification of distinctive variance associated with a specific variable to the identification of patterns of influence and outcomes. This chapter is not the place to recap the several issues involved in the analytic shift from variables to persons, patterns, and configurations. Besides, that task was confronted elsewhere (see Bergman, 1998; Cairns & Rodkin, 1998; Magnusson, 1995, 1998). Here, we examine how this shift in goals has permitted the organization of findings that otherwise seem to compete.

Virtually all longitudinal studies that have been completed identified a configuration of children who are at multiple risk for acting out–aggressive behaviors (Cairns et al., 1989; Magnusson, 1988; Pulkkinen, 1982). Two distinguishing features of children in such multiple-risk configurations are (1) high levels of aggressive behavior and (2) school failure and low levels of academic achievement. Longitudinal follow-up studies of children characterized by such configurations show they are at risk for a wide range of subsequent problems, typically, those classified as "externalizing disorders."

Aggression and low academic competence have been salient distinguishing properties of multiple-risk configuration. It is of interest that other aspects of children have been represented less consistently; that is, children in these high-risk configurations have been seen as slightly less popular than classmates, but they are as likely as peers to have reciprocal friendships and to be nuclear members in the social network of the school. Similarly, self-evaluations of members of the high-risk configuration are somewhat below those of classmates, but are not markedly different. Moreover, they are not as low as the evaluations assigned to them by teachers and peers.

As we have observed elsewhere, social support from friendship and social networks is not necessarily protective (Cairns et al., 1988). The reciprocal friendships of aggressive youth may promote antisocial behaviors because of the propensity for children and adolescents to affiliate with others who are like themselves. Although there is considerable fluidity in friendships and social networks of both aggressive and nonaggressive youth, the new friends tend to resemble the old (Neckerman, 1996). There is consistency in social influence despite changing faces.

To the extent that these social influences have been incorporated into longitudinal equations, they have helped sharpen predictions and suggested reasons for change and "turning points" in development. On this score, it has been reported that substance abuse in young adulthood is less adequately predicted for females than for males based on their substance use in adolescence. The reason seems to be that females are more likely to adopt the substance-use habits of their partners than are males (Pulkinnen, 1998). Similarly, adolescents' social networks interact with their personal configurations in determining whether or not they drop out of school, become teenage parents, or are arrested for violence (e.g., Xie et al., 1999).

Configuration analysis of longitudinal data yields two other findings that deserve special attention. First is the importance of interactions among variables. For example, extreme unpopularity or social isolation, when it appears as a distinguishing characteristic of a configuration and not associated with other problems, does not emerge as predictive of negative externalizing outcomes. Similarly, low socioeconomic status, taken alone, is not particularly predictive when it occurs independently of other features of a risk profile.

Second, the configurations indicate that there remains ample opportunity in development for change for good or for ill. A significant proportion of the subjects in the protected or nonrisk configurations develop problems in the course of development, and a significant proportion of the high-risk subjects reach tolerable levels of adolescent and adult adaptation. All this is to say that development remains a probabilistic affair, even though the field has been successful in estimating the probabilities with increasing precision.

The broader problem is whether measures of childhood aggression can predict problems of real-life adaptations in adolescence and adulthood, including antisocial and deviant sequelae of criminal arrests, violent activity, or suicide. In this regard, longitudinal samples permit us to compute the developmental probabilities on whether a person judged to be at high risk for problems of aggression in childhood and adolescence would subsequently encounter serious problems of social adaptation in late adolescence and adulthood (e.g., arrest for violence, early school dropout, hard-drug addiction, teen parenthood, residential treatment for an emotional disorder). Using these criteria for psychopathology in young adulthood, we compared the approximately one-half of the childhood-designated high-risk males and females qualified for serious problems. By contrast, roughly one-fifth (20%) of the individually matched controls encountered parallel problems of adult adaptation. Extreme aggression in childhood—or its absence—provides statistically significant but probabilistic predictions.

IMPLICATIONS FOR PREVENTION

It is a happy developmental finding that at least half of the persons who demonstrate high-risk, aggressive profiles in late childhood do not manifest disorders later in life. Development proceeds in the face of multiple interrelated constraints. The correlated nature of these constraints imposes limits on the trajectories by which development proceeds, but the correlations are not perfect. At every point, opportunity for behavioral reorganization and change is present, developmental trajectories are never frozen in time. Indeed, one feature of an interdependent, correlated system is that fundamental, lasting change in a salient aspect of that system can potentially realign other system components. This potential for reorganization of life trajectories prevents us from predicting individual outcomes with certainty, no matter how imminent they appear.

To be sure, the linkages between earlier patterns of adaptation and resulting outcomes may not be simple or direct (Sroufe & Rutter, 1984). "Single antecedents can have multiple outcomes and multiple antecedents can result in the same outcome" (Kellam & Reebok, 1992). However, there is likely to exist an underlying coherence in adaptive functioning over ontogeny such that early behavior patterns and subsequent adjustment are lawfully related. Accordingly, the identification of person-oriented configurations early on can be useful in understanding the developmental course of disorder.

Once the relation between specific configuration profiles and various mental disorders and outcomes is understood, follow-up assessments may identify "turning points" in the lives of individuals who appeared to be at high risk (Pickles & Rutter, 1991). For example, using a person analysis strategy, Mahoney and Cairns (1996) found that high-risk children who participated in one extracurricular activity in secondary school were far less likely to drop out than high-risk individuals with no extracurricular involvement (5% vs. 55% dropout rates, respectively). When these children participated in more than one activity, none of them dropped out. Moreover, the associated reduction in rates of early school dropout was most marked for students at the highest risk, a finding that was uncovered by person analysis.

The preceding discussion suggests three implications for prevention:

1. The likelihood of subsequent disorders in childhood may be reduced by taking advantage of the child's inherent behavioral bias toward health and adaptation. Specifically, the context in which development occurs serves to determine what behavior patterns are adaptive and successful among children. In this regard, providing an opportunity and rewards for children to become individually engaged and successful in conventional activities and structures may provide a safety net for some children. This net should apply particularly to children who are at risk, that is, children whose familial resources and school competencies are modest, and/or whose social behaviors are problematic. It is not merely skill mastery and personal efficacy that may be achieved through such engagement. In addition, it opens the possibility for realignment of peer relationships and relationships with teachers and other persons who can serve to provide guidance and support. At a concrete level, this refers to the importance of, say, involvement in school extracurricular activities and involvement by mentors who are committed to individual children.

2. The efficacy of any prevention or intervention program is likely to have differential influence, depending on the individual's configuration of internal and external characteristics. Attention should be given to the linkages between constraining factors such as maturational timing, social networks and peer status, school engagement, and family socioeconomic conditions. To the extent that prevention or intervention is focused on single behaviors divorced from the developmental context in which they occur, it may produce only short-lived changes.

3. Consistent with James's (1890) proposal, biographies cannot be written in advance and developmental trajectories do not appear to be fixed either by genes or early experience. Despite multiple constraints in development, reorganization can and does occur. But it is likely that all points in development are not equally vulnerable to modification. It is easier to prevent the organization of a behavior system than it is to change one once it is organized. Substance use that begins in adolescence, for example, is more readily prevented than changed. Accordingly, middle and late childhood may be particularly important as entry points for the prevention or amelioration of serious problems of living that have their onset in early and midadolescence.

SUMMARY

Significant advances have been achieved over the past half-century in defining the empirical links between childhood adaptation and later psychopathology. Recent long-term longitudinal studies have helped clarify the essential questions of continuity, change, and prevention. Furthermore, the basic empirical generalizations derived from these longitudinal investigations are basically congruent with the empirical generalizations that have been demonstrated in comparative investigations. They have also underscored the need for a holistic developmental account of aggressive behavior patterns.

Some of the generalizations about continuity are seemingly negative. For example, social interactions observed in infancy provide, at best, low levels of accuracy in the long-term prediction of behavior problems in adolescence and adulthood. By middle childhood, the predictive equations for adolescent and adult psychopathology are robust, though far from perfect. Certain behavioral measures—particularly those that involve aggressive interchanges—have been linked to a wide band of problematic adaptations in adolescence and adulthood.

The predictive validity of childhood measures of aggressive patterns seems to depend upon the configurations in which they occur. In the absence of other problem adaptations in childhood, aggression, taken alone, is not a robust predictor of subsequent problems of adaptation. This outcome is consistent with an emergent body of evidence suggesting that developmental adaptations are appropriately viewed in context. A similar conclusion holds for other single-variable measures, including the popularity–unpopularity index of sociometric status. Predictions become more stable when there are correlated constraints upon adaptation; that is, when aggression and rejection occur as part of a package of multiple problems.

In addition, the continuity of problems from childhood through adolescence reflects in part the social context in which development occurs. Bidirectional constraints exist in childhood and adolescent development whereby temperamental, cognitive, and interactional characteristics of the individual become correlated with similar characteristics of peer groups. Internal configurations are correlated with social networks. Both selection and socialization processes have been implicated in this correlation, such that intimate peer interactions both attract and shape a child's attitudes, values, and behaviors. Furthermore, social networks are essential for the deployment of indirect or "social aggression" strategies in late childhood. These strategies of social ostracization, gossip, and defamation are remarkably versatile tools for interpersonal injury and control. They appear to be used so broadly that they are normative for girls in childhood and adolescence. Unlike direct, confrontational aggression, they appear to be poorly linked to subsequent psychopathology.

In general, measures of childhood problems overpredict subsequent adolescent and adult psychopathology. Virtually all longitudinal investigations find fewer instances of subsequent problems than would be expected from the childhood assessments (e.g., Cairns & Cairns, 1994; Magnusson, 1988; Werner & Smith, 1986). Why the overprediction? While at least part of the problem lies in the assessment strategies employed, it may be speculated that the more basic problem is that the discipline has failed to consider the essential human bias toward health and adaptation. As the contexts shift over development, so should basic patterns of social adaptation. Each major developmental transition—adolescence, young adulthood, marriage, parenthood, working—affords an opportunity for change, and sometimes demands it. Failures of prediction cannot be blamed simply on our assessment instruments; they may reflect as well the positive dynamics and changing contingencies of human development.

It seems reasonable to propose that prevention and intervention programs should capitalize upon the inherent human bias toward health and adaptation. In this process, developmental time can be either an enemy or an ally. Time may be seen as an enemy, since adolescent problem behaviors become increasingly difficult to address once they have become organized and consolidated. But time can also be viewed as an ally, because an understanding of time-based processes potentially provides directions on when to begin and how long to persist in an intervention program. On this count, middle- and late-childhood seem to be especially important stages to enhance efforts to engage children in school if they have not already become engaged, or if they have experienced repeated failures. Multiple mechanisms have proved to be effective in enhancing engagement and reducing school problem behaviors in childhood and adolescence (e.g., success in extracurricular activities, successful mentoring). However, development and adaptation are progressive affairs, and they are rarely captured as single-event "turning points." Accordingly, the long-term success of prevention and intervention programs should depend upon the extent to which they are active and maintained from childhood through adolescence and maturity.

ACKNOWLEDGMENTS. The authors express their gratitude for support from the National Institute of Mental Health and the Spencer Foundation for support in the preparation of this chapter.

REFERENCES

Arendt, H. (1963). *Eichmann in Jerusalem: A report on the banality of evil.* New York: Viking Press.

Bandura, A. (1973). *Aggression: A social learning analysis.* Englewood Cliffs, NJ: Prentice-Hall.

Bandura, A. (1977). *Social learning theory.* Englewood Cliffs, NJ: Prentice Hall.

Bandura, A., & Walters, R. H. (1959). *Adolescent aggression.* New York: Ronald Press.

Bandura, A., & Walters, R. H. (1963). *Social learning and personality development.* New York: Holt, Rinehart & Winston.

Bergman, L. R. (1998). A pattern-oriented approach to studying individual development: Snapshots and processes. In R. B. Cairns, L. R. Bergman, & J. Kagan (Eds.), *The individual in developmental research: Essays in honor of Marian Radke Yarrow* (pp. 83–121). Thousand Oaks, CA: Sage.

Block, J. (1971). *Lives through time.* Berkeley: Bancroft Books.

Cairns, R. B. (1966). Attachment behavior of mammals. *Psychological Review, 72,* 409–426.

Cairns, R. B. (1973). Fighting and punishment from a developmental perspective. In J. K. Coles & D. D. Jensen (Eds.), *Nebraska Symposium on Motivation, 20,* 159–124. Lincoln: University of Nebraska Press.

Cairns, R. B. (1979). *Social development: The origins and plasticity of interchanges.* San Francisco: Freeman.

Cairns, R. B. (1983). The emergence of developmental psychology. In P. H. Mussen (Gen. Ed.) & W. Kessen (Vol. Ed.), *Handbook of child psychology: Volume 1. History, theory, and methods* (4th ed., pp. 41–102). New York: Wiley.

Cairns, R. B. (1996). Aggression from a developmental perspective: Genes, environments, and interactions. In M. Rutter (Ed.), *Genetics of criminal and antisocial behavior* (Ciba Foundation Symposium No. 194), pp. 45–60. London: Wiley.

Cairns, R. B., & Cairns, B. D. (1994). *Lifelines and risks: Pathways of youth in our time.* New York: Cambridge University Press.

Cairns, R. B., Cairns, B. D., & Neckerman, H. J. (1989). Early school dropout: Configurations and determinants. *Child Development, 60,* 1437–1452.

Cairns, R. B., Cairns, B. D., Neckerman, J. J., Gest, S., & Gariépy, J-L. (1988). Social networks and aggressive behavior: Peer support or peer rejection? *Developmental Psychology, 24,* 815–823.

Cairns, R. B., Cairns, B. D., Xie, H., Leung, M.-C., & Hearne, S. (1998). Paths across generations: Academic competence and aggressive behaviors in young mothers and their children. *Developmental Psychology, 34,* 1162–1174.

Cairns, R. B., & Lewis, M. (1962). Dependency and the reinforcement value of a verbal stimulus. *Journal of Consulting Psychology, 26,* 1–8.

Cairns, R. B., Mahoney, J. L., Xie, H., & Cadwallader, T. W. (1999). Middle childhood. In W. K. Silverman & T. H.

Ollendick (Eds.), *Developmental issues in the clinical treatment of children*. Needham Heights, MA: Allyn & Bacon.

Cairns, R. B., & Rodkin, P. C. (1998). Phenomenon regained: From variables configurations to individual pathways. In R. B. Cairns, L. R. Bergman, & J. Kagan (Eds.), *The individual in developmental research: Essays in honor of Marian Radke-Yarrow* (pp. 245–263). Thousand Oaks, CA: Sage.

Cairns, R. B., & Scholz, S. D. (1973). On fighting in mice: Dyadic escalation and what is learned. *Journal of Comparative and Physiological Psychology, 85,* 540–550.

Cairns, R. B., Xie, H., & Leung, M-C. (1998). The popularity of friendship and the neglect of social networks: Toward a new balance. *New Directions for Child Development, 80,* 25–53.

Clarke-McLean, J. (1996). Social networks among incarcerated juvenile offenders. *Social Development, 5,* 203–217.

Coie, J. D., Terry, R., Lenox, K. F., Lochman, J. E., & Hyman, C. (1995). Childhood peer rejection and aggression as predictors of stable patterns of adolescent disorder. *Development and Psychopathology, 7,* 697–713.

Crick, N. R., & Grotpeter, J. K. (1995). Relational aggression, gender, and social-psychological adjustment. *Child Development, 66,* 710–722.

Crime in the U.S. (1998). *Uniform crime reports.* Washington, DC: U.S. Department of Justice, Federal Bureau of Investigation.

Dishion, T. J., Reid, J. B., & Patterson, G. R. (1988). Empirical guidelines for a family intervention for adolescent drug use. *Journal of Chemical Dependency Treatment, 1,* 181–216.

Dollard, J., Doob, L. W., Miller, N. E., Mowrer, O. H., & Sears, R. R. (1939). *Frustration and aggression.* New Haven, CT: Yale University Press.

Eder, D., & Hallinan, M. T. (1978). Sex differences in children's friendships. *American Sociological Review, 43,* 237–250.

Edwards, C. A. (1990). *Leadership, social networks, and personal attributes in school age girls.* Unpublished doctoral dissertation, University of North Carolina at Chapel Hill.

Eibl-Eibesfeldt, I. (1961). The fighting behavior of animals. *Scientific American, 205*(6), 112–122.

Elliott, D. S., Huizinga, D., & Menard, S. (1989). *Multiple problem youth: Delinquency, substance use, and mental health problems.* New York: Springer-Verlag.

Eron, L., & Huesmann, L. R. (1987). The control of aggressive behavior by changes in attitudes, values, and the conditions of learning. In R. J. Blanchard & C. Blanchard (Eds.), *Advances in the study of aggression* (Vol. 2). New York: Academic Press.

Eron, L., Huesmann, L. R., Brice, P., Fischer, P., & Mermelstein, R. (1983). Age trends in the development of aggression, sex typing, and related television habits. *Developmental Psychology, 19,* 71–77.

Eron, L. D., Huesmann, L. R., Lefkowitz, M. M., and Walder, L. O. (1972). Does television violence cause aggression? *American Psychologist, 27,* 253–263.

Farmer, T. W., Van Acker, R. M., Pearl, R., & Rodkin, P. C. (1999). Social networks and peer-assessed problem behavior in elementary classrooms: Students with and without disabilities. *Remedial and Special Education, 20*(4), 244–256.

Farrington, D. P., & West, D. J. (1990). The Cambridge study in delinquent development: A long-term follow-up of 411 London males. In H.-J. Kerner & G. Kaiser (Eds.), *Criminality: Personality, behavior, and life history.* Berlin: Springer-Verlag.

Ferguson, T. J., & Rule, B. G. (1980). Effects of inferential set, outcome severity, and basis of responsibility on children's evaluation of aggressive acts. *Developmental Psychology, 16,* 141–146.

Feshbach, S. (1970). Aggression. In P. H. Mussen (Ed.), *Carmichael's manual of child psychology.* (3rd ed., Vol. 2). New York: Wiley.

Fingerhut, L. A., & Kleinman, J. C. (1989). Mortality among children and youth. *American Journal of Public Health, 79,* 899–901.

Gest, S. D., Mahoney, J. L., & Cairns, R. B. (1999). A developmental approach to prevention research: Early adolescence configurations associated with teenage parenthood [Special issue]. *American Journal of Community Psychology, 27*(4), 543–565.

Giordano, P. C., Cernkovich, S. A., & Pugh, M. D. (1986). Friendship and delinquency. *American Journal of Sociology, 91,* 1170–1201.

Green, J. A. (1978). Experiential determinants of postpartum aggression in mice. *Journal of Comparative and Physiological Psychology, 92,* 1179–1187.

Hirschi, T., & Gottfredson, M. (1983). Age and explanation of crime. *American Journal of Sociology, 89,* 552–584.

Holmberg, M. C. (1980). The development of social interchange patterns from 12 to 42 months. *Child Development, 51,* 448–456.

Huesmann, L. R., Lagerspetz, K., & Eron, L. D. (1984). Intervening variables in the TV violence-aggression relation: Evidence from two countries. *Developmental Psychology, 20,* 746–775.

James, W. (1890). *The principles of psychology* (Vol. 1). New York: Macmillan.

Kagan, J. (1998). *Three seductive ideas*. Cambridge, MA: Harvard University Press.

Kellam, S. G., & Reebok, G. W. (1992). Building developmental and etiological theory through epidemiologically based preventive intervention trials. In J. McCord & R. E. Tremblay (Eds), *Preventing antisocial behavior: Interventions from birth through adolescence*. New York: Guilford Press.

Kuo, Z. Y. (1967). *The dynamics of behavior development: An epigenetic view*. New York: Random House.

Kupersmidt, J. B., & Coie, J. D. (1990). Preadolescent peer status, aggression, and school adjustment as predictors of externalizing problems in adolescence. *Child Development, 61,* 1350–1362.

Lagerspetz, K. M. J., Björkqvist, K., & Peltonen, T. (1988). Is indirect aggression typical of females? Gender differences in aggressiveness in 11- to 12-year-old children. *Aggressive Behavior, 14,* 403–414.

Leung, M.-C. (1996). Social networks and self enhancement in Chinese children: A comparison of self reports and peer reports of groups membership. *Social Development, 5,* 146–157.

Lewis, M. (1997). *Altering fate: Why the past does not predict the future*. New York: Guilford Press.

Livingston, M. M., & Lee, M. W. (1992). Attitudes toward firearms and reasons for firearm ownership among nonurban youth: Salience of sex and race. *Psychological Reports, 71,* 576–578.

Loeber, R. (1982). The stability of antisocial and delinquent child behavior: A review. *Child Development, 53,* 1431–1446.

Loeber, R., & Hay, D. (1997). Key issues in the development of aggression and violence from childhood to early adulthood. *Annual Review of Psychology, 48,* 371–410.

Lorenz, K. Z. (1966). *On aggression*. New York: Harcourt, Brace, & World.

Magnusson, D. (1988). *Individual development from an interactional perspective*. Hillsdale, NJ: Erlbaum.

Magnusson, D. (1995). Individual development: A holistic integrated model. In P. Moen, G. H. Elder, Jr., & K. Lücher (Eds.), *Examining lives in context: Perspectives on the ecology of human development* (pp. 19–60). Washington, DC: American Psychological Association.

Magnusson, D. (1998). The logic and implications of a person approach. In R. B. Cairns, L. R. Bergman, & J. Kagan (Eds.), *The individual in developmental research: Essays in honor of Marian Radke Yarrow* (pp. 33–62). Thousand Oaks, CA: Sage.

Magnusson, D., & Cairns, R. B. (1996). Developmental science: Principles and illustrations. In R. B. Cairns, G. H. Elder, Jr., & J. Costello (Eds.), *Developmental science*. New York: Cambridge University Press.

Mahoney, J. L., & Cairns, R. B. (1996). Do extracurricular activities protect against early school dropout? *Developmental Psychology, 33,* 241–253.

Masten, A. S., & Braswell, L. (1991). Developmental psychopathology: An integrative framework for understanding behavior problems in children and adolescents. In P. R. Martin (Ed.), *Handbook of behavior therapy and psychological science: An integrative approach*. New York: Pergamon Press.

Maynard Smith, J. (1974). The theory of games and the evolution of animal conflict. *Journal of Theoretical Biology, 47,* 202–221.

McDougall, W. (1908). *An introduction to social psychology*. London: Methuen.

Milgram, S. (1974). *Obedience to authority: An experience view*. New York: Harper and Row.

Miller, N. E. (1941). The frustration–aggression hypothesis. *Psychological Review, 48,* 337–342.

Mills, W. (1899). The nature of animal intelligence and the methods of investigating it. *Psychological Review, 6,* 262–274.

Moffitt, T. E. (1993). Adolescence-limited and life-course-persistent antisocial behavior: A developmental taxonomy. *Psychological Review, 100,* 674–701.

Neckerman, H. J. (1996). The stability of social groups in childhood and adolescence. *Social Development, 5,* 131–145.

Olweus, D. (1979). Stability of aggressive reaction patterns in males: A review. *Psychological Bulletin, 86,* 852–875.

Olweus, D. (1994). *Bullying at school*. Cambridge, UK: Blackwell.

Parke, R. D., & Slaby, R. G. (1983). The development of aggression. In P. H. Mussen (Gen. Ed.) & M. Hetherington (Ed.), *Handbook of child psychology* (4th ed., Vol. 4, pp. 547–642). New York: Wiley.

Parker, J. G., & Asher, S. R. (1987). Peer relations and later personal adjustment: Are low accepted children at risk? *Psychological Bulletin, 102,* 537–589.

Patterson, G. R. (1982). *Coercive family systems*. Eugene, OR: Castalia.

Patterson, G. R., & Cobb, J. A. (1971). A dyadic analysis of "aggressive" behaviors. In J. P. Hill (Ed.), *Minnesota Symposium on Child Psychology* (Vol. 5). Minneapolis: University of Minnesota Press.

Patterson, G. R., Reid, J. B., & Dishion, T. J. (1992). *Antisocial boys*. Eugene, OR: Castalia.

Pickles, A., & Rutter, M. (1991). Statistical and conceptual models of "turning points" in developmental process. In D. Magnusson, L. R. Bergman, G. Rudinger, & B. Törestad (Eds.), *Problems and methods in longitudinal research* (pp. 323–336). Cambridge, UK: Cambridge University Press.

Pulkkinen, L. (1982) Self-control and continuity from childhood to late adolescence. In P. B. Baltes & O. G. Brim, Jr. (Eds.), *Life-span development and behavior* (Vol. 4, pp. 64–105). New York: Academic Press.

Pulkkinen, L. (1998). Levels of longitudinal data differing in complexity and the study of continuity in personality characteristics. In R. B. Cairns, L. R. Bergman, & J. Kagan (Eds.), *Methods and models for studying the individual* (pp. 161–182). Thousand Oaks, CA: Sage.

Radke-Yarrow, M. R., Campbell, J. D., & Burton, R. V. (1968). *Child rearing: An inquiry in research and methods.* San Francisco: Jossey-Bass.

Radke-Yarrow, M. & Zahn-Waxler, C. (1979). Observing interaction: A confrontation with methodology. In R. B. Cairns (Ed.), *The analysis of social interactions: Methods, issues, and illustrations.* Hillsdale, NJ: Erlbaum.

Robins, L. N. (1986). The consequences of conduct disorder in girls. In D. Olweus, J. Block, & M. Radke-Yarrow (Eds.), *Development of antisocial and prosocial behavior: Research, theories, and issues* (pp. 385–414). New York: Academic Press.

Rutter, M. (Ed.). (1996). *Genetics of criminal and antisocial behavior* (Ciba Foundation Symposium No. 194), pp. 45–60. London: Wiley.

Sadowski, L. S., Cairns, R. B., & Earp, J. A. (1989). Firearm ownership among nonurban adolescents. *American Journal of Diseases of Children, 143,* 1410–1413.

Schlossman, S., & Cairn, R. B. (1993). Problem girls: Observations on past and present. In G. H. Elder, Jr., R. D. Parke, & J. Modell (Eds.), *Children in time and place: Relations between history and developmental psychology* (pp. 110–130). New York: Cambridge University Press.

Scott, J. P. (1967). Comparative psychology and ethology. *Annual Review of Psychology, 18,* 65–86.

Sears, R. R., Whiting, J. W. M., Nowlis, V., & Sears, P. S. (1953). Some child-rearing antecedents of aggressive and dependency in young children. *Genetic Psychology Monographs, 47,* 135–234.

Serbin, L. A., Cooperman, J. M., Peters, P. L., Lehoux, P. M., Stack, D. M., & Swartzman, A. E. (1998). Intergenerational transfer of psychosocial risk in women with childhood histories of aggression, withdrawal, or aggression and withdrawal. *Developmental Psychology, 34,* 1246–1261.

Sherif, M., & Sherif, C. W. (1970). Motivation and intergroup aggression: A persistent problem in levels of analysis. In L. Aronson, E. Tobach, D. Lehrman, & J. Rosenblatt (Eds.), *Development and evolution of behavior.* San Francisco: Freeman.

Sroufe, L. A., & Rutter, M. (1984). The domain of developmental psychopathology. *Child Development, 55,* 17–29.

Stoff, D. M., & Cairns, R. B. (Eds.). (1996). *Aggression and violence: Neurobiological, biosocial and genetic perspectives.* Hillsdale, NJ: Erlbaum.

Stoff, D. M., Breiling, J., & Maser, J. D. (1997). *Handbook of antisocial behavior.* New York: Wiley.

Sun, S-L. (1995). *The development of social networks of Chinese children in Taiwan.* Unpublished doctoral dissertation, University of North Carolina at Chapel Hill.

Tracy, P. E., Wolfgang, M. E., & Figlio, R. M. (1990). *Delinquency careers in two birth cohorts.* New York: Plenum Press.

Werner, E. E., & Smith, R. S. (1986). *Kuai's children come of age.* Honolulu: University of Hawaii Press.

Widom, C. S. (1989). Does violence beget violence? A critical examination of the literature. *Psychological Bulletin, 106,* 3–28.

Wilson, E. O. (1975). *Sociobiology: The new synthesis.* Cambridge, MA: Harvard University Press.

Wolfgang, M. E., Figlio, R. M., & Sellin, T. (1972). *Delinquency in a birth cohort.* Chicago: University of Chicago Press.

Xie, H. (1998). *The development and functions of social aggression: A narrative analysis of social exchange in interpersonal conflicts.* Unpublished doctoral dissertation, University of North Carolina at Chapel Hill.

Xie, H., Cairns, R. B., & Cairns, B. D. (1999). Social networks and social configurations in inner-city schools: Aggression, popularity, and implications for students with EBD. *Journal of Emotional and Behavioral Disorders, 7*(3), 147–155.

Zahn-Waxler, C., Cummings, E. M., & Iannotti, R. (Eds.). (1986). *Altruism and aggression: Biological and social origins.* Cambridge, UK: Cambridge University Press.

23

Are Attention-Deficit/Hyperactivity Disorder and Oppositional Defiant Disorder Developmental Precursors to Conduct Disorder?

Benjamin B. Lahey, Keith McBurnett, and Rolf Loeber

An important goal of developmental psychopathology is the description of developmental progressions in the ontogeny of serious emotional and behavioral disorders. If milder psychopathology can be shown regularly to precede the emergence of more serious psychopathology, it may be possible to identify the factors that govern the developmental progression to the more serious problems. If some of these factors prove to be modifiable, serious disorders could be prevented to some extent. This chapter reviews what is currently known about the developmental precursors to conduct disorder (CD). Specifically, it summarizes current findings on the potential developmental relations between attention-deficit/hyperactivity disorder (ADHD) and oppositional defiant disorder (ODD) on the one hand, and CD on the other hand.

ADHD refers to developmentally inappropriate levels of attention problems, motor hyperactivity, and impulsive behavior. ODD is defined in terms of developmentally inappropriate levels of irritability, defiance, and intentional annoyance of others, and CD is characterized by persistently high levels of lying, fighting, stealing, vandalism, and other antisocial behaviors during childhood or adolescence.

Although many published studies provide evidence on possible developmental relations among ADHD, ODD, and CD, this group of studies is limited by several methodological problems. First, the constructs of ADHD, ODD, and CD have been defined in many different ways across the various studies. Some investigators have used nondiagnostic constructs, such as "conduct problems," "delinquency," and "hyperactivity," whereas other researchers have

---

Benjamin B. Lahey and Keith McBurnett • Department of Psychiatry, University of Chicago, Chicago, Illinois 60637-1470.   **Rolf Loeber** • Department of Psychiatry, University of Pittsburgh, Pittsburgh, Pennsylvania 15219.

Handbook of Developmental Psychopathology, Second Edition, edited by Arnold J. Sameroff, Michael Lewis, and Suzanne M. Miller. Kluwer Academic/Plenum Publishers, New York, 2000.

used a variety of diagnostic terms from the evolving *Diagnostic and Statistical Manual of Mental Disorders* (DSM) and the *International Classification of Diseases* (ICD). Although the core characteristics of ADHD, ODD, and CD have remained constant across the last four editions of the DSM, apparently small changes in diagnostic criteria from edition to edition have sometimes resulted in sizable changes in the prevalence of the disorders (Lahey et al., 1990). In addition, a variety of different instruments have been used to assess ADHD, ODD, and CD across the existing studies, including parent and teacher rating scales, structured diagnostic interviews, and other measures. Previous studies also differ in the informants that were assessed using these instruments (teachers in some studies, combinations of parents and teachers in other studies, etc.).

Another potential source of variation in findings among the studies reviewed in this chapter is the nature of the samples. Some studies used clinic-referred samples, whereas other studies were based on population-based samples. Although clinic samples are rich sources of youths with uncommon disorders, they are biased in some important ways. Of particular importance to the topic of this chapter, clinic studies are biased toward higher rates of comorbidity, which can exaggerate the degree of association among disorders (Goodman et al., 1997). All of the existing longitudinal studies of the developmental relation of ADHD to later CD also can be criticized on the basis of the age of the participants at the time of the baseline assessment. Because children in the existing studies were between ages 5 and 16 years in the first assessment, most participants were well into the risk period for the onset of CD, seriously limiting the value of their evidence on developmental *precursors* to CD. It also is important to note that nearly all existing studies either excluded girls or did not include enough girls to analyze their data separately. Similarly, the existing samples often did not include representative numbers of youths from the major ethnic groups in the United States. Clearly, these deficits must not only be considered in this review but also must be remedied in future studies. Because of these and other limitations on the existing database, it is not surprising that the existing studies have not always yielded consistent findings. Some findings are consistent enough, however, to generate potentially useful hypotheses about the likely developmental relations of ADHD and ODD to CD.

DEVELOPMENTAL RELATION OF ATTENTION-DEFICIT/ HYPERACTIVITY DISORDER TO CONDUCT DISORDER

Childhood ADHD has long been considered a developmental precursor to CD. Seminal prospective longitudinal studies conducted by Hechtman, Weiss, and Perlman (1984), Loney, Kramer, and Milich (1981), and Satterfield, Hoppe, and Schell (1982) showed that children with ADHD often exhibit high levels of antisocial behavior during adolescence. It is not possible to conclude on the basis of these early studies that childhood ADHD predicts the emergence of new antisocial behavior after childhood, however, as no attempt was made to exclude children with concurrent CD at the start of these studies. Gittelman Klein and her colleagues also conducted a pioneering longitudinal study of 104 clinic-referred boys who were ages 6–12 years of age at the start of the study. Boys were accepted into this study only if they were not referred primarily because of aggression and had a "primary" diagnosis of hyperkinetic reaction, but boys with "secondary" diagnoses of CD were included in this sample. Control subjects were selected from patients of other departments of the same medical center. These boys were reassessed at an average age of 18.5 years (Gittelman et al., 1985) and again at an average age of 25.5 years (Mannuzza et al., 1993). At 18 years of age, 27% of the hyperkinetic group met criteria for either CD or antisocial personality disorder, which was significantly higher than the 8% found in the control group. When these boys were reevaluated at age 23, significantly more of the formerly hyperkinetic boys met criteria for antisocial personality (16%) than the control subjects (2%). Unfortunately, the inclusion of children with secondary diagnoses of CD in the clinic group means that differences between the clinic-referred and control groups at follow-up could have been entirely due to CD during childhood among some members of the hyperkinetic group rather than to hyperkinesis.

A number of more recent longitudinal studies have investigated the possibility that childhood ADHD may be a precursor to CD using analyses that separated children with ADHD who did or did not also exhibit high levels of CD behaviors during the first assessment. These studies have failed to resolve the question of the potential role played by ADHD as a developmental precursor to CD, however. Gittelman Klein's research group recruited a second sample of 103 hyperkinetic boys and controls, ages 5–12 years at the start of the study, but in this case, only one subject in the hyperkinetic group received a secondary diagnosis of CD during childhood (Mannuzza et al., 1991). When this second sample was reassessed at an average age of 18.6 years, 32% of the hyperkinetic group met criteria for either CD or antisocial personality disorder compared to 8% of the control group. These findings suggest that ADHD may be a developmental precursor to CD and other antisocial behavior during adolescence and early adulthood, but other longitudinal studies have not yielded consistent findings.

Loeber (1988b) conducted a longitudinal study of boys who were ages 10, 13, or 16 at the start of the study. The boys were divided into four groups on the basis of parent and teacher ratings obtained during the baseline assessment: (1) high ratings on aggression only, (2) high ratings on ADHD behaviors only, (3) high ratings on both dimensions, or (4) high ratings on neither dimension. Over the next 5 years, the group that was rated high on ADHD and low on aggression had the lowest rates of offending of any group at follow-up (a rate that was even significantly lower than boys who received low ratings on both ADHD and aggression).

Loeber, Green, Keenan, and Lahey (1995) also conducted prospective analyses of data from a second longitudinal study that similarly do not support the hypothesis that ADHD is a developmental precursor to CD. The Developmental Trends Study is an ongoing longitudinal study of clinic-referred boys who were 7–12 years of age in the first year of the study (mean age 9.5 years). At the time of these analyses, data on the boys were available through Year 6, when the boys were 12–17 years old. Structured diagnostic interviews of the boys, their parent, and their teacher were conducted in Years 1–4, and the same interviews were conducted with the boys and their parent in Year 6 (a scheduled Year 5 assessment was not conducted because of a gap in funding). Although most boys in the Developmental Trends Study who met criteria for CD during any year of the 6-year study already did so during Year 1, 32 boys met criteria for CD for the first time during years 2–6. When boys with CD in Year 1 were excluded, Loeber et al. found that ADHD in Year 1 was not a significant predictor of CD in Years 2–6.

Magnusson (1984) similarly examined the possible role played by ADHD as a precursor to adult antisocial behavior in a prospective study conducted in Sweden. At age 13, 530 boys were rated on aggression and ADHD by teachers who had known them for 3 years. Boys with high ratings on ADHD and low ratings on aggression at age 13 had rates of criminal behavior in adulthood that did not differ significantly from boys who were rated low on both dimensions at age 13.

Farrington, Loeber, and Van Kammen (1990) replicated most of the findings of Loeber (1988b) using 411 boys from the longitudinal Cambridge Study in Delinquent Development. Boys were rated on ADHD behaviors during childhood by their teachers and on conduct problems by their parents, teachers, and peers. Composites of these ratings taken at ages 8 and 10 years were used to predict delinquency during adolescence and early adulthood. Using a factorial log linear analysis, high ratings of childhood conduct problems were found to be a significant predictor of self-reported delinquency during adolescence and adult criminal convictions, but high ratings of childhood ADHD were not. Thus, these findings suggest that childhood ADHD is not a predictor of later antisocial behavior when childhood conduct problems are controlled. On the other hand, Farrington et al. also found that official convictions for delinquency during adolescence (as opposed to the boys' self-report of delinquent behaviors) were significantly predicted by high ratings on both childhood ADHD and conduct problems. Thus, this study yielded mixed evidence on the potential role of ADHD as a developmental precursor to CD.

Lambert (1988) conducted a longitudinal study of 240 youths considered to be hyperactive during elementary school and 127 same-age controls until 17 or 18 years of age. Youths with high parent and teacher ratings on hyperactivity and low ratings on aggression during elementary school were more likely to exhibit symptoms of both aggressive and nonaggressive CD and to be frequent users of hard drugs in late adolescence than youths who received low ratings on both hyperactivity and aggression during childhood.

A 13-year follow-up of a group boys who had been given the diagnosis of ADHD when they were 6–12 years of age and a group of normal controls found much higher rates of felony convictions during adolescence and adulthood among boys with ADHD (Satterfield & Schell, 1997). Unlike the previous report from this study (Satterfield et al., 1982), however, Satterfield et al. distinguished boys with ADHD and comorbid conduct problems during childhood from boys with ADHD in the absence of childhood conduct problems. They found that none of the boys with ADHD and no childhood conduct problems had an adult felony conviction, whereas 82% of boys with both ADHD and conduct problems during childhood had felony convictions during adulthood.

Thus, four studies provided no support for the hypothesis that children with ADHD in the absence of childhood CD are at increased risk for later antisocial behavior when early conduct problems are controlled (Loeber, 1988b; Loeber et al., 1995; Magnusson, 1984; Satterfield & Schell, 1997). One study found support for this hypothesis on some dependent variables but not others (Farrington et al., 1990), and another study found evidence of increased risk for later CD among youths with high ratings on ADHD, but low ratings on aggression during childhood (Lambert, 1988). Interestingly, Satterfield and Schell (1997) found that covert conduct problems (lying and theft) during childhood were more predictive of adult criminality than aggression in childhood, and parent reports were better predictors than teacher reports. The fact that the study yielding the most different results from the other studies (Lambert, 1988) used teacher ratings of aggression as their measure of childhood conduct problems may explain the differences in findings to some extent.

DEVELOPMENTAL RELATION OF OPPOSITIONAL DEFIANT DISORDER TO CONDUCT DISORDER

Much less is known about the potential developmental relation of ODD to CD, but several new studies provide relevant data. As noted earlier, Loeber et al. (1995) found that ADHD in Year 1 was not a significant prospective predictor of meeting criteria for CD for the first time during Years 2–6 of the Developmental Trends Study. They did find, however, that ODD in Year 1 was a significant predictor of new cases of CD in Years 2–6. We have extended these findings by conducting new analyses of data from the Developmental Trends Study for

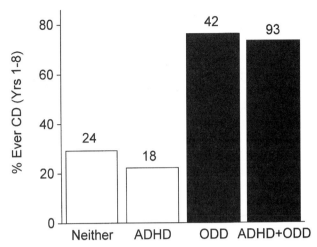

FIGURE 23.1. The percentage of boys who met DSM-III-R criteria for CD at least once during Years 1–8 of the Developmental Trends Study. Percentages are presented separately for boys who met DSM-III-R criteria in Year 1 for ADHD, ODD, both disorders, or neither disorder. The number of boys in each group is presented above the bars.

this chapter (Lahey et al., 1995; Loeber et al., 1995). At this point in the ongoing longitudinal study, interviews have been completed for Years 1–4 and Years 6–7 (the boys were 13–18 years old in Year 7). Retention of subjects has been excellent, with 97% of the sample being reinterviewed in Years 6 and 7. In addition, boys who had not yet turned 19 (83% of the sample) were interviewed again in Year 8.

As shown in Figure 23.1, 116 of the 177 boys in the study (65.5%) met criteria for DSM-III-R CD during at least one annual assessment during Years 1–8. Four groups of boys are distinguished in Figure 23.1 based on their meeting DSM-III-R criteria during Year 1 for ADHD, ODD, both disorders, or neither disorder. Nearly 80% of boys who met criteria for ODD in Year 1 also met criteria for CD at least once during Years 1–8. This proportion was significantly higher than that for boys who did not meet criteria for ODD in Year 1. In contrast, ADHD in Year 1 was not significantly associated with meeting criteria for CD during Years 1–8. Among boys who met criteria for ADHD, but not ODD in Year 1, only 22% ever met criteria for CD by Year 8. In comparison, nearly 30% of clinic-referred boys who did not meet criteria for either ADHD or ODD in Year 1 met criteria for CD during Years 1–8. These findings suggest a strong relation between ODD and CD, but not between ADHD and CD.[1]

Figure 23.2 shows the results of a similar analysis, but in this case, the 68 boys who met criteria for CD in Year 1 were deleted from the analysis to examine the relation of ADHD and ODD to CD prospectively. As before, ODD in Year 1 was significantly associated with ever meeting criteria for CD in Years 2–8, but ADHD in Year 1 was not.[2] Although one could speculate on the basis of cross-sectional studies that ODD usually precedes CD developmentally because the age of onset for ODD behaviors is recalled as being earlier than the age of

[1]Using logistic regression, ADHD in Year 1 was not associated with ever meeting criteria for CD during Years 1–8 controlling for ODD (Wald $X^2 = 1.10$, $p = .29$), but ODD in Year 1 was associated with ever meeting criteria for CD controlling for ADHD (Wald $X^2 = 10.26$, $p = .001$). The ADHD-by-ODD interaction was not statistically significant (Wald $X^2 = 0.44$, $p = .51$).

[2]ADHD in Year 1 was not associated with ever meeting criteria for CD in Years 2–8 controlling for ODD (Wald $X^2 = 0.99$, $p = .32$), but ODD in Year 1 was associated with ever meeting criteria for CD controlling for ADHD (Wald $X^2 = 4.67$, $p = .03$). The ADHD-by-ODD interaction was not statistically significant (Wald $X^2 = 0.03$, $p = .86$).

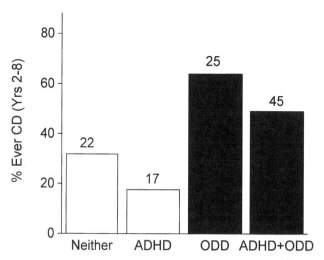

FIGURE 23.2. The percentage of boys who met DSM-III-R criteria for CD at least once during Years 2–8 of the Developmental Trends Study, when boys who met criteria for CD in Year 1 were excluded from the analysis. Percentages are presented separately for boys who met DSM-III-R criteria in Year 1 for ADHD, ODD, both disorders, or neither disorder. The number of boys in each group is presented above the bars.

onset of CD behaviors (Lahey & Loeber, 1994), it is important to show that ODD actually predicts the emergence of later CD in these prospective analyses.

Another longitudinal study of clinic-referred boys has also examined the emergence of new cases of CD in a follow-up assessment conducted 4 years after the baseline assessment among youths who met criteria at baseline for ADHD, ADHD + ODD, or were normal controls (excluding all children who met criteria for CD in the baseline assessment) (Biederman et al., 1996). The boys were 6–17 years of age at baseline and ages 10–21 years at the time of the follow-up. The rates of new diagnoses of CD in the follow-up assessment in the three groups (ADHD, 5%; ADHD + ODD, 11%; control group, 3%) were not significantly different from one another. Biederman et al. interpreted these results as not supporting the conclusion of Loeber et al. (1995) that ODD was a developmental precursor to CD. When the prevalence of new cases of CD among boys who met criteria for ODD in the baseline assessment was compared to *all* youths who did not meet criteria for ODD at baseline in this sample (those with only ADHD and the normal controls), however, CD was significantly more likely to emerge at follow-up among youths with ODD.[3] Thus, when their data were analyzed in a manner parallel to the Loeber et al. (1995) analysis, the results of the Biederman et al. study were consistent with the findings of Loeber et al. (1995) that clinic-referred boys who meet criteria for ODD are at elevated risk for meeting CD criteria at later ages.

A much lower percentage of children with ODD later developed CD in the Biederman et al. (1996) study than in the Developmental Trends Study (Loeber et al., 1995), however. This is probably due to several factors: The sample in the Biederman et al. study was an average of 1.5 years older at the time of the first assessment than the Developmental Trends Study sample. Therefore, it is likely that more of the youths who would ever progress from ODD to CD had already done so in the Biederman sample. The boys in the Biederman et al. sample also had a

---

[3]New analyses of Biederman et al.'s published data showed that the rate of new diagnoses of CD among boys with ODD at baseline (11%) were significantly higher than the rate of new diagnoses of CD among all youths without ODD at baseline (3.5% in the ADHD and control groups combined), $X^2 = 4.01$, $df = 1$, $p < .05$.

higher range of intelligence scores and were more economically advantaged, suggesting that they may have been at lower risk for CD. The most important difference between the studies, however, is that *cumulative* rates of ever meeting criteria for CD during at least one annual assessment over 7 years are reported from the Developmental Trends Study in Figure 23.2, whereas Biederman et al. reported rates of CD in a single follow-up assessment 4 years later. Because youths with CD fluctuate above and below the diagnostic criteria for the disorder from year to year (Lahey et al., 1995), rates of CD during a single assessment will be much lower than cumulative rates obtained from multiple assessments.

The analyses presented in Figures 23.1 and 23.2 suggest that ODD is a developmental precursor to later CD in clinic-referred boys, but ADHD is not. There are at least two possible explanations for the differences in findings between the Developmental Trends Study and the two previous longitudinal studies that found ADHD to be a developmental precursor to CD when childhood CD was controlled (Lambert et al., 1988; Mannuzza et al., 1991). First, the Developmental Trends Study has not yet followed all of its participants into late adolescence and early adulthood, as have some other studies. It is possible, therefore, that the findings of the Developmental Trends Study could change when the ongoing longitudinal assessments during early adulthood are completed. Second, it also is possible that previous studies mistakenly concluded that ADHD was a developmental precursor to CD because ODD was not measured in those studies and ODD was more common among children with ADHD than among children in the control groups of those studies. In the Developmental Trends Study, 84% of the boys who met full DSM-III-R criteria for ADHD in Year 1 also met criteria for ODD. If a high percentage of children with ADHD in other samples also met criteria for ODD, it seems likely that children with ADHD would be more likely to develop later CD than a control group of children without ADHD. This difference could be due to the presence of ODD in childhood rather than to the presence of ADHD in childhood, however.

Because clinic samples are biased toward higher rates of comorbidity (Goodman et al., 1997), we replicated the findings of the Developmental Trends Study using data from the NIMH Methods for the Epidemiology of Child and Adolescent Mental Disorders (MECA) Study (Lahey et al., 1996). This is a population-based household study of 1,285 girls and boys ages 9–17 years from four U.S. communities. Youths and their primary adult caretakers were interviewed using a different version of the same structured diagnostic interview used in the Developmental Trends Study and diagnoses were made in similar ways. Because the MECA Study is cross-sectional, however, it cannot shed light on the developmental relations of ADHD and ODD to CD prospectively, but these data can tell us if the cross-sectional associations among these disorders in a population-based sample resemble those found in the clinic-based Developmental Trends Study.

Because only boys participated in the Developmental Trends Study, MECA data were analyzed separately for boys and girls. As shown in Figure 23.3, ODD was significantly associated with CD when controlling for ADHD, but ADHD was not associated with CD when controlling for ODD among boys. The picture is interestingly different for girls, however. As shown in Figure 23.3, ODD was significantly associated with CD when controlling for ADHD, and ADHD was significantly associated with CD when controlling for ODD among girls.[4] This suggests that both ADHD and ODD may be independently associated with CD in girls. This finding is consistent with cross-sectional analyses of the Ontario Child Health Study

---

[4]Using logistic regression, ODD and CD were significantly associated among boys (Wald $X^2 = 4.67$, $p = .03$), but ADHD and CD were not significantly associated (Wald $X^2 = 0.61$, $p = .43$), and the ADHD-by-ODD interaction was not significant (Wald $X^2 = 0.00$, $p = .95$). Among girls, ODD and CD were significantly associated (Wald $X^2 = 12.74$, $p = .0004$), as were ADHD and CD (Wald $X^2 = 15.82$, $p = .0001$), but the ADHD-by-ODD interaction was not significant (Wald $X^2 = 2.16$, $p = .14$).

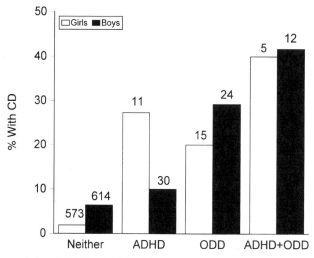

FIGURE 23.3. The association of ADHD and ODD with CD among girls and boys in the cross-sectional population-based MECA Study. The number of youths in each group is presented above the bars.

(OCHS; Szatmari, Boyle, & Offord, 1989). Szatmari et al. found that the association of ADHD with CD among girls (odds ratio 40.0) was significantly greater than among boys (odds ratio 14.7). Although ODD was not controlled in these analyses, these findings from the OCHS suggest that ADHD may be a stronger correlate of CD in girls than in boys. Unfortunately, because the data from both the MECA and OCHS studies were cross-sectional, we cannot be certain that ADHD preceded CD developmentally in these girls. For that reason, it is important that a longitudinal study by Kovacs, Paulauskas, Gatsonis, and Richards (1988) also found that ADHD was a significant predictor of later CD among girls but not boys. The generality of these findings is limited, however, by the fact that the sample consisted of clinic-referred children with depressive disorders.

Some additional comments on the findings of the present MECA analyses may be useful, however. First, because only a small percentage of children meet criteria for these disorders in population-based studies, the number of participants in most cells was small in the present analyses of MECA data. It would be of great importance, therefore, to replicate these analyses using data from a larger population-based study, particularly if that study were longitudinal rather than cross-sectional. Because little is known about the developmental precursors to CD in girls, such a study would be of particular importance to the study of antisocial behavior in girls. Second, although the strong association between ODD and CD found for both girls and boys in the MECA Study is consistent with the view that ODD is a developmental precursor to CD, this finding does not imply that most children who meet criteria for CD in the general population also meet criteria for ODD or ADHD. Consider, for example, the cell sizes for boys in Figure 23.3. Although only 6.4% of boys who did not meet criteria for either ADHD or ODD met criteria for CD, that 6.4% of 614 boys represents 72.2% of all boys who met criteria for CD in the MECA sample. Although some of these boys had numbers of ODD behaviors that were just below the diagnostic threshold for ODD, 54.6% of boys in the MECA sample who met criteria for CD exhibited no DSM-III-R symptoms of ODD. This suggests that although ODD appears to be a developmental precursor to CD, CD does not always emerge among children with ODD. Unfortunately, because the MECA Study was not longitudinal, we cannot distinguish between youths who never exhibited ODD behaviors and those who previously exhibited ODD behaviors but "outgrew" them earlier. Only a longitudinal study that began early in the risk period for CD could tell us what proportion of children who meet criteria for CD do not pass through earlier ODD behaviors.

HYPOTHESES REGARDING DEVELOPMENTAL PRECURSORS TO CONDUCT DISORDER

The present literature is not consistent enough to support any conclusions about the developmental precursors to CD, but we advance some hypotheses in this chapter that we hope will focus future research on these important topics.

1. We hypothesize that ODD behaviors are developmental precursors to CD in boys, but ADHD behaviors are not; that is, boys with high numbers of ODD behaviors in childhood are at increased risk for developing later CD behaviors whether or not they display ADHD behaviors, but boys with high numbers of ADHD behaviors are at risk for later CD only if they also display a high number of ODD behaviors.

2. Both ADHD and ODD behaviors are developmental precursors to CD in girls. Given the current paucity of data, this hypothesis is speculative, but the identification of gender differences in developmental precursors of CD would be of such great importance that this hypothesis is advanced to stimulate empirical tests.

3. Not all children who meet criteria for CD during childhood or adolescence pass through an earlier period during which they exhibit a significant number of ODD behaviors. This hypothesis also is speculative, as it is based only on the findings of the cross-sectional MECA Study, but it is possible that a substantial number of youths in the general population meets criteria for CD without exhibiting earlier ODD behaviors.

4. Regardless of whether ADHD behaviors are developmental precursors to CD when ODD behaviors are controlled, it seems likely that boys (and perhaps especially girls) with ADHD are at high risk for later CD. This may be the case only because ADHD and ODD are highly comorbid, but it would seem to be important to study the developmental progression to CD in children with ADHD for two reasons. First, because many children who develop CD have a history of ADHD, children with ADHD constitute a known high-risk population in which to study the antecedents of CD. Second, the evidence reviewed in the following section suggests that CD that emerges in children with ADHD has an earlier age of onset, is more persistent, and may be more severe. Thus, even if ODD is the developmental precursor to CD among boys, both girls and boys with ADHD are an important high-risk population that needs further study.

CHARACTERISTICS OF CONDUCT DISORDER THAT EMERGE IN CHILDREN WITH ATTENTION-DEFICIT/HYPERACTIVITY DISORDER

In this review of the current evidence on the characteristics of CD that emerge among youths with ADHD, one should keep in mind that some or all of the differences could be attributed to ODD that is comorbid with ADHD, or to interactions of ADHD and ODD, rather than ADHD per se. Unfortunately, none of the published studies reviewed here makes a distinction between ADHD that was or was not comorbid with ODD.

Attention-Deficit/Hyperactivity Disorder and the Age of Onset of Conduct Disorder

The most consistent finding in the existing literature is that ADHD is associated with the early onset of antisocial behavior. Offord, Sullivan, Allen, and Abrams (1979) found in their study of delinquent youths that the age of onset of serious delinquent behavior was significantly earlier for delinquents with ADHD. Walker, Lahey, Hynd, and Frame (1987) similarly found that children with both DSM-III CD and ADHD were significantly younger at the time of referral than children with CD but not ADHD. In a separate sample, Loeber et al. (1995) found that boys who first met criteria for CD in Years 2–6 of the Developmental Trends Study and also exhibited ADHD were significantly younger at the time they first meet criteria for CD than boys without ADHD. This latter finding is particularly important as, unlike previous studies, the Loeber et al. study did not rely on retrospective reports of the age of onset of CD.

Moffitt (1990) also used prospective longitudinal data to examine differences in the age of onset of antisocial behavior associated with ADHD. Using extensive longitudinal data gathered on a New Zealand birth cohort, she found that delinquent youths with ADHD at age 13 had exhibited high levels of behavior problems during every assessment since 3 years of age, whereas 13-year-old delinquents without ADHD exhibited normal levels of behavior problems during every assessment from ages 3 through 11 years. Thus, Moffitt also provided strong evidence from a prospective study that the onset of antisocial behavior occurred markedly later in delinquents without a history of ADHD.

Lahey and Loeber (1997) used data from the DSM-IV Field Trials for the Disruptive Behavior Disorders (Lahey et al., 1995) to replicate the relation between ADHD and ODD and the age of onset of antisocial behavior. Over 80% of youths in whom the first symptom of CD emerged between 1 through 4 years of age met DSM-III-R criteria for both ADHD and ODD, but the percentage of youths with ADHD and/or ODD declined steadily with increasing ages of onset of the first symptom of CD. When these several studies are considered together, it seems likely that ADHD is associated with an earlier age of onset of CD.

Persistence and Severity of Conduct Disorder that Co-Occurs with Attention-Deficit/Hyperactivity Disorder

Because the age of onset of CD is associated with greater persistence of CD (Loeber, 1988a) and higher levels of aggression (Lahey et al., 1998), it would not be surprising if CD that emerges in children with ADHD were more persistent and severe (because ADHD is associated with a younger age of onset of CD). There is some evidence that this is the case, but it is not consistent on all points. Schachar, Rutter, and Smith (1981) provided an important reanalysis of data from the longitudinal Isle of Wight study (Graham & Rutter, 1973), suggesting that comorbid ADHD predicts greater persistence of CD. Youths given the diagnosis of CD at ages 10–11 years were more likely to be given the same diagnosis again at ages 14–15 years if they also received high ratings from parents or teachers on motor hyperactivity at ages 10–11 years. Farrington et al. (1990) similarly found that boys rated high on both childhood conduct problems and childhood ADHD were more likely to engage in criminal behavior during adolescence and adulthood than boys rated high on only conduct problems during childhood. Indeed, Farrington et al. found that the interaction between childhood ADHD and childhood conduct problems was a significant predictor of chronic offending (defined as six or more convictions by the age of 25 years). Magnusson (1984) also found that boys who were rated high on both aggression and ADHD at age 13 years were more likely to commit crimes as adults than boys rated high on aggression only at age 13. Similarly, the follow-up study of Loeber (1988b) showed that over 5 years, boys with high baseline ratings on both aggression and ADHD exhibited significantly higher rates of criminal offending (two to three times as high) than boys rated high at baseline on aggression only. Finally, Moffitt (1990) found that 13-year-old delinquents who had been given the diagnosis of ADHD at age 11 exhibited significantly higher numbers of aggressive acts when they were reassessed at age 15 than delinquent youths without ADHD at age 11.

Thus, the results of five longitudinal studies (Farrington et al., 1990; Loeber, 1988b; Magnusson, 1984; Moffitt, 1990; Schachar et al., 1981) indicate that childhood conduct problems are more persistent when they emerge in children who also exhibit ADHD behaviors. On the other hand, the results of the prospective study of a school-based sample conducted by Lambert (1988) were not consistent with the results of these five studies. The adolescent outcomes of youths rated as exhibiting both hyperactivity and aggression during elementary school were uniformly poor, with this group differing significantly from controls on the number of symptoms of aggressive CD, nonaggressive CD, and the rate of court adjudicated delinquency during adolescence. The adolescent outcomes of youths with high ratings of aggression only during elementary school were almost as poor, however.

Two cross-sectional studies also addressed the severity of CD behaviors when CD arises in children with ADHD. Offord et al. (1979) conducted a study of adjudicated delinquent youths who were on probation to determine if delinquent youths with hyperactivity differed from those without hyperactivity. They found that the hyperactive delinquents were significantly more likely to engage in fighting, drug abuse, and reckless and irresponsible behavior than the nonhyperactive delinquents. Walker et al. (1987) similarly compared children who met DSM-III criteria for both CD and ADHD with children who met criteria for CD but not ADHD. The group with both CD and ADHD also was found to be more likely to engage in physical fighting, to exhibit a higher total number of CD symptoms, and to receive higher peer ratings of aggression and social rejection. All differences were still found when the group with CD, but not ADHD, was limited to those with at least one concurrent diagnosis, which suggests that the greater aggressiveness and severity was specific to concurrent ADHD and not simply to the presence of any concurrent disorder.

On the other hand, Lahey and Loeber (1997) attempted to replicate previously reported differences between youths with CD, with and without concurrent ADHD, in aggressive behavior by conducting new analyses of the DSM-IV Field Trials data set (Lahey et al., 1994) and the Developmental Trends Study (Lahey et al., 1995). In both analyses, youths with CD and ADHD did not differ from youths with CD but not ADHD on the number of aggressive symptoms, nonaggressive symptoms, or total number of symptoms of CD. There are many possible reasons for these failures to replicate, including differences in samples and instruments. Lahey and Loeber (1997) examined the possibility that the failure to replicate may have been due to the use of the more stringent DSM-III-R criteria but found no differences in the severity of associated CD when DSM-III criteria were used. However, they did find evidence that the effect may be dependent on the age of the subjects. Although there was not a significant difference in the number of aggressive symptoms associated with ADHD during

Year 1 of the Developmental Trends Study (when the boys were prepubertal), boys with CD and concurrent ADHD did exhibit significantly more aggressive behaviors than boys with only CD in Year 4 (when they were 10–15 years of age). Thus, it is possible that differences in the severity of CD associated with ADHD do not emerge until adolescence.

When these studies are considered together, it appears likely that CD that emerges among children with ADHD has an earlier onset and is more likely to persist into adolescence and adulthood. In addition, it is possible that youths who exhibit both CD and ADHD are more likely to engage in aggressive behavior, particularly during adolescence, than youths who meet criteria for only CD. Again, however, additional research is needed on these topics. In particular, because none of the studies of the relation of ADHD to the severity and persistence of antisocial behavior also measured ODD, it is possible that the apparent association of ADHD with greater severity and persistence of antisocial behavior could be explained by comorbid ODD instead.

SUMMARY AND DISCUSSION

The existing literature supports no conclusions but does provide the basis for a number of strong hypotheses. Although it is clear that boys with ADHD during childhood are at much higher risk for later CD than boys without childhood ADHD, we hypothesize that this is the result of the high degree of comorbidity between ADHD and ODD; that is, we hypothesize that ODD is a developmental precursor to later CD in boys, but ADHD is not. This means that we hypothesize that boys who meet criteria for ADHD in childhood, but do not exhibit high numbers of ODD behaviors, are not at increased risk for later CD. Because few data are available from prospective studies of representative samples on the base rate of meeting criteria for CD during childhood and adolescence, however, it is not possible to generate firm estimates of the lifetime prevalence of CD (through adolescence) among boys with neither ADHD nor ODD to use as standard of comparison. This weakens our confidence in the hypothesis that boys who meet criteria for ADHD are not at greater risk for later CD than youths who meet criteria for neither ADHD nor ODD. Much less evidence is available on girls, but the sparse existing data suggest that both ADHD and ODD might be developmental precursors to CD in girls. This hypothesis is quite speculative at this point, but it is advanced to stimulate research on possible gender differences in the developmental precursors to CD.

Although ODD appears to be a developmental precursor to CD in both girls and boys, the existing evidence suggests that not all children who meet criteria for CD first exhibit a significant number of ODD behaviors. Thus, it would be important to study similarities and differences between youths for whom ODD behaviors were a precursor to CD and those who developed CD without a history of ODD behaviors. It seems very likely that many factors other than ODD predispose youths to later CD (Lahey, Waldman, & McBurnett, 1999) and such studies would help to identify those factors. In addition, although it appears that many clinic-referred boys with ODD in childhood meet criteria for CD before adulthood, not all boys who meet criteria for ODD in childhood progress to CD. Paradoxically, this could make the study of developmental transitions from ODD to CD of even greater importance. If childhood ODD is a developmental precursor to CD for some boys but not others, it should be possible eventually to identify the factors that govern the developmental progression from ODD to CD. Not enough evidence is currently available on girls to speculate on the proportion of girls with ADHD or ODD who eventually meet criteria for CD, but studying the hypothesized developmental transition from ODD (and perhaps ADHD) to CD in girls would be highly informative for the same reasons.

The Developmental Trends Study (Lahey et al., 1995; Loeber et al., 1995) provides prospective data on the relation between ODD and CD in boys from middle-childhood through adolescence. Unfortunately, few published data currently are available from any longitudinal study on these developmental relations before elementary school ages. This is a serious omission, as retrospective reports of ages of onset in the Developmental Trends Study suggest that the developmental progression from ODD to CD frequently occurs during the preschool and early elementary school years. Therefore, future prospective studies of children that begin early in childhood would be of great value.

If the findings reviewed in this chapter are correct in suggesting that ODD behaviors play the role of a developmental precursor to CD, how might this happen? Although speculative at this point, we briefly advance one view in this chapter that is consistent with the existing data. ODD is characterized by frequently occurring behaviors that are defined in broad terms (e.g., "often touchy or easily annoyed by others," "often angry and resentful," and "often argues with adults"); that is, whereas CD behaviors refer to specific law-violating acts, ODD is defined in terms of broad tendencies to respond angrily and negatively that appear early in life. There is evidence that ODD behavior is highly heritable (Edelbrock, Rende, Plomin, & Thompson, 1995; Waldman, 1997), but it is undoubtedly shaped through gene–environment interactions.

There are probably many ways in which early oppositionality increases the later emergence of CD behaviors. It seems likely that ODD fosters later CD partly by evoking coercive, harsh, and inconsistent parenting behaviors (Anderson, Lytton, & Romney, 1986; Barkley, Fischer, Edelbrock, & Smallish, 1991; Loeber & Tengs, 1986). This leads to reciprocal adverse parent–child interactions that reinforce the child's disruptive behavior and interfere with parental teaching of adaptive behaviors that are incompatible with antisocial behavior (Patterson, 1982). It also seems plausible that ODD behaviors are usually evident earlier than CD behaviors, because CD behaviors require a higher level of cognitive, social, and physical development than ODD behaviors. In some cases, CD behaviors may develop directly from ODD behaviors. For example, frequent irritability and anger may often be shaped into the more complex behaviors of fighting and violence as children develop and learn through interactions with peers, siblings, and adults. Thus, early oppositionality may provide a diffuse emotional basis for the learning of aggression. ODD and fighting also appear to reduce the likelihood of friendships with well-behaved peers and increase the likelihood of associations with aggressive peers who further foster the development of other CD behaviors (Cairns & Cairns, 1994; Tremblay, Masse, Vitaro, & Dobkin, 1995).

Substantial evidence suggests that ADHD also may play a key role in the development of CD in boys, even if it is not a direct developmental precursor to CD. Nearly all existing studies suggest that when CD emerges in children with ADHD, it has an earlier age of onset and is more persistent. This means that efforts to understand the developmental relations among ADHD, ODD, and CD are of considerable scientific and practical importance. Because the most persistent CD appears to emerge earliest, it will be necessary for future studies of the potential roles of ADHD and ODD as developmental precursors of CD to begin earlier in the child's life than in previous studies. Clearly, studies that begin in the preschool period are needed. It also is possible that CD is more severe (particularly in being more likely to involve physical aggression during adolescence) when it emerges in children with ADHD, but the evidence on this point is inconclusive at present. It is possible, however, that comorbid ODD is responsible for the apparent association of ADHD with the age of onset and persistence of CD, as the studies that provide evidence on these topics did not assess ODD.

A variety of other methodological shortcomings also limit conclusions about potential developmental relations among ADHD, ODD and CD. Future research must include adequate numbers of girls to study separately and must allow separate analyses within the major ethnic groups. Because the descriptive hypotheses concerning ADHD, ODD, and CD focus on developmental sequences, prospective longitudinal studies should be the primary research strategy in the future. These future studies should use both clinic-referred and general population samples because of the advantages and disadvantages of each type of sample.

ACKNOWLEDGMENTS.   Preparation of this chapter was supported by NIMH Grant Nos. R01-MH42529, R01-MH53554, U01-MH46725, and the MECA grants. The MECA Program is an epidemiological methodology study performed by four independent research teams in collaboration with staff of the Division of Clinical Research, which was reorganized in 1992, with components now in the Division of Epidemiology and Services Research and the Division of Clinical and Treatment Research of the NIMH, Rockville, Maryland. The NIMH Principal Collaborators are Darrel A. Regier, M.D., M.P.H., Ben Z. Locke, M.S.P.H., Peter S. Jensen, M.D., William E. Narrow, M.D., M.P.H., and Donald S. Rae, M.A.; the NIMH project officer was William J. Huber. The Principal Investigators and Coinvestigators from the four sites are as follows: Emory University, Atlanta, Georgia, U01 MH46725—Mina K. Dulcan, M.D., Benjamin B. Lahey, Ph.D., Donna J. Brogan, Ph.D., Sherryl H. Goodman, Ph.D., and Elaine Flagg, Ph.D.; Research Foundation for Mental Hygiene at New York State Psychiatric Institute, New York, New York, U01 MH46718—Hector R. Bird, M.D., David Shaffer, M.D., Myrna Weissman, Ph.D., Patricia Cohen, Ph.D., Denise Kandel, Ph.D., Christina Hoven, Ph.D., Mark Davies M.P.H., Madelyn S. Gould, Ph.D., and Agnes Whitaker, M.D.; Yale University, New Haven, Connecticut, U01 MH46717—Mary Schwab-Stone, M.D., Philip J. Leaf, Ph.D., Sarah Horwitz, Ph.D., and Judith Lichtman, M.P.H.; University of Puerto Rico, San Juan, Puerto Rico, U01 MH46732—Glorisa Canino, Ph.D., Maritza Rubio-Stipec, MA, Milagros Bravo, Ph.D., Margarita Alegria, Ph.D., Julio Ribera, Ph.D., Sara Huertas, M.D., and Michel Woodbury, M.D.

REFERENCES

American Psychiatric Association. (1994). *Diagnostic and statistical manual of the mental disorders* (4th ed.). Washington, DC: Author.

Anderson, J., Williams, S., McGee, R., & Silva, P. A. (1987). The prevalence of DSM-III disorders in a large sample of preadolescent children from the general population. *Archives of General Psychiatry, 44,* 69–81.

Anderson, K. E., Lytton, H., & Romney, D. M. (1986). Mothers' interactions with normal and conduct-disordered boys: Who affects whom? *Developmental Psychology, 22,* 604–609.

Applegate, B., Lahey, B. B., Hart, E. L., Biederman, J., Hynd, G. W., Barkley, R. A., Ollendick, T., Frick, P. J., Greenhill, L., McBurnett, K., Newcorn, J. H., Kerdyk, L., Garfinkel, B., Waldman, I., & Shaffer, D. (1997). Validity of the age of onset criterion for attention-deficit/hyperactivity disorder: A report from the DSM-IV field trials. *Journal of the American Academy of Child and Adolescent Psychiatry, 36,* 1211–1221.

August, G. J., Stewart, M. A., & Holmes, C. S. (1983). A four-year follow-up of hyperactive boys with and without conduct disorder. *British Journal of Psychiatry, 143,* 192–198.

Barkley, R. A., Fischer, M., Edelbrock, C. S., & Smallish, L. (1991). The adolescent outcome of hyperactive children diagnosed by research criteria: III. Mother-child interactions, family conflicts, and maternal psychopathology. *Journal of Child Psychology and Psychiatry, 32,* 233–256.

Biederman, J., Faraone, S. V., Milberger, S., Jetton, J. G., Chen, L., Mick, E., Greene, R., & Russell, R. L. (1996). Is childhood oppositional defiant disorder a precursor to adolescent conduct disorder? Findings from a four-year follow-up of children with ADHD. *Journal of the American Academy of Child and Adolescent Psychiatry, 35*, 1193–1204.

Cairns, R. B., & Cairns, B. D. (1994). *Lifelines and risks: Pathways of youth in our time*. Cambridge, UK: Cambridge University Press.

Edelbrock, C., Rende, R., Plomin, R., & Thompson, L. E. (1995). A twin study of competence and problem behavior in childhood and early adolescence. *Journal of Child Psychology and Psychiatry, 36*, 775–785.

Farrington, D. P., Loeber, R., & Van Kammen, W. B. (1990). Long term criminal outcomes of hyperactivity-impulsivity–attention deficit and conduct problems in childhood. In L. N. Robins & M. R. Rutter (Eds.), *Straight and devious pathways to adulthood* (pp. 62–81). New York: Cambridge University Press.

Gittelman, R., Mannuzza, S., Shenker, R., & Bonagura, N., et al. (1985). Hyperactive boys almost grown up: I. Psychiatric status. *Archives of General Psychiatry, 42*, 937–947.

Goodman, S. H., Lahey, B. B., Fielding, B., Dulcan, M., Narrow, W., & Regier, D. (1997). Representativeness of clinical samples of youth with mental disorders: A preliminary population-based study. *Journal of Abnormal Psychology, 106*, 3–14.

Graham, P., & Rutter, M. (1973). Psychiatric disorder in the young adolescent: A follow-up study. *Proceedings of the Royal Society of Medicine, 66*, 58–61.

Hechtman, L., Weiss, G., & Perlman, T. (1984). Hyperactives as young adults: Past and current substance abuse and antisocial behavior. *American Journal of Orthopsychiatry, 54*, 415–425.

Kovacs, M., Paulauskas, S., Gatsonis, C., & Richards, C. (1988). Depressive disorders in childhood: III. A longitudinal study of comorbidity with and risk for conduct disorders. *Journal of Affective Disorders, 15*, 205–217.

Lahey, B. B., Applegate, B., Barkley, R. A., Garfinkel, B., McBurnett, K., Kerdyk, L., Greenhill, L., Hynd, G. W., Frick, P. J., Newcorn, J., Biederman, J., Ollendick, T., Hart, E. L., Perez, D., Waldman, I., & Shaffer, D. (1994). DSM-IV field trials for oppositional defiant disorder and conduct disorder in children and adolescents. *American Journal of Psychiatry, 151*, 1163–1171.

Lahey, B. B., Flagg, E. W., Bird, H. R., Schwab-Stone, M., Canino, G., Dulcan, M. K., Leaf, P. J., Davies, M., Brogan, D., Bourdon, K., Horwitz, S. M., Rubio-Stipec, M., Freeman, D. H., Lichtman, J., Shaffer, D., Goodman, S. H., Narrow, W. E., Weissman, M. M., Kandel, D. B., Jensen, P. S., Richters, J. E., & Regier, D. A. (1996). The NIMH Methods for the Epidemiology of Child and Adolescent Mental Disorders (MECA) Study: Background and methodology. *Journal of the American Academy of Child and Adolescent Psychiatry, 35*, 855–864.

Lahey, B. B., & Loeber, R. (1994). Framework for a developmental model of oppositional defiant disorder and conduct disorder. In D. K. Routh (Ed.), *Disruptive behavior disorders in childhood* (pp. 139–180). New York: Plenum Press.

Lahey, B. B., & Loeber, R. (1997). Attention-deficit/hyperactivity disorder, oppositional defiant disorder, conduct disorder, and adult antisocial behavior: A lifespan perspective. In D. Stoff, J. Breiling, & J. Maser (Eds.), *Handbook of antisocial behavior* (pp. 51–59). New York: Wiley.

Lahey, B. B., Loeber, R., Frick, P. J., Quay, H. C., & Grimm, J. (1992). Oppositional defiant and conduct disorders: Issues to be resolved for DSM-IV. *Journal of the American Academy of Child and Adolescent Psychiatry, 31*, 539–546.

Lahey, B. B., Loeber, R., Hart, E. L., Frick, P. J., Applegate, B., Zhang, Q., Green, S. M., & Russo, M. F. (1995). Four-year longitudinal study of conduct disorder in boys: Patterns and predictors of persistence. *Journal of Abnormal Psychology, 104*, 83–93.

Lahey, B. B., Loeber, R., Quay, H. C., Applegate, B., Shaffer, D., Waldman, I., Hart, E. L., McBurnett, K., Frick, P. J., Jensen, P., Dulcan, M., Canino, G., & Bird, H. (1998). Validity of DSM-IV subtypes of conduct disorder based on age of onset. *Journal of the American Academy of Child and Adolescent Psychiatry, 37*, 435–442.

Lahey, B. B., Loeber, R., Quay, H. C., Frick, P. J., & Grimm, J. (1992). Oppositional defiant and conduct disorders: Issues to be resolved for DSM-IV. *Journal of the American Academy of Child and Adolescent Psychiatry, 31*, 539–546.

Lahey, B. B., Loeber, R., Stouthamer-Loeber, M., Christ, M. A. G., Green, S., Russo, M. F., Frick, P. J., & Dulcan, M. (1990). Comparison of DSM-III and DSM III-R diagnoses for prepubertal children: changes in prevalence and validity. *Journal of the American Academy of Child and Adolescent Psychiatry, 29*, 620–626.

Lahey, B. B., Waldman, I. D., & McBurnett, K. (1999). The development of antisocial behavior: An integrative causal model. *Journal of Child Psychology and Psychiatry, 40*, 669–682.

Lambert, N. M. (1988). Adolescent outcomes for hyperactive children: Perspectives on general and specific patterns of childhood risk for adolescent educational, social, and mental health problems. *American Psychologist, 43*, 786–799.

Lilienfeld, B., & Waldman, I. (1990). The relationship between childhood attention-deficit hyperactivity disorder and adult antisocial behavior re-examined: The problem of heterogeneity. *Clinical Psychology Review, 10*, 699–725.

Loeber, R. (1982). The stability of antisocial and delinquent child behavior: A review. *Child Development, 53*, 1431–1446.

Loeber, R. (1988a). Natural histories of conduct problems, delinquency, and associated substance use: Evidence for developmental progressions. In B. B. Lahey & A. E. Kazdin (Eds.), *Advances in clinical child psychology* (pp. 73–124). New York: Plenum Press.

Loeber, R. (1988b). Behavioral precursors and accelerators of delinquency. In W. Buikhuisen & S.A. Mednick (Eds.), *Explaining criminal behavior* (pp. 51–67). Leiden: Brill.

Loeber, R. (1990). Development and risk factors of juvenile antisocial behavior and delinquency. *Clinical Psychology Review, 10*, 1–41.

Loeber, R. (1991). Antisocial behavior: More enduring than changeable? *Journal of the American Academy of Child and Adolescent Psychiatry, 30*, 393–397.

Loeber, R., Green, S. M., Keenan, K., & Lahey, B. B. (1995). Which boys will fare worse? Early predictors of the onset of conduct disorder in a six-year longitudinal study. *Journal of the American Academy of Child and Adolescent Psychiatry, 34*, 499–509.

Loeber, R., & Tengs, T. (1986). The analysis of coercive chains between children, mothers, and siblings. *Journal of Family Violence, 1*, 51–70.

Loney, J., Kramer, J., & Milich, R. S. (1981). The hyperactive child grows up: Predictors of symptoms, delinquency, and achievement at follow-up. In K. D. Gadow & J. Loney (Eds.), *Psychosocial aspects of drug treatment for hyperactivity* (pp. 381–415). Boulder, CO: Westview Press.

Magnusson, D. (1984). *Early conduct and biological factors in the developmental background of adult delinquency.* Henry Tajfel Memorial Lecture, Oxford University, Oxford, UK.

Magnusson, D., Stattin, H., & Duner, A. (1983). Aggression and criminality in a longitudinal perspective. In K. T. Van Dusen & S. A. Mednick (Eds.), *Antecedents of aggression and antisocial behavior* (pp. 1–54). Boston: Kluwer-Nijhoff.

Mannuzza, S., Klein, R. G., Bessler, A., Malloy, P., & LaPadula, M. (1993). Adult outcome of hyperactive boys: Educational achievement, occupational rank, and psychiatric status. *Archives of General Psychiatry, 50*, 565–576.

Mannuzza, S., Klein, R. G., Bonagura, N., Malloy, P., Giampino, T. L., & Addalli, K. A. (1991). Hyperactive boys almost grown up: Replication of psychiatric status. *Archives of General Psychiatry, 48*, 77–83.

Moffitt, T. E. (1990). Juvenile delinquency and attention deficit disorder: Boys' developmental trajectories from age 3 to 15. *Child Development, 61*, 893–910.

Moffitt, T. E. (1993). Adolescence-limited and life course persistent antisocial behavior: A developmental typology. *Psychological Review, 100*, 674–701.

Offord, D. R., Adler, R. J., & Boyle, M. H. (1986). Prevalence and sociodemographic correlates of conduct disorder. *American Journal of Social Psychiatry, 4*, 272–278.

Offord, D. R., Boyle, M. H., Szatmari, P., Rae-Grant, N. I., Links, P. S., Cadman, D. T., Byles, J. A., Crawford, J. W., Blum, H. M., Byrne, C., Thomas, H., & Woodward, C. A. (1987), Ontario Child Health Study, II: Six-month prevalence of disorder and rates of service utilization. *Archives of General Psychiatry, 44*, 832–836.

Offord, D. R., Sullivan, K., Allen, N., & Abrams, N. (1979). Delinquency and hyperactivity. *Journal of Nervous and Mental Disease, 167*, 734–741.

Osborn, S. G., & West, D. J. (1978). The effectiveness of various predictors of criminal careers. *Journal of Adolescence, 1*, 101–117.

Patterson, G. R. (1982). *Coercive family interactions.* Eugene, OR: Castalia Press.

Satterfield, J. H., Hoppe, C. M., & Schell, A. M. (1982). A prospective study of delinquency in 110 adolescent boys with attention deficit disorder and 88 normal adolescent boys. *American Journal of Psychiatry, 139*, 795–798.

Satterfield, J. H., & Schell, A. M. (1997). A prospective study of hyperactive boys with conduct problems and normal boys: Adolescent and adult criminality. *Journal of the American Academy of Child and Adolescent Psychiatry, 36*, 1726–1735.

Schachar, R., Rutter, M., & Smith, A. (1981). The characteristics of situationally and pervasively hyperactive children: Implications for syndrome definition. *Journal of Child Psychology and Psychiatry, 22*, 375–392.

Szatmari, P., Boyle, M., & Offord, D. R. (1989). ADHD and conduct disorder: Degree of diagnostic overlap and differences among correlates. *Journal of the American Academy of Child and Adolescent Psychiatry, 28*, 865–872.

Tremblay, R. E., Masse, L. C., Vitaro, F., & Dobkin, P. L. (1995). The impact of friends' deviant behavior on the early onset of delinquency: Longitudinal data from 6 to 13 years. *Development and Psychopathology, 7*, 649–667.

Waldman, I. (1997, June). *Competing models for genetic and environmental influences on childhood disruptive behavior disorders.* Paper presented to the eighth annual meeting of the International Society for Research on Child and Adolescent Psychopathology, Paris, France.

Walker, J. L., Lahey, B. B., Hynd, G. W., & Frame, C. L. (1987). Comparison of specific patterns of antisocial behavior in children with conduct disorder with or without coexisting hyperactivity. *Journal of Consulting and Clinical Psychology, 55*, 910–913.

24

Conduct Disorder

Kenneth A. Dodge

Studying conduct disorder is a bit like studying cardiovascular disease. Both constructs represent a loose collection of correlated symptoms, with subtypes, in contrast to a singular disease process. Both heart disease and conduct disorder are vaguely defined constructs with questionable validity, but both disorders have clearly identifiable referent points, such as a myocardial infarction or an act of homicide. In much of medical research, the goal is to identify a cluster of symptoms (called a "syndrome") and then to seek a single causal agent. This picture characterizes the history of research on acquired immune deficiency syndrome (AIDS). The symptoms were first noted and labeled as a syndrome in the late 1970s, and then the causal agent was identified in the form of the human immunodeficiency virus (HIV). At that point, the presence of the virus (rather than the syndrome or symptoms) became the operational definition of the disease.

With heart disease (and conduct disorder), a single causal agent will never be identified. Instead, our models of the development of heart disease include multiple diverse risk factors, such as diet, exercise, smoking, genes, arterial plaque buildup, and blood flow. These diverse factors, although correlated, suggest that there are many different ways to develop the same heart disease, a phenomenon known as *equifinality*. Also, these same risk factors have been implicated in other disease outcomes, such as cancer, lung disease, diabetes, and stroke, a phenomenon known as *multifinality*. So, too, with conduct disorder, the models that are being articulated include multiple risk factors and varying paths to conduct problems. Likewise, some of the same risk factors are being linked to other maladaptive outcomes, including adolescent pregnancy, substance abuse, and internalizing disorders.

One promising solution to the problem of heterogeneity in heart disease is to identify subtypes that have greater coherence in etiology, symptoms, course, and treatment. So, too, with conduct disorder, it appears that a promising direction will be to identify subtypes that have greater coherence. These subtypes have yet to be consensually embraced, although candidate taxonomies include the distinctions between reactive and proactive violence (Dodge, Pettit, Bates, & Valente, 1995), between life-course-persistent and adolescence-

Kenneth A. Dodge • Center for Child and Family Policy, Duke University, Durham, North Carolina 27708.

Handbook of Developmental Psychopathology, Second Edition, edited by Arnold J. Sameroff, Michael Lewis, and Suzanne M. Miller. Kluwer Academic/Plenum Publishers, New York, 2000.

limited symptoms (Moffitt, 1993), and between a pure type and a type that is comorbid with attention-deficit/hyperactivity disorder (ADHD; Hinshaw, 1987).

The risk-factor approach in developmental psychopathology has a long and rich history (Rutter & Garmezy, 1983). One limit of the risk-factor approach in developmental psycho-pathology is that it tells us little about *how* conduct problems develop or about developmental process itself. One task in understanding development is to identify major risk factors and then to weave a tapestry of development by understanding how distal risk factors (such as diet or stressful lifestyles) relate to proximal processes (such as arterial plaque buildup and blood flow) to lead over time to heart disease and to discrete events such as a heart attack.

The goal of the current chapter is to build such a developmental model of conduct disorder. We need to understand how cognitive and emotional processes during interpersonal events lead to the commission of aggressive, deviant, and violent behaviors, and we need also to understand how distal biological and social factors provide a context for these proximal processes. The proposed model is described, and this structure is buttressed by empirical findings from longitudinal inquiry. Finally, the implications of this model for intervention and prevention practice and research are summarized.

PROXIMAL PROCESSES

Consider the adolescent boy who is walking down the street and is approached by a group of peers who begin to call him names, laugh, and tease him. Some boys respond to this situation by getting angry, escalating the conflict, and perhaps reacting violently, whereas other boys are able to deflect attention to another topic, ignore it, laugh, make light of the teasing, or firmly ask that the teasing stop. The cognitive and emotional processes that occur during this situation constitute the proximal mechanisms for aggressive behavior. An adoles-cent's response in this situation can be conceptualized as occurring as a function of his emotional and mental processing of these situational cues. Processing occurs in a sequential stream across real time. Based on models of problem solving in cognitive science (Newell & Simon, 1972), Dodge (1986, 1993) and Huesmann (1988) have developed models of the information-processing steps involved in responding to social cues.

The first step of processing is to encode the presented cues through attention, sensation, and perception. Because the array of available cues is always far too complex to be encoded fully, the individual selectively attends to certain cues at the expense of attention to other cues. The individual applies a "lens" to his or her focus of attention that allows a subset of cues to be encoded more deeply. Individual differences in selective attention are likely to lead to differences in behavioral responding. For example, the boy who attends to peers' laughing at him and the inner pain that he feels will be more likely to react aggressively than the boy who attends to the police car nearby or to the hint of jocularity in the peers' voices. Gouze (1987) has found that boys who attend to hostile features of cues are more likely to behave aggres-sively than are boys who attend to nonhostile features, and Dodge et al. (1995) have found that children who attend to irrelevant stimuli are more likely to become aggressive over time than are those who attend to relevant stimuli.

The next step of processing is to interpret the encoded cues. In the preceding example, one boy might interpret the peers' teasing as a hostile sign of "dissing," whereas another boy might interpret the same cues as a harmless prank. Both deficits (inaccuracies) (Dodge, Murphy, & Buchsbaum, 1984) and biases (Dodge et al., 1995) in interpretation of others' intentions have been related to aggressive behavior. Over three dozen studies have demonstrated the hostile attributional biases of aggressive children (Coie & Dodge, 1997).

Once cues are interpreted, the individual accesses one or more possible behavioral responses from long-term memory, a process known as response generation or problem solving. Children who have available numerous aggressive and atypical responses, and who are less able to generate competent responses, are likely to demonstrate chronic aggressive behavior problems (Asher & Renshaw, 1981; Rubin, Bream, & Rose-Krasnor, 1991; Waas, 1988). Accessing a response differs from selecting that response for enactment (e.g., we all experience impulses that are withheld), so the next step of processing is response evaluation. The moral merits of a response and its probable consequences are evaluated through mental representation at this step. Children who have trouble inhibiting responses (Perry, Perry, & Rasmussen, 1986), who are able to anticipate relatively few consequences for their behaviors (Slaby & Guerra, 1988), who evaluate aggressive responses as less morally "bad" (Deluty, 1983), or who anticipate positive outcomes for aggressing (Hart, Ladd, & Burleson, 1990) are likely to display chronic aggressive behavior.

The final step of processing is to transform the cognitively selected response into behavior, called enactment. Perry et al. (1986) have found that children who report that displaying aggressive behavior would be "easy," and that they are good at it, are indeed likely to behave aggressively with great frequency.

Children's patterns of processing at these five steps significantly predict aggressive behavioral responses in specific situational episodes (Dodge, Pettit, McClaskey, & Brown, 1986) as well as chronic aggressive behavioral patterns (Dodge et al., 1995). Furthermore, they have predicted growth in aggression over time (Dodge et al., 1995). Processing patterns also distinguish subgroups of conduct problem children, in that hostile attributional biases predict reactive–angry aggressive behavior (Dodge & Coie, 1987), whereas positive evaluations of aggressive responses predict proactive–instrumental aggressive behavior (Crick & Dodge, 1996). Even though any single processing pattern predicts aggressive behavior with only modest strength, comprehensive analyses of patterns of processing at all five steps have provided fairly strong predictions of chronic aggressive behavior, with multiple correlations ranging up to .94 (Slaby & Guerra, 1988).

DISTAL RISK FACTORS

As a model of the proximal mechanisms in aggressive behavior, social information-processing analyses have proven quite useful. In addition, these analyses suggest directions to search for distal risk factors in conduct disorder; that is, the antecedents of aggressogenic processing patterns ought to be risk factors for conduct disorder as well. This analysis suggests the following three kinds of distal risk factors, all of which have been related empirically to conduct problem outcomes. These risk factors are biological predispositions, sociocultural contexts, and life experiences.

Biological Factors

We know that because of genes (Edelbrock, Rende, Plomin, & Thompson, 1992) or *in utero* experiences (Tesman & Hills, 1994), some children are born into the world with predispositions to process information in deficient ways that could, under specific environmental conditions, lead to conduct problem outcomes. Gray (1987) has hypothesized that a neural hyperpersistent behavior facilitation system (BFS), with its two major components of locomotion and drive for incentive reward, has bases in the mesolimbic dopaminergic pathway and has consequences in the cognitive emphasis on immediate gratification. In processing terms, a strong BFS would mean a focus on immediate rewards at the step of evaluating responses. Because aggressive behavior tends to produce immediate rewards (and sometimes long-term ill effects for the respondent), a strong BFS could lead to chronic instrumental aggression (Quay, 1993). A second neural system, the behavior inhibition system (BIS), stops a behavior when expectations for the outcomes of that behavior are negative. This system drives environmental signal stabilization (Spoont, 1992), which allows for impulse control (Rogeness, Javors, & Pliszka, 1992). A growing body of evidence has linked impulsive aggressive behavior to aspects of the BIS, namely, low cerebrospinal fluid concentrations of serotonin metabolites (5-HIAA; Kruesi et al., 1990), low 5-HT (5-hydroxytryptamine; Coccaro, Kavoussi, & Lesser, 1992), and low levels of norepinephrine (Rogeness et al., 1992).

Autonomic nervous system activity, in the form of low skin conductance (Hare, 1978) or low resting heart rate (Raine, 1993), has also been empirically related to chronic conduct problems. In processing terms, the function of this activity is to regulate attention to cues (Raine, 1993). Other neuropsychological deficits have been related to conduct disorder (Frost, Moffitt, & McGee, 1989), including verbal intelligence (IQ; Moffitt & Lynam, 1994), although the mechanisms have been only vaguely articulated. Pennington and Bennetto (1993) have argued that executive function deficits, which limit planning and evaluation of responses, constitute a problem distinct from verbal intelligence in the cognitive mechanisms that control aggressive behavior. Barkley (1997) has implicated executive function deficits in behavioral inhibition and has linked these deficits to both attention-deficit/hyperactivity disorder (ADHD) and conduct problems.

Individual differences in infant temperament have also been linked to later conduct problems (Bates, Bayles, Bennett, Ridge, & Brown, 1991). In a longitudinal study of 585 boys and girls followed from the preschool years through adolescence, called the Child Development Project (CDP), Bates, Pettit, Dodge, and Ridge (1997) have found that mothers' ratings of their child's difficult and hyperpersistent temperament at 6 months of age significantly and modestly predicted later teachers' ratings of externalizing conduct problems on the Child Behavior Checklist (TRF-CBC).

The magnitude of almost all of the findings relating biological dispositional characteristics at or near birth to adolescent conduct problems is modest at best, suggesting that other factors must be implicated in antisocial behavioral development. Nonetheless, this component is substantial and must not be ignored.

Sociocultural Contexts

Just as important in antisocial development is the sociocultural context into which the child is born. Children born into crowded inner-city settings are at heightened risk for violence outcomes (Hammond & Yung, 1991). Shaw and McKay (1942) argued that community structural factors of poverty, ethnic heterogeneity, and high residential mobility are risk factors for violent crime, and, more recently, Sampson, Raudenbush, and Earls (1997) have demonstrated with hierarchical linear modeling that the effects of neighborhood factors on crime persist even after individual factors are controlled. Likewise, children born into families of poverty are at risk for later peer-nominated aggression (Patterson, Kupersmidt, & Vaden, 1990) and serious violent crime (Blumstein, Farrington, & Moitra, 1985) even when community levels of poverty are controlled. Low family socioeconomic status is one of the most robust contextual risk factors for later conduct problems (Guerra, Huesmann, Tolan, Van Acker, & Eron, 1995).

Certain cultural contexts have been identified as risk factors for aggressive behavioral development. Nisbett and Cohen (1996) have compiled evidence to conclude that a "culture of honor" is responsible for the consistently higher rates of violence in the American South than in other geographic regions. Wilson (1987) has pointed toward a culture that emphasizes self-respect as a factor in violent retaliation.

Numerous other ecological conditions dispose children toward conduct problem outcomes, and these conditions exert their effects at different points in the child's development. In early life, factors such as a context of parental conflict (McCord, 1991a) and being born to a single, teenage parent in a large family (Blum, Boyle, & Offord, 1988) present significant risks. During elementary school, both classroom academic achievement levels (Werthamer-Larsson, Kellam, & Wheeler, 1991) and classroom norms for aggressive behavior (Kellam & Rebok, 1992) alter individual aggressive behavior. In adolescence and adulthood, factors such as unemployment (Farrington, Gallagher, Morley, St. Ledger, & West, 1986) enhance risk.

Life Experiences

The story is not fully told by biological and sociocultural context factors present at birth. Chronic conduct problems grow out of life experiences in multiple domains, particularly parenting and peer experiences. The specific types of experiences that have proven important in predicting later conduct problems, however, vary across development.

Parenting

In early life, insecure attachment relationships between parent and infant have been found to predict later conduct problems (Sroufe, 1983), although the effects are weak and findings have been mixed (Bates et al., 1991). Maternal negativity toward the preschool-age child has been found to predict conduct problems 4 years later (Booth, Rose-Frasnor, McKinnon, & Rubin, 1994). As children move toward the early school years, Bates and Bayles (1988) found that maternal affection and warmth are negatively related to conduct problems.

Discipline patterns by parents during the child's early school years are the hallmark of Patterson's coercion theory (1995). Inconsistent and harsh discipline, especially involving physical punishment, has been related to later conduct problems through prospective inquiry in a variety of samples, from 8-year-old boys in London (Farrington & Hawkins, 1991) to the school-age boys in the Cambridge–Somerville Youth Study (McCord, 1991a), and from children in upstate New York (Cohen & Brook, 1995) to children in the Midwest and South (Dodge et al., 1995). At the extreme of physical punishment experiences is the occurrence of physical abuse. The experience of physical abuse during the first 5 years of life is one of the most consistent distal risk factors for later conduct problems (Dodge, Bates, & Pettit, 1990), crime (Widom, 1989), and adult antisocial personality disorder (Luntz & Widom, 1994).

As children move toward adolescence, parenting becomes even more complex than employing consistent, nonviolent discipline strategies and maintaining a warm parent–child relationship. These tasks remain important predictors of antisocial growth (Hawkins & Lishner, 1987), but parental monitoring of the child's whereabouts and supervision of the child's activities become significant risk factors as well (Simons, Wu, Conger, & Lorenz, 1994).

Peer Experiences

Alongside the importance of parenting and positive parent–child relationships is the importance of positive peer relations and peer influences on antisocial development. Just as with parenting, the kinds of peer experiences that indicate risk vary across development. During the preschool years, the amount of exposure that a child has to aggressive peers in day care or preschool is predictive of later aggressive behavior, perhaps because of the modeling of this behavior (Sinclair, Pettit, Harrist, Dodge, & Bates, 1994).

During the early school years, social rejection by the classroom peer group is a marker for later conduct problems (Coie, Terry, Lenox, Lochman, & Hyman 1995). In the Child Development Project (CDP) referred to earlier, those children who have been rejected for at least 2 or 3 years by second-grade peers have a 50% chance of displaying clinically significant externalizing conduct problems later in adolescence, in contrast with only a 9% chance for those children who manage to avoid early peer rejection (Dodge, 1993). This risk holds even when controlling for any aggressive behavior that may have contributed to a child's social rejection.

As children move into adolescence, acceptance in the mainstream group remains important, but association with other, deviant, peers also becomes a risk factor for antisocial development. Deviant peer cliques exert an influence on adolescent conduct problems (Coie, Terry, & Lochman, 1993; Patterson, Capaldi, & Bank, 1991; Simons et al., 1994). It has long been recognized that membership in a gang is a risk factor for violent crime (Spergel, Ross, Curry, & Chance, 1989). Notwithstanding the effect of homophily (i.e., persons seeking association with others who are similar to them), Thornberry, Krohn, Lizotte, and Chard-Wierschem (1993) found that gang members accelerated their criminal behavior during the period of gang membership and then decelerated this behavior following termination of gang membership.

Schooling

Yet another life experience that increases risk for antisocial development is failure with competitive academic tasks in formal school (Moffitt, Gabrielli, Mednick, & Schulsinger, 1981). Early school failure, more than low intelligence (a biological predisposition risk factor), appears to endow the risk (Hinshaw, 1992). Early grade retention increases risk for later conduct problems, in spite of its immediate academic benefits (Holmes, 1989), perhaps because of peer rejection associated with being labeled as a retained child (Plummer & Graziano, 1987).

Other life experiences undoubtedly mark risk for antisocial development as well, although they have been studied less thoroughly. Preschool experience in out-of-home day care (Bates et al., 1994) and early exposure to violence on television (Huesmann & Eron, 1986) have both been identified as risk factors for later aggressive behavior.

HOW RISK FACTORS OPERATE TOGETHER

Each of the risk factors described here has been associated with conduct problem development, but the magnitude of effect for any single factor is relatively small. An important question in developmental psychopathology concerns the manner in which risk factors operate in conjunction with each other. Too many battles have been fought between those who assert that genes carry destiny and those who deny the existence of biological factors altogether. Instead, combinatory models including multiple diverse risk factors need to be examined more closely.

Additive Models

The most obvious combinatory model is an additive model. Models of cumulative risk for adolescent delinquency have been proposed by Rutter (Rutter, Cox, Tupling, Berger, & Yule, 1975), who found that the number of distal risk factors present, rather than any single risk factor, affords the strongest prediction of later antisocial behavior. This model exemplifies the principle of equifinality, and it has been supported in numerous studies.

In the CDP, 20 different biological, contextual, and life experience risk factors were assessed during preschool. Although most of these factors were significantly related to conduct problems 5 years later, the magnitude of any single factor was weak; however, the cumulative risk from all of these factors accounted for about half of the total variance in conduct problem outcomes (Deater-Deckard, Dodge, Bates, & Pettit, 1996). This cumulative effect is dramatically represented by just four diverse risk factors (difficult biological temperament, low socioeconomic status at birth, early experience of physical abuse, and peer rejection in early elementary school). Using an outcome criterion of clinically significant conduct problems in grades 6 or 7 (a teacher-rated Externalizing Problems Child Behavior Checklist T score of 70 or higher), Dodge (1996) found low risk (7% chance) for children with none of these four risk factors, moderate risk (11–30% chance) for children with any one of these factors, but high risk (57% chance) for children with all four of these risk factors.

Interactive Models

Interactive models, tested by interaction effects in analyses of variance or multiplicative terms in regression analyses, posit that certain distal risk factors operate only in the presence (or absence) of another risk factor. It may be that some life experiences increase risk for conduct problem development only for certain children (e.g., those who are genetically predisposed) or only in certain cultural contexts. These diathesis–stress models have been supported in a variety of studies and have enhanced the total predictability of conduct problem development beyond that afforded by additive models.

In the CDP, parenting effects have interacted with both biological predispositions and cultural contexts. Among families whose parents display non-restrictive parenting styles, the effects of early temperament on later conduct problems are relatively strong, whereas among families whose parents display restrictive parenting styles, the effects of temperament are muted (Bates et al., in press). It appears that a restrictive style of parenting can blunt the effects of a difficult temperament on a child's development. As another example, Pettit, Laird, Bates, and Dodge (1997) found that even though family and neighborhood poverty present risk factors for conduct problem development, the extent of this risk can be moderated by parental supervision. Among families who live in low socioeconomic class surroundings and presumably would be exposed to dangerous neighborhood influences, children who are never supervised by an adult during after-school hours during first grade receive externalizing problems scores from their sixth-grade teachers that are twice as high as those for children who spend at least some of their first-grade after-school hours with any adult supervision. In contrast, among middle-class families, close supervision is less critical: Children who spend some of their first-grade after-school hours without adult supervision fare equally as well in sixth grade as do those children who are always supervised by an adult in first grade.

In the same spirit of interaction effects, biological dispositions can alter the effects of life experiences. Recall that in the CDP, the main effects of peer social rejection during kindergarten and grades 1 and 2 were to increase the risk for conduct problem outcomes in adolescence severalfold (Dodge, 1993). It appears that social rejection acts as a stressor to increase risk of antisocial development. However, this risk is enhanced only for certain types of children, particularly those who display a difficult temperament. Among children who were below the sample median in resistant temperamental predisposition (defined as a pattern of defying maternal attempts to control behavior, as recalled by mothers when the child was age 4, using the Bates Infant Characteristics Questionnaire), the experience of peer rejection in early elementary school had no effect at all on increasing later conduct problems (Dodge, 1993). In contrast, among those children who were above the median in resistant temperament, the experience of being rejected by classroom peers had a dramatic effect on incrementing risk for conduct problem development. Those resistant-temperament children who experienced peer rejection by second grade had a three-in-five chance of clinically significant conduct problems in adolescence, which represents a sevenfold increase in risk over base rates.

Garmezy and Rutter (1983) have referred to interaction effects as depicting *protective factors* in the development of psychopathology. In the CDP example cited here, a calm temperament acts as a protective factor to buffer a child from the deleterious effects of a stressor such as chronic peer rejection. Likewise, social acceptance by the classroom peer group can be thought of as a protective factor that buffers the deleterious effects of a resistant temperament.

A crucial corollary of interaction effects is that life experiences may have very different impact on children who vary in cultural background, ethnicity, gender, or age (Deater-Deckard & Dodge, 1997). In the CDP, Deater-Deckard, Dodge, Bates, and Pettit (1997) found that physical discipline exerts different impact on European-American children and African-American children, perhaps because of the different cultural contexts in which these families reside. Among European-American children, the risk induced by the frequent experience of physical discipline is substantial, whereas among African-American children, this risk is minimal. This interaction holds even when socioeconomic status is controlled statistically.

Several hypotheses can be asserted regarding the mechanisms of this interaction effect, and they serve to draw out the possible underlying mechanisms of the effect of physical discipline itself. Physical discipline is empirically correlated with other aspects of problematic parenting (e.g., lack of monitoring and lack of parent–child warmth) among European-American families but not among African-American families, so perhaps physical discipline indexes more general problematic parenting in European-American families than African-American families. Alternately, perhaps because physical discipline is more normative among African-American families than European-American families, it is not viewed as unusual or deviant parenting by the child and thus exerts no adverse impact. Heffer and Kelly (1987) found that African-American families endorse and accept physical discipline to a greater degree than do European-American families, supporting this hypothesis. However, they found a sharp distinction among African-American families between physical discipline and physical abuse. Indeed, the major caveat on the interaction effect just described is that experience of physical abuse has equally deleterious effects on conduct problem development in both African-American and European-American children (Dodge et al., 1995).

Interaction effects between parenting and gender also occur. Using CDP data, McFadyen-Ketchum, Bates, Dodge, and Pettit (1997) found that directly observed bouts of parent–child coercion tend to accelerate aggressive behavioral development in boys (consistent with Patterson's coercion theory), but these bouts have the opposite effect on girls; that is, parental coercion decreases aggressive behavior in girls, which, of course, is the effect that parents hope it will have.

Transactional Developmental Models

Even though both additive and interactive models of risk factors in antisocial development have received empirical support and can account for large proportions of the variance in antisocial outcomes, these models tell us little about how these factors unfold over time. The developmental psychopathology of conduct disorder requires a transactional developmental understanding (Sameroff & Chandler, 1975). This understanding includes recognition of the ways that distal risk factors correlate with each other and may even cause one another across time. For example, a child with a resistant temperament might incite his or her parents to become frustrated and to employ inconsistent and harsh discipline practices. Also, a stressful context of poverty and a neighborhood offering little support for single parents might lead a parent to become less able to offer a warm relationship with his or her child. So, some life experiences for a child grow out of the sociocultural context in which that child resides, or in response to child factors.

These life experiences of parenting, peer relations, and schooling, in turn, exert an important impact on propelling a child toward specific outcomes. The fact of significant correlations between biological predispositions and life experiences of parenting does not render the life experiences as unimportant in the child's development. Consider the example of a man who might be genetically at risk for heart disease because several relatives had been diagnosed with this disease, and who exercises little and is obese. It is possible that the "genetic risk factor for heart disease" is actually a predisposition to be lethargic, and it is the fact of behavioral lethargy that alters this man's cardiovascular system in ways that lead to heart disease. The link between this man's genetic predisposition and heart disease outcome is empirical, but it is mediated by an important life experience of lethargy and lack of exercise. The behavioral lethargy is not merely epiphenomenal to the risk; rather, this life experience plays an important role in a transactional process.

With conduct problems, it is hypothesized that life experiences with parents, peers, and social institutions mediate the risks that are imposed by biological predispositions and sociocultural contexts. In the CDP (Dodge, 1996), it has been found that children with resistant temperaments are relatively likely to experience harsh physical discipline from their parents. It has already been reported that harsh discipline, in turn, predicts growth in conduct problems in early adolescence. Mediational analyses, using structural equation modeling, indicate that these life experiences account for all of the significant effects of early resistant temperament on adolescent conduct problems (Dodge, 1996).

A similar kind of mediational effect occurs with sociocultural context factors. McLoyd (1990) hypothesized that the effects of poverty on children's antisocial development are mediated primarily through problematic parenting that children in poverty experience due to the stress, lack of resources, and disorganization that poverty brings to families. In the CDP, low socioeconomic status at birth is indeed predictive of aggressive behavior in children when they reach school age, and parenting practices that are associated with poverty (especially harsh discipline) account for about 50% of the total effect of poverty on aggressive behavior (Dodge, Pettit, & Bates, 1994). Similar mediational effects have been found in Sampson and Laub's (1994) reanalysis of the Glueck and Glueck (1950) classic study of delinquency. In that reanalysis, the authors found that two-thirds of the statistical effects of family poverty on adolescent delinquency could be accounted for by three aspects of parenting: harsh discipline, poor supervision, and weak parent-child relationships.

RECIPROCAL INFLUENCES IN DEVELOPMENT

The proposed model of antisocial development is an ecosymbiotic one, meaning that a child's life experiences are influenced by biological predispositions and sociocultural contexts, but they also reciprocally influence these dispositions and contexts. For example, although testosterone levels are known to influence social behavior and dominance, numerous studies also indicate that social dominance and competitive success lead, over time, to increased levels of testosterone in adolescent males (Olweus, Mattison, Schalling, & Low, 1988). Archer (1994) has integrated this literature into a reciprocal influence model that suggests that in early childhood testosterone levels are an outcome of social competition and that later in adolescence these levels serve to organize aggressive behavior.

A body of literature (Raine, 1993) has supported the hypothesis that low resting heart rate is predictive of aggressive behavior patterns. Resting heart rate levels are presumed to occur as a function of heritable factors, as a biological predisposition. Heart rate reactivity, in contrast, may have both genetic and experiential sources. In the CDP, it was hypothesized that experiences of chronic social rejection would lead children to become psychophysiologically hyperreactive to future peer conflict cues. Rapid heart rate acceleration during social encounters, which also occurs during anxiety-provoking situations (Levenson, 1992) is known to decrease attentional capacity, leading, perhaps, to lower competence in responding. In the CDP, heart rate changes were measured while seventh-grade children watched six hypothetical social vignettes on video, imagining themselves to be the protagonist who becomes the object of peer teasing or conflict. Children who had been socially rejected during the primary grades of elementary school demonstrated significantly greater heart rate acceleration than did children who had never been socially rejected. In turn, a pattern of heart rate acceleration while observing peer conflict was correlated with later externalizing conduct problems (Dodge, 1996). It was as if a life experience of social rejection had led these children to become psychophysiologically anxious during future social encounters of potential conflict; ironically, this psychophysiological reaction, in turn, was part of a self-fulfilling-prophecy process that led to future social failure outcomes. As a caveat, because heart rate reactivity had not been measured prior to initial social rejection during early elementary school, this temporal causal conclusion must be considered as only one possible explanation for these correlations.

Early chronic social rejection might also have effects on the sociocultural context to which a child becomes exposed. Observing contrived laboratory groups of previously unacquainted peers assembled for multiple days, Dodge, Coie, Pettit, and Price (1990) found that social withdrawal is a consequence of acquired peer rejection (and not an antecedent of rejection). Kupersmidt, Coie, and Dodge (1990) suggest that painful experiences with rejection by peers might lead a child to withdraw from the classroom and either create a private lonely existence (Asher, Parkhurst, Hymel, & Williams, 1990) or become involved with deviant peer groups. Unfortunately, this reaction by the rejected child denies him or her opportunities for social and cognitive development that are derived from interaction with mainstream culture (Piaget, 1983). Instead, the child might well become influenced in antisocial directions by a deviant peer culture.

The paths described thus far imply that a few major life experiences have a one-time influence on a child's dispositions and ecology, which then exert a static and enduring influence on antisocial behavior. In fact, antisocial development involves thousands of trials in which biological dispositions, sociocultural contexts, and life experiences influence each other gradually across time, eventually canalizing particular pathways toward conduct problem outcomes. Because negative social feedback tends to amplify rather than attenuate differences among children (Zimbardo, LaBerge, & Butler, 1993), the behavior of marginally deviant children can become more extremely aggressive over time (Caprara & Zimbardo, 1996).

MEDIATION OF RISK FACTORS BY PROXIMAL PROCESSES

The model of antisocial development that has been described here includes both proximal mechanisms, in the form of cognitive and emotional processes that occur during social exchanges, and distal risk factors, involving biological dispositions, sociocultural contexts, and significant life experiences. The final task in weaving these influences together into a single tapestry is to understand how distal risk factors relate to proximal mechanisms. A body of evidence suggests that distal risk factors operate on antisocial development through the mediating mechanisms of proximal processes.

As noted earlier, a major distal risk factor for aggressive behavior is the life experience of physical abuse. Dodge, Bates, and Pettit (1990) found that early physical abuse is associated with acquisition of social information-processing patterns that include hypervigilance to hostile cues, the tendency to attribute hostile intentions to others, rapid accessing of aggressive responses during social problem-solving situations, and favorable evaluations of aggression as a reasonable response to peer conflict. These acquired processing patterns, in turn, predict growth in aggressive behavior and account for about half of the effect of physical abuse on antisocial development (Dodge et al., 1995).

In another tradition, Alessandri and Lewis (1996) found that maltreated girls who are at risk for depression outcomes display problematic emotional reactions to problem-solving tasks. Maltreated girls, relative to nonmaltreated girls, display inordinately high levels of shame in response to failure and inadequate pride in response to success. Celano (1992) found that sexually maltreated girls develop cognitive styles of attributing responsibility for negative outcomes to internal and nonchangeable sources. Celano further suggested that such cognitive–emotional reactions, in turn, will mediate deviant behavioral outcomes. Thus, the adverse early life experience of sexual maltreatment is hypothesized to lead to deviant outcomes through the mediating mechanism of acquired cognitive–emotional patterns.

A similar process has been described with respect to peer social rejection. Dodge (1993) found that early social rejection is associated with later deficits in attention to relevant social stimuli, with an increased tendency to make hostile attributions about peers' intentions, to access aggressive responses in problem-solving situations, and to evaluate aggressive responses favorably. These acquired processing patterns accounted for 51% of the effect of early peer social rejection on later aggressive behavior.

SUMMARIZED MODEL OF ANTISOCIAL DEVELOPMENT

The model described here suggests that antisocial development can occur in numerous, alternate ways, involving reciprocal influences across time among biological, contextual, life experience, and mental process factors. Common features of antisocial development appear to be as follows. First, it appears that certain children are born into the world with neural, endocrine, and psychophysiological features, or into a sociocultural context, that predispose them to develop conduct problems later in life. These dispositions and contexts could still lead to many outcomes, however. Second, these distal factors tend to lead a child toward particular life experiences that propel them further toward antisocial outcomes. These life experiences include harsh discipline, emotional neglect, and exposure to aggressive toddler peers. It may also be that these life experiences occur for a child in the absence of any biological or contextual risk. These early life experiences deny children opportunities for social growth and push them toward aggressogenic ways of processing the future social world.

The child at risk for antisocial development enters elementary school lacking in academic and social readiness and then experiences social rejection and academic failure. The child learns to react psychophysiologically with accelerated heart rate when he or she enters a new peer group or is confronted with a peer conflict. The rejected child might also shape his or her future social context by avoiding close contact with peers and adults in order to avoid overt rejection or abuse. The child's parents learn to monitor the high-risk child *less* closely in order to avoid destructive conflicts. Ironically, the kinds of experiences that the high-risk child needs to protect him or her from antisocial development, involving close supervision and monitoring from adults and access to peer groups for growth and success, are exactly the ones that the high-risk child is unlikely to get. The result is that the child never acquires the social skills and regulatory mechanisms necessary to navigate the world of adolescence. The child consistently fails to attend to relevant social cues, readily makes hostile attributions about peers and adults, accesses aggressive responses in social situations, and either impulsively performs these responses without thinking about their consequences or evaluates their likely outcomes as acceptable and selects them. By the time that he or she reaches adolescence, the probability is high that this child will react violently to a taunting peer, a hostile teacher, or a threatening policeman. Like a heart attack waiting to happen, an act of violence by this child is still only a probabilistic event, but its path is overdetermined.

IMPLICATIONS FOR INTERVENTION

The model of antisocial development presented here has numerous implications for preventive intervention and for research on prevention of conduct disorder (Conduct Problems Prevention Research Group, 1992). First, high-risk children can be identified in early life, based on difficult behaviors of the child and contextual factors of poverty, family disorganization, and neighborhood violence. This point suggests that prevention efforts can be targeted toward a subgroup of children who can be identified by the time they enter formal school but for whom neural paths can still be reversed and antisocial outcomes are not yet inevitable.

Second, prevention research designs might take any of three forms. At the most basic level, the field needs experiments in which one component of a developmental model is manipulated by intervention in order to observe whether proximal change in a particular domain is possible. For example, one might try various interventions to teach parents to employ nonviolent behavior management strategies. Long-term change from intervention in only one component of this multivariate model is unlikely because other forces are likely to counteract the positive effects of single-component interventions. However, this kind of experimental intervention is a way to build effective components of the second kind of intervention, which is a field efficacy trial.

In a field trial, which still can involve random assignment and experimental controls, one might employ multiple methods to change biological dispositions, sociocultural contexts, life experiences, and social information-processing patterns across multiple time points in development. A field trial in early elementary school might involve parent training, family management to change the child's context, peer pairing to enhance friendships, academic tutoring, social–cognitive skill training, exposure to benign rather than hostile life experiences, and classroomwide efforts to change the peer context. The trial might continue across childhood to include new components directed toward new life experience risks as they occur, such as the transition to adolescence and emergent exposure to deviant peer influences.

Because the risk factors for conduct disorder are also risk factors for other deviant outcomes, such as substance abuse, school dropout, and teen pregnancy, field trial evaluations should include a variety of outcomes. Proximal mediating processes should be measured along the way, both as a manipulation check to determine whether the intervention is operating in the hypothesized manner and as a way to test the developmental model upon which the intervention is predicated. Implementation measures are crucial for examining dose–response relations.

Once efficacy of a multicomponent program has been established in the relatively pristine world of academic research, prevention research can move toward effectiveness trials in which the crucial features of intervention are brought to a community setting for implementation by local persons. Effectiveness trials might still involve random assignment experiments, but alternate designs can still be subject to rigorous evaluation. Policy analysis can examine issues of costs versus benefits of prevention, financing of prevention, and practicality of implementation.

Finally, the model presented here suggests that there is room for optimism in prevention research. One reason that behavior geneticists are sometimes rejected in the prevention field is that preventionists read their work to imply that birth is destiny. And one reason that sociocultural theorists are sometimes ignored is that they paint a picture that requires global economic and political change in order to keep children from growing up to be violent. The model presented in this chapter fully embraces the perspectives of both biological and sociocultural theorists, but it suggests that the mechanisms of development operate through family, peer, and psychological processes. It is these processes that might be changed through prevention.

REFERENCES

Alessandri, S. M., & Lewis, M. (1996). Differences in pride and shame in maltreated and nonmaltreated preschoolers. *Child Development, 67,* 1857–1869.

Archer, J. (1994). Testosterone and aggression: A theoretical review. *Journal of Offender Rehabilitation, 21,* 3–39.

Asher, S. R., Parkhurst, J. T., Hymel, S., & Williams, G. A. (1990). Peer rejection and loneliness in childhood. In S. R. Asher & J. D. Coie (Eds.), *Peer rejection in childhood* (pp. 253–273). Cambridge, UK: Cambridge University Press.

Asher, S. R., & Renshaw, P. D. (1981). Children without friends: Social knowledge and social skill training. In S. R. Asher & J. M. Gottman (Eds.), *The development of children's friendships* (pp. 273–296). Cambridge, UK: Cambridge University Press.

Barkley, R. A. (1997). Behavioral inhibition, sustained attention, and executive function: Constructing a unified theory of ADHD. *Psychological Bulletin, 121*, 65–94.

Bates, J. E., & Bayles, K. (1988). Attachment and the development of behavior problems. In J. Belsky & T. Nezworski (Eds.), *Clinical implications of attachment*. Hillsdale, NJ: Erlbaum.

Bates, J. E., Bayles, K., Bennett, D. S., Ridge, B., & Brown, M. M. (1991). Origins of externalizing behavior problems at eight years of age. In D. J. Pepler & K. H. Rubin (Eds.), *The development and treatment of childhood aggression* (pp. 93–120). Hillsdale, NJ: Erlbaum.

Bates, J. E., Marvinney, D., Kelly, T., Dodge, K. A., Bennett, D. S., & Pettit, G. S. (1994). Child-care history and kindergarten adjustment. *Developmental Psychology, 30*, 690–700.

Bates, J. E., Pettit, G. S., Dodge, K. A., & Ridge, B. (in press). The interaction of temperamental resistance to control and restrictive parenting in the development of externalizing behavior. *Developmental Psychology*.

Blum, H. M., Boyle, M. H., & Offord, D. R. (1988). Single-parent families: Child psychiatric disorder and school performance. *Journal of the American Academy of Child and Adolescent Psychiatry, 27*, 214–219.

Blumstein, A., Farrington, D. P., & Moitra, S. D. (1985). *Delinquency careers: Innocents, desisters and persisters* (pp. 187–219). Chicago: University of Chicago Press.

Booth, C. L., Rose-Krasnor, L., McKinnon, J., & Rubin, K. H. (1994). Predicting social adjustment in middle childhood: The role of preschool attachment security and maternal style. *Social Development, 3*, 189–204.

Caprara, G. V., & Zimbardo, P. G. (1996). Aggregation and amplification of marginal deviations in the social construction of personality and maladjustment. *European Journal of Personality, 10*, 79–110.

Celano, M. (1992). A developmental model of victims' internal attributions of responsibility for sexual abuse. *Journal of Interpersonal Violence, 7*, 57–69.

Cocarro, E. F., Kavoussi, R. J., & Lesser, J. C. (1992). Self-and other-directed human aggression: The role of the central nervous system. *International Clinical Psychopharmacology, 6* (Suppl. 6), 70–83.

Cohen, P., & Brook, J. S. (1995). The reciprocal influence of punishment and child behavior disorder. In J. McCord (Ed.), *Coercion and punishment in long-term perspectives* (pp. 154–164). Cambridge, UK: Cambridge University Press.

Coie, J. D., & Dodge, K. A. (1997). Aggression and antisocial behavior. In W. Damon & N. Eisenberg (Eds.), *Handbook of child psychology* (pp. 779–862). New York: Wiley.

Coie, J. D., Terry, R., & Lochman, J. E. (1993, November). *Changing social networks and their impact on juvenile delinquency*. Paper presented at the annual meeting of the American Society of Criminology, Phoenix, AZ.

Coie, J. D., Terry, R., Zakriski, A., & Lochman, J. E. (1995). Early adolescent social influences on delinquent behavior. In J. McCord (Ed.), *Coercion and punishment in long-term perspective* (pp. 229–244). New York: Cambridge University Press.

Conduct Problems Prevention Research Group. (1992). A developmental and clinical model for the prevention of conduct disorders: The FAST Track Program. *Development and Psychopathology, 4*, 509–527.

Crick, N. R., & Dodge, K. A. (1996). Social information-processing mechanisms in reactive and proactive aggression. *Child Development, 67*, 993–1002.

Deater-Deckard, K., & Dodge, K. A. (1997). Externalizing behavior problems and discipline revisited: Nonlinear effects and variation by culture, context, and gender. *Psychological Inquiry, 8*(8), 161–175.

Deater-Deckard, K., Dodge, K. A., Bates, J. E., & Pettit, G. S. (1998). Multiple-risk factors in the development of externalizing behavior problems: Group and individual differences. *Development and Psychopathology, 10*, 469–493.

Deater-Deckard, K., Dodge, K. A., Bates, J. E., & Pettit, G. S. (1997). Physical discipline among African American and European American mothers: Links to children's externalizing behaviors. *Developmental Psychology, 32*(6), 1065–1072.

Deluty, R. H. (1983). Children's evaluations of aggressive, assertive, and submissive responses. *Journal of Clinical Child Psychology, 12*, 124–129.

Dodge, K. A. (1986). A social information processing model of social competence in children. In M. Perlmutter (Ed.). *Minnesota Symposium on Child Psychology* (pp. 77–125). Hillsdale, NJ: Erlbaum.

Dodge, K. A. (1993). Social-cognitive mechanisms in the development of conduct disorder and depression. *Annual Review of Psychology, 44*, 559–584.

Dodge, K. A. (1996, May). *Biopsychosocial perspectives on the development of conduct disorder*. Invited address to the NIMH Prevention Research Conference, McLean, VA.

Dodge, K. A., Bates, J. E., & Pettit, G. S. (1990). *How chronic conduct problems develop*. Unpublished grant proposal to the National Institute of Mental Health.

Dodge, K. A., & Coie, J. D. (1987). Social information-processing factors in reactive and proactive aggression in children's peer groups. *Journal of Personality and Social Psychology, 53*, 1146–1158.

Dodge, K. A., Coie, J. D., Pettit, G. S., & Price, J. M. (1990). Peer status and aggression in boys' groups: Developmental and contextual analyses. *Child Development, 61,* 1289–1309.

Dodge, K. A., Murphy, R. R., & Buchsbaum, K. (1984). The assessment of intention–cue detection skills in children: Implications for developmental psychopathology. *Child Development, 55,* 163–173.

Dodge, K. A., Pettit, G. S., & Bates, J. E. (1994). Socialization mediators of the relation between socioeconomic status and child conduct problems. *Child Development, 65,* 649–665.

Dodge, K. A., Pettit, G. S., Bates, J. E., & Valente, E. (1995). Social information processing patterns partially mediate the effect of early physical abuse on later conduct problems. *Journal of Abnormal Psychology, 104,* 632–643.

Dodge, K. A., Pettit, G. S., McClaskey, C. L., & Brown, M. M. (1986). Social competence in children. *Monographs of the Society for Research in Child Development, 51* (2, Serial No. 213).

Edelbrock, C., Rende, R., Plomin, R., & Thompson, L.A. (1992). *Genetic and environmental effects on competence and problem behavior in childhood and early adolescence.* Unpublished manuscript.

Farrington, D. P., Gallagher, I., Morley, R. J., St. Ledger, R. J., & West, D. J. (1986). Unemployment, school leaving, and crime. *British Journal of Criminology, 26,* 335–356.

Farrington, D. P., & Hawkins, J. D. (1991). Predicting participation, early onset and later persistence in officially recorded offending. *Criminal Behavior and Mental Health, 1,* 1–33.

Frost, L. A., Moffitt, T. E., & McGee, R. (1989). Neuropsychological correlates of psychopathology in an unselected cohort of young adolescents. *Journal of Abnormal Psychology, 98,* 307–313.

Garmezy, N., & Rutter, M. (Eds.). (1983). *Stress, coping, and development in children.* New York: McGraw-Hill.

Gouze, K. R. (1987). Attention and social problem solving as correlates of aggression in preschool males. *Journal of Abnormal Child Psychology, 15,* 181–197.

Gray, J. A. (1987). *The psychology of fear and stress.* Cambridge, UK: Cambridge University Press.

Guerra, N., Huesmann, L. R., Tolan, P. H., Van Acker, R., & Eron, L. D. (1995). Stressful events and individual beliefs as correlates of economic disadvantage and aggression among urban children. *Journal of Clinical and Consulting Psychology, 63,* 518–528.

Hammond, W. R., & Yung, B. R. (1991). Preventing violence in at-risk African-American youth. *Journal of Health Care for the Poor and Underserved, 2,* 1–16.

Hare, R. D. (1978). Electrodermal and cardiovascular correlates of psychopathy. In R. D. Hare & D. Schalling (Eds.), *Psychopathic behavior: Approaches to research* (pp. 107–144) New York: Wiley.

Hart, C. H., Ladd, G. W., & Burleson, B. (1990). Children's expectations of the outcomes of social strategies: Relations with sociometric status and maternal disciplinary styles. *Child Development, 61,* 127–137.

Hawkins, J. D., & Lishner, D. M. (1987). Schooling and delinquency. In E. H. Johnson (Ed.), *Handbook on crime and delinquency prevention* (pp. 179–221). New York: Greenwood Press.

Heffer, R. W., & Kelly, M. L. (1987). Mothers' acceptance of behavioral interventions for children: The influences of parent race and income. *Behavior Therapy, 2,* 153–163.

Hinshaw, S. P. (1987). On the distinction between attentional deficits/hyperactivity and conduct problems/aggression in child psychopathology. *Psychological Bulletin, 101,* 443–463.

Hinshaw, S. P. (1992). Externalizing behavior problems and academic underachievement in childhood and adolescence: Causal relationships and underlying mechanisms. *Psychological Bulletin, 111,* 127–155.

Holmes, C. T. (1989). Grade level retention effects: A meta-analysis of research studies. In L. A. Shepard & M. L. Smith (Eds.), *Flunking grades: Research and policies on retention* (pp. 16–33). Philadelphia: Falmer Press.

Huesmann, L. R., & Eron, L. D. (1986). *Television and the aggressive child: A cross-national perspective.* Hillsdale, NJ: Erlbaum.

Kellam, S. G., & Rebok, G. W. (1992). Building developmental and etiological theory through epidemiologically based preventive intervention trials. In J. McCord & R. Tremblay (Eds.), *Preventing antisocial behavior: Interventions from birth through adolescence* (pp. 162–195). New York: Guilford Press.

Kruesi, M. J. P., Rapoport, J. L., Hamburger, S., Hibbs, E., Potter, W. Z., Lenane, M., & Brown, G. L. (1990). Cerebrospinal fluid monoamine metabolites, aggression, and impulsivity in disruptive behavior disorders of children and adolescents. *Archives of General Psychiatry, 47,* 419–426.

Kupersmidt, J. B., Coie, J. D., & Dodge, K. A. (1990). The role of poor peer relationships in the development of disorder. In S. R. Asher & J. D. Coie (Eds.), *Peer rejection in childhood* (pp. 274–308). Cambridge, UK: Cambridge University Press.

Levenson, R. W. (1992). Autonomic nervous system differences among emotions. *Psychological Science, 3,* 23–27.

Luntz, B. K., & Widom, C. S. (1994). Antisocial personality disorders in abused and neglected children grown up. *American Journal of Psychiatry, 151,* 670–674.

McCord, J. (1991). Family relationships, juvenile delinquency, and adult criminality. *Criminology, 29,* 397–417.

McCord, J. (1991b). Questioning the value of punishment. *Social Problems, 38,* 167–179.

McFadyen-Ketchum, S. A., Bates, J. E., Dodge, K. A., & Pettit, G. S. (1997). Patterns of change in early childhood aggressive–disruptive behavior: Gender differences in predictions from early coercive and affectionate mother–child interactions. *Child Development, 67,* 2417–2433.

McLoyd, V. (1990). The impact of economic hardship on black families and children: Psychological distress, parenting, and socioemotional development. *Child Development, 61,* 311–346.

Moffitt, T. E. (1993). Adolescence-limited and life-course persistent antisocial behavior: A developmental taxonomy. *Psychological Review, 100,* 674–701.

Moffitt, T. E., Gabrielli, W. F., Mednick, S. A., & Schulsinger, F. (1981). Socioeconomic status, IQ, and delinquency. *Journal of Abnormal Psychology, 90,* 152–156.

Moffitt, T. E., & Lynam, D. R. (1994). The neuropsychology of conduct disorder and delinquency: Implications for understanding antisocial behavior. In D. C. Fowles, P. Sutker, & S. H. Goodman (Eds.), *Progress in experimental personality and psychopathology research* (pp. 233–262). New York: Springer-Verlag.

Newell, A., & Simon, H. A. (1972). *Human problem solving.* Englewood Cliffs, NJ: Prentice Hall.

Nisbett, R. E., & Cohen, D. (1996). *Culture of honor: The psychology of violence in the South.* Boulder, CO: Westview Press.

Olweus, D., Mattison, A., Schalling, D., & Low, H. (1988). Circulating testosterone levels and aggression in adolescent males: A causal analysis. *Psychosomatic Medicine, 50,* 261–272.

Patterson, C. J., Kupersmidt, J., & Vaden, N. A. (1990). Income level, gender, ethnicity, and household compositions as predictors of children's school-based competence. *Child Development, 61,* 485–494.

Patterson, G. R. (1995). Coercion—a basis for early age of onset for arrest. In J. McCord (Ed.), *Coercion and punishment in long-term perspective* (pp. 81–105). New York: Cambridge University Press.

Patterson, G. R., Capaldi, D. M., & Bank, L. (1991). An early starter model for predicting delinquency. In D. J. Pepler & K. H. Rubin (Eds.), *The development and treatment of childhood aggression* (pp. 139–168). Hillsdale, NJ: Erlbaum.

Pennington, G. B., & Bennetto, L. (1993). Main effects of transactions in the neuropsychology of conduct disorder: Commentary on "The neuropsychology of conduct disorder." *Development and Psychopathology, 5,* 153–164.

Perry, D. G., Perry, L. C., & Rasmussen, P. (1986). Cognitive social learning mediators of aggression. *Child Development, 57,* 700–711.

Pettit, G. S., Laird, R. D., Bates, J. E., & Dodge, K. A. (1997). Patterns of after-school care in middle childhood: Risk factors and developmental outcomes. *Merrill–Palmer Quarterly, 43*(3), 515–538.

Piaget, J. (1983). Piaget's theory. In W. Kesson (Vol. Ed.) & P. H. Mussen (Ed.), *Handbook of child psychology: Vol. 1. History, theory, and methods* (4th ed., pp. 104–128). New York: Wiley.

Plummer, D. L., & Graziano, W. G. (1987). Impact of grade retention on the social development of elementary school children. *Developmental Psychology, 23,* 267– 275.

Quay, H. C. (1993). The psychobiology of undersocialized aggressive conduct disorder: A theoretical perspective. *Development and Psychopathology, 5,* 165–180.

Raine, A. (1993). *The psychopathology of crime: Criminal behavior as a clinical disorder.* San Diego: Academic Press.

Rogeness, G. A., Javors, M. A., & Pliszka, S. R. (1992). Neuro-chemistry and child and adolescent psychiatry. *Journal of the American Academy of Child and Adolescent Psychiatry, 31,* 765–781.

Rubin, K. H., Bream, L. A., & Rose-Krasnor, L. (1991). Social problem solving and aggression in childhood. In D. J. Pepler & K. H. Rubin (Eds.), *The development and treatment of childhood aggression* (pp. 219–248). Hillsdale, NJ: Erlbaum.

Rutter, M., Cox, A., Tupling, C., Berger, M., & Yule, W. (1975). Attainment and adjustment in two geographical areas: I. The prevalence of psychiatric disorders. *British Journal of Psychiatry, 126,* 493–509.

Rutter, M., & Garmezy, N. (1983). Developmental psychopathology. In P. H. Mussen & E. M. Hetherington (Eds.), *Handbook of child psychology: Vol. 4. Socialization, personality and social development* (pp. 775–911). New York: Wiley.

Sameroff, A. J., & Chandler, M. J. (1975). Reproductive risk and the continuum of care-taking casualty. In F. D. Horowitz (Ed.), *Review of child development research* (Vol. 4, pp. 187–244). Chicago: University of Chicago Press.

Sampson, R. J., & Laub, J. H. (1994). Urban poverty and the family context of delinquency: A new look at structure and process in a classic study. *Child Development, 65,* 523–540.

Sampson, R. J., Raudenbush, S. W., & Earls, F. (1997). Neighborhoods and violent crime: A multilevel study of collective efficacy. *Science, 277,* 918–924.

Shaw, C., & McKay, H. (1942). *Juvenile delinquency and urban areas.* Chicago: University of Chicago Press.

Simons, R. L., Wu, C. I., Conger, R. D., & Lorenz, F. O. (1994). Two routes to delinquency: Differences between early and late starters in the impact of parenting and deviant peers. *Criminology, 32,* 247–276.

Sinclair, J. J., Pettit, G. S., Harrist, A. W., Dodge, K. A., & Bates, J. E. (1994). Encounters with aggressive peers in early childhood: Frequency, age differences, and correlates of risk for behaviour problems. *International Journal of Behavioural Development, 17*, 675–696.

Slaby, R. G., & Guerra, N. G. (1988). Cognitive mediators of aggression in adolescent offenders: I. Assessment. *Developmental Psychology, 24*, 580–588.

Spergel, I. A., Ross, R. E., Curry, G. D., & Chance, R. (1989). *Youth gangs: Problem and response*. Washington, DC: Office of Juvenile Justice and Delinquency Prevention.

Spoont, M.R. (1992). Modulating role of serotonin in neural information-processing: Implications for human psychopathology. *Psychological Bulletin, 112*, 330–350.

Sroufe, L. A. (1983). Infant caregiver attachment and patterns of adaptation in preschool: The roots of maladaptation and competence. In M. Perlmutter (Ed.), *Minnesota Symposium on Child Psychology, 16*, pp. 41–81. Hillsdale, NJ: Erlbaum.

Tesman, J. R., & Hills, A. (1994). Developmental effects of lead exposure in children. *Social Policy Report, 8*(3), 1–19.

Thornberry, T. P., Krohn, M. D., Lizotte, A. J., & Chard-Wierschem, D. (1993). The role of juvenile gangs in facilitating delinquent behavior. *Journal of Research in Crime and Delinquency, 30*, 55–87.

Waas, G. A. (1988). Social attributional biases of peer-rejected and aggressive children. *Child Development, 59*, 969–992.

Werthamer-Larsson, L., Kellam, S., & Wheeler, L. (1991). Effects of first-grade classroom environment on shy behavior, aggressive behavior, and concentration problems. *American Journal of Community Psychology, 19*, 585–602.

Widom, C. S. (1989). Does violence beget violence? A critical examination of the literature. *Psychological Bulletin, 106*, 3–28.

Wilson, W. J. (1987). *The truly disadvantaged*. Chicago: University of Chicago Press.

Zimbardo, P. G., LaBerge, S., & Butler, L. D. (1993). Psychophysiological consequences of unexplained arousal: A post-hypnotic suggestion paradigm. *Journal of Abnormal Psychology, 102*, 466–473.

VI
EMOTIONAL DISORDERS

25

Development and Depression

Judy Garber

Clinicians and researchers now generally agree that children can become depressed (Kovacs, 1989). Several important developmental questions remain, however, including whether and in what ways childhood and adult depression differ, and what accounts for these differences; that is, are there developmental differences in depression and if so, with respect to what aspects of the phenomenon?

Developmental psychopathologists have highlighted the need to consider normative developmental processes in trying to understand both the continuities and discontinuities in depressive disorder across development (Cicchetti & Schneider-Rosen, 1984; Cicchetti & Toth, 1998; Digdon & Gotlib, 1985; Herzog & Rathbun, 1982; Weiss & Garber, 2000). The present chapter reviews the literature concerning developmental differences in the epidemiology, phenomenology, course and prognosis, etiology, and treatment of nonbipolar depression. This is not intended to be an exhaustive review of both the child and adult depression literatures. Rather, this chapter highlights similarities and differences in these various aspects of depression across development from early childhood through adulthood. A discussion of differences in depression in geriatric populations, however, is beyond the scope of this chapter (for relevant literature on depression in the elderly, see Blazer, 1992; Rosenberg, Wright, & Gershon, 1992).

EPIDEMIOLOGY

Age and Sex Differences in the Prevalence of Depression

Epidemiological studies designed to determine the rates of major depressive disorder (MDD) among community samples have yielded different prevalence estimates primarily due to different methods of case ascertainment. The point prevalence for MDD among adults in

Judy Garber • Department of Psychology and Human Development, Vanderbilt University, Nashville, Tennessee 37203.
Handbook of Developmental Psychopathology, Second Edition, edited by Arnold J. Sameroff, Michael Lewis, and Suzanne M. Miller. Kluwer Academic/Plenum Publishers, New York, 2000.

Western industrialized countries is about 4.9%: for men, 2.3–3.2% and for women, 4.5–9.3%; lifetime prevalence of MDD is about 17%: for men, 12.7% and for women, 21.3% (Blazer, Kessler, McGonagle, & Swartz, 1994).

Depression occurs less frequently in young children compared to adults. Point prevalence rates of MDD in preschool children, have been found to be about 1% (Kashani & Carlson, 1987); among prepubertal children rates generally have ranged between .03% and 2.5% (Costello et al., 1996; Fleming & Offord, 1990). By adolescence, however, the prevalence estimates are about 4.3%, ranging from 0.4% to 6.4% (Fleming & Offord, 1990). Lifetime prevalence rates of MDD in adolescents range from 8.3% to 18.5%: about 24% for females and 11.6% for males (Lewinsohn, Hops, Roberts, Seeley, & Andrews, 1993).

Thus, MDD is clearly less common during childhood, but the rates become comparable to adults by middle adolescence. Indeed, compared to all other age groups studied, Blazer et al. (1994) found the 1-month prevalence rates to be highest among individuals between 15 and 24 years old. It is likely that many adults' mood disorders began during middle to late adolescence, which might be a particularly vulnerable period for first episodes of MDD (Hankin et al., 1998).

Epidemiological studies across cultures repeatedly have found approximately twice the rate of depression in women compared to men (Weissman & Olfson, 1995). This 2:1 sex ratio, however, does not become apparent until adolescence. In prepubertal children, the rate of MDD is about equal in girls and boys, and in some cases, higher among boys (Fleming & Offord, 1990). Ryan et al. (1987) reported that 62% of their depressed prepubertal patients were boys, whereas 54% of their depressed adolescents were girls.

Developmental epidemiologists (Costello, 1989; Rutter, 1988) have noted that epidemiological findings can "capitalize on developmental variations and psychopathologic variations to ask questions about mechanism and processes" (Rutter, 1988, p. 486). For example, why is MDD less common during childhood? What is it about childhood that prevents depression from occurring, or what happens during adolescence that increases individuals' risk for depression? What accounts for the change in the sex ratio of depression from childhood to adolescence?

Rutter (1986) proposed several possible mechanisms to explain the rapid rise in rates of depression and the change in the sex ratio from the pre- to postpubertal period, including (1) hormonal changes accompanying puberty, (2) genetic regulatory processes, (3) alterations in the frequency of environmental stressors, (4) developmental changes in the availability of either vulnerability or protective factors such as social support, (5) the possible role of cognitive processes such as learned helplessness and attributional style, and (6) developmental changes in children's experience and expression of emotions.

Thus, a developmental perspective leads to inquiries about why depression shows such a clear age trend in prevalence rates. The answer to this question is likely to be informative about the processes underlying the disorder. Several of these possible causal mechanisms are discussed later in the section on etiology.

Secular Trends

Depression appears to be on the increase among the young (Burke, Burke, Rae, & Regier, 1991; Klerman & Weissman, 1989); that is, depressive disorders have been found to be relatively higher among those born more recently. Burke et al. (1991) compared cohorts of individuals born between 1953 and 1966 with those born between 1937 and 1952, and between

1917 and 1936, and found an increase in depression in each young group over the older ones. Klerman and Weissman (1989) argued that such secular trends were not simply due to overreporting by the young or underreporting by older individuals, since objective indexes of distress such as suicides and hospitalizations also had been found to have increased. They also suggested that the secular trend was not a memory artifact, because studies had not found evidence that recall of more distant depressive experiences was impaired among those known to have been depressed.

Because it is unlikely that the genetic makeup of the population changed substantially during this relatively short time period, it is more probable that the secular increase resulted from environmental factors or the interaction of environmental and genetic factors (Gershon, Hamovit, Guroff, & Nurnberger, 1987). Changing cultural trends such as greater social mobility and the breakdown of the family might create more stress and reduce available resources for coping, thereby resulting in more depressions. Thus, any credible and complete theory of depression needs to account for these two important developmental epidemiological findings: (1) age differences in the rates of depression, and (2) the birth cohort effect.

PHENOMENOLOGY

The criteria outlined in the fourth edition of the *Diagnostic and Statistical Manual* (DSM-IV; American Psychiatric Association, 1994) that currently define depressive disorders are essentially the same regardless of developmental level. Two minor variations in DSM-IV are that for children and adolescents, irritability is considered a manifestation of dysphoric mood, and the duration of dysthymia is 1 rather than 2 years. Thus, according to DSM-IV, there are few real differences in the symptoms that comprise the syndrome of depression.

Developmental psychopathologists (Cicchetti & Schneider-Rosen, 1984; Weiss & Garber, 2000), however, have suggested that manifestations of depression might depend on the individual's level of cognitive, social, and physiological development; therefore, the symptoms of depression might not be isomorphic across the life span. The broad criteria that define depression in adults may "need to be translated into age-appropriate guidelines for children, sensitive to developmental changes in the children's experience and expression of depression" (Cicchetti & Schneider-Rosen, 1984, p. 7). Moreover, although there might be a core set of depressive symptoms common across all ages, there also might be other symptoms that are uniquely associated with the syndrome at different developmental levels (Carlson & Kashani, 1988).

Weiss and Garber (2000) suggested two ways in which there could be developmental differences in depressive symptoms. First, children and adults might differ in how they express particular symptoms, although the basic symptoms would be similar regardless of age. For example, dysphoric mood might be manifested by excessive crying in very young children, nonverbal sadness in school-age children, and irritability in adolescents, but the core mood symptom is essentially the same across these age-specific expressions.

Second, it is possible that the symptoms that comprise the syndrome actually differ developmentally; that is, different combinations of symptoms would define the syndrome in children versus adults. This could be because a certain level of cognitive or physiological maturation might be necessary for some depressive symptoms to occur and young children might not yet be developmentally capable of experiencing such symptoms. For example, young children think concretely and respond to their immediate circumstances, whereas adolescents and adults are more capable of thinking abstractly about themselves and about time (Piaget & Inhelder, 1969). With development comes the increasing capacity to maintain a negative self-view and negative expectations about the future, which then can sustain negative emotions beyond the immediate situation (Bemporad & Wilson, 1978; Harris, 1989). Thus, although young children might be able to experience transient sadness, particularly in response to an acute stressor, they might be less likely to experience other symptoms of depression that require a higher level of cognitive development such as guilt, worthlessness, and hopelessness (Weiner, 1985).

The primary implication of this with respect to the phenomenology of the depressive syndrome across development is that some symptoms are probably less likely than others to comprise the syndrome at different ages. This would be apparent in differences between depressed children and adults in the rates of particular depressive symptoms and in the symptom structure of the syndrome.

Weiss and Garber (2000) conducted a meta-analysis of 11 empirical studies in the literature that compared the rates of depressive symptoms in different age groups. They found that for 18 of the 29 (62%) core and associated depressive symptoms, there were developmental effects, although these effects were not consistent across studies; that is, there was significant variability in the magnitude of the developmental effects across studies that was greater than would have been expected due to random effects (Hedges & Olkin, 1985). Thus, there were developmental differences in the rates at which at least some depressive symptoms were endorsed.

Weiss and Garber (2000) also reviewed three studies that had compared the structure of depression at different age levels. One study (Smucker, Craighead, Craighead, & Green, 1986) found few differences in the item-total scores on the Children's Depression Inventory (CDI) between children and young adolescents. Another study reported that the factor structure was similar for prepubertal and pubertal children diagnosed with mood disorders (Ryan et al., 1987). A third study (Weiss et al., 1992) used confirmatory factor analysis to compare children's and adolescent's responses on the CDI and found 10 of 26 CDI item loadings on a general depression factor showed significant developmental differences, indicating some age differences in the structure of depression.

Thus, contrary to current views in the literature (Kashani, Rosenberg, & Reid, 1989; Ryan et al., 1987), the evidence does *not* support the conclusion that there are no developmental differences in the rates of depressive symptoms. Nor is it clear from the limited data currently available whether or not there are differences in the structure of depressive syndrome across development. The fact that there are not consistent findings with regard to these issues suggests that further research is needed to more adequately and completely address this important developmental question regarding the phenomenology of depressive symptoms and syndrome. Goodyer (1996) asserted, "The suggestion that the clinical presentation of major depression varies with age is far from resolved and more developmentally sensitive studies are required" (p. 407).

COURSE AND PROGNOSIS

Whereas the course of depression is concerned with the duration of an episode, prognosis refers to the extent and likelihood of recurrence of new episodes. Kovacs and colleagues (Kovacs, Feinberg, Crouse-Novak, Paulauskas, & Finkelstein, 1984a; Kovacs et al., 1984b) have conducted the most extensive studies regarding the course of mood disorders in children. They showed that, in children, major depressive disorder tends to be acute, has a mean length of episode of about 32 weeks, and the maximal recovery rate of 92% of the sample is reached at about 18 months from onset. This is similar to what has been found in adults (Coryell et al., 1994; Keller et al., 1992). Coryell et al. reported that most depressed adults recover from an episode between 6 and 12 months from onset.

With regard to a longer-term prognosis, the clinical and empirical literatures indicate that major depression is quite recurrent over the life span (Belsher & Costello, 1989; Coryell & Winokur, 1992). In children, short-term follow-up studies have shown that early-onset depressions tend to recur. Kovacs et al. (1984b) found that the cumulative probability of a recurrent episode of major depression was .72 over the course of 5 years from the onset of the disorder. Such relapse rates are comparable to what has been found in adults. In a short-term longitudinal study of adult unipolar depressives, Gonzales, Lewinsohn, and Clarke (1985) found that 57% relapsed in only 3 years. It is likely that the rates would have been even higher if the sample had been followed longer. In addition, Gonzales et al. (1985) and others (e.g., Keller, Lavori, Lewis, & Klerman, 1983) have found that younger age significantly predicts likelihood of relapse.

Longer-term prospective studies have shown continuity between childhood and adult depression. "Catch-up" longitudinal studies (e.g., Harrington, Fudge, Rutter, Pickles, & Hill, 1990) have found that individuals who are depressed as children or adolescents tend to have recurrent episodes of depression as adults. Moreover, there tends to be specificity in the continuity of mood disorders; that is, depressed children and adolescents are more likely to have subsequent episodes of depression than persons who have had other psychiatric disorders (Harrington et al., 1990). In adults, longer-term follow-up studies have indicated that relapse is quite common (Coryell & Winokur, 1992) and that about 15% of adult patients with major depressive disorders have chronic, residual symptoms after 18 years (Lee & Murray, 1988).

An important developmental question is what accounts for the observed continuity and recurrence of depression from childhood to adulthood. It could be that across the life span the same underlying processes cause depression, such as a biological propensity, chronic environmental stressors, or the interaction between the two. It also is possible that depressions that occur during different age periods are the result of correlated, although different, risk factors such as parental depression and marital discord.

Another possibility is that earlier episodes of depression create a biological or psychological scar that sensitizes the individual to later exposures to even low levels of the etiological agent(s). Post (1992) suggested a kindling hypothesis, in which prior episodes of depression "leave behind neurobiological residues that make a patient more vulnerable to subsequent episodes" (p. 1006). A related explanation is that earlier depressions change individuals in some ways that then lead to their generating the kinds of stressful environments that are likely to precipitate future episodes (Hammen, 1991a).

Finally, there is an interesting contradiction in the literature concerning the long-term outcomes of early-onset mood disorders. Harrington et al. (1990) reported that children with prepubertal onset of depression were at significantly *lower* risk of having major depression as adults than were postpubertal patients. This is in contrast to the finding that early-onset mood disorders are considered a more severe and recurrent form of the disorder that are associated with increased familial loading of depression (e.g., Weissman, Warner, Wickramaratne, & Prusoff, 1988) and with increased risk of relapse (Gonzales et al., 1985; Keller et al., 1983). Harrington et al. (1990) suggested that this finding could have been due to artifacts of their methodology, such as poor measurement of prepubertal depression or the inaccurate documentation of the onset of puberty. Nevertheless, this is an interesting result that is consistent with the view that prepubertal-onset depressions might differ from adolescent- and adult-onset depressions in several important ways, including phenomenology and outcome.

ETIOLOGY

A comprehensive review of etiological theories and the evidence supporting them is beyond the scope of this chapter. Rather, two issues are addressed here. First, should there be different theories of childhood and adult depression? Second, what is the evidence in children and adolescents supporting the leading theories of depression?

Are separate theories of depression needed for children and adults? Much of the research on the etiology of depression in youth has been based on the downward extension of theories originally developed to explain depression in adults. If MDD is essentially the same across development, then similar causal processes should underlie the disorder at any age. Therefore, it would not make sense to have different theories of childhood and adult depression. Rather, theories of depression would need to consider developmental variation in the various aspects of depression (e.g., epidemiology, phenomenology, course), and account for these differences. On the other hand, if child and adult depression are really different disorders, then different theories might be appropriate. Similar to juvenile- and adult-onset types of diabetes, which not only share some commonalities but also have important differences with regard to course, correlates, and treatment, if there are distinct child- and adult-onset types of depression, then different theories would be needed to explain them.

Cole (1991) proposed a competency-based model of childhood depression in which he hypothesized that evaluations of competence by important others (e.g., peers, teachers) predict self-perceived competence and depressive symptoms. This model has found some support when tested with children (Cole, 1991; Cole & Turner, 1993). It is possible that Cole's competency model might explain depression across the life span, although it would need to be appropriately modified and investigated with older age groups.

The converse situation has been more typical; that is, most models of depression have been proposed to explain depression in adults. The validity of these models with regard to depression in children and adolescents has been the focus of research over the last decade. Although many theories of depression have been proposed, we highlight here those for which there is the most empirical support: genetic, biological, stress, cognitive, and interpersonal theories.

Genetics

Family, twin, and adoption studies have shown that genes contribute to the risk for depression (Kendler, 1995). Familial patterns of affective illnesses appear to be about the same in children and adults. Adolescent and adult offspring of depressed parents have been found to be about three times more likely to have depressive episodes themselves compared to offspring whose parents have not had depression (Hammen, Burge, Burney, & Adrian, 1990; Weissman et al., 1987). In addition, high rates of depression in first- and second-degree relatives, particularly female relatives, have been reported in both affectively ill adults (Moldin, Reich, & Rice, 1991) and children (Kovacs, Devlin, Pollock, Richards, & Mukerji, 1997). However, the rate of familial depressive illness is higher among depressed youth than among depressed adults (Moldin et al., 1991), and early onset (i.e., ≤ 20 years old) depressions have been found to be associated with greater risk for depression in family members (e.g., Weissman et al., 1988). Kovacs et al. (1997) suggested that depressions with onset during childhood and adolescence are more familial than adult-onset depressions.

Several mechanisms could explain the high family loading of mood disorders among individuals with early-onset depressions. It might indicate the particular influence of genetic factors on childhood and adolescent depressions (Todd, Neuman, Geller, Fox, & Hickok, 1993; Weissman et al., 1988). Todd et al. (1993) argued that child probands should be used in genetic linkage studies of affective disorders because of the high rates of disorder in their family members. Thus, the association between early age of onset and family history is seen as support for genetic theories of mood disorders.

On the other hand, familiarity of mood disorders also could be due to psychosocial factors such as maladaptive parenting styles, marital dysfunction, and stress that are associated with parental psychopathology (Downey & Coyne, 1990; Hammen, 1991b). Children who are exposed to these conditions early in development might be especially vulnerable to developing mood disorders; that is, childhood-onset depressions in particular may be associated with more severe environmental stressors or traumas (Nolen-Hoeksema, Girgus, & Seligman, 1992; Post, 1992).

Depression in children is rare, but when it does occur, it likely happens to those who are either genetically vulnerable or exposed to severe trauma, or to genetically vulnerable children who experience serious stressors. Thus, both genes and environment probably increase risk for depression. Kendler (1995) suggested that persons with high genetic liability appear to be more vulnerable to adverse environments compared to individuals at lower genetic risk. Indeed, after an aversive life experience, Weller, Weller, Fristad, and Bowes (1991) found that more depression occurred among children with a personal or family history of depression than in those without such a history. Thus, genetic factors likely contribute to depression in both children and adults.

Biology

Psychobiological studies of depression in youth have attempted to replicate results of studies with adults. This research has focused on dysregulation in neuroendocrine and neuro-chemical systems, and in disturbances in sleep architecture (Dahl & Ryan, 1996; Emslie, Weinberg, Kennard, & Kowatch, 1994). Within the neuroendocrine system, depressed adults and children have abnormalities in the hypothalamic–pituitary–adrenal (HPA) axis, the hypothalamic–pituitary–thyroid (HPT) axis, and the hypothalamic–pituitary–growth hormone (HPGH) axis (Carroll & Mendels, 1976; Emslie et al., 1994).

With regard to the HPA axis, depressed adults (Carroll & Mendels, 1976) and children (Casat & Powell, 1988) show nonsuppression of cortisol production in the dexamethasone suppression test (DST). In a review of the DST results with children and adolescents, Dahl and Ryan (1996) concluded that the DST appears to be more sensitive in children (58%) than in adolescents (44%), whereas specificity tends to be higher in adolescent inpatients (85%) than in children (60%). They suggested that differences in the methods of performing the DST, in the dosage of dexamethasone, and in the severity of the disorder might have accounted for these observed age differences. DST results have been found to vary in both children and adults as a function of the severity and endogenicity of the depressive episode and suicidality (Carroll et al., 1981; Dahl & Ryan, 1996).

In studies of pharmacological challenges to the growth hormone system, both adults (Risch & Judd, 1987) and children (Ryan et al., 1994) have been found to hyposecrete growth hormone, and this tends to persist even after remission from the major depressive episode. Different patterns of results for adults and children have been found, however, with regard to levels of growth hormone secretion during sleep. In contrast to findings in adults (Jarrett,

Miewald, & Kupfer, 1990), studies of children and adolescents (Kutcher et al., 1991) have shown increased secretion of growth hormone during sleep, although Dahl et al. (1992) did find decreased nocturnal growth hormone secretion among a subgroup of suicidal, depressed adolescent inpatients. Thus, neuroendocrine studies have found some similar patterns for depressed children and adults. Nevertheless, developmental factors such as hormonal changes that occur with puberty and the uncertainty about the correct dosage for challenge tests in children add to the complexity of conducting and interpreting studies of biological processes in youth (Emslie et al., 1994).

A second important area of biological dysregulation among depressed patients is in their neurochemistry, with serotonin, norepinephrine, and acetylcholine particularly implicated in the pathophysiology of mood disorders (Gold, Goodwin, & Chrousos, 1988). Studies of depressed adults have shown dysregulation of the central serotonergic function (Maes & Meltzer, 1995). Consistent with the adult findings, one study of depressed children showed exaggerated prolactin responses to a serotonergic probe, although this was primarily in girls (Ryan et al., 1994). Dahl and Ryan (1996) suggested that changes in serotonergic regulation around the time of puberty might contribute to the abnormal 5-hydroxy-L-tryptophan (L-5HTP) response in girls. Further studies are needed to examine the extent of continuity between children and adults with respect to neurochemical dysregulation, and to identify the maturational factors that influence the onset of these problems.

Finally, several similarities and differences have been found between depressed children and adults with regard to sleep. Although the subjective report of sleep disturbance has been observed among depressed children, adolescents, and adults, there have been fewer parallels with regard to electroencephalographic (EEG) sleep changes. Depressed adults show many sleep abnormalities such as decreased sleep efficiency, reduced delta sleep, increased rapid eye movement (REM) density, and shortened REM latency (Kupfer & Reynolds, 1992). Although a few sleep studies with depressed adolescents have found some of these same kinds of sleep anomalies such as prolonged sleep latency, reduced REM latency, and decreased sleep efficiency, other studies have failed to find differences between depressed and nondepressed adolescents in EEG sleep patterns (Dahl & Ryan, 1996).

The absence of sleep abnormalities in depressed youth has been attributed to the role of maturational changes. Dahl and Ryan (1996) suggested that the sleep of young children is difficult to disrupt because they are such deep sleepers. During adolescence, however, this protective aspect of sleep decreases. Normatively, adolescents show several sleep changes, such as in the depth of sleep, REM latency, daytime sleepiness, and circadian patterns (Carskadon, Keenan, & Dement, 1987).

In depressed children, the first form of sleep disruption observed is difficulty initiating sleep. During adolescence, reduced REM latency begins to occur. It is not until adulthood, however, that delta sleep differences become evident. Thus, there are important developmental shifts in one of the core symptoms of depressive disorder (i.e., sleep). The processes underlying these differences still need to be identified.

Stressful Life Events

A clear link between stressful life events and depression has been found in both adults (Thoits, 1983) and children (Compas, 1987). In a review of the adult literature, Thoits (1983) concluded that studies have repeatedly found that persons with depressive disorders are significantly more likely than nondepressed persons to have experienced undesirable life events. Similarly, reviews of studies with children and adolescents have found that depressive symptoms and disorders are significantly associated with minor and major undesirable life events (Compas, 1987).

Various facets of stressful life events are important in the stressor–depression relation, including whether the stressors are acute versus chronic, minor hassles versus major life events, and independent of or dependent on the individual's behaviors. In addition, the type of life event, the objective degree of threat associated with the event, and the match between a particular type of stressor and the individual's specific area(s) of vulnerability have been found to be important in studies examining the link between stressors and depression (Brown & Harris, 1989; Monroe & Roberts, 1990).

For example, according to the specific vulnerability hypothesis (Beck, 1983; Blatt, Quinlan, Chevron, McDonald, & Zuroff, 1982), individuals differ in how much their self-esteem is derived from interpersonal (sociotropy) versus achievement (autonomy) goals; stressors that occur within an individual's area of particular vulnerability are likely to provoke a depressive reaction because they represent a depletion in self-worth. Several studies have found evidence consistent with this hypothesis in adults (e.g., Hammen, Marks, Mayol, & de Mayo, 1985; Segal, Shaw, Vella, & Katz, 1992), and the two studies to investigate the specific vulnerability hypothesis in children also have been supportive (Hammen & Goodman-Brown, 1990; Little & Garber, in press). Thus, there appears to be some developmental continuity with regard to this aspect of the stress–depression relation.

Another important distinction is between negative life events as distal predisposing factors that occur earlier in development but influence subsequent outcomes, and proximal precipitating factors that more immediately precede the onset of depression. As a predisposing factor, stressors such as early abuse or loss can increase an individual's vulnerability when exposed to later stressors. Brown and Harris (1978), for example, found that the experience of loss of a mother before age 11 increased the likelihood of depression among working-class women who currently were caring for three or more children at home and had a poor marital relationship. The mechanisms through which such early predisposing factors become a more stable vulnerability factor are not yet understood.

Thus, there appears to be consistent evidence of a significant association between stressful life events and depressive symptoms in children, adolescents, and adults. What might vary with development, however, is what constitutes a stressor, how individuals react to particular stressors at different ages, and in the various moderators (e.g., cognitions, coping) of the relation between stress and depression.

Stressors can be defined as circumstances characterized by either the lack or loss of a highly desirable and obtainable goal or the presence of a highly undesirable and inescapable event. Although goals are likely to change from childhood through adulthood, and the spectrum of sources of stressors grow wider with development, the fundamental definition of a stressor should remain about the same. Moreover, the basic categories of stressors are likely to be applicable across development and include interpersonal loss and separation, intrapersonal incompetence and failure, deprivation, physical incapacitation, and victimization (Garber & Kashani, 1991).

Children as young as 3 years old are aware of the emotional consequences for themselves and others of different categories of experiences (Harris, 1989). Young children reliably judge that sadness can be provoked by losing a significant person, pet, or treasured possession, experiencing failure, or receiving punishment. However, as children grow older, although they continue to acknowledge such situation–response relations, they also begin to recognize that mental processes accompany and even engender emotional reactions (Harris, 1989).

There also are notable developmental differences in how individuals respond to the same life events such as separation (Bowlby, 1980), death of a loved one (Weller et al., 1991), divorce (Wallerstein & Kelly, 1980), and failure (Heckhausen, 1982). For example, Wallerstein and Kelly (1980) reported that in reaction to parental divorce, preschool children tended to have intensified fears and sleep disturbance; 5- to 8-year-old children showed declines in schoolwork; 9- to 12-year-olds showed both anxiety and anger, and had social and academic problems; and adolescents tended to manifest the full syndrome of depression. Thus, the association between a particular life event and depressive symptoms might vary with age. This is likely due, in part, to developmental differences in the factors that moderate this relation such as individuals' appraisal of the stressor and their coping responses.

Individuals' depressive reactions to a life event will depend on their appraisal of its importance, the degree to which the event affects other aspects of their life, and their ability to alter or cope with the event and its consequences (Lazarus, 1991). These appraisals and coping responses will be a function of their prior experiences, current level of cognitive development, and the availability of external resources (e.g., social support). There likely are developmental changes in these appraisal and coping processes that will affect children's emotional reactions to life events and whether they ultimately become depressed.

Researchers who study emotional development (e.g., Harris, 1989; Lewis & Saarni, 1985) have noted that young children tend to make very rudimentary and concrete appraisals concerning the level of harm or benefit associated with negative life events. This more limited perspective can protect them from recognizing the extensive ramification of the events and from the symptoms that might accompany such realizations. With increasing cognitive development, however, children are more able to make abstract judgments regarding the globality and stability of the consequences of events for their well-being, thereby increasing their risk for a depressive reaction. On the other hand, with this increasing cognitive maturity, they also are developing a greater capacity to cope with the events they encounter.

Thus, there is continuity across development in the link between stressful life events and depression, although there is variation in how particular events impact individuals at different ages. Much of this variability is due to differences in appraisals of the meaning of the events with regard to self-worth and the future. Such appraisal processes are central to cognitive theories of depression.

Cognitions

According to cognitive theories of depression (Abramson, Metalsky, & Alloy, 1989; Beck, 1967), depressed individuals have more negative beliefs about themselves and their future, and they have the tendency to make global, stable, and internal attributions for negative events. When confronted with stressful life events, individuals who have such cognitive tendencies will appraise the stressors and their consequences more negatively, and therefore are more likely to become depressed than individuals who do not have such cognitive styles. These are essentially cognitive diathesis–stress models, because cognitions are presumed to contribute to the onset of depression primarily in the context of stressful life events.

There are three important developmental questions with regard to cognitive theories of depression

1. What is the evidence that cognitions are related to depression in children, and is this relation similar across development?

2. What is the developmental progression of this relation; that is, when do cognitions become important in predicting depression?
3. What factors contribute to the development of these cognitions?

Reviewers of the empirical literature have concluded that there is overwhelming correlational evidence of a relation between negative cognitions and depression in both adults (Haaga, Dyck, & Ernst, 1991) and children (Garber & Hilsman, 1992). Prospective studies also have found support for cognitive diathesis–stress models in adults (Metalsky & Joiner, 1992; Metalsky, Joiner, Hardin, & Abramson, 1993) and children (Hilsman & Garber, 1995; Robinson, Garber, & Hilsman, 1995). These studies have shown that individuals who have a negative cognitive style, measured prior to the onset of the stressor, report greater levels of depressive symptoms after a stressor (e.g., an exam or report card) compared to individuals who do not have such a cognitive style.

At what point in development do such cognitions matter? Some cognitions that might be precursors to depressive thinking appear to develop early. Alessandri and Lewis (1996) suggested that the cognitive capacities of mentally representing standards for comparison, self-awareness, and attributions of outcomes to personal competence, which are prerequisites for the self-conscious emotions of pride and shame, develop during the preschool years. Thus, very young children are capable of experiencing certain cognitions that might predispose them to depression.

Most studies examining the association between cognitions and depression, however, typically have not included children younger than about 8 years old. This is probably due to both methodological and developmental reasons. First, it is hard to assess depressive cognitions in children younger than age 8. Second, it is possible that some of the cognitions most relevant to depression (e.g., self-worth, attributional style) do not really emerge until around middle childhood when a more stable and less concrete sense of self is beginning to develop (Rholes, Blackwell, Jordan, & Walters, 1980). Children's views of the self become increasingly differentiated with development (Harter, 1990). Children shift their focus from concrete, behavioral characteristics in early childhood to trait-like characteristics in middle childhood, to more abstract psychological constructs during adolescence (Harter, 1986). Similarly, although very young children have a rudimentary understanding of causality (e.g., Oakes, 1994), and toddlers can engage in social-causal reasoning (Miller & Aloise, 1989), it is not until about age 8 that children's use of stable personality traits to explain behavior increases dramatically (Corrigan, 1995).

Studies examining the relations among cognitions, stress, and depression in children have found some developmental changes from middle childhood through early adolescence (Nolen-Hoeksema et al., 1992; Turner & Cole, 1994). Nolen-Hoeksema et al. (1992) showed that in 8-year-old children, negative life events, but not attributional style, significantly predicted depressive symptoms, whereas in 11- to 12-year-old children, a pessimistic explanatory style both alone and in conjunction with negative events significantly predicted depressive symptoms. Turner and Cole (1994) found an association between negative cognitions and depressive symptoms in children in grades four, six, and eight, although support for the cognitive diathesis-stress model was only found for children in eighth grade. By adolescence, the relations among cognitions and depression have been found to be relatively stable and similar to those of adults (Garber, Weiss, & Shanley, 1993). Thus, there is some normative developmental progression in children's cognitions about the self, future, and causes of events, and in the relations among these cognitions, stress, and depression. How do these cognitive patterns become negative for some children, making them more vulnerable to depression than other children?

Various theorists have speculated about the causes of the depressive cognitive style (Garber & Flynn, 1998; Kovacs & Beck, 1978; Rose & Abramson, 1992; Seligman, Kamen, & Nolen-Hoeksema, 1988). Garber and Flynn (1998) described several nonmutually exclusive processes to explain the origins of depressogenic thinking, including genetics and personality, exposure to negative life events, and such social learning processes as modeling and social feedback.

First, it is possible that cognitive style is a personality characteristic that is heritable; that is, one phenotypic expression of a depression genotype could be a depressive personality style that is characterized by negative cognitions. It also is possible that the depressive cognitive style is really a manifestation of neuroticism, which is presumably heritable (Eysenck & Eysenck, 1985).

Family studies examining intergenerational covariation in cognitive style have yielded inconsistent results (Garber & Flynn, in press; Kaslow, Rehm, Pollack, & Siegel, 1988; Seligman & Peterson, 1986). In the one twin study to compare monozygotic (MZ) and dizygotic (DZ) twins with regard to their attributional style, Schulman, Keith, and Seligman (1991) found the correlations were .48 for MZ twins and 0 for DZ twins. This study needs to be replicated, however, using more standard means of determining zygosity than the self-report method used by Schulman et al. (1991). Thus, although it is possible that depressive thinking is heritable, more systematic investigations need to be conducted.

Second, experience with chronically aversive life circumstances (e.g., abuse, poverty, parental discord) or a major traumatic life event (e.g., parental death, rape) can impact individuals' outlook on life, particularly their sense of themselves, their world, and their future (Janoff-Bulman & Hecker, 1988). When such events are uncontrollable and result in multiple and severe bad outcomes, individuals are likely to develop cognitions of universal helplessness and hopelessness (Abramson et al., 1989). Individuals who believe they are responsible for the negative events are more likely to develop a belief in personal helplessness and low self-esteem (Abramson, Seligman, & Teasdale, 1978).

Rose and Abramson (1992) suggested that children who experience severe and repetitive abuse in the context of an important interpersonal relationship are likely to develop negative self-representations, helplessness, and hopelessness about the security of important interpersonal relationships. Indeed, Feiring, Taska, and Lewis (1998) showed that the link between number of abusive events and depressive symptoms was mediated through a negative attributional style. Similarly, children who experience even less severe forms of parental criticism and rejection develop negative cognitions about themselves and others (Garber & Flynn, in press; Goodman, Adamson, Riniti, & Cole, 1994).

Third, social learning principles are likely involved in the development of the depressive cognitive style, particularly modeling and direct feedback through instruction, reinforcement, and punishment from significant others such as parents, teachers, and peers (Bandura & Walters, 1963). A modeling hypothesis is that children learn to think negatively about the causes of events, themselves, and their future by observing and imitating important people in their life.

Evidence is mixed with regard to the simple parent–child correlations of depressogenic cognitions. Whereas Seligman and Peterson (1986) found a significant correlation between mothers' and children's attributional style, two other studies (Garber & Flynn, in press; Kaslow et al., 1988) did not find such a relation. Moreover, if correlations are found between parents' and children's cognitive styles, this does not necessarily mean that this is the result of modeling, or that the direction of the relation is from parent to child; that is, parental cognitions could influence child cognitions or vice versa, or some shared third variable (e.g., genes, stressors) could contribute to the development of both parents' and children's cognitions.

Finding a significant relation between parents' and children's cognitions about the children's behavior in particular rather than in their cognitive style in general would be more consistent with a learning than a genetic perspective; that is, genetic transmission of a predisposition to make internal, global, and stable attributions for negative events should be apparent with regard to both parent- and child-focused events, and would not be specific to child behaviors. Studies (e.g., Garber & Flynn, in press; Turk & Bry, 1992), however, have shown that children's attributions correlated more closely with parents' explanations of the children's behavior than with parents' explanations of their own behavior. Thus, it is likely that children acquire at least some of their cognitive style, particularly causal inferences, from observing their parents' explanations for their children's behaviors.

Finally, children learn about themselves and their world from direct feedback from important people in their lives, including teachers (Dweck & Licht, 1980), peers (Hirsch, Engel-Levy, DuBois, & Hardesty, 1990), and parents (e.g., Goodman et al., 1994; Jaenicke et al., 1987). Children who are exposed to parenting characterized by repeated criticism and rejection, lack of warmth, and intrusiveness are likely to develop a highly self-critical and negative attitude toward themselves (McCranie & Bass, 1984).

Jaenicke et al. (1987) found a significant association between mothers' criticism of their children and children's self-blaming attributions for negative events. Goodman et al. (1994) revealed a significant association between negative affective statements of depressed mothers and lower perceived self-worth in their children. Finally, Koestner, Zuroff, and Powers (1991) showed that restrictive and rejecting parenting earlier in childhood significantly predicted self-criticism during adolescence. Thus, feedback from significant others, especially parents, can have an important and long-lasting impact on the development of children's cognitions about themselves and their world. When these communications are persistently negative, children assimilate this information into a depressive cognitive schema about themselves and the world.

Interpersonal Relationships and Attachment

Interpersonal perspectives on depression emphasize the importance of the social environment and the development of secure attachments (Cummings & Cicchetti, 1990; Gotlib & Hammen, 1992). Vulnerability to depression presumably arises in early family environments in which the child's need for security, comfort, and acceptance are not met. Bowlby (1980) argued that children with caretakers who are consistently responsive, accessible, and supportive will develop cognitive representations, or "working models," of the self and others as positive and trustworthy. In contrast, caretakers who are characterized by unresponsiveness or inconsistency will produce insecure attachments. These children will have working models that include fear of abandonment, hopelessness, and self-criticism.

Although few studies have tested Bowlby's model directly with regard to depression, some studies have reported findings consistent with it. Depressed adolescents (Kobak, Sudler, & Gamble, 1991) and adults (Rosenfarb, Becker, & Khan, 1994) report less secure attachment to parents than do nondepressed individuals. Moreover, adolescents who experienced stressful life events were more likely to become depressed if they had more insecure attachments to their parents compared to adolescents with more secure attachments (Hammen et al., 1995; Kobak et al., 1991).

Offspring of depressed caregivers also have been found to have more insecure attachments compared to offspring of well mothers (DeMulder & Radke-Yarrow, 1991; Teti, Gelfand, Messinger, & Isabella, 1995). Moreover, insecurely attached offspring of depressed mothers tend to have difficulties in their relationships with peers (Rubin, Booth, Zahn-Waxler, Cummings, & Wilkinson, 1991). Thus, there is increasing evidence of insecure attachments among offspring of depressed parents and in currently depressed youth and adults. Such insecure attachment organizations presumably produce internal representational models that are likely to "contribute to a depressotypic organization of psychological and biological systems" (Cicchetti & Toth, 1998, p. 231).

Even beyond attachment, other aspects of family relationships tend to be dysfunctional among currently depressed children (Kaslow, Deering, & Racusin, 1994), and currently depressed adults recall more family problems when they were children (Gerlsma, Emmelkamp, & Arrindell, 1990). These families tend to be characterized by high levels of criticism and overcontrol, and low levels of support and acceptance.

In addition to problems in parent–child relationships, depressed children tend to have significant peer difficulties (Panak & Garber, 1992), and depressed adults have problems with friends and marital partners (Fadden, Bebbington, & Kuipers, 1987). Moreover, negative attitudes toward depressed patients have been found to predict relapse in adults (Hooley & Teasdale, 1989) and children (Asarnow, Goldstein, Tompson, & Guthrie, 1993). Thus, depression in both children and adults is associated with high levels of interpersonal conflict, criticism, and rejection from various members in their social domain, including family, friends, and partners.

Two developmental issues are important with regard to the interpersonal perspective on depression. First, there is the problem of directionality. Most research examining the link between interpersonal problems and depression have been cross-sectional, correlational, or retrospective. Depressed individuals clearly have greater problems within the social domain than do nondepressed individuals. However, it is not clear to what extent these social difficulties precede and therefore cause the depression. Currently depressed individuals have been found to create more social stressors in their lives (Hammen, 1991a) and they tend to be rejected by others (Coyne et al., 1987). It is likely that a transactional model of mutual influence between depressed individuals and their environment is relevant here (Sameroff & Chandler, 1975). More prospective studies are needed to examine the contribution of family and peer problems to the onset of depressive disorder in both children and adults, as well as the impact of depressed individuals on their social world.

A second developmental issue is that if disrupted early parent–child relationships, particularly insecure attachments, are critical precursors to depression, then why is depression so rare in young children? Although maladaptive early relationships might be a necessary precursor to the development of a depressive vulnerability, such family dysfunction might not be sufficient to produce a depressive disorder in young children. Some other variables such as a certain level of biological or cognitive maturity and significant levels of stressful life events in the context of early family dysfunction might be necessary for the full syndrome of depression to occur.

TREATMENT

Psychopharmacological and psychosocial treatments have been found to be effective in reducing depressive symptoms in adults including tricyclic antidepressants (TCAs) and selective serotonin reuptake inhibitors (SSRIs) (Trivedi & Rush, in press), cognitive-behavioral therapy (Hollon, Shelton, & Davis, 1993), and interpersonal therapy (Klerman, Weissman,

Rounsaville, & Chevron, 1984). Studies testing the efficacy of these treatments with depressed children and adolescents have been conducted over the last decade.

Pharmacotherapy

Despite the success of TCA medications in treating depression in adults, TCAs have not been found to be as effective in the treatment of depression in children and adolescents. A meta-analysis of 12 placebo-controlled trials of TCAs in patients between 6 and 18 years old revealed that the difference between active medications and placebos was small and not clinically significant (Hazell, O'Connell, Heathcote, Robertson, & Henry, 1995). Ryan (1990) suggested that one reason for differences between adults and children's responses to medication is that the medications studied have been primarily noradrenergic or metabolized quickly to noradrenergic metabolites. Ryan noted that animal studies have found that there are differences in the rate of development of neurotransmitter systems such that the monoaminergic storage capacity and synthesis is believed to be more rapid for serotonin than for catecholamines (Goldman-Rakic & Brown, 1982). The noradrenergic system is not thought to develop fully until early adulthood; therefore, it would be less responsive to noradrenergic agents such as TCAs in children and adolescents.

Kutcher et al. (1994) similarly suggested that the central nervous system (CNS) noradrenergic receptor system would be less sensitive to TCAs because of elevated levels of gonadal steroids during adolescence. In addition, depressed and nondepressed adolescents have not been found to differ with regard to peripheral endocrine measures thought to reflect CNS noradrenergic activity, whereas they have been found to differ on other external endocrine measures that are more influenced by serotonergic CNS activity (Kutcher et al., 1991). Taken together, these findings have led researchers to suggest that serotonergic agents might be more effective than noradrenergic agents with younger individuals (Emslie et al., 1997; Kutcher et al., 1994; Ryan, 1990).

There have been relatively few controlled treatment studies of SSRIs with children and adolescents. A recent double-blind, randomized, placebo-controlled trial in children between 7 and 17 years old found that 56% of patients receiving the SSRI fluoxetine clinically improved compared to 33% receiving placebo (Emslie et al., 1997). Response rates were equivalent for boys and girls, and for both children and adolescents. The response rates were basically similar to what has been found for the treatment of adults with fluoxetine (Clinical Practice Guidelines, 1993). Thus, the use of SSRIs for treating depression in children and adolescents looks promising, although further replication is necessary. Studies also are needed to better understand the developmental factors that contribute to some medications being effective in youth, whereas others are not.

Cognitive-Behavioral Therapy

Controlled outcome studies also have found that cognitive-behavioral therapy is quite effective in treating depression in adults (Hollon et al., 1993). The aim of cognitive therapy is to teach patients to evaluate their thoughts realistically in light of evidence. Cognitive therapy should be altered developmentally to include age-appropriate materials, language, themes, and issues such as identity, individuation and separation, intimacy and sexuality, and impulsivity and aggression (Belsher & Wilkes, 1994; Lewinsohn, Clarke, Rohde, Hops, & Seeley, 1996; Stark, 1990). Belsher and Wilkes (1994) noted 10 key principles of adolescent cognitive therapy: acknowledging adolescent narcissism, adopting collaborative empiricism, being objective, including members of the social network, attending to affect, using socratic questioning, challenging all-or-none thinking, avoiding blame, operationalizing the abstract, and therapist modeling. Although most of these strategies are used in treating depressed adults also, they are particularly important when working with adolescents.

In a meta-analysis of six treatment studies involving 14 posttreatment-control comparisons and 10 follow-up comparisons that included samples of adolescents between 11 and 19 years old, Reinecke, Ryan, and DuBois (1998) found that cognitive-behavioral approaches showed both short- and long-term effectiveness in treating depressive symptoms in these populations. Reinecke et al. noted several limits to the generalizability of these findings, however, including (1) subjects were recruited primarily from school rather than clinic settings, (2) five of six studies used group rather than individual therapy, (3) self-report measures of depression were the primary dependent variables, (4) comparisons were with control groups that did not receive intervention, and (5) studies used a range of different cognitive and behavioral interventions.

A recent treatment study by Brent et al. (1997) addressed several of these limitations. Brent et al. compared individual cognitive-behavioral therapy with either systemic behavioral family (SBFT) or nondirective supportive therapy (NST) for clinically depressed adolescents ages 13 through 18. Cognitive therapy resulted in a significantly higher rate of remission (64.7%) compared to both SBFT (37.9%) and NST (39.4%). This study provided further support for the efficacy of cognitive-behavioral treatments for depression in adolescents.

Thus, there is increasing evidence of the efficacy of cognitive-behavioral approaches in the treatment of depression from adolescence through adulthood. The utility of such cognitive-behavioral approaches with depressed preadolescent children still needs to be examined. Although it is possible that the behavioral components of the therapy might be applicable to younger children, it is less likely that young children will be able to comprehend and utilize many of the more abstract cognitive procedures due to their still developing cognitive abilities. Some forms of cognitive-behavioral therapy have been shown to be effective with children who have other kinds of disorders, including impulsivity, aggression, and anxiety (Kendall, 1993), although these interventions have tended to emphasize more behavioral procedures such as self-control, self-talk, reinforcement, and modeling.

Interpersonal Psychotherapy

A second psychosocial intervention shown to be effective in the treatment of depression in adults is interpersonal psychotherapy (IPT; e.g., Klerman et al., 1984). IPT is a brief treatment that focuses on an individual's social relationships and four problem areas, including grief, role transitions, interpersonal role disputes, and interpersonal deficits. The main goals of IPT are to improve interpersonal functioning in the context of significant relationships and to reduce depressive symptoms.

Mufson, Moreau, Weissman, and Klerman (1993) modified IPT procedures to make them more appropriate for teens. They outlined special issues clinicians encounter when dealing with adolescents, including school refusal, sexuality, aggression, abuse, substance use, and nontraditional families. In an open clinical trial of 12 weeks of IPT with a sample of 10 depressed adolescents, Mufson and Fairbanks (1996) found significant improvement in 9 of the 10 patients. These results are promising, although controlled treatment trials are needed to test the efficacy of this approach with depressed adolescents and children.

CONCLUSIONS AND FUTURE DIRECTIONS

What can be concluded about the continuity of depression across development? First, the rates of depression increase from childhood to adolescence. Second, although there are many similarities in the symptoms that comprise the syndrome of depression at all ages, there also are noteworthy differences in the phenomenology and structure of depressive syndrome in children versus adults. Third, the course and outcome appear to be relatively similar across development, although earlier age of onset is associated with more severe and recurrent forms of depression and with increased risk of relapse. In general, some similar biological and psychosocial correlates have been found in depressed children and adults, although the links between these variables and the onset of depression in both children and adults need to be studied further. Finally, some of the pharmacological and psychological treatments that are effective in the treatment of depression in adults can be used to treat adolescent depression, although more controlled trials with both adolescent and child samples are needed.

Several important developmental questions were identified. With regard to epidemiology: Why are there different rates of depression from childhood to adolescence? What changes from childhood to adolescence, or what is protecting children? What accounts for the shift in the sex differences around puberty? How can the secular increase in the rates of depression be explained? With regard to phenomenology: What is the structure of depression in children, adolescents, and adults, and how does it change over time? What are the normative changes in depressive symptoms (e.g., irritability, anhedonia, fatigue), and what is the relevance of these changes for understanding changes in the rates of these symptoms among depressed youth? With regard to course and prognosis: What factors influence the course and outcome of depressive disorders across development? Are early- onset depressions more severe, recurrent, and familial than later-onset depressions? How do we account for the recurrence of depressive episodes across development? With regard to etiology: Are different theories of childhood and adult depression needed? How do existing theories of depression need to be modified to account for developmental differences? What are the risk factors that predict the onset of depression? When and how do these vulnerabilities develop and unfold? What sets off these depressive vulnerabilities (either genetic or psychosocial)? With regard to intervention: Which of the successful treatments used with depressed adults are not effective with children and adolescents, and why? How do therapies need to be modified so they can be used effectively with children and adolescents?

Finally, a point should be made about the term *developmental* because it has implications for future studies. There are at least four ways in which developmental differences have been examined in the literature, including chronological age, school grade, pubertal status, and cognitive developmental level. Although most studies have used age to examine developmental differences in the various features of depression, Weiss and Garber (2000) suggested that investigators should choose their means of defining development depending on their theory regarding the cause of the hypothesized developmental differences.

For example, one possible explanation for developmental differences in the phenomenology or treatment of depression might be the result of biological/hormonal changes that occur at puberty (Rutter, 1986, 1988). In this case, it would make sense for researchers to assess and divide their sample specifically according to pubertal status, since this would allow for the best test of this biological hypothesis. On the other hand, investigators who hypothesize that developmental differences result from differences in cognitive level should assess and divide their sample according to cognitive indices of development (e.g., Piagetian stage, mental age; see Kovacs & Paulauskas, 1984).

In contrast, dividing samples on the basis of chronological age or grade in school does not point to a particular a priori conceptualization about the processes underlying developmental differences. Age or grade cannot be direct causes of developmental differences; rather, they serve as markers of underlying processes that are correlated with age or grade (e.g., social experience, cognitive and pubertal development; Rutter, 1986, 1988). Thus, age and grade are only indirect indexes of development, although they have the advantage of being easy to measure and allow for comparisons of large samples across multiple sites (e.g., Weiss et al., 1992). Thus, using age or grade as the basis for dividing a sample might be particularly appropriate early in the process of exploring developmental differences, when investigators do not yet have a clear theory regarding the mechanisms underlying such differences.

Weiss and Garber (2000) recommended that, ideally, investigators should define developmental groups using multiple methods and then conduct separate developmental comparisons based on each method. For example, Kovacs and Paulauskas (1984) divided their sample by pubertal status as well as cognitive stage, and then conducted two sets of analyses using the two different operationalizations of developmental level. Another good example is the recent study by Angold, Costello, and Worthman (1998), in which they found that pubertal status was a better predictor than chronological age of the emergence of the expected 2:1 sex ratio in unipolar depression. Moreover, they showed that defining puberty in terms of Tanner stages rather than the onset of menarche was more precise and far more informative than simply using age to predict the transition to the adult sex ratio for depression. Although more expensive, such approaches allow for comparisons of the hypotheses upon which the developmental groupings are based; that is, the theory underlying the method that produces the larger number of developmental differences would receive more empirical support.

In summary, the answer to the question—Are there developmental differences in depression?—is that it depends on how development is defined and on what aspects of the disorder are considered (e.g., epidemiology, phenomenology, course, prognosis, etiology, treatment). There are clear and important continuities in depressive disorder across development. However, there are enough developmental differences to justify further examination of this issue. More studies that are explicitly designed to compare these various facets of depression using similar yet age-appropriate measurements and methodologies across the life span are needed.

ACKNOWLEDGMENTS: This chapter was supported in part by a grant from the National Institute of Mental Health (R01-MH57822-01A1) and a Faculty Scholar Award (88-1214-88) and grant (95173096) from the William T. Grant Foundation during its completion.

REFERENCES

Abramson, L. Y., Metalsky, G. I., & Alloy, L. B. (1989). Hopelessness depression: A theory-based subtype of depression. *Psychological Review, 96*, 358–372.

Abramson, L. Y., Seligman, M. E. P., & Teasdale, J. (1978). Learned helplessness in humans: Critique and reformulation. *Journal of Abnormal Psychology, 87*, 49–74.

Alessandri, S. M., & Lewis, M. (1996). Development of the self-conscious emotions in maltreated children. In M. Lewis & M. W. Sullivan (Eds.), *Emotional development in atypical children* (pp. 185–201), Mahwah, NJ: Erlbaum.

American Psychiatric Association. (1994). *Diagnostic and Statistical Manual of Mental Disorders* (4th ed.). Washington, DC: Author.

Angold, A., Costello, E. J., & Worthman, C. M. (1998). Puberty and depression: The roles of age, pubertal status, and pubertal timing. *Psychological Medicine, 28*, 51–61.

Asarnow, J. R., Goldstein, M. J., Tompson, M., & Guthrie, D. (1993). One-year outcomes of depressive disorders in child psychiatric in-patients: Evaluation of the prognostic power of a brief measure of expressed emotion. *Journal of Child Psychology and Psychiatry, 34*, 129–137.

Bandura, A., & Walters, R. H. (1963). *Social learning and personality development.* New York: McGraw-Hill.

Beck, A. T. (1967). *Depression: Clinical, experiential, and theoretical aspects.* New York: Harper & Row.

Beck, A. T. (1983). Cognitive therapy of depression: New perspectives. In P. J. Clayton & J. E. Barrett (Eds.), *Treatment of depression: Old controversies and new approaches* (pp. 265-290). New York: Raven Press.

Belsher, G., & Costello, C. G. (1989). Relapse after recovery from unipolar depression: A critical review. *Psychological Bulletin, 104*, 84-96.

Belsher, G., & Wilkes, T. C. R. (1994). Ten key principles of adolescent cognitive therapy. In T. C. R. Wilkes, G. Belsher, A. J. Rush, & E. Frank, (Eds.), *Cognitive therapy for depressed adolescents* (pp. 22–44). New York: Guilford Press.

Bemporad, J. R., & Wilson, A. (1978). A developmental approach to depression in childhood and adolescence. *Journal of the American Academy of Psychoanalysis, 6*, 325–352.

Birmaher, B., Ryan, N. D., Williamson, D. E., Brent, D. A., & Kaufman, J. (1996). Childhood and adolescent depression: A review of the past 10 years. Part II. *Journal of the American Academy of Child and Adolescent Psychiatry, 35*, 1575–1583.

Blatt, S. J., Quinlan, D. M., Chevron, E. S., McDonald, C., & Zuroff, D. (1982). Dependency and self-criticism: Psychological dimensions of depression. *Journal of Consulting and Clinical Psychology, 50*, 113–124.

Blazer, D. G. (1992). Geriatric psychiatry in the United States: The clinical investigation, diagnosis and treatment of late life depression as an example. *Psychiatria-Hungarica, 7*, 605-613.

Blazer, D. G., Kessler, R. C., McGonagle, K. A., & Swartz, M. S. (1994). The prevalence and distribution of major depression in a national community sample: The national comorbidity survey. *American Journal of Psychiatry, 151*, 979–986.

Bowlby, J. (1980). *Attachment and loss: Vol. 3. Loss, sadness, and depression.* New York: Basic Books.

Brent, D., Holder, D., Kolko, D., Birmaher, B., Baugher, M., Roth, C., Iyengar, S., & Johnson, B. (1997). A clinical psychotherapy trial for adolescent depression comparing cognitive, family, and supportive therapy. *Archives of General Psychiatry, 54*, 877–885.

Brown, G. W., & Harris, T. O. (1978). *Social origins of depression: A study of psychiatric disorder in women.* London: Tavistock.

Brown, G. W., & Harris, T. O. (Eds.). (1989). *Life events and illness.* New York: Guilford Press.

Burke, K. C., Burke, J. D., Rae, D., & Regier, D. A. (1991). Comparing age at onset of major depression and other psychiatric disorders by birth cohorts in five US community populations. *Archives of General Psychiatry, 48*, 789–795.

Carlson, G. A., & Kashani, J. H. (1988). Phenomenology of major depression from childhood through adulthood: Analysis of three studies. *American Journal of Psychiatry, 137*, 445–449.

Carroll, B. J., Feinberg, M., Greden, J. F., Tarika, J., Albala, A. A., Haskett, R. F., James N., Kronfol, Z., Lohr, N., de Vigne, J. P., & Young E. (1981). A specific laboratory test for the diagnosis of melancholia. *Archives of General Psychiatry, 38*, 15–22.

Carroll, B. J., & Mendels, J. (1976). Neuroendocrine regulations in affective disorders. In E. J. Scahar (Ed.), *Hormones, behavior, and psychopathology,* (pp. 193–224). New York: Raven Press.

Carskadon, M. A., Keenan, S., & Dement, W. C. (1987). Nighttime sleep and daytime sleep tendency in preadolescents. In C. Guilleminault (Ed.), *Sleep and its disorders* (pp. 43–52). New York: Raven Press.

Casat, C., & Powell, K. (1988). Utility of the dexamethasone suppression test in children and adolescents with major depressive disorder. *Journal of Clinical Psychiatry, 49*, 390–393.

Cicchetti, D., & Schneider-Rosen, K. (Eds.). (1984). Childhood depression. *New Directions in Child Development* (pp. 5–27). San Francisco: Jossey-Bass.

Cicchetti, D., & Toth, S. L. (1998). The development of depression in children and adolescents. *American Psychologist, 53*, 221–241.

Clinical Practice Guidelines. (1993). *Depression in primary care: 2. Treatment of major depression* (Health Care Policy and Research Publication, No. 5, 93-0551). Rockville, MD: U.S. Dept. of Health and Human Services, Agency for Health Care Policy and Research.

Cole, D. A. (1991). Preliminary support for a competency-based model of depression in children. *Journal of Abnormal Psychology, 100*, 181–190.

Cole, D. A., & Turner, J. E. (1993). Models of cognitive mediation and moderation in child depression. *Journal of Abnormal Psychology, 102*, 271–281.

Compas, B. E. (1987). Stress and life events during childhood and adolescence. *Clinical Psychology Review, 7*, 275–302.

Corrigan, R. (1995). How infants and young children understand the causes of events. In N. Eisenberg (Ed.), *Social development* (pp. 1–26). Thousand Oaks, CA: Sage.

Coryell, W., Akiskal, H. S., Leon, A. C., Winokur, G., Maser, J. D., Mueller, T., & Keller, M. B. (1994). The time course of nonchronic major depressive disorder: Uniformity across episodes and samples. *Archives of General Psychiatry, 51*, 405–410.

Coryell, W., & Winokur, G. (1992). Course and outcome. In E. S. Paykel (Ed.), *Handbook of affective disorders*, (pp. 89–108). New York: Guilford Press.

Costello, E. J. (1989). Developments in child psychiatric epidemiology. *Journal of the American Academy of Child and Adolescent Psychiatry, 28*, 836–841.

Costello E. J., Angold, A., Burns, B. J., Stangl, D. K., Tweed, D. L., Erkanli, A., & Worthman, C. M. (1996). The Great Smoky Mountains Study of Youth: Goals, design, methods, and prevalence of DSM-III-R disorders. *Archives of General Psychiatry, 53*, 1129–1136.

Coyne, J. C., Kessler, R. C., Tal, M., Turnbull, J., Wortman, C. B., & Greden, J. F. (1987). Living with a depressed person. *Journal of Consulting and Clinical Psychology, 55*, 347–352.

Cummings, E. M.,& Cicchetti, D. (1990). Toward a transactional model of relations between attachment and depression. In M. T. Greenberg, D. Cicchetti, & E. M. Cummings (Eds.), *Attachment in the preschool years: Theory, research and intervention* (pp. 339–372). Chicago: University of Chicago Press.

Dahl, R. E., & Ryan, N. D. (1996). The psychobiology of adolescent depression. In. D. Cicchetti & S. L. Toth (Eds.). *Adolescence: Opportunities and challenges*, (pp. 197–232). Rochester, NY: University of Rochester Press.

Dahl, R. E., Ryan, N. D., Williamson, D. E., Ambrosini, P. J., Rabinovich, H., Novacenko, H., Nelson, B., & Puig-Antich, J. (1992). The regulation of sleep and growth hormone in adolescent depression. *Journal of the American Academy of Child and Adolescent Psychiatry, 31*, 615–621.

DeMulder, E. K., & Radke-Yarrow, M. (1991). Attachment with affectively ill and well mothers: Concurrent behavioral correlates. *Development and Psychopathology, 3*, 227–242.

Digdon, N., & Gotlib, I. H. (1985). Developmental consideration in the study of childhood depression. *Developmental Review, 5*, 162–199.

Downey, G., & Coyne, J. C. (1990). Children of depressed parents: An integrative review. *Psychological Bulletin, 108*, 50–76.

Dweck, C. S., & Licht, B. (1980). Learned helplessness and intellectual achievement. In J. Garber, & M. E. P. Seligman (Eds.), *Human helplessness: Theory and applications* (pp. 197–221). New York: Academic Press.

Emslie, G. J., Rush, J. A., Weinberg, W. A., Kowatch, R. A., Hughes, C. W., Carnody, T., & Rintelmann, J. (1997). A double-blind, randomized, placebo-controlled trial of fluoxetine in children and adolescents with depression. *Archives of General Psychiatry, 54*, 1031–1037.

Emslie, G. J., Weinberg, W. A., Kennard, B. D., & Kowatch, R. A. (1994). Neurobiological aspects of depression in children and adolescents. In W. M. Reynolds & H. E. Johnston (Eds.), *Handbook of depression in children and adolescents*, (pp. 143–165). New York: Plenum Press.

Eysenck, H. J., & Eysenck, M. W. (1985). *Personality and individual difference: A natural science approach*. New York: Plenum Press.

Fadden, G., Bebbington, P. E., & Kuipers, L. (1987). Caring and its burdens: A study of the spouses of depressed patients. *British Journal of Psychiatry, 151*, 660–667.

Feiring, C., Taska, L., & Lewis, M. (1998). The role of shame and attributional style in children's and adolescents' adaptation to sexual abuse. *Child Maltreatment, 3*, 129–142.

Fleming, J. E., & Offord, D. R. (1990). Epidemiology of childhood depressive disorders: A critical review. *Journal of the American Academy of Child and Adolescent Psychiatry, 29*, 571–580.

Garber, J., & Flynn, C. (1998). Origins of depressive cognitive style. In D. Routh & R. J. DeRubeis (Eds.), *The science of clinical psychology* (pp. 53–93), Washington, DC: American Psychological Association.

Garber, J., & Flynn, C. (in press). Predictors of depressive cognitions in young adolescents. *Cognitive Theory and Research*.

Garber, J., & Hilsman, R. (1992). Cognitions, stress, and depression in children and adolescents. *Child and Adolescent Psychiatric Clinics of North America, 1*, 129–167.

Garber, J., & Kashani, J. (1991). The development of the symptom of sadness. In M. Lewis (Ed.), *Child and adolescent psychiatry: A comprehensive textbook* (pp. 293–310). Baltimore: Williams & Wilkins.

Garber, J., Weiss, B., & Shanley, N. (1993). Cognitions, depressive symptoms, and development in adolescents. *Journal of Abnormal Psychology, 102*, 47–57.

Gerlsma, C., Emmelkamp, P. M. G., & Arrindell, W. A. (1990). Anxiety, depression, and perception of early parenting: A meta-analysis. *Clinical Psychology Review, 10,* 251–277.

Gershon, E. S., Hamovit, J. H., Guroff, J. J., & Nurnberger, J. I. (1987). Birth-cohort changes in manic and depressive disorders in relatives of bipolar and schizoaffective patients. *Archives of General Psychiatry, 44,* 314–319.

Gold, P. W., Goodwin, F. K., & Chrousos, G. P. (1988). Clinical and biochemical manifestations of depression: Relation to the neurobiology of stress. *New England Journal of Medicine, 319,* 348–353.

Goldman-Rakic, C. P., & Brown, R. M. (1982). Postnatal development of monoamine content and synthesis in the cerebral cortex of rhesus monkeys. *Developmental Brain Research, 4,* 339–349.

Gonzales, L. R., Lewinsohn, P. M., & Clarke, G. N. (1985). Longitudinal follow-up of unipolar depressives: An investigation of predictors of relapse. *Journal of Consulting and Clinical Psychology, 53,* 461–469.

Goodman, S. H., Adamson, L. B., Riniti, J., & Cole, S. (1994). Mothers' expressed attitudes: Associations with maternal depression and children's self-esteem and psychopathology. *Journal of the American Academy of Child and Adolescent Psychiatry, 33,* 1265–1274.

Goodyer, I. M. (1996). Physical symptoms and depressive disorders in childhood and adolescence. *Journal of Psychosomatic Research, 41,* 405–408.

Gotlib, I. H., & Hammen, C. L. (1992). *Psychological aspects of depression: Toward a cognitive-interpersonal integration.* Chichester, UK: Wiley.

Haaga, D., Dyck, M., & Ernst, D. (1991). Empirical status of cognitive theory of depression. *Psychological Bulletin, 110,* 215–236.

Hammen, C. L. (1991a). The generation of stress in the course of unipolar depression. *Journal of Abnormal Psychology, 100,* 555–561.

Hammen, C. L. (1991b). *Depression runs in families: The social context of risk and resilience in children of depressed mothers.* New York: Springer-Verlag.

Hammen, C. L., Burge, D., Burney, E., & Adrian, C. (1990). Longitudinal study of diagnoses in children of women with unipolar and bipolar affective disorder. *Archives of General Psychiatry, 47,* 1112–1117.

Hammen, C. L., Burge, D., Daley, S. E., Davila, J., Paley, B., & Rudolph, K. D. (1995). Interpersonal attachment cognitions and prediction of symptomatic responses to interpersonal stress. *Journal of Abnormal Psychology, 104,* 436–443.

Hammen, C. L., & Goodman-Brown, T. (1990). Self-schemas and vulnerability to specific life stress in children at risk for depression. *Cognitive Therapy and Research, 14,* 215–227.

Hammen, C. L., Marks, T., Mayol, A., & deMayo, R. (1985). Depressive self-schemas, life stress, and vulnerability to depression. *Journal of Abnormal Psychology, 94,* 308–319.

Hankin, B. L., Abramson, L. Y., Moffitt, T. E., Silva, P. A., McGee, R., & Angell, K. E. (1998). Development of depression from preadolescence to young adulthood: Emerging gender differences in a 10-year longitudinal study. *Journal of Abnormal Psychology, 107,* 128–140.

Harrington, R., Fudge, H., Rutter, M., Pickles, A., & Hill, J. (1990). Adult outcomes of childhood and adolescent depression. *Archives of General Psychiatry, 47,* 465–473.

Harris, P. L. (1989). *Children and emotion: The development of psychological understanding,* Oxford, UK: Blackwell.

Harter, S. (1986). Processes underlying the construction, maintenance, and enhancement of the self-concept in children. In J. Suls & A. Greenwald (Eds.), *Psychological perspectives on the self* (Vol. 3, pp. 137–181). Hillsdale, NJ: Erlbaum.

Harter, S. (1990). Causes, correlates, and the functional role of global self-worth: A life span perspective. In J. Kolligan & R. Sternberg (Eds.), *Perception of competence and incompetence across the life span* (pp. 67–98). New Haven, CT: Yale University Press.

Hazell, P., O'Connell, D., Heathcote, D., Robertson, J., & Henry, D. (1995). Efficacy of tricyclic drugs in treating child and adolescent depression: A meta-analysis. *British Medical Journal, 310,* 897–901.

Heckhausen, H. (1982). The development of achievement motivation. In W. W. Hartup (Ed.), *Review of child development research* (pp. 600–668). Chicago: University of Chicago Press.

Hedges, L. V. & Olkin, I. (1985). *Statistical methods for meta-analysis.* Orlando, FL: Academic Press.

Herzog, D. B., & Rathbun, J. M. (1982). Childhood depression: Developmental considerations. *American Journal of Diseases in Children, 136,* 115–120.

Hilsman, R., & Garber, J. (1995). A test of the cognitive diathesis-stress model in children: Academic stressors, attributional style, perceived competence and control. *Journal of Personality and Social Psychology, 69,* 370–380.

Hirsch, B. J., Engel-Levy, A., DuBois, D. L., & Hardesty, P. H. (1990). The role of social environments in social support. In B. R. Sarason, I. G. Sarason, & G. R. Pierce (Eds.), *Social support: An interactional view* (pp. 367–393). New York: Wiley.

Hollon, S. D., Shelton, R., & Davis, D. (1993). Cognitive therapy for depression: Conceptual issues and clinical efficacy. *Journal of Consulting and Clinical Psychology, 61,* 270–275.

Hooley, J. M., & Teasdale, J. D. (1989). Predictors of relapse in unipolar depressives: Expressed emotion, marital distress, and perceived criticism. *Journal of Abnormal Psychology, 98*, 229–237.

Jaenicke, C., Hammen, C., Zupan, B., Hiroto, D., Gordon, D., Adrian, C., & Burge, D. (1987). Cognitive vulnerability in children at risk for depression. *Journal of Abnormal Child Psychology, 15*, 559–572.

Janoff-Bulman, R., & Hecker, B. (1988). Depression, vulnerability, and world assumptions. In L. B. Alloy (Ed.), *Cognitive processes in depression* (pp. 177–192). New York: Guilford Press.

Jarrett, D. B., Miewald, J. M., & Kupfer, D. J. (1990). Recurrent depression is associated with a persistent reduction in sleep-related growth hormone reduction. *Archives of General Psychiatry, 47*, 113–118.

Kashani, J. H., & Carlson, G. A. (1987). Seriously depressed preschoolers. *American Journal of Psychiatry, 144*, 348–350.

Kashani, J. H., Rosenberg, T. K., & Reid, J. C. (1989). Developmental perspectives in child and adolescent depressive symptoms in a community sample. *American Journal of Psychiatry, 146*, 871–875.

Kaslow, N. J., Deering, C. G., & Racusin, G. R. (1994). Depressed children and their families. *Clinical Psychology Review, 14*, 39–59.

Kaslow, N. J., Rehm, L. P., Pollack, S. L., & Siegel, A. W. (1988). Attributional style and self-control behavior in depressed and nondepressed children and their parents. *Journal of Abnormal Child Psychology, 16*, 163–175.

Keller, M. B., Lavori, P. W., Lewis, C. E., Klerman, G. L. (1983). Predictors of relapse in major depressive disorder. *Journal of the American Medical Association, 250*, 3299–3304.

Keller, M. B., Lavori, P. W., Mueller, T. I., Endicott, J., Coryell, W. H., Scheftner, W. A., Hirschfeld, R. M. A., & Shea, T. (1992). Time to recovery, chronicity, and levels of psychopathology in major depression: A 5-year prospective follow-up of 431 subjects. *Archives of General Psychiatry, 49*, 809–816.

Kendall, P. C. (1993). Cognitive-behavioral therapies with youth: Guiding theory, current status, and emerging developments. *Journal of Consulting and Clinical Psychology, 61*, 235–247.

Kendler, K. S. (1995). Genetic epidemiology in psychiatry. Taking both genes and environment seriously. *Archives of General Psychiatry, 52*, 895–899.

Klerman, G. L., & Weissman, M. M. (1989). Increasing rates of depression. *Journal of the American Medical Association, 261*, 2229–2235.

Klerman, G. L., Weissman, M. M., Rounsaville, B. J., & Chevron, E. S. (1984). *Interpersonal Psychotherapy of Depression.* New York: Basic Books.

Kobak, R. R., Sudler, N., & Gamble, W. (1991). Attachment and depressive symptoms during adolescence: A developmental pathways analysis. *Development and Psychopathology, 3*, 461–474.

Koestner, R., Zuroff, D. C., & Powers, T. A. (1991). Family origins of adolescent self-criticism and its continuity into adulthood. *Journal of Abnormal Psychology, 100*, 191–197.

Kovacs, M. (1989). Affective disorders in children and adolescents. *American Psychologist, 44*, 209–215.

Kovacs, M., & Beck, A. T. (1978). Maladaptive cognitive structures in depression. *American Journal of Psychiatry, 135*, 525–533.

Kovacs, M., Devlin, B., Pollock, M., Richards, C., & Mukerji, P. (1997). A controlled family history study of childhood-onset depressive disorder. *Archives of General Psychiatry, 54*, 613–623.

Kovacs, M., Feinberg, T. L., Crouse-Novak, M. A., Paulauskas, S. L., & Finkelstein, R. (1984a). Depressive disorders in childhood: I. A longitudinal prospective study of characteristics and recovery. *Archives of General Psychiatry, 41*, 229–237.

Kovacs, M., Feinberg, T. L., Crouse-Novak, M., Paulauskas, S. L., Pollock, M., & Finkelstein, R. (1984b). Depressive disorders in childhood: II. A longitudinal study of the risk for a subsequent major depression. *Archives of General Psychiatry, 41*, 653–649.

Kovacs, M., & Paulauskas, S. L. (1984). Developmental stage and the expression of depressive disorders in children: An empirical analysis. In D. Cicchetti & K. Schneider-Rosen (Eds.), *Childhood depression* (pp. 59–80). San Francisco: Jossey-Bass.

Kupfer, D. J., & Reynolds, C. F. (1992). Sleep and affective disorders. In E. S. Paykel (Ed.), *Handbook of affective disorders*, (pp. 311–326). New York: Guilford Press.

Kutcher, S. P., Boulos, C., Ward, B., Marton, P., Simeon, J., Ferguson, H. B., Szalai, J., Katic, M., Roberts, N., Dubois, C., & Reed, K. (1994). Response to desipramine treatment in adolescent depression: A fixed-dose, placebo-controlled trial. *Journal of the American Academy of Child and Adolescent Psychiatry, 33*, 686–694.

Kutcher, S. P., Malkin, D., Silverberg, J., Marton, P., Williamson, P., Malkin, A., Szalai, J., & Katic, M. (1991). Nocturnal cortisol, thyroid stimulating hormone and growth hormone secreting properties in depressed adolescents. *Journal of the American Academy of Child and Adolescent Psychiatry, 30*, 407–414.

Lazarus, R. S. (1991). *Emotion and adaptation.* New York: Oxford University Press.

Lee, A. S., & Murray, R. M. (1988). The long-term outcome of Maudsley depressives. *British Journal of Psychiatry, 153*, 741–751.

Lewinsohn, P. M., Clarke, G., Rohde, P., Hops, H., & Seeley, J. (1996). A course in coping: A cognitive-behavioral approach to the treatment of adolescent depression. In E. Hibbs, & P. Jensen (Eds.), *Psychosocial treatments for child and adolescent disorders: Empirically based strategies for clinical practice* (pp. 109–135). Washington, DC: American Psychological Association.

Lewinsohn, P. M., Hops, H., Roberts, R. E., Seeley, J. R., & Andrews, J. A. (1993). Adolescent psychopathology: I. Prevalence and incidence of depression and other DSM-III-R disorders in high school students. *Journal of Abnormal Psychology, 102*, 133–144.

Lewis, M., & Saarni, C. (1985). *The socialization of emotions*. New York: Plenum Press.

Little, S. A., & Garber, J. (in press). Interpersonal and achievement orientations and specific hassles predicting depressive and aggressive symptoms in children. *Cognitive Therapy and Research*.

Maes, M., & Meltzer, H. (1995). The serotonin hypothesis of major depression. In F. E. Bloom & D. J. Kupfer (Eds.), *Psychopharmacology: The fourth generation of progress* (pp. 933–944). New York: Raven Press.

McCranie, E. W., & Bass, J. D. (1984). Childhood family antecedents of dependency and self-criticism: Implications for depression. *Journal of Abnormal Psychology, 93*, 3–8.

Metalsky, G. I., & Joiner, T. E. (1992). Vulnerability to depressive symptomatology: A prospective test of the diathesis–stress and causal mediation components of the hopelessness theory of depression. *Journal of Personality and Social Psychology, 63*, 667–675.

Metalsky, G. I., Joiner, T. E., Hardin, T. S., & Abramson, L. Y. (1993). Depressive reactions to failure in a naturalistic setting: A test of the hopelessness and self-esteem theories of depression. *Journal of Abnormal Psychology, 102*, 101–109.

Miller, P. H., & Aloise, P. A. (1989). Young children's understanding of the psychological causes of behavior: A review. *Child Development, 60*, 257–285.

Moldin, S. O., Reich, T., & Rice, J. P. (1991). Current perspectives on the genetics of unipolar depression. *Behavior Genetics, 21*, 211–242.

Monroe, S. M., & Roberts, J. R. (1990). Definitional and conceptual issues in the measurement of life stress: Problems, principles, procedures, progress. *Stress Medicine, 6*, 209–216.

Mufson, L., & Fairbanks, J. (1996). Interpersonal psychotherapy for depressed adolescents: A one-year naturalistic follow-up study. *Journal of the Academy of Child and Adolescent Psychiatry, 35*, 1145–1155.

Mufson, L., Moreau, D., Weissman, M. M., & Klerman, G. L. (1993). *Interpersonal psychotherapy for depressed adolescents*. New York: Guilford Press.

Nolen-Hoeksema, S., Girgus, J., & Seligman, M. E. P. (1992). Predictors and consequences of childhood depressive symptoms: A 5 year longitudinal study. *Journal of Abnormal Psychology, 101*, 405–422.

Oakes, L. M. (1994). Development of infants' use of continuity cues in their perception of causality. *Developmental Psychology, 30*, 869–879.

Panak, W., & Garber, J. (1992). Role of aggression, rejection, and attributions in the prediction of depression in children. *Development and Psychopathology, 4*, 145–165.

Piaget, J., & Inhelder, B. (1969). *The psychology of the child*. New York: Basic Books.

Post, R. M. (1992). Transduction of psychosocial stress into the neurobiology of recurrent affective disorder. *American Journal of Psychiatry, 149*, 999–1010.

Reinecke, M. A., Ryan, N. E., & DuBois, D. L. (1998). Cognitive-behavioral therapy of depression and depressive symptoms during adolescence: A review and meta-analysis. *Journal of the American Academy of Child and Adolescent Psychiatry, 37*, 26–34.

Rholes, W. S., Blackwell, J., Jordan, C., & Walters, C. (1980). A developmental study of learned helplessness. *Developmental Psychology, 16*, 616–624.

Risch, S. C., & Judd, L. L. (1987). Provocative challenges of growth hormone and prolactin secretion in schizophrenic and affective disorders. In C. B. Nemeroff & P. B. Loosen (Eds.), *The handbook of clinical psychoneuroendocrinology* (pp. 36–68). New York: Guilford Press.

Robinson, N. S., Garber, J., & Hilsman, R. (1995). Cognitions and stress: Direct and moderating effects on depressive versus externalizing symptoms during the junior high school transition. *Journal of Abnormal Psychology, 104*, 453–463.

Rose, D. T., & Abramson, L. Y. (1992). Developmental predictors of depressive cognitive style: Research and theory. In D. Cicchetti & S. L. Toth (Eds.), A developmental approach to depression. *Rochester Symposium of Developmental Psychopathology, 4*, 323–349. Rochester, NY: University of Rochester Press.

Rosenberg, D. R., Wright, B., & Gershon, S. (1992). Depression in the elderly. *Dementia, 3*, 157–173.

Rosenfarb, I. S., Becker, J., & Khan, A. (1994). Perceptions of parental and peer attachments with mood disorders. *Journal of Abnormal Psychology, 103*, 637–644.

Rubin, K., Booth, L., Zahn-Waxler, C., Cummings, E. M., & Wilkinson, M. (1991). Dyadic play behaviors of children of well and depressed mothers. *Development and Psychopathology, 3*, 243–251.

Rutter, M. (1986). The developmental psychopathology of depression: Issues and perspectives. In M. Rutter, C. E. Izard & P. B. Read (Eds.), *Depression in young people: Developmental and clinical perspectives* (pp. 3–30). New York: Guilford Press.

Rutter, M. (1988). Epidemiological approaches to developmental psychopathology. *Archives of General Psychiatry, 45*, 486–495.

Ryan, N. D. (1990). Pharmacotherapy of adolescent major depression: Beyond TCAs. *Psychopharmacological Bulletin, 26*, 75–79.

Ryan, N. D., Dahl, R. E., Birmaher, B., Williamson, D. E., Iyengar, S., Nelson, B., Puig-Antich, J., & Perel, J. M. (1994). Stimulatory tests of growth hormone secretion in prepubertal major depression: Depressed versus normal children. *Journal of the American Academy of Child and Adolescent Psychiatry, 33*, 824–833.

Ryan, N. D., Puig-Antich, J., Ambrosini, P., Rabinovich, H., Robinson, D., Nelson, B., Iyengar, S., & Twomey, J. (1987). The clinical picture of major depression in children and adolescents. *Archives of General Psychiatry, 44*, 854–861.

Sameroff, A. J., & Chandler, M. J. (1975). Reproductive risk and the continuum of caretaking casualty. In F. D. Horowitz (Ed.), *Review of child development research* (Vol. 4, pp. 187–244). Chicago: University of Chicago Press.

Schulman, P., Keith, D., & Seligman, M. E. P. (1991). Is optimism heritable?: A study of twins. *Behaviour Research and Therapy, 31*, 569–574.

Segal, Z. V., Shaw, B. F., Vella, D. D., & Katz, R. (1992). Cognitive and life stress predictors of relapse in remitted unipolar depressed patients: Test of the congruency hypothesis. *Journal of Abnormal Psychology, 101*, 26–36.

Seligman, M. E. P., Kamen, L. P., & Nolen-Hoeksema, S. (1988). Explanatory style across the life span. In E. M. Hetherington, R. M. Lerner, & M. Perlmutter (Eds.), *Child development in life-span perspective* (pp. 91–114). Hillsdale, NJ: Erlbaum.

Seligman, M. E. P., & Peterson, C. (1986). A learned helplessness perspective on childhood depression: Theory and research. In M. Rutter, C. E. Izard, & P. B. Read (Eds.), *Depression in young people: Developmental and clinical perspectives* (pp. 223–249). New York: Guilford Press.

Smucker, M. R., Craighead, W. E., Craighead, L. W., & Green, B. J. (1986). Normative and reliability data for the Children's Depression Inventory. *Journal of Abnormal Child Psychology, 14*, 25–39.

Stark, K. D. (1990). *Childhood depression: School-based intervention.* New York: Guilford Press.

Teti, D., Gelfand, D., Messinger, D., & Isabella, R. (1995). Maternal depression and the quality of early attachment: An examination of infants, preschoolers, and their mothers. *Developmental Psychology, 31*, 364–376.

Thoits, P. A. (1983). Dimensions of life events that influence psychological distress: An evaluation and synthesis of the literature. In H. B. Kaplan (Ed.), *Psychosocial stress: Trends in theory and research* (pp. 33–103). New York: Academic Press.

Todd, R. D., Neuman, R., Geller, B., Fox, L. W., & Hickok, J. (1993). Genetic studies of affective disorders: Should we be starting with childhood onset probands? *Journal of the American Academy of Child and Adolescent Psychiatry, 32*, 1164–1171.

Trivedi, M. H., & Rush, A. J. (in press). Efficacy of antidepressant medication: Part 1. A meta-analysis. *Neuropsychopharmacology.*

Turk, E., & Bry, B. H. (1992). Adolescents' and parents' explanatory styles and parents' causal explanations about their adolescents. *Cognitive Therapy and Research, 16*, 349–357.

Turner, J. E., & Cole, D. A. (1994). Developmental differences in cognitive diatheses for child depression. *Journal of Abnormal Child Psychology, 22*, 15–32.

Wallerstein, J. S., & Kelly, J. B. (1980). *Surviving the breakup: How children and parents cope with divorce.* New York: Basic Books.

Weiner, B. (1985). An attributional theory of achievement motivation and emotion. *Psychological Review, 92*, 548–573.

Weiss, B., & Garber, J. (2000). *Developmental differences in the phenomenology of depression.* Manuscript under review.

Weiss, B., Weisz, J. R., Politano, M., Carey, M., Nelson, W. M., & Finch, A. J. (1992). Relations among self-reported depressive symptoms in clinic-referred children versus adolescents. *Journal of Abnormal Psychology, 101*, 391–397.

Weissman, M. M., Gammon, G. D., John, K., Merikangas, K. R., Prusoff, B. A., & Sholomskas, D. (1987). Children of depressed parents: Increased psychopathology and early onset of major depression. *Archives of General Psychiatry, 44*, 847–853.

Weissman, M. M., & Olfson, M. (1995). Depression in women: Implications for health care research. *Science, 269*, 799–801.

Weissman, M. M., Warner, V., Wickramaratne, P., & Prusoff, B. A. (1988). Early-onset major depression in parents and their children. *Journal of Affective Disorders, 15*, 269–277.

Weller, R. A., Weller, E. B., Fristad, M. A., & Bowes, J. M. (1991). Depression in recently bereaved prepubertal children. *American Journal of Psychiatry, 148*, 1536–1540.

26

A Developmental Psychopathology Perspective on the Cognitive Components of Child and Adolescent Depression

Nadine J. Kaslow, Lauren B. Adamson, and Marietta H. Collins

Multiple pathways lead to the development of depression, and myriad factors account for its maintenance and recurrence. For some youth, cognitive factors are central to the development, maintenance, and/or recurrence of their depression (e.g., Asarnow & Bates, 1988); these youth are the primary focus of this chapter. Depressed youth, even those for whom cognitive factors are not the most salient component of their presentation, typically evidence cognitive correlates of their depression; therefore, this discussion is relevant to them as well. As Garber (1992) aptly points out, it is essential that attention be paid to examining the cognitive–diathesis–stress models in children, rather than just focusing on the link between a specific cognitive process and depression. According to these models, individuals with a cognitive vulnerability to depression are most likely to evidence depression in the face of stress. This emphasis on cognitive–diathesis–stress models needs to incorporate a developmental perspective in order to ascertain the extent and nature to which there is a cognitive–diathesis × stress interaction in predicting depression for youth at different developmental stages.

To acknowledge the explanatory power of cognitive factors within the context of stress, as well as behavioral, affective, perceptual, family, interpersonal, and biological processes in the etiology and course of depression, conceptualizations of childhood depression have become multidimensional and integrative (e.g., Gotlib & Hammen, 1992). This multidimen-

Nadine J. Kaslow and Marietta H. Collins • Department of Psychiatry and Behavioral Sciences, Emory University School of Medicine, Atlanta, Georgia 30335.   **Lauren B. Adamson** • Department of Psychology, Georgia State University, Atlanta, Georgia 30303.

Handbook of Developmental Psychopathology, Second Edition, edited by Arnold J. Sameroff, Michael Lewis, and Suzanne M. Miller. Kluwer Academic/Plenum Publishers, New York, 2000.

sional nature of depression in youth makes a review of research about the cognitive aspects of depression in youth timely and difficult. The literature is replete with summaries of research data (e.g., Cole & Kaslow, 1988; Garber, 1992; Garber & Hilsman, 1992; Garber, Quiggle, & Shanley, 1990; Hammen, 1992; Kaslow, Brown, & Mee, 1994).To assess what this work indicates about cognition and depression during childhood and adolescence, the interpretation must be informed by a consideration of the core characteristics of depression and an understanding of how developmental processes qualify both cognition and depression.

There have been numerous calls for a developmental perspective. Unfortunately, few have integrated developmental theory and child clinical psychology to guide their research designs or interpret their data. Thus, it is time for us as child clinical psychologists and developmental psychologists to collaborate to reassess the vast literature on cognitive processes in depressed youth to ascertain if the adult cognitive models of depression help us understand depression from birth through adolescence. To this end, we examine what it would entail to frame the literature on adult-derived cognitive constructs of childhood depression developmentally. Then, we review studies pertinent to depressed youth who exhibit the negative cognitive styles enumerated by the major cognitive theories of depression.

ORIENTING THEMES FROM DEVELOPMENTAL PSYCHOLOGY

This chapter aims to discern if cognitive models of depression aid our understanding of depression's varied manifestations from birth to late adolescence. Cognitive constructs have fostered an understanding of adult depression, and there have been several recent attempts to extend these analyses to adolescents and children. To evaluate these efforts, it is essential to construct a frame through which to view the developmental transformation of cognitive processes. This endeavor takes us into the theoretical space of developmental psychology, which is removed from the realm of cognitive psychology that has inspired the cognitive models of adult depression. Fortunately, several trailblazers have already described the territory and located important principles. Here, we follow their lead and abstract developmental themes that can be used to frame research that probes the relevance of adult-derived cognitive models of childhood depression (e.g., Cicchetti, Rogosch, & Toth, 1994; Cole & Kaslow, 1988; Garber, 1992).

Cognition is the primary topic of several classical developmental theories, including those of Piaget, Werner, and Vygotsky. Their seminal ideas are now often grouped together to provide an organismic, integrative worldview of developmental processes that forms much of the foundation of contemporary developmental psychopathology. Although these theorists often took different stances on issues about developmental order and disorder (Adamson, 1997), for our current purpose, it is useful to blend their perspectives to abstract three developmental themes (normative shifts, directionality, relational perspective) that can orient research on cognitive processes in childhood depression.

Normative Shifts

The first orienting theme is that there is a *normative* path or expected sequence of development. Piaget sketched the details of this path, highlighting its milestones and pointing to major moments of transformation. His propensity for charting the course of development has been retained by many developmental psychopathologists. There is general agreement that the developmental path is marked by moments of transformation of the substance and/or organization of cognition. Even if a developmentalist does not endorse a stage theory, he or she tends to locate seams when novelty emerges, and there has been considerable consensus about when these seams occur. Thus, although Werner and Vygotsky did not share Piaget's enthusiasm for stages, they all were fascinated with symbol formation at the end of infancy (Piaget, 1962; Vygotsky, 1978; Werner & Kaplan, 1963) and the emergence of logical or scientific thought during early middle childhood (Inhelder & Piaget, 1969; Werner & Kaplan, 1963; Vygotsky, 1986). The theme of orderly progress through transformative moments raises issues of developmental timing and paths for cognitive models of childhood depression. In terms of developmental timing, it prompts us to ask at what point of development are the various constructs associated with cognitive models of adult depression relevant to children? A second issue that arises from a progressive view of cognition from birth to adolescence is the possibility of multiple developmental paths that challenges any neatly drawn developmental trajectory (see, e.g., Werner, 1957, for his discussion of equifinality). For our purposes, this issue is pressing because of the danger of overlooking alternative developmental routes that might increase a child's vulnerability to depression. Of particular concern is whether or not different stage-specific cognitive processes, in addition to a complex interaction of gender-related personality characteristics, biological changes, and socialization practices (Nolen-Hoeksema & Girgus, 1994), can help account for the gender-related differences in the occurrence of depression during different periods of childhood. More specifically, research reveals that in the preschool years, boys are more likely to be depressed than girls (Murray, Hipwell, Hooper, Stein, & Cooper, 1996). Data on gender differences in rates of depression during the elementary school years are inconsistent. By early to midadolescence, females evidence twice the rate of males with regard to depressive symptoms and disorders than do males (Nolen-Hoeksema & Girgus, 1994).

Directionality

The second theme is that there is an overall *direction* or sweep of development toward increasing organizational complexity. Werner (1948, 1957), in particular, focused on elaborating this claim, although Piaget and Vygotsky held similar sympathies. In both his orthogenetic principle and in his innovative theoretical vocabulary of contrastive categories (such as *syncretic–discrete* and *diffuse–articulated*), Werner (1957) tried to describe the connections, dynamics, and forces within psychological organizations. As several recent commentators have noted (e.g., Cicchetti et al., 1994; Glick, 1992), this heuristic view of developmental change raises important challenges to the assumption that the arrangement between phenomena remains constant across the developmental course. For example, Werner suggested that the clustering of processes into domains such as cognition, affect, and perception may itself reflect an advanced developmental status rather than an inevitable split that exists early in the developmental course, when processes such as cognition and affect or cognition and socialization may be inextricably intertwined (see Glick, 1983).

A number of authors have proposed integrative models that attend to the ways affective and cognitive aspects of depression become more differentiated over the course of development. Cole and Kaslow (1988) argued that depression is a failure in the regulation of negative emotions (e.g., emergence and overexpression of dysphoria, difficulties experiencing positive feelings expressed as anhedonia). These problems may reflect neurobiological vulnerability to depression, problematic family interactions in which family members fail to soothe an affectively distressed child or to teach the child skills to regulate emotional distress, failure to acquire and/or use cognitive self-regulating strategies for modulating painful emotions and negative cognitions, or a combination of factors. Difficulties in emotion regulation, which typically become evident when a child experiences stress, are manifested differently depending on the youth's developmental stage (Cole & Kaslow, 1988). In very young children, there is a general experience of sadness and affective distress that reflects an overall failure in emotion regulation. Depressed infants and preschoolers are less likely to exhibit depression as a unitary phenomenon with specific affective and cognitive symptoms, and more likely to express negative affectivity globally because they do not possess the cognitive skills to regulate and differentiate their affective distress, and they depend on significant people in their environment to help them with emotional regulation. As children mature, their depression becomes more identified as such and the affective, cognitive, and interpersonal components become more differentiated. They use cognitive strategies to regulate their affective distress relatively independently.

Relational Perspective

Developmental movement is *relational*; development occurs because of and through the interaction of different elements intrinsic and extrinsic to the child. Although Piaget, Werner, and Vygotsky agree with this claim, their analyses of what elements interact to produce changes differ. Of particular value is Vygotsky's (1978) assertion that cognitive development is related to caregivers' actions that reflect, in part, their cultural–historical context. He provides a compelling image of this relation in his discussion of *the zone of proximal development*, in which children interact with more sophisticated people who assist them so that they can act in ways they are not yet able to on their own. This image of a zone of proximal development highlights how different caregivers influence the course of a child's cognitive development. This view allows for consideration of how caregivers' depression-related cognitions, as well as their culturally informed expectations about age and gender differences in behavior, might influence how, and possibly where, they guide a child's actions.

The main thrust of the relational perspective is that the contribution of each cognitive process to the emergence of depression must be considered within the context of the entire developing system. The contribution of each component depends upon the arrangement between components, and this arrangement is dynamic. Thus, it is important to ask not only when a child has developed a cognitive capacity but also how this capacity functions in concert with currently available emotional and social processes to augment or diminish depression.

COGNITIVE CONCEPTS AND RESEARCH ON CHILD AND ADOLESCENT DEPRESSION

This section summarizes research on the relevance of the major cognitive constructs to depressed youth, with particular attention paid to the aforementioned developmental themes. We structure this review according to three overarching constructs derived from cognitive models of adult depression: cognitions about the self, information processing, and expectancies. We begin each section with a discussion of these cognitive constructs, followed by a brief review of the pertinent normative developmental literature. Then, we focus our attention on the relevant empirical literature regarding depressed youth.

Cognitions About the Self

Adult Models: Negative Self-Schemas and Views of Self

Self-schema theory holds that individuals prone to depression have pervasive negative views of the self that are represented in memory (Derry & Kuiper, 1981; Kuiper & Derry, 1982). These distorting negative schemas result in biased processing and interpretation of information in a manner that confirms negative self-perceptions and facilitates the encoding and retrieval of negative self-relevant information. As such, these negative self-schemas may account for selective attention to and personalization of salient negative events and may make the person helpless and hopeless.

Three major cognitive theories of depression highlight the role of negative views of the self. Beck (1967, 1976), in his cognitive theory, posits that depressed people exhibit a cognitive triad that includes a negative view of the self, the world, and the future. These cognitions cause the symptoms of depression. In the original learned helplessness theory (Seligman, 1975), low self-esteem is conceptualized as a helplessness deficit that results when experiences with uncontrollable events lead persons to the expectation that no response in their repertoire can control future outcomes. According to the attributional reformulation of the learned helplessness model (Abramson, Seligman, & Teasdale, 1978), low self-esteem accompanies experiences of personal helplessness in which individuals believe that the outcome of a negative event is only uncontrollable for some people including themselves.

Normative Pathways of Self-Schemas and Views of Self

Children's conceptions of self and associated affective experiences (e.g., sadness, anxiety, fear, shame, guilt) undergo qualitative transformation from infancy to adolescence (Lewis, 1992). For example, from ages 1–5, children begin to develop the capacity for self-evaluation (Stipek, Recchia, & McClintic, 1992). Initially, they lack the cognitive representational skills necessary for self-reflection and evaluation. However, they have schemas for interpersonal interactions, and the match between their schemas and an event determines some of their affective reactions. As they mature, they begin to anticipate adult reactions to their successes and attempt to avoid negative reactions to failure. Over time, they gradually internalize the reactions of others and begin to evaluate their performance and react accordingly, independent of their expectations of adult reactions. However, they have not yet developed the cognitive schemas by which they can abstract themselves from the immediate situation and observe the myriad aspects of the experiences, nor do they have the symbolic capacity to call on a stored representation of an event and reflect on the thoughts and actions of the situation. By elementary school, children manifest increasing self-awareness and the capacity to reflect on their own thoughts and feelings; they shift to having more psychological and competency-based self-assessments; they use dispositional, internal descriptors of self, and realize the constancy of themselves and the immutability of their identity; their self-evaluations become more complicated and differentiated; they make more comparative inferences about themselves; and they develop the capacity for metacognition. As a result, more stable and internally consistent self-schemas become evident; thus, more stable negative self-evaluations may emerge. As children enter adolescence, they manifest heightened self-consciousness and the capacity for abstract reasoning, further consolidating their self-schemas. Self-esteem declines during the transition from childhood to adolescence, a trend that may be more true for females than males (McCauley, Mitchell, Burke, & Moss, 1988), a trend suggesting multiple developmental pathways. Given the normative pathways in the development of self-schemas and views of self, at what stages of development are young people able to experience the symptoms of depression associated with negative self-schemas and low self-esteem?

Childhood Depression Literature

Negative Self-Schemas. Only a few studies have examined the self-schema model of depression in youth, and none of these have examined children prior to elementary school. Comparing nonreferred, mildly depressed school-age children to normal children on an incidental recall task, Hammen and Zupan (1984) found that nondepressed children recalled a higher proportion of positive self-descriptive words reflecting positive self-schemas. Zupan, Hammen, and Jaenicke (1987) expanded upon this study and compared children with a current or previous diagnosis of depression to those without a history of depression. The depressed youth viewed more of the negative content words as self-descriptive and showed greater recall for these words. Conversely, the nondepressed youth endorsed more positive-content words as apt self-descriptions and recalled more positive self-reference words. Using a different methodology, Whitman and Leitenberg (1990) found that depressed children had difficulties processing positive but not negative information, suggesting that they lack positive self-schemas. These difficulties were found on word recognition and incidental word recall measures, indicating that the problematic cognitive self-schemas of depressed youth affect both storage and accessibility of new information (Prieto, Cole, & Tageson, 1992).

Cole and Jordan (1995) examined peer nominations of a broad array of competencies and incidental recall of positive and negative self-referential adjectives in depressed and non-depressed fourth, sixth, and eighth graders. Even after controlling for depressive symptoms, positive and negative peer ratings correlated with children's capacities to recall positive and negative self-referential information respectively. Preliminary findings suggested that the cognitive processes associated with the incidental recall of negative self-descriptive information may mediate the peer evaluations–depressive symptom link (Cole & Jordan, 1995). The link between recall of negative information and depressive symptoms becomes stronger as children get older (Cole & Jordan, 1995).

Some research has compared the self-schemas of high-risk school-age children (those with depressed mothers) and low-risk children (those with nondepressed mothers). These data reveal that low-risk children have stronger positive self-schemas than high-risk children, and high-risk children with a history of mood disorders have negative self-schemas (Hammen, 1988; Jaenicke et al., 1987).

Negative Views of Self. Elevated depressive symptoms and diagnoses are associated with low self-esteem in community and clinic samples of elementary school, junior high school, and high school youth (for a review, see Garber, 1992; Kaslow, Brown, & Mee, 1994). Depressed youth display negative evaluations of themselves, their family, and their peers (Rudolph, Hammen, & Burge, 1997) and have depressive attributions (Asarnow & Bates, 1988). Negative feelings about the self decrease as a child's depressive symptoms remit (Asarnow & Bates, 1988; McCauley et al., 1988). The only study to examine the cognitive–diathesis–stress model revealed than low self-esteem combined with negative life events predicted subsequent depression in children at risk for depression; "at risk" was defined as having a depressed mother (Hammen, 1988).

Cole's (1991) competency-based model of youth depression places self-esteem in a relational framework. According to this developmental model, the study of the link between self-esteem and depression should begin in middle childhood, when children begin to use social comparison information and understand traits as stable characteristics, and when their self-concepts become more differentiated (Cole, 1991). Children gather competency-based feedback regarding their academic, social, athletic, personal, and physical characteristics from others, internalize this feedback, and develop self-schemas based on the feedback. Tests of the competency-based model reveal strong correlations between depression and academic and social competence, and the correlation between depression levels and social competence increases with age (Cole, Martin, Powers, & Truglio, 1996). Elementary school children who received high competence ratings by their peers were less likely to manifest depressive symptoms (Cole, 1991). Youth receiving low competency peer ratings in multiple domains showed more depressive symptoms than youth with fewer peer-perceived incompetencies (Cole, 1991). Finally, level of depressive symptoms was more a function of peer perceptions of incompetence than competence, particularly for girls (Cole, 1991).

Few have examined developmental differences in the link between depression and self-esteem and the extant data are contradictory (Garber, 1992). Some studies found no developmental trend; others found an age × depression interaction with regard to self-esteem. Among the studies that found an interaction, some indicated that depressed adolescents have lower self-esteem than depressed children, and this may be particularly true for females (Orvaschel, Beeferman, & Kabacoff, 1997), whereas other studies revealed the opposite (Garber, 1992).

Information Processing

Adult Models: Faulty Information Processing, Cognitive Distortions, Maladaptive Attributional Styles, and Dysfunctional Self-Control Cognitions

Theories of adult depression have offered a number of related yet distinct explanations about the information processing of depressed persons. First, information-processing models propose that depressed persons have an attentional bias toward negative stimuli (Ingram & Reed, 1986) and suggest that this bias is related to the selective attention and memory for the processing of information related to loss and failure. The etiology of this bias is explained in associative network theory (Bower, 1981), which suggests that the bias develops as a result of an associative connection of depressive memories existing within a network of emotional nodes. Second, cognitive distortion models hold that depressed people make errors in thinking that result in the systematic misinterpretation of the meaning of events, which in turn reflect and sustain the negative cognitive triad. According to Beck, Rush, Shaw, and Emery (1979), depressives make the following systematic cognitive errors: arbitrary inference, selective abstraction, overgeneralization, magnification and minimization, personalization, and absolutistic, dichotomous thinking. Third, attributional theories are based on the view that one's causal attributions or explanations for positive and negative events play a role in the development and maintenance of learned helplessness and depression (Abramson et al., 1978). Individuals who blame themselves for negative events (internal), and view the cause of these events as consistent over time (stable) and generalizable across situations (global) are at risk for developing the cluster of helplessness deficits and depressive symptoms in response to negative events. The opposite style, external–unstable–specific attributions for positive events, also is characteristic of depressive cognitions. Fourth, according to the self-control model (Rehm, 1977), depressed persons typically have maladaptive self-monitoring, self-evaluation, and/or self-reinforcement strategies for coping with stress. Specifically, they selectively attend to negative rather than positive events and to the immediate rather than the delayed consequences of behavior, have high performance standards, set overly stringent self-evaluative criteria, fail to make adaptive causal attributions, and engage in excessive self-punishment and/or fail to use appropriate and contingent positive self-reinforcement.

Normative Pathways of Information Processing, Cognitions, Attributions, and Self-Control

As early as preschool, children try to explain the causes of outcomes and their own roles in the events that transpire in their lives. They are more likely than older youth and adults to make overattributions of intentionality, to attribute greater motivation to people who are externally induced to perform and greater effort to more capable people, and they tend not to differentiate luck from skill or internal from external factors. This less differentiated thinking often results in their making inaccurate conclusions about causality, and due to their ego-centrism, they are prone to attribute negative events to internal causes even when this is not the case (e.g., abuse) and to attribute outcomes to unstable and specific causes. By middle childhood, children can invoke internal factors to explain events, reason that outer experiences may differ from inner experiences, and internally reason with themselves. They can make more stable and global attributions than their younger peers. As a result, their attributions have more effect on their behavior, expectations, and self-assessments. These patterns of increasing consistency in their understanding of events and the future are associated with the development of self-reflection and a greater sense of control over their behavior.

Childhood Depression Literature

Information Processing.   Unfortunately, no research has examined associative memory networks in depressed youth at different developmental stages. The only research on associative memory networks and depression in youth is the work of Hammen and Zupan (1984), Prieto and colleagues (1992), and Whitman and Leitenberg (1990) described earlier. These studies indicated that depressed children do not have the positive memory bias that characterizes nondepressed children.

Some researchers have examined social information processing in depressed youth (Dodge, 1993). Quiggle, Garber, Panak, and Dodge (1992) found that children with elevated levels of depressive symptoms exhibit a hostile attributional bias, in addition to a depressive attributional style. They attribute negative events to internal, stable, and global causes, and positive events to external, unstable, and specific factors, *and* attribute hostile intent to others. Compared to their nondepressed peers, depressed children more typically indicate that acting in an assertive manner is associated with less positive and more negative outcomes. These results suggest that in response to affective arousal, depressed youth often become passive, feel ineffectual, and are more likely to feel that any behavior on their part will result in negative outcomes. In addition, compared to children with few symptoms, depressed preadolescents show proportionately greater recall of negative versus positive information regarding key people in their lives and make more pessimistic predictions about the interpersonal responses of others (Rudolph et al., 1997). Finally, using structural equation modeling, Davila, Hammen, Burge, Paley, and Daley (1995) found that in 17- and 18-year-old females, initial depressive symptoms and poor interpersonal problem solving both lead to higher levels of interpersonal stress, which in turn results in an increase in depressive symptoms.

Cognitive Distortions. The research related to cognitive distortions highlights specific cognitive errors, automatic thoughts and dysfunctional attitudes, and the negative cognitive triad. These studies suggest that depressed elementary, middle, and high school youth have a distorted style of thinking rather than actual cognitive deficiencies (Kendall, Stark, & Adam, 1990).

Researchers examining cognitive errors using the Children's Negative Cognitive Error Questionnaire (CNCEQ; Leitenberg, Yost, & Carroll-Wilson, 1986) report that nonclinic youth with elevated depression scores evidence a greater tendency to personalize, catastrophize, overgeneralize, and selectively attend to negative events than do nondepressed, nonclinic youth (e.g., Leitenberg et al., 1986; Mazur, Wolchik, & Sandler, 1992; Robins & Hinkley, 1989; Turner & Cole, 1994). Such cognitive errors are evidenced more often by depressed clinic children than nondepressed clinic children (Kempton, Van Hasselt, Bukstein, & Null, 1994; Tems, Stewart, Skinner, Hughes, & Emslie, 1993). After treatment, these cognitive errors no longer differentiate depressed inpatient children and adolescents and their nondepressed inpatient peers or nonreferred control youth (Tems et al., 1993), suggesting that distorted cognitions may be state-dependent.

Studies also have been conducted using the Automatic Thoughts Questionnaire (ATQ) originally designed for adults, which assesses one's tendency to make negative and positive inferences about events. ATQ responses have discriminated between depressed and nondepressed inpatient children and adolescents (Jolly & Wiesner, 1996; Kazdin, 1990). These cognitive distortions mediate between stress and depression in adolescents (Deal & Williams, 1988). Similarly, using the Dysfunctional Attitude Scale (DAS), originally devised for adults, self-reported depression correlates in the predicted direction with cognitive distortions (Garber, Weiss, & Shanley, 1993).

Kaslow, Stark, Printz, Livingston, and Tsai (1992) devised the Cognitive Triad Inventory for Children (CTI-C) to assess all three aspects of the negative cognitive triad in youth. Children and adolescents with depressive symptoms, or those who meet criteria for depression, report low self-esteem, a negative worldview, and hopelessness on the CTI-C (Kaslow et al., 1992; Moilanen, 1995). These negative views are related to the severity of their symptoms (Stark, Schmidt, & Joiner, 1996). In addition, studies examining the negative cognitive triad from a relational perspective reveal that mothers' but not fathers' responses on a cognitive triad inventory measure are associated with children's views of self, world, and future, and children's perceptions of their parents' messages regarding self, world, and future predict children's cognitive triads and ratings of depression (Stark et al., 1996). The link between children's perceptions of their parents' messages and depressive symptoms is mediated by their CTI-C scores (Stark et al., 1996). Finally, CTI-C scores combined with responses to the ATQ for Children discriminate among depressed, anxious, and normal controls (Stark, Humphrey, Laurent, Livingston, & Christopher, 1993).

A few studies have used a developmental perspective in examining the link between cognitive distortions and depression in youth. Turner and Cole (1994), using fourth, sixth, and eighth graders, found that the role of cognitive errors as a risk factor in child depression changed over the course of development. Whereas in younger children there is no support for a cognitive–diathesis–stress model, by eighth grade, data support such a perspective, underscoring the importance of considering the directionality of development. However, Garber and colleagues (1993) found that negative cognitions were not associated with age, nor did the association between depressive symptoms and cognitive distortions (automatic thoughts, dysfunctional attitudes) change with age in a large sample of seventh through twelfth graders. Similarly, Marcotte (1996) found no age fluctuations in global scores in irrational beliefs in 11-

to 18-year-olds. But, age differences were noted in specific types of irrational beliefs. Together, these data suggest that there may be overall changes in cognitive distortions from the elementary school to the high school years, but few global changes during high school. Specific types of cognitive distortions may change within the high school years.

Maladaptive Attributional Styles.   Although research examining an attributional model of child depression does not find consistent support for this model (e.g., Cole & Turner, 1993), two recent meta-analyses (Gladstone & Kaslow, 1995; Joiner & Wagner, 1995) revealed that most cross-sectional studies find significant correlations in 6- to 18-year-olds between measures of depressive symptoms, depressive disorders, and attributional styles as measured by the Children's Attributional Style Questionnaire (CASQ). As predicted, youth with elevated depressive symptom scores tend to make more internal–stable–global attributions for negative events and more external–unstable–specific attributions for positive events than their nondepressed peers. These findings are relatively robust; they are true across age, gender, and sample type (Joiner & Wagner, 1995). Data on similarities and differences in the link between attributions and depression across age groups are contradictory. Some have found that several aspects of attributional style change with age (McCauley et al., 1988; Nolen-Hoeksema, Girgus, & Seligman, 1986; Robins & Hinkley, 1989); others have found no differences in the correlation between depressive symptoms and CASQ scores from early childhood to middle adolescence (Garber et al., 1993; Kaslow, Rehm, & Siegel, 1984). Garber and colleagues (1993) found that the age × depression interaction with regard to CASQ scores was not significant.

There is some evidence that, consistent with a diathesis–stress model, youth with a depressive attributional style are vulnerable to developing depressive symptoms, especially in response to negative events (Nolen-Hoeksema, Girgus, & Seligman, 1992; Panak & Garber, 1992; Robinson, Garber, & Hilsman, 1995). But, not all studies find that attributional style predicts later depressive symptoms (Bennett & Bates, 1995; Hammen, Adrian, & Hiroto, 1988). Some data indicate that a pessimistic explanatory style persists after remission of depressive symptoms, thus placing the youth at increased risk for future depression (Gotlib, Lewinsohn, Seeley, Rohde, & Redner, 1993; Nolen-Hoeksema et al., 1992). However, not all researchers have found this to be true (Asarnow & Bates, 1988; Benfield, Palmer, Pfefferbaum, & Stowe, 1988; McCauley et al., 1988).

As for the central hypothesis that the attributional style × negative life events interaction is associated with depression, the findings are inconclusive (Joiner & Wagner, 1995). Cole and Turner (1993), using structural equation modeling in a cross-sectional examination of the attribution × stress interaction in a large sample of elementary and high school children, found that attributional style partially mediated the effects of negative events on self-reported symptoms of depression, but no support was found for an interactive or moderator model. However, Robinson and colleagues (1995), who assessed cognitions and stress in the spring of sixth grade then again after the transition to seventh grade, found that the interaction between stressors and negative attributional style at Time 1 predicted depressive symptoms at Time 2. Further analyses revealed that self-worth moderated the negative attributional style × stress interaction, such that only those youth with low self-esteem prior to the transition to seventh grade were at risk for later depressive symptoms. These data also suggest that high self-worth may serve as a protective factor from the depressive effects of negative attributional style when children are faced with expected stress of transition to junior high school.

A key question relates to the manner in which depressed youth develop depressive attributional styles. This question has been examined from a relational perspective. Some researchers posit that these styles are acquired either via parents' modeling depressive cognitions or because depressed parents engage in faulty attribution of their child's behavior. To begin to address this question, some empirical efforts have been devoted to examining the associations between parental attributions and depression, and attributional patterns in youth. Seligman and Peterson (1986) found that in a nonclinic sample, mothers' but not fathers' attributional styles for bad events correlated with their children's attributional style and depressive symptoms. However, Kaslow, Rehm, Pollack, and Siegel (1988) did not replicate this finding in a clinic sample of depressed youth. Thus, it is premature to draw conclusions regarding the transmission of depressive attributional patterns.

Dysfunctional Self-Control Cognitions. Given that the self-control model incorporates tenets of cognitive theory of depression, the learned helplessness model, and its attributional reformulation, only findings specific to the self-control model are covered here. Data reveal that elementary and junior high school age children with elevated depressive symptoms have lower expectations for task performance, set more stringent standards for poor scores but not good scores, evaluate their performance more negatively, and punish themselves more (but do not reward themselves less) than their nondepressed counterparts (Kaslow et al., 1984). They also rate themselves more negatively than do their nondepressed peers, even when their performance is comparable (Garber, 1992). Similarly, depressed clinic children report more overall self-control difficulties as measured by the Usually That's Me self-control measure (Humphrey, 1982) than do nondepressed clinic children and normal controls. In examining self-control cognitions from a relational perspective, no differences have been found in the self-control styles of parents of depressed clinic, nondepressed clinic, and normal controls, nor has an association been found between the self-control behavior of children and their parents (Kaslow et al., 1988). However, mothers (not fathers) of depressed clinic and nonclinic children set higher criteria for providing their children with rewards when compared to mothers of clinic/nondepressed children (Cole & Rehm, 1986).

There is a relative dearth of data examining the existence of different developmental paths in the contribution of self-control cognitions to depression. However, rumination, a self-focused style of responding to distress, is one maladaptive cognitive process that may be categorized as a self-control cognition associated with depression. Nolen-Hoeksema (1994) has found that throughout childhood and into adolescence, females are more prone to ruminate than are males. In early adolescence, females are confronted with certain challenges (e.g., changes associated with puberty that may have negative societal connotations, sexual abuse, accomplishments being devalued, and constraints placed on their capacity for success in certain arenas) more often and/or to a greater degree than are males. Adolescent females with a ruminative and less active coping style may have difficulties coping with the challenges of early adolescence; this interaction may result in the increased rates of depression. These data suggest that there may be multiple pathways to depression and that these pathways may differ for males and females.

Expectancies

Adult Models: Helplessness and Hopelessness

According to Seligman's (1975) original learned helplessness model, people feel helpless and negatively about themselves and become depressed when they believe that nothing they do or do not do will change an outcome (response–outcome noncontingency). Universal helplessness, which results when one believes that neither oneself nor anyone else can control negative outcomes, is associated with the emergence of hopelessness and may be associated with the belief that the contingency of desired outcomes is at a low level. Another aspect of the learned helplessness model relates to perception of control. As a trait, locus of control refers to a generalized belief in one's ability to affect the environment to maximize rewards and minimize negative outcomes. It has been argued that depressed individuals perceive a lack of control over important events in their lives. Experiences with prior uncontrollable outcomes and the consequent expectation that future events will be uncontrollable have been linked to cognitive and motivational deficits and dysphoria.

According to the hopelessness theory of depression (Abramson, Metalsky, & Alloy, 1989), which is rooted in Seligman's learned helplessness model (1975), a person becomes hopeless and develops symptoms of hopelessness depression when they experience a negative life event, the cause of which they infer to be stable over time, generalizable across situations (global), attributable to negative aspects of the self, and likely to result in negative consequences. The theory further suggests that certain people characteristically make such causal inferences about the occurrence of negative events and thus are predisposed to hopelessness depression, while others, who are unlikely to make such inferences, are therefore at low risk for becoming hopeless and developing symptoms of hopelessness depression.

Hopelessness, or negative expectations about the future, as a core feature of depression has also been noted by Beck (1967, 1976) in his cognitive theory of depression. One aspect of Beck's negative cognitive triad, namely, the negative view of the future, has been equated with the cognitive symptom of hopelessness. According to Beck's model, the negative view of the future produces negative expectations about future outcomes and a pervasive sense of hopelessness.

Normative Pathways of Helplessness and Hopelessness

Expectant thinking is evident even in infants, so early on, there is an association between expectancies and affect (Alessandri, Sullivan, & Lewis, 1990; Lewis, Alessandri, & Sullivan, 1990; Lewis, Sullivan, Ramsay, & Alessandri, 1992; Sullivan, Lewis, & Alessandri, 1992). Infants develop an expectancy for a responsive interpersonal environment. By preschool, children have clear expectancies for mirthful and distressing situations; they seek the former and try to avoid the latter. A sizable group of preschoolers manifest achievement-based helplessness in which they believe there is a noncontingent association between their behavior and important outcomes, which results in their being less persistent in the face of failure and experiencing depressive-type affects (Burhans & Dweck, 1995; Dweck & Leggett, 1988). By middle school, children are more reflective regarding the question of whether control over an event is internally or externally determined and thus are capable of experiencing achievement-based helplessness. Children are particularly prone to experiencing helplessness in a relational context marked by criticism (Heyman, Dweck, & Cain, 1992).

It has been suggested that young children do not have the cognitive capacity to experience and manifest hopelessness because they cannot conceptualize the sequence of events or the length of time between events prior to approximately age 8. Not until adolescence does one's ability to assess probabilities emerges. It has been suggested that children cannot become hopeless or have negative expectancies about the future until they cognitively possess a future time orientation. Few studies have empirically ascertained the validity of this claim or provided data clarifying at what point in development children possess the future time perspective necessary to experience hopelessness. Despite the suggestion from developmental literature that this does not occur until adolescence, some data suggest that hopelessness does not increase from preadolescence to adolescence in the general population (Kashani, Reid, & Rosenberg, 1989).

Childhood Depression Literature

Helplessness. The lines of research pertinent to helplessness expectations in youth focus on instrumental responding, locus of control, and control-related beliefs. A few studies assessed the motivational deficit of helplessness hypothesized as central to depression. Some researchers (e.g., Kaslow, Tanenbaum, Abramson, Peterson, & Seligman, 1983; Nolen-Hoeksema et al., 1986) found that children with elevated depressive symptoms scores have deficits in instrumental responding, evidenced by difficulties on higher order cognitive tasks and tasks of reflection–impulsivity, and engage in helplessness behaviors in school. However, not all researchers find support for an association between depressive symptoms and behavioral measures of helplessness (Bodiford, Eisenstadt, Johnson, & Bradlyn, 1988).

Some investigators have examined the link between depression in children, locus of control, and perceptions of controllability. Using the Nowicki–Strickland Children's Locus of Control Scale (Nowicki & Strickland, 1973), a number of researchers have reported that children and adolescents with depressive symptoms also endorse a more external locus of control (McCauley et al., 1988; Tesiny, Lefkowitz, & Gordon, 1980). Additionally, children with an external locus of control appear to have lower self-esteem and are more likely to choose helpless, self-blaming, or externalized blaming responses. Furthermore, children who endorse high levels of depressive symptoms and an external locus of control evidence deficits in school achievement (Tesiny et al., 1980). Finally, locus of control appears to be state-dependent and little is known about developmental differences in the locus of control–depression link.

Weisz and colleagues (Weisz et al., 1989; Weisz, Sweeney, Proffitt, & Carr, 1993; Weisz, Weiss, Wasserman, & Rintoul, 1987) have used a two-dimensional model of control cognition to examine beliefs about the contingencies of outcomes (outcome contingency) and about one's own competence to perform outcome-relevant behavior (personal competence). In a series of well-designed studies, Weisz and colleagues examined control-related beliefs and cognitions in clinic-referred and inpatient children and adolescents. For clinic-referred youth (Weisz et al., 1987) who endorse high levels of depressive symptoms, low levels of perceived personal competence are also found. However, outcome contingency beliefs are not associated with depressive symptoms scores. Similar findings were reported by Weisz and co-workers in their work with inpatient samples (Weisz et al., 1989). In the most recent study in this series of investigations, Weisz and colleagues (1993) used a more psychometrically sound measure of control beliefs and studied the link between depression and control-related beliefs in a general population rather than a sample of psychiatrically defined youth. In this latter study, both perceived incompetence and perceived noncontingency were related to children's depression scores and together accounted for 40% of the variance in depressive symptom scores. Taken together, findings suggest that by late childhood, one may be susceptible to both personal and universal helplessness. However, although preliminary analyses suggest a moderate relation between contingency and competence beliefs, the findings leave open the question about whether these two forms of helplessness are associated with different constellations of symptoms (Weisz et al., 1993). Furthermore, it is still not known if perceptions of helplessness are cognitive distortions or accurate depressive perceptions of reality.

Several researchers have sought to locate the emergence of differences in children's control-related beliefs that have been related to depression in their social environment, especially in the interactions with their mothers. Their basic strategy has been to document the effect on the child of variations in maternal behavior that occur naturally as a function of depression or experimentally as a function of mothers' simulation of depression. Research with infants and toddlers has shown that depression, either real or simulated, can affect maternal responsiveness during social interactions in ways that may diminish the child's experience of responsive contingency (Murray, Fiori-Cowley, & Hooper, 1996), as well as the mothers' overall availability for sustained periods of shared attention (Goldsmith & Rogoff, 1997). Two distinct patterns have been documented, one in which the mother appears affectively flat, sad, and withdrawn, and one in which she appears angry, hostile, and intrusive (review in Cohen & Campbell, 1992), although only the former has been simulated so far in experimental studies. Moreover, infants (Cohen & Campbell, 1992) and toddlers (Seiner & Gelfand, 1995) have specific and appropriate responses to depressed maternal behavior and these responses may continue to be evident when the infant subsequently interacts with a person who is not displaying depressed behavior (for review, see Field, 1992). When infants of nondepressed mothers are unable to elicit a positive response from mothers who are simulating depressive behavior, they respond to distortions in maternal contingent responsiveness by becoming increasingly negative and unresponsive. Although this response has most often been analyzed in terms of predominantly noncognitive processes such as mirroring (Field, 1992) and self-directed regulatory behavior (Gianino & Tronick, 1988), Trad (1994) has formulated a learned helplessness model that involves relatively sophisticated cognitive processes such as discrepancy and contingency awareness, both of which have been demonstrated by infants 2–3 months of age. He contends that using these processes, even a young infant may detect disruptions of a contingency relationship and of his or her expectation of contingency that may produce negative affect that the infant may not be able to regulate successfully. He suggests in addition that infants may be prone to interpreting such negative events as a global loss of control.

There have been few efforts to relate variations in children's helpless behaviors to variations in maternal behavior. One exception is a study by Nolen-Hoeksema, Wolfson, Mumme, and Guskin (1995), in which 5- to 7-year-olds were observed with their mothers during a problem-solving task, in addition to being interviewed and being assessed by teachers to gain additional measures of helpless behavior. The results support the contention that the quality of mother–child interaction during tasks that frustrate the child is related to children's sense of helplessness. Children of mothers who were more negative and hostile and less encouraging of mastery, regardless of the mother's diagnosis, are more prone to helpless behavior.

Hopelessness. Community and clinical samples of youth with high scores on the Hopelessness Scale for Children (Kazdin, Colbus, & Rodgers, 1986; Kazdin, French, Unis, Esveldt-Dawson, & Sherick, 1983) manifest depressive symptoms and disorders (Asarnow & Bates, 1988; Benfield et al., 1988; Kashani et al., 1989; Kazdin et al., 1983; 1986; McCauley et al., 1988). Higher levels of hopelessness have been found in depressed youth than in youth with other psychiatric problems (Benfield et al., 1988; Kazdin et al., 1983; 1986). Hopeless youth are at increased risk for suicidal behavior (Kashani et al., 1989; Kazdin et al., 1983), and hopelessness is associated with low self-esteem, negative worldviews (e.g., Kaslow et al., 1992; Stark et al., 1996) and problems in school (Kashani et al., 1989). Hopelessness appears to dissipate when depressive symptoms remit (Asarnow & Bates, 1988; McCauley et al., 1988).

DISCUSSION

Available studies demonstrate that the cognitive constructs that have been helpful in conceptualizing adult depression are increasingly applicable with age during the span from infancy to adolescence. For example, as children mature, they develop more stable self-representations, become more competent in ascertaining causal relationships, possess more of a future time perspective, and are more able to engage in metacognitions. However, given the restricted age sampling of most studies, this generalization has not often been subjected to rigorous testing. In addition, it is important to determine not only whether there are higher correlations between cognitive constructs and depression over the course of development, but also whether there are qualitative differences in these links during different developmental phases.

Most studies of depression in youth have not by design spanned developmental phases or focused on points of transition (18–24 months, 5–7 shift, 11–14 shift) in cognitive processes. The initial concern has been to demonstrate that depressed children, regardless of age, differ in their cognitions from children at low risk for depression. Given that children's cognitions about the self, information processing, and expectancies develop, it is important to determine at what stage children begin to evidence the negative cognitions association with depression and how these depressive cognitive processes change over the course of development. Given the relative dearth of research on the earliest relation of cognition and depression, this research should include infants and toddlers whenever possible. Moreover, more longitudinal studies of cognitive processes and depression are needed that incorporate developmentally appropriate measures of cognitive processes that are child-friendly and take into account children's cognitive and linguistic capacities (Garber, 1992).

Given the burgeoning literature on differential expressions of depression in males and females at different developmental points, more exploration of multiple developmental pathways should be undertaken by paying more attention to gender × age interactions for cognitive processes associated with depression. This work should be conducted in a manner that takes into account the complex age × gender interactions that are pertinent to the cognitive–diathesis × stress model. Prospective and longitudinal research must address the diathesis–stress and causal mediation components of the various cognitive theories of depression in males and females at different developmental phases and from different samples (e.g., school, clinic).

The relational developmental theme also should be highlighted in future work. While a growing body of literature suggests that children of depressed parents are at risk for developing depressive cognitions, the mechanisms by which depressive cognitions are transmitted have not been studied. A number of hypotheses have been proposed to explain such transmission, notably modeling (Kaslow et al., 1988; Seligman et al., 1984), problematic parent–child attachment bonds (Hammen, 1992), perfectionistic parental standards (Cole & Rehm, 1986), critical and rejecting parents (for review, see Kaslow, Deering, & Racusin, 1994), and experiences with uncontrollable and negative life events such as child maltreatment (Garber, 1992).To understand the relational components of childhood depression, research must examine depressive cognitions in youth in the interpersonal context in which they are embedded.

A number of authors have set the stage for such an examination by proposing models that integrate cognitive and interpersonal components of depression in youth. Two of the most sophisticated models, proposed by Dodge (1993) and Hammen (1992), both may provide a framework to guide developmentally sensitive research. According to Dodge's (1993) social information-processing model, early life experiences characterized by loss or instability and/or an upbringing characterized by high and unrealistic achievement expectations may result in the development of depression via memory of negative self-schemas and low self-esteem. Such schemas combined with later experiences of loss or failure, lead the child to selectively attend to the negative features of these events and to attribute their causes to internal, stable, and global factors. When this occurs, the child readily accesses depressive responses from memory and exhibits dysphoric affect, lowered levels of activity, and anhedonia. These depressive cognitive processes impede the child's capacity to utilize helpful social resources, resulting in more chronic depressive symptoms. According to Hammen (1992), maladaptive attachment patterns with parents are reinforced by later difficulties in familial and peer interactions. In the context of impaired early social functioning, individuals develop unhealthy cognitive styles, including maladaptive models of self and others, and ineffective coping skills. These cognitive styles increase the likelihood that stressful life events will occur and are associated with difficulty managing stressful events. The presence of stressful life events and impaired coping skills contributes to the development and maintenance of depressive reactions.

In closing, data from children and adolescents are consistent with predictions based on cognitive models and suggest considerable continuity in the cognitive processes of depressed individuals from elementary school through adulthood. Despite these continuities, there are differences in the cognitive functioning of depressed infants, toddlers, elementary school children, adolescents, and adults due to cognitive developmental changes. Our effort to ascertain the utility of cognitive models for understanding depression in youth revealed that adapting adult cognitive models to children is complex. Each model must be tailored to fit within a developmental frame where cognitive processes, as well as their relation to affective and social processes, transform in ways that may qualitatively alter the child's regulation of negative affect and expression of depression.

REFERENCES

Abramson, L. Y., Metalsky, G., & Alloy, L. B. (1989). Hopelessness depression: A theory-based subtype of depression. *Psychological Review, 96,* 358–372.

Abramson, L. Y., Seligman, M. E. P., & Teasdale, J. D. (1978). Learned helplessness in humans: Critique and reformulation. *Journal of Abnormal Psychology, 87,* 49–74.

Adamson, L. B. (1997). Order and disorder: Classical developmental theories and atypical communication development. In L. B. Adamson & M. A. Romski (Eds.), *Communication and language acquisition: Discoveries from atypical development* (pp. 2–23). Baltimore: Paul H. Brookes.

Alessandri, S. M., Sullivan, M. W., & Lewis, M. (1990). Violation of expectancy and frustration in early infancy. *Developmental Psychology, 26,* 738–744.

Asarnow, J. R., & Bates, S. (1988). Depression in child psychiatric inpatients: Cognitive and attributional patterns. *Journal of Abnormal Child Psychology, 16,* 601–615.

Beck, A. T. (1967). *Depression: Clinical, experimental, and theoretical aspects.* New York: Hoeber.

Beck, A. T. (1976). *Cognitive therapy and emotional disorders.* New York: International Universities Press.

Beck, A. T., Rush, A. J., Shaw, B. F., & Emery, G. (1979). *Cognitive therapy and depression.* New York: Guilford Press.

Benfield, C. Y., Palmer, D. J., Pfefferbaum, B., & Stowe, M. L. (1988). A comparison of depressed and nondepressed disturbed children on measures of attributional style, hopelessness, life stress, and temperament. *Journal of Abnormal Child Psychology, 16,* 397–410.

Bennett, D. S., & Bates, J. E. (1995). Prospective models of depressive symptoms in early adolescence: Attributional style, stress, and support. *Journal of Early Adolescence, 15,* 299–315.

Bodiford, C. A., Eisenstadt, T. H., Johnson, J. H., & Bradlyn, A. S. (1988). Comparison of learned helpless cognitions and behavior in children with high and low scores on the Children's Depression Inventory. *Journal of Clinical Child Psychology, 17,* 152–158.

Bower, G. H. (1981). Mood and memory. *American Psychologist, 36,* 129–138.

Burhans, K. K., & Dweck, C. S. (1995). Helplessness in early childhood: The role of contingent worth. *Child Development, 66*, 1719–1738.

Cicchetti, D., Rogosch, F. A., & Toth, S. L. (1994). A developmental psychopathology perspective on depression in children and adolescents. In W. M. Reynolds & H. F. Johnston (Eds.), *Handbook of depression in children and adolescents* (pp. 123–141). New York: Plenum Press.

Cohen, J., & Campbell, S. (1992). Influence of maternal depression on infant affect regulation. In D. Cicchetti & S. L. Toth (Eds.), *Developmental perspectives on depression: Rochester symposium on developmental psychopathology* (Vol. 4, pp. 103–130). Rochester: University of Rochester Press.

Cole, D. A. (1991). Preliminary support for a competency-based model of depression in children. *Journal of Abnormal Psychology, 100*, 181–190.

Cole, D. A., & Jordan, A. E. (1995). Competence and memory: Integrating psychosocial and cognitive correlates of child depression. *Child Development, 66*, 459–473.

Cole, D. A., Martin, J. M., Powers, B., & Truglio, R. (1996). Modeling causal relations between academic and social competence and depression: A multitrait-multimethod longitudinal study of children. *Journal of Abnormal Psychology, 105*, 258–270.

Cole, D. A., & Rehm, L. P. (1986). Family interaction patterns and childhood depression. *Journal of Abnormal Child Psychology, 14*, 297–314.

Cole, D. A., & Turner, J. E. (1993). Models of cognitive mediation and moderation in child depression. *Journal of Abnormal Psychology, 102*, 271–281.

Cole, P., & Kaslow, N. J. (1988). Interactional and cognitive strategies for affect regulation: Developmental perspective on childhood depression. In L. B. Alloy (Ed.), *Cognitive processes in depression* (pp. 310–341). New York: Guilford Press.

Davila, J., Hammen, C., Burge, D., Paley, B., & Daley, S. E. (1995). Poor interpersonal problem solving as a mechanism of stress generation in depression among adolescent women. *Journal of Abnormal Psychology, 104*, 592–600.

Deal, S. L., & Williams, J. E. (1988). Cognitive distortions as mediators between life stress and depression in adolescents. *Adolescence, 23*, 477–490.

Derry, P., & Kuiper, N. (1981). Schematic processing and self-reference in clinical depression. *Journal of Abnormal Psychology, 90*, 286–297.

Dodge, K. A. (1993). Social-cognitive mechanisms in the development of conduct disorder and disorder. *Annual Review of Psychology, 44*, 559–584.

Dweck, C. S., & Leggett, E. L. (1988). A social cognitive approach to motivation and personality. *Psychological Review, 95*, 256–273.

Field, T. (1992). Infants of depressed mothers. *Development and Psychopathology, 4*, 49–66.

Garber, J. (1992). Cognitive models of depression: A developmental perspective. *Psychological Inquiry, 3*, 235–240.

Garber, J., & Hilsman, R. (1992). Cognitions, stress, and depression in children and adolescents. *Child and Adolescent Psychiatric Clinics of North America, 1*, 129–166.

Garber, J., Quiggle, N., & Shanley, N. (1990). Cognition and depression in children and adolescents. In R. E. Ingram (Ed.), *Contemporary psychological approaches to depression* (pp. 87–115). New York: Plenum Press.

Garber, J., Weiss, B., & Shanley, N. (1993). Cognitions, depressive symptoms, and development in adolescents. *Journal of Abnormal Psychology, 102*, 47–57.

Gianino, A., & Tronick, E. Z. (1988). The mutual regulation model: The infant's self and interactive regulation and coping and defensive capacities. In T. M. Field, P. M. McCabe, and N. Schniederman (Eds.), *Stress and coping across development* (pp. 47–68). Hillsdale, NJ: Erlbaum.

Gladstone, T. R. G., & Kaslow, N. J. (1995). Depression and attributions in children and adolescents: A meta-analytic review. *Journal of Abnormal Child Psychology, 23*, 597–606.

Glick, J. A. (1983). Piaget, Vygotsky, and Werner. In S. Wapner & B. Kaplan (Eds.), *Toward a holistic developmental psychology* (pp. 35–52). Hillsdale, NJ: Erlbaum.

Glick, J. A. (1992). Heinz Werner's relevance for contemporary developmental psychology. *Developmental Psychology, 28*, 558–565.

Goldsmith, D. F., & Rogoff, B. (1997). Mothers' and toddlers' coordinated joint focus of attention: Variations with maternal dysphoric symptoms. *Developmental Psychology, 33*, 113–119.

Gotlib, I. H., & Hammen, C. L. (1992). *Psychological aspects of depression: Toward a cognitive-interpersonal integration.* New York: Wiley.

Gotlib, I. H., Lewinsohn, P. M., Seeley, J. R., Rohde, P., & Redner, J. E. (1993). Negative cognitions and attributional style in depressed adolescents: An examination of stability and specificity. *Journal of Abnormal Psychology, 102*, 607–615.

Hammen, C. (1988). Self-cognitions, stressful events, and the prediction of depression in the children of depressed mothers. *Journal of Abnormal Child Psychology, 16,* 347–360.

Hammen, C. (1992). Cognitive, life stress, and interpersonal approaches to a developmental psychopathology model of depression. *Development and Psychopathology, 4,* 189–206.

Hammen, C., Adrian, C., & Hiroto, D. (1988). A longitudinal test of the attributional vulnerability model in children at risk for depression. *British Journal of Clinical Psychology, 27,* 37–46.

Hammen, C., & Zupan, B. (1984). Self-schemas, depression, and the processing of personal information in children. *Journal of Experimental Child Psychology, 37,* 598–608.

Heyman, G. D., Dweck, C. S., & Cain, K. M. (1992). Young children's vulnerability to self-blame and helplessness: Relationship to beliefs about goodness. *Child Development, 63,* 401–415.

Humphrey, L. L. (1982). Children's and teacher's perspectives on children's self-control. The development of two rating scales. *Journal of Consulting and Clinical Psychology, 50,* 624–633.

Ingram, R. & Reed, M. (1986). Information encoding and retrieval processes in depression: Findings, issues, and future directions. In R. Ingram (Ed.), *Information processing approaches to clinical psychology* (pp. 131–150). Orlando, FL: Academic Press.

Inhelder, B., & Piaget, J. (1969). *The early growth of logic in the child.* New York: Norton.

Jaenicke, C., Hammen, C., Zupan, B., Hiroto, D., Gordon, D., Adrian, C., & Burge, D. (1987). Cognitive vulnerability in children at risk for depression. *Journal of Abnormal Child Psychology, 15,* 559–572.

Joiner, T. E., & Wagner, K. D. (1995). Attributional style and depression in children and adolescents: A meta-analytic review. *Clinical Psychology Review, 15,* 777–798.

Jolly, J. B., & Wiesner, D. C. (1996). Psychometric properties of the Automatic Thoughts Questionnaire—Positive with inpatient adolescents. *Cognitive Therapy and Research, 20,* 481–498.

Kashani, J. H., Reid, J. C., & Rosenberg, T. K. (1989). Levels of hopelessness in children and adolescents: A developmental perspective. *Journal of Consulting and Clinical Psychology, 57,* 496–499.

Kaslow, N. J., Brown, R. T., & Mee, L. (1994). Cognitive and behavioral correlates of childhood depression: A developmental perspective. In W. M. Reynolds & H. F. Johnston (Eds.), *Handbook of depression in children and adolescents* (pp. 97–121). New York: Plenum Press.

Kaslow, N. J., Deering, C. G., & Racusin, G. R. (1994). Depressed children and their families. *Clinical Psychology Review, 14,* 39–59.

Kaslow, N. J., Rehm, L. P., Pollack, S. L., & Siegel, A. W. (1988). Attributional style and self-control behavior in depressed and nondepressed children and their parents. *Journal of Abnormal Child Psychology, 16,* 163–175.

Kaslow, N. J., Rehm, L. P., & Siegel, A. W. (1984). Social cognitive and cognitive correlates of depression in children. *Journal of Abnormal Child Psychology, 12,* 605–620.

Kaslow, N. J., Stark, K. D., Printz, B., Livingston, R., & Tsai, S. L. (1992). Cognitive Triad Inventory for Children: Development and relation to depression and anxiety. *Journal of Clinical Child Psychology, 21,* 339–347.

Kaslow, N. J., Tanenbaum, R. L., Abramson, L. Y., Peterson, C., & Seligman, M. E. P. (1983). Problem-solving deficits and depressive symptoms among children. *Journal of Abnormal Child Psychology, 11,* 497–502.

Kazdin, A. E. (1990). Evaluation of the Automatic Thoughts Questionnaire: Negative cognitive processes and depression among children. *Psychological Assessment: A Journal of Consulting and Clinical Psychology, 2,* 73–79.

Kazdin, A. E., Colbus, D., & Rodgers, A. (1986). Assessment of depression and diagnosis of depressive disorders among psychiatrically disturbed children. *Journal of Abnormal Child Psychology, 14,* 499–515.

Kazdin, A. E., French, N. H., Unis, A. S., Esveldt-Dawson, K., & Sherick, R. B. (1983). Hopelessness, depression, and suicidal intent among psychiatrically disturbed inpatient children. *Journal of Consulting and Clinical Psychology, 51,* 504–510.

Kempton, T., Van Hasselt, V., Bukstein, G., & Null, A. (1994). Cognitive distortions and psychiatric diagnosis in dually diagnosed adolescents. *Journal of the American Academy of Child and Adolescent Psychiatry, 33,* 217–222.

Kendall, P. C., Stark, K. D., & Adam, T. (1990). Cognitive deficit or cognitive distortion in childhood depression. *Journal of Abnormal Child Psychology, 18,* 255–270.

Kuiper, N., & Derry, P. (1982). Depressed and nondepressed content in self-reference in mild depressives. *Journal of Personality, 50,* 62–74.

Leitenberg, H., Yost, L. W., & Carroll-Wilson, M. (1986). Negative cognitive errors in children: Questionnaire development, normative data, and comparisons between children with and without self-reported symptoms of depression, low self-esteem, and evaluation anxiety. *Journal of Consulting and Clinical Psychology, 54,* 528–536.

Lewis, M. (1992). *Shame: The exposed self.* New York: Free Press.

Lewis, M., Alessandri, S. M., & Sullivan, M. W. (1990). Violation of expectancy, loss of control, and anger expressions in young infants. *Developmental Psychology, 26,* 745–751.

Lewis, M., Sullivan, M. W., Ramsay, D. S., & Alessandri, S. M. (1992). Individual differences in anger and sad expressions during extinction: Antecedents and consequences. *Infant Behavior and Development, 15*, 443–452.

Marcotte, D. (1996). Irrational beliefs and depression in adolescents. *Adolescence, 31*, 935–954.

Mazur, E., Wolchik, S. A., & Sandler, I. N. (1992). Negative cognitive errors and positive illusions for negative divorce events: Predictors of children's psychological adjustment. *Journal of Abnormal Child Psychology, 20*, 523–542.

McCauley, E., Mitchell, J. R., Burke, P., & Moss, S. (1988). Cognitive attributes of depression in children and adolescents. *Journal of Consulting and Clinical Psychology, 56*, 903–908.

Moilanen, D. L. (1995). Validity of Beck's cognitive theory of depression with nonreferred adolescents. *Journal of Counseling and Development, 73*, 438–442.

Murray, L., Fiori-Cowley, A., Hooper, R., & Cooper, P. (1996). The impact of postnatal depression and associated adversity on early mother–infant interactions and later infant outcomes. *Child Development, 67*, 2512–2526.

Murray, L., Hipwell, A., Hooper, R., Stein, A., & Cooper, P. (1996). The cognitive development of 5-year-old children of postnatally depressed mothers. *Journal of Child Psychology and Psychiatry, 37*, 927–935.

Nolen-Hoeksema, S. (1994). An interactive model for the emergence of gender differences in depression in adolescence. *Journal of Research on Adolescence, 4*, 519–534.

Nolen-Hoeksema, S., & Girgus, J. S. (1994). The emergence of gender differences in depression during adolescence. *Psychological Bulletin, 115*, 424–443.

Nolen-Hoeksema, S., Girgus, J. S., & Seligman, M. E. P. (1986). Learned helplessness in children: A longitudinal study of depression, achievement, and explanatory style. *Journal of Personality and Social Psychology, 51*, 435–442.

Nolen-Hoeksema, S., Girgus, J. S., & Seligman, M. E. P. (1992). Predictors and consequences of childhood depressive symptoms: A five year longitudinal study. *Journal of Abnormal Psychology, 101*, 405–422.

Nolen-Hoeksema, S., Wolfson, A., Mumme, D., & Guskin, K. (1995). Helplessness in children of depressed and nondepressed mothers. *Developmental Psychology, 31*, 377–387.

Nowicki, S., & Strickland, B. (1973). A locus of control scale for children. *Journal of Consulting and Clinical Psychology, 40*, 148–154.

Orvaschel, H., Beeferman, D., & Kabacoff, R. (1997). Depression, self-esteem, sex, and age in a child and adolescent clinical sample. *Journal of Clinical Child Psychology, 26*, 285–289.

Panak, W. F., & Garber, J. (1992). Role of aggression, rejection, and attributions in the prediction of depression in children. *Development and Psychopathology, 4*, 145–165.

Piaget, J. (1962). *Play, dreams, and imitation in childhood.* New York: Norton.

Prieto, S. L., Cole, D. A., & Tageson, C. W. (1992). Depressive self-schemas in clinic and nonclinic children. *Cognitive Therapy and Research, 16*, 521–534.

Quiggle, N. L., Garber, J., Panak, W. F., & Dodge, K. A. (1992). Social information processing in aggressive and depressed children. *Child Development, 63*, 1305–1320.

Rehm, L. P. (1977). A self-control model of depression. *Behavior Therapy, 8*, 787–804.

Robins, C. J., & Hinkley, K. (1989). Social-cognitive processing and depressive symptoms in children: A comparison of measures. *Journal of Abnormal Child Psychology, 17*, 29–36.

Robinson, N. S., Garber, J., & Hilsman, R. (1995). Cognitions and stress: Direct and moderating effects on depressive versus externalizing symptoms during the junior high school transition. *Journal of Abnormal Psychology, 104*, 453–463.

Rudolph, K. D., Hammen, C., & Burge, D. (1997). A cognitive-interpersonal approach to depressive symptoms in preadolescent children. *Journal of Abnormal Child Psychology, 25*, 33–45.

Seiner, S. H., & Gelfand, D. M. (1995). Effects of mothers' simulated withdrawal and depressed affect on mother–toddler interactions. *Child Development, 66*, 1519–1528.

Seligman, M. E. P. (1975). *Helplessness: On depression, development, and death.* San Francisco: Freeman.

Seligman, M. E. P., & Peterson, C. (1986). A learned helplessness perspective on childhood depression: Theory and research. In M. Rutter, C. E. Izard, & P. B. Read (Eds.), *Depression in young people: Developmental and clinical perspectives* (pp. 223–249). New York: Guilford Press.

Seligman, M. E. P., Peterson, C., Kaslow, N. J., Tanenbaum, R. L., & Abramson, L. Y. (1984). Attributional style and depressive symptoms among children. *Journal of Abnormal Psychology, 93*, 235–238.

Stark, K. D., Humphrey, L. L., Laurent, J., Livingston, R., & Christopher, J. (1993). Cognitive, behavioral, and family factors in the differentiation of depressive and anxiety disorders during childhood. *Journal of Consulting and Clinical Psychology, 61*, 878–886.

Stark, K. D., Schmidt, K. L., & Joiner, T. E. (1996). Cognitive triad: Relationship to depressive symptoms, parents' cognitive triad, and perceived parental messages. *Journal of Abnormal Child Psychology, 24*, 615–631.

Stipek, D., Recchia, S., & McClintic, S. (1992). Self-evaluation in young children. *Monographs of the Society for Research in Child Development, 57*(226), 100.

Sullivan, M. W., Lewis, M., & Alessandri, S. M. (1992). Cross-age stability in emotional expressions during learning and extinction. *Developmental Psychology, 28,* 58–63.

Tems, C. L., Stewart, S. M., Skinner, J. R., Hughes, C. W., & Emslie, G. (1993). Cognitive distortions in depressed children and adolescents: Are they state dependent or traitlike? *Journal of Clinical Child Psychology, 22,* 316–326.

Tesiny, E. P., Lefkowitz, M. M., & Gordon, N. H. (1980). Childhood depression, locus of control, and school achievement. *Journal of Educational Psychology, 12,* 506–510.

Trad, P. V. (1994). Depression in infants. In W. M. Reynolds & H. F. Johnston (Eds.), *Handbook of depression in children and adolescents* (pp. 401–426). New York: Plenum Press.

Turner, J. E., Jr., & Cole, D. A. (1994). Developmental differences in cognitive diatheses for child depression. *Journal of Abnormal Child Psychology, 22,* 15–32.

Vygotsky, L. S. (1978). *Mind in society: The development of higher psychological processes.* Cambridge, MA: Harvard University Press.

Vygotsky, L. S. (1986). *Thought and language.* Cambridge, MA: MIT Press.

Weisz, J. R., Stevens, J. S., Curry, J. F., Cohen, R., Craighead, E., Burligame, W. V., Smith, A., Weiss, B., & Parmalee, D. X. (1989). Control-related cognitions and depression among inpatient children and adolescents. *Journal of the American Academy of Child and Adolescent Psychiatry, 28,* 358–363.

Weisz, J. R., Sweeney, L., Proffitt, V., & Carr, T. (1993). Control-related beliefs and self-reported depressive symptoms in late childhood. *Journal of Abnormal Psychology, 102,* 411–418.

Weisz, J. R., Weiss, B., Wasserman, A., & Rintoul, B. (1987). Control-related beliefs and depression among clinic-referred children and adolescents. *Journal of the Abnormal Psychology, 96,* 58–63.

Werner, H. (1948). *Comparative psychology of mental development.* New York: International Universities Press.

Werner, H. (1957). The concept of development from a comparative and organismic point of view. In D. Harris (Ed.), *The concept of development* (pp. 125–148). Minneapolis: University of Minnesota Press.

Werner, H., & Kaplan, B. (1963). *Symbol formation.* New York: Wiley.

Whitman, P. B., & Leitenberg, H. (1990). Negatively biased recall in children with self-reported symptoms of depression. *Journal of Abnormal Child Psychology, 18,* 15–27.

Zupan, B. A., Hammen, C., & Jaenicke, C. (1987). The effects of current mood and prior depressive history on self-schematic processing in children. *Journal of Experimental Child Psychology, 43,* 149–158.

27

Anxiety

Michael W. Vasey and Thomas H. Ollendick

Anxiety problems are among the most common forms of emotional disturbance in childhood and adolescence (Anderson, 1994; Hagopian & Ollendick, 1997). Furthermore, although mild anxiety problems are often short-lived, childhood anxiety disorders are often chronic, interfering substantially with children's adaptive functioning and persisting into adulthood (Keller et al., 1992; Ollendick & King, 1994). Indeed, many adult anxiety disorders appear to have their onset in childhood (Burke, Burke, Regier, & Rae, 1990; Öst, 1987). Thus, there is a clear need for improved understanding of the factors contributing to the development, persistence, and remission of such problems to guide efforts at their early detection, prevention, and treatment. Unfortunately, only recently have discussions and studies of the developmental psychopathology of anxiety begun to appear (Daleiden, Vasey, & Brown, 1999). This chapter is meant to provide a roadmap to extant research on the central issues in understanding the developmental psychopathology of childhood anxiety. The chapter begins with a discussion of issues in the definition of childhood anxiety disorders, followed by epidemiological issues, etiological factors, and illustrations of how development affects and is affected by these issues and factors. Unfortunately, space does not permit discussion of developmental issues in the assessment, treatment, and prevention of childhood anxiety disorders. The interested reader is directed to recent developments regarding these issues (e.g., Daleiden et al., 1999; Hagopian & Ollendick, 1997; Ollendick, Hagopian, & King, 1998).

DEFINITIONAL ISSUES

The definition of childhood anxiety disorders is complicated by several issues. First, the high normative frequency of anxiety in childhood raises questions about how to distinguish pathological anxiety from normal forms of anxiety. The clinical manifestations of anxiety

Michael W. Vasey • Department of Psychology, Ohio State University, Columbus, Ohio 43210.   **Thomas H. Ollendick** • Child Study Center, Virginia Polytechnic Institute and State University, Blacksburg, Virginia 24061-0355.

Handbook of Developmental Psychopathology, Second Edition, edited by Arnold J. Sameroff, Michael Lewis, and Suzanne M. Miller. Kluwer Academic/Plenum Publishers, New York, 2000.

disorders are likely to show considerable developmental variation in focus, severity, and form (Albano, Chorpita, & Barlow, 1996). Continuity from early childhood through adolescence at the level of molecular anxiety symptoms is unlikely. Instead, symptoms are likely to change as children's ways of experiencing, interpreting, and expressing anxiety change due to cognitive, social, and emotional developmental advances (Garber & Strassberg, 1991). For these reasons, diagnostic criteria that are valid for adults or adolescents may be invalid when applied to children. Definitions must reflect developmental changes in the content of children's fears, as well as their severity, to determine if they are to be judged outside the normal range of anxiety. Age-related changes in the normative base rates of potentially symptomatic behavior present serious problems for definitions of childhood anxiety disorders because what is abnormal among older children, adolescents, or adults may be normal among young children (see, e.g., Evans et al., 1997). Although current diagnostic systems, for example, the fourth edition of the *Diagnostic and Statistical Manual of Mental Disorders* (DSM-IV; American Psychiatric Association, 1994), suggest developmental variations in the criteria that define most anxiety disorders, rarely are these variations grounded in research, leaving their validity open to question. Clearly, further research is needed on developmental variations in childhood anxiety disorder manifestations.

A second definitional issue concerns the distinction between childhood anxiety and depression. Studies consistently find moderate to high correlations and comorbidity between anxious and depressive symptoms and disorders in childhood (see Seligman & Ollendick, 1999). Based on such findings, some researchers have suggested that the two constructs constitute a single dimension (e.g., Achenbach, 1991), whereas others suggest that, despite their overlap, critical differences remain between the two constructs (e.g., Brady & Kendall, 1992). Because this issue is the focus of a separate chapter in this volume (see Chapter 28), it is not considered further here.

A third definitional issue concerns the structure of childhood anxiety disorders. In the DSM-IV, the general category of anxiety disorder is divided into at least six subcategories (see below). However, it is unclear whether the structure of anxiety disorder in childhood is best represented by the DSM-IV subcategories or whether there may be developmental variations in the structure of such disorders. More fundamental still is the question of whether childhood anxiety disorders should be conceptualized as categorical or dimensional constructs. This question is dealt with more generally elsewhere in this volume (see Chapter 3). However, it is noteworthy that many studies of childhood anxiety problems have represented anxiety as a continuous dimension rather than categorical diagnoses. Caution is required in generalizing findings from dimensional studies to clinical groups.

Returning to the question of how many categories best represent the structure of anxiety disorders in childhood, doubt about current diagnostic categories is raised by high levels (about 50%) of comorbidity among the childhood anxiety disorders (Anderson, 1994). This has led several researchers to conclude that the current diagnostic categories lack discriminant validity and reflect artificial boundaries (e.g., Perrin & Last, 1995). Spence (1997) similarly suggested that this level of comorbidity may mean that the symptoms of anxiety disorder in childhood do not covary in a manner consistent with current diagnostic categories. However, she also noted that the categories may be valid but co-occur frequently because they stem from common etiological factors or reflect the existence of a higher order pattern. This latter possibility would be consistent with the DSM-IV view of anxiety disorder as a broad category comprised of a number of related subcategories.

Few studies have evaluated the discriminant validity of the DSM-IV (or its predecessors) anxiety disorder subcategories when they are applied to children (Silverman, 1992). Most of these subcategories have their origin in clinical observations rather than theory or research, and the field trials needed to validate them for use with children are lacking. Previous efforts to find continuous dimensions analogous to DSM anxiety disorder subcategories among children have generally failed. As noted earlier, factor-analytic studies typically yield a single anxiety–depression factor or, at most, separate anxiety and depression factors (e.g., Achenbach, 1991; Joiner, Catanzaro, & Laurent, 1996). However, Spence (1997) argued that such studies have used narrow item sets that do not include sufficient symptoms of each subcategory of anxiety disorder to provide a valid test of their discriminant validity. To provide a more sensitive test, Spence used confirmatory factor analysis of children's self-reports regarding the major symptoms of each of six DSM-IV anxiety disorder subcategories: Panic–Agoraphobia, Separation Anxiety Disorder (SAD), Social Phobia, Obsessive–Compulsive Disorder (OCD), Generalized Anxiety Disorder (GAD), and a Specific Phobia (i.e., fear of injury). The best-fitting model was a single, higher order anxiety factor associated with these six anxiety subdimensions. These findings are consistent with the DSM-IV model in which these six anxiety disorders are viewed as subcategories of a broader category of anxiety disorder. Spence also found some evidence for the invariance of this factor structure among boys and girls and in children ages 8–10 versus those ages 11–12. However, the correlations between the six first order factors were higher for younger than older children, suggesting that the structure of anxiety may become increasingly differentiated with age.

Spence's (1997) study offers some support for the discriminant validity of these six anxiety disorders; however, it has several limitations. First, it was based exclusively on children's self-reports; the generalizability of the findings to other information sources is open to question. Second, it focused on a community sample; thus, results cannot be generalized to clinical samples. Third, because the study did not include symptoms of other internalizing or externalizing disorders, it is unclear whether the observed factors would be obtained using a broader set of items. Finally, the study approached anxiety disorders dimensionally, and we must be cautious in generalizing to categorical clinical diagnoses. Nevertheless, the study lends support to a number of the DSM-IV anxiety disorder subcategories in childhood.

DIAGNOSTIC CATEGORIES

The DSM-III (American Psychiatric Association, 1980) introduced three anxiety disorders that were specific to children: SAD, Overanxious Disorder (OAD), and Avoidant Disorder. Additionally, DSM-III introduced a wide range of adult anxiety disorders that were also applicable to children. As defined in DSM-IV (American Psychiatric Association, 1994), the major members of this group include Specific Phobia (formerly Simple Phobia), Social Phobia, Panic Disorder (PD) with and without Agoraphobia, GAD, OCD, and Posttraumatic Stress Disorder (PTSD). To a greater extent than its predecessors, DSM-IV specifies developmental variations in diagnostic criteria for most anxiety disorders that should be considered when applying them to children. Although this was a positive step toward developmentally appropriate diagnostic constructs, the validity of many of the suggested developmental variations remains unknown.

With the publication of DSM-IV, the childhood anxiety disorder categories of OAD and avoidant disorder were subsumed, respectively, under the categories of GAD and Social Phobia. OAD was dropped from DSM-IV, largely because studies consistently failed to support its validity. For example, Beidel (1991) compared nonreferred samples of children with OAD, social phobia, or no diagnosis, and found that, in marked contrast to those with social phobia, children with OAD did not differ from children with no diagnosis on a variety of measures. Similarly, Beidel, Silverman, and Hammond-Laurence (1996) compared clinic- and nonreferred samples of children with OAD to normal controls. Although the clinic- and non-referred OAD samples differed on a number of measures, this was attributable largely to greater prevalence of comorbid diagnoses in the clinic-referred sample. Such evidence has led Beidel et al. to suggest that the criteria for OAD represent behaviors that are too common for their presence, even in combination, to indicate functional impairment. Unfortunately, the replacement of OAD with GAD in DSM-IV may not resolve the problem of overdiagnosis because a clear set of functional criteria defining clinical levels of impairment necessary in childhood are also lacking for GAD. Given the apparently high base rate of worries in childhood (see Silverman, La Greca, & Wasserstein, 1995), it may be that higher levels of impairment must be specified for the criteria of GAD to be valid when applied to children.

Regarding avoidant disorder and social phobia, it remains unclear whether the former is best conceptualized as a developmentally earlier form of the latter or as a distinct disorder. Although a study by Francis, Last, and Strauss (1992) suggests that these disorders are similar on the global characteristics of gender, race, and comorbid diagnoses, a potentially important difference was also reported. Specifically, children with pure avoidant disorder were significantly younger than children with either social phobia alone or the comorbid combination of avoidant disorder and social phobia. Similarly, other studies have found that social phobia typically has its onset in early adolescence (Giaconia et al., 1994), whereas the onset of avoidant disorder typically falls in childhood (Cantwell & Baker, 1987). This pattern parallels closely the pattern seen in oppositional defiant disorder (ODD) and conduct disorder (CD) (see Loeber, Lahey, & Thomas, 1991). Despite sharing many correlates in common, ODD and CD have remained distinct disorders within DSM-IV, in part, because ODD has a substantially earlier age of onset. In that case, there is also longitudinal evidence showing that, although most children with CD met criteria for ODD when they were younger, most children with ODD do not develop CD. In the absence of similar longitudinal data regarding avoidant disorder and social phobia, the decision to subsume the former under the latter may be premature. It may be that these two categories are merely different developmental manifestations of the same basic phenomenon, with the expression of the central problem evolving from avoidance of unfamiliar people in childhood to fear of negative social evaluation in early adolescence (Francis et al., 1992). However, they may instead be distinct disorders characterized by meaningfully different phobic objects (i.e., unfamiliar people in the case of avoidant disorder, and negative social evaluation in the case of social phobia). Prospective and retrospective studies focused on the relationship between these two syndromes are needed to resolve this question. However, several recent studies suggest that shyness and behavioral inhibition in childhood may predict later social phobia (Kagan, 1997; Stemberger, Turner, Beidel, & Calhoun, 1995). Thus, to the extent that such constructs are similar to the central feature of avoidant disorder, avoidant disorder may indeed develop into social phobia in some cases. However, it would seem prudent for researchers to continue to collect information that allows a distinction to be made between these disorders if desired. Only in this way can important questions regarding the continuity between these two disorders be adequately answered.

EPIDEMIOLOGICAL ISSUES

Prevalence

The prevalence of anxiety disorders in childhood has been evaluated in community and clinical samples. Studies of community samples generally find anxiety disorders to be common among children, with estimates of overall population prevalence ranging from 12% to 17.3% (Anderson, Williams, McGee, & Silva, 1987; Kashani & Orvaschel, 1988), although Anderson (1994) noted that rates fall to 2.4–8.7% when only confirmed disorders or those meeting minimal requirements for dysfunction are considered. Averaged for boys and girls across age (see below), prevalence estimates for nonclinical samples range from 0.7% to 12.9% for SAD, 2.7% to 12.4% for OAD (rates for GAD are unavailable), 2.4% to 9.2% for specific phobias, and 1% to 1.1% for social phobia (Anderson, 1994). Only one population study has considered avoidant disorder, finding its prevalence to be 1.6% (Costello et al., 1988). Prevalence rate estimates vary from 0.3% to 3% for OCD (Albano et al., 1996) and, in studies of adolescents only, rates for panic disorder vary from 1% to 4.7% (Albano et al., 1996).

Rates for these disorders among clinic-referred samples of anxious children vary from 11.4% to 33% for SAD, 15% to 17.5% for OAD, and 15% to 25.3% for social phobia (Albano et al., 1995, as cited in Albano et al., 1996; Last et al., 1987). Albano and colleagues also reported that 13.3% of their sample of 7- to 17-year-olds presented with OCD, 9.6% for specific phobia, and 6% for panic disorder.

Age and Gender Differences

Age of onset varies widely across the anxiety disorders. Similarly, the prevalence of such disorders varies with age and gender. Such differences in the prevalence of childhood anxiety disorders may provide important clues regarding the role of developing biological, social, cognitive, and emotional capacities in the etiology of these disorders. Moreover, such differences raise questions about the validity of diagnostic categories at different ages and suggest that the etiological pathways to such disorders may differ for girls and boys. For example, the discriminant validity of childhood anxiety disorder categories will be supported to the extent that different disorders exhibit divergent prevalence patterns across age and gender. Age changes in the prevalence of a disorder may suggest an increase in the occurrence of causal factors or may suggest the emergence of a new etiological pathway among older children (Angold, 1993).

A number of anxiety disorders typically first appear early in childhood. For example, SAD is most common prior to puberty (Bowen, Offord, & Boyle, 1990; Kashani, Orvaschel, Rosenberg, & Reid, 1989). Although SAD can occur at any age, its prevalence appears to decline with age (Cohen et al., 1993; Kashani & Orvaschel, 1990; Strauss & Last, 1993). According to retrospective reports of adult phobics, specific phobias also tend to have their onset in early childhood, with mean age of onset between 6 and 8 years of age (Burke et al., 1990; Giaconia et al., 1994; Merckelbach, de Jong, Muris, & Hout, 1996). Unlike SAD, specific phobias do not appear to decline in prevalence across the age span.

Some evidence suggests that OAD may have its onset as early as 4 years of age (Beitchman, Wekerle, & Hood, 1987), but most studies suggest an average age of onset between 11 and 13 years of age (Last, Hersen, Kazdin, Finkelstein, & Strauss, 1987), with its prevalence increasing with age. For example, based on their cross-sectional community sample, Kashani and Orvaschel (1990) reported that the prevalence of OAD rose from 8.6% at age 8 years to 17.1% at age 17 years. It remains unknown whether similar age of onset and patterns of prevalence occur for GAD.

Social phobia appears to have its average age of onset in midadolescence, although some socially phobic adults report onset as early as 5–9 years of age (Öst, 1987). However, it appears to be rare prior to preadolescence. For example, Kashani and Orvaschel (1990) found no cases of social phobia among 8-year-olds, but among 12-year-olds, it was present in 1% of children. The prevalence of social phobia appears fairly stable subsequent to the preadolescent period (Anderson et al., 1987; Kashani & Orvaschel, 1990).

Despite past suggestions that panic disorder does not occur in childhood (see Nelles & Barlow, 1988), recent evidence suggests that children may experience panic attacks and panic disorder (see Ollendick, Mattis, & King, 1994). This ongoing controversy is discussed further in reference to cognitive factors in the etiological influences section below. Clear estimates of the prevalence and mean age of onset are unavailable due to the lack of adequate research on panic disorder in youth (Albano et al., 1996). However, Ollendick et al. (1994) reported that panic disorder becomes considerably more prevalent in adolescence than during childhood.

Regarding the remaining anxiety disorders, OCD has a mean age of onset of about 10 years of age (Albano et al., 1996), although it has been reported in children as young as 5–9 years of age (Burke et al., 1990; Swedo, Rapoport, Leonard, Lenane, & Cheslow, 1989). PTSD appears to have a mean age of onset between 14 and 15 years (Giaconia et al., 1994), although it has been reported in children as young as 6–7 years of age (Fletcher, 1996; Giaconia et al., 1994; Shannon, Lonigan, Finch, & Taylor, 1994). Finally, PTSD appears to be more common subsequent to major trauma among younger than older children (Shannon et al., 1994).

As in adulthood, there appear to be substantial sex differences in the prevalence of some childhood anxiety disorders. Like age-related differences in prevalence, gender differences may provide important clues regarding the factors that contribute to the etiology of these disorders. However, such differences have not been adequately studied, and considerable ambiguity remains in this area, particularly regarding the possibility of changes in gender ratios across age, such as those seen in childhood depression. Such age-by-gender interactions are particularly interesting because they may offer important clues regarding etiological factors and developmental pathways (see Nolen-Hoeksema & Girgus, 1994).

Evidence suggests that girls are approximately three times more likely than boys to manifest SAD (Bowen et al., 1990; Kashani & Orvaschel, 1990; McGee et al., 1990), although not all studies find this difference (e.g., Anderson et al., 1987). Similarly, panic attacks and panic disorder appear to be more prevalent among girls than boys (see Ollendick et al., 1994) and this pattern appears to hold across age (Hayward et al., 1992). Most epidemiological studies of social phobia suggest that its prevalence is comparable among boys and girls (e.g., Kashani & Orvaschel, 1990; Last, Perrin, Hersen, & Kazdin, 1992; McGee et al., 1990). However, specific phobias appear to be more prevalent among girls than boys by a 2:1 margin (see Anderson, 1994), although Strauss and Last (1993) reported equal frequency among boys and girls in their clinic-referred sample. There is some evidence that gender differences in the prevalence of OAD change as a function of age, similar to the pattern seen in childhood depression (see Nolen-Hoeksema & Girgus, 1994). Among children, studies suggest that OAD is either more prevalent among boys than girls (e.g., Anderson et al., 1987; Cantwell & Baker, 1987) or equally prevalent across genders (e.g., Cohen et al., 1993). In contrast, among adolescents, evidence consistently finds OAD (and GAD) to be more prevalent among girls than boys (Bowen et al., 1990; McGee et al., 1990). With respect to OCD, evidence suggests that boys predominate in younger samples (Swedo et al., 1989) but that relatively equal gender ratios are evident in older samples (Valleni-Basile et al., 1994). Finally, according to large-scale studies of traumatized children, PTSD appears to be more prevalent among girls than boys (Shannon et al.,1994), although this difference does not appear to be large when other factors, such as severity of trauma exposure, are considered (Vernberg, La Greca, Silverman, & Prinstein, 1996).

ETIOLOGICAL FACTORS

This section provides an overview of the major factors that may predispose to, protect against, precipitate, maintain, intensify, or ameliorate clinical forms of anxiety in childhood. Where extant data and theory permit, we consider developmental variations in these factors, their operation, and the roles they may play. Although we discuss each factor separately, there are likely to be multiple pathways to any given anxiety disorder in childhood, each reflecting complex transactions among multiple factors (Cicchetti & Cohen, 1995). For example, evidence suggests there are at least two pathways to social phobia (Stemberger et al., 1995). Similarly, depending on the configuration of other factors with which it occurs, any given factor may lead to several different anxiety disorders, to other forms of psychopathology, or to no disorder. Only rarely should factors produce the same outcomes regardless of the influence of other factors. This fact is illustrated by the shortcomings of the strong classical conditioning main effect model of the etiology of specific phobias (see Menzies & Clarke, 1995; Merckelbach et al., 1996).

Biological Factors

Genetic Factors

Family history studies consistently show substantial familial risk for anxiety disorders (see Silverman, Cerny, & Nelles, 1988). This risk has been reported among children of clinically anxious parents (Turner, Beidel, & Costello, 1987) as well as parents of clinically anxious children (Last, Hersen, Kazdin, Orvaschel, & Perrin, 1991). Although such findings suggest the possibility of genetic influences, they may also reflect the influence of the family environment. Twin or adoption studies are necessary to resolve this ambiguity.

Although there are no adoption studies relevant to this issue, numerous twin studies of anxiety are now available. Twin studies of anxiety disorders among adults generally indicate significant genetic influence, with most recent studies suggesting both general and disorder-specific genetic risk (Kendler, Neale, Kessler, Heath, & Eaves, 1992a). However, the relevance of these findings for childhood anxiety disorders is unclear because genetic effects are often not constant across the developmental span. Recent reports suggest that childhood anxiety symptoms, like those in adulthood, are moderately heritable (Eley & Stevenson, 1997; Stevenson, Batten, & Cherner, 1992; van den Oord, Verhulst, & Boomsma, 1996). However, it must be noted that such studies have not always found genetic effects (Thapar & McGuffin, 1995) and twin studies of clinical forms of childhood anxiety remain lacking.

Among adults, there is growing evidence that these genetic influences, at least in part, may not be specific to anxiety but include depression as well, with their differentiation influenced primarily by environmental factors (Kendler et al., 1992b; Roy, Neale, Pedersen, Mathe, & Kendler, 1995). Limited evidence suggests this may also be the case among children. Eley and Stevenson (1997) found that anxiety and depression in children were associated with a common genetic factor, with the difference between the two types of symptoms determined by environmental factors. Specifically, Eley (1996, as cited in Eley & Stevenson, 1997) found that environmental events involving loss were related to depression, whereas events involving danger were related to anxiety.

The findings of Eley and Stevenson (1997) also suggest that the type of environmental factors associated with anxiety symptoms in childhood may differ in important ways from those operating in adulthood. With the exception of certain situational phobias (see Kendler et al., 1992a), twin studies of adults have generally failed to find evidence for the influence of shared environmental factors. Instead, such studies reveal the substantial influence of non-shared environmental factors. As noted by Kendler et al., the absence of such effects raises questions for etiological theories involving intrafamilial features that should affect all children in the family. Thus, it is noteworthy that there is *some* evidence of shared environmental influences on childhood anxiety symptoms (Edelbrock, Rende, Plomin, & Thompson, 1995; Eley & Stevenson, 1997; Thapar & McGuffin, 1995). This evidence is tempered by other studies of anxiety and anxiety-related constructs in children that have failed to find significant shared environmental influences (Plomin & Rowe, 1979; Robinson, Kagan, Reznick, & Corley, 1992; van den Oord et al., 1996). However, these negative studies all pertain to very young children whereas the studies finding such effects involved children in middle childhood and adolescence. Perhaps shared environmental factors contribute only during a limited portion of the developmental span.

Temperamental Factors

Eley and Stevenson (1997) suggest that the genetically mediated shared variance between symptoms of anxiety and depression in their sample was accounted for largely by symptoms that fall on the temperamental dimension of negative affectivity (NA; Watson & Clark, 1984). NA and similar temperamental dimensions, including neuroticism (Eysenck & Eysenck, 1985) and behavioral inhibition (BI) to the unfamiliar (Reznick, Hegeman, Kaufman, Woods, & Jacobs, 1992) have been shown to increase risk for both depression and anxiety, and to be moderately heritable (Eaves, Eysenck, & Martin, 1989; Robinson et al., 1992; Tellegen et al., 1988). Of these overlapping constructs, BI has received the most attention as a risk factor for childhood anxiety disorders.

BI appears to be associated with heightened risk for anxiety disorders in childhood, particularly in that subset of children who show stable BI from infancy through middle childhood (see Turner, Beidel, & Wolff, 1996). However, because studies also show that many BI children do not develop anxiety disorders and uninhibited children sometimes do, BI can be neither sufficient nor necessary to produce such disorders (Turner et al., 1996). Instead, in keeping with the findings from behavioral genetics research, paths to anxiety disorders involving BI or similar anxiety-prone temperamental factors also involve shared and unshared environmental factors (Eley & Stevenson, 1997). It is also unclear whether BI poses a general risk for anxiety or, rather, a specific risk for social phobia (see Kagan, 1997).

Environmental Factors

Exposure to Stressful Events and Uncontrollable Environments

In interaction with other factors, stressful life events appear to be associated with anxiety symptoms and their onset in childhood (see Albano et al., 1996; Hagopian & Ollendick, 1997). One pathway linking stressful events to anxiety is traumatic respondent conditioning; however, considerable evidence suggests that anxiety disorders also often appear subsequent to exposure to unrelated stressful events (Barlow, 1988). For example, the onset of SAD often follows a major stressor such as a move to a new school (Gittelman-Klein & Klein, 1980).

The controllability of environmental events, especially early in childhood, may be particularly important in the development of anxiety disorders. Specifically, early exposure to controllable environments appears to protect against anxiety, whereas uncontrollable environments predispose to it. For example, infant rhesus monkeys exposed to chronically uncontrollable environments responded to novel stimuli with greater fear and less exploration (Mineka, Gunnar, & Champoux, 1986), and higher cortisol levels (Insel, Scanlan, Champoux, & Suomi, 1988) than monkeys who had control over their environment. Comparisons to normally reared monkeys suggested that the difference was at least partly due to the protective effects of exposure to controllable environments (i.e., mastery experiences; Mineka et al., 1986). Evidence from studies of children also supports the predisposing role of uncontrollability and the protective role of controllable experiences (e.g., Kohlmann & Krohne, 1988; Krohne & Hock, 1991).

The predisposing effects of uncontrollable environments may be mediated, in part, by biological changes. Gunnar (1980) reviewed evidence from studies of human infants that exposure to uncontrollable experiences leads to changes in the endocrine systems associated with stress responses that may increase physiological reactivity to stressful events (see also Nachmias, Gunnar, Mangelsdorf, Parritz, & Buss, 1996). Similarly, Insel et al. (1988) suggest that the anxiety-related effects of early exposure to controllable or uncontrollable environments may be mediated by changes in the benzodiazepine receptor system. However, such effects are also likely to be mediated by control-related cognitions formed through experiences with controllable and uncontrollable events (Skinner, 1995).

Learning Influences

The principles of respondent conditioning suggest several mechanisms by which environmental experiences may predispose to, precipitate, or protect against the development of anxiety disorders. Such conditioning processes are most commonly discussed as precipitating factors: Direct and indirect (i.e., modeling or verbal information) conditioning episodes are presumed to spark the onset of phobic anxiety (see Davey, 1992). Consistent with this view, evidence suggests that a substantial percentage of children with fears and phobias have a history of direct or indirect conditioning (Merckelbach et al., 1996; Ollendick & King, 1991). However, even severely traumatic episodes are not always sufficient to produce phobic anxiety (e.g., Lonigan, Shannon, Taylor, Finch, & Sallee, 1994; Vernberg et al., 1996). Similarly, traumatic conditioning episodes may not be necessary given that phobic anxiety may develop in their absence (see Menzies & Clarke, 1995). Traumatic conditioning episodes appear to interact with predisposing factors such as temperament and prior learning history to produce heightened risk for phobic responses in vulnerable individuals (see, e.g., Lonigan et al., 1994; Zinbarg & Revelle, 1989).

Growing evidence suggests that direct conditioning experiences may account for only a small percentage of childhood phobias, with vicarious modes of acquisition (and nonassociative paths, see below) being more common. For example, Ollendick and King (1991) found that modeling and information transmission were the most common modes of acquisition reported by children, with a minority reporting direct conditioning experiences. As they grow, children undoubtedly encounter many opportunities for vicarious learning about anxious emotion and the situations that may produce it. Experimental evidence for observational learning of fear in children is limited by ethical constraints, but animal studies show that modeling can create intense and persistent fears (see Mineka & Zinbarg, 1995). Nonexperimental studies of anxious children suggest that observational learning has substantial potential to precipitate problematic anxiety or to protect against it (Muris, Steerneman, Merckelbach, & Meesters, 1996; Windheuser, 1977).

In addition to precipitating anxiety, respondent conditioning mechanisms may play predisposing and protective roles. The phenomenon of sensory preconditioning may explain why some children develop phobias despite lacking any apparent history of direct conditioning involving the feared stimulus (see Davey, 1992). Similarly, to the extent that children have nontraumatic experiences with a stimulus, they may be resistant to acquiring a fear of that stimulus subsequent to a conditioning episode (i.e., latent inhibition; see Davey, 1992). Finally, respondent conditioning processes may contribute to the maintenance and intensification of childhood anxiety responses through unconditioned stimulus (UCS) inflation (Davey, 1992). Evidence suggests that children as young as 5 years of age are capable of worrying in ways that could potentially foster UCS inflation and heightened expectancy (Vasey, Crnic, & Carter, 1994).

Although respondent conditioning is clearly important in understanding many phobias, Menzies and Clarke (1995) have offered a model that suggests some phobic anxiety is due to failure of the processes by which children normally master childhood fears or to the dishabituation of previously mastered fears rather than reflecting the learning of maladaptive associations. For example, Menzies and Clarke (1993) found little evidence for any of the three modes of respondent conditioning in the etiology of children's water phobia. Instead, parents of water phobic children generally reported that their children had always feared water since their first contact with it, a pattern that Menzies and Clarke (1995) argue cannot be explained through respondent conditioning mechanisms.

There are certain categories of fear that occur among many, if not most children, as part of normal development (Ollendick et al., 1998). From the perspective of Menzies and Clarke's (1995) nonassociative model, any of these normal childhood fears could serve as the starting point for a phobia. They suggest that such fears are normally mastered through habituation that occurs in the context of repeated, nontraumatic exposure to the feared object or situation. Clarke and Jackson (1983) suggested two reasons why this process may fail. First, some children may fail to show normal habituation despite being exposed with normative frequency to the feared stimulus. In other words, these "poor habituators" are temperamentally prone to anxiety (a construct that shares much in common with BI temperament). Second, some children may not be given sufficient opportunities for safe exposure. Specifically, Clarke and Jackson suggested that this may occur because some parents fail to provide normal exposure to such feared stimuli because they themselves are phobic.

Historically, anxious parents, specifically mothers, have been viewed as primary sources of childhood anxiety (Gittelman, 1986). Evidence suggests that fearful parents do indeed contribute to their children's fears (Engfer, 1993; Muris et al., 1996; Silverman et al., 1988; Windheuser, 1977). One way anxious parents may foster anxiety in their children is by limiting their exposure to fear-provoking stimuli and thereby interfering with the normal process of fear habituation or mastery (Menzies & Clarke, 1995; Silverman et al., 1988; Windheuser, 1977). Reduced demand for contact with challenging situations has long been thought to contribute to the development of children's anxiety (Andrews, 1966) and retrospective and prospective studies support this view (Engfer, 1993; Gerlsma, Emmelkamp, & Arrindell, 1990; Klonsky, Dutton, & Liebel, 1991). However, parents need not be anxious themselves to contribute to their child's anxiety by inadvertently fostering limited exposure to fear mastery situations. Parents' responses to their child's anxiety are likely to shape and be shaped by their child's anxiety through operant conditioning mechanisms.

Operant conditioning may play a role in the acquisition of anxiety disorders (e.g., inept social behavior may bring negative social evaluation and thus lead to social anxiety), but the impact of such factors is perhaps greatest with regard to the maintenance and intensification of anxiety. Once children exhibit anxious behavior, there are likely to be numerous opportunities for such behavior to be influenced by its consequences and to shape the behavior of parents and others. For example, by virtue of anxious children's extreme distress, they are likely to be effective at punishing their caregivers and others around them for insisting on exposure to feared stimuli or for not accommodating their desire for avoidance of such stimuli. Simultaneously, relief from their children's intense negative reactions is likely to be a potent source of reinforcement for parents and others (e.g., teachers) when they allow the child to escape or avoid the feared situation. Thus, the behavior of parents and others may come to be controlled by its short-term reduction of the child's anxiety, at the expense of the child's ultimate mastery of anxiety and the demands of anxiety-provoking situations. In addition, parents may supply various tangible rewards to make up for the child's inability to attend the avoided situation. For example, tangible rewards appear to play a major role in one form of school-refusal behavior (Kearney & Silverman, 1990).

In addition to directly limiting the situations their children encounter, parents may also protect their anxious children by fostering their selection of avoidance as a means of coping with anxiety-provoking situations. Barrett, Rapee, Dadds, and Ryan (1996) found that anxious children chose avoidant solutions to vignettes describing challenging situations more often than normal controls. More importantly, this tendency was fostered by their parents in family problem-solving discussions. Dadds, Barrett, Rapee, and Ryan (1996) found that parents of anxious children were significantly more likely than parents of normal controls to reinforce differentially their children's mention of avoidance during problem-solving discussions. Furthermore, rates of such reinforcement were positively correlated with the children's selection of avoidant responses following the discussion. Similarly, restrictive and overcontrolling parental behavior also appears to be related to childhood anxiety. For example, Krohne and Hock (1991) reported that mothers of high-anxious girls were more restrictive than mothers of low-anxious girls during a problem-solving task, suggesting that child anxiety may be negatively related to the extent to which parents teach their child to problem-solve and positively related to parents' restrictiveness and overcontrol. Although it remains unclear whether such parental behaviors are a cause of, or a response to, childhood anxiety, in either case, once present, they may contribute to the maintenance and intensification of childhood anxiety over time.

In summary, parents and others may contribute to the maintenance and intensification of children's anxiety in a variety of ways, perhaps most directly by fostering their child's reliance on avoidance as a primary means of coping with anxiety-provoking situations. As noted earlier, much of parents' anxiety-fostering behavior may be a response to punishment and negative reinforcement associated with the child's anxious behavior. Thus, just as antisocial children are architects of the coercive environments that foster their antisocial behavior (Patterson, Reid, & Dishion, 1992), anxious children may foster their own anxiety by shaping the behavior of their caregivers and by virtue of their tendency to avoid anxiety-provoking situations.

To the extent that anxious children avoid contact with important developmental contexts, they should be at-risk for gradually growing incompetence that in turn may foster the maintenance and further intensification of anxiety as well as leading to additional problems (e.g., depression; see Brady & Kendall, 1992). This is similar to the notion of "limited shopping" in Patterson's theory of antisocial behavior (Patterson et al., 1992). Avoiding challenges such as those in academic and social domains should ultimately lead to growing incompetence. Consistent with such predictions, evidence shows that anxiety is associated with incompetence in academic (Dweck & Wortman, 1982) and social contexts (Evans, 1993;

Rubin, 1993; Strauss, Frame, & Forehand, 1987; Vernberg, Abwender, Ewell, & Beery, 1992). For example, social avoidance appears to interfere with the correction of socially anxious children's distorted beliefs about social situations (Hauck, Martens, & Wetzel, 1986). Furthermore, because of their failure to acquire important skills and because anxiety may interfere with performance, anxious children face increased risk of failure or other punishing outcomes when they encounter threatening situations. Such punishing outcomes and cumulative incompetence are exemplified by the consequences of social withdrawal. There is substantial evidence that social anxiety and withdrawal lead to peer rejection and unpopularity by mid- to late childhood (see Rubin & Stewart, 1996).

Cognitive and Emotional Factors

Cognitive Biases and Distortions

Childhood anxiety disorders appear to be associated with a variety of information-processing biases (see Daleiden & Vasey, 1997; Vasey & Daleiden, 1996). For example, clinically anxious and high-test-anxious children show an attentional bias in favor of threat relevant stimuli (Vasey, Daleiden, Williams, & Brown, 1995; Vasey, El-Hag, & Daleiden, 1996). Compared to normal controls, clinically anxious children also show a bias toward interpreting ambiguous information as threatening (Barrett et al., 1996; Chorpita, Albano, & Barlow, 1996).

To the extent that biases are shown by children prior to the onset of problematic anxiety, they may contribute significantly to risk for its development. For example, preliminary evidence of threat-related information-processing biases among BI children when they were followed-up at 13 years of age (Schwartz, Snidman, & Kagan, 1996) and among insecurely attached children (Kirsch & Cassidy, 1998) suggests that such biases may mediate the risk for anxiety disorders that is associated with these other factors. However, because many in the BI or insecurely attached groups in these studies may also have shown high levels of anxiety, it is unclear whether such biases represent risk factors for, or a consequence of, anxiety. Only prospective studies of at-risk children can adequately resolve this question.

Whether such cognitive biases predispose to or result from anxiety, once present, they may foster the maintenance and intensification of anxiety (see Vasey & Daleiden, 1996). By virtue of their tendency to show attentional biases toward threat cues and to interpret ambiguous information as threatening, anxious children construct their own anxiogenic experiences. In essence, they must cope with a world that is more threatening than that experienced by nonanxious children. Because of such biases, anxious children may be more likely to engage in avoidance even when faced with situations that pose no objective threat. Thus, such biases may foster increased incompetence. Furthermore, because they draw attentional resources away from coping with the situation at hand, they may also increase the likelihood of failure and punishment when the child faces challenges (see Vasey & Daleiden, 1996). In turn, such failures are likely to intensity further anxiogenic information-processing biases.

How cognitive developmental changes impact the operation of anxiety-related cognitive factors is an important question. Nelles and Barlow (1988) considered this question in the context of panic disorder, a problem in which cognitive misinterpretations of bodily sensations appear to play an important role. They argued that panic disorder should not occur prior to early adolescence because younger children lack the cognitive abilities required to support the requisite catastrophic misinterpretations. Thus, although younger children may have panic attacks and hyperventilation, because cognitive limitations prevent them from misinterpreting these symptoms as signaling impending death, they should not develop panic disorder. This conclusion has proved controversial and several issues merit further consideration. First, even if children do not develop panic disorder, this may have little to do with their level of cognitive development or their illness concepts. Age is a nonspecific variable that leaves unclear the specific physical, psychological, or social changes that are responsible for age-related differences (Rutter, 1989). Although panic disorder appears to be rare prior to adolescence, this may stem more from physical than cognitive developmental factors. For example, evidence that pubertal status is related to increased prevalence of panic attacks, especially in females, led Hayward et al. (1992) to suggest this increase may be linked to biological changes. Furthermore, there is growing evidence that children are capable of making internal causal attributions about panic symptoms considerably earlier than Nelles and Barlow suggested. For example, Mattis and Ollendick (1997) found that even children in third grade were able to formulate catastrophic attributions about panic symptoms. Indeed, as Ollendick et al. (1994) noted in their review, it is important to remember that although panic disorder is less common in children than adolescents, some children do experience panic attacks, develop panic disorder, and report both the physical and cognitive symptoms of that disorder.

Emotion Regulation Deficits

Children who fail to develop the skills for, or believe themselves incapable of, regulating their anxious emotion should be at risk for anxiety disorders. Furthermore, perceived uncontrollability of anxiety may lead to hypervigilance for stimuli signaling the likelihood of anxiety, thus serving as one pathway to the development of the attentional bias toward threat cues seen among anxious children (Thompson & Calkins, 1996). Also, beliefs that anxiety is uncontrollable may increase risk for further anxiety dysregulation by virtue of their effect on the strategies children choose to regulate their anxiety (e.g., avoidance), which may further increase their contact with factors leading to problematic anxiety.

Emotion regulation skills, as well as beliefs about control and self-efficacy, are a central part of what is learned in the attachment relationship. Because the internal working models of insecurely attached children are likely to represent others and the world in general as unpredictable or uncontrollable and themselves as lacking the resources to regulate anxiety, they should predispose to the development of problematic anxiety (Cassidy, 1996). In contrast, to the extent that secure attachment relationships foster effective anxiety regulation skills as well as a sense of control, they may protect against anxiety disorders. Consistent with such predictions, children with insecure attachments do indeed show higher levels of fearfulness than securely attached children in laboratory situations as well as a variety of information-processing biases similar to those seen among anxious children (Cassidy, 1996; Kirsh & Cassidy, 1998). However, the risk associated with insecure attachment status is likely to depend on the co-occurrence of other predisposing factors such as BI temperament. For example, Nachmias et al. (1996) examined the interaction of BI and attachment status, and found that only BI children in insecure attachment relationships showed elevated levels of cortisol when exposed to the Strange Situation task. Clearly, more research on these important factors is needed.

SUMMARY

In this chapter, we have provided a glimpse into the complex, unfolding nature of anxiety and its disorders in children and adolescents. This is a particularly exciting time in the study of anxiety insofar as much has been learned in recent years. Development in its many forms is at center stage in this quickly evolving and exciting area of study.

We began this chapter with a brief foray into definitional issues associated with the study of anxiety in children. The definition of childhood anxiety disorders is made difficult by three major issues. First, anxiety—at least in its mild forms—is part of normal development and, as such, it is frequently difficult to differentiate between normal forms of anxiety and pathological states. As we noted, clinical manifestations of anxiety disorders in children are likely to show considerable variation in focus, severity, and form as a function of development, making our definitional task most difficult. A second issue concerns the basic structure of childhood anxiety disorders. At this time, it is unclear whether anxiety disorders in childhood should even be conceptualized as categorical constructs. Moreover, it is unclear whether they should be conceptualized differently depending upon the developmental status of the growing child. For example, some findings suggest that the structure of anxiety may be more diffuse in younger children and become increasingly differentiated with age. Finally, a third definitional issue concerns the comorbidity of anxiety disorders with other disorders, including both internalizing and externalizing disorders (see Chapter 28). Interestingly, some findings indicate that the pattern of comorbidity may vary as a function of development. As is evident, definitional issues are abundant and not easily resolved; quite obviously, these issues have implications for the study and diagnosis of anxiety disorders in children.

Similarly, development plays a central role in the etiology and epidemiology of anxiety disorders. Age of onset varies greatly across the anxiety disorders, as does prevalence of the various disorders. Such differences in age of onset and prevalence of childhood anxiety disorders may provide important clues regarding the role of developing biological, social, cognitive, and emotional capacities in the etiology and maintenance of these disorders. In short, these developmental factors may predispose toward, precipitate, or protect against various disorders in a complex and transactive manner. Depending upon the configuration with which these factors occur, any given factor may lead to several different anxiety disorders, to other forms of psychopathology, or to no disorder at all! Moreover, there are likely to be multiple pathways to any anxiety disorder in childhood. As one example, we reviewed evidence for two different pathways to social phobia, suggesting that these different pathways might have important implications for assessment and treatment. Although these findings are exciting, they are at the same time disconcerting. Prediction of onset of disorder is difficult under such circumstances, and understanding of causal pathways under such conditions or "rules" is quixotic indeed. The challenge is before us.

Although space limitations did not permit us to examine the implications of development for the assessment, treatment, and prevention of anxiety disorders in children, we have explored these issues in some detail elsewhere (e.g., Daleiden et al., 1999; Hagopian & Ollendick, 1997; Ollendick et al., 1998). Suffice it to indicate that development and all that it portends raises equally exciting issues in these areas as well. Having noted this, however, we must assert that a "developmentally informed" study of childhood anxiety disorders is really in its own stage of infancy at this time. We have learned much, but much more remains to be mastered.

REFERENCES

Achenbach, T. M. (1991). Integrative guide for the 1991 CBCL/4–18, YSR, and TRF profiles. Burlington: Department of Psychiatry, University of Vermont.

Albano, A. M., Chorpita, B. F., & Barlow, D. H. (1996). Anxiety disorders in children and adolescents. In E. J. Mash & R. A. Barkley (Eds.), *Child psychopathology* (pp. 196–241). New York: Guilford Press.

American Psychiatric Association. (1980). *Diagnostic and statistical manual of mental disorders* (3rd ed.). Washington, DC: Author.

American Psychiatric Association. (1994). *Diagnostic and statistical manual of mental disorders* (4th ed.). Washington, DC: Author.

Anderson, J. C. (1994). Epidemiological issues. In T. H. Ollendick, N. J. King, & W. Yule (Eds.), *International handbook of phobic and anxiety disorders in children and adolescents* (pp. 43–66). New York: Plenum Press.

Anderson, J. C., Williams, S., McGee, R., & Silva, P. A. (1987). DSM-III disorders in preadolescent children: Prevalence in a large sample from the general population. *Archives of General Psychiatry, 44*, 69–76.

Andrews, J. D. (1966). Psychotherapy of phobias. *Psychological Bulletin, 66*, 455–480.

Angold, A. (1993). Why do we not know the causes of depression in children? In D. F. Hay & A. Angold (Eds.), *Precursors and causes in development and psychopathology* (pp. 265–292). Chichester, UK: Wiley.

Barlow, D. A. (1988). *Anxiety and its disorders: The nature and treatment of anxiety and panic.* New York: Guilford Press.

Barrett, P. M., Rapee, R. M., Dadds, M. R., & Ryan, S. M. (1996). Family enhancement of cognitive style in anxious and aggressive children: Threat bias and the FEAR effect. *Journal of Abnormal Child Psychology, 24*, 187–203.

Beidel, D. C. (1991). Social phobia and overanxious disorder in school-age children. *Journal of the American Academy of Child and Adolescent Psychiatry, 30*, 545–552.

Beidel, D. C., Silverman, W. K., & Hammond-Laurence, K. (1996). Overanxious disorder: Subsyndromal state or specific disorder? A comparison of clinic and community samples. *Journal of Clinical Child Psychology, 25*, 25–32.

Beitchman, J. H., Wekerle, C., & Hood, J. (1987). Diagnostic continuity from preschool to middle childhood. *Journal of the American Academy of Child and Adolescent Psychiatry, 26*, 694–699.

Bowen, R. C., Offord, D. R., & Boyle, M. H. (1990). The prevalence of overanxious disorder and separation anxiety disorder: Results from the Ontario Child Health Study. *Journal of the American Academy of Child and Adolescent Psychiatry, 29*, 753–758.

Brady, E. U., & Kendall, P. C. (1992). Comorbidity of anxiety and depression in children and adolescents. *Psychological Bulletin, 111*, 244–255.

Burke, C. B., Burke, J. D., Regier, D. A., & Rae, D. S. (1990). Age at onset of selected mental disorders in five community populations. *Archives of General Psychiatry, 47*, 511–518.

Cantwell, D. P., & Baker, L. (1987). The prevalence of anxiety in children with communication disorders. *Journal of Anxiety Disorders, 1*, 239–248.

Cassidy, J. (1996). Attachment and generalized anxiety disorder. In D. Cicchetti & S. Toth (Eds.), *Rochester Symposium on Developmental Psychopathology: Emotion, cognition, and representation* (Vol. 6, pp. 343–370). Rochester, NY: University of Rochester Press.

Chorpita, B. F., Albano, A. M., & Barlow, D. H. (1996). Cognitive processing in children: Relationship to anxiety and family influences. *Journal of Clinical Child Psychology, 25*, 170–176.

Cicchetti, D., & Cohen, D. J. (1995). Perspectives on developmental psychopathology. In D. Cicchetti & D. Cohen (Eds.), *Developmental psychopathology: Vol. 1. Theory and methods* (pp. 3–20). New York: Wiley.

Clarke, J. C., & Jackson, J. A. (1983). *Hypnosis and behavior therapy: The treatment of anxiety and phobias.* New York: Springer.

Cohen, P., Cohen, J., Kasen, S., Velez, C., Hartmark, C., Johnson, J., Rojas, M., Brook, J., & Streuning, E. L. (1993). An epidemiological study of disorders in late childhood and adolescence: I. Age- and gender-specific prevalence. *Journal of Child Psychology and Psychiatry and Allied Disciplines, 34*, 851–867.

Costello, E. J., Costello, A. J., Edelbrock, C. S., Burns, B. J., Dulcan, M. J., Brent, D., & Janiszewski, S. (1988). DSM-III disorders in pediatric primary care: Prevalence and risk factors. *Archives of General Psychiatry, 45*, 1107–1116.

Dadds, M. R., Barrett, P. M., Rapee, R. M., & Ryan, S. (1996). Family process and child psychopathology: An observational analysis of the FEAR effect. *Journal of Abnormal Child Psychology, 24*, 715–734.

Daleiden, E. L., & Vasey, M. W. (1997). An information-processing perspective on childhood anxiety. *Clinical Psychology Review, 17*, 407–429.

Daleiden, E. L., Vasey, M. W., & Brown, L. M. (1999). Internalizing disorders. In W. K. Silverman & T. H. Ollendick (Eds.), *Developmental issues in the clinical treatment of children and adolescents.* New York: Allyn & Bacon.

Davey, G. C. L. (1992). Classical conditioning and the acquisition of human fears and phobias: A review and synthesis of the literature. *Advances in Behaviour Research and Therapy, 14*, 29–66.

Dumas, J. E., LaFreniere, P. J., & Serketich, W. J. (1995). "Balance of power": A transactional analysis of control in mother–child dyads involving socially competent, aggressive, and anxious children. *Journal of Abnormal Psychology, 104*, 104–113.

Dweck, C., & Wortman, C. (1982). Learned helplessness, anxiety, and achievement. In H. Krohne & L. Laux (Eds.), *Achievement, stress, and anxiety*. New York: Hemisphere.

Eaves, L. J., Eysenck, H., & Martin, N. G. (1989). *Genes, culture, and personality: An empirical approach*. London: Academic Press.

Edelbrock, C., Rende, R., Plomin, R., & Thompson, L. A. (1995). A twin study of competence and problem behavior in childhood and early adolescence. *Journal of Child Psychology and Psychiatry and Allied Disciplines, 36*, 775–785.

Eley, T., & Stevenson, J. (1997). *Using genetic analyses to clarify the distinction between depressive and anxious symptoms in children*. Unpublished manuscript.

Engfer, A. (1993). Antecedents and consequences of shyness in boys and girls: A 6-year longitudinal study. In K. H. Rubin & J. B. Asendorpf (Eds.), *Social withdrawal, inhibition, and shyness in childhood* (pp. 49–79). Hillsdale, NJ: Erlbaum.

Evans, D. W., Leckman, J. F., Carter, A., Reznick, J. S., Henshaw, D., King, R. A., & Pauls, D. (1997). Ritual, habit, and perfectionism: The prevalence and development of compulsive-like behavior in normal young children. *Child Development, 68*, 58–68.

Evans, M. A. (1993). Communication competence as a dimension of shyness. In K. H. Rubin & J. B. Asendorpf (Eds.), *Social withdrawal, inhibition, and shyness in childhood* (pp. 189–212). Hillsdale, NJ: Erlbaum.

Eysenck, H. J., & Eysenck, M. W. (1985). *Personality and individual differences*. New York: Plenum Press.

Fletcher, K. E. (1996). Childhood posttraumatic stress disorder. In E. J. Mash & R. A. Barkley (Eds.), *Child psychopathology* (pp. 242–276). New York: Guilford Press.

Francis, G., Last, C. G., & Strauss, C. C. (1992). Avoidant disorder and social phobia in children and adolescents. *Journal of the American Academy of Child and Adolescent Psychiatry, 31*, 1086–1089.

Garber, J., & Strassberg, Z. (1991). Construct validity: History and applications to developmental psychopathology. In W. M. Grove & D. Cicchetti (Eds.), *Thinking clearly about psychology: Vol. 2. Personality and psychopathology* (pp. 219–258). Minneapolis: University of Minnesota Press.

Gerlsma, C., Emmelkamp, P. M. G., & Arrindell, W. A. (1990). Anxiety, depression, and perception of early parenting: A meta-analysis. *Clinical Psychology Review, 10*, 251–277.

Giaconia, R. M., Reinherz, H. Z., Silverman, A. B., Pakiz, B., Frost, A. K., & Cohen, E. (1994). Ages of onset of psychiatric disorders in a community population of older adolescents. *Journal of the American Academy of Child and Adolescent Psychiatry, 33*, 706–717.

Gittelman, R. (1986). Childhood anxiety disorders: Correlates and outcome. In R. Gittelman (Ed.), *Anxiety disorders of childhood* (pp. 101–125). New York: Guilford Press.

Gittelman-Klein, R., & Klein, D. F. (1980). Separation anxiety in school refusal and its treatment with drugs. In L. Hersov & I. Berg (Eds.), *Out of school* (pp. 321–341). New York: Wiley.

Gunnar, M. (1980). Contingent stimulation: A review of its role in early development. In S. Levine & H. Ursin (Eds.), *Coping and health* (pp. 101–119). New York: Plenum Press.

Hagopian, L. P., & Ollendick, T. H. (1997). Anxiety disorders in children. In T. Ammerman and M. Hersen (Eds.), *Handbook of prevention and treatment with children and adolescents*. New York: Wiley.

Hauck, W. E., Martens, M., & Wetzel, M. (1986). Shyness, group dependence and self-concept: Attributes of the imaginary audience. *Adolescence, 21*, 529–534.

Hayward, C., Killen, J. D., Hammer, L. D., Litt, I. F., Wilson, D. M., Simmonds, B., & Taylor, C. B. (1992). Pubertal stage and panic attack history in sixth- and seventh-grade girls. *American Journal of Psychiatry, 149*, 1239–1243.

Insel, T. R., Scanlan, J., Champoux, M., & Suomi, S. J. (1988). Rearing paradigm in a nonhuman primate affects response to β-CCE challenge. *Psychopharmacology, 96*, 81–86.

Joiner, T. E., Jr., Catanzaro, S. J., & Laurent, J. (1996). Tripartite structure of positive and negative affect, depression, and anxiety in child and adolescent psychiatric inpatients. *Journal of Abnormal Psychology, 105*, 401–409.

Kagan, J. (1994). *Galen's prophecy: Temperament in human nature*. New York: Basic Books.

Kagan, J. (1997). Temperament and the reactions to unfamiliarity. *Child Development, 68*, 139–143.

Kashani, J. H., & Orvaschel, H. (1988). Anxiety disorders in mid-adolescence: A community sample. *American Journal of Psychiatry, 145*, 960–964.

Kashani, J. H., & Orvaschel, H. (1990). A community study of anxiety in children and adolescents. *American Journal of Psychiatry, 147*, 313–318.

Kashani, J. H., Orvaschel, H., Rosenberg, T. K., & Reid, J. C. (1989). Psychopathology in a community sample of children and adolescents: A developmental perspective. *Journal of the American Academy of Child and Adolescent Psychiatry, 28*, 701–706.

Kearney, C. A., & Silverman, W. K. (1990). A preliminary analysis of a functional model of assessment and treatment for school refusal behavior [Special Issue: Child abuse and neglect]. *Behavior Modification, 14,* 340–366.

Keller, M. B., Lavori, P. W., Wunder, J., Beardslee, W. R., Schwartz, C. E., & Roth, J. (1992). Chronic course of anxiety disorders in children and adolescents. *Journal of the American Academy of Child and Adolescent Psychiatry, 31,* 595–599.

Kendler, K. S., Neale, M. C., Kessler, R. C., Heath, A. C., & Eaves, L. J. (1992a). The genetic epidemiology of phobias in women: The interrelationship of agoraphobia, social phobia, situational phobia, and simple phobia. *Archives of General Psychiatry, 49,* 273–281.

Kendler, K. S., Neale, M. C., Kessler, R. C., Heath, A. C., & Eaves, L. J. (1992b). Major depression and generalized anxiety disorder: Same genes, (partly) different environments? *Archives of General Psychiatry, 49,* 716–722.

Kirsch, S., & Cassidy, J. (1998). Preschoolers' attention to and memory for attachment-relevant information. *Child Development, 68,* 1143–1153.

Klonsky, B. G., Dutton, D. L., & Liebel, C. N. (1991). Developmental antecedents of private self-consciousness, public self-consciousness, and social anxiety. *Genetic, Social, and General Psychology Monographs, 117,* 275–297.

Kohlmann, C. W., & Krohne, H. W. (1988). Erziehungsstildeterminanten schulischer Leistung und Leistungsangstlichkeit (Child-rearing antecedents of school performance and test anxiety). *Zeitschrift fur Padagogische Psychologie, 2,* 271–279.

Krohne, H. W., & Hock, M. (1991). Relationships between restrictive mother–child interactions and anxiety of the child. *Anxiety Research, 4,* 109–124.

Last, C. G., Hersen, M., Kazdin, A. E., Finkelstein, R., & Strauss, C. C. (1987). Comparison of DSM-III separation anxiety and overanxious disorders: Demographic characteristics and patterns of comorbidity. *Journal of the American Academy of Child and Adolescent Psychiatry, 26,* 527–531.

Last, C. G., Hersen, M., Kazdin, A., Orvaschel, H., & Perrin, S. (1991). Anxiety disorders in children and their families. *Archives of General Psychiatry, 48,* 928–934.

Last, C. G., Perrin, S., Hersen, M., & Kazdin, A. E. (1992). DSM-III-R anxiety disorders in children: Sociodemographic and clinical characteristics. *Journal of the American Academy of Child and Adolescent Psychiatry, 31,* 1070–1076.

Loeber, R., Lahey, B. B., & Thomas, C. (1991). Diagnostic conundrum of oppositional defiant disorder and conduct disorder. *Journal of Abnormal Psychology, 100,* 379–390.

Lonigan, C. J., Shannon, M. P., Taylor, C. M., Finch, A. J., & Sallee, F. R. (1994). Children exposed to disaster: II. Risk factors for the development of post-traumatic symptomatology. *Journal of the American Academy of Child and Adolescent Psychiatry, 33,* 94–105.

Mattis, S. G., & Ollendick, T. H. (1997). Children's cognitive responses to the somatic symptoms of panic. *Journal of Abnormal Child Psychology, 25,* 47–57.

McGee, R., Fehan, M., Williams, S., Partridge, F., Silva, P. A., & Kelly, J. (1990). DSM-III disorders in a large sample of adolescents. *Journal of the American Academy of Child and Adolescent Psychiatry, 29,* 611–619.

Menzies, R. G., & Clarke, J. C. (1993). The etiology of childhood water phobia. *Behaviour Research and Therapy, 31,* 499–501.

Menzies, R. G., & Clarke, J. C. (1995). The etiology of phobias: A nonassociative account. *Clinical Psychology Review, 15,* 23–48.

Merckelbach, H., de Jong, P. J., Muris, P., & Hout, M. A. (1996). The etiology of specific phobias: A review. *Clinical Psychology Review, 16,* 337–361.

Merckelbach, H., Muris, P., & Schouten, E. (1996). Pathways to fear in spider phobic children. *Behaviour Research and Therapy, 34,* 935–938.

Miller, S. M., Boyer, B. A., & Rodoletz, M. (1990). Anxiety in children: Nature and development. In M. Lewis & S. M. Miller (Eds.), *Handbook of developmental psychopathology* (pp. 191–207). New York: Plenum Press.

Mineka, S., Gunnar, M., & Champoux, M. (1986). Control and early socioemotional development: Infant rhesus monkeys reared in controllable versus uncontrollable environments. *Child Development, 57,* 1241–1256.

Mineka, S., & Zinbarg, R. (1995). Conditioning and ethological models of social phobia. In R. G. Heimberg, M. R. Liebowitz, D. A. Hope, & F. R. Schneier (Eds.), *Social phobia: Diagnosis, assessment, and treatment* (pp. 135–210). New York: Guilford Press.

Muris, P., Steerneman, P., Merckelbach, H., & Meesters, C. (1996). Parental modeling and fearfulness in middle childhood. *Behaviour Research and Therapy, 34,* 265–268.

Nachmias, M., Gunnar, M., Mangelsdorf, S., Parritz, R. H., & Buss, K. (1996). Behavioral inhibition and stress reactivity: The moderating role of attachment security. *Child Development, 67,* 508–522.

Nelles, W. B., & Barlow, D. H. (1988). Do children panic? *Clinical Psychology Review, 8,* 359–372.

Nolen-Hoeksema, S., & Girgus, J. S. (1994). The emergence of gender differences in depression during adolescence. *Psychological Bulletin, 115,* 424–443.

Ollendick, T. H., Hagopian, L. P., & King, N. J. (1998). Specific phobias in children. In G. C. L. Davey (Ed.), *Phobias: A handbook of theory, research and treatment* (pp. 201–226). Chichester, UK: Wiley.

Ollendick, T. H., & King, N. J. (1991). Origins of childhood fears: An evaluation of Rachman's theory of fear acquisition. *Behaviour Research and Therapy, 29,* 117–123.

Ollendick, T. H., & King, N. J. (1994). Diagnosis, assessment, and treatment of internalizing problems in children: The role of longitudinal data. *Journal of Consulting and Clinical Psychology, 62,* 918–927.

Ollendick, T. H., Mattis, S. G., & King, N. J. (1994). Panic in children and adolescents: A review. *Journal of Child Psychology and Psychiatry, 35,* 113–134.

Öst, L. G. (1987). Age of onset in different phobias. *Journal of Abnormal Psychology, 96,* 223–229.

Patterson, G. R., Reid, J. B., & Dishion, T. J. (1992). *Antisocial boys.* Eugene, OR: Castalia.

Perrin, S., & Last, C. G. (1995). Dealing with comorbidity. In A. R. Eisen, C. A. Kearney, & C. A. Schaefer (Eds.), *Clinical handbook of anxiety disorders in children and adolescents* (pp. 412–435). Northvale, NJ: Aronson.

Philips, K., Fulker, D. W., & Rose, R. J. (1987). Path analysis of seven fear factors in adult twin and sibling pairs and their parents. *Genetic Epidemiology, 4,* 345–355.

Plomin, R., & Rowe, D. C. (1979). Genetic and environmental etiology of social behavior in infancy. *Developmental Psychopathology, 15,* 62–72.

Reznick, J. S., Hegeman, I. M., Kaufman, E. R., Woods, S. W., & Jacobs, M. (1992). Retrospective and concurrent self-report of behavioral inhibition and their relation to adult mental health. *Development and Psychopathology, 4,* 301–321.

Robinson, J. L., Kagan, J., Reznick, J. S., & Corley, R. (1992). The heritability of inhibited and uninhibited behavior: A twin study. *Developmental Psychology, 28,* 1030–1037.

Roy, M. A., Neale, M. C., Pedersen, N. L., Mathe, A. A., & Kendler, K. S. (1995). A twin study of generalized anxiety disorder and major depression. *Psychological Medicine, 25,* 1037–1049.

Rubin, K. H. (1993). The Waterloo longitudinal project: Correlates and consequences of social withdrawal from childhood to adolescence. In K. H. Rubin & J. B. Asendorpf (Eds.), *Social withdrawal, inhibition, and shyness* (pp. 291–314). Hillsdale, NJ: Erlbaum.

Rubin, K. H., & Stewart, S. L. (1996). Social withdrawal. In E. Mash & R. Barkley (Eds.), *Child psychopathology* (pp. 277–307). New York: Guilford Press.

Rutter, M. (1989). Age as an ambiguous variable in development research: Some epidemiological considerations from developmental psychopathology. *International Journal of Behavioral Development, 12,* 1–34.

Schwartz, C. E., Snidman, N., & Kagan, J. (1996). Early temperamental predictors of Stroop interference to threatening information at adolescence. *Journal of Anxiety Disorders, 10,* 89–96.

Seligman, L. D., & Ollendick, T. H. (1999). Comorbidity of anxiety and depression in children and adolescents: A critical review and integration. *Clinical Child and Family Psychology Review, 1,* 125–144.

Shannon, M. P., Lonigan, C. L., Finch, A. J., & Taylor, C. M. (1994). Children exposed to disaster: I. Epidemiology of post-traumatic symptoms and symptoms profiles. *Journal of the American Academy of Child and Adolescent Psychiatry, 33,* 80–93.

Silove, D., Manicavasagar, V., Curtis, J., & Blaszczynski, A. (1996). Is early separation anxiety a risk factor for adult panic disorder? A critical review. *Comprehensive Psychiatry, 37,* 167–179.

Silverman, W. K. (1992). Taxonomy of anxiety disorders in children. In G. D. Burrows, R. Noyes, & S. M. Roth (Eds.), *Handbook of anxiety* (Vol. 5, pp. 281–308). Amsterdam: Elsevier.

Silverman, W. K., Cerny, J. A., & Nelles, W. B. (1988). The familial influence in anxiety disorders: Studies on the offspring of patients with anxiety disorders. In B. B. Lahey & A. E. Kazdin (Eds.), *Advances in Clinical Child Psychology* (Vol. 11, pp. 223–248). New York: Plenum Press.

Silverman, W. K., La Greca, A. M., & Wasserstein, S. (1995). What do children worry about? Worries and their relation to anxiety. *Child Development, 66,* 671–686.

Skinner, E. A. (1995). *Perceived control, motivation, and coping.* Thousand Oaks, CA: Sage.

Spence, S. H. (1997). Structure of anxiety symptoms among children: A confirmatory factor-analytic study. *Journal of Abnormal Psychology, 106,* 280–297.

Stemberger, R. T., Turner, S. M., Beidel, D. C., & Calhoun, K. S. (1995). Social phobia: An analysis of possible developmental factors. *Journal of Abnormal Psychology, 104,* 526–531.

Stevenson, J., Batten, N., & Cherner, M. (1992). Fears and fearfulness in children and adolescents: A genetic analysis of twin data. *Journal of Children Psychology and Psychiatry, 33,* 977–985.

Strauss, C. C., Frame, C. L., & Forehand, R. (1987). Psychosocial impairment associated with anxiety in children. *Journal of Clinical Child Psychology, 16,* 235–239.

Strauss, C. C., & Last, C. G. (1993). Social and simple phobias in children. *Journal of Anxiety Disorders, 7,* 141–152.

Swedo, S. E., Rapoport, J. L., Leonard, H., Lenane, M., & Cheslow, D. (1989). Obsessive-compulsive disorder in children and adolescents: Clinical phenomenology of 70 consecutive cases. *Archives of General Psychiatry, 46,* 335–341.

Tellegen, A., Lykken, D.T., Bouchard, T.J., Wilcox, K.J., Segal, N.L., & Rich, S. (1988). Personality similarity in twins reared apart and together. *Journal of Personality and Social Psychology, 54,* 1031–1039.

Thapar, A., & McGuffin, P. (1995). Are anxiety symptoms in childhood heritable? *Journal of Child Psychology and Psychiatry and Allied Disciplines, 36,* 439–447.

Thompson, R. A., & Calkins, S. D. (1996). The double-edged sword: Emotional regulation for children at risk. *Development and Psychopathology, 8,* 163–182.

Turner, S. M., Beidel, D. C., & Costello, A. (1987). Psychopathology in the offspring of anxiety disorders patients. *Journal of Consulting and Clinical Psychology, 55,* 229–235.

Turner, S. M., Beidel, D. C., & Wolff, P. L. (1996). Is behavioral inhibition related to the anxiety disorders? *Clinical Psychology Review, 16,* 157–172.

Valleni-Basile, L. A., Garrison, C. Z., Jackson, K. L., Waller, J. L., McKeown, R. E., Addy, C. L., & Cuffe, S. P. (1994). Frequency of obsessive-compulsive disorder in a community sample of young adolescents. *Journal of the American Academy of Child and Adolescent Psychiatry, 33,* 782–791.

van den Oord, E. J., Verhulst, F. C., & Boomsma, D. I. (1996). A genetic study of maternal and paternal ratings of problem behaviors in 3-year-old twins. *Journal of Abnormal Psychology, 105,* 349–357.

Vasey, M. W. (1993). Development and cognition in childhood anxiety: The example of worry. In T. H. Ollendick & R. Prinz (Eds.), *Advances in clinical child psychology* (Vol. 15, pp. 1–39). New York: Plenum Press.

Vasey, M. W., Crnic, K. A., & Carter, W. G. (1994). Worry in childhood: A developmental perspective. *Cognitive Therapy and Research, 18,* 529–549.

Vasey, M. W., & Daleiden, E. L. (1996). Information-processing pathways to cognitive interference in childhood. In I. G. Sarason, G. Pierce, & B. Sarason (Eds.), *Cognitive interference: Theory, methods, and findings* (pp. 117–138). Hillsdale, NJ: Erlbaum.

Vasey, M. W., Daleiden, E. L., Williams, L. L., & Brown, L. M. (1995). Biased attention in childhood anxiety disorders: A preliminary study. *Journal of Abnormal Child Psychology, 23,* 267–279.

Vasey, M. W., El-Hag, N., & Daleiden, E. L. (1996). Anxiety and the processing of emotionally-threatening stimuli: Distinctive patterns of selective attention among high- and low-test-anxious children. *Child Development, 67,* 1173–1185.

Vernberg, E. M., Abwender, D. A., Ewell, K. K., & Beery, S. H. (1992). Social anxiety and peer relationships in early adolescence: A prospective analysis. *Journal of Clinical Child Psychology, 21,* 189–196.

Vernberg, E. M., La Greca, A. M., Silverman, W. K., & Prinstein, M. J. (1996). Prediction of posttraumatic stress symptoms in children after Hurricane Andrew. *Journal of Abnormal Psychology, 105,* 237–248.

Watson, D., & Clark, L. A. (1984). Negative affectivity: The predisposition to experience aversive emotional states. *Psychological Bulletin, 96,* 465–490.

Windheuser, H. J. (1977). Anxious mothers as models for coping with anxiety. *Behavioral Analysis and Modification, 1,* 39–58.

Zinbarg, R., & Revelle, W. (1989). Personality and conditioning: A test of four models. *Journal of Personality and Social Psychology, 57,* 301–314.

28

Mixed Anxiety/Depression in Childhood and Adolescence

Bruce E. Compas and Gerri Oppedisano

Depression and anxiety are recognized as significant mental health problems during childhood and adolescence. The prevalence of symptoms of anxiety and depression increases during development, these problems are associated with impaired social and school functioning, and anxiety and depression symptoms or disorders early in development are predictive of similar problems in adulthood (Hammen & Rudolph, 1996). In spite of the overall significance of these problems for the well-being and development of children and adolescents, several issues about the conceptualization and basic nature of anxiety and depression in young people remain unresolved (Compas, Connor, & Hinden, 1998). Most importantly, the conceptualization of the nature and developmental course of depression and anxiety in young people remains open to debate. On the one hand, these problems have been conceptualized as discrete disorders that adhere to criteria that were originally developed for adults and have been extended down, with minor modifications, to children and adolescents (American Psychiatric Association, 1994). On the other hand, quantitative approaches to child and adolescent psychopathology have not identified distinct syndromes that reflect anxiety and depression, but have consistently revealed a syndrome that includes a mixture of anxious and depressed symptoms (Achenbach, 1991; Achenbach, Verhulst, Baron, & Akkerhuis, 1987; Verhulst & van der Ende, 1992).

Further clarification of the relationship between anxiety and depression has implications for understanding basic emotions and emotional problems in development, while at the applied level the association between anxiety and depression has implications for the assessment and treatment of these problems in children and adolescents. At least four relationships are possible between depression and anxiety in young people. First, anxiety and depression may be two separate disorders that have a strong tendency co-occur or to be comorbid. Second, anxiety and depression may be two aspects of a single syndrome that is best conceptualized as mixed anxiety/depression. Third, both a general syndrome of mixed anxiety/depression and

Bruce E. Compas and Gerri Oppedisano • Department of Psychology, University of Vermont, Burlington, Vermont 05405.

Handbook of Developmental Psychopathology, Second Edition, edited by Arnold J. Sameroff, Michael Lewis, and Suzanne M. Miller. Kluwer Academic/Plenum Publishers, New York, 2000.

distinct disorders could be manifested concurrently in the presentation of symptoms or longitudinally/sequentially in the development of symptoms and disorders. Fourth, some symptoms of anxiety and depression may reflect a common syndrome, while other symptoms represent the distinct features of separate syndromes or disorders. An integrative perspective on anxiety and depression in children and adolescents suggests that these perspectives are not mutually exclusive and each may be correct to some degree (Compas, Ey, & Grant, 1993; Compas et al., 1998). The goals of this chapter are to provide a brief review of empirical research on the relationship between depression and anxiety in young people, to consider the evidence in support of each of these four perspectives on depression and anxiety, and to outline directions for future research to clarify the association between these two problems in children and adolescents.

NATURE OF DEPRESSION AND ANXIETY IN YOUNG PEOPLE

Conceptualizations of Depression and Anxiety

Defining and understanding depression and anxiety during childhood and adolescence are dependent on the paradigms one uses for the *assessment* and *taxonomy* of psychopathology. Broadly defined, assessment is concerned with the identification of distinguishing features of individual cases, whereas taxonomy is concerned with the grouping of cases according to their distinguishing features (Achenbach, 1985, 1993). Assessment and taxonomy are linked to one another in that the grouping of cases in a taxonomic system should be based on clearly defined criteria and procedures for identifying the central features that distinguish between cases. Similarly, assessment procedures should reflect certain basic assumptions of the underlying system for classifying the phenomena of interest.

One of the major challenges facing researchers and clinicians concerned with depression and anxiety during childhood and adolescence involves operationally defining and measuring these constructs. Researchers and clinicians have drawn upon different definitions of depression and anxiety, different taxonomic systems, and have used different measures, including a focus on (1) depressed and anxious mood, (2) empirically derived syndromes that include depressive and anxious symptoms, and (3) symptoms that meet diagnostic criteria for categorical disorders (e.g., Angold, 1988; Cantwell & Baker, 1991; Compas et al., 1993; Kovacs, 1989). These three approaches to depressive and anxious phenomena during childhood and adolescence have all been included under the general labels of "depression" or "anxiety," leading to confusion and miscommunication. The accompanying debate about the most appropriate way to conceptualize depression and anxiety (and other forms of psychopathology) has often been reflected in polarized views on the nature of this problem (e.g., Coyne & Downey, 1991). Unfortunately, this polarization of views has diverted attention from a richer understanding of the relationship between depressive or anxious symptoms on a continuum and categorical diagnosis of depression, or anxiety disorders (for an attempt to reconcile these two approaches, see Jensen et al., 1996). In addition to confusion regarding taxonomic issues, the assessment of depression and anxiety during childhood and adolescence has also been problematic. A wide variety of assessment and diagnostic tools have been used in the measurement of child and adolescent depression. These measures have varied in the breadth versus specificity of the symptoms that are assessed, in their source of information (children/adolescents, parents, teachers, clinicians), whether they involve interviews or checklists, and in their psychometric quality (Barrios & Hartmann, 1997; Compas, 1997).

Heterogeneity in the conceptualization and measurement of depression and anxiety during childhood and adolescence has resulted in a fragmentation of research efforts and has impeded determination of the prevalence of depressive and anxious phenomena, understanding of their developmental course, and identification of etiological factors. Therefore, clarifying the relations among the three taxonomic approaches is the first step toward understanding the nature of depression and anxiety in childhood and adolescence.

The study of *depressed and anxious mood* during childhood and adolescence has emerged from developmental research in which depressive and anxious emotions are studied along with other features of biological, cognitive, and social development (e.g., Kandel & Davies, 1982; Petersen, Sarigiani, & Kennedy, 1991). The depressed/anxious mood approach is concerned with depression and anxiety as symptoms or emotional states, and refers to the presence of sadness, unhappiness, blue feelings, worry, or anxiety for an unspecified period of time. No assumptions are made regarding the presence or absence of other symptoms that may or may not be associated with these emotions (e.g., concentration problems, poor appetite, insomnia). Widely used measures at the general level of depressed or anxious mood, or general symptoms of depression and anxiety include the Children's Depression Inventory (CDI; Kovacs, 1980) and the Revised Children's Manifest Anxiety Scale (R-CMAS; Reynolds & Richmond, 1978). Measures of positive and negative emotions or affect in adults, such as the Positive and Negative Affect Scale (PANAS; Watson, Clark, & Carey, 1988), have been adapted for use with children and adolescents (e.g., Joiner, Catanzaro, & Laurent, 1996; Rudolph, Osborne, Lambert, & Gathright, 1998).

The second approach, the study of an *anxious/depressed syndrome*, is concerned with depression and anxiety as a constellation of behaviors and emotions identified empirically through the reports of children/adolescents and other informants (e.g., parents, teachers). This strategy involves the use of multivariate statistical methods in the assessment and taxonomy of child and adolescent psychopathology, represented by the empirically based taxonomy of Achenbach (1985, 1993). Within this approach, a syndrome of anxiety and depression refers to a set of emotions and behaviors that have been found statistically to occur together in an identifiable pattern at a rate that exceeds chance, without implying any particular model for the nature or causes of these associated symptoms. Differences between individuals are viewed in terms of quantitative deviations in levels of symptoms. An empirically deprived syndrome of anxious and depressive symptoms is best represented in the research of Achenbach and colleagues (e.g., Achenbach, 1993). Most pertinent here is the syndrome labeled Anxious/Depressed, comprised of symptoms reflecting a mixture of anxiety and depression (see Table 28.1). The syndrome has been replicated in large samples in both the United States and the Netherlands (Achenbach, McConaughy, & Howell, 1987). A more "pure" depressive or anxious syndrome did not emerge in the reports of parents, teachers, and adolescents, despite the availability of items reflecting all but one of the symptoms (anhedonia) of major depression, and most of the symptoms of anxiety disorders. It is noteworthy that symptoms of sleep disturbance, appetite problems, and concentration difficulties were included in these measures but did not load on the Anxious/Depressed syndrome.

The *categorical/diagnostic* approach is based on assumptions of a disease or disorder model of psychopathology as reflected in the categorical diagnostic system of the DSM-IV (American Psychiatric Association, 1994) and the International Classification of Diseases and Health-Related Problems (ICD-10) of the World Health Organization (1990). This approach views depression and anxiety as psychiatric disorders that include the presence of an identifiable set of symptoms associated with significant levels of current distress or disability, and with increased risk for impairment in the individual's current functioning (American Psychiatric Association, 1994).

**Table 28.1. Symptoms of the Anxious/Depressed Syndrome
Based on Parent (CBCL) and Adolescent (YSR) Reports**

Parent report	Adolescent report
Complains of loneliness	I feel lonely.
Cries a lot	I cry a lot.
Fears s/he might do something bad	I am afraid I might think or do something bad.
Feels s/he has to be perfect	
Feels or complains that no one loves	I feel that no one loves me.
Feels others are out to get him/her	I feel that others are out to get me.
Feels worthless or inferior	I feel worthless or inferior.
Nervous, highstrung, or tense	I am nervous or tense.
Too fearful or anxious	I am too fearful or anxious.
Feels too guilty	I feel too guilty.
Self-conscious or easily embarrassed	I am self-conscious or easily embarrassed.
Suspicious	I am suspicious.
Unhappy, sad, or depressed	I am unhappy, sad, or depressed.
Worrying	I worry a lot.
	I deliberately try to hurt or kill myself.
	I think about killing myself.

Depressive disorders are classified under the broad category of Mood Disorders. Within the Mood Disorders, depression is divided into two categories: Bipolar Disorders and Depressive Disorders. In distinguishing between Bipolar and Depressive Disorders, Bipolar Disorders are defined by the presence of manic or hypomanic symptoms that may alternate with depression. As this chapter is concerned with Depressive Disorders without manic or hypomanic episodes, the reader is referred to the DSM-IV for more information regarding Bipolar Disorders (see also, Carlson, 1994). Differences between individuals are considered in terms of quantitative and qualitative differences in the pattern, severity, and duration of symptoms. With only a few exceptions, child/adolescent depression is diagnosed according to the same DSM-IV criteria as adult depression.

To meet the criteria for major depressive disorder (MDD), the child or adolescent must have experienced *five or more* of the specified symptoms for at least a 2-week period at a level that differs from prior functioning, and at least one of the symptoms includes either (1) depressed or irritable mood, or (2) anhedonia (see Table 28.2). Irritable mood may be observed in lieu of depressed mood in children/adolescents and is believed to be more common in this age group than in adults. A range of mild, moderate, and severe diagnoses, with or without psychotic features, is applied. The criteria for diagnosis of Dysthymic Disorder (DY) in childhood and adolescence are that for at least a period of 1 year (as compared to 2 years for adults), an individual must display depressed or irritable mood for more days than not, without more than 2 months symptom free, along with additional symptoms specified in Table 28.2.

Anxiety disorders of childhood and adolescence are represented by several diagnostic categories in the DSM-IV, including Separation Anxiety Disorder, Generalized Anxiety Disorder, Obsessive–Compulsive Disorder, Posttraumatic and Acute Stress Disorder, and various specific phobias. Presentation of the specific criteria for all of the anxiety disorders is beyond the scope of this discussion; however, the criteria for Generalized Anxiety Disorder (GAD) are presented in Table 28.3. The primary criteria include the presence of excessive anxiety and worry, accompanied by at least one additional symptom in children (as compared

Table 28.2. DSM-IV Criteria for Major Depressive Episode and Dysthymic Disorder

Major depressive episode

A. Five (or more) of the following symptoms during the same 2-week period; at least one of the symptoms is depressed mood or loss of interest or pleasure.
   1. Depressed mood most of the day, nearly every day, as indicated by subjective report or observation by others. *Note.* In children and adolescents, this can be irritable mood.
   2. Markedly diminished interest or pleasure in all or almost all activities most of the day, nearly every day, as indicated by subjective account or observation by others.
   3. Significant weight loss when not dieting or weight gain (e.g., a change of more than 5% body weight in a month), or decrease or increase in appetite nearly every day. *Note.* In children, consider failure to make expected weight gains.
   4. Insomnia or hypersomnia nearly every day.
   5. Psychomotor agitation or retardation nearly every day (observable by others).
   6. Fatigue or loss of energy nearly every day.
   7. Feelings of worthlessness or excessive or inappropriate guilt nearly every day.
   8. Diminished ability to think or concentrate, or indecisiveness, nearly every day (either subjective or observed by others).
   9. Recurrent thoughts of death (not just fear of dying), recurrent suicidal ideation without a specific plan, or a suicide attempt or a specific plan for committing suicide.

Major depressive episode (unipolar) can be further specified as mild, moderate, severe (based on functional impairment and severity of symptoms), with or without psychotic features, with or without melancholic features, whether or not recurrent, or chronic.

Dysthymic disorder

A. Depressed mood for most of the day, for more days than not, as indicated either by subjective account or observation by others, for at least 2 years. *Note.* In children and adolescents, mood can be irritable and duration must be at least 1 year.
B. Presence, while depressed, of two or more of the following:
   1. Poor appetite or overeating
   2. Insomnia or hypersomnia
   3. Low energy or fatigue
   4. Low self-esteem.
   5. Poor concentration or difficulty making decisions.
C. During period of depression, the person has never been without symptoms A or B for more than 2 months at a time. Also, the disturbance must not be accounted for by major depressive disorder (or major depressive disorder in partial remission), that is, no major depressive disorder in the first 2 years of the disturbance (1 year for children and adolescents).

with at least three symptoms among adults) from the following: restlessness, fatigue, concentration problems, irritability, muscle tension, and sleep disturbance.

The overlap between the symptoms of MDD and DY with GAD is striking. Symptoms that appear for both mood disorders and generalized anxiety include problems with concentration, fatigue, irritability (in children and adolescents), sleep disturbance, and restlessness or agitation—fully half of the symptoms of MDD and over half of the symptoms of DY are also symptoms of GAD. The overlap of symptoms is most pronounced for DY and GAD, as a child or adolescent who meets criteria for GAD would also meet criteria for DY if he or she was experiencing irritability, and two or more symptoms among fatigue, sleep difficulties, or concentration problems.

Among the disorders listed in the DSM-IV as under consideration and warranting further study is Mixed Anxiety-Depression Disorder (see Table 28.4). The proposed category of

Table 28.3. DSM-IV Criteria for Generalized Anxiety Disorder

A. Excessive anxiety and worry (apprehensive expectations), occurring more days than not for at least 6 months, about a number of events or activities (such as work or school performance).

B. The person finds it difficult to control the worry.

C. Anxiety and worry are associated with three (or more) of the following six symptoms (with at least some symptoms present for more days than not for the past 6 months). *Note.* Only one item is required in children.
   1. Restlessness or feeling keyed up or on edge
   2. Being easily fatigued
   3. Difficulty concentrating or mind going blank
   4. Irritability
   5. Muscle tension
   6. Sleep disturbance (difficulty falling or staying asleep, or restless, unsatisfying sleep)

Additional criteria (D, E, F) rule out other Axis I disorders, effects of substance use or a general medical condition, and specify that clinically significant impairment must be present.

mixed anxiety-depression would be precluded by any history of MDD, DY, Panic Disorder, or GAD, or if criteria for any other mood or anxiety disorder were currently met. Therefore, there is an implicit assumption about the developmental sequence of the proposed Mixed Anxiety/Depression Disorder and other mood and anxiety disorders: The mixed disorder is assumed to occur before or independent of these other disorders. As is evident from a review of the proposed criteria, this disorder would be characterized by depressed or dysphoric mood, and might or might not include worry or anxiety, as worry is included as one of 10 possible symptoms, of which four are required to meet criteria for the disorder. Therefore, although the DSM-IV conceptualizes anxiety and depression as separate diagnoses, there is ample evidence of the overlap of these two conditions, even at that categorical/diagnostic level.

ASSOCIATION OF DEPRESSION AND ANXIETY: EMPIRICAL EVIDENCE

Symptoms, syndromes, or disorders of psychopathology rarely occur alone during childhood and adolescence. Nowhere is this phenomenon, referred to as the covariation or co-

Table 28.4. DSM-IV Research Criteria for Mixed Anxiety–Depressive Disorder

A. Persistent or recurrent dysphoric mood lasting at least 1 month.

B. The dysphoric mood is accompanied by at least 1 month of four (or more) of the following symptoms:
   1. Difficulty concentrating or mind going blank
   2. Sleep disturbance (difficulty falling or staying asleep, or restless unsatisfying sleep)
   3. Fatigue or low energy
   4. Irritability
   5. Worry
   6. Being easily moved to tears
   7. Hypervigilance
   8. Anticipating the worst
   9. Hopelessness (pervasive pessimism about the future)
   10. Low self-esteem or feelings or worthlessness

occurrence of symptoms and the comorbidity of disorders, more evident than for symptoms of depression and anxiety in children and youth (e.g., Angold & Costello, 1993; Brady & Kendall, 1992; Compas & Hammen, 1994). This is true across all three levels of depressive and anxious problems discussed earlier—depressed mood and anxious mood are strongly correlated, the Anxious/Depressed syndrome reflects the covariation of these symptoms, and MDD and DY are highly comorbid with anxiety disorders.

Correlation of Symptoms of Depression and Anxiety

A series of studies has shown that during childhood and adolescence, as in adulthood, depressed and anxious mood are closely related. Monomethod studies (i.e., studies relying on a single method, such as child/adolescent self-reports) have found a strong association between depressed mood (and other symptoms of depression) and anxiety (and other negative emotions, such as anger and hostility). For example, Saylor, Finch, Spirito, and Bennett (1984) found that children and adolescents classified as "high" or "low" in depressive symptoms on the CDI also differed significantly on self-reported anxiety. Furthermore, multitrait–multimethod validity studies examining reports from different informants (e.g., children/adolescents, teachers, parents) of various negative emotions (depression, anxiety, anger) have found that strong associations between child/adolescent depressed mood and other negative emotions, especially anxiety, are not limited to child/adolescent self-reports of emotions; that is, reports of child/adolescent depressed mood by each informant are correlated more highly with reports of other negative emotions by that same informant than they are correlated with reports of depressed mood obtained by other informants (e.g., Wolfe et al., 1987).

It is noteworthy that parent and teacher reports of child/adolescent emotions and behaviors also show considerable covariance in levels of depressed and anxious mood (Finch, Lipovsky, & Casat, 1989). Thus, the association of depressed mood with other elements of the broader construct of negative affectivity is not the result of a simple bias in child/adolescent reports about their internal emotional states. Finch et al. (1989) suggested that anxiety and depression are not separable in children and adolescents and that the distinction between these two forms of negative affect should be put to rest. These findings must be interpreted with a level of caution, however, as there is some item contamination between measures of depressed and anxious mood, as in several items that are included on the CDI and standard self-report scales of anxiety such as the R-CMAS (Brady & Kendall, 1992). The extent to which item similarity on these measures accounts for the degree of association between the scales was not accounted for in these early studies.

A recent study by Cole, Truglio, and Peeke (1997) addressed the problem of confounded items on measures of depressed and anxious symptoms, and also provided evidence of developmental changes in the association of these symptoms. In analyses of self-, parent, teacher, and peer reports, these authors found that a single trait model of anxiety and depression was the best fit with the data for a sample of third graders, whereas a two-factor model was a better fit than a single-factor model for a sample of sixth-grade children. Furthermore, Cole et al. (1997) found that these results held even after removing overlapping items on the measures of depressive and anxious symptoms. Thus, after controlling for confounded items, these data suggest that anxiety and depression symptoms are highly correlated and that there may be greater differentiation between anxiety and depression with age.

Anxious/Depressed Syndrome

The findings from studies using measures of symptoms of depression and anxiety are generally consistent with the results of principal components analyses of reports of parents, teachers, and adolescents that revealed the syndrome of mixed anxiety and depression symptoms discussed earlier (Achenbach, 1991). This research differs from the studies described earlier in several ways, however. First, the measures that were used (Child Behavior Checklist, CBCL; Teacher Report Form, TRF; Youth Self-Report, YSR) include a wide range of both internalizing and externalizing behavioral and emotional problems. Second, principal components analyses were conducted on large samples of clinically referred children and adolescents, with separate analyses conducted for different sex and age groups, and for each measure. Core syndromes were derived from items that were common to the versions of syndromes found for most age and sex groups for each instrument. Cross-informant syndrome constructs were then derived from the items that were common to the core syndromes for at least two informants/instruments. Eight cross-informant syndromes were derived: Withdrawn, Anxious/Depressed, Somatic Complaints, Social Problems, Thought Problems, Attention Problems, Delinquent Behavior, and Aggressive Behavior. In addition, a large number of items that are relevant to most conceptualizations of anxiety and depression did not load on any of these factors (e.g., overeating or not eating, sleep problems), while other items loaded on syndromes other than the Anxious/Depressed syndrome (e.g., "can't concentrate" loaded on the Attention Problems syndrome, and "clings to adults" loaded on the Social Problems syndrome).

Several features of these findings are noteworthy when considering the association of anxiety and depression. A syndrome of mixed symptoms of anxiety and depression was present for both boys and girls across a wide age range from childhood through adolescence, and across the reports of parents, teachers and adolescents. These findings were also replicated in a large sample of clinically referred children and youth in the Netherlands (Achenbach et al., 1987; de Groot, Koot, & Verhulst, 1994). Thus, the identification of a mixed syndrome was replicable and robust across age, sex, informant, and culture. Additional factor analyses of the items on the Anxious/Depressed syndrome have revealed interpretable factors, but these third-order factors do not correspond with traditional notions of depression and anxiety per se (Oppedisano, Compas, & Achenbach, 1998). Thus, it does not appear that the Anxious/Depressed syndrome is simply the co-occurrence of two more discrete factors that reflect anxiety and depression as conceptualized, for example, in the DSM-IV.

Subsequent research has found that the Anxious/Depressed syndrome covaries or co-occurs with other internalizing and externalizing syndromes, above and beyond the effects of informant or method variance (Hinden, Compas, Achenbach, & Howell, 1997). As expected, scores on the Anxious/Depressed syndrome are greater for girls than for boys, although this difference is far more pronounced in clinically referred than in nonreferred youth (Compas et al., 1997). Thus, gender differences, developmental changes, referral status differences, and patterns of comorbidity of the Anxious/Depressed syndrome all correspond with findings on depressive and anxious symptoms and disorders when they are measured separately.

Comorbidity of Depression and Anxiety Disorders

When depression and anxiety are measured as categorical disorders using structured diagnostic interviews to assess DSM criteria, there is considerable evidence for the comorbidity of these disorders (see reviews by Angold & Costello, 1993; Brady & Kendall, 1992;

Hammen & Compas, 1994). The rates of comorbidity have varied widely across studies, however, perhaps as a function of the type sample and the specific interview that was used. For example, Brady and Kendall (1992) reviewed seven studies (five clinic samples, one community sample, one pediatric sample) and found that among clinic samples comorbidity of depression and anxiety ranged from 28% to 62%; comorbidity in the community sample was 16%; and in the pediatric sample the comorbidity was only 1%. Angold and Costello (1993) reviewed eight studies in the United States and New Zealand, and found rates of comorbidity of anxiety and depression ranging from 30% to 75%. In a community study of 1,709 adolescents in Oregon, Lewinsohn, Rohde, Seeley, and Hops (1991) reported a 21% rate of lifetime comorbidity of depression and anxiety, which was significantly greater than chance based on prevalence odds ratios.

In spite of the wide range in estimates of comorbidity, these studies highlight three important findings. First, DSM criteria (DSM-III and DSM-III-R criteria in most studies) can be reliably applied to children and adolescents to identify individuals who meet criteria for MDD, DY, and various anxiety disorders; that is, these disorders can be reliably measured as discrete categories. Second, mood disorders and anxiety disorders are highly comorbid, with some studies suggesting that more than half of individuals with one disorder will also be positive for the other. Third, in spite of these high rates of comorbidity, the overlap between these disorders is imperfect and a significant number of children and youth can be identified with only one disorder or the other. Therefore, findings from studies of categorical diagnoses of mood and anxiety disorders suggest that these disorders are discrete and co-occur in many but not all cases.

MODELS OF THE ASSOCIATION
BETWEEN DEPRESSION AND ANXIETY

What are the implications of research on the association of anxiety and depression? Do these findings support the notion of separate constructs or disorders? Or does the evidence indicate that anxiety and depression are inseparable in young people? Several perspectives have been offered to synthesize and interpret these findings.

Separate but Comorbid Disorders

One perspective on anxiety and depression in children and adolescents is that these are in fact distinct disorders with a tendency to co-occur in many but not all affected individuals. This position is supported by findings that diagnoses of mood and anxiety disorders can be reliably applied to children and adolescents, and that the rates of comorbidity, although high, still suggest that a sizable number of young people can be identified with only one of these disorders (Hammen & Compas, 1994). When bidirectional patterns of comorbidity are considered (McConaughy & Achenbach, 1994), there is evidence that anxiety disorders in children and adolescents are more likely to co-occur with depression, while depression is less likely to co-occur with anxiety. Furthermore, longitudinal studies with clinical samples of children and youth suggest that a depressive disorder is more likely to follow than to precede an anxiety disorder (e.g., Kovacs, Gatsonis, Paulauskas, & Richards, 1989). Therefore, there is some support for the categorical perspective on depression and anxiety as separate but related disorders.

A Single, Mixed Syndrome

A second perspective is that depression and anxiety are not discrete disorders, but are shared elements of a single syndrome. The support for this perspective comes from studies of depressed and anxious mood, depressed and anxious symptoms, and mutivariate studies that have identified a syndrome of mixed anxiety and depression (Achenbach, 1991; Achenbach, Verhulst, Baron, & Akkerhuis, 1987; Verhulst & van der Ende, 1992). Evidence of a mixed syndrome is found in studies that have controlled for confounded items in measures of depression and anxiety, across different informants, and across cultures or countries. This perspective holds that although depression and anxiety are distinct in terms of their phenomenology (i.e., feeling depressed is different from feeling anxious), the occurrence of these emotions and symptoms is so strong that they are indistinguishable.

The notion of a single syndrome is also represented in the proposed category of Mixed Anxiety and Depression that was presented for consideration in the DSM-IV. This approach differs from the findings from multivariate empirical studies, however, in that depressed or dysphoric mood is proposed as a necessary symptom in the mixed category proposed in DSM-IV, accompanied by at least four of 10 other symptoms, only two of which (worry and hypervigilance) are typically associated with anxiety. Furthermore, only four of the 11 symptoms included in the proposed disorder have a counterpart on the empirically derived Anxious/Depressed syndrome (sad or unhappy mood, worrying, crying, worthlessness). Therefore, this proposed category represents a relatively different constellation of symptoms than the symptoms that have been identified in empirical analyses.

Sequential and Hierarchical Relationship

The categorical diagnostic perspective and the empirical syndrome perspective are not incompatible. They may represent different manifestations of depression and anxiety that occur in a hierarchical and sequential fashion (Compas et al., 1993). Correspondence among measures of depressed mood, the Anxious/Depressed syndrome, and mood disorders has been examined by using diagnostic interviews to assign DSM-III-R or DSM-IV diagnoses of MDD and obtaining questionnaire or behavior checklist data on the same sample of individuals. This method has been applied in several studies using self-report inventories of depressive symptoms and diagnostic interviews (e.g., Garrison, Addy, Jackson, McKeown, & Waller, 1991; Gotlib, Lewinsohn, & Seeley, 1995; Kazdin, Esveldt-Dawson, Unis, & Rancurello, 1983; Roberts, Lewinsohn, & Seeley, 1991), and studies in which behavior checklists and diagnostic interviews or other measures of DSM criteria were examined (Edelbrock & Costello, 1988; Gerhardt, Compas, Connor, & Achenbach, 1999; Rey & Morris-Yates, 1991, 1992; Weinstein, Noam, Grimes, Stone, & Schwab-Stone, 1990). Each study provides some evidence for the convergence of these different approaches; that is, all of these studies found that there was some degree of overlap, although imperfect, between children/adolescents who were elevated on measures of anxious/depressed symptoms and those who met criteria for MDD.

These studies indicate that diagnoses of MDD and DY derived from clinical interviews are related, albeit imperfectly, to both scores on self-report inventories of depressive symptoms (including depressed mood) and depressive syndrome scores from multivariate checklists. Compas et al. (1993) have proposed a hierarchical and sequential model to describe the association among depressed mood (as measured by self-report questionnaires), depressive syndromes (as measured by behavior checklists), and depressive disorders (as measured by diagnostic interviews). Each of these three levels of depressive phenomena is hypothesized to reflect a more severe manifestation of depressive problems, with depressed mood functioning as a risk for the development of the syndrome, and the syndrome functioning as a risk factor for the disorder. These data described are generally consistent with this model, although the overlap of the three levels of depressive problems is imperfect. Moreover, it is important to recognize that children/adolescents who obtain high depressive symptom scores on self-report questionnaires, who score in the clinical range on the Anxious/Depressed syndrome, or who meet DSM-IV criteria for MDD or DD, all experience significant clinical problems; that is, all of these groups are experiencing significant levels of emotional distress and substantial levels of impairment in social functioning (Gerhardt et al., 1999; Gotlib et al., 1995).

Several explanations for the relationship between the empirically derived Anxious/Depressed syndrome and a categorical diagnosis of MDD are plausible. First, anxiety and depression may be less well differentiated in children and adolescents than in adults (Cole et al., 1997). Categorical diagnoses, such as Attention-Deficit/Hyperactivity Disorder (ADHD), that have been derived specifically for children and adolescents show close correspondence with empirically derived syndromes. The empirically derived syndrome, Attention Problems, that reflects symptoms of ADHD has shown excellent sensitivity and specificity with regard to a diagnosis of ADHD (Chen, Faraone, Biederman, & Tsuang, 1994). In contrast, MDD is based on criteria derived for adults and may be less representative of disorders in adolescents. Second, the measures used to derive the empirically based syndromes may be less sensitive than clinical interviews to important variations in onset, duration, and severity of symptoms. Third, base rates of mood and anxiety disorders may be sufficiently low that they are difficult to detect using multivariate statistical methods even in relatively large samples of clinic-referred youth. Fourth, there may be subtypes of mood and anxiety disorders among adolescents, with one subtype developing out of a syndrome of mixed anxiety and depression symptoms, and a second that follows a different etiological course that is qualitatively distinct from the first subtype.

Common and Distinct Features

Findings from research on anxiety and depression in young people can be considered within the broader framework of theories of emotion (e.g., Watson & Tellegen, 1985; Watson & Clark, 1992). Extensive evidence from studies of the structure of emotions in children, adolescents, college students, and adults indicates that self-rated mood is dominated by two broad factors: *negative affect*, which is comprised of negative emotions and distress, and *positive affect* which is made up of positive emotions (King, Ollendick, & Gullone, 1991; Watson & Tellegen, 1985). Depressed and anxious mood are components of the broader construct of *negative affectivity*, whereas positive emotions are important in distinguishing among subtypes of negative emotion (Watson & Clark, 1984).

Research with adults indicates that although depressed mood is strongly intercorrelated with other negative emotions, it appears to be distinguishable from anxiety, if not other forms of negative affect, on the basis of its association with positive emotion (e.g., happiness, excitement, pride, contentment). Specifically, whereas anxiety is typically uncorrelated with positive affect, depressed mood shows a consistent inverse relationship with positive mood (Watson & Kendall, 1989). Thus, highly anxious individuals may be low, moderate, or high in positive affect, as anxiety and positive emotions can co-occur. In contrast, highly depressed individuals are likely to experience low levels of positive emotion (i.e., anhedonia). The relation between positive affect and depressed mood during adolescence warrants further research. In general, research suggests that sad or depressed mood is a phenomenologically distinct emotional state that, although closely related to the experience of other forms of negative affect, is distinguished by its relation to positive emotion (Watson & Clark, 1992).

At least two versions of a "tripartite" model of depression and anxiety have been proposed to integrate theories on the structure of emotions with findings on the covariation and co-occurrence of symptoms of depression and anxiety, and the comorbidity of depression and anxiety disorders. In the most extensively developed and researched model, Watson and Clark have proposed three components: (1) symptoms of general distress or negative affect that are relatively nonspecific—that is, they are commonly experienced by both depressed and anxious individuals; (2) symptoms of anhedonia and the absence of positive emotional experiences that are relatively specific to depression; (3) manifestations of somatic tension and arousal that are relatively specific to anxiety. All three types of symptoms must be included in a comprehensive assessment of these constructs. However, a key implication of the tripartite model is that depression and anxiety can be differentiated better by deemphasizing the importance of the nonspecific symptoms and by focusing on the two unique symptom clusters. Factor-analytic studies of this model in adults have yielded three broad factors: General distress that includes "general distress: mixed symptoms" (e.g., worried, trouble concentrating, confused irritable), "general distress: depressive symptoms" (e.g., depressed, discouraged, sad hopeless), and "general distress: anxious symptoms" (e.g., tense, uneasy, nervous, afraid); Anhedonia–Positive Affect that includes "loss of interest" (e.g., nothing enjoyable, withdrawn from others, bored, nothing interesting or fun); and "high positive affect" (e.g., happy, lot of energy, having a lot of fun, confident, hopeful about the future); and Somatic Anxiety that includes "anxious arousal" (e.g., dizzy, trembling, shaking, short of breath, dry mouth) (Watson, Weber, et al., 1995).

A slightly different perspective on the tripartite notion has been offered by Barlow and colleagues (Barlow, Chorpita, & Turovsky, 1996; Chorpita, Albano, & Barlow, 1998; Chorpita & Barlow, 1998). They proposed a 3-factor model of negative emotions, including Fear (similar to autonomic arousal), Anxiety (similar to negative affect), and Depression (similar to negative affect and depression). Chorpita et al. (1998) tested this model based on child reports on the CDI and R-CMAS and parent reports on the CBCL in a sample of children who met DSM-III-R criteria for a mood or anxiety disorder. Symptoms of fear were assessed on the CBCL (dizzy, overtired, nausea, stomach aches, vomiting) and the R-CMAS (breathlessness, tired, mad easily, poor sleep, wiggle in seat, upset stomach); symptoms of anxiety were measured on the CBCL (worries, fears impulses, needs to be perfect, nervous, tense, self-conscious), the R-CMAS (nervous, worry about harm, worry about future, worry about bedtime), and the CDI (indecision, somatic worries, worry about harm); and symptoms of depression were measured on the CBCL (rather be alone, stares blankly, sulks, underactive, unhappy, withdrawn) and the CDI (dislike being with others, feel alone, no fun at school, no friends, must push self to work, nothing is fun). A 3-factor solution that was consistent with the hypothesized model and provided the best fit with the data as compared with either 1- or 2-factor solutions (Chorpita et al., 1998).

The symptoms that comprise the Anxious/Depressed syndrome and those included in the proposed version of Mixed Anxiety/Depression in the DSM-IV correspond imperfectly with the symptoms included in the general negative affect or mixed distress factors in the tripartite models. For example, six of 12 symptoms on the Anxious/Depressed syndrome are included in the general distress factors reported by Watson et al. (1995a, 1995b; cries, nervous, fearful, guilty, sad, worries), while six items do not have counterparts (fears doing bad things, needs to be perfect, feels unloved, feels others are out to him/her, suspicious). Similarly, the items included in the Anxiety factor reported by Chorpita et al. (1998) correspond with five of the items on the Anxious/Depressed syndrome (worries, fears own impulses, needs to be perfect, nervous, self-conscious). The Depression factor reported by Chorpita et al. (1998) includes items from both the Anxious/Depressed syndrome (sad) and all of the items on this scale loaded significantly on the Withdrawn syndrome (rather be alone, stares blankly, sulks, under-active, sad, withdrawn). Similarly, all of the items on the Fear factor reported by Chorpita et al. loaded on the Somatic Complaints syndrome (dizzy, overtired, nausea, stomach aches, vomit-ing). Therefore, there appears to be some correspondence between the 3-factor model as proposed by Chorpita et al. (1998) and the three internalizing syndromes (Withdrawn, Anxious/Depressed, Somatic Complaints) identified by Achenbach (1991). This suggests that the 3-factor model proposed by Chorpita and colleagues captures the three narrowband syndromes that are part of a broadband syndrome of internalizing problems.

Weiss, Susser, and Catron (1998) have emphasized the importance of considering both the specific and nonspecific characteristics of psychopathology. The expression of any syn-drome is the combination of features common to all forms of psychopathology, features that are specific to a broadband category, features that are specific to a narrowband syndrome, and error (individual differences). Within this model, "(a) common features differentiate psycho-pathology from normality; (b) broadband-specific features differentiate the broadband syn-dromes (i.e., internalizing vs. externalizing) from each other but are common to the narrow-band syndromes within a broadband syndrome; (c) narrowband-specific features differentiate the narrowband within each of the broadband syndromes from each other (e.g., anxiety vs. depression vs. somatization); and (d) error again represents individual differences" (Weiss et al., 1998, p. 119). Therefore, negative affect may comprise a narrowband syndrome, and it may combine with somatic problems or hyperarousal, and with social withdrawal or anhedonia to form the broadband syndrome of internalizing problems.

Most recently, Rudolph et al. (1998) addressed the symptom structure of anxiety and depression using a Youth Mood and Anxiety Symptom Questionnaire (Y-MASQ), an adapta-tion of the Mood and Anxiety Symptom Questionnaire (MASQ; Watson et al., 1995) for use with children and adolescents. Using both exploratory and confirmatory factor analyses, Rudolph et al. found support for a 5-factor model of mood and anxiety symptoms in the self-reports of a community sample of over 500 nine- to 15-year-olds. The five factors included anxious arousal (e.g., dizzy, light headed; trouble getting breath), anxious apprehension (e.g., nervous, afraid), negative self-focus (e.g., "felt like other kids were better than me; felt like I was no good"), general depression (e.g., sad or down; hopeless), and positive affect (e.g., "really happy; had a lot of energy"). These findings are consistent with the tripartite model but offer further discrimination among the dimensions of mood and anxiety; that is, the physiolog-ical component of anxiety can be distinguished from worry or apprehension, and general depressive symptoms can be distinguished from the presence or absence of positive affect.

MOVING TOWARD A DEVELOPMENTAL MODEL OF ANXIETY AND DEPRESSION

An important next step in the understanding the relationship between anxiety and depression in young people involves closer consideration of developmental processes that may be involved in this relationship. Two issues are most salient. First, does the relationship between anxiety and depression change with development? And second, what are the biolog-ical, psychological, and environmental factors involved in this relationship over the course of childhood and adolescence?

The data that support the sequential–hierarchical model relationship between anxiety and depression and those that support the common and distinct features models can be combined when viewed from a developmental perspective; that is, there may be developmental changes in the capacity to experience anxiety and depression, with capacity for anxiety emerging early in development, followed by the capacity for mixed anxiety and depression, and finally for a syndrome that is reflected primarily in symptoms of depression (Chorpita & Barlow, 1998; Rudolph, 1998). Although evidence for this developmental sequence is still preliminary, some findings suggest that the common features of anxiety and depression may emerge before the distinct expression of these separate disorders occurs. For example, Cole et al. (1997) found that a single, mixed factor of anxiety and depression provides the best fit for younger children, and a 2-factor solution provides a better fit with older children. However, the data on such a developmental progression in symptom expression are far from consistent. For example, Achenbach (1991) did not find developmental differences in the structure of the Anxious/Depressed syndrome in children and adolescents. This issue remains a high priority for future research.

Recent conceptualizations of depression and anxiety have pointed to several processes that may influence the developmental course of mood and anxiety symptoms, and disorders during childhood and adolescence. Rudolph (1998) has proposed that, for example, helplessness/hopelessness theory can be used to derive hypotheses regarding the sequence of anxiety and depression during childhood and adolescence. Early stressful experiences that occur under conditions of uncontrollability and uncertain helplessness may contribute to the development of anxiety during early childhood (Alloy, Kelly, Mineka, & Clements, 1990; Chorpita & Barlow, 1998). These early experiences may be followed by a sense of certain helplessness and uncertain hopelessness that is associated with the experience of mixed anxiety and depression (Alloy et al., 1990; Rudolph, 1998). Finally, after repeated stressful experiences and the development of patterns of negative cognitive interpretations of these events, a sense of certain helplessness combined with certain hopelessness may emerge, leading to a more purely depressive syndrome (Alloy et al., 1990; Rudolph, 1998). Consistent with this model, Cole et al. (1998) found that in a community sample of school-age children, symptoms of anxiety predicted subsequent symptoms of depression even after controlling for initial levels of depressive symptoms. This pattern held up in both children's self-reports and in parents' reports of their children's symptoms.

Recent evidence also points to the role of both biological and environmental factors in the relationship between anxiety and depression. Using behavioral genetics methods in analyzing data from a large twin study, Eley (1997a, 1997b) reported that shared and nonshared environmental factors, as well as genetic factors, are involved in the development of symptoms of anxiety and depression, as well as in the correlation between these symptoms. Specifically, nonshared environmental factors accounted for the majority of the variance ($>$ 50%) in both anxiety and depression symptoms. Genes accounted for a greater portion of the variance in depressive symptoms (approximately 30%) than anxiety symptoms (approximately 10%); conversely, shared environmental factors accounted for more of the variance in anxiety ($>$ 30%) than depressive symptoms (between 10% and 20%). However, genes accounted for the vast majority (approximately 80%) of the correlation between anxiety and depression symptoms (Eley, 1997b). These analyses suggest that both environmental and genetic factors play a role in the development of depression and anxiety, and an even greater role in the association between these symptoms. Therefore, there may be genetic factors that account for nonspecific effects in the development of internalizing symptoms of both anxiety and depression, while exposure to certain types of environmental experiences may determine the degree to which symptoms of anxiety, depression, or both, are manifested. This suggests that there may be developmental differences in exposure to environmental factors that contribute to depression as opposed to anxiety, and/or in the cognitive processes that lead to the interpretation of environmental experiences that lead to one or the other type of symptoms. Further research is needed to determine if the effects of genes and environment on the expression of anxiety and depression vary with development. Furthermore, behavioral genetic research using measures of the unique and shared features of anxiety and depression should be a high priority.

SUMMARY AND CONCLUSIONS

The research reviewed here clearly indicates that a significant number of children and adolescents are likely to experience and to present clinically with a mixture of symptoms of anxiety and depression. Several initial conclusions can be drawn from the research to date. The meaning of this mixture of symptoms is far from clear, however, in terms of its implications for understanding the structure of psychopathology in young people or for the assessment and treatment of child/adolescent psychopathology, and further research is needed.

A significant number of children and adolescents can be identified who meet DSM-IV diagnostic criteria for mood and anxiety disorders using structured diagnostic interviews. Moreover, these disorders are highly comorbid, with anxiety disorders likely to precede major depression in initial onset. In spite of evidence that mood and anxiety disorders can be identified in young people, it is also clear that an even larger number of children and adolescents can be identified who are characterized by a mixture of symptoms of anxiety and depression that do not conform to DSM-IV criteria. This syndrome of mixed anxiety and depression is associated with impairment in social and academic functioning, and is strongly associated with referral for mental health services. Therefore, mixed anxiety and depression symptoms are highly prevalent and clinically significant in their impact on children's functioning and well being.

The tripartite model of depression and anxiety proposed by Watson, Clark, and colleagues, and a similar model investigated by Chorpita et al. (1998), appears to be promising in increasing our understanding of the shared and unique features of anxiety and depression. A core syndrome of negative affect may represent the shared component of anxiety and depression, while other symptoms may distinguish between them. Anxiety may be associated with physiological arousal or somatic symptoms, while depression may be associated with anhedonia or social withdrawal. Furthermore, anxiety and depression may become increasingly differentiated with age, and symptoms of mixed anxiety and depression may precede the onset of the full manifestation of an anxiety disorder or major depression, or may represent a link between the early development of anxiety and the later development of depression. These processes warrant continued research to clarify the role of mixed anxiety and depression in developmental psychopathology.

REFERENCES

Achenbach, T. M. (1985). *Assessment and taxonomy of child and adolescent psychopathology*. Newbury Park, CA: Sage.

Achenbach, T. M. (1991). *Integrative guide for the 1991 CBCL/4–18, YSR, and TRF profiles*. Burlington: University of Vermont, Department of Psychiatry.

Achenbach, T. M. (1993). *Empirically based taxonomy*. Burlington: University of Vermont, Department of Psychiatry.

Achenbach, T. M., McConaughy, S. H., & Howell, C. T. (1987). Child/adolescent behavioral and emotional problems: Implications of cross-informant correlations for situational specificity. *Psychological Bulletin, 101*, 213–232.

Achenbach, T. M., Verhulst, F. C., Baron, D. C., & Akkerhuis, G. W. (1987). Epidemiological comparisons of American and Dutch children: I. Behavioral/emotional problems and competencies reported by parents for ages 4 to 16. *Journal of the American Academy of Child and Adolescent Psychiatry, 26,* 317–325.

Alloy, L. B., Kelly, K. A., Mineka, S., & Clements, C. M. (1990). Comorbidity of anxiety and depressive disorders: A helplessness-hopelessness perspective. In J. D. Maser & R. C. Cloninger (Eds.), *Comorbidity of mood and anxiety disorders* (pp. 499–543). Washington, DC: American Psychiatric Association.

American Psychiatric Association. (1994). *Diagnostic and statistical manual of mental disorders* (4th ed.). Washington, DC: Author.

Angold, A. (1988). Childhood and adolescent depression: I. Epidemiological and aetiological aspects. *British Journal of Psychiatry, 152,* 601–617.

Angold, A., & Costello, E. J. (1993). Depressive comorbidity in children and adolescent: Empirical, theoretical, and methodological issues. *American Journal of Psychiatry, 150,* 1779–1791.

Angold, A., & Rutter, M. (1992). Effects of age and pubertal status on depression in a large clinical sample. *Development and Psychopathology, 4,* 5-28.

Barlow, D. H., Chorpita, B. F., & Turovsky, J. (1996). Fear, panic, anxiety, and the disorders of emotion. In D. A. Hope (Ed.), *Nebraska Symposium on Motivation: Perspectives on anxiety, panic, and fear* (Vol. 43, pp. 251–328). Lincoln: University of Nebraska Press.

Barrios, B. A., & Hartmann, D. P. (1997). Fears and anxieties. In E. J. Mash & L. G. Terdal, (Eds.) *Assessment of childhood disorders* (3rd ed., pp. 230–327). New York: Guilford Press.

Brady, E. U., & Kendall, P. C. (1992). Comorbidity of anxiety and depression in children and adolescents. *Psychological Bulletin, 111,* 244–255.

Cantwell, D. P., & Baker, L. (1991). Manifestations of depressive affect in adolescence. *Journal of Youth and Adolescence, 20,* 121–133.

Carlson, G. A. (1994). Adolescent bipolar disorder: Phenomenology and treatment implications. In W. M. Reynolds & H. F. Johnston (Eds.), *Handbook of depression in children and adolescents* (pp. 41–60). New York: Plenum Press.

Chen, W. J., Faraone, S. V., Biederman, J., & Tsuang, M. T. (1994). Diagnostic accuracy of the Child Behavior Checklist scales for attention-deficit hyperactivity disorder: A receiver-operating characteristic analysis. *Journal of Consulting and Clinical Psychology, 62,* 1017-1025.

Chorpita, B. F., Albano, A. M., & Barlow, D. H. (1998). The structure of negative emotions in a clinical sample of children and adolescents. *Journal of Abnormal Psychology, 197,* 74–85.

Chorpita, B. F., & Barlow, D. H. (1998). The development of anxiety: The role of control in the early environment. *Psychological Bulletin, 124,* 3–21.

Cole, D., Martin, J., Powers, B., & Truglio, R. (1996). Modeling causal relations between academic and social competence and depression: A multitrait–multimethod longitudinal study of children. *Journal of Abnormal Psychology, 105,* 258–270.

Cole, D. A., Peeke, L. G., Lachlan, G., Martin, J. M., Truglio, R., & Seroczynski, A. D. (1998). A longitudinal look at the relation between depression and anxiety in children and adolescents. *Journal of Consulting and Clinical Psychology, 66,* 451–460.

Cole, D. A., Truglio, R., & Peeke, L. (1997). Relation between symptoms of anxiety and depression in children: A multitrait–multimethod–multigroup investigation. *Journal of Consulting and Clinical Psychology, 65,* 110–119.

Compas, B. E. (1997). Depression in children and adolescents. In E. J. Mash & L. G. Terdal (Eds.), *Assessment of childhood disorders* (3rd ed., pp. 190–229). New York: Guilford Press.

Compas, B. E., Connor, J. K., & Hinden, B. R (1998). New perspectives on depression during adolescence. In R. Jessor (Ed.), *New perspectives on problem behavior in adolescence* (pp. 319–362). New York: Cambridge University Press.

Compas, B. E., Ey, S., & Grant, K. E. (1993). Taxonomy and assessment of depression during adolescence. *Psychological Bulletin, 114,* 323–344.

Compas, B. E., & Hammen, C. L. (1994). Child and adolescent depression: Covariation and comorbidity in development. In R. J. Haggerty, L. R. Sherrod, N. Garmezy, & M. Rutter (Eds.), *Stress, risk, and resilience in children and adolescents: Processes, mechanisms, and interventions* (pp. 225–267). New York: Cambridge University Press.

Compas, B. E., Oppedisano, G., Connor, J. K., Gerhardt, C. A., Hinden, B., Achenbach, T. M., & Hammen, C. (1997). Gender differences in depressive symptoms in adolescence: Comparison of national samples of clinically-referred and non-referred youth. *Journal of Consulting and Clinical Psychology, 65,* 617–626.

Coyne, J. C., & Downey, G. (1991). Social factors and psychopathology: Stress, social support, and coping processes. *Annual Review of Psychology, 42,* 401–425.

de Groot, A., Koot, H. M., & Verhulst, F. C. (1994). Cross-cultural generalizability of the Child Behavior Checklist cross-informant syndromes. *Psychological Assessment, 6,* 225–230.

Edelbrock, C., & Costello, A. J. (1988). Convergence between statistically derived behavior problem syndromes and child psychiatric diagnoses. *Journal of Abnormal Child Psychology, 16,* 219–231.

Eley, T. C. (1997a). Depressive symptoms in children and adolescents: Etiological links between normality and abnormality. *Journal of Child Psychology and Psychiatry and Allied Disciplines, 38,* 861–866.

Eley, T. C. (1997b). General genes: A new theory in developmental psychopathology. *Current Directions in Psychological Science, 6,* 90–95.

Fechner-Bates, S., Coyne, J. C., & Schwenk, T. L. (1994). The relationship of self-reported distress to depressive disorders and other psychopathology. *Journal of Consulting and Clinical Psychology, 62,* 550–559.

Finch, A. J., Lipovsky, J. A., & Casat, C. D. (1989). Anxiety and depression in children and adolescents: Negative affectivity or separate constructs? In P. C. Kendall & D. Watson (Eds.), *Anxiety and depression: Distinctive and overlapping features* (pp. 171–202). New York: Academic Press.

Garrison, C. Z., Addy, C. L., Jackson, K. L., McKeown, R. E., & Waller, R. (1991). The CES-D as a screen for depression and other psychiatric disorders in adolescents. *Journal of the American Academy of Child and Adolescent Psychiatry, 30,* 636–641.

Garrison, C. Z., Jackson, K. L., Marstellar, F., McKeown, R. E., & Addy, C. (1990). A longitudinal study of depressive symptomatology in young adolescents. *Journal of the American Academy of Child and Adolescent Psychiatry, 29,* 581–585.

Gerhardt, C., Compas, B. E., Connor, J., & Achenbach, T. M. (1999). Association of a mixed anxiety-depression syndrome and symptoms of major depressive disorder during adolescence. *Journal of Youth and Adolescence, 28,* 305–323.

Gotlib, I. H., Lewinsohn, P. M., & Seeley, J. R. (1995). Symptoms versus diagnosis of depression: Differences in psychosocial functioning. *Journal of Consulting and Clinical Psychology, 65,* 90–100.

Hammen, C. & Compas, B. E. (1994). Unmasking unmasked depression in children and adolescents: The problem of comorbidity. *Clinical Psychology Review, 14,* 585–603.

Hammen, C. L., & Rudolph, K. (1996). Childhood depression. In E. J. Mash & R. A. Barkley (Eds.), *Child psychopathology.* New York: Guilford Press.

Hinden, B., Compas, B. E., Achenbach, T. M., Hammen, C., Oppedisano, G., Connor, J. K., & Gerhardt, C. A. (1998). *Charting the course of depressive symptoms during adolescence: Do we have the right map?* Manuscript submitted for publication.

Hinden, B., Compas, B. E., Howell, D. C., & Achenbach, T. M. (1997). Comorbidity of depression during adolescence: Separating fact from artifact. *Journal of Consulting and Clinical Psychology, 65,* 6–14.

Jensen, P. S., Watanabe, H. K., Richters, J. E., Roper, M., Hibbs, E. D., Salzberg, A. D., & Liu, S. (1996). Scales, diagnoses, and child psychopathology: II. Comparing the CBCL and DISC against external validators. *Journal of Abnormal Child Psychology, 24,* 151–168.

Joiner, T. E., Catanzaro, S. J., & Laurent, J. (1996). Tripartite structure of positive and negative affect, depression, and anxiety in child and adolescent psychiatric inpatients. *Journal of Abnormal Psychology, 105,* 401–409.

Kandel, D. B., & Davies, M. (1982). Epidemiology of depressive mood in adolescents. *Archives of General Psychiatry, 39,* 1205–1212.

Kandel, D. B., & Davies, M. (1986). Adult sequelae of adolescent depressive symptoms. *Archives of General Psychiatry, 43,* 255–262.

Kashani, J. H., Carlson, G. A., Beck, N. C., Hoeper, E. W., Corcoran, C. M., McAllister, J. A., Fallahi, C., Rosenberg, T. K., & Reid, J. C. (1987). Depression, depressive symptoms, and depressed mood among a community sample of adolescents. *American Journal of Psychiatry, 144,* 931–934.

Kazdin, A. E. (1994). Informant variability in the assessment of childhood depression. In W. M. Reynolds & H. F. Johnston (Eds.), *Handbook of depression in children and adolescents* (pp. 249–271). New York: Plenum Press.

Kazdin, A. E., Esveldt-Dawson, K., Unis, A. S., & Rancurello, M. D. (1983). Child and parent evaluations of depression and aggression in psychiatric inpatient children. *Journal of Abnormal Child Psychology, 11,* 401–413.

King, N. J., Ollendick, T. H., & Gallone, E. (1991). Negative affectivity in children and adolescents: Relations between anxiety and depression. *Clinical Psychology Review, 11,* 441–460.

Kovacs, M. (1980). Rating scales to assess depression in school-aged children. *Acta Paedopsychiatrica, 46,* 305–315.

Kovacs, M. (1989). Affective disorders in children and adolescents. *American Psychologist, 44,* 209–215.

Kovacs, M., Akiskal, H. S., Gatsonis, C., & Parrone, P. L. (1994). Childhood-onset dysthymic disorder: Clinical features and prospective naturalistic outcome. *Archives of General Psychiatry, 51,* 365–374.

Kovacs, M., Feinberg, T. L., Crouse-Novak, M. A., Paulauskas, S. L., & Finkelstein, R. (1984). Depressive disorders in childhood: I. A longitudinal prospective study of Characteristics and recovery. *Archives of General Psychiatry, 41,* 229–237.

Kovacs, M., Gatsonis, C., Paulauskas, S. L., & Richards, C. (1989). Depressive disorders in childhood: IV. A longitudinal study of comorbidity with and risk for anxiety disorders. *Archives of General Psychiatry, 46,* 776–782.

Lewinsohn, P. M., Hops, H., Roberts, R. E., Seeley, J. R., & Andrews, J. A. (1993). Adolescent Psychopathology: I. Prevalence and incidence of depression and other DSM-III-R disorders in high school students. *Journal of Abnormal Psychology, 102,* 133–144.

Lewinsohn, P. M., Rohde, P., Seeley, J. R., & Hops, H. (1991). Comorbidity of unipolar depression: I. Major depression with dysthymia. *Journal of Abnormal Psychology, 100,* 205–213.

McConaughy, S. H., & Achenbach, T. M. (1994). Comorbidity of empirically based syndromes in matched general population and clinical samples. *Journal of Clinical Child Psychology and Psychiatry and Allied Disciplines, 35,* 1141–1157.

McGee, R., Feehan, M., Williams, S., Partridge, F., Silva, P., & Kelly, J. (1990). DSM-III disorders in a large sample of adolescents. *Journal of the American Academy of Child and Adolescent Psychiatry, 29,* 611–619.

Nurcombe, B., Seifer, R., Scioli, A., Tramontana, M. G., Grapentine, W. L., & Beauchesne, H. C. (1989). Is major depressive disorder in adolescence a distinct entity? *Journal of the American Academy of Child and Adolescent Psychiatry, 28,* 333–342.

Oppedisano, G., Compas, B. E., & Achenbach, T. M. (1998). *Further analysis of the structure of the anxious/ depressed syndrome of the Child Behavior Checklist and Youth Self-Report.* Unpublished manuscript.

Petersen, A. C., Compas, B. E., Brooks-Gunn, J., Stemmler, M., Ey, S., & Grant, K. E. (1993). Depression in adolescence. *American Psychologist, 48,* 155–168.

Petersen, A. C., Sarigiani, P. A., & Kennedy, R. E. (1991). Adolescent depression: Why more girls? *Journal of Youth and Adolescence, 20,* 247–271.

Rey, J. M., & Morris-Yates, A. (1991). Adolescent depression and the Child Behavior Checklist. *Journal of the American Academy of Child and Adolescent Psychiatry, 30,* 423–427.

Rey, J. M., & Morris-Yates, A. (1992). Diagnostic accuracy in adolescents of several depression rating scales extracted from a general purpose behavior checklist. *Journal of Affective Disorders, 27,* 281–287.

Reynolds, C. R., & Richmond, B. O. (1978). What I think and feel: A revised measure of children's manifest anxiety. *Journal of Abnormal Child Psychology, 6,* 271–280.

Roberts, R. E., Lewinsohn, P. M., & Seeley, J. R. (1991). Screening for adolescent depression: A comparison of depression scales. *Journal of the American Academy of Child and Adolescent Psychiatry, 30,* 58–66.

Rohde, P., Lewinsohn, P. M., & Seeley, J. R. (1991). Comorbidity of unipolar depression: II. Comorbidity with other mental disorders in adolescents and adults. *Journal of Abnormal Psychology, 100,* 214–222.

Rudolph, K. D. (1998). *An integrative, developmental conceptualization of the relationship between anxiety and depression.* Manuscript submitted for publication.

Rudolph, K. D., Osborne, L., Lambert, S., & Gathright, T. (1998). *A developmental analysis of symptom structure of anxiety and depression.* Manuscript submitted for publication.

Saylor, C. F., Finch, A. J., Spirito, A., & Bennett, B. (1984). The Children's Depression Inventory: A systematic evaluation of psychometric properties. *Journal of Consulting and Clinical Psychology, 52,* 955–967.

Verhulst, F. C., & van der Ende, J. (1992). Six-year developmental course of internalizing and externalizing problem behaviors. *Journal of the American Academy of Child and Adolescent Psychiatry, 31,* 924–931.

Watson, D., & Clark, L. (1984). Negative affectivity: The disposition to experience aversive emotional states. *Psychological Bulletin, 96,* 465–490.

Watson, D., & Clark, L. A. (1992). Affects separable and inseparable: On the hierarchical arrangement of the negative affects. *Journal of Personality and Social Psychology, 62,* 489–505.

Watson, D., Clark, L. A., & Carey, G. (1988). Positive and negative affectivity and their relation to anxiety and depressive disorders. *Journal of Abnormal Psychology, 97,* 346–353.

Watson, D. & Kendall, P. C. (1989). Common and differentiating features of anxiety and depression: Current findings and future directions. In P. C. Kendall & D. Watson (Eds.), *Anxiety and depression: Distinctive and overlapping features* (pp. 493–508). New York: Academic Press.

Watson, D. & Tellegen, A. (1985). Toward a consensual structure of mood. *Psychological Bulletin, 98,* 219–235.

Watson, D., Weber, K., Assenheimer, J. S., Clark, L. A., Strauss, M. E., & McCormick, R. A. (1995). Testing a tripartite model: I. Evaluating the convergent and discriminant validity of mood and anxiety scales. *Journal of Abnormal Psychology, 104,* 3–14.

Weinstein, S. R., Noam, G. G., Grimes, K., Stone, K., & Schwab-Stone, M. (1990). Convergence of DSM-III diagnoses and self-reported symptoms in child and adolescent inpatients. *Journal of the American Academy of Child and Adolescent Psychiatry, 29,* 627–634.

Weiss, B., Susser, K., & Catron, T. (1998). Common and specific features of childhood psychopathology. *Journal of Abnormal Psychology, 107,* 118–127.

Wolfe, V. V., Finch, A. J., Saylor, C. F., Blount, R. L., Pallmeyer, T. P., & Carek, D. J. (1987). Negative affectivity in children: A multitrait–multimethod investigation. *Journal of Consulting and Clinical Psychology, 55,* 245–250.

World Health Organization. (1990). *International classification of diseases and health related problems (ICD-10).* Geneva: Author.

29

Obsessions and Compulsions

The Developmental and Familial Context

Alice S. Carter and Rachel A. Pollock

In this chapter we describe developmental and clinical characteristics of obsessionality and ritualistic behaviors, highlighting both pathologic and nonpathological expressions in childhood and adolescence. We define and discuss obsessional thoughts and compulsions, ritualistic behavior, and obsessive compulsive disorder (OCD) from a developmental perspective that places these behaviors in the familial context. With respect to OCD, we review empirical and theoretical literature that addresses clinical characteristics and phenomenology, observed age and gender effects in clinical populations, epidemiological studies, and issues of comorbidity. Finally, we propose a developmental model that begins with the emergence of early ritualistic behavior and suggests pathways to normative and maladaptive obsessional outcomes.

Despite the increased research attention on obsessionality in adult clinical populations (e.g., Jenike, 1989), we focus on studies that pertain to children and adolescents. Similar to the adult literature, the vast majority of information derives from research on the disordered state; however, we review the current knowledge about OCD in childhood and adolescence as well as the limited number of studies that address typical variation. Though obsessive compulsive personality disorder (OCPD) has often been described along a continuum of obsessionality, there is good evidence to suggest that OCD and OCPD are distinct clinical entities and that obsessionality is not a hallmark feature of OCPD (Carter, Pauls & Leckman, 1995). Moreover, given our focus on children and adolescents, and on the fact that personality disorders are not typically diagnosed in younger populations (DSM-IV; American Psychiatric Association, 1994), OCPD will not be discussed.

Alice S. Carter and Rachel A. Pollock • Department of Psychology, Yale University, New Haven, Connecticut 06520-8205.

Handbook of Developmental Psychopathology, Second Edition, edited by Arnold J. Sameroff, Michael Lewis, and Suzanne M. Miller. Kluwer Academic/Plenum Publishers, New York, 2000.

OBSESSIONS

Obsessions are repetitive, intrusive thoughts, images, and ideational impulses that can lead to significant subjective distress. Obsessions are typically experienced as uncontrollable. The content of obsessions may appear pointless, out of sync with day-to-day tasks, and/or bizarre, inappropriate, violent, repulsive, or obscene (Rachman, 1985). The obsessional thoughts are unwanted, and individuals with frequent obsessions commonly attempt to resist or dismiss the obsessions or to neutralize them with another thought or action (e.g., compulsion) (Hoogduin, 1986; Insel, 1984; Rachman, 1985).

Obsessions are not unique to individuals suffering from OCD. Rather, they are experienced by a majority of individuals in the general population and across numerous forms of psychopathology (March, Leonard, & Swedo, 1995a; Riddle et al., 1990; Turner, Beidel, & Stanley, 1992). Obsessional ideation can be distinguished from cognitions or cognitive styles that are characteristic of other psychiatric disorders. In contrast to unwanted and disturbing thoughts observed in psychotic processes (e.g., thought insertion), obsessions are understood and experienced as being internally produced rather than externally imposed. For example, in a psychotic process, an individual may experience distress from hearing "critical" voices and believing that the voices are emanating from real and outside sources. An obsessional thought about needing to confess any and every rule violation may also cause distress, though in this case, the individual is usually aware that the thought is a production of his or her own thinking. Obsessions are also distinct from the excessive worries that typify generalized anxiety disorder (GAD) (e.g., worry about finances, completing daily tasks, getting to appointments on time). The cognitions associated with GAD are future oriented and usually lack the stereotyped or ritualistic behaviors often complementing obsessions. Furthermore, obsessionality is often about feared consequences that are immediate and time-limited. It is not uncommon to observe both patterns of anxious cognitions in the same individual. As discussed later, OCD and other anxiety psychopathology often co-occur.

While the content of some obsessions may be extremely anxiety provoking (e.g., sexual or aggressive images involving loved ones), the content of obsessions does not appear to discriminate between pathological and nonpathological obsessions. In the adult literature, the major distinction between nonimpairing and pathological obsessions involves the degree of distress and amount of time that is associated with efforts to resist, regulate, neutralize, and/or suppress the intrusive thoughts (Rachman & Hodgson, 1978; Salkovskis & Harris, 1984). In nonpathological forms, an occasional disturbing thought may be intrusive or invasive, but it may be dismissed without lasting consequences and persistent anxiety. Similar findings have been reported for adolescents (Flament et al., 1990). There is some evidence that the degree of distress caused by intrusive thoughts is influenced by cognitive information processing, which includes attentional biases, appraisal processes, attributions about the content of the thoughts, and the role of the self in relation to these thoughts (Bolton, 1996; England & Dickerson, 1988; Leonard, Goldberger, Rapoport, Cheslow, & Swedo, 1990; Parkinson & Rachman, 1981; Salkovskis, 1985). For example, investigators have argued that perceived controllability, assumed (and overestimated) responsibility, self-criticism and blame for thought content, and the unacceptability of thoughts or images distinguish pathological and nonpathologic forms of obsessions (e.g., Rachman & Hodgson, 1978; Salkovskis, 1985; Turner, Beidel & Stanley, 1992). Thus, a better understanding of normative developmental processes regarding attributions of responsibility (i.e., internal–external), controllability, and stability should inform our understanding of a child's or adolescent's risk for specific maladaptive obsessions. Fearful and particularly salient attributions, such as potential harm to a family member, are likely to influence the appraisal and subsequent degree of interference associated with obsessional ideation in childhood. In addition, information-processing styles may be associated with cognitive distortions that give rise to feelings of helplessness about pathological obsessions and may contribute to risk for maintained rumination and concomitant disorders such as depression (Rehm & Carter, 1990).

As young children depend on parents and other caregivers for interpreting their experiences, parental reactions may influence a child's cognitive and affective interpretation of intrusive ideation. This may be particularly true for very young children who have not developed metacognitive capacities. Thus, studying parental cognitive information-processing styles may help to identify critical predictors of later child adaptation and information-processing styles. Parental response to and management of early emerging and potentially maladaptive ideation may influence the subsequent severity and maintenance of similar thoughts in the child. For example, a parent who reacts to a child's sharing of an unwanted, intrusive thought with extreme distress may heighten the child's own sense of distress about the thought. Similarly, through repeated inquiry about the presence of certain thoughts, a parent may focus the child's attention on the specific intrusive thoughts and may subsequently create a hypervigilance and heightened awareness regarding such thoughts. Children may then withdraw for fear of the consequences (real or imagined) of sharing disturbing imagery with parents. Parental response to withdrawal may be as critical to later functioning as the more overt response to a shared image or thought. A parent who accepts the withdrawal may unintentionally communicate disinterest or corroborate evidence of the cognition's deviance to the child. In contrast, a parent may recognize a child's withdrawal behavior as a function of distress, draw out the problematic thought, and normalize or minimize the salience of the negative experience and feared consequences.

COMPULSIONS AND RITUALISTIC BEHAVIORS

Compulsions involve repetitive behaviors or mental activities that are employed to diminish anxiety, distress, or tension (DSM-IV; American Psychiatric Association, 1994). Typical pathological compulsions involve perseverative checking, hand washing, hoarding, and cleaning. Common mental activities include counting and/or repetitively chanting specific words. The particular compulsive behaviors and mental activities are not inherently goal directed or rewarding. In older children and adolescents, compulsions are commonly employed in response to a specific and significant anxiety-generating obsession. The performance of overt or covert mental rituals may serve to relieve anxiety, restore safety in a perceived dangerous state, or prevent harm when harm is the believed inevitable outcome (Rachman, 1976). However, even in these instances, maladaptive compulsive behaviors may not be functionally related to an obsessive thought (e.g., hand washing in response to an obsessional thought about being exposed to germs). It has been suggested that belief in the efficacy of the compulsion to ward off or minimize anxiety associated with an obsession is akin to the kind of magical thinking that is observed in the preschool years (e.g., "If I sit very still, no one will see me") and/or superstitious beliefs typical of children in the early school years (e.g., "Step on a crack and break your mother's back") (Bolton, 1996). While a child's use of magical thinking, often associated with game playing, appears developmentally appropriate, individuals engaging in compulsions are usually aware that the behaviors and mental activities are not realistically linked to the source of distress, and the compulsions are viewed neither as fun nor as a game.

Pathological compulsions are performed to excess and inflexible, and the repetition appears purposeless to an observer. Many individuals with pathological obsessions need to begin a very specific sequence of behaviors (compulsions) repeated over multiple trials, until the sequence is performed perfectly, or until it feels "just right" (e.g., dressing, making a bed, brushing teeth, applying makeup). To the child, the rituals are of great importance; if done incompletely or out of order, the ramifications are likely quite malignant, requiring repetition until performance is "just so." In pathological forms, the behaviors and mental activities can consume hours of the child's or adolescent's day and can disrupt interpersonal relationships, physical health, and occupational functioning. For example, a parent of a 4-year-old at familial risk for OCD described her daughter's recent visit to a relative's home, where she repeatedly and incessantly checked under the bed to ensure that there were no monsters. This behavior endured for 7 hours. Visual feedback and parental assurance that there were in fact no monsters present proved ineffective in diminishing the checking behavior.

In nonpathological forms, there is a lack of subjective distress associated with the compulsions, and the rituals are typically related to functionally realistic obsessions. Moreover, nonpathological compulsions are brief in duration and not performed in a repetitive or redundant manner, and may result in an experience of relief or pleasure. These behaviors may serve an adaptive and goal-directed function. For example, a child may always check all of his or her math problems once again, prior to moving on to the next page of a test, minimizing careless errors or skipped problems. An individual may have repetitive thoughts associated with safety and health concerns that are connected to engaging in protective checking, cleaning, or hoarding activities. Such activities may serve the beneficial role of engendering a sense of safety and security in family members or the broader community. When these behaviors begin to impair the child in daily activities, an adaptive routine becomes pathological. If a child were to check each math problem seven times, he or she would likely not complete the test. An adaptive tooth brushing ritual (e.g., once after every meal) may serve to minimize cavities and promote oral hygiene. However, a child who brushes his or her teeth for 2 hours in the morning and 2 hours at night is likely to suffer damage to the gums. It has been suggested that nonpathological forms of checking reflect an effort to establish control over the environment (Frost, Sher, & Geen, 1986), while nonpathological cleaning behaviors may involve restorative efforts rather than a concern with controlling future harm (Rachman & Hodgson, 1980). This understanding of nonpathological obsessions may inform our understanding of cognitive biases that may be associated with pathological forms as well.

COGNITIVE DEVELOPMENTAL PERSPECTIVES

From a cognitive developmental perspective, repeating behaviors and activities, adhering to rules, and enacting rituals are important components of typical development. Piaget (1962) discussed the critical role that repetition serves in the first year of life with respect to creating and maintaining new schemata (i.e., integrated perceptual and motor action patterns). Piaget described developmentally appropriate repetition as pursuit of a concrete and obtainable goal. Piaget also suggested that when infants begin to have the capacity for imitation, repetition forms the basis for many novel reciprocal games (e.g., waving bye-bye). Viewing adaptive, repetitive behaviors as goal oriented allows a definition of maladaptive obsessional behavior to emerge. In this light, and independent of subjective accounts of distress or interference, the detection of maladaptive repetitive behaviors in younger children may be enhanced, as rituals lacking goal direction are identified.

More recent cognitive developmental studies of repetition or response inhibition have viewed perseveration as a component of the broader set of executive functions associated with frontal lobe development and dysfunction (e.g., Diamond & Taylor, 1996; Welsh, Pennington, & Groisser, 1991; Zelazo, Carter, Reznick, & Frye, 1997). For example, in a card-sorting task, preschoolers often fail to inhibit the motor response of pointing to an incorrect response. Specifically, when sorting by shape after several trials of sorting by color, children may perseverate and continue to employ the previously learned color rule despite their ability to verbalize the correct rule and response (Zelazo & Frye, 1996). It is not clear whether individual variation in the acquisition of these normative cognitive and motor inhibition skills is associated with the development of obsessions and compulsions. Of interest around this age, when children typically show a dissociation between rule knowledge and rule use, they are at the same time exploring and rehearsing the use of rules in their everyday environments. It is common that at approximately age 2.5 years, children often insist on or become rigid regarding food habits, dressing, and bedtime routines.

Anna Freud (1965) noted the emergence of repetitive behaviors while observing young children. Furthermore, and consistent with Freud's early observations, Gesell, Ames, and Ilg (1974) noted that at 2.5 years of age, there appears a qualitative shift in toddlers' interest in maintaining routines. The authors described a toddler's use of rituals (e.g., insisting a bedtime story be read "just so" or requiring that the stuffed animals be lined up in a specific way prior to a kiss good night) to minimize anxiety and heighten feelings of mastery and control. In addition, Geselle and colleagues observed that toddlers were most likely to insist on "sameness" during potentially stressful transitions or separations (e.g., bedtime). Adams (1973), similarly supported the view that early rituals were adaptive for warding off uncertainty and unpredictability. In the same manner that young children's rituals serve to organize a sense of efficacy in the environment, adult obsessions and compulsions may be employed adaptively to gain control over the environment (Frost et al., 1986) and prevent future harm (Rachman & Hodgson, 1978).

Recently, an empirical study of rituals and repetitive behavior examined developmental changes between 8 and 72 months of age and addressed questions regarding the frequency, intensity, and age of onset of specific ritualistic behaviors (Evans, Leckman, King, Henshaw, & Alsobrook, 1995). Supporting Geselle et al.'s (1974) observations, children ages 2, 3, and 4 years had significantly higher frequency/intensity ratings than either younger or older children. Indeed, approximately 62% of parents of children between the ages of 24 and 35 months indicated that their children were engaging in repetitive behaviors in contrast to 27% of the youngest and 49% of the oldest age group. Results highlight the presence of two salient features of childhood routines: (1) a dimension related to things being "just right" (e.g., "seems very aware of how certain clothes feel," "arranges objects in straight lines or symmetrical patterns"), and (2) a dimension including items related to repetitive behaviors and insistence on sameness (e.g., "acts out the same thing over and over in pretend play," "prefers the same household schedule or routine every day"). Of interest, ritualistic behaviors were associated with adaptive outcomes in younger children and negative outcomes in older children (Evans et al., 1995). These findings suggest that repetitive behavior may serve different functions at different ages and may be associated with both adaptive and maladaptive outcomes.

In summary, preschoolers may have difficulty disengaging from or inhibiting repetitive patterns that are not enacted in the service of enhancing mastery, control, or self-efficacy. Notwithstanding that young children may have difficulty reflecting on their own behaviors or concomitant distress; some children often appear to be stuck performing non-goal-directed, uncontrollable, perseverative action sequences that resemble maladaptive adult compulsions. Repetitive behaviors that are employed in the service of acquisition of new skills or in play activities will likely be accompanied by expressions of positive affect or interest. In contrast, perseverative behaviors that are not goal directed may manifest in a resigned, neutral affective expression or be a source of marked frustration in a child. The preschool years are a time of dramatic change in cognitive aspects of inhibition and perseveration (Zelazo et al., 1997). In typical development, a significant increase in the performance of repetitive behaviors during these years is followed by a decrease in the ensuing developmental time period (Evans et al., 1995). Attention to adaptive and maladaptive perseveration in the preschool years is warranted, as this distinction of behavior may predict later developmental pathology.

As children enter elementary school, they engage in complex rule-based games and superstitious behaviors (Carter et al., 1995; King, 1991). Normally emerging superstitious beliefs appear similar to adaptive compulsions in that they may minimize anxiety associated with disturbing thoughts or impulses (Leonard et al., 1990). Superstitious behaviors, ritualistic play, and rule-governed games may also be viewed on a continuum with the maladaptive variants more characteristic of OCD. However, several distinctions between typical superstitions and maladaptive compulsions are evident, again with the primary divergence considering duration, distress, and interference with routine activities (Leonard et al., 1990; Nemiah, 1985; Peller, 1955). A single study hypothesized that children with OCD would have more superstitious behaviors than unaffected children; however, results were not confirmed (Leonard et al., 1990). As we continue to view these patterns of behavior as part of typical development, the obsessive and compulsive behaviors that appear common in school-age children further decline as children approach puberty (Zohar & Bruno, 1997).

The mean age of onset for childhood OCD is 9–10 years of age (Pauls, Alsobrook, Goodman, Rasmussen, & Leckman, 1995; Riddle et al., 1990; Swedo, Rapoport, Leonard, Lenane, & Cheslow, 1989). Zohar and Bruno (1997) noted significant developmental changes in patterns of obsessions between 8 and 14 years of age. They focused on this particular age range to capture the period of highest risk for the emergence of pathological forms of obsessions. Zohar and Bruno reported that while mean rates of obsessions appeared to be higher in 4th and 6th grades relative to 8th grade, the number of children with very high obsessionality scores was significantly higher in 8th grade as compared to 4th and 6th grades. Furthermore, while the level of obsessive symptoms was significantly lower in older children, associations with anxiety symptoms were higher in 8th grade than in either 6th or 4th grades. This pattern is similar to that reported by Evans and colleagues in a study of younger children (Evans, E. W., personal communication, March 16, 1997). The increased percentage of children in the extreme group and the strong association with anxiety symptoms suggests that the stressful transition from childhood to adolescence may trigger the onset of more severe pathology.

Just as patterns of parental information processing and behavioral reactions may shape the developmental course of obsessions, they also may be involved in the unfolding of normative and pathological compulsive behaviors. Parents may become incorporated into a child's or adolescent's ritual, serving either an active or passive role ranging from facilitation to resistance. In addition, both facilitation and resistance can assume active and passive dimensions. Active participation may involve a parent affected with OCD or maladaptive compulsions, where both child and parent collaborate in the successful completion of a repetitive sequence of behaviors. For instance, prior to the child leaving home on the way to school, a parent involves him or her in a sequence of checking behaviors, assigning a specific task to the child such as checking the bathroom lights. After time and practice, the child initiates independently the checking ritual with the parent, and possibly generalizes the behavior to other contexts. Alternatively, the well-intentioned parent of a child who exhibits marked anxiety may comply with the request to participate in a ritual to pacify the distressed child. When family members scaffold a child's safety and avoidance rituals in reaction to his or her suffering, they are likely not only to reinforce the behavior through attention allocation but also to buttress the child's belief in the potency of the ritual. On the other hand, the parent or family member who resists involvement, perhaps by distracting a child from engaging in a ritual or suggesting alternative activities, may in fact be applying naturalistic exposure and response prevention. An extreme example of passive participation can occur when parents are not aware that they have become a part of an elaborate ritual. For example, as part of a long sequence of behaviors, a child may require a parent to provide a goodnight kiss on the cheek. Unbeknownst to the parent, prior to requesting the kiss, the child may have rearranged his or her bedding, checked under the bed, flipped the lights on and off seven times, put clothing out for the next morning, and set up stuffed animals in a very particular, "just right" arrangement. Once the child completes this sequence of events in a satisfactory manner, the ritual is sealed for the night with a good night kiss.

OBSESSIVE COMPULSIVE DISORDER

Diagnosis and Phenomenology

When the frequency, intensity, duration and/or distress associated with obsessions and compulsions begin to interfere with developmental progress and day-to-day functioning, the possibility of a disordered state must be considered. OCD is the psychiatric diagnostic category that is assigned to individuals with pathological or impairing obsessions and/or compulsions. OCD is classified as an anxiety disorder. The DSM-IV (American Psychiatric Association, 1994) criteria specify that the obsessions and/or compulsions must be experienced as inappropriate and be of sufficient frequency, intensity, or duration to cause a significant degree of distress. Related to the issue of impairment, the individual must report ineffective efforts to resist, neutralize, or suppress obsessions and compulsions, or GAD (i.e., excessive worries about real-life issues), and must acknowledge that the thoughts are a product of his or her own mind. Very young children can obtain a diagnosis despite an inability to describe the unwanted or intrusive nature of obsessions. Finally, the DSM-IV excludes obsessions that are secondary to another psychiatric disorder (e.g., intrusive thoughts about food or dieting associated with an Axis I eating disorder).

The DSM-IV considers compulsions to be impairing when they are performed in response to an obsession or in accordance with rigid or inflexible rules that must be followed in an exacting manner. Performing the compulsion is not experienced as gratifying. Rather, the compulsion is performed to reduce anxiety or distress associated with a dreaded consequence. To be considered a compulsion, the DSM-IV requires that the behavior or mental activity be either excessive or functionally unrelated to the dreaded event or situation.

In contrast to earlier psychiatric nosological systems, the DSM-IV has diminished the importance of resistance for assigning a diagnosis of OCD. This shift is in part due to the recognition that patterns of responding to obsessions or other internal anxiety triggers with compulsions can change over time as they become overlearned through practice and/or automatic. Thus, in some individuals, the compulsive response occurs so quickly (e.g., automatic processing) that the awareness of anxiety or efforts to resist the compulsion are minimal.

The most frequent symptoms reported by children with OCD are washing and cleaning, followed by checking, counting, repeating, and touching (March, Leonard, & Swedo, 1995b). The endurance of symptoms that are common at an earlier developmental phase (e.g., checking, cleaning) appears to implicate later pathology. More research in community samples is needed to confirm this hypothesis, as Rettew, Swedo, Leonard, Lenane, and Rapoport (1992) report that symptoms in clinically referred children with OCD often change over time, with no apparent age progression or age-related patterns.

Although OCD often makes its first appearance in childhood or adolescence, OCD is not considered a "developmental disorder" (Bolton, 1996). The DSM-IV does, however, acknowledge the role of development in assigning a diagnosis of OCD. Specifically, the DSM-IV has added a caveat that children need not acknowledge that their obsessions and compulsions are either excessive or senseless. As the definitive symptoms of OCD involve cognitive ideation, the clinician determining whether an individual meets criteria for a diagnosis of OCD must obtain subjective accounts of the individual's cognitive and affective experiences. With young children, obtaining information about mental processes such as resistance, interference, and ego-dystonicity (i.e., whether or not the thoughts are part of the self) can be extremely difficult (Carter et al., 1995; King, 1991). Indeed, even children who exhibit severe obsessive–compulsive symptoms may have no explanation for the source(s) of their compulsions; the obsessions they report subsequent to the onset of the compulsions may serve to give meaning to their otherwise senseless behavior (Carter et al., 1995; King, 1991). Young children may have difficulty answering questions that require them to reflect on their own behaviors, cognitions, and emotions, and may not fully grasp the meaning of relevant but abstract constructs (e.g., interference). With development, the child's cognitive structures undergo significant qualitative shifts that will impact the manner in which he or she construes and organizes information in the external world, self-perception, as well as how he or she integrates cognitive, emotional, and behavioral experiences.

EPIDEMIOLOGICAL STUDIES OF NORMATIVE AND PATHOLOGICAL OBSESSIONS AND COMPULSIONS

While once believed to be an extremely rare disorder in children and adults, recent estimates based on community studies of adolescents indicate that the disorder is not infrequent, with prevalence estimates of OCD ranging from 1% to 4% (Flament et al., 1990; Valleni-Basile et al., 1994; Zohar et al., 1992). Moreover, at least one-third to one-half of adult patients reports onset in childhood or adolescence (Black, Noyes, Rise, Goldstein, & Blum, 1992; Rasmussen & Eisen, 1991). Unfortunately, the majority of studies reporting prevalence rates in younger children are based on clinically referred samples that are subject to ascertainment biases.

Problems with obtaining reliable information based on self-reports from young children limit our knowledge of obsessions prior to school age. However, anecdotal reports can be obtained from clinic-referred or high-risk children who are as young as 4 years of age (e.g., "I keep seeing a racetrack in my head with a car going around and around, and I can't make it stop"). Thus, while clinical examples suggest that preschool-age children may be distressed by obsessions, empirical studies have not addressed the prevalence of obsessions or compulsions in children younger than school age. Prevalence data are available for nonclinic referred children and adolescents based on epidemiological studies that have employed obsessionality symptom checklists such as the Leyton Obsessional Inventory—Child Version (or the Maudsley

Obsessive–Compulsive Inventory (MOCI; Berg, Whitaker, Davies, Flament, & Rapoport, 1988; Zohar & Bruno, 1997; Zohar et al., 1992).

Zohar and Bruno (1997) reported no gender differences in total MOCI scores in non-referred children ages 8–14 years. However, boys scored significantly higher than girls on symptoms involving checking, while girls scored significantly higher on symptoms involving cleaning. This finding is consistent with patterns reported for adult OCD. Although equal numbers of men and women suffer from OCD, a higher percentage of affected women report cleaning obsessions and compulsions, while a higher percentage of affected men report checking obsessions and compulsions (Holzer et al., 1994; Noshirvani, Kasvikis, Marks, Tsarkiris, & Montiero, 1991). A final important finding reported by Zohar and Bruno (1997) was that the pattern of specific obsessive and compulsive behaviors varied with age; 4th graders were more likely to endorse items dealing with checking, cleanliness, and guilt about lying, whereas 8th graders were more likely to endorse what may be considered age-appropriate concerns about sexuality, bodily cleanliness, and personal appearance.

Thomsen and Mikkelsen (1993) used the short form of the Leyton in a sample of Danish children (ages 11–17 years) and found an elevation of interference symptoms in the older children. This pattern suggests that some children had OCD onset in adolescence (Thomsen & Mikkelsen, 1993). This is not surprising given the aforementioned prevalence estimates. Prevalence information is also available about nonpathological obsessive symptoms in high school students. In a study by Berg et al. (1988), 46% of students endorsed items that are considered to be obsessive (e.g., thinking repetitive thoughts and words, hating dirt and dirty things, being fussy about keeping one's hands clean, and having trouble making decisions). In contrast to the lack of gender differences in extreme scores in this sample and total scores for the school-age sample, female high school students were more likely to report a greater number of obsessional symptoms and also to endorse significantly higher interference scores. This finding is consistent with evidence that female adolescents are more likely than their male counterparts to engage in ruminative responses when depressed and that these responses tend to interfere with functioning (Nolen-Hoeksema, 1990). In contrast to Zohar and Bruno's (1997) study of school-age children, no associations were observed between symptom levels and age between 9th and 12th grades. It is clear that longitudinal, epidemiological studies identifying risk factors and predictors of OCD course and outcome are needed.

ASSOCIATED CONDITIONS

Based on both clinically referred and epidemiological samples of OCD, there is evidence for increased rates of comorbid depression, anxiety disorders, tic disorders, and substance dependence (Flament et al., 1990; March & Leonard, 1996; Riddle et al., 1990). In studies that address associated conditions, the majority of individuals who meet criteria for OCD also meet criteria for at least one other diagnosis (for review, see March, 1995). Rasmussen and Eisen (1991) suggest that individuals with OCD may be particularly vulnerable to anxiety disorders. This may be due in part to shared genetic etiology (Alsobrook & Pauls, 1997) and/or to common cognitive information-processing patterns. The typical course of onset of associated disorders provides some clues to etiology. For example, in at least of half of child-referred cases, a major episode of depression follows the onset of OCD (Swedo et al., 1989). Given the debilitating and uncontrollable nature of OCD symptoms (i.e., OCD is an uncontrollable, negative event), OCD can be considered depressogenic. In contrast, anxiety disorders typically emerge prior to the diagnosis of OCD (e.g., Rasmussen & Eisen, 1991). Family studies provide additional information regarding the etiology of associated conditions, demonstrating elevated anxiety but not depressive disorders in family members of OCD probands (Black et al, 1992). Furthermore, Rachman and Hodgson (1980) described levels of somatic arousal in individuals with OCD that are comparable to those present in other anxiety disorders. Although a similar early course across multiple anxiety disorders may be construed as evidence of a common etiological pathway, it is also possible that multiple genetic and environmental risk factors share an early phenotypic expression that becomes more differentiated through development (Carter et al., 1995).

DEVELOPMENTAL MODEL

Both normative and pathological variants of obsessions and compulsions are influenced by biological and environmental factors (Carter et al., 1995). Yet the specific mechanisms determining the emergence, maintenance, and exacerbation of obsessions and compulsions are unknown. Also unrevealed is whether typical variation in obsessive and compulsive behaviors lies on the same continuum as maladaptive forms. Evidence suggesting that the same factors predispose individuals to develop both adaptive and maladaptive obsessions and compulsions would support the existence of a continuum. Identifying independent etiological agents would imply a discontinuous model. In this section, we highlight some of the factors that may influence the course of obsessions and compulsions through development.

Bolton (1996), advocating a developmental model of OCD, has argued that many aspects of OCD phenomenology are similar to typical processes observed in the prerational child. Specifically, he highlights adult features of the disorder that are relevant to cognitive models such as overattribution of personal responsibility, fusion of thoughts and actions, and the functional anxiety-reducing goal of compulsions. His model postulates that a significant psychosocial stress or perceived threat may result in the adoption of a prerational or magical system of cognition, in which compulsions or ritualized behaviors are viewed as an effective solution to the threat. Bolton acknowledges that the mechanism that would lead an individual to resort to prerational strategies has yet to be identified. Moreover, the cognitive risk factors presented in the model appear nonspecific to OCD as distinct from other anxiety disorders. While the lack of specificity in this model is problematic, the focus on cognitive distortion provides exciting avenues for future research.

Biology and Temperament

As noted earlier, there is increasing evidence that at least some forms of OCD are genetic (Alsobrook & Pauls, 1997). Specifically, tic-related OCD may be more familial than non-tic-related OCD. Moreover, recent work addressing components of the OCD phenotype suggests that some dimensions of OCD may be more heritable than others (Alsobrook, Leckman, Goodman, Rasmussen, & Pauls, 1998). A subset of adult OCD symptoms involving symmetry and ordering appears to show stronger patterns of genetic transmission than other symptom subsets. Developmental components of the OCD phenotype have yet to be similarly addressed.

Investigators studying nonclinical populations from infancy through high school demonstrate the wide individual variation in the normative expression of obsessive and compulsive behaviors (Evans et al., 1997; Flament et al., 1990; Zohar & Bruno, 1997). In addition to a specific predisposition to the expression of obsessional ideation or ritualistic behaviors, some temperamental styles may bias a child toward maladaptive variants of obsessions and compulsions. This may be due in part to the influence of temperament on the appraisal of unwanted or intrusive thoughts and the ability to inhibit ritualistic behaviors. Specifically, highly emotionally reactive children (Rothbart, 1989) may become more distressed when confronted by anxiety provoking ideation and/or more frustrated when unable to inhibit a repetitive behavior. As level of disturbance or distress is one of the dimensions that distinguishes nonpathological and pathological forms of obsessionality (Rachman & Hodgson, 1978), heightened reactivity may determine a child's crossing the threshold to maladaptation. Similarly, behavioral inhibition, a temperamental style associated with extreme shyness, behavioral restraint, retreat from novelty, and increased sympathetic activity (Kagan, 1989a,b; Kagan et al., 1988; Kagan & Snidman, 1991), has been associated with non-OCD forms of anxiety disorders (Biederman et al., 1993a,b; Rosenbaum et al., 1988; Rosenbaum et al., 1991; Rosenbaum, Beiderman, Hirshfeld, Bolduc, & Kagan et al., 1990). Children who are behaviorally inhibited may be hypervigilant in their response to fear-eliciting thoughts or images and may have more intense physiological consequences that maintain a state of alertness and negative expectancy consistent with patterns observed in adults with OCD. It is also important to note that children's temperamental styles may influence and be influenced by their parenting environments (Arcus & McCartney, 1989; Kagan, 1994; Rosenbaum et al., 1993; Sameroff, 1995; Sameroff & Seifer, 1983).

Developmental Transitions

In addition to evidence of individual variation from infancy through adolescence, obsessions and compulsions are more likely to emerge at specific stages in development. This is true for typically occurring obsessions and compulsions, as well as for disordered states. Specifically, young children appear to exhibit an increase in ritualistic behaviors between 2 and 3 years of age (Evans et al., 1997), and there is a decrease in obsessional thoughts between the 4th and 8th grade (Zohar & Bruno, 1997). The most common age of onset for OCD in childhood is between 9 and 10 years of age (Riddle et al., 1990). Other developmental transitions that stress the child's or adolescent's sense of felt security, control, or mastery may elicit maladaptive coping with obsessional ideation and ritualistic behaviors that were previously in the normative range of functioning. Alternatively, developmental transitions may be marked by biological changes that even in the absence of perceived psychosocial stress will lead to the emergence of a disordered state. A developmental stress–diathesis model that includes both biological and psychosocial factors is implicated. However, empirical support for this synthesis specific to OCD is lacking.

The Familial Context

The familial context must be understood both with respect to parental psychopathology and with regard to parenting behaviors and parental cognitive information-processing styles. The presence of psychopathology in the immediate family should be considered a risk factor in the development and course of a child's or adolescent's maladaptive obsessionality not only in terms of genetic contribution but also with respect to familial experiences. Parental psychopathology may interfere with adaptive parenting in many different ways, including increasing intrusiveness, expressed hostility, and overprotection, as well as decreasing emotional availability and structuring of developmentally appropriate activities. Parents may also unwittingly model fear and avoidance responses or encourage the use of maladaptive coping strategies (e.g., rituals) in response to anxiety-provoking stimuli, including unwanted or intrusive thoughts (Pollock, Rosenbaum, Marrs, Miller, & Biederman, 1995).

To date, research has not addressed whether obsessive–compulsive pathology in children and adolescents is associated with cognitive errors including overattributions of controllability and responsibility or catastrophic misinterpretation of the likelihood that the feared negative outcome associated with the obsession will occur. These factors appear to be important to OCD pathology in adults and adolescents (McNally & Kohlbeck, 1993; Rachman, 1985; Rachman & Hodgson, 1978; Salkovskis, 1985). A child's general cognitive development must also be taken into consideration when interpreting cognitive styles or obsessional thoughts and rituals. Even before children are capable of reporting on their own thought processes, studying parental cognitive styles may inform our understanding of the development and maintenance of obsessive–compulsive pathology in children. Specifically, parental attributions about children's typical ritualistic behavior are likely to influence parenting practices. Parenting practices will in turn contribute to the child's interpretation of the salience and deviance of the ritualistic behavior. Thus, a parent who has a dramatic response may heighten the child's anxiety about the behavior. Moreover, children may model the cognitive strategies observed in their parents. The interaction among affected family members, parenting style, and perpetuation of disordered states of obsessionality in children and adolescents cannot be divorced.

In summary, children who have a biological predisposition to either nonpathological or pathological obsessionality are likely to exhibit obsessional behaviors at specific developmental transitions. Their own and family members' responses to the initial emergence of these behaviors may influence the subsequent trajectory toward a disordered state (i.e., OCD). Temperament, cognitive level, cognitive style, and the experience of the family environment will color children's responses to the emergence of ritualistic or obsessional behaviors.

TREATMENT OF CHILD AND ADOLESCENT OBSESSIVE–COMPULSIVE DISORDER

The treatment of child and adolescent OCD has received increased attention in the literature (March, 1995; March, Leonard, & Swedo, 1995; March & Mulle, 1998; Rapoport, Leonard, Swedo, & Lenane, 1993; Riddle, 1996). Both pharmacological and cognitive-behavioral interventions have demonstrated efficacy in symptom reduction. With respect to pharmacology, the majority of clinical trials have involved selective serotonin reuptake inhibitors (SSRIs), which have been shown to be effective in adult populations, and in adolescents and older children, though less is known about their efficacy in preschoolers and younger school-age children. The side-effect profile observed in children and adolescents is consistent with that observed in adults. Thus, the most common and problematic side effects for children and adolescents include weight gain, hyperarousal, and gastrointestinal distress. Due to the possibility of side effects, as well as interest in promoting feelings of self-efficacy and the use of adaptive coping strategies in symptom management, expert consensus recommends that the first line of intervention should involve cognitive-behavioral therapy (CBT) (March, 1995).

CBT in children and adolescents with OCD is relatively new on the scene. Only very recently has a protocol-driven manual been established and tested empirically (March &

Mulle, 1998). Results demonstrate good outcome and maintenance of treatment gains. Information gathering, cognitive restructuring and skills building, therapist-assisted exposure and response prevention, and homework assignments are integrated components in CBT. Though research suggests that cognitive components of treatment may be of less importance than exposure and response prevention (Emmelkamp & Beens, 1991), cognitive restructuring, particularly for the older child and adolescent, may be beneficial. As compared to younger children, adolescents typically demonstrate the capacity to identify their obsessions and verbalize feared negative consequences. Greater self-reflective capacities facilitate therapists' ability to target negative or ambiguous automatic thoughts that interfere with adaptive coping responses and/or perpetuate maladaptive behaviors. Thought stopping and satiation have also been used as cognitive treatment components for OCD (Kellerman, 1981; March et al., 1994; Neziroglu & Neuman, 1990).

Exposure and response prevention involve presenting the feared stimulus to the child or adolescent while preventing the ritualized response. Response inhibition will initially increase anxiety; in the absence of the ritualized response, habituation and fear extinction are facilitated. This is typically done in a graduated manner, in which increasingly feared stimuli are introduced and the child or adolescent gains skill at managing anxiety during response inhibition. For example, in collaboration with his or her therapist, a child who fears contamination and engages in compulsive hand washing will develop a hierarchy of increasingly distressing contaminants (i.e., dirty and yucky things) that have previously led to hand washing. The child will then be encouraged to touch the least upsetting contaminant and tolerate the level of anxiety while inhibiting the hand-washing compulsion until the urge or perceived need to wash is gone. Subsequently, more challenging contaminants are introduced. Flooding techniques, where the child is exposed initially to the *most* feared stimuli until anxiety decreases, have also demonstrated efficacy (Marks, 1987). For a comprehensive review of CBT in children and adolescents, the reader is referred to March (1995).

Depending on the individual child's or adolescent's response to CBT, pharmacological agents can be combined with CBT approaches. If the child or adolescent does not respond to augmentation with a particular SSRI [e.g., clomipramine (Anafranil), fluoxetine (Prozac), sertraline (Zoloft), fluvoxamine (Luvox)], or only has a partial response, alternative SSRI medications and/or benzodiazepines can be employed (March & Mulle, 1998). Case reports suggest that concurrent administration of low-dose benzodiazepines may be particularly effective with highly anxious children and adolescents (Leonard, Topol, Bukstein, Hindmarsh, Allen, & Swedo, 1992).

As mentioned earlier in this chapter, it is critical for families to be educated about the interventions that their children are receiving. When family members have been actively involved in a child's or adolescent's rituals, it may be necessary to involve the parents as well in response prevention efforts. They may also experience some loss as the child gains more independence, hence subjecting the child–parent relationship to change. To maximize parental support of the intervention, it may be necessary to encourage alternative, adaptive parent–child activities.

RECOMMENDATIONS AND IMPLICATIONS

A promising avenue of research involves identifying reliable components of OCD phenomenology (Leckman et al., 1997). One identified factor, comprised of aggressive cognitions (i.e., fear of harming another), sexual and somatic obsessions, and checking compulsions, appears to be most strongly associated with an increase in OCD in family members (Alsobrook et al., 1998), earlier age of onset, female gender, and an increase in anxiety in family members (Carter, Pollock, Alsobrook, & Pauls, 1998).

Although not reviewed in this chapter, recent studies demonstrate the importance of genetic factors (for review, see Alsobrook & Pauls, 1997) and neurobiology (e.g., brain structures and neurochemical processes) in the etiology of OCD (e.g., Baxter, Schwartz, & Guze, 1991). The current salience of biological theories does not undermine the importance of etiological cognitive-behavioral models. In light of biological etiology and the typical chronicity of the disorder (March et al., 1995b), it is critical to examine the course of OCD behaviors in the context of developmental shifts in biological systems and relevant psychosocial environments (Carter et al., 1995; Cicchetti, 1993).

An excellent research tool for examining questions of continuity among normally emerging ritualistic behavior and later obsessionality, as well as continuity in the phenomenology of child, adolescent, and adult forms of pathological obsessive and compulsive behaviors, involves the high-risk longitudinal prospective design, which, ideally, can be embedded within larger family genetic studies to address multiple levels and domains of assessment.

Given the high prevalence of obsessions and compulsions reported in nonclinical studies and the association at particular ages of elevated symptoms with greater anxiety (e.g., Zohar & Bruno, 1997), it would be useful to assess children with subclinical manifestations of OCD prior to significant developmental transitions and follow them through periods of highest risk. These children and family members could be assessed on multiple occasions, with particular attention to temperament, information processing, and parent–child interactions to determine predictors of pathological obsessional states and appropriate windows of opportunity for prevention and intervention. For example, the transition to middle school or high school presents unique challenges with increased responsibility and unpredictability, as well as a wide range of other stressors that may lower an individual's threshold for obsessionality. Such high-risk studies may also improve the early identification of children who are suffering, which is critical due to the secretiveness typically associated with obsessive–compulsive pathology, chronicity of symptoms, and individuals' vulnerability to impairment in multiple developmental domains.

Addressing the familial context of childhood maladaptive obsessionality is critical for developing appropriate interventions. Based on genetic evidenced at a higher rate of OCD, other anxiety disorders are expected in parents of children and adolescents who meet criteria for OCD (Alsobrook & Pauls, 1997). In addition, parents affected with OCD are at much higher risk for depression and other anxiety disorders. Severity and chronicity of parental psychopathology may interfere with parental availability, positive emotional expressivity, appropriate structuring, and response to the child's difficulties more than any specific disorder (March & Curry, 1998). When parents are suffering from a clinical disorder, it is necessary to involve them in the treatment of their own psychopathology as well as their child's intervention. Irrespective of parental diagnostic status, psychoeducation of parents is a critical component of any child or adolescent interventions for OCD.

In conclusion, obsessionality reflects a heterogeneous pattern of repetitive and intrusive thoughts and behaviors. Throughout development, both pathological and nonpathological repetitive forms are observed, with maladaptive behaviors characterized by heightened distress and an inability to suppress or inhibit thoughts and actions, leading to significant interference with daily functioning. Studies are only beginning to address the developmental course of typical obsessive behaviors. These preliminary studies indicate several developmental periods, such as the early preschool years, in which these behaviors are common. Although obsessional behaviors appear quite common at various points in childhood and adolescence, extreme rates of these behaviors are usually associated with anxiety and most likely reflect a disordered state. Further attention to the developmental and familial context of obsessionality is warranted in both research and clinical endeavors.

REFERENCES

Adams, P. (1973). *Obsessive children*. New York: Penguin Books.

Alsobrook, J. I., Leckman, J., Goodman, W., Rasmussen, S., & Pauls, D. (1999). Segregation analysis of obsessive–compulsive disorder using symptom-based factors. *Journal of Medical Genetics (Neuropsychiatric Genetics)*, 88, 669–675.

Alsobrook, J. I., & Pauls, D. (1998). The genetics of obsessive–compulsive disorder. In M. Jenike, L. Baer, & W. Minichiello (Eds.), *Obsessive–compulsive disorders: Theory and management* (3rd ed., pp. 276–288). Littleton, MA: Medical Publishers, Inc.

American Psychiatric Association. (1994). *Diagnostic and statistical manual of mental disorders* (4th ed.). Washington, DC: Author.

Arcus, D., & McCartney, K. (1989). When baby makes four: Family influences in the stability of behavioral inhibition. In J. Reznick (Ed.), *Perspectives on behavioral inhibition* (pp. 197–218). Chicago: University of Chicago Press.

Baxter, L., Schwartz, J., & Guze, B. (1991). Brain imaging: Toward a neuroanatomy of OCD. In J. Zohar, T. Insel, & S. Rasmussen (Eds.), *The psychobiology of obsessive-compulsive disorder* (pp. 101–125). New York: Springer.

Berg, C., Whitaker, A., Davies, M., Flament, M., & Rapoport, J. (1988). The survey form of the Leyton Obsessional Inventory—Child Version: Norms from an epidemiological study. *Journal of the American Academy of Child and Adolescent Psychiatry, 27*, 759–763.

Biederman, J., Rosenbaum, J. F., Bolduc-Murphy, E. A., Faraone, S. V., Chaloff, J., Hirshfeld, D. R., & Kagan, J. (1993a). Behavioral inhibition as a temperamental risk factor for anxiety disorders. *Child Adolescent Psychiatric Clinics of North America, 2*, 667–683.

Biederman, J., Rosenbaum, J. F., Bolduc-Murphy, E. A., Faraone, S. V., Hirshfeld, D. R., Chaloff, J., & Kagan, J. (1993b). A three year follow-up of children with and without behavioral inhibition. *Journal of the American Academy of Child and Adolescent Psychiatry, 32*, 814–821.

Black, D., Noyes, R., Rise, B., Goldstein, R., & Blum, N. (1992). A family study of obsessive–compulsive disorder. *Archives of General Psychiatry, 49*, 362–368.

Bolton, D. (1996). Annotation: Developmental issues in obsessive compulsive disorder. *Journal of Child Psychology and Psychiatry, 37*, 131–137.

Carter, A., Pauls, D., & Leckman, J. (1995). The development of obsessionality: Continuities and discontinuities. In D. Cicchetti & D. Cohen (Eds.), *The manual of developmental psychopathology* (pp. 609–632). New York: Wiley.

Carter, A., Pollock, R., Alsobrook, J. I., & Pauls, D. (1998, November). *Early-onset obsessive–compulsive disorder: Anxiety comorbidity and phenomenology*. Paper presented at the Association for the Advancement of Behavior Therapy, Washington, DC.

Cicchetti, D. (1993). Developmental psychopathology: Reactions, reflections, and projections. *Developmental Review, 13*, 471–502.

Diamond, A., & Taylor, C. (1996). Development of an aspect of executive control: Development of the abilities to remember what I said and to "Do as I say, not as I do." *Developmental Psychobiology, 29*, 315–334.

Emmelkamp, P., & Beens, H. (1991). Cognitive therapy with obsessive compulsive disorder: A comparative evaluation. *Behaviour Research and Therapy, 27*, 89–93.

England, S., & Dickerson, M. (1988). Intrusive thoughts: Unpleasantness not the major cause of uncontrollability. *Behaviour Research and Therapy, 26*, 279–282.

Evans, D., Leckman, J., Carter, A., Reznick, J., Henshaw, D., & Pauls, D. (1997). Ritual, habit and perfectionism: The prevalence and development of compulsive-like behavior in normal young children. *Child Development, 68*, 58–68.

Evans, D., Leckman, J., King, R., Henshaw, D., & Alsobrook, K. (1995, April). *The development of compulsive-like behaviors in young children*. Paper presented at the Society for Research in Child Development, Indianapolis, IN.

Flament, M., Koby, E., Rapoport, J., Berg, C., Zahn, T., Cox, C., et al., (1990). Childhood obsessive compulsive disorder: A prospective follow-up study. *Journal of Child Psychology and Psychiatry and Allied Disciplines, 13*, 363–380.

Freud, A. (1965). *Normality and pathology in childhood*. New York: International Universities Press.

Frost, R., Sher, K., & Geen, T. (1986). Psychopathology and personality characteristics of nonclinical compulsive checkers. *Behaviour Research and Therapy, 24*, 133–143.

Gesell, A., Ames, L., & Ilg, F. (1974). *Infant and child in the culture of today*. New York: Harper & Row.

Holzer, J., Goodman, W., McDougle, C., Baer, L., Boyarsky, B., Leckman, J., & Price, L. (1994). Obsessive compulsive disorder with and without a chronic tic disorder: A comparison of symptoms in 70 patients. *British Journal of Psychiatry, 164*, 469–473.

Hoogduin, K. (1986). On the diagnosis of obsessive–compulsive disorder. *American Journal of Psychotherapy, 40*, 36–51.

Insel, T. (1984). Obsessive compulsive disorder: The clinical picture. In T. Insel (Ed.), *New findings in obsessive compulsive disorder* (pp. 2–22). Washington, DC: American Psychiatric Press.

Jenike, M. (1989). Obsessive–compulsive and related disorders: A hidden epidemic. *New England Journal of Medicine, 321*, 539–541.

Kagan, J. (1989a). The concept of behavioral inhibition to the unfamiliar. In J.S. Reznick (Eds.), *Perspectives on behavioral inhibition* (pp. 1–23). Chicago: University of Chicago Press.

Kagan, J. (1989b). Temperamental contributions to social behavior. *American Psychologist, 44*, 668–674.

Kagan, J. (1994). *Galen's prophecy*: Biological bases of childhood shyness. *Science, 240*, 167–171.

Kagan, J., Reznick, J. S., & Snidman, N. (1987). The physiology and psychology of behavioral inhibition in children. *Child Development, 58*, 1459–1473.

Kagan, J., Reznick, J. S., & Snidman, N. (1988). Biological bases of childhood shyness. *Science, 240*, 167–171.

Kagan, J., & Snidman, N. (1991). Infant predictors of inhibited and uninhibited profiles. *Psychological Science, 2*, 40–44.

Kellerman, J. (1981). Hypnosis as an adjunct to thought stopping and covert reinforcement in the treatment of homicidal obsession in a twelve-year-old boy. *International Journal of Clinical and Experimental Hypnosis, 29*, 129–135.

King, R. (1991). Obsessive–compulsive disorder. In R. King and J. Noshpitz (Eds.), *Pathways of growth: Essentials of child psychiatry* (pp. 265–298). New York: Wiley.

Leckman, J. F., Grice, D. E., Boardman, J., Zhang, H., Vitale, A., Bondi, C., Alsobrook, J., Peterson, B. S., Cohen, D. J., Rasmussen, S. A., Goodman, W. K., McDougle, C. J., & Pauls, D. L. (1997). Symptoms of obsessive–compulsive disorder. *American Journal of Psychiatry, 154*(7), 911–917.

Leonard, H., Goldberger, E., Rapoport, J., Cheslow, D., & Swedo, S. (1990). Childhood rituals: Normal development or obsessive–compulsive symptoms? *Journal of the American Academy of Child and Adolescent Psychiatry, 29*, 17–23.

Leonard, H. L., Topol, D., Bukstein, O., Hindmarsh, D., Allen, A. J., & Swedo, S. E. (1994). Clonazepam as an augmenting agent in the treatment of childhood-onset obsessive–compulsive disorder. *Journal of the American Academy of Child and Adolescent Psychiatry, 33*, 792–794.

March, J., (1995). Cognitive-behavioral psychotherapy for children and adolescents with OCD: A review and recommendations for treatment. *Journal of the American Academy of Child and Adolescent Psychiatry, 34*, 7–18.

March, J. S., & Curry, J. F. (1998). Predicting the outcome of treatment. *Journal of Abnormal Child Psychology, 26*, 39–51.

March, J., & Leonard, H. (1996). Obsessive–compulsive disorder in children and adolescents: A review of past 10 years. *Journal of the American Academy of Child and Adolescent Psychiatry, 35*(10), 1265–1273.

March, J., Leonard, H., & Swedo, S. (1995a). Neuropsychiatry of obsessive-compulsive disorder in children and adolescents. *Comprehensive Therapy, 21*, 507–512.

March, J., Leonard, H., & Swedo, S. (1995b). Obsessive–compulsive disorder. In J. March (Ed.), *Anxiety disorders in children and adolescents* (pp. 251–275). New York: Guilford Press.

March, J. S., & Mulle, K. (1998). *OCD in children and adolescents: A cognitive–behavioral treatment manual*. New York: Guilford Press.

March, J., Mulle, K., and Herbel, B. (1994). Behavioral psychotherapy for children and adolescents with obsessive–compulsive disorder: An open trial of a new protocol-driven treatment package. *Journal of the American Academy of Child and Adolescent Psychiatry, 33*, 333–341.

Marks, I. (1987). *Fears, phobias, and rituals*. New York: Oxford University Press.

McNally, R., & Kohlbeck, P. (1993). Reality monitoring in obsessive–compulsive disorder. *Behaviour Research and Therapy, 31*, 249–253.

Nemiah, J. (1985). Obsessive compulsive neurosis. In A. Freedman, H. Kaplan, & B. Sadock (Eds.), *A comprehensive textbook of psychiatry* (pp. 1241–1255). Baltimore: Williams & Wilkins.

Neziroglu, F., & Neuman, J. (1990). Three treatment approaches for obsessions. *Journal of Cognitive Psychotherapy, 4*, 377–392.

Noshirvani, H., Kasvikis, Y., Marks, I., Tsarkiris, F., & Montiero, W. (1991). Gender-divergent factors in obsessive–compulsive disorder. *British Journal of Psychiatry, 158,* 260–263.

Parkinson, L., & Rachman, S. (1981). The nature of intrusive thoughts. *Advances in Behavior Research and Therapy, 3,* 101–110.

Pauls, D., Alsobrook, J. I., Goodman, W., Rasmussen, S., & Leckman, J. (1995). A family study of obsessive–compulsive disorder. *American Journal of Psychiatry, 143,* 76–84.

Peller, L. (1955). Libidinal phases, ego development and play. *Psychoanalytic Study of the Child, 10,* 178–199.

Piaget, J. (1962). *Play, dreams and imitation in childhood.* New York: Norton.

Pollock, R., Rosenbaum, J., Marrs, A., Miller, B., & Biederman, J. (1995). Anxiety disorders of childhood: Implications for adult psychopathology. *Psychiatric Clinics of North America, 18,* 745–766.

Rachman, S. (1976). The modification of obsessions: A new formulation. *Behaviour Research and Therapy, 14,* 437–443.

Rachman, S. (1985). An overview of clinical and research issues in obsessive–compulsive disorders. In M. Mavissakalian, S. Turner, & L. Michelson (Eds.), *Obsessive–compulsive disorders: Psychological and pharmacological treatment* (pp. 1–47). New York: Plenum Press.

Rachman, S., & Hodgson, R. (1978). Abnormal and normal obsessions. *Behaviour Research and Therapy, 16,* 233–248.

Rachman, S., & Hodgson, R. (1980). *Obsessions and compulsions.* Englewood Cliffs, NJ: Prentice Hall.

Rapoport, J. L., Leonard, H. L., Swedo, S. E., & Lenane, M. C. (1993). Obsessive–compulsive disorder in children and adolescents: Issues in management. *Journal of Clinical Psychiatry, 54,* 27–29.

Rasmussen, S., & Eisen, J. (1991). Phenomenology of OCD: Clinical subtypes, heterogeneity and coexistence. In J. Nohar, T. Insel, & S. Rasmussen (Eds.), *The psychobiology of obsessive–compulsive disorder* (pp. 13–43). New York: Springer.

Rehm, L., & Carter, A. (1990). Cognitive components of depression. In M. Lewis & S. Miller (Eds.), *Handbook of developmental psychopathology* (pp. 341–351). New York: Plenum Press.

Rettew, D., Swedo, S., Leonard, H., Lenane, M., & Rapoport, J. (1992). Obsessions and compulsions across time in 79 children and adolescents with obsessive–compulsive disorder. *Journal of the American Academy of Child and Adolescent Psychiatry, 31,* 1050–1056.

Riddle, M., Scahill, L., King, R., Hardin, M., Towbin, K., Ort, S., Leckman, J., & Cohen, D. (1990). Obsessive–compulsive disorder in children and adolescents: Phenomenology and family history. *Journal of the American Academy of Child and Adolescent Psychiatry, 29,* 766–772.

Rosenbaum, J., Biederman, J., Bolduc-Murphy, E., Faraone, S., Chaloff, J., Hirshfeld, D., & Kagan, J. (1993). Behavioral inhibition in childhood: A risk factor for anxiety disorders. *Harvard Review of Psychiatry, 1,* 2–16.

Rosenbaum, J. F., Biederman, J., Gersten, M., Hirshfeld, D. R., Meminger, S. R., Herman, J. B., Kagan, J., Reznick, J. S., & Snidman, N. (1988). Behavioral inhibition in children of parents with panic disorder and agoraphobia: A controlled study. *Archives of General Psychiatry, 45,* 463–470.

Rosenbaum, J. F., Biederman, J., Hirshfeld, D. R., Bolduc, E. A., & Chaloff, J. (1991). Behavioral inhibition in children: A possible precursor to panic disorder or social phobia. *Journal of Clinical Psychiatry, 52,* 5–9.

Rosenbaum, J. F., Biederman, J., Hirshfeld, D. R., Bolduc, E. A., Faraone, S. V., Kagan, J., Snidman, N., & Reznick, J. S. (1991). Further evidence of an association between behavioral inhibition and anxiety disorders: Results from a family study of children from a non-clinical sample. *Journal of Psychiatric Research, 25,* 49–65.

Rosenbaum, J. F., Biederman, J., Hirshfeld, D. R., Bolduc, E. A., & Kagan, J. (1990). *Behavioral inhibition and risk for anxiety disorders.* Paper presented at the American Psychiatric Association (New Research Section-Risk Factors in Childhood Psychopathology), New York, NY.

Rothbart, M. K. (1989a). Behavioral approach and inhibition. In J. Reznick (Ed.), *Perspectives on behavioral inhibition* (p. 1167). Chicago: University of Chicago Press.

Rothbart, M. K. (1989b). Temperament in childhood: A framework. In G. A. Kohnstamm, J. E. Bates, & M. K. Rothbart (Eds.), *Temperament in childhood* (pp. 59–76). Chichester, UK: Wiley.

Salkovskis, P. (1985). Obsessional–compulsive problems: A cognitive–behavioural analysis. *Behaviour Research and Therapy, 23,* 571–583.

Salkovskis, P., & Harris, J. (1984). Abnormal and normal obsessions—a replication. *Behaviour Research and Therapy, 22,* 549–552.

Sameroff, A. (1995). General systems theories and developmental psychopathology. In D. Cicchetti & D. Cohen (Eds.), *Developmental psychopathology: Theory and methods* (pp. 659–695). New York: Wiley.

Sameroff, A. J., & Seifer, R. (1983). Familial risk and child competence. *Child Development, 54,* 1254–1268.

Swedo, S., Rapoport, J., Leonard, H., Lenane, M., & Cheslow, D. (1989). Obsessive-compulsive disorder in children and adolescents: Clinical phenomenology of 70 consecutive cases. *Archives of General Psychiatry, 46,* 335–341.

Thomsen, P., & Mikkelsen, H. (1993). Development of personality disorders in children and adolescents with obsessive–compulsive disorder: A 6- to 22-year follow-up study. *Acta Psychiatric Scandinavica, 87,* 456–462.

Turner, S., Beidel, D., & Stanley, M. (1992). Are obsessional thoughts and worry different cognitive phenomena? *Clinical Psychology Review, 12*, 257–270.

Valleni-Basile, L., Garrison, C., Jackson, K., Waller, J., McKewown, R., Addy, C., & Cuffe, S. (1994). Frequency of obsessive–compulsive disorder in a community sample of young adolescents. *Journal of the American Academy of Child and Adolescent Psychiatry, 33*, 782–791.

Welsh, M., Pennington, B., & Groisser, D. (1991). A normative–developmental study of executive functioning: A window on prefrontal function in children. *Developmental Neuropsychology, 7*, 131–149.

Zelazo, P., & Frye, D. (1996). An age-related dissociation between knowing rules and using them. *Cognitive Development, 11*, 37–63.

Zelazo, P., Carter, A., Reznick, J., & Frye, D. (1997). Early development of executive function: A problem-solving framework. *Review of General Psychology, 1*, 198–226.

Zohar, A., & Bruno, R. (1997). Normative and pathological obsessive–compulsive behavior and ideation in childhood: A question of timing. *Journal of Child Psychology and Psychiatry and Allied Disciplines, 38*, 993–999.

Zohar, A., Ratzoni, G., Pauls, D., Apter, A., Bleich, A., Kron, S., Rapoport, M., Weizman, A., & Cohen, D. (1992). An epidemiological study of obsessive–compulsive behavior and related disorder in Israeli adolescents. *Journal of the American Academy of Child and Adolescent Psychiatry, 31*, 1057–1061.

VII
CONTROL DISORDERS

30

Alcoholism

A Life Span Perspective on Etiology and Course

Robert A. Zucker, Steven T. Chermack,
and Geoffrey M. Curran

INTRODUCTION

From the perspective of the developmental psychopathologist, the understanding of alcoholism (or alcohol abuse and dependence, if one uses the most recent diagnostic parlance of the DSM-IV (American Psychiatric Association, 1994) occupies a special place among the psychopathologies for three reasons.

The first is shared in common with all other addictive disorders but not other forms of psychopathology, namely, that the deviant behavior occurs in conjunction with an external object. Thus, availability and regulation issues of the object (in the present instance, alcohol), as well as ongoing patterns of use in the peer structure, have direct implications for the manner in which the disorder can and will develop. Consequently, alcohol dependence is not a high-prevalence disorder in abstinent Muslim countries, although it may become a problem for individuals with high-risk profiles who happen to emigrate or travel. Related to this availability issue, prevalence of the disorder has been shown to vary with the overall use structure of the larger social system in which it is embedded (Reich, Cloninger, Van Eerdewegh, Rice, & Mullaney, 1988). Thus, when consumption rates have been higher, the threshold for moving into problem activity is easier to approach because availability is more omnipresent, and the cue structure for continued use is also more common. Under these circumstances population rates of the disorder have been observed to increase. Conversely, when social controls are

Robert A. Zucker • Alcohol Research Center, University of Michigan, Ann Arbor, Michigan 48108-3318. Steven T. Chermack • Detroit–VA Medical Center, Wayne State University School of Medicine, Detroit, Michigan 48201-1932. Geoffrey M. Curran • Central Arkansas Veterans Healthcare System, University of Arkansas for Medical Sciences, Little Rock, Arkansas 72205.

Handbook of Developmental Psychopathology, Second Edition, edited by Arnold J. Sameroff, Michael Lewis, and Suzanne M. Miller. Kluwer Academic/Plenum Publishers, New York, 2000.

tighter and the normative structure has been more abstinence oriented (as has been true in the United States until the last 2–3 years), alcoholism rates decrease (Department of Health and Human Services, 1997).

Second, alcohol, as a drug of everyday use, occupies a special place in the social order that makes patterns of both use and abuse more heavily tied to other life-cycle variations than is true of other forms of psychopathology. Ethanol happens to be the world's most domesticated psychoactive drug. It is heavily sought after for its pharmacological attributes, and also, in the form of beer, is one of the world's most common foods. And in the form of wine, it is one of the world's major celebratory substances. Thus, alcohol's use structure is heavily embedded in the life fabric of the majority of modern societies. It is a drug of courting, recreation, and relaxation, and it is also a drug with which we sometimes bury people.

Third, but related to point two, because alcohol is so heavily embedded in the fabric of everyday life, not only use but also abuse is to a degree superimposed upon the ongoing life structure. Therefore, patterns of abuse and dependence are likely to differ as a function of the life course variations upon which the alcohol involvement is overlaid (Jackson, Williams, & Gomberg, 1998; Zucker, 1998). An understanding of alcohol problems and development needs to take account of the life-cycle variations that co-occur with the age variation, that make availability greater or lesser, and that to a degree either proscribe or prescribe use with the shifts in role structure that occur. This issue is relevant for all parts of the life cycle, although it has been more commonly applied to the earlier parts of the life cycle. Thus, much of the patterning variation that is evident in the existing epidemiological data, of course, is explainable by way of these variations, but this underlying variation has been insufficiently appreciated. This point is revisited at a number of points throughout the chapter.

Conversely, this pattern of life course interrelatedness has been tantalizing from an explanatory perspective because it means that there will be many apparent associations of interest that are life-course connected. Thus, the proliferation of grand theories of alcoholism (e.g., Chaudron & Wilkinson, 1988) may be seen as an effort by different disciplinary specialists to claim the disorder as their own, out of a belief that it is in fact "capturable" even though the explanatory structures typically embrace only a small part of the causal matrix of the disorder, or else are relevant only to a small segment of the life course of the disorder.

To do justice to the complexity of this biopsychosocial matrix obviously requires more space than is available here. To manage this limitation, after a brief review of the epidemiology of the disorder, we have addressed four topics that we regard as critical to a developmental understanding of origins and course, with brief commentaries along the way about other important points that would need attention in any more comprehensive review of this area. The topics we have chosen are phenotypic heterogeneity, the diversity of developmental trajectories, causal structure across the life span, and the relationship of individual risk structure to context structure.

EPIDEMIOLOGY

Table 30.1 summarizes the National Comorbidity Study (NCS) data on 12-month and lifetime prevalence rates (percentages) for DSM-III-R alcohol abuse and dependence (Kessler et al., 1994). This project was the first to administer a structured psychiatric interview to a national probability sample and has been able to provide projections for rates of psychiatric disorder for the noninstitutionalized civilian population between the ages of 15 and 54 years.

Table 30.1. Lifetime and 12-Month Prevalence of UM-CIDI/DSM-III-R Substance Use Disorders

Disorder	Total		Male		Female	
	Lifetime	12 months	Lifetime	12 months	Lifetime	12 months
Alcohol abuse without dependence	9.4	2.5	12.5	3.4	6.4	1.6
Alcohol dependence	14.1	7.2	20.1	10.7	8.2	3.7
Alcohol abuse/dependence combined	23.5	9.7	32.5	14.1	14.6	5.3
Other drug abuse without dependence	4.4	0.8	5.4	1.3	3.5	0.3
Other drug dependence	7.5	2.8	9.2	3.8	5.9	1.9
Other drug abuse/dependence combined	11.9	3.6	14.6	5.1	9.4	2.1
Any substance abuse/dependence	26.6	11.3	35.4	16.1	17.9	6.6

Source: from Kessler et al. (1994), National Comorbidity Study, and are weighted noninstitutionalized U.S. population percentage estimates for persons 15 to 54 years of age.

To give a larger perspective on the problem, rates for other drug abuse and dependence are also presented.

A number of points about these rate variations are of relevance to this chapter:

1. Alcohol abuse and dependence are the most common of the substance use disorders.
2. Among males, one in three adults have at some point in their lives met either abuse or dependence criteria.
3. Gender differences are significant, and are of the order of 2:1 for abuse, and 3:1 for dependence.
4. Abuse without dependence (involving a pattern of repeated use paired with harmful consequences) represents 40% of the life-course problem, and 24% of the current (12-month prevalence) problem. Or, to put this figure slightly differently, 40% of the lifetime problem is of subclinical proportions but nonetheless may involve socially and personally significant misbehavior (e.g., compromised driving, risky sex, date rape, job absenteeism, neglect of household responsibilities).
5. In addition, because of the gender differences in abuse versus dependence, abuse is a relatively greater problem among females, accounting for 30% of the 12-month total problem, while only accounting for 24% among males.
6. Other drug disorders are substantially less of an issue than alcohol abuse/dependence, with a ratio of 12-month alcohol to drug disorder of 2.7.
7. Other drug disorders are to a large degree superimposed upon alcohol use disorders given that only 14% of 12-month drug disorders occur without a concomitant alcohol diagnosis.
8. The visibility of other drug disorders is likely because the disorders are more dramatic, hence socially compelling, because they appear to be more of a threat to the social order (e.g., because of their links with crime and the belief that they may be less responsive to treatment), and because the social costs involved in interdiction and treatment are proportionately much larger. The lay view, as well, is that the disorders

occur in isolation, which heightens the differentiation between the different types of drug involvement.

Related to these points but not shown in Table 30.1, from the perspective of lifetime rates of disorder, alcohol abuse/dependence is the nationally most prevalent disorder, with 23.5% of the population reporting symptomatology that qualifies them for an abuse or dependence diagnosis at some point during their lives (Kessler et al., 1994). So this set of problems is a large one, and its magnitude is to a degree understandable within the framework we presented in the previous section, namely, that alcohol is the world's most domesticated psychoactive drug.

A major premise of this volume, as well as the authors of this chapter, is that adult disorder does not emerge full-blown in adulthood, but rather is a process that emerges over time, and for which childhood precursors are likely to be identifiable. In that spirit, Table 30.2 presents data from the time frame of childhood and adolescence on onset of drunkenness as one of the first potential markers of the problem alcohol involvement whose adult rates are depicted in Table 30.1.

These data straightforwardly make the case that there is a small subset of individuals who have begun their excessive involvement with alcohol by age 10, and that by age 16, almost half the population has had some problem experiences in this realm. Again, consistent with both the adult data and the framework we have described, beginning signs of problem development are large in a population sense even though it would be a mistake to presume that everyone with early signs of problem use will go on to develop an alcohol use disorder. In fact, for a generation now, the adolescent developmental literature has been clear that early alcohol use as well as alcohol problems need to be regarded as one component part of a deviance syndrome. The syndrome emerges in adolescence and is adolescence-specific in the sense that the majority of individuals with such problems do not go on to develop adult disorder, although some may reach diagnosable levels during their adolescent years (Donovan & Jessor, 1985; Jessor & Jessor, 1977; Zucker, 1987).

This issue of differences in course and a related set of questions about how many different variations there may be, what their determinants are, how best to describe and understand them, has become a major set of questions for the field because it encompasses issues of phenotypic heterogeneity as well as definitional issues about what the "true" nature of alcoholic disorder might be. We turn to that set of questions now.

Table 30.2. Grade of First Drunkeness as Retrospectively Reported by Tenth Graders (Percentage of U.S. Population)

	Grade	Approximate age	First time drunk	Cumulative drunk population
Grade school	4	10	1.3	1.3
	5	11	1.1	2.4
Middle school	6	12	3.2	5.6
	7	13	7.0	12.6
	8	14	11.1	23.7
High school	9	15	16.0	39.7
	10	16	8.0	47.7

Source: 1992 national survey from *Monitoring the Future* (Johnston, O'Malley, & Bachman, 1993, Table 18b, p. 135).

DEFINITIONAL ISSUES AND PROBLEMS
OF PHENOTYPIC HETEROGENEITY

For at least a century now, there have been periodic attempts to classify the diverse array of alcohol-related problems, and probably because of their visibility as well as their greater social impact, the bulk of this attention has focused upon those severe and chronic forms of the problem that are lumped under the rubric of alcoholism (Babor & Lauerman, 1986). Within the last half century, the most visible of these efforts has been Jellinek's (1960) *The Disease Concept of Alcoholism*, which characterized five forms of problem alcohol use but concluded that only two of them fulfilled sufficient addictive criteria (involving physical as well as psychological dependence) to warrant a disease label. Jellinek called these two forms gamma and delta alcoholism.

This envelope of difficulties and symptoms has been variously described over the last generation, and the most recent version, contained in the *Diagnostic and Statistical Manual of Mental Disorders* (DSM-IV; American Psychiatric Association, 1994), differentiates between problems of compulsive use (dependence) and problems of repeated use and harmful consequences (abuse). Dependence includes symptoms related to tolerance and withdrawal, compulsive use, substantial psychosocial consequences, continued use despite significant negative consequences, and is more chronic in nature. Alcohol abuse is a less severe syndrome, characterized by drinking patterns that produce recurrent adverse psychosocial consequences. Abuse is not necessarily prodromal to dependence, and in fact, an increasing literature continues to suggest that the two have different natural histories (Goodwin, Schulsinger, Knop, Mednick, & Guze, 1973; Hasin, Grant, & Endicott, 1990; Vaillant, 1995). At the same time, given that alcohol dependence does not emerge full-blown, a subset of those with abuse is "traveling through," while another subset has reached the end of the line.

In a backhanded way, the DSM nosology has begun to acknowledge developmental variation, if only by providing formal criteria for levels of symptomatic/diagnostic remission that imply there is diagnostic change over time. But the bigger leap—to acceptance that the symptomatology itself may vary with developmental stage—has not yet taken place (Zucker, Davies, Kincaid, Fitzgerald, & Reider, 1997). Thus, commentators have criticized the scheme for inadequately assessing the manner in which alcohol problems show themselves in both adolescents (Pandina, White, & Milgram, 1991), and in the elderly (Beresford & Gomberg, 1995). But the next step, involving the description of dependence as a developmental disorder or even a family of developmental disorders, is only beginning to take place (Zucker, Fitzgerald, & Moses, 1995).

The classification problem is further complicated by the fact that the causal structure driving the emergence of the phenotype is multifactorial (Zucker, Boyd, & Howard, 1994). Differential risk for dependence involves appetitive differences in the reinforcing nature of ethanol and the manner in which intoxication proves to be an energizing versus sedating experience (Newlin & Thomson, 1990; Sher, 1991), as well as a variety of nonalcohol specific factors that are marked by differences in age of onset and the presence versus absence of other psychiatric comorbidity. Thus, significant comorbid psychiatric symptomatology is found in 45% of men and in 65% of women with alcohol use disorders (Helzer, Burnam, & McEvoy, 1991), and the comorbidity increases with the greater severity of the alcohol involvement (Kessler et al., 1997). The strongest coassociation is with antisocial personality disorder, where the ratio of prevalence in alcoholics to prevalence in nonalcoholics (i.e., the odds ratio) is 12:1 for men and 29:1 for women. Although the antisocial comorbidity is by no means the only one that is heavily connected, it is clinically and socially the most visible. More generally, this heterogeneity of alcoholic adaptation would be less of a descriptive issue if it always were secondary to the development of the primary substance use disorder, but a substantial literature indicates this is not always the case (Zucker, 1994).

HOW MANY ALCOHOLISMS?

How is one to make sense out of this diversity? On the basis of the existing literature on comorbidity and course, six different subtypes of adult disorder are easily differentiated. An extended discussion of these subtypes is not possible within the space limitations of this chapter, but a brief recapitulation of that work is provided here. Our summary follows closely on Zucker et al. (1995). The reader is also referred to two earlier papers (Zucker, 1987, 1994) for more extensive discussions of these types and the rationale for their derivation.

Making use of the proposition that stability of behavioral organization in adulthood is a marker that identifies outcomes that, a priori, must be reflective of earlier developmental differences in process, the argument has been made that the clustering of adult symptomatology among alcoholics is likewise a set of midstage markers of trajectory variation that have had a substantial backward span. Utilizing U.S. population estimates of alcoholic comorbidity (cf. Regier et al., 1990) as a route to identification of these major types of behavioral covariation, six adult types have been described in which the evidence is indicative of major differences in developmental trajectory, as well as major differences in adult function, course, and prognosis.

Figure 30.1 provides graphic representations of the trajectories of the different types. Three types are characterized by way of their association with specific forms of psychiatric comorbidity (Figure 30.1a), and the other three, as a group, are differentiated by their lack of significant comorbidity (see Figure 30.1b). One of the comorbid forms, the *antisocial alcoholic* type, involves a coassociation of long standing between alcohol problems and antisocial behavior in its developmentally progressing forms; that is, the antisocial behavior first shows as conduct problems, later emerges into delinquent activity, and ultimately shows as antisocial personality disorder. Or to frame the epigenetic pattern somewhat differently, the antisocial behavior is a central part of the emergence of the alcoholism, and the alcohol problems and alcoholism are an essential piece in the emergence of the antisocial adaptation (cf. Zucker, Ellis, Bingham, Fitzgerald, & Sanford, 1996a, for a fuller description of this type). A second type, *developmentally limited alcoholism*, likewise involves a comorbid antisocial connection, but the conduct disorder is stage-limited (i.e., this is the stage-specific delinquent and impulsive activity of the adolescent problem behavior syndrome [cf. Donovan & Jessor, 1985] that is coupled with the problem alcohol use endemic to adolescence). The third type involves the emergence in childhood and adolescence of internalizing symptomatology in high-risk populations (e.g., Colder & Chassin, 1993; Earls, Reich, Jung, & Cloninger, 1988; Rolf, Johnson, Israel, Baldwin, & Chandra, 1988; Sher, Walitzer, Wood, & Brent, 1991) but appears to be linked to a trajectory of severe and sustained alcohol-related difficulty only in adulthood. This third pattern, termed *negative affect alcoholism*, is more common among women (Schuckit, Pitts, & Reich, 1969; Turnbull & Gomberg, 1990) and has also been tied to the special role demands that women face (Wilsnack, Klassen, Schur, & Wilsnack, 1991), as well as to the influence of genetic factors common to both major depression and alcoholism (Kendler, Heath, Neale, Kessler & Eaves, 1993; Merikangas, Leckman, Prusoff, Pauls, & Weissman, 1985).

The trajectories illustrated in Figure 30.1b depict a subset, alcoholisms that have no

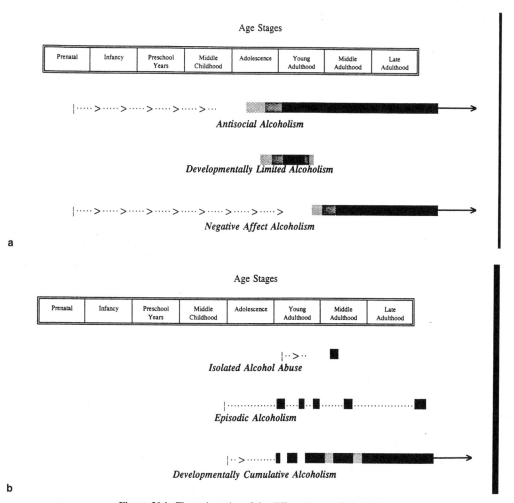

Figure 30.1. The trajectories of the different types of alcoholisms.

clearly demarcated childhood antecedents. They involve sustained alcohol intake, which leads to severe, alcohol-related symptomatology. No other behavioral covariation is known to have linkages to their onset. The hypothesis, still relatively untested, is that these trajectories are driven by the presence of elevated environmental stress, occurring in a social context that provides a support and value structure for alcohol as the drug of choice for tension reduction. When these two conditions are met, and are coupled with a third set of risk factors involving alcohol-specific vulnerabilities that make the consumption of this drug even more reinforcing (or less aversive), then the best-fit scenario exists for alcohol abuse. Under circumstances of nonsustained stress (e.g., immediately preceding or following the breakup of a marriage; cf. Cahalan, 1970), *isolated abuse* may occur. Under circumstances of recurring stress (e.g., times of heightened stress related to periodic job layoffs; cf. Brenner, 1972), or for those in intermittently high-stress occupations, the pattern may become *episodic*. For those whose contextual and individual vulnerability match is greatest, the pattern would eventually move into a chronic adaptation. This latter trajectory has been termed *developmentally cumulative alcoholism.* There are obvious parallels between these latter three trajectories and the developmentally limited but antisocially comorbid pattern of adolescence. Although the form of all four types is similar, for the developmentally limited pattern, individual level etiological risk factors have already been identified, but the onset and termination of the disorder is bounded by nonindividual level contextual factors. This may ultimately also be the case for the episodic and developmentally cumulative variants; in fact, both Schuckit and Moos, and their colleagues have been specially focused upon this issue (e.g., Moos, Brennan, & Schutte, 1998; Schuckit, 1988, 1994). But at the moment, their causal structure has been less well charted.

DEVELOPMENTALLY EARLIER EVIDENCE FOR TRAJECTORY VARIATION: CONVERGING LINES OF WORK

Until recently, with one exception (Zucker et al., 1996b), the evidence for different pathways into disorder for the three comorbid trajectories has been based upon studies either within adolescence or spanning the interval between adolescence and early adulthood. Within this somewhat limited developmental purview, the work has documented both the antisocial trajectory and the developmentally limited one (Schulenberg, O'Malley, Bachman, Wadsworth, & Johnston, 1996a; Schulenberg, Wadsworth, O'Malley, Bachman, & Johnston, 1996b; Zucker, 1987, 1994). However, a new study out of the Dunedin (New Zealand) cohort has now established a direct link between behavioral undercontrol at age 3 and alcohol dependence at age 21 (Caspi, Moffit, Newman, & Silva, 1996), thus affirming the connection between an ontogenetically much earlier, and also more rudimentary form of conduct disruption, and the adult outcome. Furthermore, the Dunedin study documents a link between a rudimentary form of social and behavioral inhibition and fear, and the adult outcome of alcohol problems at age 21. In other words, a connection exists between negative affectivity in early life and problem-alcohol outcome in adulthood. Whether this second pattern of relationships can be specifically tied to anxious or depressive comorbidity in adulthood remains to be demonstrated.

Microclimates and Developmental Variation

The line of reasoning being followed here is that as one disaggregates the variability of drinking behavior and its symptomatic correlates over time, it becomes apparent that multiple pathways of onset, stability, and change are present that have different time courses connected to their flow, and that in some but not all instances, have different process structures regulating their variability. Thus, the two major tasks for the developmental psychopathologist are to (1) refine the nosology, and (2) specify those aspects of etiology that are uniform across trajectories but only vary in presence (amount) and timing of appearance, and those that are reflective of different causal structures. Clearly, these are interactive problems, since greater nosological clarity brings with it the greater ability to specify etiological similarity and variation. Conversely, greater etiological clarity brings with it the ability to make more accurate, and previously ignored, diagnostic specifications that refine the definition of the phenomena. In this spirit, we move again to the epidemiological data in order to highlight the importance of microsystems for trajectory variation. To illustrate the point, we focus upon drinking practices in the second half of the life cycle, with the caveat that a similar point could be made for younger populations, but the data are not as dramatic.

Recent surveys show that patterns of alcohol use among older adults are changing. The 1980s saw a significant decline in the level of alcohol use in the U.S. population, and the 1984 and 1990 National Alcohol Surveys (NAS) bear this out, with 70% of the population reporting current (past year) drinking in 1984 and 65% in 1990 (Midanik & Clark, 1994). However, these general population figures obscure significant subgroup variability. Thus, the same data bases show 59% of men age 60 and over to be current drinkers in 1984, but the figure changes to 66% for 1990. Comparable figures for women in this age group are 49% in 1984 and 37% in 1990, a significant decline. This age and gender variation that on the one hand moves in opposition to the overall population trend of decline in level of drinking, and on the other hand moves in consonance with it, not only reinforces the point about subgroup variation, but also under-scores another especially relevant principle for older populations—that there is substantial across-group heterogeneity (Hertzman et al., 1994). Thus, for some segments of the population the stereotype of low levels of drinking and low levels of problem is accurate, and for others, disaggregated figures indicate that it is less so.

Cross-sectional but age-graded data from both the NAS and other recent surveys illus-trate major across-age variations in patterns of alcohol use that vary not only by gender but also by ethnic group membership and cohort (cf. the National Longitudinal Alcohol Epidemi-ologic Survey, NLAES; Grant, 1997; Grant et al. 1994). Jackson et al.'s (1998) disaggregation of the Substance Abuse and Mental Health Services Administration (SAMHSA) National Household Surveys of 1991 and 1993 (Gerstein et al., 1996) by age and ethnic group also makes this case strongly, albeit with a cross-sectional sample, and shows that the trajectory of peak use, as well as the slope of change over the life span, varies across groups. We reproduce the 1991 problem indicator data in Figures 30.2 and 30.3 to give some sense of this variability.

The specificity argument for developmental variation is central to an appreciation that even though overall alcohol problems may be a comparatively lower level phenomenon in one macrosystem (e.g., the elderly), microsystem figures may show a different pattern. Thus, again with regard to the elderly, the relatively higher patterns of consumption and problems of the Boomer generation (Grant, 1997) are another overlay on the moving cohort that will become aged over the next generation. The concomitants of these population shifts are likely to produce patterns of alcohol use that are not comparable to the nation's past experience with earlier cohorts, because the newer elderly are beginning to involve different value structures that drive different alcohol use structures (Zucker, 1998).

Two subpopulations are particularly implicated in these anticipated changes: The Euro-American subpopulation, although decreasing in proportion among the elderly, over the next generation will remain the largest subset of the elderly. This subgroup will have a higher educational level and greater financial resources than was true for earlier generations of the elderly, and the likelihood of sustained leisure-time activity as well as a style of health monitoring that is related to successful aging should lead both to increased longevity and to a style of recreational living that welcomes moderate alcohol use. The other subgroup is the Hispanic subpopulation, which is increasing at the largest rate of all elderly subgroups. This subpopulation has a more disenfranchised opportunity structure, concomitant lower levels of education, and a machismo set of values about alcohol use for men. These factors in turn are anticipated to produce substantially greater problem use among the elderly than in past generations (Zucker, 1998).

CAUSAL STRUCTURE ACROSS THE LIFE SPAN

In constructing a model of causal process that is pertinent across the life span, we need to return to a theme with which we began this chapter, concerning the special role of context structure in the emergence of this particular form of psychopathology. Given the centrality of

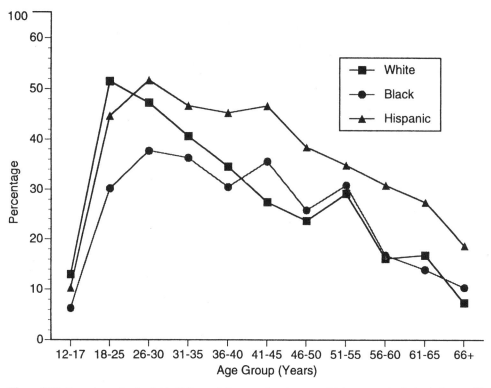

Figure 30.2. Percentage of males in the U.S. population reporting 4 or more drinks on any single day in the past 30 days, by age group and race. (*Sources*: Gerstein et al. [1996]; Jackson et al. [1998])

the object (alcohol) to the problem behavioral repertoire, any full model needs to take account of "object presence." Thus, use and, ultimately, abuse/dependence are modulated by drug availability, which is culturally regulated by differences in relative "wetness" of the social structure, as well as legally regulated by laws about places of sale and use, level of alcohol in the beverages being sold, and age of legal consumption (Edwards et al., 1994). Social regulation also occurs by way of the normative availability of alcohol in some settings (e.g., near college campuses and military bases), and its relative unavailability in others (e.g., offices, public schools). Thus, at a structural level, much of the informal regulation of patterns of abuse can be related to the age-gradedness of patterns of use, with heaviest use and heaviest problems peaking around age 20 and declining thereafter. Prevalence rates for disorder (i.e., dependence) follow a similar pattern, with median age of onset reported to be age 18, at least based upon retrospective report of symptom clustering (Kessler et al., 1997). From a developmental perspective, it is therefore important to underscore that settings sometimes have an age-gradedness associated with them, and the availability of alcohol as well as the encouragement of alcohol use, can be a part of that. Our college campuses and sports arenas until very recently have had this attribute.

Concurrent with the sociolegal control structure is another set of structures pertaining to the unique pharmacology of this drug. So far, the literature has pointed to mechanisms that are (1) appetitive, that is, relating to craving, to the reinforcing properties of ethanol's drug effects

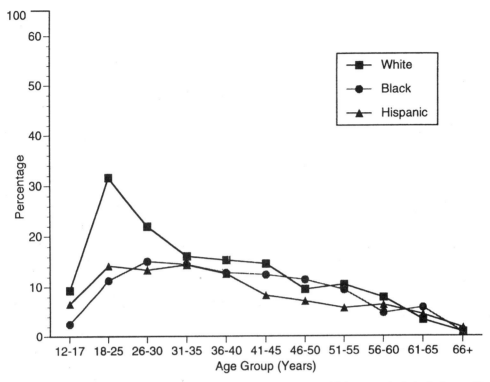

Figure 30.3. Percentage of females in the U.S. population reporting 4 or more drinks on any single day in the past 30 days, by age group and race. (*Sources*: Gerstein et al. [1996]; Jackson et al. [1998])

(Newlin & Thomson, 1990) and to the changes in sensitization occurring over time, what Robinson and Berridge (1993) call "sensitized wanting" rather than "liking"; (2) connected to affect regulation, as well as (3) structures relating to impulsivity and control. Mechanisms having specially to do with the neuroanatomic structures underlying reward, such as the nucleus accumbens (Koobs, Rassnick, Heinrichs, & Weiss, 1994), as well as chemoarchitectural structures involving the serotonergic and the dopaminergic neurotransmitter systems, have been especially implicated in these processes. A full exposition of these mechanisms is beyond the scope of this chapter but the interested reader is referred to the most recent NIAAA Report to Congress for a summary of this work (National Institute on Alcohol Abuse and Alcoholism, 1997).

Behavioral undercontrol has been repeatedly postulated as the precursor of an impulsivity-to-aggression pathway (Sher, 1991; Tarter & Vanukov, 1994), but it also can be posited as an early vulnerability precursor to poorer capacity in monitoring and decision-making functions. This vulnerability has been specifically connected with frontal lobe deficits, which in turn have been hypothesized to underlie deficits in executive function (cf. Pihl & Bruce, 1995; Pihl & Peterson, 1991; Tarter, Alterman, & Edwards, 1985). The pathway is as follows: Executive function deficits lead to attentional deficits, which in turn lead to poorer decision making, which has implications for (1) poor judgment in choosing peers, and (2) less ability to monitor and desist from drinking when drunkenness and other drinking consequences commence.

A Multidomain, Probabilistic Framework for the Causal Matrix

A number of very different regulatory structures are operating, some "top-down," others "bottom-up," and the environment in which they interact is modified as the individual organism moves into new contexts that shift the social control structure, on the one hand, that encourage or suppress the impulsivity, and choice structure on the other, and that play upon the epigenetic balance that the individual has already achieved. This three-way interplay is what makes this developmental problem not only so interesting but also so complex. There is also increasing evidence that the same control structures do not operate in the same manner at different points in the life cycle, partly out of population selectivity with age (Baltes, 1997), partly out of differences in life-stage challenges presented at different points in the life course (Moos et al., 1998), and partly because the varying context structures that turn genes on and off produce different levels of heritability over the life course (Heller & McClearn, 1995; Jazwinski, 1996).

A multidomain probabilistic model involving both risk aggregation and risk dilution is necessary to account for these different variable networks. For the same reason, it is likely that different causal matrices need to be invoked at different points in the life cycle given the increasing importance of individual control and guidance structures as the individual ages (Baltes, 1997; Bergman & Magnusson, 1997). Until now, this point has not explicitly been made in the etiological literature, but it is a logical proposition on the basis of both the existing evidence and epigenetic theory. We follow now with a multidomain cumulation model of the emergence of risk and eventual symptom onset that invokes a shifting variable structure as development proceeds.

The Emergence of Early-Stage Alcohol Problems and Early-Onset Dependence

A plausible cumulation sequence is as follows: (1) the development of aggressive behavior and negative affect, and alcohol use, in a familial structure that genetically transmits vulnerability to these attributes, then models as well as shapes them, (2) coupled with individual biological constitutional vulnerability in these areas, (3) will cumulate into an adaptation that moves the child into peer networks that are high in aggression and negative mood, and substance use; (4) social support structure, family level, and individual level religious, school, and work involvement are mediators (1, 2, and 3) as well as moderators (4) of this process. At the same time, it needs to be clear that these variable structures are all nonspecific to alcohol and are more likely contributory to the emergence of behavioral repertoires high in impulsivity, undercontrol, and affect dysregulation.

A parallel social structure that shapes the emergence of early encounters with alcohol likewise needs to be in place; that is, we return again to the need to specify an availability and encouragement matrix for the object (the drug and drug-using behavior) as a necessary ingredient in any full model of alcoholic etiology. The drug-using social structure (5) first shapes the development of rudimentary drug schemas that allow earlier identification of drugs (alcohol) as desirable objects and also shapes an awareness of the usefulness of these objects as producers of change of state (6) later shapes the development of expectancies that are positive toward use and relatively less negative toward abuse of alcohol and other drugs (Zucker et al., 1995); (7) as with (3), this expectancy structure encourages earlier involvement with alcohol using peers; (8) alcohol nonspecific factors and alcohol specific factors, when operating in concert, produce the outcome of earlier onset of alcohol use and heavier drinking (quantity and frequency). The development of alcohol abuse, as well as the earlier and more problematic involvement with other drugs, follows as a result of these cumulations; (9) when the factors remain in place, progression will continue; (10) when (if) progression continues long enough, the outcome will be the clinical one of alcohol abuse/dependence, with comorbid antisociality and depression. In other words, the outcome is an early-onset diagnosis coupled with extensive but specialized psychiatric comorbidity. Other drug abuse/dependence diagnoses are also likely to occur at greater frequency and with earlier onset than in individuals lacking such a cumulation history. Conversely, when fewer of these factors are present, the process takes longer, or requires higher levels of a smaller number of variables, in order to sustain progression.

Utilizing the same variable network and risk-cumulation model as a framework for influencing structure, gender differences are easily derivable from differences in proximal exposure to these risk factors. The model, along with a substantial amount of recent data (Anthony et al., 1993; Chassin et al., 1995), suggests that process is similar across the sexes; that is, only when socialization structure has more risk aggregation (availability, modeling, shaping), and when there is an individual background of vulnerability, should there be earlier use and abuse. Thus, assuming the context structure remains in place, an early end point of abuse/dependence with comorbidity in late adolescence and early adulthood is anticipatable for girls as well as boys (Moses, 1996).

This is a multidomain cumulation model of the emergence of risk and eventual symptom onset that involves a shifting variable structure as development proceeds. Each of the steps described is separately testable, and the earlier steps, involving (1) and (2) have already been tested and confirmed among boys (Zucker, Ellis, Bingham, & Fitzgerald, 1996b), and early work tends to be confirmatory for girls (Puttler, Zucker, Fitzgerald, & Bingham, 1998). There has also been some confirmation of (4), albeit at a very early way point (i.e., among preschoolers).

Age-Related Variability in Causal Structure

Alcohol involvement and problem alcohol involvement are both endemic to, and epidemic in, adolescence, and an elaborate and well-elaborated theory of problem behavior has been articulated to account for the age-related variation (Jessor, Donovan & Costa, 1991; Jessor & Jessor, 1977). Also endemic is the age-related transitioning away from alcohol problems in the early twenties. Peak alcohol problem rates occur in the 18–22 years age range, and as noted earlier, median onset for abuse/dependence is age 18. Moreover, 80% of abuse/ dependence has been estimated to have onset prior to age 30 (Helzer et al., 1991). For these reasons, few studies have examined the course of alcohol disorders into later phases of adulthood, and information regarding both the incidence and causal structure for new cases of alcohol problems/abuse/dependence in both middle adulthood and among older adults is sparse. Moreover, as we have described earlier in this chapter, what information there is indicates that the alcohol abuse/dependence of later onset is of different type as well as of different longevity than that which has an adolescent onset (Zucker, 1994; Zucker et al., 1995).

The retrospectively based epidemiological data on this issue indicate that abuse/ dependence commencing in later life is more likely without psychiatric comorbidity and is of shorter duration than the earlier-onset forms (Helzer et al., 1991). The symptom picture that is presented also implies that this later emerging form has a different causal structure, involving those with an initially higher functioning social adaptation, and where the alcohol problems are driven by relatively immediate loss (of job, marriage, spouse) (Brenner, 1972; Brennan & Moos, 1991; Sobell, Sobell, Toneatto, & Leo, 1993). However, the jury is still out regarding the degree to which a different causal structure needs to be invoked for this later-onset subset.

In the last decade, a number of studies have suggested that still another later-onset type is identifiable, involving the first onset of alcohol problems in midlife or thereafter (what may developmentally be termed a *late-onset* type). Rates of "late onset" have been estimated to range from 10% (Chermack, Blow, Walton, Mudd, & Hill, 1997) to 41% of those with problems/dependence (Finlayson, Hurt, Davis, & Morse, 1988). However, the true prevalence is difficult to estimate for a number of reasons. First, studies have used widely divergent definitions of what constitutes late onset, ranging from onset after age 40 (Adams & Waskel, 1993), after age 50 (Blow et al., 1998; Chermack et al., 1997; Schonfeld & Dupree, 1991), age 60 (Atkinson, Tolson, & Turner, 1990), and even after age 65 (Finlayson et al., 1988). Second, the definitional issue of what constitutes alcoholism and what constitutes "hazardous" or problem use has not been clearly enough demarcated. This is a particularly relevant developmental issue given that what constitutes problem use, but not dependence, for a woman over age 65 may be as little as 10 drinks per week because of lower body weight and higher alcohol absorption rates of females, coupled with the greater likelihood that the ethanol may interact with ongoing medical conditions (Barry, 1997). Conversely, the figure may be 21 drinks per week for a healthy young adult male. Third, a good deal of the work has either used brief, unstructured measures of lifetime alcohol problems and alcohol symptoms (Atkinson et al., 1990), or did not appear to assess lifetime alcohol consumption patterns (Schonfeld & Dupree, 1991). And most importantly, population studies that would allow unbiased estimates of true prevalence have not yet been utilized to characterize this phenomenon.

Understanding of causal structure is similarly not well documented given the problems of retrospective distortion (Henry, Moffitt, Caspi, Langley, & Silva, 1994) and the fact that no one has yet tracked the natural history of these phenomena from childhood to old age with a sufficiently broadly defined population sample to ensure generalizability of findings. A number of the earlier studies on "late-onset" alcoholism have suggested that these late-onset problem drinkers and alcoholics have less severe alcohol problems, less family history of alcoholism, greater social stability, lower current alcohol consumption levels, and a more positive prognosis for their drinking problems than do participants with an earlier onset (Atkinson et al., 1990; Brennan & Moos, 1991; Schonfeld & Dupree, 1991). However, more recent studies using more structured and comprehensive assessment techniques have yielded divergent findings. For example, Chermack et al. (1997) found that late-onset alcoholics (onset after age 50) did not differ from earlier-onset alcoholics in current alcohol consumption levels but had more current alcohol-related diagnostic symptoms. Thus, at present, it is not possible to offer a definitive summary of process. At the same time, these phenomena are of increasing salience given that they are heavily linked to population changes taking place over the next generation (Gomberg, Hegedus, & Zucker, 1998). Thus, it is likely that this situation will be addressed in substantially greater detail in the not too distant future.

THE CORRELATION OF CONTEXTS AND INDIVIDUAL RISK, AND THE NESTING OF RISK STRUCTURE

From an etiological perspective, there is special interest in the degree to which risk aggregation is correlated, both at the individual and familial levels, as well as at the neighborhood level. At the individual level, the literature has increasingly acknowledged the clustering of comorbid symptomatology, social dysfunction, and alcoholism severity among adults (Babor, 1996); in fact, such assortment has been one of the driving forces for the notion that subtypes of disorder need to be demarcated. In the same vein, the association of severe alcoholism with poverty has a long and visible history (Fitzgerald & Zucker, 1995), and recent analyses at the microenvironmental level have documented a clear association between neighborhood disadvantage and alcoholism rates (Zucker et al., in press). The most common explanation of this has been that poverty, and the neighborhood structure in which it is embedded, drive the alcoholism (i.e., a top-down explanation; Curran & Zucker, 1998). What has been less clear is the degree to which individual processes are also at work here. Some evidence suggests the work of individual processes, at least for those with the antisocial subtype. Thus, antisocial alcoholic men are more likely to marry/couple with antisocial and heavy drinking/alcoholic women (Ellis et al., 1998; Zucker et al. 1996a). Thus, the families they create are more likely to be disadvantaged in their capacity to socialize offspring. Antisocial alcoholism is also associated with downward social mobility (Zucker et al., 1996b), and offspring in these families, even early in life, appear to be developmentally more disadvantaged; that is, they have more learning disabilities and intellectual deficits than do offspring from alcoholic but not antisocial families (Poon, Ellis, Zucker, & Fitzgerald, 1998). A risk cumulation theory would suggest that as these factors continue to cumulate, they produce a risk structure that moves the child into peer networks high in aggression, negative mood, and substance use, thus providing a familial, a neighborhood, and a peer structure, all of which act in concert in encouraging the development of (1) an expectancy structure that is positive toward use and abuse of alcohol and other drugs, (2) very early onset for such use, and (3) a stable repertoire of behaviors that are prototypical for the eventual emergence of abuse/ dependence.

We have elsewhere suggested that this risk aggregation in certain ecological and familial microenvironments needs to be regarded as a "nesting structure" (Zucker et al., 1995) that makes stability of psychopathological outcome much more likely and therefore encourages the view that a trajectory of development exists. We have also argued (Ellis et al., 1998) that this aggregation structure changes the process model of risk, because the variable network determining the effective causal structure has become sufficiently different; it initially contains more variance pertaining to parental and child psychopathology, social deviance, and neurobiological vulnerability than is true of other nonaggregated structures, and the nested nature of these different risks is therefore more likely to produce a coalescence and overlearning of the risky behavioral repertoire than would be anticipated in a less densely risk-laden system. In contrast, when the microenvironment has less "collinearity," then developmental course should be more fluid and also apparently more probabilistic. This line of reasoning is consistent with normative studies of adolescence that have shown the enhanced effects upon drug use and timing of onset when family conflict, association with deviant peers, and poor academic performance are clustered (Duncan, Duncan, Biglan, & Ary, 1998).

TRAJECTORIES OR PATHWAYS?

Webster's dictionary defines trajectory as "The curve which a body describes in space, as a planet or comet in its orbit, or a projectile in passing from the muzzle to the first point of impact" (G. & C. Merriam, 1943). In short, a trajectory is a pathway through space that is primarily determined at the time either the "orbit" is established or the projectile is fired. Only very major planetary events (or for projectiles, major obstacles) are capable of altering course once the trajectory is established. We suggest that this metaphor is probably not appropriate as an accurate general descriptor of developmental course for disordered outcome in this area. It fits best in the circumstances of nested risk, but in other circumstances, where context is not so densely risk laden, the probabilistic nature of risk variation implies that course will vary from one life stage to the next. On these grounds, the "pathway" metaphor is more descriptive: It allows for "trajectory" over shorter distances (after all, pathways are more likely the route of choice when compared to their adjacent surroundings, and pathways are also predetermined routes), but it also allows for branching and choice points. In the framework of our earlier descriptions, "course" comes closest to a trajectory for antisocial alcoholics and their high-risk offspring, but the metaphor is not useful for others. In the same vein, the late-onset alcoholic subtype provides an example of a pathway bifurcation. And perhaps most important of all, preventive intervention as well as remedial intervention activities are deliberate, socially engineered efforts to modify course. When successful, they likewise provide alternative pathways (Steinman, Kloska, Schulenberg, & Zucker, 1998; Steinman & Schulenberg, 1997).

ACKNOWLEDGMENTS.   Preparation of this chapter was supported by several grants from the National Institute on Alcohol Abuse and Alcoholism (2P50 AA07378, 2R01 AA07065, and T32 AA 07477).

REFERENCES

Adams S. L., & Waskel S.A. (1993). Late onset alcoholism: Stress or structure. *Journal of Psychology, 127,* 329–334.

American Psychiatric Association. (1994). *Diagnostic and statistical manual of mental disorders* (4th ed.; DSM-IV). Washington, DC: Author.

Atkinson, R. M., Tolson, R. L., & Turner, J. A. (1990). Late versus early onset problem drinking in older men. *Alcoholism: Clinical and Experimental Research, 14,* 574–579.

Babor, T. F. (1996). The classification of alcoholics: Typology theories from the 19th century to the present. *Alcohol Health and Research World, 20,* 6–17.

Babor, T. F., & Lauerman, R. J. (1986). Classification and forms of inebriety: Historical antecedents of alcohol typologies. In M. Galanter (Ed.), *Recent developments in alcoholism* (Vol. 4, pp. 113–144). New York: Plenum Press.

Baltes, P. B. (1997). On the incomplete architecture of human ontogeny. *American Psychologist, 52,* 366–380.

Barry, K. L. (1997). Alcohol and drug abuse. In M. Mengel & W. Holleman (Eds.), *Fundamentals of clinical practice: A textbook on the patient, doctor, and society.* New York: Plenum Medical Book Co.

Beresford, T. P., & Gomberg, E. S. L. (Eds.). (1995). *Alcohol and aging.* New York: Oxford University Press.

Bergman, L. R., & Magnusson, D. (1997). A person-oriented approach in research on developmental psychopathology. *Development and Psychopathology, 9,* 291–320.

Blow, F. C., Walton, M. A., Chermack, S. T., Mudd, S. A., Brower, K. J., & Comstock, M. A. (1998). *Treatment outcome for elderly alcoholics following elder-specific inpatient treatment.* Unpublished manuscript, University of Michigan Alcohol Research Center, Ann Arbor, MI.

Brennan, P., & Moos, R. H. (1991). Functioning, life context, and help seeking among late-onset problem drinkers: Comparisons with nonproblem and early-onset problem drinkers. *British Journal of Addiction, 86,* 1139–1150.

Brenner, M. H. (1972). *Mental illness and the economy.* Cambridge, MA: Harvard University Press.

Cahalan, D. (1970). *Problem drinkers.* San Francisco: Jossey-Bass.

Caspi, A., Moffitt, T. E., Newman, D. L., & Silva, E. A. (1996). Behavioral observations at age 3 years predict adult psychiatric disorders: Longitudinal evidence from a birth cohort. *Archives of General Psychiatry, 53,* 1033–1039.

Chaudron, C. D., & Wilkinson, D. A. (Eds.). (1988). *Theories on alcoholism.* Toronto: Addiction Research Foundation.

Chermack, S. T., Blow, F. C., Walton, M. A., Mudd, S. A., & Hill, E. M. (1997). Older adults with alcohol diagnoses: An examination of early and late onset (abstract). *Alcoholism: Clinical and Experimental Research, 22,* 574.

Colder, C. R., & Chassin, L. (1993). The stress and negative affect model of adolescent alcohol use and the moderating effects of behavioral under control. *Journal of Studies on Alcohol, 54,* 326–334.

Department of Health and Human Services. (1997). *Ninth Special Report to the U.S. Congress on Alcohol and Health.* Bethesda, MD: Author (National Institutes of Health, National Institute on Alcohol Abuse and Alcoholism, NIH Publication No. 97-4017).

Donovan, J. E., & Jessor, R. (1985). Structure of problem behavior in adolescence and young adulthood. *Journal of Consulting and Clinical Psychology, 53,* 890–904.

Duncan S. C., Duncan, T. E., Biglan, A., & Ary, D. (1998). Contributions of the social context to the development of adolescent substance use: A multivariate latent growth modeling approach. *Drug and Alcohol Dependence, 50,* 57–71.

Earls, F., Reich, W., Jung, K. G., & Cloninger, C. R. (1988). Psychopathology in children of alcoholic and antisocial parents. *Alcohol: Clinical and Experimental Research, 12,* 481–487.

Edwards, G., Arif, A., & Hodgson, R. (1981). Nomenclature and classification of drug-and alcohol-related problems. A WHO memorandum. *Bulletin of the World Health Organization, 99,* 225.

Edwards, G., et al. (1994). *Alcohol policy and the public good.* New York: Oxford University Press.

Ellis, D. A., Zucker, R. A., Von Eye, A., Fitzgerald, H. E., Bingham, C. R., & Naud, S. (1998). *Typological differences in patterns of risk load and child adaptation among young alcoholic families.* (MSU–UM Longitudinal Study and University of Michigan Alcohol Research Center, Ann Arbor. Manuscript under review.

Fils-Aime, M., Eckardt, M., George, D., Brown, G., Mefford, M., & Linnoila, M. (1996). Early-onset alcoholics have lower CSF 5-HIAA than late-onset alcoholics. *Archives of General Psychiatry, 53,* 211–216.

Finlayson, R. E., Hurt, R. D., Davis, L. R., Jr., & Morse, R. M. (1988). Alcoholism in elderly persons: A study of psychiatric and psychosocial features of 216 inpatients. *Mayo Clinic Proceedings, 63,* 761–768.

Fitzgerald, H. E., & Zucker, R. A. (1995). Socioeconomic status and alcoholism: Structuring developmental pathways to addiction. In H. E. Fitzgerald, B. M. Lester, & B. Zuckerman (Eds.), *Children of poverty* (pp. 125–147). New York: Garland Press.

G. & C. Merriam Co. (1943). *Webster's collegiate dictionary, Fifth edition.* Springfield, MA: Author.

Gerstein, D. R., Gray, F., Epstein, J., & Ghadialy, R. (1996). *Mental health estimates from the 1994 National Household Survey on Drug Abuse.* Advance Report Number 16: DHHS Publication No. (SMA) 36-3103. Substance Abuse and Mental Health Services Administration. Washington, DC: U.S. Government Printing Office.

Gomberg, E. S. L. (1995). Black and white older men: Alcohol use and abuse. In T. P. Beresford & E. S. L. Gomberg (Eds.), *Alcohol and aging.* New York: Oxford University Press.

Gomberg, E. S. L., Hegedus, A. M., & Zucker, R. A. (Eds.). (1998). *Alcohol problems and aging* (NIAAA Research Monograph No. 33). Rockville, MD: U.S. Department of Health and Human Services.

Goodwin, D. W., Schulsinger, F., Knop, J., Mednick, S., & Guze, S. B. (1973). Alcohol problems in adoptees raised apart from alcoholic biological parents. *Archives of General Psychiatry, 28,* 238–243.

Grant, B. F. (1997). Prevalence and correlates of alcohol use and DSM-IV alcohol dependence in the United States: Results of the National Longitudinal Epidemiologic Survey. *Journal of Studies on Alcohol, 58,* 464–473.

Grant, B. F., Harford, T. C., Dawson, D. A., Chou, P., Dufour, M., & Pickering, R. (1994). Prevalence of DSM-IV alcohol abuse and dependence. United States, 1992. *Alcohol Health and Research World, 18,* 243–248.

Hasin, D. S., Grant, B., & Endicott, J. (1990). The natural history of alcohol abuse: Implications for definitions of alcohol use disorders. *American Journal of Psychiatry, 147,* 1537–1541.

Heller, D. A., & McClearn, G. E. (1995). Alcohol, aging, and genetics. In T. P. Beresford & E. S. L. Gomberg (Eds.), *Alcohol and aging* (pp. 99–114). New York: Oxford University Press.

Helzer, J. E., Burnam, A., & Mc Evoy, L. T. (1991). Alcohol abuse and dependence. In L. N. Robins & D. A. Regier (Eds.), *Psychiatric disorders in America: The epidemiologic catchment area studies* (pp. 81–115). New York: Free Press.

Henry, B., Moffitt, T. E., Caspi, A., Langley, J., & Silva, P. A. (1994). On the "Remembrance of things past": A longitudinal evaluation of the retrospective method. *Psychological Assessment, 6,* 92–101.

Hertzman, C., Frank, J., & Evans, R. G. (1994). Heterogeneities in health status and the determinants of population health. In R. Evans, M. Barer, & T. Marmor (Eds.), *Why are some people healthier than others?* (pp. 67–92). New York: Aldine.

Jackson, J. S., Williams, D. R., & Gomberg, E. S. L. (1998). Aging and alcohol use and abuse among African-Americans: A life-course perspective. In E. S. L. Gomberg, A. M. Hegedus, & R. A. Zucker (Eds.), *Alcohol problems and aging* (pp. 63–87). (NIAAA Research Monograph No. 33). NIH Publication No. 98-4163. Bethesda, MD: NIAAA.

Jazwinski, S. M. (1996). Longevity, genes, and aging. *Science, 273,* 54–59.

Jellinek, E. M. (1960). *The disease concept of alcoholism.* New Haven, CT: Hillhouse Press.

Jessor, R., Donovan, J. E., & Costa, F. M. (1991). *Beyond adolescence: Problem behavior and young adult development.* New York: Cambridge University Press.

Jessor, R., & Jessor, S. L. (1977). *Problem behavior and psychosocial development: A longitudinal study of youth.* New York: Academic Press.

Johnston, L. D., O'Malley, P. M., & Bachman, J. G. (1993). *National survey results on drug use from the Monitoring the Future study, 1975–1992: Vol. 1. Secondary school students.* Rockville, MD: National Institute on Drug Abuse.

Kendler, K. S., Heath, A. C., Neale, M. C., Kessler, R. C., & Eaves, L. J. (1993). Alcoholism and major depression in women: A twin study of the causes of comorbidity. *Archives of General Psychiatry, 50,* 690–698.

Kessler, R. C., Crum, R. M., Warner, L. A., Nelson, C. B., Schulenberg, J., & Anthony, J. C. (1997). Lifetime co-occurrence of DSM-III-R alcohol abuse and dependence with other psychiatric disorders in the National Comorbidity Survey. *Archives of General Psychiatry, 54,* 313–321.

Kessler, R. C., McGongale, K. A., Zhao, S., Nelson, C. B., Hughs, M., Eshleman, S., Wittchen, H. U., & Kendler, K. S. (1994). Lifetime and 12-month prevalence of DSM-III-R psychiatric disorders in the United States. *Archives of General Psychiatry, 51,* 8–19.

Koob, G. F., Rassnick, S., Heinrichs, S., & Weiss, F. (1994). Alcohol, the reward system and dependence. In B. Jansson, H. L. Jornvall, U. Rydberg, L. Terenius, & B. L. Vallee (Eds.), *Toward a molecular basis of alcohol use and abuse* (pp. 103–114). Boston: Birkhauser Verlag.

Merikangas, K. R., Leckman, J. F., Prusoff, B., Pauls, D. L., & Weissman, M. M. (1985). Familial transmission of depression and alcoholism. *Archives of General Psychiatry, 42,* 367–371.

Midanik, L. T., & Clark, W. B. (1994). Demographic distribution of US drinking patterns in 1990: Description and trends from 1984. *American Journal of Public Health, 84,* 1218–1222.

Moos, R., Brennan, P., & Schutte, K. (1998). Life context factors, treatment, and late-life drinking behavior. In E. S. L. Gomberg, A. M. Hegedus, & R. A. Zucker (Eds.), *Alcohol problems and aging* (NIAAA Research Monograph No. 33). Rockville, MD: U.S. Department of Health and Human Services.

Moses, H. D. (1996). *Subtypes of alcoholic women.* Unpublished doctoral dissertation, Department of Psychology, Michigan State University, East Lansing.

National Institute on Alcohol Abuse and Alcoholism. (1997). Neurobehavioral effects of alcohol consumption. In the NIAAA *Ninth Special Report to the U.S. Congress on Alcohol and Health* (pp. 99–113). Bethesda, MD: National Institutes of Health.

Newlin, D. B., & Thomson, J. B. (1990). Alcohol challenge with sons of alcoholics: A critical review and analysis. *Psychological Bulletin, 108,* 383–402.

Pandina, R. A., White, H. R., & Milgram, G. G. (1991). Assessing youthful drinking patterns. In D. J. Pittman & H. R. White (Eds.), *Society, culture, and drinking patterns reexamined* (pp. 221–241). New Brunswick, NJ: Rutgers Center of Alcohol Studies.

Pihl, R. O., & Bruce, K. P. (1995). Cognitive impairment in children of alcoholics. *Alcohol Health and Research World, 19,* 142–147.

Pihl, R. O., & Peterson, J. B. (1991). Attention deficit hyperactivity disorder, childhood conduct disorders and alcoholism: Is there an association? *Alcohol Health and Research World, 15,* 25–31.

Poon, E., Ellis, D. A., Zucker, R. A., & Fitzgerald, H. E. (1998). Academic under achievement in elementary school children of alcoholics as related to familial alcoholism subtype (Abstract). *Alcoholism: Clinical and Experimental Research, 22,* 27A.

Puttler, L. I., Zucker, R. A., Fitzgerald, H. E., & Bingham, C. R, (1998). Behavioral outcomes among children of alcoholics during thte early and middle childhood years: Familial subtype variations. *Alcoholism: Clinical and Experimental Research, 22,* 1962–1972.

Reich, T. R., Cloninger, C. R., Van Eerdewegh, P., Rice, J. P., & Mullaney, J. (1988). Secular trends in the familial transmission of alcoholism. *Alcoholism: Clinical and Experimental Research, 12,* 458–464.

Robinson, T. E., & Berridge, K. C. (1993). The neural basis of drug craving: An incentive-sensitization theory of addiction. *Brain Research Reviews, 18,* 247–291.

Rolf, J. E., Johnson, J. L., Israel, E., Baldwin, J., & Chandra, A. (1988). Depressive affect in school-aged children of alcoholics. *British Journal of Addiction, 83,* 841–848.

Schonfeld, L., & Dupree, L. W. (1991). Antecedents of drinking for early- and late-onset elderly alcohol abusers. *Journal of Studies on Alcohol, 52,* 587–592.

Schuckit, M. A., Pitts, F. N., & Reich, T. (1969). Alcoholism: I. Two types of alcoholism in women. *Archives of General Psychiatry, 20,* 301–306.

Schulenberg, J., O'Malley, P. M., Bachman, J. G., Wadsworth, K. N., & Johnston, L. D. (1996a). Getting drunk and growing up: Trajectories of frequent binge drinking during the transition to early adulthood. *Journal of Studies on Alcohol, 57,* 289–304.

Schulenberg, J., Wadsworth, K. N., O'Malley, P. M., Bachman, J. G., & Johnston, L. D. (1996b). Adolescent risk factors for binge drinking during the transition to young adulthood: Variable- and pattern-centered approaches to change. *Developmental Psychology, 32,* 659–674.

Sher, K. (1991). *Children of alcoholics: A critical appraisal of theory and research.* Chicago: Univerisity of Chicago Press.

Sher, K. J., Walitzer, K. S., Wood, P. K., & Brent, E. E. (1991). Characteristics of children of alcoholics: Putative risk factors, substance use and abuse, and psychopathology. *Journal of Abnormal Psychology, 100,* 427–448.

Sobell, L. C., Sobell, M. B., Toneatto, T., & Leo, G. (1993). What triggers the resolution of alcohol problems without treatment? *Alcoholism: Clinical and Experimental Research, 17,* 217–224.

Steinman, K. J., & Schulenberg, J. (1997, November). Predicting trajectories of alcohol overindulgence in adolescence. Poster presented at the 125th Annual Meeting of the American Public Health Association, Indianapolis, IN.

Steinman, K. J., Kloska, D. D., Schulenberg, J., & Zucker, R. A. (1998, February). *The onset of alcohol misuse in adolescence: Defining trajectories of alcohol overindulgence.* Paper presented at the annual meeting of the Society for Research in Adolescence, San Diego, CA.

Tarter, R. E., Alterman, A. L., & Edwards, K. L. (1985). Vulnerability to alcoholism in men: A behavior–genetic perspective. *Journal of Studies on Alcohol, 46*(4), 329–356.

Tarter, R. E., & Vanukov, M. (1994). Stepwise developmental model of alcoholism etiology. In R. A. Zucker, J. Howard, & G. M. Boyd (Eds.), *The development of alcohol problems: Exploring the biopsychosocial matrix of risk* (NIAAA Research Monograph No. 26, pp. 303–330). Rockville, MD: U.S. Department of Health and Human Services.

Turnbull, J. E., & Gomberg, E. S. L. (1990). The structure of depression in alcoholic women. *Journal of Studies on Alcohol, 51,* 148–154.

Vaillant, G. E. (1995). *The natural history of alcoholism revisited.* Cambridge, MA: Harvard University Press.

Wilsnack, S. C., Klassen, A. D., Schur, B. E., & Wilsnack, R. W. (1991). Predicting onset and chronicity of women's problem drinking: A five-year longitudinal analysis. *American Journal of Public Health, 81,* 305–318.

Zucker, R. A. (1987). The four alcoholisms: A developmental account of the etiologic process. In P. C. Rivers (Ed.), *Alcohol and addictive behaviors: Nebraska Symposium on Motivation, 34* (pp. 27–83). Lincoln: University of Nebraska Press.

Zucker, R. A. (1994). Pathways to alcohol problems and alcoholism: A developmental account of the evidence for multiple alcoholisms and for contextual contributions to risk. In R. A. Zucker, J. Howard, & G. M. Boyd (Eds.), *The development of alcohol problems: Exploring the biopsychosocial matrix of risk* (NIAAA Research Monograph No. 26, pp. 255–289). Rockville, MD: U.S. Department of Health and Human Services.

Zucker, R. A. (1998). Developmental aspects of aging, alcohol involvement, and their inter-relationship. In E. S. L. Gomberg, A. M. Hegedus, & R. A. Zucker (Eds.), *Alcohol problems and aging* (NIAAA Research Monograph No. 33). Rockville, MD: U.S. Department of Health and Human Services.

Zucker, R. A., Boyd, G. M., & Howard, J. (Eds.). (1994). *The development of alcohol problems: Exploring the biopsychosocial matrix of risk* (NIAAA Research Monograph No. 26). Rockville, MD: Department of Health and Human Services.

Zucker, R. A., Davies, W. H., Kincaid, S. B., Fitzgerald, H. E., & Reider, E. E. (1997). Conceptualizing and scaling the developmental structure of behavior disorder. The lifetime alcohol problems score as an example. *Development and Psychopathology, 9,* 453–471.

Zucker, R. A., Ellis, D. A., Bingham, C. R., Fitzgerald, H. E., & Sanford, K. (1996a). Other evidence for at least two alcoholisms: II. Life course variation in antisociality and heterogeneity of alcoholic outcome. *Development and Psychopathology, 8,* 831–848.

Zucker, R. A., Ellis, D. A., Bingham, C. R., & Fitzgerald, H. E. (1996b). The development of alcoholic subtypes: Risk variation among alcoholic families during the early childhood years. *Alcohol Health and Research World, 20,* 46–54.

Zucker, R. A., Fitzgerald, H. E., & Moses, H. D. (1995). Emergence of alcohol problems and the several alcoholisms: A developmental perspective on etiologic theory and life course trajectory. In: D. Cicchetti & D. J. Cohen (Eds.). *Developmental psychopathology: Vol. 2. Risk, disorder and adaptation* (pp. 677–711). New York: Wiley.

Zucker, R. A., Fitzgerald, H. E., Refior, S. K., Puttler, L. I., Pallas, D. M., & Ellis, D. A. (in press). The clinical and social ecology of childhood for children of alcoholics: Description of a study and implications for a differentiated social policy. In H. E. Fitzgerald, B. M. Lester, & B. S. Zuckerman (Eds.), *Children of addiction.* New York: Garland Press.

31

Adolescent Drug Use Development
A Social Interactional and Contextual Perspective

Hyman Hops, Judy A. Andrews, Susan C. Duncan, Terry E. Duncan, and Elizabeth Tildesley

INTRODUCTION

Drug use, both licit and illicit, has become increasingly normative among adolescents over the past two to three decades, with increases in both quantity and variability in substances (Johnston, O'Malley, & Bachman, 1998). With the advent of the 1960s and '70s, the use and abuse of substances such as marijuana, cocaine, and amphetamines have supplemented the traditional licit substances of alcohol and tobacco, although the latter two continue to have the highest prevalence rates. In the 1960s, much of this drug use occurred among adults or on college campuses, with some dispersion to high schools. Today, drug use in high schools can be considered endemic and cause for concern because many teens become young adults with a history of drug-use experiences. Although trends over the past 20 years have varied, current use is relatively high (for complete data, see Johnston et al., 1998). For example, during the 1990s, the 30-day prevalence of any illicit drug increased from approximately 6% to nearly 15% among eighth graders. Among seniors, the same prevalence rates increased from approximately 16% to 26%. Examining the most recent evidence for alcohol, the most prevalent substance, by eighth grade, about 25% have had a drink in the last 30 days. By 12th grade, the prevalence was doubled, and more than half also reported being drunk. Although, a downturn in prevalence rates occurred during the early 1980s, the trend for the '90s has been increasing, with some leveling off in the past couple of years. Thus, these data highlight the normative existence of drug use among adolescents and also indicate the need to carefully assess its possible effects over the short and long run.

From a developmental perspective, adolescence has been characterized as a period of adaptation and change in individual and family processes and the accompanying transitions. It

Hyman Hops, Judy A. Andrews, Susan C. Duncan, Terry E. Duncan, and Elizabeth Tildesley • Oregon Research Institute, Eugene, Oregon 97403.

Handbook of Developmental Psychopathology, Second Edition, edited by Arnold J. Sameroff, Michael Lewis, and Suzanne M. Miller. Kluwer Academic/Plenum Publishers, New York, 2000.

is a period defined by significant physical development coupled with increases in aggressive behavior, conflicts with parents, an orientation away from family toward peers, and experimentation (Collins, 1990; Gjerde, 1986; Magnusson, Stattin, & Allen, 1985; Montemayor, 1982). Experimentation with substances, much like experimentation with other adult-oriented, unconventional, or deviant activities, has been a hallmark of adolescent cultures for generations. Because experimentation per se is normative, it does not necessarily portend later problems, since many adolescents progress through this period and into adulthood with relative ease (Offer & Offer, 1975). Nevertheless, a number of adolescents do experience problems with drug use and abuse, delinquency, depression, and other psychological difficulties. What factors lead some adolescents not to experiment, others to experiment with substances and yet continue to function competently, and others to go on to more regular use and perhaps abuse, has been a focus of our research effort for the past 15 years (Andrews, Hops, Ary, Lichtenstein, & Tildesley, 1991; Duncan, Duncan, & Hops, 1994; Hops, Tildesley, Lichtenstein, Ary, & Sherman, 1990). Although a variety of factors such as advertising, availability, and genetics, to mention a few, can contribute to the onset, maintenance, use, and abuse of substances, we have focused on the social ecology of adolescents and young adults, primarily that of the family and the peer group, with some attention to larger ecological variables such as socioeconomic status (SES). Both familial and peer influences have been identified as major contributors to adolescent drug use and abuse. In the present chapter, we present the results of longitudinal studies that our group has conducted.

More specifically, we first discuss the structure and sequencing of adolescent drug-use involvement and identify patterns of onset and use over time. Next, we examine whether substance use or misuse is part of larger repertoire of problematic behaviors, such as delinquency and precocious sex. Third, we examine the social influences that could be contributing to these results. To, this end, we focus on a range of family influences, including parent and sibling use, and relationships, peer influences, and the confluence of peer and family effects. Because of the longitudinal nature of our data, we examine both the predictors of substance use and its consequences in late adolescence and young adulthood, including the effect on intimate relationships. In general, these results are presented within a contextual and developmental framework so that we can explore not only the predictors of substance use but also the social processes that contribute to its onset, maintenance, and long-term use as individuals move through adolescence and into young adulthood at various rates and with various competencies.

Our conceptual position is based primarily on social interactional theory (e.g., Cairns, 1979; Patterson, 1982), which has been useful in investigating socialization practices and developmental trends, as well as problematic behavior patterns (e.g., Patterson, Reid, & Dishion, 1992). With the emphasis on behavior within a responsive social environment, social interactional theory suggests that interactional patterns within salient contexts are critical areas of study and key targets for change (Cairns, 1979; Lamb, Suomi, & Stephenson, 1979; Patterson & Reid, 1984). Social interactional theory is supplemented by social learning theory (Bandura, 1977, 1986; Bandura & Walters, 1963) to account for behavior learned as a function of modeling or imitation. Within this framework, we have attempted to identify the specific processes wherein conflict in the home and coercive family interactions, along with poor parental monitoring, lead to an association with deviant peers and subsequent substance use. That substance use appears to be part of a general problem behavior construct is consistent with other research on various forms of deviant behavior such as delinquency or aggression. Our overall goal is to incorporate all of the findings into a meaningful, consistent, comprehensive model of substance use development and its consequences. To conclude, we discuss the implications of these results for prevention and intervention efforts.

THE STRUCTURE AND SEQUENCE
OF ADOLESCENT DRUG-USE INVOLVEMENT

Several investigators have postulated an underlying dimension of drug-use involvement along a Guttman scale, which assumes that use along any point of the scale was preceded by use at all previous points. In a classic study, Kandel (1980) found that licit substances (alcohol and/or tobacco) preceded the use of marijuana and a series of other illicit drugs. Donovan and Jessor (1983) similarly found that marijuana use was preceded by alcohol. Why is it that some teens move on the next stage and become polydrug users, whereas others do not? This is one of the questions that we attempted to answer. It is also important to understand the sequence of drug-use involvement and identify the predictors of the transition to each stage. Adolescents who remain at one stage, or who use a single substance, may be different than those who are more variable in their use patterns. Such information could provide critical knowledge necessary for effective prevention or intervention tactics. In these studies, we focused on the sequence of substance-use initiation (Andrews et al., 1991), the development of substance-use patterns over time (e.g., Duncan et al., 1996), as well as a description of the growth in substance use at both the group and the individual level (Duncan, Alpert, & Hops, 1997; Duncan & Duncan, 1994, 1996; Duncan et al., 1996; Duncan, Tildesley, Duncan, & Hops, 1995).

We extended the previous work on the sequence of substance-use initiation by developing a Guttman Scale that examined cigarettes and alcohol separately within a 2-year prospective design (Andrews et al., 1991). A Guttman scale fit over 90% of the sample with the temporal sequence of drug-use involvement, proceeding in cumulative fashion from no use, to alcohol, to tobacco, to marijuana, and finally to other illicit substances. Moreover, the validity of this sequence was supported by significant covariation with both adolescents and parents reports of the child's level of deviance, similar to that found by Donovan and Jessor (1983).

In a more precise examination of the sequence, Duncan et al. (1997), using latent growth modeling (LGM), determined whether the level of these precedent substances influenced the development of use among never users of the next substance in the sequence. LGM allows us to examine the mean level of change as well as individual trajectories over time. Gender, age, and precedent substance use were included as predictors of both initial status and development, and changes in use of each precedent substance were included as predictors of development. Here, we found that only change in *alcohol* use predicted the development of cigarette use among never smokers. Analyses of the next transition included both alcohol and cigarettes; however, only level and rate of change in *cigarette* use predicted the initial status and development of marijuana use. These results not only provide further support for the more refined stages of Andrews et al. (1991) but also demonstrate a significant relationship between cigarette and marijuana use, attributable in part to similar manner of ingestion, or to a further step along the dimension of deviant behavior (see Donovan & Jessor, 1983; Hops, Davis, & Lewin, 1999). On the whole, however, the results highlight cigarettes as the most likely gateway drug to illegal substances.

We also examined whether trends or trajectories of each of these substances varied by age, gender, and their relationship with each other over time. Using LGM within our cohort-sequential design for approximating longitudinal data analysis (Duncan et al., 1994), we combined information from the five overlapping age cohorts (11–15 years at Time 1) across four annual assessment periods to see whether they would form a single developmental trajectory for alcohol use spanning the ages 11–18. Results indicated a common trajectory across the 8 years represented by this cohort-sequential analysis, with alcohol use increasing more rapidly during the transition to high school. This may not be surprising, since the high school setting is more problematic, with its older students, higher levels of use, and increased availability and influence. Minimal gender differences were noted; boys levels were generally higher in the younger cohorts, but girls showed faster acceleration rates over time. This is consistent with other studies showing junior high boys reporting proportionally more drinking as well as greater earlier increases compared to girls (Donovan & Jessor, 1978; Downs & Robertson, 1982; Sutker, McCleary, & Allain, 1986). Follow-up analyses (Duncan & Duncan, 1994) expanded the model to an associative model that included the simultaneous analysis of alcohol, cigarette, and marijuana use. These findings show very similar development in all of these substances, with only differences in levels, consistent with our previous work on the sequencing of drug-use involvement (Andrews et al., 1991). Moreover, similarities in changes over time for all substances were also demonstrated (Duncan & Duncan, 1996). Thus, once initiation begins, the rate of acquisition is similar across substances. Although gender was not a significant predictor of initial status or slope (development), females were found to demonstrate greater cigarette-use development across time and especially at the earlier years. This is consistent with other data showing higher rates of smoking for females during the 1980s, when this study was conducted (Johnston et al., 1998).

Taken together, these findings suggest that it may be practical to treat substance use as a unitary construct, for example, when designing general prevention and intervention strategies for younger and older adolescents (Hansen, Malotte, Collins, & Fielding, 1987). The parallel accelerating trends shown for the three primary substances are remarkably similar except for time of onset and level of use. These data also show that despite initial gender differences, older adolescent females appear to be catching up in their use of these substances, although differences remain. And entry into high school, when dramatic changes in the social environment occur, appears to have an additional impact on level of use. Next, we examine whether the substance-use construct is independent of other deviant or problematic behaviors.

Is Substance Use Part of a Problem Behavior Pattern?

From various theoretical perspectives, researchers have considered substance use and abuse to be part of a larger behavioral syndrome or class of responses. For example, in a large epidemiological study of adolescent pathology, Lewinsohn, Hops, Roberts, Seeley, and Andrews (1993) showed that lifetime substance-use disorder was comorbid with several other disorders, including unipolar depression, anxiety, and disruptive behavior disorder. Jessor (1987), in his problem behavior theory, assumes a stable relation between substance use and a variety of other problematic behaviors. In the Oregon Social Learning Center's coercion model, based on social interactional theory, Patterson, Reid, and Dishion (1992) have shown that antisocial boys display a range of problematic behaviors, including substance use. Knowing whether substance use and abuse is part of a larger response class or group of problem behaviors is important for designing intervention and prevention activities, because behavioral targets for programmatic efforts may differ. To explore these possibilities, we examined the relationships between substance use and a range of problem and nonproblem behaviors.

Tildesley, Hops, Ary, and Andrews (1995) used a multitrait multimethod design to examine the relation among seven problem behaviors. Results from hierarchical confirmatory factor analyses supported a correlated two-factor, second-order model of problem behavior. The first factor, problem behavior, consisted of delinquency, precocious sexual behavior, and low academic motivation; the second, general drug use, was made up of alcohol, cigarette, marijuana, and other illicit substance use. Nevertheless, the two lower order factors were also related, indicating that they are not completely orthogonal.

Next, we examined the influence of specific types of antisocial behavior on later substance use (Loeber, 1988; Windle, 1990). We chose only this direction of influence because younger children are more likely to show other forms of misbehavior, with substance use entering their repertoires later on. Duncan and Tildesley (1996) investigated the influence of four types of deviant behavior—aggressive conduct, property damage, theft, and rule violations—on 1-year lagged changes in the alcohol, cigarette, and marijuana use of adolescents over a 4-year period. As expected, rule violations, most typical of adolescent development, predicted increased use of all three substances 1 year later for both males and females. More interesting, however, were the findings by gender. Female adolescents' aggressive behavior and higher levels of involvement in theft predicted higher levels of cigarette use 1 year later. In addition, younger females' aggressive behavior predicted higher levels of alcohol use, although the results approached significance for older girls. These results show that, first, there were no specific effects for boys. Second, the effects for girls are consistent with the sequence of substance-use involvement noted earlier, with older girls showing higher levels of cigarette use and younger girls more alcohol use, both of which are associated with deviant activities. This suggests that the sequence of greater movement along the drug-use Guttman scale also indicates greater deviant behavior patterns for females. These data may be interpreted in several ways. First, they suggest that early problematic behavior among females poses a significant risk for increased deviance and later substance use. Second, they are consistent with a view of gender differences that has been associated with culturally prescribed practices and socialization efforts. Aggression is less acceptable for females; thus, early indications are more powerful predictors of later problematic behavior than they are for males.

In a further investigation of substance-use relations with other behaviors, Andrews and Duncan (1997) used general estimating equation (GEE) analyses within a lagged design to examine the reciprocal relation between academic motivation and cigarette, alcohol, and marijuana use across four annual assessments. GEE allows us to examine the covariation of variables over time and the lagged design provides greater credibility of the direction of influence. The results suggested inverse reciprocal relations across time between academic motivation and both cigarette and marijuana use. In other words, lower levels of academic motivation resulted in greater use of these substances in the following year, but the inverse was true as well. Furthermore, we found that a general deviance factor mediated the relation between marijuana use and academic motivation in both directions, suggesting that adolescents who use marijuana or are not academically motivated are likely to become involved in deviant activities, furthering the problematic behavior. Among younger adolescents, general deviance mediated the relation between cigarette use and academic motivation. This relation among the younger teens also suggests that the deviant practices had already begun, making cigarette use a marker for later problems. Interestingly, reciprocal relations between academic motivation and alcohol use were not found, consistent with our earlier suggestion that alcohol use per se is a poor predictor of later problems because of its normative nature.

In summary, it appears that substance use may be considered to be part of a larger class of deviant or problem behaviors. If so, it is likely that the different components of this class of behaviors may have common antecedents. Thus, prevention activities could be aimed more efficiently at the earlier events that are the markers for deviant behavior in general. In the next section, we present some of the results evaluating these early predictors and the processes that may be involved.

ECOLOGICAL INFLUENCES
ON ADOLESCENT SUBSTANCE USE

Family Influences

The importance of parental influence and specifically parents' own drug use has had a late start in the literature (e.g., Brook, Whiteman, Gordon, & Brook, 1985). The significance of the family cannot be overemphasized. The current generation of adolescents may be the first whose parents grew up during the 1960s and 1970s (Fisher, MacKinnon, Anglin, & Thompson, 1987), a time during which the rates of illicit drug use were increasing. Parents of present-day adolescents may be the first to have provided models and offers of or encouragement for the use of substances such as marijuana. In our work, we examined the effects of the family structure (i.e., parent marital status, the relation between parent and adolescent use of alcohol, cigarettes, and marijuana as well as some of the processes involved).

In several studies, we found that being a single parent is a risk factor for adolescent substance use (e.g., Hops, Duncan, Duncan, & Stoolmiller, 1996). Similar effects have been found by other investigators (e.g., Byram & Fly, 1984). We showed this effect in both cross-sectional and longitudinal studies (Hops et al., 1990; Andrews, Hops, Ary, Tildesley, & Harris, 1993). Similarly, Burnside, Baer, McLaughlin, and Pokorny (1986) found higher levels of alcohol use by both adolescents and parents in nonintact families and a significant relation between parent and adolescent alcohol use. Adolescents from single-parent homes may be at risk for several reasons. As we shall note later, the SES of single parents is likely to be low, and economic hardship and low education have been known risk factors. Also, adolescents may be more susceptible to peer pressure for deviant behavior (Dornbusch et al., 1985; Steinberg, 1987) because single parents may find it more difficult to monitor their behavior. Monitoring, a critical component of effective parenting behavior, reduces the likelihood of adolescent problem behavior within the context of a deviant peer group (Patterson et al., 1992).

Parent and Sibling Use

From our perspective, parents' substance use represents a class of possible influences, ranging from the simple modeling of substances (Bandura, 1977, 1986), which may indicate parents' tacit acceptance or the availability of substances in the home, to disrupted parenting practices or lax control as a result of their use (Conger, Reuter, & Conger, 1994; Dishion & Loeber, 1985). However, we sought first simply to examine the relation between use of substances by family members and that of their adolescent offspring or siblings.

In several studies, we focused on the influence of parents' use on use by the target adolescent. Duncan and Duncan (1996) showed that parents' substance use influences the initial levels of adolescent substance use. Next, we used GEE to examine the annual time-varying influence of parents' use, using a 1-year lagged analysis (Hops et al., 1996); that is, does parents' use of a specific substance predict use by their adolescent of that same substance 1 year later, and does this hold over a 6-year period? We repeated the analyses for the effects of parents' alcohol, marijuana, and cigarette use, and examined each parent's individual contribution as well as their interaction. Parental influence was demonstrated for all substances. For marijuana use, we found significant positive and additive effects of mother and father use, age, and single-parent mother use on their adolescent's use of marijuana; that is, use by either parent was independent of the other, so that families in which both parents were marijuana users doubled the likelihood of the teen's use of marijuana. In contrast, for alcohol and tobacco use, high use by one parent was sufficient to affect the patterns of their offspring. Additionally, we found significant interactions among mother use, father use, age, and gender in the prediction of alcohol and cigarette use. With a single exception, adolescents less than 14 years of age were particularly susceptible to the influence of alcohol use by either parent. In addition, alcohol use, especially by older boys, was influenced primarily by fathers, suggesting that fathers may have a more generalized effect on their offspring's drinking behavior, and it is their drinking that sets the stage for the acquisition of drinking habits by both male and female offspring at all ages.

In a 1-year prospective study, Ary, Tildesley, Hops, and Andrews (1993) showed that parental alcohol use, although not related to concurrent adolescent use, predicted adolescent use in the following year. In contrast, sibling alcohol use was related concurrently but not prospectively. These data suggest a more complex interplay of parent and sibling use that may be influencing adolescent drinking behavior. We followed this study with several others that were designed to examine the social context in more precise detail. Duncan, Duncan, and Hops (1998), using multilevel LGM, found significant homogeneity in level and development of alcohol use among family members that included parents, adolescents, and older siblings. In other words, members within each family demonstrated similar trends over a 4-year period. Moreover, parents have been shown to have an indirect effect via the older siblings' influence on younger ones (Duncan, Duncan, & Hops, 1996). Family trends were consistent with previous research showing an increase in alcohol use from adolescence into young adulthood, with a gradual decline from then on (Johnston, O'Malley, & Bachman, 1997). And as with other studies on gender effects, males had consistently higher levels of use (Johnston et al., 1997; Sutker et al., 1986). These data provide strong support for the influence of the family unit on an adolescent's propensity to drink. We also examined family-level covariates for possible explanatory mechanisms. Single-parent families had consistently higher levels of use consistent with previous findings (e.g., Burnside et al., 1986; Hops et al., 1990). However, the highest levels were found among stepparent families. Both of these results suggest that a stressful family context may place families at higher risk for increased alcohol consumption. Stress can occur in the form of economic disadvantage (Conger et al., 1991), as is usually the case with single-parent families, or with conditions associated with multiple transitions, as in the case of divorce and remarriage (Capaldi & Patterson, 1991; Hetherington, 1991, 1993). Finally, we found that the greatest amount of variation in family-level effects was accounted for by biological parents; parents who consume more alcohol relative to other parents have adolescents who are likely to be using more alcohol relative to their own age group. These latter data suggest that genetic factors may play a role as well (Bierut, Dinwiddie, & Reich, 1998).

In summary, our data have shown that (1) parent use is indeed a risk factor that increases the likelihood of adolescent use, (2) high use of alcohol or cigarettes by one parent is sufficient to influence use by the adolescent, (3) siblings in the family may have both direct effects and mediate the effect of the parents, (4) mothers and fathers have an additive effect on marijuana use, (5) children younger that age 14 are particularly vulnerable to parent use of alcohol, (6) adolescents in a home with single mothers are likely to be in a particularly problematic situation, and (7) parent use can generalize across subjects. As we have noted, however, parent or sibling use is a limited concept for understanding the processes by which intergenerational transfer occurs.

The Influence of Family Relationships

Parent or sibling use only accounts for part of the family influence. In addition, positive family relationships have generally been regarded as important for healthy development. We found some support in Andrews et al. (1991), who demonstrated that poorer family relationships were predictive of several transitions along the Guttman scale, especially for females. Poor family relations were a risk factor for females' transition to alcohol and cigarette use, and for males' transition to marijuana and hard drugs.

From a social learning perspective, one would expect the following: (1) Adolescents model or imitate the substance-use behavior and attitudes of family members and peers; (2) they model not only the specific behavior that they see (i.e., the use of the specific substance) but also behavior that is functionally similar (i.e., the use of other substances); and (3) adolescents imitate the behavior of individuals they value. In two studies, we examined several of these assumptions. In concurrent and prospective studies, Hops et al. (1990) and Andrews et al. (1993), respectively, showed this to be the case; parent use was related to the teen's use of a specific substance as well as others. In the Andrews et al. (1993) study, parental influence was defined as a combination of use and a group of parenting behaviors, such as parental attitude toward use, cautionary statements regarding use, and consequences following use. The differences between mothers' and fathers' influence was minimal. Fathers' substance-specific influence predicted the initiation of all three substances, whereas mothers' influence predicted the adolescent's initiation of alcohol and marijuana, but the maintenance of cigarettes. After controlling for the specific influences, both parents' influence generalized to the onset and maintenance of other substances.

The modeling hypothesis is supported by the relationships shown between parent and adolescent use as we have shown here. However, social learning theory is based on the premise that imitation or modeling is more likely to occur if the model is valued. Testing of this theory had not been previously done in substance-use studies. Andrews, Hops, and Duncan (1997) found that adolescents are more likely to model the substance use of their parents *if* their relationship is characterized by low conflict. Using GEE to examine the covariation of parent and adolescent use over time, we found that adolescents' substance use was related to their mother's concurrent use of cigarettes and marijuana and their father's use of alcohol and marijuana *only if* their relationship was characterized by low to moderate conflict. There was no such relationship in high conflict families. The implications of this study are twofold. First, it demonstrates that modeling of parent use, per se, is an insufficient explanation of the effect on adolescent use, and that the relationship process moderates this influence. This probably accounts for the consistently low relationship generally found between parent and adolescent use (for review, see Ary et al., 1993), especially when the variables are obtained from independent sources. Furthermore, it provides indirect support for the social interactional model (Patterson et al., 1992), suggesting that conflictual relations with parents may make adolescents more susceptible to peer influence. Whether this acts as a protective factor in families in conflict, with drug using parents, is yet to be determined.

The Influence of Peers

Although families are an important socializing influence, and parenting practices account for a considerable amount of variance in the prediction of problem behavior, the literature suggests that peer influence on substance use is at least equal to, if not greater than, that of parents and other family influences, especially at more proximal points in time (Kandel, 1985). As children grow older, they spend increasing amounts of time with the peer group (Montemayor, 1983), increasing the potential for peer influence. There is also evidence that peers are particularly influential in the early stages of drug use (Coombs, Paulson, & Richardson, 1991;

Kandel, 1985; Quine & Stephenson, 1990) and this increases with age. In several studies, we examined the peer group's effect on the acquisition and maintenance of substance use. Peer attitude and substance use was shown to be predictive of current alcohol use (Ary et al., 1993). Using LGM, Duncan et al. (Duncan, Duncan, & Hops 1994, 1996; Duncan, Tildesley, Duncan, & Hops, 1995) demonstrated that peer encouragement to use substances affects not only the initial level of use but also its growth over time. In one study, we examined the substance-specific relation between adolescent use along the Guttman scale and the teen's reports of friends' use (Hops & Davis, 1998). The findings were quite consistent; teens who reported being abstinent, using only alcohol, alcohol and cigarettes, alcohol, cigarettes, and marijuana, and all three plus other substances, reported having friends whose use patterns were very similar. In previous work, Kandel (1985) and Cohen (1977) showed that individuals within adolescent cliques tend to become more similar over the course of the school year. This increase in similarity could be due to repeating behavior patterns that promote the relationship, as well as mutual reinforcement, as Dishion, Andrews, and Crosby (1995) have demonstrated.

Family and Peer Influence Processes

It is generally assumed that family and peer influences are antagonistic. As family influences wane, peers take over. The change in influence, of course, is not that dramatic and occurs more gradually over time. In several studies (Duncan et al., 1994, 1995), we examined how these two major influences may interact with one another. We examined the influence of family cohesion and peer encouragement to use substances over several years within a longitudinal design covering the age range from 11–18. In general, family cohesion was related to the adolescent's initial levels of alcohol, cigarette, and marijuana use. In contrast, peer encouragement to use substances was related not only to initial levels but also to increases over time. Duncan and Duncan (1996) showed similarly that parent use, familial conflict, and peer encouragement were related to initial levels of use, and that an increase in peer encouragement was related to increases in substance use across time. Thus, family influences appear to be critical early on in setting the stage to ward off or temper later peer influences.

Using data from coded parent–adolescent problem-solving interactions, Hops et al. (1990) showed that aversive affective behavior (negative tone of voice, eye rolling, grimacing) predicts adolescent substance use. Andrews et al. (1993) showed that aversive consequences do not always have the desired effect; parents' reports of coercive consequences for the use of a substance predicted the initiation of another substance by the adolescent.

Taken together, these results are consistent with Patterson's (1982) coercion model, showing that conflict in the home and coercive family interactions, along with poor parental monitoring, lead to an association with deviant peers and subsequent substance use and other problem behaviors. Ary, Duncan, Duncan, and Hops (1999), in a direct test of the coercion developmental model of antisocial behavior, found that families experiencing high levels of conflict were more likely to have low levels of parent–child involvement. Moreover, these family conditions led to less adequate parental monitoring of adolescent behavior and subsequent higher levels of association with deviant peers. Poor parental monitoring and associations with deviant peers were strong proximal predictors of engagement in adolescent problem behavior that included substance use, antisocial behavior, academic failure, and risky sexual behavior. This was demonstrated over a 3-year period.

SUMMARY

The results of our studies show that modeling, per se, is an insufficient explanation for the mechanism that governs the relation between parent and adolescent use of substances. Older siblings may play a unique role in the family, with parents unaware of their indirect impact. Moreover, parenting skills, as well as the relationship between parents and children, need to be considered. In addition to the family's social setting, larger contextual variables that impact the family, including SES, marital status, and other stressors, indicate that a child's substance-use pattern is determined by a complex arrangement of factors within the family constellation. Of course, peers have also been shown to make significant contributions to the onset and maintenance of substance-use patterns, but as shown in the coercion model, it depends in part on the earlier relationships within the family unit.

Predictors and Consequences of Adolescent Substance Use

Predictors or Correlates of Adult Substance Abuse and Dependence

Even among young adults, we have found similarities in the substance use of friends (Andrews et al., 1999). Regression analyses showed that for each substance, the use of *both* the same- and opposite-sex friend/partner *independently* predicted the substance use of the young adult. Congruence of marijuana use between young adults' same-sex friends and themselves was significantly higher for males than females. Again, consistent with social learning theory, we found that for females, congruence between the same-sex peer's and the young adult's alcohol use increased as a function of the quality of their relationship. Thus, for these women, the more intimate their relationship, the more their substance use was like that of their female friend.

Demographic variables (including age, gender, and SES), family conflict, and parent substance use were evaluated as predictors of a diagnosis of lifetime abuse or dependence according to DSM-III-R criteria (derived from the Composite International Diagnostic Interview–Substance Abuse Schedule [CIDI-SAM]; Cottler, Robins, & Helzer, 1989). Cigarette dependence was predicted only by family conflict. Gender and parental alcohol use significantly predicted the presence of alcohol abuse or dependence. Similarly, gender, SES, and parent marijuana use significantly predicted marijuana abuse or dependence. The results showed that being male and having parents who use alcohol or marijuana significantly increases the likelihood of problems with the respective substances.

Consequences of Adolescent Substance Use

Because of the longitudinal nature of our studies, we also examined the consequences of adolescent substance use on outcomes in late adolescence and young adulthood. As a starting point, we examined the level of adult use as a function of early ($\leq$ age 14) versus mid (ages 15 to 17) versus late starting ($\geq$ age 18) adolescents. Use was defined as the onset of (at least tried or experimented with) two of three substances (alcohol, cigarettes, and marijuana) (Hops & Alpert, 1997). We found that those who had used at least two substances by age 14 had a significantly higher rate of alcohol, cigarette, and marijuana use as young adults than those who started after age 14. In addition, users of two or more substances prior to age 18 had significantly higher rates of adult substance use than those beginning after age 18. Specifically, multiple substance use is particularly problematic for cigarettes, with three times the difference between those starting early and late. Female early starters are more likely to use more alcohol as adults than males. These data suggest that early substance use is a major risk factor for increased adult use of any substance, and that the earlier this occurs, the more problematic the later consequences. These results are quite consistent with the work of Patterson and colleagues on early starters for antisocial behavior. They found that arrest prior to age 14 was one of the best markers of a later antisocial career (Patterson, 1996).

We examined the effects of the use of cigarettes, alcohol, and marijuana in early adolescence (ages 11 to 15) on functioning 4 years later, in mid- to late adolescence (Andrews et al., 1992) . Frequency of substance use in early adolescence was associated with both future health problems and problem substance use. Frequency of cigarette use was also related to an increase in general deviance from early to late adolescence.

Duncan, Alpert, Duncan, and Hops (1997) used LGM to model the effects of level and development of adolescent alcohol use on young adult outcomes. Chronicity of adolescent alcohol use was related to higher alcohol use, alcohol-related problems, aggressive behavior, theft, and suicide ideation 5–6 years later in young adulthood, with no gender differences. But with increasing use of alcohol during adolescence, males were more likely to use higher levels during young adulthood and engage in aggressive behavior. These results suggest that rates of development in alcohol use, as well as level of alcohol use in adolescence, are important for future adjustment outcomes. These results also indicate that normative drinking behavior, although illegal during adolescence, may not be problematic, but high levels of use, as well as an increasing rate, relative to others, is particularly symptomatic of later problems and may also indicate more movement along a deviancy dimension (Hops et al., 1999).

We also examined the relation of substance use in early adolescence to the assumption of young adult roles (Andrews, 1996; Andrews & Alpert, 1997). The literature has been somewhat inconsistent, with results supporting competing theories, in part due to varying methodologies such as cross-sectional or retrospective studies, or not controlling for demographics. For example, Newcomb and Bentler (1988) provided support for their pseudomaturity hypothesis, which predicts a positive relation between drug use and early entry into adult roles, whereas Yamaguchi and Kandel (1985) demonstrated a negative relation in support of their role incompatibility hypothesis. Still, Jessor, Donovan, and Costa (1991) have argued that early adolescent use may not predict adult role assumption because it is dependent upon the more proximal effects of adult substance use. We did find that early substance use predicted early marriage, having children, living independently, and not working or attending school. However, after controlling for age, gender, and SES, early marriage and parenthood were no longer significant. Moreover, after controlling for adult substance use, only independent living remained significant. Our interpretation of these data takes a broader perspective and focuses on the processes producing these outcomes. Our earlier analyses showed early substance use related to family conflict, increased deviant peer influences, less academic motivation, as well as more adult substance use. Thus, difficulties in adolescence which are likely to result in less competent social and academic functioning, forcing the adolescent into the workplace, low paying jobs, and more adult influences, with greater use of substances. One plausible theoretical perspective is Caspi and Elder's (1988a,b) theory of cumulative continuity, which suggests that events—whether adaptive or maladaptive—are maintained by the progressive accumulation of their own consequences, the basic "law of effect." For example, high levels of maladaptive behavior may channel an individual into environments that sustain the behavior. Individuals may choose to enter settings that are compatible with their interaction style or attempt to change incompatible settings in ways that will maximize the reinforcement therein that maintains their behavior. Similarly, Patterson has suggested that at-risk boys are rejected by conventional peers and "shop" around for peer groups that will reinforce antisocial behavior (Patterson, 1996; Dishion, Patterson, & Griesler, 1994; for a similar theoretical point of view, see Lewis, 1997, 1998).

More evidence was seen in cross-sectional analyses. Young adults who lived away from their parents' home were twice as likely to use more alcohol and less likely to use hard drugs. But if they were married, and further along the transition, they tended to use more cigarettes and less alcohol. On the other hand, working and/or attending school was associated with less cigarette use. Finally, we found that the relation between substance use in adolescence and both early parenthood and nonattendance at school were mediated by the substance use of the young adult, thus completing the process.

Focusing on intimate relationships, we investigated the relation between early adolescent substance use and parenting satisfaction, parenting efficacy, and the quality of intimate relationships, controlling for demographics (Hops & Li, 1999). Substance use in adolescence was not related to parenting satisfaction or efficacy. However, the extent of cigarette use in early adolescence predicted the amount of verbal aggression given to and received from the partner/opposite-sex friend even after controlling for substance use in young adulthood. Similarly, cigarette, alcohol, and marijuana use in young adulthood independently predicted both verbal aggression and violent acts given and received from a partner/spouse, and the level of intimacy experienced with the partner/spouse. We continued the study of the relation of substance use in young adulthood to conflictual behavior between participants and their opposite-sex peers. The latent construct of dyadic conflict included a measure of the aggressive behavior of each member of the dyad observed during their problem-solving interactions, as well as each member's report of their own aggressive behavior directed toward the other member of the dyad. Using structural equation modeling, we found a significant association between dyadic conflict and a young adult substance use construct, measured by the participant's self-report of number of cigarettes per week, drinks per week, and total amount of marijuana used in a month. This association remained after controlling for whether the other member of the dyad was a partner or friend. Taken together, the current data suggest a link between adult conflict with intimate relations, current substance use, and historical antecedents.

Developmental Implications for Prevention and Intervention

These results show clearly the substance-use trajectories that begin in early adolescence, continuing through the teens and into young adulthood. We have tried to show that specific substance use may not be a unitary construct and that there is a predictable sequence of drug-use involvement for some children, from alcohol use to cigarettes, marijuana, and on to other illicit substances. We have also tried to show that the further along the sequence an adolescent might progress, the more likely that substance use is part of a larger set of behaviors that are problematic, such as aggression and antisocial behavior, but include low levels of academic and social competencies. This behavior pattern not only predicts difficulties in later adolescence but also in young adulthood, including substance-related problems as well as difficulties in interpersonal relationships.

From one perspective, this set of behaviors can be conceptualized as fitting Jessor, Donovan, and Jessor's (1985) problem behavior theory, suggesting that a subset of individuals displays a group of deviant behaviors. From a psychiatric perspective, these data suggest comorbidity of specific disorders, although we did not obtain information sufficient for diagnostic purposes across all years of the study. However, neither of these speak to the developmental process by which these behaviors are learned and expressed over time. A more cogent conceptualization has been offered by Patterson and colleagues (Patterson, 1982; Patterson & Capaldi, 1991) in their coercion model within a social interactional framework. They have shown that such processes may begin within the family unit when parenting skills are poorly performed, so that children are disciplined and monitored inadequately. Under these conditions, there is a high probability that children will be rejected in school and seek from among deviant peer groups similar children who will teach them a new set of skills. These skills include breaking rules, a variety of antisocial delinquent behaviors, such as stealing and aggressive behavior to deal with interpersonal problems. Thus, the set of deviant behaviors that has been referred to as a problem behavior syndrome and that accounts for the comorbidity of disorders is the result of a very precise developmental process beginning in the family unit. As noted earlier, this process is also consistent with Caspi and Elder's (1988a,b) conceptualization of life's trajectories as a function of the consequences of individual behaviors and the selective demands of the environments in which they occur (cf. Lewis, 1997).

In our work, we have provided further evidence for the coercion model and its developmental trajectories in several ways. We have shown the protective effects of good family relationships and effective parenting skills. We have also shown the power of the peer group to increase the rate at which adolescents acquire drug-use habits. By age 14, adolescents who have begun to use substances, and have friends who use, are more likely to increase their use beyond that of normative patterns. Experimentation in adolescence is a normal procedure. Shedler and Block (1990) have provided data suggesting that not to experiment may predict more difficulties than actually trying marijuana. We have shown that alcohol use, for example, is not predictive of further movement along the drug sequence. However, higher levels of drinking, beyond normative patterns, are more likely to predict onset and development of cigarettes, the gateway substance, which is, in turn, closely tied to the onset of marijuana use and, potentially, other illicit substances.

How do these data speak to prevention and intervention activities? To begin with, they stress the importance of early programmatic efforts, before the onset of substance use and related problematic behaviors. In the past, prevention efforts have focused too heavily on proximal targets such as the child's own use and peer group influences during early to middle adolescence. The late timing of the program when the child is well along a drug use/abuse trajectory will likely limit the effectiveness of these procedures.

Additionally, we need to stress the importance of good family relations early on in a child's life, well in advance of adolescence, when peers take on greater influence. Family influences need to be directed toward a set of behaviors or skills that also teach the child competent social skills to function well within the peer group, and academic skills to function competently in the classroom. We must also be aware of gender similarities and differences due to culturally proscribed behavioral expectations. We expect girls to be more prosocial and meet or excel academically, and slight deviations from these expectations may be seen as deviant (Kavanagh & Hops, 1994). At the same time, we have seen that, similar to the results for boys, delinquent antisocial activities among girls are also predictors of later problem behaviors.

Interventions for high-risk adolescents and those well along the substance-use trajectory, are essential and need to focus on the whole family unit to ensure that both parents and siblings, as well as the identified child, are working together to attain the treatment goals (e.g., Dishion, Andrews, Kavanagh, & Soberman, 1996; Waldron & Slesnick, 1998). Focusing primarily on the problem adolescent ignores the family influences that may be contributing to the situation, such as the effects of the older siblings.

Finally, more research is needed to explore the contributions of some of the larger contextual factors such as the school and the neighborhood, within which individual and family processes occur, and which also contribute to the onset and maintenance of drug use and other problematic behaviors. The people with whom the child interacts, and who determines their activities are also influenced by the ecology of the school and neighborhood (Dishion et al., 1994). More studies would explore the processes in these settings by which support or encouragement of prosocial or deviant behaviors is enhanced. Future prevention work needs to take into account these contexts to maximize the likelihood of children turning out to be happy and productive citizens (e.g., Biglan, 1995; Sanders, 1992).

ACKNOWLEDGMENTS. The preparation of this chapter was supported by grants from the National Institute of Drug Abuse, Grant Nos. DA03707 and DA10324.

We would like to acknowledge the contributions of many ORIers over the life of these projects that made this chapter possible. We deeply thank the monitors, schedulers, observers, research assistants, and data analysts. We also express our thanks to the many loyal participants, without whom studies like these could not be carried out. Finally, we would like to thank Elizabeth Mondulick for her efforts in the preparation of this manuscript.

REFERENCES

Andrews, J. A. (1996, August). *Predictors and consequences of substance use: Adolescence through young adulthood.* Paper presented at the Annual Meeting of the American Psychological Association, Toronto, Canada.

Andrews, J. A., & Alpert, A. (1997, March). *The relation of substance use in early adolescence to the acquisition of social roles in young adulthood.* Paper presented at the biennial meeting of the Society for Research in Child Development, Washington, DC.

Andrews, J. A., & Duncan, S. C. (1997). Examining the reciprocal relation between academic motivation and substance use: Effects of family relationships, self-esteem and general deviance. *Journal of Behavioral Medicine, 20,* 523–549.

Andrews, J. A., Foster, S. L., Capaldi, D., & Hops, H. (in press). *Adolescent and family predictors of physical aggression, communication, and satisfaction in young adult couples: A prospective analysis.*

Andrews, J. A., Hops, H., Ary, D., Lichtenstein, E., & Tildesley, E. (1991). The construction, validation and use of a Guttman scale of adolescent substance use: An investigation of family relationships. *Journal of Drug Issues, 21,* 557–572.

Andrews, J. A., Hops, H., Ary, D., Tildesley, E., & Harris, J. (1993). Parental influence on early adolescent substance use: Specific and nonspecific effects. *Journal of Early Adolescence, 13,* 285–310.

Andrews, J. A., Hops, H., & Duncan, S. C. (1997). Adolescent modeling of parent substance use: The moderating effect of the relationship with the parent. *Journal of Family Psychology, 11,* 259–270.

Andrews, J. A., Hops, H., Duncan, S. C., Tildesley, E., Ary, D., & Smolkowski, K. (1992). *Long-term consequences of level of substance use in adolescence.* Poster presented at the fourth biennial meetings of the Society for Research on Adolescence, Washington, DC.

Ary, D. V., Duncan, T. E., Duncan, S. C., & Hops, H. (1999). Adolescent problem behavior: The influence of parents and peers. *Behaviour Research and Therapy, 37,* 217–230.

Ary, D. V., Tildesley, E., Hops, H., & Andrews, J. (1993). The influence of parent, sibling and peer modeling and attitudes on adolescent use of alcohol. *International Journal of the Addictions, 28,* 853–880.

Bandura, A. (1977). *Social learning theory.* Englewood Cliffs, NJ: Prentice Hall.

Bandura, A. (1986). *Social foundations of thought and action: A social cognitive theory.* Englewood Cliffs, NJ: Prentice Hall.

Bandura, A., & Walters, R. H. (1963). *Social learning and personality development.* New York: Holt, Rinehart & Winston.

Bierut, L. J., Dinwiddie, S. H., & Reich, T. (1998). Familial transmission of substance dependence: Alcohol, marijuana, cocaine, and habitual smoking: A report from the collaborative study on the genetics of alcoholism. *Archives of General Psychiatry*, *55*, 982.

Biglan, A. (1995). *Changing cultural practices: A contextualist framework for intervention research*. Reno, NV: Context Press.

Brook, J. S., Brook, D. W., Gordon, A. S., Whiteman, M., & Cohen, P. (1990). The psychosocial etiology of adolescent drug use: A family interactional approach. *Genetic, Social, and General Psychology Monographs*, *116*, 111–267.

Brook, J. S., Whiteman, M., Gordon, A. S., & Brook, D. W. (1985). Father's influence on his daughter's marijuana use viewed in a mother and peer context. In J. Brook, D. Lettieri, D. W. Brook, & B. Stimmel (Eds.), *Alcohol and substance abuse in adolescence* (Vol. 4, pp. 165–190). New York: Haworth Press.

Burnside, M. A., Baer, P. E., McLaughlin, R. J., & Pokorny, A. D. (1986). Alcohol use by adolescents in disrupted families. *Alcoholism: Clinical and Experimental Research*, *10*, 274–278.

Byram, O. W., & Fly, J. W. (1984). Family structure, race, and adolescent alcohol use: A research note. *American Journal of Drug and Alcohol Abuse*, *11*, 11–25.

Cairns, R. B. (1979). *The analysis of social interaction: Methods, issues, and illustrations*. Hillsdale, NJ: Erlbaum.

Capaldi, D. M., & Patterson, G. R. (1991). Relation of parental transitions to boys' adjustment problems: I. A linear hypothesis. II. Mothers at risk for transitions and unskilled parenting. *Developmental Psychology*, *27*, 489–504.

Caspi, A., & Elder, G. H. (1988a). Childhood precursors of the life course: Early personality and life disorganization. In E. M. Hetherington, R. M. Lerner, & M. Perlmutter (Eds.), *Child development in life-span perspective* (pp. 115–142). Hillsdale, NJ: Erlbaum.

Caspi, A., & Elder, G. H. (1988b). Emergent family patterns: The intergenerational construction of problem behavior and relations. In R. Hinde & J. Stevenson-Hinde (Eds.), *Relationships within families* (pp. 218–240). Oxford, UK: Clarendon Press.

Cohen, J. (1977). *Statistical power analysis for the behavioral sciences*. New York: Academic Press.

Collins, W. A. (1990). Parent–child relationships in the transition to adolescence: Continuity and change in inter-action, affect, and cognition. In R. Montemayor, G. R. Adams & P. Gullotta (Eds.), *From childhood to adolescence: A transitional period?* (pp. 85–106). Newbury Park, CA: Sage.

Conger, R. D., Lorenz, F. O., Elder, G. H., Jr., Melby, J. N., Simons, R. L., & Conger, K. J. (1991). A process model of family economic pressure and early adolescent alcohol use. *Journal of Early Adolescence*, *11*, 430–449.

Conger, R. D., Rueter, M. A., & Conger, K. J. (1994). The family context of adolescent vulnerability and resilience to alcohol use and abuse. *Sociological Studies of Children*, *6*, 55–86.

Coombs, R. H., Paulson, M. J., & Richardson, M. A. (1991). Peer vs. parental influence in substance use among Hispanic and Anglo children and adolescents. *Journal of Youth and Adolescence*, *20*, 73–88.

Cottler, L. B., Robins, L. N., & Helzer, J. E. (1989). The reliability of the CIDI-SAM: A comprehensive substance abuse interview. *British Journal of Addiction*, *84*, 801–814.

Dishion, T. J., Andrews, D. W., & Crosby, L. (1995). Antisocial boys and their friends in early adolescence: Relationship characteristics, quality, and interactional processes. *Child Development*, *66*, 139–151.

Dishion, T., Andrews, D., Kavanagh, K., & Soberman, L. (1996). Preventive interventions for high-risk youth: The adolescent transitions program. In B. McMahon & R. D. Peters (Eds.), *Childhood disorders, substance abuse and delinquency: Prevention and early intervention approaches*. Newbury Park, CA: Sage.

Dishion, T. J., & Loeber, R. (1985). Adolescent marijuana and alcohol use: The role of parents and peers revisited. *American Journal of Drug and Alcohol Abuse*, *11*, 11–25.

Dishion, T. J., Patterson, G. R., & Griesler, P. C. (1994). Peer adaptations in the development of antisocial behavior. In L. R. Huesmann (Ed.), *Aggressive behavior: Current perspectives* (pp. 61–95). New York: Plenum Press.

Donovan, J. E., & Jessor, R. (1978). Adolescent problem drinking: Psychosocial correlates in a national sample study. *Journal of Studies on Alcohol*, *39*(9), 1506–1524.

Donovan, J. E., & Jessor, R. (1983). Problem drinking and the dimension of involvement with drugs: A Guttman scalogram analysis of adolescent drug use. *American Journal of Public Health*, *73*, 543–552.

Donovan, J. E., & Jessor, R. (1985). Structure of problem behavior in adolescence and young adulthood. *Journal of Consulting and Clinical Psychology*, *53*, 890–904.

Dornbusch, S. M., Carlsmith, J. M., Bushwall, S. J., et al. (1985). Single parents, stepparents, and the susceptibility of adolescents to antisocial peer pressure. *Child Development*, *58*, 269–275.

Downs, W. R., & Robertson, J. F. (1982). Adolescent alcohol consumption by age and sex of respondent. *Journal of Studies on Alcohol*, *43*, 1027–1032.

Duncan, S. C., Alpert, A., Duncan, T. E., & Hops, H. (1997). Adolescent alcohol use development and young adult outcomes: A cohort-sequential latent growth curve analysis. *Drug and alcohol dependence*, *49*, 39–48.

Duncan, S. C., & Duncan, T. E. (1994). Modeling incomplete longitudinal substance use data using latent variable growth curve methodology. *Multivariate Behavioral Research*, *29*, 313–338.

Duncan, S. C., & Duncan, T. E. (1996). A multivariate latent growth curve analysis of adolescent substance use. *Structural Equation Modeling, 3,* 323–347.

Duncan, S. C., Duncan, T. E., & Hops, H. (1996). Analysis of longitudinal data within accelerated longitudinal designs. *Psychological Methods, 1,* 236–248.

Duncan, S. C., Duncan, T. E., & Hops, H. (1998). Progressions of alcohol, cigarette, and marijuana use in adolescence. *Journal of Behavioral Medicine, 21,* 375–388.

Duncan, S. C., & Tildesley, E. (1996, March). *Adolescent substance use types of deviance and gender: A lagged analysis using GEE.* Poster presented at the annual meeting of the Society for Research on Adolescence, Boston, MA.

Duncan, T. E., Duncan, S. C., Alpert, A., & Hops, H. (1997). Latent variable modeling of longitudinal and multilevel substance use data. *Multivariate Behavioral Research, 32,* 275–318.

Duncan, T. E., Duncan, S. C., & Hops, H. (1994). The effect of family cohesiveness and peer encouragement on the development of adolescent alcohol use: A cohort-sequential approach to the analysis of longitudinal data. *Journal of Studies on Alcohol, 55,* 588–599.

Duncan, T. E., Duncan, S. C., & Hops, H. (1996). The role of parents and older siblings in predicting adolescent substance use: Modeling development via structural equation latent growth methodology. *Journal of Family Psychology, 10*(2), 158–172.

Duncan, T. E., Duncan, S. C., & Hops, H. (1998). Latent variable modeling of longitudinal and multilevel alcohol use data. *Journal of Studies on Alcohol, 59,* 399–408.

Duncan, T. E., Tildesley, E., Duncan, S. C., & Hops, H. (1995). The consistency of family and peer influences on the development of substance use in adolescence. *Addiction, 90,* 1647–1660.

Fisher, D. G., MacKinnon, D. P., Anglin, M. D., & Thompson, J. P. (1987). Parental influences on substance use: Gender differences and stage theory. *Journal of Drug Education, 17*(1), 69–85.

Gjerde, P. F. (1986). The interpersonal structure of family interaction settings: Parent–adolescent relations in dyads and triads. *Developmental Psychology, 22,* 297–304.

Hansen, W. B., Malotte, C., Collins, L., & Fielding, J. E. (1987). Dimensions and psychosocial correlates of adolescent alcohol use. *Journal of Alcohol and Drug Education, 32,* 19–31.

Hetherington, E. M. (1991). Presidential address: Families, lies, and videotapes. *Journal of Research on Adolescence, 1,* 323–348.

Hetherington, E. M. (1993). An overview of the Virginia longitudinal study of divorce and remarriage with a focus on early adolescence. *Journal of Family Psychology, 7*(1), 39–56.

Hops, H., & Alpert, A. (1997). *The maintenance of substance use in young adulthood by early, middle, and late onset adolescents.* Paper presented at the annual meeting of the Society for Prevention Research, Baltimore, MD.

Hops, H., Alpert, A., & Davis, B. (1997). The development of same- and opposite-sex social relations among adolescents: An analogue study. *Social Development, 6,* 165–183.

Hops, H., & Davis, B. (1998, November). *Longitudinal and developmental perspective on drug use development: Family and peer influences.* Paper presented at the NIAAA Workshop on Research on Treatment for Adolescent Alcohol Problems: Methodological Issues, Bethesda, MD.

Hops, H., Davis, B., & Lewin, L. M. (1999). The development of alcohol and other substance use: A gender study of family and peer context. *Journal of Studies on Alcohol,* (Suppl. 13), 22–31.

Hops, H., Duncan, T. E., Duncan, S., & Stoolmiller, M. (1996). Parent substance use as a predictor of adolescent use: A six-year lagged analysis. *Annals of Behavioral Medicine, 18,* 157–164.

Hops, H., & Li, F. (1999). *Adolescent alcohol use as predictors of adult use and intimate relationships.* Paper presented at the annual meeting of the Research Society on Alcoholism, Santa Barbara, CA.

Hops, H., Tildesley, E., Lichtenstein, E., Ary, D., & Sherman, L. (1990). Parent-adolescent problem-solving interactions and drug use. *American Journal of Drug and Alcohol Abuse, 16,* 239–258.

Jessor, R. (1987). Problem behavior theory, psychosocial development, and adolescent problem drinking. *British Journal of Addiction, 82,* 331–342.

Jessor, R., Donovan, J. E., & Costa, F. M. (1991). *Beyond adolescence: Problem behavior and young adult development.* New York: Cambridge University Press.

Johnston, L. D., O'Malley, P. M., & Bachman, J. G. (1997). *National survey results on drug use from* Monitoring the Future Study, 1975–1996. Rockville, MD: National Institute on Drug Abuse.

Johnston, L. D., O'Malley, P. M., & Bachman, J. G. (1998). *National survey results on drug use from* Monitoring the Future Study, 1975–1997. Rockville, MD: National Institute on Drug Abuse.

Kandel, D. B. (1980). Drug and drinking behavior among youth. *Annual Review of Sociology, 6,* 235–285.

Kandel, D. B. (1985). On processes of peer influences in adolescent drug use: A developmental perspective. In J. S. Brook, D. J. Lettiere, D. W. Brook, & B. Stimmel (Eds.), *Alcohol and substance abuse in adolescence* (pp. 139–163). New York: Haworth Press.

Kavanagh, K., & Hops, H. (1994). Good girls? Bad boys? Gender and development as contexts for diagnosis and treatment. In T. H. Ollendick & R. J. Prinz (Eds.), *Advances in clinical child psychology* (Vol. 16, pp. 45–79). New York: Plenum Press.

Lamb, M. E., Suomi, S., & Stephenson, G. (1979). *Social interaction analysis.* Madison: University of Wisconsin Press.

Lewinsohn, P. M., Hops, H., Roberts, R. E., Seeley, J. R., & Andrews, J. A. (1993). Adolescent psychopathology: I. Prevalence and incidence of depression and other DSM-III-R disorders in high school students. *Journal of Abnormal Psychology, 102,* 133–144.

Lewis, M. (1997). *Altering fate: Why the past does not predict the future.* New York: Guilford Press.

Lewis, M. (1998). Altering fate: Why the past does not predict the future. *Psychological Inquiry, 2,* 105–108.

Loeber, R. (1988). Natural histories of conduct problems, delinquency, and associated substance abuse: Evidence for developmental progressions. In B. B. Lahey & A. E. Kazdin (Eds.), *Advances in clinical child psychology* (Vol. 11, pp. 73– 124). New York: Plenum Press.

Magnusson, D., Stattin, H., & Allen, V. L. (1985). Biological maturation and social development: A longitudinal study of some adjustment processes from mid-adolescence to adulthood. *Journal of Youth and Adolescence, 14,* 267–283.

Montemayor, R. (1982). The relationship between parent–adolescent conflict and the amount of time adolescents spend alone and with parents and peers. *Child Development, 53,* 1512–1519.

Montemayor, R. (1983). Parents and adolescents in conflict: All of the families some of the time and some families most of the time. *Journal of Early Adolescence, 3,* 83–103.

Newcomb, M. D., & Bentler, P. M. (1988). *Consequences of adolescent drug use: Impact on the lives of young adults.* Newbury Park, CA: Sage.

Offer, D., & Offer, J. (1975). Three developmental routes through normal male adolescence. *Adolescent Psychiatry, 4,* 121–141.

Patterson, G. R. (1982). *A social learning approach to family intervention: Vol. 3. Coercive family process.* Eugene, OR: Castalia.

Patterson, G. R. (1996). Some characteristics of a developmental theory for early-onset delinquency. In M. F. Lenzenweger & J. J. Haugaard (Eds.), *Frontiers of developmental psychology* (pp. 81–124). New York: Oxford University Press.

Patterson, G. R., & Capaldi, D. M. (1991). Antisocial parents: Unskilled and vulnerable. In P. A. Cowan & E. M. Hetherington (Eds.), *Advances in family research: Vol. II. Family transitions* (pp. 173–218). Hillsdale, NJ: Erlbaum.

Patterson, G. R., & Reid, J. B. (1984). Social interactional processes within the family: The study of the moment-by-moment family transactions in which human social development is imbedded. *Journal of Applied Developmental Psychology, 5,* 237–262.

Patterson, G. R., Reid, J. B., & Dishion, T. J. (1992). *A social interactional approach: IV. Antisocial boys.* Eugene, OR: Castalia.

Quine, S., & Stephenson, J. A. (1990). Predicting smoking and drinking intentions and behavior of pre-adolescents: The influence of parents, siblings, and peers. *Family Systems Medicine, 8,* 191–200.

Sanders, M. R. (1992). New directions in behavioral family interventions with children: From clinical management to prevention [Special Issue: Behavioral family therapy and the wider social context]. *New Zealand Journal of Psychology, 21,* 25–36.

Shedler, J., & Block, J. (1990). Adolescent drug use and psychological health: A longitudinal inquiry. *American Psychologist, 45,* 612–630.

Steinberg, L. (1987). Single parents, stepparents, and the susceptibility of adolescents to antisocial peer pressure. *Child Development, 58,* 269–275.

Sutker, P. B., McCleary, G. E., & Allain, A. N., Jr. (1986). Adolescent alcohol abuse. In R. A. Feldman & A. R. Stiffman (Eds.), *Advances in adolescent mental health* (Vol. 1, Part B, pp. 195–253). Greenwich, CT: JAI Press.

Tildesley, E., Hops, H., Ary, D., & Andrews, J. A. (1995). A multitrait–multimethod model of adolescent deviance, drug use, academic and sexual behaviors. *Journal of Psychopathology and Behavioral Assessment, 17,* 185–215.

Waldron, H. B., & Slesnick, N. (1998). Treating the family. In W. R. Miller & N. Heather (Eds.), *Treating addictive behaviors: Processes of change* (2nd ed., pp. 271–285). New York: Plenum Press.

Windle, M. (1990). A longitudinal study of antisocial behaviors in early adolescence as predictors of late adolescent substance use: Gender and ethnic group differences. *Journal of Abnormal Psychology, 99,* 86–91.

Yamaguchi, K., & Kandel, D. B. (1985). Dynamic relationships between premarital cohabitation and illicit drug use: An event-history analysis of role selection and role socialization. *American Sociological Review, 50,* 530–546.

32

The Development of Disordered Eating

Correlates and Predictors of Eating Problems in the Context of Adolescence

Audrey R. Tyrka, Julia A. Graber, and Jeanne Brooks-Gunn

An enormous amount of research has been directed toward identifying the social, psychological, and biological correlates of anorexia nervosa and bulimia nervosa. The goal of these efforts is to elucidate factors that predispose individuals to the development of eating disorders and may influence the course of these disorders. However, as most investigations have involved cross-sectional, concurrent or retrospective approaches with college student samples or eating-disordered patients, they offer little information about risk factors and the developmental course of eating problems and disorders. A developmental approach is critical to the study of these disorders, as eating problems commonly emerge during adolescence and are likely to be linked to the biological, social, and psychological transformations inherent to this period. Moreover, there appears to be a broad spectrum of eating disturbances, with relatively common eating problems such as dieting and binge eating arrayed along a continuum with the more severe clinical eating disorders. Finally, considerable change occurs over time, with individuals moving to more or less severe positions along this continuum.

The perspective of developmental psychopathology is well suited for research on eating problems and disorders, as this paradigm seeks to elucidate the relations between normal developmental processes and the emergence of psychopathology within sociocultural, biological, personality, family, and behavioral contexts. Individual differences in coping with transitional events of adolescence, such as pubertal and social role changes, are considered to be especially important for understanding the course of normal development and of psycho-

Audrey R. Tyrka • Department of Psychiatry and Human Behavior, Brown University School of Medicine, Butler Hospital, Providence, Rhode Island 02906.   **Julia A. Graber and Jeanne Brooks-Gunn** • Center for Study of Children and Families, Teachers' College, Columbia University, New York, New York 10027.

Handbook of Developmental Psychopathology, Second Edition, edited by Arnold J. Sameroff, Michael Lewis, and Suzanne M. Miller. Kluwer Academic/Plenum Publishers, New York, 2000.

pathology (Graber & Brooks-Gunn, 1996b; Rutter, 1994). The developmental approach to psychopathology involves cross-sectional and longitudinal studies of individuals who are at high and low risk for developing a disorder to identify internal and external sources of competence and vulnerability in relation to developmental transitions, and to delineate patterns of continuity and discontinuity between normal development and psychopathology and between behaviors across development (Cicchetti & Schneider-Rosen, 1986).

Efforts to apply a developmental psychopathology framework to the investigation of the emergence of eating problems and disorders have been initiated. However, the developmental viewpoint in research on eating is still not well articulated, particularly in comparison with developmental work on depression and conduct disorder. In this chapter, we review several developmental issues of importance to eating disorder research. First, the spectrum of eating problems in adolescence is explored, including dieting and dissatisfaction with weight and shape, as well as binge eating, purging, and partial- and full-syndrome forms of bulimia and anorexia nervosa. The significance of reports of these eating problems and the possibility of age- and gender-related differences in their meaning is considered. Next, the continuum hypothesis, which holds that concerns with weight and dieting are temporally and perhaps causally related to clinical eating disorders, is presented, and evidence regarding the course of dieting and eating problems and disorders is considered. We then focus on the nature of adolescent development, as adolescence is the period of greatest risk for the development of eating problems and is a transition characterized by a convergence of physical transformations and changes in social roles and relationships. Next, precursors of disordered eating identified in prospective investigations are discussed. Finally, we address the question of whether subtypes of eating problems based on differences in severity or duration, coexisting depression, social context, age, and gender, may have unique developmental trajectories for the emergence or course of eating problems. We emphasize investigations of nonclinical adolescent samples that are most relevant to a developmental perspective (for an extensive review of the theoretical and empirical literature on clinical populations, see Attie & Brooks-Gunn, 1995).

THE SPECTRUM OF EATING DISTURBANCE IN ADOLESCENCE

Dieting and body dissatisfaction are pervasive among adolescent girls and young women. Little is known about the meaning of these attitudes and behaviors for adolescents, and their precise role in the development of eating disorders is not well understood. An understanding of the significance of these behaviors requires an appreciation of their character, prevalence, and course during late childhood and adolescence.

Satisfaction with Body Weight and Dieting

A large number of Western adolescent girls report dissatisfaction with their weight and body shape, with surveys finding that more than one-half of girls 7–13 years old (Maloney, McGuire, Daniels, & Specker, 1989) and one-half to two-thirds of middle school and high school girls report often feeling fat or wanting to lose weight (e.g., Childress, Brewerton, Hodges, & Jarrell, 1993; Pike, 1995). Girls who are dissatisfied with their bodies commonly attempt to lose weight through dieting; large surveys of adolescent girls have found that 30–45% report current dieting and 11–12% report chronic dieting (Serdula et al., 1993; Story et al., 1991). High rates of purging and other unhealthy dieting behaviors have also been found, with 4–11% of adolescent girls reporting vomiting, 4–8% using diet pills, 2–7% using laxatives, and 1–4% using diuretics (e.g., Childress et al., 1993; Killen et al., 1986).

The data on weight dissatisfaction and dieting behaviors have largely been garnered from self-report surveys or single questions assessing dieting status, ideal weights, or figures. It is possible that the responses of young adolescent girls, who strive to exhibit appropriate sex-role behavior as they become young women (Hill & Lynch, 1983), may reflect identification with feminine concerns rather than genuine attitudes or behaviors. Indeed, there is some evidence that girls experience cultural pressure to say that they feel fat and are dieting (Nichter & Vuckovic, 1994). However, reports of dieting by adolescent girls have been validated with assessments by parents and friends, and reports on food and exercise diaries (Rosen & Poplawski, 1987).

Another important issue concerns the definition of a standard for normal or expected weight. It is often reported that the majority of girls who are dissatisfied with their weight or dieting are of normal weight (e.g., Rosen, Gross, & Vara, 1987); however, cultural weight standards depicted in the media may be more salient to adolescents than average weights. Among dieters, girls who are of average weight but heavier than this cultural ideal may differ in important ways from those who are thin according to any measure. Little is known about the weight standards adolescents adopt, the degree to which such ideals influence their attitudes about their own weight, and how these standards change over the course of development.

A few investigators have begun to study the development of eating attitudes and behaviors in adolescence. Our group conducted a maximum likelihood analysis with a large sample of girls to determine whether the constructs underlying problem eating change with development. While the latent construct underlying reports of dieting and bulimic behavior was similar for 7th- to 8th-, 9th- to 10th-, and 11th- to 12th-grade girls, the salience of these constructs, as indicated by the size of absolute factor loadings, increased with grade in school (Brooks-Gunn, Rock, & Warren, 1989). Additionally, Green and McKenna (1993) found an age difference in the selective attention of girls to shape- and "fattening"-food-related words in the Stroop test. The performance of both 11- and 14-year-old girls declined with fattening-food words, suggesting concern about such foods. For 14-year-old girls, an effect of shape-related words also emerged. These results could indicate that cultural attitudes about "fattening" foods are assimilated independently of concerns about weight and shape, with the latter achieving full expression subsequent to the pubertal fat spurt.

Thus, it appears that the expression and meaning of attitudes and behaviors related to body image and eating may evolve over the course of adolescence. A developmental understanding of these issues will be necessary for an appreciation of the role of weight dissatisfaction and dieting in the emergence of more severe eating problems.

Eating Disorder, Subclinical Disorder, and Eating Problems

Anorexia nervosa and bulimia nervosa are the two primary eating disorders of adolescence and adulthood (American Psychiatric Association, 1994). The diagnosis of anorexia nervosa is based on the refusal to maintain a minimally normal body weight, intense fear of gaining weight or becoming fat, amenorrhea for 3 consecutive months, and a disturbance in body image. Bulimia nervosa is characterized by binge eating (i.e., consuming an abnormally large amount of food in a short period of time accompanied by a sense of lack of control over the behavior) and compensatory behaviors intended to prevent weight gain, such as self-induced vomiting and use of laxatives, diuretics, enemas, fasting, or excessive exercise. As some individuals who meet criteria for anorexia nervosa also engage in bulimic behaviors; restricting and binge-eating/purging subtypes of anorexia have been specified. Finally, binge eating disorder, a syndrome involving binge eating but not purging, has been proposed as a new diagnostic category requiring further study (American Psychiatric Association, 1994).

Individuals with partial syndrome eating disorders, which may be alternately referred to as atypical or subclinical eating disorder, or eating disorder not otherwise specified, meet many, but not all, of the diagnostic criteria for an eating disorder. This category includes those who meet most of the criteria for anorexia nervosa but, despite low weight or significant weight loss, do not meet the weight or amenorrhea criteria, or for bulimia, those who binge and purge but do not meet the frequency criteria (American Psychiatric Association, 1994).

Self-report instruments with established reliability and validity are commonly used to detect partial syndrome eating problems. "Eating problems" or "disordered eating" are usually defined by scores above a cut-point on a self-report measure such as the Eating Attitudes Test (EAT, Garner & Garfinkel, 1979), which assesses a broad range of eating disorder symptoms.

Epidemiology

The prevalence of eating disorders in adolescent and young-adult Western females has been reported to be 0.2–0.8% for anorexia nervosa and 1–2% for bulimia nervosa (Hoek, 1993). As nonrespondents in studies of eating problems are overrepresented by individuals with such problems, these rates are likely underestimates of actual prevalence (e.g., Childress et al., 1993; Johnson-Sabine, Wood, Patton, & Mann, 1988). Moreover, there are concerns about the veracity of reports by individuals with eating disorders who do participate, as denial and secrecy are often components of these disorders (Vandereycken & Vanderlinden, 1983).

Partial syndrome eating disorders are more common than anorexia or bulimia, with estimates based on interview studies of young Western females of 3–6% (e.g., Kendler et al., 1991; Killen, Hayward, et al., 1994). Self-report measures have yielded rates of 6–15% (e.g., Dancyger & Garfinkel, 1995; Gross & Rosen, 1988; Whitaker, et al., 1989); this figure may be as high as 19–27% among girls in private schools (Graber, Brooks-Gunn, Paikoff, & Warren, 1994; Hesse-Biber, 1992; Rosen, Compas, & Tacy, 1993).

Binge eating has been documented in 7–25% of adolescent girls and has been found to be even more prevalent in adolescent boys in some large self-report surveys (e.g., Childress et al., 1993; Whitaker et al., 1989). However, some studies suggest that reports of binge eating by males, in contrast to females, reflect consumption that does not involve negative emotion and stops short of causing a feeling of physical illness (e.g., LaPorte, 1997; Whitaker et al., 1989).

Anorexia nervosa and bulimia nervosa are far more common in females than males, with ratios between 10:1 and 20:1, and have previously been reported to be overrepresented in the middle and upper classes (Hoek, 1993). Notably, population studies (Whitaker et al., 1989) have found little or no association of socioeconomic status (SES) with eating disorder symptoms, possibly because of biases in prior studies due to selective referral practices (Wakeling, 1996) or change in demographic characteristics. Eating disorders are reportedly rare in non-Western countries, and those who immigrate to Western countries appear to have increased risk (Hoek, 1993), perhaps because the "slim ideal" and dieting are largely Western phenomena (McCarthy, 1990). It is possible that such environmental sources of vulnerability interact with a genetic predisposition to produce eating problems and disorders. Family studies and investigations of twins who were reared together have provided preliminary evidence of a genetic contribution to risk for both anorexia and bulimia (for a review, see Attie & Brooks-Gunn, 1995).

THE CONTINUUM HYPOTHESIS

As indicated, girls and young women commonly experience a wide range of eating problems, including dieting, binge eating, and partial- and full-syndrome eating disorders. This had led many researchers to assert that eating pathology is arrayed along a continuum as a dimensional variable (Nylander, 1971). The significance of such a continuum depends on whether the elements are causally, as well as phenomenologically and developmentally, related. If dieting and other eating problems are causally implicated in the development of eating disorders, additional factors must be involved, as the vast majority of those with less severe problems do not develop anorexia or bulimia.

Developmental Continuity

Some evidence suggests that childhood feeding difficulties may be related to the development of eating problems or disorders in adolescence (Shisslak, Crago, & Estes, 1995). In a prospective epidemiological interview study of eating patterns from early childhood to late adolescence, childhood difficulty at mealtimes and pica (a childhood disorder involving consumption of nonnutritive substances) were predictive of the development of bulimic symptoms in adolescence. The development of anorexic symptoms was predicted by digestive difficulties and picky eating in childhood but not weight concerns or dieting (Marchi & Cohen, 1990).

Other longitudinal studies have focused on the developmental relations among dieting, disordered eating attitudes, and behaviors in adolescence. Studies with follow-up periods of 1–2 years have reported that dieters and those with weight concerns (King, 1989; Patton, Johnson-Sabine, Wood, & Mann, 1990; Vollrath, Koch, & Angst, 1992) were at increased risk for developing subclinical eating problems. Finally, longitudinal studies with follow-up periods of 20–41 months have found that 13–45% of individuals with partial eating disorders progressed to full syndrome anorexia or bulimia during the course of the investigation (e.g., King, 1989; Thelen, Kanakis, Farmer, & Pruitt, 1993).

Developmental continuity has also been documented in studies examining the histories of individuals with eating problems. Patton and colleagues (1990) found that 81% of girls with onset of partial syndrome eating disorder at 1-year follow-up had initially been categorized as dieters. Additionally, several studies of the development of bulimia found that all cases had reported symptoms of bulimia 12–18 months earlier, and all initial cases that no longer qualified for a diagnosis still reported bulimic symptoms at follow-up (Drewnowski, Yee, & Krahn, 1988; King, 1989; Striegel-Moore, Silberstein, Frensch, & Rodin, 1989).

DIETARY RESTRAINT

Some authors have argued that dieting, or restrained eating, is causally implicated in the development of binge eating. Restrained eating refers to chronic dieting associated with overconcern with weight and sometimes includes a history of weight fluctuation. It has been well established that restrained eaters overeat following consumption of an ostensibly high-calorie food, or when they experience an anxious or depressed mood (Beebe, 1994). This phenomenon has been termed "counterregulation" (in contrast to the decrease, or regulation, of intake by nondieters seen in such experimental situations), and has been likened to binge eating (Tuschl, 1990). The classic semistarvation study by Keys, Brozek, Henschel, Michelsen, and Taylor (1950), in which 36 male conscientious objectors lost an average of 25% of their body weight over 6 months, found that as weight loss increased, the men became obsessed with food and engaged in abnormal food rituals commonly seen in anorexia nervosa. During refeeding, most men overate, several gorged themselves to the point of nausea and vomiting, and many reported relentless hunger even following very large meals.

Despite the compelling evidence linking restrained eating to binge eating, significant gaps in this association remain. It is important to note that few of the men in the study by Keys and colleagues experienced what could be considered bulimic episodes. Moreover, counterregulation in the laboratory rarely resembles binge eating in terms of the amount eaten and loss of control over the consumption, and some restrained eaters do not counterregulate at all (Cooper & Charnock, 1990; Kirkley & Burge, 1989). It is not known what factors might distinguish restrained eaters who consistently regulate their intake from those who lose control over eating (Kirkley & Burge, 1989). Multivariate, prospective studies comparing the developmental course and risk factors for dieting, eating problems, and disorders will be necessary for a full understanding of the links between these problems and their correlates. (Existing cross-sectional studies are discussed in a later section of this chapter.)

ADOLESCENT CHALLENGES AND CORRELATES OF EATING PROBLEMS

Adolescence, the period of greatest vulnerability to the development of eating disorders (Hoek, 1993), is characterized by dramatic physical and psychosocial changes. For Western girls, this transition involves changes in body shape and fat composition that occur within a cultural context that devalues such changes (Attie & Brooks-Gunn, 1987). In addition, adolescents experience alterations of the power structure and emotional bonds within the family, increases in social stressors, and the maturation of a psychological framework for the regulation of mood, impulse, and self-esteem (e.g., Brooks-Gunn, 1991).

Physical Changes and Body Image

The female pubertal "fat spurt" results in a profound change in body shape and composition, adding an average of 24 pounds of body fat (Warren, 1983). This alteration in body shape and the concomitant change in reproductive status may require a fundamental reorganization of body image. Girls appear to evaluate their bodies largely in aesthetic rather than functional terms, and weight is a primary component of body image for girls and young women (e.g., Attie & Brooks-Gunn, 1987). Adolescent girls who perceive themselves to be underweight are more satisfied with their bodies than those who think they are average weight, who in turn are more satisfied than those who perceive themselves to be overweight (Tobin-Richards, Boxer, & Petersen, 1983). While girls with eating problems do tend to be heavy for their height, as a group, they would not be characterized as overweight (e.g., Johnson-Sabine et al., 1988;

Killen, Hayward, et al., 1994). Wichstrom (1995) found that body mass accounted for only 23% of the variance in perceived obesity, which was the best of several predictors of eating pathology. There is also evidence that young women with dieting and bulimic behavior place more importance on appearance and thinness than do others (e.g., Hart & Kenny, 1997).

Pubertal Timing

Several studies have found that girls who mature early are more likely than on-time or late-maturing girls to report body dissatisfaction and eating problems (Killen et al., 1992), even after their peers have reached puberty (e.g., Graber et al., 1994). This association may be partially explained by the tendency for such girls to be heavier than their peers (Faust, 1983). In addition, early-maturing girls have less time and perhaps less social support with which to develop strategies for coping with pubertal changes (Brooks-Gunn, 1991). Early menarche has also been associated with major depressive disorder and conduct disorder in girls (Graber, Lewinsohn, Seeley, & Brooks-Gunn, 1997). Clarification of the nature of the relations among early maturation, eating problems, and related difficulties will require further study.

Sociocultural Influences

In recent decades there has been an increase in the cultural obsession with thinness and a change to a slimmer, prepubertal "ideal" feminine shape (Garner, Garfinkel, Schwartz, & Thompson, 1980; Wiseman, Gray, Mosimann, & Ahrens, 1992). This redefinition of the "ideal" female form projects an image that is unhealthy or unattainable for most postpubertal females (Garner et al., 1980). Adolescence is a vulnerable time regarding such pressures, as it is a period in which conformity peaks (Hill & Lynch, 1983) and girls' bodies begin to defy cultural standards.

The potential influence of sociocultural factors on eating disorders has been suggested in studies of girls who are under vocational pressure to maintain low body weight, such as ballet dancers and fashion models. These young women have substantially elevated rates of eating problems and disorders (Attie & Brooks-Gunn, 1992).

Gender Role

The increase in emphasis on thinness in this country has occurred in the context of dramatic changes in the female gender role. With movement into previously male-dominated fields, women may experience pressure to mimic male behavior and appearance (Attie & Brooks-Gunn, 1987) while still exhibiting a feminine focus on attractiveness and interpersonal relationships. Disordered eating may represent an ambivalent response to this complex gender role; a number of studies offer support for this association in young women (Hart & Kenny, 1997; Silverstein, Carpman, Perlick, & Perdue, 1990; Steiner-Adair, 1986).

Some evidence suggests that eating disorders are associated with stereotypical feminine traits such as passivity. In their review of the literature, Lancelot and Kaslow (1994) concluded that empirical investigations of the link between femininity and eating disorders per se have suffered from methodological limitations and yielded inconsistent findings; however, positive associations between femininity and both dieting and appearance concern, and negative associations between masculinity and eating problems have been consistently demonstrated.

Such correlations may be mediated by links between gender roles and self-esteem or other psychological factors.

Stress and Stressors

Stress has been defined as a negative emotional or physical response to a stressor, which is an event that is perceived as threatening, important, and requiring a novel coping strategy (Brooks-Gunn, 1991). Adolescence is replete with such events, including moving to a less personal, more demanding school, and possibly smoking, drinking, and sexual behavior.

Investigations of community and clinical samples have found individuals with disordered eating to report high levels of perceived stress (e.g., Rosen et al., 1993) The nature of a link between stress and eating problems remains to be elucidated. Dieting, or purging following binge eating, could be used as a coping mechanism to enhance a sense of self-control or mastery in the face of threatening experiences. Conversely, the psychological or physiological effects of dieting or the binge–purge cycle may increase stress levels (Rosen, Tacy, & Howell, 1990).

Dating

Interest in opposite-sex popularity emerges in adolescence and is strongly associated with concerns about appearance and weight (e.g., Gargiulo, Attie, Brooks-Gunn, & Warren, 1987). Girls who begin dating early have been found to be more likely than their peers to have eating problems (e.g., Dykens & Gerrard, 1986), even after accounting for the effects of pubertal maturation (Cauffman & Steinberg, 1996). Moreover, the simultaneous experience of dating and menarche has been associated with dieting and eating problems in adolescent girls (Cauffman & Steinberg, 1996; Levine, Smolak, Moodey, Shuman, & Hessen, 1994; Smolak, Levine, & Gralen, 1993). In one study, girls with simultaneous onset of dating and menarche who also reported high levels of academic stress and a thin ideal body image had the highest levels of disturbed eating (Levine et al., 1994). The link between early dating and eating problems may be further mediated by associations with such factors as sex roles, family functioning, or other forms of psychopathology.

Family Relationships

Establishing psychological autonomy presents one of the most fundamental challenges of the adolescent period, one that requires a renegotiation of the parent–child relationship (for a review, see Graber & Brooks-Gunn, 1996a). While most adolescents and parents report feeling close to one another during early adolescence, in early to middle adolescence, time spent together decreases and conflict increases. Conflict in mother–daughter relationships may be especially pronounced.

The literature on family functioning of girls with eating disorders has been reviewed by Attie and Brooks-Gunn (1995). Families of girls with anorexia have been portrayed as enmeshed and overprotective, and those of girls with bulimia have been described as under-involved and lacking in nurturance. Some clinical investigations have provided support for these characterizations, but results have been inconsistent (Strober & Humphrey, 1987).

Several studies of adolescent girls have identified low family cohesion as a correlate of eating problems (e.g., Attie & Brooks-Gunn, 1989; Wertheim et al., 1992). In our study of adolescent girls and their mothers, daughter dieting was associated with a divergence in mother and daughter ratings of cohesion, independent of overall cohesion (Paikoff, Carlton-Ford, & Brooks-Gunn, 1993), perhaps reflecting differences in perception of family functioning, or more general contention in the mother–daughter relationship.

Family Modeling and Communication about Weight and Dieting

The attitudes and behaviors of mothers have been hypothesized to play an important role in the development of eating problems because the mother–daughter relationship may be particularly influential, and because mothers often struggle with weight and body image themselves. A recent prospective study found that maternal body dissatisfaction and eating problems were predictive of the emergence of eating disturbances in young children (Stice, Agras, & Hammer, 1999). Several studies have found an association between eating problems or disorders in female relatives (Attie & Brooks-Gunn, 1995; Pike, 1995; Pike & Rodin, 1991). This may in part be accounted for by overt parental disapproval regarding weight. A survey of high school girls (Paxton et al., 1991) and a study of fourth-grade girls and their parents (Thelen & Cormier, 1995) found that parental encouragement to diet was associated with daughter dieting, irrespective of body mass. Pike and Rodin (1991) reported that the mothers of girls with eating problems thought that their daughters should lose more weight and rated them as less attractive than did other mothers, even after controlling for daughters' body mass.

Eating Problems in the Peer Group

As adolescents separate from the family, peer relationships increase in importance and conformity to the attitudes of the peer group peaks (Brooks-Gunn & Attie, 1995). Body image, dieting, binge eating, and purging may be influenced by the attitudes and behaviors of peers. In a survey of sorority members, Crandall (1988) found that while at the beginning of the school year, severity of binge eating was uncorrelated among friends within a sorority, after 7 months, it was more uniform. Additionally, eating problems have been linked to reports of dieting and eating disorders among friends (Levine et al., 1994; Pike, 1995).

Related Psychopathology

In addition to eating problems, the transitions of adolescence have been associated with several other domains of psychopathology (e.g., Petersen et al., 1993). Successful coping with this transition requires development of social and psychological foundations for the regulation of mood, impulse, and self-esteem. Studies of eating disorder patients have documented disturbances in these domains, including depressive symptoms, perfectionist strivings, feelings of ineffectiveness, and deficits in the regulation of affect and impulse (Attie & Brooks-Gunn, 1995). Girls with eating problems have also been found to have low self-esteem, depressed affect, feelings of ineffectiveness, perfectionism, difficulty with identifying emotions, and impulsivity (e.g., Graber et al., 1994; Killen, Taylor, et al., 1994; Leon, Fulkerson, Perry, & Early-Zald, 1995; Pike, 1995; Wichstrom, 1995).

PROSPECTIVE STUDIES OF RISK FACTORS
FOR EATING PROBLEMS AND DISORDERS

Cross-sectional designs, such as those employed in most of the investigations cited thus far, do not allow delineation of the direction of causal effects. Moreover, links with such factors as perfectionism or even body image may not be specific to eating problems but may be indicative of more generalized psychopathology. In response to these concerns, a number of prospective studies of the development of eating problems and disorders in adolescent girls and young adult women have been undertaken. In these prospective analyses, putative risk factors measured at an initial assessment are used to predict problems found to occur at follow-up; the possibility that predictive relationships are due to concurrent effects of initial eating problems is excluded, either by studying only those with onset of symptoms at follow-up or by statistically controlling for the effect of initial symptoms. These investigations have provided support for many of the factors reviewed earlier; however, few findings are consistent across studies.

Turning first to short-term investigations, in a 5-week prospective study of college women, Greenberg and Harvey (1986) found that an interaction of initial depression and dietary restraint predicted bulimic symptomatology at follow-up, after controlling for initial bulimic symptoms, restraint, and depression. Other short-term (Rosen et al., 1993) and long-term (Cattarin & Thompson, 1994) investigations found that initial eating problems led to increased stress (Rosen et al., 1993) and poor psychological functioning (Cattarin & Thompson, 1994) whereas neither stress nor psychological symptoms predicted later eating problems (Rosen et al., 1993).

Several investigations of 1–4 years' duration have explored putative risk factors for the development of disordered eating. One study of British schoolgirls (Patton et al., 1990) and another of Polish schoolgirls (Wlodarczyk-Bisaga & Dolan, 1996) were unable to identify prospective predictors of the onset of partial syndrome eating disorders. A number of multivariate prospective studies of maturational, familial, and personality factors in females have found that only initial dieting, weight concerns, or high body mass (Keel, Fulkerson, & Leon, 1997; Killen, Hayward, et al., 1994; Killen, Taylor, Hayward, & Haydel, et al., 1996) and body image (Attie & Brooks-Gunn, 1989; Cattarin & Thompson, 1994) were uniquely predictive of disordered eating at follow-up. In a large prospective study of 7th- to 10th-grade students, Leon and colleagues (1995) found that among several psychosocial and behavioral measures collected in 3 consecutive years, Caucasian race and interoceptive awareness, a measure of difficulty identifying emotions, were significant predictors of subsequent eating disorder risk status, after controlling for the significant associations with prior eating disorder symptoms.

Other studies have explored more specific models of the development of eating attitudes and behaviors. Smolak and colleagues (1993) investigated the impact of experiencing menarche and beginning to date within the same year in a longitudinal study of middle school girls. Girls who had simultaneous onset of menses and dating reported more dieting and body dissatisfaction and had higher Child EAT scores in 8th grade than other girls, after controlling for 6th-grade EAT scores. Those with early (i.e., prior to 7th grade) and simultaneous onset appeared to be at highest risk; these girls also experienced a change to middle school in the same year.

Swarr and Richards (1996) studied working- and middle-class white girls in 5th–9th grades and again 2 years later. Somewhat different effects were found for the younger (5th–6th grade) versus older (7th–9th grade) girls; however, taken together, the findings indicated that normative timing of pubertal maturation, spending time with parents, the quality of relationships with parents, and particularly the interaction of these factors, led to healthier eating attitudes and behaviors.

Stice and Agras (1998) conducted a 9-month study of bulimic symptomatology in high school girls. Body dissatisfaction, dieting, and negative affect were predictive of the later onset of binge eating and of compensatory purging behaviors. Additionally, low initial levels of body dissatisfaction and dieting were associated with cessation of compensatory purging at follow-up.

Members of our group have used the longitudinal approach to explore whether there are unique correlates of transient compared to recurrent eating problems in an 8-year study of white private-school girls (Graber et al., 1994). Girls were classified according to whether they scored in the disordered range on the EAT-26 initially (grades 7–10) and at the second assessment 2 years later. In general, girls who did not have an eating problem had more positive feelings about their bodies and less psychopathology than those with an eating problem. In addition, girls with recurrent eating problems were differentiated from those with a transient problem by earlier ages at menarche, higher body mass, and more disturbed psychosocial functioning.

In summary, the prospective studies that have been conducted to date have identified some possible risk factors for the development of eating problems. Not surprisingly, weight concerns, dieting, and eating problems have been found to be strong predictors of later disordered eating. Studies investigating the influence of physical and psychosocial factors point to pubertal timing, body mass, poor body image, negative affect, and difficulty identifying emotions as possible risk factors for the development of disordered eating. Interactions of depression with dietary restraint, and of pubertal timing with early dating and with relationships with parents have also been found to predict the development of eating problems. Because many individuals exhibited weight and eating problems at the initial assessment in each of these studies, it is possible that other predictors exerted an influence on initial problem eating, but no longer had unique effects on later onset or worsening of symptoms in subsequent assessments. Furthermore, the work by Rosen and colleagues indicates that dieting and eating problems may result in increased negative impact of reported stressful life events. Overall, prospective studies have yet to address differences in onset, course, and recovery from eating problems; our longitudinal study provides evidence that girls with chronic or recurrent eating problems may be distinguished from those with transient problems on the basis of pubertal maturation and psychosocial functioning.

HETEROGENEITY AMONG INDIVIDUALS WITH EATING PROBLEMS AND DISORDERS

Most existing prospective and cross-sectional studies have investigated simple associations between eating problems and putative risk factors. More complex models might specify the links between dieting and other eating problems or explore the possibility that alternate developmental pathways exist for groups with coexisting psychopathology, weight-related pressures, or differences in the age of onset or duration of eating problems. Comparative studies of the antecedents, correlates, and outcomes of disordered eating in such groups could elucidate specific risk factors for different developmental trajectories.

Unique and Shared Correlates of Different Elements of the Eating Problem "Continuum"

A few studies have compared the psychological functioning of dieters and those who have more severe eating disturbances. There is some evidence that dieting is associated with psychological difficulty that in some respects may resemble that of eating disordered subjects (e.g., Dykens & Gerrard, 1986). Nutritional deprivation (Keys et al., 1950) or other stressful effects of dieting (Rosen et al., 1990) could be responsible for this association; alternatively, emotional problems may lead to dieting, perhaps because of disturbances in self-perceptions, coping mechanisms, or self-control.

Overall, however, findings suggest that individuals with eating problems such as bulimic symptomatology experience more profound psychological, familial, and behavioral disturbances than do dieters (e.g., Dykens & Gerrard, 1986; Laessle, Tuschl, Waadt, & Pirke, 1989; Attie & Brooks-Gunn, 1992). Additionally, studies comparing individuals with full-syndrome eating disorders compared to partial-syndrome disorders or eating problems indicate that psychological correlates may be arrayed on a continuum, with severity corresponding to that of the eating disturbance (Dancyger & Garfinkel, 1995; Garner, Olmsted, Polivy, & Garfinkel, 1984). Heterogeneity among those with eating problems may account for these findings. Garner and colleagues (1984) conducted a cluster analysis with their weight-preoccupied students and identified one group with psychopathology resembling that of anorexic patients, and a second group with high scores only on measures of drive for thinness, body dissatisfaction, and perfectionism. Olmsted and Garner (1986) found comparable subgroups among purging college women. These results suggest the possibility that one subtype of partial-syndrome eating disturbance may comprise part of an eating disorder spectrum, while another group of extreme dieters may not be at risk for more severe disorders.

These comparative studies represent preliminary steps in defining risk groups and specifying the relations among them. That dieters or individuals with eating problems have intermediate or equivalent levels of psychopathology, however, does not inform us as to the direction of a causal association between eating problems and other psychopathology. The existence of a group of individuals with eating problems that does not report psychological distress indicates that eating problems do not inevitably lead to other psychopathology. This group also appeared to have less eating-related pathology than the other group in these studies; hence, the possibility that psychological difficulty was due to severe eating disturbances remains. Additionally, the group with significant psychopathology may have had another primary disorder such as depression, may have been in a partial-syndrome phase prior to developing full-blown disorder, or may have required the experience of some other factor(s) to develop a clinical eating disorder.

Comorbidity

In addition to symptoms of psychopathology, clinical disorders such as depression and certain personality disorders have been reported to be overrepresented among individuals with eating disorders (for a review, see Attie & Brooks-Gunn, 1995). Thus, it is possible that the developmental precursors or consequences of eating problems in adolescence differ for individuals who have co-occurring conditions, or that the correlates of eating problems discussed earlier are primarily associated with the coexisting disorders.

Coexisting depression, in particular, may account for some of the links between psychosocial factors and eating problems noted earlier, as depression has been associated with such correlates of eating problems as perfectionism, anxiety, body dissatisfaction, self-esteem, feminine sex-role behavior, stress and major stressful events, and poor peer and family relationships (Petersen et al., 1993). Some evidence suggests that coexisting depression may be responsible for the association between eating problems and poor family functioning (e.g., Thienemann & Steiner, 1993; Wonderlich & Swift, 1990). Investigations of the developmental relations among eating and depressive problems, with attempts to elucidate shared and specific precursors of each problem and of their co-occurrence, will be necessary for a more complete understanding of this association.

Subgroups with Different Correlates

While eating problems and disorders are commonly associated with other psychological disturbances, psychopathology may not be a feature of eating problems for all adolescents. For example, members of our group found that among girls with eating problems, dancers were less likely to report signs of psychopathology than nondancers (e.g., Lancelot, Brooks-Gunn, Warren, & Newman, 1991). This finding suggests that extraordinary pressure to maintain thinness may take the place of psychosocial risk factors in this population. Similarly, some studies have found that dieting and eating problems in boys are not associated with the psychological correlates identified for girls (Leon et al., 1995; Rosen et al., 1987; Wertheim et al., 1992), and that male, but not female, adolescents with eating problems have higher body mass than other adolescents (e.g., Childress et al., 1993; Killen et al., 1986; Richards, Casper, & Larson, 1990).

Our longitudinal study discussed earlier (Graber et al., 1994) also found differences among subgroups of girls; those with recurrent eating problems had earlier menarche, higher body mass, and more disturbed psychosocial functioning than girls who had a transient eating problem.

Age-Related Differences in Correlates of Eating Problems

Results of a few longitudinal and cross-sectional investigations suggest that the correlates of eating problems may change with age or development. Factors such as grade (Attie & Brooks-Gunn, 1989), body mass (Attie & Brooks-Gunn, 1989; Richards et al., 1990), and age of menarche and dating status (Gralen, Levine, Smolak, & Murnen, 1990) have been associated with dieting or eating problems in early, but not later, adolescence. It is likely that factors associated with age, such as the changes that occur with pubertal maturation, age of onset, or course of eating disturbances are responsible for these associations.

SUMMARY AND FUTURE DIRECTIONS

Reports of weight dissatisfaction and eating disturbances are exceedingly common among adolescent girls and young women; little is known about developmental changes in the meaning and actual behaviors associated with these reports. There is a spectrum of eating problems, from mild dieting to clinical eating disorders, that appears to exhibit phenomenological and developmental continuity. In addition, dieting behavior, or some latent factor that predisposes individuals to diet, may be causally implicated in the development of eating problems; additional risk factors, such as maturational or personality factors, or psychological disturbances, must also be involved, as only a small proportion of dieters develop further eating problems.

Prospective studies have begun to identify risk factors for the development of disordered eating, but results thus far have been sporadic, with little consistency across studies. Although a number of prospective studies have been conducted in recent years, few have utilized the same measures, and replications have not been attempted thus far. Moreover, many putative risk factors and nonlinear models remain to be explored. That prior eating problems are the strongest predictors of later eating problems and that there are different correlates of eating problems in early compared to later adolescence suggest that ongoing eating problems may be somewhat independent of the factors that initiate them, or that the variance accounted for by initiating factors is shared by initial eating problems. Moreover, heterogeneity with regard to the duration of eating problems, coexisting psychopathology, age of onset, and social pressure could also result in an inability to detect longitudinal predictors, as different subgroups may be associated with different risk factors (Graber et al., 1994). Future prospective studies should investigate subgroups based on differences in phenomenological characteristics such as binge-eating–purging and restricting subtypes of anorexia or family history of eating problems, as well as age of onset, duration, and presence of coexisting conditions.

A central focus of developmental psychopathology concerns the elucidation of the characteristics of persons and their environments that act individually and interactively to increase risk for the emergence of disorders. O'Connor and Rutter (1996) discuss two important issues in risk research: (1) elucidation of the proximal effects of environmental factors, such as changes in cognitive, biological, psychological, or behavioral functioning, that confer risk for psychopathology; and (2) specification of the pathways by which these effects ultimately result in disorder. In some cases, the connections between early experience and later disorder may be direct. For example, experience may lead to changes in biology or behavior that result in disorder. Other pathways may consist of multiple, indirect links. For example, experience could influence self concept, coping styles, or the selection of future environments; these changes may lead to disorder if other relevant experiences are encountered (Sroufe & Rutter, 1984).

In this chapter, we have reviewed several domains of adolescent transition that appear to be compromised in girls with eating problems and disorders. Identification of correlates represents an initial step in the process of specifying risk pathways; these factors are likely to interact with other maturational or psychosocial processes and may additionally be affected by the presence of the eating problem. For example, while the family environment undoubtedly impacts individual functioning, family interactions are shaped by individual behavior; eating problems, particularly dangerous behaviors such as extreme caloric restriction or purging, may provoke strong reactions in family members. Moreover, when a factor is found to be predictive of eating problems in prospective work, it remains possible that the association is indirect and another factor is more proximally involved. Many putative risk factors, rather than having a specific association with eating problems, likely place individuals at risk for depression or for psychiatric problems in general. When general risk factors are involved, other individual or environmental characteristics may function interactively to confer specificity for eating problems and disorders. Future efforts should attempt to disentangle reciprocal effects of putative risk factors and eating disturbances and explore the specific direct or indirect pathways by which such factors may lead to the development of eating problems and disorders.

ACKNOWLEDGMENTS: This project was supported by grants from the National Institute of Child Health and Human Development, the W. T. Grant Foundation, and the National Institute of Mental Health.

REFERENCES

American Psychiatric Association. (1994). *Diagnostic and statistical manual of mental disorders* (4th ed.). Washington, DC: Author.

Attie, I., & Brooks-Gunn, J. (1987). Weight concerns as chronic stressors in women. In R. C. Barnett, L. Biener & G. K. Baruch (Eds.), *Gender and stress* (pp. 218–254). New York: Free Press.

Attie, I., & Brooks-Gunn, J. (1989). Development of eating problems in adolescent girls: A longitudinal study. *Developmental Psychology, 25*, 70–79.

Attie, I., & Brooks-Gunn, J. (1992). Developmental issues in the study of eating problems and disorders. In J. H. Crowther, S. E. Hobfoll, M. A. P. Stephens & D. L. Tennenbaum (Eds.), *The etiology of bulimia: The individual and familial context* (pp. 35–58). Washington, DC: Hemisphere.

Attie, I., & Brooks-Gunn, J. (1995). The development of eating regulation across the life span. In D. Cicchetti & D. J. Cohen (Eds.), *Developmental psychopathology* (Vol. 2. pp. 332–368). New York: Wiley.

Beebe, D. W. (1994). Bulimia nervosa and depression: A theoretical and clinical appraisal in light of the binge–purge cycle. *British Journal of Clinical Psychology, 33*, 259–276.

Brooks-Gunn, J. (1991). How stressful is the transition to adolescence for girls? In M. E. Colten & S. Gore (Eds.), *Adolescent stress: Causes and consequences* (pp. 131–149). Hawthorne, NY: Aldine de Gruyter.

Brooks-Gunn, J., & Attie, I. (1995). Developmental psychopathology in the context of adolescence. In J. J. Haugaard & M. F. Lenzenweger (Eds.), *Frontiers of developmental psychopathology* (pp. 148–189). New York: Oxford University Press.

Brooks-Gunn, J., Rock, D., & Warren, M. P. (1989). Comparability of constructs across the adolescent years. *Developmental Psychology, 25*, 51–60.

Cattarin, J. A., & Thompson, J. (1994). A three-year longitudinal study of body image, eating disturbance, and general psychological functioning in adolescent females. *Eating Disorders: The Journal of Treatment and Prevention, 2*, 114–125.

Cauffman, E., & Steinberg, L. (1996). Interactive effects of menarcheal status and dating on dieting and disordered eating among adolescent girls. *Developmental Psychology, 32*, 631–635.

Childress, A. C., Brewerton, T. D., Hodges, E. L., & Jarrell, M. P. (1993). The Kids' Eating Disorders Survey (keds): A study of middle school students. *Journal of the American Academy of Child and Adolescent Psychiatry, 32*, 843–850.

Cicchetti, D., & Schneider-Rosen, K. (1986). An organizational approach to childhood depression. In M. Rutter, C. E. Izard, & P. B. Read (Eds.), *Depression in young people: Clinical and developmental perspectives* (pp. 71–134). New York: Guilford Press.

Cooper, P. J., & Charnock, D. (1990). From restraint to bulimic episodes: A problem of some loose connections. *Appetite, 14*, 120–122.

Crandall, C. S. (1988). Social contagion of binge eating. *Journal of Personality and Social Psychology, 55*, 588–598.

Dancyger, I. F., & Garfinkel, P. (1995). The relationship of partial syndrome eating disorders to anorexia and bulimia nervosa. *Psychological Medicine, 25*, 1019–1025.

Drewnowski, A., Yee, D., & Krahn, D. (1988). Bulimia in college women: Incidence and recovery rates. *American Journal of Psychiatry, 145*, 401–408.

Dykens, E. M., & Gerrard, M. (1986). Psychological profiles of purging bulimics, repeat dieters, and controls. *Journal of Consulting and Clinical Psychology, 54*, 283–288.

Faust, M. S. (1983). Alternative constructions of adolescent growth. In J. Brooks-Gunn & A. C. Petersen (Eds.), *Girls at puberty* (pp. 105–125). New York: Plenum Press.

Gargiulo, J., Attie, I., Brooks-Gunn, J., & Warren, M. P. (1987). Girls' dating behavior as a function of social context and maturation. *Developmental Psychology, 23*, 730–737.

Garner, D. M., & Garfinkel, P. E. (1979). The Eating Attitudes Test: An index of symptoms of anorexia nervosa. *Psychological Medicine, 9*, 273–279.

Garner, D. M., Garfinkel, P. E., Schwartz, D., & Thompson, M. (1980). Cultural expectations of thinness in women. *Psychological Reports, 47*, 483–491.

Garner, D. M., Olmsted, M. P., Polivy, J., & Garfinkel, P. E. (1984). Comparison between weight-preoccupied women and anorexia nervosa. *Psychosomatic Medicine, 46,* 255–266.

Graber, J. A., & Brooks-Gunn, J. (1996a). Reproductive transitions: The experience of mothers and daughters. In C. D. Ryff & M. M. Seltzer (Eds.), *The parental experience in midlife* (pp. 255–299). Chicago: University of Chicago Press.

Graber, J. A., & Brooks-Gunn, J. (1996b). Transitions and turning points: Navigating the passage from childhood through adolescence. *Developmental Psychology, 32,* 768–776.

Graber, J. A., Brooks-Gunn, J., Paikoff, R. L., & Warren, M. P. (1994). Prediction of eating problems: An 8-year study of adolescent girls. *Developmental Psychology, 30,* 823–834.

Graber, J. A., Lewinsohn, P. M., Seeley, J. R., & Brooks-Gunn, J. (1997). Is psychopathology associated with the timing of pubertal development? *Journal of the American Academy of Child and Adolescent Psychiatry, 36,* 1768–1776.

Gralen, S. J., Levine, M. P., Smolak, L., & Murnen, S. K. (1990). Dieting and disordered eating during early and middle adolescence: Do the influences remain the same? *International Journal of Eating Disorders, 9,* 501–512.

Green, M. W., & McKenna, F. P. (1993). Developmental onset of eating related color-naming interference. *International Journal of Eating Disorders, 13,* 391–397.

Greenberg, B. A., & Harvey, P. D. (1986). The prediction of binge eating over time. *Addictive Behaviors, 11,* 383–388.

Gross, J., & Rosen, J. C. (1988). Bulimia in adolescents: Prevalence and psychosocial correlates. *International Journal of Eating Disorders, 7,* 51–61.

Hart, K., & Kenny, M. E. (1997). Adherence to the super woman ideal and eating disorder symptoms among college women. *Sex Roles, 36,* 461–478.

Hesse-Biber, S. (1992). Report on a panel longitudinal study of college women's eating patterns and eating disorders: Noncontinuum versus continuum measures. *Health Care for Women International, 13,* 375–391.

Hill J. P., & Lynch M. E. (1983). The intensification of gender-related role expectations during early adolescence. In J. Brooks-Gunn & A. C. Petersen (Eds.), *Girls at puberty: Biological and psychosocial perspectives* (pp. 201–228). New York: Plenum Press.

Hoek, H. W. (1993). Review of the epidemiological studies of eating disorders. *International Review of Psychiatry, 5,* 61–74.

Johnson-Sabine, E., Wood, K., Patton, G., & Mann, A. (1988). Abnormal eating attitudes in London schoolgirls: A prospective epidemiological study: Factors associated with abnormal response on screening questionnaires. *Psychological Medicine, 18,* 615–622.

Keel, P. K., Fulkerson, J. A., & Leon, G. R. (1997). Disordered eating precursors in pre- and early adolescent girls and boys. *Journal of Youth and Adolescence, 26,* 203.

Kendler, K. S., MacLean, C., Neale, M., Kessler, R., Heath, S., & Eaves, L. (1991). The genetic epidemiology of bulimia nervosa. *American Journal of Psychiatry, 148,* 1627–1637.

Keys, A., Brozek, J., Henschel, A., Michelsen, O., & Taylor, H. L. (1950). *The biology of human starvation.* Minneapolis, MN: University of Minneapolis Press.

Killen, J. D., Hayward, C., Litt, I., Hammer, L. D., Wilson, D. M., Miner, B., Taylor, B., Varady, A., & Shisslak, C. (1992). Is puberty a risk factor for eating disorders. *American Journal of Diseases of Children, 146,* 323–325.

Killen, J. D., Hayward, C., Wilson, D. M., Taylor, C. B., Hammer, L. D., Litt, I., Simmonds, B., & Haydel, F. (1994). Factors associated with eating disorder symptoms in a community sample of 6th and 7th grade girls. *International Journal of Eating Disorders, 15,* 357–367.

Killen, J. D., Taylor, C. B., Hayward, C., Haydel, K. F., Wilson, D. M., Hammer, L., Kraemer, H., Blair-Greiner, A., & Strachowski, D. (1996). Weight concerns influence the development of eating disorders: A 4-year prospective study. *Journal of Consulting & Clinical Psychology, 64,* 936–940.

Killen, J. D., Taylor, C. B., Hayward, C., Wilson, D. M., Haydel, K. F., Hammer, L. D., Simmonds, B., Robinson, T. N., Litt, I., Varady, A., & Kraemer, H. (1994). Pursuit of thinness and onset of eating disorder symptoms in a community sample of adolescent girls: A three-year prospective analysis. *International Journal of Eating Disorders, 16,* 227–238.

Killen, J. D., Taylor, C. B, Telch, M. J., Saylor, K. E., Maron, D. J., & Robinson, T. N. (1986). Self-induced vomiting and laxative and diuretic use among teenagers: Precursors of the binge-purge syndrome? *Journal of the American Medical Association, 255,* 1447–1449.

King, M. B. (1989). Eating disorders in a general practice population: Prevalence, characteristics and follow-up at 12 to 18 months. *Psychological Medicine, Monograph Suppl. 14,* 1–34.

Kirkley, B. G., & Burge, J. C. (1989). Dietary restriction in young women: Issues and concerns. *Annals of Behavioral Medicine, 11,* 66–72.

Laessle, R. G., Tuschl, R. J., Waadt, S., & Pirke, K. M. (1989). The specific psychopathology of bulimia nervosa: A comparison with restrained and unrestrained (normal) eaters. *Journal of Consulting and Clinical Psychology, 57,* 772–775.

Lancelot, C., Brooks-Gunn, J., Warren, M. P., & Newman, D. L. (1991). Comparison of DSM-III and DSM-III-R bulimia nervosa classifications for psychopathology and other eating behaviors. *International Journal of Eating Disorders, 10*, 57–66.

Lancelot, C., & Kaslow, N. J. (1994). Sex role orientation and disordered eating in women: A review. *Clinical Psychology Review, 14*, 139–157.

LaPorte, D. J. (1997). Gender differences in perceptions and consequences of an eating binge. *Sex Roles, 36*, 479–489.

Leon, G. R., Fulkerson, J. A., Perry, C. L., & Early-Zald, M. B. (1995). Prospective analysis of personality and behavioral vulnerabilities and gender influences in the later development of disordered eating. *Journal of Abnormal Psychology, 104*, 140–149.

Levine, M. P., Smolak, L., Moodey, A. F., Shuman, M. D., & Hessen, L. D. (1994). Normative developmental challenges and dieting and eating disturbances in middle school girls. *International Journal of Eating Disorders, 15*, 11–20.

Maloney, M. J., McGuire, J., Daniels, S. R., & Specker, B. (1989). Dieting behavior and eating attitudes in children. *Pediatrics, 84*, 482–487.

Marchi, M., & Cohen, P. (1990). Early childhood eating behaviors and adolescent eating disorders. *Journal of the American Academy of Child and Adolescent Psychiatry, 29*, 112–117.

McCarthy, M. (1990). The thin ideal, depression and eating disorders in women. *Behaviour Research and Therapy, 28*, 205–215.

Nichter, M., & Vuckovic, N. (1994). Fat talk: Body image among adolescent females. In N. Sault (Ed.), *Many mirrors: Body image and social relations* (pp. 109–131). New Brunswick, NJ: Rutgers University Press.

Nylander, I. (1971). The feeling of being fat and dieting in a school population. *Acta Socio-Medica Scandinavica, 1*, 17–26.

O'Connor, T. G., & Rutter, M. (1996). Risk mechanisms in development: Some conceptual and methodological considerations. *Developmental Psychology, 32*, 787–795.

Olmsted, M. P., & Garner, D. M. (1986). The significance of self-induced vomiting as a weight control method among non-clinical samples. *International Journal of Eating Disorders, 5*, 683–700.

Paikoff, R. L., Carlton-Ford, S., & Brooks-Gunn, J. (1993). Mother–daughter dyads view the family: Associations between divergent perceptions and daughter well-being. *Journal of Youth and Adolescence, 22*, 473–492.

Patton, G., Johnson-Sabine, E., Wood, K., & Mann, A. (1990). Abnormal eating attitudes in London schoolgirls: A prospective epidemiological study: Outcome at twelve month follow-up. *Psychological Medicine, 20*, 383–394.

Paxton, S. J., Wertheim, E. H., Gibbons, K., Szmukler, G. I., Hillier, L., & Petrovich, J. L. (1991). Body image satisfaction, dieting beliefs, and weight loss behaviors in adolescent girls and boys. *Journal of Youth and Adolescence, 20*, 361–379.

Petersen, A. C., Compas, B. E., Brooks-Gunn, J., Stemmler, M., Ey, S., & Grant, K. E. (1993). Depression in adolescence. *American Psychologist, 48*, 155–168.

Pike, K. M. (1995). Bulimic symptomatology in high school girls. *Psychology of Women Quarterly, 19*, 373–396.

Pike, K. M., & Rodin, J. (1991). Mothers, daughters, and disordered eating. *Journal of Abnormal Psychology, 100*, 198–204.

Richards, M. H., Casper, R. C., & Larson, R. W. (1990). Weight and eating concerns among pre- and young adolescent boys and girls. *Journal of Adolescent Health Care, 11*, 203–209.

Rosen, J. C., Compas, B. E., & Tacy, B. (1993). The relation among stress, psychological symptoms, and eating disorder symptoms: A prospective analysis. *International Journal of Eating Disorders, 14*, 153–162.

Rosen, J. C., Gross, J., & Vara, L. (1987). Psychological adjustment of adolescents attempting to lose or gain weight. special issue: Eating disorders. *Journal of Consulting and Clinical Psychology, 55*, 742–747.

Rosen, J. C., & Poplawski, D. (1987). The validity of self-reported weight loss and weight gain efforts in adolescents. *International Journal of Eating Disorders, 6*, 515–523.

Rosen, J. C., Tacy, B., & Howell, D. (1990). Life stress, psychological symptoms and weight reducing behavior in adolescent girls: A prospective analysis. *International Journal of Eating Disorders, 9*, 17–26.

Rutter, M. (1994). Continuities, transitions and turning points in development. In M. Rutter & D. F. Hay (Eds.), *Development through life: A handbook for clinicians* (pp. 1–25). London: Blackwell Scientific.

Serdula, M. K., Collins, M. E., Williamson, D. F., Anda, R. F., Pamuk, E. R., & Byers, T. E. (1993). Weight control practices of U.S. adolescents and adults. *Annals of Internal Medicine, 119*, 667–671.

Shisslak, C. M., Crago, M., & Estes, L. S. (1995). The spectrum of eating disturbances. *International Journal of Eating Disorders, 18*, 209–219.

Silverstein, B., Carpman, S., Perlick, D., & Perdue, L. (1990). Nontraditional sex role aspirations, gender identity conflict, and disordered eating among college women. *Sex Roles, 23*, 687–695.

Smolak, L., Levine, M. P., & Gralen, S. (1993). The impact of puberty and dating on eating problems among middle school girls. *Journal of Youth and Adolescence, 22*, 355–368.

Sroufe, L. A., & Rutter, M. (1984). The domain of developmental psychopathology. *Child Development, 55*, 17–29.

Steiner-Adair, C. (1986). The body politic: Normal female adolescent development and the development of eating disorders. *Journal of the American Academy of Psychoanalysis, 14*, 95–114.

Stice, E., & Agras, W. S. (1998). Predicting onset and cessation of bulimic behaviors during adolescence: A longitudinal grouping analysis. *Behavior Therapy, 29*, 257–276.

Stice, E., Agras, W. S., & Hammer, L. D. (1999). Risk factors for the emergence of childhood eating disturbances: A five-year prospective study. *International Journal of Eating Disorders, 25*, 375–387.

Story, M., Rosenwinkel, K., Himes, J. H., Resnick, M., Harris, L. J., & Blum, R. W. (1991). Demographic and risk factors associated with chronic dieting in adolescents. *American Journal of Diseases in Children, 145*, 994–998.

Striegel-Moore, R. H., Silberstein, L. R., Frensch, P., & Rodin, J. (1989). A prospective study of disordered eating among college students. *International Journal of Eating Disorders, 8*, 499–509.

Strober, M., & Humphrey, L. L. (1987). Familial contributions to the etiology and course of anorexia nervosa and bulimia. *Journal of Consulting and Clinical Psychology, 55*, 654–659.

Swarr, A. E., & Richards, M. H. (1996). Longitudinal effects of adolescent girls' pubertal development, perceptions of pubertal timing, and parental relations on eating problems. *Developmental Psychology, 32*, 636–646.

Thelen, M. H., & Cormier, J. F. (1995). Desire to be thinner and weight control among children and their parents. *Behavior Therapy, 26*, 85–99.

Thelen, M. H., Kanakis, D. M., Farmer, J., & Pruitt, J. (1993). Bulimia and interpersonal relationships: An extension of a longitudinal study. *Addictive Behaviors, 18*, 145–150.

Thienemann, M., & Steiner, H. (1993). Family environment of eating disordered and depressed adolescents. *International Journal of Eating Disorders, 14*, 43–48.

Tobin-Richards, M. H., Boxer, A. M., & Petersen, A. C. (1983). The psychological significance of pubertal change: Sex differences in perceptions of self during early adolescence. In J. Brooks-Gunn & A. C. Petersen (Eds.), *Girls at puberty: Biological and psychosocial perspectives* (pp. 127–154). New York: Plenum Press.

Tuschl, R. J. (1990). From dietary restraint to binge eating: Some theoretical considerations. *Appetite, 14*, 105–109.

Vandereycken, W., & Vanderlinden, J. (1983). Denial of illness and the use of self-reporting measures in anorexia. *International Journal of Eating Disorders, 2*, 101–108.

Vollrath, M., Koch, R., & Angst, J. (1992). Binge eating and weight concerns among young adults: Results from the Zurich cohort study. *British Journal of Psychiatry, 160*, 498–503.

Wakeling, A. (1996). Epidemiology of anorexia nervosa. *Psychiatry Research, 62*, 3–9.

Warren, M. P. (1983). Physical and biological aspects of puberty. In J. Brooks-Gunn & A. C. Petersen (Eds.), *Girls at puberty: Biological and psychosocial perspectives* (pp. 3–28). New York: Plenum Press.

Wertheim, E. H., Paxton, S. J., Maude, D., Szmukler, G. I., Gibbons, K., & Hiller, L. (1992). Psychosocial predictors of weight loss behaviors and binge eating in adolescent girls and boys. *International Journal of Eating Disorders, 12*, 151–160.

Whitaker, A., Davies, M., Shaffer, D., Johnson, J., Abrams, S., Walsh, B. T., & Kalikow, K. (1989). The struggle to be thin: A survey of anorexic and bulimic symptoms in a non-referred adolescent population. *Psychological Medicine, 19*, 143–163.

Wichstrom, L. (1995). Social, psychological and physical correlates of eating problems: A study of the general adolescent population in Norway. *Psychological Medicine, 25*, 567–579.

Wiseman, C. V., Gray, J. J., Mosimann, J. E., & Ahrens, A. H. (1992). Cultural expectations of thinness in women: An update. *International Journal of Eating Disorders, 11*, 85–89.

Wonderlich, S. A., & Swift, W. J. (1990). Perceptions of parental relationships in the eating disorders: The relevance of depressed mood. *Journal of Abnormal Psychology, 99*, 353–360.

33

Disorders of Elimination

Janet E. Fischel and Robert M. Liebert

Every one of us began life wetting the bed and making a "mess" of diapers on a daily basis. Our parents and others then imposed some form of toilet training on us. By various means, they taught us when to eliminate and when to withhold urine and feces, and they insisted that we learn to comply with the rules. We were not alone. In a classic study of 22 cultures, Whiting and Child (1953) concluded that toilet training is the most basic and universal target of socialization everywhere. Furthermore, virtually every culture appears to succeed in toilet training 80–90% of its new members within the expected time limit. The few who remain untrained, or who become trained but then relapse, are said to have a disorder of elimination.

Our goal in this chapter is to summarize what is known about the origins, diagnosis, and treatment of children who do not achieve continence at the culturally expected time, or who revert to incontinence after training has apparently been successful.

PHYSIOLOGICAL AND DEVELOPMENTAL MECHANISMS

In order to fully explain the elimination disorders and the methods used to treat them, we begin with a general description of the physiological mechanisms underlying urination and defecation.

The Physiology of Urination

The human bladder is actually a stretchy, hollow muscle (the detrusor vesicae) in which urine is collected continuously. As urine accumulates, the bladder stretches, producing an initial urge to urinate that must be voluntarily suppressed until reaching a toilet. *Enuresis* is defined as passing urine anywhere except into a toilet (DSM-IV Code 307.6; American

Janet E. Fischel • Department of Pediatrics, State University of New York at Stony Brook, Stony Brook, New York 11794-8111.   **Robert M. Liebert** • Department of Psychology, State University of New York at Stony Brook, Stony Brook, New York 11794-2500.

Handbook of Developmental Psychopathology, Second Edition, edited by Arnold J. Sameroff, Michael Lewis, and Suzanne M. Miller. Kluwer Academic/Plenum Publishers, New York, 2000.

Psychiatric Association, 1994). Successful treatment of enuresis is presumed to involve increasing the individual's sensitivity to appropriate body signals and/or increasing voluntary control over the relevant muscles.

The Physiology of Defecation

The digestive tract is a long hollow tube, with the colon and the rectum at the distal end. After food is digested in the stomach and small intestine, the remaining waste products move through the colon and gradually shift from a liquid state to a semisolid one. When sufficient waste accumulates, muscle contractions move it down the colon and into the rectum. The resultant stretching of the walls of the rectum leads to the urge to defecate. Unless voluntarily controlled, this urge will lead to a relaxation of the external and internal sphincters and subsequent evacuation. Those who fail to exhibit such control are said to have *encopresis*, defined as passing feces anywhere but into a toilet (without constipation and overflow incontinence, DSM-IV Code 307.7; with constipation and overflow incontinence, DSM-IV Code 787.6; American Psychiatric Association, 1994).

Developmental Considerations

Before a child can achieve independent toileting, there must have been adequate development in five domains: communication skills, social and emotional development, fine motor development, gross motor development, and cognitive development. Specifically, communication skills are required to convey to caretakers that an elimination need is present. Social and emotional development must have reached the point where the child recognizes the necessity of adhering to certain parental/societal expectations. Fine motor skills are needed to manipulate clothing, use toilet paper, and so on. Gross motor skills are needed to assume the required body postures/positions for using toilet facilities, and, not least, cognitive skills are needed to understand the meaning of relevant bodily sensations, and to exhibit planfulness and self-control when it comes to satisfying elimination needs. Thus, an overall evaluation of developmental readiness is the first step in assessing any child's toileting problems.

NOMENCLATURE AND PREVALENCE

Most children in the United States are completely toilet trained before their fourth birthdays, so children over this age who are still wetting or soiling are said to have a disorder of elimination. In other cultures, expectations are different. For example, the Bena of Africa do not begin toilet training until their children are almost 5 years old, and often the children are not completely trained until they are 6 or 7; the Tanala of Madagascar, on the other hand, begin toilet training when their infants are only a few months old and expect full continence by the sixth month (Whiting & Child, 1953).

The Functional–Organic Distinction

In diagnosing elimination disorders, a fundamental distinction is made between those that are functional and those that are organic. Organic disorders are caused by an underlying physical illness or abnormality, whereas functional disorders have no identifiable physical basis. Although organically caused elimination disorders are quite rare (accounting for less than 10% of all cases), they can be extremely serious. Therefore, every child with an elimination disorder should be checked by a physician before a functional diagnosis is given or any form of treatment is begun.

Prevalence and Distribution

Table 33.1 presents a summary of some of what is known about the prevalence and distribution of the elimination disorders. Note the very high prevalence of primary nocturnal enuresis (bedwetting by children who have never been dry at night for a substantial period of time) relative to the other forms of elimination disorder. (The maximum period of continuous dryness permitted in applying the diagnosis "primary" is neither fully standardized in the literature nor stated in the DSM-IV, but it varies between 2 and 6 months.) Note, too, that more boys than girls suffer from these disorders. Finally, because it has been suggested that enuresis and encopresis may stem from one or more common causes (e.g., struggles with parents over toilet training), it is of interest that enuretic children are more likely to be encopretic than are other children.

Spontaneous Remission versus Treatment

Virtually all of the parents with whom we deal have already spoken to a pediatrician about their child's elimination problem. Once organic causes have been ruled out, the usual

**Table 33.1. Descriptive Data
Regarding the Elimination Disorders[a]**

	Enuresis	Encopresis[b]
Prevalence at age 5	33%	2%
Prevalence at age 7	25%	1.5%
Prevalence at age 9	15%	1%
Prevalence at age 11	8%	< 1%
Prevalence at age 13	4%	< 1%
Prevalence at age 15	2%	< 1%
Prevalence at age 17	1%	< 1%
Male/female ratio	60/40[c]	75/25
Primary/secondary ratio	80/20	50/50
Percentage nocturnal only	75%	0%
Percentage diurnal[d]	25%	100%

[a]Compiled from data reported by Achenbach and Edelbrock (1981), Bellman (1966), Byrd, Weitzman, Lanphear, and Auinger (1966), Forsythe and Redmond (1974), Levine (1975), and Miller (1973).
[b]About one-third of all encopretics are also enuretic.
[c]The sex difference is due almost entirely to primary nocturnal enuretics; there are no sex differences for other types.
[d]Diurnal enuresis almost invariably involves some nighttime wettings; diurnal encopresis virtually never involves nighttime soiling.

advice they have gotten is to be patient, because the child will eventually outgrow the problem. Is this advice sound? As Table 33.1 shows, barely more than half of those suffering from an elimination disorder at age 5 will have it "take care of itself" by age 9. On the average, an elementary school-age child with a toileting problem has only about a 15% chance of seeing it resolved by itself within the succeeding 12 months. The best guess is that from any hypothetical starting age in middle childhood, it will take, on average, more than 3 years before the child becomes fully continent. Left untreated, a few unfortunate individuals will still be wetting or soiling in their late teens.

Given this information, we firmly believe most parents and children should *not* wait for a spontaneous remission to occur. This is especially so because the evidence is overwhelming that elimination disorders *cause* serious embarrassment, lowered self-esteem, social withdrawal, and other psychological problems, whereas successful treatment does *not* lead to symptom substitution (e.g., Butler, 1993; Houts, Berman, & Abramson, 1994; Moffatt, 1989; Mowrer & Mowrer, 1938; Strömgren & Thomsen, 1990; Warzak & Friman, 1994).

Nonretentive versus Retentive Encopresis

With encopresis, an important distinction is made between its nonretentive and retentive forms. *Nonretentive encopresis* is the diagnosis given to individuals who simply defecate in inappropriate places. *Retentive encopresis* is the term applied to those whose soiling is related to withholding stool; a history of constipation is common among these individuals. Most encopretic children are retentive and can be treated successfully (Levine, 1992); unfortunately, nonretentive encopresis has been associated with poorer treatment outcome (Rockney, McQuade, Days, Linn, & Alario, 1996).

Retentive encopresis can become a vicious circle. In its normal state, the rectum is empty. However, when a person withholds stool voluntarily, the rectum and lower colon become filled with fecal material. If withholding continues, a huge quantity of stool will accumulate, and, as a result, the lower colon will become very distended. Concurrently, the body will absorb almost all the moisture from the fecal mass, leaving hard, impacted stool. In this condition, passing stool is extremely painful or impossible. The urge and ability to defecate are therefore significantly reduced. Fresh, moist stool from the upper colon now can no longer be passed at all, but a brown liquid from the fresh stool almost invariably leaks around the impacted mass, producing soiled underwear and a fecal smell.

Accompanying the retentive pattern may also be inappropriate closure of the external anal sphincter precisely at times when its relaxation is necessary for proper defecation. This "paradoxical constriction" of the sphincter can delay defecation or truncate the experience, yielding only partial defecation. So it should not be surprising that a history of painful defecation is present in the majority of children who suffer from fecal soiling (Partin, Hamill, Fischel, & Partin, 1992). Furthermore, fear of painful defecation is implicated among the top causes of encopresis, based on a questionnaire of parent and child perceptions of causal factors (Bernard-Bonnin, Haley, Belanger, & Nadeau, 1993).

CLINICAL DIAGNOSIS

Thus far, the elimination disorders have been described in abstract terms. The data, however, are only as good as the clinical diagnoses on which they are based. The enuresis/

encopresis program at Stony Brook is a collaborative effort of the departments of psychology and pediatrics. The approach to clinical diagnosis that we have evolved over the years is briefly summarized here.

Intervention begins with a highly structured initial consultation, including a thorough toileting history and a determination of whether parents or other family members have experienced similar problems. (Rushton [1993a] estimated that when both parents have a history of enuresis, the child has an enuresis risk of almost 80%; when one parent has such a history, the child's risk is about 45%; the risk is less than 15% for children with no family history of enuresis.) We also ask for such details as age of onset of the disorder, correlates of onset (e.g., parental divorce, start of school, illness), and frequency of wetting or soiling.

Perhaps the most important question to ask is whether the problem has been brought to the attention of a physician. A physical examination is always requested if the child has not had one within the past year. It is also essential to learn what the family is doing about the problem right now, and require discontinuation of any treatments or practices that seem inappropriate. (According to Miller [1993], almost 40% of all parents with bedwetting children report using punishment; for parents with only a grade-school education, the figure is above 70%.)

CONCOMITANT PROBLEMS

Psychological and behavioral problems often co-occur with elimination disorders. For example, attentional problems and, most specifically, hyperactivity appear to occur in unusually high proportions among children with encopresis (e.g., Johnston & Wright, 1993) and enuresis (e.g., Ornitz, Hanna, & Traversay, 1992). Elevated behavioral and social competence problems are also found in children with either or both disorders (Houts et al., 1994; Young, Brennen, Baker, & Baker, 1995). Such problems appear to reduce after behavioral treatment (e.g., Butler, 1993; Moffatt, 1989; Young et al., 1995). On the other hand, the presence of behavioral and emotional problems in the child tends to decrease the likelihood of treatment success (Stark, Spirito, Lewis, & Hart, 1990). So, appropriate treatment of an elimination disorder in some cases will require concurrent or antecedent attention to other behavioral problems.

ETIOLOGICAL ISSUES

At least three broad models have been put forth as general explanations of functional (nonorganic) elimination disorders. These are structured along parallel paths for enuresis and encopresis. While there are variations within each of the following approaches, no causal model of the elimination disorders is complete without acknowledgment of the familial nature of the disorders; that is, the disorders run in families (Bellman, 1966).

The Psychodynamic Model

According to the psychodynamic formulation, toilet training is a psychological battle between child and parents; the battle must be resolved in the child's psyche before he or she becomes or remains fully continent. Inspired by psychodynamic thinking, researchers have shown that parent–child conflict is characteristic of the family with an incontinent child (e.g., Baird, 1975). Although one can interpret the correlation between parent–child conflict and elimination disorders in psychodynamic terms by assuming that the interpersonal conflicts cause the elimination disorders, the preponderance of evidence suggests that such conflicts are most often the effects rather than the cause of incontinence (Houts et al., 1994; Vivian, Fischel, & Liebert, 1986).

The Learning/Skills Deficit Model

According to the learning/skills deficit model, individuals with elimination disorders have not received the amount or kind of training they need to become continent. Within this model, the focus is on toilet training per se, rather than on broader or "deeper" aspects of the parent–child relationship. The conceptualization of toilet training is that the parents and therapists are teachers and the child is a learner. A child's failure to become continent may occur because the parents used inadequate teaching methods and/or because the child was an unusually slow learner or learned faulty elimination patterns. In either event, the child is presumed to have not yet learned to notice and respond appropriately to bodily cues indicating the need to eliminate. When applied to the case of nocturnal enuresis, the learning/skills deficit model may be exemplified in a hypothesis that involves inadequate learned arousal from sleep in response to cues of a full bladder (Moffatt, 1997).

An alternative theoretical formulation, applicable specifically to retentive encopresis, involves escape and avoidance learning. Whether initial toilet training was "complete" or not, the child who experiences repeated episodes of highly effortful and uncomfortable stool passage gradually learns to avoid defecating. Whatever the cause of painful defecation may have been initially, the acquired tendency to inappropriately suppress the urge to defecate by stopping the necessary sphincter relaxation eventually leads to stool retention, overdistension of the rectum, and inordinately hard and large fecal matter in the rectum. Subsequent attempts to defecate will then bring renewed discomfort, which the child avoids or escapes by further stool retention.

The Improper Diet Hypothesis

The third etiological model of elimination disorders is the improper diet hypothesis. According to this view, dietary excesses or deficits, or food allergies, cause problems with voiding or defecating. The food allergy hypothesis, sometimes discussed in causal considerations of nocturnal enuresis, currently has weak scientific support at best (Moffatt, 1997). In the case of retentive encopresis, diets with inadequate roughage are considered to potentiate constipation and effortful, painful stools, with the eventual development of withholding. In parallel fashion, enuresis is sometimes blamed on excess fluid intake during the hours just before bedtime.

TREATMENT

In establishing treatment goals and evaluating treatments, an important distinction must be made between a treatment's ability to stop wetting or soiling (initial arrest) and its ability to overcome the problem permanently (lasting cure). Some treatments are initially quite effective but are associated with high relapse rates; others work only as long as they are being actively administered.

Enuresis

Treatments Prior to the Twentieth Century

Several writers have described cruel and barbarous methods of treating enuresis before the current century (e.g., Bloom, 1993; Mishne, 1993). Two of the most ancient treatments were consuming the boiled crop of a hen in tepid water and drinking a glass of red wine in which the testicle of a hare had been soaking for 24 hours. Pliny the Elder (77 A.D.) prescribed the ingestion of boiled mice and the urine of spayed swine. A pediatric textbook written in 1544 prescribed the ingestion of hedgehog testicles. Other texts written in the same period recommended sleeping on mattresses with protruding metal spikes; one advised that enuretic girls have rubber bags inserted into their vaginas and inflated with air to compress the bladder neck and urethra. Penile tourniquets were in common use to treat enuresis in boys during the eighteenth century, but the practice was discontinued because it led to numerous cases of gangrene. Among the treatments recommended in an 1897 pediatric textbook were circumcision and strychnine. All these practices attest to the fact that enuresis has long been considered a sufficiently serious problem or unacceptable behavior to warrant powerful intervention.

Drug Treatment for Enuresis

A remarkable array of powerful, controlled substances have been held out as possible treatments for enuresis. These include stimulants, monoamine oxidase inhibitors, sedative hypnotics, major tranquilizers, anticholinergics, tricyclic antidepressants, synthetic hormones, and even pituitary snuff (Blackwell & Currah, 1973). The only pharmaceuticals shown to be superior to placebo preparations in double-blind controlled drug studies are the tricyclic antidepressants and desmopressin acetate (DDAVP) for nocturnal enuresis, and oxybutynin for diurnal enuresis.

For years imipramine hydrochloride, a tricyclic antidepressant, was by far the most widely prescribed medication for bedwetting. Imipramine produces a noticeable reduction in bedwetting for between 30% and 50% of enuretic children but rarely produces complete arrest; the therapeutic effect usually appears within 10 days or less (Black, 1983). Unfortunately, as many as 90% of all bedwetters treated with these drugs will relapse completely to premedication levels of nocturnal wetting when their medication is withdrawn (Blackwell & Currah, 1973).

Recent research has shown that at night, nonbedwetters produce more of a natural antidiuretic, arginine vasopressin (AVP), than do bedwetters (e.g., Nørgaard & Djurhuus, 1993). With this fact in mind, the synthetic antidiuretic hormone DDAVP was recently marketed in the United States as a treatment for nocturnal enuresis (Rushton, 1993b). It can be administered either intranasally as a nose spray or it can be ingested orally (Stenberg & Läckgren, 1993).

Desmopressin sometimes produces immediate, complete cessation of bedwetting while it is being used, and in this sense is superior to either other pharmacological or behavioral treatments (e.g., Houts et al., 1994). However, desmopressin virtually never cures enuresis; wetting almost immediately resumes when medication stops, and this expensive substance can cause nasal polyps, water intoxication, headache, abdominal pain, wheezing, nosebleed, anorexia, and sight disturbance (Bloom, 1993).

Fluid and/or Food Restriction and Enuresis

Restriction of liquids for one to several hours before bedtime is the remedy most parents seize on first to treat their enuretic children. Ninety percent of the parents in the Stony Brook Enuresis Project who reported trying a restriction of liquids concluded that it did not help. The consensus among researchers is that fluid restriction is of no value and should be avoided (Houts & Liebert, 1984; Houts et al., 1994; Nørgaard & Djurhuus, 1993).

The Urine Alarm

For enuresis, the core of all the successful behavior management plans is the urine alarm, a device that sounds an alarm to wake the sleeping bedwetter as soon as a drop or two of urine is passed. Although the idea was first introduced in the nineteenth century, Mowrer and Mowrer (1938) are often credited with developing the urine alarm and are certainly the ones responsible for popularizing the "bell-and-pad" version. (Today, a wearable alarm is available, which weighs less than an ounce, is smaller than a package of gum, and operates with almost complete reliability on hearing-aid batteries.[1]) In general, 65–75% of bedwetters can expect to be dry within 3 months of conscientious application of the urine alarm, without any concurrent behavioral or pharmacological treatment (Doleys, 1977; Moffatt, 1989); success with the urine alarm is higher for primary enuretics than for secondary enuretics (Said, Wilson, & Hensley, 1991).

One basic limitation of the urine alarm has been the long time required to achieve initial arrest; not only must the child and parents endure a treatment that often lasts 12 weeks or more, but also it is typical for no progress at all to occur during the first month of treatment. (Failure to comply with the procedures in a diligent manner on a continuing basis appears to be the single biggest reason for the failure of urine alarm treatment.)

A second problem with the urine alarm is a high relapse rate. As many as 40% of those bedwetters who are seemingly cured will relapse within the year after treatment and require retreatment (e.g., Butler, 1993; Bollard, 1982).

Overlearning

Young and Morgan (1972) introduced an adjunctive antirelapse procedure to urine alarm training that they called overlearning. The procedure requires children who have achieved a preset criterion of dryness with the urine alarm (e.g., 14 dry nights in a row) to drink a significant quantity of water every night in the hour before retiring, while continuing to use the alarm. Overlearning continues until the child is able to remain consistently dry through the night even with the liquid overload. In their experimental comparison, Young and Morgan found a relapse rate of about 35% for those who had not received overlearning as opposed to a relapse rate of less than 15% for those who had; similar results have more recently been reported by Butler (1993).

[1]We have been using the Wetstop alarm, manufactured and distributed by Palco Labs, 1595 Soquel Drive, Santa Cruz, California 95065.

Bladder Stretching and Retention Control Training

On the average, bedwetting children have smaller functional bladder capacities than nonwetters (Rushton, 1993a; Starfield, 1967). Inasmuch as the bladder is a "stretchy" material, bladder capacity can be increased by regularly filling the bladder to its greatest capacity and keeping it full for longer and longer periods of time. Exercises requiring children to drink and then hold substantial quantities of water (called retention control training, or RCT) can help some of them to achieve dryness (Kimmel & Kimmel, 1970); used by itself, RCT has a cure rate of less than 30%, but it appears to enhance the urine alarm significantly (Houts & Liebert, 1984).

Dry-Bed Training

Dry-bed training (Azrin, Sneed, & Foxx, 1974) is a very intensive procedure employing the urine alarm, a demanding "nightly waking schedule," and a response cost component called "positive practice," which is invoked whenever the child wets the bed. Children are also made responsible for their wet clothing and linens and are required to make their own beds, a component of the program that is called "cleanliness training." The price paid for an accident is being made to lie on the bed and count to 50, and then to get up and go to the bathroom and try to urinate. Children are made to repeat this sequence 20 times in a row whenever they wet their beds. Positive practice is also required of the child 20 times just before going to bed on nights following a night in which an accident has occurred.

The nightly waking schedule requires that the child be awakened every hour during the first night of training, taken to the bathroom, asked to urinate, and then be "loaded" with fluids before returning to bed. On the second night, the child is awakened 3 hours after going to bed; if dry, the child is awakened 2 hours after going to bed on the third night; if dry, he or she is awakened 1 hour after going to bed on the fourth night, and so on; thus, the nightly waking schedule terminates itself as long as the child remains dry. If the child wets twice in one week, however, the entire schedule starts over again.

Averaging across a number of studies, the complete dry-bed program (whether administered by a professional home trainer or by parents themselves) produces initial arrest in about 90% of all cases, requires an average treatment time of about 6 weeks, and has about a 25% relapse rate. When dry-bed training is employed without a urine alarm, however, initial arrest occurs in only about 60% of all cases, and typical length of treatment is extended to 10 weeks. Therefore, without the urine alarm, dry-bed training appears to be not much quicker and somewhat less effective than a urine alarm alone (for a complete review of the literature, see Houts & Liebert, 1984).

Combination Treatments with Urine Alarm

Many researchers and clinicians have now concluded that the urine alarm can be enhanced by the addition of adjunct procedures. The resulting "packages" enjoy higher success rates, more rapid effects, and lower relapse levels than have been found with the urine alarm alone.

Among the first such packages to be described was full-spectrum home training (FSHT; Houts & Liebert, 1984; Houts, Liebert, & Padawer, 1983). The treatment is built around a parent manual and incorporates retention control training and overlearning procedures, as well as an Azrin-type cleanliness training component. These components are organized into a contract between parents and children ("the family support agreement"); all procedures are home-implemented by parents, following a single 1 hour training session, which can be administered individually or in groups. FSHT has been shown to produce an initial arrest of slightly more than 80% in an average of less than 10 weeks; the relapse rate is under 25% (Houts et al., 1983). Direct experimental comparison has shown it to produce significantly more rapid initial arrest and a lower relapse rate than a urine alarm alone (Houts, Peterson, & Whelan, 1986).

The single easiest (and perhaps most important) complement to the urine alarm is to instruct the child in how to behave after the alarm goes off. Ronen, Rahav, and Wozner (1995) urge that bedwetting children not only be told but actually rehearse the activities to be engaged in after the alarm goes off: turning off the alarm, going to the toilet to complete voiding, changing the wet sheets and clothes, remaking the bed, putting the alarm back on, and going back to sleep.

Another recent development is the addition of cognitive techniques, including self-statements and visualization, to enhance urine alarm treatment. For example, Miller (1993) has had success teaching bedwetters to repeat to themselves such statements as the following: "When I need to urinate, I will wake up all by myself, urinate in the toilet, and return to my nice, dry bed" (p. 35). Similarly, Butler (1993) recommends visualization as an adjunct to urine alarm treatment. Visualization is picturing oneself as if being filmed; the child imagines him- or herself sleeping, increasing body movements when the bladder becomes full, and waking to use the toilet. Internal visualization involves imagining the bladder filling and stretching like a balloon, and thinking of sensations of bladder fullness as beeper signals being transported to the brain, followed by the brain buzzing the child to wake up and go to the toilet.

Encopresis

Although a variety of treatments have been tried for encopresis (for a review of the treatment spectrum, from psychotherapy and play therapy to hypnosis and behavioral interventions, see Howe & Walker, 1992), the most successful efforts to treat encopresis appear to be founded on behavior management principles used in conjunction with laxative and dietary prescriptions (for examples of comprehensive management programs, see Levine 1992; Stark, Owens-Stively, Spirito, Lewis, & Guevremont, 1990). In the last decade, there has been a good deal of attention paid to "combination" treatments, meaning the union of behavioral management with medical management (see, e.g., Dawson, Griffith, & Boeke, 1990; Reimers, 1996).

The following treatment methods, sometimes in a treatment "package" combining two or more interventions, are current: (1) medical clean out plan followed by use of a laxative or stool softener; (2) a prescribed toilet-sitting schedule as a behavioral adjunct to medical management; (3) a dietary program (both educational and behavioral) to enhance fiber consumption; (4) education about the disorder and its management steps and expectations; (5) behavioral programs targeted to increase stooling frequency, increase toilet use, and decrease soiling; and (6) behavioral programs to train more healthful defecation dynamics through one or another form of biofeedback. Detailed training protocols may be found in the literature (e.g., Levine, 1992), but some degree of custom-tailoring is often required for each family, because every child has his or her individual training needs.

Behavioral management strategies aimed at enhancing soft stools and regular defecation differ from one another in their particulars, but all seem to include the same five components, namely, record keeping, scheduled toilet sitting, structured toilet-skills training with systematic reinforcement of appropriate behaviors, family education about the problem, and laxative, stool softener, and/or dietary intervention.

Ensuring Soft and Frequent Stool Passage

For retentive children, the first goal is to clear the rectum and lower colon, using enemas or suppositories as needed. Dietary changes to increase fiber or bulk are frequently established to ensure soft stool and to enhance the urge to defecate. Options regarding stool softener or laxative choices and dosages should be chosen in consultation with a pediatrician or pediatric gastroenterologist. Loening-Baucke (1993) offers a table of the most common choices, emphasizing that family compliance with the management plan to prevent reaccumulation of stools takes priority over precisely which medicine is chosen.

Record Keeping

As with enuresis, record keeping for encopresis is instituted at the end of the first visit and is continued throughout treatment. The record is usually in the form of a daily calendar on which the parent and child monitor two things: (1) the occurrence and time of day of soiling incidents and (2) the occurrence of each successful toileting episode. The child and parent are asked to do all record keeping together.

Scheduled Toilet Sitting

It is important to establish a daily schedule of toilet sitting times for the child. Ordinarily, two to four sits per day are required. The first daily sit should occur just after breakfast. In scheduling the others, attention should be given to relevant aspects of the child's routine. For example, if a laxative is given in the morning, a toilet sit in the middle or late afternoon is usually desirable.

Systematic Reinforcement

The primary behavioral technique for controlling encopresis is systematic reinforcement of appropriate behaviors. The preferred reward is immediate social praise, which is always given for successful stool passage on the toilet and for appropriate toilet sitting, including both scheduled and spontaneous sits. For nonretentive encopretic children, days of no soiling may also be rewarded, but it is important not to reward retentive children for "no soiling" days alone, as this may only exacerbate retention. Social praise is important as a reinforcer for children.

With severely retentive preschool children who have a history of fear or pain when attempting to defecate, it is helpful to reward any and all stool passage initially, even when the toilet is not used. In these cases, actual toilet training is not begun until softer, painless stools are experienced frequently and without emotionality.

Warm Evening Baths

A day of soiling should conclude with a warm bath in the evening, because soiling often signals incomplete evacuation of feces. The bath should be followed promptly by a toilet sit, which will often result in a successful bowel movement, especially for younger children.

Cleanliness Training

Cleanliness training for encopresis parallels that in our enuresis program. From the time treatment begins, children are expected to be responsible for taking off soiled undergarments and putting them in an appropriate place. Older children are expected to change themselves.

Providing Appropriate Expectancies

Unlike management plans for enuresis, a dramatic initial reduction in soiling behavior in the early weeks after the behavior training session for encopresis is frequently noted. This initial arrest is often not maintained over the longer term, however, without continued use of the plan's several components.

Two General Treatment Considerations

Monitoring for Compliance

In treating any of the elimination disorders, the most important role for the therapist is to assure that the entire family faithfully maintains all aspects of the plan until treatment has been successfully completed.

Follow-Up

Children should be followed in an office visit within 6 weeks after treatment is initiated; during these visits, we review daily records and troubleshoot any further problems or issues that have arisen for either the parents or the child. We also conduct longer-term telephone follow-ups every 3 months for at least a year after initial arrest of the disorder. Relapses are given prompt attention.

A Final Word about Treatment

The most encouraging fact about the functional elimination disorders is that successful treatments exist for the most common forms, especially those that fit one of the specific learning models. On the other hand, cases involving intermittent secondary enuresis or encopresis that persists in the face of adequate diet and structured behavioral guidance tend to be unresponsive to either verbal psychotherapy, play therapy, or behavioral techniques (e.g., Warzak & Friman, 1994; Werry & Cohrssen, 1965).

REFERENCES

Achenbach, T. M., & Edelbrock, C. S. (1981). Behavioral problems and competencies reported by parents of normal and disturbed children aged four through sixteen. *Monographs of the Society for Research in Child Development, 46* (Serial No. 188). Chicago: University of Chicago Press.

American Psychiatric Association. (1994). *Diagnostic and statistical manual of mental disorders* (4th ed.). Washington, DC: Author.

Azrin, N. H., Sneed, T. J., & Foxx, R. M. (1974). Dry-bed training: Rapid elimination of childhood enuresis. *Behaviour Research and Therapy, 12,* 147–156.

Baird, M. (1975). Characteristic interaction patterns in families of encopretic children. *Bulletin of the Menninger Clinic, 38*, 144–153.

Bellman, M. (1966). Studies on encopresis. *Acta Paediatrica Scandinavica,* (Suppl.) *170*, 1–151.

Bernard-Bonnin, A., Haley, N., Belanger, S., & Nadeau, D. (1993). Parental and patient perceptions about encopresis and its treatment. *Journal of Developmental and Behavioral Pediatrics, 14*, 397–400.

Black, J. (1983). Nocturnal enuresis. *Journal of the Royal Society of Medicine, 76*, 622–623.

Blackwell, B., & Currah, J. (1973). The psychopharmacology of nocturnal enuresis. In I. Kolvin, R. C. MacKeith, & S. R. Meadow (Eds.), *Bladder control and enuresis* (pp. 231–257). Philadelphia: Lippincott.

Bloom, D. A. (1993). The American experience with desmopressin. *Clinical Pediatrics, Special Edition*, 28–31.

Bollard, J. (1982). A 2-year follow-up of bedwetters treated with dry-bed training and standard conditioning. *Behaviour Research and Therapy, 20*, 571–580.

Butler, R. J. (1993). Establishing a dry run: A case study in securing bladder control. *British Psychological Society, 32*, 215–217.

Byrd, R. S., Weitzman, M., Lanphear, N. E., & Auinger, P. (1996). Bed-wetting in U.S. children: Epidemiology and related behavior problems. *Pediatrics, 98*, 414–419.

Dawson, P. M., Griffith, K., & Boeke, K. M. (1990). Combined medical and psychological treatment of hospitalized children with encopresis. *Child Psychiatry and Human Development, 20*, 181–190.

Doleys, D. M. (1977). Behavioral treatments for nocturnal enuresis in children: A review of the recent literature. *Psychological Bulletin, 84*, 30–54.

Forsythe, W., & Redmond, A. (1974). Enuresis and spontaneous cure rate: Study of 1,129 enuretics. *Archives of Disease in Childhood, 49*, 259–263.

Houts, A. C., Berman, J. S., & Abramson, H. (1994). Effectiveness of psychological and pharmacological treatments for nocturnal enuresis. *Journal of Consulting and Clinical Psychology, 62*, 737–745.

Houts, A. C., & Liebert, R. M. (1984). *Bedwetting*. Springfield, IL: Charles C. Thomas.

Houts, A. C., Liebert, R. M., & Padawer, W. (1983). A delivery system for the treatment of primary enuresis. *Journal of Abnormal Child Psychology, 11*, 513–520.

Houts, A. C., Peterson, J. K., & Whelan, J. P. (1986). Prevention of relapse in full spectrum home training for primary enuresis: A components analysis. *Behavior Therapy, 17*, 462–469.

Howe, A. C., & Walker, C. E. (1992). Behavioral management of toilet training, enuresis and encopresis. *Pediatric Clinics of North America, 39*, 413–432.

Johnston, B. D., & Wright, J. A. (1993). Attentional dysfunction in children with encopresis. *Journal of Developmental and Behavioral Pediatrics, 14*, 381–385.

Kimmel, H. D., & Kimmel, E. (1970). An instrumental conditioning method for the treatment of enuresis. *Journal of Behavior Therapy and Experimental Psychiatry, 1*, 121–123.

Levine, M. D. (1975). Children with encopresis: A descriptive analysis. *Pediatrics, 56*, 412–416.

Levine, M. D. (1992). Encopresis. In M. D. Levine, W. B. Carey, & A. C. Crocker (Eds.), *Developmental–behavioral pediatrics* (pp. 389–397). Philadelphia: Saunders.

Loening-Baucke, V. (1993). Chronic constipation in children. *Gastroenterology, 105*, 1557–1564.

Miller, F. J. W. (1973). Children who wet the bed. In I. Kolvin, R. C. MacKeith, & S. R. Meadow (Eds.), *Bladder control and enuresis* (pp. 47–52). Philadelphia: Lippincott.

Miller, K. (1993). Concomitant nonpharmacologic therapy in the treatment of primary nocturnal enuresis. *Clinical Pediatrics, Special Edition*, 32–37.

Mishne, J. M. (1993). Primary nocturnal enuresis: A psychodynamic clinical perspective. *Child and Adolescent Social Work Journal, 10*, 469–495.

Moffatt, M. E. K. (1989). Nocturnal enuresis: Psychologic implications of treatment and nontreatment. *Journal of Pediatrics, 114* (Suppl.), 697–704.

Moffatt, M. E. K. (1997). Nocturnal enuresis: A review of the efficacy of treatments and practical advice for clinicians. *Journal of Developmental and Behavioral Pediatrics, 18*, 49–56.

Mowrer, O. H., & Mowrer, W. M. (1938). Enuresis: A method for its study and treatment. *American Journal of Orthopsychiatry, 8*, 436–459.

Nørgaard, J. P., & Djurhuus, J. C. (1993). The pathophysiology of enuresis in children and young adults. *Clinical Pediatrics, Special Edition*, 5–8.

Ornitz, E. M., Hanna, G. L., & Traversay, J. D. (1992). Prestimulation-induced startle modulation in attention-deficit hyperactivity disorder and nocturnal enuresis. *Psychophysiology, 29*, 437–451.

Partin, J. C., Hamill, S. K., Fischel, J. E., & Partin, J. S. (1992). Painful defecation and fecal soiling in children. *Pediatrics, 89*, 1007–1009.

Reimers, T. M. (1996). A biobehavioral approach toward managing encopresis. *Behavior Modification, 20*, 469–479.

Rockney, R. M., McQuade, W. H., Days, A. L., Linn, H. E., & Alario, A. J. (1996). Encopresis treatment outcome: Long-term follow-up of 45 cases. *Journal of Developmental and Behavioral Pediatrics, 17,* 380–385.

Ronen, T., Rahav, G., & Wozner, Y. (1995). Self-control and enuresis. *Journal of Cognitive Psychotherapy: An International Quarterly, 9,* 249–258.

Rushton, H. G. (1993a). Evaluation of the enuretic child. *Clinical Pediatrics, Special Edition,* 14–18.

Rushton, H. G. (1993b). Older pharmacologic therapy for nocturnal enuresis. *Clinical Pediatrics, Special Edition,* 10–13.

Said, J. A., Wilson, P. H., & Hensley, V. R. (1991). Primary versus secondary enuresis: Differential response to urine-alarm treatment. *Child and Family Behavior Therapy, 13,* 1–12.

Starfield, B. (1967). Functional bladder capacity in enuretic and nonenuretic children. *Journal of Pediatrics, 70,* 777–781.

Stark, L. J., Owens-Stively, J., Spirito, A., Lewis, A., & Guevremont, D. (1990). Group behavioral treatment of retentive encopresis. *Journal of Pediatric Psychology, 15,* 659–671.

Stark, L. J., Spirito, A., Lewis, A. V., & Hart, K. J. (1990). Encopresis: Behavioral parameters associated with children who fail medical management. *Child Psychiatry and Human Development, 20,* 169–179.

Stenberg, A., & Läckgren, G. (1993). Treatment with oral desmopressin in adolescents with primary nocturnal enuresis. *Clinical Pediatrics, Special Edition,* 25–27.

Strömgren, A., & Thomsen, P. H. (1990). Personality traits in young adults with a history of conditioning-treated childhood enuresis. *Acta Psychiatrica Scandinavica, 81,* 538–541.

van Londen, A., van Londen-Barentsen, M. W. M., van Son, M. J. M., & Mulder, G. A. L. A. (1993). Arousal training for children suffering from nocturnal enuresis: A 2½ year follow-up. *Behaviour Research and Therapy, 31,* 613–615.

van Londen, A., van Londen-Barentsen, M. W. M., van Son, M. J. M., & Mulder, G. A. L. A. (1995). Relapse rate and subsequent parental reaction after successful treatment of children suffering from nocturnal enuresis: A 2½ year follow-up of bibliotherapy. *Behaviour Research and Therapy, 33,* 309–311.

Vivian, D., Fischel, J. E., & Liebert, R. M. (1986). Effect of "wet nights" on daytime behavior during concurrent treatment of enuresis and conduct problems. *Journal of Behavior Therapy and Experimental Psychiatry, 17,* 301–303.

Warzak, W. J., & Friman, P. C. (1994). Current concepts in pediatric primary nocturnal enuresis. *Child and Adolescent Social Work Journal, 11,* 507–523.

Werry, J. S., & Cohrssen, J. (1965). Enuresis: An etiologic and therapeutic study. *Journal of Pediatrics, 67,* 423–431.

Whiting, J. W. M., & Child, I. L. (1953). *Child training and personality: A cross-cultural study.* New Haven, CT: Yale University Press.

Young, G. C., & Morgan, R. T. T. (1972). Overlearning in the conditioning treatment of enuresis. *Behaviour Research and Therapy, 10,* 147–151.

Young, M. H., Brennen, L. C., Baker, R. D., & Baker, S. S. (1995). Functional encopresis: Symptom reduction and behavioral improvement. *Journal of Developmental and Behavioral Pediatrics, 16,* 226–232.

VIII
PERVASIVE DEVELOPMENTAL DISORDERS

34

A Developmental Approach to Autism

Lisa L. Travis and Marian D. Sigman

INTRODUCTION

Autism is one of the most well-investigated developmental disorders. The reasons for the intensive research effort are easy to grasp for those with interests in cognition, language, development, or psychopathology. Autism presents a truly puzzling, sometimes even paradoxically uneven profile of abilities. Because it is uneven, this profile holds promise for revealing surprising insights into the functioning of both normal and abnormal minds.

Autism is best known for presenting a dissociation between social and cognitive functioning, with social abilities being more impaired than cognitive ones. Recent research has begun to reveal that autism is also characterized by many other more specific dissociations in functioning. One way that these dissociations are brought into sharper relief is through the application of a developmental perspective. This involves considering how different abilities are related to each other at different points in development both in autistic and in typically developing individuals. By applying this approach, researchers have uncovered finer level dissociations in functioning that offer both a clearer picture of autism and intriguing clues into the nature of normal development. This chapter emphasizes the functional dissociations in autism that are apparent from a developmental perspective.

Classification and Diagnosis of Autism

Identifying criteria for classification of autism involve separating core symptoms, those that are universal and specific to autism, from associated or secondary symptoms. The current consensus in the field, reflected in the current diagnostic standard, the fourth edition of the

Lisa L. Travis and Marian D. Sigman • Child and Adolescent Psychiatry, Neuropsychiatric Institute, University of California at Los Angeles, Los Angeles, California 90024-1759.

Handbook of Developmental Psychopathology, Second Edition, edited by Arnold J. Sameroff, Michael Lewis, and Suzanne M. Miller. Kluwer Academic / Plenum Publishers, New York, 2000.

Diagnostic and Statistical Manual of Mental Disorders (DSM-IV; American Psychiatric Association, 1994), identifies three core sets of symptoms in autism: impaired reciprocal social interaction, delayed language, and aberrant activities. Aberrant activities include an abnormally restricted range of interests, rigid adherence to routines, and motor stereotypies. Epidemiological research reveals that these three core impairments are associated (Wing & Gould, 1979), indicating that autism thus defined is a true syndrome and not simply a conjunction of independent symptoms. Symptoms that are characteristic of autism, but not considered to be core, are mental retardation, uneven profiles on IQ test batteries, savant abilities, abnormalities of attention, impaired cross-modal integration, and self-injurious behavior. One associated symptom, that of mental retardation, bears special consideration. Approximately 75% of individuals with autism exhibit some degree of mental retardation (Rutter, 1979).

Although autism represents a true syndrome, the boundaries separating it from other disorders are by no means clear. For example, the distinctions between autism, Asperger's syndrome, and semantic–pragmatic disorder are still a matter of debate (Happé, 1995). Also, many individuals who fail to meet diagnostic criteria for autism nevertheless present many autistic symptoms. These individuals are typically classified as having Pervasive Developmental Disorder (PDD). The term *autistic spectrum* is sometimes used to signify the range of disorders that share symptoms with autism.

Etiology

The etiology of autism is not yet well understood. Research has established that psychological or social stressors do not cause autism, focusing attention squarely on biological underpinnings. However, it now appears unlikely that autism is caused by any single organic factor. Rather, there is probably a heterogeneous set of biological factors and multiple causal paths that may result in autism. The search for biological underpinnings has revealed that autism is associated with a number of other organic conditions, such as prenatal and obstetric complications, the onset of epilepsy in adolescence or adulthood, and two genetic disorders, tuberous sclerosis and Fragile X syndrome (for a review, see Gilberg & Coleman, 1992). The reasons for these links are not yet understood.

In contrast, twin and family studies show clear evidence for a genetic component to autism (for a review, see Bailey et al., 1995). Monozygotic twins are much more likely to be concordant for autism than dizygotic twins, and siblings of children with autism have an increased risk of developing autism. There is also evidence that symptoms characteristic of autism, such as language and communication impairments, are more common in families of children with autism. No specific genes have yet been identified as potential candidates for links to autism, though researchers are actively pursuing this goal.

Whatever the original causes of autism, they are undoubtedly tied to behavior through abnormalities in brain structure and function. Almost every major brain structure has been suggested as a possible mediator of the particular patterns of behavior seen in autism, and a wide variety of brain abnormalities have been identified (for a review, see Waterhouse, Fein, & Modahl, 1996). The challenge in this area of research is to identify which brain dysfunctions are causally and developmentally primary. Complicating the issue is the fact that brain abnormalities may arise from aberrant input from other structures, or as a secondary consequence of aberrant experiences during development. For example, the basic social impairments in autism may result in quite different kinds and amounts of social experience for people with autism starting early in childhood. The lack of this "expected" input may play a role in brain organization. Researchers are actively attempting to tease apart the primary and secondary brain abnormalities in autism, and significant progress in this area is likely to be forthcoming in the near future as a result of advances in brain imaging technology.

SOCIAL AND EMOTIONAL DEVELOPMENT

Although social functioning is the area of most severe impairment in autism, research has revealed that not all aspects of social functioning are equally affected. Surprising dissociations in social abilities are evident from an early age. For example, important early social achievements that are largely spared in autism are attachment relationships and self-recognition. However, other achievements normally linked to these behaviors are disrupted.

Early Responsiveness

From birth, human infants are particularly responsive to human faces and voices. In the first months of life, they begin to engage in face-to-face affective sharing and turn-taking episodes that are thought to lay the foundations for later communication and social relationships. Because autism is typically not diagnosed until the third or fourth year, we do not yet know whether these early forms of social exchange are disrupted in autism. Although researchers are actively seeking to fill this gap, the low incidence of autism in the population makes this task extremely difficult. Retrospective examination of home videotapes of children later diagnosed as autistic suggests that there may be early appearing deficits; however, this database is currently very small (Kubicek, 1980; Osterling & Dawson, 1993). Whether children with autism engage in normal social interactions during infancy and only display aberrant social functioning later on, or whether their social interactions are disrupted from the start, is a critical issue for theories of autism. The answer to this question would also provide information about continuity in normal social development.

Early Social Relationships and Communicative Behaviors

Toward the end of the first year, there is a fundamental reorganization in a typically developing child's social and emotional life. One important change is that the child begins to participate more actively in the attachment relationship. The child begins to show distress in the absence of the primary caregiver, to show greater comfort in her presence, and to seek actively to maintain contact. A second important change is that a new form of communicative behavior emerges, in which the infant begins to communicate with a partner about aspects of the world external to the dyad. This newfound communicative skill takes three distinct forms: requesting or eliciting aid in obtaining objects, affiliative interactions in which the aim is to achieve or maintain ongoing interaction, and joint attention. Joint attention involves the use of eye contact and gestures to coordinate the attention of oneself and another with respect to a third object or event. In addition, the infant starts to use social referencing, utilizing the emotional expressions of other people as sources of information about objects and events in the world.

In autism, this developmental reorganization is clearly disrupted. Indeed, the first clear signs of autism involve the failure to show the patterns of social, communicative, and emotional responses that typically emerge at this time. It is not that children with autism fail to make advances in social and communicative functioning at this point in development. Rather, it appears that their achievements in these areas are not integrated with each other as they are in typical development.

There is now clear evidence that children with autism establish attachment relationships. In separation–reunion episodes designed to assess attachment, children with autism are like typically developing children in seeking contact and comfort from their caregivers on reunion, and in directing more behavior to their caregivers than to strangers (e.g., Rogers, Ozonoff, & Maslin-Cole, 1991; Sigman & Ungerer, 1984a). This preservation of the attachment relationship in the face of severe disruption in other areas of social functioning is good evidence for its status as a fundamental behavioral system.

However, children with autism appear to be particularly dependent on their caregivers to initiate and structure their interactions. When caregivers are instructed to play with their children with autism as they normally would, surprisingly few differences are found between their interactions and those of caregivers with mental age (MA) matched children. They engage in similar amounts of looking, smiling, vocalizing, and mutual play. In contrast, when caregivers are instructed not to initiate interactions, differences become very apparent. While most typically developing and mentally retarded (MR) children will spontaneously engage their caregivers in play, children with autism are typically content to play alone (Kasari, Sigman, & Yirmiya, 1993). These studies suggest that children with autism are socially responsive when adults engage them in interactions, but they may have particular difficulties initiating interactions.

In interactions with their caregivers and with other adults, abnormalities in social communication are also apparent. For example, children with autism are less likely to coordinate expressions of positive affect with communicative behaviors such as looking at the caregiver (Dawson, Hill, Spencer, Galpert, & Watson, 1990; Snow, Hertzig, & Shapiro, 1987). Children with autism have great difficulty establishing joint attention. This difficulty is manifested both in children's failure to initiate joint attention with others and to respond to others' initiation attempts (Mundy, Sigman, Ungerer, & Sherman, 1986). When children with autism do engage in joint attention, they are less likely to engage in eye contact and to display positive affect than are MA matched controls (Kasari, Sigman, Mundy, & Yirmiya, 1990).

In contrast, requesting is a communicative function that is relatively intact in autism. Although children with autism show some deficits in requesting relative to typically developing and developmentally delayed controls, these deficits are much smaller than those in joint attention (e.g., Loveland & Landry, 1986; Mundy et al., 1986; Mundy, Sigman, & Kasari, 1994; Sigman & Ruskin, 1999). Not only do children with autism generate requests spontaneously, but also their requests are well organized in that they are just as likely as control subjects to establish eye contact while requesting (Mundy et al., 1986). They are also as compliant as control samples in responding to simple requests made by others (Mundy et al., 1986). Thus, one communicative function, requesting, appears to be relatively intact in children with autism, while another, joint attention, is severely affected.

Another aspect of social communication that is impaired in autism is social referencing. Typically developing infants begin to use the emotional expressions of adults as sources of information about their environments toward the end of the first year (e.g., Campos & Sternberg, 1981; Gunnar & Stone, 1984). A parent's expression of fear or pleasure toward an ambiguous object will influence whether a child approaches or withdraws from it. Sigman, Kasari, Kwon, and Yirmiya (1992) compared autistic, typically developing, and MR children's responses to an ambiguous object, in this case, a mechanical robot. They found large differences between autistic and other children in the amount of time spent looking at adults' faces in this situation. In fact, the majority of children with autism did not look even once to the adult. Probably as a result of failing to encounter the emotional signals expressed by adults, they were also more likely than the other groups to approach the robot.

Self-Awareness

In typically developing children, the second and third years of life involve a second substantial reorganization in social and emotional functioning. One aspect of this reorganization is the emergence of self-recognition, as measured by the ability to self-identify from a mirror image (Brooks-Gunn & Lewis, 1984). At about the same time, children develop increasing awareness of their own behavior and its relation to social standards (Bullock & Lutkenhaus, 1988). These developments give rise to new emotions. Self-recognition ability is associated with the emergence of self-conscious emotions, such as embarrassment (Lewis, Sullivan, Stanger, & Weiss, 1989), and the realization that others evaluate one's behavior against standards gives rise to the complex emotions of shame and pride (Lewis, 1992). These advances bring a concomitant increase in socialization pressure from parents, who require children to take increasing responsibility for regulating their own behavior. At the same time, more sophisticated understanding of emotional states in others gives rise to behavior that is aimed at influencing these states, including both prosocial behavior, such as comforting, and deliberate attempts to hurt.

Again, in autism, the aspects of functioning that are normally integrated at this point in development appear to be dissociated. Although self-recognition is not delayed in relation to other cognitive abilities, complex emotions, self-regulation, and prosocial and antisocial behavior are all affected by autism.

In the classic test of self-recognition ability, an experimenter surreptitiously dabs some rouge on a child's nose and later exposes the child to a mirror to see whether the child responds by touching his or her nose. Although children with autism show evidence of self-recognition by touching their noses in this situation, they fail to exhibit the coy behavior and positive affect that typically developing children exhibit when discovering the unexpected spot (e.g., Dawson & McKissick, 1984; Spiker & Ricks, 1984). One interpretation of this behavior is that children with autism lack awareness of, or concern for, other people's perceptions of them.

Such lack of regard for others' evaluations of their behavior is also evident in situations where children with autism are involved in mastering challenging tasks. Kasari, Sigman, Baumgartner, and Stipek (1993) studied the behavior of autistic, MR, and typically developing children as they completed puzzles in the presence of their caregivers and an experimenter. All groups smiled equally in response to completing a challenging task. However, children with autism were significantly less likely to combine smiling with looking to an adult.

Prosocial Behaviors and Peer Interactions

Clinical reports suggest that both prosocial and antisocial behavior are less common in children with autism than in other groups (Lord, 1993). Although children may learn to engage in routines that comprise prosocial acts, spontaneous demonstrations of prosocial behavior are rare. One laboratory study of prosocial behavior in older individuals with autism found support for these observations. They were less likely to cooperate and share than control subjects, though they were equally likely to help in cleaning up, a more routine task (Sigman & Ruskin, 1999). Older children with autism also show less empathy than other children, although the differences are small (Yirmiya, Sigman, Kasari, & Mundy, 1992). They may occasionally do things that are hurtful to others, but these actions are usually attributed to lack of understanding rather than to malice. Clinical reports and laboratory research also indicate that children with autism fail to engage in deceit, though one study has demonstrated that they are capable of deliberately acting to sabotage another's goals (Sodian & Frith, 1992).

One common form of prosocial behavior is attempting to comfort another in distress. Even before children become competent at comforting, they find displays of distress captivating and disturbing. Sigman et al. (1992) found striking differences between children with autism and typically developing and MR children in their responses to displays of distress by their parents or by an experimenter. Children with autism attended much less to the person exhibiting distress than did typically developing and MR children. Some children with autism failed to look even once at the adult who was displaying distress, while all of the other children looked.

An important developmental task of the preschool and school years is forming relationships with peers and acquiring skills for successful peer interaction. Observations of teachers and parents suggest that children with autism interact very little with their peers and tend to be socially inept. A recent study of the peer interactions of children with autism on the playground provides support for these clinical impressions (Sigman & Ruskin, 1999). Children with autism were found to spend less time in social play than other developmentally delayed children. This finding primarily reflected their failure to approach others. Their approaches were not more likely to be rejected by peers, and once they entered interactions, children with autism were as able as their peers to maintain them.

Emotional Expressiveness and Understanding

The ability to display clear emotions also appears to be impaired in autism. Yirmiya, Kasari, Sigman, and Mundy (1989) found that children with autism were more likely to show expressions that were mixtures of two emotions than were other children. They also occasionally showed blends of positive and negative emotions, which never occurred in the comparison groups. When older children with autism are instructed to assume a particular expression, or to imitate the expression of another, their displays are rated as poorer examples of the expression than are those of control subjects (Macdonald et al., 1989; Loveland et al., 1994). People with autism also appear to have difficulty integrating various aspects of emotional expression, such as gestures, vocalizations, and facial expressions into meaningful wholes (Hobson, 1986a,b).

As children grow older, they become capable of reflecting on and verbalizing their knowledge of emotions and the circumstances that give rise to them. High-functioning children with autism also make substantial gains in this area. Older high-functioning children with autism are able to demonstrate understanding of emotion words by describing instances in which they have experienced a particular emotion (Capps, Yirmiya, & Sigman, 1992; Jaedicke, Storoschuk, & Lord, 1994). However, their descriptions appear to lack spontaneity and are more general than those of nonautistic control subjects.

With increasing age, individuals with autism tend to develop increasing social interest. However, even the most intelligent individuals with autism are socially odd throughout their lives. Conversational exchanges pose difficulties even for highly able adults with autism, as will be described in more detail in the section on language. They have difficulty following subtle rules of social engagement, such as those concerning politeness, familiarity, and status. While typically developing individuals require some tutoring regarding these social rules in childhood, they use them quite flexibly and productively in novel situations in adulthood. By contrast, individuals with autism appear to learn social rules by rote, with the result that they apply them inflexibly and often incorrectly. As Frith (1989) points out, these social impairments also have a positive side: They can be described as honesty, innocence, or guilelessness. Nevertheless, these characteristics are signs that individuals with autism never achieve normal levels of social competence.

In summary, the course of social development in autism deviates from normal development in several ways. Major reorganizations occurring in the first and second years in normal development are altered in autism. Not all forms of social functioning are impaired. For example, self-recognition and the attachment relationship are mostly spared. In contrast, social emotions such as pride and empathy do not appear to emerge at all normally. Like typically developing children, older individuals with autism acquire the ability to reflect on their emotional and social lives, but their skills in this area may never equal those of typically developing individuals.

COGNITIVE DEVELOPMENT

As in the case of social development, cognitive development in autism proceeds unevenly. The most severe impairments appear in social cognitive abilities such the understanding of false beliefs. However, cognitive deficits in autism are not restricted to the domain of social cognition, and not all aspects of social cognition are impaired.

Early Representation

The nature and timing of early developmental milestones in representational ability are important issues in cognitive development that are still actively debated. Although we do not yet have a firmly grounded, widely accepted account of representational change in normal development, recent research has focused attention on major shifts occurring at about 9 and 18 months of age. At about age 9 months, a number of changes signal the emergence of newfound representational competence, roughly corresponding to declarative memory. More evidence for recall memory, as opposed to recognition, is apparent in infants' everyday behavior (Ashmead & Perlmutter, 1980). At this stage, infants' representations appear to include more spatial and contextual information, and to accommodate cross-modal associations more effectively (Schacter & Moscovitch, 1984). The increasing ability to maintain nonperceptual representations of events over time is also evident in the emergence of deferred imitation (Meltzoff, 1988). Although the earliest forms of these abilities are evident prior to 9 months of age, the improvement at 9 months is rapid and dramatic (Mandler, 1988). At about 18 months, a second shift is evident in infants' representational competence. Perhaps the clearest sign of this shift is the rapid increase in use of communicative symbols, including words and gestures. Other signs of this change are increase in the amount of pretend play and the ability to solve object-permanence tasks involving invisible displacement. Meltzoff and Gopnik (1989) suggest that these changes represent the emergence of a "hypothetical" representational ability, which allows infants to manipulate their representations in order to go beyond remembering what was in order to make inferences about what must have occurred and to consider what might be.

We have relatively little evidence regarding early representational development in autism. Because autism is not diagnosed until relatively late, the youngest subjects studied typically have mental ages of at least 18 months, with the result that there is little information regarding delay or disruption of the 9-month shift. The fact that the youngest samples studied perform as well as MA-matched controls on tests of object permanence and mental problem solving (Sigman & Ungerer, 1984b) suggests that children with autism do not have long-lasting impairments in abilities that normally emerge around 9 months.

In contrast, there is reason to believe that the representational abilities that normally emerge at 18 months may be impaired in autism, because the two major advances associated with these abilities, pretend play and communicative words and gestures, are at least substantially delayed or, in some cases, completely absent (e.g., Mundy, Sigman, Ungerer, & Sherman, 1987; Riguet, Taylor, Benaroya, & Klein, 1981; Sigman & Ungerer, 1984b). Imitation, another key indicator of early representational ability, is also impaired in autism (for a review, see Smith & Bryson, 1994).

Concrete Operational Abilities

Children with autism perform as well as MA matched controls on tests of seriation, conservation, and hierarchical classification (Shulman, Yirmiya, & Greenbaum, 1995; Yirmiya, Sigman, & Zacks, 1994; Yirmiya & Shulman, 1996), but they are impaired on class-inclusion problems (Shulman et al., 1995) and appearance–reality problems (Baron-Cohen, 1989a). This particular pattern of strengths and weaknesses is not well understood. What has attracted much more attention are the striking deficits of people with autism in certain kinds of perspective taking, specifically those requiring understanding of false belief.

Perspective Taking

Perspective taking takes many forms, from the very simple, such as assessing whether or not an object is visible to another, to the complex, such as understanding that another person is likely to have a false belief. Somewhat surprisingly, children with autism do not have general problems with perspective taking. Individuals with autism are not impaired in their ability to assess how a simple visual array appears to another person, although they show some impairments in tasks involving more complex arrays (Baron-Cohen, 1989b; Tan & Harris, 1991; Yirmiya et al., 1994). These strengths indicate that not all aspects of perspective-taking ability are impaired in autism, contrary to what would be expected if individuals with autism failed to appreciate the fact that different people represent the world in different ways.

In contrast, one particular kind of perspective-taking task, the false-belief task, is especially difficult for people with autism. In one of the classic versions of this task, the subject is introduced to two characters, Sally and Ann. Sally puts a marble in a basket and then leaves the room. While she is gone, Ann moves the marble to a new location. The subject is then asked where Sally will look for the marble when she returns. The correct answer is that Sally will look where she hid the marble, and not where the subject knows it to be truly located. This presents a challenging task, because it requires a firm understanding of the fact than another person can have a mental representation that is both different from reality and different from one's own. This task is not mastered by typically developing children until they are about 4 years of age. However, children with autism with mental ages well above 4 years perform poorly on false-belief tasks. Many carefully controlled studies have attempted to isolate the source of their difficulty, and have produced results suggesting that the problem is specific to the understanding of mental states (for a review, see Happé & Frith, 1995; for an alternative interpretation, see Hughes & Russell, 1993).

Categorization

A number of the characteristic behaviors of autism suggest abnormalities in categorization. Clinicians are acutely aware that people with autism often have great difficulty generalizing from training experiences. For example, they may fail to generalize a newly learned skill across settings or trainers. They also tend to exhibit an insistence on sameness in daily routines, and overly narrow interests. For example, Francesca Happé describes one high-functioning man with autism who had an extreme interest in the color of the doors of juvenile courts in different towns in England. When asked why he did not inquire about the door colors of adult courts, he responded, "They bore me to tears" (Happé, 1995, p. 37). Such peculiarities suggest that people with autism may be "carving the world at its joints" in an abnormal manner.

If this is true, it does not appear to be based on a failure to develop natural object categories. Children with autism show MA-appropriate performance on tasks assessing their understanding of basic and superordinate level categories (Tager-Flusberg, 1985; Ungerer & Sigman, 1987) and can demonstrate a grasp of even more abstract ontological distinctions, such as the difference between animates and inanimates (Baron-Cohen, 1991). The database on categorization in autism is still rather slim, but it suggests that any impairments are likely to be subtle.

Executive Function

Executive function (EF) is a general term referring to a broad set of abilities. Two underlying themes in EF are organization of goal-directed behavior and integration of information from a variety of sources, such as perception and memory, in order to select an appropriate response. Thus, EF abilities include planning, inhibiting prepotent responses, controlling impulses, engaging in an organized search, and maintaining or flexibly switching response sets. Although EF is typically associated with the frontal lobes, damage to other brain areas can also affect EF.

Investigations of EF in subjects with autism of various ages and abilities have found deficits in the use of a number of different tasks (for a review, see Pennington & Ozonoff, 1996). For example, subjects with autism are more prone to perseverative responding and have difficulty inhibiting prepotent responses. An excellent illustration of this problem is found in a task devised by Hughes and Russell (1993). Children with autism were simply asked to point to an empty box in order to win a candy contained in another box. They were unable to inhibit their tendency to point to the desired candy, in spite of showing evidence of understanding the task and repeatedly failing to win it in this manner. Hughes and Russell attributed this pattern to the inability of children with autism to disengage from the object and use internal rules to guide behavior. Other EF impairments include attention shifting (Courchesne et al., 1994) and working memory (Bennetto, Pennington, & Rogers, 1996).

Not only are EF deficits found consistently, but they are also usually quite large. Because the effects are large and consistent, EF tasks are better than other tasks, including false-belief tasks, at differentiating between persons with autism and other groups (Ozonoff, Pennington, & Rogers, 1991). In addition, EF impairments in autism are not ameliorated by development (Ozonoff & McEvoy, 1994).

Taken as a whole, the pattern of cognitive deficits in autism presents a puzzling profile. Specific deficits are clearly found in social cognition, namely, in imitation and perspective taking. However, closer examination of these deficits does not support the view that they are simply due to the fact that social information processing is involved. For example, children with autism seem to do well on simple visual perspective-taking tasks but poorly on false-belief tasks. Some nonsocial, concrete operational abilities are also more impaired than others. Because EF is implicated in nearly every cognitive task, it is somewhat surprising that children with autism, who have substantial EF deficits, exhibit as much competence as they do on a variety of cognitive tasks. Many different explanations for this uneven profile are offered by competing theories of autism, as will be discussed in the concluding section of this chapter.

LANGUAGE DEVELOPMENT

Language and communication problems are one of the hallmark characteristics of autism. As in other domains of functioning, impairments are not uniform: Certain aspects of language are more affected than others. The pattern of unevenness in functioning is quite consistent with the unevenness found in social and cognitive abilities. Essentially, those aspects of language that involve an appreciation of its social, communicative function pose the most difficulty for individuals with autism.

About half of children with autism never develop functional language. Language development is correlated with intelligence; thus, children in the normal or near-normal range of intelligence are most likely to develop language (Stone & Caro-Martinez, 1990). Even people with autism who eventually achieve good language are substantially delayed in their language development.

For the most part, acquisition of vocabulary and grammar in autism proceeds normally (e.g., Tager-Flusberg, 1993; Tager-Flusberg, Calkins, Nolin, Anderson, & Chadwick-Dias, 1990). For example, in a longitudinal study of early language in autistic and Down's children, Tager-Flusberg found that distribution of form classes in spontaneous speech, and order of emergence of grammatical morphemes in both groups were like that of typically developing children. However, she found some evidence of a lack of flexibility in language use in the sample with autism, a characteristic that appears to persist throughout development in autistic language.

In spite of the relatively normal course of vocabulary and grammatical development, the language system in autism is far from intact. The missing ingredient in the system is pragmatics—the integration of language with the social context in order to achieve effective communication. Autistic speech exhibits some characteristic peculiarities that are related to a fundamental pragmatic deficit. These include echolalia, pronoun reversals, and lack of appropriate prosody. People with autism engage in stilted, awkward conversations. Although they may be fairly effective in transmitting and receiving bare facts, they do not achieve the smooth exchange of information that is characteristic of normal conversations. As a result, conversational flow is disrupted and misinterpretations are frequent. The nonautistic partner is often left with the feeling that communication was not achieved.

For those individuals with autism who do develop language, grammar and vocabulary develop quite normally, though slowly, but the ability to engage in conversational exchanges is impaired from the earliest stages of development onward. Some aspects of conversational impairment are inability to master rules of politeness, and difficulty maintaining conversational flow and constructing informative messages. The particulars of autistic language have many parallels in the social and cognitive deficits described earlier.

THEORIES OF AUTISM

Throughout this review, five themes are apparent in many of the phenomena observed in autism: disorders of affect, attention, initiation, integration, and representation. For example, initiation problems are evident in children's interactions with peers and caregivers, and in a tendency toward perseverative responding in nonsocial contexts. Failures of attention are apparent in social contexts such as in lack of joint attention, in failure to respond to distress and to engage in social referencing, and in nonsocial contexts such as overly narrow interests. Individuals with autism appear to have difficulty processing and conveying emotional information in both verbal and nonverbal channels. Integration difficulties are apparent in the lack of ability to combine displays of affect with other communicative behavior, and in difficulty appreciating the relationships between gestural, vocal, and facial displays in others. Representational difficulties are suggested by the lack of pretend play and difficulties with understanding false belief. These themes are representative not only of the major phenomena to be explained in autism, but also of the major theoretical accounts of autism. Each theory of autism tends to emphasize one theme as primary, with causal and developmental links from the primary deficit to the other themes.

For example, according to Peter Hobson (1989, 1993), the primary deficit in autism is an inability to make affective contact with other people. This deficit is present from early in infancy, and precludes experiences that are essential for normal social and cognitive development. An alternative account, proposed by Courchesne and his colleagues (1994), is that attentional impairments are primary causes of autism. In support of this position, Courchesne presents data from adolescents and adults with autism in a variety of attention shifting tasks showing that individuals with autism take longer to disengage and refocus attention than control subjects but are not impaired in maintaining attentional focus. Ozonoff (1995) suggests that EF impairments consisting of an inability use an on-line mental representation in order to guide behavior may be primary causes of autism. She links this impairment to a variety of deficits found in autism, including emotion perception, imitation, and pretend play.

The accounts discussed so far are in agreement that autism involves failure to develop normal representations in both social and cognitive domains. They explain this failure in terms of lower-level dysfunctions that disrupt the input from which these representations are derived. In contrast, two additional theories propose that in autism, the innate capacity to form certain specifically social representations is lacking.

One of the most influential accounts is Leslie's "theory of mind" proposal, which centers around a modular theory of mind mechanism (ToMM), specialized for the processing representations of mental states (Leslie, 1987; Leslie & Roth, 1993). These mental state representations are called *metarepresentations*. According to Leslie, autism involves an inability to form metarepresentations, resulting in a failure to appreciate mental states in oneself and others. An indirect consequence is that the ToMM lacks its proper input, and thus cannot derive a "theory of mind," which is an unconscious appreciation of the relation between mental states and behavior. The child with autism is stuck with behaviorist interpretations of the social world. Although these interpretations are adequate for some purposes, they are incapable of dealing with cases such as false belief and pretend play.

A second representational account of autism centers around a proposed disruption of representations underlying imitation (Meltzoff & Gopnik, 1993; Rogers & Pennington, 1991). According to these accounts, autism may result from developmental consequences of an inability to perceive self–other correspondences.

Uta Frith offers an information-processing account of autism that is not dependent on specific forms of representation, but rather on a general information-processing force that applies very broadly to a variety of cognitive operations (Frith, 1989). Frith argues that typically developing individuals have a strong drive to seek underlying patterns and regularities in all kinds of information. According to Frith, in autism, the drive for coherence is unusually weak. In support of this theory are findings showing that children with autism excel in tasks requiring the suppression of information about global organization such as block design and searching for embedded figures (Shah & Frith, 1983; Asarnow, Tanguay, Bott, & Freeman, 1987). According to Frith, a weak drive for central coherence would naturally impede progress toward developing a theory of mind, because the achievement of a theory of mind is dependent on drawing exceptionally broad and abstract generalizations.

CONCLUSIONS

Research on autism has often been described as exemplifying the usefulness of the developmental psychopathology approach to understanding typical and atypical development. The primary reason is that the bidirectional flow of ideas and information between the domains of autism and normal development is particularly clear. This bidirectional flow has been particularly useful in identifying unexpected dissociations in functioning in autism. Investigators have identified important normal developmental achievements, such as attachment, self-recognition, object permanence, conservation, acquisition of grammatical morphemes, and so on, and have gone on to investigate whether these achievements are spared or disrupted in autism. This has allowed the identification of unexpected dissociations between abilities that normally develop together, such as requesting and joint attention, self-recognition and the self-conscious emotions, and the pragmatic and grammatical aspects of language. In turn, these dissociations provide a particularly valuable window onto normal development by suggesting that some relationships among normally coincident developmental achievements may be more fundamental than others.

ACKNOWLEDGMENTS.   Some of the research from this laboratory cited in this chapter has been supported by grant NS25243 from the National Institute of Neurological Disorders and Stroke and grants HD35470 and HD12662 from the National Institute of Child Health and Human Development.

REFERENCES

American Psychiatric Association. (1994). *Diagnostic and statistical manual of mental disorders* (4th ed.). Washington, DC: Author.

Asarnow, R. F., Tanguay, P. E., Bott, L., & Freeman, B. J. (1987). Patterns of intellectual functioning in non-retarded autistic and schizophrenic children. *Journal of Child Psychology and Psychiatry, 28,* 273–280.

Ashmead, D. H., & Perlmutter, M. (1980). Infant memory in everyday life. In M. Perlmutter (Ed.), *New directions for child development: Children's memory* (Vol. 10, pp. 1–16). San Francisco: Jossey-Bass.

Bailey, A., LeCouteur, A., Gottesman, I., Bolton, P., Simonoff, E., Yuzda, E., & Rutter, M. (1995). Autism as a strongly genetic disorder: Evidence from a British twin study. *Psychological Medicine, 25*, 63–78.

Bailey, A., Phillips, W., & Rutter, M. (1996). Autism: Towards an integration of clinical, genetic, neuropsychological, and neurobiological perspectives. *Journal of Child Psychology and Psychiatry, 37*, 89–126.

Baron-Cohen, S. (1987). Autism and symbolic play. *British Journal of Developmental Psychology, 5*, 139–148.

Baron-Cohen, S. (1989a). Are autistic children "behaviorists"? An examination of their mental-physical and appearance–reality distinctions. *Journal of Autism and Developmental Disorders, 19*, 579–600.

Baron-Cohen, S. (1989b). Perceptual role taking and protodeclarative pointing in autism. *British Journal of Developmental Psychology, 7*, 113–127.

Baron-Cohen, S. (1991). The theory of mind deficit in autism: How specific is it? *British Journal of Developmental Psychology, 9*, 301–314.

Bennetto, L., Pennington, B. F., & Rogers, S. J. (1996). Intact and impaired memory functions in autism. *Child Development, 67*, 1816–1835.

Brooks-Gunn, J. & Lewis, M. (1984). The development of early visual self-recognition. *Developmental Review, 4*, 215–239.

Bullock, M. & Lutkenhaus, P. (1988). The development of volitional behavior in the toddler years. *Child Development, 59* 664–674.

Campos, J. J., & Sternberg, C. R. (1981). *Perception, appraisal, and emotion: The onset of social referencing.* Hillsdale, NJ: Erlbaum.

Capps, L., Yirmiya, N., & Sigman, M. (1992). Understanding of simple and complex emotions in non-retarded children with autism. *Child Psychology and Psychiatry, 33*, 1169–1182.

Courchesne, E., Townsend, J. P., Akshoomoff, N. A., Yeung-Courchesne, R. Y., Press, G. A., Murakama, J. W., Lincoln, A., James, H., Saitoh, O., Egaas, B., Haas, R. H., & Schreibman, L. (1994). A new finding: Impairment in shifting attention in autistic and cerebellar patients. In S. H. Broman & J. G. Grafman (Eds.), *Atypical cognitive deficits in developmental disorders: Implications for brain function* (pp. 101–137). Hillsdale, NJ: Erlbaum.

Dawson, G., & Adams, A. (1984). Imitation and social responsiveness in autistic children. *Journal of Abnormal Child Psychology, 12*, 209–226.

Dawson, G., Hill, D., Spencer, A., Galpert, L., & Watson, L. (1990). Affective exchanges between young autistic children and their mothers. *Journal of Abnormal Child Psychology, 18*, 335–345.

Dawson, G., & McKissick, F. C. (1984). Self-recognition in autistic children. *Journal of Autism and Developmental Disorders, 14*, 383–394.

Frith, U. (1989). *Autism: Explaining the enigma.* Oxford, UK: Blackwell.

Gilberg, C., & Coleman, M. (1992). *The biology of autistic syndromes* (2nd ed.). London: MacKeith Press.

Gunnar, M. R., & Stone, C. (1984). The effects of positive maternal affect on infant responses to pleasant, ambiguous, and fear-provoking toys. *Child Development, 55*, 1231–1236.

Happe, F., & Frith, U. (1995). Theory of mind in autism. In E. Schopler & G. Mesibov (Eds.), *Learning and cognition in autism* (pp. 172–197). New York: Plenum Press.

Happe, F. G. E. (1995). *Autism: An introduction to psychological theory.* Cambridge, MA: Harvard University Press.

Hobson, R. P. (1986a). The autistic child's appraisal of expressions of emotion. *Journal of Child Psychology and Psychiatry, 27*, 321–342.

Hobson, R. P. (1986b). The autistic child's appraisal of expressions of emotion: A further study. *Journal of Child Psychology and Psychiatry, 27*, 671–680.

Hobson, R. P. (1989). Beyond cognition: A theory of autism. In G. Dawson (Ed.), *Autism: Nature, diagnosis and treatment* (pp. 22–48). New York: Guilford Press.

Hobson, R. P. (1993). Understanding persons: The role of affect. In S. Baron-Cohen, H. Tager-Flusberg, & D. J. Cohen (Eds.), *Understanding other minds: Perspectives from autism* (pp. 204–224). Oxford, UK: Oxford University Press.

Hughes, C. H., & Russell, J. (1993). Autistic children's difficulty with mental disengagement from an object: Its implications for theories of autism. *Developmental Psychology, 29*, 498–510.

Jaedicke, S., Storoschuk, S., & Lord, C. (1994). Subjective experience and causes of affect in high-functioning children and adolescents with autism. *Development and Psychopathology, 6*, 273–284.

Kanner, L. (1943). Autistic disturbances of affective contact. *Nervous Child, 2*, 217–250.

Kasari, C., Sigman, M., Baumgartner, P., & Stipek, D. J. (1993). Pride and mastery in children with autism. *Journal of Child Psychology and Psychiatry, 34*, 353–362.

Kasari, C., Sigman, M., Mundy, P., & Yirmiya, N. (1988). Caregiver interactions with autistic children. *Journal of Abnormal Child Psychology, 16*, 45–46.

Kasari, C., Sigman, M., Mundy, P., & Yirmiya, N. (1990). Affective sharing in the context of joint attention interactions of normal, autistic, and mentally retarded children. *Journal of Autism and Developmental Disorders, 20*, 87–100.

Kasari, C., Sigman, M., & Yirmiya, N. (1993). Focused and social attention of autistic children in interactions with familiar and unfamiliar adults: A comparison of autistic, mentally retarded, and normal children. *Development and Psychopathology, 5*, 403–414.

Kubicek, L. F. (1980). Organization in two mother–infants interactions involving a normal infant and his fraternal twin brother who was later diagnosed as autistic. In T. M. Field, S. Goldberg, D. Stern, & A. M. Sostek (Eds.), *High-risk infants and children: Adult and peer interactions* (pp. 99–110). New York: Academic Press.

Leslie, A. M. (1987). Pretense and representation: The origins of "theory of mind." *Psychological Review, 94*, 412–426.

Leslie, A. M., & Roth, D. (1993). What autism teaches us about metarepresentation. In S. Baron-Cohen, H. Tager-Flusberg, & D. J. Cohen (Eds.), *Understanding other minds: Perspectives from autism* (pp. 83–111). Oxford, UK: Oxford University Press.

Lewis, M. (1992). *Shame: The exposed self*. New York: Free Press.

Lewis, M., Sullivan, M. W., Stanger, C., & Weiss, M. (1989). Self development and self-conscious emotions. *Child Development, 60*, 146–156.

Lord, C. (1993). The complexity of social behavior in autism. In S. Baron-Cohen, H. Tager-Flusberg, & D. Cohen (Eds.), *Understanding other minds: Perspectives from autism* (pp. 292–316). Oxford, UK: Oxford University Press.

Loveland, K., & Landry, S. (1986). Joint attention and language in autism and developmental language delay. *Journal of Autism and Developmental Disorders, 16*, 335–349.

Loveland, K., Turali-Kotoski, B., Pearson, D. A., Belsford, K. A., Ortegon, J., & Chen, R. (1994). Imitation and expression of facial affect in autism. *Development and Psychopathology, 6*, 433–443.

Macdonald, H., Rutter, M., Howlin, P., Rios, P., Le Couteur, A., Evered, C., & Folstein, S. (1989). Recognition and expression of emotional cues by autistic and normal adults. *Journal of Child Psychology and Psychiatry, 30*, 865–877.

Mandler, J. (1988). How to build a better baby: On the development of an accessible representational system. *Cognitive Development, 3*, 113–136.

Meltzoff, A. N. (1988). Infant imitation and memory: Nine-month-olds in immediate and deferred tests. *Child Development, 59*, 217–225.

Meltzoff, A. N., & Gopnik, A. (1989). On linking nonverbal imitation, representation, and language learning in the first two years of life. In G. E. Speidel & K. E. Nelson (Eds.), *The many faces of imitation in language learning* (pp. 23–51). New York: Springer-Verlag.

Meltzoff, A. N., & Gopnik, A. (1993). The role of imitation in understanding persons and developing a theory of mind. In S. Baron-Cohen, H. Tager-Flusberg, & D. Cohen (Eds.), *Understanding other minds: Perspectives from autism* (pp. 335–366). Oxford, UK: Oxford University Press.

Mundy, P., Sigman, M., & Kasari, C. (1994). Joint attention, developmental level and symptom presentation in autism. *Development and Psychopathology, 6*, 389–401.

Mundy, P., Sigman, M., Ungerer, J., & Sherman, T. (1986). Defining the social deficits of autism: The contribution of nonverbal communication measures. *Journal of Child Psychology and Psychiatry, 27*, 657–669.

Mundy, P., Sigman, M., Ungerer, J. A., & Sherman, T. (1987). Nonverbal communication and play correlates of language development in autistic children. *Journal of Autism and Developmental Disorders, 17*, 349–364.

Osterling, J., & Dawson, G. (1993, March). *Early recognition of children with autism: A study of first year birthday home video tapes*. Paper presented at the annual meeting of the Society for Research in Child Development, New Orleans, LA.

Ozonoff, S. (1995). Executive functions in autism. In E. Schopler & G. B. Mesibov (Eds.), *Learning and cognition in autism* (pp. 199–219). New York: Plenum Press.

Ozonoff, S., & McEvoy, R. E. (1994). A longitudinal study of executive function and theory of mind development in autism. *Development and Psychopathology, 6*, 415–431.

Ozonoff, S., Pennington, B. F., & Rogers, S. J. (1991). Executive function deficits in high-functioning autistic children: Relationship to theory of mind. *Journal of Child Psychology and Psychiatry, 32*, 1081–1106.

Pennington, B. F., & Ozonoff, S. (1996). Executive functions and developmental psychopathology. *Journal of Child Psychology and Psychiatry, 37*, 51–87.

Riguet, C. B., Taylor, N. D., Benaroya, S., & Klein, L. S. (1981). Symbolic play in autistic, Down's, and normal children of equivalent mental age. *Journal of Autism and Developmental Disorders, 11*, 439–448.

Rogers, S. J., Ozonoff, S., & Maslin-Cole, C. (1991). A comparative study of attachment behavior in young children with autism or other psychiatric disorders. *Journal of the American Academy of Child and Adolescent Psychiatry, 30*, 483–488.

Rogers, S. J., & Pennington, B. F. (1991). A theoretical approach to the deficits in infantile autism. *Development and Psychopathology, 3*, 137–162.

Rutter, M. (1979). Language, cognition and autism. In R. Katzman (Ed.), *Congenital and acquired cognitive disorders* (pp. 247–264). New York: Raven Press.

Schacter, D. L., & Moscovitch, M. (1984). Infants, amnesics and dissociable memory systems. In M. Moscovitch (Ed.), *Infant memory : Its relation to normal and pathological memory in humans and animals* (pp. 173–216). New York: Plenum Press.

Shah, A., & Frith, U. (1983). An islet of ability in autistic children: A research note. *Journal of Child Psychology and Psychiatry, 24*, 613–620.

Shulman, C., Yirmiya, N., & Greenbaum, C. W. (1995). From categorization to classification: A comparison among individuals with autism, mental retardation, and normal development. *Journal of Abnormal Psychology, 104*, 601–609.

Sigman, M., Mundy, P., Sherman, T., & Ungerer, J. (1986). Social interactions of autistic, mentally retarded and normal children and their caregivers. *Journal of Child Psychology and Psychiatry, 27*, 647–656.

Sigman, M. & Ruskin, E. (1999). Social competence in children with autism, Down Syndrome and other developmental delays: A longitudinal study. *Monographs of the Society for Research in Child Development*, Serial No. 256, *64*(1). Chicago, IL: University of Chicago Press.

Sigman, M., & Ungerer, J. A. (1984a). Attachment behaviors in autistic children. *Journal of Autism and Developmental Disorders, 14*, 231–244.

Sigman, M., & Ungerer, J. A. (1984b). Cognitive and language skills in autistic, mentally retarded, and normal children. *Developmental Psychology, 20*, 293–302.

Sigman, M. D., Kasari, C., Kwon, J., & Yirmiya, N. (1992). Responses to the negative emotions of others by autistic, mentally retarded, and normal children. *Child Development, 63*, 796–807.

Smith, I. M., & Bryson, S. E. (1994). Imitation and action in autism: A critical review. *Psychological Bulletin, 116*, 259–273.

Snow, M. E., Hertzig, M. E., & Shapiro, T. (1987). Expression of emotion in young autistic children. *Journal of the American Academy of Child and Adolescent Psychiatry, 26*, 836–838.

Sodian, B., & Frith, U. (1992). Deception and sabotage in autistic, retarded and normal children. *Journal of Child Psychology and Psychiatry, 33*, 591–605.

Spiker, D., & Ricks, M. (1984). Visual self-recognition in autistic children: Developmental relationships. *Child Development, 55*, 214–225.

Stone, W. L., & Caro-Martinez, L. M. (1990). Naturalistic observations of spontaneous communication in autistic children. *Journal of Autism and Developmental Disorders, 20*, 437–453.

Tager-Flusberg, H. (1985). Basic level and superordinate level categorization in autistic, mentally retarded and normal children. *Journal of Experimental Child Psychology, 40*, 450–469.

Tager-Flusberg, H. (1993). What language reveals about the understanding of minds in children with autism. In S. Baron-Cohen, H. Tager-Flusberg, & D. Cohen (Eds.), *Understanding other minds: Perspectives from autism* (pp. 138–157). Oxford, UK: Oxford University Press.

Tager-Flusberg, H., Calkins, S., Nolin, T. L., Anderson, M. J., & Chadwick-Dias, A. M. (1990). A longitudinal study of language acquisition in autistic and Down syndrome children. *Journal of Autism and Developmental Disorders, 20*, 1–20.

Tan, J., & Harris, P. (1991). Autistic children understand seeing and wanting. *Development and Psychopathology, 3*, 163–174.

Ungerer, J. A., & Sigman, M. (1981). Symbolic play and language comprehension in autistic children. *Journal of the American Academy of Child Psychiatry, 20*, 318–338.

Ungerer, J. A., & Sigman, M. (1987). Categorization skills and language development in autistic children. *Journal of Autism and Developmental Disorders, 17*, 3–16.

Waterhouse, L., Fein, D., & Modahl, C. (1996). Neurofunctional mechanisms in autism. *Psychological Review, 103*, 457–489.

Wing, L., & Gould, J. (1979). Severe impairments of social interaction and associated abnormalities in children: Epidemiology and classification. *Journal of Autism and Developmental Disorders, 9*, 11–29.

Yirmiya, N., Kasari, C., Sigman, M., & Mundy, P. (1989). Facial expressions of affect in autistic, mentally retarded and normal children. *Journal of Child Psychology and Psychiatry, 30*, 725–735.

Yirmiya, N., & Shulman, C. (1996). Seriation, conservation, and theory of mind abilities in individuals with autism, individuals with mental retardation, and normally developing children. *Child Development, 67*, 2045–2059.

Yirmiya, N., Sigman, M., Kasari, C., & Mundy, P. (1992). Empathy and cognition in high-functioning children with autism. *Child Development, 63*, 150–160.

Yirmiya, N., Sigman, M., & Zacks, D. (1994). Perceptual perspective-taking and seriation abilities in high functioning children with autism. *Development and Psychopathology, 6*, 263–272.

35

Psychopathology in Individuals with Mental Retardation

Henry T. Sachs and Rowland P. Barrett

INTRODUCTION

Mental retardation is a categorization for a heterogeneous group of individuals with deficits in cognitive and adaptive functioning manifest prior to their 18th birthday. Those presenting with mental retardation display individual patterns of strengths and weaknesses across academic, language, social, emotional, and physical skills performances. The developmental course for individuals with mental retardation is not as inflexible as once thought. Multiple, unique developmental challenges face these children and their caregivers alike. How these challenges are resolved contributes significantly to the eventual developmental outcomes of children with mental retardation.

Mental retardation is not a disorder. Instead, it is a deviation in development that increases the risk of mental disorder. Until recently, mental retardation was wrongly viewed as a protective or exclusionary factor in mental disorders. "Diagnostic overshadowing" (Reiss, Levitan, & Szyszko, 1982) attributed most behavioral and emotional abnormalities in those with mental retardation to their cognitive limitations or underlying medical condition. However, it is now clear that individuals with mental retardation have three to four times the general population risk for the full range of psychiatric disorders (cf. Matson & Barrett, 1993). This is not surprising when one considers the factors contributing to developmental psychopathology: biology, learned behavior, psychodynamic issues, social factors, family systems functioning, and cognitive abilities. Mental retardation and its various etiologies are likely to impact on most or all of these components. In this regard, individuals with mental retardation and psychiatric disorder represent a unique population requiring the integration of numerous treatment modalities.

Henry T. Sachs and Rowland P. Barrett • Department of Psychiatry and Human Behavior, Brown University School of Medicine, Emma Pendleton Bradley Hospital, East Providence, Rhode Island 02915.

Handbook of Developmental Psychopathology, Second Edition, edited by Arnold J. Sameroff, Michael Lewis, and Suzanne M. Miller. Kluwer Academic/Plenum Publishers, New York, 2000.

DIAGNOSIS OF MENTAL RETARDATION

Diagnostic Criteria

There are several different diagnostic criteria for mental retardation. The *International Classification of Diseases*, 10th edition (ICD-10; World Health Organization, 1992) identifies mental retardation as "arrested or incomplete development of the brain … during the developmental period," leading to the impairment of specific skills. The American Association of Mental Retardation (1992) emphasizes limitations in current adaptive functioning combined with subaverage intellectual functioning.

The *Diagnostic and Statistical Manual for Mental Disorders*, 4th edition (DSM-IV; American Psychiatric Association, 1994) contains the most widely used clinical definition in the United States. The three criteria for mental retardation include (1) significantly subaverage intellectual functioning as represented by an IQ of approximately 70 or below; (2) concurrent deficits or impairment in adaptive functioning in at least two of the following areas: communication, self-care home living, social/interpersonal skills, use of community resources, self-direction, functional academic skills, work, leisure, health, and safety; and (3) onset before the age of 18 years.

Subtypes

DSM-IV categorizes four subtypes of mental retardation (mild, moderate, severe, profound) based on intellectual impairment that is accompanied by commensurate deficits in adaptive behavior. Those with *mild* mental retardation constitute a vast majority of individuals with mental retardation and are characterized by an IQ between 55 and 70. Individuals with mild mental retardation typically develop social and communication skills by age 4, and eventually achieve academic skills approximating the sixth-grade level. For many children with mild mental retardation, cognitive deficits will be misinterpreted as decreased motivation, oppositionality, or attentional deficits, and appropriate special education interventions will not be sought. Many will eventually become self-supportive, but some may need assistance when facing unusual personal and social stressors. Some also will require ongoing vocational, social, and self-care support.

Individuals with *moderate* mental retardation have an IQ between 40 and 55, and usually develop communication skills in early childhood. They may obtain academic skills commensurate with the second-grade level and might have great difficulty with abstract concepts. They will usually be able to interpret social cues but may have difficulty organizing a timely and appropriate response to social interactions. Even as adults, individuals with moderate mental retardation will likely require increased supervision and supportive vocational and living arrangements in comparison with their mildly affected counterparts.

Severe mental retardation implies an IQ of 25–40. Individuals in this diagnostic category develop very limited language and self-care skills. They often have concurrent medical problems and may require significant professional supervision throughout life.

An IQ of below 25 signifies *profound* mental retardation and considerable impairment requiring lifelong supervision. Neurological impairments are most common in this group. Skills for simple tasks, such as basic communication, may be learned with frequent repetition and dedicated individual attention.

Instead of IQ-derived (i.e., mild, moderate, severe, profound) levels of mental retardation, as characterized by the ICD-10 and DSM-IV, the AAMR definition emphasizes identification of an individual's specific areas of "ability" rather than "disability," and then classifies the intensity of needed support services in various cognitive and adaptive behavioral domains. The intent is to drive recognition of the relative strengths of individuals with mental retardation and create an awareness among service providers, researchers, and policymakers that the population is vastly heterogeneous, even within sets of individuals possessing a common IQ.

Epidemiology

The statistical component of the definition of mental retardation would presume a population prevalence of approximately 3% (2 standard deviations below the mean in a normal distribution of intelligence). However, studies (cf. Murphy, Boyle, Schendel, Decoufle, & Yeargin-Allsopp, 1998) have repeatedly demonstrated a prevalence rate equal to or less than 1% (Baird & Sadovnick, 1985), with males being 50% more likely to have mental retardation. Males also are at greater risk of genetic abnormality (McLaren & Bryson, 1987) and are more likely to come to professional attention for psychiatric (i.e., aggressive, disruptive behaviors) disorders. Approximately 2.5 million individuals in the United States have mental retardation (Centers for Disease Control, 1996), which is identified as the largest categorical disability among children. The prevalence rate of mental retardation in children between the ages of 6 and 17 is 11.4/1,000.

The reasons for the apparent overestimation of mental retardation prevalence is probably multifactorial. The mortality rate for those with moderate-profound mental retardation is elevated (McLaren & Bryson, 1987). Genetic counseling and prenatal testing have decreased the likelihood of children with chromosomal abnormalities. Newborn screening, hormone replacement, vaccination, and immunotherapy have nearly eliminated some causes of mental retardation (Alexander, 1998). Finally, improvements in early childhood nutrition and education have decreased the rate of mild mental retardation, the classification most likely impacted by environmental variables associated with poverty (Thompson & Hupp, 1992).

Undiagnosed mental retardation also plays a role in suppressing prevalence rates. As individuals become adults and function independently in society, they no longer meet the adaptive impairment criteria of mental retardation. If mental retardation is not identified during the school years, when academic expectations are more stringent and objective, it is much less likely that a person will be seen as mentally retarded in the working world.

Etiology

The potential etiologies for mental retardation are as diverse as they are numerous (Accardo & Capute, 1998). Chromosomal abnormalities, deficits of metabolism, intrauterine infections, and toxic exposures or brain developmental errors are among the prenatal causes of mental retardation. Normally developed fetuses may experience perinatal insult. Toxemia, obstetrical trauma, intracranial hemorrhage, hydrocephalus, seizures, and infections may create permanent deficits. Throughout the child's development, head injuries, infections, seizure disorders, genetic disorders, toxic exposures and/or environmental deprivation may contribute to a presentation consistent with mental retardation.

Specific etiologies are most frequently uncovered in individuals with severe and profound mental retardation. Early studies (e.g., Zigler, 1967) emphasize the role of cultural and familial factors, and social and sensory deprivation in children with mild mental retardation. Low socioeconomic status, maternal education, positive family histories of mental retardation, consanguinity, child abuse, and child neglect have been identified as risk factors for mild mental retardation. More recent studies, however, have found the majority of children with mild mental retardation to have some associated medical risk (Murtiaro, 1990; Al-Ansari, 1993).

Associated Disabilities

In comparison to the general population, children with mental retardation are more likely to have significant disabilities (Frazier, Barrett, Feinstein, & Walters, 1997). The frequency of associated physical disabilities increases in proportion to the level of cognitive and adaptive delay. Blindness and hearing impairment occur at 30 and 20 times the rate of the general population, respectively (Baroff, 1986), in those with severe to profound mental retardation. Cerebral palsy, scoliosis, kyphosis, and other impairments of motor functioning are much more frequent. Even constipation, enuresis, and encopresis have significant impacts on social and life skills development in those with mental retardation.

CULTURAL INFLUENCES

The societal perception of those with mental retardation has changed dramatically over the past 30 years. Deinstitutionalization, academic mainstreaming, increased respect for individual rights, and the deemphasis of chemical restraint have required shifting paradigms for treatment and support that are still evolving. Increased societal acceptance has been gradual, but many obstacles still face individuals with mental retardation and their families.

FAMILY STRESS

Family stress is often significantly increased while parents care for a child with mental retardation. These children will often have coexisting conditions requiring frequent medical involvement (Knoll, 1992). The paroxysmal nature of seizures, the loss of functioning in numerous associated degenerative genetic disorders, and the monitoring of multiple medications and their potential side effects contribute to heightened parental vigilance and a perception of greater fragility in the child.

The normal maturation of the family is inhibited or may even regress as the child fails to meet developmental milestones. Constant advocacy for special education and support services diverts energy from other family responsibilities. Parental career progress may be impacted. Siblings often feel ignored or overburdened and may exhibit problematic behaviors (Lobato, 1990; Stoneman & Berman, 1993). The family's sense of loss and guilt in not having the anticipated "perfect child" cannot be overlooked (Lewis, 1998).

The parents may have to master many skills unique to their situation (Baker, 1989). More intensive behavioral management techniques or medical care interventions may be needed. Up to 80% of children with developmental delays have significant sleep difficulties (Quine, 1989). This may lead to pervasive family sleep deprivation that further increases stress and limits adaptability. There is also an increased incidence of mental retardation and illiteracy in family members of probands with mental retardation. This may impact on a family's coping ability in the face of the unique demands associated with raising a child with mental retardation (Knoll, 1992).

DEVELOPMENTAL CHALLENGES OF MENTAL RETARDATION

Children and adolescents with mental retardation encounter many developmental challenges unique to the population. The great variety of challenges children may face is dictated by the extent of their cognitive and adaptive limitations, any associated disabilities or medical problems, and their support network's ability to assist them in addressing these challenges. While the developmental course of these children is influenced by the inherent limitations of their mental retardation, how these developmental challenges are addressed contributes to any subsequent developmental psychopathology.

Infancy

Infancy is characterized by the development of attachment, self-regulation, and environmental awareness and exploration (Lieberman & Pawl, 1988). Mental retardation and associated disorders may disrupt mastery in each of these areas. Many developmental processes in infancy focus on strengthening attachment. Eye contact, a social smile, and cooing and other vocalizations are often delayed or nonexistent in children with mental retardation. For infants with significant neurological or physical disabilities, uncertainty about their survival or prognosis, long-term hospitalization postnatally, or prolonged intrusive medical interventions also inhibit normal attachment.

Families often experience anger, denial, sorrow, and a prolonged grieving process (Lewis & McLean, 1982) in response to having a child with developmental delays. This may also interfere with the attachment process. In children with more subtle delays, the inability to achieve milestones at expected intervals may lead to misgivings about parental skills and increasing frustration. Pervasive Developmental Disorders (American Psychiatric Association, 1994), often associated with mental retardation, create further obstacles to attachment.

Delays in motor coordination and exploration of the environment often create a greater dependence on caregivers that is a harbinger of future interactive patterns. This may be enhanced by comorbid medical disorders, such as seizures, that enhance parental vigilance. Conversely, social withdrawal and isolation are frequent presentations.

Early Childhood

Many children's developmental delays are identified during this period. Parental response, both emotionally and in terms of expectations, impact on this period of personal mastery. Maintaining unrealistic expectations of trying to "prove the experts wrong" leads to increasing frustration and tension in the parent–child relationship. Conversely, removing or minimizing expectations may inhibit the development of many key skills. This may create an environment of overprotection or chronic parental apathy that squelches individual initiative.

Language development is usually delayed in persons with mental retardation. Mild delays are often overlooked or misinterpreted. Early intervention, which can be very helpful, is often unintentionally delayed. Deficits in language and communication development are some of the best predictors of behavioral difficulties in children with developmental disabilities (Carr & Durand, 1985). Frustration at not being able to communicate needs or desires may lead to disruptive, aggressive, or self-injurious behavior. Social failures are often the result of an inability to follow the flow of communication and basic interpersonal cues. Isolation or increased reliance on selected caregivers may be inadvertently reinforced. In this regard, it is important to recognize that children with specific language disorders may develop effective alternative communication systems to express their needs (Bondy & Frost, 1994).

Self-care skills are frequently delayed. Associated fine and gross motor delays may prevent children from successfully dressing, going to the toilet, or feeding themselves. Children with less severe delays may express the desire to perform these tasks without the requisite skills. This may lead to increasing conflict with caregivers. For those with severe or profound mental retardation, there is often a lifelong inability to contribute effectively to activities of daily living. Opportunities for child care may be greatly reduced by the child's lack of self-care skills. Unfortunately, it is just those parents who must continue providing their children with intensive assistance who would benefit most from more readily available child care.

Spontaneous, meaningful play may be delayed or missing. Children with severe and profound mental retardation may engage in seemingly undirected or self-stimulatory behavior instead of appropriate play. Children with lesser delays may only develop some symbolic play as they are about to enter school. Isolated or parallel play may predominate, especially when communicative skills are significantly impaired.

As with all children, many factors during this formative period contribute to personality development. The challenges of skills mastery, communication, emotional and physiological self-regulation, and how caregivers address these issues have significant implications. For children with mild and moderate mental retardation, self-esteem, trust, and perceived competence form the basis of interpersonal relationships and a sense of self in the world. For those with more severe delays, the caregiver's ability to assist the child effectively in regulating responses to internal and environmental stimuli helps create a lifelong style of behavior.

Childhood

For many children with mental retardation, beginning school is the first exposure to a large number of children without disabilities. It may be the first time descriptors such as "mentally retarded," "slow learner," or other pejorative terms are encountered. This may be particularly challenging to children with mild mental retardation. While increased academic mainstreaming has elevated the awareness of many children regarding disabilities, children with mental retardation often are still perceived as different and are the target of peer taunting and rejection. As importantly, they perceive themselves as different. This becomes particularly challenging in the later elementary grades as peers become less tolerant of anyone seen as different. It is also a time when children with mild and moderate mental retardation become increasingly aware of their limitations. Social withdrawal, isolation, and depression are often manifest during this period. Some children display externalizing or acting-out behavior as an increasing desperation to be socially accepted coincides with peers increased willingness to use them as a foil.

Participation in extracurricular and community activities is a hallmark of this age. Athletics may be inaccessible for some with significant associated physical handicaps. The nationwide Special Olympics initiative and greater understanding and support from many school districts have increased the participation rate of children with developmental delays in athletics. Group activities such as scouting have created subgroups that are more geared toward children with special needs but may isolate them from the mainstream, increasing their awareness of perceived differences. Dance and martial arts classes are often very well received by parents and children alike.

Most children with mental retardation need support in the classroom in terms of either special resource support or placement in a self-contained special education classroom. As peers tackle more demanding language and abstract concepts, children with mild mental retardation increasingly struggle to keep up. Academic failures are common. For children with more severe delays, the goals of education often change from preparation for higher education to life skills and vocational activities, further differentiating them from peers. The rigid demands of an academic schedule may be very different from the previous flexibility of home. Children with mental retardation will have greater difficulty adapting to this change. This difficulty will often be expressed behaviorally as they are unable to convey via communicative skills the ensuing frustration and confusion. The subtleties of communication and behavioral routines, well learned by families, may be lost on teachers caring for numerous children with varying special needs.

Adolescence

Adolescence is a challenging period for everyone. Physical changes, striving for greater independence and social acceptance, are even more difficult for those with cognitive and adaptive skills deficits.

Increasing sensitivity of the erogenous zones may lead to inappropriate touching in children unable to master social rules. Some females with moderate to profound mental retardation may be unable to understand the physical sensations of menstruation. Physical discomfort may lead to increased irritability, self-injury, and aggression (Kaminer, Feinstein, Barrett, Tylenda, & Hole, 1988). Personal hygiene may also be a problem.

The commonly held prejudice that those with mental retardation are likely perpetrators of sexual assaults belies the reality that they more likely may be victims of sexual mistreatment or abuse (Ammerman, Hersen, van Hasselt, Lubetsky, & Sieck, 1994). Adolescence is a particularly risky period. Many children at this age are living in institutional settings, such as group homes, which may further increase the risk of abuse.

Deficits in social skills are particularly debilitating during this period (Borden, Walters, & Barrett, 1995). Complex social interactions, rapidly changing trends, and group cohesiveness are the norm. It is very challenging for adolescents with mild mental retardation to keep up with their developmentally intact age-mates. Friendships with nondelayed peers, which may have flourished for years, are strained as these peers begin dating, working, and expressing their own independence. Children with developmental delays may have the same dreams and expectations as their peers. Status symbols such as driving or a "cool" job may be out of reach. Medical or neurological conditions may contribute to physical abnormalities at an age when personal appearance has heightened significance. Depression and withdrawal are common as social failures accumulate. Suicidal ideation is not unusual (Walters, Barrett, Knapp, & Borden, 1995). Relationships with adults are often more rewarding. Somatization or creative storytelling may increase as a means of soliciting professional help or to otherwise fill the void of loneliness.

Academic challenges often change during this period. Vocational skills development predominates. Those with severe or profound mental retardation will frequently be taught repetitive "prevocational" tasks that are often minimally rewarding. For adolescents with mild to moderate delays, attending vocational classes may be stigmatizing and a source of shame (Lewis, 1998). Self-worth may diminish rapidly as teens with mental retardation come to blame themselves for having a developmental disability.

Families face different stressors. Parents are aging and may feel increasingly overwhelmed by the demands of a child with developmental delays. The normal cycle of increasing child independence may be disrupted, forcing families to face issues that have previously been avoided. The opportunity for increasing freedom for the couple as the children leave the nest may be illusory. Issues of long-term care arise when parents are no longer able to support more seriously delayed children. This is frequently a period when agencies become involved in an individual's life to plan vocational, social, and residential opportunities. Many families find it stressful to relinquish some or all of the care of their children to others. Brothers and sisters may be overprotective or resentful of a sibling with special needs and find that the changes of adolescence have a greater impact on family functioning.

Adulthood

As many with mild developmental delays and some with moderate developmental delays reach adulthood, they no longer are considered mentally retarded. Relieved of the imposed structure of academics, many find appropriate jobs and housing arrangements that allow them to live independently. Unfortunately, stressors around child rearing, social relationships, and occupational or financial matters may lead to minor or major regression that requires additional family or professional support. Others with mild to moderate mental retardation receive support around occupational, residential, and social issues as needed. Self-motivation and time management may be a challenge when rewards (i.e., a paycheck) are not immediate. In less supported worksites, relationships with co-workers can be challenging. Being criticized or taken advantage of is common.

Managing the home finances, food shopping, laundry, and other life skills may be daunting tasks (Antonello, 1996). Those with mild to moderate delays are more at risk for con artists and "scams." Some engage in inappropriate or illegal activities without understanding the full import of their actions. Many have guardians. Sometimes individuals and guardians disagree on issues, which may lead to tension and frustration. All of these factors may contribute to greater dependence on others than the individual desires.

Those with developmental delays may have physical handicaps, limited mobility, or limited access to transportation. This enhances difficulties in keeping appointments and job expectations, and creates further isolation. Individuals with severe to profound mental retardation in adulthood often work in a very structured and supportive environment. Behavioral issues such as aggression, self-injury, compulsions, and opposition are common and limit productivity. Ongoing assistance around self-care skills requires close supervision by family or agencies.

COMORBID PSYCHOPATHOLOGY

The incidence of psychopathology in those with mental retardation is elevated above the rate observed in nonretarded individuals (Reiss, 1990). One study (Einfield & Tonge, 1996) found that 20% of children with an IQ less than 70 had severe emotional or behavioral disorders, and only 1 in 10 of these children and adolescents with major psychiatric disorders had received specialized psychiatric care. Individual and family stress, neurological impairment, sensory deficits, and limited adaptive skills increase the risk of developing psychopathology.

Controversy persists as to the efficacy of DSM-IV diagnoses in those with severe to profound mental retardation. It is not clear if abnormal behaviors seen in this population meet the specific criteria for psychiatric disorders. However, in those with mild to moderate mental retardation, presentations meeting DSM-IV diagnostic criteria are readily apparent (Harden & Sahl, 1997; Szymanski, 1994).

Abnormal behaviors are often the presenting complaint of dually diagnosed individuals and a functional analysis of behaviors, including a review of antecedent issues and behavioral consequences, is necessary to better understand the etiology of a given behavior.

Self-Injurious Behavior

Self-injurious behavior (SIB) is common in persons with mental retardation, occurring in 11% of persons in community residences and 22% in state institutions (Hill, Balow, & Bruininks, 1985). Self-injurious responses may range from skin picking and headbanging to severe self-mutilation. There is an inverse correlation between the amount and severity of SIB and expressive language and cognitive development (Schroeder, Schroeder, Smith, & Dalldorf, 1978). Self-injury may be a final common pathway for several psychiatric and behavioral phenomena. Identifying specific etiologies will presumably dictate appropriate treatment interventions.

Inadvertently reinforced self-injury may occur in children with limited communication skills or sensory deficits. These children appear to learn rapidly that engaging in self-mutilating behaviors commands instant and close attention from caregivers. Often, these behavioral patterns arise from periods of physical discomfort such as headaches, earaches, dental pain, menstrual periods, constipation, or eczema. The child's inability to describe discomfort leads to physical expression of pain and frustration.

For some children, self-injury appears to be internally reinforced by the release of endogenous opiates (Barrett, Feinstein, & Hole, 1989). Repeated self-injury apparently induces endorphin release and a temporarily favorable sensory consequence. In these situations, medications that inhibit the effectiveness of endogenous opiates effectively extinguish the drive to self-injury (Sandman et al., 1998).

Some SIBs suggest an underlying affective disorder or obsessive–compulsive disorder (Matson, 1986). Cyclic presentations, co-occurring vegetative symptoms, and associated affective changes may indicate a mood disorder. In mild to moderate mental retardation, a child or adolescent will often be able to describe depressed mood, anhedonia, or even manic symptoms. The apparent ego-dystonic nature of self-injury and the desire for imposed physical restraint to prevent the acts in some are consistent within a compulsive drive. This may be difficult to differentiate from stereotypical behaviors often seen in individuals with severe developmental delays. Interestingly, medications that address mood disorders and obsessive–compulsive behaviors have diminished SIB in some individuals (Cook, 1992; Kastner, Finesmith, & Walsh, 1993). Mental disorders such as Lesch–Nyhan syndrome, and chromosomal abnormalities such as Cornelia de Lange syndrome (Opitz, 1985), have phenotypic presentations that include severe self-injury.

Abnormal Movements

Individuals with mental retardation and associated neurological impairments are at increased risk for movement disorders. Motor tics and Tourette's syndrome are common in this population. Differentiating motor tics from stereotypies and vocal tics from echolalia is challenging and impacts treatment recommendations. Vocal and complex motor tics often are misdiagnosed as oppositional, aggressive, and disruptive behavior.

Many adolescents and young adults with mental retardation have been on neuroleptics for extended periods, targeting aggression or disruptive behavior. Comorbid neurological abnormalities increase the risk of tardive dyskinesia, involuntary muscle movements often centering on the oral musculature. The neuroleptics also may increase a sense of restlessness known as akathesia. This may present as hyperactivity, irritability, or dysphoria and, if not properly diagnosed, could lead to a cascade of inappropriate psychopharmacological and behavioral interventions (Wilson, Lott, & Tsai, 1998).

Aggressive/Destructive Behaviors

Aggressive behaviors appear in approximately 20% of the community sample of children and adolescents with developmental disabilities (Quine, 1986). These behaviors contribute significantly to the social isolation and institutional placement of this population (Hill & Bruininks, 1981). Frustration stemming from communicative deficits is a common source of aggressive and destructive behaviors. Adjustment difficulties created by environmental changes may be expressed aggressively. Disruption in living arrangements, support staff, or routine that is not understood or explained can lead to significant outbursts. If these outbursts lead to the reinstatement of the status quo, such behavioral patterns are strongly reinforced.

Mood disorders, both major depression (Dosen, 1984) and mania (Sovner, 1989), may present as disruptive behavior. This is especially challenging to diagnose in nonverbal children. Associated changes in sleep, appetite, and energy patterns are frequently seen. There is also often an ebb and flow to the presenting symptoms.

Previous traumatic events including abuse and neglect may create a long-standing pattern of disruptive behaviors in an attempt at self-protection. Withdrawal and social isolation may often be seen in these situations. The interictal, or between-seizure, phase in some seizure disorders may increase aggressive tendencies. Comorbid schizophrenia or substance abuse may lead to increased confusion and poor impulse control, exacerbating aggressive tendencies.

Attentional and Motivational Deficits

Attentional difficulties and motivational deficits are found as common presentations for numerous disorders, including attention-deficit/hyperactivity disorder (ADHD), depression, mania, anxiety, and hyperthyroidism. Differentiation of these disorders in cognitively limited and often medically complicated populations is particularly challenging but important. There is evidence that treatments helpful to otherwise intact children with ADHD are useful for those with mild mental retardation (Payton, Burkhart, Hersen, & Helsel, 1989). Those with severe to profound cognitive delays are more resistant to standard pharmacological intervention (Aman, Marks, Turbott, Wilsher, & Merry, 1991). The symptom presentation in these individuals may represent underlying neurocognitive deficits in attention and arousal, or other psychiatric disorders, and not ADHD per se. Medications for seizures or other medical conditions as well as sensory deficits may also diminish attention (cf. Aman & Singh, 1988; Reiss & Aman, 1998).

Anxiety

Rates of significant anxiety symptoms appear to be much higher in children with mental retardation, approximately 25% (Benson, 1985), than the general population estimate of 2–5% (Clum & Picket, 1984). The typical predominance of females is not seen. It remains unclear if an individual's level of cognitive delay contributes to the severity and frequency of anxiety disorders.

The inability of many with developmental delays to describe internal states accurately is particularly problematic around anxiety disorders. Careful observation is often the most helpful diagnostic tool. One must differentiate general anxiety, avoidance, panic, posttraumatic stress, and obsessive–compulsive behaviors from several other diagnoses. This list should include mania, ADHD, stereotypical movements, akathesia, hyperthyroidism, and seizures.

Limited adaptability, sensory deficits, concrete thought processes, and increased family stress may also contribute to an increased rate of anxiety symptoms in this population. If identified, these symptoms are frequently responsive to typical interventions (cf. Barlow, 1993; Reiss & Aman, 1998; Werry & Aman, 1993).

Adjustment Disorders

Those with mental retardation often thrive and rely on consistency in routine. Even minor changes in the environment can have a disproportionately significant impact on behavior and mood. Careful analysis of recent changes in living situation, education, or caretaker interaction is necessary when sudden changes in behavior are seen. The DSM-IV criteria of resolution of symptoms in 6 months is not always relevant in this population. It is not unusual for children with mental retardation to be excluded from full or partial explanations for the sudden disappearance of a relative from death or moving. Entering the school situation where one is teased or ignored can lead to withdrawal or provocative behaviors across settings. Entering or leaving institutions may create changes in mood or behavior as long-standing routines are disrupted. Understanding underlying issues is essential for efficacious treatment.

CONCLUSIONS

Individuals with mental retardation have a high incidence and wide variety of psychopathological presentations. Many biological, social, and psychological factors contribute to this increased susceptibility. These persons present unique challenges in diagnosis and treatment. However, long-held prejudices as to the immutability of their life circumstance are unfounded and detrimental. The tendency of professionals to deny the independent existence of psychopathology in this population perpetuates the wrongful notion that emotional and behavioral disorders are a base component of mental retardation. This is particularly harmful, first, because it is not true, and second, because it results in diminished attempts to identify and secure proper treatment. Although mental retardation may be correctly viewed as confounding the diagnosis and treatment of psychiatric illness in this population, it is important for professionals to acknowledge that early and accurate mental health intervention may have a profound impact on the quality of life of the individuals involved as well as that of their families.

REFERENCES

Accardo, P. J., & Capute, A. J. (1998). Mental retardation. *Mental Retardation and Developmental Disabilities Research Reviews, 4,* 2–5.

Al-Ansari, A. (1993). Etiology of mild mental retardation among Bahmani children: A community-based case control study. *Mental Retardation, 31*(3), 140–143.

Alexander, D. (1998). Prevention of mental retardation: Four decades of research. *Mental Retardation and Developmental Disabilities Research Reviews, 4,* 50–58.

Aman, M. G., Marks, R. E., Turbott, S. H., Wilsher, C. P., & Merry, S. N. (1991). The clinical effect of methylphenidate and thioridazine in intellectually sub-average children. *Journal of the American Academy of Child and Adolescent Psychiatry, 30,* 246–256.

Aman, M. G., & Singh, N. N. (Eds.). (1988). *Psychopharmacology of the developmental disabilities.* New York: Springer-Verlag.

American Association of Mental Retardation. (1992). *Mental retardation: Definition, classification and systems of support, Special 9th Edition.* Washington, DC: Author.

American Psychiatric Association. (1994). *Diagnostic and statistical manual of mental disorders* (4th ed.). Washington, DC: Author.

Ammerman, R. T., Hersen, M., van Hasselt, V., Lubetsky, M. J., & Sieck, W. R. (1994). Maltreatment in psychiatrically hospitalized children and adolescents with developmental disabilities: Prevalence and correlates. *Journal of the American Academy of Child and Adolescent Psychiatry, 33,* 567–576.

Antonello, S. J. (1996). *Social skills development: Practical strategies for adolescents and adults with developmental disabilities.* Boston: Allyn & Bacon.

Baird, P. A., & Sadovnick, A. D. (1985). Mental retardation in over half a million consecutive live births: An epidemiologic study. *American Journal of Mental Deficiency, 89,* 323.

Baker, B. L. (1989). *Parent training and developmental disabilities.* Washington, DC: American Association of Mental Retardation.

Barlow, D. (Ed.). (1993). *Clinical handbook of psychological disorders* (2nd ed.). New York: Guilford Press.

Baroff, G. S. (1986). *Mental retardation: Nature, causes, and management* (2nd ed.). Washington, DC: Hemisphere.

Barrett, R. P., Feinstein, C., & Hole, W. (1989). Effects of naloxone and naltrexone on self-injury in autism: A double blind, placebo controlled analysis. *American Journal on Mental Retardation, 93,* 644–651.

Benson, B. A. (1985). Behavior disorders in mental retardation: Associations with age, sex, and level of functioning in an outpatient clinic sample. *Applied Research in Mental Retardation, 6,* 79–85.

Bondy, A. S., & Frost, L. A. (1994). The picture exchange communication system. *Focus on Autistic Behavior, 9,* 1–19.

Borden, M. C., Walters, A. S., & Barrett, R. P. (1995). Mental retardation and developmental disabilities. In V. van Hasselt & M. Hersen (Eds.), *Handbook of adolescent psychopathology: A guide to diagnosis and treatment* (pp. 497–524). New York: Lexington Books.

Carr, E. G., & Durand, V. M. (1985). Reducing behavior problems through functional communication. *Journal of Applied Behavior Analysis, 18,* 111–126.

Center for Disease Control. (1996). State-specific rates of mental retardation—United States, 1993. *Morbidity Mortality Weekly Report, 45,* 61–65.

Clum, G. A., & Pickett, L. (1984). Panic disorder and generalized anxiety disorders. In P. B. Sutkon & H. Adams (Eds.), *Comprehensive handbook of psychopathology* (pp. 123–146). New York: Plenum Press.

Cook, E. H., Rowlett, R., Jaselskis, C., & Leventhal, B. L. (1992). Fluoxetine treatment of children and adults with autistic disorder and mental retardation. *Journal of the American Academy of Child and Adolescent Psychiatry, 31,* 739–745.

Corbett, J. A. (1979). Psychiatric morbidity and mental retardation. In F. E. James & R. P. Snaith (Eds.), *Psychiatric illness and mental handicap* (pp. 11–25). London: Gaskell Press.

Dosen, A. (1984). Depressing conditions in mentally handicapped children. *Acta Paedopsychiatrica, 50,* 29–40.

Einfield, L. F., & Menolascino, F. J. (1992). Clinical assessment of psychiatric symptoms in mentally retarded individuals. *Australian New Zealand Journal of Psychiatry, 26,* 48–63.

Einfield, S. L., & Tonge, B. J. (1996). Population prevalence of psychopathology in children and adolescents with intellectual disability: II. Epidemiological findings. *Journal of Intellectual Disabilities Research, 40,* 99–109.

Frazier, J., Barrett, R. P., Feinstein, C. B., & Walters, A. S. (1997). Moderate to profound mental retardation. In J. Noshpitz (Ed.), *Handbook of child and adolescent psychiatry* (Vol. 4, pp. 397–408). New York: Wiley.

Harden, A., & Sahl, R. (1997). Psychopathology in children and adolescents with developmental disorders. *Research in Developmental Disabilities, 18,* 369–382.

Harris, J. C. (1995). *Developmental neuropsychiatry* (Vol. 2). New York: Oxford University Press.

Hill, B. K., Balow, E. A., & Bruininks, R. H. (1985). A national study of prescribed drugs in institutions and community residential facilities for mentally retarded people. *Psychopharmacology Bulletins, 21,* 279–284,

Hill, B. K., & Bruininks, R. H. (1981). *Physical and behavioral characteristics and maladaptive behavior of mentally retarded individuals in residential facilities.* Minneapolis: University of Minnesota, Department of Psychoeducational Studies.

Kaminer, Y., Feinstein, C., Barrett, R. P., Tylenda, B., & Hole, W. (1988). Menstrually related mood disorders in developmentally disabled adolescents: Review and current status. *Child Psychiatry and Human Development, 18,* 239–249.

Kastrom, T., Finesmith, R., & Walsh, K. (1993). Long-term administration of valproic acid in the treatment of affective symptoms in people with mental retardation. *Journal of Clinical Psychopharmacology, 15,* 448–451.

Knoll, J. (1992). Being a family: The experience of raising a child with a disability or chronic illness. In V. J. Bradley, J. Knoll, & J. M. Agosta (Eds.), *Emerging issues in family support* (pp. 9–56). Washington, DC: American Association of Mental Retardation.

Lewis, M. (1998). Shame and stigma. In P. Gilbert & B. Andrews (Eds.), *Shame: Interpersonal behavior, psychopathology, and culture* (pp. 126–140). New York: Oxford University Press.

Lewis, M. H., & MacLean, W. E., Jr. (1982). Issues in treating emotional disorders of the mentally retarded. In J. L. Matson & R. P. Barrett (Eds.), *Psychopathology in the mentally retarded* (pp. 1–36). New York: Grune & Stratton.

Lieberman, A. F., & Pawl, J. H. (1988). Clinical applications of attachment theory. In M. Greenberg (Ed.), *Attachment beyond infancy* (pp. 327–351). Chicago: University of Chicago Press.

Lobato, D. J. (1990). *Brothers, sisters, and special needs: Information and activities for helping young siblings of children with chronic illnesses and developmental disabilities.* Baltimore: Paul H. Brookes.

Matson, J. L. (1986). Self-injury and its relationship to diagnostic schemes in psychopathology. *Applied Research in Mental Retardation, 7,* 223–227.

Matson, J. L., & Barrett, R. P. (Eds.). (1993). *Psychopathology in the mentally retarded* (2nd ed.). Boston: Allyn & Bacon.

McLaren, J., & Bryson, S. E. (1987). Review of recent epidemiological studies of mental retardation: Prevalence associated disorders and etiology. *American Journal of Mental Retardation, 92*(5), 243–254.

Murphy, C. C., Boyle, C., Schendel, D., Decoufle, P., & Yeargin-Allsopp, M. (1998). Epidemiology of mental retardation in children. *Mental Retardation and Developmental Disabilities Research Reviews, 4,* 6–13.

Murtiaro, R. J. (1990). A population based study of mild mental retardation in children: Preliminary analysis of obstetric associations. *Journal of Mental Deficiency Research, 34,* 59–65.

Opitz, J. M. (1985). The Brachmann–deLange syndrome. *American Journal of Medical Genetics, 22,* 89–102.

Payton, J. B., Burkhart, J. E., Hersen, M., & Helsel, W. J. (1989). Treatment of ADHD in mentally retarded children: A preliminary study. *Journal of the American Academy of Child and Adolescent Psychiatry, 28,* 761–767.

Quine, L. (1986). Behavior problems in severely mentally handicapped children. *Psychological Medicine, 16,* 895–901.

Reiss, S. (1990). Prevalence of dual diagnosis in community-based day programs in the Chicago metropolitan area. *American Journal of Mental Retardation, 94,* 578–585.

Reiss, S., & Aman, M. G. (Eds.). (1998). *Psychotropic medications and developmental disabilities.* Columbus: Ohio State University Press.

Reiss, S., Levitan, G. W., & Szyszko, J. (1982). Emotional disturbance and mental retardation: Diagnostic overshadowing. *American Journal of Mental Deficiency, 86,* 567–574.

Rutter, M., Tizard, J., & Whitmore, K. (1970). *Education, health, and behavior.* London: Longman.

Sandman, C. A., Thompson, T. T., Barrett, R. P., Verhoeven, W. M., McCubbin, J. A., Schroeder, S. R., & Hetrick, W. P. (1998). Opiate blockers. In S. Reiss & M. G. Aman (Eds.), *Psychotropic medications and developmental disabilities* (pp. 291–302). Columbus: Ohio State University Press.

Schroeder, S. R., Schroeder, C. S., Smith, B., & Dalldorf, J. (1978). Prevalence of self-injurious behaviors in a large state facility for the retarded: A three year follow-up study. *Journal of Autism and Childhood Schizophrenia, 8,* 261–269.

Sovner, R. (1989). The use of valproate in the treatment of mentally retarded persons with typical and atypical bipolar disorders. *Journal of Clinical Psychiatry, 50,* 40–43.

Stoneman, Z., & Berman, P. W. (Eds.). (1993). *The effects of mental retardation, disability, and illness on sibling relationships: Research issues and challenges.* Baltimore: Paul H. Brookes.

Szymanski, L. S. (1994). Mental retardation and mental health: Concepts, aetiology, and incidence. In N. Bouras (Ed.), *Mental health in mental retardation: Recent advances and practices* (pp. 19–33). Cambridge, UK: Cambridge University Press.

Thompson, T., & Hupp, S. C. (Eds.). (1992). *Saving children at risk: Poverty and disabilities.* London: Sage.

Walters, A. S., Barrett, R. P., Knapp, L., & Borden, M. C. (1995). Suicidal behavior in children and adolescents with mental retardation. *Research in Developmental Disabilities, 16,* 85–96.

Werry, J. S., & Aman, M. G. (Eds.). (1993). *Practitioner's guide to psychoactive drugs for children and adolescents.* New York: Plenum Press.

Wilson, J. G., Lott, R. S., & Tsai, L. (1998). Side effects: Recognition and management. In S. Reiss & M. G. Aman (Eds.), *Psychotropic medications and developmental disabilities* (pp. 95–114). Columbus: Ohio State University Press.

World Health Organization. (1992). *The ICD-10 classification of mental and behavioral disorders: Clinical descriptions and diagnostic guideline.* Geneva, Switzerland: Author.

Zigler, E. (1967). Familial mental retardation: A continuing dilemma. *Science, 155,* 292–298.

36

Gender Identity Disorder

Kenneth J. Zucker

Because gender identity disorder (GID) in children is relatively uncommon, most child clinicians and researchers are likely to have had very little direct experience with it. In this chapter, I provide a selective overview of our knowledge about children with GID. In keeping with the general mission of this volume, where appropriate, I focus on the interface between typical and atypical development in my consideration of children with GID.

Some of the material in this chapter comes from our own Child and Adolescent Gender Identity Clinic. Between 1978 and 1997, 277 boys and 45 girls were referred, a sex ratio of 6.2:1. At referral, the mean age of the children was about 7 years, with a range of 3–12 years. Their mean Full-Scale IQ was at the high end of the *Average* range, with a range from the *Intellectually Deficient* to the *Very Superior*. Parents' were, on average, middle-class, with a range that fully covered the socioeconomic spectrum. About two-thirds of the children lived with both of their parents; the remaining one-third came from single-parent or reconstituted families (Zucker, Bradley, & Sanikhani, 1997). Relative to the general population, there was a disproportionate number of referred boys who were adopted in the first year of life (7.6%), mainly at birth (Zucker & Bradley, 1998).

PHENOMENOLOGY

The following two vignettes illustrate the basic phenomenology of GID.

Nathan, a 6-year-old boy with an IQ of 106, was referred at the request of his mother, who had spoken informally with a friend who was a therapist. He lived with his mother, who had a lower-middle-class socioeconomic background. Nathan was the product of a planned, but anonymous, sexual encounter. Nathan's mother was "desperate" to have a child with whom she could spend "the rest of her life" (indeed, during the assessment, Nathan's mother commented that she would rather "date" him than adults). As a consequence,

Kenneth J. Zucker • Child and Adolescent Gender Identity Clinic, Child and Family Studies Centre, Clarke Institute of Psychiatry, Toronto, Ontario M5T 1R8 Canada.

Handbook of Developmental Psychopathology, Second Edition, edited by Arnold J. Sameroff, Michael Lewis, and Suzanne M. Miller. Kluwer Academic/Plenum Publishers, New York, 2000.

Nathan's biological father was unknown to him, although he often asked his mother to marry and thus provide him with a dad.

Nathan's mother stated that he was happy in every way except in one respect: "He desperately wants to be a girl and to cut off his penis." Of particular concern to his mother was that, of late, Nathan would sing himself to sleep with a sad song: "My dreams will never come true." Nathan's mother had noted signs of cross-gender behavior since he was under 2 years of age. At that time, he began to cross-dress in an intense and compulsive way, using items such as towels and aprons.

At the time of assessment, Nathan preferred girls as playmates but complained that some of them would tease him because he acted like a girl. He was also teased quite intensely by other boys because of his cross-gender behavior. Nathan's favorite toys were Barbie dolls, of which he had "dozens," and he would spend hours enacting nurturant, benevolent female icons, such as Snow White, Sleeping Beauty, and Cinderella. During the clinical assessment, Nathan's capacity to "flip" into female roles was striking. It was as if Nathan had become another person. In fact, Nathan had brought to the assessment some of his feminine dress-up apparel. In the presence of his mother and the two interviewers, Nathan removed all of his outer clothing and put these on, commenting somewhat sadly that he hoped that if he was "good enough," we might be able to give him a "[sex change] operation" that day. Nathan's mother reported that he had no interest in athletics or rough-and-tumble play and that they were both very "frightened" by a boy they had known who had intense temper tantrums.

Aimee, a 4½-year-old girl with an IQ of 117, was referred at her mother's request. The parents were of a lower-middle-class socioeconomic background. Aimee's mother was extremely concerned about her gender identity development, but her father was not.

During an intake telephone interview, Aimee's mother was tearful as she recounted her concerns. She remarked that she had always planned not to "[sex] stereotype," as this was part of her child-rearing philosophy, but that she was now "very worried" about Aimee. She indicated that, since around the age of 2, Aimee referred to herself with stereotypical boys' names such as Johnny or Stevie. She preferred to play with swords and guns, particularly squirt guns, although it was noted that Aimee also played with dolls but that these incidents were "few and far between." In role play, Aimee was never the "mommy" but rather was one male or another, such as the "daddy," and during such enactments, she would "put on" a deeper voice. Aimee would often imitate her father by carrying around a portable phone or pretending to use a pager. Aimee was "very adamant" about not wearing dresses or skirts and, in fact, if required to, would not attend special occasions. When Aimee would don masculine dress-up apparel, she made remarks such as "I look like a great man." Regarding peer relations, Aimee's mother was not sure if she played more with girls or with boys although she noted that in the day care she attended, Aimee wanted to be with the boys "but they weren't interested." Aimee frequently expressed a wish to be a boy, or, at other times, actually insisted that she was a boy. She also expressed the desire to grow a penis and was interested in standing to urinate.

During an interview, Aimee's parents placed the onset of Aimee's cross-gender behavior at around 27 months, while she was away from her father. At this time, Aimee began to refer to herself with boys' names. Aimee's father attributed her conflicts to her desire to be like him—wanting her hair cut short like his and to wear what he wore.

Apart from Aimee's gender identity development, the parents did not report other major concerns about her socioemotional functioning. It was, however, apparent from the clinical assessment that the marital relationship was quite conflicted and at times involved physical altercations. Aimee's mother was clinically depressed and had a behavioral history consistent with borderline personality and dependent personality traits. Because Aimee's father would not agree to be interviewed alone, only aspects of his life history could be ascertained. By maternal report, he had had a marked history of sexual promiscuity and recreational drug use, the latter of which had resulted in some rather severe physical health problems. It was also apparent that there was a lot of disagreement about parenting issues: Mother saw father as very permissive ("Everything with him is a day on the beach"), and father saw mother as rigid and controlling.

Aimee was clearly quite sensitive to her mother's unpredictable mood states and would get very agitated when her mother was angry. She would tell her mother that she hated her, and call her "poo-poo, cacky, throw-up." Aimee's sensitivity to interpersonal conflict was also apparent on the Rorschach test. Several of the blots were perceived as quite threatening (e.g., sharp objects, sharks). On Card X, Aimee commented, "Dangerous stuff that can kill you. ... They look so dangerous to me. They might not to you, but they do to me." Regarding her parents' relationship, Aimee would tell her mother quite directly, "You don't like him" (i.e., her father).

These vignettes illustrate that boys and girls with GID display an array of sex-typed behavior signaling a strong psychological identification with the opposite sex and a rejection or avoidance of sex-typed behaviors more characteristic of their own sex. The behaviors occur in concert, not in isolation, and it is this behavioral patterning that is of clinical significance. From a developmental perspective, it is also important to note that the age of onset of these cross-gender behaviors is typically during the toddler and preschool years (Green, 1976), the same time period in which more normative or typical signs of gender identity development are first expressed. This suggests that the mechanisms or processes that underlie the development of GID may resemble the same processes that account for normative psychosexual differentiation, albeit in inverted form.

DIAGNOSIS, ASSESSMENT, AND REASONS FOR REFERRAL

Diagnosis

DSM-IV Diagnostic Description and Changes from DSM-III-R

In the DSM-IV (American Psychiatric Association, 1994), there were some changes in the conceptualization of GID and in the diagnostic criteria. For example, there was a reduction of diagnoses from three to one between the DSM-III-R (American Psychiatric Association, 1987) and the DSM-IV. The DSM-IV Subcommittee on Gender Identity Disorders (hereafter, the DSM-IV Subcommittee; Bradley et al., 1991) took the position that the DSM-III-R diagnoses of GID of childhood, transsexualism, and GID of adolescence or adulthood, nontranssexual type, were not qualitatively distinct disorders but reflected differences in both developmental and severity parameters. As a result, the DSM-IV Subcommittee recommended one overarching diagnosis, GID, that could be used, with appropriate variations in criteria, across the life cycle. Table 36.1 shows the DSM-IV criteria for GID. It can be seen that three criteria (Points A, B, and D) are required for the diagnosis and that Point C is an exclusion criterion.

Compared to the DSM-III and DSM-III-R, there were five main changes in the criteria for use with children:

1. The A criterion reflects the child's cross-gender identification, indexed by a total of five behavioral characteristics, of which at least four must be present. These characteristics had been listed in either the A or B criterion in the DSM-III-R.

Table 36.1. DSM-IV Diagnostic Criteria for Gender Identity Disorder

A. A strong and persistent cross-gender identification (not being merely a desire for any perceived cultural advantages of being the other sex).

In children, the disturbance is manifested by at least four (or more) of the following:

1. Repeatedly stated desire to be, or insistence that he or she is, the other sex.
2. In boys, preference for cross-dressing or simulating female attire; in girls, insistence on wearing only stereotypical masculine clothing.
3. Strong and persistent preferences for cross-sex roles in make-believe play or persistent fantasies of being the other sex.
4. Intense desire to participate in the stereotypical games and pastimes of the other sex.
5. Strong preference for playmates of the other sex.

B. Persistent discomfort with his or her sex, or a sense of inappropriateness in the gender role of that sex.

In children, the disturbance is manifested by any of the following: In boys, assertion that the penis or testes are disgusting or will disappear, or that it would be better not to have a penis, or an aversion toward rough-and-tumble play and rejection of male stereotypical toys, games, and activities; in girls, rejection of urinating in a sitting position, the assertion that she has or will grow a penis, or that she does not want to grow breasts or menstruate, or a marked aversion toward normative feminine clothing.

C. The disturbance is not concurrent with a physical intersex condition.

D. The disturbance causes clinically significant distress or impairment in social, occupational, or other important areas of functioning.

Source: Reprinted with permission of the American Psychiatric Association. Only criteria for children are listed.

2. The B criterion reflects the child's rejection of his or her anatomic status and/or rejection of same-sex stereotypical activities and behaviors. In the DSM-III-R, the B criterion had also included some behavioral signs of cross-gender identification, which are now restricted to the A criterion.

3. The criteria for boys and girls are more similar than they were in the DSM-III-R. For example, in the DSM-III-R, girls had to have a "stated" desire to be a boy, whereas boys had to have only an "intense" desire to be a girl. Moreover, the passage referring to girls in the DSM-III-R contained no reference to intensity or chronicity. In the DSM-IV, both boys and girls must manifest a "repeatedly" stated desire to be of the other sex.

4. In the DSM-III-R, a girl's desire to be of the other sex could not be "merely ... for any perceived cultural advantages from being a boy" (p. 73), whereas this proviso was not included for boys. In the DSM-IV, the proviso applies to both boys and girls.

5. In the DSM-III-R, the A criterion specified that a child must show a "persistent and intense distress" about being a boy or a girl. This phrase has been deleted from the DSM-IV A criterion; however, Point D specifies that the "disturbance ... causes clinically significant distress or impairment in social, occupational, or other important areas of functioning" (p. 538).

Reliability and Validity

Can the DSM-IV diagnosis of GID be made reliably? Because the criteria have changed, and because no field trials were conducted, this question cannot yet be answered; however, previous versions of the criteria have shown strong evidence for both reliability and validity (Zucker & Bradley, 1995).

Distress and Impairment

As noted by Zucker (1992), the DSM-III-R did not provide guidelines regarding the assessment of distress in the A criterion ("persistent and intense distress" about being a boy or a girl) or the ways in which it might be distinct from other operationalized components in the criteria (namely, the "desire" to be of the other sex). In the DSM-IV, this problem persists (except that it is now located in Point D), and there is the additional problem of defining impairment.

The inclusion of a distress/impairment criterion ("a clinical significance criterion"; American Psychiatric Association, 1994, p. 7) is not unique to GID; in fact, this criterion now appears in most of the DSM-IV diagnoses. Very little empirical work preceded the introduction of the criterion (see Spitzer & Wakefield, 1999). Indeed, the DSM-IV states that assessment of distress and impairment "is an inherently difficult clinical judgment" (p. 7).

For children with GID, we need to ask two interrelated questions: Are they distressed by their condition, and, if so, what is the source of the distress? Regarding these questions, there are two broad views. One view is that children with GID become distressed about their cross-gender behavior only after it has been interfered with (Stoller, 1975). Stoller took the position that marked cross-gender identification (in boys) was ego-syntonic because the putative familial psychodynamics that produced it were systemically syntonic.

The other view is that the distress is caused by psychopathology in the child and in the family. Coates and Person (1985) claimed that GID is a "solution" to specific forms of psychopathology in the child, particularly separation anxiety and "annihilation" anxiety, that were induced by familial psychopathology.

It is conceivable that both views are correct or that one or the other better fits individual cases. The latter view, however, is more compatible with the notion of inherent distress, whereas the former is more compatible with the notion that social pathology creates individual pathology. From a clinical standpoint, it has been my experience that from a very early age, many youngsters with GID feel a sense of discomfort regarding their status as boys or girls, which matches nicely with the DSM notion of distress. Nevertheless, in my view, there are youngsters in whom the behavioral characteristics of GID appear to be ego-syntonic, and who experience distress only when their cross-gender behavior is interfered with by others. The exact manner in which we should measure the putative distress of children with GID has not been worked out (Zucker, 1999a); however, this holds true not only for GID but also for all of the other childhood psychiatric conditions that include the distress/impairment criterion.

Regarding impairment, there are several domains in which it might be manifest in children with GID. For example, children with GID seem to have more trouble than other children with basic cognitive concepts concerning their gender. Zucker et al. (1993) found that children with GID were more likely than controls to misclassify their own gender. Zucker et al. (1999) provided additional evidence that children with GID appear to have a "developmental lag" in the acquisition of gender constancy. Given the ubiquity of gender as a social category (Lewis, 1980), this may well lead to affective confusion in self-representation and in social interactions.

There is also evidence that children with GID have poorer peer relations than controls and more general behavioral problems, possible indices of impairment (although the evidence for their relation to the GID itself is open to debate, an issue that is discussed further later) (Zucker & Bradley, 1995; Zucker et al., 1997).

Assessment

Biomedical Tests

There are no known biological markers that can identify children with GID. Gross parameters of biological sex, such as the sex chromosomes and the appearance of the external genitalia, are invariably normal (Green, 1976).

Because gender identity conflict is overrepresented among specific physical intersex conditions (Zucker, 1999c), particularly congenital adrenal hyperplasia (CAH) in genetic females (Meyer-Bahlburg et al., 1996), partial androgen-insensitivity syndrome in genetic males reared as girls, and in genetic males with cloacal exstrophy reared as girls (Meyer-Bahlburg, Ehrhardt, Pinel, & Gruen, 1989), it is important to inquire about any physical signs of these conditions; however, it is rare that these conditions have not already been diagnosed prior to a clinical assessment for GID.

In our sample of children, physical intersex conditions were present in 7 (15.5%) of the 45 girls; in contrast, only 1 (0.0036%) of the 277 boys had such a condition. This finding is consistent with Meyer-Bahlburg's (1994) observation that gender identity conflict is most prominent among genetic females with atypical exposure to prenatal androgens or among genetic males with partial or typical exposure to prenatal androgens but who are reared as girls.

Psychological Tests

A number of parent-report and behavioral measures can be used to assess sex-typed behavior in children with GID (Zucker, 1992; Zucker & Bradley, 1995). From a diagnostic standpoint, it should be recognized that no one test is a replacement for a diagnosis that is established by a clinical interview that covers the behavioral signs for GID. Nevertheless, these measures have strong discriminant validity and constitute one strong line of evidence that GID is, in fact, a distinct syndrome. As reviewed elsewhere, data from psychological tests show a consistent pattern in that the percentage of false positives appears to be lower than the percentage of false negatives (Zucker, 1992; Zucker & Bradley, 1995).

Parent-report data can illustrate the sometimes dramatic differences in sex-typed behavior between children referred for gender identity concerns and controls. Let us consider four of the five diagnostic signs in Point A of the DSM-IV criteria for GID (Table 36.1, A1–A3, A5). It should, of course, be well known to developmentalists that the sex-typed behaviors concerning choice of clothing in dress-up play, roles in fantasy play, and peer affiliation preference show, on average, substantial sex differences in the general population of boys and girls. Table 36.2 shows maternal ratings for these four behaviors in gender-referred children and controls. It can be seen that the differences between the two groups are quite dramatic. There is, however, evidence for more "false negatives" than "false positives"; for example, 11.0% of the gender-referred children were judged to have same-sex friends as favorite playmates but only 3.7% of the controls were judged to have cross-sex friends as favorite playmates.

Reasons for Referral

Because parents, not children, generally make the decision to seek out an assessment, one might ask what reasons parents provide regarding their request for an assessment of their child with GID—reasons that are not necessarily mutually exclusive.

Table 36.2. Maternal Ratings
of Specific Sex-Typed Behaviors

	Group	
	Gender Identity Disorder	Controls
Wish to be opposite sex[a]	(N = 201)	(N = 380)
Frequently/every day	23.4%	0.3%
Once-in-a-while	35.8%	3.2%
Very rarely	16.9%	4.2%
Never	23.9%	92.4%
Dress-up play[b]	(N = 165)	(N = 250)
Same-sex	10.9%	87.2%
Equal	16.4%	9.6%
Cross-sex	72.7%	3.2%
Role in fantasy play[c]	(N = 180)	(N = 300)
Same-sex	20.6%	93.0%
Equal	21.7%	5.7%
Cross-sex	57.8%	1.3%
Favorite playmates[d]	(N = 200)	(N = 378)
Same-sex	11.0%	66.7%
Equal	37.0%	29.6%
Cross-sex	52.0%	3.7%

Note. Controls consisted of three groups of children: siblings, clinic-referred, and nonreferred ("normals"). Preliminary analyses showed no differences among the three types of controls, so their data were collapsed. Same-sex and cross-sex categories combined the response options of *Usually* and *Always*. For dress-up play, role play, and playmates, there was a *Not applicable* option (e.g., "doesn't dress up"). Children whose mothers endorsed this option had their data exluded from these analyses; hence, the Ns vary from item to item. The four items are from a 16-item parent-report questionnaire (Zucker, 1992, pp. 332–334).
[a]X^2 (3) = 296.5, $p < .00001$
[b]X^2 (2) = 261.2, $p < .00001$
[c]X^2 (2) = 273.7, $p < .00001$
[d]X^2 (2) = 237.1, $p < .00001$

Phase-Specific Notions Regarding Gender Identity Differentiation

As noted earlier, the initial behavioral signs of GID most often appear during the toddler and preschool years, just like the behavioral signs of more typical gender identity development. In my experience, it has been extremely common for parents to report that when their child's cross-behavior first began, they viewed it as developmentally normal or typical, a "phase" that most or all children "go through." Some parents consulted their pediatrician or family doctor, who would provide reassurance that the behavior was, in fact, developmentally normal or phase-specific. Similar reassurance is often also provided by nursery school teachers or day care workers.

From a normative developmental perspective (i.e., a purely statistical approach), it should be possible to answer the question of whether cross-gender behavior is common enough at certain ages to be considered (statistically) typical or phase-specific. Although it is beyond the scope of this chapter to review the relevant data in detail, a number of normative studies point to the conclusion that cross-gender behavior is relatively uncommon among nonreferred populations of boys and girls, even during the preschool years (Zucker, 1985; Zucker &

Bradley, 1995; Zucker et al., 1997). Although these normative studies provide evidence for an age-related decrease in the occurrence of some specific cross-gender behaviors, none of the studies suggest that cross-gender behavior is ever common or frequent enough to be considered "normative" in a statistical sense. Given that this is the case for specific cross-gender behaviors, it is certainly the case for patterns of cross-gender behavior.

Social Thresholds for Cross-Gender Behavior

Parental tolerance of cross-gender behavior, independent of the issue of its commonness, can be considered under the rubric of the "social thresholds" concept. For example, many parents will go along with, if not encourage, a child's cross-gender behavior during the toddler and preschool years (Green, 1974). From a "motivational" perspective, some parents will report that they were attempting to raise their child in a non-sex-stereotypic or nonsexist manner, which is surely part of a cultural *Zeitgeist*, at least in segments of contemporary Western society (see, e.g., Bem, 1998). Indeed, some parents of boys will comment that nursery school teachers or day care workers are "delighted" to see a young male engage in cross-dressing and female doll play, interpreting it along the lines of nurturant or creative behavior ("role" flexibility). Eventually, however, some threshold for the extent of cross-gender behavior is crossed, which activates parental concern.

Social Ostracism

A very common reason for referral concerns social ostracism, particularly in the peer group, but also from siblings, relatives, and other adults known to the child. From the normative developmental literature, there is, however, considerable evidence that cross-gender behavior elicits more disapproval in boys than it does in girls, from both peers and parents (Fagot, 1985), which may be one factor in explaining the sex difference in referral rates described earlier.

Family Dynamics

Some parents believe that various factors within the family have contributed to their child's sense of unhappiness about being a boy or a girl. This attributional bias is part of the motivation to seek out an assessment.

Long-Term Psychosexual Differentiation

A final concern pertains to the relationship between marked cross-gender behavior in childhood and postpubertal gender identity and sexual orientation. Some parents are concerned that their child might grow up to be "transsexual"; other parents are concerned that their child will grow up to be gay or homosexual—indeed, many parents appear to "condense" concerns about their child's gender identity and sexual orientation development such that these two aspects of psychosexual development are viewed as isomorphic, rather than as correlated, phenomena (for further discussion, see Bailey & Zucker, 1995; Zucker, 1999b).

ASSOCIATED FEATURES

Apart from the behavioral characteristics that define GID, children with this disorder have other sex-dimorphic traits that distinguish them from control children. For example, masked adult raters judged boys with GID to have a physical appearance that was more stereotypically feminine and less stereotypically masculine than same-sex controls, whereas the converse was found for girls with GID (Fridell, Zucker, Bradley, & Maing, 1996; McDermid, Zucker, Bradley, & Maing, 1998; Zucker, Wild, Bradley, & Lowry, 1993). Other research showed that boys with GID were perceived by their parents as having been particularly "beautiful" and "feminine" during their infancy compared to control boys (Green, 1987). Boys with GID have a lower parent-rated activity level than same-sex controls, whereas girls with GID have a higher parent-rated activity level than same-sex controls. Indeed, boys with GID have a lower activity level than girls with GID (Zucker & Bradley, 1995). Finally, boys with GID have a relative deficit in spatial ability whereas same-sex controls do not (Zucker & Bradley 1995).

General Behavior Problems

On measures such as the Child Behavior Checklist (CBCL) and the Teacher's Report Form, clinic-referred boys and girls with GID show significantly more general behavior problems than their siblings and nonreferred ("normal") children (Zucker & Bradley, 1995). Given that the siblings and nonreferred children do not engage, on average, in marked cross-gender role behavior, this might be construed as evidence for a relation between cross-gender role behavior and general behavior problems. The situation, however, is clearly more complicated than this, because demographically matched clinical controls (who, on average, show typical gender role behavior) show comparable levels of behavior problems to the children with GID (Zucker & Bradley, 1995). Thus, the relation between childhood sex-typed behavior patterns and general adjustment is complex (cf. Lewis, 1987).

On the CBCL, boys with GID have a predominance of internalizing behavioral difficulties, whereas girls with GID do not (Zucker & Bradley, 1995). Boys with GID have also been found to show high rates of separation anxiety traits (Coates & Person, 1985; Zucker, Bradley, & Lowry Sullivan, 1996).

At present, reasons for this associated behavioral psychopathology have been best studied in boys with GID (Zucker & Bradley, 1995). It is positively associated with age, which may reflect the results of increasing social ostracism, particularly in the peer group. It is also associated with a composite index of maternal psychopathology, which may reflect generic, nonspecific familial risk factors in producing behavior problems in general. The predominance of internalizing psychopathology may reflect familial risk for affective disorders and temperamental features of the boys. The extent to which aspects of the behavioral psychopathology may actually induce the emergence of the GID itself remains unresolved.

Family Demographics

Two family demographic variables—sibling sex ratio and birth order—are associated with GID. Boys with GID come from families with a significant excess of brothers, not sisters (Blanchard, Zucker, Bradley, & Hume, 1995; Zucker, Green, et al., 1997). In a study by Blanchard et al. (1995), a matched clinical control group of boys did not show a significant excess of brothers and, in both studies, the sibling sex ratio of the probands was elevated when compared to the known secondary sex ratio at birth (the ratio of male live births to female live births) in the general population. Blanchard et al. (1995) also showed that boys with GID have a later birth order than clinical control boys. Both Blanchard et al. and Zucker, Green, et al. (1997) also provided evidence suggesting that boys with GID are born later primarily in relation to their brothers, not their sisters. Because of small sample size, only birth order could be examined in girls with GID. Zucker, Lightbody, Pecore, Bradley, and Blanchard (1998) found that girls with GID have an earlier birth order than clinical control girls, and there was some evidence suggesting that they were born early primarily in relation to their sisters, but not their brothers.

Both biological and psychosocial explanations of these familial demographic patterns have been proposed, but none have yet been tested empirically. For example, in boys, one possible biological explanation pertains to maternal immune reactions during pregnancy. Because the male fetus is experienced by the mother as more "foreign" (antigenic) than the female fetus, it has been suggested that the production of maternal antibodies has the (inadvertent) consequence of demasculinizing or feminizing the male fetus. Because the mother's antigenicity increases with each successive male pregnancy, the model predicts that males born later in a sibline would be more affected, which is consistent with the finding that boys with GID are later born, and that this birth order effect occurs largely in relation to the number of older brothers, not older sisters. Among the varied psychosocial accounts, one explanation pertains to differential parental attention to a later-born son who has one or more older brothers; for example, a father may spend less time with a later-born son because he has already invested heavily in relating to his older sons and thus is less available as an object of masculine identification. It has also been argued that mothers who had desired a daughter might be particularly prone to feminize a later-born son (for a more detailed review, see Blanchard, 1997; Blanchard & Klassen, 1997; Blanchard et al., 1995; Zucker, Green, et al., 1997).

ETIOLOGICAL INFLUENCES

Both biological and psychosocial factors have been proposed to account for the development of GID in children. In the biological arena, several domains of inquiry have been deemed relevant: both molecular and behavior genetics, the roles of both prenatal maternal stress and immune reactions (as discussed earlier), prenatal sex hormones, and temperament. In the psychosocial arena, other domains have been deemed relevant: prenatal gender preference of the parents, social reinforcement of cross-gender behavior, quantitative and qualitative aspects of mother–child and father–child relationships, self-socialization, and traumata within the family matrix. All of these domains of putative influence have been reviewed in detail elsewhere (Zucker & Bradley, 1995).

Biological Influences

Lines of biological inquiry have been relatively limited in the study of children with GID. For example, molecular genetic and postmortem neuroanatomical studies have been conducted in relation to other aspects of psychosexual differentiation (namely, sexual orientation), but comparable studies have not been carried out with regard to GID. There is reasonable consensus that gross prenatal hormonal anomalies do not account for the development of GID in the majority of cases. However, it is conceivable that more subtle variations in patterns of prenatal hormonal secretion play a predisposing role. For example, in experimental studies of female rhesus monkey offspring, it has been possible, by varying the timing of exogenous administration of hormones during the pregnancy, to alter the normal patterning of sex-dimorphic behavior but to keep normal genital differentiation intact (Goy, Bercovitch, & McBrair, 1988). This animal model, which shows a *dissociation* between sex-dimorphic behavioral differentiation and genital differentiation, has the most direct relevance for explaining the marked cross-gender behavior of children with GID, since their genitalia are invariably normal.

Psychosocial Influences

Psychosocial factors, to truly merit causal status, must be able to influence the emergence of marked cross-gender behavior in the first few years of life. Parental tolerance or encouragement of early cross-gender behavior appears to be one such candidate; it is a factor that has been reported on by clinicians of diverse theoretical persuasions and has also marshaled some degree of empirical support (Green, 1987; Zucker & Bradley, 1995).

The reasons why parents might tolerate, if not encourage, early cross-gender behaviors appear to be quite diverse, suggesting that the antecedents to this "end state" are multiple in origin. As noted earlier, for example, some parents report being influenced by ideas regarding nonsexist child rearing. In other parents, the antecedents seem to be rooted in pervasive conflict that revolves around gender issues. For example, a small subgroup of mothers (about 10%) of boys with GID appear to experience something akin to what I have termed *pathological gender mourning* (Zucker, 1996). During the pregnancy, there is a strong desire for a girl; in all of the cases, the mother had already borne at least one other son, but no daughter—except in three instances in which the daughter was given up for adoption (one case) or had died in infancy (two cases). After the birth of the "nonpreferred" son, this wish seems to color strongly the mother's perception and relationship with her newborn, and there are strong signs of ambivalence about his gender status. This ambivalence has been manifested in several ways, including marked jealousy of friends with daughters, assignment of a gender-ambiguous or neutral given name, delayed naming of the newborn, severe postpartum depression, replacement and adoption fantasies, recurrent nightdreams about being pregnant with a girl, conscious preoccupations (e.g., diary entries about the unmet "need" to have a daughter), and active cross-dressing of the boy during infancy and toddlerhood.

Green (1987) examined quantitative and qualitative aspects of the father–son relationship, including amount of shared time. Green found that the amount of time the fathers of the feminine boys recalled spending with their sons during the second year of life, years 3 to 5, and at the time of assessment was less than the amount of time that the fathers of the controls recalled spending with their sons during the same periods. The difference in recalled shared time occurred in both two-parent families and in the families in which the parents had separated. The fathers of the feminine boys also recalled spending less time with the feminine boy than with a male sibling (when there was one) during these periods. This last finding is of interest in light of the birth order data reviewed earlier, suggesting that boys with GID, on average, tend to be later born relative to their brothers. Perhaps fathers of later-born sons are prone to spend less time with them, and this interactional pattern functions as a predisposing factor for their sons' behavioral femininity.

Another emerging line of psychosocial data concerns the extent of psychological and psychiatric disorder among the parents of children with GID. Although there is variation, the evidence suggests that these parents have rates of psychopathology that are greater than those of parents of "normal" children and at least commensurate with those of parents of clinical control children (Marantz & Coates, 1991; Zucker & Bradley, 1995). For example, among mothers of boys with GID, over half had two or more psychiatric disorders on the Diagnostic Interview Schedule, with major depressive episode and recurrent major depression being the most common (Zucker & Bradley, 1995). Among fathers of boys with GID, depression and alcohol abuse have also been quite common. What needs to be resolved and worked out is whether parental impairment, when it is present, impacts directly on the genesis of GID or whether it functions more as a perpetuating factor. Other evidence suggests that parental impairment is associated with the extent of general behavior problems seen in children with GID (Zucker & Bradley, 1995) and thus may function as a general risk factor.

PSYCHOSEXUAL DIFFERENTIATION: FOLLOW-UP

Green (1987) has conducted the most extensive long-term follow-up of boys with GID. This study can be used as a benchmark for the other published follow-up reports, which have been summarized in detail elsewhere (Zucker, 1985, 1990). At the moment, insufficient numbers of girls have been followed prospectively to draw conclusions about long-term outcome.

Green's (1987) study contained 66 feminine boys and 56 control boys assessed initially at a mean age of 7.1 years (range, 4–12). Forty-four feminine boys and 30 control boys were available for follow-up at a mean age of 18.9 years (range, 14–24). The majority of the boys were not in therapy between assessment and follow-up.

Sexual orientation in fantasy and behavior was assessed by means of a semistructured clinical interview. Kinsey ratings were made on a 7-point continuum, ranging from exclusive heterosexuality to exclusive homosexuality. Depending on the measure (fantasy or behavior), 75–80% of the previously feminine boys were either bisexual or homosexual at follow-up versus 0–4% of the control boys.

Green also reported on the gender identity status of the 44 previously feminine boys. He found that 1 youngster, at the age of 18 years, was gender-dysphoric to the extent of considering sex-reassignment surgery.

The prospective data are consistent with retrospective studies of adults with a homosexual sexual orientation, which have repeatedly shown that homosexual men and women recall more cross-gender behavior in childhood than heterosexual men and women (Bailey & Zucker, 1995). Thus, there is now sufficient evidence from both retrospective and prospective studies to conclude that childhood sex-typed behavior is strongly associated with later sexual orientation, which represents one of the more powerful illustrations of developmental continuity to emerge from research in developmental psychiatry.

Recall interviews with adult transsexuals with a "homosexual" sexual orientation almost invariably document a childhood cross-gender history. The prospective studies of children with GID, however, have yielded only a handful of transsexual outcomes. Thus, the convergence between prospective and retrospective studies is far less for transsexualism than for homosexuality.

Where have all the transsexuals gone? There are at least three possibilities. First, as Weinrich (1985) argued, the reason may be a simple statistical one. Because the base rate of transsexualism is so low, even within the population of cross-gender-identified children, large sample sizes would be required to "scoop in" the few transsexual patients. A second possibility concerns referral bias. As Green (1974) argued, it is conceivable that transsexuals grow up in families in which the cross-gender behavior is never experienced as "dystonic"; hence, a clinical assessment is not sought. Thus, clinic-referred samples may not perfectly reflect the universe of children with GID. Finally, as Green (1974) also pointed out, the natural history of cross-gender identification may be altered by the assessment process itself, with or without therapy. Reductions in cross-gender identity during childhood may well lower the risk for subsequent transsexualism.

Childhood Sex-Typed Behavior and Sexual Orientation: Explaining the Linkage

Both biological and psychosocial perspectives have been invoked to account for the association between childhood sex-typed behavior and sexual orientation. The most prominent biological explanation is that both sex-typed behavior and sexual orientation are joined together by some common factor or set of factors; for example, regarding genetic females with CAH, excessive prenatal exposure to androgens has been posited as the linkage factor that explains the higher rates of both behavioral masculinity during childhood (Berenbaum & Hines, 1992) and bisexuality/homosexuality in adulthood (Zucker, Bradley, Oliver, et al., 1996).

Psychosocial perspectives have been varied. For example, Green (1987) conjectured that compared to control boys, a feminine boy's lack of close relationships with other boys and with his father might result in "male affect starvation." Thus, in adolescence and adulthood, homoerotic contact is used in some compensatory manner to achieve closeness with other males. This scenario is an example of accounting for a within-sex difference in a behavioral outcome (in this instance, sexual orientation). It is not clear if "male affect starvation" during childhood would also account for a girl's later sexual attraction to males.

In Bem's (1996) developmental theory of sexual orientation, it is, in fact, proposed that similar mechanisms are operative in the sexual object choice of feminine boys and feminine girls (and masculine boys and masculine girls). Bem's account is not so much a "deficit" model, as is implied by the term "affect starvation," as a "difference" model. Bem proposed that variations in childhood "temperaments" influence a child's preference for sex-typical or sex-atypical activities and peers:

> These preferences lead children to feel different from opposite-sex or same-sex peers—to perceive them as dissimilar, unfamiliar, and exotic. This, in turn, produces heightened nonspecific autonomic arousal that subsequently gets eroticized to that same class of dissimilar peers: Exotic becomes erotic. (p. 320)

For feminine boys and feminine girls, males are "exotic," whereas for masculine boys and masculine girls, females are "exotic."

Bem's (1996) theory of sexual orientation represents a prototype in trying to unite typical and atypical development. There are, however, many unanswered questions and alternative interpretations raised by the theory. For example, Bem places great emphasis on temperamental factors that affect a child's preference for sex-typical or sex-atypical activities and friendships—an emphasis that might be disputed by some developmentalists (Ruble & Martin, 1998). Empirical evidence for the emergence of specific erotic feelings following "heightened nonspecific autonomic arousal" is scant, although it is quite likely that the relevant tests can be obtained through an analysis of emerging sexual interactions within the preadolescent peer group.

Bem's theory is intriguing in that it implies a greater potential for malleability in sexual-orientation development than is apparent in some of the biological theories. For example, if a feminine boy becomes more masculine in the course of his childhood, does this imply that the likelihood of later homoeroticism decreases? Conversely, if a feminine girl becomes more masculine in the course of her childhood, does this imply that the likelihood of later homo-eroticism increases?

Unfortunately, there is not much information available to answer these questions. Green (1987) compared on a number of childhood variables the feminine boys who were subsequently classified as bisexual or homosexual with the feminine boys who were subsequently classified as heterosexual. Although some feminine behaviors distinguished the two subgroups, a composite extent of femininity‑ score only approached conventional levels of significance, and only for the rating of sexual orientation in fantasy, not behavior. The lack of a stronger correlation is somewhat surprising, since one might have expected an association between the degree of cross-gender identification and long-term outcome; however, Green (1987) did find that the continuation of certain feminine behaviors throughout childhood was associated with later homosexuality. Thus, it may be that the persistence of these feminine behaviors is more important than their extent during the early childhood years.

SUMMARY

In this chapter, I have reviewed aspects of the core phenomenology, diagnostic and assessment issues, associated features, selected etiological factors, and long-term follow-up data pertaining to GID in children. Some matters have been more easily settle than others; for example, the phenomenology of GID is now well described, and extant assessment procedures are available to conduct a thorough diagnostic evaluation (see Zucker, 1992; Zucker & Bradley, 1995). Like other psychiatric disorders of childhood, however, it is apparent that complexity, not simplicity, is the guiding rule-of-thumb in any effort to make sense of the origins of GID. From an etiological standpoint, perhaps the most vexing issue is to make progress in solving the problem of specificity. It is likely that both biological and psychosocial factors will be implicated, and a model of cumulative risk (partly sex-specific) will be required to understand this relatively uncommon psychiatric disorder of childhood.

REFERENCES

American Psychiatric Association. (1987). *Diagnostic and statistical manual of mental disorders* (3rd ed., rev.). Washington, DC: Author.

American Psychiatric Association. (1994). *Diagnostic and statistical manual of mental disorders* (4th ed.). Washington, DC: Author.

Bailey, J. M., & Zucker, K. J. (1995). Childhood sex-typed behavior and sexual orientation: A conceptual analysis and quantitative review. *Developmental Psychology, 31*, 43–55.

Bem, D. J. (1996). Exotic becomes erotic: A developmental theory of sexual orientation. *Psychological Review, 103*, 320–335.

Bem, S. L. (1998). *An unconventional family.* New Haven, CT: Yale University Press.

Berenbaum, S. A., & Hines, M. (1992). Early androgens are related to childhood sex-typed toy preferences. *Psychological Science, 3*, 203–206.

Blanchard, R. (1997). Birth order and sibling sex ratio in homosexual versus heterosexual men and women. *Annual Review of Sex Research, 8*, 27–67.

Blanchard, R., & Klassen, P. (1997). H-Y antigen and homosexuality in men. *Journal of Theoretical Biology, 185*, 373–378.

Blanchard, R., Zucker, K. J., Bradley, S. J., & Hume, C. S. (1995). Birth order and sibling sex ratio in homosexual male adolescents and probably prehomosexual feminine boys. *Developmental Psychology, 31*, 22–30.

Bradley, S. J., Blanchard, R., Coates, S., Green, R., Levine, S. B., Meyer-Bahlburg, H. F. L., Pauly, I. B., & Zucker, K. J. (1991). Interim report of the DSM-IV subcommittee for gender identity disorders. *Archives of Sexual Behavior*, *20*, 333–343.

Coates, S., & Person, E. S. (1985). Extreme boyhood femininity: Isolated behavior or pervasive disorder? *Journal of the American Academy of Child Psychiatry*, *24*, 702–709.

Fagot, B. I. (1985). Beyond the reinforcement principle: Another step toward understanding sex role development. *Developmental Psychology*, *21*, 1097–1104.

Fridell, S. R., Zucker, K. J., Bradley, S. J., & Maing, D. M. (1996). Physical attractiveness of girls with gender identity disorder. *Archives of Sexual Behavior*, *25*, 17–31.

Goy, R. W., Bercovitch, F. B., & McBrair, M. C. (1988). Behavioral masculinization is independent of genital masculinization in prenatally androgenized female rhesus macaques. *Hormones and Behavior*, *22*, 552–571.

Green, R. (1974). *Sexual identity conflict in children and adults*. New York: Basic Books.

Green, R. (1976). One-hundred ten feminine and masculine boys: Behavioral contrasts and demographic similarities. *Archives of Sexual Behavior*, *5*, 425–446.

Green, R. (1987). *The "sissy boy syndrome" and the development of homosexuality*. New Haven, CT: Yale University Press.

Lewis, M. (1980). Self-knowledge: A social cognitive perspective on gender identity and sex-role development. In M. E. Lamb & L. R. Sherrod (Eds.), *Infant social cognition* (pp. 395–414). Hillsdale, NJ: Erlbaum.

Lewis, M. (1987). Early sex role behavior and school age adjustment. In J. M. Reinisch, L. A. Rosenblum, & S. A. Sanders (Eds.), *Masculinity/femininity: Basic perspectives* (pp. 202–226). New York: Oxford University Press.

Marantz, S., & Coates, S. (1991). Mothers of boys with gender identity disorder: A comparison of matched controls. *Journal of the American Academy of Child and Adolescent Psychiatry*, *30*, 310–315.

McDermid, S. A., Zucker, K. J., Bradley, S. J., & Maing, D. M. (1998). Effects of physical appearance on masculine trait ratings of boys and girls with gender identity disorder. *Archives of Sexual Behavior*, *27*, 253–267.

Meyer-Bahlburg, H. F. L. (1994). Intersexuality and the diagnosis of gender identity disorder. *Archives of Sexual Behavior*, *23*, 21–40.

Meyer-Bahlburg, H. F. L., Ehrhardt, A. A., Pinel, A., & Gruen, R. (1989, September). *Gender identity development in two 46,XY individuals with normal gonads raised female because of severe genital abnormalities*. Paper presented at the meeting of the Harry Benjamin International Gender Dysphoria Association, Cleveland, OH.

Meyer-Bahlburg, H. F. L., Gruen, R. S., New, M. I., Bell, J. J., Morishima, A., Shimshi, M., Bueno, Y., Vargas, I., & Baker, S. W. (1996). Gender change from female to male in classical congenital adrenal hyperplasia. *Hormones and Behavior*, *30*, 319–332.

Ruble, D. N., & Martin, C. L. (1998). Gender development. In W. Damon (Sr. Ed.) and N. Eisenberg (Vol. Ed.), *The handbook of child psychology: Vol. 3. Social, emotional, and personality development* (5th ed., pp. 933–1016). New York: Wiley.

Spitzer, R. L., & Wakefield, J. C. (1999). DSM-IV diagnostic criterion for clinical significance: Does it help solve the false positives problem? *American Journal of Psychiatry*, *156*, 1856–1864.

Stoller, R. J. (1975). *Sex and gender: Vol. II. The transsexual experiment*. London: Hogarth Press.

Weinrich, J. D. (1985). Transsexuals, homosexuals, and sissy boys: On the mathematics of follow-up studies. *Journal of Sex Research*, *21*, 322–328.

Zucker, K. J. (1985). Cross-gender-identified children. In B. W. Steiner (Ed.), *Gender dysphoria: Development, research, management* (pp. 75–174). New York: Plenum Press.

Zucker, K. J. (1990). Gender identity disorders in children: Clinical descriptions and natural history. In R. Blanchard & B. W. Steiner (Eds.), *Clinical management of gender identity disorders in children and adults* (pp. 1–23). Washington, DC: American Psychiatric Press.

Zucker, K. J. (1992). Gender identity disorder. In S. R. Hooper, G. W. Hynd, & R. E. Mattison (Eds.), *Child psychopathology: Diagnostic criteria and clinical assessment* (pp. 305–342). Hillsdale, NJ: Erlbaum.

Zucker, K. J. (1996, March). *Pathological gender mourning in mothers of boys with gender identity disorder: Clinical evidence and some psychocultural hypotheses*. Paper presented at the meeting of the Society for Sex Therapy and Research, Miami Beach, FL.

Zucker, J. J. (1999a). Commentary on Richardson's (1996) "Setting Limits on Gender Health." *Harvard Review of Psychiatry*, *7*, 37–42.

Zucker, K. J. (1999b). Gender identity disorder in the DSM-IV [Letter to the editor]. *Journal of Sex and Marital Therapy*, *25*, 5–9.

Zucker, K. J. (1999c). Intersexuality and gender identity differentiation. *Annual Review of Sex Research*, *10*, 1–69.

Zucker, K. J., & Bradley, S. J. (1995). *Gender identity disorder and psychosexual problems in children and adolescents*. New York: Guilford Press.

Zucker, K. J., & Bradley, S. J. (1998). Adoptee overrepresentation among clinic-referred boys with gender identity disorder. *Canadian Journal of Psychiatry, 43*, 1040–1043.

Zucker, K. J., Bradley, S. J., Kuksis, M., Pecore, K., Birkenfeld-Adams, A., Doering, R. W., Mitchell, J. N., & Wild, J. (1999). Gender constancy judgments in children with gender identity disorder: Evidence for a developmental lag. *Archives of Sexual Behavior, 28*, 475–502.

Zucker, K. J., Bradley, S. J., & Lowry Sullivan, C. B. (1996). Traits of separation anxiety in boys with gender identity disorder. *Journal of the American Academy of Child and Adolescent Psychiatry, 35*, 791–798.

Zucker, K. J., Bradley, S. J., Lowry Sullivan, C. B., Kuksis, M., Birkenfeld-Adams, A., & Mitchell, J. N. (1993). A gender identity interview for children. *Journal of Personality Assessment, 61*, 443–456.

Zucker, K. J., Bradley, S. J., Oliver, G., Blake, J., Fleming, S., & Hood, J. (1996). Psychosexual development of women with congenital adrenal hyperplasia. *Hormones and Behavior, 30*, 300–318.

Zucker, K. J., Bradley, S. J., & Sanikhani, M. (1997). Sex differences in referral rates of children with gender identity disorder: Some hypotheses. *Journal of Abnormal Child Psychology, 25*, 217–227.

Zucker, K. J., Green, R., Coates, S., Zuger, B., Cohen-Kettenis, P. T., Zecca, G. M., Lertora, V., Money, J., Hahn-Burke, S., Bradley, S. J., & Blanchard, R. (1997). Sibling sex ratio of boys with gender identity disorder. *Journal of Child Psychology and Psychiatry, 38*, 543–551.

Zucker, K. J., Lightbody, S., Pecore, K., Bradley, S. J., & Blanchard, R. (1998). Birth order in girls with gender identity disorder. *European Child and Adolescent Psychiatry, 7*, 30–35.

Zucker, K. J., Wild, J., Bradley, S. J., & Lowry, C. B. (1993). Physical attractiveness of boys with gender identity disorder. *Archives of Sexual Behavior, 22*, 23–36.

IX
TRAUMA DISORDERS

37

An Ecological–Transactional Model of Child Maltreatment

Dante Cicchetti, Sheree L. Toth, and Angeline Maughan

> We stand today ... as American families and as an American community to commit ourselves to putting our children first, to building a just America that leaves no child behind, and to ensuring all children healthy and safe passage to adulthood.... And we stand to affirm our belief that each of us individually and collectively as citizens of a great nation can do better in protecting and improving the quality of life for all children.... While we do not agree on everything, we do agree on one crucial thing: that no one in America should harm children and that every one of us can do more to ensure our children grow up safe, healthy, and educated in nurturing families and in caring communities.... Together we can give our children back their childhoods' safety, and hope and improve millions of young lives right now. (Marian Wright Edelman, 1998, pp. 1–2, emphasis in the original).

Although community efforts to protect America's children have grown, the stark reality that confronts us as a nation is that 1 out of every 43 children in the United States has experienced some form of maltreatment at the hands of a parent or primary caregiver. More alarming, according to the National Incidence Study completed in 1993 (NIS-III; United States Department of Health and Human Services, 1996), since 1980, the American public has witnessed and/or contributed to a 149% increase in the number of children reported for alleged maltreatment, with estimates rising from 625,100 to more than 1.5 million children nationally. When the definition of maltreatment is expanded to include children at risk for maltreatment who may not yet have suffered harm, estimates rise to over 2.8 million cases nationwide. Out of these 1993 incident reports, 1,500 children died due to fatal wounds and over 36% of these children experienced serious injuries (i.e., loss of consciousness, stopping breathing, broken bones, and/or third-degree burns).

One might question whether these estimates of child maltreatment are reflective of a nation's commitment to the protection and promotion of its children's safety and well-being.

Dante Cicchetti, Sheree L. Toth, and Angeline Maughan • Mt. Hope Family Center, University of Rochester, Rochester, New York 14608.

Handbook of Developmental Psychopathology, Second Edition, edited by Arnold J. Sameroff, Michael Lewis, and Suzanne M. Miller. Kluwer Academic/Plenum Publishers, New York, 2000.

As a society, we are faced with an increasing number of children who are suffering the deleterious effects of having been maltreated. Since the identification of the *battered child syndrome* (Kempe, Silverman, Steele, Droegemueller, & Silver, 1962), diligent efforts have been made to understand the causes and consequences of child maltreatment, as well as to intervene and prevent this human tragedy. It is only by continuing to refine our definition of child maltreatment, enhance our understanding of etiology, and build upon our knowledge of the effects of maltreatment on the process of development, that a unified, comprehensive plan of action capable of addressing the complexity of child maltreatment will emerge.

GOALS OF THIS CHAPTER

In this chapter, we provide a perspective on child maltreatment that is derived from a developmental psychopathology framework. After addressing epidemiological and definitional aspects of child maltreatment, we describe an organizational perspective on development and its application to conceptualizing the impact of maltreatment experiences on the developmental process. In so doing, we present an ecological–transactional model to guide our review of the maltreatment literature. Specifically, we discuss how forces from each level of the ecology (i.e., macrosystem, exosystem, and microsystem), as well as characteristics of the individual, influence the development of adaptive and maladaptive developmental outcomes in maltreated children.

EPIDEMIOLOGICAL AND DEFINITIONAL ISSUES

Incidence and prevalence rates of child maltreatment within the United States are integrally related to criteria that are used to define an act as maltreatment. Therefore, it is important to examine how definitional decisions have affected epidemiological estimates of maltreatment. Historically, legislative officials have struggled over whether the government has the right to dictate parenting practices and to determine what is and is not considered abusive behavior toward children. Shifts between liberal and conservative views with regard to appropriate government involvement have had a significant impact on decisions and policies regarding definitions of child maltreatment (Barnett, Manly, & Cicchetti, 1993), as well as on service availability. Typically, those with liberal philosophies have maintained that it is the responsibility of the State to protect minors from being oppressed by their families. This philosophical orientation results in a broad definition of child maltreatment. Conversely, those having more conservative persuasions have advocated for restricted definitions of maltreatment, arguing for families' right to privacy and patriarchal authority (Goldstein, Freud, & Solnit, 1973). Despite disparate views among liberal and conservative legislators, the Child Abuse Prevention and Treatment Act that was passed in 1974 included the adoption of a national definition of child maltreatment, as well as the establishment of a National Center on Child Abuse and Neglect (NCCAN) that is responsible for the establishment of a federal administrative center for research aimed at the elucidation and prevention of child maltreatment.

Since the center's establishment, the National Incidence Studies (NIS), compiled by the NCCAN, provide the most comprehensive source of information regarding the epidemiology of child abuse and neglect within the United States (U.S. Department of Health and Human Services, NIS-I, 1981; NIS-II, 1988; NIS-III, 1996). Epidemiological estimates contained in the NIS are based on incident reports collected from child protective services agencies (CPS), as well as maltreatment cases identified by community professionals (i.e., physicians, social workers, teachers, and day care providers) that either were not reported or went unrecognized by CPS agencies. The NIS reports use two definitions of child maltreatment: the Harm Standard, which requires that children are considered to have been maltreated if they have experienced demonstrable harm at the hands of a parent or primary caregiver; and the Endangerment Standard, which includes children who have experienced maltreatment that puts them at risk of demonstrable harm.

Despite consensus among researchers, lawmakers, and clinicians that child maltreatment is a major societal problem that requires immediate attention, discordance on what constitutes maltreatment and how it should be defined continues. Historically, social scientific approaches to defining child maltreatment have evolved based on the theoretical conceptualizations and purpose for which the definition was being used (Aber & Zigler, 1981). For example, the key criteria for the medical–diagnostic definition are on the individual abuser (i.e., parental adjustment); parental acts and society's role in perpetuating maltreatment are central to the sociological definition; the legal definition emphasizes physical and emotional harm incurred by children; and evidence of environmental and familial contributors to the occurrence of maltreatment are necessary elements of the ecological approach. In view of these varied foci, uncertainty arises over whether similar definitions should be used for scientific, legal, and clinical purposes. Zuravin (1991) suggests that for researchers, definitions of maltreatment need to focus on the specific acts that endanger children, thereby allowing researchers to concentrate on identifiable behaviors that comprise the child's maladaptive caretaking environment.

The maltreatment literature has witnessed methodological advances devoted to the operationalization and quantification of acts of child maltreatment. In general, four putative categories of child maltreatment are distinguished from each other: (1) *physical abuse*, which involves the infliction of bodily injury on a child by other than accidental means; (2) *sexual abuse*, which includes sexual contact or attempted sexual contact between a caregiver or other responsible adult and a child for purposes of the caregiver's sexual gratification or financial benefit; (3) *neglect*, which includes both the failure to provide minimum care and the lack of supervision; and (4) *emotional maltreatment*, which involves persistent and extreme thwarting of a child's basic emotional needs. McGee and Wolfe (1991) have subsequently augmented the definition of emotional maltreatment to include both psychologically abusive and psychologically neglectful caretaking behaviors. Investigators have identified a high degree of comorbidity among maltreatment subtypes, indicating that many maltreated children experience more than one type of maltreatment (Cicchetti & Barnett, 1991b; Cicchetti & Rizley, 1981). In many instances, it may be necessary to focus on the most heinous subtypes of maltreatment in a particular case, but the actual experience of many children is much more complicated, thus presenting significant challenges for researchers and clinicians.

In order to address additional definitional considerations, Cicchetti and Barnett (1991b) proposed a nosology that attempts to provide a complete account of each child's maltreatment experience. They incorporate many salient features of maltreatment, including the severity of the incident, the frequency and chronicity of the maltreating acts, who the perpetrator is, and the developmental period of the child during which the maltreatment occurred. These authors consider each aspect of maltreatment influential in specifying the nature of the environmental failure. By quantifying the major components of maltreatment, researchers can capture the qualitative meaning of the experience for the child and can then apply these powerful independent variables in investigations aimed at elucidating the consequences of maltreatment. For example, Manly, Cicchetti, and Barnett (1994) investigated the relationship among the subtype, severity, frequency, and chronicity of maltreatment and child outcome among a sample of 235 low socioeconomic status (SES) families. Findings indicated that the type of maltreatment experienced significantly influences a child's level of functioning, with physically abused children exhibiting higher rates of behavior problems than nonmaltreated comparisons, and sexually abused children scoring higher on social competence ratings than other maltreated children. Additionally, the severity of the maltreatment, the frequency of CPS reports, and the interaction between frequency and severity contributed significant variance in predicting both social competence and behavior problems among maltreated children. The chronicity of the maltreatment also predicted peer ratings of aggression.

In another examination of the various components of the maltreatment experience and how they relate to child outcome, Wolfe and McGee (1994) found significant differences in adjustment patterns among maltreated children depending on the developmental period during which the maltreatment occurred, the type of maltreatment experienced, and the gender of the victim. In males, the relationship between early maltreatment and adjustment is strengthened when interactions between physical and psychological abuse and between partner abuse and neglect are entered into the analysis. Current adjustment of females is significantly related to the developmental period during which neglect or psychological abuse occurs, with elevated adjustment problems occurring when maltreatment increases during midchildhood relative to early childhood.

An Organizational Perspective on Development

Although developmental psychopathology is not characterized by the acceptance of any unitary theoretical approach, the organizational perspective on development (Cicchetti, 1993; Sroufe & Rutter, 1984) offers a powerful theoretical framework for conceptualizing the intricacies of the life-span perspective on risk and psychopathology, as well as on normal ontogenesis. The organizational perspective attends to the quality of integration both within and among the behavioral and biological systems of the individual. This focus on variations in the quality of integration provides the foundation on which the developmental psychopathologist characterizes heterogeneous developmental outcomes.

At each juncture of reorganization in development, the concept of hierarchical motility specifies that prior developmental structures are incorporated into later ones by means of hierarchical integration. In this way, early experience and its effects on the individual are carried forward within the individual's organization of systems through subsequent developmental stages and across the life span rather than having reorganizations override previous organizations. Based on this hierarchical picture of adaptation, the successful resolution of an early stage-salient issue increases the probability of subsequent successful adjustment (Sroufe & Rutter, 1984). Conversely, failure on early stage-salient issues increases the likelihood of continued difficulties. This is not to say that early adaptation ensures successful later adaptation, or that early maladaptation destines an individual to future failure. Factors in the internal and external environment have the potential to alter subsequent adaptational capacities. Thus, an ever-changing model of development is portrayed in which newly formed competencies or maladaptations may surface throughout the life course (Cicchetti & Tucker, 1994; Lewis, 1997).

Developmental Pathways

One of the hallmarks of the developmental psychopathology perspective is an acceptance and appreciation of diversity in process and outcome among high-risk and normal populations

(Cicchetti & Rogosch, 1996). It is believed that there is heterogeneity among individuals who develop a specific disorder with respect to the features of their disturbance, as well as among individuals who evidence maladaptation but who do not develop a disorder. Based on this understanding, developmental psychopathologists agree that multiple pathways to any particular manifestation of disordered behavior exist.

In accord with this view, the principles of equifinality and multifinality, derived from general systems theory (von Bertalanffy, 1968), are germane. Equifinality refers to the observation that in any open system, a diversity of pathways, including chance events, or what biologists refer to as nonlinear epigenesis, may lead to the same outcome. Consequently, a variety of developmental progressions may end in a given disorder. The principle of multifinality suggests that any one component may function differently depending on the organization of the system in which it operates. Multifinality states that a particular adverse event should not necessarily be seen as leading to the same outcome in every individual. For example, decades of research on the etiology of maltreatment have demonstrated that single-variable cause-and-effect models designed to explain the occurrence of maltreatment are too simplistic (Belsky, 1980; Cicchetti & Rizley, 1981; Wolfe, 1985). Furthermore, years of research on the consequences of maltreatment clearly indicate that all maltreated children do not evidence the same psychological and behavioral profile, and that social, biological, and experiential factors all contribute to how children cope with the stressors associated with maltreatment (Cicchetti, Ganiban, & Barnett, 1991; Cicchetti & Tucker, 1994).

ETIOLOGY OF MALTREATMENT

According to the developmental psychopathology perspective, a recognition of the developmental and contextual aspects of maltreatment is a requisite for understanding its causes and consequences. Discussion of the etiology of maltreatment is complicated by the recognition that most forms of maltreatment are part of a pattern of maladaptive behavior that emerges over time. Because no single risk factor or set of risk factors have been identified as providing a necessary or sufficient cause of maltreatment, a number of interactive etiological models have evolved historically. In accord with the framework proposed by Bronfenbrenner (1977), in which equal emphasis is placed on the role of environmental, contextual, and family factors, a consensus has emerged regarding the contributions made by a variety of transacting factors operating at various levels of individual, family, and societal ecologies.

Belsky (1980) proposed an ecological model to account for the etiology of child maltreatment. This model provides a framework for defining and understanding the "ecology" or broader environment in which child maltreatment occurs. Belsky views child maltreatment as being influenced by forces within the individual, the family, the community, and the culture. Four levels of analysis are addressed in this model: (1) *ontogenic* development, which includes factors within the individual that are associated with being a perpetrator of child maltreatment; (2) the *microsystem*, which includes factors within the family that contribute to the occurrence of child maltreatment; (3) the *exosystem*, which includes aspects of the communities in which families and individuals live that contribute to child maltreatment; and (4) the *macrosystem*, which includes the beliefs and values of the culture that contribute to the perpetuation of child maltreatment.

Cicchetti and Rizley (1981) developed a transactional approach to address the causes, consequences, and mechanisms through which maltreatment is propagated. In their transactional model, environmental forces, caregiver characteristics, and child characteristics are seen as mutually influencing each other, thereby making reciprocal contributions to the events and outcomes of child development (Sameroff & Chandler, 1975). Cicchetti and Rizley (1981) focus on the transactions of four primary risk factors that may contribute to the occurrence of maltreatment. The first set of risk factors include enduring *vulnerability* factors, which are considered to be relatively long-lasting factors, conditions, or attributes that serve to potentiate maltreatment. These may involve parental, child, or environmental characteristics. Vulnerability factors may be biological in nature, historical (e.g., a parent with a history of being maltreated), psychological, and sociological. Second, Cicchetti and Rizley (1981) propose that *transient challengers* within an individual's environment have the potential to increase maltreatment acts. These include short-term conditions and stresses such as loss (of status, a job, or a loved one), physical injury or illness, legal difficulties, marital or family problems, discipline problems with children, and the emergence of a child into a new and more difficult developmental period. Third, *enduring protective factors* exist that decrease the risk of maltreatment. These include relatively permanent conditions such as a parent's own history of good parenting and a secure quality of intimate relationships between the parent figures. And last, *transient buffers* include factors in an individual's environment that may protect a family from stress, such as sudden improvement in financial conditions, periods of marital harmony, and a child's transition out of a difficult developmental period. These risk factors are divided into two broad categories: potentiating factors, which increase the probability of maltreatment (i.e., enduring vulnerability factors and transient challengers); and compensatory factors, which decrease the risk of maltreatment (i.e., enduring protective factors and transient buffers). According to Cicchetti and Rizley's (1981) transactional model, maltreatment occurs only when potentiating factors outweigh compensatory ones.

Drawing from the work of Belsky (1980) and Cicchetti and Rizley (1981), Cicchetti and Lynch (1993) have proposed an ecological–transactional model (see Figure 37.1) that will

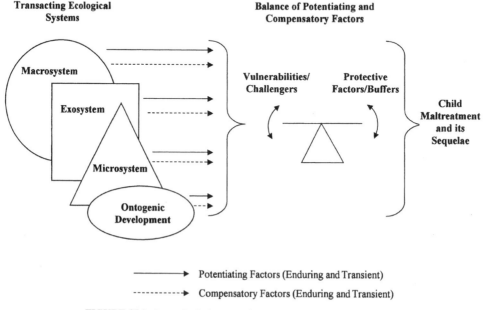

FIGURE 37.1. An ecological–transactional model of child maltreatment.

guide our examination of the processes associated with child maltreatment and their implications for children's development.

AN ECOLOGICAL–TRANSACTIONAL MODEL OF CHILD MALTREATMENT

The ecological–transactional model provides a more contextualized approach to understanding the effects of child maltreatment by examining multiple risk factors simultaneously. Specifically, this model explains how transacting cultural, community, and family factors (i.e., macro-, exo-, and microsystems), in conjunction with characteristics of the individual, exert reciprocal influences on each other and shape the course of child development (cf. Cicchetti & Lynch, 1993; Sameroff & Chandler, 1975). Thus, the multilevel ecology of child maltreatment proposed by an ecological–transactional framework can be seen as demonstrating broad-based environmental failure.

According to this conceptualization, risk factors can be present at each level of the ecology noted by Belsky (1980). Potentiating and compensatory risk factors within a given level of the model can influence outcomes and processes in surrounding levels of the environment. At higher, more distal levels of the ecology, potentiating factors increase the likelihood of child maltreatment. Occurrences in these environmental systems also influence what takes place in more proximal ecological levels, such as when potentiating and compensatory factors determine the presence or absence of maltreatment within the family environment. Overall, concurrent risk factors in the various ecological levels (e.g., cultural sanction of violence, community violence, low SES, loss of job, divorce, parental substance abuse, maladaptation, and/or child psychopathology) act to increase or decrease the likelihood that abuse will occur.

The manner in which children handle the challenges associated with maltreatment is seen in their own ontogenic development, which shapes their ultimate adaptation or maladaptation. Despite the conceptualization that levels of the environment are mutually influencing entities on developmental processes, we believe that factors associated with a child's more proximal ecologies exert the most direct contributions to the outcomes of child development. Research conducted from a developmental psychopathology perspective can assist in elucidating how mechanisms operative in more distal ecological levels impact upon the more proximal environments, thereby exerting a more direct influence on child ontogeny and ultimate adaptation.

In order to investigate how various levels of the ecology contribute to the causes and consequences of child maltreatment, we next examine factors within the macro-, exo-, and microsystem. Table 37.1 outlines the multiple vulnerability and protective factors contained within each level of the ecological–transactional model that will be addressed in our review of maltreatment during childhood and adolescents.

The Macrosystem

The macrosystem represents the set of cultural values and beliefs that may promote the occurrence of child maltreatment within families and communities. It is in the macrosystem that overarching values permeate individual and family lifestyles. The American society's acceptance of violence has been identified as a significant precipitating force behind the increase in abusive acts within our nation. Compared with other Western countries, the level of violence observed in the United States is high (Christoffel, 1990; Fingerhut & Kleinman,

Table 37.1. Examples of Risk and Protective Factors in an Ecological–Transactional Model of Child Maltreatment

	Ontogenic	Microsystem	Exosystem	Macrosystem
Vulnerability factors (enduring)	Difficult infant temperament Physiological dysregulation Dysregulated affect Limited cognitive abilities Insecure attachments Low self-esteem Poor peer relations School difficulties Psychopathology	Domestic violence Financial hardship Chronic unemployment Chronic stress conditions Hostile family environment Intergenerational abuse Parental psychopathology Maladaptive child-rearing skills	Community violence Crime in neighborhood Social isolation Impoverished community	Violent culture Parenting customs Racism Social acceptance of violence
Challengers (transient)	Physical illness Transient stressors Task failures	Job loss Divorce Daily hassles	Losing community resources Lack of community services	Recession
Protective factors (enduring)	Easy infant temperament Adaptive physiological regulation Adaptive affect regulation High intelligence Secure attachments High self-esteem Positive peer relations Positive adaptation to school Good mental health	Good marital relations Consistent employment Positive family relations Good parental mental health Positive child-rearing skills	Supportive social network Good community resources Supportive church	National support for education Beliefs in children's rights National commitment to rehabilitating substance abusers
Buffers (transient)	Pride over personal accomplishment Positive relationship with current teacher	Getting a job Finding adequate housing Accessing child care	Gaining community resources Accessing social support networks	Lower unemployment rate Elected officials committed to improving the plight of the disadvantaged Reducing availability of illegal drugs

1990). The Justice Department estimates that 1 out of every 10 American households has fallen victim to a violent crime (i.e., robbery, assault, or rape) (U.S. Department of Justice, 1991). Also, the United States has witnessed an increase in gang warfare, where it is estimated that African American adolescent males are more likely to die from a gunshot wound than from any other cause. In addition, observation of films and television programs that contain excessive acts of violence has become customary among family households, supporting Straus's (1974) and Zigler's (1976) claims that violence is condoned in this country.

Issues of race also have been identified as factors within the macrosystem that pose potential influences on the perpetration of parental violence toward children. The stressors associated with racism (i.e., lack of educational and job opportunities), undermine the ability of many ethnic minority families to support their children financially. The lack of resources necessary to maintain a household places increasing stress on the whole family and on the primary caregiver in particular. In view of our ecological–transactional model of child maltreatment, societal tolerance of violent acts and issues of racism act as enduring vulnerability factors that serve to potentiate maltreatment and set the stage for continued maladaptation in the exosystem, microsystem, and on ontogenic development among children.

The Exosystem

The exosystem subsumes formal and informal social structures that make up the immediate environment in which children and families function. These social structures include neighborhoods, formal and informal support groups, the availability of employment, social service opportunities, and SES. The exosystem also encompasses Bronfenbrenner's proposed "mesosystem" of interconnecting community settings, which include school, peer group, church, and employment environments (Bronfenbrenner, 1977).

Several aspects of the exosystem have been associated with child maltreatment. Investigators have identified four primary potentiating factors within the exosystem that exert significant influences on the family microsystem: poverty, unemployment, neighborhood status, and social isolation. Poverty is an enduring vulnerability factor that frequently distinguishes maltreating families from nonmaltreating families. Although maltreatment permeates all levels of society, the majority of maltreated children are from families that reside below the poverty level. Concurrent economic, sociocultural, and interpersonal factors create for these families a milieu of economic stress and hardship that threatens overall family functioning (Garbarino & Gilliam, 1980). In fact, a number of studies have demonstrated the independent additive and interactive effects of low SES and maltreatment on children's development, thus placing low SES maltreated children at increased risk for maladaptive ontogenic outcomes (see, e.g., Okun, Parker, & Levendosky, 1994; Trickett, Aber, Carlson, & Cicchetti, 1991).

Unemployment and the stress that accompany it are another aspect of the exosystem that has been associated with maltreatment (see, e.g., Gelles & Hargreaves, 1981; Light, 1973; Whipple & Webster-Stratton, 1991). Unemployment represents a transient challenger that has the potential to stimulate maltreatment and family dysfunction through the pressure and stress it places on families. In fact, Steinberg, Catalano, and Dooley (1981) demonstrated that periods of high unemployment correlated with an increase in incident reports of child abuse. Specifically, investigations identified that the relationship between unemployment and violent behavior toward children appears to be strongest among fathers (Straus & Kaufman-Kantor, 1986; Wolfner & Gelles, 1993). Such studies lend credence to an ecological–transactional framework in explaining how the lack of employment can lead to family stress that may precipitate acts of maltreatment toward children.

The neighborhoods in which families reside represent an additional enduring vulnerability factor that promotes the occurrence of child maltreatment. Neighborhoods with high rates of violence, for example, undoubtedly are stressful environments for individual and family functioning, and represent a significant potentiating force for the proliferation of spousal violence and child maltreatment in the family. For example, poverty and unemployment, which are often concentrated in inner-city neighborhoods, can produce increased stress and frustration that lead to violence at both the broader community level and the narrower family level. In fact, Richters and Martinez (1993) found that a significant number of children who lived in violent neighborhoods had themselves been victims of violence, including abuse. Unfortunately, maltreating families may have few real opportunities to move out of violent neighborhoods because of limited financial resources.

In addition to the negative influences of violence in neighborhood settings, Garbarino and his colleagues (Garbarino & Crouter, 1978; Garbarino & Sherman, 1980) also have found that the availability of social resources significantly influences child abuse rates. Higher rates of maltreatment characterized neighborhoods that lacked adequate social resources compared to equally disadvantaged neighborhoods whose resources were more easily attainable. What differentiated these neighborhoods was not only the accessibility of social resources but also the manner in which these resources were used. Parents residing in these high-abuse-rate neighborhoods do not use resources preventively, they do not use informal supports such as scouting or youth groups, and they usually rely on formal public agencies when intervention is necessary. In general, parents who report dissatisfaction with the resources and support provided by friends and neighbors likewise tend to be dissatisfied with their roles as caregivers, to engage in less optimal interactions with their children, and to provide poor-quality home environments (Corse, Schmid, & Trickett, 1990). In contrast, parents in neighborhoods with lower than expected abuse rates make more constructive use of resources to cope successfully with challenges from the exosystem. By employing more achievement-oriented socialization practices with their children, these parents are attempting to protect their families from the dangers of their surrounding environment (Dubrow & Garbarino, 1989; Jayaratne, 1993).

Social isolation from neighborhood networks, support groups, and extended family also has been associated with maltreatment (Garbarino, 1977; Hunter & Kilstrom, 1979; Kempe, 1973). In particular, physically abusing mothers have been characterized as having fewer peer relationships, more troubled relationships with relatives, and more limited contact with the wider community than nonabusing mothers (Corse et al., 1990), thus lacking a necessary "lifeline" to emotional and material support during times of stress (Kempe, 1973). Maltreating mothers report less enjoyment of and openness in parenting (Corse et al., 1990) and, because of their isolation from the broader community, employ child-rearing practices that lack the positive influences of educational and societal informants that promote new strategies to improve overall parenting skills and practices (Belsky, 1984; Garbarino & Gilliam, 1980; Sigel, 1986; Trickett & Susman, 1988).

In discussing the association between social isolation and maltreatment, it is necessary to distinguish between lack of support and failure to use available support (Garbarino, 1977). Maltreating families commonly ignore or fail to use social supports or resources even when they are readily available. Studies indicate that an interaction between characteristics of individual families and characteristics of the environment may serve as a possible cause of social isolation among maltreating households. Relevant factors include the stresses that cut families off from supports, developmental histories of the parents, characteristics of the family that alienate others, increased mobility that disrupts social networks, the ability of social service systems to identify and monitor high-risk families, and the ability of neighborhoods to provide feedback and adequate resources (Crittenden, 1985; Crittenden & Ainsworth, 1989; Garbarino, 1977).

Within an ecological–transactional framework, the presence of social networks in an individual's exosystem has been regarded as a protective factor against child maltreatment (Garbarino, 1977). Religious affiliation and participation, in particular, have been identified as countering social isolation and having important influences in protecting against child maltreatment, especially among African Americans (Garbarino, 1977; Giovannoni & Billingsley, 1970). In addition, if a maltreated child can attain support at school or through participation in a youth group, the adverse sequelae of the maltreatment may be reduced (Cicchetti, Toth, & Hennessy, 1993; Lynch & Cicchetti, 1992).

Overall, to the extent that stress within the family is already high, the presence of any of these negative exosystem factors, whether a transient challenger (i.e., social isolation and recent unemployment) or an enduring vulnerability factor (i.e., persistent poverty and background community violence), may increase the likelihood of child maltreatment. Also, if the parent's developmental history predisposes him or her to respond to stress with aggression (another enduring vulnerability factor), then the probability of child maltreatment increases even further.

The Microsystem

Following Belsky's (1980) usage, the microsystem represents the family environment. This is the immediate context in which child maltreatment takes place. The ecological–transactional model, influenced by Bronfenbrenner (1977), extends the conceptualization of the microsystem to include any environmental setting that contains the developing person, such as the home, school, or workplace. In addition, family dynamics and parenting styles, and the developmental histories and psychological resources of the maltreating parents are all incorporated in an analysis of microsystem influences on child maltreatment.

The field has witnessed a surge in investigative efforts to elucidate the potentiating factors contributing to the breakdown of competent parenting among these high-risk families. A parent's prior developmental history may be the first contributor that can influence a family's microsystem. There is considerable support for the claim that maltreating parents are more likely than nonmaltreating parents to have had a history of abuse (Hunter & Kilstrom, 1979; Kaufman & Zigler, 1989). In fact, it has been estimated that approximately one-third of all maltreating parents were maltreated themselves as children (Kaufman & Zigler, 1989; Oliver, 1993). Nonetheless, it is important to recognize that not all parents who maltreat their children were themselves maltreated. As we noted earlier, maltreatment can occur in response to acute environmental challengers, especially in an unsupportive ecology, even if the parent has no personal history of abuse. Moreover, not all adults who were maltreated as children become abusive parents. Studies have identified some possible protective factors in breaking the cycle of maltreatment. These include social support structures (i.e., a supportive spouse); formation of a positive relationship with a significant adult during childhood; and participation in therapy, either as an adolescent or an adult, to enable childhood maltreatment experiences to be appropriately processed and addressed.

The psychological and biological resources that maltreating parents bring with them to the family ecology also distinguish them from nonmaltreating parents. In general, maltreating parents have been found to be depressed (Lahey, Conger, Atkeson, & Treiber, 1984), socially isolated and with few social supports (Egeland & Brunquell, 1979; Garbarino, 1976), and lacking in impulse control, especially when aroused and stressed (Altemier, O'Connor, Vietze, Sandler, & Sherrod, 1982). Furthermore, in a prospective study, Brunquell, Crichton, and Egeland (1981) have shown that parents who later became abusive were less psychologically complex and personally integrated, receiving more negative scores on summary scales of anxiety, locus of control, aggression, and dependence than nonmaltreating parents. In addition, Dinwiddie and Bucholz (1993) demonstrated that self-identified child maltreaters have increased lifetime rates of alcoholism, depression, and antisocial personality disorder.

Physiological findings extend our knowledge on the resources of maltreating parents by providing insights into how they cope with stressful life events. Studies indicate that maltreating parents may be biologically predisposed to overreact to stressful stimuli (McCanne & Milner, 1991). For example, Frodi and Lamb (1980) have shown that abusive mothers report more aversion to infant cries than nonabusers, and that they are more physiologically aroused. Subsequently, Wolfe and colleagues demonstrated, based on skin conductance and respiration data, that abusive mothers displayed greater emotional arousal in response to stressful stimuli than nonabusive mothers, and that abusive mothers remained more aroused during both stressful and nostressful stimuli (Wolfe, Fairbank, Kelly, & Bradlyn, 1983).

Conflict and disruption among family members may be another particularly salient feature of abusive family functioning. Trickett and Susman (1988) found that maltreating parents report more anger and conflict in the family than nonmaltreating parents. Specifically, maltreating parents, interact with their children less and display more negative affect toward them (Burgess & Conger, 1978). Moreover, husbands and wives in maltreating families are less warm and supportive, less satisfied with their spouses, and more aggressive and violent with their marital partners than are parents in nonabusive households (Howes & Cicchetti, 1993; Rosenberg, 1987; Straus, Gelles, & Steinmetz, 1980). Overall, chaos, instability, and unsupportive relations characterize family interactions in maltreating families (Cicchetti & Howes, 1991). Thus, it is not surprising that pervasive family dysfunction compounds the experience of child maltreatment.

Finally, parents labeled as maltreating engage in a host of interactions and other parental practices with their children that directly impact on a child's ontogenic development (Rogosch, Cicchetti, Shields, & Toth, 1995). Specifically, studies indicate that maltreating parents appear to be less likely to appreciate and accept their children's unique experience and perspective (Kavanagh, Youngblade, Reid, & Fagot, 1988; Pianta, Egeland, & Erickson, 1989), and are less prone to encourage independence and openness to new experiences (Susman, Trickett, Ianotti, Hollenbeck, & Zahn-Waxler, 1985). In addition, maltreating parents often have expectations of their children that are unrealistic, and they are also less likely to have their parenting guided by developmentally appropriate expectations (Pianta et al., 1989). Maltreating caregivers also tend to be less reciprocal (Crittenden, 1981) and more egocentric (Newberger & Cook, 1983), and as such, they generally place their needs and wishes above those of their children. This process is evident in the role reversal often witnessed in maltreating dyads, in which the children, rather than the parents, frequently serve as the sensitive and nurturing caregivers (Carlson, Cicchetti, Barnett, & Braunwald, 1989b). Moreover, maltreating parents utilize authoritarian control, inconsistent discipline, and anxiety and guilt induction, by beating, threatening, and coercing compliance, rather than by setting clear contingencies and limits, offering explanations, or eliciting ideas from their children (Trickett & Kuczynski, 1986; Trickett & Susman, 1988).

Now that we have discussed aspects of the macro-, exo-, and microsystems that can contribute to child maltreatment, we turn our attention specifically to ontogenic development.

Ontogenic Development

At the level of ontogenic development, the most critical determinant of eventual competence or incompetence is the negotiation of the salient tasks of each developmental period (Cicchetti, 1989). Although certain issues may be central at particular periods in time and subsequently decrease in importance, each issue must be coordinated and integrated with the environment as well as with subsequently emerging issues across the life span (Cicchetti & Lynch, 1993; Sroufe & Rutter, 1984). Accordingly, each new developmental task builds upon and incorporates previous issues. The manner in which these issues are resolved plays a pivotal role in determining subsequent adaptation. Although the previously described features of the macro-, exo-, and microsystems continue to transact with the individual to influence overall development, poor resolution of these issues ultimately may contribute to the development of maladaptation and/or psychopathology.

Most of the existing research relevant to an ecological–transactional perspective on child maltreatment has focused on the ontogenic level. When studying developmental processes among high-risk samples, the processes contributing to adaptive or maladaptive outcome must be elucidated. Because high-risk populations, such as maltreated youngsters, typically are confronted with a matrix of negative life events (i.e., poverty, low SES, traumatic experiences), the relative role that each exerts on development must be identified. Therefore, one is confronted with the question of how to tease out the unique developmental influences of child maltreatment from the effects of other stressful demographic and experiential circumstances. In order to disentangle respective influences, nonmaltreated comparison groups that are matched with the maltreatment groups on variables such as SES, race, family structure, education, and public assistance must be utilized (Okun et al., 1994). Such methodologies and strategies have resulted in the identification of significant differences between abused and nonabused children living within comparable environments (e.g., Cicchetti & Toth, 1995; Dodge, Pettit, & Bates, 1994; Toth & Cicchetti, 1996a,b).

We approach our review of the consequences of maltreatment with an organizational framework that necessitates an examination of adaptation on stage-salient issues. Our review focuses on issues of physiological regulation, affect differentiation and the modulation of attention and arousal, the development of attachment relationships and of self-system processes, peer relations, and adaptation to school among maltreated children. Each issue, while salient during a given period of development, also continues to be important to adaptation across the life course. Thus, relevant research is reported for each stage-salient issue even if the issue is beyond its period of apogee. Moreover, because research with maltreated children is not available for each issue at its most salient point, some issues only include research that is beyond the point of developmental salience. Although by no means reflecting a comprehensive review of the sequelae of maltreatment literature, these issues encompass areas that forebode later maladaptation in the absence of intervention. Furthermore, in accordance with the ecological–transactional framework, we identify possible potentiating and compensatory factors from varying ecological levels that compound, complement, or offset the deleterious effects of abuse on development, and thus account for the heterogeneity in functioning among samples of maltreated children. Additionally, specific deviant developmental trajectories among maltreated children are highlighted.

Physiological Regulation

One of the first tasks of development is the maintenance of physiological or homeostatic regulation (Emde, Gaensbauer, & Harmon, 1976; Greenspan, 1981; Sroufe, 1979). The goal of a homeostatic system is to maintain a "set point" of functioning or homeostatic equilibrium. Departure from this point introduces tension into the system, which serves as the motivation for behavioral systems that subsequently act to dissipate tension and return the system once more to a state of homeostasis (Bischof, 1975). Tension during the first months of life is defined in terms of changes in the infant's arousal level and the physiological discomfort caused by these experiences. Thus, overarousal or physical discomfort generates homeostatic tension in infancy.

Throughout the first months of life, caregivers and infants develop their own system of signals or language through which infants can effectively communicate their needs and caregivers can sensitively respond to them (Sroufe, 1979). Miscommunication between an infant and caregiver can potentially produce homeostatic tension within the infant's physiological system. Therefore, an infant's homeostatic system is viewed as an open system, in which the caregiver plays an integral role in (1) helping the infant modulate states and reduce internal tension; (2) assisting in the establishment of basic cycles and rhythms of balance between inner need states and external stimuli (Hofer, 1987); and (3) guiding the maturation and development of physiological regulation (Sander, 1962). By directly aiding infants in the maintenance of physiological homeostasis in the early weeks of life, caregivers may also influence the development and organization of neurological systems (Black & Greenough, 1986). Such influences on the part of the caregiver during a period of rapid neurological growth and maturation may have long-term effects on the organization and development of the infant's central nervous system.

A paucity of evidence exists that delineates how stressful rearing environments impact psychophysiological and neurological development among children. Adverse life circumstances, exemplified by maltreatment, can be viewed as potentially chronic stressors to a child's physiological processes, and are expected to negatively influence early physiological regulation and development. Although the impact of maltreatment on physiological regulation has not received any attention, examination of the neurobiological sequelae of child abuse and neglect may enhance our understanding of the mechanisms contributing to pathological development in maltreated children (Cicchetti & Tucker, 1994).

The studies on physiological regulation that have been conducted beyond infancy reveal atypical physiological processes in maltreated children. In particular, noradrenergic, dopaminergic, and glucocorticoid systems, which are activated by stress, may be affected. For example, Rogeness (1991) has found abnormal noradrenergic activity, as indicated by lower urinary norepinephrine, in children who have been abused and neglected. This finding is significant because noradrenergic functions are believed to be associated with attention, conditioning, internalization of values, anxiety, and inhibition (Rogeness, Javors, & Pliszka, 1992). In addition, sexually abused girls have been shown to excrete significantly greater amounts of the dopamine metabolite homovanillac acid (DeBellis, Lefter, Trickett, & Putnam, 1994). Furthermore, abnormal cortisol levels have been found in sexually abused girls, implicating altered glucocorticoid functions in the hypothalamic–pituitary–adrenal axis. Relatedly, the attenuated plasma adrenocorticotropic hormone (ACTH) responses to the ovine corticotropin-releasing hormone (CRH) stimulation test in sexually abused girls further suggests a dysregulatory disorder of the hypothalamic–pituitary–adrenal axis (DeBellis et al., 1993).

Information is accumulating on the functioning of the hypothalamic–pituitary–adrenocortical (HPA) system in maltreated children (Hart, Gunnar, & Cicchetti, 1995, 1996). Hart and colleagues (1995) examined the salivary cortisol concentrations and social behavior (via observations and teacher reports) of maltreated and nonmaltreated children. Results indicated a reduction in cortisol reactivity in maltreated children related to the impairment in social competence frequently noted among these children.

Hart et al. (1996) also examined the effects of maltreatment on physiological and affective functioning in a large group of school-age maltreated and nonmaltreated children attending a summer day camp. These investigators discovered that maltreated children had slightly elevated afternoon cortisol concentrations, whereas their morning concentrations did not differ significantly from those of nonmaltreated children. Neither clinical levels of depression, nor internalizing or externalizing problems were predictive of these elevated afternoon values. Depression among maltreated children was, however, associated with altered activity of the HPA system. Specifically, depressed maltreated children displayed lower morning cortisol concentrations compared with nondepressed maltreated children and were more likely to show a rise rather than the expected decrease in cortisol from morning to afternoon. In addition, there was no evidence that depressed, nonmaltreated children exhibited this change in diurnal cortisol activity.

Investigations aimed at elucidating how the timing of maltreatment impacts physiological development suggest that maltreatment at developmentally critical points may have particular effects on the noradrenergic system. Specifically, Galvin and colleagues (1991) have focused on serum dopamine beta hydroxylase (DBH), an enzyme involved in the conversion of dopamine to norepinephrine. In general, boys who were abused and/or neglected early in life (i.e., before 36 months of age) revealed lower DBH activity than those who were abused later in life or who were never maltreated (Galvin et al., 1991). Based on previous primate and human studies that suggest serious disruptions in the formation of attachment relationships during developmentally sensitive or critical periods may result in regulatory failure of the noradrenergic system (Kandel, 1983; Sapolsky, Krey, & McEwen, 1984), Galvin and his colleagues interpret their low DBH findings among young maltreated boys as indicative of a biological sequela of abuse and neglect brought about by an early impairment in the parent–child attachment relationship.

Other biological studies have examined the effects of different types of maltreatment. For example, Jensen and his colleagues studied the growth hormone (GH) response patterns of sexually and physically abused boys (Jensen, Pease, Ten Bensel, & Garfinkel, 1991). These investigators discovered that, compared with psychiatric controls and normal comparisons, boys who had experienced different types of abuse developed disparate patterns of neuroendocrine dysregulation. Specifically, sexually abused boys showed an increased GH response to clonidine and a decreased response to L-dopa. This pattern may be linked to feelings of anxiety, isolation, mistrust, and depression, and a tendency toward revictimization and self-destructive behavior among sexually abused boys (Jensen et al., 1991; van der Kolk, 1987). On the other hand, physically abused boys showed a decreased GH response to clonidine and an increased response to L-dopa. The pattern for physically abused boys may be associated with behavioral lessening of activity, increased learning or "overlearning," and increased fear and enhanced startle response (Jensen et al., 1991). This pattern among physically abused boys may suggest a prelude to hypervigilance in some maltreated children (see, e.g., Hill, Bleichfeld, Brunstetter, Hebert, & Steckler, 1989).

Maltreated children also evidence different cognitive event-related potentials (ERPs) to positive and negative affective stimuli than do nonmaltreated youngsters (Pollak, Cicchetti, Klorman, & Brumaghim, 1997). Specifically, maltreated children had larger P300 amplitudes in the angry than in the happy target conditions as compared to nonmaltreated children, who displayed equivalent response amplitudes in both target conditions. The authors interpret the greater P300 amplitude findings among maltreated children as indicative of more efficient cognitive organization in the anger condition than during the happy condition. Such patterns of activation suggest that the increased neurophysiological reactivity of maltreated children may be reflective of their affective representation of their prior experiences with their caregivers.

Affect Differentiation and the Modulation of Attention and Arousal

An early stage-salient developmental task in infancy involves the ability to regulate and differentiate affective experience. Affect regulation pertains to the internal and external organismic factors by which emotional arousal is redirected, controlled, modulated, and modified to enable an individual to optimize performance and function adaptively in emotionally arousing situations (Cicchetti et al., 1991; Thompson, 1990). Because affect-regulatory processes emerge within the context of early caregiving experiences, maltreatment poses a significant threat to a child's affective development (cf. Lewis, 1992). Child maltreatment represents a profound disturbance in parent–child relationships that is likely to lead to maladaptive deviations in affective processing abilities. In accord with an organizational and developmental psychopathology perspective, early affect-regulatory failures among maltreated children place them at risk for future maladaptive peer relations, including later relationship difficulties (Howes & Cicchetti, 1993; Shields, Cicchetti, & Ryan, 1994).

Maltreated infants also exhibit distortions in their early patterns of affect differentiation (Gaensbauer & Hiatt, 1984). Specifically, they manifest either excessive amounts of negative affect or, in contrast, blunted patterns of affect, where they express neither positive nor negative emotions.

Deviations in the development of emotion expression among maltreated children have been noted as early as 3 months of age. Gaensbauer (1980) demonstrated that physically abused infants develop negative affects such as fear, anger, and sadness earlier than is the case with nonabused infants, where these negative affects do not appear until approximately 7–9 months of age (Sroufe, 1996). It is conceivable that early maltreatment experiences accelerate the development of negative affect in infancy, and that these maltreatment experiences contribute to the development of corresponding neurobiological changes in the negative affect pathways in the brain (cf. Cicchetti & Tucker, 1994; Eisenberg, 1995; Pollak et al., 1997). Izard and Harris (1995) suggested that the innate response of anger to pain is obstructed in maltreated children, with fear rather than anger being exhibited in the context of a physically abusive parent. Thus, normal emotional reactions in maltreated children tend to be undermined, resulting in an atypical organization of emotions and their experiences. Gaensbauer, Mrazek, and Harmon (1981) delineated four affective patterns that appeared to be relatively consistent and that could represent the predominant dysfunctional communicative patterns between maltreated mothers and their infants. *Affectively retarded* behavior patterns demonstrated a lack of social responsiveness, with emotional blunting and inattentiveness to the environment. *Depressed* affective patterns involve inhibition, withdrawal, aimless play, and sad and depressed facial expressions. *Ambivalent* or *affectively labile* patterns show sudden shifts from engagement and pleasure to withdrawal and anger. *Angry* behavior patterns manifest active disorganized play and a low frustration tolerance, with frequent angry outbursts. Although the direction of causality of these atypical communication patterns remains to be ascertained, it is apparent that deviant styles of affective displays, decreased responsivity, and poor quality interactions tend to characterize maltreating dyads.

A spectrum of affect-regulatory deficits also have been identified among maltreated children. Specifically, these children evidence a greater prevalence of anxiety, depression, aggression, impulsivity, inattentiveness, and social withdrawal in comparison to equally disadvantaged nonmaltreated peers (Erickson, Egeland, & Pianta, 1989; Toth, Manly, & Cicchetti, 1992). The emotional self-regulatory deficits identified among maltreated children have been attributed to aberrant modulation of positive and negative affects. Because serotonin is the neurotransmitter involved in the fine-tuning of arousal and aggression (Spoont, 1992), it is conceivable that maltreatment experiences bring about a dysregulation of the neuromodulating serotonergic system.

Research indicates that early maladaptive processing of stimuli that induce negative affect in infancy may lay the foundation for future problems in modulating powerful negative affect. For example, physically abused preschool boys who witnessed an angry simulated interaction directed at their mothers by an adult female evinced greater aggressiveness and more coping responses aimed at alleviating the distress of their mothers than did nonabused boys (Cummings, Hennessy, Rabideau, & Cicchetti, 1994). Rather than habituating to others' hostility as a result of their history of exposure to familial violence, these abused children appeared more aroused and angered by it and more motivated to intervene. Moreover, because level of arousal is related to one's subsequent propensity for aggression, heightened arousal in abused children could contribute to the development of aggressive patterns, particularly if conflict in the home is chronic (cf. Lewis, 1992).

In a related line of inquiry, Hennessy, Rabideau, Cicchetti, and Cummings (1994) presented physically abused and nonabused boys with videotaped vignettes of adults in angry and friendly interactions. After viewing the vignettes, abused boys reported experiencing more distress than nonabused boys in response to interadult hostility, especially when the hostility involved unresolved anger between adults. Moreover, physically abused boys reported more fear in response to different forms of angry adult behavior. These findings support a sensitization model whereby repeated exposure to anger and familial violence leads to greater emotional reactivity. Similarly, the distress responses to interadult anger that abused children display may provide an early indication of an increased potential for developing internalizing problems among children exposed to high levels of familial violence.

A number of cross-sectional investigations provide evidence for specific developmental trajectories from affect-regulatory problems to behavioral dysregulation among maltreated children. Maltreated preschool- (Alessandri, 1991; Haskett & Kistner, 1991) and school-age children (Shields et al., 1994) have been found to exhibit a range of dysregulated behaviors that are frequently characterized by disruptive and aggressive actions. Maltreated toddlers also have been shown to react to peer distress with poorly regulated and situationally inappropriate affect and behavior, including anger, fear, and aggression, as opposed to the more normatively expected response of empathy and concern (Howes & Eldredge, 1985; Main & George, 1985; Troy & Sroufe, 1987). Moreover, Erickson et al. (1989) found that during the preschool years, maltreated toddlers were rated by teachers as more hyperactive, distractible, lacking in self-control, and evidencing a higher level of negative affect than nonmaltreated peers. In kindergarten, the maltreated children were viewed as more inattentive, aggressive, and overactive by their teachers.

Additional evidence about the affective coping strategies of maltreated children can be seen in studies of cognitive control functioning. Rieder and Cicchetti (1989) have found that maltreated children are more hypervigilant to aggressive stimuli and recall a greater number of distracting aggressive stimuli than do nonmaltreated children. Maltreated children also assimilate aggressive stimuli more readily even though this impairs their efficiency on cognitive control tasks. Hypervigilance and ready assimilation of aggressive stimuli may develop originally as an adaptive coping strategy in the maltreating environment, alerting the child to signs of imminent danger and keeping affects from rising so high that they would incapacitate the child. Although hypervigilance and quick assimilation of aggressive stimuli may emerge as an adaptive coping response in a maltreating environment, this strategy becomes less adaptive when children are faced with nonthreatening situations.

Development of Attachment Relationships

Since the advent of Bowlby's (1969/1982) seminal exposition on attachment theory, there has been assent among developmental psychologists and psychopathologists that the establishment of a secure attachment relationship between an infant and his or her caregiver is one of the primary tasks during the first year of life. Achieving security in the attachment relationship provides the infant with a secure base from which to explore his or her environment (Bowlby, 1969/1982; Sroufe, 1979). As development proceeds, attachment theorists (Bowlby, 1969/1982, 1973, 1980) have delineated how cognition, emotion, and behavior are integrated and influence ongoing and future relationships with others, as well as the understanding of the self. In recent years, the principles of attachment theory have had a major impact on efforts to provide a framework within which to conceptualize, treat, and understand the impact of maltreatment on child development. In view of the extreme relational dysfunction that occurs in maltreating families, attachment theorists maintain that maladaptive attachment processes exert a substantial effect on the development of the psychopathological symptoms and disorders that have been associated with child maltreatment. Thus, efforts aimed at delineating the attachment processes in children who have been maltreated represent an important area of inquiry.

The main issue concerning researchers relates to the quality of attachment among maltreated children and the nature of their internal representational models of attachment figures, the self, and the self in relation to others. Since the 1980s, investigators have utilized the Ainsworth and Wittig (1969) Strange Situation paradigm to study the attachment organization of maltreated infants and toddlers. A number of studies have shown that maltreated children are more likely to form insecure attachments with their caregivers than are nonmaltreated children. Using traditional attachment classification schemes (cf. Ainsworth, Blehar, Waters, & Wall, 1978), approximately two-thirds of maltreated children have insecure attachments to their mothers (either anxious–avoidant Type A or anxious–resistant Type C), while the remaining one-third of these children have secure attachments (Type B). The reverse pattern is observed in nonmaltreated children. In addition, both cross-sectional and longitudinal studies that employ only the traditional ABC attachment typology reveal that, with increasing age, maltreated infants' attachments are more likely to be classified as insecure-avoidant (see, e.g., Cicchetti & Barnett, 1991a; Schneider-Rosen, Braunwald, Carlson, & Cicchetti, 1985).

Over the years, a number of investigators have observed unusual patterns of attachment behavior that cannot be easily captured by the traditional attachment classification system (e.g., Crittenden, 1988; Egeland & Sroufe, 1981; Main & Solomon, 1990). Unlike infants from nonrisk samples who fit within the original attachment ratings of secure (Type B), anxious-avoidant (Type A), and anxious-resistant (Type C), infants from high-risk and maltreating populations often lack organized strategies for dealing with separations from and reunions with their caregiver. Crittenden (1988) found that many children who had been both abused and neglected could be classified as having avoidant–resistant (A/C) patterns of attachment. Main and Solomon (1990) describe this pattern of attachment as disorganized/disoriented (Type D). In addition to presenting unorganized attachment strategies with primary caregivers, maltreated children manifest other bizarre symptoms in the presence of their caregiver such as interrupted movements and expressions, dazing, freezing and stilling behaviors, and apprehension. With the incorporation of the Type D and A/C atypical attachment patterns, insecure attachment rates among maltreated infants and toddlers have increased dramatically, with percentages averaging around 90% (Crittenden, 1988; Lyons-Ruth, Connell, Zoll, & Stahl, 1987). For example, Carlson, Cicchetti, Barnett, and Braunwald (1989a) found that more than 80% of the maltreated infants in their study had atypical, disorganized/disoriented attachments compared with less than 20% of a demographically comparable nonmaltreated comparison group.

Several explanations have been proposed to account for the preponderance of atypical attachment relations in maltreated infants. Because inconsistent care is a hallmark of maltreating families, combinations of insensitive overstimulation, which has been linked to avoidant attachment, and insensitive understimulation, which has been associated with resistant attachment, are likely to be present (Belsky, Rovine, & Taylor, 1984; Crittenden, 1985; Lyons-Ruth et al., 1987). The combination of these caregiving styles could lead to the contradictory features associated with Type D attachments. The fear that pervades maltreating families also has been viewed as central to the emergence of the disorganized/disoriented attachment (Main & Hesse, 1990). Finally the common pattern of child parentification in maltreating families, where role reversal results in the child caring for the parent, may reflect an underlying disorganized/disoriented attachment relationship (Carlson et al., 1989b; Howes & Cicchetti, 1993).

Even though attachment has been conceived as being most salient during infancy and toddlerhood, the importance of attachment beyond the early years of life has begun to receive increased attention in the literature (see, e.g., Ainsworth, 1989; Bretherton, 1985; Main, Kaplan, & Cassidy, 1985). Because the developmental capacities that emerge during the preschool period allow the attachment relationship to become more interpersonally connected while the child simultaneously evidences increased autonomy, this period of transition is especially important. Consistent with attachment patterns identified in infancy, maltreated children are more likely than nonmaltreated children to have insecure attachments throughout the preschool years (Cicchetti & Barnett, 1991b). However, when attachment patterns are examined beyond the toddler period, it appears that fewer maltreated children manifest an atypical pattern of attachment (i.e., Type D or A/C). For example, in a cross-sectional/longitudinal investigation of attachment organization in preschool-age maltreated children (Cicchetti & Barnett, 1991a), 30-, 36-, and 48-month-old children evidenced higher rates of insecure attachments than nonmaltreated children, with only 30-month-old children differing significantly from nonmaltreated children in the formation of atypical attachment patterns. Consistent with the findings on attachment stability during infancy and toddlerhood (Schneider-Rosen, et al., 1985), the longitudinal data presented by Cicchetti and Barnett (1991a) revealed that the insecure attachments of maltreated children remained stable across each of the three age groups studied (30, 36, and 48 months), while the attachments of maltreated preschoolers who were classified as secure tended to be unstable. In contrast, securely attached nonmaltreated comparison children showed stability of attachment across the subsequent age periods studied, whereas insecurely attached comparisons revealed an instability in their attachment classification. Although the rates of atypical attachments among maltreated children appear to decrease to approximately 30% after infancy and toddlerhood (Cicchetti & Barnett, 1991a), the continued prevalence of insecure attachment patterns underscores the risk that maltreated children face in achieving adaptive outcomes.

As the examination of attachment approaches the school-age years, investigators have needed to develop alternate strategies for assessing internalized representations or internal working models of the caregiving relationship. One recent method that has emerged involves the use of a self-report measure, the Relatedness Scales (Connell & Wellborn, 1991; Lynch & Cicchetti, 1991), in which the child is asked to rate the quality of his or her relationship to various partners (i.e., mother, teacher, and peers). In exploring the patterns of relatedness among school-aged maltreated children, Lynch and Cicchetti (1991) found a preponderance of nonoptimal (i.e., insecure) patterns of relatedness, indicating continued maladaptation in the representations of their relationships. Approximately 30% of these maltreated children, between the ages of 7 and 13 years, reported having a "confused" pattern of relatedness to their mothers. This pattern is characterized by children reporting that they feel warm and secure with their mothers despite not feeling psychologically close to them. The identification of a confused pattern of relatedness may be consistent with accounts that some maltreated children manifest a basic confusion, disorganization, or disorientation in how they mentally represent their relationship with their mothers.

More recently, Toth and Cicchetti (1996a) investigated the link between nonoptimal patterns of relatedness among maltreated and nonmaltreated school-age children and the emergence of depressive symptomatology. Findings indicated that maltreated children with nonoptimal or confused patterns of relatedness with their mothers reported higher rates of depressed symptomatology than maltreated children with optimal or adequate relatedness to their mother. These findings are significant in that the formation of an adequate pattern of relatedness with a primary caregiver in the school-age years may buffer or mitigate against the deleterious effects of maltreatment. Within an ecological–transactional framework, optimal patterns of relatedness represent a compensatory factor that assists in the moderation of pathological processes in ontogenic development. This finding is consistent with research that has found that resilient individuals frequently report a positive relationship history with a significant adult during childhood (Masten, Best, & Garmezy, 1990).

The Development of Self-System Processes

After the consolidation of the attachment relationship, the succeeding stage-salient issue for children is the establishment of a sense of self as separate from the caregiver and as capable of autonomous functioning (Lewis & Brooks-Gunn, 1979). The development of an autonomous self occurs during the 18 to 36-month period, when toddlers become increasingly able to construct differentiated and sophisticated representations of the self in relation to others (Greenspan & Porges, 1984). Increasingly during this period, responsibility for self-regulation and the regulation of affect is transferred from the caregiver–child dyad to the child alone. The caregiver's sensitivity to, and tolerance of, the toddler's strivings for autonomy, in addition to the caregiver's ability to set age-appropriate limits, are necessary for the successful resolution of this issue. Caregivers who feel rejected as a result of their toddler's increasing independence, or who are stressed by their child's new demands, may inhibit the emergence of autonomy in their children.

As self-capacities emerge, children raised within maltreating environments are at heightened risk for maladaptive self-development. Knowing that maltreated children receive chronically insensitive care from parents (Crittenden, 1991; Trickett & Susman, 1988) and that they are likely to form insecure attachment relationships, one would expect that children who have been maltreated will manifest disturbances in their self-system processes. Studies on the visual self-recognition of maltreated children provide some insight into their emerging self-concepts. An examination of visual self-recognition in maltreated toddlers revealed no differences between maltreated and nonmaltreated youngsters, suggesting that this aspect of self-development is maturationally based (cf. Kagan, 1981; Mans, Cicchetti, & Sroufe, 1978; Schneider-Rosen & Cicchetti, 1984, 1991). However, differences were detected with regard to affective responsivity. Maltreated toddlers were more likely than comparison children to display either neutral or negative affect upon seeing their rouge-marked images in a mirror, possibly indicating an early precursor to a generalized low sense of self-worth. In contrast, nonmaltreated toddlers were more likely to evince positive affective reactions.

Other delays in maltreated children's self-system have been noted in their ability to talk about the internal states and feelings of self and other. Because socialization plays a significant role in a child's expression of affect, caregivers can directly influence a child's ability to express various emotions. In doing so, a caregiver's ability to talk about his or her own feelings and to use emotion words during interactions teaches the children adaptive or maladaptive forms of affective expression. Beeghly and Cicchetti (1994) examined the internal-state language that maltreated and nonmaltreated toddlers used with their mothers. Although children did not differ on receptive vocabulary, significant group differences on productive and internal-state language variables emerged. Maltreated toddlers used proportionately fewer internal-state words, showed less differentiation in their attributional focus, and were more context-bound in their use of internal-state language than their nonmaltreated peers. Whereas the maltreated and nonmaltreated children generally did not differ significantly in the categorical context of their internal-state language (i.e., words about perception, volition, etc.), there were two notable exceptions. Nonmaltreated children produced proportionately more utterances about physiological states (hunger, thirst, state of consciousness) and more utterances about negative affect (hate, disgust, anger, bad feelings). Results suggest that the use of negative emotion words, references to the self, and the self's desires may provoke responses in the mother that generate anxiety in the child that necessitate regulation and control. Therefore, the tendency for maltreated children to use fewer negative internal-state words may represent an adaptive coping strategy. By modifying their language (and perhaps even their thinking), maltreated children are able to escape the anxiety engendered by certain aspects of language and discourse in parent–child dyads.

In addition, Alessandri and Lewis (1996) studied the expression of self-conscious emotions among a sample of 84 maltreated and nonmaltreated preschool children. The investigators were interested in examining the presence of pride and shame behavior as elicited through problem-solving tasks between mother and child. Differences were found between maltreated and nonmaltreated preschoolers in the expression of both pride and shame. Specifically, findings indicated significant sex differences, with maltreated girls showing less pride and more shame as compared to both maltreated boys and nonmaltreated comparisons. Also, the responses of maltreating mothers during problem-solving tasks contained more negative comments, especially among mother–daughter dyads, as compared to the feedback of non-maltreating mothers.

Moving beyond infancy and toddlerhood, studies with school-age youngsters continue to identify abnormalities in the self-system of maltreated children. In general, maltreated children show deficits in self-esteem when compared with nonabused children. However, consistent with the work of Katz and Zigler (1967), there appear to be different patterns of findings for children of different ages. Young maltreated children actually have been shown to overrate their level of competence and peer acceptance in comparison to nonmaltreated children (Vondra, Barnett, & Cicchetti, 1989). Alternatively, by the age of 8 to 9 years, when the self-esteem is more consolidated, maltreated children evidence lower rates of self-esteem and perceive themselves as being less competent than do nonmaltreated children. The overinflated or "false" self-representations exhibited by the younger maltreated children are viewed as a compensatory strategy, or defense mechanism, to minimize the experience of self-deprecating emotions precipitated by their dysfunctional home environments. Consistent with this conceptualization, maltreated children often act compulsively compliant with their caregivers and display insincere positive affect (Crittenden & DiLalla, 1988). Aberrations in the self-system also have been reported in chronic cases of sexual abuse. Fragmentations in self-organization were found among a sample of sexually abused adolescent females, who demonstrated deviant splitting between both positive and negative self-references (Calverley, Fischer, & Ayoub, 1994). For example, the sexually abused girls described discrepant aspects of their core selves without seeming to recognize the disparity among their self-descriptions.

Peer Relations

The development of peer relationships is yet another important stage-salient task of ontogenic development. Many important issues of social and emotional development are directly influenced by a child's exposure to the peer system. Because family and peer relationships have been described as interacting "synergistically" (Hartup, 1983), maltreated children are at risk for developing dysfunctional peer relations. Unfortunately, maltreated children's history of insecure attachment patterns and maladaptive representational models of self and other hamper their ability to form adaptive peer relationships. Those children who perform poorly with peers, especially when their ecologies are unsupportive, are at heightened risk to experience continued incompetence and maladaptation. Conversely, the presence of positive peer relations among children who have experienced maltreatment could facilitate the promotion of adaptive development (see, e.g., Cowen, Pederson, Babigian, Izzo, & Trost, 1973).

Two main themes have emerged across studies in the literature on peer relations in maltreated children (Mueller & Silverman, 1989), with maltreated children manifesting either elevated aggression toward or withdrawal from peers (Dodge, et al., 1994; George & Main, 1979; Hoffman-Plotkin & Twentyman, 1984; Rogosch, Cicchetti, & Aber, 1995; Salzinger, Feldman, Hammer, & Rosario, 1993). Some of the most salient findings indicate that (1) maltreated children evidence more antisocial behaviors, that is, agressiveness, meanness, and disruptiveness, and fewer prosocial behaviors such as leadership and sharing in their interaction with peer groups (Salzinger et al., 1993); and (2) abused preschoolers are more likely to cause distress in their peers than are nonabused children (Klimes-Dougan & Kistner, 1990). In a longitudinal study, Dodge et al. (1994) found that maltreated children were more disliked, less popular, and more socially withdrawn, based on peer, teacher, and mother evaluations, than nonmaltreated comparisons. Moreover, rejection of maltreated children by peers was found to increase over a 5-year period, where by grades 3 and 4, maltreated children received social preference scores that were two-thirds of a standard deviation below the scores of nonmaltreated children.

Furthermore, Rogosch and Cicchetti (1994) have identified a subgroup of maltreated and nonmaltreated children who are perceived by their peers as demonstrating a combination of aggressive and withdrawn behavior. In particular, maltreated children who were perceived as relatively high on both aggression and withdrawal by their peers evidence substantially lower social effectiveness than is the case for nonmaltreated comparison children. This co-occurrence of aggression and withdrawal may represent the continued operation of disorganized representational models of relationships carried forward from the attachment relationship into new social encounters, resulting in disturbances in social adaptation. The aggressive–withdrawn strategy may be used protectively to diminish the anticipated negative aspects of interpersonal relations; aggression may be employed to terminate perceived interpersonal threats, while isolation may be utilized to avoid threats.

Significant difficulties in developing and maintaining friendships also have been found in physically abused children (Parker & Herrera, 1996). In an investigation of preadolescent and young adolescent physically abused children, physically abused children and their friends were found to display less intimacy in their interactions than nonabused children and their friends. Friendships of physically abused children also were more conflictual, especially during situations where emotion regulation skills were taxed, such as during competitive activities (Parker & Herrera, 1996).

Adaptation to School

The final task of ontogenic development that we address involves adaptation to school. School represents the major extrafamilial environment in which children are exposed to a novel community of unfamiliar peers and adults, and are presented with a new set of stage-salient tasks that include integration into the peer group, acceptable performance in the classroom, and appropriate motivational orientations for achievement.

Because a child's experience in the home serves as the foundation on which the transition to the school setting is built, it is not surprising that children who have been maltreated are at extremely high risk for failure in school. Eckenrode and his colleagues have shown that maltreated children, in comparison with nonmaltreated children, perform worse on standardized tests, obtain lower grades, and are more likely to repeat a grade (Eckenrode, Laird, & Doris, 1993). In addition, maltreated children receive significantly more discipline referrals and suspensions than nonmaltreated peers (Eckenrode et al., 1993). Furthermore, Rogosch and Cicchetti (1994) found that teachers consistently perceive maltreated children as evidencing greater maladaptation in social functioning than nonmaltreated children. Specifically, teachers evaluate maltreated children as less socially competent, as less socially accepted by their peers, and as displaying higher levels of behavioral disturbance, particularly externalizing problems.

An especially important factor in resolving the task of adaptation to school may be "secure readiness to learn." Aber, Allen, Carlson, and Cicchetti (1989) have proposed that effectance motivation, which is the intrinsic desire to deal competently with one's environment (see, e.g., Zigler, Abelson, Trickett, & Seitz, 1982), and successful relations with novel adults (i.e., relations that are characterized by neither dependency nor wariness; cf. Zigler &

Balla, 1982) are important factors related to children's being able to adapt to their first major out-of-home environment. "Secure readiness to learn" is characterized by high effectance motivation and low dependency. Maltreated children consistently score lower than comparison children on secure readiness to learn (Aber et al., 1989). Secure readiness to learn appears to represent a dynamic balance between establishing secure relationships with adults and feeling free to explore the environment in ways that will promote cognitive competence. The findings of Aber and his colleagues with school-age children are particularly compelling because the results are congruent with prior research on how maltreatment affects development in infants and toddlers. At both of these developmental periods, preschool and school-age, maltreatment interferes with the balance between the motivation to establish secure relationships with adults and the motivation to explore the world in competency-promoting ways.

In addition, Trickett, McBride-Chang, and Putnam (1994) examined the impact of sexual abuse on academic performance and achievement in a group of 16-year-old females. These investigators were interested in elucidating the role of possible factors that might buffer or exacerbate the negative influences of sexual abuse on school performance. The findings indicated that previous abuse predicted lower teacher ratings of classroom social competence, competence in learning, and overall academic performance. The sexually abused females also exhibited higher levels of anxious depression, bizarre destructiveness patterns, and dissociation than nonabused comparisons. Overall, cognitive ability and perceived competence were identified as having direct mediating effects on overall academic performance and achievement, while dissociative and destructive behaviors exacerbated the child's level of school success.

Furthermore, Okun and colleagues (1994) examined the independent and interactive effects of physical abuse, recent exposure to additional negative life events (i.e., death, illness, or divorce), and a composite of social disadvantage or stress measures (i.e., SES, family size and structure, housing conditions, and minority status) on children's social, cognitive, and affective adjustment in middle childhood. Results indicated that abused children, in comparison to nonabused children, evidenced significant difficulties in three areas: peer adjustment, self-perceptions, and depression. Further analyses identified unique effects of negative events and socioeconomic disadvantage on children's adjustment: (1) Cumulative negative life events predicted lower rates of self-perception and depression; and (2) deficits in peer-adjustment and cognitive maturity were independently related to socioeconomic disadvantage. Also, additive contributions of abuse and socioeconomic disadvantage predicted behavior problems at school and in the home. By differentiating between the unique and interactive effects of multiple environmental influences (i.e., physical abuse, negative life events, and socioeconomic disadvantage) on child development, Okun and colleagues support the claim that maltreatment may not be the only or even primary contributing factor in the manifestation of problems among abused and neglected children (Wolfe, 1987). Exposure to various concomitant potentiating factors can help to explain the diversity of developmental pathways that maltreated children take.

In a further examination of possible links between relationship patterns and school adaptation, Toth and Cicchetti (1996a) found that the security that a child experienced in relation to his or her mother, in interaction with maltreatment status, significantly affected school functioning. Nonmaltreated children who reported secure patterns of relatedness to their mothers exhibited less externalizing symptomatology, more ego resilience, and fewer school-record risk factors (e.g., attendance problems, poor achievement test performance, suspensions, failure in 50% of courses, grade retention) than did maltreated children who reported insecure patterns of relatedness. Additionally, nonmaltreated children with secure patterns of relatedness to their mothers exhibited more positive adaptation in school than did nonmaltreated children who reported insecure patterns of relatedness. The investigations conducted by Trickett et al. (1994), Okun et al. (1994), and Toth and Cicchetti (1996a) all underscore the importance of identifying potentiating and compensatory factors within a child's microsystem that can significantly influence ontogenic success on stage-salient issues.

CHILD MALTREATMENT AND PSYCHOPATHOLOGY

As we have illustrated, maltreated children manifest deviant patterns of functioning across all stage-salient issues of early development. Within an ecological–transactional framework, the deviant developmental profiles characteristic of maltreated children represent significant vulnerability factors that increase the risk of the emergence of psychopathology. The presence of various forms of behavioral disturbance and psychopathology among maltreated children (Aber et al., 1989; Erickson et al., 1989) support developmental psychopathology's concept of multifinality, in that the experience of maltreatment can result in a diversity of outcomes, depending on the child's accomplishment of stage-salient tasks and influences within his or her own ecology.

In general, the literature on maltreated children reveals a greater prevalence of psychiatric symptoms and diagnoses in these youngsters than in nonmaltreated children. Some of these include anxiety disorders, eating disorders, somatic complaints, sexual dysfunction, and affective disorders (Browne & Finkelhor, 1986; Green, 1993; Merry & Andrews, 1994; Wolfe & Jaffe, 1991). For example, maltreatment has been associated with increased rates of child depressive symptomatology (Allen & Tarnowski, 1989; Kaufman, 1991; Toth & Cicchetti, 1996b; Toth et al., 1992). Moreover, in an investigation aimed at elucidating the effects of domestic violence on children's behavior problems and depression, physically abused children were found to manifest higher rates of behavioral problems and depression than did children who had witnessed spousal abuse or who had experienced no known domestic violence (Sternberg et al., 1993). Moreover, in comparing 5- to 10-year-old maltreated and nonmaltreated children on child and parent interviews assessing child disturbances, Famularo, Kinscherff, and Fenton (1992) found significantly higher rates of diagnosis for attention-deficit/hyperactivity disorder, oppositional disorder, and posttraumatic stress disorder (PTSD) among maltreated children.

Research also has been devoted to examining the prevalence of PTSD and dissociative symptomatology in sexually abused children. Sexually abused children have been shown to be at greater risk of developing PTSD symptoms than both nonmaltreated controls and children experiencing other forms of abuse (McLeer, Callaghan, Henry, & Wallen, 1994). Specific aspects of the abuse, such as penetration, duration and frequency of the abuse, the use of force, and the perpetrator's relationship to the child, all have been shown to affect the degree of PTSD symptomatology (Alexander, 1993; Kendall-Tackett, Williams, & Finkelhor, 1993; Kiser, Heston, Millsap, & Pruitt, 1991).

In addition, Nash and colleagues found that sexually abused children also are more vulnerable to dissociative symptoms (i.e., disturbances in soma and self) than children who experienced other forms of maltreatment or nonmaltreated comparisons (Nash, Hulsey, Sexton, Harralson, & Lambert, 1993). Investigators suggest that dissociative symptomatology is used as a defense against the overwhelming trauma the sexually abused children have experienced. Furthermore, disturbances in self-functioning evidenced by maltreated children may be especially apparent in problems with self-definition and integration, and in problems with self-regulatory processes (Cole & Putnam, 1992).

Finally, increased rates of depression (Bemporad & Romano, 1992) and higher rates of violence toward other adults, dating partners, and spouses (Malinosky-Rummell, & Hansen, 1993) also have been documented in adults with histories of childhood maltreatment. Although generalizations from existing research data must be made cautiously because of the varying modes of sampling employed and the presence of co-occurring risk factors, childhood maltreatment also has been linked to antisocial personality disorder, substance abuse, suicidal and self-injurious behavior, somatization, anxiety, and depression (Luntz & Widom, 1994; Malinosky-Rummell & Hansen, 1993). Thus, across childhood and into adulthood, maltreatment poses increased risk for a wide range of disturbances in functioning and varied forms of psychopathology.

CONCLUSIONS

In this chapter, we have utilized a developmental psychopathology approach and an ecological–transactional model to provide a framework for understanding the causes and consequences of child maltreatment. By highlighting the risk and protective factors associated with each level of an ecological–transactional model, multiple pathways toward diverse developmental outcomes among maltreated children begin to emerge.

Our review of the sequelae of maltreatment conveys the negative and often lifelong effects of child abuse and neglect. In the absence of intervention, victims of maltreatment frequently evidence failure on a range of stage-salient issues and are at risk for the emergence of various types of psychopathology. In addition, the inadequate caregiving histories of maltreated children increase the likelihood that they will continue to form maladaptive relationships, often resulting in the cross-generational perpetuation of maltreatment.

Investigative efforts to elucidate the causes and consequences of child maltreatment can play a critical role in enhancing the quality of clinical, legal, and policy-making decisions for maltreated children and their families. Aber and Cicchetti (1984) stated that decisions such as whether to remove a child from the home, how to develop prevention and intervention services to meet the specific needs of maltreated children, and how to evaluate these services would all benefit from a sophisticated database on the sequelae of maltreatment. As funding for a myriad of social ills becomes increasingly competitive, allocation of limited resources is likely to be directed toward those concerns that have the most solid base of popular support and whose intervention services have been documented to be the most effective.

In the past decade, remarkable advancements have been made in our understanding of child maltreatment. We believe that the ecological–transactional model of child maltreatment provides an integrative framework that will assist intervention and prevention efforts, as well as suggest necessary directions for social policies on behalf of children and families. In particular, the ecological–transactional approach requires that we cease searching for simple and direct relations between cause and effect with respect to maltreatment and direct our efforts toward the elucidation of a multilevel ecological perspective. Preventive interventions must occur at all levels of the ecology in order to ameliorate the harmful effects of child maltreatment. The development and implementation of policies that will facilitate the attainment of the goals embodied by an ecological–transactional model will provide the tools necessary to ensure that each child has a "healthy and safe passage to adulthood" (Edelman, 1998, p. 2).

ACKNOWLEDGMENTS.   Our work on this chapter was supported by grants from the National Center on Child Abuse and Neglect and the Spunk Fund, Inc.

REFERENCES

Aber, J. L., Allen, J. P., Carlson, V., & Cicchetti, D. (1989). The effects of maltreatment on development during early childhood: Recent studies and their theoretical, clinical, and policy implications. In D. Cicchetti & V. Carlson (Eds.), *Child maltreatment: Theory and research on the causes and consequences of child abuse and neglect* (pp. 579–619). New York: Cambridge University Press.

Aber, J. L., & Cicchetti, D. (1984). Socioemotional development in maltreated children: An empirical and theoretical analysis. In H. Fitzgerald, B. Lester, & M. Yogman (Eds.), *Theory and research in behavioral pediatrics: Vol. II* (pp. 147–205). New York: Plenum Press.

Aber, J. L., & Zigler, E. (1981). Developmental considerations in the definition of child maltreatment. *New Directions for Child Development, 11*, 1–29.

Ainsworth, M. D. S. (1989). Attachments beyond infancy. *American Psychologist, 44*, 709–716.

Ainsworth, M. D. S., Blehar, M. C., Waters, E., & Wall, S. (1978). *Patterns of attachment: A psychological study of the Strange Situation.* Hillsdale, NJ: Erlbaum.

Ainsworth, M. D. S., & Wittig, B. A. (1969). Attachment and the exploratory behavior of one-year-olds in a Strange Situation. In B. M. Foss (Ed.), *Determinants of infant behavior* (Vol. 4, pp. 113–136). London: Methuen.

Alessandri, S. M. (1991). Play and social behaviors in maltreated preschoolers. *Development and Psychopathology, 3*, 191–206.

Alessandri, S. M., & Lewis, M. (1996). Differences in pride and shame in maltreated and nonmaltreated preschoolers. *Child Development, 67*, 1857–1869.

Alexander, P. C. (1993). The differential effects of abuse characteristics and attachment in the prediction of long-term effects of sexual abuse. *Journal of Interpersonal Violence, 8*, 346–362.

Allen, D., & Tarnowski, K. (1989). Depressive characteristics of physically abused children. *Journal of Abnormal Child Psychology, 17*, 1–11.

Altemeier, W., O'Connor, S., Vietze, P., Sandler, H., & Sherrod, L. (1982). Antecedents of child abuse. *Journal of Pediatrics, 100*, 823–829.

Barnett, D., Manly, J. T., & Cicchetti, D. (1993). Defining child maltreatment: The interface between policy and research. In D. Cicchetti & S. L. Toth (Eds.), *Child abuse, child development, and social policy* (pp. 7–73). Norwood, NJ: Ablex.

Beeghly, M., & Cicchetti, D. (1994). Child maltreatment, attachment and the self system: Emergence of an internal state lexicon in toddlers at high social risk. *Development and Psychopathology, 6*, 5–30.

Belsky, J. (1980). Child maltreatment: An ecological integration. *American Psychologist, 35*, 320–335.

Belsky, J. (1984). The determinants of parenting: A process model. *Child Development, 55*, 83–96.

Belsky, J., Rovine, M., & Taylor, D. G. (1984). The Pennsylvania Infant and Family Development Project, 3: The origins of individual differences in infant–mother attachment: Maternal and infant contributions. *Child Development, 55*, 718–728.

Bemporad, J. R., & Romano, S. J. (1992). Childhood maltreatment and adult depression: A review of research. In D. Cicchetti & S. L. Toth (Eds.), *Rochester Symposium on Developmental Psychopathology: Vol. 4. Developmental perspectives on depression* (pp. 351–376). Rochester, NY: University of Rochester Press.

Bischof, N. (1975). A systems approach toward the functional connections of attachment and fear. *Child Development, 46*, 801–817.

Black, J., & Greenough, W. (1986). Induction of pattern in neural structure by experience: Implications of cognitive development. In M. Lamb, A. Brown, & B. Rogoff (Eds.), *Advances in developmental psychology* (Vol. 4, pp. 1–44). Hillsdale, NJ: Erlbaum.

Bowlby, J. (1982). *Attachment and loss* (Vol. 1). New York: Basic Books. (Original published in 1969)

Bowlby, J. (1973). *Attachment and loss: Vol. 2. Separation.* New York: Basic Books.

Bowlby, J. (1980). *Attachment and loss: Vol. 3. Loss, sadness, and depression.* New York: Basic Books.

Bretherton, I. (1985). Attachment theory: Retrospect and prospect. In I. Bretherton & E. Waters (Eds.), Growing points of attachment theory and research. *Monographs of the Society for Research in Child Development, 50*, 3–38.

Bronfenbrenner, U. (1977). Toward an experimental ecology of human development. *American Psychologist, 32*, 513–531.

Browne, A., & Finkelhor, D. (1986). Initial and long-term effects: A review of the research. In D. Finkelhor (Ed.), *A sourcebook on child sexual abuse* (pp. 143–179). Beverly Hills, CA: Sage.

Brunquell, D., Crichton, L., & Egeland, B. (1981). Maternal personality and attitude in disturbances of child rearing. *American Journal of Orthopsychiatry, 51*, 680–690.

Burgess, R. L., & Conger, R. D. (1978). Family interaction in abusive, neglectful, and normal families. *Child Development, 49*, 1163–1173.

Calverley, R. M., Fischer, K. W., & Ayoub, C. (1994). Complex affective splitting in sexually abused adolescent girls. *Development and Psychopathology, 6*, 195–213.

Carlson, V., Cicchetti, D., Barnett, D., & Braunwald, K. (1989a). Disorganized/disoriented attachment relationships in maltreated infants. *Deveopmental Psychology, 25*, 525–531.

Carlson, V., Cicchetti, D., Barnett, D., & Braunwald, K. (1989b). Finding order in disorganization: Lessons from research in maltreated infants' attachments to their caregivers. In D. Cicchetti & V. Carlson (Eds.), *Child maltreatment: Theory and research on the causes and consequences of child abuse and neglect* (pp. 494–528). New York: Cambridge University Press.

Christoffel, K. K. (1990). Violence death and injury in U.S. children and adolescents. *American Journal of Disease Control, 144*, 697–706.

Cicchetti, D. (1989). How research on child maltreatment has informed the study of child development: Perspectives from developmental psychopathology. In D. Ciccheti & V. Carlson (Eds.), *Child maltreatment: Theory and research on the causes and consequences of child abuse and neglect* (pp. 377–431). New York: Cambridge University Press.

Cicchetti, D. (1993). Developmental psychopathology: Reactions, reflections, projections. *Developmental Review, 13*, 471–502.

Cicchetti, D., & Barnett, D. (1991a). Attachment organization in preschool aged maltreated children. *Development and Psychopathology, 3*, 397–411.

Cicchetti, D., & Barnett, D. (1991b). Toward the development of a scientific nosology of child maltreatment. In W. Grove & D. Cicchetti (Eds.), *Thinking clearly about psychology: Essays in honor of Paul E. Meehl: Vol. 2. Personality and psychopathology* (pp. 346–377). Minneapolis: University of Minnesota Press.

Cicchetti, D., Ganiban, J., & Barnett, D. (1991). Contributions from the study of high risk populations to understanding the development of emotion regulation. In J. Garber & K. Dodge (Eds.), *The development of emotion regulation* (pp. 15–48). New York: Cambridge University Press.

Cicchetti, D., & Howes, P. (1991). Developmental psychopathology in the context of the family: Illustrations from the study of child maltreatment. *Canadian Journal of Behavioural Science, 23*, 257–281.

Cicchetti, D., & Lynch, M. (1993). Toward an ecological/transactional model of community violence and child maltreatment: Consequences for children's development. *Psychiatry, 56*, 96–118.

Cicchetti, D., & Rizley, R. (1981). Developmental perspectives on the etiology, intergenerational transmission, and sequelae of child maltreatment. *New Directions for Child Development, 11*, 31–55.

Cicchetti, D., & Rogosch, F. A. (1996). Equifinality and multifinality in developmental psychopathology. *Development and Psychopathology, 8*, 597–600.

Cicchetti, D., & Toth, S. L. (1995). A developmental psychopathology perspective on child abuse and neglect. *Journal of American Academy of Child and Adolescent Psychiatry, 34*, 541–565.

Cicchetti, D., Toth, S. L., & Hennessy, K. (1993). Child maltreatment and school adaptation: Problems and promises. In D. Cicchetti & S. L. Toth (Eds.), *Child abuse, child development, and social policy* (pp. 301–330). Norwood, NJ: Ablex.

Cicchetti, D., & Tucker, D. (1994). Development and self-regulatory structures of the mind. *Development and Psychopathology, 6*, 533–549.

Cole, P., & Putnam, F. (1992). Effect of incest on self and social functioning: A developmental psychopathology perspective. *Journal of Clinical and Consulting Psychology, 60*, 174–184.

Connell, J. P., & Wellborn, J. G. (1991). Competence, autonomy and relatedness: A motivational analysis of self-system processes. In M. Gunnar & L. A. Sroufe (Eds.), *Minnesota Symposia on Child Psychology: Vol. 23: Self Processes and Development* (pp. 43–78). Hillsdale, NJ: Erlbaum.

Corse, S. J., Schmid, K., & Trickett, P. K. (1990). Social network characteristics of mothers in abusing and nonabusing families and their relationships to parenting beliefs. *Journal of Community Psychology, 18*, 44–59.

Cowen, E., Pederson, A., Babigian, H., Izzo, L., & Trost, M. (1973). Long-term follow-up of early detected vulnerable children. *Journal of Consulting and Clinical Psychology, 41*, 438–446.

Crittenden, P. M. (1981). Abusing, neglecting, problematic, and adequate dyads: Differentiating by patterns of interaction. *Merrill–Palmer Quarterly, 27*, 201–208.

Crittenden, P. M. (1985). Maltreated infants: Vulnerability and resilience. *Journal of Child Psychology and Psychiatry and Allied Disciplines, 26*, 85–96.

Crittenden, P. M. (1988). Relationships at risk. In J. Belsky & T. Nezworski (Eds.), *Clinical implications of attachment theory* (pp. 136–174). Hillsdale, NJ: Erlbaum.

Crittenden, P. M., & Ainsworth, M. D. S. (1989). Attachment and child abuse. In D. Cicchetti & V. Carlson (Eds.), *Child maltreatment: Theory and research on the causes and consequences of child abuse and neglect* (pp. 432–463). New York: Cambridge University Press.

Crittenden, P. M., & DiLalla, D. (1988). Compulsive compliance: The development of an inhibitory coping strategy in infancy. *Journal of Abnormal Child Psychology, 16,* 585–599.

Cummings, E. M., Hennessy, K., Rabideau, G., & Cicchetti, D. (1994). Responses of physically abused boys to interadult anger involving their mothers. *Development and Psychopathology, 6,* 31–42.

DeBellis, M. D., Chrousos, G., Dorn, L., Burke, L., Helmers, K., Kling, M., Trickett, P., Putnam, F. (1993). Hypothalamic–pituitary–adrenal axis dysregulation in sexually abused girls. *Journal of Clinical Endocrinology and Metabolism, 77,* 1–7.

DeBellis, M. D., Lefter, L., Trickett, P. K., & Putnam, F. W. (1994). Urinary catecholamine excretion in sexually abused girls. *Journal of the American Academy of Child and Adolescent Psychiatry, 33,* 320–327.

Dinwiddie, S., & Bucholz, K. (1993). Psychiatric diagnoses of self-reported child abuses. *Child Abuse and Neglect, 17,* 465–476.

Dodge, K. A., Pettit, G. S., & Bates, J. E. (1994). Effects of physical maltreatment on the development of peer relations. *Development and Psychopathology, 6,* 43–55.

Dubrow, N. F., & Garbarino, J. (1989). Living in the war zone: Mothers and young children in a public housing project. *Child Welfare, 68,* 3–20.

Eckenrode, J., Laird, M., & Doris, J. (1993). School performance and disciplinary problems among abused and neglected children. *Developmental Psychology, 29,* 53–62.

Edelman, M. W. (1998). *Stand for children.* Washington, DC: Hyperion.

Egeland, B., & Brunquell, D. (1979). An at-risk approach to the study of child abuse: Some preliminary findings. *Journal of the American Academy of Child Psychiatry, 18,* 219–235.

Egeland, B., & Sroufe, L. A. (1981). Developmental sequelae of maltreatment in infancy. *New Directions for Child Development, 11,* 77–92.

Eisenberg, L. (1995). The social construction of the human brain. *American Journal of Psychiatry, 152,* 1563–1575.

Emde, R. N., Gaensbauer, T., & Harmon, R. (1976). *Emotional expression in infancy: A biobehavioral study.* New York: International Universities Press.

Erickson, M., Egeland, B., & Pianta, R. (1989). The effects of maltreatment on the development of young children. In D. Cicchetti & V. Carlson (Eds.), *Child maltreatment: Theory and research on the causes and consequences of child abuse and neglect* (pp. 647–684). New York: Cambridge University Press.

Famularo, R., Kinscherff, R., & Fenton, T. (1992). Psychiatric diagnoses of maltreated children: Preliminary findings. *Journal of the American Academy of Child and Adolescent Psychiatry, 31,* 863–867.

Fingerhut, L. A., & Kleinman, J. C. (1990). International and interstate comparisons of homicide among young males. *Journal of the American Medical Association, 263,* 3292–3295.

Frodi, A., & Lamb, M. (1980). Child abusers' responses to infant smiles and cries. *Child Development, 51,* 238–241.

Gaensbauer, T. (1980). Anaclitic depression in a three-and-one-half-month-old child. *American Journal of Psychiatry, 137,* 841–842.

Gaensbauer, T., & Hiatt, S. (1984). Facial communication of emotion in early infancy. In N. A. Fox & R. J. Davidson (Eds.), *The psychobiology of affective development* (pp. 207–230). Hillsdale, NJ: Erlbaum.

Gaensbauer, T., Mrazek, D., & Harmon, R. (1981). Emotional expression in abused and/or neglected infants. In N. Frude (Ed.), *Psychological approaches to child abuse* (pp. 120–135). Totowa, NJ: Rowman & Littlefield.

Galvin, M. R., Shekar, A., Simon, J., Stilwell, B., Ten Eyck, R., Laite, G., Karwisch, G., & Blix, S. (1991). Low opamine beta hydroxylase: A biological sequela of abuse and neglect? *Psychiatry Research, 39,* 1–11.

Garbarino, J. A. (1976). A preliminary study of some ecological correlates of child abuse: The impact of socioeconomic stress on mothers. *American Journal of Orthopsychiatry, 47,* 372–381.

Garbarino, J. (1977). The human ecology of child maltreatment: A conceptual model for research. *Journal of Marriage and the Family, 39,* 721–732.

Garbarino, J., & Crouter, A. (1978). Defining the community context for parent–child relations: The correlates of child maltreatment. *Child Development, 49,* 604–616.

Garbarino, J., & Gilliam, G. (1980). *Understanding abusive families.* Lexington, MA: Lexington Press.

Garbarino, J., & Sherman, D. (1980). High-risk neighborhoods and high-risk families: The human ecology of child maltreatment. *Child Development, 51,* 188–198.

Gelles, R. J., & Hargreaves, E. F. (1981). Maternal employment and violence toward children. *Journal of Family Issues, 2,* 509–530.

George, C., & Main, M. (1979). Social interactions of young abused children: Approach, avoidance, and aggression. *Child Development, 50,* 306–318.

Giovannoni, J., & Billingsley, A. (1970). Child neglect among the poor: A study of parental adequacy in families of three ethnic groups. *Child Welfare, 49,* 196–204.

Goldstein, J., Freud, A., & Solnit, A. (1973). *Beyond the best interests of the child.* New York: Free Press.

Green, A. (1993). Child sexual abuse: Immediate and long-term effects and intervention. *Journal of the American Academy of Child and Adolescent Psychiatry, 35,* 890–902.

Greenspan, S. I. (1981). *Psychopathology and adaptation in infancy and early childhood.* New York: International Universities Press.

Greenspan, S. I., & Porges, S. W. (1984). Psychopathology in infancy and early childhood: Clinical perspectives on the organization of sensory and affective–thematic experience. *Child Development, 55,* 49–70.

Hart, J., Gunnar, M., & Cicchetti, D. (1995). Salivary cortisol in maltreated children: Evidence of relations between neuroendocrine activity and social competence. *Development and Psychopathology, 7,* 11–26.

Hart, J., Gunnar, M., & Cicchetti, D. (1996). Altered neuroendocrine activity in maltreated children related to depression. *Development and Psychopathology, 8,* 201–214.

Hartup, W. (1983). Peer relations. In P. Mussen (Ed.), *Handbook of child psychology* (4th ed., pp. 103–196). New York: Wiley.

Haskett, M. E., & Kistner, J. A. (1991). Social interactions and peer perceptions of young physically abused children. *Child Development, 62,* 979–990.

Hennessy, K., Rabideau, G., Cicchetti, D., & Cummings, E. M. (1994). Responses of physically abused children to different forms of interadult anger. *Child Development, 65,* 815–828.

Hill, S. D., Bleichfeld, B., Brunstetter, R. D., Hebert, J. E., & Steckler, S. (1989). Cognitive and physiological responsiveness of abused children. *Journal of the American Academy of Child and Adolescent Psychiatry, 28,* 219–224.

Hofer, M. A. (1987). Early social relationships: A psychobiologist's view. *Child Development, 58,* 633–647.

Hoffman-Plotkin, D., & Twentyman, C. T. (1984). A multimodal assessment of behavioral and cognitive deficits in abused and neglected preschoolers. *Child Development, 55,* 794–802.

Howes, C., & Eldredge, R. (1985). Responses of abused, neglected, and non-maltreated children to the behaviors of their peers. *Journal of Applied Developmental Psychology, 6,* 261–270.

Howes, P., & Cicchetti, D., (1993). A family/relational perspective on maltreating families: Parallel processes across systems and social policy implications. In D. Cicchetti & S. L. Toth (Eds.), *Child abuse, child development and social policy* (pp. 249–300). Norwood, NJ: Ablex.

Hunter, R. S., & Kilstrom, N. (1979). Breaking the cycle in abusive families. *American Journal of Psychiatry, 136,* 1320–1322.

Izard, C. E., & Harris, P. (1995). Emotional development and developmental psychopathology. In D. Cicchetti & D. J. Cohen (Eds.), *Developmental psychopathology: Vol. 1. Theory and methods* (pp. 467–503). New York: Wiley.

Jayaratne, T. E. (1993, March). *Neighborhood quality and parental socialization among single, African American mothers: Child gender differences.* Paper presented at the biennial meeting of the Society for Research in Child Development, New Orleans, LA.

Jensen, J. B., Pease, J. J., Ten Bensel, B. S., & Garfinkel, B. D. (1991). Growth hormone response patterns in sexually or physically abused boys. *Journal of the American Academy of Child and Adolescent Psychiatry, 30,* 784–790.

Kagan, J. (1981). *The second year: The emergence of self-awareness.* Cambridge, MA: Harvard University Press.

Kandel, E. (1983). From metapsychology to molecular biology: Explorations into the nature of anxiety. *American Journal of Psychiatry, 140,* 1277–1293.

Katz, P., & Zigler, E. (1967). Self-image disparity: A developmental approach. *Journal of Personality and Social Psychology, 5,* 186–195.

Kaufman, J. (1991). Depressive disorders in maltreated children. *Journal of the American Academy of Child and Adolescent Psychiatry, 30,* 257–265.

Kaufman, J., & Zigler, E. (1989). The intergenerational transmission of child abuse and the prospect of predicting future abusers. In D. Cicchetti & V. Carlson (Eds.), *Child maltreatment: Research and theory on consequences of child abuse and neglect* (pp. 129–150). New York: Cambridge University Press.

Kavanagh, K. A., Youngblade, L., Reid, J. B., & Fagot, B. I. (1988). Interactions between children and abusive versus control parents. *Journal of Clinical Child Psychology, 17,* 137–142.

Kempe, C. (1973). A practical approach to the protection of the abused child and rehabilitation of the abusing parent. *Pediatrics, 51,* 804–812.

Kempe, C. H., Silverman, F. N., Steele, B. B., Droegemueller, W., & Silver, H. K. (1962). The battered child syndrome. *Journal of the American Medical Association, 181,* 17–24.

Kendall-Tackett, K. A., Williams, L. M., & Finklehor, D. (1993). The impact of sexual abuse on children: A review and synthesis of recent empirical studies. *Psychological Bulletin, 113,* 164–180.

Kiser, L. J., Heston, J., Millsap, P. A., & Pruitt, D. B. (1991). Physical and sexual abuse in childhood: Relationship with post-traumatic stress disorder. *Journal of the American Academy of Child and Adolescent Psychiatry, 30,* 776–783.

Klimes-Dougan, B., & Kistner, J. (1990). Physically abused preschoolers' responses to peer distress. *Developmental Psychology, 26,* 599–602.

Lahey, B., Conger, R., Atkeson, B., & Treiber, F. (1984). Parenting behavior and emotional status of physically abused mothers. *Journal of Consulting and Clinical Psychology, 52,* 1062–1071.

Lewis, D. O. (1992). From abuse to violence: Psychophysiological consequences of maltreatment. *Journal of the American Academy of Child and Adolescent Psychiatry, 31,* 383–391.

Lewis, M. (1997). *Altering fate.* New York: Guilford Press.

Lewis, M., & Brooks-Gunn, J. (1979). *Social cognition and the acquisition of self.* New York: Plenum Press.

Light, R. (1973). Abused and neglected children in America: A study of alternative policies. *Harvard Educational Review, 43,* 556–598.

Luntz, B., & Widom, C. (1994). Antisocial personality disorder in abused and neglected children grown up. *American Journal of Psychiatry, 151,* 670–674.

Lynch, M., & Cicchetti, D. (1991). Patterns of relatedness in maltreated and nonmaltreated children: Connections among multiple representational models. *Development and Psychopathology, 3,* 207–226.

Lynch, M., & Cicchetti, D. (1992). Maltreated children's reports of relatedness to their teachers. *New Directions for Child Development, 57,* 81–107.

Lyons-Ruth, K., Connell, D., Zoll, D., & Stahl, J. (1987). Infants at social risk: Relationships among infant maltreatment, maternal behavior, and infant attachment behavior. *Developmental Psychology, 23,* 223–232.

Main, M., & George, C. (1985). Response of abused and disadvantaged toddlers to distress in agemates: A study in the day care setting. *Developmental Psychology, 21,* 407–412.

Main, M., & Hesse, E. (1990). Parents' unresolved traumatic experiences are related to infant disorganized attachment status: Is frightened and/or frightening parent behavior the linking mechanism? In M. Greenberg, D. Cicchetti, & E. M. Cummings (Eds.), *Attachment in the preschool years* (pp. 161–182). Chicago: University of Chicago Press.

Main, M., Kaplan, N., & Cassidy, J. C. (1985). Security in infancy, childhood and adulthood: A move to the level of representation. In I. Bretherton & E. Waters (Eds.), Growing points of attachment theory and research. *Monographs of the Society for Research in Child Development, 50* (Serial No. 209, Nos. 1–2), 66–104.

Main, M., & Solomon, J. (1990). Procedures for identifying infants as disorganized/disoriented during the Ainsworth Strange Situation. In M. Greenberg, D. Cicchetti, & E. M. Cummings (Eds.), *Attachment during the preschool years* (pp. 121–160). Chicago: University of Chicago Press.

Malinosky-Rummell, R., & Hansen, D. (1993). Long-term consequences of childhood physical abuse. *Psychological Bulletin, 114,* 68–79.

Manly, J. T., Cicchetti, D., & Barnett, D. (1994). The impact of maltreatment on child outcome: An exploration of dimensions within maltreatment. *Development and Psychopathology, 6,* 121–143.

Mans, L., Cicchetti, D., & Sroufe, L. A. (1978). Mirror reactions of Down's syndrome infants and toddlers: Cognitive underpinnings of self-recognition. *Child Development, 49,* 1247–1250.

Masten, A., Best, K., & Garmezy, N. (1990). Resilience and development: Contributions from the study of children who overcome adversity. *Development and Psychopathology, 2,* 425–444.

McCanne, T. R., & Milner, J. S. (1991). Physiological reactivity of physically abusive and at-risk subjects to child-related stimuli. In J. S. Milner (Ed.), *Neuropsychology of aggressioin* (pp. 147–166). Boston: Kluwer Academic.

McGee, R. A., & Wolfe, D. A. (1991). Between a rock and a hard place: Where do we go from here in defining psychological maltreatment? *Development and Psychopathology, 3,* 119–124.

McLeer, S. V., Callaghan, M., Henry, D., & Wallen, J. (1994). Psychiatric disorders in sexually abused children. *Journal of the American Academy of Child and Adolescent Psychiatry, 33,* 313–319.

Merry, S., & Andrews, L. (1994). Psychiatric status of sexually abused children 12 months after disclosure of abuse. *Journal of the American Academy of Child and Adolescent Psychiatry, 33,* 939–944.

Mueller, E., & Silverman, N. (1989). Peer relations in maltreated children. In D. Cicchetti & V. Carlson (Eds.), *Child maltreatment: Theory and research on the causes and consequences of child abuse and neglect* (pp. 529–578). New York: Cambridge University Press.

Nash, M. R., Hulsey, T. L., Sexton, M. C., Harralson, T. L., & Lambert, W. (1993). Long-term sequelae of childhood sexual abuse: Perceived family environment, psychopathology, and dissociation. *Journal of Consulting and Clinical Psychology, 61,* 276–283.

Newberger, C. M., & Cook, S. J. (1983). Parental awareness and child abuse: A cognitive developmental analysis of urban and rural samples. *American Journal of Orthopsychiatry, 53,* 512–524.

Okun, A., Parker, J. G., & Levendosky, A. A. (1994). Distinct and interactive contributions of physical abuse, socioeconomic disadvantage, and negative life events to children's social, cognitive, and affective adjustment. *Development and Psychopathology, 6,* 77–98.

Oliver, J. E. (1993). Intergenerational transmission of child abuse: Rates, research, and clinical implications. *American Journal of Psychiatry, 150*, 1315–1324.

Parker, J. G., & Herrera, C. (1996). Interpersonal processes in friendship: A comparison of maltreated and nonmaltreated children's experiences. *Developmental Psychology, 32*, 1025–1038.

Pianta, R., Egeland, B., & Erickson, M. (1989). The antecedents of child maltreatment: Results of the mother–child interaction research project. In D. Cicchetti & V. Carlson (Eds.), *Child maltreatment: Theory and research on the causes and consequences of child abuse and neglect* (pp. 203–252). New York: Cambridge University Press.

Pollak, S., Cicchetti, D., Klorman, R., & Brumaghim, J. (1997). Cognitive brain event-related potentials and emotion processing in maltreated children. *Child Development, 5*, 773–787.

Richters, J. E., & Martinez, P. (1993). The NIMH community violence project: I. Children as victims and witnesses to violence. *Psychiatry, 56*, 7–21.

Rieder, C., & Cicchetti, D. (1989). Organizational perspective on cognitive control functioning and cognitive–affective balance in maltreated children. *Developmental Psychology, 25*, 516.

Rogeness, G. A. (1991). Psychosocial factors and amine systems. *Psychiatry Research, 39*, 215–217.

Rogeness, G. A., Javors, M. A., & Pliszka, S. R. (1992). Neurochemistry and child and adolescent psychiatry. *Journal of the American Academy of Child and Adolescent Psychiatry, 31*, 765–781.

Rogosch, F. A., & Cicchetti, D. (1994). Illustrating the interface of family and peer relations through the study of child maltreatment. *Social Development, 3*, 291–308.

Rogosch, F. A., Cicchetti, D., & Aber, J. L. (1995). The role of child maltreatment in early deviations in cognitive and affective processing abilities and later peer relationship problems. *Development and Psychopathology, 7*, 591–609.

Rogosch, F. A., Cicchetti, D., Shields, A., & Toth, S. L. (1995). Facets of parenting disturbance in child maltreatment. In M. H. Bornstein (Ed.), *Handbook of parenting* (Vol. 4, pp. 127–159). Hillsdale, NJ: Erlbaum.

Rosenberg, M. S. (1987). New directions for research on the psychological maltreatment of children. *American Psychologist, 42*, 166–171.

Salzinger, S., Feldman, R. S., Hammer, M., & Rosario, M. (1993). The effects of physical abuse on children's social relationships. *Child Development, 64*, 169–187.

Sameroff, A., & Chandler, M. (1975). Reproductive risk and the continuum of caretaking casualty. In F. Horowitz (Ed.), *Review of child development research* (Vol. 4, pp. 187–244). Chicago: University of Chicago Press.

Sander, L. (1962). Issues in early mother–child interaction. *Journal of the American Academy of Child Psychiatry, 1*, 141–166.

Sapolsky, R., Krey, L., & McEwen, B. (1984). Glucocorticoid-sensitive hippocampal neurons are involved in terminating the adrenal stress response. *Proceedings of the National Academy of Sciences of the United States, 81*, 6174–6177.

Schneider-Rosen, K., Braunwald, K., Carlson, V., & Cicchetti, D. (1985). Current perspectives in attachment theory: Illustration from the study of maltreated infants. In I. Bretherton & E. Waters (Eds.), Growing points in attachment theory and research. *Monographs of the Society for Research in Child Development, 50* (Serial No. 209), 194–210.

Schneider-Rosen, K., & Cicchetti, D. (1984). The relationship between affect and cognition in maltreated infants: Quality of attachment and the development of visual self-recognition. *Child Development, 55*, 648–658.

Schneider-Rosen, K., & Cicchetti, D. (1991). Early self-knowledge and emotional development: Visual self-recognition and affective reactions of mirror self-image in maltreated and nonmaltreated toddlers. *Developmental Psychology, 27*, 481–488.

Shields, A. M., Cicchetti, D., & Ryan, R. M. (1994). The development of emotional and behavioral self regulation and social competence among maltreated school-age children. *Development and Psychopathology, 6*, 57–75.

Sigel, I. E. (1986). Reflections on the belief–behavior connection: Lessons learned from a research program on parental belief systems and teaching strategies. In R. D. Ashmore & D. M. Brodzinsky (Eds.), *Thinking about the family: Views of parents and children* (pp. 35–65). Hillsdale, NJ: Erlbaum.

Spoont, M. (1992). Modulatory role of serotonin in neural information processing: Implications for human psychopathology. *Psychological Bulletin, 112*, 330–350.

Sroufe, L. A. (1979). The coherence of individual development: Early care, attachment, and subsequent developmental issues. *American Psychologist, 34*, 834–841.

Sroufe, L. A. (1996). *Emotional development: The organization of emotional life in the early years.* New York: Cambridge University Press.

Sroufe, L. A., & Rutter, M. (1984). The domain of developmental psychopathology. *Child Development, 55*, 17–29.

Steinberg, L., Catalano, R., & Dooley, D. (1981). Economic antecedents of child abuse and neglect. *Child Development, 52*, 975–985.

Sternberg, K., Lamb, M., Greenbaum, C., Cicchetti, D. Dawud, S., Cortes, R., & Krispin, O. (1993). Effects of domestic violence on children's behavior problems and depression. *Developmental Psychology, 29*, 44–52.

Strauss, M. A. (1974). Cultural and social organizational influences on violence between family members. In R. Prince & D. Barried (Eds.), *Configurations: Biological and cultural factors in sexuality and family life*. Lexington, MA: Heath.

Straus, M. A., Gelles, R. J., & Steinmetz, S. K. (1980). *Behind closed doors: Violence in the American family*. New York: Anchor Books.

Straus, M. A., & Kaufman-Kantor, G. (1986). Stress and physical child abuse. *Child Abuse and Neglect, 4*, 75–88.

Susman, E. J., Trickett, P. K., Iannotti, R. J., Hollenbeck, B. E., & Zahn-Waxler, C. (1985). Childrearing patterns in depressed abusive, and normal mothers. *American Journal of Orthopsychiatry, 55*, 237–251.

Thompson, R. (1990). Emotions and self-regulation. In R. Thompson (Ed.), *Nebraska Symposium on Motivation: Vol. 36. Socioemotional development* (pp. 367–467). Lincoln: University of Nebraska Press.

Toth, S. L., & Cicchetti, D. (1996a). Patterns of relatedness, depressive symptomatology, and perceived competence in maltreated children. *Journal of Consulting and Clinical Psychology, 64*, 32–41.

Toth, S. L., & Cicchetti, D. (1996b). The impact of relatedness with mother on school functioning in maltreated children. *Journal of School Psychology, 3*, 247–266.

Toth, S. L., Manly, J. T., & Cicchetti, D. (1992). Child maltreatment and vulnerability to depression. *Development and Psychopathology, 4*, 97–112.

Trickett, P. K., Aber, J. L., Carlson, V., & Cicchetti, D. (1991). The relationship of socioeconomic status to the etiology and development sequelae of physical child abuse. *Developmental Psychology, 27*, 148–158.

Trickett, P. K., & Kuczyinski, L. (1986). Children's misbehaviors and parental discipline strategies in abusive and nonabusive families. *Developmental Psychology, 22*, 115–123.

Trickett, P., McBride-Chang, C., & Putnam, F. (1994). The classroom performance and behavior of sexually abused females. *Development and Psychopathology, 6*, 183–194.

Trickett, P. K., & Susma, E. J. (1988). Parental perceptions of childrearing practices in physically abusive and nonabusive families. *Developmental Psychology, 24*, 270–276.

Troy, M., & Sroufe, L. A. (1987). Victimization among preschoolers: The role of attachment relationship history. *Journal of the American Academy of Child and Adolescent Psychiatry, 26*, 166–172.

United States Department of Health and Human Services. (1981). *Study findings: National Study of incidence and severity of child abuse and neglect* (DHHS Publication No. [OHDS] 81-30325). Washington, DC: U.S. Government Printing Office.

United States Department of Health and Human Services. (1988). *Study findings: Study of national incidence and prevalence of child abuse and neglect* (DHHS Publication No. [OHDS] 20-01099). Washington, DC: U.S. Government Printing Office.

United State Department of Health and Human Services, National Center on Child Abuse and Neglect. (1996). *Child abuse and neglect case-level data 1993: Working Paper 1*. Washington, DC: U.S. Government Printing Office.

United States Department of Justice. (1991). *Criminal victimization, 1990* (Special Report No. NCJ-122743). Washington, DC: Author.

Van der Kolk, B. (1987). The compulsion to repeat the trauma: Re-enactment, revictimization, and masochism. *Psychiatric Clinics of North America, 12*, 389–411.

Von Bertalanffy, L. (1968). *General system theory*. New York: Braziller.

Vondra, J., Barnett, D., & Cicchetti, D. (1989). Perceived and actual competence among maltreated and comparison school children. *Development and Psychopathology, 1*, 237–255.

Vondra, J., Barnett, D., & Cicchetti, D. (1990). Self-contempt, motivation, and competence among preschoolers from maltreating and comparison families. *Child Abuse and Neglect, 14*, 525–540.

Whipple, E. E., & Webster-Stratton, C. (1991). The role of parental stress in physically abusive families. *Child Abuse and Neglect, 15*, 279–291.

Wolfe, D. A. (1985). Prevention of child abuse through the development of parent and child competencies. In R. J. McMahon & R. Peters (Eds.), *Childhood disorders: Behavioral–developmental approaches* (pp. 195–217). New York: Brunner/Mazel.

Wolfe, D. A. (1987). *Child abuse: Implications for child development and psychopathology*. Newbury Park, CA: Sage.

Wolfe, D. A., Fairbank, J. A., Kelly, J. A., & Bradlyn, A. S. (1983). Child abusive parents' physiological response to stressful and non-stressful behavior in children. *Behavioral Assessment, 5*, 363–371.

Wolfe, D. A., & Jaffe, P. (1991). Child abuse and family violence as determinants of child psychopathology. *Canadian Journal of Behavioural Science, 23*, 282–299.

Wolfe, D. A., & McGee, R. (1994). Dimensions of child maltreatment and their relationship to adolescent adjustment. *Development and Psychopathology, 6*, 165–181.

Wolfner, G. D., & Gelles, R. J. (1993). A profile of violence toward children: A national study. *Child Abuse and Neglect, 17*, 197–212.

Zigler, E. (1976). Controlling child abuse in America: An effort doomed to failure? In W. A. Collins (Ed.), *Newsletter of the division on developmental psychology, American Psychological Association* (pp. 17–30). Washington, DC: American Psychological Association.

Zigler, E., Abelson, W., Trickett, P., & Seitz, V. (1982). Is an intervention program necessary in order to improve economically disadvantaged children's IQ scores? *Child Development, 53,* 340–348.

Zigler, E., & Balla, D. (1982). Atypical development: Personality determinants in the behavior of the retarded. In E. Zigler, M. Lamb, & I. Child (Eds.), *Socialization and personality development* (pp. 238–245). New York: Oxford University Press.

Zuravin, S. J. (1991). Research definitions of child abuse and neglect: Current problems. In R. Starr & D. Wolfe (Eds.), *The effects of child abuse and neglect: Issues and research* (pp. 100–128). New York: Guilford Press.

38

Traumatic Stress and Posttraumatic Stress Disorder among Children and Adolescents

Laura M. Davidson, Sabra S. Inslicht, and Andrew Baum

Children are exposed to traumatic events at alarming rates, and evidence suggests that this exposure may have profound effects on development and well-being. The events that evoke stress responses, the responses that are evoked, and the conditions that are protective or that may enhance vulnerability have received research attention, but long-term consequences and outcomes of trauma are less clear. Most research on the sequelae of traumatic stress has been on adults, but evidence suggests that children are exposed and react similarly to threatening events and experience mild and severe symptoms of stress as well. In this chapter, we discuss the consequences of stress and trauma among children. Precipitating events and mediating variables are considered as well as common symptoms of distress along a developmental continuum. Parallels with adults' responses to stress and with posttraumatic stress syndromes are also considered.

Posttraumatic Stress Disorder (PTSD) is among the most profound consequences of exposure to a stressor. It is one of the few diagnoses in the *Diagnostic and Statistical Manual of Mental Disorders* that is recognized as a response to specific environmental events (DSM-IV; American Psychiatric Association, 1994). Long recognized in war, after serious accidents, or in the wake of other life-threatening events, PTSD is a syndrome of hypersensitivity and exaggerated stress responses, characterized by reexperiencing the stressor, avoidance, and hyperarousal. Since the first publication of this book, the study of posttraumatic stress in children has developed rapidly. By 1995, the PILOTS database, an index to trauma-related literature maintained by the National Center for PTSD, catalogued more than 7,500 trauma-related references. Of these, more than 2,400 were relevant to children and published after

Laura M. Davidson and Andrew Baum • Behavioral Medicine and Oncology, University of Pittsburgh Cancer Institute, Pittsburgh, Pennsylvania 15219.   **Sabra S. Inslicht** • Department of Psychology, University of Pittsburgh, Pittsburgh, Pennsylvania 15219.

Handbook of Developmental Psychopathology, Second Edition, edited by Arnold J. Sameroff, Michael Lewis, and Suzanne M. Miller. Kluwer Academic / Plenum Publishers, New York, 2000.

1986. There is considerable research interest in this area and existing research needs to be systematized to facilitate future research and clinical activities.

To accomplish this and produce more relevant, applicable research, investigators have applied conceptual models to studies of childhood trauma that focus on an interaction among characteristics of the event, the environment, and variables describing victims. We use this framework to discuss the consequences of stress and trauma among children and adolescents, using the more extensive literature of research and experience in adult victims to provide a context for the reporting of data and speculation.

POSTTRAUMATIC STRESS DISORDER AND TRAUMATIC STRESSORS

Exposure to a traumatic event is a defining characteristic of PTSD. Traumatic events have been characterized by the DSM-IV as involving the experience, witnessing, or confrontation of actual or threatened death, serious injury, or threat to the physical integrity of self or others. The stressor can be a natural event, such as a flood, earthquake, or tornado, or it can be of human origin (i.e., wars, accidents, violence, sexual abuse, invasive medical procedures). Human-caused events seem particularly likely to cause psychiatric problems (e.g., Baum, 1987). These stressors can have an intensity that seems near-universal in its threat, and are experiences that tend to disrupt the behavior of most individuals irrespective of their role, status, geographical locale, or perhaps even the historical era in which they occur (Garmezy, 1983, p. 46).

Not all victims of traumatic events experience pathological outcomes. Stress and stress-related outcomes are products of an interaction among characteristics of the person (e.g., styles of coping, social support, and preexisting psychopathology) and characteristics of the event and environment or setting. Features of traumatic events that have been associated with negative outcomes in adults include loss and bereavement, displacement, life threat, and exposure to the grotesque (Gleser, Green, & Winget, 1981). However, even when these stressors are involved many or most survivors recover readily and with little or no long-term loss.

Prevalence of Traumatic Stressors

There are no studies that look broadly at the prevalence of PTSD in children. One reason for this is that identification of victims of trauma can be difficult and sampling bias is likely. Although many traumatic events can be documented during childhood, victims of some stressors (e.g., sexual and physical abuse) often remain hidden or hard to identify (Foy, Madvig, Pynoos, & Camilleri, 1996). However, estimates can be made, based on exposure to traumatic stressors, and when one considers these data, childhood trauma seems alarmingly common. For example, Perry (1994) hypothesized that the number of children at risk for PTSD exceeds 15 million. If one takes a conservative position and assumes that only 10% of children exposed to traumatic events since 1964 will develop PTSD, there would be more than 4.5 million veterans of childhood PTSD today (Perry, 1994).

Norris (1992) reported that 70% of the population is exposed to trauma at some time in their lives, but lifetime prevalence rates of PTSD vary. The DSM-IV reports rates ranging from 3% to 58% for exposed groups, and studies of disasters, motor vehicle accidents, combat, and other stressors are consistent with this estimated range (e.g., Delahanty et al., 1997; Kulka et al., 1990; McNally, 1993). Among children, similar circumstances are true; most children exposed to trauma should recover without lasting harm, but some of them will inevitably show signs of long-term disruption and disorganization.

A major source of trauma exposure for children is warfare or civil unrest. UNICEF estimated that in the last 10 years, 2 million children have been killed, 4–5 million have been disabled, 12 million have been left homeless, more than 1 million have been orphaned or separated from their parents, and 10 million have been "psychologically traumatized" (UNICEF, 1996). Accidents are another important source of trauma among children. Almost 9 million children under the age of 15 were seen in emergency departments for injuries in the United States in 1992 (Burt, 1995). Within the family, parent-to-child violence was more than twice as common as violence between spouses (Straus, Gelles, & Steinmetz, 1980).

Poststressor Syndromes

Following traumatic exposure, clinical manifestation of distress among children is varied and may include conduct disorder, borderline personality, major affective disorder, attention-deficit/hyperactivity, phobic disorder, and adjustment disorder, in addition to PTSD (Terr, 1991). Disordered behavior is characterized by a high level of comorbidity (up to 85%; Perry, 1994). However, PTSD is a distinctive response to trauma and should be considered separately from these other disturbances. Symptoms of PTSD are typically divided into three clusters: reexperiencing symptoms, avoidance and numbing symptoms, and symptoms reflecting hyperarousal.

The reexperiencing cluster reflects the fact that traumatic events may be reexperienced through intrusive and recurrent recollections of the events and dreams, or through dissociative states. Intense psychological distress or physiological reactivity may accompany internal or external cues that symbolize the trauma. In children, these symptoms can be expressed through repetitive play symbolizing the trauma, frightening dreams with recognizable content, and reenactments of the events. Avoidance of reminders of the event and emotional "anesthesia" also occur following exposure to traumatic events. Symptoms included in this cluster include diminished affect, or an inability to feel emotions, and a loss of interest in previously significant activities or people. Unlike adults, children do not express feeling "numb," but they may withdraw from previously enjoyed activities (Pelcovitz & Kaplan, 1996). Victims may also avoid reminders of the traumatic event because their symptoms may intensify when they encounter these stimuli. Symptoms reflecting autonomic arousal include difficulty sleeping, irritability and anger, memory impairment, and exaggerated startle response or hyperalertness.

Terr (1991) described four symptoms of victimization unique to all children exposed to trauma: strongly visualized or repeatedly perceived memories, repetitive behaviors, trauma-specific fears, and changes in attitudes about life. Memories occur during leisure rather than as a disruptive event. Young children without verbal memories may draw or play out portions of the traumatic event, and repetitive behavior may be manifest as posttraumatic play (Terr, 1983, 1985). The themes of this type of play link it to the traumatic event, and it appears compulsive and repetitive in nature. Trauma-related fears appear to be more persistent outcomes of victimization, often generalizing into adulthood. Reinforcement of these fears through selective attention and sensitization of threat, or by applying effective avoidance coping, may be responsible for this chronic outcome. Nonspecific fears such as the fear of the dark or of being alone are also common but these are likely to be shorter-lived. Feelings of a limited future are often expressed by children, perhaps because the typical feelings of invincibility have been shattered.

Stress and Biological Responses

Since stress and PTSD reflect integrated psychobiological disturbances, neurodevelopmental consequences of traumatic exposure may be profound as well. Changes that are adaptive during acute stress do not remain adaptive if they extend beyond the period of danger. Physiological systems may be permanently affected by traumatic experiences and may have profound effects if they occur during critical periods of development (Perry, 1993). Sensitization of neurochemical systems that mediate the stress response may cause the system to be more vigilant and sensitive to future stressors that relate to the trauma. Changes in this system may also cause alterations in sensation, perception, and information processing.

In adults, stress appears to be accompanied by alterations in adrenergic systems, the hypothalamic–pituitary–adrenal (HPA) axis, and the benzodiazepine and endogenous opioid systems. These changes in the brain, peripheral sympathetic nervous system, and neuroendocrine pathways appear to occur in traumatized children as well. For example, sexually abused girls had increased 24-hour urinary catecholamine (epinephrine, norepinephrine, and dopamine) excretion compared to controls (DeBellis & Putnam, 1994). Sexually abused girls who were diagnosed with PTSD also had higher 24-hour levels of urinary epinephrine than girls with overanxious disorders or controls (DeBellis, Lefter, Trickett, & Putnam, 1994). A study of neglected and clinically depressed boys showed that they also had higher concentrations of norepinephrine in 24-hour urine samples (Queiroz, Lombardi, Furtado, Basques, & Lippi, 1991). Other studies have found increased sympathetic reactivity, reductions of alpha-2 adrenergic receptors, and greater heart rate liability in children with PTSD compared with controls (e.g., Perry, 1994).

Additionally, Perry (1993) suggested that a neurohormonal cascade caused by stressful experiences may alter the pattern and quantity of neurotransmitter release and of second and third messengers and gene transcription. These could also produce permanent structural alterations that can affect sensitization, learning, memory, and differentiation (Kandel & Schwartz, 1982). Bremner, Davis, Southwick, Krystal, and Charney (1994) hypothesized that "neurotransmitters and neuropeptide-mediated alterations in memory acquisition may underlie PTSD symptoms related to abnormal memory, such as intrusive memories, flashbacks, and amnesia for traumatic memories" (p. 55). This relationship between biological changes and memories may be particularly salient for children, because a child's thoughts about a stressor remain active long after the initial event (Pynoos & Nader, 1993). Different meaning may be assigned to events as the reprocessing occurs, and the child may remember real or imagined actions. Interviewing may affect recall, because it can provide markers for stored memories.

Traumatized children also show evidence of changes in the HPA axis (DeBellis et al., 1994; Kaufman, 1991). Survivors of the Armenian earthquake who were more symptomatic and lived closer to the earthquake's epicenter exhibited lower mean baseline morning cortisol and greater cortisol suppression by dexamethasone (Goenjian et al., 1996). These HPA alterations could affect a number of systems, including thyroid control of metabolism, brain growth, and cognitive development (for review, see DeBellis & Putnam, 1994). They may alter the secretion of growth hormone, which could affect skeletal growth and protein synthesis, nonorganic failure to thrive, and the growth spurt in puberty. Finally, HPA alterations could affect the hypothalamic–pituitary–gonadal axis and alter menarche, menstruation, ovulation, the development of secondary sex characteristics, and libido. Physiological alterations seen in traumatized children may mediate many of the emotional, cognitive, and behavioral effects that have been observed, and may affect other physiological systems responsible for normal growth, development, and functioning.

SOURCES OF TRAUMATIC STRESS

Responses during stress can be thought of as involving the entire body and approximating adaptive responses for an undefined period of adjustment and/or accommodation. One can also view responses and consequences of stress as ranging from minimal to profound; in cases characterized by successful adaptation or by transient, resolvable stressors, impact is likely to be relatively small. For those instances featuring more intense and/or prolonged threat, responses may be exaggerated or drawn out over time. PTSD represents a particularly profound consequence of exposure to very intense stressors that threaten life and limb and that stretch the envelope of normal coping responses. Research has considered the impact of several events in this latter category, examining human and naturally caused stressors that vary in the nature, time course and intensity of threat, harm, or loss they pose.

There are fundamental differences between trauma caused by natural forces (e.g., storms, earthquakes) and those of human origin. Whether these differences are reflected in different levels of stress or dysfunction is not clear, but accounts suggest that among adults, events of human origin tend to be associated with more persistent distress and more long-term emotional consequences (Baum, Fleming, & Davidson, 1983). Recent work suggests that this is true for children as well and that events of human origin are more likely to cause PTSD (Green, 1990). However, traumatic events may have different meanings for adults and children, and the mechanisms by which emotional disturbances are generated may differ depending on the age of the victim.

Human- and natural-caused trauma share many characteristics. They are both powerful stressors that threaten one's life or long-term well-being, and they can be sudden and destructive. However, the psychological impact associated with events appears to differ in significant ways. One can argue that natural disasters, for example, are generally predictable and that they follow a predictable course. A flood may destroy homes and property, and disrupt power and sanitation, and these events are relatively predictable. Some human-made events such as airplane disasters or war may also cause visible destruction, but other disasters of human origin, such as assaults, abuse, or "technological" mishaps involving leaks of toxic chemicals or radiation, may pose risks that are less visible but more insidious and more harmful in the long term (Baum, 1987). If they become commonplace or come to characterize normal daily experience, these events can disrupt basic psychological assumptions and processes. Related to this, some human-caused traumas are not characterized by a clear low point, marking the beginning of recovery (Baum, 1987). There may never be a time when the victims can say that the worst is over.

When human-made traumas occur, they can erode people's confidence in their ability to control what should be under control, and even people not directly affected by a disaster may feel more vulnerable because of it. Thus, trauma of human origin may represent a loss of control over a situation in which someone is supposed to have had control, rather than an instance of lack of control over natural forces. Situations like this are more likely to lead to an altered worldview, and normal feelings of invincibility may be compromised, making depression a likely outcome (Janoff-Bulman, 1989).

Although the distinction between natural and human-made trauma provides a useful framework for predicting the long-term consequences of events for adults, its usefulness for children appears to be more limited. It is possible that the greater destructive power of some types of natural disasters may be more threatening to children. Nir (1985) concluded, for example, that the diagnosis of cancer was accompanied by posttraumatic stress symptoms in children almost without exception, but that worries about developing cancer while healthy were less likely to affect children.

Technological Disasters

Technological disasters refer to accidents and other threatening events that reflect a failure of the technological systems that support our way of life. Some, such as air disasters, motor vehicle accidents, and railroad accidents, often involve a combination of human error and mechanical failure, and represent acute, intense life threat. Others develop more slowly and may involve exposure to radiation or toxic chemicals. A study of 87 children (ages 3–11 years) who were evacuated from their homes because of a fire in a PCB warehouse found evidence of distress in older children (Breton, Valla, & Lambert, 1993). Symptoms of distress were observed in older (6- to 11-year-old) children who exhibited more internalizing and PTSD symptoms than did controls. Closer proximity to the fire and being female predicted symptoms. Parental reactions were also correlated with children's reactions, and parents' psychological adjustment was a significant predictor of internalizing and PTSD symptoms in their children.

Studies of survivors of more destructive human-caused disasters such as the dam collapse and deadly flood at Buffalo Creek, West Virginia, have suggested that about 37% of the affected children had "probable PTSD" 2 years after the disaster. Symptoms were associated with threat to life, gender (females had more symptoms than males), age (the younger children were more severely affected), and parental adjustment and family functioning (Green et al., 1991). A 17-year follow-up of survivors suggested that these children had recovered; PTSD rates were down to 7% (Green et al., 1994).

Not all technological catastrophes are large-scale disasters. Many involve serious accidents, often in transportation settings. A study of survivors of the sinking of a cruise ship indicated that distress was present in nearly half the survivors more than 1 year after this accident (Yule, 1992). Similarly, the accident at the Pittsburgh Regatta (Martini, Ryan, Nakayama, & Ramenofsky, 1990) resulted in PTSD in 3 of 5 injured spectators assessed. Medical trauma may also be an important source of stress among children. The combination of threat to life and invasive medical procedures may result in PTSD in children with chronic illnesses. Stoddard, Norman, Murphy, and Beardslee (1989) evaluated 30 burn victims (ages 7–19) and found a 30% lifetime prevalence of PTSD. Investigation of children undergoing bone marrow transplantation suggest that these children report moderate levels of PTSD symptoms after the procedure, but the acute phase of treatment is not associated with PTSD (Stuber, Nader, Houskamp, & Pynoos, 1996). Leukemia survivors were not more likely to have PTSD than controls, although their parents had more symptoms than control parents (Kazak et al., 1997).

War

War-related stressors involve direct threat of death and injury and indirect threats due to parental separation, loss, and absence (Jensen & Shaw, 1993). However, coping is often effective, and children in war situations develop much less psychopathology than one might expect (Jensen & Shaw, 1993). World War II led to victimization of many children, but most emerged from bombings and warfare relatively unscathed (e.g., Freud & Burlingham, 1943). Robinson and Hemmendinger (1982) found no evidence of psychoses among a sample of Holocaust survivors. Some reported depression, insomnia, and nightmares, and children who were hospitalized did not fare as well. Half of those who were hospitalized and younger than 17 years of age showed evidence of psychoses, 78% under age 7 were psychotic, and all under age 3 were severely debilitated. Inclusion in a functioning social group seemed to be important in preventing later symptom formation (Robinson & Hemendinger, 1982). A 1992 survey of 103 childhood survivors indicated that death camp survivors still suffer more than do victims of other forms of Nazi persecution; mental suffering was positively correlated with trauma intensity (Robinson, Rapaport-Bar-Sever, & Rapaport, 1994).

The continuing conflict in the Middle East has also resulted in trauma exposure for many children. Milgrim and Milgrim (1976) administered a general anxiety scale to Israeli children 4 months before the Yom Kippur War and then again afterward, but while the army was still mobilized. Levels of anxiety nearly doubled after the war. Kristal (1978) also found that children exposed to shelling in Lebanon had a higher incidence of anxiety and behavior problems as well as PTSD than their less exposed counterparts (Macksoud & Aber, 1996).

Although children in this country are largely spared the effects of war and political violence, community violence is epidemic. Almost three-fourths of 10- to 19-year-olds who live in high-crime neighborhoods report that they have witnessed a robbery, stabbing, shooting, and/or killing, and almost half are personally victimized (Vehara, Chalmers, Jenkins, & Shakoor, 1996). Children exposed to community and domestic violence are at increased risk for developing PTSD (Eth & Pynoos, 1994; Horowitz, Weine, & Jekel, 1995). A survey of community violence in and around Cleveland indicated that 26–44% of adolescents reported being slapped, hit, or punched at school, up to 22% were beaten or mugged in their own neighborhoods, up to one-third were shot at or shot within the past year, and about 16% were attacked or stabbed with a knife (Singer, Anglin, Song, & Lunghofer, 1995). Adolescent males from large-city high schools experienced the greatest violence exposure, but adolescent males from small-city schools also experienced a significant number of violent experiences. Females had more PTSD symptoms than boys, regardless of exposure level. Witnessing or experiencing home violence, sexual abuse/assault, past threats, slaps/hits/punches, beatings, or muggings were most likely to produce distress.

Child Abuse

Childhood physical and sexual abuse are strongly related to PTSD (McLeer, Deblinger, Atkins, Foa, & Ralphe, 1988; Deblinger et al., 1989). The relationship of the child to the perpetrator is highly correlated with prevalence rates, suggesting that one toxic element of this stressor is the violation of basic trust and expectations based on relationships (e.g., McLeer et al., 1988; McLeer, Deblinger, Henry, & Orvaschel, 1992). McLeer et al. (1992) studied 92 sexually abused children. Approximately 44% of the sample met PTSD criteria: 10% of those abused by a stranger, 42.4% abused by a trusted adult, and 53.8% abused by a father.

Several factors predict the impact of sexual abuse. One study found that 55% of 163 physically and/or sexually abused children had PTSD and that concerns over school achievement, intellectual functioning, and severity and duration of abuse predicted PTSD (Kiser, Heston, Millsap, & Pruitt, 1991). Studies of adult survivors of childhood sexual abuse suggest that long-term symptoms are common (Roway, Rodriguez, & Ryan, 1994). Level of overall exposure, high exposure to penetration and physical force, or penetration and perceived life threat were significantly related to PTSD status.

Natural Disasters

Natural disasters appear to be associated with PTSD, and the development of PTSD symptoms in childhood appears to be moderated by level of exposure to the stressor. Armenian children (8–16 years old) who experienced effects of the Spitak earthquake, an unusually severe and destructive disaster, were studied 18 months after the earthquake (Goenjian et al., 1995). Distance from the epicenter and extent of loss of family members were correlated with severity of PTSD and depressive reactions. Prevalence of PTSD was higher (95%) among children who lived in Spitak, the city closest to the epicenter, than in cities further from the epicenter (71% and 26%, respectively).

Closer to home, studies of children following the devastating trek of Hurricane Andrew across south Florida produced evidence of severe or very severe PTSD symptoms in 18% of the children 3 months after the hurricane (LaGreca, Silverman, Vernberg, & Prinstein, 1996). Scores declined over time, but 12% of the sample still showed PTSD 1 year later. Perceived life threat, number of life-threatening events during the hurricane, and number of loss and disruption events during the hurricane predicted long-term distress. More distress was seen in African American and Hispanic American children than in white children, and social support from parents and classmates also predicted symptoms (LaGreca et al., 1996). Interestingly, most of the variance in symptoms of PTSD was predicted by characteristics of the child (e.g., age or gender), degree of exposure, access to social support, and coping styles used (Vernberg et al., 1996). Another study of children after Hurricane Andrew used a random-digit telephone survey to interview 400 parent–adolescent (12–17 years old) pairs living in high- and low-impact areas 6 months after Hurricane Andrew (Garrison et al., 1995). Rates of PTSD were lower than in reports by LaGreca and her colleagues; females and minorities, again, experienced more PTSD symptoms. Disaster exposure, lifetime exposure to trauma, and life events following the storm were correlated with PTSD symptoms.

MEDIATING CONDITIONS

This brief review of traumatic stress suggests that several factors mediate the short- and long-term impact of trauma. Exposure, or the degree to which one is affected, is an important predictor of outcomes, and family cohesion, support outside the family (e.g., church, school), and person variables (e.g., flexibility, gender) are major determinants of appraisal and responses to stress (Rutter, Cox, Tupling, Berger, & Yule, 1975). Family influences appear to be particularly important in predicting the behavior of children. Children are so sensitive to the behavior of their parents that they can exhibit symptoms of PTSD even when they have not been directly exposed to a stressor. Children of Vietnam War veterans exhibit symptoms of PTSD, and may experience fantasies and flashbacks in the same way as their parents (Rosenheck & Nathan, 1985). Parental PTSD is often a significant predictor of morbidity in children following traumatic exposure (McFarlane, Blumbergs, Policansky, & Irwin, 1985). In Israel, children of Holocaust survivors were more likely than children without such a family history to develop PTSD following participation in the 1982 Lebanon War (Solomon, Kotler, & Mikulincer, 1988).

Another important factor for children is separation from their primary caregiver (Garmezey, 1983). Even for adults, separation during a crisis may make the situation more frightening and stressful. Brief separations from parents may have serious psychological consequences and are most dramatic for younger children, because they are the most dependent on their primary care providers for support.

Gender may also play a role in symptom formation in children following trauma, but findings are mixed. Boys appear more adversely affected by events such as hospitalization, divorce, and parental discord (Hetherington, Cox, & Cox, 1980; Rutter, 1970). Elder (1979) suggested that parents may have different expectations for boys and may not be as willing to provide additional support for them during times of need, heightening their distress. Alternatively, stressors may be more salient to boys (Block, Block, & Morrison, 1981). However, more recent research has produced inconsistent results, with some researchers reporting no association between gender and symptoms (Bloch, Silber, & Perry, 1956) and others reporting that girls or boys were more distressed (Gleser et al., 1981; Milgrim & Milgrim, 1976). Some have found that girls exhibit more symptoms than boys (Foy et al., 1996). However, Garbarino and Kostelny (1996) found more symptoms in boys under conditions of high accumulated risk. The difference in early work and more recent reports may be explained in part by assessment techniques and the types of symptoms displayed by boys and girls. Early assessments relied primarily on parental reports, but more recent studies have used interviews with children. Female children may be more likely to report these internal states.

Age also affects vulnerability to traumatic stress. Pynoos and Eth (1985) found age-dependent differences in PTSD among a sample of children who had witnessed a murder. In general, younger children had the most difficulty and required the most assistance in assimilating traumatic events. Davidson and Smith (1990) report that PTSD is three times more likely in children younger than age 11 and that preschoolers are particularly vulnerable. These findings are similar to results of studies of children undergoing the stress of hospitalization or parental divorce. Again, younger children were the most severely affected (Rutter, 1966, 1983). With increasing age, children develop a greater repertoire of coping responses, making them increasingly competent and self-reliant in the face of threat (Maccoby, 1983).

Styles of coping appear to change with age and influence the impact of trauma. Problem-focused coping is acquired earlier than emotion-focused coping, and more complex coping strategies also appear to develop later (Compas & Epping, 1993). Depending on the exact nature of the trauma, some types of coping may be more effective than others (although the greater repertoire in older children is probably of benefit). Some debate has arisen over self-blame coping; some clinicians have suggested that any form of self-blame is harmful to children who have experienced trauma, but others have argued that while attributing blame to others diminishes feelings of self-efficacy, that behavioral self-blame can be beneficial (Lamb, 1986). Celano (1992) suggests that children cannot distinguish among complex types of self-blame.

The role of stigmatization in development of posttraumatic stress syndromes is not well established, though recent work in this area suggests that it may form an important basis of these disorders in children (Feiring, Taska, & Lewis, 1996). Some sources of victimization may be likely to contribute to distress through this pathway, particularly if they induce shame or guilt (Lewis, 1998). Childhood sexual abuse, for example, may be particularly likely to induce negative self-evaluations and a sense of responsibility associated with shame and stigmatization. Fiering et al. (1996) argued that victimization can cause shame as a direct result of attributions about the source or circumstances of the victimizing event; self-blame and other control-enhancing attributions may contribute indirectly to shame, which then affects or determines adjustment. To the extent to which this process of stigmatization affects the duration and intensity of poststressor syndromes, shame should predict more persistent and/or upsetting sequelae. Of particular interest are associations between shame and self-blame, the factors that balance control-enhancing and stigmatizing attributions, and the possibility that shame may occur more widely and lead to stigmatization in situations or settings not commonly associated with shame.

Finally, personality characteristics also influence response to victimization. Finkelhor (1995) estimated that one-tenth of the population is chronically victimized; "chronic" victims are either distinctively aggressive or passive. Intelligence has been proposed as a resiliency factor, but Foy et al. (1996) disputed the scientific basis of this assertion. Pynoos (1994) suggested that intelligence may put the child at greater risk if cognitive abilities result in more accurate but disturbing risk perceptions. Psychiatric comorbidity increases the likelihood of PTSD (March & Amaya-Jackson, 1993). Depressed children, for example, may experience more guilt and hence exacerbation of PTSD symptoms.

CONCLUSIONS

Children are exposed to a variety of sources of traumatic stress and appear to respond in ways that parallel adult responses. The dependent nature of children may put them at greater risk for exposure to some traumatic stressors and may exacerbate the impact of others. Also, like adults, children show considerable variability in their vulnerability to trauma. General effects of extreme stressors are negative, and many children are resilient in the face of such stress. However, some experience stress and develop PTSD or other poststressor syndromes. Of particular concern among young children and adolescents is the possibility that trauma can have broader, systemic effects, sensitizing them to stressors, altering belief systems and worldview, and affecting their sexual and maturational progress in critical phases of development. For children in particular, a traumatic stressor may disrupt normal development or functioning, resulting in lifelong consequences.

It may be difficult to predict responses in children based on stressor criteria such as chronic or acute stress, or human-made or natural origins of stress. Although research suggests that human-made stressors are more likely to result in lasting pathological changes for adults than acute natural events (Baum, 1987), other event characteristics may be more important in determining outcomes among children. Level of exposure to trauma, proximity to danger, amount of personal loss, and perceptions of threat appear to affect risk of an untoward reaction. Other life events and family factors, such as parental distress or loss of income, and social support, also appear to be important. Finally, characteristics that appear to place children at greater risk include younger age and minority status.

Responses to trauma may be mild and short-lived or chronic and pathological. Common symptoms include depression, anger, anxiety, dissociation, and posttraumatic stress. If posttraumatic stress does develop during childhood, it is typically of long duration (Terr, 1983) and it closely resembles the syndrome in adults. However, correct diagnoses may be obscured by the inability of children to articulate the nature of their distress and its cause, the high degree of symptom overlap with other disorders, and because PTSD symptoms such as sleep disturbances may make a child appear as though he or she is suffering from other disorders (e.g., depression), and finally because PTSD frequently occurs comorbidly with other disorders. For example, researchers have noted symptoms of trauma-related distress that "go beyond the DSM-IV criteria for PTSD" (Stuber, Kazak, Meeske, & Barakat, 1998, p. 173). Although genetic vulnerabilities are almost certainly involved, current research does not adequately explain why some children develop PTSD, others become depressed or anxious, and still others are resilient to these stressors.

Assessing PTSD in children is more difficult than in adults. Ethical problems associated with child research include mandated reporting of abuse, confidentiality in areas in which children are not protected, confusion about definitions of "minimal risk," and hesitancy to probe sensitive areas in children (Putnam, 1996). In addition, developmental issues may complicate assessments because changes that have no relationship to the traumatic events may confound research. Instruments and measures that are appropriate for one age group may not be appropriate for another, and there is such a wide variation in development that age may not even be the best criterion to use in picking the suitability of an instrument. Gender and cultural factors also influence symptom reporting in children (Putnam, 1996).

Perhaps the most difficult issues characterizing work in this area reflect the need to integrate developmental perspectives into models describing traumatic stress syndromes in children and adolescents, and the difficulties in doing so. For example, Stuber and her colleagues (1997) found that primary predictors of PTSD in childhood cancer survivors were not exposure variables but, rather, were subjective reports of distress. Exposure measures, frequently used in adults as a primary marker for risk for posttraumatic stress, were not strong predictors of mental health outcomes in this sample. In addition, these investigators have argued that chronic effects of traumatic events would be manifest not as psychopathology but as changes in personality or temperament instead (Stuber et al., 1998). These changes, which may be subtle and difficult to detect, may have long-term effects on interpersonal relationships and regulation of emotion (Stuber et al., 1998).

Relative to research on adult populations, research on children and adolescents exposed to traumatic stressors has been slower to develop, partly because of difficulties inherent in assessing children. More importantly, there was no single event like the Vietnam War that mobilized research efforts. To develop more rapidly, the field must establish prevalence estimates for childhood PTSD in the general population, and longitudinal research aimed at understanding the disorder from a developmental perspective should be initiated. Standardization of assessment tools will facilitate comparisons across trauma types, and multimethod assessment strategies like those used to assess adults exposed to trauma should enhance our understanding of the interplay among emotional, behavioral, and biological changes that accompany traumatic exposure. Because biological changes that accompany stress exposure in children occur in the context of developmental changes, the potential for permanent alterations in regulatory and neurological systems is enhanced. It is crucial that these biological changes be a focus of future research in children.

REFERENCES

American Psychiatric Association. (1980). *Diagnostic and statistical manual of mental disorders* (3rd ed.). Washington, DC: Author.

American Psychiatric Association. (1994). *Diagnostic and statistical manual of mental disorders* (4th ed.). Washington, DC: Author.

Baum, A. (1987). Toxins, technology, and natural disasters. In G. R. Van denBos & B. K. Bryant (Eds.), *Cataclysms, crises, and catastrophes: Psychology in action* (pp. 5–53). Washington, DC: American Psychological Association.

Baum, A., Fleming, R., & Davidson, L. M. (1983). Natural disasters and technological catastrophe. *Environment and Behavior, 15,* 333–354.

Bloch, D., Silber, E., & Perry, S. (1956). Some factors in the emotional reactions of children to disaster. *American Journal of Psychiatry, 113,* 416–422.

Block, J. H., Block, J., & Morrison, A. (1981). Parental agreement–disagreement on childbearing orientations and gender-related personality correlates in children. *Child Development, 52,* 965–974.

Bremner, J. D., Davis, M., Southwick, S. M., Krystal, J. H., & Charney, D. S. (1994). Neurobiology of posttraumatic stress disorder. In R. S. Pynoos (Ed.), *Posttraumatic stress disorder: A clinical review* (pp. 43–64). Lutherville, MD: Sidran.

Breton, J., Valla, J., Lambert, J. (1993). Industrial disaster and mental health of children and their parents. *Journal of the American Academy of Child and Adolescent Psychiatry, 32,* 438–444.

Burt, C. W. (1995). *Injury-related visits to hospital emergency departments: United States, 1992* (Advance Data No. 261). Vital and Health Statistics of the Centers for Disease Control and Prevention, National Center for Health Statistics.

Butterfield, P. T., & Wright, H. H. (1984). Children's emotional response to disasters. *Journal of the South Carolina Medical Association, 80,* 567–570.

Celano, M. P. (1992). A developmental model of victims' internal attributions of responsibility for sexual abuse. *Journal of Interpersonal Violence, 7,* 57–69.

Compas, B. E., & Epping, J. E. (1993). Stress and coping in children and families. In C. Saylor (Ed.), *Children and disasters* (pp. 11–28). New York: Plenum Press.

Davidson, J., & Smith, R. (1990). Traumatic experiences in psychiatric outpatients. *Journal of Traumatic Stress Studies, 3,* 459–475.

DeBellis, M. D., Chrousos, G. P., Dorn, L. D., Burke, L., Helmers, K., Kling, M. A., Trickett, P. K., & Putnam, F. W. (1994). Hypothalamic–pituitary–adrenal axis dysregulation in sexually abused girls. *Journal of Clinical Endocrinology and Metabolism, 78,* 249–255.

DeBellis, M. D., Lefter, L., Trickett, P. K., & Putnam, F. W. (1994). Urinary catecholamine excretion in sexually abused girls. *Journal of the American Academy of Child and Adolescent Psychiatry, 33,* 320–327.

DeBellis, M. D., & Putnam, F. W. (1994). The psychobiology of childhood maltreatment. *Child and Adolescent Psychiatric Clinics of North America, 3,* 663–678.

Deblinger, E., McLeer, S. V., Atkins, M. S., Ralph, D., & Foa, E. (1989). Post-traumatic stress disorder in sexually abused, physically abused, and nonabused children. *Child Abuse and Neglect, 13,* 403–408.

Delahanty, D., Herberman, H. B., Craig, K. J., Hayward, M. C., Fullerton, C. S., Ursano, R. J., & Baum, A. (1997). Acute and chronic distress and posttraumatic stress disorder as a function of responsibility for serious motor vehicle accidents. *Journal of Consulting and Clinical Psychology, 65*(4), 560–567.

Elder, G. H. (1979). Historical change in life patterns and personality. In P. B. Baltes & O. G. Brim (Eds.), *Life-span development and behavior* (Vol. 2, pp. 117–159). New York: Academic Press.

Eth, S., & Pynoos, R. S. (1994). Children who witness the homicide of a parent. *Psychiatry, 57,* 287–306.

Feiring, C., Taska, L., & Lewis, M. (1996). A process model for understanding adaptation to sexual abuse: The role of shame in defining stigmatization. *Child Abuse and Neglect, 20,* 767–783.

Finkehor, D. (1995). The victimization of children: A developmental perspective. *American Journal of Orthopsychiatry, 65,* 177–193.

Foy, D. W., Madvig, B. T., Pynoos, R. S., & Camilleri, A. J. (1996). Etiologic factors in the development of posttraumatic stress disorder in children and adolescents. *Journal of School Psychology, 34,* 133–145.

Freud, A., & Burlingham, P. T. (1943). *War and children.* London: Medical War Books.

Garbarino, J., & Kostelny, K. (1996). The effects of political violence on Palestinian children's behavior problems: A risk accumulation model. *Child Development, 67,* 33–45.

Garmezy, N. (1983). *Stress, coping, and development in children.* New York: McGraw-Hill.

Garrison, C., Bryant, E. S., Addy, C. L., Spurrier, P. G., Freedy, J. R., & Kilpatrick, D. G. (1995). Posttraumatic stress disorder in adolescents after Hurricane Andrew. *Journal of the American Academy of Child and Adolescent Psychiatry, 34,* 1193–1201.

Gleser, G. C., Green, B. L., & Winget, C. N. (1981). *Prolonged psychosocial effects of disaster: A study of Buffalo Creek.* New York: Academic Press.

Goenjian, A. K., Pynoos, R. S., Steinberg, A. M., Najarian, L. M., Asarnow, J. R., Karayan, I., Ghurabi, M., & Fairbanks, L. A. (1995). Psychiatric comorbidity in children after the 1988 earthquake in Armenia. *Journal of the American Academy of Child and Adolescent Psychiatry, 34,* 1174–1184.

Goenjian, A. K., Yehuda, R., Pynoos, R. S., Steinberg, A. M., Tashijian, M., Yang, R. K., Najarian, L. M., & Fairbanks, L. A. (1996). Basal cortisol, dexamethasone suppression of cortisol, and MHPG in adolescents after the 1988 earthquake in Armenia. *American Journal of Psychiatry, 153,* 929–934.

Green, B. (1990). Defining trauma: Terminology and generic stressor dimensions. *Journal of Applied Social Psychology, 20,* 1632–1642.

Green, B., Grace, M. C., Vary, M. G., Kramer, T. L., Gleser, G. C., & Leonard, A. C. (1994). Children of disaster in the second decade: A 17-year follow-up of Buffalo Creek survivors. *Journal of the American Academy of Child and Adolescent Psychiatry, 33,* 71–79.

Green, B., Korol, M., Grace, M. C., Vary, M. G., Leonard, A. C., Gleser, G. C., & Smitson-Cohen, S. (1991). Children and disaster: Age, gender, and parental effects on PTSD symptoms. *Journal of the American Academy of Child and Adolescent Psychiatry, 30,* 945–951.

Hetherington, E. M., Cox, M., & Cox, R. (Ed.). (1980). Aftermath of divorce. In J. H. Steners, Jr., and M. Matthews (Eds.), *Mother–child relations.* Washington, DC: National Association for the Education of Young Children.

Horowitz, K., Weine, S., & Jekel, J. (1995). PTSD symptoms in urban adolescent girls: Compounded community trauma. *Journal of the American Academy of Child and Adolescent Psychiatry, 34,* 1353–1361.

Janoff-Bulman, R. (1989). Assumptive worlds and the stress of traumatic events: Applications of the schema construct. *Social Cognition, 7,* 113–136.

Jensen, P. S., & Shaw, J. (1993). Children as victims of war: Current knowledge of future needs. *Journal of the American Academy of Child and Adolescent Psychiatry, 32,* 697–709.

Kandel, E. R., & Schwartz, J. H. (1982). Molecular biology of an elementary form of learning: Modulation of transmitter release by cyclic AMP. *Science, 218,* 433–443.

Kaufman, J. (1991). Depressive disorders in maltreated children. *Journal of the American Academy of Child and Adolescent Psychiatry, 30,* 257–265.

Kazak, A., Barakat, L., Meeske, K., Christakis, D., Meadows, A., Casey, R., Penati, B., & Stuber, M. (1997). Posttraumatic stress, family functioning, and social support in survivors of childhood leukemia and their mothers and fathers. *Journal of Consulting and Clinical Psychology, 65,* 120–129.

Kiser, L. J., Heston, J., Millsap, P., & Pruitt, D. B. (1991). Physical and sexual abuse in childhood: Relationship with posttraumatic stress disorder. *Journal of the American Academy of Child and Adolescent Psychiatry, 30,* 776–783.

Kristal, L. (1978). *Bruxism: An anxiety response to environmental stress* (Vol. 5). New York: Halsted Press.

Kulka, R. C., Schlenger, W. E., Fairbank, J. A., Hough, R. L., Jordan, B. K., Marmar, C. R., & Weiss, P. S. (1990). *Trauma and the Vietnam generation: Report of findings from the National Vietnam Veterans Readjustment Study.* New York: Brunner/Mazel.

LaGreca, A. M., Silverman, W. K., Vernberg, E. M., & Prinstein, M. J. (1996). Symptoms of posttraumatic stress in children after Hurricane Andrew: A prospective study. *Journal of Consulting and Clinical Psychology, 64,* 712–723.

Lamb, S. (1986). Treating sexually abused children: Issues of blame and responsibility. *American Journal of Orthopsychiatry, 56,* 303–307.

Lewis, M. (1998). Shame and stigma. In P. Gilbert & B. Andrews (Eds.), *Shame: Interpersonal behavior, psychopathology, and culture* (pp. 126–140). New York: Oxford University Press.

Maccoby, E. E. (1983). Social–emotional development and response to stressors. In N. Garmezy & M. Rutter (Eds.), *Stress, coping, and development in children* (pp. 217–264). New York: McGraw-Hill.

Macksoud, M., & Aber, J. L. (1996). The war experiences and psychosocial development of children in Lebanon. *Child Development, 67,* 70–88.

March, J. D., & Amaya-Jackson, L. (1993, Spring). Post-traumatic stress disorder in children and adolescents. *PTSD Research Quarterly, 4,* 1–7.

Martini, D. R., Ryan, C., Nakayama, D., & Ramenofsky, M. (1990). Psychiatric sequelae after traumatic injury: The Pittsburgh Regatta accident. *Journal of the American Academy of Child and Adolescent Psychiatry, 29,* 70–75.

McFarlane, A. C., Blumbergs, V., Policansky, S. K., & Irwin, C. (1985). *A longitudinal study of psychological morbidity in children due to natural disasters.* Unpublished manuscript.

McLeer, S. V., Deblinger, E., Atkins, M. S., Foa, E. B., & Ralphe, D. L. (1988). Post-traumatic stress disorder in sexually abused children. *American Academy of Child and Adolescent Psychiatry, 27,* 650–654.

McLeer, S. V., Deblinger, E., Henry, D., & Orvaschel, H. (1992). Sexually abused children at high risk for posttraumatic stress disorder. *Journal of the American Academy of Child and Adolescent Psychiatry, 27,* 650–654.

McNally, R. J. (1993). Stressors that produce posttraumatic stress disorder in children. In J. R. T. Davidson & E. B. Foa (Eds.), *Posttraumatic stress disorder: DSM-IV and beyond* (pp. 57–74). Washington, DC: American Psychiatric Press.

Milgrim, R., & Milgrim, N. (1976). The effects of the Yom Kippur War on the anxiety level in Israeli children. *Journal of Psychology, 94,* 107–113.

Nader, K., Pynoos, R., Fairbanks, L., & Frederick, C. (1990). Children's PTSD reactions one year after a sniper attack at their school. *American Journal of Psychiatry, 147,* 1526–1530.

Nir, Y. (1985). Post-traumatic stress disorder in children with cancer. In S. Eth & R. S. Pynoos (Eds.), *Post-traumatic stress disorder in children* (pp. 121–132). Washington, DC: American Psychiatric Press.

Norris, F. M. (1992). Epidemiology of trauma: Frequency and impact of different potentially traumatic events. *Journal of Consulting and Clinical Psychology, 60*, 409–418.

Pelcovitz, D., & Kaplan, S. (1996). Post-traumatic stress disorder in children and adolescents. *Child and Adolescent Psychiatric Clinics of North America, 5*, 449–470.

Perry, B. D. (1993). Neurodevelopment and the neurophysiology of trauma: I. Conceptual considerations for clinical work with maltreated children. *The Advisor, 6*(1), 1–18.

Perry, B. D. (1994). Neurobiological sequelae of childhood trauma: PTSD in children. In C. F. Saylor (Ed.), *Children and disasters* (pp. 233–255). New York: Plenum Press.

Putnam, F. W. (1996). Special methods for trauma research with children. In E. B. Carlson (Ed.), *Trauma research methodology* (pp. 153–173). Lutherville, MD: Sidran.

Pynoos, R. S. (1994). Traumatic stress and developmental psychopathology in children and adolescents. In R. S. Pynoos (Ed.), *Posttraumatic stress disorder a clinical review* (pp. 65–98). Lutherville, MD: Sidran.

Pynoos, R. S., & Eth, S. (1984). The child as witness to homicide. *Journal of Social Issues, 40*(2), 87–108.

Pynoos, R. S., & Eth, S. (1985). Developmental perspective on psychic trauma in childhood. In C. R. Figley (Ed.), *Trauma and its wake* (pp. 36–52). New York: Brunner/Mazel.

Pynoos, R. S., Frederick, C., Arroyo, W., Nader, K., Eth, S., Lyon-Levine, M., Silverstein, S., & Nunez, F. (1985, May). *Life-threat and posttraumatic stress in school age children.* Paper presented at the Annual Meeting of the American Psychiatric Association, Dallas, TX.

Pynoos, R. S., & Nader, K. (1993). Issues in the treatment of posttraumatic stress in children and adolescents. In J. P. Wilson & B. Raphael (Eds.), *International handbook of traumatic stress syndromes* (pp. 535–549). New York: Plenum Press.

Querioz, E. A., Lombardi, A. B., Furtado, A. B., Basques, J. C., & Lippi, J. R. S. (1991). Biochemical correlates of depression in children. *Arquivos de Neuro-Psiquiatria, 49*, 418–425.

Robinson, S., & Hemmendinger, J. (1982). Psychosocial adjustment 30 years later of people who were in Nazi concentration camps. In N. A. Milgram (Ed.), *Stress and anxiety* (pp. 397–404). New York: Hemisphere.

Robinson, S., Rapaport-Bar-Sever, M., & Rapaport, J. (1994). The present state of the people who survived the Holocaust as children. *Acta Psychiatrica Scandinavica, 89*, 242–245.

Rosenheck, R., & Nathan, P. (1985). Secondary traumatization in children of Vietnam veterans. *Hospital and Community Psychiatry, 36*, 538–539.

Rowan, A. B., Foy, D. W., Rodriguez, N., and Ryan, S. (1994). Posttraumatic stress disorder in a clinical sample of adults sexually abused as children. *Child Abuse and Neglect, 18*, 51–61.

Rutter, M. (1966). *Children of sick parents: An environmental and psychiatric study.* Maudsley Monographs No. 16. London: Oxford University Press.

Rutter, M. (1970). Sex differences in children's responses to family stress. In E. J. Anthony & C. Koupernick (Eds.), *The child and his family.* New York: Wiley.

Rutter, M. (1983). Stress, coping, and development: Some issues and some questions. In N. Garmezy & M. Rutter (Ed.), *Stress, coping, and development in children* (pp. 1–41). New York: McGraw-Hill.

Rutter, M., Cox, A., Tupling, C., Berger, M., & Yule, W. (1975). Attainment and adjustment in two geographic areas: I. The prevalence of psychiatric disorder. *British Journal of Psychiatry, 126*, 493–509.

Shannon, M. P., Lonigan, C. J., Finch, A. J., & Taylor, C. M. (1994). Children exposed to disaster: I. Epidemiology of post-traumatic symptoms and symptom profiles. *Journal of the American Academy of Child and Adolescent Psychiatry, 33*, 80–93.

Singer, M. I., Anglin, T. M., Song, L. Y., & Lunghofer, L. (1995). Adolescents' exposure to violence and associated symptoms of psychological trauma. *Journal of the American Medical Association, 273*, 477–482.

Solomon, Z., Kotler, M., & Mikulincer, M. (1988). Combat-related posttraumatic stress among second-generation Holocaust survivors: Preliminary findings. *American Journal of Psychiatry, 145*, 865–868.

Stoddard, F. J., Norman, D. K., Murphy, J. M., & Beardslee, W. R. (1989). Psychiatric outcome of burned children and adolescents: Annual meeting of the American Academy of Child and Adolescent Psychiatry. *Journal of the American Academy of Child and Adolescent Psychiatry, 28*, 589–595.

Straus, M. A., Gelles, R., & Steinmetz, S. K. (1980). *Behind closed doors: Violence in the American family.* Garden City, NY: Anchor Press.

Stuber, M. L., Kazak, A. E., Meeske, K., & Barakat, L. (1998). Is post-traumatic stress a viable model for understanding responses to childhood cancer? *Child and Adolescent Psychiatric Clinics of North America, 7*, 169–182.

Stuber, M., Kazak, A. E., Meeske, K., Barakat, L. P., Guthrie, D., Garnier, H., Pynoos, R. S., & Meadows, A. (1997). Predictors of posttraumatic stress symptoms in childhood cancer survivors. *Pediatrics, 100*, 958–964.

Stuber, M. L., Nader, K. O., Houskamp, B. M., & Pynoos, R. S. (1996). Appraisal of life threat and acute trauma responses in pediatric bone marrow transplant patients. *Journal of Traumatic Stress, 9*, 674–686.

Terr, L. C. (1983). Chowchilla revisited: The effects of psychic trauma four years after a school-bus kidnapping. *American Journal of Psychiatry, 140*, 1543–1550.

Terr, L. C. (1985). Psychic trauma in children and adolescents. *Psychiatric Clinics of North America, 8*, 815–835.

Terr, L. C. (1991). Childhood traumas: An outline and overview. *American Journal of Psychiatry, 148*, 10–20.

UNICEF, United Nations Children's Research Fund. (1996). The state of the world's children 1996 (on line). http://www.unicef.org/sowc96.

Vehara, E., Chalmers, D., Jenkins, E. J., & Shakoor, B. (1996). Youth encounters with violence: Results from the Chicago Community Mental Health Council violence screening project. *Journal of Black Studies, 26*, 768–781.

Vernberg, E. M., LaGreca, A. M., Silverman, U. K., et al. (1996). Prediction of post-traumatic stress symptoms in children after Hurricane Andrew. *Journal of Abnormal Psychology, 105*, 237–248.

Yule, W. (1992). Post-traumatic stress disorder in child survivors of shipping disasters: The sinking of the "Jupiter". *Journal of Psychotherapy and Psychosomatics, 576*, 200–205.

Ziv, A., Kruglanski, A. W., & Shulman, S. (1974). Children's psychological reactions to wartime stress. *Journal of Personality and Social Psychology, 40*, 287–291.

39

Dissociative Disorders

Frank W. Putnam

INTRODUCTION

Definitions of dissociation as a psychological process converge around the observation that profound levels of dissociation are characterized by a discernible failure in the integration of memory, information, perception, and experience (Putnam, 1997). Dissociative disorders are characterized by profound alterations in memory and identity that are not the result of organic brain injury or a toxic or metabolic condition (American Psychiatric Association, 1994). The DSM-IV recognizes five types of dissociative disorders: Dissociative Amnesia, Dissociative Fugue, Depersonalization Disorder, Dissociative Identity Disorder (DID, also known as multiple personality disorder, MPD); and Dissociative Disorder Not Otherwise Specified (DDNOS).

Specific types of disturbances in memory and identity serve as common features grouping these disorders together. Dissociative memory disturbances are understood to be "functional amnesias"; that is, these amnesias *cannot* be attributed to any detectable organic cause. Dissociative amnesias are typically manifest as an inability of an individual to recall complex behavior in which he or she has engaged. Frequently, this involves extensive periods of time and complex interactions with others. Under certain circumstances, these previously inaccessible memories may become available to the individual. Dissociative amnesias typically involve autobiographical information rather than general fund of knowledge, which usually remains intact. Dissociative disturbances of identity typically involve partial or sometimes complete amnesia for a primary identity, and sometimes adoption of a secondary identity that is often at odds with the primary identity.

In Dissociative Amnesia, individuals becomes amnesic for core aspects of their personal identity such as their name or whether or not they are married, have a job, or children. Dissociative Fugue is manifest by travel while in a dissociative amnesia, or while in a secondary identity. In both Dissociative Amnesia and Dissociative Fugue, when the individual recovers his or her primary identity, there is often an inability to recall events experienced in

Frank W. Putnam • Mayerson Center for Safe and Healthy Children, Children's Hospital Medical Center, Cincinnati, Ohio 45219-3039.

Handbook of Developmental Psychopathology, Second Edition, edited by Arnold J. Sameroff, Michael Lewis, and Suzanne M. Miller. Kluwer Academic/Plenum Publishers, New York, 2000.

the dissociative state. Multiple personality disorder is manifest by the existence of distinct alter personality states that recurrently exchange executive control of an individual's behavior. There are often reciprocal amnesias compartmentalizing the individual's awareness of his or her behavior while in different personality states. DDNOS is mixed category, including culture-specific dissociative variants as well as responses to extreme stressors, such as being held hostage. Many individuals diagnosed with DDNOS appear clinically similar to MPD patients except that they lack the overt appearance of discrete alter personality states. Depersonalization Disorder is characterized by profound feelings of being unreal or dead. There are often subtle memory disturbances, but the gross functional amnesias found in the other dissociative disorders are absent.

History

Clinical descriptions of dissociative disorders date to the seventeenth century and become relatively plentiful by the nineteenth century. Many individuals prominent in the history of psychology and psychiatry—Benjamin Rush, known as the father of American psychiatry; Pierre Janet, the great French clinician; Morton Prince, founder of the *Journal of Abnormal Psychology*, and William James, the renowned American psychologist—contributed case reports and essays on the nature of these unusual disorders. Most of their cases were adults, who recurrently manifest distinctly different personality states, usually accompanied by reciprocal amnesias for their behavior while in different personality states. By the end of the nineteenth century, most of the theories in vogue today had been proposed in one form or another (Putnam, 1986).

The diagnosis of MPD fell out of favor in the early 1920s, with most of these cases being rediagnosed as a form of schizophrenia. A variety of reasons have been offered for the abandonment of the diagnosis of MPD, including the rise of psychoanalysis, with its emphasis on repression theory; the popularity of the then broadly defined diagnosis of schizophrenia; and allegations that MPD was iatrogenically created by unwitting clinicians fascinated by the bizarreness of such patients. Similar challenges to the credibility of MPD continue today (McHugh & Putnam, 1995).

Beginning in the mid-1970s, the adoption of criterion-based diagnostic systems for schizophrenia and other psychiatric disorders highlighted the differences between dissociative patients and other disorders, and thus increased their recognition. Diagnostic criteria were formalized with the publication of the DSM-III in 1980, although MPD was described in earlier versions. By the early to mid-1980s, clinical reports describing hundreds of cases were appearing in reputable journals and a new understanding of the etiology of MPD was emerging. This was based on the discovery that the vast majority of such patients reported histories of severe early trauma, particularly child abuse. Most adult patients reported the onset of dissociative symptoms in childhood, although, typically, a dissociative disorder diagnosis was not made until the third or fourth decade following a long and complicated psychiatric history.

The growing acceptance of adult dissociative disorders, coupled with the recognition of the role of childhood trauma, has spurred the identification of child and adolescent cases in recent years. Although lagging behind the adult literature in time and scope, clinical research on child and adolescent dissociative disorders has followed a similar progression from scattered single case reports to statistical analyses of 50 or more cases. These studies find strong parallels between core dissociative symptoms in children and adults, although their behavioral expression evolves with age. This research has also begun to grapple with the thorny issue of determining when certain "dissociative" behaviors (e.g., the existence of vivid imaginary companionship) is developmentally appropriate or inappropriate.

Measurement of Dissociation

Both adult and child research has benefitted from the development of reliable and valid measures of dissociation. Self-report measures such as the Dissociative Experiences Scale (DES) have operationalized dissociation in terms of subjective experiences (Carlson & Putnam, 1993), whereas observer report measures such as the Child Dissociative Checklist (CDC) score a set of dissociative behaviors manifest by the subject (Putnam, Helmers, & Trickett, 1993). As with many psychological assessments, the former approach is preferred for adults and the latter for children, with adolescents not fitting neatly within either format. Hundreds of empirical studies have been published and the psychometrics of these instruments scrutinized (van IJzendoorn & Schuengel, 1996; Waller, 1995). Reviews and meta-analyses indicate that the reliability and validity of leading dissociation measures are equivalent to measurement of other clinical constructs, such as depression or anxiety.

This growing body of empirical research encompasses a range of clinical and general population samples, including dozens of international data sets using translations of standard measures. By and large, the results of these studies are highly congruent and robustly support the association between traumatic antecedents and pathological dissociation suggested in clinical reports (van IJzendoorn & Schuengel, 1996). These measures have also helped to identify other correlates of dissociation, including family process variables independent of maltreatment experiences.

Modern research with dissociation measures has reopened a question that dates back to the nineteenth-century debate between Morton Prince and Pierre Janet. Prince's position was that pathological dissociation is the extreme end of a normal continuum of dissociative experiences; whereas Janet believed that pathological dissociation occurred in a certain type of individual who differed significantly from normal individuals. Until recently, the continuum model dominated. Taxometric statistical approaches (Putnam, Carlson, et al., 1996; Waller & Ross, 1997; Waller, Putnam, & Carlson, 1996) and psychophysiological approaches (Griffin, Resick, & Mechanic, 1997), however, call the continuum model into question. In aggregate, these studies suggest that individuals with high levels of dissociation respond to stimuli such as traumatic stressors significantly differently than the general population and thus constitute a distinct "dissociative type."

The existence of a distinct pathological dissociative "type" of cognitive organization implies a different developmental process from a continuum model in which an individual simply exceeds some clinical threshold. A distinct dissociative type should also have a different response to treatment compared with an individual suffering from a higher than "normal" level of dissociation. In the typological model, successful treatment should be manifest by a significant reorganization of cognitive structure and sense of self, whereas clinical improvement in the continuum model would be expected to proceed by degree. At present, it is not clear which of these two models better characterizes the data.

Prevalence

Few data exist on the prevalence of dissociative disorders. The most systematic studies have examined the prevalence rates of these disorders in clinical samples, typically evaluating consecutive admissions to inpatient units or clinics. These studies indicate that between 5% and 17% of psychiatric admissions in North American settings meet criteria for a dissociative disorder (e.g., Horen, Leichner, & Lawson, 1995; Latz, Kramer, & Hughes, 1995; Ross, Anderson, Fleisher, & Norton, 1991; Saxe et al., 1993). European studies have found similar prevalence rates (e.g., Darves-Bornoz, Degiovanni, & Gaillard, 1995; Modestin, Ebner, Junghan, & Erni, 1996). The most rigorous general population study to date was conducted by Ross and colleagues using the DES, with a large stratified sample from Winnipeg, Canada (Ross, Joshi, & Currie, 1989). A follow-up structured diagnostic interview of about 40% of the sample found that 3.1% of subjects met criteria for MPD, with about 11% of the sample having significant dissociative symptoms (Ross, 1991). Waller and Ross subsequently reanalyzed the DES data using the DES-T, a subscale optimized for detection of pathological levels of dissociation. They calculated a base rate of 3.3% for pathological dissociation in this general population sample (Waller & Ross, 1997). Although not definitive, these preliminary studies indicate that pathological dissociation is not a rare event, and patients meeting DSM diagnostic criteria for MPD or DDNOS are routinely encountered in psychiatric settings.

DEVELOPMENTAL ANTECEDENTS OF PATHOLOGICAL DISSOCIATION

The clinical recognition that significant childhood trauma is often associated with pathological dissociation initiated research on the developmental antecedents of dissociative disorders. This research is in its infancy and much of the variance in who develops pathological dissociation and who does not cannot be explained. Nonetheless, a number of variables have been identified as contributing sources to pathological dissociation. These are discussed below.

Trauma

Pierre Janet was the first to forcefully articulate the relationship between trauma and dissociation (van der Hart & Friedman, 1989). Kardiner's (1941) work with World War I veterans and classic studies by Abeles and Schilder (1935) and Kanzer (1939) between the world wars reinforced Janet's observations. During World War II, symptoms such as dissociative amnesias and fugue reactions were recognized as common sequelae of intense combat and routinely treated with hypnosis or sodium amytal abreaction, rest, and brief supportive therapy. The majority of such cases were returned to their units within 3–7 days. Postwar psychiatry, however, moved away from this approach, particularly with the advent of the psychopharmacological revolution. The recent rediscovery of the role of trauma in pathological dissociation resulted from studies of large numbers of MPD patients, beginning in the early 1980s. There are now several well-established lines of evidence that document the association between trauma and dissociation.

The first line of evidence comes from research on case series of dissociative disorder patients. To date, every study that has systemically evaluated MPD and DDNOS patients for histories of trauma has found extremely high rates (85–100%) of maltreatment, often together with subsequent adult trauma such as rape (e.g., Coons, Bowman, & Milstein, 1988; Loewenstein & Putnam, 1990; Ross, Miller, et al., 1991; Ross, Norton, & Wozney, 1989; Schultz, Braun, & Kluft, 1989). The first retrospective studies of traumatic histories were criticized for their lack of corroboration (Frankel, 1993), but more recent studies have included good documentation (e.g., Coons, 1994; Swica, Lewis, & Lewis, 1996). The second line of evidence comes from research within a variety of trauma populations, including combat veterans and disaster, rape, and maltreatment victims. These studies find evidence of a rough dose–response relationship between the degree of trauma and level of dissociation (e.g., Anderson, Yasenik, & Ross, 1993; Branscomb, 1991; Carlson & Rosser-Hogan, 1991; Chu & Dill, 1990; Kirby, Chu, & Dill, 1993; Sandberg & Lynn, 1992). It is clear from the moderate correlations, however, that other factors beyond trauma contribute to increased dissociation.

The third line of evidence emerges from studies that have compared levels of dissociation between traumatized and nontraumatized subjects. As with the within-trauma sample studies, a variety of different types of trauma have been investigated. In virtually every study to date, the traumatized group had significantly higher levels of dissociation than the comparison group (for a table of these studies, see Putnam & Carlson, 1997). The fourth line of evidence is the now well replicated finding that high levels of dissociation proximal to a traumatic experience (peritraumatic dissociation) predispose an individual to the subsequent development of posttraumatic stress disorder (PTSD) (Bremner et al., 1992; Koopman, Classen, & Spiegel, 1994; Marmar et al., 1994; Weiss, Marmar, Metzler, & Ronfeldt, 1995). This is proving to be an especially important finding, as it allows clinicians to prospectively identify individuals at risk for the development of serious posttraumatic complications. A promising fifth line of evidence, the correlation between traumatic biological alterations and levels of dissociation, is emerging from recent investigations (Griffin et al., 1997; Stein, Koverola, Hanna, Torchia, & McClarty, 1997).

Dissociation as a "Defense" against Trauma

Increased levels of dissociation in the context of immediate trauma are widely regarded as serving a defensive function in the classic psychoanalytic sense of an unconscious process acting to decrease anxiety and psychological conflict. Enumerations of the defensive functions of dissociation usually emphasize the role of dissociative compartmentalization, which separates conflicting information and minimizes cognitive dissonance (Ludwig, 1983). Dissociative alterations of identity are regarded as an expression of forbidden affects and impulses that are unacceptable to the individual, or the assumption of context-dependent roles or aspects of self that are in opposition to the primary identity. Recent research identifying the contribution of peritraumatic dissociation to the subsequent development of PTSD has called into question the adaptive nature of traumatic dissociation. Psychophysiological studies, however, indicate that dissociative states evoked by traumatic reminders do decrease hyperarousal and autonomic dysregulation (Griffin et al., 1997). The current view of many authorities is that increased dissociation in a traumatic context is transiently adaptive but also likely to subsequently predispose an individual to serious posttraumatic sequelae.

Age at Onset of Trauma

The age of the individual at the time of the onset of severe trauma appears to be an important variable influencing the form of the dissociative response. Numerous studies using dissociation measures in different populations have consistently found moderate negative correlations between age of trauma onset and increased dissociation scores (van IJzendoorn & Schuengel, 1996). Two chronic dissociative disorders, DID/MPD, and DDNOS, are strongly associated with childhood onsets of trauma. In contrast, transient dissociative disorders, such as dissociative amnesia or fugue, typically occur in adults subjected to acute stressors (Loewenstein, 1991b; Putnam, 1985).

Early childhood trauma may produce chronic dissociative disorders such as MPD through several mechanisms. Clinical experience and empirical research with dissociation measures in clinical and normal samples indicate that, as a group, younger individuals are more dissociative. Typically, there is a small to moderate decline in dissociation scores with increasing age (van IJzendoorn & Schuengel, 1996). Thus, it is hypothesized that early childhood trauma occurs during a critical developmental period, when an individual is "more dissociative" and thus more likely to cope with stress through dissociative defenses. If this proves to be the case, then sustained levels of increased dissociation associated with chronic repetitive traumas such as child abuse may disrupt critical developmental processes associated with the consolidation of a unified sense of identity. If these dissociative disruptions in development of memory and identity functions span a sufficient length of time, a different "type" of cognitive organization may emerge. This could account for the "dissociative type" phenomena discussed earlier. Understanding the effects of increased dissociation on critical developmental processes, such as the elaboration and consolidation of a unified sense of self and the development of emotional regulation and impulse control, appears to be a key area for future research.

Gender

Research has not found evidence of significant gender effects on dissociation scores. For example, a meta-analysis of 19 DES studies found no gender differences (van IJzendoorn & Schuengel, 1996). Yet most clinical studies find six to nine times more females than males in adult dissociative disorder samples (e.g., Coons et al., 1988; Putnam, Guroff, Silberman, Barban, & Post, 1986; Ross, Miller, et al., 1991). A cross-sectional analysis of gender ratios in different age groups in a large juvenile sample ($n = 177$) of dissociative disorder cases found a steady increase in the percentage of females with increasing age (Putnam, Hornstein, & Peterson, 1996). Preschool cases were almost evenly divided by gender, but by late adolescence, the ratio was more than 8:1 female to male cases. Whether this developmental shift in gender ratio reflects a differential vulnerability of females or a sampling bias has not been established. Most authorities believe that many older male MPD cases are being missed, either because they have entered non-mental-health systems (e.g., the criminal justice system) or because male dissociative patients present differently from female cases and are being overlooked.

Cultural Influences

Cultural factors undoubtedly play a role in the expression of dissociative symptoms, just as they do for the manifestation of virtually all other psychiatric disorders (Kleinman, Fabrega, & Parron, 1996). For example, MPD is relatively rare in India, but "Brief Dissociative Stupor" is frequently diagnosed (Alexander, Joseph, & Das, 1997). Research with translations of measures such as the DES, however, indicate that core pathological dissociative features such as disturbances in memory and identity are remarkably similar across diverse cultures (e.g., Berger, Onon, Nakajima, & Suematsu, 1994; Boon & Draijer, 1993; Carlson & Putnam, 1993; Park et al., 1995; Yargic, Tutkun, & Sar, 1995). When ethnic or racial differences have been found in North American samples, they appear to be largely accounted for by differences in life experiences. For example, initial differences in DES scores among African American, Hispanic American, and European American combat veterans disappeared when level of combat exposure was controlled (Zatzick, Marmar, Weiss, & Metzler, 1994).

Family Environment Effects

Clinical recognition that dissociative disorders tend to run in families emerged during the 1980s. These case reports characterized dissociative families as authoritarian and patriarchal with inconsistent parenting and harsh discipline. More systematic support for this position accrued with the advent of larger case series studies in the late 1980s and early 1990s. Dissociation-measure-based research has found moderate correlations between dissociation and inconsistent parental disciplinary practices (Mann & Sanders, 1994). Studies of abusive families have found that patients with dissociative disorders tend to come from families characterized by severe abuse, conflict, and controlling and extremely violent parents (Alexander & Schaeffer, 1994). Most recently, Yeager and Lewis (1996), studied the families of 11 children and adolescents diagnosed with dissociative disorders. They documented considerable psychopathology and violence in the parents, including numerous parental cases of dissociative disorders as well as frequent histories of child abuse. Sixty percent of the siblings evaluated also suffered from dissociative disorders. Only one sibling was judged free of serious psychopathology.

Attachment

One of the earliest signs of the effects of inconsistent or aversive parenting is manifest in abnormal attachment behaviors. Attachment theory has been applied to dissociative disorders by several investigators (Alexander & Schaeffer, 1994; Barach, 1991; Liotti, 1992; Main & Hesse, 1996). Recent efforts have focused on the association of a specific infant/toddler attachment response, Type D, with high levels of maternal dissociation (Main & Hesse, 1996). Type D attachment responses, first described by Main and Solomon (1986), are characterized by disorganized and conflicting movement patterns, contradictions in intention, poor orientation to environment, and periods of sudden immobility associated with dazed expressions or trance-like states. Type D attachment responses are common in maltreated infants and toddlers (Cicchetti & Nurcombe, 1994). Liotti (1992) proposes several theoretical pathways through which Type D attachment behaviors could evolve into MPD, although an alternative hypothesis is that both are the results of abusive parenting. The increasing inclusion of child and parental dissociation measures in studies of child development promises to inform us about the relationship of dissociation to critical early parent–child interactions.

Transgenerational Transmission of Abusive Behavior

The role of pathological dissociation in the transgenerational transmission of abusive behaviors was first raised by clinicians in the early 1980s (e.g., Brown, 1983). In a unique prospective study investigating the contribution of parental dissociation to child maltreatment in a sample of high-risk mothers with histories of their own maltreatment, Egeland and Susman-Stillman (1996) found that mothers who maltreated their children had DES scores twice as high as nonmaltreating mothers. They also manifest more dissociation on rater-scored interviews. Nonmaltreating, low dissociation mothers were better able to discuss their own maltreatment experiences suggesting that these memories were more available for psychological processing than the childhood experiences of the high-dissociation mothers. High levels of parental dissociation may prove to be a useful predictor of maltreatment risk, permitting better screening and early preventative interventions for high-risk parents.

Genetic Predisposition

The clinical recognition of the frequent transgenerational transmission of pathological dissociation naturally led to speculation on the importance of a genetic predisposition (Kluft, 1986). Modest correlations between dissociation scores in parents and their children could also be interpreted as evidence of genetic contributions (Mann & Sanders, 1994; Putnam, 1996). A recent DES study of 280 (140 pairs) identical and 148 (74 pairs) fraternal adolescent twins, however, found no evidence of heritability of pathological dissociation. About one-third to one-half of the variance was accounted for by shared environmental experiences, with the remaining variance attributable to nonshared environmental experiences (Waller & Ross, 1997). Additional twin studies in progress should shed further light on the magnitude, if any, of genetic contributions to pathological dissociation.

HYPNOTIZABILITY, SUGGESTIBILITY, AND FANTASY PRONENESS

The constructs of hypnotizability, suggestibility, and fantasy proneness are frequently loosely equated and have often been invoked individually or in combination as "explanations" for pathological dissociation. Empirical research, however, suggests that the overlaps among these constructs are not as extensive as is often assumed (Putnam & Carlson, 1997). Nor do these processes provide a satisfactory mechanistic explanation for many dissociative phenomena (Putnam & Carlson, 1997).

Hypnotizability

Hypnotic explanations of MPD can be traced back to eighteenth-century clinical formulations. The autohypnotic model of MPD continues to be the most widely accepted theory for the disorder. Elsewhere, I critique these hypnotic formulations in detail (Putnam, 1997; Putnam & Carlson, 1997). Correlations between a range of hypnosis and dissociation measures have been examined in a score of studies (for a table of the findings, see Putnam & Carlson, 1997). Low, generally nonsignificant correlations have been consistently reported by numerous investigators across a range of traumatized and nontraumatized clinical and population samples. If one narrowly restricts subjects to highly traumatized individuals, then moderate correlations between hypnotizability and dissociation measures emerge (Putnam & Carlson, 1997; Putnam, Helmers, Horowitz, & Trickett, 1994). The absence of the expected robust association between measures of dissociation and hypnosis indicates that increased hypnotizability is not a simple, direct mechanism for pathological dissociation, although a more complex, nonlinear relationship has not been ruled out (Putnam & Carlson, 1997).

Suggestibility

Increased "suggestibility" has been postulated to predispose an individual to MPD. Critics allege that highly suggestible individuals are iatrogenically susceptible to zealous therapists who suggest the existence of alter personalities (McHugh & Putnam, 1995). Suggestibility is a poorly operationalized construct, and few empirical studies are available to test this hypothesis. The existent data, however, indicate that there is little or no positive relationship between accepted measures of suggestibility, such as the Gudjonsson Suggestibility Scale, and dissociation scores in traumatized patients (Leavitt, 1997). Indeed, clinicians working with MPD patients often lament their lack of responsiveness to therapists' suggestions.

Fantasy Proneness

At least two lines of evidence indicate that fantasy proneness may be related to dissociative behaviors and perhaps dissociative disorders. The first involves the apparent increased frequency and vividness of imaginary companion (IC) phenomena in dissociative patients. When systematic questions are included as part of a clinical evaluation, as many as 80% of dissociative children and adolescents report the existence of vivid imaginary companion-like entities (Putnam, 1997). Sanders has studied the frequency and characteristics of ICs retrospectively reported by adult MPD patients (Sanders, 1992). Sixty-four percent of the MPD patients remembered one or more ICs between the ages of 2 and 13 years, compared with 10% of male and 19% of female college student comparison subjects. The most striking difference was the degree of reported vividness of the IC experience. All of the MPD patients recalling ICs reported seeing or hearing their ICs and believing that they were real and separate entities, whereas only 25% of comparison subjects with an IC reported a similar degree of vividness. Trujillo, Lewis, Yeager, and Gidlow (1996) compared IC phenomena in normal boys and maltreated boys in residential treatment, including seven boys diagnosed with MPD. Fifty-seven percent of the residential treatment group reported ICs, with an average of 6.4 entities, compared with 30% of normal boys averaging 2.5 entities. The ICs of the normal boys were benign, experienced as volitional, and typically served as playmates during periods of loneliness. In addition to serving as playmates and comforters, the ICs of the maltreated children functioned as protectors and as introjected family members. Protector ICs were often associated with aggressive behavior in the maltreated boys.

Over the years, a number of clinical theorists have proposed that imaginary companionship capacities provide the developmental kernel for the elaboration of MPD in maltreated children (see review in Putnam, 1997). Differentiation between normal, benign imaginary companionship and the potentially more pathological IC phenomena of dissociative children can be difficult. Important clinical features are (1) the degree of vividness of the IC experience; (2) the degree volition experienced by the child (i.e., whether the child experiences "being controlled" by the IC); and (3) the playful versus protective or aggressive nature of the IC. Dissociative ICs appear to be considerably more vivid, usually including visual and auditory hallucinations of an external entity. Dissociative children often report being "made to do" aggressive, impulsive, or self-destructive acts by their ICs. The ICs of dissociative or traumatized children often appear in contexts other than play, especially when the child feels threatened.

The second line of evidence connecting pathological dissociation with fantasy capacities emerges from research on fantasy proneness. First described by Wilson and Barber (1983), fantasy proneness has been operationalized as a construct by Lynn, Rhue, and Green (1988). Measures of fantasy proneness are moderately to strongly correlated with dissociation scores. Individuals meeting criteria for fantasy proneness frequently have histories of childhood mal-treatment (Lynn et al., 1988). Further research is necessary to determine the overlap between pathological dissociation and fantasy proneness, but preliminary studies suggest that high levels of fantasy proneness may be related to the development of pathological dissociation.

DISSOCIATION AND PSYCHOPATHOLOGY

Dissociative Disorders

As discussed in the introduction, the dissociative disorders share common features with regard to functional disturbances of memory and identity. In the modern era, the clinical phenomenology of MPD is the best delineated with more than a dozen replications of the core syndromal profile. Indeed, this repeated replication provides an important source of construct validity for the diagnosis (McHugh & Putnam, 1995). Specific dissociative symptoms are often grouped together under the larger categories of dissociative memory symptoms and dissociative process symptoms (Loewenstein, 1991a; Putnam, 1997).

Dissociative memory symptoms include amnesias for complex behaviors ("time loss" or "blackouts"), fugue episodes, fragmentary recall of autobiographical information, difficulty in determining the original source of recalled information (source amnesias), and difficulty in determining if recalled memories represent actual life experiences. Dissociative process symptoms include depersonalization, derealization, trance-like states, passive-influence/ interference experiences such as possession, and vivid auditory and visual hallucinations. The alter identities seen in MPD, and sometimes in dissociative fugue, are usually included under this category.

The alter personalities of MPD patients have received considerable attention in the popular media. Popular portrayals often promulgate the misleading stereotype that the alter personalities of MPD patients are as different from one another as are separate people. In contrast, experienced clinicians working with these entities describe them as narrowly circum-scribed behaviorally, with each usually only capable of a limited range in one prevailing affect (Kluft, 1991; Putnam, 1992). They fall far short of the depth, breadth, and complexity that is generally deemed to constitute "personality." Psychophysiological and neuropsychological studies have documented alter personality state differential responsivity for some measures, but these studies also find important continuities across the alter personality states of a given MPD patient (Putnam, 1991; Zahn, Moraga, & Ray, 1996). For example, habituation to a noxious stimulus generalizes across different alter personalities at the same rate as it does for normal control subjects (Putnam, Zahn, & Post, 1990). Authorities recommend that clinicians avoid overfascination with these entities and focus instead on the underlying conflicts that they personify.

Dissociation and General Psychopathology

Increased levels of dissociation are linked to broadly increased general psychopathology by several lines of evidence. The first is the well-replicated finding that adult dissociative disorder patients manifest extensive psychiatric comorbidity, most commonly including depression, suicide and self-mutilation behaviors, panic and anxiety symptoms, posttraumatic symptoms, eating disorders, conversion and somatoform symptoms (e.g., Coons et al., 1988; Putnam et al., 1986; Ross, Norton, et al., 1989; Schultz et al., 1989). Similar polysymptomatic clinical profiles are emerging from more recent studies of child and adolescent dissociative patients (Coons, 1996; Hornstein & Putnam, 1992).

The second source of evidence emerges from dissociation measure research with clinical and nonclinical samples. These studies uniformly find significant correlations between dissociation measures and dimensional measures of depression, anxiety, PTSD, self-mutilation behavior, and somatization in adults (e.g., Nemiah, 1991; Reiter, Shakerin, Gambone, & Milburn, 1990; Saxe et al., 1994; van der Kolk et al., 1996). In a parallel fashion, similar findings are beginning to be reported for child and adolescent samples (Putnam, 1996).

In our prospective longitudinal study of sexually abused and comparison girls, we have found moderate to strong correlations between total and subscale scores of the Child Behavioral Checklist (Putnam & Peterson, 1994) and the CDC (Putnam, 1996). Dissociation scores were also predictive of significant school problems as rated by teachers (Trickett, McBride-Chang, & Putnam, 1994). Dissociation scores at the first evaluation point most proximal to the child's disclosure of sexual abuse are predictive of psychopathology and psychophysiological responsivity to stressors at the Time 4 evaluation point, more than 6 years later on average (Putnam & Trickett, 1997, unpublished data). These findings underscore the importance of routinely assessing dissociation in developmental and clinical studies of child and adolescent psychopathology.

Plausible Developmental Psychopathological Mechanisms

The broad and robust associations between dissociation and general psychopathology as documented in clinical and nonclinical studies have led some to speculate that dissociation measures such as the DES might really be nonspecific measures of psychopathology (e.g., van IJzendoorn & Schuengel, 1996). There are several arguments against this conclusion, including the finding that large numbers of seriously ill psychiatric patients nonetheless have low DES scores (e.g., see DES score distributions in Putnam, Carlson, et al., 1996). An alternative interpretation is that increased dissociation represents a fundamental form or developmental layer of psychopathology that has multiple, long-term negative effects on cognition and adaptation, and thus contributes to multiple forms of psychopathology as well as to the dissociative disorders. Several theorists have detailed plausible dissociative developmental effects on the maturation of cognition, consolidation of a unified sense of self, acquisition of emotional regulation and impulse control, and the development of interpersonal skills (Fink, 1988; Kluft, 1985; Putnam, 1996). Elsewhere, I detail a mechanistic model through which increased dissociation would lead to increased general psychopathology as well as to DSM dissociative disorders (Putnam, 1997).

Treatment

Most treatment approaches to adult dissociative patients emphasize psychotherapy (Putnam & Loewenstein, 1993). A considerable number of therapists augment psychotherapy with hypnotherapy (Putnam & Loewenstein, 1993). Some critics charge that hypnosis is iatrogenic, but comparisons of MPD patients treated with and without hypnosis find no significant differences in symptom patterns (Putnam et al., 1986; Ross, 1989). Psychopharmacotherapy is an important adjunctive treatment, primarily for depressive, anxiety, and posttraumatic symptoms (Loewenstein, 1991c; Putnam & Loewenstein, 1993). At present, no medications appear specific for treatment of dissociative symptoms, although several experimental or illicit drugs produce dissociative symptoms (Good, 1989; Krystal, Bennett, Bremner, Southwick, & Charney, 1995).

Adult psychotherapy treatment models generally emphasize a staged approach (Kluft, 1991; Loewenstein, 1993; Putnam, 1989). Initial efforts are focused on crisis intervention and stabilization of the patient, development of rapport, and, in the case of MPD, the identification of the issues and conflicts personified by dissociative personality states. The middle stages of therapy focus on psychological processing of dissociated traumatic or affective experiences and their transformation of meaning for the individual. There is an emphasis on the integration of these experiences into the autobiographical schema of the individual and on resolution of cognitive distortions associated with traumatic life experiences. The final stages of therapy are usually directed toward a more formal integration of dissociated aspects of self and substitution of nondissociative coping responses to life stressors. Recent treatment outcome studies document significant gains on standard measures for many dissociative patients, although controlled clinical trials have yet to be conducted (Choe & Kluft, 1995; Ellason & Ross, 1997).

Child treatment models are less well developed and tested. One common approach has been the application of a more or less standard adult model to children (Silberg, 1997). Others have taken issue with the developmental appropriateness of the adult model, especially for younger children (Putnam, 1997). In particular, the emphasis in the adult model on explicit psychological processing of traumatic contents and affects is considered beyond the capacities of younger children. The emphasis in the adult model on directly interacting with alter personality states is also considered problematic for dissociative children whose identity states are more ambiguous, and who often do not have a crystallized sense of individuality. It is believed that it is important not to socialize the child as a multiple but rather to emphasize the integration of different aspects of behavior. There is, however, at present only anecdotal evidence on which to judge one approach against another. The lack of treatment outcome data plagues the child abuse field as a whole and must be addressed in future research.

REFERENCES

Abeles, M., & Schilder, P. (1935). Psychogenic loss of personal identity. *Archives of Neurological Psychiatry, 34*, 587–604.

Alexander, P. C., & Schaeffer, C. M. (1994). A typology of incestuous families based on cluster analysis. *Journal of Family Process, 8*, 458–470.

Alexander, P. J., Joseph, S., & Das, A. (1997). Limited utility of ICD-10 and DSM-IV classification of dissociative and conversion disorders in India. *Acta Psychiatrica Scandinavica, 95*, 177–182.

American Psychiatric Association. (1994). *Diagnostic and statistical manual of mental disorders* (4th ed.). Washington, DC: Author.

Anderson, G., Yasenik, L., & Ross, C. A. (1993). Dissociative experiences and disorders among women who identify themselves as sexual abuse survivors. *Child Abuse and Neglect, 17*, 677–686.

Barach, P. M. (1991). Multiple personality disorder as an attachment disorder. *Dissociation, 4*, 117–123.

Berger, D., Onon, Y., Nakajima, K., & Suematsu, H. (1994). Dissociative symptoms in Japan. *American Journal of Psychiatry, 151*, 148–149.

Boon, S., & Draijer, N. (1993). *Multiple personality disorder in the Netherlands*. Amsterdam: Swets & Zeitlinger.

Branscomb, L. (1991). Dissociation in combat-related post-traumatic stress disorder. *Dissociation, 4*, 13–20.

Bremner, J. D., Southwick, S., Brett, E., Fontana, A., Rosenheck, R., & Charney, D. S. (1992). Dissociation and posttraumatic stress disorder in Vietnam combat veterans. *American Journal of Psychiatry, 149*, 328–332.

Brown, G. W. (1983). Multiple personality disorder as perpetrator of child abuse. *Child Abuse and Neglect, 7*, 123–126.

Carlson, E. B., & Putnam, F. W. (1993). An update on the Dissociative Experiences Scale. *Dissociation, 6*, 16–27.

Carlson, E. B., & Rosser-Hogan, R. (1991). Trauma experiences, posttraumatic stress, dissociation, and depression in Cambodian refugees. *American Journal of Psychiatry, 148*, 1548–1551.

Choe, B., & Kluft, R. (1995). The use of the DES in studying treatment outcome with dissociative identity disorder: A pilot study. *Dissociation, 8*, 160–174.

Chu, J. A., & Dill, D. L. (1990). Dissociative symptoms in relation to childhood physical and sexual abuse. *American Journal of Psychiatry, 147*, 887–892.

Cicchetti, D., & Nurcombe, B. (1994). Advances and challenges in the study of sequelae of child maltreatment. In D. Cicchetti (Ed.), *Development and psychopathology* (Vol. 6, pp. 1–3). New York: Cambridge University Press.

Coons, P. (1996). Clinical phenomenology of 25 children and adolescents with dissociative disorders. *Child and Adolescent Psychiatric Clinics of North America, 5*, 361–374.

Coons, P. M. (1994). Confirmation of childhood abuse in child and adolescent cases of multiple personality disorder and dissociative disorder not otherwise specified. *Journal of Nervous and Mental Disease, 182*, 461–464.

Coons, P. M., Bowman, E. S., & Milstein, V. (1988). Multiple personality disorder: A clinical investigation of 50 cases. *Journal of Nervous and Mental Disease, 176*, 519–527.

Darves-Bornoz, J., Degiovanni, A., & Gaillard, P. (1995). Why is dissociative identity disorder infrequent in France? [Letter]. *American Journal of Psychiatry, 152*, 1530–1531.

Egeland, B., & Susman-Stillman, A. (1996). Dissociation as a mediator of child abuse across generations. *Child Abuse and Neglect, 20*, 1123–1132.

Ellason, J., & Ross, C. (1997). Two year follow-up of inpatients with dissociative identity disorder. *American Journal of Psychiatry, 154*, 832–839.

Fink, D. L. (1988). The core self: A developmental perspective on the dissociative disorders. *Dissociation, 1*, 43–47.

Frankel, F. H. (1993). Adult reconstruction of childhood events in the multiple personality literature. *American Journal of Psychiatry, 150*, 954–958.

Good, M. I. (1989). Substance-induced dissociative disorders and psychiatric nosology. *Journal of Clinical Psychopharmacology, 9*, 88–93.

Griffin, M., Resick, P., & Mechanic, M. (1997). Objective assessment of peritraumatic dissociation: Psychophysiological indicators. *American Journal of Psychiatry, 154*, 1081–1088.

Horen, S. A., Leichner, P. P., & Lawson, J. S. (1995). Prevalence of dissociative symptoms and disorders in an adult psychiatric inpatient population in Canada. *Canadian Journal of Psychiatry, 40*, 185–191.

Hornstein, N., & Putnam, F. W. (1992). Clinical phenomenology of child and adolescent dissociative disorders. *Journal of the American Academy of Child and Adolescent Psychiatry, 31*, 1077–1085.

Kanzer, M. (1939). Amnesia: A statistical study. *American Journal of Psychiatry, 96*, 711–716.

Kardiner, A. (1941). *The traumatic neuroses of war.* New York: Paul B. Hoeber.

Kirby, J. S., Chu, J. A., & Dill, D. L. (1993). Correlates of dissociative symptomatology in patients with physical and sexual abuse histories. *Comprehensive Psychiatry, 34*, 258–263.

Kleinman, A., Fabrega, H., & Parron, D. (Eds.). (1996). *Culture and psychiatric diagnosis: A DSM-IV perspective.* Washington, DC: American Psychiatric Press.

Kluft, R. P. (1985). Childhood multiple personality disorder: Predictors, clinical findings, and treatment results. In R. P. Kluft (Ed.), *Childhood antecedents of multiple personality* (pp. 167–196). Washington, DC: American Psychiatric Press.

Kluft, R. P. (1986). Treating children who have multiple personality disorder. In B. G. Braun (Ed.), *Treatment of multiple personality disorder* (pp. 81–105). Washington, DC: American Psychiatric Press.

Kluft, R. P. (1991). Multiple personality disorder. In A. Tasman & S. Goldfinger (Eds.), *American Psychiatric Press Annual Review of Psychiatry* (Vol. 10, pp. 161–181). Washington, DC: American Psychiatric Press.

Koopman, C., Classen, C., & Spiegel, D. (1994). Predictors of posttraumatic stress symptoms among survivors of the Oakland/Berkeley, Calif., firestorm. *American Journal of Psychiatry, 151*, 888–894.

Krystal, J. H., Bennett, A. L., Bremner, D. J., Southwick, S. M., & Charney, D. S. (1995). Towards a cognitive neuroscience of dissociation and altered memory function in post-traumatic stress disorder. In M. J. Friedman, D. S. Charney, & A. Y. Deutch (Eds.), *Neurobiological and clinical consequences of stress: From normal adaptation to post-traumatic stress disorder* (pp. 239–269). Philadelphia: Lippincott-Raven.

Latz, T., Kramer, S., & Hughes, D. (1995). Multiple personality disorder among female inpatients in a state hospital. *American Journal of Psychiatry, 152*, 1343–1348.

Leavitt, F. (1997). False attribution of suggestibility to explain recovered memory of childhood sexual abuse following extended amnesia. *Child Abuse and Neglect, 21*, 265–272.

Liotti, G. (1992). Disorganized/disoriented attachment in the etiology of dissociative disorders. *Dissociation, 5*, 196—204.

Loewenstein, R. (1993). Posttraumatic and dissociative aspects of transference and countertransference in the treatment of multiple personality disorder. In R. Kluft & C. Fine (Eds.), *Clinical perspectives on multiple personality disorder* (pp. 51–85). Washington, DC: American Psychiatric Press.

Loewenstein, R., & Putnam, F. (1990). The clinical phenomenology of males with multiple personality disorder: A report of 21 cases. *Dissociation, 3*, 135–143.

Loewenstein, R. J. (1991a). An office mental status examination for complex chronic dissociative symptoms and multiple personality disorder. *Psychiatric Clinics of North America, 14*, 567–604.

Loewenstein, R. J. (1991b). Psychogenic amnesia and psychogenic fugue: A comprehensive review. In A. Tasman & S. M. Goldfinger (Eds.), *American psychiatric press review of psychiatry* (Vol. 10, pp. 189–221). Washington, DC: American Psychiatric Press.

Loewenstein, R. J. (1991c). Rational psychopharmacology in the treatment of multiple personality disorder. *Psychiatric Clinics of North America, 14*, 721–740.

Ludwig, A. M. (1983). The psychobiological functions of dissociation. *American Journal of Clinical Hypnosis, 26*, 93–99.

Lynn, S. J., Rhue, J. W., & Green, J. P. (1988). Multiple personality and fantasy proneness: Is there an association or dissociation. *British Journal of Experimental and Clinical Hypnosis, 5*, 138–142.

Main, M., & Hesse, E. (1996). Disorganization and disorientation in infant Strange Situation behavior: Phenotypic resemblance to dissociative states. In L. Michelson & W. Ray (Eds.), *Handbook of dissociation: Theoretical, empirical, and clinical perspectives* (pp. 107–138). New York: Plenum Press.

Main, M., & Solomon, J. (1986). Discovery of a new, insecure-disorganized/disoriented attachment pattern. In T. B. Brazelton & M. Yogman (Eds.), *Affective development in infancy* (pp. 95–124). Norwood, NJ: Ablex.

Mann, B. J., & Sanders, S. (1994). Child dissociation and the family context. *Journal of Abnormal Child Psychology, 22*, 373–388.

Marmar, C. R., Weiss, D. S., Schlenger, W. E., Fairbank, J. A., Jordan, B. K., Kulka, R. A., & Hough, R. L. (1994). Peritraumatic dissociation and posttraumatic stress in male Vietnam theater veterans. *American Journal of Psychiatry, 151*, 902–907.

McHugh, P., & Putnam, F. (1995). Resolved: Multiple personality disorder is an individually and socially created artifact. *Journal of the American Academy of Child and Adolescent Psychiatry, 34*, 957–963.

Modestin, J., Ebner, G., Junghan, M., & Erni, T. (1996). Dissociative experiences and dissociative disorders in acute psychiatric patients. *Comprehensive Psychiatry, 37*, 355–361.

Nemiah, J. C. (1991). Dissociation, conversion and somatization. In A. Tasman & S. M. Goldfinger (Eds.), *American Psychiatric Press annual review of psychiatry* (Vol. 10, pp. 248–260). Washington, DC: American Psychiatric Press.

Park, J., Choe, B., Kim, M., Hnan, H., Yoo, S., Kim, S., & Joo, Y. (1995). Standardization of the Dissociative Experiences Scale—Korean Version (I). *Korean Journal of Psychopathology, 4*, 105–125.

Putnam, F. (1996). Child development and dissociation. *Child and Adolescent Psychiatric Clinics of North America, 5*, 285–302.

Putnam, F. (1997). *Dissociation in children and adolescents: A developmental approach.* New York: Guilford Press.

Putnam, F. W. (1985). Dissociation as a response to extreme trauma. In R. P. Kluft (Ed.), *Childhood antecedents of multiple personality* (pp. 66–97). Washington, DC: American Psychiatric Press.

Putnam, F. W. (1986). The scientific investigation of multiple personality. In J. M. Quen (Ed.), *Split minds, split brains* (pp. 109–126). New York: New York University Press.

Putnam, F. W. (1989). *Diagnosis and treatment of multiple personality disorder.* New York: Guilford Press.

Putnam, F. W. (1991). Recent research on multiple personality disorder. *Psychiatric Clinics of North America, 14*, 489–502.

Putnam, F. W. (1992). Are alter personalities fragments or figments? *Psychoanalytic Inquiry, 12*, 95–111.

Putnam, F. W., & Carlson, E. B. (1997). Dissociation, hypnosis and trauma: Myths, metaphors and mechanisms. In D. Bremner & C. Marmar (Eds.), *Dissociation, memory and trauma* (pp. 27–55). Washington, DC: American Psychiatric Press.

Putnam, F. W., Carlson, E. B., Ross, C. A., Anderson, G., Clark, P., Torem, M., Bowman, E., Coons, P., Chu, J., Dill, D., Loewenstein, R. J., & Braun, B. G. (1996). Patterns of dissociation in clinical and non-clinical samples. *Journal of Nervous and Mental Disease, 184*, 673–679.

Putnam, F. W., Guroff, J. J., Silberman, E. K., Barban, L., & Post, R. M. (1986). The clinical phenomenology of multiple personality disorder: Review of 100 recent cases. *Journal of Clinical Psychiatry, 47*, 285–293.

Putnam, F. W., Helmers, K., Horowitz, L. A., & Trickett, P. K. (1994). Hypnotizability and dissociativity in sexually abused girls. *Child Abuse and Neglect, 19*, 645–655.

Putnam, F. W., Helmers, K., & Trickett, P. K. (1993). Development, reliability and validity of a child dissociation scale. *Child Abuse and Neglect, 17*, 731–741.

Putnam, F. W., Hornstein, N., & Peterson, G. (1996). Clinical phenomenology of child and adolescent dissociative disorders: Gender and age effects. *Child and Adolescent Psychiatric Clinics of North America, 5*, 351–360.

Putnam, F. W., & Loewenstein, R. J. (1993). Treatment of multiple personality disorder: A survey of current practices. *American Journal of Psychiatry, 150*, 1048–1052.

Putnam, F. W., & Peterson, G. (1994). Further validation of the child dissociative checklist. *Dissociation, 7*, 204–211.

Putnam, F. W., & Trickett, P. K. (1997). Dissociation as predictor of psychopathology. Unpublished manuscript.

Putnam, F. W., Zahn, T. P., & Post, R. M. (1990). Differential autonomic nervous system activity in multiple personality disorder. *Psychiatric Research, 31*, 251–260.

Reiter, R. C., Shakerin, L. R., Gambone, J. C., & Milburn, A. K. (1990). Correlation between sexual abuse and somatization in women with somatic and nonsomatic pelvic pain. *American Journal of Obstetrics and Gynecology, 165*, 104–109.

Ross, C., Anderson, G., Fleisher, W., & Norton, G. (1991). The frequency of multiple personality disorder among psychiatric inpatients. *American Journal of Psychiatry, 148*, 1717–1720.

Ross, C., & Norton, G. (1989). Effects of hypnosis on features of multiple personality disorder. *American Journal of Clinical Hypnosis, 32*, 99–106.

Ross, C. A. (1991). Epidemiology of multiple personality disorder. *Psychiatric Clinics of North America, 14*, 503–518.

Ross, C. A., Joshi, S., & Currie, R. (1989). Dissociative experiences in the general population. *American Journal of Psychiatry, 147*, 1547–1552.

Ross, C. A., Miller, S. D., Bjornson, L., Reagor, P., Fraser, G. A., & Anderson, G. (1991). Abuse histories in 102 cases of multiple personality disorder. *Canadian Journal of Psychiatry, 36*, 97–101.

Ross, C. A., Norton, G. R., & Wozney, K. (1989). Multiple personality disorder: An analysis of 239 cases. *Canadian Journal of Psychiatry, 34*, 413–418.

Sandberg, D. A., & Lynn, S. J. (1992). Dissociative experiences, psychopathology and adjustment, and child and adolescent maltreatment in female college students. *Journal of Abnormal Psychology, 101*, 717–723.

Sanders, B. (1992). The imaginary companion experience in multiple personality disorder. *Dissociation, 5*, 159–162.

Saxe, G. N., Chinman, G., Berkowitz, R., Hall, K., Lieberg, G., Schwartz, J., & van der Kolk, B. A. (1994). Somatization in patients with dissociative disorders. *American Journal of Psychiatry, 151*, 1329–1334.

Saxe, G. N., van der Kolk, B. A., Berkowitz, R., Chinman, G., Hall, K., Lieberg, G., & Schwartz, J. (1993). Dissociative disorders in psychiatric inpatients. *American Journal of Psychiatry, 150*, 1037–1042.

Schultz, R., Braun, B. G., & Kluft, R. P. (1989). Multiple personality disorder: Phenomenology of selected variables in comparison to major depression. *Dissociation, 2*, 45–51.

Silberg, J. (Ed.). (1997). *The dissociative child.* Lutherville, MD: Sidran.

Stein, M., Koverola, C., Hanna, C., Torchia, M., & McClarty, B. (1997). Hippocampal volume in women victimized by childhood sexual abuse. *Psychological Medicine, 27*, 951–959.

Swica, Y., Lewis, D., & Lewis, M. (1996). Child abuse and multiple personality: The objective documentation of childhood maltreatment. *Child and Adolescent Psychiatric Clinics of North America, 5*, 431–448.

Trickett, P., McBride-Chang, C., & Putnam, F. (1994). The classroom performance and behavior of sexually abused females. *Development and Psychopathology, 6*, 183–194.

Trujillo, K., Lewis, D. O., Yeager, C. A., & Gidlow, B. (1996). Imaginary companions of school boys and boys with dissociative identity disorder: A normal to pathological continuum. *Child and Adolescent Psychiatric Clinics of North America, 5*, 375–392.

van der Hart, O., & Friedman, B. (1989). A reader's guide to Pierre Janet on dissociation: A neglected intellectual heritage. *Dissociation, 2*, 3–16.

van der Kolk, B., Pelcovitz, D., Roth, S., Mandel, F., McFarlane, A., & Herman, J. (1996). Dissociation, somatization, and affect dysregulation: The complexity of adaptation to trauma. *American Journal of Psychiatry, 153* (Festschrift in Honor of John C. Nemiah, M.D.), 83–93.

van IJzendoorn, M., & Schuengel, C. (1996). The measurement of dissociation in normal and clinical populations: Meta-analytic validation of the Dissociative Experiences Scale (DES). *Clinical Psychology Review, 16*, 365–382.

Waller, N., & Ross, C. (1997). The prevalence and biometric structure of pathological dissociation in the general population: Taxometric and behavior genetic findings. *Journal of Abnormal Psychology, 106*, 499–513.

Waller, N. G. (1995). The Dissociative Experiences Scale. In J. Conley & J. Impola (Eds.), *Twelfth mental measurements yearbook* (p. 122). Lincoln, NE: Buros Institute of Mental Measurement.

Waller, N. G., Putnam, F. W., & Carlson, E. B. (1996). Types of dissociation and dissociative types: A taxometric analysis of dissociative experiences. *Psychological Methods, 1*, 300–321.

Weiss, D. S., Marmar, C. R., Metzler, T. J., & Ronfeldt, H. M. (1995). Predicting symptomatic distress in emergency services personnel. *Journal of Consulting and Clinical Psychology, 63*, 361–368.

Wilson, S. C., & Barber, T. X. (1983). The fantasy-prone personality: Implications for understanding imagery, hypnosis, and parapsychological phenomena. In A. A. Sheikh (Ed.), *Imagery: Current theory, research, and application* (pp. 340–387). New York: Wiley.

Yargic, L., Tutkun, H., & Sar, V. (1995). Reliability and validity of the Turkish version of the Dissociative Experiences Scale. *Dissociation, 8,* 10–13.

Yeager, C. A., & Lewis, D. O. (1996). The intergenerational transmission of violence and dissociation. *Child and Adolescent Psychiatric Clinics of North America, 5,* 393–430.

Zahn, T. P., Moraga, R., & Ray, W. J. (1996). Psychophysiological assessment of dissociative disorders. In L. Michelson & W. Ray (Eds.), *Handbook of dissociation: Theoretical, empirical, and clinical perspectives* (pp. 269–287). New York: Plenum Press.

Zatzick, D. F., Marmar, C. R., Weiss, D. S., & Metzler, T. (1994). Does trauma-linked dissociation vary across ethnic groups. *Journal of Nervous and Mental Disease, 182,* 576–582.

Author Index

Page numbers in boldface type indicate occurrences of names within reference lists.

Subject Index

ISBN 0-306-46275-3

90000

9 780306 462757